EUROPEAN COMPETITION LAW

ELGAR COMMENTARIES

Titles in the series include:

Intellectual Property Enforcement
A Commentary on the Anti-Counterfeiting Trade Agreement (ACTA)
Michael Blakeney

The WTO Agreement on Trade-Related Aspects of Intellectual Property Rights
A Commentary
Justin Malbon, Charles Lawson and Mark Davison

EU Copyright Law
A Commentary
Edited by Irini Stamatoudi and Paul Torremans

European Competition Law
A Case Commentary
Edited by Weijer VerLoren van Themaat and Berend Reuder

EU Regulation of E-Commerce
A Commentary
Edited by Arno R. Lodder and Andrew D. Murray

European Competition Law
A Case Commentary, Second Edition
Edited by Weijer VerLoren van Themaat and Berend Reuder

EUROPEAN COMPETITION LAW

A Case Commentary, Second Edition

Edited by

WEIJER VERLOREN VAN THEMAAT

Advocaat, Houthoff, Amsterdam, the Netherlands

BEREND REUDER

Advocaat, Houthoff, Amsterdam, the Netherlands

ELGAR COMMENTARIES

Edward Elgar
PUBLISHING

Cheltenham, UK • Northampton, MA, USA

Published by
Edward Elgar Publishing Limited
The Lypiatts
15 Lansdown Road
Cheltenham
Glos GL50 2JA
UK

Edward Elgar Publishing, Inc.
William Pratt House
9 Dewey Court
Northampton
Massachusetts 01060
USA

A catalogue record for this book
is available from the British Library

Library of Congress Control Number: 2017950459

This book is available electronically in the **Elgar**online
Law subject collection
DOI 10.4337/9781786435477

ISBN 978 1 78643 546 0 (cased)
ISBN 978 1 78643 547 7 (eBook)

Typeset by Columns Design XML Ltd, Reading
Printed on FSC approved paper
Printed and bound in Great Britain by Marston Book Services Ltd, Oxfordshire

CONTENTS

List of contributors   xxii
Preface   xxiii
Table of cases   xxv

**PART 1   TREATY ON EUROPEAN UNION (TEU), TREATY ON THE
FUNCTIONING OF THE EUROPEAN UNION (TFEU) AND REGULATIONS**

Section 1   Treaty on European Union (TEU)

1 Article 3 TEU – Objectives of the Union   5
2 Article 4 TEU – Relations between the Union and the Member
   States; Principles of subsidiarity, equality and sincere co-operation   7
3 Article 6 TEU – The Charter and the ECHR   15

Section 2   Treaty on the Functioning of the European Union (TFEU)

4 Article 101 TFEU – Cartel prohibition   27
5 Article 102 TFEU – Abuse of dominance   141
6 Article 103 TFEU – Regulation regarding the application of Arts
   101 and 102   204
7 Article 104 TFEU – Competence of authorities in Member States   207
8 Article 105 TFEU – Application of Arts 101 and 102 by the
   Commission   208
9 Article 106 TFEU – Public undertakings   211
10 Article 107 TFEU – General rule: Prohibition of aid   232
11 Article 108 TFEU – Procedure before the Commission: Notification
   of aid   279
12 Article 109 TFEU – Determination of Regulations regarding the
   application of Arts 107 and 108   319

Section 3   Regulations

13 Regulation (EC) No 1/2003 on the implementation of the rules
   on competition   323
14 Regulation (EC) No 139/2004 on the control of concentrations
   between undertakings   490

15 Regulation (EU) No 330/2010 on vertical agreements   639
16 Regulation (EU) No 461/2010 on vertical agreements in the
    motor vehicles sector   663
17 Regulation (EU) No 1308/2013 establishing a common
    organisation of the markets in agricultural products and
    repealing council regulations   682

**PART 2   EUROPEAN CONVENTION ON HUMAN RIGHTS (ECHR)
AND CHARTER OF FUNDAMENTAL RIGHTS OF THE
EUROPEAN UNION (CHARTER)**

Section 1   European Convention on Human Rights

18 Article 1 ECHR – Obligation to respect human rights   703

Section 2   Charter of Fundamental Rights of the European Union

19 Article 7 Charter – Respect for private and family life   715
20 Article 16 Charter – Freedom to conduct a business   755
21 Article 17(1) Charter – Right to property   757
22 Article 20 Charter – Equality before the law   759
23 Article 41 Charter – Right to good administration   762
24 Article 47 Charter – Right to an effective remedy and to an
    impartial tribunal   777
25 Article 48 Charter – Presumption of innocence and rights of the
    defence   840
26 Article 49 Charter – Principles of legality and proportionality of
    criminal offences and penalties   857
27 Article 50 Charter – Right not to be tried or punished twice in
    criminal proceedings for the same criminal offence   875
28 Article 51 Charter – Field of application   882
29 Article 52 Charter – Scope and interpretation of rights and
    principles   885
30 Article 53 Charter – Level of protection   891

Annex   893
Index   895

EXTENDED TABLE OF CONTENTS

List of contributors		xxii
Preface		xxiii
Table of cases		xxv

PART 1 TREATY ON EUROPEAN UNION (TEU), TREATY ON THE FUNCTIONING OF THE EUROPEAN UNION (TFEU) AND REGULATIONS

SECTION 1 TREATY ON EUROPEAN UNION (TEU)

1. ARTICLE 3 TEU – OBJECTIVES OF THE UNION

2. ARTICLE 4 TEU – RELATIONS BETWEEN THE UNION AND THE MEMBER STATES; PRINCIPLES OF SUBSIDIARITY, EQUALITY AND SINCERE CO-OPERATION

A. Duty not to jeopardise Union objectives Re. Arts 101 and 102 TFEU		2.01
B. Duty not to jeopardise Union objectives Re. Arts 107 and 108 TFEU		2.14
C. Procedural aspects		2.15

3. ARTICLE 6 TEU – THE CHARTER AND THE ECHR

A. The Charter		3.01
B. Application of the ECHR by the EU Courts		3.03
1. The ECHR as a source of law		3.03
(a) Prior to the entry into force of the Lisbon Treaty		3.03
(b) Following the entry into force of the Lisbon Treaty but prior to accession to the ECHR		3.09
2. Direct effect		3.11
(a) In relation to EU law		3.11
(b) In relation to national law		3.12
C. Position of Poland and the UK		3.15

SECTION 2 TREATY ON THE FUNCTIONING OF THE EUROPEAN UNION (TFEU)

4. ARTICLE 101 TFEU – CARTEL PROHIBITION

A. General		4.01
1. Direct effect		4.01
2. *Ratione personae*		4.03
3. *Ratione materiae*		4.07
(a) Coal and steel		4.07
(b) Atomic energy		4.07
(c) Agriculture		4.07
(d) Transport		4.08

	(e) Books	4.10
	(f) Banks	4.11
	(g) Insurance	4.12
	(h) Motor vehicles	4.13
	(i) Postal services	4.13
	(j) Social policy	4.14
	(k) Sports	4.18
	(l) Telecommunications	4.18
4.	*Ratione loci*	4.19
5.	*Ratione temporis*	4.25
6.	Concepts	4.28
	(a) Concept of 'competition'	4.28
	(b) Concept of 'undertaking'	4.38
	(c) Concept of 'association of undertakings'	4.63
	(d) Concept of 'agreement'	4.68
	(e) Concept of 'concerted practice'	4.95
	(f) Concept of 'decision of associations of undertakings'	4.125
7.	Relationship between national law and Article 101 TFEU	4.130
B.	Restriction of competition	4.141
1.	Object to prevent, restrict or distort competition	4.141
2.	Effect to prevent, restrict or distort competition	4.156
3.	Appreciable restriction of competition	4.165
4.	Rule of reason	4.176
5.	Restrictions inherent to an object of (non) economic interest	4.179
C.	Effect upon trade between Member States	4.183
D.	Paragraph 2: Nullity	4.201
E.	Paragraph 3: Exemption	4.210
1.	General	4.210
2.	Four cumulative conditions	4.218
	(a) Improvement of the production and distribution, promotion of technical and economic progress	4.218
	(b) Direct benefit for consumers	4.228
	(c) Proportionality	4.232
	(d) No elimination of competition	4.237
F.	Types of conduct falling under Article 101 TFEU	4.243
1.	Horizontal agreements	4.243
	(a) Agreements concerning prices and other trading conditions	4.243
	(b) Sharing of markets	4.253
	(c) Certification systems and standards	4.258
	(d) Exchange of information	4.260
	(e) Non-competition clauses	4.269
	(f) Pay-for-delay	4.272
2.	Vertical agreements	4.273
	(a) General	4.273
	(b) Agency	4.276
	(c) Block exemption regulations	(p.130)
	(d) Resale price restrictions	(p.130)
	(e) Selective distribution	4.282
	(f) Exclusive distribution	4.306
	(g) Single branding	4.310
	(h) Franchising	4.312

5. ARTICLE 102 TFEU – ABUSE OF DOMINANCE

A.	General	5.01
1.	Direct effect	5.01
2.	*Ratione personae*	(p.142)
	(a) Undertaking	(p.142)
	(b) Economic activity	(p.142)
3.	*Ratione materiae*	5.03

		(a) Agriculture	5.03
		(b) Transport	5.03
	4.	*Ratione loci* (Territorial jurisdiction)	5.04
B.	Dominance		5.07
	1.	General	5.07
	2.	Market definition	5.12
		(a) Relevant product market	5.13
		(b) Relevant geographic market	5.22
		(c) Temporal markets	5.26
	3.	Market power	5.27
		(a) Market share	5.27
		(b) Barriers to entry	5.34
		(c) Vertical integration	5.44
		(d) Unavoidable trading partner	5.45
		(e) Countervailing buyer power	5.48
	4.	Collective dominance	5.49
C.	Substantial part of the internal market		5.57
D.	Abuse		5.60
	1.	The objective concept of abuse	5.60
	2.	Capability of restricting competit on	5.66
	3.	Categories of abuses	5.70
		(a) General	5.70
		(b) Exclusive dealing	5.71
		(c) Tying and bundling	5.84
		(d) Predatory pricing	5.88
		(e) Refusal to supply	5.92
		(f) Margin squeeze	5.113
		(g) Unfair conditions	5.116
		(h) Price discrimination	5.124
		(i) Limitations on trade between Member States	5.129
		(j) Lack of transparency	5.132
		(k) 'Sham action'	5.133
	4.	Abuse on secondary markets	5.134
	5.	Abuse of collective dominance	5.136
	6.	Justification	5.137
		(a) General	5.137
		(b) Objective necessity	5.139
		(c) Protecting commercial interests	5.141
		(d) Efficiencies	5.145
		(e) Contestable market	5.147
		(f) Intellectual property rights	5.148
		(g) State action defence	5.149
E.	Effect on trade between Member States		5.150
F.	Relation to Articles 101 and 106 TFEU		5.152
	1.	Article 101 TFEU	5.152
		(a) Application of Art. 101(3) does not preclude applicability of Art. 102	5.152
		(b) Individual exemption under Art. 101(3) does not preclude applicability of Art. 102	5.154
		(c) Simultaneous application of Arts 101 and 102 TFEU	5.155
	2.	Article 106 TFEU	5.157

6. ARTICLE 103 TFEU – REGULATION REGARDING THE APPLICATION OF ARTS 101 AND 102

7. ARTICLE 104 TFEU – COMPETENCE OF AUTHORITIES IN MEMBER STATES

8. ARTICLE 105 TFEU – APPLICATION OF ARTS 101 AND 102 BY THE COMMISSION

9. ARTICLE 106 TFEU – PUBLIC UNDERTAKINGS
   A. Article 106(1): Obligations of Member States regarding public undertakings ... 9.01
      1. General ... 9.01
      2. Examples of (prohibited) measures ... 9.11
   B. Article 106(2) TFEU: Exceptional derogation from Treaty rules ... 9.26
      1. General ... 9.26
      2. Definition of 'undertakings entrusted with the operation of services of general economic interest' ... 9.31
      3. Proportionality test ... 9.36
   C. Article 106(3) TFEU: Commission powers ... 9.46
   D. Relation to Article 107 TFEU ... 9.55

10. ARTICLE 107 TFEU – GENERAL RULE: PROHIBITION OF AID
   A. Criteria: Art. 107(1) ... 10.01
      1. Granted by a Member State or through State resources ... 10.01
         (a) State resources ... 10.01
         (b) Imputability ... 10.12
         (c) Trade association governed by public law ... 10.17
      2. Advantage ... 10.19
         (a) Market economy investor principle ... 10.19
         (b) Services of general economic interest ... 10.30
      3. Selectivity ... 10.36
         (a) General ... 10.36
         (b) Regional selectivity ... 10.40
         (c) Selectivity in the context of taxation ... 10.41
      4. Distortion of competition ... 10.54
      5. Effect on trade between Member States ... 10.58
         (a) General ... 10.58
         (b) Amount of aid/de minimis ... 10.65
         (c) No effect on trade between Member States – examples ... 10.67
   B. Direct effect ... 10.71
   C. Article 107(1) in relation to other Treaty provisions ... 10.75
      1. General ... 10.75
      2. Free movement of goods ... 10.80
      3. Competition rules ... 10.81
      4. Social measures ... 10.82
   D. Form in which the aid is provided ... 10.83
      1. Aim of the measure ... 10.83
      2. Margin of appreciation ... 10.85
      3. Concept of 'subsidy' ... 10.89
      4. Capital injections ... 10.91
      5. Debt arrangement ... 10.102
      6. Loans ... 10.103
      7. Guarantees ... 10.104
      8. Cross-subsidisation ... 10.105
      9. Operating aid ... 10.106
      10. Sale of land ... 10.107
      11. Privatisation ... 10.114
         (a) General ... 10.114
         (b) Privatisation by tendering ... 10.114
      12. Reductions and non-payment of social security ... 10.115
      13. Fiscal measures ... 10.116
      14. Non-financial regulatory measures ... 10.121
      15. Minimum retail prices ... 10.123
      16. Fixing of tariffs by Member State ... 10.124

17.	Compensation for damages	10.125
E.	Article 107(2): 'Shall be compatible with the internal market'	10.126
F.	Article 107(3): 'May be considered to be compatible with the internal market'	10.127
1.	Article 107(3)(a)	10.131
2.	Article 107(3)(b)	10.138
	(a) Financial crisis	10.141
3.	Article 107(3)(c)	10.142
4.	Article 107(3)(d)	10.145

11. ARTICLE 108 TFEU – PROCEDURE BEFORE THE COMMISSION: NOTIFICATION OF AID

A.	Article 108(1): Constant review and appropriate measures	11.01
1.	New aid and existing aid	11.01
	(a) Existing aid	11.04
	(b) New aid	11.12
2.	'Appropriate measures'	11.16
B.	Article 108(2): Formal investigation	11.18
1.	Formal investigation procedure	11.18
	(a) Obligation on Commission to initiate the formal investigation procedure	11.18
	(b) The concept of 'serious difficulties'	11.24
	(c) Procedure between the Commission and the Member State granting the aid	11.32
	(d) Decision to initiate the formal investigation procedure	11.35
2.	Interested parties	11.39
	(a) The concept of 'interested party'	11.39
	(b) The rights of interested parties	11.44
	(c) Limited role of interested parties	11.48
	(d) Obligation of Commission to address complaints parties	11.51
C.	Article 108(3): Requirement to notify and standstill obligation	11.52
1.	Notification	11.52
	(a) Only in case of State aid	11.52
	(b) In case of alterations to existing aid	11.55
	(c) Notification of aid and the method of financing the aid (taxes)	11.56
	(d) Obligation of the Member State	11.60
	(e) When to notify	11.62
	(f) Notification after the implementation of the aid measure	11.63
2.	Examination of unlawful aid	11.68
3.	Standstill obligation	11.70
	(a) Only in case of State aid	11.70
	(b) Scope of the standstill obligation	11.72
	(c) Injunction to suspend	11.73
4.	Direct applicability of Article 108(3) TFEU	11.74
5.	Preliminary examination	11.75
	(a) Request for information	11.75
	(b) Assessment of the aid measure	11.76
6.	The role of the national courts	11.77
	(a) No ruling on the compatibility of the aid	11.89
	(b) Deggendorf-doctrine	11.90
D.	Other subjects	11.91
1.	Action for annulment (Art. 263 TFEU)	11.91
	(a) Admissibility	11.91
	(b) Assessment by the Union courts	11.96
2.	Recovery of aid	11.100
	(a) Objective of recovery	11.108
	(b) Recovery in accordance with national law	11.110
	(c) Duty of genuine cooperation	11.111
	(d) Absolutely impossible	11.113
	(e) Legitimate expectations	11.116
	(f) Recovery and bankruptcy	11.121
3.	Complaints received by the Commission	11.123

12. ARTICLE 109 TFEU – DETERMINATION OF REGULATIONS REGARDING THE APPLICATION OF ARTS 107 AND 108

SECTION 3 REGULATIONS

13. REGULATION (EC) NO 1/2003 ON THE IMPLEMENTATION OF THE RULES ON COMPETITION

Article 1 – Application of Articles 81 and 82 of the Treaty		(p.332)
Article 2 – Burden of proof		(p.333)
A.	Burden and standard of proof	13.01
	1. General	13.01
	2. Undertaking publicly distancing itself from agreement or concerted practice	13.06
	3. Limitation defence/duration	13.10
B.	Nature of evidence	13.12
C.	Single and continuous or repeated infringement	13.16
	1. General	13.16
	2. Continuous vs. repeated infringement	13.19
Article 3 – Relationship between Articles 81 and 82 of the Treaty and national competition laws		13.21
Article 4 – Powers of the Commission		(p.347)
Article 5 – Powers of the competition authorities of the Member States		13.23
Article 6 – Powers of the national courts		(p.350)
Article 7 – Finding and termination of infringement		13.25
Article 8 – Interim measures		(p.353)
A.	Prima facie case	13.26
B.	Threat of irreperable damage	13.27
Article 9 – Commitments		(p.355)
A.	Period of validity of commitment decisions	13.29
B.	Proportionality	13.30
Article 10 – Finding of inapplicability		(p.358)
Article 11 – Cooperation between the Commission and the competition authorities of the Member States		(p.359)
Article 12 – Exchange of information		13.33
Article 13 – Suspension or termination of proceedings		(p.362)
Article 14 – Advisory Committee		(p.363)
Article 15 – Cooperation with national courts		13.34
Article 16 – Uniform application of community competition law		13.36
Article 17 – Investigations into sectors of the economy and into types of agreements		(p.369)
Article 18 – Requests for information		(p.370)
A.	General	13.38
B.	Paragraph 1: Powers of the Commission to request information	13.39
C.	Paragraph 3: Information request by decision	13.42
D.	Paragraph 4: Obligation to cooperate	13.44
Article 19 – Power to take statements		(p.377)
Article 20 – The Commission's powers of inspection		(p.378)
A.	General	13.46
B.	Paragraph 2: Legal privilege	13.51
	1. General	13.51
	2. Documents other than privileged correspondence between lawyer and client	13.53
	3. Procedure protection confidentiality	13.55
	4. Limitation of legal privilege for in-house lawyers	13.57
C.	Paragraphs 3 and 4: Choice between investigation by authorisation and investigation ordered by decision	13.58
D.	Paragraph 4: Motivation inspection decision	13.59
E.	Paragraphs 5 to 8: Granting assistance to Commission officials	13.61
Article 21 – Inspection of other premises		(p.392)
Article 22 – Investigations by competition authorities of Member States		(p.393)

Article 23 – Fines (p.394)
  A.   General 13.62
  B.   Paragraph 1: Fines for incorrect or misleading information etc. 13.66
  C.   Paragraph 3: Fixing the amount of the fine 13.68
      1. General 13.68
      2. Legal framework 13.71
      3. Guidelines on the method for setting the fine 13.76
      4. Factors of assessment 13.82
         (a) General 13.82
         (b) Repeat infringements 13.85
         (c) Turnover 13.88
         (d) Market share 13.103
         (e) Size of geographic market 13.105
         (f) Gravity of the infringement 13.107
         (g) Duration of the infringement 13.113
         (h) Consequences of the infringement 13.116
         (i) Deterrence 13.120
      5. Mitigating circumstances 13.123
      6. Aggravating circumstances 13.138
      7. Principle of proportionality 13.146
         (a) Profit derived from (illegal) practices 13.146
         (b) Assessment conduct undertaking in relation to gravity infringement 13.148
         (c) Relation fine undertakings involved in the same infringement 13.154
         (d) New calculation method for fine 13.158
      8. Equality of treatment 13.159
      9. *Ne bis in idem* 13.164
      10. Leniency 13.171
      11. Ability to pay 13.175
  D.   Paragraph 4: Associations of undertakings 13.177
      1. Calculation turnover associations of undertakings 13.177
  E.   Liability 13.178
      1. General 13.178
      2. Imputability of infringement on parent company/companies 13.181
      3. Joint and several liability 13.189
      4. Legal and economic links 13.194
      5. Legal and economic continuity 13.197
      6. Representation in administrative procedure 13.204
      7. Vertical relation 13.206
Article 24 – Periodic penalty payments (p.447)
Article 25 – Limitation periods for the imposition of penalties (p.448)
  A.   Applicable limitation periods 13.207
  B.   Principle of legal certainty 13.211
  C.   Burden of proof: Single and continuous infringement 13.213
  D.   Paragraph 3: Interruption of limitation period 13.215
  E.   Paragraph 6: Proceedings pending before the Court of Justice 13.217
Article 26 – Limitation period for the enforcement of penalties 13.218
Article 27 – Hearing of the parties, complainants and others (p.456)
Article 28 – Professional secrecy 13.232
Article 29 – Withdrawal in individual cases (p.464)
Article 30 – Publication of decisions 13.234
Article 31 – Review by the Court of Justice (p.469)
  A.   General 13.240
  B.   Exercise of unlimited jurisdiction 13.247
  C.   No unlimited jurisdiction in appeal 13.249
Article 32 (p.474)
Article 33 – Implementing provisions (p.475)
Article 34 – Transitional provisions 13.251
Article 35 – Designation of competition authorities of Member States 13.252
Article 36 – Amendment of Regulation (EEC) No 1017/68 (p.479)
Article 37 – Amendment of Regulation (EEC) No 2988/74 (p.480)

Article 38 – Amendment of Regulation (EEC) No 4056/86 (p.481)
Article 39 – Amendment of Regulation (EEC) No 3975/87 (p.483)
Article 40 – Amendment of Regulations No 19/65/EEC, (EEC) No 2821/71
    and (EEC) No 1534/91 (p.484)
Article 41 – Amendment of Regulation (EEC) No 3976/87 (p.485)
Article 42 – Amendment of Regulation (EEC) No 479/92 (p.486)
Article 43 – Repeal of Regulations No 17 and No 141 (p.487)
Article 44 – Report on the application of the present regulation (p.488)
Article 45 – Entry into force (p.489)

14. REGULATION (EC) NO 139/2004 ON THE CONTROL OF CONCENTRATIONS BETWEEN UNDERTAKINGS

Article 1 – Scope (p.500)
  A. General (p.501)
  B. Extraterritorial application 14.01
  C. Competence of the European Commission in case of an amendment of the
      proposed concentration 14.02
  D. Notion of 'undertakings concerned' 14.03
Article 2 – Appraisal of concentrations (p.503)
  A. General (p.504)
  B. General considerations for appraisal of concentrations 14.04
    1. Standard of proof 14.04
    2. Parallel notifications 14.08
    3. Counterfactual in case of change from joint to sole control 14.11
  C. Paragraphs 2 and 3: Substantive analysis 14.14
    1. Relevant market 14.14
       (a) Trade patterns 14.15
       (b) Price differences 14.17
       (c) (National) preferences 14.18
       (d) Transportation costs and distances 14.20
       (e) Regulatory differences and other trade barriers 14.24
       (f) Chain of substitution 14.27
    2. Horizontal mergers 14.29
       (a) Non-coordinated effects 14.29
       (b) Coordinated effects 14.56
       (c) Countervailing buyer power 14.61
    3. Non-horizontal mergers 14.62
       (a) Vertical mergers 14.62
       (b) Conglomerate mergers 14.64
    4. Failing firm defence 14.70
    5. Efficiency defence 14.74
  D. Paragraphs 4 and 5: Assessment of coordinated effects JV 14.78
  E. Procedural aspects 14.79
    1. Liability of the European Commission in case of annulment of a decision 14.79
Article 3 – Definition of concentration (p.541)
  A. General (p.542)
  B. Paragraphs 1 and 2: Concentration as a result of a structural change in control 14.82
    1. De facto control 14.82
    2. Sole control 14.88
       (a) General 14.88
       (b) Negative sole control 14.92
    3. Joint control 14.95
    4. Interrelated transactions 14.99
    5. Acquisition of control by the State 14.109
    6. Scope of 'undertakings concerned' in case of acquisition of control by
       state-owned enterprises (SOE) 14.111
    7. No control/concentration 14.113
    8. Lasting structural change 14.120
  C. Paragraph 4: The creation of a joint venture 14.121

D. Paragraph 5: Credit institutions, financial institutions or insurance companies   14.127

Article 4 – Prior notification of concentrations and pre-notification referral at the
request of the notifying parties   (p.566)
  A. General   (p.568)
  B. Paragraph 1: 'Suspensive effect' and 'gun jumping'   14.128
  C. Paragraph 2: Good faith intention to conclude agreement   14.129

Article 5 – Calculation of turnover   (p.570)
  A. General   (p.572)
  B. Geographic allocation of turnover   14.130
  C. Paragraph 2: Consecutive acquisitions   14.132
  D. Paragraph 4: Attribution of turnover   14.136

Article 6 – Examination of the notification and initiation of proceedings   (p.576)
  A. General   (p.577)
  B. Paragraph 1: Investigation by the Commission   14.139
  C. Commitments   14.141
  D. Ancillary restraints   (p.581)

Article 7 – Suspension of concentrations   (p.582)
  A. General   14.148
  B. Derogation   14.149

Article 8 – Powers of decision of the Commission   (p.585)
  A. General   14.153
  B. Article 102 TFEU versus remedies   14.154
  C. Paragraph 1: Assessment of ancillary restraints   14.155
  D. Paragraphs 4 and 5: Restorative measures   14.156
    1. General   14.156
    2. Meaning of 'Implementation'   14.160

Article 9 – Referral to the competent authorities of the Member States   (p.591)
  A. General   14.161
  B. Paragraph 2: Significant effect within a Member State   14.162
  C. Paragraph 3: Commission decision regarding request for referral   14.163

Article 10 – Time limits for initiating proceedings and for decisions   (p.597)
  A. General   (p.598)
  B. Paragraph 2: Time-limit for clearance decision   14.169
  C. Paragraph 4: Exceptional circumstances for suspension   14.170

Article 11 – Requests for information   (p.600)
Article 12 – Inspections by the authorities of the Member States   (p.602)
Article 13 – The Commission's powers of inspection   (p.603)

Article 14 – Fines   (p.605)
  A. General   (p.606)
  B. Paragraph 1: Providing incorrect or misleading information   14.173
  C. Paragraph 2: Failure to notify a concentration   14.176

Article 15 – Periodic penalty payments   (p.609)
Article 16 – Review by the Court of Justice   14.178

Article 17 – Professional secrecy   (p.612)
  A. Paragraph 1: Use of incidentally gained information   14.180
  B. Paragraph 2: Scope of non-disclosure obligation   14.181

Article 18 – Hearing of the parties and of third persons   (p.614)
  A. Statement of objections   14.182
  B. Right to be heard   14.187
  C. Access to files   14.189

Article 19 – Liaison with the authorities of the Member States   (p.620)
Article 20 – Publication of decisions   (p.622)
Article 21 – Application of the Regulation and jurisdiction   (p.623)
  A. General   (p.624)
  B. Paragraph 1: Exclusive competence for the Commission   14.190
    1. General   14.190
    2. European merger control without prejudice to separate assessment under
State aid rules   14.191
  C. Paragraph 3: Applicability of national competition law   14.192
  D. Paragraph 4: Competences of *Commission v. Member States*   14.193

Article 22 – Referral to the Commission (p.628)
    A. General 14.196
    B. Paragraph 1: Influence of trade between Member States 14.197
Article 23 – Implementing provisions (p.631)
Article 24 – Relations with third countries 14.200
Article 25 – Repeal (p.633)
Article 26 – Entry into force and transitional provisions (p.634)
Annex (p.635)

15. REGULATION (EU) NO 330/2010 ON VERTICAL AGREEMENTS

Article 1 – Definitions (p.642)
Article 2 – Exemption (p.645)
Article 3 – Market share threshold (p.647)
Article 4 – Restrictions that remove the benefit of the block exemption – hardcore
    restrictions (p.649)
    A. General (p.650)
    B. Resale price clauses 15.04
    C. Resale price clauses in vertical agreements for petroleum products 15.05
    D. De facto prohibition on sales via internet in selective distribution agreements 15.06
        1. General 15.06
        2. Integrity of selective distribution system 15.07
        3. Territorial restrictions 15.08
Article 5 – Excluded restrictions (p.655)
    A. General 15.13
    B. Non-compete and exclusivity clauses in vertical agreements for petroleum
      products 15.14
Article 6 – Non-application of this Regulation (p.658)
Article 7 – Application of the market share threshold (p.659)
Article 8 – Application of the turnover threshold (p.660)
Article 9 – Transitional period 15.19
Article 10 – Period of validity (p.662)

16. REGULATION (EU) NO 461/2010 ON VERTICAL AGREEMENTS IN THE MOTOR VEHICLES SECTOR

Article 1 – Definitions (p.669)
Article 2 – Application of Regulation (EC) No 1400/2002 (p.672)
Article 3 – Application of Regulation (EU) No 330/2010 (p.674)
Article 4 – Exemption 16.02
Article 5 – Restrictions that remove the benefit of the block exemption – hardcore
    restrictions 16.09
Article 6 – Non-application of this Regulation (p.679)
Article 7 – Monitoring and Evaluation Report (p.680)
Article 8 – Period of validity (p.681)

17. REGULATION (EU) No 1308/2013 ESTABLISHING A COMMON ORGANISATION OF THE MARKETS IN AGRICULTURAL PRODUCTS AND REPEALING COUNCIL REGULATIONS

Article 206 (p.684)
    A. Scope of Regulation No 1184/2006 vs. Regulation No 1308/2013 and Regulation
      No 1379/2013 17.01
    B. Scope of Articles 206 and 209 17.03
        1. General 17.03
        2. Article 1A Regulation No 1184/2006 17.04
Article 209 (p.688)
    A. Paragraph 1: Farmers, Farmers' Associations 17.05
    B. Division of competence in Article 2(2) of Regulation No 1184/2006 17.14
Article 210 (p.695)
Article 222 (p.697)

PART 2   EUROPEAN CONVENTION ON HUMAN RIGHTS (ECHR) AND CHARTER OF FUNDAMENTAL RIGHTS OF THE EUROPEAN UNION (CHARTER)

SECTION 1   EUROPEAN CONVENTION ON HUMAN RIGHTS

18. ARTICLE 1 ECHR – OBLIGATION TO RESPECT HUMAN RIGHTS

A.	General	(p.703)
B.	The ECHR: A supra-national human rights treaty	18.01
C.	Methods of interpretation	18.02
	1. General	18.02
	2. The ECHR as a living instrument	18.04
	3. The Vienna Treaty on the Law of Treaties, Sens Clair and Purposive Construction	18.06
	4. Member State practice	18.12
	5. Other sources of International Law	18.13
D.	No direct binding effect vis-à-vis the EU prior to accession	18.15
	1. No binding effect vis-à-vis the EU as such	18.15
	2. No binding effect vis-à-vis the EU as holder of powers which have been deferred to it by the Member States	18.16
E.	EU Member State responsibility when deferring powers to the EU	18.17
	1. General	18.17
	2. Equivalent guarantees	18.21
	(a) General	18.21
	(b) Two-step test: General level and protection in the individual case concerned	18.22
	(c) Finding of equivalence	18.23
	(d) In relation to the grant of an exequatur for a Commission Decision imposing a fine	18.24
	(e) In relation to the preliminary reference procedure	18.25

SECTION 2   CHARTER OF FUNDAMENTAL RIGHTS OF THE EUROPEAN UNION

19. ARTICLE 7 CHARTER – RESPECT FOR PRIVATE AND FAMILY LIFE

A.	Explanation relating to Article 7 Charter	(p.716)
B.	Scope of application	19.01
	1. Respect for the home	19.01
	(a) Eur. Court H.R.	19.01
	(b) EU Courts	19.05
	2. Respect for correspondence	19.09
	3. Respect for privacy of telephone calls	19.11
C.	Interference	19.12
D.	Justification for the interference	19.14
	1. General	19.14
	2. In accordance with the law	19.17
	(a) General	19.17
	(b) In accordance with national laws	19.19
	(c) Accessible	19.22
	(d) Foreseeable	19.23
	(e) Compatible with the rule of law	19.24
	3. Legitimate aim	19.29
	4. Necessary in a democratic society	19.31
	(a) General	19.31
	(b) Adequate safeguards	19.33
	(c) Two-step test	19.35
	(d) Importance of prior judicial authorisation	19.37
	(e) Disproportionate national systems	19.39

(f) Proportionate national systems 19.48
5. Assessment of the EU System 19.53
E. Legal privilege 19.56
1. Eur. Court H.R. 19.56
2. EU Courts 19.57
F. Exclusionary rule (p.754)

20. ARTICLE 16 CHARTER – FREEDOM TO CONDUCT A BUSINESS
A. Explanation relating to Article 16 Charter (p.755)
B. General 20.01

21. ARTICLE 17(1) CHARTER – RIGHT TO PROPERTY
A. Explanation relating to Article 17(1) Charter (p.757)
B. General 21.01

22. ARTICLE 20 CHARTER – EQUALITY BEFORE THE LAW
A. Explanation relating to Article 20 Charter (p.759)
B. General 22.01
C. In relation to the finding of an infringement 22.02
D. In relation to a leniency rebate 22.03
E. In relation to the calculation of a fine by the European Commission 22.04
F. In relation to the review of a fine by the EU Courts 22.05

23. ARTICLE 41 CHARTER – RIGHT TO GOOD ADMINISTRATION
A. Explanation relating to Article 41 Charter (p.763)
B. Reasonable period 23.01
1. General 23.01
2. Test 23.02
3. Assessment in respect of administrative proceedings 23.07
4. Consequences of a failure to adopt a decision within a reasonable period 23.09
(a) EU Courts 23.09
(b) EFTA Court 23.09
C. Rights of the defence 23.10
1. Applicability to preliminary inquiries 23.13
2. Right to be heard 23.14
3. Statement of objections 23.16
4. Access to the file 23.25

24. ARTICLE 47 CHARTER – RIGHT TO AN EFFECTIVE REMEDY AND TO AN IMPARTIAL TRIBUNAL
A. Explanation relating to Article 47 Charter (p.778)
B. General 24.01
1. Relationship between the principles of effective remedy (para. 1) and fair trial (para. 2) 24.01
2. General principles 24.02
(a) European Court of Human Rights (Eur. Court H.R.) 24.02
(b) European Union (EU) Courts 24.03
C. Scope of application of Articles 47 Charter and Articles 6 and 13 ECHR 24.07
1. General applicability of Article 47 Charter 24.07
2. Civil rights and obligations within the meaning of Article 6 ECHR 24.08
3. Criminal charge within the meaning of Article 6 ECHR 24.14
(a) Concept 24.14
(b) Distinction between hard core criminal law and other criminal charges 24.22
(c) Moment when the charge is brought 24.23
D. Independent and impartial tribunal 24.28
1. Concept of 'Tribunal' 24.28

		(a) European Court of Human Rights	24.28
		(b) European Union Courts	24.32
	2.	Independence	24.35
		(a) European Court of Human Rights	24.35
		(b) European Union Courts	24.36
	3.	Impartiality	24.37
		(a) General	24.37
		(b) Objective and subjective test	24.38
		(c) Following remandment	24.40
E.	Full jurisdiction		24.43
	1.	Legal standard	24.43
	2.	Assessment	24.46
		(a) Insufficiency of a pure constitutionality review	24.46
		(b) Insufficiency of a review restricted to points of law	24.47
		(c) Insufficiency in case of deference of the court to decisions of the executive	24.49
		(d) Full review of sanctions by an administrative court	24.51
F.	Access		24.57
	1.	General	24.57
	2.	Effet utile	24.58
	3.	Restrictions	24.60
G.	Effective remedy		24.62
	1.	Legal standard	24.62
	2.	In relation to dawn raids	24.63
		(a) European Court of Human Rights	24.63
		(b) European Union Courts	24.65
H.	Fair trial		24.66
	1.	Applicability to pre-trial proceedings	24.66
		(a) European Court of Human Rights	24.66
		(b) European Union Courts	(p.810)
	2.	Imposition of fines by an administrative body	24.69
		(a) An administrative body may impose a sanction, provided that such sanction is open to appeal	24.69
		(b) Except in relation to serious charges	24.73
		(c) Lawfulness of having one and the same body investigate and fine	24.74
		(d) No obligation to remand to a different body following annulment	24.75
	3.	Principle of adversarial proceedings	24.76
		(a) General	24.76
		(b) Applicability when the court applies grounds of its own motion	24.84
		(c) Exceptions	24.87
	4.	Equality of arms	24.88
		(a) General	24.88
	5.	Access to the file in criminal proceedings	24.92
	6.	Exclusionary rule	24.95
	7.	Obligation to state the grounds of a judgment	24.97
	8.	Waiver of rights	24.100
I.	Reasonable period		24.102
	1.	General	24.102
		(a) European Court of Human Rights	24.102
		(b) European Union Courts	24.103
	2.	Relevant period	24.104
		(a) Start	24.104
		(b) End	24.104
	3.	Legal standard	24.108
	4.	Assessment	24.110
	5.	Consequences of a failure to adjudicate within a reasonable period	24.113
		(a) European Court of Human Rights	24.113
		(b) European Union Courts	24.115
J.	Public hearing		24.118
K.	Access to a lawyer		24.119
	1.	General	24.119

	2.	During an interrogation	24.121
	3.	Legal privilege	(p.837)
L.	Legal aid		24.126
	1.	Scope	24.126
	2.	Assistance by a lawyer and dispensation of the cost of proceedings	24.127
	3.	Grant procedure	24.128
	4.	Availability to a legal person	24.129

25. ARTICLE 48 CHARTER – PRESUMPTION OF INNOCENCE AND RIGHTS OF THE DEFENCE

A.	Explanation relating to Article 48 Charter		(p.841)
B.	Presumption of innocence		25.01
	1.	General	25.01
		(a) Eur. Court H.R.	25.01
		(b) EU Courts	25.09
	2.	In relation to parental liability	25.15
	3.	In relation to the causal link in case of a concerted practice	25.18
	4.	In relation to participation in a meeting with an anti-competitive character	25.21
C.	Rights of the defence – General		25.22
D.	Privilege against self-incrimination and right to remain silent		25.25
	1.	Intrinsic to the concept of 'fair trial'	25.25
	2.	Scope	25.28
	3.	Test	25.30
	4.	Right to remain silent stricto sensu	25.33
	5.	Order to submit information or documents	25.36
		(a) Eur. Court H.R.	25.36
		(b) EU Courts	25.40
	6.	Inferences which may be drawn from the exercise of the right to remain silent	25.44
E.	Obligation to mention the privilege against self-incrimination and the right to remain silent		25.46
F.	Access to legal assistance and legal aid		(p.856)

26. ARTICLE 49 CHARTER – PRINCIPLES OF LEGALITY AND PROPORTIONALITY OF CRIMINAL OFFENCES AND PENALTIES

A.	Explanation relating to Article 49 Charter		(p.858)
B.	Legality principle		26.01
	1.	Eur. Court H.R.	26.01
	2.	EU Courts	26.05
C.	Concept of 'penalty'		26.08
D.	Non-retroactivity of criminal sanctions		26.09
E.	Retroactivity of the more lenient sanction		26.11
	1.	Eur. Court H.R.	26.11
	2.	EU Courts	26.12
F.	Foreseeability		26.13
	1.	Eur. Court H.R.	26.13
	2.	EU Courts	26.15
G.	Proportionality		26.19
H.	Principle of personal liability		26.24

27. ARTICLE 50 CHARTER – RIGHT NOT TO BE TRIED OR PUNISHED TWICE IN CRIMINAL PROCEEDINGS FOR THE SAME CRIMINAL OFFENCE

A.	Explanation relating to Article 50 Charter	(p.876)
B.	Principle	27.01
C.	Criminal proceedings	27.03
D.	Same offence	27.06

    E. Final acquittal or conviction in the first proceedings   27.07
    F. Tried or punished again   27.09

28. ARTICLE 51 CHARTER – FIELD OF APPLICATION
    A. Explanation relating to Article 51 Charter   (p.882)
    B. Applicability to the Member States when they are implementing Union law   28.01
    C. Ability of the Member States to apply national fundamental rights   28.02

29. ARTICLE 52 CHARTER – SCOPE AND INTERPRETATION OF RIGHTS AND PRINCIPLES
    A. Explanation relating to Article 52 Charter   (p.886)
    B. Exceptions   29.01
    C. Explanations   29.04

30. ARTICLE 53 CHARTER – LEVEL OF PROTECTION
    A. Explanation relating to Article 53 Charter   (p.891)
    B. General   30.01

Annex   893
Index   895

CONTRIBUTORS

Jacques Derenne
Avocat, Sheppard, Mullin, Richter & Hampton LLP, Brussels, and Professor, University of Liège, and Brussels School of Competition

Greetje van Heezik
Advocaat, Houthoff, Brussels

Mats Johnsson
Advokat, Hamilton Advokatbyrå, Stockholm

Karsten Metzlaff
Rechtsanwalt, Noerr LLP, Hamburg, and Professor at the Europa-Universität Viadrina, Frankfurt/Oder

Edmon Oude Elferink
Advocaat, CMS, Brussels

Alvaro Pliego Selie
Advocaat, Freshfields Bruckhaus Deringer LLP, Amsterdam

Herman Speyart
Advocaat, NautaDutilh, Amsterdam

Peter Stauber
Rechtsanwalt, Noerr LLP, Berlin

PREFACE

There are probably few rules that have provoked so much thought, arguments and, ultimately, judgments as the European Treaty rules on competition. This book aims to explain those rules by presenting them and the related European (human rights) legislation together with case extracts from the most important Commission decisions and court cases pertaining to those provisions.

The book is divided into two parts. Part 1 deals with the competition provisions of the EU Treaties and the main EU regulations on competition. Part 2 discusses the relevant provisions of the Charter of Fundamental Rights of the EU and the European Convention on Human Rights.

The case extracts were selected for their interpretative value for the relevant provision. The extracts originate mostly from decisions of the European Commission and judgments of the Court of Justice of the European Union and the European Court of Human Rights. Although most come from landmark cases, some have been taken from decisions or judgments that are less well known but shed new light on the interpretation of the Treaty or that otherwise fill a gap of some kind. In all instances, however, it is the extract that explains the law, rather than the authors of this book. To that end, the ambition of the authors is to present a compilation of concise extracts that are both objective and comprehensible. For the convenience of the reader, the references in the case extracts to the articles of the various treaties have been renumbered so that they are in accordance with the Lisbon Treaty. The new numbering has been placed between brackets.

The documents and case extracts reproduced in this second edition are current up to and including 31 August 2016. In some instances, however, it has been possible to include more recent material.

The scope of European competition law and the volume of the case law require a large team to keep track of all the developments. We wish to acknowledge the invaluable contributions of the following contributors:

- Jacques Derenne on state aid;
- Greetje van Heezik on agriculture;
- Mats Johnsson on Articles 3 and 4 TEU and Regulation 1/2003;
- Karsten Metzlaff and Peter Stauber on merger control;
- Edmon Oude Elferink on cartels;
- Alvaro Pliego Selie on abuse of dominance and public undertakings;
- Herman Speyart on human rights.

The final editing was ours. We welcome any suggestions for amendments or improvements. Please send these to us by e-mail at w.verloren@houthoff.com or b.reuder@houthoff.com.

Weijer VerLoren van Themaat and Berend Reuder

Amsterdam, 28 March 2017

TABLE OF CASES

European Commission

ABB/Renault Automation (M.409), OJ 1994 C 80/0, 9 March 1993 .... 14.99
ABF/Azucarera (M.5449), 30 March 2009 .... 14.25
ABF/GBI Business (M.4980), 23 September 2008 .... 14.60
Advent/Maxam (M.6411), 6 February 2012 .... 14.03
AEE/Lentjes (M.4647), 5 December 2007 .... 14.38
Aegean/Olympic II (M.6796), 9 October 2013 .... 14.73
Air Liquide/BOC (M.1630), OJ 2002 L 92/16, 18 January 2001 .... 14.50
Alpha Flight Services v. Aéroports de Paris (IV/35.613), OJ 1998 L 230/10,
    11 June 1998 .... 5.59, 5.124
Amer/Salomon (M.3765), 12 May 2005 .... 14.42
Anglo Irish Bank/RBS/Arnotts (M.5826), 9 August 2010 .... 14.91
ArcelorMittal/Miglani/JV (M.5643), 30 November 2009 .... 14.86
Atos Origin/Siemens IT Solutions & Services (M.6127), 25 March 2011 .... (p.581), 14.155
Bananas (COMP/39188), 15 October 2008 .... 17.13
Barilla/BPL/Kamps (M.2817), OJ 2002 C 198/4, 25 June 2002 .... 14.41
BASF/Eurodiol/Pantochim (M.2314), OJ 2001 L 132/45, 11 July 2001 .... 14.71
Belgacom/BICS/MTN (M.5584), 26 October 2009 .... 14.92
Bertelsmann/Kirch/Premiere (M.993), OJ 1999 L 53/1 (Press release IP/97/953),
    27 May 1998 .... 14.128
Blokker/Toys 'R' Us (M.890), OJ 1998 L 316/1, 26 June 1997 .... 14.19
Boeing/Hughes (M.1879), OJ 2004 L 63/53, 29 September 2000 .... 14.130
Boeing/McDonnell Douglas (M.877), OJ 1997 L 336/16, 30 July 1997 .... 14.200
BP/Erdölchemie (M.2624), OJ 2004 L 91/48, 19 June 2002 .... 14.175
BP/E.ON (M.2533), OJ 2002 C 276/31, 20 December 2001 .... 14.08
BP/JV Dissolution (M.1820), OJ 2000 C 98/9, 22 November 1999 .... 14.152
British Airways/Dan Air (M.278), OJ 1996 L 134/32, 17 February 1993 .... 14.197
British Airways/TAT (M.259), OJ 1992 C 326, 27 November 1992 .... 14.113
BritishTelecom/MCI (M.353), OJ 1993 C 253/0, 13 September 1993 .... 14.114
Carnival Corporation/P&O Princess (M.2706), OJ 2005 C 318/6, 24 July 2002 .... 14.32
CASC/JV (M.5154), 14 August 2008 .... 14.122
Cauliflowers (IV/28.948), OJ 1978 L 21/23, 2 December 1977 .... 17.05
CCI (IV/30.211), OJ 1981 L 27/31, 17 November 1981 .... 13.38
Charterhouse/Porterbrook (M.669), OJ 1995 C 350/18, 11 December 1995 .... 14.127
China National Bluestar/Elkem (M.6082), 31 March 2011 .... 14.111
Comcast/NBC Universal (M.5779), 13 July 2010 .... 14.90
CVC/Lenzing (M.2187), OJ 2004 L 82/2017, October 2001 .... 14.29
CVC/Virgin Group Holdings/Virgin Active Group (M.6354), 14 October 2011 .... 14.98
Dana/GKN (M.1587), OJ 2000 C 9/10, 4 November 1999 .... 14.101
Danisco/Abitec (M.5109), 17 April 2008 .... 14.199
Danish Crown/Steff Houlberg (M.2662), OJ 2002 C 114/22, 14 February 2002 .... 14.71,
    14.163

Deloitte Touche/Andersen (UK) (M.2810), OJ 2002 C 200/8, 1 July 2002 .... 14.71
DSM/Sinochem/JV (M.6113), 19 May 2011 .... 14.112
Deutsche Bank/Actavis (M.5949), 22 September 2010 .... 14.93
Deutsche Post/Securicor (M.3155), OJ 2003 C 222/4, 19 June 2003 .... 14.11
Dolby/Doremi (M.7297), C(2014) 5984 final, 14 August 2014 .... 14.196
EDF/TXU Europe/Westburton Power Station and EDF/TXU Europe/24 (M.2679),
    OJ 2002 C 43/21, 20 December 2001 .... 14.103
Electrabel/Compagnie Natiale du Rhone (M.4994), 10 June 2009 .... 14.86, 14.176
ENI Spa (COMP/39.315), 29 September 2010 .... 5.96
ENW/Eastern (M.1315), OJ 1998 C 344/7, 15 October 1998 .... 14.121
E.ON/TXU-Europe Group plc (M.3007), OJ 2003 C 14/8, 15 November 2002 .... 14.152
Ernst & Young France/Andersen France (M.2816), OJ 2002 C 232/6,
    5 September 2002 .... 14.71
F2i/AXA Funds/G6 Rete Gas (M.6302), 24 August 2011 .... 14.120
Facebook/Whatsapp (M.7217), 3 October 2014 .... 14.55
Faurecia/Plastal (M.5977), 30 September 2010 .... 14.134
Ford/Hertz (M.397), OJ 1994 C 121/00, 7 March 1994 .... 14.82
Fortis/ABN AMRO Assets (M.4844), 3 October 2007 .... 14.47
Fortis/CGER (M.342), OJ 1993 C 23, 15 November 1993 .... 14.24
Friesland Foods/Campina (M.504617) December 2008 .... 14.34
Geely/Daqiing/Volvo Cars (M.5789), 1 July 2010 .... 14.191
Germany – Leisure pool Dorsten, State aid (N.258/2000), 12 January 2001 .... 10.67
Google/DoubleClick (M.4731), 11 March 2008 .... 14.62
Hutchison 3G Austria/Orange Austria (M.6437), 12 December 2012 .... 14.53
Hutchison 3G UK/Telefonica Ireland (M.6992), 28 May 2015 .... 14.30, 14.48
IAG/BMI (M.6447), 30 March 2012 .... 14.138
IBM/Telelogic (M.4747), 5 March 2008 .... 14.39
IF P&C/TopDanmark (M.6957), 12 March 2004 .... 14.84
Inco/Falconbridge (M.4000), 4 July 2006 .... 14.74
ING v. Barings (M.573), OJ 1995 C114/6, 11 April 1995 .... 14.150
Intel (COMP/C-3 /37.990), 13 May 2009 .... 5.42, 5.48
Ireland – Capital allowances for hospitals, State aid (N.543/010, 27 February 2002 ..... 10.68
Ireland – Seed and Venture Capital Fund Scheme (N.172/2000, SG(2000)
    D/107/07595), 17 October 2000 .... 10.27
Italy – Local Museums – Region of Sardinia, State aid (N.630/2003),
    18 February 2004 .... 10.70
Itema/Barcovision (M.4874), 4 August 2008 .... 14.62
Kali-Salz/MdK/Treuhand (M.308), OJ 1994 L 186/38, 14 December 1993 .... 14.52
KarstadtQuelle/MyTravel (M.4601), 4 May 2007 .... 14.09
Kingfisher/Wegert/Promart (M.1188), OJ 1998 C 342/3, 18 June 1998 .... 14.100
Kirch/Richemont/MultiChoice/Telepiu (M.584), OJ 1995 C 82/5, 5 May 1995 .... 14.18
KLM/Air UK (M.967), OJ 1997 C 372/20, 22 September 1997 .... 14.86
KLM/Martinair III (M.1608), OJ 2005 L 50/10, 14 December 1999 .... 14.173
KLM-Martinair (M.5141), 17 December 2008 .... 14.13, 14.76
Knorr Bremse/Vossloh (M.7538), 14 September 2015 .... 14.87
Koninklijke Philips Electronics/Saeco International Group (M.5547), 17 July 2009 ..... 14.43
Kraft Foods/Cadbury (M.5644), 6 January 2010 .... 14.44

Kronospan/Constantia (M.4525), 19 September 2007 .... 14.20

Kühne/HGV/TUI/Hapag-Lloyd (M.5450), 6 February 2009 .... 14.95

Lagardere/Natexis/VUP (M.2978), OJ 2004 L 125/54, 7 January 2004 .... 14.166

Linde/BOC (M.4141), 6 June 2006 .... 14.46

Mannesmann/Vallourec/Ilva (M.315), OJ 1994 L 102/15, 31 January 1994 .... 14.17

Matra Marconi Space/Satcomms (M.497), OJ 1994 C 307/3, 14 October 1994 .... 14.152

Mauser Holding International/Reyde/JV (M.5394), 21 January 2009 .... 14.22, 14.106

Measures in favour of non-profit harbours for recreational crafts, the Netherlands,
    OJ 2004 L 34/63, 29 October 2003 .... 10.69

Meldoc (IV/31.204), OJ 1986 L 348/50, 26 November 1986 .... 17.07

Milchförderungsfonds (IV/ 28.930), OJ 1985 L 35/35, 7 December 1984 .... 17.06

Mitsubishi Heavy Industries (M.1634), OJ 2001 L 4/31, 14 July 2000 .... 14.174

Mubadala/Rolls Royce/JV (M.5399), 16 February 2009 .... 14.78, 14.96, 14.123

Mytilineos/Motor Oil/Corinthos Power (M.5445), 30 March 2009 ..... 14.97, 14.107, 14.124

NEC/BULL/PBN (M.1095), OJ 1998 C 53/07, 6 February 1998 .... 14.115

Neste/IVO (M.931), OJ 1998 C 218/4, 2 June 1998 .... 14.109

Neste Markkinionti Oy v. Yötuuli Ky e.a. (C-214/99) [2000] ECR I-11121,
    7 December 2000 .... 15.14

News Corp/BSkyB (M.5932), 21 December 2010 .... 14.129

Newscorp/Telepiù (M.2876), OJ 2004 L 110/73, 2 April 2003 .... 14.71

Nokia/Navteq (M.4942), 2 July 2008 .... 14.10, 14.62, 14.63, 14.75

Nokia/Siemens (M.4297), 13 November 2006 .... 14.39

Norddeutsche Affinerie/Cumerio (M.4781), 23 January 2008 .... 14.16, 14.21, 14.28, 14.58

Novartis/Glaxosmithkline Oncology Business (M.7275), 28 January 2015 .... 14.14, 14.145

Nynas/Shell/Harburg Refinery (M.6360), 2 September 2013 .... 14.72

NXP Semiconductors/Freescale Semiconductor (M.7585), 17 September 2015 .... 14.147

Omnitel (M.538), OJ 1995 C96/3, 27 March 1995 .... 14.149

Oracle/Sun Microsystems (M.5529), 21 January 2010 .... 14.77

Pepsico/Pepsi Americas (M.5632), 26 October 2009 .... 14.86

Philips/Lucent Technologies II (M.1358), OJ 1999 C 39/13, 6 January 1999 .... 14.152

Pilkington/SIV (M.358), OJ 1994 L 15/24, 21 December 1993 .... 14.27

Plastic Omnium/Faurecia Exterior Automotive Business (M.7893), 11 July 2016 .... 14.23,
                                                                                                                          14.61

PO/Royal Nedlloyd/Po Nedlloyd (M.3379), 29 March 2004 .... 14.12

Post Danmark A/S v. Konkurrencerâdet (C-23/14), ECLI:EU:C:2015:651,
    6 October 2015 .... 5.69, 5.83

Posten AB/Post Danmark A/S (M.5152), 21 April 2009 .... 14.26, 14.51, 14.69

Pre-Insulated Pipe Cartel (IV/35.691), OJ 1999 L 24/1, 21 October 1998 .... 13.108, 13.125

Privatisation of Automobile Craiova (former Daewoo), State aid (NN.59/2000),
    27 February 2008 .... 10.114

Rambus (COMP/38.636), 9 December 2009 .... 5.43, 5.111

Raw Tobacco Spain (COMP/C.38.238/B.2), 20 October 2004 .... 17.11, 17.12

Renova Industries/Sulzer (M.5469), 17 June 2009 .... 14.85

Repsol Butano/Shell Gas (LPG) (M.3664), 2 March 2005 .... 14.132

RTL/M6 (M.3330), OJ 2004 C 95/35, 12 March 2004 .... 14.83

RTL/Veronica/Endemol (M.553), OJ 1996 L 134/32, 20 September 1995 ...... 14.18, 14.198

Ryanair/Aer Lingus (M.4439), 27 June 2007 .... 14.131

Ryanair/Aer Lingus III (M.6663), 27 February 2013 .... 14.142–14.144, 14.169, 14.172

Sampo/Varma Samp/IF Holding (M.2676), OJ 2002 C 145/8, 18 December 2001 ..... 14.31

Sanofi/Synthélabo (M.1543), 28 July 1999 .... 14.175

Scandlines Sverige AB v. Port of Helsingborg (COMP/A.36.568), 23 July 2004 .... 5.119

SEB/Moulinex (M.2621), OJ 2005 L 138/18, 27 September 2001 .... 14.151

SevenOne Media/G+J Electronic Media Sales/Tomorrow Focus Portal/IP
    Deutschland/JV (M.5676), 21 January 2010 .... 14.125

Shell/Dea (M.2389), OJ 2003 L 15/35, 20 December 2001 .... 14.08

Siemens/Alstom Gas and Steam Turbines (M.3148), OJ 2003 C 207/25,
    10 July 2003 .... 14.37

Siemens/Dresser-Rand (M.7429), 29 June 2015 .... 14.40

Slovakian postal legislation (C(2008) 5912), 7 October 2008 .... 9.09

SoFFin/Hypo Real Estate (M.5508), 14 May 2009 .... 14.110

Sony/Mubadala/EMI Music Publishing (M.6459), 19 April 2012 .... 14.94

STX/Aker Yards (M.4956), 5 May 2008 .... 14.51

Sugar beet (IV/32.414), OJ 1990 L 31/32, 19 December 1989 .... 17.15

Tech Data Europe/Brightstar Europe/Triade Holding (M.5903), 22 September
    2010 .... 14.108

Telefónica Deutschland/E-Plus (M.7018), 2 July 2015 .... 14.168

Telia/Telenor (M.1439), OJ 2001 L 40/01, 13 October 1999 .... 14.49

Telos (IV/29.895), OJ 1981 L 58/19, 25 November 1981 .... 13.66

Tetra Laval/Sidel (M.2416), OJ 2004 L 038/01, 30 January 2002 .... 14.156

Tetra Laval/Sidel (M.3255), 7 July 2004 .... 14.175

Thomas Cook Group/Gold Medal International (M.5462), 30 March 2009 .... 14.88

T-Mobile Austria – Tele.ring (M.3916) (Press release IP/06/535; IP/06/1417),
    26 April 2006 .... 14.45

TPV/Philips monitors and colour TVs (M.5964), 9 November 2010 .... 14.135

TomTom/Tele Atlas (M.4854), 14 May 2008 .... 14.10, 14.62, 14.63, 14.75

Total Produce/Haluco/JV (M.5201), 11 August 2006 .... 14.105

Tui/First Choice (M.4600), 4 June 2007 .... 14.09

UBS/Mister Minit (M.940), OJ 1997 C 232/5, 9 July 1997 .... 14.136, 14.137

Universal Music Group/EMI (M.6458), 21 September 2012 .... 14.35, 14.54

UPS/TNT Express (M.6570), 30 January 2013 .... 14.141

Valeo/Robert Bosch/JV (M.2046), OJ 2001 C 270/6, 28 July 2000 .... 14.102

Various measures and the State aid invested by Spain in 'Terra Mítica SA', a theme
    park near Benidorm (Alicante), OJ 2003 L 91/23, 2 August 2002 .... 10.107

Welded steel mesh (31.553), OJ 1989 L 260, 2 August 1989 .... 13.178

Whirlpool/Privileg Rights (M.5859), 7 July 2010 .... 14.89

WPP v. Cordiant (M.3209), OJ 2003 C 212/9, 23 June 2003 .... 14.152

Zimmer/Biomet (M.7265), 30 March 2015 .... 14.146

European Commission Human Rights cases

CFDT v. European Communities (no 8030/77), DR 13, 10 July 1978 .... 18.15, 18.16

M&Co v. Germany (no 13258/87), DR 64, 9 February 1990 .... 18.17, 18.19, 18.21, 18.24

European Court of Human Rights

Airey v. Ireland (no 6289/73), Series A no 32, 9 October 1979 .... 18.07, 24.127, 24.129, 25.46

Al-Adsani v. the United Kingdom (no 35763/97) EHRC 2001-XI, 21 November 2001 ....18.14

Albert and Le Compte v. Belgium (no 7299/75 and 7496/76), Series A no 58, 10 February 1983 .... 24.48, 24.69

Allenet de Ribemont v. France (no 15175/89), Series A no 308, 10 February 1995 ..... 25.01, 25.05, 25.06

Ankerl v. Switzerland, ECHR 1996-V, 23 October 1996 .... 24.88

A.P., M.P. and T.P. v. Switzerland (no 41545/98), ECHR 1997-V, 29 August 1997 ..... 24.18

Artico v. Italy (no 6694/74), Series A no 37, 13 May 1980 .... 18.07, 25.23

Ashingdane v. the United Kingdom (no 8225/78), Series A no. 93, 28 May 1985 ...... 24.58, 24.61

Axen v. Germany, Series A no 72, 8 December 1983 .... 24.118

Baokaya and Okçuoglu v. Turkey, ECHR 1999-IV, 8 July 1999 .... 26.18

Barberà, Messegué and Jabardo v. Spain (no 10590/83), Series A no 146, 6 December 1988 .... 25.04

Bendenoun v. France, Series A no 284, 24 February 1994 .... 24.70

Benthem v. the Netherlands (no 8848/80), Series A no 97, 23 October 1985 .... 24.10

Bernh Larsen Holding AS a.o. v. Norway (no. 24117/08), unreported, 14 March 2013 .... 19.04

Borgers v. Belgium (Series A no 214-B), 30 October 1991 .... 24.77

Bosphorus Hava Yollari v. Ireland (no 45036/98), ECHR 2005-VI, 30 June 2005 .... 18.17–18.23

Brandstetter v. Austria (no 11170/84, 12876/87 and 13468/87), Series A no 211, 28 August 1991 .... 24.76

Brusco v. France (no 1466/07), 14 October 2010 .... 24.125, 25.35

Bryan v. the United Kingdom, Series A no 335-A, 22 November 1995 .... 24.35

Buscemi v. Italy (no 29569/95), ECHR 1999-VI, 16 September 1999 .... 24.39

Camenzind v. Switzerland (no 136/96), ECHR 1997-VIII, 16 December 1997 .... 19.12, 19.16, 19.31, 19.35, 19.37, 19.49

Campbell v. the United Kingdom (no 13590/88), Series A no 233, 25 March 1992 .... 19.56

Campbell and Fell v. the United Kingdom, Series A no 80, 28 June 1984 .... 19.56, 24.17, 24.19, 24.22

Cantoni v. France, ECHR 1996-V, 15 November 1996 .... 26.16, 26.18

Chappell v. UK (no 10461/83), Series A no 152-A, 30 March 1989 ...... 19.20, 19.22, 19.23, 19.48

Chevrol v. France (no 49636/99), ECHR 2003-III, 13 February 2003 .... 24.44, 24.50

Clinique des Acacias and others v. France (65399/01, 65406/ 01, 65405/01 and 65407/01), 13 October 2005 .... 24.84, 24.86

Coëme and others v. Belgium, nos. 32492/96, 32547/96, 32548/96, 33209/ 96 and 33210/96) ECHR 2000-VII, 22 June 2000 .... 26.01, 26.03, 26.16, 26.18

Comingersoll S.A. v. Portugal (no 35382/97), ECHR 2000-IV, 6 April 2000 .... 24.109

Compagnie des Gaz de Pétrole Primagaz v. France (no. 29613/08), 21 December 2010 .... 24.64

Coöperatieve Producentenorganisatie van de Nederlandse Kokkelvisserij U.A. v.
  The Netherlands (no 13645/05), unreported, 20 January 2009 .... 18.15, 18.16, 18.25
Colas Est v. France (no 37971/97), ECHR 2002-III, 16 April 2002 ...... 18.04, 19.02, 19.06,
  19.13, 19.21, 19.29, 19.41
Corigliano v. Italy (no 8304/78), Series A no 57, 10 December 1982 .... 24.26
Cossey v. the United Kingdom, Series A no 184, 27 September 1990 .... 18.04
C.R. v. the United Kingdom, Series A no 335-C, 22 November 1995 .... 26.01, 26.16
De Cubber v. Belgium, Series A no 86, 26 October 1984 .... 24.73
Delcourt v. Belgium (no. 2689/65), Series A no. 11,17 January 1970 .... 24.106
Del Sol v. France (no 46800/99), 26 February 2002 .... 24.128
Delta Pekárny v. Czech Republic (no. 97/11), unreported, 2 October 2014 .... 19.30, 19.46
Demebukov v. Bulgaria (no 68020/01), 28 February 2008 .... 24.119
Deweer v. Belgium (no 6903/75), Series A no 35, 27 February 1980 ..... 18.08, 24.15, 24.25,
  25.01, 25.22
Diennet v. France (no 25/1994), Series A no 325 A, 26 September 1995 .... 24.41
Dombo Beheer v. the Netherlands (no. 14448/88), Series A no. 274,
  27 October 1993 .... 24.88
Doorson v. the Netherlands (no 20524/92), ECHR 1996-II, 26 March 1996 .... 24.93
Eckle v. Germany (no. 8130/78), 15 July 1982 .... 24.107
E.K. v. Turkey (no 28496/95), 7 February 2002 .... 26.17, 26.18
Engel and others v. the Netherlands (no 5100/71, 5101/71, 5102/71, 5354/72 and
  5370/72), Series A no 22-1, 8 June 1976 .... 24.14, 27.03, 27.04
Ernst and others v. Belgium (no 33400/96), unreported, 15 July 2003 .... 19.42
Ezeh and Connors v. the United Kingdom (nos. 39665/98 and 40086/98), ECHR 2003-X,
  9 November 2003 .... 24.14, 24.19
Fayed v. United Kingdom (no 17101/90), Series A no 294-B, 21 September 1994 ...... 24.68
Ferrazzini v. Italy (no. 44759/98), ECHR 2001-VII, 12 July 2001 .... 24.12
Fey v. Austria, Series A no 255-A, 24 February 1993 .... 24.38
Findlay v. United Kingdom (no 22107/93) ECHR 1997-I, 25 February 1997 ... 24.38, 24.73
Fischer v. Austria, Series A no 312, 26 April 1995 .... 24.46, 24.51
Funke v. France (no 10828/84), Series A no 256-A, 5 February 1993 .... 19.14, 19.31, 19.33,
  19.40, 19.43, 25.25, 25.30, 25.36
G. v. France, Series A no 325-B, 27 September 1995 .... 26.07, 26.17, 26.18
Gäfgen v. Germany (no 22978/05), 1 June 2010 .... 24.96
Göç v. Turkey (no 36590/97), ECHR 2002-V 24.118
Golder v. the United Kingdom (no 4451/70), Series A no 18, 21 February 1975 .... 18.06,
  18.13, 24.57, 24.60
Gradinger v. Austria (no 15963/90), Series A no 328-C, 23 October 1995 .... 24.46, 24.52,
  24.70
Grieves v. the United Kingdom (no 57067/00), ECHR 2003-XII, 16 December
  2003 .... 24.38
Guisset v. France (no 33933/96), ECHR 2000-IX 24.22
Hadjianastassiou v. Greece, Series A No 252, 16 December 1992 .... 24.98
Haralampiev v. Bulgaria (no 29648/03), 24 April 2012 .... 24.101
Harju v. Finland (no. 56716/09), 15 February 2011 .... 19.28, 19.55
Heaney and McGuiness v. Ireland (no 4720/97), ECHR 2000-XII,
  21 December 2000 .... 25.34

Heino v. Finland (no 56720/09), ECHR 2011, 15 February 2011 ..... 19.03, 19.18, 19.28, 19.55

Imbrioscia v. Switzerland (no 13972/88), Series A no 275,
24 November 1993 .... 24.67, 24.120

Ireland v. the United Kingdom, Series A no 25, 18 January 1978 .... 18.01

Jalloh v. Germany (no 54810/00), 11 July 2006 .... 25.31, 25.32

James and others v. the United Kingdom (no 8793/79), Series A no 98,
21 February 1986 .... 24.11

Janosevic v. Sweden (no 34619/97), ECHR 2002-VII, 23 July 2002 .... 25.17

J.B. v. Switzerland (no 31827/96), ECHR 2001-VI, 3 May 2001 .... 24.18, 25.38, 25.42

John Murray v. the United Kingdom, ECHR 1996-I, 8 February 1996 .... 24.121, 24.122,
25.07, 25.26, 25.30, 25.44

Johnston a.o. v. Ireland, Series A no 112, 18 December 1986 .... 18.09

Jussila v. Finland (no 73053/01), ECHR 2006-XIV, 23 November 2006 .... 24.14, 24.22

Kafkaris v. Cyprus (no 21906/04), 12 February 2008 .... 26.01, 26.03, 26.04, 26.08

Khan v. the United Kingdom (no 35394/97), 12 May 2000 .... 24.95

Klass and others v. Germany (no 5029/71), Series A no. 28,
6 September 1978 .... 19.11, 19.14, 19.31, 19.33

Kokkinakis v. Greece, Series A no 260-A, 25 May 1993 .... 26.13, 26.18

König v. Germany (no 6232/73), Series A no 27, 28 June 1978 .... 24.09, 24.107, 24.108

Kopp v. Switzerland (no 13/1997), ECHR 1998-II, 25 March 1998 .... 19.25

Kraska v. Switzerland, Series A no 254-B, 19 April 1993 .... 24.90

Kress v. France (no 39594/98), 7 June 2001 .... 24.90

Kreuz v. Poland, ECHR 2001-VI, 19 June 2001 .... 24.127

Kruslin v. France (no 11801/85), Series A no 176-A, 24 April 1990 .... 19.17, 19.21

Kudla v. Poland (no 30210/96), ECHR 2000-XI, 26 October 2000 .... 24.01, 24.113

Langborger v. Sweden, Series A no 155, 22 June 1989 .... 24.35

Lavents v. Latvia (no 58442/00), 28 November 2002 .... 24.39

Leander v. Sweden (no 9248/81), Series A no 116, 26 March 1987 .... 19.19

Le Compte and others v. Belgium (no 6878/75 and 7238/ 75), Series A no 43,
23 June 1981 .... 24.29, 24.43, 24.47, 24.48, 24.66

Lobo Machado v. Portugal (no 15764/89), ECHR 1996-I, 20 February 1996 .... 24.78

Loizidou v. Turkey (no 15318/89), Series A no 310, 23 March 1995 ...... 18.02, 18.05, 18.12

Lutz v. Germany (no 9912/82), Series A no 123, 25 August 1987 .... 24.17

Magyar Helsinki Bizottság v. Hungary (no. 18030/11), unreported,
8 November 2016 .... 18.03

Malone v. the United Kingdom (no 8691/79), Series A no 82, 2 August 1984 .... 19.24

Mamidakis v. Greece (no 35533/04), 11 January 2007 .... 21.01, 26.23

Margareta and Roger Andersson v. Sweden, Series A no 226-A, 25 February 1992 .... 26.07,
26.17

Martinie v. France (no 58675/00), 12 April 2006 .... 24.118

Mastepan v. Russia (no 3708/03), 14 January 2010 .... 19.51

Matthews v. the United Kingdom (no 24833/94), ECHR 1999-I, 18 February 1999 ... 18.20

McVicar v. the United Kingdom (no 6311/99), 7 May 2002 .... 24.126

Menarini Diagnostics v. Italy, unreported, 27 September 2011 .... 24.20, 24.45, 24.54,
24.71

Medenica v. Switzerland (no 20491/92), ECHR 2001-VI, 14 June 2001 .... 24.101

Minelli v. Switzerland (no 8660/79), Series A no 62, 25 March 1983 .... 25.01, 25.02

Neumeister v. Austria (no 1936/6), Series A no 87, p. 26, 27 June 1968 .... 24.23, 24.105

Nideröst-Huber v. Switzerland (no. 18990/91), ECHR Reports 1997-I
    18 February 1997 .... 24.78, 24.88

Niemietz v. Germany (no 13710/88), Series A No. 251-B,
    16 December 1992 .... 19.01, 19.06, 19.09, 19.15, 19.39

O'Halloran and Francis v. the United Kingdom (nos 15809/02 and 25624/02),
    29 June 2007 .... 25.32, 25.38, 25.39

Olsson v. Sweden (no 10465/83), Series A no 130, 24 March 1988 .... 19.32

Olujic v. Croatia (no 22330/05), ECHR 2009, 5 February 2009 .... 24.31, 24.35, 24.38,
    24.39

Ortenberg v. Austria, Series A no 295-B, 25 November 1994 .... 24.46

Öztürk v. Germany (no 8544/79), Series A no 73, 21 February 1984 ...... 24.16, 24.27, 24.70

P., C. and S. v. the United Kingdom, ECHR 2002-VI, 16 July 2002 .... 24.127

Padovani v. Italy, Series A no 257-B, 26 February 1993 .... 24.38

Pedro Ramos v. Switzerland (no 10111/06), 14 October 2010 .... 24.128

Petri Sallinen and others v. Finland (no 50882/99), ECHR 2005-VIII,
    27 September 2005 .... 19.26, 19.27, 19.28

Pham Hoang v. France (no 13191/87), Series A no 243, 25 September 1992 .... 15.03

Piersack v. Belgium, Series A no 53, 1 October 1982 .... 24.38

Pizzati v. Italy (no 62361/00), 29 March 2006 .... 24.114

Poitrimol v. France, Series A no 277-A, 23 November 1993 .... 24.119

Prikyan and Angelova v. Bulgaria (no 44624/99), 16 February 2006 .... 24.81

Puscasu v. Germany (no 45793/07), 29 September 2009 .... 24.128

Quaranta v. Switzerland (no 12744/87), Series A no 205, 24 May 1991 .... 24.02

Ravon v. France (no 18497/03), ECHR 2008, 21 February 2008 .... 24.13, 24.30, 24.59,
    24.63

Remli v. France (no 16839/90), ECHR 1996, 23 April 1996 .... 24.37

Ringeisen v. Austria (no 2614/65), Series A no 13, 16 July 1971 .... 24.08, 24.28, 24.40

Rolf Gustafson v. Sweden, ECHR 1997-IV, 1 July 1997 .... 24.31

Rowe and Davis v. the United Kingdom (no 11170/84, 12876/87 and 13468/87),
    ECHR 2000-II, 16 February 2000 .... 24.80, 24.92, 24.93, 24.94

S v. Switzerland, Series A no 220, 28 November 1991 .... 19.56

Saadi v. the United Kingdom (no. 13229/03), ECHR 2008, 29 January 2008 .... 18.11

Salduz v. Turkey (no 36391/02), unreported, 27 November 2008 .... 18.07, 24.67, 24.100,
    24.122, 24.123

Saunders v. the United Kingdom (no 43/1994), ECHR 1996-VI, 17 December
    1996 .... 25.27, 25.29, 25.33, 25.37, 25.42

Schenk v. Switzerland (no 10862/84), Series A no 140, 12 July 1988 .... 24.95

Scoppola v. Italy (no. 10249/03), unreported, 17 September 2009 .... 26.01, 26.11, 26.13,
    26.14

Scordino v. Italy (no 1) (no 36813/97), ECHR 2006-V 23.09

Sejdovic v. Italy (no 56581/00), ECHR 2006-II, 1 March 2006 .... 24.101

Sergey Zolotukhin v. Russia (no 14939/03), 10 February 2009 .... 27.03, 27.04, 27.06,
    27.08, 27.09

Silver a.o. v. the United Kingdom (no 5947/72), Series A no 61, 25 March 1983 .... 24.62

Silvester's Horeca Service v. Belgium (no 47650/99), 4 March 2003 .... 24.45, 24.53, 24.70

Skondrianos v. Greece (no 63000/00, 74291/01 and 74292/01), 18 December 2003 .... 24.84

Smirnov v. Russia (no 71362/01), 7 June 2007 .... 19.36, 19.43

Société Bouygues Télécom (no 2324/08), 13 March 2012 .... 24.90

Société Canal Plus v. France (no 29408/0/8), 21 December 2010 .... 24.64

Sociéteté Métallurgique Liotard Frères v. France (no 29598/0890), 5 May 2011 .... 24.64

Société Stenuit v. France, Series A no 232-A), 27 February 1992 .... 24.22

Soering v. the United Kingdom, Series A no 161, 7 July 1989 .... 18.10

Sorvisto v. Finland (no 19348/04), 13 January 2009, ECHR 2009 .... 19.25, 19.27

Steel and Morris v. the United Kingdom, ECHR 2005-II, 15 February 2005 .... 24.126

Stubbings and others v. the United Kingdom, ECHR 1996-IV, 22 October 1996 .... 24.61

S.W. v. the United Kingdom, Series A no 335-B, 22 November 1995 ... 26.01, 26.02, 26.16,
26.18

Swedish Engine Drivers' Union, Series A no 20, 6 February 1976 .... 24.62

Tamosius v. the United Kingdom (no 62002/00), ECHR 2002-VIII,
19 September 2002 .... 19.38, 19.50

Telfner v. Austria (no 33501/96), ECHR 2001-V, 20 March 2001 .... 25.45

Terra Woningen B.V. v. the Netherlands, ECHR 1996-VI, 17 December 1996 .... 24.44,
24.49

Tolstoy Miloslavsky v. the United Kingdom, Series A no 316-B, 13 July 1995 .... 24.61

T.P. and K.M. v. the United Kingdom (no. 28945/95), 10 May 2001 .... 24.61

Tyrer v. the United Kingdom, Series A no 26, 25 April 1978 .... 18.04

United Communist Party of Turkey and others v. Turkey (no 133/1996), ECHR 1998-I,
30 January 1998 .... 18.18

V. v. Finland (no 40412/98), unreported, 24 April 2007 .... 24.94

Van Droogenbroeck v. Belgium, Series A no 50, 24 June 1982 .... 24.62

Van Leuven and De Meyere v. Belgium (no. 6878/75; 7238/75), 23 June 1981 .... 24.29,
24.43, 24.47, 24.66

Varga v. Romania (no 73957/01), 1 April 2008 .... 19.45

Vermeulen v. Belgium (no 19075/91), ECHR 1996-I, 20 February 1996 .... 24.77, 24.79

Vinci Construction and GTM Génie Civil et Services v. France (nos 63629/10 and
60567/10), unreported, 2 April 2015 .... 19.30, 19.47

Waite and Kennedy v. Germany (no 26083/94), ECHR 1999-I, 18 February 1999 .... 24.61

Wemhoff v. Germany (no. 2122/64), Series A no. 7, 27 June 1968 ...... 24.24, 24.102, 24.104

Wieser and Bicos v. Austria (no 74336/01), unreported, 16 October 2007 .... 19.10, 19.34,
19.44

X v. the United Kingdom, Series A no 46, 5 November 1981 .... 24.62

Yvon v. France (no. 44962/98), unreported, 24 April 2003 .... 24.89

Zaichenko v. Russia (no 39660/02), 18 February 2010 .... 24.124, 25.46

Zlinsat, spol. s.r.o., v. Bulgaria (no 57785/00, 15 June 2006 .... 24.31

Zumtobel v. Austria, Series A no 268-A, 21 September 1993 .... 24.46

European Court of Justice

3F v. Commission (T-30/03 RENV) [2011] ECR II-6651, 27 September
2011 .... 11.22

A. Brünsteiner GmbH, Autohaus Hilgert GmbH v. Bayerische Motorenwerke AG (BMW)
(Joined Cases C-376/05 and C-377/05) [2006] ECR I-11383,
30 November 2006 .... 15.19, (p.672)

Aalberts Industries NV (T-385/06) [2011] ECR II-1223, 24 March 2011 .... 13.16
Aalborg Portland a.o. v. Commission (Joined Cases C-204/00, C-205/00, C-211/00,
    C-213/00, C-217/00 and C-219/00 P) [2004] ECR I-123, 7 January 2004 .... 4.03,
        4.117, 13.03, 13.83, 13.167, 13.202, 13.214, 23.12, 23.15, 23.29,
        23.30, 24.97, 25.10, 25.11, 25.24, 27.02
AC-Treuhand v. Commission (T-99/04) [2008] ECR II-1501,
    8 July 2008 .... 4.06, 4.76, 13.42, 13.59, 13.248, 26.18
Accession ECHR, Opinion 2/94 [1996] ECR 1759, 28 March 1996 .... 3.03–3.06, 3.11
ACF Chemiefarma v. Commission (41/69) [1970] ECR 661, 15 July 1970 .... 4.68, 4.243,
        4.253, 13.222, 13.224, 23.16
Activision Blizzard Germany v. Commission (C-260/09 P) [2011] ECR I-419,
    10 February 2011 .... 4.77, 13.02
Administración del Estado v. Xunta de Galicia (C-71/04) [2005] ECR I-7419,
    21 July 2005 .... 11.54, 11.83
Adria-Wien Pipeline (C-143/99) [2001] ECR I-8365, 8 November 2001 .... 10.39, 10.42
Adriatica di Navigazione (T-61/99) [2003] ECR II-5349, 11 December 2003 .... 13.08,
        13.94
Adriatica di Navigazione (C-111/04 P) [2006] ECR I-22, 16 February 2006 .... 13.94
AEG -Telefunken v. Commission (107/82) [1983] ECR 3151, 25 October 1983 .... 4.79,
        4.188, 4.284, 4.295, 4.299
Aer Lingus v. Commission (T-411/07R) [2008] ECR II-411,
    18 March 2008 .... 5.156, 13.28, 14.160
Aer Lingus Group v. Commission (T-411/07) [2010] ECR II-03691,
    6 July 2010 .... 14.116–14.119, 14.148, 14.158, 14.159, 14.192
Aéroports de Paris v. Commission (T-128/98) [2000] ECR II-3929,
    12 December 2000 .... 4.45
Aéroports de Paris v. Commission (C-82/01) [2002] ECR I-9297, 24 October 2002 ... 5.47
AG2R Prévoyance v. Beaudout Père et Fils SARL (C-437/09) [2011] ECR I-973,
    3 March 2011 .... 4.16, 9.45
Agrofert Holding v. Commission (T-111/07) [2010] ECR II-00128, 7 July 2010 ...... 14.181
Ahlström Osakeyhtiö and others v. Commission (Joined Cases C-89/85, C-104/85,
    C-114/85, C-116/85, C-117/85, C-125/85 and C-129/85) [1993] ECR I-1307,
    31 March 1993 .... 13.160
Ahlström Osakeythoe and others v. Commission (Joined Cases 89, 104, 114, 116, 117 and
    125–129/85) [1988] ECR 5193, 27 September 1988 .... 4.22, 4.105, 4.107
Ahlströ, Osakeyhtiö (Joined Cases C-89/85 C-104/85, C-114/85, C-116/85, C-117/85,
    C-125/85, C-126/85, C-127/85, C-128/85 and C-129/85) [1993] ECR I-1307,
    31 March 1993 .... 22.02
Air France (II) (T-358/94) [1996] ECR II-2109, 12 December 1996 .... 10.07, 10.12,
        10.100, 10.101
Air France (T-371/94 and T-394/94) [1998] ECR II-2405, 25 June 1998 .... 10.101
Air One SpA v. Commission (T-395/04) [2006] ECR II-1343, 10 May 2006 .... 11.41
Air Tours v. Commission (T-342/99) [2002] ECR II-2585, 6 June 2002 ... 5.54, 5.56, 14.56,
        14.64, 14.65
Aiscat v. Commission (T-182/10), ECLI:EU:T:2013:9, 15 January 2013 .... 10.08
Åkerberg Fransson (C-617/10), ECLI:EU:C:2013:105, 26 February 2013 ... 3.02, 3.10, 3.14,
        27.05, 28.01, 28.02

Aktionsgemeinschaft Recht und Eigentum eV (ARE) (C-78/03)[2005] ECR I-10737,
        13 December 2005 .... 11.91
AKZO Chemie v. Commission (53/85) [1986] ECR 1965, 24 June 1986 ..... 13.232, 13.234
AKZO Chemie v. Commission (C-62/86) [1991] ECR I-3359, 3 July 1991 .... 5.14, 5.30,
                                                                                                        5.88
AkzoNobel Chemicals Ltd and Akcros Chemicals Ltd v. Commission (T-1125/05) [2007]
        ECR II-5049, 17 September 2007 .... 13.181
Akzo Nobel Chemicals Ltd v. Commission (C-97/08 P) [2009] ECR I-8237, 23 April 2009
        (opinion of AG Kokott) 25.15
Akzo Nobel Chemicals Ltd v. Commission (C-97/08 P) [2009] ECR I-8237,
        10 September 2009 .... 4.57, 13.180, 13.181, 25.16, 25.17, 26.25
AkzoNobel Chemicals Ltd and Akcros Chemicals Ltd v. Commission (Joined Cases
        T-125/03 and T-253/03) [2007] ECR II-3523, 17 September 2007 .... 13.52, 13.54,
                                                                                        13.56, 13.57, 13.142, 19.59
Akzo Nobel Chemicals Ltd and Akcros Chemicals Ltd v. Commission (C-550/07 P) [2010]
        ECR I-08301, 14 September 2010 .... 6.03, 8.02, 19.59
Albany International BV v. Stichting Bedrijfspensioenfonds Textielindustrie (C-67/96)
        [1999] ECR I-5751, 21 September 1999 .... 4.43, 9.23, 9.42
Alcan Deutschland (C-24/95) [1997] ECR I-1591, 20 March 1997 .... 11.102, 11.110,
                                                                                                11.119, 11.120
Alcoa Trasformazioni v. Commission (C-194/09 P) [2011] ECR I-6311,
        21 July 2011 .... 11.03
Alitalia v. Commission (T-296/97) [2000] ECR II-3871, 12 December 2000 .... 10.28,
                                                                                                10.101
Alliance One International v. Commission (T-41/05) [2011] ECR II-7101,
        12 October 2011 ....13.163, 13.192
Alliance One International v. Commission (C-679/11 P), ECLI:EU:C:2013:606,
        26 September 2013 .... 13.122, 13.185
Allianz Hungária Biztosító and others (C-32/11), ECLI:EU:2013:160,
        14 March 2013 .... 4.11, 4.275
Almamet GmbH v. Commission (T-410/09), ECLI:EU:T:2012:676,
        12 December 2012 .... 13.12, 13.49
Alouminion v. Commission (T-542/11), ECLI:EU:T:2014:859, 8 October 2014 .... 11.14
Alrosa v. Commission (T-170/06) [2007] ECR II-2601, 11 July 2007 .... 5.72, 13.29, 13.226
Alrosa v. Commission (C-441/07) [2010] ECR I-05949, 29 June 2010 .... 5.72, 13.30,
                                                                                                13.229
Alsatel (247/86) [1988] ECR 5987, 5 October 1988 .... 5.24
AltmarkTrans (C-280/00) [2003] ECR I-7747, 24 July 2003 .... 10.31, 10.32, 10.63, 10.66
Amann & Söhne and Cousin Filterie v. Commission (T-446/05) [2010] ECR II-1255,
        28 April 2010 .... 4.119, 13.45, 13.65, 13.69, 13.97
AM&S Europe Ltd v. Commission (C-155/79) [1982] ECR 1575, 18 May 1982 ...... 13.51,
                                                                        13.55, 13.57, 19.57, 19.59, 23.13, (p. 888)
Ambulanz Glöckner v. Landkreis Südwestpfalz (C-475/99) [2001] ECR I-8089,
        25 October 2001 .... 9.16, 9.24, 9.43
Anic v. Commission (T-6/89) [1991] ECR II-1623, 17 December 1991 .... 13.199
Annibaldi (C-309/96) [1997] ECR I-7493, 18 December 1997 .... (p. 883)

AOK Bundesverband and others (Joined Cases C-261, 306, 354 and 355/01) [2004] ECR
I-2493, 16 March 2004 .... 4.49
Archer Daniels Midland v. Commission (T-224/00) [2003] ECR II-2597,
9 July 2003 .... 13.138, 13.165
Archer Daniels Midland v. Commission (C-397/03 P) [2006] ECR I-4429,
18 May 2006 .... 13.166, 26.10, 26.22
Archer Daniels Midlands v. Commission (C-511/06 P) [2009] ECR I-5843,
9 July 2009 .... 23.22, 23.23
ArcelorMittal Luxemburg and others v. Commission (T-405/06) [2009] ECR II-789,
31 March 2009 .... 4.07
ArcelorMittal Luxembourg SA v. Commission (C-201/09 P and C-216/09 P) [2011]
ECR I-2239, 29 March 2011 .... 13.217
ARD v. Commission (T-158/00) [2003] ECR II-3825, 30 September 2003 .... 14.154
Aristrain v. Commission (T-156/94) [1999] ECR II-645, 11 March 1999 .... 13.92
Arkema France v. Commission (T-343/08) [2011] ECR II-2287, 17 May 2011 .... 13.167
Arnold André (C-434/02) [2004] ECR I-11825, 14 December 2004 .... 26.20
Asjes (Joined Cases 209–213/84) [1986] ECR 1425, 30 April 1986 .... 2.06, 4.06. 7.01, 7.02
ASM Brescia SpA v. Comune di Rodengo Saiano (C-347/06) [2008] ECR I-5641,
17 July 2008 .... 9.08
ASML (C-283/05) [2006] ECR I-12041, 14 December 2006 .... 24.98
Asnef-Equifax (C-238/05) [2006] ECR I-11125, 23 November 2006 .... 4.215, 4.230, 4.267
Asociación de Estaciones de Servicio de Madrid and Federación Catalana de Estaciones de
Servicio v. Commission (T-95/03) [2006] ECR II-4739, 12 December 2006 ...... 11.27
Asociación Nacional de Empresas Forestales (Asemfo) v. Transformación Agraria SA
(Tragsa) and Administración del Estado (C-295/05) [2007] ECR I-2999,
19 April 2007 .... 9.07
Association Belge des Consommateurs test-chats ASBL v. Commission (T-224/10) [2011]
ECR II-07177, 12 October 2011 .... 14.167, 14.187, 14.188
Association Vent De Colère! Fédération nationale and others v. Ministre de l'Écologie
(C-262–12), ECLI:EU:C:2013:851, 19 December 2013 .... 10.10
Asteris and others v. Greece and EEC (Joined Cases 106–120/87) [1988] ECR 5515,
27 September 1988 .... 10.125
AstraZeneca v. Commission (T-321/05) [2010] ECR II-02805, 1 July 2010 .... 5.21, 5.65,
5.132, 5.144, 13.70
AstraZeneca v. Commission (C-457/10 P), ECLI:EU:C:2012:770,
6 December 2012 .... 5.21, 5.65, 5.132, 5.144
Athinaïki Techniki v. Commission (C-362/09 P) [2010] ECR I-13275,
16 December 2010 .... 11.37
Atlantic Container Line and others v. Commission (T-395/94) [2002] ECR II-875,
28 February 2002 .... 4.242
Atlantic Container Line and others v. Commission (Joined Cases T-191 and
T-212–214/98) [2003] ECR II-3275, 30 September 2003 .... 4.138
Austria v. Commission (C-99/98) [2001] ECR I-1101, 15 February 2001 .... 11.20
Auto 24 SARL v. Jaguar Land Rover France SAS (C-158/11), ECLI:EU:C:2012:351,
14 June 2012 .... 4.298, 15.01, 16.01
Automec v. Commission (II) (T-24/90) [1992] ECR II-2223,
18 September 1992 .... 4.207, 16.04

Automobiles Peugeot and others v. Commission (T-23/90) [1990] ECR II-195,
    21 May 1990 .... 4.13, 16.03
Automobiles Peugeot SA and Peugeot SA v. Commission (T-23/90) [1991]
    ECR II-653, 12 July 1991 .... (p.672)
Automobiles Peugeot v. Commission (T-9/92) [1993] ECR II-493, 22 April 1993 ..... 4.213,
                                                                                    (p.672)
Automobiles Peugeot SA and Peugeot SA v. Commission (C-322/93 P) [1994]
    ECR I-2727, 16 June 1994 .... (p.672)
Auto Peter Petschenig GmbH v. Toyota Frey Austria GmbH (C-273/06) [2007]
    ECR I-14, 26 January 2007 .... (p.672)
Banco de Crédito Industrial v. Ayuntamiento de Valencia (C-387/92) [1994]
    ECR I-877, 15 March 1994 .... 10.119, 11.05
Banco Exterior de Espaæa (C-387/92) [1994] ECR I-877, 15 March 1994 .... 10.90
Bank Austria Creditanstalt AG v. Commission (T-198/03) [2006] ECR II-01429,
    30 May 2006 .... 13.232, 13.237, 13.238, 14.181
Banks (C-390/98) [2001] ECR I-6117, 20 September 2001 .... 11.121
BASF v. Commission (T-4/89) [1991] ECR II-1523, 12 December 1991 .... 4.106
BASF v. Commission (T-15/02) [2006] ECR II-497, 15 March 2006 .... 13.123
BASF and UCB v. Commission (Joined Cases T-101/05 and T-11/05) [2007]
    ECR II-4949, 12 December 2007 .... 13.123, 13.247
BAT v. Commission (35/83) [1985] ECR 363, 30 January 1985 .... 4.220
BAT and Reynolds v. Commission (Joined Cases 142 and 156/84) [1987] ECR 4487,
    17 November 1987 .... 4.160
Baustahlgewebe v. Commission (C-185/95 P) [1998] ECR I-8417,
    17 December 1998 .... 13.103, 23.02, 23.03, 23.26, 24.05, 24.103, 24.110, 24.115
Bayer v. Commission (T-41/96) [2000] ECR II-3383, 26 October 2000 .... 4.72, 4.84
Bayerische Motorenwerke AG v. ALD Auto-Leasing D GmbH (C-70/93) [1995]
    ECR I-3439, 24 October 1995 .... 15.10
BBC v. Commission (T-70/89) [1991] ECR II-535, 10 July 1991 .... 5.20
Béguelin Import (22/71) [1971] ECR 949, 25 November 1971 .... 4.19, 4.91, 4.158, 4.203
Belasco and others v. Commission (246/86) [1989] ECR 2117, 11 July 1989 .... 4.247
Belgian Sewing Thread (BST) v. Commission (T-452/05) [2010] ECR II-1373,
    28 April 2010 .... 13.136, 13.152
Belgische Radio en Televisie and société belge des auteurs, compositeurs et éditeurs v. SV
    SABAM and NV Fonior (SABAM) (C-127/73) [1974] ECR 51,
    30 January 1974 .... 5.01
Belgische Radio en Televisie and société belge des auteurs, compositeurs et éditeurs v.
    SV SABAM and NV Fonior (SABAM) (C-127/73) [1974] ECR 313,
    21 March 1974 .... 5.100, 9.26, 9.32
Belgium v. Commission (234/84) [1986] ECR 2263, 10 July 1986 .... 10.59, 10.92, 11.32
Belgium v. Commission (142/87) [1990] ECR I-959, 21 March 1990 .... 10.61, 11.110
Belgium v. Commission (C-56/93) [1996] ECR I-723, 29 February 1996 .... 10.21
Belgium v. Commission (Joined Cases C-356/90 and C-180/91) [1993] ECR I-2323,
    18 May 1993 .... 10.145
Belgium v. Deutsche Post and DHL International (C-148/09 P) [2011] ECR I-8573,
    22 September 2011 .... 11.28, 11.38
Belgium v. Commission (C-75/97) [1999] ECR I-03671, 17 June 1999 .... 10.41, 10.62

Benzine en Petroleum Handelsmaatschappij BV and others v. Commission (77/77)
[1978] ECR 1513, 29 June 1978 .... 5.74
Berlusconi a.o. (Joined Cases C-387/02, C-391/02 and C-403/02) [2005] ECR I-3565,
3 May 2005 .... 26.12
Bertelsmann and Sony Corporation of America v. Impala (Impala) (C-413/06)
[2008] ECR I-4951, 10 July 2008 .... 5.56, 14.06, 14.59, 14.65, 14.184, 14.185
BEUC v. Commission (T-256/97) [2000] ECR II-101, 27 January 2000 .... 14.187
Binon v. AMP (243/83) [1985] ECR 2015, 3 July 1985 .... 4.290, 4.295
BMW Belgium and others v. Commission (Joined Cases 32 and 36–82/78)
[1979] ECR 2435, 12 July 1979 .... 4.78, 15.08
BMW (C-70/93) [1985] ECR I-3439, 24 October 1995 .... 4.83
BNIC/Aubert (136/86) [1987] ECR 4789, 3 December 1987 .... 2.08
BNIC v. Clair (123/83) [1985] ECR 391, 30 January 1985 .... 2.05, 4.132, 4.144, 17.03
BNP Paribas and BNL v. Commission (C-452/10 P), ECLI:EU:C:2012:366,
21 June 2012 .... 10.47
Bodson v. Pompes funèbres (30/87) [1988] ECR 2479, 4 May 1988 .... 9.12
Boehringer Mannheim (45/69) [1970] ECR 769, 15 July 1970 .... 13.62, 13.63
Bolloré v. Commission (T-109/02) [2007] ECR II-947, 26 April 2007 .... 24.32
Bonda (C-489/10), ECLI:EU:C:2012:319, 5 June 2012 .... 27.04
BPB Industries and British Gypsum v. Commission (T-65/89) [1993] ECR II-389,
1 April 1993 .... 5.46, 5.76, 5.141
BPB Industries and British Gypsum v. Commission (C-310/93 P) [1995] ECR I-865,
6 April 1995 .... 23.14, 23.25
BPB v. Commission (T-53/03) [2008] ECR II-1333, 8 July 2008 .... 4.118, 4.268
Brasserie De Haecht (23/67) [1967] ECR 511, 12 December 1967 .... 4.157, 4.185, 4.310
Brasserie De Haecht II (48/72) [1973] ECR 77, 6 February 1973 .... 4.204
Brasserie Nationale and others v. Commission (Joined Cases T-49 and 51/02)
[2005] ECR II-3033, 27 July 2005 .... 4.74, 13.111
Borelli (C-97/91) [1992] ECR I-63133 December 1992 .... (p.779), 24.03
Brentjens' Handelsonderneming BV v. Stichting Bedrijfspensioenfonds voor de Handel in
Bouwmaterialen (Joined Cases C-115 and 117/97) [1999] ECR I-6025,
21 September 1999 .... 9.23, 9.42
British Aggregates a.o. v. Commission (T-359/04) [2010] ECR II-4227,
9 September 2010 .... 11.31
British Aggregates v. Commission (C-487/06 P) [2008] ECR I-0505,
22 December 2008 .... 10.45, 11.92
British Aggregates v. Commission (T-210/02), ECLI:EU:T:2012:110, 7 March 2012 .. 10.46
British Airways and others v. Commission (T-371/94 and T-394/94) [1998] ECR II-2405,
25 June 1998 .... 11.51
British Airways v. Commission (T-219/99) [2003] ECR II-5917, 17 December 2003 ... 5.11
British Airways v. Commission (C-95/04) [2007] ECR I-2331,
15 March 2007 .... 5.80, 5.125, 5.146
British American Tobacco Co Ltd v. Commission (Joined Cases 142 and 156/84) [1986]
ECR 1899, 18 June 1986 .... 13.221
British Leyland v. Commission (226/84) [1986] ECR 3263, 11 November 1986 .... 5.16,
5.118
British Telecommunications (C-302/94) [1996] ECR I-6417, 12 December 1996 .... 9.19

Bronner (Oscar) v. Mediaprint (C-7/97) [1998] ECR I-7791, 26 November 1998 .... 5.41,
5.95, 5.115

BRT I (127/73) [1974] ECR 51, 30 January 1974 .... 4.01

Buchmann v. Commission (T-295/94) [1998] ECR II-813, 14 May 1998 .... 4.262

Bulk Oil (174/84) [1986] ECR 559, 18 February 1986 .... 4.21

Bundeskartellamt v. Volkswagen and VAG Leasing (C-266/93) [1995] ECR I-3477,
24 October 1995 .... 4.277, (p.673)

Bundesverband der Arzneimittel-Importeure eV and others v. Bayer (Joined Cases C-2
and 3/01 [2004] ECR I-23, 6 January 2004 .... 4.86, 13.06

Bundesverband der Bilanzbuchhalter eV v. Commission (C-107/95 P) [1997]
ECR I-947, 20 February 1997 .... 9.50

Bundesverband deutscher Banken v. Commission (T-36/06) [2010] ECR II-537,
3 March 2010 .... 11.29, 11.30, 11.31

Bundeswettbewerbsbehörde v. Donau Chemie and others (C-536/11),
ECLI:EU:C:2013:366, 6 June 2013 .... 13.22

Bundeswettbewerbsbehörde and Bundeskartellanwalt v. Schenker & Co. AG and others
(C-681/11), ECLI:EU:C:2013:404, 18 June 2013 .... 13.24

BUPA v. Commission (T-289/03) [2008] ECR II-81, 12 February 2008 .... 9.35, 10.34

Burban (C-255/90) [1992] ECR I-2253, 31 March 1992 .... (p.763)

Cabour and others v. Arnor (C-230/96) [1998] ECR I-2055, 30 April 1998 .... 16.07,
(p.673)

Cantiere navale De Poli v. Commission (C-167/11 P), ECLI:EU:C:2012:164,
22 March 2012 .... 11.62

Capolongo v. Maya (77/72) [1973] ECR 611, 19 June 1973 .... 10.01, 10.71

Carra and others (C-258/98) [2000] ECR I-4217, 8 June 2000 .... 9.06

Cascades v. Commission (T-308/94) [1998] ECR II-931, 14 May 1998 .... 4.249, 13.223,
19.59

Cascades v. Commission (C-279/98 P) [2000] ECR I-9693, 16 November 2000 .... 13.200

CB and Europay v. Commission (Joined Cases T-39/92 and T-40/92) [1994] ECR II-49,
23 February 1994 .... 13.177

CBEM v. CLT and IPB (311/84) [1985] ECR 3261, 3 October 1985 .... 5.35, 5.134

CBI v. Commission (T-137/10) [2012] ECLI:EU:T:2012:584, 7 November 2012 .... 10.35

CELBI SA v. Fazenda Pública (C-266/91) [1993] ECR I-4337, 2 August 1993 .... 10.118

CELF v. SIDE (C-199/06) [2008] ECR I-469, 12 February 2008 .... 11.67

CELF and Ministre de la Culture and de la Communication (C-1/09)
[2010] ECR I-2099, 11 March 2010 .... 11.84, 11.85

Cementbouw Handel Industrie v. Commission (T-282/02) [2006] ECR II-319,
23 February 2006 .... 14.104, 14.133

Cementbouw Handel Industrie v. Commission (C-202/06 P) [2007] ECR I-12129,
18 December 2007 .... 14.02

Centrafarm and Adriaan de Peijper (15/74) [1974] ECR 1147, 31 October 1974 .... 4.92

CEPSA Estaciones de Servicio SA v. LVTobar e Hijos SL (C-279/06)
[2008] ECR I-6681, 11 September 2008 .... 4.281, 15.05, 15.15

Cewal (Joined Cases T-24–26/93 and T-28/93) [1996] ECR II-1201,
8 October 1996 .... 5.09, 5.32

Chalkor AE Epexergasias Metallon v. Commission (T-21/05) [2010] ECR II-1895,
19 May 2010 .... 13.157

Chalkor AE Epexergasias Metallon v. Commission (C-386/10 P) [2011]
    ECR I-13085, 8 December 2011 .... 3.09, 13.242, 24.07, 24.72
Cheil Jedang v. Commission (T-220/00) [2003] ECR II-2473, 9 July 2003 ..... 4.252, 13.76,
                                                                13.93, 13.126, 13.236, 13.240
Chemische Afvalstoffen Dusseldorp and Others v. Minister van Volkshuisvesting,
    Ruimtelijke Ordening en Milieubeheer (Dusseldorp) (C-203/96) [1998]
    ECR I-4075, 25 June 1998 .... 9.22, 9.41
Chronopost SA and La Poste (Joined Cases C-341/06 P and C-342/06 P)
    [2008] ECR I-4777, 1 July 2008 .... 24.42
CIF (C-198/01) [2003] ECR I-8055, 9 September 2003 .... 4.137
Cimenteries CBR and others v. Commission (Joined Cases T-25, 26, 30, 32, 34, 39, 42,
    46, 48, 50, 65, 68, 71, 87, 88, 103 and 104/95) [2000] ECR II-491,
    15 March 2000 .... 4.99
Cinéthèque v. Fédération Natinoale des Cinémas Français (Joined Cases 60/84 and 61/84)
    [1987] ECR 3719, 11 July 1985 .... 3.12
Cisal (C-218/00) [2002] ECR I-1691, 22 January 2002 .... 4.46
Cisco Systems and Messagenet v. Commission (T-79/12), ECLI:EU:T:2013:635,
    11 December 2013 .... 14.07, 14.36, 14.65, 14.178
City Motors Groep NV v. Citroën Benelux NV (C-421/05) [2007] ECR I-653,
    18 January 2007 .... (p.672)
Cityflier Express Ltd v. Commission (T-214/95) [1998] ECR II-717,
    30 April 1998 .... 10.103
Clearstream v. Commission (T-301/04) [2009] ECR II-03155, 9 September 2009 .... 5.94,
                                                                          5.126, 13.181
CMA CMG v. Commission (T-213/00) [2003] ECR II-913, 19 March 2003 .... 4.251,
                                                                  13.92, 13.211, 13.215
Coca-Cola v. Commission (Joined Cases T-125/97 and T-127/97) [2000] ECR II-1733,
    22 March 2000 .... 5.10
Cofaz and others v. Commission (C-169/84) [1986] ECR 391, 28 January 1986 .... 11.91
Commission v. Anic Partecipazioni (C-49/92 P) [1999] ECR I-4125, 8 July 1999 .... 4.95,
                                                       4.110, 4.116, 13.149, 13.200, 25.18, 26.24
Commission v. Belgium (52/84) [1986] ECR 89, 15 January 1986 .... 2.14, 11.113
Commission v. Council (C-122/94) [1996] ECR I-881, 29 February 1996 .... 10.77
Commission v. Deutsche Post (C-399/08 P) [2010] ECR I-7831,
    2 September 2010 .... 24.56
Commission v. EDF (C-124/10 P), ECLI:EU:C:2012:318, 5 June 2012 .... 10.26
Commission v. Éditions Odile Jacob (C-404/10 P), ECLI:EU:C:2012:393,
    28 June 2012 .... 14.189
Commission v. EnBW (C-365/12 P), ECLI:EU:C:2014:112, 27 February 2014 .... 14.189
Commission v. France (Joined Cases 6 and 11/69) [1969] ECR 523,
    10 December 1969 .... 10.116
Commission v. France (52/83) [1983] ECR 3707, 15 November 1983 .... 11.97
Commission v. France (C-159/94) [1997] ECR I-2461, 23 October 1997 .... 9.40
Commission v. French Republic (C-261/99) [2001] ECR I-2537, 22 March 2001 .... 2.14,
                                                                              11.115
Commission v. Germany (70/72) [1973] ECR 813, 12 July 1973 .... 11.68, 11.96, 11.100
Commission v. Germany (94/87) [1989] ECR 175, 2 February 1989 .... 11.111, 11.114

Commission v. Germany (C-5/89) [1990] ECR I-3437, 20 September 1990 .... 11.117

Commission v. Germany (C-62/90) [1992] ECR I-2575, 8 April 1992 .... 29.01

Commission v. Ireland and others, Aluminiumoxide excise duties (C-89/08)
[2009] ECR I-11245, 2 December 2009 .... 24.83, 24.86

Commission v. Italy (103/84) [1986] ECR 1759, 5 June 1986 .... 10.80

Commission v. Italy (118/85) [1987] ECR 2599, 16 June 1987 .... 4.38

Commission v. Italy (C-348/93) [1995] ECR I-673, 4 April 1995 .... 11.109

Commission v. Italy (C-350/93) [1995] ECR I-699, 4 April 1995 .... 11.108, 11.109

Commission v. Italy (C-280/95) [1998] ECR I-259, 29 January 1998 .... 10.116

Commission v. Italy (C-35/96) [1998] ECR I-3851, 18 June 1998 .... 2.16, 4.42, 4.64

Commission v. Italy and Wam SpA (C-494/06 P) [2009] ECR I-3639,
30 April 2009 .... 10.64

Commission v. Italy (C-496/09) [2011] ECR I-11483, 17 November 2011 .... 1.03

Commission v. Kingdom of the Netherlands (C-157/94) [1997] ECR I-5699,
23 October 1997 .... 9.40

Commission v. Kronoply (C-83/09 P) [2011] ECR I-4441, 24 May 2011 .... 11.43

Commission v. Lisrestal (C-32/95 P) [1996] ECR I-5387, 24 October 1996 .... 23.11

Commission v. Parker Hannifin Manufacturing Srl (C-434/13), ECLI:EU:C:2014:2456,
18 December 2014 .... 4.60

Commission v. Schneider Electric (C-440/07 P) [2009] ECR I-6413,
16 July 2009 .... 14.80, 14.186

Commission v. SGL Carbon AG (C-301/04) [2006] ECR I-5915, 29 June 2006 .... 13.44,
25.43

Commission v. Siemens AG Österreich e.a. (Joined Cases C-231/11 P to C-233/11 P),
ECLI:EU:C:2014:256, 10 April 2014 .... 26.25, 26.27

Commission v. Stichting Administratiekantoor Portielje and others (C-440/11),
ECLI:EU:C:2013:514, 11 July 2013 .... 4.58, 4.197

Commission v. Sytraval (C-367/95 P) [1998] ECR I-1719, 27 May 1997 .... 11.39

Commission v Technische Glaswerke Ilmenau (C-139/07 P) [2010] ECR I-05885,
29 June 2010 .... 14.189

Commission v. Tetra Laval (C-12/03 P) [2008] ECR I-987, 15 February 2005 .... 14.04,
14.68, 14.178

Commission v. TF1 (C-302 and C-308/99 P) [2001] I-5603, 12 July 2001 ...... 9.52, 10.126

Commission v. T-Mobile Austria GmbH (C-141/02 P) [2005] ECR I-1283,
22 February 2005 .... 9.54

Commission v. Verhuizingen Coppens NV (C-441/11 P), ECLI:EU:C:2012:778,
6 December 2012 .... 13.18, 13.113, 22.07

Commission v. Volkswagen (C-74/04 P) [2006] ECR I-6585, 13 July 2006 .... 4.87, 4.274

Commission and others v. Ladbroke Racing (Joined Cases C-359 and 379/95 P) [1997]
ECR I-6265, 11 November 1997 .... 4.136

Communauté de communes de Lacq v. Commission (T-132/10) [2011] ECR II-00254,
1 September 2011 .... 14.153

Compañía Española de Comercialización de Aceite SA (C-505/07) [2009] ECR I-08963,
12 February 2009 .... 17.01, 17.17

Compagnie Générale Maritime and others v. Commission (T-86/95) [2002] ECR II-1011,
28 February 2002 .... 4.225, 4.236, 13.222, 13.223, 13.224, 14.182

Compagnie Maritime Belge Transports and others v. Commission (T-24/93-T-26/93 and
    T-28/93) [1996] ECR II-1201, 8 October 1996 .... 13.224
Compagnie Maritime Belge Transports and others v. Commission (C-395/96 and C-396/96)
    [2000] ECR I-1365, 16 March 2000 .... 5.39, 5.53, 5.89, 5.155, 23.20
Compagnie Maritime Belge v. Commission (T-276/04) [2008] ECR II-1277,
    8 July 2008 .... 13.211
Compass-Datenbank (C-138/11), ECLI:EU:C:2012:449, 12 July 2012 .... 4.52
Competition Authority Ireland (C-209/07) [2008] ECR I-8637, 20 November
    2008 .... 4.146
Confederación Espaæola de Empresarios de Estaciones de Servicio v. Compaæía Espaæola
    de Petróleos SA (C-217/05) [2006] ECR I-11987, 14 December 2006 .... 4.280
Confédération européenne des associations d'horlogers-réparateurs (CEAHR) v. Commission
    (T-427/08) [2010] ECR II-05865, 15 December 2010 .... 15.03
Consiglio nazionale dei geologi (C-136/12) ECLI:EU:C:2013:489, 18 July 2013 .... 4.67
Consten and Gründig v. Commission (Joined Cases 56 and 58/64) [1966] ECR 340,
    13 July 1966 .... 4.89, 4.142, 4.184, 4.202, 4.218
Cook v. Commission (C-198/91) [1993] ECR I-2487, 19 May 1993 .... 11.18, 11.91
Coop de France bétail et viande (C-101/07P and C-110/07 P) [2008] ECR I-10193,
    18 December 2008 .... 13.168
Coöperatieve Stremsel en Kleurselfabriek v. Commission (61/80) [1980] ECR 851,
    25 March 1981 .... 4.233, 17.03
Corbeau, Paul, Criminal proceedings against (C-320/91) [1993] ECR I-2533,
    19 May 1993 .... 9.38, 9.43
Corsica Ferries France v. Commission (T-565/08), ECLI:EU:T:2012:415, 11 September
    2012 .... 10.26
Corsica Ferries (C-18/93) [1994] ECR I-1783, 17 May 1994 .... 9.18
Corsica Ferries v. Gruppo Antichi Ormoggiatori (C-266/96) [1998] ECR I-3949,
    18 June 1998 .... 2.16
Corus UK v. Commission (C-199/99 P) [2003] ECR I-11177, 2 October 2003 .... 23.26,
    23.27
Costa v. ENEL (6/64) [1964] ECR 585, 15 July 1964 .... 11.74
Courage and Crehan (C-543/99) [2000] ECR I-6297, 20 September 2000 .... 4.209
CRAM and Rheinzink v. Commission (Joined Cases 29 and 30/83) [1984] ECR 1699,
    28 March 1984 .... 4.104, 4.143, 4.167, 13.198
Cullet v. Leclerc (231/83) [1985] ECR 305, 29 January 1985 .... 2.04
Currà and others (C-466/11), ECLI:EU:T:2012:465, 12 July 2012 .... 28.01
Daiichi Pharmaceutical v. Commission (T-26/02) [2006] ECR II-713,
    15 March 2006 .... 13.96, 13.133
DaimlerChrysler AG v. Commission (T-325/01) [2005] ECR II-3319,
    15 September 2005 .... 4.278, 4.279, 13.205, 15.07
Dansk Pelsdyravlerforening (T-61/89) [1992] ECR II-1931, 2 July 1992 .... 17.03
Dansk Rørindustri v. Commission (T-21/99) [2002] ECR II-1681,
    20 March 2002 .... 13.154
Dansk Rørindustrie and others v. Commission (Joined Cases C-189/02, C-202/02,
    C-205/02–208 and C-213/02 P) [2005] ECR I-5425, 28 June 2005 ..... 4.145, 13.109,
        13.130, 13.141, 13.154, 13.250, 22.04, 22.06, 23.21, 26.09, 26.10, 26.16, 26.18

DEB (C-279/09) [2010] ECR I-13849, 22 December 2010 .... 3.01, 24.126, 24.127, 24.128, 24.129, 29.04

De Bie and others v. Campina Melkunie (C-224/94) [1995] ECR I-4471, 12 December 1995 ...... 17.09, 17.16

Degussa AG v. Commission (T-279/02) [2006] ECR II-897, 5 April 2006 ... 13.64, 13.134, 13.162

Delimitis (C-234/89) [1991] ECR I-935, 28 February 1991 ...... 4.161, 4.206, 4.311

Delta Schiffahrts-und Speditionsgesellschaft (C-153/93) [1994] ECR I-2517, 9 June 1994 ...... 2.12

Deltafina v. Commission (T-29/05) [2010] ECR II-4077, 8 September 2010 ...... 4.196, 13.80, 13.105, 13.137, 13.145, 13.230

Deufil GmbH & Co v. Commission (310/85) [1987] ECR 901, 24 February 1987 ... 10.128

Deutsche Bahn v. Commission (T-229/94) [1997] ECR II-1689, 21 October 1997 ...... 5.16

Deutsche Bahn v. Commission (T-351/02) [2006] ECR II-1047, 5 April 2006 ...... 10.15

Deutsche Bahn AG and others v. Commission (Joined Cases T-289/11, T-290/11 and T-521/11), ECLI:EU:T:2013:404, 6 September 2013 ...... 13.50, 19.55, 24.65

Deutsche Bahn a.o. v. Commission (C-583/13 P), EU:C:2013:404, 18 June 2015 ...... 19.08, 24.60

Deutsche Börse v. Commission (T-175/12), ECLI:EU:T:2015:148, 9 March 2015 ...... 14.77

Deutsche Grammophon v. Metro-SB-Großmärkte GmbH & Co. KG (78/70) [1971] ECR 487, 8 June 1971 ...... 5.99, 5.127

Deutsche Lufthansa AG v. Flughafen Frankfurt-Hahn GmbH (C-284/12), ECLI:EU:2013:755, 21 November 2013 ...... 11.71, 11.87

Deutsche Post v. Commission (T-266/02) [2008] ECR II-1233, 1 July 2008 ...... 10.32

Deutsche Telekom v. Commission (T-271/03) [2008] ECR II-477, 10 April 2008 ...... 5.64

Deutsche Telekom v. Commission (C-280/08) [2010] ECR I-09555, 14 October 2010 ...... 5.64. 5.67, 5.113, 5.149

DHL Express (Italy) Srl and DHL Global Forwarding (Italy) SpA v. Autorità Garante della Concorrenza e del Mercato (C-428/14), ECLI:EU:C:2016:27, 20 January 2016 ...... 13.37

Diamanthandel A. Spira BVBA v. Commission (T-108/07 and T-354/08), ECLI:EU:T:2013:367, 11 July 2013 ...... 8.05, 13.41

Diego Calí (C-343/95) [1997] ECR I-1545, 18 March 1997 ...... 4.41

Dijkstra and others v. Friesland Frico Domo (C-319/93) [1995] ECR I-4471, 12 December 1995 ...... 17.09, 17.16

Diputación Foral de Álava and others v. Commission (T-127/99, T-129/99 and T-148/99) [2002] ECR II-1275, 6 March 2002 ...... 10.37, 10.108

Djebel – SGPS, Sa v. Commission (T-422/07), ECLI:EU:T:2012:11, 18, 12 January 2012 ...... 10.130

Dole Foods Company, Inc v. Commission (C-286/13), ECLI:EU:C:2015:184, 19 March 2015 ...... 4.153

Doux Élevage and Coopérative agricole UKL-ARREE (C-677/11), ECLI:EU:C:2013:348, 30 May 2013 ...... 10.09, 10.16

Dow Chemical Company, The v. Commission (T-42/07) [2011] ECR II-4531, 13 July 2011 ...... 13.183

Dow Chemical Company, The v. Commission (T-77/08), ECLI:EU:T:2012:47, 2 February 2012 ...... 13.81, 14.126

Dow Chemical Company, The v. Commission (C-499/11 P), ECLI:EU:C:2013:482,
    18 July 2013 .... 8.04, 13.121, 13.163
Dow Chemical Company, The v. Commission (C-179/12 P), ECLI:EU:C:2013:605,
    26 September 2013 .... 13.186
Dow Chemical Ibérica a.o. v. Commission (Joined Cases 97/87–99/87) [1989] ECR 3165,
    17 October 1989 .... 19.05, 23.13
Dresdner Bank AG and Others (Joined Cases T-44/02 OP, T-54/02 OP, T-56/02 OP,
    T-60/02 OP and T-61/02 OP) [2006] ECR II-3567, 27 September 2006 .... 13.06,
                                                                                        25.12, 25.13
Drijvende Bokken v. Stichting Pensioenfonds (C-219/97) [1999] ECR I-6121,
    21 September 1999 .... 2.16, 4.14, 9.23, 9.42
DSD Der Grüne Punkt v. Commission (T-151/01) [2007] ECR II-1607,
    24 May 2007 .... 5.123
DSD Der Grüne Punkt v. Commission (C-385/07) [2009] ECR I-06155,
    16 July 2009 .... 5.123, 23.02, 23.03, 23.05, 24.111, 24.116
DSG v. Commission (T-234/95) [2000] ECR II-2603, 29 June 2000 .... 10.22
Dunlop Slazenger International v. Commission (T-43/92) [1984] ECR II-441,
    7 July 1994 .... 4.82, 13.213
Du Pont de Nemours Italiana SpA v. Unità sanitaria locale No 2 di Carrar (C-21/88)
    [1990] ECR I-889, 20 March 1990 .... 10.80
EARL (C-15/95) [1997] ECR I-1961, 17 April 1997 .... (p.759)
easyJet Airline Co. Ltd v. European Commission (T-335/13), ECLI:EU:T:2015:36,
    21 January 2015 .... 8.05
EC v. Otis a.o. (C-199/11), ECLI:EU:C:2012:684, 6 November 2012 .... 3.09, 24.07, 24.36,
                                                                                        24.91
Eco Swiss (C-126/97) [1999] ECR I-3055, 1 June 1999 .... 4.208
EDF v. Commission (T-156/04) [2009] ECR II-4503, 15 December 2009 .... 10.26
Éditions Odile Jacob v. Commission (T-471/11), ECLI:EU:T:2014:739, 5 September
    2014 .... 14.179
EI du Pont de Nemours and Co v. Commission (T-76/08), ECLI:EU:T:2012:46,
    2 February 2012 .... 14.126
EI du Pont de Nemours and Co v. Commission (C-172/12 P), ECLI:EU:C:2013:601,
    26 September 2013 .... 4.59, 13.193
Elf Aquitaine SA v. Commission (C-521/09 P) [2011] ECR I-08947 .... 25.17, 26.26
Emanuela Sbarigia v. Azienda USL RM/A, Comune di Roma, Assiprofar – Associazione
    Sindacale Proprietari Farmacia, Ordine dei Farmacisti della Provincia di Roma
    (C-393/08) [2010] ECR I-06337, 1 July 2010 .... 6.02, 8.01
EMC Development v. Commission (T-432/05) [2010] ECR II-1629, 12 May 2010 .. 4.259,
                                                                                        13.25
Emesa Sugar (C-17/98) [2000] ECR I-665, 4 February 2000 .... 3.08
EMI (51/75) [1976] ECR 811, 15 June 1976 .... 4.20, 4.69, 4.187
Enirisorse (Joined Cases C-34/01 to C-38/01) [2003] ECR I-14243, 27 November
    2003 .... 10.33
ENI SpA v. Commission (C-508/11 P), ECLI:EU:C:2013:289, 8 May 2013 .... 13.184
Enso Española v. Commission (T-348/94) [1998] ECR II-1875, 14 May 1998 .... 13.92,
                                                                13.175, 13.223, 24.04, 24.33, 24.74

E.ON Energie AG v. Commission (T-141/08) [2010] ECR II-5761,
    15 December 2010 .... 13.67
E.ON Energie AG v. Commission (C-89/11 P), ELI:EU:C:2012:738,
    22 November 2012 .... 13.04, 26.23
E.ON Ruhrgas and others v. Commission (T-360/09), ECLI:EU:T:2012:332,
    29 June 2012 .... 4.270
Erste Group Bank and others v. Commission (Joined Cases C-125/07, C-133/07, C-135/07
    and C-137/07 P) [2009] ECR I-8681, 24 September 2009 .... 4.195
ERT v. DEP (C-260/89) [1991] ECR I-2925, 18 June 1991 .... 3.07, 3.13, 9.14, 9.29,
                                                                                                             (p.883)
Estación de Servicio Pozuelo (4 SL, C-384/13), ECLI:EU:C:2014:2425,
    4 December 2014 .... 4.308, 15.20
ETI and others v. Autorità Garante della Concorrenza e del Mercato and Others
    (C-280/06) [2007] ECR I-10893, 11 December 2007 .... 13.203
Eturas (C-74/14), ECLI:EU:C:2016:42 .... 4.113
Europemballage Corporation and Continental Company Inc. v. Commission of the
    European Communities (Continental Can) (6/72) [1973] ECR 215,
    21 February 1973 ....5.04, 5.13, 5.60
European Night Services Ltd (ENS) and others v. Commission (Joined Cases T-374/94,
    T-375/94, T-384/94 and T-388/94) [1998] ECR II-3141, 15 September 1998 ..... 4.33,
                                                                                                             4.170
Europese Gemeenschap v. Otis NV and others (C-199/11), ECLI:EU:C:2012:684,
    6 November 2012 .... 13.36
Evonik Degussa GmbH and AlzChem AG, formerly AlzChem Trostberg GmbH, formerly
    AlzChem Hart GmbH v. European Commission (C-155/14 P),
    ECLI:EU:C:2016:446, 16 June 2016 .... 13.187, 13.188
Evonik Degussa (C-266/06 P) [2008] ECR I-81, 22 May 2008 .... 26.05, 26.06, 26.07
Expedia v. Autorité de la concurrence and others (C-226/11), ECLI:EU:C:2012:795,
    13 December 2012 .... 4.174, 4.175, 13.21
Falck and Acciaierie di Bolzano v. Commission (C-74/00 P and C-75/00 P) [2002] ECR
    I-7869, 24 September 2002 .... 13.207
Falles Fagligt Forbund (3F) v. Commission (C-319/07) [2009] ECR I-5963,
    9 July 2009 .... 11.42, 11.93
Falles Fagligt Forbund (3F) v. Commission (C-646/11 P), ECLI:EU:2013:36,
    24 January 2013 .... 11.23
FEDECOM v. Commission (T-243/09), ECLI:EU:T:2012:497,
    27 September 2012 .... 10.106
Fédération nationale du commerce extérieur des produits alimentaires (C-354/90)
    [1991] ECR I-5505, 21 November 1991 .... 11.63, 11.80, 11.89
FEG v. Commission (T-5/00) [2003] ECR II-5761, 16 December 2003 ...... 13.129, 13.160,
                                                                                                             13.212, 23.07
FENIN v. Commission (T-319/99) [2003] ECR II-357, 4 March 2003 .... 4.48
Ferriere Nord SpA v. Commission (C-219/95) [1997] ECR I-4411, 17 July 1997 .... 13.83
Ferriere Nord SpA v. Commission (T-153/04) [2006] ECR II-3889,
    27 September 2006 .... 13.220
Ferriere Nord SpA v. Commission (C-516/06 P) [2007] ECR I-10685,
    6 December 2007 .... 13.209

FFAD v. Københavns Kommune (C-209/98) [2000] ECR I-3743,
    23 May 2000 .... 9.30, 9.38
FFSA and others v. Commission (T-106/95) [1997] ECR II-229, 27 February 1997 ... 9.51,
    9.55
Fiskano v. Commission (C-135/92) [1994] ECR I-2899, 29 June 1994 .... 23.15
Fiskeby Board v. Commission (T-319/94) [1998] ECR II-1331, 14 May 1998 .... 13.175
Fleuren Compost v. Commission (T-109/01) [2004] ECR II-127, 14 January 2004 .... 11.33
Fluorsid SpA and Minmet Financing Co. v. Commission (T-404/08), ECLI:EU:T:
    2013:321, 18 June 2013 .... 13.112
FNV Kiem (C-413/13), ECLI:EU:C:2014:2411, 4 December 2014 .... 4.17
Football Association Premier League and others v. QC Leisure and others (Joined Cases
    C-403 and 429/08) [2011] ECR I-9083, 4 October 2011 .... 4.149
Ford-Werke and others v. Commission (Joined Cases 25 and 26/84) [1985] ECR 2725,
    17 September 1985 .... 4.80, 15.09
France v. Commission (47/69) [1970] ECR 487, 25 June 1970 .... 10.117
France v. Commission (259/85) [1987] ECR 4393, 11 November 1987 .... 10.17
France v. Commission (102/87) [1988] ECR 4067, 13 July 1988 .... 10.60
France v. Commission (C-301/87) [1990] ECR I-307, 14 February 1990 .... 10.93, 10.142,
    11.09, 11.48, 11.69, 11.73
France v. Commission (C-241/94) [1996] ECR I-4551, 26 September 1996 ..... 10.36, 10.84
France v. Commission (C-482/99) [2002] ECR I-4397, 13 December 2001 .... 11.52
France v. Commission (Stardust Marine) (C-482/99) [2002] ECR I-4397,
    16 May 2002 .... 10.13, 10.14
France v. Ladbroke Racing and Commission (C-83/98 P) [2000] ECR I-3271,
    16 May 2000 .... 10.07, 10.85, 10.86
France Télécom v. Commission C-81/10 P) [2011] ECR II-12899, 8 December
    2011 .... 11.103, 11.106
France Télécom (Wanadoo) v. Commission (T-340/03) [2007] ECR II-107,
    30 January 2007 .... 5.142, 13.223, 13.225
France Télécom v. Commission (T-340/04) [2007] ECR II-573, 8 March 2007 .... 13.40,
    13.32, 13.58
France Télécom v. Commission (C-202/07) [2009] ECR I-2369, 2 April 2009 .... 5.91
Fred Olsen (T-17/02) [2005] ECR II-02031, 15 June 2005 .... 9.34
Freistaat Sachsen and Others v. Commission (T-443/08 and T-455/08) [2011]
    ECR II-1311, 24 March 2011 .... 11.02
Freistaat Thüringen v. Commission (T-318/00) [2005] ECR II-4179,
    19 October 2005 .... 11.35
French Republic v. Commission (C-202/88) [1991] ECR I-1223, 19 March 1991 .... 9.04,
    9.28, 9.47
French Republic, Italian Republic and United Kingdom of Great Britain and Northern
    Ireland v. Commission (Joined Cases 188–190/80) [1982] ECR 2545,
    6 July 1982 .... 9.46
Fresh Del Monte Produce Inc. v. Commission (Joined Cases C-293/13 and 294/13),
    ECLI:EU:C:2015:416, 24 June 2015 .... 4.67
Frubo v. Commission (71/74) [1975] ECR 563, 15 May 1975 .... 17.14

Frucona Košice v. Commission (T-11/07) [2010] ECR II-5453, 7 December 2010 ... 10.102

Fuji Electric Co (T-132/07) [2011] ECR II-4091, 12 July 2011 .... 13.03, 13.231

Galec (T-88/92) [1996] ECR II-1961, 12 December 1996 .... 4.287, 4.291, 4.296, 4.297

Galp Energía España SA and Others v. European Commission (C-603/13 P),
    ECLI:EU:C:2016:38, 21 January 2016 .... 13.245

Gascogne Sack Deutschland v. Commission (C-40/12 P), ECLI:EU:C:2013:768,
    26 November 2013 .... 23.02, 23.03, 23.05, 24.112, 24.117

GB-INNO-BM/ATAB (13/77) [1977] ECR 2115, 16 November 1977 .... 2.01, 9.02

Geigy v. Commission (52/69) [1972] ECR 787, 14 July 1972 .... 13.218

Gencor v. Commission (T-102/96) [1999] ECR II-753, 25 March 1999 .... 5.52, 14.01

General Electric v. Commission (T-210/01) [2005] ECR II-5575,
    14 December 2005 .... 14.33, 14.66, 14.68

General Motors v. Commission (C-551/03 P) [2006] ECR I-3173, 6 April 2006 .... 13.73

General Motors and Opel v. Commission (T-368/00) [2003] ECR II-4491,
    21 October 2003 .... 4.172

General Motors Continental (26/75) [1975] ECR 1367, 13 November 1975 .... 5.16

General Motors Nederland BV and Opel Nederland BV v. Commission (T-368/00) [2003]
    ECR II-4491, 21 October 2003 .... 13.73

General Motors Nederland BV and Opel Nederland BV v. Commission (C-551/03 P)
    [2006] ECR I-3173, 6 April 2006 .... 15.12

General Química SA v. Commission (C-90/09 P) [2011] ECR I-0001,
    20 January 2011 .... 13.183

Germany v. Commission (84/82) [1984] ECR 1451, 20 March 1984 .... 11.21, 11.44

Germany v. Commission (248/84) [1987] ECR 4013, 14 October 1987 .... 10.03, 10.131

Germany v. Commission, Bremer Vulkan (Joined Cases C-329/93, C-62/95 and C-63/95)
    [1996] ECR I-5151, 24 October 1996 .... 10.62, 10.99

Germany v. Commission (C-288/96) [2000] ECR I-8237, 5 October 2000 .... 10.77, 10.104

Germany v. Commission (SMI) (C-277/00) [2004] ECR I-3925, 29 April 2004 .... 11.121

Germany v. Commission (T-47/15), ECLI:EU:T:2016:281, 10 May 2016 .... 10.07

Gibraltar v. Commission (T-195/01) [2002] ECR II-2309, 30 April 2002 .... 11.10, 11.55

Gibraltar v. Commission (T-211/04 and T-215/04) [2008] ECR II-3745,
    18 December 2008 .... 10.44

GIL Insurance and others (C-308/01) [2004] ECR I-4777, 29 April 2004 .... 10.39

Giovanni Carra (C-258/98) [2000] ECR I-4217, 8 June 2000 .... 9.13

GlaxoSmithKline Services and others v. Commission (T-168/01) [2006] ECR II-2969,
    27 September 2006 .... 4.75, 13.07

GlaxoSmithKline Services and others v. Commission and others (Joined Cases C-501/06,
    C-513/06 and C-519/06 P) [2009] ECR I-9291, 6 October 2009 .... 4.148, 4.216,
                                                                                        4.226

Gøttrup-Klim (C-250/92) [1994] ECR I-5641, 15 December 1994 .... 4.179, 5.31, 17.03

Gözütok (C-187/01) [2003] ECR I-1345, 11 February 2003 .... (p.876)

Grant (C-249/96) [1998] ECR I-621, 17 February 1998 .... (p.883)

Greenwich Film Production v. SACEM (SACEM) (22/79) [1979] ECR 3275,
    25 October 1979 .... 5.102

Group Danone v. Commission (T-38/02) [2005] ECR II-4407, 25 October 2005 ...... 13.05,
                                                                                        26.21

Groupe Danone v. Commission (C-3/06 P) [2007] ECR I-1331,
    8 February 2007 .... 13.208, 13.241, 26.09, 26.10
Groupement des cartes bancaires (CB) (T-266/03) [2007] ECR II-83, 12 July 2007 ... 13.40
Groupement des Cartes Bancaires (CB) vs. Commission (C-67/13),
    ECLI:EU:C:2014:2204, 11 September 2014 .... 4.152
Groupement des fabricants des Papier Peints v. Commission (73/74) [1975] ECR 1491,
    26 November 1975 .... 4.246
Gruber + Weber v. Commission (T-310/94) [1998] ECR II-1043, 14 May 1998 .... 4.263
GT-Link v. De Danske Stadbaner (C-242/95) [1997] ECR I-4449, 17 July 1997 .... 9.20
Gütermann and Zwicky v. Commission (Joined Cases T-456 and 457/05) [2010] ECR
    II-1443, 28 April 2010 .... 4.24, 13.158, 13.172
Gutmann v. Commission (Joined Cases 18/65 and 35/65) [1966] ECR 149,
    5 May 1966 .... (p.876)
GVL v. Commission (7/82) [1983] ECR 483, 2 March 1983 .... 5.103, 9.33
H. Lundbeck A/S and others v. Commission (T-472/13), ECLI:EU:T:2016:449,
    8 September 2016 .... 4.37, 4.155, 4.272
Hasselblad (86/82) [1984] ECR 883, 21 February 1984 .... 4.294, 4.300, 4.301
Hauer (44/79) [1979] ECR 3727, 13 December 1979 .... 3.06, (p.758), (p.888)
HeidelbergCement AG v. European Commission (C-247/14 P), ECLI:EU:C:2016:149,
    10 March 2016 .... 13.43
Heineken (Joined Cases 91/93 and 127/93) [1984] ECR 3435, 9 October 1984 .... 11.60,
                                                                                    11.72
Heineken v. Commission (T-240/07) [2011] ECR II-3355, 16 June 2011 .... 23.07
Hellenic Republic v. Commission (C-263/12), ECLI:EU:2013:673, 17 October
    2013 .... 11.107
Hercules Chemicals v. Commission (T-7/89) [1991] ECR II-1711,
    17 December 1991 .... 4.114, 4.260, 13.123, 13.150
Hercules Chemicals v. Commission (C-51/92 P) [1999] ECR I-4235,
    8 July 1999 .... 23.26, 23.28
Hermann Schräder HS Kraftfutter v. Hauptzollamt Gronau (265/87) [1989] ECR 2237,
    11 July 1989 .... 29.01
Heubach GmbH & Co. KG v. Commission (T-64/02) [2005] ECR II-5137,
    29 November 2005 .... 13.147
Heylens (222/86) [1987] ECR 4097, 15 October 1987 .... (p.763), 24.03
HFB Holding für Fernwärmetechnik and others v. Commission (T-9/99) [2002] ECR
    II-1487, 20 March 2002 .... 4.73
Hilti v. Commission (T-30/89) [1990] ECR II-163, 4 April 1990 .... 13.53, 19.58
Hilti v. Commission (T-30/89) [1991] ECR II-1439, 12 December 1991 .... 5.25, 5.85,
                                                                                5.107, 5.139
Hilti v. Commission (C-53/92) [1994] ECR I-667, 2 March1994 .... 5.85
Hoechst v. Commission (Joined Cases 46/87 and 227/88) [1989] ECR 2859,
    21 September 1989 .... 13.44, 13.61, 19.05, 19.06, 19.59, 23.13, 25.40
Hoechst v. Commission (T-10/89) [1992] ECR II-629, 10 March 1992 .... 4.115
Hoechst v. Commission (T-410/03) [2008] ECR II-881, 18 June 2008 .... 13.167
Hoek Loos v. Commission (T-304/02) [2006] ECR II-1887, 4 July 2006 .... 13.156
Hoffmann-La Roche v. Centrafarm (102/77) [1978] ECR 1139, 23 May 1978 .... 5.101

Hoffmann-La Roche v. Commission (85/76) [1979] ECR 461, 13 February 1979 .... 5.08,
        5.18, 5.29, 5.45, 5.62, 5.71, 5.80, 5.152, 19.59, 23.14, 23.17, 23.18, 23.25
Höfner and Elser v. Macroton (C-41/90) [1991] ECR I-1979, 23 April 1991 ..... 4.39, 5.36,
        9.13
Honeywell v. Commission (T-209/01) [2005] ECR II-5527, 14 December 2005 .... 14.05
Hugin v. Commission (22/78) [1979] ECR 1869, 31 May 1979 .... 5.17, 5.84, 5.150
Hüls v. Commission (C-199/02 P) [1999] ECR I-4287, 8 July 1999 ..... 4.109, 13.08, 24.21,
        25.09, 25.18, 25.21
Huawei Technologies Co. Ltd v. ZTE Corp., ZTE Deutschland GmbH (C170/13),
        ECLI:EU:C:2015:477, 16 July 2015 .... 5.112
Hydrotherm (170/83) [1984] ECR 2999, 12 July 1984 .... 4.55
Iannelli and Volpi v. Meroni (74/76) [1977] ECR 557, 22 March 1977 .... 10.73, 10.75
IAZ and others v. Commission (Joined Cases 96–102, 104, 105, 108 and 110/82) [1983]
        ECR 3369, 8 November 1983 .... 4.126, 13.175
ICI v. Commission (48/69) [1972] ECR 619, 14 July 1972 .... 4.28, 4.96, 4.101, 4.244,
        13.218
ICI v. Commission (T-30/91) [1995] ECR II-1775, 29 June 1995 .... 4.98
IJssel-Vliet Combinatie BV v. Minister van Economische Zaken (C-311/94) [1996] ECR
        I-5023, 15 October 1996 .... 10.78, 11.17
IMI v. Commission (T-18/05) [2010] ECR II-1769, 19 May 2010 .... 13.157, 13.228
Impala v. Commission (T-464/04) [2006] ECR II-02289, 13 July 2006 .... 14.57
IMS Health Inc. v. Commission (T-184/01R) [2001] ECR II-2349,
        10 August 2001 .... 13.28
IMS Health GmbH Co. OHG v. NDC Health GmbH Co. KG (C-418/01) [2004] ECR
        I-5039, 29 April 2004 .... 5.109, 5.148
ING Pensii Societate de Administrare a unui Fond de Pensii Administrat Privat SA v.
        Consiliul Concurenței. (C-172/14), ECLI:EU:C:2015:484, 16 July 2015 .... 4.256
Inspecteur van de Belastingdienst v. X BV (C-429/07) [2009] ECR I-4833,
        11 June 2009 .... 6.01, 13.34, 13.35
Intel Corp. v. European Commission (T-286/09), ECLI:EU:T:2014:547, 12 June
        2014 .... 5.82
Inter-Huiles (172/82) [1983] ECR I-555, 10 March 1983 .... 9.03
Intermills SA v. Commission (323/82) [1984] ECR 3809, 14 November 1984 .... 10.91,
        11.40
International Power and others/NALOO (C-172/01P, C-175/01P, C-176/01P and
        C-180/01 P) [2003] ECR I-11421, 2 October 2003 .... 13.207
Internationale Handelsgesellschaft (11/70) [1970] ECR 1125, 17 December 1970 .... 3.04,
        30.01
Ioannis Doulamis (C-446/05) [2008] ECR I-1377, 13 March 2008 .... 2.04
Ireland v. Commission (325/85) [1987] ECR 5041, 15 December 1987 .... 26.15
Iride & Iride Energia v. Commission (T-25/07) [2009] ECR II-245, 11 February
        2009 .... 10.05, 10.07
Irish Sugar v. Commission (T-228/97) [1999] ECR II-2969, 7 October 1999 .... 5.77, 5.136
Istituto Chemioterapico Italiano S.p.A. et Commercial Solvents Corporation v. Commission
        of the European Communities (Commercial Solvents) (Joined Cases 6/73 and 7/73)
        [1974] ECR 223, 6 March 1974 .... 5.05, 5.15, 5.92
Italy v. Commission (173/73) [1974] ECR I-709, 2 July 1974 .... 10.41, 10.83

Italy v. Commission (C-303/88) [1991] ECR I-1433, 21 March 1991 .... 10.19, 10.94, 11.101

Italy v. Commission (C-261/89) [1991] ECR I-4437, 3 October 1991 .... 10.95

Italy v. Commission (Italgrani) (C-47/91) [1994] ECR I-4635, 5 October 1994 .... 11.06, 11.09, 11.12

Italy v. Commission (C-66/02) [2005] ECR I-10901, 15 December 2005 .... 11.76

Italy v. Commission (T-379/09), ECLI:EU:T:2012:422, 13 September 2012 .... 10.144

Italy v. Council and Commission (32/65) [1996] ECR 389, 13 July 1966 .... 4.90

Italy and SIM 2 Multimedia v. Commission (C-328/99) [2003] ECR I-4035,
    8 May 2003 .... 11.104, 11.121

ITP v. Commission (T-76/89) [1991] ECR II-575, 10 July 1991 .... 5.20

ITT Promedia v. Commission (111/96) [1998] ECR II-2937, 17 July 1998 .... 5.133

Jager (C-420/06) [2008] ECR I-1315, 11 March 2008 .... 26.12

Javico (C-306/96) [1998] ECR I-1983, 28 April 1998 .... 4.23, 4.193

JCB v. Commission (T-67/01) [2004] ECR II-49, 13 January 2004 .... 13.74

JFE Engineering v. Commission (T-67/00) [2004] ECR II-2501, 8 July 2004 .... 13.151

Job-centre coop. arl. (C-55/96) [1997] ECR I-7119, 11 December 1979 .... 5.151

John Deere v. Commission (T-35/92) [1994] ECR II-957, 27 October 1994 .... 4.261

John Deere v. Commission (C-7/95 P) [1998] ECR I-3111, 28 May 1998 .... 4.162, 4.264

Johnston (C-222/84) [1986] ECR 1651, 15 May 1986 .... 3.06, (p.779), 24.03

Jørgen Andersen v. Commission (T-92/11), ECLI:EU:T:2013:143, 20 March 2013 ..... 10.87

Jungbunzlauer v. Commission (T-43/02) [2006] ECR II-3435, 27 September 2006 ..... 26.17

Kali and Salz and others v. Commission (Joined Cases 19/74 and 20/74) [1975] ECR 499,
    14 May 1975 .... 4.237

Kali and Salz and others v. Commission (Joined Cases C-68/94 and C-30/95) [1998] ECR
    I-1375, 31 March 1998 .... 5.51, 5.56, 14.15, 14.70, 14.71

Kamberaj (Case C-571/10), ECLI:EU:C:2012:233 .... 3.14

Kanal 5 Ltd and TV 4 AB v. STIM (C-52/07) [2008] ECR I-9275,
    11 December 2008 .... 5.12, 5.120

Karlsson (C-292/97) [2000] ECR 2737, 13 April 2000 .... (p.759), (p.883), (p.886)

Kendrion v. Commission (C-50/12 P), ECLI:EU:C:2013:771, 26 November 2013 ..... 23.03, 23.05, 24.112, 24.117

Keramag Keramische Werke AG and others v. Commission (Joined Cases T-379/10 and
    T-381/10) [2013] ECLI:EU:T:2013:457, 16 September 2013 .... 13.13

Kingdom of Spain v. Commission (T-398/07), ECLI:EU:T:2013:457,
    29 March 2012 .... 5.115, 6.04

Kirsammer v. Sidal (C-189/91) [1993] ECR I-6185, 30 November 1993 .... 10.06

Klausner Holz Niedersachsen (C-505/14), ECLI:EU:C:2015:742,
    11 November 2015 .... 11.88

Kledingverkoopbedrijf De Geus and Uitdenboogerd (13/61) [1962] ECR 93,
    6 April 1962 .... 4.25

KME Germany AG v. Commission (T-25/05) [2010] ECR II-91, 19 May 2010 ..... 13.153, 13.173, 13.176

KME Germany AG, KME France SAS and KME Italy SpA (C-272/09 P) [2011] ECR
    I-12789, 8 December 2011 .... 13.84, 13.243

KME Germany AG, KME France SAS and KME Italy SpA (C-389/10 P) [2011] ECR
    I-13125, 8 December 2011 .... 13.101, 13.119, 24.55

Knauf Gips v. Commission (C-407/08 P) [2010] ECR I-6375, 1 July 2010 .... 25.14

KNP BT v. Commission (T-309/94) [1998] ECR II-1007, 14 May 1998 .... 13.195

KNP BT v. Commission (C-248/98 P) [2000] ECR I-9641, 16 November 2000 ...... 13.236

Kone Oyj, Kone GmbH and Kone BV v. Commission (T-151/07) [2011] ECR II-5313,
    13 July 2011 .... 13.174

Kone Oyj, Kone GmbH and Kone BV v. Commission (C-510/11 P),
    ECLI:EU:C:2013:696, 24 October 2013 .... 13.244, 22.03, 24.56

Koninklijke PTT Nederland NV and PTT Post BV v. Commission (Joined Cases 48/90
    and 66/90) [1992] ECR I-565, 12 February 1992 .... 9.48, 9.49

KoninklijkeWegenbouw Stevin v. Commission (T-357/06), ECLI:EU:T:2012:488,
    27 September 2012 .... 13.47

Konkurrensverket v. TeliaSonera Sverige AB (C-52/09) [2011] ECR I-00527,
    17 February 2011 .... 1.02, 5.114

Konsum Nord ekonomisk förening v. Commission (T-244/08) [2011] ECR II-00444,
    13 December 2011 .... 10.113

Kremikovtzi (C-262/11), ECLI:EU:C:2012:760, 29 November 2012 .... 11.11

Krupp Stahl AG v. Commission (C-183/83) [1985] ECR 3609, 12 November 1985 ... 13.89

Kuwait Petroleum v. Commission (T-354/99) [2006] ECR II-1475, 31 May 2006 ...... 11.36

La Cinq v. Commission (T-44/90) [1992] ECR II-1, 24 January 1992 .... 13.26, 13.27

Ladbroke v. Commission (T-504/93) [1997] ECR II-00923, 12 June 1997 .... 5.108

Ladbroke v. Commission (T-67/94) [1998] ECR II-1, 27 January 1998 .... 10.85

Lafarge SA v. Commission (C-413/08 P) [2010] ECR I-5361, 17 June 2010 ... 13.86, 26.07

Lancôme v. Etos and Albert Heijn (99/70) [1980] ECR 2511, 10 July 1980 .... 4.283

Land Burgenland and Austria v. Commission (T-268/08 and T-281/08),
    ECLI:EU:T:2012:90, 28 February 2012 .... 10.29

Land Burgenland & GrazerWechselseitige Versicherung AG v. Commission (Joined Cases
    C-214/12 P, C-215/12 P and C-223/12 P), ECLI:EU:C:2013:682,
    24 October 2013 .... 10.114

Land Rheinland-Pfalz v. Alcan Deutschland GmbH (C-24/95) [1997] ECR I-1591,
    20 March 1997 .... 11.110

Leclerc v. Au blé vert (229/83) [1985] ECR 1, 10 January 1985 .... 2.02, 2.03

Le Levant 001 and others v. Commission (T-34/02) [2006] ECR II-267,
    22 February 2006 .... 11.45

'Les Verts' v. European Parliament (294/83) [1986] ECR 1339, 23 April 1986 .... (p.779)

Limburgse Vinyl Maatschappij and others v. Commission (Joined Cases T-305–307,
    313–316, 318, 325, 328, 329 and 335/94) [1999] ECR II-931, 20 April 1999 ... 4.163,
                                                                                                                    4.250, (p.876)

Limburgse Vinyl Maatschappij NV v. Commission (C-23/99 P) [2002] ECR I-8375,
    15 October 2002 .... 13.05, 13.109, 22.06, 23.02, 23.04, 23.05, 23.26, 23.29, 25.42,
                                                                                                                    27.01, 27.07

Lisrestal (T-450/93) [1994] ECR II-1177, 6 December 1994 .... (p.763)

L'Oréal NV v. De Nieuwe AMCK (31/80) [1980] ECR 3775, 11 December 1980 ..... 4.289

Lorenz v. Germany (120/73) [1973] ECR 1471, 11 December 1973 ...... 10.72, 11.04, 11.77

LR AF 1998 formerly Løgstør Rør A/S v. Commission (T-23/99) [2002] ECR II-1705,
    20 March 2002 .... 13.72, 13.146, 13.159, 13.175

LTM v. MBU (56/65) [1966] ECR 235, 30 June 1966 .... 4.88, 4.141, 4.156, 4.183, 4.202, 4.306

Lubricantes y Carburantes Galaicos SL v. GALP Energía Espaæa SAU (C-506/07) [2009] ECR I-00134, 3 September 2009 .... 15.18

M6 & TF1 v. Commission (T-568/08 and T-573/08) [2010] ECR II-3397, 1 July 2010 .... 11.31

Manfredi and others (Joined Cases C-295 and 298/04) [2006] ECR I-6619, 13 July 2006 .... 4.140, 15.05

Mannesmannröhren-Werke v. Commission (T-112/98) [2001] ECR II-729, 20 February 2001 .... 25.41

Mannesmannröhren-Werke v. Commission (T-44/00) [2004] ECR II-2223, 8 July 2004 .... 4.173, 13.77

Manuli Rubber Industries SpA (MRI) v. Commission (T-154/09), ECLI:EU:T:2013:260, 17 May 2013 .... 13.20, 13.210

Marchandise (C-332/89) [1991] ECR I-1027, 28 February 1991 .... 2.11

Mastercard Inc. and others v. Commission (T-111/08), ECLI:EU:T:2012:260, 24 May 2012 .... 4.127, 4.217

MasterCard Inc. and others v. Commission (C-382/12), ECLI:EU:C:2014:2201, 11 September 2014 .... 4.129, 4.227, 4.231, 4.271

Masterfoods and HB (C-344/98) [2000] ECR I-11369, 14 December 2000 .... 17.17

Matra Hachette v. Commission (T-17/93) [1994] ECR II-595, 15 July 1994 .... 4.214, 4.223, 4.234

Matra SA v. Commission (C-225/91) [1993] ECR I-3203, 15 June 1993 .... 10.81, 10.132, 11.91

Maxicar v. Renault (53/87) [1988] ECR 6211, 5 October 1988 .... 5.104

Mayr-Melnhof v. Commission (T-347/94) [1998] ECR II-1751, 14 May 1998 .... 13.72

MCI v. Commission (T-310/00) [2004] ECR II-3253, 28 September 2004 .... 14.140

Meca-Medina and Majcen v. Commission (C-519/04 P) [2006] ECR I-6991, 18 July 2006 .... 4.18, 4.182

Mediaset (C-69/13), ECLI:EU:C:2014:71, 13 February 2014 .... 11.112

Melloni v. Ministerio Fiscal (C-399/11), ECLI:EU:C:2013:107, 26 February 2013 .... 24.101, 28.02, 30.01

Meng (C-2/91) [1993] ECR I-575, 17 November 1993 .... 2.16

Metro v. Cartier (C-376/92) [1994] ECR I-15, 13 January 1994 .... 4.134, 4.302, 4.303

Metro v. Commission I (26/76) [1977] ECR 1875, 25 October 1977 .... 4.30, 4.210, 4.228, 4.232, 4.238, 4.282, 4.283, 4.288, 4.292, 5.27

Metro v. Commission II (75/84) [1986] ECR 3021, 22 October 1986 .... 4.241, 4.286

Métropole and others v. Commission (T-112/99) [2001] ECR II-2459, 18 September 2001 .... 4.178

Metsä-Serla and others v. Commission (Joined Cases T-339/94 and T-342/94) [1998] ECR II-1727, 14 May 1998 .... 13.194

Metsä-Serla and others v. Commission (C-294/98 P) [2000] ECR I-10065, 16 November 2000 .... 13.196

Michelin v. Commission (C-322/81) [1983] ECR 3461, 9 November 1983 .... 5.19, 5.63, 5.75, 5.80

Michelin v. Commission (T-203/01) [2003] ECR II-4071, 30 September 2003 .... 5.33, 5.79, 13.72, 13.120, 13.139

Microsoft v. Commission (T-201/04) [2007] ECR II-3601, 17 September 2007 .... 5.66, 5.87, 5.110, 5.137, 5.148, 13.79, (p.447)

Miller International Schallplatten (19/77) [1978] ECR 131, 1 February 1978 .... 4.284

Milk Marque and National Farmers' Union (C-137/00) [2003] ECR I-7975, 9 September 2003 .... 17.17

Ministère public v. Guy Blanguernon (C-38/89) [19990] ECR I-83, 11 January 1990 .... 9.53

Ministère public v. Jean-Louis Tournier (Tournier) (395/87) [1989] ECR 2521, 13 July 1989 .... 5.121

Ministero dello Sviluppo economico e.a (C-327/12), ECLI:EU:C:2013:827, 12 December 2013 .... 4.54

Minoan Lines SA v. Commission (T-66/99) [2003] ECR II-5515, 11 December 2003 .... 13.117, 13.127, 13.140, 13.206

Minoan Lines SA v. Commission (C-121/04 P) not published, 17 November 2005 .... 13.127

Mitsubishi Electric Corp v. Commission (T-133/07) [2011] ECR II-4219, 12 July 2011 .... 13.11, 13.75

Montedipe SpA (T-14/89) [1992] ECR II-1155, 10 March 1992 .... 13.71

Montecatini v. Commission (C-235/92 P) [1999] ECR I-4539, 8 July 1999 .... 4.177, 13.08, 24.21, 25.21

Mo och Domsjö v. Commission (T-352/94) [1998] ECR II-1989, 14 May 1998 ..... 13.124, 13.223

Motosykletistiki Omospondia Ellados NPID (MOTOE) v. Elliniko Dimosio (C-49/07) [2008] ECR I-4863, 1 July 2008 .... 4.43, 5.40, 9.25

Municipality of Almelo and others v. NV Energiebedrijf IJsselmij (C-393/92) [1994] ECR I-1477, 27 April 1994 .... 5.50, 9.39

Musique Diffusion française and Others v Commission (Joined Cases 100/80 to 103/80) [1983] ECR 1825, 7 June 1983 .... 26.19

MyTravel Group v. Commission (T-212/03) [2008] ECR II-1967, 9 September 2008 ....14.81

Namur-Les Assurances du Crédit SA v. Office National du Ducroire and the Belgian Stat (C-44/93) [1994] ECR 3829, 9 August 1994 .... 11.55

National Panasonic v. Commission (136/79) [1980] ECR 2033, 26 June 1980 .... 13.58

Nationale Delcrederedienst (C-44/93) [1994] ECR I-3829, 9 August 1994 ..... 11.07, 11.08, 11.73

Nazairdis SAS, now Distribution Casino France SAS and others (Joined Cases C-266/04, C-270/04, C-276/04, C-321/04–325/04) [2005] ECR I-9481, 27 October 2005 .... 11.59

NDC Health GmbH Co. KG and NDC Health Corporation v. Commission and IMS Health Inc (C-481/01 P(R)) [2002] ECR I-3401, 11 April 2002 .... 13.28

NDSHT v. Commission (C-322/09 P) [2010] ECR I-11911, 18 November 2010 ...... 11.94

Nederlandse Federatieve Vereniging voor de Groothandel op Elektrotechnisch Gebied v. Commission (C-105/04 P) [2006] ECR I-8725, 21 September 2006 .... 23.01

Netherlands & NOS v. Commission (T-231/06 and T-237/06) [2010] ECR II-05993, 16 December 2010 .... 10.56, 11.10

New Europe Consulting and others (T-231/97) [1999] ECR II-2403, 9 July 1999 ... (p.763)

Nexans France SAS and Nexans SA v. Commission (T-135/09), ECLI:EU:T:2012:596,
    14 November 2012 .... 13.48
Niki Luftfahrt v. Commission (T-162/10), ECLI:EU:T:2015:283, 13 May 2015 .... 14.178
Nissan v. Dupasquier (C-309/94) [1996] ECR I-677, 15 February 1996 .... 16.05
Nold (4/73) [1974] ECR 491, 14 May 1974 .... 3.05, 3.11, (p.755)
Nölle (T-167/94) [1995] ECR II-2589, 18 September 1995 .... (p.763)
Norddeutsches Vieh-und Fleischkontor (Joined Cases 213–215/81) [1982] ECR 3583,
    13 October 1982 .... 10.02
NS a.o. (Joined Cases C-411/10 and C-493/10) [2011] ECR I-13905,
    21 December 2011 .... 3.15
NSO v. Commission (260/82) [1985] ECR 3801, 10 December 1985 .... 4.168
Nungesser and Eisele v. Commission (258/78) [1982] ECR 2015, 8 June 1982 .... 4.240
Nynäs Petroleum and Nynas Petróleo v. Commission (T-482/07), ECLI:EU:T:2013:437,
    16 September 2013 .... 13.14
O2 (Germany) v. Commission (T-328/03) [2006] ECR II-1231, 2 May 2006 .... 4.164,
                                                                                                                        13.251
Ohra (C-245/91) [1993] ECR I-5851, 17 November 1993 .... 2.13
Okley Threads Ltd v. Commission (T-448/05) [2010] ECR II-69, 28 April 2010 ...... 13.98,
                                                                                                                        13.99, 13.171
Omya v. Commission (T-145/06) [2009] ECR II-145, 4 February 2009 .... 14.171
Opinion of the Court 1/91 [1991] ECR I-6079, 14 December 1991 .... 30.01
Opinion of the Court 1/09 [2011] ECR I-1137, 8 March 2011 .... 30.01
Orange v. European Commission (T-402/13), ECLI:EU:T:2014:991, 25 November
    2014 .... 8.05
Ordem dos Técnicos Oficiais de Contas (C-1/12), ECLI:EU:C:2013:127,
    28 February 2013 .... 4.53, 4.66
Ordre des barreaux francophones et germanophone and others (C-305/05) [2007] ECR
    I-05305, 26 June 2007 .... 24.06
Orkem v. Commission (374/87) [1989] ECR 3283, 18 October 1989 .... 13.39, 13.44,
                                                                                        (p.763), 25.28, 25.40, 25.42, 25.43
Otto v. Postbank (C-60/92) [1993] ECR I-5683, 10 November 1993 .... 25.28, 25.40
Oude Luttikhuis v. Coberco (C-399/93) [1995] ECR I-4515, 12 December 1995 ...... 17.10,
Outokumpu Oyj v. Commission (T-20/05) [2010] ECR II-89, 19 May 2010 .... 13.85,
                                                                                                                        13.100, 13.144
P Oy (C-6/12) ECLI:EU:C:2013:525, 18 July 2013 .... 10.48, 11.86
P TWD v. Commission (Case C-355/95) [1997] ECR I-2549, 15 May 1997 .... 10.138
Pape v. Minister van Landbouw, Natuurbeheer en Visserij (C-175/02) [2005] ECR I-127,
    13 January 2005 .... 11.58
Papierfabrik August Koehler AG, Bolloré, Distibuidora Vizcaína de Papeles SL v.
    Commission (Joined Cases C-322/07 P, C-327/07 P and C-328/07 P) [2009] ECR
    I-07191, 3 September 2009 .... 13.227, 23.24
Parke, Davis Co v. Probel (24/67) [1968] ECR 81, 29 February 1968 .... 5.97
Parker Hannifin Manufacturing Srl, formerly Parker ITR Srl and Parker-Hannifin Corp. v.
    European Commission (T-146/09 RENV), ECLI:EU:T:2016:411, 14 July
    2016 .... 13.91, 13.145, 13.192, 13.203
Parker ITR Srl, Parker-Hannifin Corp. v. Commission (T-146/09), ECLI:EU:T:2013:258,
    17 May 2013 .... 13.203

Pavlov and others (Joined Cases C-180–184/98) [2000] ECR I-6451,
    12 September 2000 .... 4.15, 4.44, 4.171, 4.180

Pearle BV and others v. Hoofdbedrijfschap Ambachten (C-345/02) [2004] ECR I-7139,
    15 July 2004 .... 10.18, 11.53, 11.70

Pedro IV Servicios SL v. Total Espaæa SA (C-260/07) [2009] ECR I-2437,
    2 April 2009 .... 15.04, 15.16, 15.17

Pegler Ltd v. Commission (T-386/06) [2011] ECR I-1267, 24 March 2011 .... 13.191

PerganHilffstoffe für industrielle Prozesse (T-474/04) [2007] ECR II-4225,
    12 October 2007 .... 13.232, 13.233, 13.239, 14.181

Peróxidos Orgánicos, SA v. Commission (T-120/04) [2006] ECR II-4441,
    16 November 2006 .... 13.10, 13.214, 13.216

Petrofina v. Commission (T-2/89) [1991] ECR II-1087, 24 October 1991 .... 4.191

Petrolessence and SG2R v. Commission (T-342/00), EU:T:2003:97, 3 April 2003 ..... 14.179

Pfizer v. Council (T-13/99) [2002] ECR II-3305, 11 September 2002 .... (p.888)

Pfleiderer (C-360/09) [2011] ECR II-5161, 14 June 2011 .... 13.33

Philip Morris Holland BV v. Commission (730/79) [1980] ECR 2671,
    17 September 1980 .... 10.58, 10.127

Philips v. Commission (T-119/02) [2003] ECR II-1433, 3 April 2003 .... 14.139, 14.161,
                                                                14.162, 14.164, 14.165, 14.178

Piau (Laurent) v. Commission (T-193/02) [2005] ECR II-209, 26 January 2005 .... 4.128,
                                                                                    4.139, 5.55

Pierre Fabre Dermo-Cosmétique v. Président de l'Autorité de la concurrence and Ministre
    de l'Économie, de l'Industrie et de l'Emploi (C-439/09) [2011] ECR I-9419,
    13 October 2011 .... 4.217, 4.305, 15.06

Pigs and Bacon Commission v. Redmond (177/78) [1979] ECR 2161,
    26 June 1979 .... 10.76, 17.01

Plant and others v. Commission (C-480/99 P) [2002] ECR I-265, 10 January 2002 ... 24.82

Port de Mertert (10/71) [1971] ECR 723, 14 July 1971 .... 9.31

Porto di Genova (C-179/90) [1991] ECR I-5889, 10 December 1991 .... 5.02, 5.37, 5.58,
                                                                                    9.15

Portugal v. Commission (C-88/03) [2006] ECR I-7115, 6 September 2006 .... 10.40

Portugal v. Commission (C-163/99) [2001] ECR I-02613, 29 March 2001 .... 5.78, 9.53

Portugal v. Commission (C-204/97) [2001] ECR I-3175, 3 May 2001 .... 11.21

Portugal Telecom SGPS, SA v. European Commission (T-208/13), ECLI:EU:T:2016:368,
    28 June 2016 .... 4.36, 13.102

Postbank v. Commission (T-353/94) [1996] ECR II-921, 18 September 1996 .... 13.235

Post Danmark v. Konkurrencerådet (C-209/10), ECLI:EU:T:2013:481,
    27 March 2012 .... 5.68

Post Danmark A/S v. Konkurrencerådet (C-23/14), ECLI:EU:C:2015:651,
    6 October 2015 .... 5.69, 5.83

Poste Italiane SpA v. Commission (T-525/08), ECLI:EU:T:2013:481,
    13 September 2013 .... 10.88

Poucet and Pistre (Joined Cases C-159 and 160/91) [1993] ECR I-637,
    17 February 1993 .... 4.40

Prayon-Rupel v. Commission (T-73/98) [2001] ECR II-867, 15 March 2001 .... 11.21,
                                                                        11.24, 11.25, 11.26

Président de l'Autorité de la concurrence v. Association des producteurs vendeurs d'endives
and others (Case C-671/15) OJ C 90 of 07.03.2016, p. 7) 17.02, 17.04
PreussenElektra (C-379/98) [2001] ECR I-2099, 13 March 2001 .... 10.05, 10.79
Prezes Urzedu Ochrony Konkurencji i Konsumentów v. Tele2 Polska (C-375/09) [2011]
ECR I-3055, 3 May 2011 .... 13.23
Procureur du Roi v. Benoît and Gustave Dassonville (8/74) [1974] ECR 837,
1 July 1974 .... 4.307
Procureur du Roi v. Jean-Marie Lagauche and others (Joined Cases C-46/90 and C-93/91)
[1993] ECR I-5267, 27 October 1993 .... 9.17
Prodifarma (T-116/89) [1990] ECR II-843, 13 December 1990 .... 2.15
Pronuptia (161/84) [1986] ECR 353, 28 January 1986 .... 4.189, 4.211, 4.312, 4.313
Protimonopolný úrad Slovenskej republiky and others (C-68/12), ECLI:EU:C:2013:71,
7 February 2013 .... 4.05, 4.150, 13.09
Prysmian v. Commission (T-140/09), ECLI:EU:T:2012:597, 14 November 2012 .... 19.07,
19.54
Publishers Association v. Commission (C-360/92) [1995] ECR I-23,
17 January 1995 .... 4.229
Quinn Barlo Ltd and others v. Commission (T-208/06) [2011] ECR II-7953,
30 November 2011 .... 13.08
Quinn Barlo Ltd and others v. Commission (C-70/12), ECLI:EU:C:2013:351,
30 May 2013 .... 13.114
Racke v. Hauptzollamt Mainz (283/83) [1984] ECR 379113 November 1984 .... 22.01
Raiffeisen Zentralbank Österreich and others v. Commission (Joined Cases T-259–264 and
271/02) [2006] ECR II-5169, 14 December 2006 .... 4.194
Raso, Silvano and others, Criminal Proceedings against (C-163/96) [1998] ECR I-533,
12 February 1998 .... 5.38, 9.21
Rau v. BALM (Joined Cases 133–136/85) [1987] ECR 2289, 21 May 1987 .... 11.79
Regione autonoma della Sardegna and Others v. Commission (T-394/08, T-408/08,
T-453/08 and T-454/08) [2011] ECR II-6255, 20 September 2011 .... 11.13, 11.22,
11.105
Reiff (C-185/91) [1993] ECR I-5801, 17 November 1993 .... 2.12
Remia v. Commission (C-42/84) [1985] ECR 2545, 11 July 1985 .... 4.159, 4.221, 4.269
Repsol Lubricantes y Especialidades, SA and Others v. European Commission
(C-617/13 P), ECLI:EU:C:2016:416, 9 June 2016 .... 13.246
Reynolds Tobacco and others v. Commission (C-131/03 P) [2006] ECR I-7795,
12 September 2006 .... 13.219
Riviera Auto Service Etablissements Dalmasso and others v. Commission (Joined Cases
T-185 and 190/96) [1999] ECR II-93, 21 January 1999 .... 4.02, 16.08
Roquette Frères (C-94/00) [2002] ECR I-9011, 22 October 2002 .... 13.46, 13.58, 19.06,
19.53
Royal Philips Electronics v. Commission (T-119/02) [2003] ECR II-1433,
3 April 2003 .... 14.139, 14.161, 14.162, 14.164, 14.165, 14.178
RSV (223/85) [1987] ECR 4617, 24 November 1987 .... 11.116
RTE v. Commission (T-69/89) [1991] ECR II-485, 10 July 1991 .... 5.20, 5.106, 5.148
RTT v. GB-Inno-BM (C-18/88) [1991] ECR I-5941, 13 December 1991 .... 5.158, 9.05,
9.37

Ryanair Ltd v. Commission (T-196/04) [2008] ECR II-3643, 17 December 2008 ..... 10.23, 10.24, 10.25

Sacchi (155/73) [1974] ECR 409, 30 April 1974 .... 5.157, 9.01, 9.27

Saeed Flugreisen (66/86) [1989] ECR 803, 11 April 1989 .... 2.10, 4.09, 5.03, 5.153, 9.36

SA Musique Diffusion Française v. Commission (Joined Cases 100–103/80) [1983] ECR 1825, 7 June 1983 .... 13.68, 13.83, 13.88, 13.107, 13.148, 13.150, 13.224, 23.14, 23.17, 23.18, 23.19, 23.25

Sandoz v. Commission (C-277/87) [1990] ECR I-45, 11 January 1990 .... 4.81

Sarrió v. Commission (C-291/98 P) [2000] ECR I-9991, 16 November 2000 .... 22.05

Scandinavian Airlines System v. Commission (T-241/01) [2005] ECR II-2917, 18 July 2005 .... 4.254, 13.78, 13.131

Schemaventotto v. Commission (T-58/09) [2010] ECR II-03863, September 2010 .... 14.193, 14.194, 14.195

Schenker Ltd. v. Commission (T-265/12), ECLI:EU:T:2016:111, 29 February 2016 .... 4.200, 13.15

Scheucher-Fleisch GmbH and Others v. Commission (T-375/04) [2009] ECR II-4155, 18 November 2009 .... 11.28

Schlüsselverlag J.S. Moser and others v. Commission (C-170/02) [2003] ECR I-9889, 25 September 2003 .... 14.190

Schindler v. Commission (C-501/11 P), ECLI:EU:C:2013:522, 18 July 2013 .... 3.10, 21.01, 24.72, 25.17, 26.07, 26.10, 26.23, 26.26

Schneider Electric v. Commission (T-310/01) [2002] ECR II-4071 22 October 2002 .... 13.223, 13.225, 14.170, 14.183

Schneider Electric v. Commission (T-351/03) [2007] ECR II-2237, 11 July 2007 ...... 14.79, 14.80, 24.34, 24.75

Schunk GmbH, Schunk Kohlenstoff-Technik GmbH (T-69/04) [2008] ECR II-2567, 8 October 2008 .... 1.01, 13.118, 13.143, 13.247

SCK and FNK v. Commission (Joined Cases T-213 and 218/96) [1997] ECR II-1739, 22 October 1997 .... 4.224, 4.258

Scott v. Commission (C-276/03) [2005] ECR I-8437, 6 October 2005 .... 11.34, 11.50

Scott v. Commission (T-366/00) [2007] ECR II-797, 29 March 2007 .... 10.109, 10.110, 11.46

Secop v. Commission (T-79/14), ECLI:EU:T:2016:118, 1 March 2016 .... 14.180

Selex Sistemi Integrati v. Commission and others (C-113/07 P) [2009] ECR I-2207, 26 March 2009 .... 4.51

SEP v. Commission (T-39/90) [1991] ECR II-1497, 12 December 1991 .... 13.42

Servizi Ausiliari Dottori Commercialisti Srl v. Giuseppe Calafiori (C-451/03) [2006] ECR I-2941, 30 March 2006 .... 9.16

Seydaland v. BVVG (C-239/09) [2010] ECR I-13083, 16 December 2010 ... 10.111, 10.112

SFEI v. La Poste (C-39/94) [1996] ECR I-3547, 11 July 1996 .... 10.105, 11.81, 11.82

Shell International v. Commission (T-11/89) [1992] ECR II-757, 10 March 1992 .... 4.56, 13.179

SIA Maxima Latvija (C-345/14), ECLI:EU:C:2015:784, 26 November 2015 .... 4.154

SIA 'VM Remonts' and others (C-542/14), ECLI:EU:C: 2016:578, 21 July 2016 .... 4.62

SIC – Sociedade Independente de Comunicaço, SA v. Commission (T-46/97) [2000] ECR II-2125, 10 May 2000 .... 10.30, 11.19

SIC – Sociedade Independente de Comunicaço, SA v. Commission (T-442/03)
[2008] ECR II-1161, 26 June 2008 .... 9.56, 10.14

Siemens v. Commission (T-459/93) [1995] ECR II-1675, 8 June 1995 .... 10.106, 10.129

Siemens AG Österreich and others v. Commission (Joined Cases T-122/07–T-124/07)
[2011] ECR II-793, 3 March 2011 .... 13.190

Siemens and others v. Commission (Joined Cases C-239/11 P, C-489/11 P and C-498/11
P), ECLI:EU:C:2013:866, 19 December 2013 .... 4.122

Simmenthal (106/77) [1978] ECR 629, 9 March 1978 .... 3.02

Si.mobil telekomunikacijske storitve d.d. v. European Commission (T-201/11),
ECLI:EU:T:2014:1096, 17 December 2014 .... 8.06

Sirena v. Eda (40/70) [1971] ECR 69, 18 February 1971 .... 4.26, 5.98, 5.116

SIV and others v. Commission (T-68/89, T-77/89 and T-78/89) [1992] ECR II-1403,
10 March 1992 .... 5.49, 5.52

Skibsværftsforeningen and others v. Commission (T-266/94) [1996] ECR II-1399,
22 October 1996 .... 11.44

Sky Österreich (C-283/11) ECLI:EU:2013:28, 22 January 2013 .... 20.01, 29.02, 29.03

Sloman Neptun v. Bodo Ziesemer (Joined Cases C-72/91 and C-73/91) [1993] ECR I-887,
17 March 1993 .... 10.04, 10.05, 10.121

Smurfit Kappa Group plc v. Commission (T-304/08), ECLI:EU:T:2012:351,
10 July 2012 .... 10.136

SNCM & France v. Corsica Ferries France (C-533/12 P & C-536/12 P),
ECLI:EU:C:2014:2142, 4 September 2014 .... 10.26

SNCZ v. Commission (T-52/02) [2005] ECR II-5005, 29 November 2005 .... 4.04, 13.95,
13.132, 13.154

SNCF v. Commission (T-242/12), ECLI:EU:T:2015:1003, 17 December 2015 .... 10.20

S.N.U.P.A.T. v. High Authority (42/59 and 49/59) [1961] ECR 103,
22 March 1961 .... 24.82

Societa Italiana Vetro and others v. Commission (Joined Cases T-68/89, T-77/89 and
T-78/89) [1992] ECR II-1403, 10 March 1992 .... 4.93

Société civile agricole d'insémination de la Crespelle v. Département de la Mayenne (La
Crespelle) (C-323/93) [1994] ECR I-5077, 5 October 1994 .... 9.16

Société de Vente de Ciments et Bétons (319/82) [1983] ECR 4173,
14 December 1983 .... 4.205

Société Générale v. Commission (T-34/93) [1995] ECR II-545, 8 March 1995 .... 13.42

Soliver NV v. Commission (T-68/09), ECLI:EU:T:2014:867, 10 October 2014 .... 4.123

Solvay v. Commission (C-110/10 P) [2011] ECR I-10439, 25 October 2011 .... 23.05,
23.09, 23.12, 23.14, 23.25, 23.28, 23.29, 23.30

Solvay v. Commission (C-455/11 P), ECLI:EU:C:2013:796, 5 December 2013 .... 4.112

Sot. Lélos kai Sia EE and Others v. GlaxoSmithKline AEVE Farmakeftikon Proïonton
(Joined Cases C-468/06–C-478/06) [2008] ECR I-07139,
16 September 2008 .... 5.131, 5.143

Spain v. Commission (C-42/93) [1994] ECR I-4175, 14 September 1994 .... 10.20, 10.96

Spain v. Commission (C-135/93) [1995] ECR I-1651, 29 July 1995 .... 11.16

Spain v. Commission (C-169/95) [1997] ECR I-135, 14 January 1997 .... 10.134, 10.135,
11.118

Spain v. Commission (Joined Cases C-278–280/92) [1994] ECR I-4103,
14 September 1994 .... 10.97, 10.98, 10.133, 10.143, 11.99

Spain v. Commission (C-342/96) [1999] ECR I-2459, 29 April 1999 .... 10.82, 10.103
Spain v. Commission (C-480/98) [2000] ECR I-8717, 12 October 2000 .... 10.84, 10.115,
11.103
Spain v. Commission (C-351/98) [2002] ECR I-8031, 26 September 2002 ..... 10.38, 10.43,
10.65
Spector Photo Group and Van Raemdonck (C-45/08) [2009] ECR I-12073,
23 December 2009 .... 25.17
SPO and others v. Commission (C-137/95 P) [1996] ECR I-1611,
25 March 1996 .... 13.116
Stauder (29/69) [1969] ECR 419, 12 November 1969 .... 3.03
Steenkolenmijnen in Limburg v. High Authority of the European Coal and Steel
Community (30/59) [1961] ECR 3, 23 February 1961 .... 10.89
Steinike and Weinlig v. Federal Republic of Germany (78/76) [1997] ECR 595,
22 March 1977 .... 10.01, 10.74, 11.78
Stora v. Commission (C-286/98) [2000] ECR I-9925, 16 November 2000 ... 13.201, 13.204
Stora Kopparbergs Bergslags v. Commission (T-354/94) [1989] ECR II-2111,
14 May 1998 .... 13.74
Stora Kopparbergs Bergslags v. Commission (C-286/98 P) [2008] ECR I-9925,
16 November 2000 .... 25.17
Streekgewest Westelijk Noord-Brabant (C-174/02) [2005] ECR I-85,
13 January 2005 .... 11.57, 10.120
Suiker Unie and others v. Commission (Joined Cases 40/73–48/73, 50/73, 54/73–56/73,
111/73, 113/73 and 114/73) [1975] ECR 1663, 16 December 1975 .... 4.29, 4.97,
4.102, 4.130, 5.22, 5.57, 5.73, 5.122, 5.129, 13.82, 13.197
Sumitomo and Nippon Steel v. Commission (Joined Cases C-403, C-404/04 P) [2007]
ECR I-729, 25 January 2007 .... 4.255
Sun Chemical Group and Others v. Commission (T-282/06) [2007] ECR II-02149,
9 July 2007 .... 14.178
Sytraval (C-367/95 P) [1998] ECR I-1719, 2 April 1998 .... 11.123, 11.124
T-Mobile a.o. (C-8/08) [2009] ECR I-4529, 19 February 2009 .... 4.111, 4.147, 25.19
T-Mobile Netherlands BV and others v. RvB NMa (C-8/08) [2009] ECR I-4529,
4 June 2009 .... 13.01, 25.18, 25.20
Team Relocations NV (T-204/08 and T-212/08) [2011] ECR II-3569,
16 June 2011 .... 13.17
Team Relocations and others v. Commission (C-444/111 P), ECLI:EU:C:2013:464,
11 July 2013 .... 4.120
Technische Unie v. Commission (C-113/04 P) [2006] ECR I-8831,
21 September 2006 .... 23.04
Telefónica SA v. Commission (C-274/12 P), ECLI:EU:2013:852, 19 December
2013 .... 11.95
Tepea v. Commission (28/77) [1978] ECR 1391, 20 June 1978 .... 4.166, 4.219
Territorio Histórico de Álava – Diputación Foral de Álava and Others v. Commission
(Joined Cases T-227/01–229/01, T-265/01, T-266/01 and T-270/01) [2009] ECR
II-3029, 9 September 2009 .... 11.01, 11.47
Tetra Laval v. Commission (T-5/02) [2002] ECR II-4381, 25 October 2002 ... 14.66, 14.67,
Tetra Laval v. Commission (T-80/02) [2002] ECR II-4519, 25 October 2002 .... 14.157

Tetra Pak International SA v. Commission (T-51/89) [1990] ECR II-309,
   10 July 1990 .... 5.154
Tetra Pak International SA v. Commission (T-83/91) [1994] ECR I-755,
   6 October 1994 .... 5.140
Tetra Pak International SA v. Commission (C-333/94 P) [1996] ECR I-5951,
   14 November 1996 .... 5.70, 5.86, 5.90, 5.135
Textilwerke Deggendorf (C-188/92) [1994] ECR I-833, 9 March 1994 .... 11.90
TF1 v. Commission (T-17/96) [1999] ECR II-1757, 3 June 1999 .... 9.52
ThyssenKrupp Liften Ascenseurs NV and others v. Commission (T-144/07) [2011] ECR
   II-5129, 13 July 2011 .... 13.87
ThyssenKrupp Stainless AG v. Commission (T-24/07) [2009] ECR II-2309,
   1 July 2009 .... 13.135, 13.169
Thyssen Stahl v. Commission (T-141/94) [1999] ECR II-347, 11 March 1999 ... 4.32, 4.71,
                                                                                                           4.108
Thyssen Stahl v. Commission (C-194/99) [2003] ECR I-10821, 2 October 2003 ...... 4.266,
                                                                                                          13.110
Tipp-Ex v. Commission (C-279/87) [1990] ECR I-261, 8 February 1990 .... 13.90
TNT Traco SpA v. Poste Italiane SpA and others (C-340/99) [2001] ECR I-4109,
   17 May 2001 .... 9.44
Tokai Carbon and others v. Commission (T-236/01) [2004] ECR II-1181,
   29 April 2004 .... 13.156, 13.161, 13.162
Tomra v. Commission (T-155/06) [2010] ECR II-04361, 9 September 2010 ..... 5.81, 5.138,
                                                                                                          5.147
Tomra v. Commission (C-549/10 P), ECLI:EU:C:2012:221, 19 April 2012 ..... 5.138, 5.147
Toshiba Corporation (17/10), ECLI:EU:C:2012:72, 14 February 2012 .. 4.27, 13.170, 26.12,
                                                                                                   27.01, 27.02
Toshiba Corporation v. Commission (C-373/14), ECLI:EU:C:2016:26, 20 January
   2016 .... 4.35, 4.257
Total Raffinage Marketing v. Commission (T-566/08), ECLI:EU:T:2013:423,
   13 September 2013 .... 3.115
Trade Agency v. Seramico (C-619/10) [2012] ECLI:EU:C:2012:531, 6 September
   2012 .... 24.99
Trade-Stomil (T-53/07) [2011] ECR II-4657, 13 July 2011 .... 13.11
Transalpine Ölleitung (C-368/04) [2006] ECR I-9957, 5 October 2006 .... 11.65, 11.66
Transocean Marine Paint Association v. Commission (17/74) [1974] ECR 1063,
   23 October 1974 .... 23.17
Tréfilunion v. Commission (T-148/89) [1995] ECR II-1063, 6 April 1995 ...... 4.135, 4.176,
                                                                                                           13.91
Trelleborg Industrie SAS and Trelleborg AB v. Commission (T-147/09 and T-148/09),
   ECLI:EU:T:2013:259, 17 May 2013 .... 13.19, 4.120
Trioplast v. Commission (T-40/06) [2010] ECR II-4893, 13 September 2010 .... 13.189
TU München (C-269/90) [1991] ECR I-5469, 21 November 1991 .... (p.763)
TV2/Denmark v. Commission (T-674/11), ECLI:EU:T:2015:684, 24 September
   2015 .... 10.11, 10.33, 11.15
Ufex v. Commission (T-613/97) [2000] ECR II-4055, 14 December 2000 .... 10.105
Unilever Bestfoods (Ireland) Ltd v. Commission (C-552/03 P) [2006] ECR I-9091,
   28 September 2006 .... 15.13

Union Pigments (T-62/02) [2005] ECR II-5057, 29 November 2005 .... 13.155
United Brands v. Commission (27/76) [1978] ECR 207, 14 February 1978 .... 5.06, 5.07,
                    5.23, 5.26, 5.28, 5.34, 5.61, 5.93, 5.117, 5.119, 5.128, 5.130
United Kingdom v. Commission (C-46/03) [2005] ECR I-10167,
    1 December 2005 .... 13.219
UTi Worldwide, Inc. and others v. Commission (T-264/12), ECLI:EU:T:2016:112 .... 4.100
VAG France SA v. Établissements Magne (C-10/86) [1986] ECR 4071,
    18 December 1986 .... 15.02, 16.02
VAG Händlerbeirat eV v. SYD Consult (C-41/96) [1997] ECR I-3123,
    5 June 1997 .... 4.304, 16.06
Valmont v. Commission (T-274/01) [2004] ECR II-3145, 16 September 2004 .... 10.31,
                                                                                10.32, 10.108
Van Ameyde (90/76) [1977] ECR I-1091, 9 June 1977 .... 9.11
Van Calster and Cleeren (C-261/01 and C-262/01) [2003] ECR I-12249,
    21 October 2003 .... 11.56, 11.64
Van den Berg (265/85) [1987] ECR 1155, 31 January 1985 .... (p.889)
Van der Kooy (Joined Cases 67/85, 68/75 and 70/85R) [1985] ECR 1315,
    3 May 1985 .... 11.98
Van der Kooy (Joined Cases 67/85, 68/75 and 70/85) [1988] ECR 219,
    2 February 1988 .... 10.124
Van Eycke (267/86) [1988] ECR 4769, 21 September 1988 .... 2.09
Van Landewyck and others v. Commission (Joined Cases 209–215 and 218/78) [1980] ECR
    3125, 29 October 1980 .... 4.63, 4.70, 4.125, 4.239, 24.32
Van Roessel and others v. Campina Melkunie (C-40/94) [1995] ECR I-4471,
    12 December 1995 .... 17.07, 17.16
Van Schijndel (Joined Cases C-430/93 and C-431/93) [1995] ECR I-4705,
    14 December 1995 .... 2.16
Van Tiggele (82/77) [1978] ECR 25, 24 January 1978 .... 10.123
Varec SA v. Belgian State (C-450/06) [2008] ECR I-581, 14 February 2008 .... 24.85, 24.87
VBVB and VBBB (Joined Cases 4/82 and 63/82) [1984] ECR 19,
    17 January 1984 .... 4.10, 4.131
Ventouris SA (T-59/99) [2003] ECR II-5257, 11 December 2003 .... 13.128, 13.150
Verband der Sachversicherer v. Commission (45/85) [1987] ECR 405,
    27 January 1987 .... 4.12, 4.127, 4.133, 4.212
Vereniging van Cementhandelaren v. Commission (8/72) [1972] ECR 977,
    17 October 1972 .... 4.186, 4.245
Vereniging van Vlaamse Reisbureaus (C-311/85) [1987] ECR 3801,
    1 October 1987 .... 2.07, 4.276
Vichy v. Commission (T-19/91) [1991] ECR II-415, 27 February 1992 .... 4.169, 4.222
Viho v. Commission (T-102/92) [1995] ECR II-17, 12 January 1995 .... 4.94
Villeroy & Boch Austria Gmbh v. Commission (C-626/13), ECLI:EU:C:2017:54, 26
    January 2017 .... 4.124
Visa Europe Ltd and others v. Commission (T-461/07) [2011] ECR II-1729, 14 April
    2011 .... 4.34
Viscido and others v. Ente Poste Italiane (Joined Cases 52/97, C-53/97 and C-54/97)
    [1998] ECR I-2629, 7 May 1998 .... 10.122

Vizcaya v. Commission (P & O European Ferries) (T-116/01 and T-118/01) [2003] ECR
    II-2957, 5 August 2003 .... 11.75
Vizcaya v. Commission (P & O European Ferries) (C-442/03 P and C-471/03 P) [2006]
    ECR I-4845, 1 June 2006 .... 11.61
Vlaamse federatie van verenigingen van Brood-en Banketbakkers, Ijsbereiders en
    Chocoladebewerkers (VEBIC) (C-439/08) [2010] ECR I-12471,
    7 December 2010 .... 13.252
Vlaamse Gewest (Flemish Region) v. Commission (T-214/95) [1998] ECR II-717,
    30 April 1998 .... 10.54, 10.55
Voelk v. Vervaecke (C-5/69) [1969] ECR 295, 9 July 1969 .... 4.165
voestalpine AG and others v. Commission (T-418/10), ECLI:EU:T:2015:516, 15 July
    2015 .... 4.61
Volkswagen AG and others v. Commission (Joined Cases T-132/96 and T-143/96)
    [1999] ECR II-3663, 15 December 1999 .... 10.126, 10.139, 10.142
Volkswagen AG v. Commission (C-338/00 P) [2003] ECR I-9189,
    18 September 2003 .... 4.273, 13.249, 15.11, 22.06
Volkswagen AG v. Commission (T-208/01) [2003] ECR II-5141, 3 December 2003 .... 4.85
Volvo, AB v. Erik Veng (UK) Ltd (238/87) [1988] ECR 6211, 5 October 1988 .... 5.105,
    16.09
VSPOB v. Commission (T-29/92) [1995] ECR II-289, 21 February 1995 .... 4.31, 4.192,
    4.235, 4.248
VW-Audi Forhandlerforeningen, acting on behalf of Vulcan Silkeborg A/S/ Skandinavisk
    Motor Co. A/S v. Skandinavisk Motor Co. A/S (C-125/05) [2006] ECR I-7637,
    7 September 2006 .... (p.672)
Waalse Gewestexecutive and Glaverbel (Joined Cases 62/87 and 72/87) [1988] ECR 1573,
    8 March 1988 .... 10.138
Wabco Europe and others v. Commission (T-380/10), ECLI:EU:T:2013:449,
    16 September 2013 .... 13.05
Wachauf (C-5/88) [1989] ECR 2609, 13 July 1989 .... 3.11, (p.883)
Walt Wilhelm v. Bundeskartellamt (14/68) [1969] ECR 1, 13 February 1969 .... 13.164
Waterleidingmaatschappij Noord-West Brabant v. Commission (T-188/95) [1998] ECR
    II-3713, 16 September 1998 .... 11.62
Westdeutsche Landesbank Girozentrale v. Commission (T-228/99 and T-233/99)
    [2003] ECR II-435, 6 March 2003 .... 11.49
William Prym GmbH Co.KG, Prym Consumer GmbH Co. KG v. Commission (C-534/07
    P) [2009] ECR I-7415, 3 September 2009 .... 13.104, 13.222
Windsurfing International v. Commission (193/83) [1986] ECR 611,
    25 February 1986 .... 4.190
Winner Wetten (C-409/06) [2010] ECR I-8015, 8 September 2010 .... 30.01
Wirtschaftsvereinigung Stahl and others v. Commission (T-16/98) [2001] ECR II-1207,
    5 April 2001 .... 4.265
Wouters and others (C-309/99) [2002] ECR I-1577, 19 February 2002 .... 4.47, 4.65,
    4.181
Ziegler SA v. Commission (T-199/08) [2011] ECR II-3507, 16 June 2011 .... 4.198, 13.106
Ziegler SA v. Commission (C-439/11 P), ECLI:EU:C:2013:513, 11 July 2013 .... 8.03
Züchner (172/80) [1981] ECR 1981 2021, 14 July 1981 .... 4.11, 4.103

European Free Trade Association Court

Posten Norge AS v. EFTA Surveillance Authority (E-15/10) [2012] EFTACR 246,
     18 April 2012 .... 23.06, 23.08, 23.09

Part 1

TREATY ON EUROPEAN UNION (TEU), TREATY ON THE FUNCTIONING OF THE EUROPEAN UNION (TFEU) AND REGULATIONS

Section 1

TREATY ON EUROPEAN UNION (TEU)

1

ARTICLE 3 TEU[*]

OBJECTIVES OF THE UNION

1. The Union's aim is to promote peace, its values and the well-being of its peoples.

2. The Union shall offer its citizens an area of freedom, security and justice without internal frontiers, in which the free movement of persons is ensured in conjunction with appropriate measures with respect to external border controls, asylum, immigration and the prevention and combating of crime.

3. The Union shall establish an internal market. It shall work for the sustainable development of Europe based on balanced economic growth and price stability, a highly competitive social market economy, aiming at full employment and social progress, and a high level of protection and improvement of the quality of the environment. It shall promote scientific and technological advance.

   It shall combat social exclusion and discrimination, and shall promote social justice and protection, equality between women and men, solidarity between generations and protection of the rights of the child.

   It shall promote economic, social and territorial cohesion, and solidarity among Member States.

   It shall respect its rich cultural and linguistic diversity, and shall ensure that Europe's cultural heritage is safeguarded and enhanced.

4. The Union shall establish an economic and monetary union whose currency is the euro.

5. In its relations with the wider world, the Union shall uphold and promote its values and interests and contribute to the protection of its citizens. It shall contribute to peace, security, the sustainable development of the Earth, solidarity and mutual respect among peoples, free and fair trade, eradication of poverty and the protection of human rights, in particular the rights of the child, as well as to the strict observance and the development of international law, including respect for the principles of the United Nations Charter.

---

[*] This chapter was written by Mats Johnsson.

6.   **The Union shall pursue its objectives by appropriate means commen-
     surate with the competences which are conferred upon it in the Treat-
     ies. (TEU 4; Protocol (No 27) on the internal market and competition)**

*The Treaty of Lisbon removed the former Article 3(g) from the Treaty establishing the
European Community. This provision provided that the activities of the Community
included 'a system ensuring that competition in the internal market is not distorted'.
After this provision was removed, 'Protocol (no 27) on the internal market and
competition' was adopted. In the Protocol, it is stated 'that the internal market as set
out in Article 3 of the Treaty on European Union includes a system ensuring that
competition is not distorted'.*

1.01   [I]t must be observed that the penalties laid down in Article 15(2) of Regulation No 17
       [now Article 23(2) Regulation No 1/2003] in the event of infringement of Articles [101
       and 102 TFEU] are a key instrument available to the Commission for ensuring that 'a
       system ensuring that competition in the internal market is not distorted' (Article
       3(1)(g) EC [cf. Protocol (no 27) on the internal market and competition]) is established
       within the Community. That system enables the Community to fulfil its task which
       consists, by means of the establishment of a common market, in promoting throughout
       the Community a harmonious, balanced and sustainable development of economic
       activities and a high degree of competitiveness (Article 2 EC [cf. Art. 3 TEU]).
       Furthermore, that system is necessary for the adoption, within the Community, of an
       economic policy conducted in accordance with the principle of an open market
       economy with free competition (Article [119(1) and (2) TFEU]). […]
       General Court 8 October 2008 (Schunk, T-69/04) [2008] ECR II-2567, para. 39.

1.02   […] Article 3(3) TEU states that the European Union is to establish an internal
       market, which, in accordance with Protocol No 27 on the internal market and
       competition, annexed to the Treaty of Lisbon (OJ 2010 C 83, p. 309), is to include a
       system ensuring that competition is not distorted.
       *CoJ 17 February 2011 (Konkurrensverket v. TeliaSonera Sverige AB, C-52/09)
       [2011] ECR I-00527, para. 20.*

1.03   As to the seriousness of the infringement, the vital nature of the Treaty rules on
       competition must be recalled, in particular those on State aid, which are the expression of
       one of the essential tasks with which the European Union is entrusted. At the time of the
       Court's assessment of the appropriateness and the amount of the present penalty
       payment, that vital nature is apparent from Article 3(3) TEU, namely the establishment
       of an internal market, and from Protocol No 27 on the internal market and competition,
       which forms an integral part of the Treaties in accordance with Article 51 TEU, and
       states that the internal market includes a system ensuring that competition is not
       distorted.
       *CoJ 17 November 2011 (Commission v. Italian Republic, C-496/09) [2011] ECR
       I-11483, para. 60.*

2

ARTICLE 4 TEU[*]

RELATIONS BETWEEN THE UNION AND THE MEMBER STATES; PRINCIPLES
OF SUBSIDIARITY, EQUALITY AND SINCERE CO-OPERATION

1. In accordance with Article 5, competences not conferred upon the Union in the Treaties remain with the Member States.

2. The Union shall respect the equality of Member States before the Treaties as well as their national identities, inherent in their fundamental structures, political and constitutional, inclusive of regional and local self-government. It shall respect their essential State functions, including ensuring the territorial integrity of the State, maintaining law and order and safeguarding national security. In particular, national security remains the sole responsibility of each Member State.

3. Pursuant to the principle of sincere cooperation, the Union and the Member States shall, in full mutual respect, assist each other in carrying out tasks which flow from the Treaties.
    The Member States shall take any appropriate measure, general or particular, to ensure fulfilment of the obligations arising out of the Treaties or resulting from the acts of the institutions of the Union.
    The Member States shall facilitate the achievement of the Union's tasks and refrain from any measure which could jeopardise the attainment of the Union's objectives. (TEU 3; TFEU 101, 102, 107, 108; Protocol (No 27) on the internal market and competition)

OVERVIEW

A. DUTY NOT TO JEOPARDISE UNION
    OBJECTIVES RE. ARTS 101 AND 102 TFEU 2.01

B. DUTY NOT TO JEOPARDISE UNION
    OBJECTIVES RE. ARTS 107 AND 108 TFEU 2.14

C. PROCEDURAL ASPECTS   2.15

---

[*] This chapter was written by Mats Johnsson.

A. DUTY NOT TO JEOPARDISE UNION OBJECTIVES RE. ARTS 101 AND 102 TFEU

2.01   The second paragraph of Article 5 of the [EEC Treaty, cf. third paragraph of Art. 4(3) TEU] provides that Member States shall abstain from any measure which could jeopardize the attainment of the objectives of the Treaty.

Accordingly, while it is true that Article [102] is directed at undertakings, none the less it is also true that the Treaty imposes a duty on Member States not to adopt or maintain in force any measure which could deprive that provision of its effectiveness. *CoJ 16 November 1977 (GB-INNO-BM/ATAB, 13/77) [1977] ECR 2115, paras 30 and 31.*

2.02   Whilst it is true that the rules on competition are concerned with the conduct of undertakings and not with national legislation, Member States are none the less obliged under the second paragraph of Article 5 [EEC Treaty, cf. third paragraph of Art. 4(3) TEU] not to detract, by means of national legislation, from the full and uniform application of community law or from the effectiveness of its implementing measures; nor may they introduce or maintain in force measures, even of a legislative nature, which may render ineffective the competition rules applicable to undertakings [...]. *CoJ 10 January 1985 (Leclerc v. Au blé vert, 229/83) [1985] ECR 1, para. 14.*

2.03   [T]he question arises as to whether national legislation which renders corporate behaviour of the type prohibited by Article [101(1) TFEU] superfluous, by making the book publisher or importer responsible for freely fixing binding retail prices, detracts from the effectiveness of Article [101 TFEU] and is therefore contrary to the second paragraph of Article 5 [EEC Treaty, cf. third paragraph of Art. 4(3) TEU]. [...]

It is thus apparent that the purely national systems and practices in the book trade have not yet been made subject to a community competition policy with which the Member States would be required to comply by virtue of their duty to abstain from any measure which might jeopardise the attainment of the objectives of the Treaty. It follows that, as community law stands, Member States' obligations under Article 5 [EEC] Treaty, in conjunction with articles 3(f) [EEC Treaty, cf. Protocol (No 27) on the internal market and competition] and [101 TFEU], are not specific enough to preclude them from enacting legislation of the type at issue on competition in the retail prices of books, provided that such legislation is consonant with the other specific Treaty provisions, in particular those concerning the free movement of goods. It is therefore necessary to consider those provisions. *CoJ 10 January 1985 (Leclerc v. Au blé vert, 229/83) [1985] ECR 1, paras 15 and 20.*

2.04   [R]ules such as those concerned in this case are not intended to compel suppliers and retailers to conclude agreements or to take any other action of the kind referred to in Article [101(1) TFEU]. On the contrary, they entrust responsibility for fixing prices to the public authorities, which for that purpose consider various factors of a different kind. The mere fact that the ex-refinery price fixed by the supplier – which, moreover, may not exceed the ceiling price fixed by the competent authorities – is one of the factors taken into account in fixing the retail selling price does not prevent rules such as those concerned here from being state rules and is not capable of depriving the rules on competition applicable to undertakings of their effectiveness.

CoJ 29 January 1985 (Cullet v. Leclerc, 231/83) [1985] ECR 305, para. 17.

See also CoJ 13 March 2008 (Ioannis Doulamis, C-446/05) [2008] ECR I-1377.

[T]he adoption of a measure by a public authority making an agreement binding on all **2.05** the traders concerned, even if they were not parties to the agreement, cannot remove the agreement from the scope of Article [101(1) TFEU].

The fact that the chairman or director of a body within which an agreement intended to prevent free competition is concluded places his signature at the foot of the agreement, even though national law does not provide for such a signature, does not affect the applicability to the agreement of the provisions of Article [101(1) TFEU].

It follows from the foregoing that the reply which must be given to the first question is that Article [101(1) TFEU] must be taken to apply to an inter-trade agreement fixing a minimum price for a product such as cognac concluded by two groups of traders within the framework of, and in accordance with the procedures of, a body such as the Bureau National Interprofessionnel du Cognac.

CoJ 30 January 1985 (BNIC v. Clair, 123/83) [1985] ECR 391, paras 23, 25 and 26.

[It] is contrary to the obligations of the Member States under Article 5 [EEC Treaty, cf. **2.06** Art. 4(3) TEU], read in conjunction with Article 3(f) [EEC Treaty, cf. Protocol (No 27) on the internal market and competition'] and Article [101 TFEU], in particular paragraph (1) [...] to approve air tariffs and thus to reinforce the effects thereof, where, in the absence of any rules adopted by the council in pursuance of Article [103 TFEU], it has been found in accordance with the forms and procedures laid down in Article [104 TFEU] or Article [105(2)] TFEU that those tariffs are the result of an agreement, a decision by an association of undertakings, or a concerted practice contrary to Article [101 TFEU].

CoJ 30 April 1986 (Asjes, Joined Cases 209–213/84) [1986] ECR 1425, para. 77.

See to the contrary the subsequent Council Regulation (EEC) No 3975/87 of 14 December 1987 laying down the procedure for the application of the rules on competition to undertakings in the air transport sector (OJ 1987 L 374/1).

[Certain legislative provisions or regulations of Belgium required] travel agents to **2.07** observe the prices and tariffs for travel set by tour operators, prohibiting them from sharing commissions paid in respect of the sale of such travel with their customers or granting rebates to their customers and regarding such acts as contrary to fair commercial practice. [The question is whether these legislative provisions or regulations] are [in]compatible with the obligations of the Member States pursuant to Article 5 [EEC Treaty, cf. Art. 4(3) TEU], in conjunction with Articles 3(f) [EEC Treaty, cf. Protocol (No 27) on the internal market and competition'] and [101 TFEU].

[W]hile it is true that Articles [101 and 102 TFEU] concern the conduct of undertakings and not laws or regulations of the Member States, the Treaty nevertheless imposes a duty on Member States not to adopt or maintain in force any measure which could deprive those provisions of their effectiveness. The Court has held that that would be the case, in particular, if a Member State were to require or favour the adoption of agreements, decisions or concerted practices contrary to Article [101] or to reinforce their effects.

[I]t is necessary first of all to determine whether the documents before the Court disclose the existence of agreements, decisions or concerted practices of that kind in the area of activities concerned by the question referred, and then to determine whether provisions such as the Belgian provisions at issue are intended to reinforce the effects of such agreements, decisions or concerted practices, or have that effect.

The documents before the Court show that the Belgian provisions form part of a structure involving agreements at various levels intended to oblige travel agents to observe the prices of tours fixed by tour operators [and that these] agreements [...] are incompatible with Article [101(1) TFEU].

It remains to be determined whether provisions such as those at issue before the national court, viewed in this context, are of such a nature as to reinforce the effects of the agreements between travel agents and tour operators.

First of all, by transforming an originally contractual prohibition into a legislative provision such as [the relevant provision] reinforces the effect of the agreements in question between the parties, inasmuch as the rule acquires a permanent character and can no longer be rescinded by the parties. Secondly, by treating the failure to observe agreed prices and tariffs or the prohibition on the sharing of commissions with clients as contrary to fair commercial practice it allows travel agents who comply with the agreed rules of commercial practice to bring proceedings for a restraining order against travel agents who are not party to the agreement and do not comply with those rules. Thirdly, with regard both to parties to the agreements and to third parties the possible withdrawal of the licence to operate as a travel agent in the event of failure to observe the agreed rules of commercial practice constitutes a highly effective sanction.

The answer [...] must therefore be that [the relevant legislative provisions or regulations] are incompatible with the obligations of the Member States pursuant to Article 5 [EEC Treaty, cf. Art. 4(3) TEU], in conjunction with Articles 3(f) [EEC Treaty, cf. Protocol (No 27) on the internal market and competition'] and [101 TFEU], where the object or effect of such national provisions is to reinforce the effects of agreements, decisions or concerted practices which are contrary to Article [101(1) TFEU].

CoJ 1 October 1987 (Vereniging van Vlaamse Reisbureaus, C-311/85) [1987] ECR 3801, paras 9–12 and 21–24.

2.08   A ministerial order which makes [an agreement contrary to Art. 101(1) TFEU] generally binding is contrary to the obligations imposed on the Member States by Article 5 [EEC Treaty, cf. Art. 4(3) TEU] read together with article 3(f) [EEC Treaty, cf. Protocol (No 27) on the internal market and competition] and [101 TFEU].

CoJ 3 December 1987 (BNIC/Aubert, 136/86) [1987] ECR 4789, para. 25.

[...] In order to assess the true scope of that legislation in the light of the criteria laid **2.09** down by the Court in its case-law it is therefore necessary merely to ascertain, first, whether it may be regarded as intended to reinforce the effects of pre-existing agreements and, secondly, whether there are circumstances capable of depriving the legislation of its official character.

With regard to the first point it is sufficient to note that, as the Court has consistently held, legislation may be regarded as intended to reinforce the effects of pre-existing agreements, decisions or concerted practices only if it incorporates either wholly or in part the terms of agreements concluded between undertakings and requires or encourages compliance on the part of those undertakings. [...]. Although the prospect of losing the entire benefit of the preferential tax treatment for savings deposits constitutes a significant inducement to comply with the legislation in question, it is not apparent from any of the findings made by the national court in its judgment that such legislation merely confirmed both the method of restricting the yield on deposits and the level of maximum rates adopted under pre-existing agreements, decisions or practices. However, it is for the national court to enquire further into that point if it considers that there may be doubts in that regard.

With regard to the second point, it is apparent from the legislation in question that the authorities reserved to themselves the power to fix the maximum rates of interest on savings deposits and did not delegate that responsibility to any private trader. That legislation thus has an official character which cannot be called in question by the mere fact, emphasized by the plaintiff in the main proceedings, that according to the preamble to the Royal Decree of 13 March 1986 the decree was adopted following consultations with the representatives of associations of credit establishments.

CoJ 21 September 1988 (Van Eycke, 267/86) [1988] ECR 4769, paras 17–19.

[T]he approval by the aeronautical authorities of tariff agreements contrary to Article **2.10** [101(1)] is not compatible with Community law and in particular with Article 5 [EEC Treaty, cf. Art. 4(3) TEU]. It also follows that the aeronautical authorities must refrain from taking any measure which might be construed as encouraging airlines to conclude tariff agreements contrary to the Treaty. [...]

Whilst [...] new rules laid down by the Council and the Commission leave the Community institutions and the authorities in the Member States free to encourage the airlines to organize mutual consultations on the tariffs to be applied on certain routes served by scheduled flights [...] the Treaty nevertheless strictly prohibits them from giving encouragement, in any form whatsoever, to the adoption of agreements or concerted practices with regard to tariffs contrary to Article [101(1)] or Article [102], as the case may be.

CoJ 11 April 1989 (Saeed Flugreisen, 66/86) [1989] ECR 803, paras 49 and 52.

In the present case there is no evidence before the Court to support the conclusion that **2.11** the legislation at issue seeks to reinforce the effects of pre-existing agreements, decisions or concerted practices. Moreover, no aspect of the legislation is liable to deprive it of its official character.

CoJ 28 February 1991 (Marchandise, C-332/89) [1991] ECR I-1027, para. 23.

2.12   [...] Article 3(f) [EEC Treaty, cf. Protocol (No 27) on the internal market and competition], the second paragraph of Article 5 [EEC Treaty, cf. the third paragraph of Art. 4(3) TEU] and Article [101 TFEU] do not preclude rules of a Member State which provide that tariffs for the long-distance transport of goods by road are to be fixed by tariff boards and are to be made compulsory for all economic agents, after approval by the public authorities, if the members of those boards, although chosen by the public authorities on a proposal from the relevant trade sectors, are not representatives of the latter called on to negotiate and conclude an agreement on prices but are independent experts called on to fix the tariffs on the basis of considerations of public interest and if the public authorities do not abandon their prerogatives but in particular ensure that the boards fix the tariffs by reference to considerations of public interest and, if necessary, substitute their decision for that of the boards.

CoJ 17 November 1993 (Reiff, C-185/91) [1993] ECR I-5801, para. 24.

See also CoJ 9 June 1994 (Delta Schiffahrts-und Speditionsgesellschaft, C- 153/93) [1994] ECR I-2517.

2.13   It must first be observed in that regard that the Netherlands rules on insurance agencies neither require nor favour the conclusion of any unlawful agreement, decision or concerted practice by insurance intermediaries, since the prohibition which they lay down is self-sufficient.

It must then be determined whether the rules have the effect of reinforcing an anti-competitive agreement. In that regard, it is common ground that the rules at issue were not preceded by any agreement in the sectors to which they relate.

Finally, it must be observed that the rules themselves prohibit the grant of financial advantages to policyholders and beneficiaries of policies and do not delegate to private traders responsibility for taking decisions affecting the economic sphere.

It follows that rules like those at issue in the main proceedings do not fall within the categories of State rules which, according to the case-law of the Court of Justice, undermine the effectiveness of Article 3(f) [EEC Treaty, cf. Protocol (No 27) on the internal market and competition], the second paragraph of Article 5 [EEC Treaty, cf. the third paragraph of Art. 4(3) TEU] and Article [101 TFEU].

CoJ 17 November 1993 (Ohra, C-245/91) [1993] ECR I-5851, paras 11–14.

B. DUTY NOT TO JEOPARDISE UNION OBJECTIVES RE. ARTS 107 AND 108 TFEU

2.14   [T]he fact that the only defence which a Member State to which a decision has been addressed can raise in legal proceedings such as these is that implementation of the decision is absolutely impossible does not prevent that state – if, in giving effect to the decision, it encounters unforeseen or unforeseeable difficulties or perceives consequences overlooked by the Commission – from submitting those problems for consideration by the Commission, together with proposals for suitable amendments. In such a case the Commission and the Member State concerned must respect the principle underlying Article 5 [EEC Treaty, cf. Art. 4(3) TEU] which imposes a duty of genuine cooperation on the Member States and Community institutions; accordingly, they must work together in good faith with a view to overcoming difficulties whilst fully observing the Treaty provisions, and in particular the provisions on aid. [...]

CoJ 15 January 1986 (Commission v. Belgium, 52/84) [1986] ECR 89, para. 16.

See also CoJ 22 March 2001 (Commission v. French Republic, C-261/99) [2001] ECR I-2537.

C. PROCEDURAL ASPECTS

[...] Article 5 [EEC Treaty, cf. Art. 4(3) TEU] does not confer on the Commission the **2.15** power to address binding decisions to the Member States prescribing a course to be followed in conformity with Community law [...]. Nor, in consequence, can it serve as the legal basis for a decision authorizing a Member State to adopt a given course. It is for the Member States to ensure that their conduct meets their obligations under Articles 3(f) [EEC Treaty, cf. Protocol (No 27) on the internal market and competition], 5 [EEC Treaty, cf. Art. 4(3) TEU] and [101 TFEU], subject to the review which the Court may subsequently undertake in the context of the procedures provided for in Articles [258 and 267 TFEU] [...]. In contrast, a prior check as to whether national measures are in conformity with Community law, in the form of authorization given by the Commission, is not consistent with the division of powers between the Community and national authorities in this area as laid down by the Treaty.

General Court 13 December 1990 (Prodifarma, T-116/89) [1990] ECR II-843, para. 79.

The competition rules mentioned by the national court are binding rules, directly **2.16** applicable in the national legal order. Where, by virtue of domestic law, courts or tribunals must raise of their own motion points of law based on binding domestic rules which have not been raised by the parties, such an obligation also exists where binding Community rules are concerned [...].

The position is the same if domestic law confers on courts and tribunals a discretion to apply of their own motion binding rules of law. Indeed, pursuant to the principle of cooperation laid down in Article 5 [EEC Treaty, cf. Art. 4(3) TEU], it is for national courts to ensure the legal protection which persons derive from the direct effect of provisions of Community law [...].

[I]n proceedings concerning civil rights and obligations freely entered into by the parties, it is for the national court to apply Articles 3(f) [EEC Treaty, cf. Protocol (No 27) on the internal market and competition], [101, 102 and 106 TFEU] even when the party with an interest in application of those provisions has not relied on them, where domestic law allows such application by the national court.

CoJ 14 December 1995 (Van Schijndel, Joined Cases C-430/93 and C-431/93) [1995] ECR I-4705, paras 13–15.

See also CoJ 17 November 1993 (Meng, C-2/91) [1993] ECR I-575; CoJ 18 June 1998 (Corsica Ferries v. Gruppo Antichi Ormoggiatori, C-266/96) [1998] ECR I-3949; CoJ 18 June 1998 (Commission v. Italian Republic, C-35/96) [1998] ECR I-385; CoJ 21 September 1999 (Drijvende Bokken v. Stichting Pensioenfonds, C-219/97) [1999] ECR I-6121.

3

ARTICLE 6 TEU*

THE CHARTER AND THE ECHR

1. The Union recognises the rights, freedoms and principles set out in the Charter of Fundamental Rights of the European Union of 7 December 2000, as adapted at Strasbourg, on 12 December 2007, which shall have the same legal value as the Treaties. The provisions of the Charter shall not extend in any way the competences of the Union as defined in the Treaties. The rights, freedoms and principles in the Charter shall be interpreted in accordance with the general provisions in Title VII of the Charter governing its interpretation and application and with due regard to the explanations referred to in the Charter, that set out the sources of those provisions.

2. The Union shall accede to the European Convention for the Protection of Human Rights and Fundamental Freedoms. Such accession shall not affect the Union's competences as defined in the Treaties.

3. Fundamental rights, as guaranteed by the European Convention for the Protection of Human Rights and Fundamental Freedoms and as they result from the constitutional traditions common to the Member States, shall constitute general principles of the Union's law.

OVERVIEW

A. THE CHARTER	3.01	1.	The ECHR as a source of law	3.03
		2.	Direct effect	3.11
B. APPLICATION OF THE ECHR BY THE EU COURTS	3.03	C.	POSITION OF POLAND AND THE UK	3.15

---

*   This chapter was written by Herman Speyart.

GENERAL

Protocols TEU and TFEU

Protocol (No 8) relating to Article 6(2) of the Treaty on European Union on the accession of the Union to the European Convention on the Protection of Human Rights and Fundamental Freedoms

Article 1

The agreement relating to the accession of the Union to the European Convention on the Protection of Human Rights and Fundamental Freedoms (hereinafter referred to as the 'European Convention') provided for in Article 6(2) of the Treaty on European Union shall make provision for preserving the specific characteristics of the Union and Union law, in particular with regard to:

(a)   the specific arrangements for the Union's possible participation in the control bodies of the European Convention;

(b)   the mechanisms necessary to ensure that proceedings by non–Member States and individual applications are correctly addressed to Member States and/or the Union as appropriate.

Article 2

The agreement referred to in Article 1 shall ensure that accession of the Union shall not affect the competences of the Union or the powers of its institutions. It shall ensure that nothing therein affects the situation of Member States in relation to the European Convention, in particular in relation to the Protocols thereto, measures taken by Member States derogating from the European Convention in accordance with Article 15 thereof and reservations to the European Convention made by Member States in accordance with Article 57 thereof.

Article 3

Nothing in the agreement referred to in Article 1 shall affect Article 344 of the Treaty on the Functioning of the European Union.

Protocol (No 30) on the Application of the Charter of Fundamental Rights of the European Union to Poland and to the United Kingdom

WHEREAS in Article 6 of the Treaty on European Union, the Union recognises the rights, freedoms and principles set out in the Charter of Fundamental Rights of the European Union,

WHEREAS the Charter is to be applied in strict accordance with the provisions of the aforementioned Article 6 and Title VII of the Charter itself,

WHEREAS the aforementioned Article 6 requires the Charter to be applied and interpreted by the courts of Poland and of the United Kingdom strictly in accordance with the explanations referred to in that Article,

WHEREAS the Charter contains both rights and principles,

WHEREAS the Charter contains both provisions which are civil and political in character and those which are economic and social in character,

WHEREAS the Charter reaffirms the rights, freedoms and principles recognised in the Union and makes those rights more visible, but does not create new rights or principles,

RECALLING the obligations devolving upon Poland and the United Kingdom under the Treaty on European Union, the Treaty on the Functioning of the European Union, and Union law generally,

NOTING the wish of Poland and the United Kingdom to clarify certain aspects of the application of the Charter,

DESIROUS therefore of clarifying the application of the Charter in relation to the laws and administrative action of Poland and of the United Kingdom and of its justiciability within Poland and within the United Kingdom,

REAFFIRMING that references in this Protocol to the operation of specific provisions of the Charter are strictly without prejudice to the operation of other provisions of the Charter,

REAFFIRMING that this Protocol is without prejudice to the application of the Charter to other Member States,

REAFFIRMING that this Protocol is without prejudice to other obligations devolving upon Poland and the United Kingdom under the Treaty on European Union, the Treaty on the Functioning of the European Union, and Union law generally,

Article 1

1. *The Charter does not extend the ability of the Court of Justice of the European Union, or any court or tribunal of Poland or of the United Kingdom, to find that the laws, regulations or administrative provisions, practices or action of Poland or of the United Kingdom are inconsistent with the fundamental rights, freedoms and principles that it reaffirms.*

2. *In particular, and for the avoidance of doubt, nothing in Title IV of the Charter creates justiciable rights applicable to Poland or the United Kingdom except in so far as Poland or the United Kingdom has provided for such rights in its national law.*

Article 2

To the extent that a provision of the Charter refers to national laws and practices, it shall only apply to Poland or the United Kingdom to the extent that the rights or principles that it contains are recognised in the law or practices of Poland or of the United Kingdom.

Declarations annexed to the Final Act of the Intergovernmental Conference which adopted the Treaty of Lisbon

Declaration 1 concerning the Charter of Fundamental Rights of the European Union (first sentence)

The Charter of Fundamental Rights of the European Union, which has legally binding force, confirms the fundamental rights guaranteed by the European Convention for the Protection of Human Rights and Fundamental Freedoms and as they result from the constitutional traditions common to the Member States.

Declaration 2 on Article 6(2) of the Treaty on European Union

The Conference agrees that the Union's accession to the European Convention for the Protection of Human Rights and Fundamental Freedoms should be arranged in such a way as to preserve the specific features of Union law. In this connection, the Conference notes the existence of a regular dialogue between the Court of Justice of the European Union and the European Court of Human Rights; such dialogue could be reinforced when the Union accedes to that Convention.

Declaration 53 by the Czech Republic on the Charter of Fundamental Rights of the European Union

1. *The Czech Republic recalls that the provisions of the Charter of Fundamental Rights of the European Union are addressed to the institutions and bodies of the European Union with due regard for the principle of subsidiarity and division of competences between the European Union and its Member States, as re-affirmed in Declaration (No 18) in relation to the delimitation of competences. The Czech Republic stresses that its provisions are addressed to the Member States only when they are implementing Union law, and not when they are adopting and implementing national law independently from Union law.*

2. *The Czech Republic also emphasises that the Charter does not extend the field of application of Union law and does not establish any new power for the Union. It does not diminish the field of application of national law and does not restrain any current powers of the national authorities in this field.*

3. *The Czech Republic stresses that, in so far as the Charter recognises fundamental rights and principles as they result from constitutional traditions common to the Member States, those rights and principles are to be interpreted in harmony with those traditions.*

4. *The Czech Republic further stresses that nothing in the Charter may be interpreted as restricting or adversely affecting human rights and fundamental freedoms as recognised, in their respective field of application, by Union law and by international agreements to which the Union or all the Member States are party, including the European Convention for the Protection of Human Rights and Fundamental Freedoms, and by the Member States' Constitutions.*

Declaration 61 by the Republic of Poland on the Charter of Fundamental Rights of the European Union

The Charter does not affect in any way the right of Member States to legislate in the sphere of public morality, family law, as well as the protection of human dignity and respect for human physical and moral integrity.

Declaration 62 by the Republic of Poland concerning the Protocol on the application of the Charter of Fundamental Rights of the European Union in relation to Poland and the United Kingdom

Poland declares that, having regard to the tradition of social movement of 'Solidarity' and its significant contribution to the struggle for social and labour rights, it fully respects social and labour rights, as established by European Union law, and in particular those reaffirmed in Title IV of the Charter of Fundamental Rights of the European Union.

A. THE CHARTER

3.01   As regards fundamental rights, it is important, since the entry into force of the Lisbon Treaty, to take account of the Charter, which has 'the same legal value as the Treaties' pursuant to the first subparagraph of Article 6(1) TEU.
CoJ 22 December 2010 (DEB, C-279/09) [2010] ECR I-13849, para. 30.

3.02   As regards […] the conclusions to be drawn by a national court from a conflict between provisions of domestic law and rights guaranteed by the Charter, it is settled case-law that a national court which is called upon, within the exercise of its jurisdiction, to apply provisions of European Union law is under a duty to give full effect to those provisions, if necessary refusing of its own motion to apply any conflicting provision of national legislation, even if adopted subsequently, and it is not necessary for the court to request or await the prior setting aside of such a provision by legislative or other constitutional means […]
CoJ (Grand Chamber) 26 February 2013 (Åkerberg Fransson, C-617/10), ECLI:EU:C:2013:105, para. 45.

See also CoJ 9 March 1978 (Simmenthal, 106/77) [1978] ECR 629, paras 21 and 24.

B. APPLICATION OF THE ECHR BY THE EU COURTS

1. The ECHR as a source of law

(a)   Prior to the entry into force of the Lisbon Treaty

3.03   Fundamental rights are an integral part of the general principles of law the observance of which the Court ensures.
CoJ 12 November 1969 (Stauder, 29/69) [1969] ECR 419, para. 7.

See also CoJ 28 March 1996 (Accession ECHR, Opinion 2/94) [1996] ECR 1759, para. 33.

3.04   [T]he protection of such rights, whilst inspired by the constitutional traditions common to the Member States, must be ensured within the framework of the structure and objectives of the Community.
CoJ 17 December 1970 (Internationale Handelsgesellschaft, 11/70) [1970] ECR 1125, para. 4.

See also CoJ 28 March 1996 (Accession ECHR, Opinion 2/94) [1996] ECR 1759, para. 33.

[I]nternational treaties for the protection of human rights on which the Member States **3.05** have collaborated or of which they are signatories, can supply guidelines which should be followed within the framework of Community law.
CoJ 14 May 1974 (Nold, 4/73) [1974] ECR 491, para. 13.

See also CoJ 28 March 1996 (Accession ECHR, Opinion 2/94) [1996] ECR 1759, para. 33.

The Convention has special significance in that respect. **3.06**
CoJ 13 December 1979 (Hauer, 44/79) [1979] ECR 3727, para. 4.

See also CoJ 15 May 1986 (Johnston, C-222/84) [1986] ECR 1651, para. 18; CoJ 28 March 1996 (Accession ECHR, Opinion 2/94) [1996] ECR 1759, para. 33.

[T]he Court [...] has no power to examine the compatibility with the [ECHR] of **3.07** national rules which do not fall within the scope of Community law. On the other hand, where such rules do fall within the scope of Community law, and reference is made to the Court for a preliminary ruling, it must provide all the criteria of interpretation needed by the national court to determine whether those rules are compatible with the fundamental rights the observance of which the Court ensures and which derive in particular from the [ECHR].
CoJ 18 June 1991 (ERT, C-260/89) [1991] ECR I-2925, para. 42.

Moreover, those principles have been incorporated in Article 6(2) of the TEU [pre- **3.08** Lisbon version], according to which The Union shall respect fundamental rights, as guaranteed by the European Convention for the Protection of Human Rights and Fundamental Freedoms signed in Rome on 4 November 1950 and as they result from the constitutional traditions common to the Member States, as general principles of Community law. According to Article 46(d) of the Treaty on European Union [pre-Lisbon version], the Court is to ensure that this provision is applied with regard to action of the institutions, in so far as [it] has jurisdiction under the Treaties establishing the European Communities and under [the] Treaty [old].
Order CoJ 4 February 2000 (Emesa Sugar, C-17/98) [2000] ECR I-665, para. 9.

(b) *Following the entry into force of the Lisbon Treaty but prior to accession to the ECHR*

[Application, first, of the Charter, as the internal provision, before looking at the **3.09** ECHR] Article 47 of the Charter secures in EU law the protection afforded by Article 6(1) of the ECHR. It is necessary, therefore, to refer only to Article 47.
CoJ 8 December 2011 (Chalkor v. Commission, C-386/10 P) [2011] ECR I-13085, para. 51.

See also CoJ 6 November 2012 (EC v. Otis a.o., C-199/11), ECLI:EU:C: 2012:684, para. 47.

3.10   [W]hilst, as Article 6(3) TEU confirms, fundamental rights recognised by the ECHR constitute general principles of the European Union's law and whilst Article 52(3) of the Charter requires rights contained in the Charter which correspond to rights guaranteed by the ECHR to be given the same meaning and scope as those laid down by the ECHR, the latter does not constitute, as long as the European Union has not acceded to it, a legal instrument which has been formally incorporated into European Union law.

CoJ (Grand Chamber) 26 February 2013 (Åkerberg Fransson, C-617/10), ECLI:EU:C:2013:105, para. 44.

See also CoJ 18 July 2013 (Schindler v. Commission, C-501/11 P), ECLI: EU:C:2013:522, para. 32.

2.   Direct effect

(a)   In relation to EU law

3.11   Fundamental rights form an integral part of the general principles of law, the observance of which [the Court] ensures. In safeguarding these rights, the Court is bound to draw inspiration from constitutional traditions common to the Member States, and it cannot therefore uphold measures which are incompatible with fundamental rights recognized and protected by the constitutions of those states.

CoJ 14 May 1974 (Nold, 4/73) [1974] ECR 491, para. 13.

See also CoJ 13 July 1989 (Wachauf, C-5/88) [1989] ECR 2609, para. 19; CoJ 28 March 1996 (Accession, ECHR Opinion 2/94) [1996] ECR I-1759.

(b)   In relation to national law

3.12   Although it is true that it is the duty of this Court to ensure the observance of fundamental rights in the field of Community law, it has no power to examine the compatibility with the Europan Convention of national legislation which concerns, as in this case, an area which falls within the jurisdiction of the national legislator.

CoJ 11 July 1985 (Cinéthèque v. Fédération Natinoale des Cinémas Français, Joined Cases 60/84 and 61/84) [1987] ECR 3719, para. 28.

3.13   [W]here such rules do fall within the scope of Community law, and reference is made to the Court for a preliminary ruling, it must provide all the criteria of interpretation needed by the national court to determine whether those rules are compatible with the fundamental rights the observance of which the Court ensures and which derive in particular from the [ECHR].

CoJ 18 June 1991 (ERT, C-260/89) [1991] ECR I-2925, para. 42.

As regards, first, the conclusions to be drawn by a national court from a conflict between **3.14** national law and the ECHR, it is to be remembered that whilst, as Article 6(3) TEU confirms, fundamental rights recognised by the ECHR constitute general principles of the European Union's law and whilst Article 52(3) of the Charter requires rights contained in the Charter which correspond to rights guaranteed by the ECHR to be given the same meaning and scope as those laid down by the ECHR, the latter does not constitute, as long as the European Union has not acceded to it, a legal instrument which has been formally incorporated into European Union law. Consequently, European Union law does not govern the relations between the ECHR and the legal systems of the Member States, nor does it determine the conclusions to be drawn by a national court in the event of conflict between the rights guaranteed by that convention and a rule of national law (see, to this effect, *Case C-571/10 Kamberaj*, ECLI:EU:C: 2012:233, para. 62).

CoJ (Grand Chamber) 26 February 2013 (Åkerberg Fransson, C-617/10), ECLI:EU:C:2013:105, para. 44.

C. POSITION OF POLAND AND THE UK

By its seventh question in Case C-411/10, the Court of Appeal (England & Wales) **3.15** (Civil Division) asks, in essence, whether, in so far as the preceding questions arise in respect of the obligations of the United Kingdom, the answers to the second to sixth questions should be qualified in any respect so as to take account of Protocol (No 30).

As noted by the ECHR, that question arises because of the position taken by the Secretary of State before the High Court of Justice (England & Wales) (Administrative Court) that the provisions of the Charter do not apply in the United Kingdom.

Even if the Secretary of State no longer maintained that position before the Court of Appeal (England & Wales) (Civil Division), it must be noted that Protocol (No 30) provides, in Article 1(1), that the Charter is not to extend the ability of the Court of Justice or any court or tribunal of Poland or of the United Kingdom, to find that the laws, regulations administrative provisions, practices or action of Poland or of the United Kingdom are inconsistent with the fundamental rights, freedoms and principles that it affirms.

According to the wording of that provision, as noted by the Advocate General in points 169 and 170 of her Opinion in Case C-411/10, Protocol (No 30) does not call into question the applicability of the Charter in the United Kingdom or in Poland, a position which is confirmed by the recitals in the preamble to that protocol. Thus, according to the third recital in the preamble to Protocol (No 30), Article 6 TEU requires the Charter to be applied and interpreted by the courts of Poland and of the United Kingdom strictly in accordance with the explanations referred to in that article. In addition, according to the sixth recital in the preamble to that protocol, the Charter reaffirms the rights, freedoms and principles recognised in the Union and makes those rights more visible, but does not create new rights or principles.

In those circumstances, Article 1(1) of Protocol (No 30) explains Article 51 of the Charter with regard to the scope thereof and does not intend to exempt the Republic of Poland or the United Kingdom from the obligation to comply with the provisions of the

Charter or to prevent a court of one of those Member States from ensuring compliance with those provisions.

CoJ 21 December 2011 (NS a.o., Joined Cases C–411/10 and C–493/10) [2011] ECR I–13905, paras 116–120.

Part 1

Section 2

TREATY ON THE FUNCTIONING OF THE EUROPEAN UNION (TFEU)

4

ARTICLE 101 TFEU*

CARTEL PROHIBITION

1. The following shall be prohibited as incompatible with the internal market: all agreements between undertakings, decisions by associations of undertakings and concerted practices which may affect trade between Member States and which have as their object or effect the prevention, restriction or distortion of competition within the internal market, and in particular those which:

    (a) directly or indirectly fix purchase or selling prices or any other trading conditions;

    (b) limit or control production, markets, technical development, or investment;

    (c) share markets or sources of supply;

    (d) apply dissimilar conditions to equivalent transactions with other trading parties, thereby placing them at a competitive disadvantage;

    (e) make the conclusion of contracts subject to acceptance by the other parties of supplementary obligations which, by their nature or according to commercial usage, have no connection with the subject of such contracts.

2. Any agreements or decisions prohibited pursuant to this Article shall be automatically void.

3. The provisions of paragraph 1 may, however, be declared inapplicable in the case of:

    – any agreement or category of agreements between undertakings,

    – any decision or category of decisions by associations of undertakings,

    – any concerted practice or category of concerted practices, which contributes to improving the production or distribution of goods or to promoting technical or economic progress, while allowing consumers a fair share of the resulting benefit, and which does not:

---

* This chapter was written by Edmon Oude Elferink.

(a) **impose on the undertakings concerned restrictions which are not indispensable to the attainment of these objectives;**

(b) **afford such undertakings the possibility of eliminating competition in respect of a substantial part of the products in question.**

OVERVIEW

A. GENERAL   4.01
   1. Direct effect   4.01
   2. *Ratione personae*   4.03
   3. *Ratione materiae*   4.07
   4. *Ratione loci*   4.19
   5. *Ratione temporis*   4.25
   6. Concepts   4.28
   7. Relationship between national law and Article 101 TFEU   4.130

B. RESTRICTION OF COMPETITION   4.141
   1. Object to prevent, restrict or distort competition   4.141
   2. Effect to prevent, restrict or distort competition   4.156
   3. Appreciable restriction of competition   4.165

   4. Rule of reason   4.176
   5. Restrictions inherent to an object of (non) economic interest   4.179

C. EFFECT UPON TRADE BETWEEN MEMBER STATES   4.183

D. PARAGRAPH 2: NULLITY   4.201

E. PARAGRAPH 3: EXEMPTION   4.210
   1. General   4.210
   2. Four cumulative conditions   4.218

F. TYPES OF CONDUCT FALLING UNDER ARTICLE 101 TFEU   4.243
   1. Horizontal agreements   4.243
   2. Vertical agreements   4.273

A. GENERAL

1. Direct effect

4.01   As the prohibitions of Articles [101(1) TFEU and 102 TFEU] tend by their very nature to produce direct effects in relations between individuals, these Articles create direct rights in respect of the individuals concerned which the national courts must safeguard.
CoJ 30 January 1974 (BRT I, 127/73) [1974] ECR 51, para. 16.

4.02   Moreover, where, as in the present case, the Commission does not have exclusive competence to find contractual clauses to be incompatible with Article [101](1) of the Treaty, national courts also having such competence owing to the fact that that provision has direct effect, a complainant does not have the right to obtain from the Commission a decision under Article [288 TFEU] regarding the existence or otherwise of the infringements alleged.
General Court 21 January 1999 (Riviera Auto Service Etablissements Dalmasso and others v. Commission, Joined Cases T-185 and 190/96) [1999] ECR II-93, para. 48.

2. *Ratione personae*

It is appropriate, in that context, to observe that Article [101] of the Treaty refers to the **4.03**
activities of undertakings. For that provision to apply, a change in the legal form and
name of an undertaking does not necessarily have the effect of creating a new
undertaking free of liability for the anti-competitive behaviour of its predecessor when,
from an economic point of view, the two are identical.
*CoJ 7 January 2004 (Aalborg Portland a.o. v. Commission, Joined Cases C-204,
205, 211, 213, 217 and 219/00P) [2004] ECR I-123, para. 59.*

Apart from those considerations concerning size, there is no reason to treat SMEs **4.04**
differently from other undertakings. The fact that the undertakings concerned are
SMEs does not exempt them from their duty to comply with the competition
rules [...].
*General Court 29 November 2005 (SNCZ v. Commission, T-52/02) [2005] ECR
II-5005, para. 84.*

[A]rticle 101 TFEU must be interpreted as meaning that the fact that an undertaking **4.05**
that is adversely affected by an agreement whose object is the restriction of competition
was allegedly operating illegally on the relevant market at the time when the agreement
was concluded is of no relevance to the question whether the agreement constitutes an
infringement of that provision.
*CoJ 7 February 2013 (Protimonopolný úrad Slovenskej republiky, C-68/12), ECLI:
EU:C:2013:71, para. 21.*

Moreover, it cannot be inferred from the Court's case-law that Article [101(1) TFEU] **4.06**
concerns only either (i) the undertakings operating on the market affected by the
restrictions of competition or indeed the markets upstream or downstream of that
market or neighbouring markets or (ii) undertakings which restrict their freedom of
action on a particular market under an agreement or as a result of a concerted practice.

Indeed, it is apparent from the Court's well established case-law that the text of
Article [101(1) TFEU] refers generally to all agreements and concerted practices
which, in either horizontal or vertical relationships, distort competition on the common
market, irrespective of the market on which the parties operate, and that only the
commercial conduct of one of the parties need be affected by the terms of the
arrangements in question [...].

It should also be noted that the main objective of Article [101(1) TFEU] is to ensure
that competition remains undistorted within the common market. The interpretation
of that provision advocated by AC-Treuhand would be liable to negate the full
effectiveness of the prohibition laid down by that provision, in so far as such an
interpretation would mean that it would not be possible to put a stop to the active
contribution of an undertaking to a restriction of competition simply because that
contribution does not relate to an economic activity forming part of the relevant market
on which that restriction comes about or is intended to come about. [...]

It follows that the conduct adopted by AC-Treuhand is directly linked to the efforts made by the producers of heat stabilisers, as regards both the negotiation and monitoring of the implementation of the obligations entered into by those producers in connection with the cartels, the very purpose of the services provided by AC-Treuhand on the basis of service contracts concluded with those producers being the attainment, in full knowledge of the facts, of the anticompetitive objectives in question, namely [...] price-fixing, market-sharing and customer-allocation and the exchange of commercially sensitive information.

In those circumstances, [...] even though those service contracts were formally concluded separately from the commitments entered into by the producers of heat stabilisers among themselves, and notwithstanding the fact that AC-Treuhand is a consultancy firm, it cannot be concluded that the action taken by AC-Treuhand in that capacity constituted mere peripheral services that were unconnected with the obligations assumed by the producers and the ensuring restrictions of competition.

CoJ 22 October 2015 (AC-Treuhand AG v. Commission, C-194/14), ECLI: EU:C:2015:717, paras 34–36, 38 and 39.

3.   *Ratione materiae*

(a)   *Coal and steel*

4.07   The Court points out that the Community Treaties established a single legal order [...], in which, as reflected in Article 305(1) EC, the ECSC Treaty constituted a specific regime derogating from the rules of general application established by the EC Treaty.

Pursuant to Article 97, the ECSC Treaty expired on 23 July 2002. Consequently, on 24 July 2002 the scope of the general regime resulting from the EC Treaty extended to the sectors which were initially governed by the ECSC Treaty. [...]

[...] Thus, the pursuit of the aim of undistorted competition in the sectors which initially fell within the common market in coal and steel is not suspended by the fact that the ECSC Treaty has expired, since that objective is also pursued in the context of the EC Treaty, by the same institution, namely the Commission, the administrative authority responsible for implementing and developing competition policy in the general interest of the Community.

General Court 31 March 2009 (ArcelorMittal Luxemburg and others v. Commission, T-405/06) [2009] ECR II-789, paras 57, 58 and 61.

(b)   *Atomic energy*

The rules on competition apply to this sector, notwithstanding the Euratom Treaty.

(c)   *Agriculture*

See Chapter 17 on Regulation No 1184/2006 and Regulation No 1234/2007 of 22 October 2007, known as the 'Single Common Market Organisation (CMO) Regulation' (OJ 2007 L 299/1).

(d) Transport

It is clear […] that the objectives of the Treaty, including that set out in Article 3(g) [cf. **4.08**
Protocol No 27 on the internal market and competition], namely the institution of a
system ensuring that competition in the common market is not distorted, are equally
applicable to the transport sector. […]

It must therefore be concluded that the rules in the Treaty on competition in
particular Articles [101 TFEU] to [106 TFEU], are applicable to transport. […]

It follows that air transport remains, on the same basis as the other modes of
transport, subject to the general rules of the Treaty, including the competition rules.

*CoJ 30 April 1986 (Asjes and others, Joined Cases 209–213/84) [1986] ECR 1425,
paras 36, 42 and 45.*

[T]he Community rules which have been adopted with regard to air transport apply **4.09**
only to international air transport services between Community airports. It must be
inferred from this that domestic air transport and air transport to and from airports in
non-member countries continue to be subject to the transitional provisions laid down in
Articles [104 TFEU] and [105 TFEU], and that with respect to those air transport
services the system described in the judgment of 30 April 1986 still applies.

CoJ 11 April 1989 (Saeed Flugreisen, 66/86) [1989] ECR 803, para. 21.

(e) Books

Its view is however that the special features of that market [for books] do not permit the **4.10**
two associations to set up, in their mutual relations, a restrictive system whose effect is
to deprive distributors of all freedom of action as regards the fixing of the selling price
up to the level of the final price to the consumer. Such an arrangement would indeed
infringe Article [101(1)(a) TFEU].

*CoJ 17 January 1984 (VBVB and VBBB, Joined Cases 4 and 63/82) [1984]
ECR 19, para. 45.*

(f) Banks

Although the transfer of customers' funds from one member state to another normally **4.11**
performed by banks is an operation which falls within the special task of banks,
particularly in conne[ct]ion with international movements of capital, that is not
sufficient to make them undertakings within the meaning of Article [106(2) TFEU]
unless it can be established that in performing such transfers the banks are operating a
service of general economic interest with which they have been entrusted by a measure
adopted by the public authorities.

As to Article 104 et seq. [EEC], those provisions in no way have the effect of
exempting banks from the competition rules of the [EEC-]Treaty. They appear in
Chapter 2 of Title II of the [EEC-]Treaty, which concerns 'balance of payments', and
are restricted to stipulating that there must be coordination between the Member States
on economic policy, and to that end they provide for collaboration between the

appropriate national administrative departments and the central banks of the Member States in order to attain the objectives of the [EEC-]Treaty.

CoJ 14 July 1981 (Züchner, 172/80) [1981] ECR 2021, paras 7 and 8.

(g) Insurance

See Council Regulation 1534/91 of 31 May 1991, the enabling regulation (OJ 1991 L 143/2) and Commission Regulation No 267/2010 of 24 March 2010 on the application of Article 101(3) of the Treaty to certain categories of agreements, decisions and concerted practices in the insurance sector (OJ 2010 L 83/1), as well as the explanatory communication from the Commission (OJ 2010 C 82/20).

4.12 Consequently, it must be concluded that the Community competition system, as set out in particular in Articles [101 and 102 TFEU] and in the provisions of Regulation No 17 [now Regulation No 1/2003], applies without restriction to the insurance industry.

That conclusion in no way implies that Community competition law does not permit the special characteristics of certain branches of the economy to be taken into account. It is for the Commission, within the framework of its power under Article [101(3) TFEU] to grant exemption from the prohibitions contained in Article [101(1) TFEU], to take account of the particular nature of different branches of the economy and the problems peculiar to them.

CoJ 27 January 1987 (Verband der Sachversicherer v. Commission, 45/85) [1987] ECR 405, paras 14 and 15.

(h) Motor vehicles

See Chapter 16 on Regulation No 461/2010 and the Supplementary guidelines on vertical restraints in agreements for the sale and repair of motor vehicles and for the distribution of spare parts for motor vehicles (OJ 2010 C 138/16).

4.13 It follows that, contrary to what the applicants maintain, it cannot be said, in general terms, that motor-vehicle distribution has been exempted from the application of Article [101(1) TFEU] [...].

Pres. General Court 21 May 1990 (Automobiles Peugeot and others v. Commission, T-23/90) [1990] ECR II-195.

(i) Postal services

See Commission Notice on the application of the competition rules to the postal sector (OJ 1998 C 39/2).

(j) Social policy

4.14 Next, it is important to bear in mind that, under Article 3(g) EC [cf. Protocol No 27 on the internal market and competition] and 3(i) EC [cf. Article 4(2)(c) TFEU], the activities of the Community are to include not only a 'system ensuring that competition in the internal market is not distorted' but also 'a policy in the social sphere'. Article 2 of the EC Treaty [cf. Article 3 TEU] provides that a particular task of the Community is 'to promote throughout the Community a harmonious and balanced development of economic activities' and 'a high level of employment and of social protection'.

In that connection, Article [153 TFEU] provides that the Commission is to promote close cooperation between Member States in the social field, particularly in matters relating to the right of association and collective bargaining between employers and workers.

Article [155 TFEU] adds that the Commission is to endeavour to develop the dialogue between management and labour at European level which could, if the two sides consider it desirable, lead to relations based on agreement. [...]

It is beyond question that certain restrictions of competition are inherent in collective agreements between organisations representing employers and workers. However, the social policy objectives pursued by such agreements would be seriously undermined if management and labour were subject to Article [101(1) TFEU] in seeking jointly to adopt measures to improve conditions of work and employment.

It therefore follows from an interpretation of the provisions of the Treaty as a whole which is both effective and consistent that agreements concluded in the context of collective negotiations between management and labour in pursuit of such objectives must, by virtue of their nature and purpose, be regarded as not falling within the scope of Article [101(1) TFEU].

CoJ 21 September 1999 (Drijvende Bokken and others, C-219/97) [1999] ECR I-6121, paras 41–43, 46 and 47.

It should be borne in mind that, at paragraphs 64, 61 and 51 respectively of the **4.15** judgments in *Albany*, *Brentjens'* and *Drijvende Bokken*, the Court held that agreements concluded in the context of collective bargaining between employers and employees and aimed at improving employment conditions are not, by reason of their nature and purpose, to be regarded as falling within the scope of Article [101(1) TFEU].

Such exclusion from the scope of Article [101(1) TFEU] cannot be applied to an agreement which, whilst being intended, like the agreement at issue in the main proceedings, to guarantee a certain level of pension to all the members of a profession and thus to improve one aspect of their working conditions, namely their remuneration, is not concluded in the context of collective bargaining between employers and employees.

On this point, it should be emphasised that the Treaty contains no provisions, like Articles [153 and 155 TFEU] [...] or Articles 1 and 4 of the Agreement on social policy (OJ 1992 C 191/91), encouraging the members of the liberal professions to conclude collective agreements with a view to improving their terms of employment and working conditions and providing that, at the request of members of the professions, such agreements be made compulsory by the public authorities, for all the members of the profession in question.

That being so, Article [101(1) TFEU] must be interpreted as meaning that a decision taken by the members of a liberal profession to set up a pension fund responsible for managing a supplementary pension scheme and to request the public authorities to make membership of that fund compulsory for all the members of that profession does not, by reason of its nature or purpose, fall outside the scope of that provision.

CoJ 12 September 2000 (Pavlov and others, Joined Cases C-180–184/98) [2000] ECR I-6451, paras 67–70.

4.16   [A]rticle 101 TFEU, read in conjunction with Article 4(3) TEU, must be interpreted as not precluding the decision by the public authorities to make compulsory, at the request of the organizations representing employers and employees within a given occupational sector, an agreement which is the result of collective bargaining and which provides for compulsory affiliation to a scheme for supplementary reimbursement of healthcare costs for all undertakings within the sector concerned, without any possibility of exception.

CoJ 3 March 2011 (AG2R Prévoyance, C-437/09) [2011] ECR I-973, para. 39.

4.17   In the case in the main proceedings, the agreement concerned was concluded between an employers' organisation and employees' organisations of mixed composition, which negotiated, in accordance with national law, not only for employed substitutes but also for affiliated self-employed substitutes.

Therefore, it is necessary to examine whether the nature and purpose of such an agreement enable it to be included in collective negotiations between employers and employees and justify its exclusion, as regards minimum fees for self-employed substitutes, from the scope of Article 101(1) TFEU.

First, as regards the nature of that agreement, it is clear from the findings of the referring court that the agreement was concluded in the form of a collective labour agreement. However, that agreement, specifically as regards the provision in Annex 5 thereto on minimum fees, is the result of negotiations between an employers' organisation and employees' organisations which also represent the interests of self-employed substitutes who provide services to orchestras under a works or service contract.

It must be held in that regard that, although they perform the same activities as employees, service providers such as the substitutes at issue in the main proceedings, are, in principle, 'undertakings' within the meaning of Article 101(1) TFEU, for they offer their services for remuneration on a given market [...] and perform their activities as independent economic operators in relation to their principal [...].

It is clear, [...] that, in so far as an organisation representing workers carries out negotiations acting in the name, and on behalf, of those self-employed persons who are its members, it does not act as a trade union association and therefore as a social partner, but, in reality, acts as an association of undertakings.

It should also be added that, although the Treaty encourages dialogue between management and labour, it does not, however, contain provisions, like Articles 153 TFEU and 155 TFEU or Articles 1 and 4 of the Agreement on social policy [...], encouraging self-employed service providers to open a dialogue with the employers to which they provide services under a works or service contract and, therefore, to conclude collective agreements with a view to improving their terms of employment and working conditions [...].

In those circumstances, it follows that a provision of a collective labour agreement, such as that at issue in the main proceedings, in so far as it was concluded by an employees' organisation in the name, and on behalf, of the self-employed services providers who are its members, does not constitute the result of a collective negotiation between employers and employees, and cannot be excluded, by reason of its nature, from the scope of Article 101(1) TFEU.

CoJ 4 December 2014 (FNV Kiem, C-413/13), ECLI:EU:C:2014:2411, paras 24–30.

(k) Sports

Thus, where engagement in the sporting activity must be assessed in the light of the Treaty provisions relating to freedom of movement for workers or freedom to provide services, it will be necessary to determine whether the rules which govern that activity satisfy the requirements of Articles [45 and 56 TFEU], that is to say do not constitute restrictions prohibited by those articles […].

4.18

Likewise, where engagement in the activity must be assessed in the light of the Treaty provisions relating to competition, it will be necessary to determine, given the specific requirements of Articles [101 and 102 TFEU], whether the rules which govern that activity emanate from an undertaking, whether the latter restricts competition or abuses its dominant position, and whether that restriction or that abuse affects trade between Member States.

Therefore, even if those rules do not constitute restrictions on freedom of movement because they concern questions of purely sporting interest and, as such, have nothing to do with economic activity […], that fact means neither that the sporting activity in question necessarily falls outside the scope of Articles [101 and 102 TFEU] nor that the rules do not satisfy the specific requirements of those articles.

However, in […] of the contested judgment, the [General Court] held that the fact that purely sporting rules may have nothing to do with economic activity, with the result that they do not fall within the scope of Articles [45 and 56 TFEU], means, also, that they have nothing to do with the economic relationships of competition, with the result that they also do not fall within the scope of Articles [101 and 102 TFEU].

In holding that rules could thus be excluded straightaway from the scope of those articles solely on the ground that they were regarded as purely sporting with regard to the application of Articles [45 and 56 TFEU], without any need to determine first whether the rules fulfilled the specific requirements of Articles [101 and 102 TFEU], as set out in […] the present judgment, the [General Court] made an error of law.

CoJ 18 July 2006 (Meca-Medina and Majcen v. Commission, Case C-519/04P) [2006] ECR I-6991, paras 29–33.

(l) Telecommunications

See Commission guidelines on market analysis and the assessment of significant market power under the Community regulatory framework for electronic communications networks and services (OJ 2002 C 165/6), the notice on the application of the competition rules to access agreements in the telecommunications sector framework, relevant markets and principles (OJ 1998 C 265/2) and the guidelines on the application of EEC competition rules in the telecommunications sector (OJ 1991 C 233/2).

4. Ratione loci

See Guidelines on the effect on trade concept contained in Articles [101] and [102 TFEU] (OJ 2004 C 101/81).

4.19   To be incompatible with the common market and prohibited under Article [101 TFEU], an agreement must be one which 'may affect trade between Member States' and have 'as (its) object or effect' an impediment to 'competition within the common market'.

The fact that one of the undertakings which are parties to the agreement is situated in a third country does not prevent application of that provision since the agreement is operative on the territory of the common market.

An exclusive dealing agreement entered into between a producer who is subject to the law of a third country and a distributor established in the common market fulfils the two aforementioned conditions when, de jure or de facto, it prevents the distributor from re-exporting the products in question to other Member States or prevents the products from being imported from other Member States into the protected area and from being distributed therein by persons other than the exclusive dealer or his customers.

CoJ 25 November 1971 (Béguelin Import, 22/71) [1971] ECR 949, paras 10–12.

4.20   A restrictive agreement between traders within the common market and competitors in third countries that would bring about an isolation of the common market as a whole which, in the territory of the Community, would reduce the supply of products originating in third countries and similar to those protected by a mark within the Community, might be of such a nature as to affect adversely the conditions of competition within the common market.

In particular if the proprietor of the mark in dispute in the third country has within the Community various subsidiaries established in different Member States which are in a position to market the products at issue within the common market such isolation may also affect trade between Member States.

CoJ 15 June 1976 (EMI, 51/75) [1976] ECR 811, paras 28 and 29.

4.21   As has just been stated, a measure such as that in question which is specifically directed at exports of oil to a non-member country is not in itself likely to restrict or distort competition within the common market. It cannot therefore affect trade within the Community and infringe Articles 3(f) EC [cf. Protocol No 27 on the internal market and competition], [4(3) TEU] and [101 TFEU].

CoJ 18 February 1986 (Bulk Oil, 174/84) [1986] ECR 559, para. 44.

It should be observed that an infringement of Article [101 TFEU], such as the **4.22** conclusion of an agreement which has had the effect of restricting competition within the common market, consists of conduct made up of two elements, the formation of the agreement, decision or concerted practice and the implementation thereof. If the applicability of prohibitions laid down under competition law were made to depend on the place where the agreement, decision or concerted practice was formed, the result would obviously be to give undertakings an easy means of evading those prohibitions. The decisive factor is therefore the place where it is implemented.

The producers in this case implemented their pricing agreement within the common market. It is immaterial in that respect whether or not they had recourse to subsidiaries, agents, sub-agents, or branches within the Community in order to make their contacts with purchasers within the Community.

Accordingly the Community's jurisdiction to apply its competition rules to such conduct is covered by the territoriality principle as universally recognized in public international law.

CoJ 27 September 1988 (Ahlström Osakeythoe and others v. Commission, Joined Cases 89, 104, 114, 116, 117 and 125–129/85) [1988] ECR 5193, paras 16–18.

It follows that an agreement in which the reseller gives to the producer an undertaking **4.23** that he will sell the contractual products on a market outside the Community cannot be regarded as having the object of appreciably restricting competition within the common market or as being capable of affecting, as such, trade between Member States.

Consequently, the agreements at issue, in that they prohibit the reseller Javico from selling the contractual product outside the contractual territory assigned to it, do not constitute agreements which, by their very nature, are prohibited by Article [101(1) TFEU]. Similarly, the provisions of the agreements in question, in that they prohibit direct sales within the Community and re-exports of the contractual product to the Community, cannot be contrary, by their very nature, to Article [101(1) TFEU].

Although the contested provisions of those agreements do not, by their very nature, have as their object the prevention, restriction or distortion of competition within the common market within the meaning of Article [101(1) TFEU], it is, however, for the national court to determine whether they have that effect. Appraisal of the effects of those agreements necessarily implies taking account of their economic and legal context [...] and, in particular, of the fact that YSLP has established in the Community a selective distribution system enjoying an exemption.

CoJ 28 April 1998 (Javico, C-306/96) [1998] ECR I-1983, paras 20–22.

Moreover, in so far as Zwicky's complaint is to be understood as meaning that only **4.24** undertakings which are active in the geographic market in the Nordic countries as competitors, or on the side of supply or demand, are capable of coordinating their conduct as undertakings which are the (co-) perpetrators of an infringement, it must be pointed out that an undertaking can infringe the prohibition laid down in Article [101 TFEU] where the purpose of its conduct, as coordinated with that of other undertakings, is to restrict competition on a specific relevant market within the common market, and that does not mean that the undertaking has itself to be active on that relevant market [...].

General Court 28 April 2010 (Gütermann and Zwicky v. Commission, Joined Cases T-456 and 457/05) [2010] ECR II-1443, para. 53.

5. Ratione temporis

4.25   [The question is] whether Article [101 TFEU] has been applicable from the time of entry into force of the Treaty. The answer to this question must in principle be in the affirmative. Articles [104 TFEU] and [105 TFEU], which confer powers on the national authorities and on the Commission respectively for the application of Article [101 TFEU], presuppose its applicability from the time of entry into force of the Treaty.
CoJ 6 April 1962 (Kledingverkoopbedrijf De Geus and Uitdenboogerd, 13/61) [1962] ECR 93.

4.26   If the restrictive practices arose before the Treaty entered into force, it is both necessary and sufficient that they continue to produce their effects after that date.
CoJ 18 February 1971 (Sirena, 40/70) [1971] ECR 69, para. 12.

4.27   However, in the present case, neither the wording, nor the purpose, nor the general system of Article [101 TFEU], Article 3 of Regulation No 1/2003 and the Act of Accession contain any clear indications that those two provisions should be applied retroactively. [...]

The answer to the first question is therefore that the provisions of Article [101 TFEU] and Article 3(1) of Regulation No 1/2003 must be interpreted as meaning that, in the context of a proceeding initiated after 1 May 2004, they do not apply to a cartel which produced effects, in the territory of a Member State which acceded to the Union on 1 May 2004, during periods prior to that date.
CoJ 14 February 2012 (Toshiba Corporation, Case 17/10), ECLI:EU:C:2012:72, paras 52 and 67.

6. Concepts

(a) Concept of 'competition'

(i) Competition

4.28   The function of price competition is to keep prices down to the lowest possible level and to encourage the movement of goods between the Member States, thereby permitting the most efficient possible distribution of activities in the matter of productivity and the capacity of undertakings to adapt themselves to change.

Differences in rates encourage the pursuit of one of the basic objectives of the Treaty, namely the interpenetration of national markets and, as a result, direct access by consumers to the sources of production of the whole Community.
CoJ 14 July 1972 (ICI v. Commission, 48/69) [1972] ECR 619, paras 115 and 116.

The criteria of coordination and cooperation [...], which in no way require the working out of an actual plan, must be understood in the light of the concept inherent in the provisions of the Treaty relating to competition that each economic operator must determine independently the policy which he intends to adopt on the common market including the choice of the persons and undertakings to which he makes offers or sells.

CoJ 16 December 1975 (Suiker Unie and others v. Commission, Joined Cases 40–48, 50, 54–56, 111, 113 and 114/73) [1975] ECR 1663, para. 173.

4.29

The requirement contained in Articles 3 [EC, cf. Protocol No 27 on the internal market and competition] and [101 TFEU] that competition shall not be distorted implies the existence on the market of workable competition, that is to say the degree of competition necessary to ensure the observance of the basic requirements and the attainment of the objectives of the Treaty, in particular the creation of a single market achieving conditions similar to those of a domestic market. In accordance with this requirement the nature and intensiveness of competition may vary to an extent dictated by the products or services in question and the economic structure of the relevant market sectors.

CoJ 25 October 1977 (Metro v. Commission, 26/76) [1977] ECR 1875, para. 20.

4.30

The applicants' response that such negotiations would necessarily lead to ruinous competition which would ultimately have adverse repercussions on contract awarders themselves is not right. As the Commission observed, it is impossible to distinguish between normal competition and ruinous competition. Potentially, any competition is ruinous for the least efficient undertakings. That is why, by taking action to counteract what they regard as ruinous competition, the applicants necessarily restrict competition and therefore deprive consumers of its benefits.

General Court 21 February 1995 (VSPOB v. Commission, T-29/92) [1995] ECR II-289, para. 294.

4.31

It follows from that case-law that the idea that every undertaking must determine independently the market policy which it intends to pursue, without collusion with its competitors, is inherent to the ECSC Treaty and in particular Articles 4(d) and 65(1) thereof [regarding competition].

General Court 11 March 1999 (Thyssen Stahl v. Commission, T-141/94) [1999] ECR II-347, para. 265.

4.32

(ii)   Potential competition

[T]he examination of conditions of competition is based not only on existing competition between undertakings already present on the relevant market but also on potential competition, in order to ascertain whether, in the light of the structure of the market and the economic and legal context within which it functions, there are real concrete possibilities for the undertakings concerned to compete among themselves or for a new competitor to penetrate the relevant market and compete with the undertakings already established [...].

4.33

General Court 15 September 1998 (European Night Services Ltd (ENS) and others v. Commission, Joined cases T-374, 375, 384 and 388/94) [1998] ECR II-3141, para. 137.

4.34   [A]s regards the legal tests which should be applied in order to determine whether Morgan Stanley was a potential competitor in the market in question […] the Commission was required to determine whether, if the Rule had not been applied to Morgan Stanley, there would have been real concrete possibilities for it to enter the United Kingdom acquiring market and to compete with established undertakings.

[S]uch a demonstration must not be based on a mere hypothesis, but must be supported by evidence or an analysis of the structures of the relevant market […]. Accordingly, an undertaking cannot be described as a potential competitor if its entry into a market is not an economically viable strategy […].

It necessarily follows that, while the intention of an undertaking to enter a market may be of relevance in order to determine whether it can be considered to be a potential competitor in that market, nonetheless the essential factor on which such a description must be based is whether it has the ability to enter that market.

It should, in that regard, be recalled that whether potential competition – which may be no more than the existence of an undertaking outside that market – is restricted cannot depend on whether it can be demonstrated that that undertaking intends to enter that market in the near future. The mere fact of its existence may give rise to competitive pressure on the undertakings currently operating in that market, a pressure represented by the likelihood that a new competitor will enter the market if the market becomes more attractive.

[…] Recourse should […] be had to the […] definition of 'potential competitor' in the […] 'Guidelines on cooperation agreements'.

It is stated in [paragraph 10] in the Guidelines on cooperation agreements that '[a] [company] is treated as a potential competitor if [, in the absence of] the agreement, [in case of] a small and permanent increase in relative prices [it is likely that the former, within a short period of time, would undertake the necessary additional investments or other necessary switching costs to enter the relevant market on which the latter is active]'. Moreover, '[t]his assessment has to be based on realistic grounds, the mere theoretical possibility to enter a market is not sufficient'. […]

It is clear that such a definition reproduces, and clarifies, the tests deriving from the case-law. Consequently, since that definition does not appear to be inconsistent with the relevant case-law, it can be taken into account in order to determine whether the Commission was justified in describing Morgan Stanley as a potential competitor.

General Court 14 April 2011 (Visa Europe Ltd and others v. Commission, T-461/07) [2011] ECR II- 1729, paras 166–172.

4.35   [I]t should be observed that the General Court examined Toshiba's argument that the Gentlemen's Agreement was not capable of restricting competition within the EEA due to the fact that the European and Japanese producers were not competitors on the European market. It is in that context that the General Court found, first, […], that, since Article 101 TFEU also concerns potential competition, the Gentlemen's Agreement was capable of restricting competition, unless insurmountable barriers to entry to the European market existed that ruled out any potential competition from Japanese producers.

Secondly, [...], the General Court held that those barriers could not be classified as insurmountable, which was shown by the fact that Hitachi had accepted projects coming from customers situated in Europe.

The General Court also held, [...] that the Gentlemen's Agreement represented a 'strong indication that a competitive relationship existed' between the two categories of producers, which, [...], constitutes an element of the relevant economic and legal context.

The analysis which the General Court thus carried out is in accordance with the criteria set out in [...] this judgment in order to establish an infringement of Article 101(1) TFEU as a restriction by object, without a more detailed analysis of the relevant economic and legal context being necessary.

[E]ven if the General Court had distorted the content of the Hitachi letter, that would not be capable of calling into question the conclusion that the Commission demonstrated to the requisite legal standard that the barriers to entry to the European market were not insurmountable.

That conclusion is not based exclusively on the Hitachi statements, but also on other evidence. Thus, the General Court stated, [...] that the Commission set out, [...], the reasons why the barriers to entry to the market were not insurmountable, namely that the Korean undertaking Hyundai had recently entered the European market, and that the Japanese producers had recorded considerable sales in the United States, the undertakings concerned not having produced any evidence showing that the barriers to entry to the US market were very different to the barriers to entry to the European market. [...]

Moreover, [...], the General Court held that the very existence of the Gentlemen's Agreement constituted an argument which seriously calls into question the plausibility of the appellant's argument that the barriers to entry to the European market were insurmountable. As the General Court correctly noted [...] it is unlikely that the Japanese and European producers would have entered into a market-sharing agreement if they had not considered themselves to be at least potential competitors.

CoJ 20 January 2016 (Toshiba Corporation v. Commission, C-373/14 P), ECLI: EU:C:2016:26, paras 31–34 and 45–47.

[L]e fait de conclure un accord de non-concurrence constitue une reconnaissance par les **4.36** parties du fait qu'elles sont, pour le moins, des concurrentes potentielles concernant certains services. [...]

[S]i l'intention qu'a une entreprise d'intégrer un marché est éventuellement pertinente aux fins de vérifier si elle peut être considérée comme un concurrent potentiel sur ledit marché, l'élément essentiel sur lequel doit reposer une telle qualification est cependant constitué par sa capacité à intégrer ledit marché [...].

General Court 28 June 2016 (Portugal Telecom SGPS SA v. Commission, T-208/ 13), ECLI:EU:T:2016:368, paras 180 and 186.

Although it follows from that case-law that the Commission may rely inter alia on the **4.37** perception of the undertaking present on the market in order to assess whether other undertakings are potential competitors, nevertheless, the purely theoretical possibility of market entry is not sufficient to establish the existence of potential competition. The Commission must therefore demonstrate, by factual evidence or an analysis of the structures of the relevant market, that the market entry could have taken place sufficiently quickly for the threat of a potential entry to influence the conduct of the participants in the market, on the basis of costs which would have been economically viable [...].

[I]t would be surprising if an undertaking as experienced as Lundbeck would have decided to pay several million euros to the generic undertakings in exchange for their commitment not to enter the market during a certain period if the possibility that those generic undertakings could enter the market was purely theoretical. [...]

[I]n order to establish the existence of potential competition, the case-law requires only that the entry to the market take place within a reasonable period, without fixing a specific limit in that respect. The Commission therefore does not need to demonstrate with certainty that the entry of the generic undertakings to the market would have taken place before the expiry of the agreements at issue in order to be able to establish the existence of potential competition in the present case, particularly since, [...], potential competition may be exerted long before the expiry of a patent [...].

[P]otential competition already exists before the expiry of patents protecting a medicinal product [...]. [T]he steps taken before that expiry are relevant in assessing whether that competition was restricted.

General Court 8 September 2016 (H. Lundbeck A/S and others v. Commission, T-472/13), ECLI:EU:T:2016:449, paras 104, 161, 163 and 164.

(b) Concept of 'undertaking'

(i) Economic activity

4.38 The distinction provided [...] flows from the recognition of the fact that the state may act either by exercising public powers or by carrying on economic activities of an industrial or commercial nature by offering goods and services on the market. In order to make such a distinction, it is therefore necessary, in each case, to consider the activities exercised by the state and to determine the category to which those activities belong.

It must be observed that for that purpose, it is of no importance that the state carries out the said economic activities by way of a distinct body over which it may exercise, directly or indirectly, a dominant influence [...] or that it carries out the activities directly through a body forming part of the state administration.

CoJ 16 June 1987 (Commission v. Italy, 118/85) [1987] ECR 2599, paras 7 and 8.

4.39 It must be observed, in the context of competition law, first that the concept of an undertaking encompasses every entity engaged in an economic activity, regardless of the legal status of the entity and the way in which it is financed and, secondly, that employment procurement is an economic activity.

CoJ 23 April 1991 (Höfner and Elser, C-41/90) [1991] ECR I-1979, para. 21.

Sickness funds, and the organizations involved in the management of the public social **4.40** security system, fulfil an exclusively social function. That activity is based on the principle of national solidarity and is entirely non-profit-making. The benefits paid are statutory benefits bearing no relation to the amount of the contributions.

Accordingly, that activity is not an economic activity and, therefore, the organizations to which it is entrusted are not undertakings within the meaning of Articles [101] and [102 TFEU].

CoJ 17 February 1993 (Poucet and Pistre, Joined Cases C-159 and 160/91) [1993] ECR I-637, paras 18 and 19.

[T]he main proceedings concern the payment to be made by Calì for anti-pollution **4.41** surveillance exercised by SEPG in relation to the loading and unloading of acetone products transported by Calì in the oil port of Genoa.

[T]he main proceedings do not concern the invoicing of any action by SEPG necessitated by pollution actually produced during loading or unloading operations.

[The relevant regulation] expressly distinguishes, moreover, between surveillance intended to prevent pollution and intervention in a case where pollution has occurred and it provides [...] that those responsible for the pollution are to bear the costs arising from any action deemed necessary or advisable.

The anti-pollution surveillance for which SEPG was responsible in the oil port of Genoa is a task in the public interest which forms part of the essential functions of the State as regards protection of the environment in maritime areas and is to be interpreted as not being applicable to anti-pollution surveillance with which a body governed by private law has been entrusted by the public authorities in an oil port of a Member State, even where port users must pay dues to finance that activity.

CoJ 18 March 1997 (Diego Calì, C-343/95) [1997] ECR I-1545, paras 19–22 and 25.

The activity of customs agents has an economic character. They offer, for payment, **4.42** services consisting in the carrying out of customs formalities, relating in particular to the importation, exportation and transit of goods, as well as other complementary services such as services in monetary, commercial and fiscal areas. Furthermore, they assume the financial risks involved in the exercise of that activity [...]. If there is an imbalance between expenditure and receipts, the customs agent is required to bear the deficit himself.

In those circumstances, the fact that the activity of customs agent is intellectual, requires authorisation and can be pursued in the absence of a combination of material, non-material and human resources, is not such as to exclude it from the scope of Articles [101] and [102 TFEU].

CoJ 18 June 1998 (Commission v. Italy, C-35/96) [1998] ECR I-3851, paras 37 and 38.

The sectoral pension fund itself determines the amount of the contributions and **4.43** benefits and the Fund operates in accordance with the principle of capitalisation.

Accordingly, by contrast with the benefits provided by organisations charged with the management of compulsory social security schemes of the kind referred to in *Poucet and Pistre* [...] the amount of the benefits provided by the Fund depends on the financial results of the investments made by it, in respect of which it is subject, like an insurance company, to supervision by the Insurance Board.

In addition, as is apparent from Article 5 of the BPW and Articles 1 and 5 of the Guidelines for exemption from affiliation, a sectoral pension fund is required to grant exemption to an undertaking where the latter has already made available to its workers for at least six months before the request was lodged on the basis of which affiliation to the fund was made compulsory, a pension scheme granting them rights at least equivalent to those which they would acquire if affiliated to the fund. Moreover, under Article 1 of the abovementioned Guidelines, that fund is also entitled to grant exemption to an undertaking which provides its workers with a pension scheme granting them rights at least equivalent to those deriving from the Fund, provided that, in the event of withdrawal from the Fund, compensation considered reasonable by the Insurance Board is offered for any damage suffered by the Fund, from the actuarial point of view, as a result of the withdrawal.

It follows that a sectoral pension fund of the kind at issue in the main proceedings engages in an economic activity in competition with insurance companies.

CoJ 21 September 1999 (Albany, C-67/96) [1999] ECR I-5751, paras 81–84.

4.44   In the present cases, the medical specialists who are members of the LSV provide, in their capacity as self-employed economic operators, services on a market, namely the market in specialist medical services. They are paid by their patients for the services they provide and assume the financial risks attached to the pursuit of their activity.

The self-employed medical specialists who are members of the LSV therefore carry on an economic activity and are thus undertakings within the meaning of Articles [101, 102 and 106 TFEU]. The complexity and technical nature of the services they provide and the fact that the practice of their profession is regulated cannot alter that conclusion.

CoJ 12 September 2000 (Pavlov and others, Joined Cases C-180–184/98) [2000] ECR I-6451, paras 76 and 77.

4.45   It is therefore necessary first to determine what the relevant activities are and then to consider whether or not they constitute economic activities.

ADP is a public corporation enjoying financial autonomy, registered in the Paris register of companies; it is engaged in the planning, operation and development of all civil air transport installations in the Paris region that are designed to facilitate the arrival and departure of aircraft, and it supervises air-traffic control, and the embarkation, disembarkation and moving on land of passengers, cargo and air mail [...]. [...]

Through its activity as manager of the airport infrastructures, ADP determines the procedures and conditions on which suppliers of ground-handling services carry out their activities and in return levies the fee at issue. Such an activity on the part of ADP cannot be classified as a supervisory activity. The existence under domestic law of a system of special supervision of publicly owned property is not in any way incompatible with the exercise in public places or on public land of activities of an economic nature. Thus, the provision of airport facilities by ADP contributes to the performance, on publicly owned property, of a range of services of an economic nature and so forms part of its economic activity. Accordingly, the fact that the agreements between ADP and the ground handlers were concluded under French law applicable to agreements for the occupation of publicly owned property, even if that were proved to be the case, is not capable of calling in question the reasoning on which the contested decision is based.

The provision of airport facilities to airlines and the various service providers, in return for a fee at a rate freely fixed by ADP, must be regarded as an economic activity.

Similarly, the facilities within the Paris airports are essential, since their use is indispensable to the provision of various services, in particular ground handling. The management and provision of those facilities for the supply of such services constitute an economic activity.

General Court 12 December 2000 (Aéroports de Paris v. Commission, T-128/98) [2000] ECR II-3929, paras 110, 111 and 120–122.

However, as is clear from the case-law of the Court, the social aim of an insurance **4.46** scheme is not in itself sufficient to preclude the activity in question from being classified as an economic activity. [...]

In summary, it is clear from the foregoing that the amount of benefits and the amount of contributions, which are two essential elements of the scheme managed by the INAIL, are subject to supervision by the State and that the compulsory affiliation which characterises such an insurance scheme is essential for the financial balance of the scheme and for application of the principle of solidarity, which means that benefits paid to insured persons are not strictly proportionate to the contributions paid by them.

In conclusion, it may be stated that in participating in this way in the management of one of the traditional branches of social security, in this case insurance against accidents at work and occupational diseases, the INAIL fulfils an exclusively social function. It follows that its activity is not an economic activity for the purposes of competition law and that this body does not therefore constitute an undertaking within the meaning of Articles [101] and [102 TFEU].

CoJ 22 January 2002 (Cisal, C-218/00) [2002] ECR I-1691, paras 37, 44 and 45.

According to the case-law of the Court, the Treaty rules on competition do not apply to **4.47** activity which, by its nature, its aim and the rules to which it is subject does not belong to the sphere of economic activity [...] or which is connected with the exercise of the powers of a public authority [...].

CoJ 19 February 2002 (Wouters and others, C-309/99) [2002] ECR I-1577, para. 57.

In this connection, it is the activity consisting in offering goods and services on a given **4.48** market that is the characteristic feature of an economic activity [...], not the business of purchasing, as such. Thus, as the Commission has argued, it would be incorrect, when determining the nature of that subsequent activity, to dissociate the activity of purchasing goods from the subsequent use to which they are put. The nature of the purchasing activity must therefore be determined according to whether or not the subsequent use of the purchased goods amounts to an economic activity.

Consequently, an organisation which purchases goods – even in great quantity – not for the purpose of offering goods and services as part of an economic activity, but in order to use them in the context of a different activity, such as one of a purely social nature, does not act as an undertaking simply because it is a purchaser in a given market. Whilst an entity may wield very considerable economic power, even giving rise to a monopsony, it nevertheless remains the case that, if the activity for which that entity purchases goods is not an economic activity, it is not acting as an undertaking for the purposes of Community competition law and is therefore not subject to the prohibitions laid down in Articles [101(1) and 102 TFEU].

General Court 4 March 2003 (FENIN v. Commission, T-319/99) [2003] ECR II-357, paras 36 and 37.

4.49   Sickness funds in the German statutory health insurance scheme, like the bodies at issue in *Poucet and Pistre* [...] are involved in the management of the social security system. In this regard they fulfil an exclusively social function, which is founded on the principle of national solidarity and is entirely non-profit-making.

It is to be noted in particular that the sickness funds are compelled by law to offer to their members essentially identical obligatory benefits which do not depend on the amount of the contributions. The funds therefore have no possibility of influence over those benefits.

It follows from those characteristics that the sickness funds are similar to the bodies at issue in *Poucet and Pistre* and *Cisal* and that their activity must be regarded as being non-economic in nature.

The latitude available to the sickness funds when setting the contribution rate and their freedom to engage in some competition with one another in order to attract members does not call this analysis into question. As is apparent from the observations submitted to the Court, the legislature introduced an element of competition with regard to contributions in order to encourage the sickness funds to operate in accordance with principles of sound management, that is to say in the most effective and least costly manner possible, in the interests of the proper functioning of the German social security system. Pursuit of that objective does not in any way change the nature of the sickness funds' activity.

CoJ 16 March 2004 (AOK Bundesverband and others, Joined Cases C-261, 306, 354 and 355/01) [2004] ECR I-2493, paras 51, 52, 55 and 56.

4.50   As regards the effect that the fact that ELPA does not seek to make a profit may have on that classification, it should be noted that [...] the Court stated that the fact that the offer of goods or services is made without profit motive does not prevent the entity which carries out those operations on the market from being considered an undertaking, since that offer exists in competition with that of other operators which do seek to make a profit.

That is the case of activities engaged in by a legal person such as ELPA. The fact that MOTOE, the applicant in the main proceedings, is itself a non-profit-making association has, from that point of view, no effect on the classification as an undertaking of a legal person such as ELPA. First, it is not inconceivable that, in Greece, there exist, in addition to the associations whose activities consist in organising and commercially exploiting motorcycling events without seeking to make a profit, associations which are engaged in that activity and do seek to make a profit and which are thus in competition with ELPA. Second, non-profit-making associations which offer goods or services on a given market may find themselves in competition with one another. The success or economic survival of such associations depends ultimately on their being able to impose, on the relevant market, their services to the detriment of those offered by the other operators.

CoJ 1 July 2008 (MOTOE, C–49/07) [2008] ECR I-4863, paras 27 and 28.

The [General Court] therefore made an assessment that was erroneous in law in finding   **4.51**
that the activity of assisting the national administrations was separable from Eurocontrol's tasks of air space management and development of air safety by considering that that activity had an indirect relationship with air navigation safety, on the ground that the assistance provided by Eurocontrol covered only technical specifications in the implementation of tendering procedures and therefore affected air navigation safety only as a result of those procedures.

The other grounds set out in the judgment under appeal in that connection, to the effect that Eurocontrol provides assistance to the national administrations only on their request and the activity is therefore not essential or indispensable to ensuring the safety of air navigation, are not capable of demonstrating that the activity in question is not connected with the exercise of public powers.

The fact that the assistance provided by Eurocontrol is optional and that, as the case may be, only certain Member States have recourse to it cannot preclude such a connection or alter the nature of the activity. Moreover, in order for there to be a connection with the exercise of public powers, it is not necessary for the activity concerned to be essential or indispensable to ensuring the safety of air navigation, since what matters is that the activity is connected with the maintenance and development of air navigation safety, which constitute public powers.

It follows from all the foregoing considerations that the [General Court] erred in law by regarding Eurocontrol's activity of assisting the national administrations as an economic activity and, as a consequence, on the basis of grounds that were erroneous in law, considering that Eurocontrol was, in the exercise of that activity, an undertaking within the meaning of Article [102 TFEU] [and, thus, within the scope of Article 101 TFEU] [...].

CoJ 26 March 2009 (Selex Sistemi Integrati v. Commission and others, C–113/07P) [2009] ECR I-2207, paras 77–80.

[T]he activity of a public authority consisting in the storing, in a database, of data which   **4.52**
undertakings are obliged to report on the basis of statutory obligations, in permitting interested persons to search for that data and/or in providing them with print-outs thereof does not constitute an economic activity, and that public authority is not, therefore, to be regarded, in the course of that activity, as an undertaking, within the meaning of Article 102 TFEU. The fact that those searches and/or that provision of print-outs are carried out in consideration for remuneration provided for by law and not determined, directly or indirectly, by the entity concerned, is not such as to alter the legal classification of that activity. In addition, when such a public authority prohibits any other use of the data thus collected and made available to the public, by relying upon the *sui generis* protection granted to it as maker of the database at issue pursuant to Article 7 of Directive 96/9 or upon any other intellectual property right, it also does not

exercise an economic activity and is not therefore to be regarded, in the course of that activity, as an undertaking, within the meaning of Article 102 TFEU.

CoJ 12 July 2012 (Compass-Datenbank, C-138/11), ECLI:EU:C:2012:449, para. 51.

4.53   In the present case, it is apparent from the file before the Court that the chartered accountants offer, for remuneration, accounting services consisting in particular, pursuant to Article 6 of the Statute of the OTOC, of planning, organising and coordinating the accounts of entities, signing their financial statements and tax declarations, acting as consultants in the fields of accounting, taxation and social security and representing the taxpayers whose accounting they perform at the administrative stage of the taxation procedure. In addition, it is common ground that chartered accountants assume, as members of a liberal profession, the financial risks related to the exercise of those activities, since, where there is an imbalance between outgoings and revenue, a chartered accountant is required to bear the deficit personally.

That being so, chartered accountants, having regard to the manner in which their profession is regulated in Portugal, carry on an economic activity and are, therefore, undertakings for the purposes of Article 101 TFEU. The complexity and technical nature of the services they provide and the fact that the practice of their profession is regulated cannot alter that conclusion [...].

CoJ 28 February 2013 (Ordem dos Técnicos Oficiais de Contas, C-1/12), ECLI:EU:C:2013:127, paras 37 and 38.

4.54   In this case, the Italian legislature introduced, in accordance with Article 52(1) of Directive 2004/18, a certification scheme to be carried out by private bodies, namely SOAs. The latter are commercial undertakings entrusted with supplying certification services, the receipt of an appropriate certificate being a necessary condition in order for interested persons to participate in public works contracts in accordance with national legislation.

However, SOAs' activities have an economic character. They issue certificates in return for remuneration and exclusively on the basis of actual market demand. Furthermore, they assume the financial risks involved in the exercise of that activity.

The national legislation provides, inter alia, that the SOAs are to check the technical and financial capacity of the undertakings subject to certification, the contents of the declarations, certificates and documents presented by the persons to whom the certification is issued and compliance with the conditions relating to the personal situation of the candidate or tenderer.

In the context of that check, SOAs are required to send the relevant information to the Autorità, which is to review the lawfulness of the certification activities, with penalties capable of being imposed on companies in the event of an infringement of their obligations under the national legislation in force.

In contrast to the situation which was at issue in *Case C-113/07 P* [...], SOAs do not perform standardisation tasks. Those undertakings do not have any power to make decisions connected with the exercise of public powers.

As is apparent from the file in the present case, the undertakings carrying out certification activities, namely SOAs, operate [...] in conditions of competition.

Undertakings seeking to participate in procedures for the award of public works contracts are not legally obliged to use the certification services of a specific SOA.

In those circumstances, it should be held that, in the same way as the Court found that a motor vehicle manufacturer constituted an undertaking in so far as it operated on the market for certification of motor vehicles by issuing certificates of conformity necessary for their registration [...], SOAs must be considered, in the context of their certification activities, as 'undertakings' within the meaning of Articles 101 TFEU, 102 TFEU and 106 TFEU.

CoJ 12 December 2013 (Ministero dello Sviluppo economico e.a, C-327/12.), ECLI:EU:C:2013:827, paras 28–35.

(ii)   Economic unit

In competition law, the term 'undertaking' must be understood as designating an economic unit for the purpose of the subject-matter of the agreement in question even if in law that economic unit consists of several persons, natural or legal. **4.55**

CoJ 12 July 1984 (Hydrotherm, 170/83) [1984] ECR 2999, para. 11.

The Court considers that in prohibiting undertakings inter alia from entering into agreements or participating in concerted practices which may affect trade between Member States and have as their object or effect the prevention, restriction or distortion of competition within the common market, Article [101(1) TFEU] is aimed at economic units which consist of a unitary organization of personal, tangible and intangible elements which pursues a specific economic aim on a long-term basis and can contribute to the Commission of an infringement of the kind referred to in that provision. **4.56**

The Court holds that Shell and the Shell group operating companies which produce and market chemical products constitute a single unitary organization of personal, tangible and intangible elements which pursues, on a long-term basis, the objective inter alia of producing and selling polypropylene with a view to maximizing profits, even, in some cases, to the detriment of the individual profits of its various components. In that organization, each company plays a specific role. The operating companies produce or sell polypropylene, while the applicant plays a stimulating and coordinating role between the various operating companies of the group. Consequently, Shell and the Shell group operating companies constitute a single undertaking.

General Court 10 March 1992 (Shell International v. Commission, T-11/89) [1992] ECR II-757, paras 311 and 312.

It must be observed, from a preliminary point, that Community competition law refers to the activities of undertakings [...], and that the concept of an undertaking covers any entity engaged in an economic activity, regardless of its legal status and the way in which it is financed [...]. **4.57**

The Court has also stated that the concept of an undertaking, in the same context, must be understood as designating an economic unit even if in law that economic unit consists of several persons, natural or legal [...].

CoJ 10 September 2009 (Akzo Nobel v. Commission, C-97/08P) [2009] ECR I-8237, paras 54 and 55.

4.58   It follows […] that where the issue is whether an undertaking is to be penalised for infringement of competition law on the basis of Article [101 TFEU] in conjunction with Article 23(2) of Regulation No 1/2003, it is also irrelevant whether each individual legal entity comprising the undertaking is itself economically active and therefore individually constitutes an undertaking […].

   The only decisive factor for the purpose of the penalty is that all the legal entities which are held jointly and severally liable, in whole or in part, for payment of the same fine together constitute with the entity whose direct involvement in the infringement has been established ('the author of the infringement') a single undertaking for the purpose of Article [101 TFEU]. According to the case-law […], it is the actual exercise by the holding entity of decisive influence over the author of the infringement which is important in that regard.

   It follows from the foregoing that the General Court erred in law in finding, first, […] that the concept of an undertaking must be considered separately from the concept that the conduct of the author of the infringement is to be imputed to its holding entity and, second, […] that 'the parent company of an undertaking which has infringed Article [101 TFEU] cannot be penalised by a decision implementing Article [101 TFEU], if it is not an undertaking itself' and by consequently verifying, […] whether the Commission had established that Portielje, by itself, was an undertaking for the purpose of Article [101 TFEU].

CoJ 11 July 2013 (Commission v. Stichting Administratiekantoor Portielje and others, C-440/11), ECLI:EU:C:2013:514, paras 43–45.

4.59   Where two parent companies each have a 50 per cent shareholding in the joint venture which committed an infringement of the rules of competition law, it is only for the purposes of establishing liability for participation in the infringement of that law and only in so far as the Commission has demonstrated, on the basis of factual evidence, that both parent companies did in fact exercise decisive influence over the joint venture, that those three entities can be considered to form a single economic unit and therefore form a single undertaking for the purposes of Article [101 TFEU].

CoJ 26 September 2013 (EI du Pont de Nemours and Company v. Commission, Case C-172/12P), ECLI:EU:C:2013:601, para. 47.

4.60   [I]t must be concluded that, for the purpose of establishing the existence of economic continuity, the relevant date for assessing whether the transfer of activities is within a group or between independent undertakings must be that of the transfer itself.

CoJ 18 December 2014 (Commission v. Parker Hannifin Manufacturing Srl, C-434/13), ECLI:EU:C:2014:2456, para. 50.

4.61   In fact, instead of representing one principal for business purposes, Mr G. represented two, namely, essentially, CB, which generated the bulk of Studio Crema's income (around 75 per cent during the period of the infringement which the applicants are found to have committed), but also Austria Draht, which also generated a not insignificant proportion of that income (around 25 per cent during that period).

In such a situation, in order to determine the existence of an economic unit between the agent and one of his principals, it is necessary to ascertain whether that agent is in a position, as regards the activities entrusted to him by that principal, to act as an independent trader free to determine his own business strategy. If the agent is not in a position to act in that way, the functions which he carries out on behalf of the principal form an integral part of the latter's activities.

Thus, [...] the decisive factor in determining the existence of an economic unit between Mr G. and Austria Draht lies in the assessment of the financial risks associated with sales or the performance of the contracts concluded with third parties through Mr G. If Mr G. acts as an emanation of Austria Draht, he may then be treated as an 'auxiliary organ forming an integral part of Austria Draht's undertaking and thus [as] a commercial employee', which would not be the case if he acted as an independent trader.

General Court 15 July 2015 (voestalpine AG and others v. Commission, T-418/10), ECLI:EU:T:2015:516, paras 152–154.

[...] An employee performs his duties for and under the direction of the undertaking for **4.62** which he works and, thus, is considered to be incorporated into the economic unit comprised by that undertaking [...].

For the purposes of a finding of infringement of EU competition law any anti-competitive conduct on the part of an employee is thus attributable to the undertaking to which he belongs and that undertaking is, as a matter of principle, held liable for that conduct.

However, where a service provider offers, in return for payment, services on a given market on an independent basis, that provider must be regarded, for the purpose of applying rules aimed at penalizing anti-competitive conduct, as a separate undertaking from those to which it provides services and the acts of such a provider cannot automatically be attributed to one of those undertakings.

The relationship between an undertaking and its employees is thus not, in principle, comparable to the relationship between that undertaking and the service providers which supply services to it [...].

Nonetheless, it is possible that, in certain circumstances, a service provider which presents itself as independent is in fact acting under the direction or control of an undertaking that is using its services. That would be the case, for example, in circumstances in which the service provider had only little or no autonomy or flexibility with regard to the way in which the activity concerned was carried out, its notional independence disguising an employment relationship [...]. Furthermore, such direction or control might be inferred from the existence of particular organizational, economic and legal links between the service provider in question and the user of the services, just as with the relationship between parent companies and their subsidiaries [...]. In such circumstances, the undertaking using the services could be held liable for the possible unlawful conduct of the service provider.

It must be stated, secondly, that, assuming the service provider concerned to be genuinely independent (a matter which falls to be determined by the national court), in circumstances such as those in the main proceedings the concerted practice involving that provider may be attributed to the undertaking using that provider's services only under certain conditions. [...]

Accordingly, the concerted practice at issue may be attributed to the undertaking using the services, inter alia, if the undertaking was aware of the anti-competitive objectives pursued by its competitors and the service provider and intended to contribute to them by its own conduct. Whilst it is true that such a condition is met when that undertaking intended, through the intermediary of its service provider, to disclose commercially sensitive information to its competitors, or when it expressly or tacitly consented to the provider sharing that commercially sensitive information with them [...]. The condition is not met when that service provider has, without informing the undertaking using its services, used the undertaking's commercially sensitive information to complete those competitors' tenders.

The concerted practice at issue may also be attributed to the undertaking using those services if the latter could reasonably have foreseen that the service provider retained by it would share its commercial information with its competitors and if it was prepared to accept the risk which that entailed. [...]

Having regard to all the foregoing considerations, [...], Article 101(1) TFEU must be interpreted as meaning that an undertaking may, in principle, be held liable for a concerted practice on account of the acts of an independent service provider supplying it with services only if one of the following conditions is met: the service provider was in fact acting under the direction or control of the undertaking concerned, or that undertaking was aware of the anti-competitive objectives pursued by its competitors and the service provider and intended to contribute to them by its own conduct, or that undertaking could reasonably have foreseen the anti-competitive acts of its competitors and the service provider and was prepared to accept the risk which they entailed.

CoJ 21 July 2016 (SIA 'VM Remonts' and others, C-542/14), ECLI:EU:C: 2016:578, paras 23–28, 30–31 and 33.

(c) Concept of 'association of undertakings'

4.63   Certain applicants [...] complain [...] that the Commission wrongly treated the recommendation as a decision of an association of undertakings within the meaning of Article [101(1) TFEU]. The recommendation is said to have been made by FEDETAB, a non-profit-making association which as such does not trade.

That argument cannot be accepted either. [...] Article [101(1) TFEU] also applies to associations in so far as their own activities or those of the undertakings belonging to them are calculated to produce the results which it aims to suppress.

CoJ 29 October 1980 (Van Landewyck and others v. Commission, Joined Cases 209–215 and 218/78) [1980] ECR 3125, paras 87 and 88.

4.64   The next point to be considered is the extent to which a professional body such as the CNSD is acting as an association of undertakings, within the meaning of Article [101(1) TFEU], when compiling the tariff.

In this connection, it must be borne in mind that the public law status of a national body such as the CNSD does not preclude the application of Article [101 TFEU]. According to its wording, that provision applies to agreements between undertakings and decisions by associations of undertakings. Accordingly, the legal framework within which such agreements are made and such decisions are taken and the classification given to that framework by the various national legal systems are irrelevant as far as the applicability of the Community rules on competition, and in particular Article [101 TFEU], are concerned [...].

Moreover, the members of the CNSD are the representatives of professional customs agents and nothing in the national legislation concerned prevents the CNSD from acting in the exclusive interest of the profession.

CoJ 18 June 1998 (Commission v. Italy, C-35/96) [1998] ECR I-3851, paras 39–41.

When it adopts a regulation such as the 1993 Regulation, a professional body such as **4.65** the Bar of the Netherlands is neither fulfilling a social function based on the principle of solidarity, unlike certain social security bodies [...], nor exercising powers which are typically those of a public authority [...]. It acts as the regulatory body of a profession, the practice of which constitutes an economic activity.

In that respect, the fact that Article 26 of the Advocatenwet also entrusts the General Council with the task of protecting the rights and interests of members of the Bar cannot a priori exclude that professional organisation from the scope of application of Article [101 TFEU], even where it performs its role of regulating the practice of the profession of the Bar [...].

Next, other indications support the conclusion that a professional organisation with regulatory powers, such as the Bar of the Netherlands, cannot escape the application of Article [101 TFEU].

First, it is clear from the Advocatenwet that the governing bodies of the Bar are composed exclusively of members of the Bar elected solely by members of the profession. The national authorities may not intervene in the appointment of the members of the Supervisory Boards, College of Delegates or the General Council [...].

Second, when it adopts measures such as the 1993 Regulation, the Bar of the Netherlands is not required to do so by reference to specified public-interest criteria. Article 28 of the Advocatenwet, which authorises it to adopt regulations, does no more than require that they should be in the interest of the proper practice of the profession [...].

Lastly, having regard to its influence on the conduct of the members of the Bar of the Netherlands on the market in legal services, as a result of its prohibition of certain multi-disciplinary partnerships, the 1993 Regulation does not fall outside the sphere of economic activity.

In light of the foregoing considerations, it appears that a professional organisation such as the Bar of the Netherlands must be regarded as an association of undertakings within the meaning of Article [101(1) TFEU] where it adopts a regulation such as the 1993 Regulation. Such a regulation constitutes the expression of the intention of the delegates of the members of a profession that they should act in a particular manner in carrying on their economic activity.

CoJ 19 February 2002 (Wouters and others, C-309/99) [1999] ECR I-1577, paras 58–64.

4.66   [T]he obligation on chartered accountants to undertake training in accordance with the rules laid down by that regulation is closely linked to the practice of their profession [...]. Failure to comply with that obligation can therefore lead to disciplinary sanctions under Articles 57(1)(a), 59(2), 63 and 64 of the Statute of the OTOC, such as suspension for a maximum period of three years or expulsion from that professional association.

De even if that regulation did not directly affect the economic activity of the chartered accountants themselves, as the referring court appears to suggest in its third question, that fact cannot, of itself, remove a decision of an association of undertakings from the scope of Article 101 TFEU.

Such a decision can be such as to prevent, restrict or distort competition within the meaning of Article 101(1) TFEU, not only on the market on which the members of a professional association practise their profession, but also on another market on which that professional association itself has an economic activity.

CoJ 28 February 2013 (Ordem dos Técnicos Oficiais de Contas, C-1/12), ECLI: EU:C:2013:127, paras 43–45.

4.67   As regards the question referred to in paragraph 38 above, it is appropriate to examine to what extent a professional organisation such as the National Association of Geologists in Italy should be regarded as an association of undertakings within the meaning of Article 101(1) TFEU when adopting rules such as those laid down by the Code of Conduct.

In that examination, it is necessary to verify whether, when it adopts rules such as those at issue in the main proceedings, a professional association is to be treated as an association of undertakings or, on the other hand, as a public authority, on the ground that its activity is connected with the exercise of the powers of a public authority [...].

As regards the nature of CNG's activities, it is apparent from Articles 8 and 9 of Law No 112/1963 that all geologists entered in the register established by that provision constitute the Association and elect the CNG, the latter being responsible for ensuring compliance with the rules regulating the profession and all other provisions concerning the profession and for adopting disciplinary measures.

It should be noted that, when it adopts a measure such as the Code of Conduct, a professional organisation such as the National Association of Geologists is neither fulfilling a social function based on the principle of solidarity, nor exercising powers which are typically those of a public authority. It acts as the regulatory body of a profession, the practice of which constitutes an economic activity [...].

In the light of those considerations, the Court finds therefore that a professional organisation such as the National Association of Geologists acts as an association of undertakings within the meaning of Article 101(1) TFEU when drawing up rules of professional conduct such as those at issue in the main proceedings.

CoJ 18 July 2013 (Consiglio nazionale dei geologi, Case C-136/12), ECLI:EU:C: 2013:489, paras 41–45.

(d) Concept of 'agreement'

(i) Concurrence of wills

The parties to the export agreement mutually declared themselves willing to abide by **4.68**
the gentlemen's agreement and concede that they did so until the end of October 1962.
    This document thus amounted to the faithful expression of the joint intention of the
parties to the agreement with regard to their conduct in the common market.
CoJ 15 July 1970 (ACF Chemiefarma v. Commission, 41/69) [1970] ECR 661,
paras 111 and 112.

For Article [101 TFEU] to apply to a case [...] of agreements which are no longer in **4.69**
force it is sufficient that such agreements continue to produce their effects after they
have formally ceased to be in force.
    An agreement is only regarded as continuing to produce its effects if from the
behaviour of the persons concerned there may be inferred the existence of elements of
concerted practice and of coordination peculiar to the agreement and producing the
same result as that envisaged by the agreement.
CoJ 15 June 1976 (EMI, 51/75) [1976] ECR 811, paras 30 and 31.

[T]o constitute such an agreement the recommendation would have had to involve **4.70**
features making it a binding contract under national law. [...]
    That argument cannot be accepted. In the present case the applicant members of
FEDETAB informed the Commission that they wished to be party to the notification
of the recommendation and during the proceedings before the Court they admitted
that they had complied with it [...]. It follows that the recommendation is a faithful
expression of the applicants' intention to conduct themselves [...] in conformity with
the terms of the recommendation.
CoJ 29 October 1980 (Van Landewyck and others v. Commission, Joined Cases
209–215 and 218/78) [1980] ECR 3125, paras 85 and 86.

In the present case, the conduct objected to [...] is characterised by the Commission as **4.71**
'agreements' to fix prices within the meaning of that provision [Article 65(1) ECSC
Treaty]. It is clear from the facts now found by the [General Court] that, on each of the
occasions referred to by those recitals of the Decision, the undertakings in question,
including the applicant, did not confine themselves to merely exchanging information
on their price 'forecasts' or 'estimates' but expressed their common desire to conduct
themselves on the market in a particular manner in regard to prices, that is to say, to act
in such a way as to ensure that the prices agreed at the meetings in question would be
achieved or, in some cases, maintained. The [General Court] finds that such a common
intention constitutes an 'agreement' within the meaning of Article 65(1) [ECSC
Treaty]. Moreover, the [General Court] sees no reason here to interpret the concept of
'agreement' in Article 65(1) [ECSC Treaty] differently from the concept of 'agreement'
in Article [101(1) TFEU] [...].
General Court 11 March 1999 (Thyssen Stahl v. Commission, T-141/94) [1999]
ECR II-347, para. 262.

4.72   It follows that the concept of an agreement within the meaning of Article [101(1)
             TFEU] [...] centres around the existence of a concurrence of wills between at least two
             parties, the form in which it is manifested being unimportant so long as it constitutes
             the faithful expression of the parties' intention.

*General Court 26 October 2000 (Bayer v. Commission, T-41/96) [2000] ECR
II-3383, para. 69.*

4.73   [T]he facts relied on by the Commission cannot be characterised as merely an
             attempted agreement. It is apparent from the series of meetings at which market-
             sharing was discussed that, at least at a certain time, the undertakings in question
             expressed their joint intention to conduct themselves on the market in a specific
             manner. As observed [...] above, it must be held that, even if there was not an
             agreement on all the matters forming the subject-matter of the negotiations, a joint
             intention to restrict competition on the German market by means of fixed market
             shares for each operator governed the negotiations during a certain period in 1993.
                 In that context, the Commission's assertion [...] that it may well be true that [the
             arrangements] were inchoate, loose and often fragmentary cannot be taken to mean
             that, in respect of the facts characterised as an agreement by the Commission, there was
             not yet a joint intention on the part of the undertakings concerned to conduct
             themselves on the market in a specific way. The Commission's assertion, although it
             states that the arrangements were not always concluded for all the matters forming the
             subject-matter of the negotiations or for all the foreseeable details and that they were
             sporadic and non-continuous, does not in any way mean that the undertakings
             concerned did not reach agreement on one or more matters intended to restrict
             competition on the market in question.

*General Court 20 March 2002 (HFB Holding für Fernwärmetechnik and others v.
Commission, T-9/99) [2002] ECR II-1487, paras 206 and 207.*

4.74   It is of little relevance who originated the proposal to extend the scope of the
             Agreement (the cartel agreement), since a concurrence of wills can be established [...].

*General Court 27 July 2005 (Brasserie Nationale and others v. Commission, Joined
Cases T-49 and 51/02) [2005] ECR II-3033, para. 130.*

4.75   In order for there to be an agreement, it is sufficient that at least two undertakings have
             expressed their joint intention to conduct themselves on the market in a specific way
             [...].
                 While it is therefore essential that the decisions in which the Commission applies
             Article [101(1) TFEU] show the existence of a joint intention to act on the market in a
             specific way, those decisions [...] are not required to establish the existence of a joint
             intention to pursue an anti-competitive aim.

*General Court 27 September 2006 (GlaxoSmithKline Services and others v. Com-
mission, T-168/01) [2006] ECR II-2969, paras 76 and 77.*

4.76   In that regard, the formulations used in the case-law – the 'joint intention of conducting
             themselves on the market in a specific way' [...] or 'expression of the joint intention of
             the parties to the agreement with regard to their conduct in the common market' [...]

stress the element of 'joint intention' and do not require the relevant market on which the undertaking which is the 'perpetrator' of the restriction of competition is active to be exactly the same as the one on which that restriction is deemed to materialise. […].

General Court 8 July 2008 (AC–Treuhand v. Commission, T-99/04) [2008] ECR II-1501, para. 122.

As regards […] the assessment as to whether CD-Contact Data accepted, at least tacitly, **4.77** Nintendo's invitation to participate in an agreement to restrict parallel trade, it should, first of all, be pointed out that it is apparent […] that […] the General Court's finding that CD-Contact Data had accepted that invitation was based not on the fact that CD-Contact Data did not protest against Nintendo's anti-competitive policy, but on the correspondence relied on by the Commission and, in particular, on the fact that the faxes of 4 September 1997 and of 3 and 12 November 1997, which were sent by CD-Contact Data to NOE or to Nintendo France, were intended to denounce the parallel imports carried out in Belgium, a territory which had been assigned to CD-Contact Data.

Next, it is important to point out that the General Court in no way erred in law by concluding, […] that the fact that CD-Contact Data had, in practice, participated in passive parallel trade by exporting goods to customers outside Belgium and Luxembourg was not capable of calling in question the existence of a concurrence of wills.

Although it is true that that fact constitutes one of the relevant factors to be taken into consideration in assessing whether CD-Contact Data accepted Nintendo's invitation, the fact remains that it is not, in itself, decisive and it cannot automatically preclude the possibility of such acceptance. Thus, […] an exclusive distributor may have an interest, not only in entering into an agreement with the manufacturer to limit parallel trade, as a means of further protecting its own distribution area, but also in secretly making sales contrary to that agreement in an attempt to use the agreement for its exclusive benefit. Consequently, it was open to the General Court to conclude, without erring in law, that it was apparent from an overall assessment of all the relevant factors and in particular of the correspondence relied on by the Commission, read in the specific context of the case, that CD-Contact Data had in fact accepted Nintendo's invitation to collaborate in limiting parallel trade.

CoJ 10 February 2011 (Activision Blizzard Germany v. Commission, C-260/09P) [2011] ECR I-419, paras 80–82.

(ii) Unilateral conduct and apparently unilateral conduct

[T]he circular from BMW Belgium […] and the circular from the Belgian dealers […], **4.78** considered according to their tenor and in relation to the legal and factual context in which they are set and in relation to the conduct of the parties, indicate an intention to put an end to all exports of new BMW vehicles from Belgium.

In sending those circulars to all the Belgian dealers, BMW Belgium played the leading role in the conclusion with those dealers of an agreement designed to halt such exports completely.

The Belgian dealers […] did, by virtue of that consent, subscribe to such an agreement, the detailed content of which is determined by the said circulars.

CoJ 12 July 1979 (BMW Belgium and others v. Commission, Joined Cases 32 and 36–82/78) [1979] ECR 2435, paras 28–30.

4.79   Such an attitude on the part of the manufacturer does not constitute, on the part of the undertaking, unilateral conduct which [...] would be exempt from the prohibition contained in Article [101(1) TFEU]. On the contrary, it forms part of the contractual relations between the undertaking and resellers. Indeed, in the case of the admission of a distributor, approval is based on the acceptance, tacit or express, by the contracting parties of the policy pursued by AEG which requires inter alia the exclusion from the network of all distributors who are qualified for admission but are not prepared to adhere to that policy.

CoJ 25 October 1983 (AEG v. Commission, 107/82) [1983] ECR 3151, para. 38.

4.80   It must be observed in this regard that agreements which constitute a selective distribution system and which [...] seek to maintain a specialized trade capable of providing specific services for high-technology products are normally concluded in order to govern the distribution of those products for a certain number of years. Because technological developments are not always foreseeable over such a period of time, those agreements necessarily have to leave certain matters to be decided later by the manufacturer. [...]

Such a decision on the part of the manufacturer does not constitute, on the part of the undertaking, a unilateral act which [...] would be exempt from the prohibition contained in Article [101(1) TFEU]. On the contrary, it forms part of the contractual relations between the undertaking and its dealers. Indeed, admission to the Ford AG dealer network implies acceptance by the contracting parties of the policy pursued by Ford with regard to the models to be delivered to the German market.

CoJ 17 September 1985 (Ford Werke and others v. Commission, Joined Cases 25 and 26/84) [1985] ECR 2725, paras 20 and 21.

4.81   The systematic dispatching by a supplier to his customers of invoices bearing the words 'Export prohibited' constitutes an agreement prohibited by Article [101(1) TFEU], and not unilateral conduct, when it forms part of a set of continuous business relations governed by a general agreement drawn up in advance, based on the consent of the supplier to the establishment of business relations with each customer prior to any delivery and the tacit acceptance by the customers of the conduct adopted by the supplier in their regard, which is attested by renewed orders placed without protest on the same conditions.

CoJ 11 January 1990 (Sandoz v. Commission, C-277/87) [1990] ECR I-45.

4.82   The [General Court] considers that [...] the Commission, clearly [demonstrated] the existence of a general prohibition on the re-export of the goods in question, imposed by the applicant on its exclusive distributors.

In this case, the Court considers that that general prohibition on re-exporting the applicant's goods cannot be attributed to unilateral action by the applicant which as such would not be caught by Article [101(1) TFEU], which solely concerns agreements, decisions by associations of undertakings and concerted practices. A contractual provision which is contrary to Article [101(1) TFEU] does not have to be recorded in writing [...], but may form a tacit part of the contractual relations between an undertaking and its commercial partners [...].

Furthermore, the [General Court] finds that the applicant, while emphasizing that the agreements with its exclusive distributors did not contain a clause prohibiting exports, designed to give them absolute territorial protection, admits that its exclusive distributors complained to it 'when affected by sales under its special relationship with Newitt', and that those complaints evidenced 'that they believed that the applicant was in breach of the legitimate exclusivity provisions under their exclusive distribution agreements' [...].

The [General Court] holds that the fact that the applicant's exclusive distributors interpreted their contracts with it in that way, considered in conjunction with the general export ban referred to by the applicant in its abovementioned correspondence with Newitt, means either that there was already a tacit provision in its contracts with its distributors guaranteeing them absolute territorial protection or that they accepted the applicant's policy as manufacturer not to allow its products to be exported to any world market where it had a distributor [...].

General Court 7 July 1994 (Dunlop Slazenger International v. Commission, T-43/92) [1994] ECR II-441, paras 53–56.

According to the documents in the present case, the call to refrain from supplying **4.83** independent leasing companies contained in the circular of 12 February 1988 was made in the context of the contractual relations between BMW and its dealers. Furthermore, the circular expressly refers to the dealership agreement on numerous occasions. The call which it contains therefore forms part of a set of continuous business relations governed by a general agreement drawn up in advance.

That call must therefore be regarded as an agreement within the meaning of Article [101(1) TFEU]. In order to determine whether that agreement is prohibited by Article [101(1) TFEU], it must be considered whether the ban on supplies resulting from the agreement has as its object or effect the restriction to an appreciable extent of competition within the common market and whether it may affect trade between Member States.

CoJ 24 October 1995 (BMW, C-70/93) [1995] ECR I-3439, paras 17 and 18.

In certain circumstances, measures adopted or imposed in an apparently unilateral **4.84** manner by a manufacturer in the context of his continuing relations with his distributors have been regarded as constituting an agreement within the meaning of Article [101(1) TFEU] [...].

That case-law shows that a distinction should be drawn between cases in which an undertaking has adopted a genuinely unilateral measure, and thus without the express or implied participation of another undertaking, and those in which the unilateral character of the measure is merely apparent. Whilst the former do not fall within Article [101(1) TFEU], the latter must be regarded as revealing an agreement between undertakings and may therefore fall within the scope of that article. That is the case, in particular, with practices and measures in restraint of competition which, though apparently adopted unilaterally by the manufacturer in the context of its contractual relations with its dealers, nevertheless receive at least the tacit acquiescence of those dealers.

The proof of an agreement between undertakings within the meaning of Article [101(1) TFEU] must be founded upon the direct or indirect finding of the existence of the subjective element that characterises the very concept of an agreement, that is to say a concurrence of wills between economic operators on the implementation of a policy, the pursuit of an objective, or the adoption of a given line of conduct on the market, irrespective of the manner in which the parties' intention to behave on the market in accordance with the terms of that agreement is expressed […]. The Commission misjudges that concept of the concurrence of wills in holding that the continuation of commercial relations with the manufacturer when it adopts a new policy, which it implements unilaterally, amounts to acquiescence by the wholesalers in that policy, although their de facto conduct is clearly contrary to that policy.

General Court 26 October 2000 (Bayer v. Commission, T-41/96) [2000] ECR II-3383, paras 70, 71 and 173.

4.85 [T]he Commission cannot hold that apparently unilateral conduct on the part of a manufacturer, adopted in the context of the contractual relations which it maintains with its dealers, in reality forms the basis of an agreement between undertakings within the meaning of Article [101(1) TFEU] if the Commission does not establish the existence of an acquiescence by the other partners, express or implied, in the attitude adopted by the manufacturer […]. […]

It can […] be envisaged that a contractual variation could be regarded as having been accepted in advance, upon and by the signature of a lawful dealership agreement, where it is a lawful contractual variation which is foreseen by the contract, or is a variation which, having regard to commercial usage or legislation, the dealer could not refuse. By contrast, it cannot be accepted that an unlawful contractual variation could be regarded as having been accepted in advance, upon and by the signature of a lawful distribution agreement. In that case, acquiescence in the unlawful contractual variation can occur only after the dealer has become aware of the variation desired by the manufacturer.

General Court 3 December 2003 (Volkswagen v. Commission, T-208/01) [2003] ECR II-5141, paras 36 and 45.

4.86 For an agreement within the meaning of Article [101(1) TFEU] to be capable of being regarded as having been concluded by tacit acceptance, it is necessary that the manifestation of the wish of one of the contracting parties to achieve an anti-competitive goal constitute an invitation to the other party, whether express or implied, to fulfil[l] that goal jointly, and that applies all the more where, as in this case, such an agreement is not at first sight in the interests of the other party, namely the wholesalers.

[…] The mere concomitant existence of an agreement which is in itself neutral and a measure restricting competition that has been imposed unilaterally does not amount to an agreement prohibited by that provision [101(1) TFEU]. Thus, the mere fact that a measure adopted by a manufacturer, which has the object or effect of restricting competition, falls within the context of continuous business relations between the manufacturer and its wholesalers is not sufficient for a finding that such an agreement exists.

CoJ 6 January 2004 (Bundesverband der Arzneimittel-Importeure and others v. Bayer, Joined Cases C-2 and 3/01P) [2004] ECR I-23, paras 102 and 141.

The [General Court] rightly noted […] that, in order to constitute an agreement within **4.87** the meaning of Article [101(1) TFEU], it is sufficient that an act or conduct which is apparently unilateral be the expression of the concurrence of wills of at least two parties, the form in which that concurrence is expressed not being by itself decisive.

CoJ 13 July 2006 (Commission v. Volkswagen, C-74/04 P) [2006] ECR I-6585, para. 37.

(iii)   Between two or more undertakings

In order to fall within this prohibition [of Article 101 TFEU], an agreement must have **4.88** been made between undertakings.

CoJ 30 June 1966 (LTM, 56/65) [1966] ECR 235.

The wording of Article [101 TFEU] causes the prohibition to apply, provided that the **4.89** other conditions are met, to an agreement between several undertakings. Thus it does not apply where a sole undertaking integrates its own distribution network into its business organization.

CoJ 13 July 1966 (Consten and Gründig v. Commission, Joined Cases 56 and 58/64) [1966] ECR 340.

Thus it cannot be denied that an agreement between a producer undertaking and a **4.90** distributor undertaking is an example of 'agreements between undertakings'.

CoJ 13 July 1966 (Italy v. Council and Commission, 32/65) [1966] ECR 389.

Article [101(1) TFEU] prohibits agreements which have as their object or effect an **4.91** impediment to competition.

   This is not the position in the case of an exclusive sales agreement when in fact the concession granted under that agreement is in part transferred from the parent company to a subsidiary which, although having separate legal personality, enjoys no economic independence.

CoJ 25 November 1971 (Béguelin Import, 22/71) [1971] ECR 949, paras 7 and 8.

Article [101 TFEU] is not concerned with agreements or concerted practices between **4.92** undertakings belonging to the same concern and having the status of parent company and subsidiary, if the undertakings form an economic unit within which the subsidiary has no real freedom to determine its course of action on the market, and if the agreements or practices are concerned merely with the internal allocation of tasks as between the undertakings.

CoJ 31 October 1974 (Centrafarm and Adriaan de Peijper, 15/74) [1974] ECR 1147, para. 41.

[T]he concept of agreement or concerted practice between undertakings does not cover **4.93** agreements or concerted practices among undertakings belonging to the same group if the undertakings form an economic unit […]. It follows that when Article [101 TFEU]

61

refs to agreements or concerted practices between 'undertakings', it is referring to relations between two or more economic entities which are capable of competing with one another.

General Court 10 March 1992 (Societa Italiana Vetro and others v. Commission, Joined Cases T-68, 77 and 78/89) [1992] ECR II-1403, para. 357.

4.94   It follows that, where there is no agreement between economically independent entities, relations within an economic unit cannot amount to an agreement or concerted practice between undertakings which restricts competition within the meaning of Article [101(1) TFEU]. Where, as in this case, the subsidiary, although having a separate legal personality, does not freely determine its conduct on the market but carries out the instructions given to it directly or indirectly by the parent company by which it is wholly controlled, Article [101(1) TFEU] does not apply to the relationship between the subsidiary and the parent company with which it forms an economic unit. [...]

Article [101(1)(d) TFEU] prohibits agreements between undertakings, decisions by associations of undertakings and concerted practices which apply dissimilar conditions to equivalent transactions with other trading parties, thereby placing them at a competitive disadvantage. The discrimination at which Article [101(1) TFEU] is aimed must therefore be the result of an agreement, a decision or a concerted practice between separate and autonomous economic entities and not the result of unilateral conduct by a single undertaking. [...]

Moreover, the [General Court] has held above [...] that Parker and its subsidiaries form a single economic unit whose unilateral conduct is not prohibited by Article [101(1)(d) TFEU]. Consequently, in this case there is no discrimination against Viho which is capable of being the subject of sanctions for breach of Article [101(1)(d) TFEU].

General Court 12 January 1995 (Viho v. Commission, T-102/92) [1995] ECR II-17, paras 51, 61 and 63.

(e)   Concept of 'concerted practice'

(i)   General

4.95   It follows that, as is clear from the very terms of Article [101(1) TFEU], a concerted practice implies, besides undertakings' concerting together, conduct on the market pursuant to those collusive practices, and a relationship of cause and effect between the two.

CoJ 8 July 1999 (Commission v. Anic Partecipazioni, C-49/92 P) [1999] ECR I-4125, para. 118.

(ii)   Concertation

4.96   Article [101 TFEU] draws a distinction between the concept of 'concerted practices' and that of 'agreements between undertakings' or of 'decisions by associations of undertakings'; the object is to bring within the prohibition of that article a form of coordination between undertakings which, without having reached the stage where an agreement properly so-called has been concluded, knowingly substitutes practical cooperation between them for the risks of competition.

By its very nature, then, a concerted practice does not have all the elements of a contract but may inter alia arise out of coordination which becomes apparent from the behaviour of the participants. [...]

Although every producer is free to change his prices, taking into account in so doing the present or foreseeable conduct of his competitors, nevertheless it is contrary to the rules on competition contained in the treaty for a producer to cooperate with his competitors, in any way whatsoever, in order to determine a coordinated course of action relating to a price increase and to ensure its success by prior elimination of all uncertainty as to each other's conduct regarding the essential elements of that action, such as the amount, subject-matter, date and place of the increases.

CoJ 14 July 1972 (ICI v. Commission, 48/69) [1972] ECR 619, paras 64, 65 and 118.

The concept of a 'concerted practice' refers to a form of coordination between **4.97** undertakings, which, without having been taken to the stage where an agreement properly so-called has been concluded, knowingly substitutes for the risks of competition, practical cooperation between them which leads to conditions of competition which do not correspond to the normal conditions of the market, having regard to the nature of the products, the importance and number of the undertakings as well as the size and nature of the said market. [...]

The criteria of coordination and cooperation laid down by the case-law of the Court, which in no way require the working out of an actual plan, must be understood in the light of the concept inherent in the provisions of the treaty relating to competition that each economic operator must determine independently the policy which he intends to adopt on the common market including the choice of the persons and undertakings to which he makes offers or sells.

Although it is correct to say that this requirement of independence does not deprive economic operators of the right to adapt themselves intelligently to the existing and anticipated conduct of their competitors, it does however strictly preclude any direct or indirect contact between such operators, the object or effect whereof is either to influence the conduct on the market of an actual or potential competitor or to disclose to such a competitor the course of conduct which they themselves have decided to adopt or contemplate adopting on the market.

The documents quoted show that the applicants contacted each other and that they in fact pursued the aim of removing in advance any uncertainty as to the future conduct of their competitors.

CoJ 16 December 1975 (Suiker Unie and others v. Commission, Joined Cases 40–48, 50, 54–56, 111, 113 and 114/73) [1975] ECR 1663, paras 26, 173–175.

[A] concerted practice is characterized by the fact that it substitutes for the risks of **4.98** competition cooperation between undertakings, which lessens each undertaking's uncertainty as to the future attitude of its competitors. If that uncertainty is not lessened, there is no concerted practice [...].

General Court 29 June 1995 (ICI v. Commission, T-30/91) [1995] ECR II-1775, para. 66.

4.99 Any direct or indirect contact between economic operators of such a nature as to disclose to a competitor the course of conduct which they themselves have decided to adopt or contemplate adopting on the market constitutes a concerted practice prohibited by Article [101(1) TFEU] where the object or effect of such contact is to create conditions of competition which do not correspond to the normal conditions of the market in question.

General Court 15 March 2000 (Cimenteries CBR and others v. Commission, Joined Cases T-25, 26, 30, 32, 34, 39, 42, 46, 48, 50, 65, 68, 71, 87, 88, 103 and 104/95) [2000] ECR II–491, para. 1852.

4.100 [T]he concerted action on an element of the composition of the final price can have an impact on the conduct of the undertakings on the market, especially in sectors with low margins […].

[T]he collusive conduct caught by Article 101(1) TFEU also includes conduct which relates to practices to be adopted in the future, which is, moreover, generally the case where price-fixing cartels are concerned.

Moreover, […] the mere exchange of commercial information between competitors in order to prepare an anticompetitive agreement may already be enough to prove the existence of a concerted practice within the meaning of Article 101(1) TFEU […]. A fortiori, the conclusion of an anticompetitive agreement which relates to the future is caught by that provision.

Accordingly, […] the question of whether the United States authorities had not yet officially adopted the AMS rules during a part of the period of the infringement is not decisive where it is established that the freight forwarders agreed to a restriction of competition in the future.

General Court 29 February 2016 (UTi Worldwide, Inc. and others v. Commission, T-264/12), ECLI:EU:T:2016:112, paras 61 and 65–67.

(iii) Conduct on the market and a relationship of cause and effect with the concertation

4.101 Although parallel behaviour may not by itself be identified with a concerted practice, it may however amount to strong evidence of such a practice if it leads to conditions of competition which do not correspond to the normal conditions of the market, having regard to the nature of the products, the size and number of the undertakings, and the volume of the said market.

This is especially the case if the parallel conduct is such as to enable those concerned to attempt to stabilize prices at a level different from that to which competition would have led, and to consolidate established positions to the detriment of effective freedom of movement of the products in the common market and of the freedom of consumers to choose their suppliers.

CoJ 14 July 1972 (ICI v. Commission, 48/69) [1972] ECR 619, paras 66 and 67.

4.102 The documents referred to earlier only deal with white sugar so that, so far as transactions in raw sugar are concerned, it is necessary to consider whether the conduct which the Commission alleges and regards as a constituent part of the concerted practice can only reasonably be explained by the existence of a concerted action.

CoJ 16 December 1975 (Suiker Unie and others v. Commission, Joined Cases 40–48, 50, 54–56, 111, 113 and 114/73) [1975] ECR 1663, para. 301.

Parallel conduct in the debiting of a uniform bank charge on transfers by banks from **4.103** one Member State to another of sums of similar amount from their customers' funds amounts to a concerted practice prohibited by Article [101(1) TFEU] if it is established that such parallel conduct exhibits the features of coordination and cooperation characteristic of such a practice and if that practice is capable of significantly affecting conditions of competition in the market for the services connected with such transfers.

CoJ 14 July 1981 (Züchner, 172/80) [1981] ECR 2021, para. 4.

The Commission's reasoning is based on the supposition that the facts established **4.104** cannot be explained other than by concerted action by the two undertakings. Faced with such an argument, it is sufficient for the applicants to prove circumstances which cast the facts established by the Commission in a different light and which thus allow another explanation of the facts to be substituted for the one adopted by the contested decision.

CoJ 28 March 1984 (CRAM and Rheinzink v. Commission, Joined Cases 29 and 30/83) [1984] ECR 1699, para. 16.

It follows that where those producers concert on the prices to be charged to their **4.105** customers in the Community and put that concertation into effect by selling at prices which are actually coordinated, they are taking part in concertation which has the object and effect of restricting competition within the common market within the meaning of Article [101 TFEU].

CoJ 27 September 1988 (Ahlström Osakeyhtiö and others v. Commission, Joined Cases 89, 104, 114, 116, 117 and 125–129/85) [1988] ECR 5193, para. 13.

Accordingly, not only did the applicant pursue the aim of eliminating in advance **4.106** uncertainty about the future conduct of its competitors but also, in determining the policy which it intended to follow on the market, it could not fail to take account, directly or indirectly, of the information obtained during the course of those meetings. Similarly, in determining the policy which they intended to follow, its competitors were bound to take into account, directly or indirectly, the information disclosed to them by the applicant about the course of conduct which the applicant itself had decided upon or which it contemplated adopting on the market.

General Court 12 December 1991 (BASF v. Commission, T-4/89) [1991] ECR II-1523, para. 242.

Since the Commission has no documents which directly establish the existence of **4.107** concertation between the producers concerned, it is necessary to ascertain whether the system of quarterly price announcements, the simultaneity or near-simultaneinity of the price announcements and the parallelism of price announcements as found during the period from 1975 to 1981 constitute a firm, precise and consistent body of evidence of prior concertation. [...]

Following that analysis, it must be stated that, in this case, concertation is not the only plausible explanation for the parallel conduct. To begin with, the system of price announcements may be regarded as constituting a rational response to the fact that the pulp market constituted a long-term market and to the need felt by both buyers and sellers to limit commercial risks. Further, the similarity in the dates of price announcements may be regarded as a direct result of the high degree of market transparency, which does not have to be described as artificial. Finally, the parallelism of prices and the price trends may be satisfactorily explained by the oligopolistic tendencies of the market and by the specific circumstance prevailing in certain periods. Accordingly, the parallel conduct established by the Commission does not constitute evidence of concertation.

CoJ 31 March 1993 (Ahlström Osakeyhtiö and others v. Commission, Joined Cases 89, 104, 114, 116, 117 and 125–129/85) [1993] ECR I-1307, paras 70 and 126.

4.108   As regards the applicant's argument that the concept of a 'concerted practice' Article 65(1) of the [ECSC] Treaty presupposes that the undertakings have engaged in the practices which were the subject of their concertation, in particular by uniformly increasing their prices, it follows from the Court's case-law concerning the [ECSC] Treaty that, in order to be able to conclude that a concerted practice existed, it is not necessary for the concertation to have had an effect, in the sense understood by the applicant, on the conduct of competitors on the market. It suffices to find that each undertaking was bound to take into account, directly or indirectly, the information obtained during its contacts with its competitors [...].

CoJ 11 March 1999 (Thyssen Stahl v. Commission, T-141/94) [1999] ECR II-347, para. 269.

4.109   Next, although the very concept of a concerted practice presupposes conduct by the participating undertakings on the market, it does not necessarily mean that that conduct should produce the specific effect of restricting, preventing or distorting competition.

CoJ 8 July 1999 (Hüls v. Commission, C-199/02P) [1999] ECR I-4287, para. 165.

4.110   [A]s is clear from the very terms of Article [101(1) TFEU], a concerted practice implies, besides undertakings' concerting together, conduct on the market pursuant to those collusive practices, and a relationship of cause and effect between the two.

The [General Court] therefore committed an error of law in relation to the interpretation of the concept of concerted practice in holding that the undertakings' collusive practices had necessarily had an effect on the conduct of the undertakings which participated in them. [...]

For one thing, subject to proof to the contrary, which it is for the economic operators concerned to adduce, there must be a presumption that the undertakings participating in concerting arrangements and remaining active on the market take account of the information exchanged with their competitors when determining their conduct on that market, particularly when they concert together on a regular basis over a long period, as was the case here, according to the findings of the [General Court].

CoJ 8 July 1999 (Commission v. Anic Partecipazioni, C-49/92 P) [1999] ECR I-4125, paras 118, 119, and 121.

As regards the presumption of a causal connection formulated by the Court in **4.111** connection with the interpretation of Article [101 TFEU], it should be pointed out, first, that the Court has held that the concept of a concerted practice, as it derives from the actual terms of that provision, implies, in addition to the participating undertakings concerting with each other, subsequent conduct on the market and a relationship of cause and effect between the two. However, the Court went on to consider that, subject to proof to the contrary, which the economic operators concerned must adduce, it must be presumed that the undertakings taking part in the concerted action and remaining active on the market take account of the information exchanged with their competitors in determining their conduct on that market. That is all the more the case where the undertakings concert together on a regular basis over a long period. Lastly, the Court concluded that such a concerted practice is caught by Article [101 TFEU], even in the absence of anti-competitive effects on the market [...].

In those circumstances, it must be held that the presumption of a causal connection stems from Article [101 TFEU], as interpreted by the Court, and it consequently forms an integral part of applicable [EU] law.

[W]hat matters is not so much the number of meetings held between the participating undertakings as whether the meeting or meetings which took place afforded them the opportunity to take account of the information exchanged with their competitors in order to determine their conduct on the market in question and knowingly substitute practical cooperation between them for the risks of competition. Where it can be established that such undertakings successfully concerted with one another and remained active on the market, they may justifiably be called upon to adduce evidence that that concerted action did not have any effect on their conduct on the market in question.

In the light of the foregoing, the answer to the third question must be that, in so far as the undertaking participating in the concerted action remains active on the market in question, there is a presumption of a causal connection between the concerted practice and the conduct of the undertaking on that market, even if the concerted action is the result of a meeting held by the participating undertakings on a single occasion.

CoJ 4 June 2009 (T-Mobile and others, C-8/08) [2009] ECR I-4529, paras 51, 52, 61 and 62.

[A]s regards Solvay's argument that the General Court failed to take account of its **4.112** observations that the information exchanged was not sufficient to have negative effects on competition, it should be borne in mind that the Court of Justice has held that, subject to proof to the contrary, which the economic operators concerned must adduce, it must be presumed that the undertakings taking part in the concerted action and remaining active on the market take account of the information exchanged with their competitors in determining their conduct on that market. That is all the more the case where the undertakings concert together on a regular basis over a long period [...].

In order to rebut that presumption, it is for the undertaking concerned to prove that the concerted action did not have any influence whatsoever on its own conduct on the market [...]. The proof to the contrary must therefore be such as to rule out any link between the concerted action and the determination, by that undertaking, of its conduct on the market.

In that regard, it must be stated that probative data illustrating the competitive nature of the market and, in particular, the decrease of prices during the period concerned cannot suffice, of itself, to rebut that presumption. That data does not of itself make it possible to prove that that undertaking did not take account of the information exchanged with its competitors in determining its conduct on the market. It follows that that data does not of itself preclude the presumption that the concerted action enabled that undertaking to eliminate uncertainties regarding its conduct on the market, so that normal competition might as a result have been prevented, restricted or distorted.

CoJ 5 December 2013 (Solvay v. Commission, C-455/11P), ECLI:EU:C: 2013:796, paras 42–44.

4.113   The Court has indeed held that the presumption of a causal connection between a concertation and the market conduct of the undertakings participating in the practice, according to which those undertakings, where they remain active on that market, take account of the information exchanged with their competitors in determining their conduct on that market, follows from Article 101(1) TFEU and consequently forms an integral part of the EU law which the national court is required to apply [...].

However, in contrast to that presumption, the answer to the question whether the mere dispatch of a message, such as that at issue in the main proceedings, may, having regard to all of the circumstances before the referring court, constitute sufficient evidence to establish that its addressees were aware, or ought to have been aware, of its content, does not follow from the concept of a 'concerted practice' and is not intrinsically linked to that concept. That question must be regarded as relating to the assessment of evidence and to the standard of proof, with the result that it is governed – in accordance with the principle of procedural autonomy and subject to the principles of equivalence and effectiveness – by national law.

In that regard, the referring court cannot require that those agencies take excessive or unrealistic steps in order to rebut that presumption. The travel agencies concerned must have the opportunity to rebut the presumption that they were aware of the content of the message at issue in the main proceedings as from the date of that message's dispatch, for example by proving that they did not receive that message or that they did not look at the section in question or did not look at it until some time had passed since that dispatch.

[A]s regards the participation of the travel agencies concerned in a concerted practice within the meaning of Article 101(1) TFEU, it must be recalled, first, that under that provision, the concept of a concerted practice implies, in addition to the participating undertakings concerting with each other, subsequent conduct on the market and a relationship of cause and effect between the two [...].

Secondly, it must be pointed out that the case at issue in the main proceedings, as presented by the referring court, is characterized by the fact that the administrator of the information system at issue sent a message concerning a common anticompetitive action to the travel agencies participating in that system, a message which could only be consulted in the 'Notices' section of the information system in question and to which those agencies did not expressly respond. Following the dispatch of that message, a technical restriction was implemented which limited the discounts that could be applied to bookings made via that system to 3%. Although that restriction did not prevent the travel agencies concerned from granting discounts greater than 3% to their customers, it nevertheless required them to take additional technical steps in order to do so.

Those circumstances are capable of justifying a finding of a concertation between the travel agencies which were aware of the content of the message at issue in the main proceedings, which could be regarded as having tacitly assented to a common anti-competitive practice, provided that the two other elements constituting a concerted practice, [...], are also present. Depending on the referring court's assessment of the evidence, a travel agency may be presumed to have participated in that concertation if it was aware of the content of that message.

CoJ 21 January 2016 (Eturas, C-74/14), ECLI:EU:C:2016:42, paras 33, 34 and 41–44.

(iv) Relationship between 'agreement' and 'concerted practice' – single continuous infringement

Those schemes were part of a series of efforts made by the undertakings in question in pursuit of a single economic aim, namely to distort the normal movement of prices on the market in polypropylene. It would thus be artificial to split up such continuous conduct, characterized by a single purpose, by treating it as consisting of a number of separate infringements. The fact is that the applicant took part – over a period of years – in an integrated set of schemes constituting a single infringement, which progressively manifested itself in both unlawful agreements and unlawful concerted practices.

4.114

General Court 17 December 1991 (Hercules v. Commission, T-7/89) [1991] ECR II-1711, para. 263.

As regards the question whether the Commission was entitled to find that there was a single infringement, described in Article 1 of the Decision as 'an agreement and concerted practice', the Court points out that, in view of their identical purpose, the various concerted practices followed and agreements concluded formed part of schemes of regular meetings, target-price fixing and quota fixing.

4.115

Those schemes were part of a series of efforts made by the undertakings in question, in pursuit of a single economic aim, namely to distort the normal movement of prices on the market in polypropylene. It would thus be artificial to split up such continuous conduct, characterized by a single purpose, by treating it as consisting of a number of separate infringements. The fact is that the applicant took part – over a period of years – in an integrated set of schemes constituting a single infringement, which progressively manifested itself in both unlawful agreements and unlawful concerted practices.

The Commission was also entitled to characterize that single infringement as 'an agreement and a concerted practice', since the infringement involved at one and the same time factual elements to be characterized as 'agreements' and factual elements to be characterized as 'concerted practices'. Given such a complex infringement, the dual characterization by the Commission in Article 1 of the Decision must be understood not as requiring, simultaneously and cumulatively, proof that each of those factual elements presents the constituent elements both of an agreement and of a concerted practice, but rather as referring to a complex whole comprising a number of factual elements some of which were characterized as agreements and others as concerted practices for the purposes of Article [101(1) TFEU], which lays down no specific category for a complex infringement of this type.

General Court 10 March 1992 (Hoechst v. Commission, T-10/89) [1992] ECR II-629, paras 293–295.

4.116   It follows that, whilst the concepts of an agreement and of a concerted practice have partially different elements, they are not mutually incompatible. Contrary to Anic's allegations, the [General Court] did not therefore have to require the Commission to categorise either as an agreement or as a concerted practice each form of conduct found but was right to hold that the Commission had been entitled to characterise some of those forms of conduct as principally 'agreements' and others as 'concerted practices'.

[I]t must be pointed out that this interpretation is not incompatible with the restrictive nature of the prohibition laid down in Article [101(1) TFEU] [...]. Far from creating a new form of infringement, the arrival at that interpretation merely entails acceptance of the fact that, in the case of an infringement involving different forms of conduct, these may meet different definitions whilst being caught by the same provision and being all equally prohibited.

[I]t must be observed that, contrary to Anic's allegations, such an interpretation does not have an unacceptable effect on the question of proof and does not infringe the rights of defence of the undertakings concerned.

On the one hand, the Commission must still establish that each form of conduct found falls under the prohibition laid down in Article [101(1) TFEU] as an agreement, a concerted practice or a decision by an association of undertakings.

On the other hand, the undertakings charged with having participated in the infringement have the opportunity of disputing, for each form of conduct, the characterisation or the characterisations applied by the Commission by contending that the Commission has not adduced proof of the constituent elements of the various forms of infringement alleged.

CoJ 8 July 1999 (Commission v. Anic Partecipazioni, C-49/92 P) [1999] ECR I-4125, paras 132–136.

4.117   An infringement of Article [101(1) TFEU] may result not only from an isolated act but also from a series of acts or from continuous conduct. That interpretation cannot be challenged on the ground that one or several elements of that series of acts or continuous conduct could also constitute in themselves and taken in isolation an infringement of that provision [...]. When the different actions form part of an 'overall plan', because their identical object distorts competition within the common market, the Commission is entitled to impute responsibility for those actions on the basis of participation in the infringement considered as a whole.

CoJ 7 January 2004 (Aalborg Portland and others v. Commission, Joined Cases C-204, 205, 211, 213, 217 and 219/00P) [2004] ECR I-123, para. 258.

4.118   [I]t is sufficient to recall that the notion of a single infringement covers precisely a situation in which several undertakings participated in an infringement in which continuous conduct in pursuit of a single economic aim was intended to distort competition, and also individual infringements linked to one another by the same object (all the elements sharing the same purpose) and the same subjects (the same undertakings, who are aware that they are participating in the common object).

General Court 8 July 2008 (BPB v. Commission, T-53/03) [2008] ECR II-1333, para. 273.

It must also be made clear that the concept of a single objective cannot be determined by **4.119** a general reference to the distortion of competition on the market concerned by the infringement, since an impact on competition, whether it is the object or the effect of the conduct in question, constitutes an element consubstantial with any conduct covered by Article [101 TFEU]. Such a definition of the concept of a single objective is likely to deprive the concept of a single and continuous infringement of part of its meaning, since it would have the consequence that different instances of conduct which relate to a particular economic sector and are prohibited under Article [101 TFEU] would have to be systematically characterised as constituent elements of a single infringement. Thus, for the purposes of characterising various instances of conduct as a single and continuous infringement, it is necessary to establish whether they display a link of complementarity in that each of them is intended to deal with one or more consequences of the normal pattern of competition and whether, through interaction, they contribute to the attainment of the set of anti-competitive effects desired by those responsible, within the framework of a global plan having a single objective. In that regard, it will be necessary to take into account any circumstance capable of establishing or of casting doubt on that link, such as the period of implementation, the content (including the methods used) and, correlatively, the objective of the various agreements and concerted practices in question [...].

General Court 28 April 2010 (Amann & Söhne and Cousin Filterie v. Commission, T-446/05) [2010] ECR II-1255, para. 92.

[T]he notion of a single infringement covers a situation in which several undertakings **4.120** participated in an infringement in which continuous conduct in pursuit of a single economic aim was intended to distort competition and also individual infringements linked to one another by the same object and the same undertakings [...].

In other words, the way in which the infringement was committed determines whether it may be categorized as a single, continuing infringement or a single, repeated infringement.

Furthermore, it must be borne in mind, as regards a continuing infringement, that the notion of an overall plan means that the Commission may assume that an infringement has not been interrupted even if, in relation to a specific period, it has no evidence of the participation of the undertaking concerned in that infringement, provided that that undertaking participated in the infringement prior to and after that period and provided that there is no proof or indicia that the infringement was interrupted so far as concerns that undertaking. In that case, it will be able to impose a fine in respect of the whole of the period of infringement, including the period in respect of which it does not have evidence of the participation of the undertaking concerned [...].

By contrast, if the participation of an undertaking in the infringement may be regarded as having been interrupted and the undertaking may be regarded as having participated in the infringement prior to and after that interruption, that infringement may be categorized as repeated if – as in the case of a continuing infringement [...] – there is a single objective which it pursued both before and after the interruption, a circumstance which may be deduced from the identical nature of the objectives of the practices at issue, of the goods concerned, of the undertakings which participated in the collusion, of the main rules for its implementation, of the natural persons involved on behalf of the undertakings and, lastly, of the geographical scope of those practices. The infringement is then single and repeated and, although the Commission may impose a fine in respect of the whole of the period of the infringement, it may not do so for the period during which the infringement was interrupted.

Consequently, separate periods of infringement in which the same undertaking takes part, but in respect of which a common objective cannot be established, cannot be categorized as a single infringement – continuing or repeated – and constitute separate infringements.

General Court 17 May 2013 (Trelleborg Industries and others v. Commission, Joined Cases T-147/09 and 148/09), ECLI:EU:T:2013:259, paras 85–89.

4.121   In the present case, the General Court [...] inferred [...] that 'three conditions must be met in order to establish participation in a single and continuous infringement, namely the existence of an overall plan pursuing a common objective, the intentional contribution of the undertaking to that plan, and its awareness (proved or presumed) of the offending conduct of the other participants'.

The General Court undertook [...] an examination of whether each of those conditions was met in the present case. It held, following an analysis of the facts stated by the Commission in the contested decision and the arguments made before it by Team Relocations, that that was the case. It stated, first, inter alia, [...] that the commissions agreement and the cover quotes agreement pursued the same objective as the price-fixing agreement, that common objective being 'to establish and maintain a high price level for the provision of international removal services in Belgium and to share this market'. It then stated that it was common ground that Team Relocations had participated in two out of the three agreements described in the contested decision. It then, finally, held that in the light of the functioning of the cartel in question, Team Relocations must have been aware of the offending conduct of the other participants in the cartel since 1997. It concluded from this, [...] that 'the Commission was fully entitled to find that Team Relocations had been a party to the single and continuous infringement described in the [contested decision]'.

That analysis does not contain any of the alleged errors of law. The conditions which the General Court considered, [...] must be satisfied in order that an undertaking can be held responsible for a single and continuous infringement are in fact compatible with the case-law of the Court referred to [...].

CoJ 11 July 2013 (Team Relocations and others v. Commission, C-444/111P), ECLI:EU:C:2013:464, paras 51–53.

4.122   The fact that the evidence of the existence of a continuous infringement was not adduced for certain specific periods does not preclude the infringement from being regarded as having been established during a more extensive overall period than those periods, provided that such a finding is based on objective and consistent indicia. In the context of an infringement extending over a number of years, the fact that the agreement is shown to have applied during different periods, which may be separated by longer or shorter periods, has no effect on the existence of the agreement, provided that the various actions which form part of the infringement pursue a single purpose and fall within the framework of a single and continuous infringement [...].

CoJ 19 December 2013 (Siemens and others v. Commission, Joined Cases C-239, 489 and 498/11P), ECLI:EU:C:2013:866, para. 264.

It follows, [...] that, in order to establish the applicant's participation in the single and **4.123** continuous infringement to which the contested decision relates, the Commission must show not only the anti-competitive nature of the applicant's contacts with AGC/Splintex and with Saint-Gobain between November 2001 and March 2003, but also that the applicant was aware or could reasonably be expected to be aware of, first, the fact that those contacts were intended to contribute to achieving the cartel's overall plan and, secondly, the general scope and the essential characteristics of the cartel [...]. [...]

[I]n accordance with the principles set out [...], the finding that the applicant had bilateral contacts of an anti-competitive nature with AGC/Splintex and with Saint-Gobain between November 2001 and the March 2003 is not, however, sufficient to conclude that it participated in the single and continuous infringement which forms the subject-matter of the contested decision. Since it is not disputed that the applicant did not participate in any of the actual club meetings, it must be examined, first, whether it knew, or should have known, that the collusion in which it was invited to participate formed part of the overall plan of that single and continuous infringement [...] and, secondly, whether it was aware, or should have been aware, of the general scope and the essential characteristics of the cartel as a whole.

CoJ 10 October 2014 (Soliver NV v. Commission, T-68/09), ECLI:EU:T: 2014:867, paras 67 and 82.

Moreover, for the purpose of characterizing various instances of conduct as a single and **4.124** continuous infringement, it is not necessary to ascertain whether they present a link of complementarity, in the sense that each of them is intended to deal with one or more consequences of the normal pattern of competition, and, through interaction, contribute to the attainment of the set of anti-competitive effects desired by those responsible, within the framework of a global plan having a single objective. By contrast, the condition relating to a single objective requires that it be ascertained whether there are any elements characterizing the various instances of conduct forming part of the infringement which are capable of indicating that the instances of conduct in fact implemented by other participating undertakings do not have an identical object or identical anticompetitive effect and, consequently, do not form part of an 'overall plan' as a result of their identical object distorting the normal pattern of competition within the internal market [...].

Furthermore, it cannot be inferred from the Court's case-law that Article 101(1) TFEU concerns only either (i) the undertakings operating on the market affected by the restrictions of competition or indeed on the markets upstream or downstream of that market or neighbouring markets or (ii) undertakings which restrict their freedom of action on a particular market under an agreement or as a result of a concerted practice. Indeed, it is apparent from the Court's well-established case-law that the text of Article 101(1) TFEU refers generally to all agreements and concerted practices which, in either horizontal or vertical relationships, distort competition on the internal market, irrespective of the market on which the parties operate, and that only the commercial conduct of one of the parties need be affected by the terms of the arrangements in question [...].

CoJ 26 January 2017 (Villeroy & Boch Austria Gmbh v. Commission, C-626/13), ECLI:EU:C:2017:54, paras 63 and 64.

(f) Concept of 'decision of associations of undertakings'

4.125   The recommendation [...] of which notice was given by FEDETAB to the Commission on 1 December 1975 concerns only the cigarette sub-sector. It is common ground that the other applicants informed the Commission that they intended to comply with the recommendation and wished to be party to the notification. According to the reasons stated in the Commission decision the firms in FEDETAB had a great influence on other manufacturers and importers and on wholesalers and retailers. The recommendation therefore operates as a genuine mandatory rule of conduct for all firms in the industry. It constitutes a decision of an association of undertakings and an agreement between them the object and effect of which are appreciably to restrict competition between manufacturers and alternatively between wholesalers within the common market.

CoJ 29 October 1980 (Van Landewyck and others v. Commission, Joined Cases 209–215 and 218/78) [1980] ECR 3125, para. 102.

4.126   As the Court has already held [...], Article [101(1) TFEU] applies also to associations of undertakings in so far as their own activities or those of the undertakings affiliated to them are calculated to produce the results which it aims to suppress. [...] That a recommendation, even if it has no binding effect, cannot escape Article [101(1) TFEU] where compliance with the recommendation by the undertakings to which it is addressed has an appreciable influence on competition in the market in question.

CoJ 8 November 1983 (IAZ and others v. Commission, Joined Cases 96–102, 104, 105, 108 and 110/82) [1983] ECR 3369, para. 20.

4.127   As the Court has consistently held, it is unnecessary to consider the actual effects of an agreement if it is apparent that it has the object of preventing, restricting or distorting competition. The same principle applies to a decision of an association of undertakings. The Commission was consequently correct in limiting its examination initially to the objective of the recommendation without considering what were its effects.

CoJ 27 January 1987 (Verband der Sachversicherer v. Commission, 45/85) [1987] ECR 405, para. 39.

4.128   On the other hand, since they are binding on national associations that are members of FIFA, which are required to draw up similar rules that are subsequently approved by FIFA, and on clubs, players and players' agents, those regulations are the reflection of FIFA's resolve to coordinate the conduct of its members with regard to the activity of players' agents. They therefore constitute a decision by an association of undertakings within the meaning of Article [101(1) TFEU] [...], which must comply with the Community rules on competition, where such a decision has effects in the Community. [...]

A decision like the FIFA Players' Agents Regulations may, where it is implemented, result in the undertakings operating on the market in question, namely the clubs, being so linked as to their conduct on a particular market that they present themselves on that market as a collective entity vis-à-vis their competitors, their trading partners and consumers [...].

General Court 26 January 2005 (Piau v. Commission, T-193/02) [2005] ECR II-209, paras 75 and 113.

In the present case, [...], it is undisputed that, before the IPO, MasterCard could be **4.129** considered to be an 'association of undertakings' within the meaning of Article [101 TFEU]. It is also apparent from that paragraph that, in the context of their third plea at first instance, the appellants complained that the Commission, in particular, had not taken into account the changes made by the IPO to MasterCard's structure and governance. In those circumstances, [...] the third plea before the General Court concerned the issue whether MasterCard could still be considered to be 'an institutionalised form of coordination of the banks' conduct' after the changes made by the IPO. [...]

In that regard, [...] the General Court essentially found in its definitive assessment of the facts, first, that, at the time of the adoption of the decision at issue, even though the MasterCard member banks were no longer taking part in the decision-making process within the bodies of that organization in relation to the MIF, 'MasterCard ... seemed instead to be continuing to operate in Europe as an association of undertakings, in which the banks were not merely customers for the services provided but participated collectively and in a decentralized manner in all essential elements of the decision-making power'. It should be emphasized in that regard that, notwithstanding the General Court's inappropriate use of the word 'seemed' in that context, it is evident from a reading of the whole of paragraphs 245 to 249 of the judgment under appeal that the General Court did ascertain that, at the date of the decision at issue, the banks were continuing, collectively, to exercise decision-making powers in respect of the essential aspects of the operation of the MasterCard payment organization after the IPO, which meant that the conclusions to be drawn from the IPO were very much to be set in perspective. Secondly, in paragraphs 250 to 258 of the judgment under appeal, the General Court also found, in essence, that the Commission had been able properly to conclude that the MIF reflected the banks' interests, because there was, on that point, a commonality of interests between MasterCard, its shareholders and the banks.

Taken together, those two factors, [...], effectively explain why, according to the General Court, the setting of the MIF by MasterCard continued to operate, notwithstanding the changes arising from the IPO, as 'an institutionalised form of coordination of the conduct of the banks'. According to the logic of the General Court in the judgment under appeal, given that MasterCard's interests and those of the shareholders of MasterCard Inc. converged with regard to the setting of the MIF, the participating banks were in a position to delegate the setting of those fees, while retaining decision-making powers in many other respects.

CoJ 11 September 2014 (MasterCard Inc. and others v. Commission, C-382/12), ECLI:EU:C:2014:2201, paras 64, 68 and 69.

7. Relationship between national law and Article 101 TFEU

4.130   All these considerations show that Italian regulations and the way in which they have been implemented had a determinative effect on some of the most important aspects of the course of conduct of the undertakings concerned which the Commission criticizes, so that it appears that, had it not been for these regulations and their implementation, the cooperation, which is the subject-matter of these proceedings, either would not have taken place or would have assumed a form different from that found to have existed by the Commission.

It emerges from the contested decision that the Commission has not made sufficient allowance for the effect of those regulations and has consequently overlooked a crucial factor in the evaluation of the infringements which it alleges. [...]

Although [...], the system of national quotas, by tending to partition national markets, only leaves a residual field for the operation of the rules of competition, that field is in turn to a great extent fundamentally restricted in its scope by the special organization of the Italian market.

These considerations show that the conduct complained of could not appreciably impede competition and does not therefore come within the prohibition of Article [101(1) TFEU].

CoJ 16 December 1975 (Suiker Unie and others v. Commission, Joined Cases 40, 48, 50, 54–56, 111, 113 and 114/73) [1975] ECR 1663, paras 65, 66, 71 and 72.

4.131   National legislative or judicial practices, even on the supposition that they are common to all the Member States, cannot prevail in the application of the competition rules set out in the Treaty. The same reasoning must apply with even greater force in relation to practices of private undertakings, even where they are tolerated or approved by the authorities of a Member State.

CoJ 17 January 1984 (VBVB and VBBB v. Commission, Joined Cases 43 and 63/82) [1984] ECR 19, para. 8.

4.132   [T]he adoption of a measure by a public authority making an agreement binding on all the traders concerned, even if they were not parties to the agreement, cannot remove the agreement from the scope of Article [101(1) TFEU].

CoJ 30 January 1985 (BNIC, 123/83) [1985] ECR 391, para. 23.

4.133   It must be added that, whilst it is true that the legislation of a Member State may establish a close link between the application of competition law and the law relating to the supervision of the insurance industry, Community law does not, however, make the implementation of the provisions of Articles [101 and 102 TFEU] dependent upon the manner in which the supervision of certain areas of economic activity is organized by national legislation.

CoJ 27 January 1987 (Verband der Sachversicherer v. Commission, 45/85) [1987] ECR 405, para. 23.

Nor can the application of the prohibition on agreements, decisions and concerted **4.134** practices laid down by Community law depend on a condition which is peculiar to a national system.

CoJ 13 January 1994 (Metro, C-376/92) [1994] ECR I-15, para. 25.

Finally, the [General Court] points out that the applicant is not entitled to rely on **4.135** provisions of national law authorizing price controls since, first, it is settled law that the fact that conduct on the part of undertakings was known, authorized or even encouraged by national authorities has no bearing, in any event, on the applicability of Article [101 TFEU] or, where appropriate, Article [102 TFEU] [...] and, secondly, as the Commission rightly emphasized, the period in which prices were frozen was not included in the period of infringement determined by the Decision.

General Court 6 April 1995 (Tréfilunion v. Commission, T-148/89) [1995] ECR II-1063, para. 118.

However, the compatibility of national legislation with the Treaty rules on competition **4.136** cannot be regarded as decisive in the context of an examination of the applicability of Articles [101 and 102 TFEU] to the conduct of undertakings which are complying with that legislation.

Although an assessment of the conduct of the racing companies and the PMU in the light of Articles [101 and 102 TFEU] requires a prior evaluation of the French legislation, the sole purpose of that evaluation is to determine what effect that legislation may have on such conduct.

Articles [101 and 102 TFEU] apply only to anti-competitive conduct engaged in by undertakings on their own initiative [...]. If anti-competitive conduct is required of undertakings by national legislation or if the latter creates a legal framework which itself eliminates any possibility of competitive activity on their part, Articles [101 and 102 TFEU] do not apply. In such a situation, the restriction of competition is not attributable, as those provisions implicitly require, to the autonomous conduct of the undertakings [...].

Articles [101 and 102 TFEU] may apply, however, if it is found that the national legislation does not preclude undertakings from engaging in autonomous conduct which prevents, restricts or distorts competition [...].

CoJ 11 November 1997 (Commission and others v. Ladbroke Racing, Joined Cases C-359 and 379/95 P) [1997] ECR I-6265, paras 31–34.

[W]here undertakings engage in conduct contrary to Article [101(1) TFEU] and **4.137** where that conduct is required or facilitated by national legislation which legitimises or reinforces the effects of the conduct, specifically with regard to price-fixing or market-sharing arrangements, a national competition authority, one of whose responsibilities is to ensure that Article [101(1) TFEU] is observed:

- has a duty to disapply the national legislation;

- may not impose penalties in respect of past conduct on the undertakings concerned when the conduct was required by the national legislation;
- may impose penalties on the undertakings concerned in respect of conduct subsequent to the decision to disapply the national legislation, once the decision has become definitive in their regard;
- may impose penalties on the undertakings concerned in respect of past conduct where the conduct was merely facilitated or encouraged by the national legislation, whilst taking due account of the specific features of the legislative framework in which the undertakings acted.

[I]t is for the referring court to assess whether national legislation such as that at issue in the main proceedings, under which competence to fix the retail selling prices of a product is delegated to a ministry and power to allocate production between undertakings is entrusted to a consortium to which the relevant producers are obliged to belong, may be regarded, for the purposes of Article [101(1) TFEU], as precluding those undertakings from engaging in autonomous conduct which remains capable of preventing, restricting or distorting competition.

CoJ 9 September 2003 (CIF, C-198/01) [2003] ECR I-8055, paras 58 and 80.

4.138   [A]rticles [101 and 102 TFEU] apply only to anti-competitive conduct in which undertakings engage on their own initiative. If anti-competitive conduct is required of undertakings by national law or if the latter creates a legal framework eliminating any possibility of competitive conduct on their part, Articles [101 and 102 TFEU] do not apply. In such a situation, the restriction of competition is not attributable, as is implied by those provisions, to the autonomous conduct of the undertakings. Articles [101 and 102 TFEU] may apply, by contrast, if it is found that the national legislation does not preclude undertakings from engaging in autonomous conduct which prevents, restricts or distorts competition [...]. Consequently, if a national law merely allows, encourages or makes it easier for undertakings to engage in autonomous anti-competitive conduct, those undertakings remain subject to the Treaty competition rules [...].

General Court 30 September 2003 (Atlantic Container Line and others v. Commission, Joined Cases T-191 and 212–214/98) [2003] ECR II-3275, para. 1130.

4.139   Since the national associations constitute associations of undertakings and also, by virtue of the economic activities that they pursue, undertakings, FIFA, an association grouping together national associations, also constitutes an association of undertakings within the meaning of Article [101 TFEU]. That provision applies to associations in so far as their own activities or those of the undertakings belonging to them are calculated to produce the results to which it refers [...]. The legal framework within which decisions are taken by undertakings and the classification given to that framework by the various national legal systems are irrelevant as far as the applicability of the Community rules on competition is concerned [...].

General Court 26 January 2005 (Piau v. Commission, T-193/02) [2005] ECR II-209, para. 72.

4.140   It should also be borne in mind that Articles [101(1) and 102 TFEU] produce direct effects in relations between individuals and create rights for the individuals concerned which the national courts must safeguard [...] and that the primacy of Community law requires any provision of national law which contravenes a Community rule to be disapplied, regardless of whether it was adopted before or after that rule [...].

CoJ 13 July 2006 (Manfredi and others, Joined Cases C-295 and 298/04) [2006] ECR I-6619, para. 39.

B. RESTRICTION OF COMPETITION

1. Object to prevent, restrict or distort competition

See also the Guidelines on the application of Article [101(3) TFEU] (OJ 2004 C 101/97).

[F]or the agreement at issue to be caught by the prohibition contained in Article **4.141** [101(1) TFEU] it must have as its 'object or effect the prevention, restriction or distortion of competition within the common market'.

The fact that these are not cumulative but alternative requirements, indicated by the conjunction 'or', leads first to the need to consider the precise purpose of the agreement, in the economic context in which it is to be applied. This interference with competition referred to in Article [101(1) TFEU] must result from all or some of the clauses of the agreement itself. Where, however, an analysis of the said clauses does not reveal the effect on competition to be sufficiently deleterious, the consequences of the agreement should then be considered and for it to be caught by the prohibition it is then necessary to find that those factors are present which show that competition has in fact been prevented or restricted or distorted to an appreciable extent. The competition in question must be understood within the actual context in which it would occur in the absence of the agreement in dispute.

CoJ 30 June 1966 (LTM, 56/65) [1966] ECR 235.

Besides, for the purpose of applying Article [101(1) TFEU], there is no need to take **4.142** account of the concrete effects of an agreement once it appears that it has as its object the prevention, restriction or distortion of competition.

CoJ 13 July 1966 (Consten and Grundig v. Commission, Joined Cases 56 and 58/64) [1966] ECR 450.

In order to determine whether an agreement has as its object the restriction of **4.143** competition, it is not necessary to inquire which of the two contracting parties took the initiative in inserting any particular clause or to verify that the parties had a common intent at the time when the agreement was concluded. It is rather a question of examining the aims pursued by the agreement as such, in the light of the economic context in which the agreement is to be applied.

CoJ 28 March 1984 (CRAM and Rheinzink v. Commission, Joined Cases 29 and 30/83) [1984] ECR 1679, para. 26.

4.144   It must be pointed out in that respect that for the purposes of Article [101(1) TFEU] it is unnecessary to take account of the actual effects of an agreement where its object is to restrict, prevent or distort competition. By its very nature, an agreement fixing a minimum price for a product which is submitted to the public authorities for the purpose of obtaining approval for that minimum price, so that it becomes binding on all traders on the market in question, is intended to distort competition on that market.

CoJ 30 January 1985 (BNIC, 123/83) [1985] ECR 391, para. 22.

4.145   For the purposes of applying Article [101(1) TFEU], it is sufficient that the object of an agreement should be to restrict, prevent or distort competition irrespective of the actual effects of that agreement. Consequently, in the case of agreements reached at meetings of competing undertakings, that provision is infringed where those meetings have such an object and are thus intended to organise artificially the operation of the market. In such a case, the liability of a particular undertaking in respect of the infringement is properly established where it participated in those meetings with knowledge of their object, even if it did not proceed to implement any of the measures agreed at those meetings. The greater or lesser degree of regular participation by the undertaking in the meetings and of completeness of its implementation of the measures agreed is relevant not to the establishment of its liability but rather to the extent of that liability and thus to the severity of the penalty [...].

CoJ 28 June 2005 (Dansk Rørindustrie and others v. Commission, Joined Cases C-189, 202, 205–208 and 213/02P) [2005] ECR I-5425, para. 145.

4.146   The distinction between 'infringements by object' and 'infringements by effect' arises from the fact that certain forms of collusion between undertakings can be regarded, by their very nature, as being injurious to the proper functioning of normal competition.

[...] BIDS submits that those arrangements do not come within the category of infringements by object, but should, on the contrary, be analysed in the light of their actual effects on the market. It argues that the BIDS arrangements, first, are not anti-competitive in purpose and, second, do not entail injurious consequences for consumers or, more generally, for competition. It states that the purpose of those arrangements is not adversely to affect competition or the welfare of consumers, but to rationalise the beef industry in order to make it more competitive by reducing, but not eliminating, production overcapacity.

That argument cannot be accepted.

In fact, to determine whether an agreement comes within the prohibition laid down in Article [101 (1) TFEU], close regard must be paid to the wording of its provisions and to the objectives which it is intended to attain. In that regard, even supposing it to be established that the parties to an agreement acted without any subjective intention of restricting competition, but with the object of remedying the effects of a crisis in their sector, such considerations are irrelevant for the purposes of applying that provision. Indeed, an agreement may be regarded as having a restrictive object even if it does not have the restriction of competition as its sole aim but also pursues other legitimate objectives [...]. It is only in connection with Article [101(3) TFEU] that matters such as those relied upon by BIDS may, if appropriate, be taken into consideration for the purposes of obtaining an exemption from the prohibition laid down in Article [101(1) TFEU]. [...]

The BIDS arrangements are intended therefore, essentially, to enable several under-takings to implement a common policy which has as its object the encouragement of some of them to withdraw from the market and the reduction, as a consequence, of the overcapacity which affects their profitability by preventing them from achieving economies of scale.

That type of arrangement conflicts patently with the concept inherent in the [TFEU] provisions relating to competition, according to which each economic opera-tor must determine independently the policy which it intends to adopt on the common market. Article [101(1) TFEU] is intended to prohibit any form of coordination which deliberately substitutes practical cooperation between undertakings for the risks of competition.

CoJ 20 November 2008 (Competition Authority Ireland, C-209/07) [2008] ECR I-8637, paras 17, 19–21 and 33–34.

[A]s to whether a concerted practice may be regarded as having an anti-competitive **4.147** object even though there is no direct connection between that practice and consumer prices, it is not possible on the basis of the wording of Article [101(1) TFEU] to conclude that only concerted practices which have a direct effect on the prices paid by end users are prohibited.

On the contrary, it is apparent from Article [101(1)(a) TFEU] that concerted practices may have an anti-competitive object if they 'directly or indirectly fix purchase or selling prices or any other trading conditions'. In the present case […] as far as concerns post-paid subscriptions, the remuneration paid to dealers is evidently a decisive factor in fixing the price to be paid by the end user.

In any event […] Article [101 TFEU], like the other competition rules of the Treaty, is designed to protect not only the immediate interests of individual competitors or consumers but also to protect the structure of the market and thus competition as such.

Therefore, contrary to what the referring court would appear to believe, in order to find that a concerted practice has an anti-competitive object, there does not need to be a direct link between that practice and consumer prices […].

However, as the Advocate General observed […], while not all parallel conduct of competitors on the market can be traced to the fact that they have adopted a concerted action with an anti-competitive object, an exchange of information which is capable of removing uncertainties between participants as regards the timing, extent and details of the modifications to be adopted by the undertaking concerned must be regarded as pursuing an anti-competitive object, and that extends to situations, such as that in the present case, in which the modification relates to the reduction in the standard commission paid to dealers.

CoJ 4 June 2009 (T-Mobile and others, C-8/08) [2009] ECR I-4529, paras 36–39 and 41.

With respect to the [General Court's] statement that, while it is accepted that an **4.148** agreement intended to limit parallel trade must in principle be considered to have as its object the restriction of competition, that applies in so far as it may be presumed to deprive final consumers of the advantages of effective competition in terms of supply or price, the Court notes that neither the wording of Article [101(1) TFEU] nor the case-law lend support to such a position.

First of all, there is nothing in that provision to indicate that only those agreements which deprive consumers of certain advantages may have an anti-competitive object. Secondly, it must be borne in mind that the Court has held that, like other competition rules laid down in the Treaty, Article [101 TFEU] aims to protect not only the interests of competitors or of consumers, but also the structure of the market and, in so doing, competition as such. Consequently, for a finding that an agreement has an anti-competitive object, it is not necessary that final consumers be deprived of the advantages of effective competition in terms of supply or price [...].

It follows that, by requiring proof that the agreement entails disadvantages for final consumers as a prerequisite for a finding of anti-competitive object and by not finding that that agreement had such an object, the [General Court] committed an error of law.

CoJ 6 October 2009 (GlaxoSmithKline Services and others v. Commission and others, Joined Cases C-501, 513 and 519/06 P) [2009] ECR I-9291, paras 62–64.

4.149 In the main proceedings, the actual grant of exclusive licences for the broadcasting of Premier League matches is not called into question. Those proceedings concern only the additional obligations designed to ensure compliance with the territorial limitations upon exploitation of those licences that are contained in the clauses of the contracts concluded between the right holders and the broadcasters concerned, namely the obligation on the broadcasters not to supply decoding devices enabling access to the protected subject-matter with a view to their use outside the territory covered by the licence agreement.

Such clauses prohibit the broadcasters from effecting any cross-border provision of services that relates to those matches, which enables each broadcaster to be granted absolute territorial exclusivity in the area covered by its licence and, thus, all competition between broadcasters in the field of those services to be eliminated.

Also, FAPL and others and MPS have not put forward any circumstance falling within the economic and legal context of such clauses that would justify the finding that, despite the considerations set out in the preceding paragraph, those clauses are not liable to impair competition and therefore do not have an anticompetitive object.

Accordingly, given that those clauses of exclusive licence agreements have an anticompetitive object, it is to be concluded that they constitute a prohibited restriction on competition for the purposes of Article 101(1) TFEU.

CoJ 4 October 2011 (Football Association Premier League and others, Joined Cases C-403 and 429/08) [2011] ECR I-9083, paras 141–144.

4.150 For the purpose of applying Article 101(1) TFEU, there is no need to take account of the concrete effects of an agreement once it appears that it has as its object the prevention, restriction or distortion of competition [...].

Article 101 TFEU is intended to protect not only the interests of competitors or consumers but also the structure of the market and thus competition as such [...].

In that regard, it is apparent from the order for reference that the agreement entered into by the banks concerned specifically had as its object the restriction of competition and that none of the banks had challenged the legality of Akcenta's business before they were investigated in the case giving rise to the main proceedings. The alleged illegality of Akcenta's situation is therefore irrelevant for the purpose of determining whether the conditions for an infringement of the competition rules are met.

Moreover, it is for public authorities and not private undertakings or associations of undertakings to ensure compliance with statutory requirements. The Czech Government's description of Akcenta's situation is evidence enough of the fact that the application of statutory provisions may call for complex assessments which are not within the area of responsibility of those private undertakings or associations of undertakings.

It follows from those considerations [...] that Article 101 TFEU must be interpreted as meaning that the fact that an undertaking that is adversely affected by an agreement whose object is the restriction of competition was allegedly operating illegally on the relevant market at the time when the agreement was concluded is of no relevance to the question whether the agreement constitutes an infringement of that provision.

CoJ 7 February 2013 (Protimonopolný úrad Slovenskej republiky and others, C-68/12), ECLI:EU:C:2013:71, paras 17–21.

In order to determine whether an agreement involves a restriction of competition 'by object', regard must be had to the content of its provisions, its objectives and the economic and legal context of which it forms a part [...]. When determining that context, it is also appropriate to take into consideration the nature of the goods or services affected, as well as the real conditions of the functioning and structure of the market or markets in question [...]. [...] **4.151**

Concerning the agreements referred to in the question submitted, it should be noted that they relate to the hourly charge to be paid by the insurance company to car dealers, acting as repair shops, for the repair of cars in the event of accidents. They provide that that charge is increased in accordance with the number and percentage of insurance contracts that the dealer sells for that company.

Such agreements therefore link the remuneration for the car repair service to that for the car insurance brokerage. The linkage of those two different services is possible because of the fact that the dealers act in relation to the insurers in a dual capacity, namely as intermediaries or brokers, offering car insurance to their customers at the time of sale or repair of vehicles, and as repair shops, repairing vehicles after accidents on behalf of the insurers.

However, while the establishment of such a link between two activities which are in principle independent does not automatically mean that the agreement concerned has as its object the restriction of competition, it can nevertheless constitute an important factor in determining whether that agreement is by its nature injurious to the proper functioning of normal competition, which is the case, in particular, where the independence of those activities is necessary for that functioning.

Moreover, it is necessary to take account of the fact that such an agreement is likely to affect not only one, but two markets, in this case those of car insurance and car repair services, and that its object must be determined with respect to the two markets concerned.

In that regard, it must, first, be noted that [...] the fact that both cases concern vertical relationships in no way excludes the possibility that the agreement at issue in the main proceedings constitutes a restriction of competition 'by object'. While vertical agreements are, by their nature, often less damaging to competition than horizontal agreements, they can, nevertheless, in some cases, also have a particularly significant restrictive potential. The Court has thus already held on several occasions that a vertical agreement had as its object the restriction of competition [...].

Next, with regard to determining the object of the agreements at issue in the main proceedings with respect to the car insurance market, it should be noted that, by such agreements, insurance companies such as Allianz and Generali aim to maintain or increase their market shares.

It is not disputed that, if there was a horizontal agreement or a concerted practice between those two companies designed to partition the market, such an agreement or practice would have to be treated as a restriction by object and would also result in the unlawfulness of the vertical agreements concluded in order to implement that agreement or practice. Allianz and Generali dispute however that they acted in agreement or concert and claim that the contested decision found that there was no such agreement or practice. It is for the referring court to check the accuracy of those claims and, to the extent that it is enabled under domestic law, to determine whether there is enough evidence to establish the existence of an agreement or concerted practice between Allianz and Generali.

Nevertheless, even if there is no agreement or concerted practice between those insurance companies, it will still be necessary to determine whether, taking account of the economic and legal context of which they form a part, the vertical agreements at issue in the main proceedings are sufficiently injurious to competition on the car insurance market as to amount to a restriction of competition by object.

CoJ 14 March 2013 (Allianz Hungária Biztosító and others, C-32/11), ECLI: EU:C:2013:160, paras 36 and 39–46.

4.152   First, [...], when the General Court defined the concept of the restriction of competition 'by object' within the meaning of that provision, it did not refer to the settled case-law of the Court of Justice [...] thereby failing to have regard to the fact that the essential legal criterion for ascertaining whether coordination between undertakings involves such a restriction of competition 'by object' is the finding that such coordination reveals in itself a sufficient degree of harm to competition.

Secondly, [...], the General Court erred in finding [...] that the concept of restriction of competition by 'object' must not be interpreted 'restrictively'. The concept of restriction of competition 'by object' can be applied only to certain types of coordination between undertakings which reveal a sufficient degree of harm to competition that it may be found that there is no need to examine their effects, otherwise the Commission would be exempted from the obligation to prove the actual effects on the market of agreements which are in no way established to be, by their very nature, harmful to the proper functioning of normal competition. The fact that the types of agreements covered by Article [101(1) TFEU] do not constitute an exhaustive list of prohibited collusion is, in that regard, irrelevant.

It is, however, necessary to examine whether those errors of law were capable of vitiating the General Court's analysis as regards the characterization of the measures at issue in the light of Article [101(1) TFEU]. [...]

In so doing, the General Court confused the issue of the definition of the relevant market and that of the context which must be taken into account in order to ascertain whether the content of an agreement or a decision by an association of undertakings reveals the existence of a restriction of competition 'by object' within the meaning of Article [101(1) TFEU].

In order to assess whether coordination between undertakings is by nature harmful to the proper functioning of normal competition, it is necessary, [...], to take into consideration all relevant aspects – having regard, in particular, to the nature of the services at issue, as well as the real conditions of the functioning and structure of the markets – of the economic or legal context in which that coordination takes place, it being immaterial whether or not such an aspect relates to the relevant market.

CoJ 11 September 2014 (Groupement des Cartes Bancaires (CB) vs. Commission, C-67/13), ECLI:EU:C:2014:2204, paras 57–59, 77 and 78.

In the present case, the General Court examined, [...], the Dole companies' arguments **4.153** concerning the relevance of quotation prices in the banana sector and the responsibility of the Dole Food employees involved in the pre-pricing communications.

As observed by the Advocate General [...], it is apparent from the extremely detailed findings of the General Court, first, that bilateral pre-pricing communications were exchanged between the Dole companies and other undertakings in the banana sector and, as part of those communications, the undertakings discussed their own quotation prices and certain price trends. Moreover, the Dole companies do not contest that finding.

Second, the General Court found, [...], that quotation prices were relevant to the market concerned, since, on the one hand, market signals, market trends or indications as to the intended development of banana prices could be inferred from those quotation prices, which were important for the banana trade and the prices obtained and, on the other, in some transactions the actual prices were directly linked to the quotation prices.

Third, [...], the General Court found that the Dole employees involved in the pre-pricing communications participated in the internal pricing meetings.

Furthermore, those findings of the General Court are to a large extent based on statements made by Dole Food and the Dole companies have not alleged any form of distortion in that regard.

Accordingly, the General Court was entitled to take the view, without erring in law, that the conditions for the application of the presumption referred to at paragraph 127 above were fulfilled in the present case, with the result that the Dole companies' claims that that court infringed the principle governing the burden of proof and the presumption of innocence are unfounded.

It also follows that the General Court was entitled to take the view, [...], without erring in law, that it was permissible for the Commission to conclude that, as they made it possible to reduce uncertainty for each of the participants as to the foreseeable conduct of competitors, the pre-pricing communications had the object of creating conditions of competition that do not correspond to the normal conditions on the market and therefore gave rise to a concerted practice having as its object the restriction of competition within the meaning of Article [101 TFEU].

CoJ 19 March 2015 (Dole Foods Company Inc. v. Commission, C-286/13), ECLI:EU:C:2015:184, paras 128–134.

[T]he referring court asks, in essence, whether Article 101(1) TFEU must be inter- **4.154** preted as meaning that the mere fact that a commercial lease agreement for the letting of a large shop or hypermarket located in a shopping centre contains a clause granting the lessee the right to oppose the letting by the lessor, in that centre, of commercial premises to other tenants, means that the object of that agreement is to restrict competition within the meaning of that provision. [...]

In the present case, it is apparent from the documents submitted to the Court that Maxima Latvija is not in a competitive situation with the shopping centres with which it has concluded the agreements at issue in the main proceedings. Although the Court has already held that a fact of that nature in no way precludes an agreement from containing a restriction of competition 'by object' [...], it must, however, be stated that the agreements at issue in the main proceedings are not among the agreements which it is accepted may be considered, by their very nature, to be harmful to the proper functioning of competition.

Even if the clause at issue in the main proceedings could potentially have the effect of restricting the access of Maxima Latvija's competitors to some shopping centres in which that company operates a large shop or hypermarket, such a fact, if established, does not imply clearly that the agreements containing that clause prevent, restrict or distort, by the very nature of the latter, competition on the relevant market, namely the local market for the retail food trade.

Taking account of the economic context in which agreements, such as those at issue in the main proceedings are to be applied, the analysis of the content of those agreements would not, in the light of the information provided by the referring court, show, clearly, a degree of harm with regard to competition sufficient for those agreements to be considered to constitute a restriction of competition 'by object' within the meaning of Article 101(1) TFEU.

CoJ 26 November 2015 (SIA Maxima Latvija, C–345/14), ECLI:EU:C: 2015:784, paras 15 and 21–23.

4.155 In any event, even if the restrictions contained in the agreements at issue potentially fell within the scope of Lundbeck's patents, in that they could also have been obtained through litigation, the contested decision rightly finds that this was merely a possibility at the time the agreements at issue were concluded. Replacing that uncertainty in relation to whether or not the generic undertakings were infringing and to the validity of the applicants' patents with the certainty that the generic undertakings would not enter the market during the term of the agreements at issue constitutes, as such, a restriction on competition by object in the present case, since that result was obtained through a reverse payment [...].

[T]he agreements at issue were comparable to market exclusion agreements, which are among the most serious restrictions of competition. The exclusion of competitors from the market constitutes an extreme form of market sharing and of limitation of production. [...]

Moreover, [...], it is not necessary that the same type of agreement have already been censured by the Commission in order for them to constitute a restriction of competition by object. The role of experience, mentioned by the Court of Justice in paragraph 51 of the judgment in CB v Commission [...], does not concern the specific category of an agreement in a particular sector, but rather refers to the fact that it is established that certain forms of collusion are, in general and in view of the experience gained, so likely to have negative effects on competition that it is not necessary to demonstrate that they had such effects in the particular case at hand. The fact that the Commission has not, in the past, considered that a certain type of agreement was, by its very object, restrictive of competition is therefore not, in itself, such as to prevent it from doing so in the future following an individual and detailed examination of the measures in question having regard to their content, purpose and context […].

[T]he case-law relied on by the applicants, according to which it does not matter, as far as the existence of the infringement is concerned, whether or not the conclusion of the agreement was in the commercial interests of the parties concluding that agreement […], means only that the parties to an agreement cannot maintain that that agreement was the most cost-effective option in order to circumvent the prohibition laid down in Article 101 TFEU […]. It does not, however, prevent the Commission from taking account of the content of an agreement, as well as its purpose and the context in which it was concluded – such as, in the present case, the presence of significant reverse payments –in order to establish the existence of a restriction by object.

The examination of a hypothetical counterfactual scenario – besides being impracticable since it requires the Commission to reconstruct the events that would have occurred in the absence of the agreements at issue, whereas the very purpose of those agreements was to delay the market entry of the generic undertakings […] – is more an examination of the effects of agreements at issue on the market than an objective examination of whether they are sufficiently harmful to competition. Such an examination of effects is not required in the context of an analysis based on the existence of a restriction of competition by object […].

Accordingly, even if some generic undertakings would not have entered the market during the term of the agreements at issue, as a result of infringement actions brought by Lundbeck, or because it was impossible to obtain an [market authorization] within a sufficiently short period, what matters is that those undertakings had real concrete possibilities of entering the market at the time the agreements at issue were concluded with Lundbeck, with the result that they exerted competitive pressure on the latter. That competitive pressure was eliminated for the term of the agreements at issue, which constitutes, by itself, a restriction of competition by object, for the purpose of Article 101(1) TFEU.

Although it is true that settlements are often intended to reduce the uncertainty inherent in litigation, such settlements are not exempt from the application of competition law […]. In addition, as the Commission found in the contested decision, settlements are particularly problematic when they are intended to pay potential competitors to stay out of the market for a certain period, without, however, resolving the underlying patent dispute, as in the present case.

Accordingly, the Commission rightly considered that the agreements at issue were akin to market exclusion agreements between competitors and that they were liable to have negative effects on competition, without it being necessary, for the purpose of Article 101(1) TFEU, to demonstrate that they had had such effects.

General Court 8 September 2016 (H. Lundbeck A/S and others v. Commission, T-472/13), ECLI:EU:T:2016:449, paras 401, 435, 438, 445 and 473–476.

2. Effect to prevent, restrict or distort competition

See also the Guidelines on the application of Article [101(3) TFEU] (OJ 2004 C 101/97).

4.156   Where an analysis of the said clauses does not reveal the effect on competition to be sufficiently deleterious, the consequences of the agreement should then be considered, and for it to be caught by the prohibition it is then necessary to find that those factors are present which show that competition has in fact been prevented or restricted or distorted to an appreciable extent. The competition must be understood within the actual context in which it would occur in the absence of the agreement in dispute.
CoJ 30 June 1966 (LTM, 56/65) [1966] ECR 235.

4.157   Furthermore, by basing its application to agreements, decisions or practices not only on their subject-matter but also on their effects in relation to competition, Article [101(1) TFEU] implies that regard must be had to such effects in the context in which they occur, that is to say, in the economic and legal context of such agreements, decisions or practices and where they might combine with others to have a cumulative effect on competition. [...] The existence of similar contracts [exclusive supply agreements between brewery and café owners] may be taken into consideration for this objective to the extent to which the general body of contracts of this type is capable of restricting the freedom of trade.
CoJ 12 December 1967 (Brasserie De Haecht, 23/67) [1967] ECR 511.

4.158   [I]n order to come within the prohibition imposed by Article [101 TFEU], the agreement must affect trade between Member States and the free play of competition to an appreciable extent.
In order to establish whether this is the case, these factors must be considered in the light of the situation which would have existed but for the agreement in question.
CoJ 25 November 1971 (Béguelin Import, 22/71) [1971] ECR 949, paras 16 and 17.

4.159   The fact that non-competition clauses are included in an agreement for the sale of an undertaking is not of itself sufficient to remove such clauses from the scope of Article [101(1) TFEU].
In order to determine whether or not such clauses come within the prohibition in Article [101(1) TFEU], it is necessary to examine what would be the state of competition if those clauses did not exist.
CoJ 11 July 1985 (Remia v. Commission, C–42/84) [1985] ECR 2545, paras 17 and 18.

4.160   Although the acquisition by one company of an equity interest in a competitor does not in itself constitute conduct restricting competition, such an acquisition may nevertheless serve as an instrument for influencing the commercial conduct of the companies in question so as to restrict or distort competition on the market on which they carry on business.
[...] That may also be the case where the agreement gives the investing company the possibility of reinforcing its position at a later stage and taking effective control of the other company. Account must be taken not only of the immediate effects of the agreement but also of its potential effects and of the possibility that the agreement may be part of a long-term plan.

CoJ 17 November 1987 (BAT and Reynolds v. Commission, Joined Cases 142 and 156/84) [1987] ECR 4487, paras 37 and 39.

The existence of a bundle of similar contracts, even if it has a considerable effect on the **4.161** opportunities for gaining access to the market, is not, however, sufficient in itself to support a finding that the relevant market is inaccessible, inasmuch as it is only one factor, amongst others, pertaining to the economic and legal context in which an agreement must be appraised [...]. The other factors to be taken into account are, in the first instance, those also relating to opportunities for access.

In that connection it is necessary to examine whether there are real concrete possibilities for a new competitor to penetrate the bundle of contracts by acquiring a brewery already established on the market together with its network of sales outlets, or to circumvent the bundle of contracts by opening new public houses. For that purpose it is necessary to have regard to the legal rules and agreements on the acquisition of companies and the establishment of outlets, and to the minimum number of outlets necessary for the economic operation of a distribution system. The presence of beer wholesalers not tied to producers who are active on the market is also a factor capable of facilitating a new producer's access to that market since he can make use of those wholesalers' sales networks to distribute his own beer.

Secondly, account must be taken of the conditions under which competitive forces operate on the relevant market. In that connection it is necessary to know not only the number and the size of producers present on the market, but also the degree of saturation of that market and customer fidelity to existing brands, for it is generally more difficult to penetrate a saturated market in which customers are loyal to a small number of large producers than a market in full expansion in which a large number of small producers are operating without any strong brand names [...]

If an examination of all similar contracts entered into on the relevant market and the other factors relevant to the economic and legal context in which the contract must be examined shows that those agreements do not have the cumulative effect of denying access to that market to new national and foreign competitors, the individual agreements comprising the bundle of agreements cannot be held to restrict competition within the meaning of Article [101(1) TFEU]. They do not, therefore, fall under the prohibition laid down in that provision.

If, on the other hand, such examination reveals that it is difficult to gain access to the relevant market, it is necessary to assess the extent to which the agreements entered into by the brewery in question contribute to the cumulative effect produced in that respect by the totality of the similar contracts found on that market. Under the Community rules on competition, responsibility for such an effect of closing off the market must be attributed to the breweries which make an appreciable contribution thereto. Beer supply agreements entered into by breweries whose contribution to the cumulative effect is insignificant do not therefore fall under the prohibition under Article [101(1) TFEU].

CoJ 28 February 1991 (Delimitis, C-234/89) [1991] ECR I-935, paras 20–24.

In this regard, it must be stated first of all that the [General Court] was right to consider **4.162** [...], that since it was not contended that the agreement had an anti-competitive object, the effects of the agreement had to be evaluated in order to determine whether it prevented, restricted or distorted competition to an appreciable degree.

According to the settled case-law of the Court, in order to determine whether an agreement is to be considered to be prohibited by reason of the distortion of competition which is its effect, the competition in question should be assessed within the actual context in which it would occur in the absence of the agreement in dispute [...].

Article [101(1) TFEU] does not restrict such an assessment to actual effects alone; it must also take account of the agreement's potential effects on competition within the common market [...].

CoJ 28 May 1998 (John Deere v. Commission, C-7/95P) [1998] ECR I-3111, paras 75–77.

4.163   The objective findings of the producers themselves at the time of the facts thus show that the price initiatives affected market prices.

Moreover, as the Commission pointed out [...], the practices in question were decided upon over a period of more than three years. It is thus hardly likely that, at that time, the producers considered them wholly ineffective.

It follows that the Commission correctly assessed the effects of the infringement. Therefore, and bearing in mind in particular the objective findings of the producers themselves at the time of the facts, the Commission was not required to carry out a detailed economic analysis of the effects of the cartel on the market. [...].

General Court 20 April 1999 (Limburgse Vinyl Maatschappij and others v. Commission, Joined Cases T-305–307, 313–316, 318, 325, 328, 329 and 335/94) [1999] ECR II-931, paras 747–749.

4.164   In order to assess whether an agreement is compatible with the common market in the light of the prohibition laid down in Article [101(1) TFEU], it is necessary to examine the economic and legal context in which the agreement was concluded [...], its object, its effects, and whether it affects intra-Community trade taking into account in particular the economic context in which the undertakings operate, the products or services covered by the agreement, and the structure of the market concerned and the actual conditions in which it functions [...].

That method of analysis is of general application and is not confined to a category of agreements [...].

Moreover, in a case such as this, where it is accepted that the agreement does not have as its object a restriction of competition, the effects of the agreement should be considered and for it to be caught by the prohibition it is necessary to find that those factors are present which show that competition has in fact been prevented or restricted or distorted to an appreciable extent. The competition in question must be understood within the actual context in which it would occur in the absence of the agreement in dispute; the interference with competition may in particular be doubted if the agreement seems really necessary for the penetration of a new area by an undertaking [...].

Such a method of analysis, as regards in particular the taking into account of the competition situation that would exist in the absence of the agreement, does not amount to carrying out an assessment of the pro- and anti-competitive effects of the agreement and thus to applying a rule of reason, which the Community judicature has not deemed to have its place under Article [101(1) TFEU] [...].

In this respect, to submit, as the applicant does, that the Commission failed to carry out a full analysis by not examining what the competitive situation would have been in the absence of the agreement does not mean that an assessment of the positive and negative effects of the agreement from the point of view of competition must be carried out at the stage of Article [101(1) TFEU]. Contrary to the defendant's interpretation of the applicant's arguments, the applicant relies only on the method of analysis required by settled case-law.

The examination required in the light of Article [101(1) TFEU] consists essentially in taking account of the impact of the agreement on existing and potential competition [...] and the competition situation in the absence of the agreement [...], those two factors being intrinsically linked. [...]

In order to take account of the two parts which this plea actually contains, it is therefore necessary to examine, first, whether the Commission did in fact consider what the competition situation would have been in the absence of the agreement and, second, whether the conclusions which it drew from its examination of the impact of the agreement on competition are sufficiently substantiated. [...]

It follows from the foregoing that the Decision, in so far as it concerns the application of Article [101(1) TFEU] and Article 53(1) of the EEA Agreement, suffers from insufficient analysis, first, in that it contains no objective discussion of what the competition situation would have been in the absence of the agreement, which distorts the assessment of the actual and potential effects of the agreement on competition and, second, in that it does not demonstrate, in concrete terms, in the context of the relevant emerging market, that the provisions of the agreement on roaming have restrictive effects on competition, but is confined, in this respect, to a petitio principii and to broad and general statements.

General Court 2 May 2006 (O2 v. Commission, T-328/03) [2006] ECR II-1231, paras 66–71, 73 and 116.

3. Appreciable restriction of competition

See Guidelines on the effect on trade concept contained in Articles [101] and [102 TFEU] (OJ 2004 C 101/81) and the Commission Notice on agreements of minor importance which do not appreciably restrict competition under Article [101(1) TFEU] (de minimis) (OJ 2001 C 368/13).

Moreover the prohibition in Article [101 (1) TFEU] is applicable only if the agreement **4.165** in question also has as its object or effect the prevention, restriction or distortion of competition within the common market. Those conditions must be understood by reference to the actual circumstances of the agreement. Consequently, an agreement falls outside the prohibition of Article [101 (1) TFEU] when it has only an insignificant effect on the markets taking into account the weak position which the persons have on the market of the product in question. Thus an exclusive dealing agreement, even with absolute territorial protection, may, having regard to the weak position of the persons

concerned on the market in question in the area covered by the absolute protection, escape the prohibition laid down in Article [101 (1) TFEU].
CoJ 9 July 1969 (Voelk, C-5/69) [1969] ECR 295, para 5–7.

4.166   Consideration of the specific effects of these agreements shows that they restricted intra-Community trade appreciably since the sale of appliances of the Watts brand in the Netherlands accounted for 15 per cent of the market for appliances for cleaning gramophone records.
CoJ 20 June 1978 (Tepea v. Commission, 18/77) [1978] ECR 1391, para. 50.

4.167   It does not however contest that, as far as production of zinc sheet is concerned, there are only six rolling mills of various sizes in the common market, of which Rheinzink is the only one in the Federal Republic of Germany. In that kind of market situation, it is impossible to accept the argument that a restriction of competition consisting of the isolation of the German market would not be appreciable.
CoJ 28 March 1984 (CRAM and Rheinzink v. Commission, Joined Cases 29 and 30/83) [1984] ECR 1679, para. 30.

4.168   In that respect it is sufficient to hold that an agreement which restricts competition between most manufacturers and importers carrying on business in a particular sector and establishes a rebate amounting to 7 per cent of retailers' profit margins must be assumed to result in an appreciable restriction of competition.
CoJ 10 December 1985 (NSO v. Commission, 260/82) [1985] ECR 3801, para. 49.

4.169   [...] In that connection, it must also be borne in mind that whilst any adverse effect on competition within the common market resulting from such a distribution system must be sufficiently appreciable [...], it is certainly not necessary for it to be effective. The adverse effect on competition in the common market may be merely potential [...]. [...]
         The [General Court] observes [...], that, according to the terms of the contested decision, which has not been challenged on this point, the differences in average selling prices charged by general agents or wholesalers to retailers vary by as much as 30 per cent from one Member State to another. It follows that [...] effective competition between the pharmaceutical distribution network and the other distribution channels which, in the present case, would be particularly propitious to the development of Inter-State trade by activating, for the same product, competition between the distribution channels – in particular price competition – is restricted to a sufficiently appreciable extent for the purposes of Article [101(1) TFEU].
General Court 27 February 1992 (Vichy v. Commission, T-19/91) [1991] ECR II-415, paras 59 and 79.

4.170   That being so, where, as in the present case, horizontal agreements between undertakings reach or only very slightly exceed the 5 per cent threshold regarded by the Commission itself as critical and such as to justify application of Article [101(1) TFEU], the Commission must provide an adequate statement of its reasons for considering such agreements to be caught by the prohibition in Article [101(1) TFEU]. Its obligation to do so is all the more imperative here, where, as the applicants stated in their notification, ENS has to operate on markets largely dominated by other modes of transport, such as air transport, and where, on the assumption of an increase in demand on the relevant markets and having regard to the limited possibilities for ENS to increase its capacity, its market shares will either fall or remain stable. In addition, such a statement of reasons is necessary in the present instance in view of the fact that [...] an agreement is capable of exercising an appreciable influence on the pattern of trade between Member States even where the market shares of the undertakings concerned do not exceed 3 per cent, provided that those market shares exceed those of most of their competitors.

General Court 15 September 1998 (European Night Services Ltd (ENS) and others v. Commission, Joined Cases T-374, 375, 384 and 388/94) [1998] ECR II-3141, para. 103.

The conclusion must be that such a decision, which standardises in part the costs and **4.171** supplementary pension benefits of medical specialists, restricts competition as far as concerns one cost factor of specialist medical services, inasmuch as one of its effects is that those medical practitioners do not compete with one another to obtain less costly insurance for that part of their pension.

[T]he restrictive effects of such a decision on the specialist medical services market are limited.

The decision in question produces restrictive effects only in relation to one cost factor of the services offered by self-employed medical specialists, namely the supplementary pension scheme, which is insignificant in comparison with other factors, such as medical fees or the cost of medical equipment. The cost of the supplementary pension scheme has only a marginal and indirect influence on the final cost of the services offered by self-employed medical specialists.

Furthermore, it should be observed that the implementation of a supplementary pension scheme managed by a single fund allows self-employed medical specialists to share the risks insured against whilst achieving economies of scale in the management of contributions and payment of pensions and in the investment of assets.

It follows from the foregoing that a decision by the members of a profession to set up a pension fund entrusted with the management of a supplementary pension scheme does not appreciably restrict competition within the common market.

CoJ 12 September 2000 (Pavlov and others, Joined Cases C-180–184/98) [2000] ECR I-6451, paras 93–97.

[T]he Commission rightly argues that an agreement to stop exporting of relatively **4.172** short duration may, in the course of its application, involve a significant restriction on competition and significantly affect trade between Member States, and that the duration of the infringement is a factor to be taken into consideration in calculating the amount of the fine. In this case, having regard to the position of the Opel brand on automobile markets, notably those of the Netherlands and Germany, the number of vehicles sold for export from the Netherlands in 1996, and the fact that the nine dealers accounted for about 65 per cent of exports, the effect of the measure on trade between Member States and the operation of competition was not, in any event, insignificant [...].

General Court 21 October 2003 (General Motors and Opel v. Commission, T-368/00) [2003] ECR II-4491, para. 153.

4.173   In that regard, undertakings which conclude an agreement whose purpose is to restrict competition cannot, in principle, avoid the application of Article [101(1) TFEU] by claiming that their agreement should not have an appreciable effect on competition.

General Court 8 July 2004 (Mannesmannröhren-Werke v. Commission, T-44/00) [2004] ECR II-2223, para. 130.

4.174   Moreover the prohibition in Article [101(1) TFEU] is applicable only if the agreement in question also has as its object or effect the prevention, restriction or distortion of competition within the common market. Those conditions must be understood by reference to the actual circumstances of the agreement. Consequently an agreement falls outside the prohibition in Article [101 TFEU] when it has only an insignificant effect on the markets, taking into account the weak position which the persons concerned have on the market of the product in question.

CoJ 13 December 2012 (Expedia, C-226/11), ECLI:EU:C:2012:795, paras 23, 32 and 34–47.

4.175   It is apparent from paragraphs 1 and 2 of the *de minimis* notice [Commission Notice on agreements of minor importance which do not appreciably restrict competition under Article [101(1) TFEU] (*de minimis*), OJ 2001 C 368/13] that the Commission intends to quantify therein, with the help of market share thresholds, what is not an appreciable restriction of competition within the meaning of Article 101 TFEU and the case-law cited in paragraphs 16 and 17 of the present judgment. [...]

[I]n order to determine whether or not a restriction of competition is appreciable, the competition authority of a Member State may take into account the thresholds established in paragraph 7 of the *de minimis* notice but is not required to do so. Such thresholds are no more than factors among others that may enable that authority to determine whether or not a restriction is appreciable by reference to the actual circumstances of the agreement [...].

In so far as Expedia, the French Government and the Commission have, in their written observations or during the hearing, questioned the finding made by the national court that it is not disputed that the agreement at issue in the main proceedings had an anti-competitive object, it should be remembered that, in proceedings under Article 267 TFEU, which is based on a clear separation of functions between the national courts and the Court of Justice, any assessment of the facts in the main proceedings is a matter for the national court [...].

Moreover, it should be noted that, according to settled case-law, for the purpose of applying Article 101(1) TFEU, there is no need to take account of the concrete effects of an agreement once it appears that it has as its object the prevention, restriction or distortion of competition [...].

In that regard, the Court has emphasised that the distinction between 'infringements by object' and 'infringements by effect' arises from the fact that certain forms of collusion between undertakings can be regarded, by their very nature, as being injurious to the proper functioning of normal competition […].

It must therefore be held that an agreement that may affect trade between Member States and that has an anti-competitive object constitutes, by its nature and independently of any concrete effect that it may have, an appreciable restriction on competition.

CoJ 13 December 2012 (Expedia, C-226/11), ECLI:EU:C:2012:795, paras 23, 32 and 34–37.

4. Rule of reason

It must be borne in mind that the Commission has established to the requisite legal standard that the object of the agreements was anti-competitive within the meaning of Article [101 TFEU]. Moreover, the fact that the infringement of Article [101 TFEU], in particular subparagraphs (a) and (c), is a clear one necessarily precludes the application of a rule of reason, assuming such a rule to be applicable in Community competition law, since in that case it must be regarded as an infringement per se of the competition rules […].   **4.176**

General Court 6 April 1995 (Tréfilunion v. Commission, T-141/89) [1995] ECR II-1063, para. 109.

On this point, it need merely be stated that, even if the rule of reason did have a place in the context of Article [101 TFEU], in no event may it exclude application of that provision in the case of a restrictive arrangement involving producers accounting for almost all the Community market and concerning price targets, production limits and sharing out of the market. The [General Court] did not therefore commit an error of law when it considered that the clear nature of the infringement in any event precluded the application of the rule of reason.   **4.177**

CoJ 8 July 1999 (Montecatini v. Commission, C-235/92P) [1999] ECR I-4539, para. 133.

According to the applicants, as a consequence of the existence of a rule of reason in Community competition law, when Article [101(1) TFEU] is applied it is necessary to weigh the pro- and anti-competitive effects of an agreement in order to determine whether it is caught by the prohibition laid down in that article. It should, however, be observed, first of all, that contrary to the applicants' assertions the existence of such a rule has not, as such, been confirmed by the Community courts. Quite to the contrary, in various judgments the Court of Justice and the [General Court] have been at pains to indicate that the existence of a rule of reason in Community competition law is doubtful […].   **4.178**

Next, it must be observed that an interpretation of Article [101(1) TFEU], in the form suggested by the applicants, is difficult to reconcile with the rules prescribed by that provision.

Article [101 TFEU] expressly provides, in its third paragraph, for the possibility of exempting agreements that restrict competition where they satisfy a number of conditions, in particular where they are indispensable to the attainment of certain objectives and do not afford undertakings the possibility of eliminating competition in respect of a substantial part of the products in question. It is only in the precise framework of that provision that the pro- and anti-competitive aspects of a restriction may be weighed [...]. Article [101(3) TFEU] would lose much of its effectiveness if such an examination had to be carried out already under Article [101(1) TFEU].

It is true that in a number of judgments the Court of Justice and the [General Court] have favoured a more flexible interpretation of the prohibition laid down in Article [101(1) TFEU] [...].

Those judgments cannot, however, be interpreted as establishing the existence of a rule of reason in Community competition law. They are, rather, part of a broader trend in the case-law according to which it is not necessary to hold, wholly abstractly and without drawing any distinction, that any agreement restricting the freedom of action of one or more of the parties is necessarily caught by the prohibition laid down in Article [101(1) TFEU]. In assessing the applicability of Article [101(1) TFEU] to an agreement, account should be taken of the actual conditions in which it functions, in particular the economic context in which the undertakings operate, the products or services covered by the agreement and the actual structure of the market concerned [...].

General Court 18 September 2001 (Métropole and others v. Commission, T-112/99) [2001] ECR II-2459, paras 72–76.

5. Restrictions inherent to an object of (non) economic interest

4.179   In the [...] set of questions, the national court seeks to ascertain whether a provision in the statutes of a cooperative purchasing association, the effect of which is to forbid its members to participate in other forms of organized cooperation which are in direct competition with it, is caught by the prohibition in Article [101(1) TFEU].

It follows that such dual membership would jeopardize both the proper functioning of the cooperative and its contractual power in relation to producers. Prohibition of dual membership does not, therefore, necessarily constitute a restriction of competition within the meaning of Article [101(1) TFEU] and may even have beneficial effects on competition. Nevertheless, a provision in the statutes of a cooperative purchasing association, restricting the opportunity for members to join other types of competing cooperatives and thus discouraging them from obtaining supplies elsewhere, may have adverse effects on competition. So, in order to escape the prohibition laid down in Article [101(1) TFEU], the restrictions imposed on members by the statutes of cooperative purchasing associations must be limited to what is necessary to ensure that the cooperative functions properly and maintains its contractual power in relation to producers.

CoJ 15 December 1994 (Gøttrup-Klim, C-250/92) [1994] ECR I-5641, paras 28 and 35.

As for the request, made to the public authorities by an organisation representing the members of a profession, to make membership of the occupational pension fund it has set up compulsory, it is made under a scheme identical to those existing under the national law of a number of countries concerning the exercise of regulatory authority in the social domain. Such regimes are designed to promote the creation of supplementary pensions of the second type and include a number of safeguards whose observance the competent Minister must ensure, so that a request by the members of a profession for membership to be made compulsory cannot constitute an infringement of Article [101(1) TFEU]. **4.180**

That being so, it must be held that a decision by the members of a profession to set up a pension fund entrusted with the management of a supplementary pension scheme and to request the public authorities to make membership of that fund compulsory for all members of the profession, is not contrary to Article [101(1) TFEU].

CoJ 12 September 2000 (Pavlov and others, Joined Cases C-180–184/98) [2000] ECR I-6451, paras 98 and 99.

However, not every agreement between undertakings or every decision of an association of undertakings which restricts the freedom of action of the parties or of one of them necessarily falls within the prohibition laid down in Article [101(1) TFEU]. For the purposes of application of that provision to a particular case, account must first of all be taken of the overall context in which the decision of the association of undertakings was taken or produces its effects. More particularly, account must be taken of its objectives, which are here connected with the need to make rules relating to organisation, qualifications, professional ethics, supervision and liability, in order to ensure that the ultimate consumers of legal services and the sound administration of justice are provided with the necessary guarantees in relation to integrity and experience [...]. It has then to be considered whether the consequential effects restrictive of competition are inherent in the pursuit of those objectives. **4.181**

CoJ 19 February 2002 (Wouters and others, C-309/99) [1999] ECR I-1577, para. 97.

Therefore, even if the anti-doping rules at issue are to be regarded as a decision of an association of undertakings limiting the appellants' freedom of action, they do not, for all that, necessarily constitute a restriction of competition incompatible with the common market, within the meaning of Article [101 TFEU], since they are justified by a legitimate objective. Such a limitation is inherent in the organisation and proper conduct of competitive sport and its very purpose is to ensure healthy rivalry between athletes. **4.182**

CoJ July 2006 (Meca-Medina and Majcen v. Commission, C-519/04P) [2006] ECR I-6991, para. 45.

C. EFFECT UPON TRADE BETWEEN MEMBER STATES

See Guidelines on the effect on trade concept contained in Articles [101] and [102 TFEU] (OJ 2004 C 101/81).

4.183   The agreement must also be one which 'may affect trade between Member States'.

This provision, clarified by the introductory words of [Article 101 TFEU] which refers to agreements in so far as they are 'incompatible with the common market', is directed to determining the field of application of the prohibition by laying down the condition that it may be assumed that there is a possibility that the realization of a single market between Member States might be impeded. It is in fact to the extent that the agreement may affect trade between Member States that the interference with competition caused by that agreement is caught by the prohibitions in Community law found in Article [101 TFEU], whilst in the converse case it escapes those prohibitions. For this requirement to be fulfilled it must be possible to foresee with a sufficient degree of probability on the basis of a set of objective factors of law or of fact that the agreement in question may have an influence, direct or indirect, actual or potential, on the pattern of trade between Member States.

CoJ 30 June 1966 (LTM, 56/65) [1966] ECR 235.

4.184   The defendant replies that this requirement in Article [101(1) TFEU] is fulfilled once trade between Member States develops, as a result of the agreement, differently from the way in which it would have done without the restriction resulting from the agreement, and once the influence of the agreement on market conditions reaches a certain degree. Such is the case here, according to the defendant, particularly in view of the impediments resulting within the common market from the disputed agreement as regards the exporting and importing of Grundig products to and from France.

The concept of an agreement 'which may affect trade between Member States' is intended to define, in the law governing cartels, the boundary between the areas respectively covered by Community law and national law. It is only to the extent to which the agreement may affect trade between Member States that the deterioration in competition caused by the agreement falls under the prohibition of Community law contained in Article [101 TFEU]; otherwise it escapes the prohibition.

In this connection, what is particularly important is whether the agreement is capable of constituting a threat, either direct or indirect, actual or potential, to freedom of trade between Member States in a manner which might harm the attainment of the objectives of a single market between states. Thus the fact that an agreement encourages an increase, even a large one, in the volume of trade between states is not sufficient to exclude the possibility that the agreement may 'affect' such trade in the abovementioned manner.

CoJ 13 July 1966 (Grundig and Consten v. Commission, Joined Cases 56 and 58/64) [1966] ECR 450.

4.185   [It] is only to the extent to which agreements, decisions or practices are capable of affecting trade between Member States that the alteration of competition comes under Community prohibitions. In order to satisfy this condition, it must be possible for the agreement, decision or practice, when viewed in the light of a combination of the objective, factual or legal circumstances, to appear to be capable of having some influence, direct or indirect, on trade between Member States, of being conducive to a partitioning of the market and of hampering the economic interpenetration sought by the Treaty. When this point is considered the agreement, decision or practice cannot therefore be isolated from all the others of which it is one.

The existence of similar contracts is a circumstance which, together with others, is capable of being a factor in the economic and legal context within which the contract must be judged. Accordingly, whilst such a situation must be taken into account it should not be considered as decisive by itself, but merely as one among others in judging whether trade between Member States is capable of being affected through any alteration in competition.

CoJ 12 December 1967 (Brasserie De Haecht, 23/67) [1967] ECR 511.

An agreement extending over the whole of the territory of a Member State by its very nature has the effect of reinforcing the compartmentalization of markets on a national basis, thereby holding up the economic interpenetration which the Treaty is designed to bring about and protecting domestic production. **4.186**

CoJ 17 October 1972 (Vereniging van Cementhandelaren v. Commission, 8/72) [1972] ECR 977, para. 29.

A restrictive agreement between traders within the common market and competitors in third countries that would bring about an isolation of the common market as a whole which, in the territory of the Community, would reduce the supply of products originating in third countries and similar to those protected by a mark within the Community, might be of such a nature as to affect adversely the conditions of competition within the common market. **4.187**

In particular if the proprietor of the mark in dispute in the third country has within the Community various subsidiaries established in different Member States which are in a position to market the products at issue within the common market such isolation may also affect trade between Member States.

CoJ 15 June 1976 (EMI, 51/75) [1976] ECR 811, paras 28 and 29.

[T]he mere fact [that] at a certain time traders applying for admission to a distribution network or who have already been admitted are not engaged in intra-Community trade cannot suffice to exclude the possibility that restrictions on their freedom of action may impede intra-Community trade, since the situation may change from one year to another in terms of alterations in the conditions or composition of the market both in the common market as a whole and in the individual national markets. **4.188**

CoJ 25 October 1983 (AEG v. Commission, 107/82) [1983] ECR 3151, para. 60.

[I]t must be added that franchise agreements for the distribution of goods which contain provisions sharing markets between the franchisor and the franchisees or between the franchisees themselves are in any event liable to affect trade between Member States, even if they are entered into by undertakings established in the same **4.189**

Member State, in so far as they prevent franchisees from establishing themselves in another Member State.

CoJ 28 January 1986 (Pronuptia, 161/84) [1986] ECR 353, para. 26.

4.190   It follows from the foregoing that […] imports have always represented an appreciable percentage of the sailboards supplied to the market in each Member State. This is all the more true as the significance of the intra-Community trade in sailboards must be evaluated in relation to the whole of the common market and not to individual national markets.

[…] Article [101(1) TFEU] does not require that each individual clause in an agreement should be capable of affecting intra-Community trade. Community law on competition applies to agreements between undertakings which may affect trade between Member States; only if the agreement as a whole is capable of affecting trade is it necessary to examine which are the clauses of the agreement which have as their object or effect a restriction or distortion of competition.

CoJ 25 February 1986 (Windsurfing International v. Commission, 193/83) [1986] ECR 611, paras 22 and 96.

4.191   [T]he Commission was not required to demonstrate that its participation in an agreement and a concerted practice had had an appreciable effect on trade between Member States. All that is required by Article [101(1) TFEU] is that anti-competitive agreements and concerted practices should be capable of having an effect on trade between Member States. In this regard, it must be concluded that the restrictions on competition found to exist were likely to distort trade patterns from the course which they would otherwise have followed […].

It follows that the Commission has established to the requisite legal standard […] that the infringement in which the applicant participated was apt to affect trade between Member States, and it is not necessary for it to demonstrate that the applicant's individual participation affected trade between Member States.

General Court 24 October 1991 (Petrofina v. Commission, T-2/89) [1991] ECR II-1087, paras 226 and 227.

4.192   As the Commission rightly states, the applicants are not entitled to invoke the limited extent of trade between the Member States in seeking to reject that analysis since they do not contest the figures produced by the Commission in the decision which show that, although limited, there is indeed real trade between Member States. […] The Court of Justice has held that, for restrictive arrangements to be prohibited by Article [101(1) TFEU], it is not necessary for them appreciably to affect trade between Member States but merely to be capable of having that effect […]. Since a potential effect is sufficient, future development of trade may be taken into account in assessing the effect of the restrictive arrangements on trade between Member States, whether or not it was foreseeable. Finally, as regards the appreciable nature of that effect, it must be noted, as the Commission observes, that the more limited the trade the greater is the likelihood that it will be affected by the restrictive arrangements.

General Court 21 February 1995 (VSPOB v. Commission, T-29/92) [1995] ECR II-289, para. 235.

If an agreement, decision or practice is to be capable of affecting trade between Member **4.193**
States, it must be possible to foresee with a sufficient degree of probability, on the basis
of a set of objective factors of law or of fact, that they may have an influence, direct or
indirect, actual or potential, on the pattern of trade between Member States in such a
way as to cause concern that they might hinder the attainment of a single market
between Member States. Moreover, that effect must not be insignificant.

CoJ 28 April 1998 (Javico, C-306/96) [1998] ECR I-1983, para. 16.

It is of little importance in that regard that the influence of a cartel on trade is **4.194**
unfavourable, neutral or favourable. A restriction of competition is liable to affect trade
between Member States when it is likely to divert trade patterns from the course which
they would otherwise have followed [...]. Therefore, the argument put forward by
certain of the applicants in this case, to the effect that only the effects of partitioning of
the markets may be taken into consideration in concluding that a cartel is capable of
affecting trade between Member States, must be rejected.

That broad interpretation of the criterion of the capability of affecting trade between
Member States is not contrary to the principle of subsidiarity invoked by RLB. [T]he
Treaty provides that any conflicts between maintaining undistorted competition and
other legitimate objectives of economic policy are to be resolved by the application of
Article [101(3) TFEU]. That provision may therefore be regarded as a special provision
giving effect to the principle of subsidiarity in the sphere of cartels. That principle
cannot therefore be invoked in order to restrict the scope of Article [101 TFEU] [...].

*General Court 14 December 2006 (Raiffeisen Zentralbank Österreich and others v.
Commission, Joined Cases T-259–264 and 271/02) [2006] ECR II-5169, paras
164 and 165.*

The Court has already held that the fact that a cartel relates only to the marketing of **4.195**
products in a single Member State is not sufficient to preclude the possibility that trade
between Member States might be affected. A cartel extending over the whole of the
territory of a Member State has, by its very nature, the effect of reinforcing the
partitioning of markets on a national basis, thus impeding the economic interpenetration which the Treaty is designed to bring about [...].

It follows that, contrary to the appellants' assertion, the [General Court] was right
[...] to take as the starting-point of its reasoning of the existence of a strong
presumption that trade between Member States is affected, going on to say that '[t]hat
presumption can only be rebutted if an analysis of the characteristics of the agreement
and its economic context demonstrates the contrary'.

[T]he [General Court] did not reverse the burden of proof but, exercising its power
to assess the facts, found, after analysis, that the applicants had not overturned the
presumption that the cartel as a whole, extending as it did to Austria in its entirety, had
been capable of affecting trade between States.

*CoJ 24 September 2009 (Erste Group Bank and others v. Commission, Joined Cases
C-125, 133, 135 and 137/07P) [2009] ECR I-8681 paras 38, 40 and 43.*

101

4.196   It is true that, in assessing whether the condition relating to effects on trade between Member States is met, the Commission took account of a product – processed tobacco – on a market situated downstream of the relevant market. However, as Deltafina expressly acknowledges in the application, that approach is consistent not only with case-law, which considers that the effect on the pattern of trade between Member States may be indirect […], but also the Guidelines on the effect on trade concept in Articles [101 and 102 TFEU]. Thus, paragraph 38 of the Guidelines states, inter alia, that '[i]ndirect effects often occur in relation to products that are related to those covered by an agreement or practice', that '[i]ndirect effects may … occur where an agreement or practice has an impact on cross-border economic activities of under-takings that use or otherwise rely on the products covered by the agreement or practice' and that '[s]uch effects can, for instance, arise where the agreement or practice relates to an intermediate product, which is not traded, but which is used in the supply of a final product, which is traded'.

General Court 8 September 2010 (Deltafina v. Commission, T-29/05) [2010] ECR II-4077, para. 173.

4.197   [T]he description of the market in the contested decision is […] sufficient for the purpose of determining whether the cartel in question may have an effect on trade between Member States. Furthermore, contrary to what is claimed by Portielje, there are no grounds for concluding that the Commission omitted to define the relevant market because […] it defined the size of the product market and of the geographic market affected by the cartel, namely the international Belgian removal services market. That description was therefore sufficient to enable it to ascertain the market share threshold referred to in point 53 of the Guidelines on the effect on trade.

Next, first, it is apparent from the file on the case before the General Court that the total relevant market share held by the members of the cartel is considerably in excess of 5 per cent. Second, in the light of both the case-law […] and the characteristics of the infringement at issue […], the requirement laid down in point 53 of the Guidelines on the effect on trade relating to the nature of the cartel in question is clearly fulfilled.

In those circumstances and bearing in mind in particular the fact that the 5 per cent market share threshold laid down at point 53 of the Guidelines on the effect on trade was clearly exceeded, the Commission was justified in concluding that the agreements in question were capable of having an appreciable effect on trade between Member States for the purpose of Article [101(1) TFEU].

CoJ 11 July 2013 (Commission v. Stichting Administratiekantoor Portielje and others, C-440/11), ECLI:EU:C: 2013:514, paras 103–105.

4.198   As regards, first of all, the cross-border nature of the relevant removals, it is clear that that cross-border nature – which is not disputed – is not identical to the issue of whether trade between Member States was 'appreciably' affected.

If every cross-border transaction were automatically capable of appreciably affecting trade between Member States, the concept of appreciability, which is, however, a condition for the application of Article [101(1) TFEU] established by case-law, would be devoid of meaning. In that connection, the Commission also acknowledged, at the hearing, that even in the case of an infringement by object, the infringement must be capable of affecting intra-Community trade appreciably. That is, moreover, also apparent from the 2004 Guidelines, since the positive presumption, laid down in point 53 thereof, applies only to agreements or practices that by their very nature are capable of affecting trade between Member States.

General Court 16 June 2011 (Ziegler SA v Commission, T-199/08), [2011] ECR II-3507, paras 52 and 53.

[I]t must be observed that the concept of trade for the purposes of Article 101 TFEU **4.199** also encompasses services. That is stated in paragraph 19 of the 2004 Effects Notice where it is explained that that concept is not limited to traditional exchanges of goods and services across borders, but covers all cross-border economic activity, including establishment, in accordance with the fundamental objective of the Treaty to promote free movement of goods, services, persons and capital.

General Court 29 February 2016 (EGL Inc. and others v. Commission, T-251/12), ECLI:EU:T:2016:114, para. 68.

[T]he application of the presumption provided for in paragraph 53 of the 2004 Effects **4.200** Notice does not necessarily require that the cartel cover several Member States. As is apparent from the use of the words 'for example', that is no more than one example of the agreements that are covered by that paragraph. [...]

General Court 29 February 2016 (Schenker Ltd. and others v. Commission, T-265/12), ECLI:EU:T:2016:111, para. 175.

D. PARAGRAPH 2: NULLITY

See also Chapter 13 on Regulation No 1/2003.

Article [101(2) TFEU] provides that 'any agreements or decisions prohibited pursuant **4.201** to this article shall be automatically void'.

This provision, which is intended to ensure compliance with the Treaty, can only be interpreted with reference to its purpose in Community law, and it must be limited to this context. The automatic nullity in question only applies to those parts of the agreement affected by the prohibition, or to the agreement as a whole if it appears that those parts are not severable from the agreement itself. Consequently any other contractual provisions which are not affected by the prohibition, and which therefore do not involve the application of the Treaty, fall outside Community law.

CoJ 30 June 1966 (LTM, 56/65) [1966] ECR 235.

The provision in Article [101(2) TFEU] that agreements prohibited pursuant to **4.202** Article [101 TFEU] shall be automatically void applies only to those parts of the agreement which are subject to the prohibition, or to the agreement as a whole if those parts do not appear to be severable from the agreement itself.

CoJ 13 July 1966 (Grundig and Consten v. Commission, Joined Cases 56 and 58/64) [1966] ECR 450.

4.203   Article [101(2) TFEU]: 'any agreements or decisions prohibited pursuant to this article shall be automatically void'.

Accordingly, an agreement falling under Article [101(1) TFEU] which has not been declared inapplicable under Article [101(3 TFEU)] as an agreement or a category of agreements becomes null and void in so far as its object or effect is incompatible with the prohibition in Article [101(1) TFEU]. [...]

Since the nullity referred to in Article [101(2) TFEU] is absolute, an agreement which is null and void by virtue of this provision has no effect as between the contracting parties and cannot be set up against third parties.

CoJ 25 November 1971 (Béguelin Import, 22/71) [1971] ECR 949, paras 25, 26 and 29.

4.204   [...] Article [101(2) TFEU] renders agreements and decisions prohibited pursuant to that article automatically void.

Such nullity is therefore capable of having a bearing on all the effects, either past or future, of the agreement or decision.

Consequently, the nullity provided for in Article [101(2)] is of retroactive effect.

CoJ 6 February 1973 (Brasserie De Haecht (II), 48/72) [1973] ECR 77, paras 25–27.

4.205   In its judgment of 25 November 1971, [...] the Court ruled that an agreement falling under the prohibition imposed by Article [101(1) TFEU] is void and that, since the nullity is absolute, the agreement has no effect as between the contracting party. It also follows from previous judgments of the Court [...] that the automatic nullity decreed by Article [101(2) TFEU] applies only to those contractual provisions which are incompatible with Article [101(1) TFEU]. The consequences of such nullity for other parts of the agreement are not a matter for Community law. The same applies to any orders and deliveries made on the basis of such an agreement and to the resulting financial obligations. [...].

CoJ 14 December 1983 (Société de Vente de Ciments et Bétons, 319/82) [1983] ECR 4173, para. 11.

4.206   The reply [...] should therefore be that a national court may not extend the scope of Regulation No 1984/83 [now Regulation No 330/2010] to beer supply agreements which do not explicitly meet the conditions for exemption laid down in that regulation. Nor may a national court declare Article [101(1) TFEU] inapplicable to such an agreement under Article [101(3)]. It may, however, declare the agreement void under Article [101(2)] if it is certain that the agreement could not be the subject of an exemption decision under Article [101(3)].

CoJ 28 February 1991 (Delimitis, C-234/89) [1991] ECR I-935, para. 55.

Article [101(1) TFEU] prohibits certain anti-competitive agreements or practices. **4.207** Among the consequences which an infringement of that prohibition may have in civil law, only one is expressly provided for in Article [101(2) TFEU], namely the nullity of the agreement. The other consequences attaching to an infringement of Article [101 TFEU], such as the obligation to make good the damage caused to a third party or a possible obligation to enter into a contract [...] are to be determined under national law. Consequently, it is the national courts which, where appropriate, may, in accordance with the rules of national law, order one trader to enter into a contract with another.

    Although the national courts do not have the power to order any infringement found by them to be brought to an end and to impose fines on the undertakings responsible, as the Commission can, it is nevertheless for the national courts to apply Article [101(2) TFEU] in relations between individuals. In making express provision for that civil sanction, the Treaty presupposes that national law gives the national courts the power to safeguard the rights of undertakings which have been subjected to anti-competitive practices.

General Court 18 September 1992 (Automec v. Commission (II), T-24/90) [1992] ECR II-2223, paras 50 and 93.

However, according to Article 3(g) EC [cf. Protocol (No 27) on the internal market and **4.208** competition], Article [101 TFEU] constitutes a fundamental provision which is essential for the accomplishment of the tasks entrusted to the Community and, in particular, for the functioning of the internal market. The importance of such a provision led the framers of the Treaty to provide expressly, in Article [101(2) TFEU], that any agreements or decisions prohibited pursuant to that article are to be automatically void.

    It follows that where its domestic rules of procedure require a national court to grant an application for annulment of an arbitration award where such an application is founded on failure to observe national rules of public policy, it must also grant such an application where it is founded on failure to comply with the prohibition laid down in Article [101(1) TFEU].

CoJ 1 June 1999 (Eco Swiss, C-126/97) [1999] ECR I-3055, paras 36 and 37.

It follows from the foregoing considerations that any individual can rely on a breach of **4.209** Article [101 (1) TFEU] before a national court even where he is a party to a contract that is liable to restrict or distort competition within the meaning of that provision.

CoJ 20 September 2000 (Courage and Crehan, C-543/99) [2000] ECR I-6297, para. 24.

E. PARAGRAPH 3: EXEMPTION

See also Guidelines on the application of Article [101(3) TFEU] (OJ 2004 C 101/97).

1. General

4.210   The powers conferred upon the Commission under Article [101(3) TFEU] show that the requirements for the maintenance of workable competition may be reconciled with the safeguarding of objectives of a different nature and that to this end certain restrictions on competition are permissible, provided that they are essential to the attainment of those objectives and that they do not result in the elimination of competition for a substantial part of the common market. [...].
CoJ 25 October 1977 (Metro v. Commission, 26/76) [1977] ECR 1875, para. 21.

4.211   It is of course possible that a prospective franchisee would not take the risk of becoming part of the chain, investing his own money, paying a relatively high entry fee and undertaking to pay a substantial annual royalty, unless he could hope, thanks to a degree of protection against competition on the part of the franchisor and other franchisees, that his business would be profitable [motive for inclusion of potentially restrictive clauses in a franchise agreement]. That consideration, however, is relevant only to an examination of the agreement in the light of the conditions laid down in Article [101(3) TFEU].
CoJ 28 January 1986 (Pronuptia, 161/84) [1986] ECR 353, para. 24.

4.212   It is for the Commission, within the framework of its power under Article [101(3) TFEU] to grant exemption from the prohibitions contained in Article [101(1) TFEU], to take account of the particular nature of different branches of the economy and the problems peculiar to them.
CoJ 27 January 1987 (Verband der Sachversicherer v. Commission, 45/85) [1987] ECR 415, para. 15.

4.213   In this respect the [General Court] stresses that, regard being had to the general principle of the prohibition of agreements restricting competition in Article [101(1) TFEU], provisions derogating there from in a regulation on exemption by categories cannot be interpreted widely or so as to extend the effects of the regulation further than is necessary for the protection of the interests which they are intended to safeguard [...].
General Court 22 April 1993 (Automobiles Peugeot v. Commission, T-9/92) [1993] ECR II-493, para. 37.

4.214   The [General Court] considers that, at this stage in the examination of the case, the first limb of the plea, as put forward by the applicant, can only be rejected. That first limb consists [...] in the contention, first, that the Commission did not adequately evaluate the anti-competitive effects of that agreement and, secondly, that a correct evaluation of those effects would have shown that competition in the common market would be so undermined that no individual exemption could be granted in respect of the agreement in question.

The [General Court] observes that such reasoning presumes that there are adverse effects on competition which, by their nature cannot qualify for an exemption under Article [101(3) TFEU]. In other words [...], such reasoning presumes acceptance of the view that there are infringements which are inherently incapable of qualifying for an exemption but Community competition law, the applicability of which is subject to the existence of a practice which is anti-competitive in intent or has an anti-competitive effect on a given market, certainly does not embody that principle. On the contrary, the [General Court] considers that, in principle, no anti-competitive practice can exist which, whatever the extent of its effects on a given market, cannot be exempted, provided that all the conditions laid down in Article [101(3) TFEU] are satisfied and the practice in question has been properly notified to the Commission.

General Court 15 July 1994 (Matra Hachette v. Commission, T-17/93) [1994] ECR II-595, paras 84 and 85.

Only if the referring court finds [...] that there is indeed in the dispute before it a restriction of competition within the meaning of Article [101(1) TFEU] will it be necessary for that court to carry out an analysis by reference to Article [101(3) TFEU] in order to resolve that dispute. **4.215**

CoJ 23 November 2006 (Asnef-Equifax, C-238/05) [2006] ECR I-11125, para. 64.

The [General Court] referred to the case-law, principles and criteria governing the burden of proof and standard of proof required in relation to requests for exemptions under Article [101(3) TFEU]. It correctly stated that a person who relies on that provision must demonstrate, by means of convincing arguments and evidence, that the conditions for obtaining an exemption are satisfied [...]. **4.216**

The burden of proof thus falls on the undertaking requesting the exemption under Article [101(3) TFEU]. However, the facts relied on by that undertaking may be such as to oblige the other party to provide an explanation or justification, failing which it is permissible to conclude that the burden of proof has been discharged [...].

CoJ 6 October 2009 (GlaxoSmithKline Services and others v. Commission and others, Joined Cases C-501, 513 and 519/06 P) [2009] ECR I-9291, paras 82 and 83.

[I]t should be noted, that, as an undertaking has the option, in all circumstances, to assert, on an individual basis, the applicability of the exception provided for in Article 101(3) TFEU, thus enabling its rights to be protected, it is not necessary to give a broad interpretation to the provisions which bring agreements or practices within the block exemption. **4.217**

CoJ 13 October 2011 (Pierre Fabre Dermo-Cosmétique, C-439/09) [2011] ECR I-9419, para. 57.

2. Four cumulative conditions

(a) *Improvement of the production and distribution, promotion of technical and economic progress*

4.218   The question whether there is an improvement in the production of distribution of the goods in question, which is required for the grant of exemption, is to be answered in accordance with the spirit of Article [101 TFEU].

This subjective method, which makes the content of the concept of 'improvement' depend upon the special features of the contractual relationships in question, is not consistent with the aims of Article [101 TFEU]. [...]

In its evaluation of the relative importance of the various factors submitted for its consideration, the Commission on the other hand had to judge their effectiveness by reference to an objectively ascertainable improvement in the production and distribution of the goods, and to decide whether the resulting benefit would suffice to support the conclusion that the consequent restrictions upon competition were indispensable.

CoJ 13 July 1966 (Grundig and Consten v. Commission, Joined Cases 56 and 58/64) [1966] ECR 450.

4.219   Furthermore these agreements, which by preventing parallel imports secured for Theal absolute territorial protection which was made still more effective by the prohibition on exports imposed by Watts, did not contribute either to improving the production or distribution of goods or to promoting technical or economic progress and could not [...] be exempted as provided for in Article [101(3) TFEU] since the requisite conditions for the application of that article do not exist.

CoJ 20 June 1978 (Tepea v. Commission, 28/77) [1978] ECR 1391, para. 57.

4.220   It adds that the agreement contributed to an improvement in tobacco distribution on the German market and that without the agreement Segers would have found it impossible to market his product under the Toltecs brand.

That line of argument is clearly contradicted both by the content of the agreement of 16 January 1975 [...] and by the conduct of BAT, the sole purpose of which was to prevent Segers' tobacco from being sold on the German market. It is therefore clear that the agreement did not fulfil the conditions laid down in Article [101(3) TFEU].

CoJ 30 January 1985 (BAT v. Commission, 35/83) [1985] ECR 363, paras 40 and 41.

4.221   In connection with the argument to the effect that the survival of the undertaking and the preservation of jobs are only possible if the non-competition clause applies for a period of 10 years, it must indeed be admitted that [...] the provision of employment comes within the framework of the objectives to which reference may be had pursuant to Article [101(3) TFEU] because it improves the general conditions of production, especially when market conditions are unfavourable.

CoJ 11 July 1985 (Remia v. Commission, 42/84) [1985] ECR 2545, para. 42.

[T]he profitability of an investment made by a producer in connection with the launch **4.222** of a product or range of new products may also, depending on the specific circumstances of the case in question, be one of the advantages which may be taken into account as regards the contribution made to economic progress. Although the Commission maintained that that could not be the case, that approach forms part of its practice [...] in which the Commission expressly takes account of the optimization of investment expenses in exempting a research and development agreement in the sphere of space communication techniques. But, in the present case, the applicant has not in any event produced any evidence to show that the profitability of the investment involved in the launching of a product or range of products is greater, in the case of retail pharmacies, than that which might be achieved through another distribution channel. Moreover, the contested decision correctly emphasizes [...] that, by opening its distribution network to holders of diplomas in pharmacy, Vichy would in no way be deprived of the assistance of pharmacists in ensuring the successful launch of innovative products.

General Court 27 February 1992 (Vichy v. Commission, T-19/91) [1992] ECR II-415, para. 94.

As regards, first, the manufacturing process, it is clear from the unambiguous state- **4.223** ments from the intervener, Ford [...], that the manufacturing process to be used [...] constitutes the first application by a European car manufacturer of the enhanced form of the manufacturing process recommended in 1990 by the most authoritative research- ers in the field of technological development, such as the Massachusetts Institute of Technology (MIT). The [General Court] considers, despite the applicant's assertions to the contrary, that an optimization of the manufacturing process of that kind is in conformity with the meaning and purpose of the first of the four conditions laid down by Article [101(3) TFEU].

As regards, secondly, the technical improvements made to the product, described as 'cosmetic' by the applicant, they must be assessed in relation to the state of development of car construction techniques in Europe when the Decision was adopted. Adopting that approach, the [General Court] considers that, as maintained by the Commission, the technical improvements made to the vehicle fall within the scope of Article [101(3) TFEU], since they bring together in a single product techniques which, where they exist, are at present used in isolation, on different models.

General Court 15 July 1994 (Matra Hachette v. Commission, T-17/93) [1994] ECR II-595, paras 109 and 110.

An increase in market transparency is in fact inherent in any system of recommended **4.224** rates set and published by an association which represents a significant proportion of undertakings operating in a given market. Accordingly, demonstrating an increase in market transparency linked to a system of recommended rates is not sufficient proof that the first condition in Article [101(3) TFEU] is satisfied.

General Court 22 October 1997 (SCK and FNK v. Commission, Joined Cases T-213 and 218/96) [1997] ECR II-1739, para. 210.

For the purposes of examining the merits of the Commission's findings as to the various **4.225** requirements of Article [101(3) TFEU] and Article 5 of Regulation No 1017/68,

[Regulation applying rules of competition to transport by rail, road and inland waterways now repealed by Regulation No 169/2009 with the exception of Article 13(3)] regard should naturally be had to the advantages arising from the agreement in question, not only for the relevant market, namely that for inland transport services provided as part of intermodal transport, but also, in appropriate cases, for every other market on which the agreement in question might have beneficial effects, and even, in a more general sense, for any service the quality or efficiency of which might be improved by the existence of that agreement. Both Article 5 of Regulation No 1017/68 and Article [101(3) TFEU] envisage exemption in favour of, amongst others, agreements which contribute to promoting technical or economic progress, without requiring a specific link with the relevant market.

General Court 28 February 2002 (Compagnie Générale Maritime and others v. Commission, T-86/95) [2002] ECR II-1011, para. 343.

4.226   [T]he [General Court] rightly observed that, in order to be capable of being exempted under Article [101(3) TFEU], an agreement must contribute to improving the production or distribution of goods or to promoting technical or economic progress. That contribution is not identified with all the advantages which the undertakings participating in the agreement derive from it as regards their activities, but with appreciable objective advantages of such a kind as to compensate for the resulting disadvantages for competition […].

As the Advocate General observed […], an exemption granted for a specified period may require a prospective analysis regarding the occurrence of the advantages associated with the agreement, and it is therefore sufficient for the Commission, on the basis of the arguments and evidence in its possession, to arrive at the conviction that the occurrence of the appreciable objective advantage is sufficiently likely in order to presume that the agreement entails such an advantage.

The [General Court] therefore committed no error of law […] in holding that the Commission's approach may entail ascertaining whether, in the light of the factual arguments and the evidence provided, it seems more likely either that the agreement in question must make it possible to obtain appreciable advantages or that it will not.

Moreover, the [General Court] made no error of law […] in observing that it was necessary to determine whether the Commission was entitled to conclude that GSK's factual arguments and evidence, examination of which entailed a prospective analysis, did not demonstrate with a sufficient degree of probability that Clause 4 of the agreement would, by encouraging innovation, make it possible to obtain an appreciable objective advantage of such a kind as to offset the disadvantage which it entailed for competition. […]

The Court notes that the examination of an agreement for the purposes of determining whether it contributes to the improvement of the production or distribution of goods or to the promotion of technical or economic progress, and whether that agreement generates appreciable objective advantages, must be undertaken in the light of the factual arguments and evidence provided in connection with the request for exemption under Article [101(3) TFEU].

Such an examination may require the nature and specific features of the sector concerned by the agreement to be taken into account if its nature and those specific features are decisive for the outcome of the analysis. Taking those matters into account, moreover, does not mean that the burden of proof is reversed, but merely ensures that the examination of the request for exemption is conducted in the light of the appropriate factual arguments and evidence provided by the party requesting the exemption.

CoJ 6 October 2009 (GlaxoSmithKline Services and others. v. Commission and others, Joined Cases C-501, 513 and 519/06P) [2009] ECR I-9291, paras 92–95, 102 and 103.

It follows from this that, in the case of a two-sided system such as the MasterCard **4.227** scheme, in order to assess whether a measure which in principle infringes the prohibition laid down in Article [101(1) TFEU] – in so far as it creates restrictive effects in regard to one of the two groups of consumers associated with that system – can fulfil the first condition laid down in Article [101(3) TFEU], it is necessary to take into account the system of which that measure forms part, including, where appropriate, all the objective advantages flowing from that measure not only on the market in respect of which the restriction has been established, but also on the market which includes the other group of consumers associated with that system, in particular where, as in this instance, it is undisputed that there is interaction between the two sides of the system in question. To that end, it is necessary to assess, where appropriate, whether such advantages are of such a character as to compensate for the disadvantages which that measure entails for competition.

CoJ 11 September 2014 (MasterCard Inc. and others vs. Commission, C-382/12) ECLI:EU:C:2014:2201, para. 237.

(b) Direct benefit for consumers

[T]he conditions of supply for wholesalers under the cooperation agreement are such as **4.228** to provide direct benefit for consumers in that they ensure continued supplies and the provision of a wider range of goods by retailers for private customers.

Even if it is doubtful whether the requirement in this conne[ct]ion of Article [101(3) TFEU] can be said to be satisfied by the assumption that the pressure of competition will be sufficient to induce SABA and the wholesalers to pass on to consumers a part of the benefit derived from the rationalization of the distribution network, the grant of exemption may, however, in the present case be considered as sufficiently justified by the advantage which consumers obtain from an improvement in supplies.

CoJ 25 October 1977 (Metro v. Commission, 26/76) [1977] ECR 1875, paras 47 and 48.

Nothing in the wording or the spirit of Article [101(3) TFEU] allows that provision to **4.229** be interpreted as meaning that the possibility for which it provides, of declaring the provisions of paragraph 1 inapplicable in the case of certain agreements which contribute to improving the production or distribution of goods or to promoting technical or economical progress, is subject to the condition that those benefits should occur only on the territory of the Member State or States in which the undertakings who are parties to the agreement are established and not in the territory of other Member States. Such an

interpretation is incompatible with the fundamental objectives of the Community and with the very concepts of common market and single market.
CoJ 17 January 1995 (Publishers Association v. Commission, C–360/92) [1995] ECR I–23, para. 29.

4.230   In order for the condition that consumers be allowed a fair share of the benefit to be satisfied, it is not necessary, in principle, for each consumer individually to derive a benefit from an agreement, a decision or a concerted practice. However, the overall effect on consumers in the relevant markets must be favourable.
CoJ 23 November 2006 (Asnef-Equifax, C–238/05) [2006] ECR I–11125, para. 72.

4.231   [I]n so far as the appellants complain that the General Court did not explain why all the categories of consumers must benefit from the same share of the profit resulting from the MIF, suffice it to note that that complaint is based on a misreading of the judgment under appeal. The General Court did not in any way find that each group of consumers should benefit from the same share of that profit, but merely indicated that, as merchants constitute one of the two groups of users affected by payment cards, they should also enjoy appreciable objective advantages attributable to the MIF. Thus, by using the word 'also' in paragraph 228 of its judgment, the General Court correctly indicated that merchants had to enjoy the MIF 'as well as' cardholders, and not 'to the same extent' as them.
CoJ 11 September 2014 (MasterCard Inc. and others v. Commission, C–382/12), ECLI:EU:C:2014:2201, para. 248.

(c)   Proportionality

4.232   [I]t must be considered whether the restrictions imposed on wholesalers under the cooperation agreement are indispensable to the attainment of the objectives in view.
   If there were no undertakings covering a period of a given duration the relationship between the producer and appointed wholesalers could only take the form of occasional contact which would not make it possible to achieve the stability necessary to enable specialist wholesalers and producers to undertake the other obligations which guarantee improved supplies.
   In considering that the cooperation agreement, by restricting the period covered by the supply contract to six months, remained within the limits of what is necessary the Commission clearly did not exceed the margin of discretion which it possesses in this sphere.
CoJ 25 October 1977 (Metro v. Commission, 26/76) [1977] ECR 1875, paras 44 and 45.

4.233   [I]t is necessary to recall once again the factor of assessment contributed by the cooperative's position on the Netherlands market in the products in question. It is accepted that the members of the cooperative account for more than 90 per cent of cheese output in the Netherlands and that non-member Netherlands producers also buy virtually all the rennet which they need from the cooperative. In those circumstances provisions of such a constraining nature as a 100 per cent purchasing obligation, reinforced by an obligation to pay a not inconsiderable sum in the event of a resignation or expulsion, are not indispensable for the attainment of the objects referred to in Article [101(3) TFEU]. What is more, it follows from the foregoing that those provisions in any event contribute to maintaining a situation in which competition is eliminated in respect of a substantial part of the products in question. The Commission was therefore right to find that the last two conditions for the application of Article [101(3) TFEU] are not fulfilled.

CoJ 25 March 1981 (Coöperatieve Stremsel en Kleurselfabriek v. Commission, 61/80) [1980] ECR 851, para. 18.

The [General Court] considers that, as the Commission maintains, the central question **4.234** to be answered, in assessing the legality of the Decision in relation to the third of the four conditions laid down in Article [101(3) TFEU], is whether the joint venture is strictly indispensable to enable the founders to penetrate the market in question. If that question is answered in the affirmative, it will ipso facto be established that the restrictions of competition deriving from the agreement are indispensable in order to attain the objectives pursued by the two conditions examined above, in particular the first one. The answer is indeed affirmative, since the Commission maintains [...] that, if each of the founders actually was technically and financially capable of penetrating the market individually, such penetration could be achieved only at a loss, in view of the particularly high level of the joint venture's 'break-even point' and of the information available concerning forecasts of sales and market shares.

General Court 15 July 1994 (Matra Hachette v. Commission, T-17/93) [1994] ECR II-595, para. 138.

Since the [General Court] has found that the Commission was right to consider that **4.235** the notified rules did not fulfil the second and third conditions for the grant of an exemption under Article [101(3) TFEU], there can be no question of any breach of the principle of proportionality, particularly since the applicants emphasized, during the administrative procedure and the procedure before the [General Court], that the rules constitute a single whole from which the various component parts cannot be artificially isolated.

General Court 21 February 1995 (VSPOB v. Commission, T-29/92) [1995] ECR II-289, para. 327.

It is for the undertakings claiming an exemption under Article [101(3) TFEU] to **4.236** provide documentary evidence to establish the justification for an exemption. In particular, it is for those undertakings to show that the restrictions of competition arising from the agreement in question meet the objectives referred to by that provision and that those objectives could not be attained without the introduction of those restrictions.

General Court 28 February 2002 (Compagnie Générale Maritime and others. v. Commission, T-86/95) [2002] ECR II-1011, para. 381.

113

(d)   No elimination of competition

4.237   The arguments on which the Commission has [...] based its case, show that there is competition between the two products which is effected by their prices and their intrinsic advantages for the consumer. The figures mentioned in the decision show a considerable increase in consumption of compound potash fertilizers which however has not eliminated straight potash. The decision challenged stated, it is true, that such considerations as the state of the soil, the availability of labour and the weather, point in certain cases to the desirability of using straight potash, but it is not shown that the two types of fertilizers constitute different markets. The decision itself makes a point of the fact that a small number of farmers may in some years buy straight fertilizer and in others compound fertilizer.

In these circumstances the conclusion of the decision that 'the declaration of inapplicability of Article [101(1) TFEU] must in any case be refused because the agreement affords the undertakings the possibility of eliminating competition in respect of a substantial part of the products in question' is not valid.

CoJ 14 May 1975 (Kali und Salz and others v. Commission, Joined Cases 19 and 20/74) [1975] ECR 499, paras 6 and 7.

4.238   [I]t must be considered whether the obligations contained in the cooperation agreement do not afford the undertakings concerned the possibility of eliminating competition in respect of a substantial part of the products in question.

It is clear from the foregoing considerations that the conditions laid down by SABA for appointment as a wholesaler may largely be fulfilled without inconvenience by self-service wholesale undertakings. Nevertheless, although the supply estimates which wholesalers are obliged to sign under the cooperation agreements in all probability constitute an element foreign to the methods appropriate to that distribution channel, it does not appear that, in weighing up, in the context of the electronic leisure equipment sector, the relative importance of the need for cooperation agreements, giving sufficient coherence to SABA's marketing network [...], on the one hand, and the surmountable difficulties which that involves for self-service wholesale traders, on the other, and deciding in favour of the former, the Commission exceeded its discretionary power in this sphere. [...] Accordingly, that decision is not manifestly based on a mistaken appraisal of the economic factors conditioning competition in the sector in question.

CoJ 25 October 1977 (Metro v. Commission, 26/76) [1977] ECR 1875, paras 49 and 50.

4.239   For the provisions of the recommendation to enjoy exemption they must not afford the members of FEDETAB the possibility of eliminating competition in respect of a substantial part of the products in question.

In that respect it must be remembered, as the Commission pointed out [...], that FEDETAB member firms produce or import roughly 95 per cent of the cigarettes sold in Belgium and that ten FEDETAB members, who also import foreign branded products, imported in 1974 51 per cent of the cigarettes imported into Belgium, or about 5 per cent of the cigarettes sold there. [...]

As has already been stated, the provisions of the recommendation to which the applicant companies agreed have as their object, by means of a collective agreement, the restriction on competition in which those companies might engage between themselves. Having regard to the very large share of the Belgian cigarette market held by the FEDETAB members and in particular by the applicant companies, there must be a finding that the recommendation has the effect of affording the applicants the possibility of eliminating competition in respect of a substantial part of the products in question. It follows that the recommendation cannot in any event have exemption under Article [101(3) TFEU].

CoJ 29 October 1980 (Van Landewyck and others v. Commission, Joined Cases 209–215 and 218/78) [1980] ECR 3125, paras 187–189.

However, the Commission rightly stated in reply that that view [...] concerns the **4.240** problem of the demarcation of the market; that is a problem which arises when the Commission has to examine whether an agreement affords 'the possibility of eliminating competition in respect of a substantial part of the products in question' (Article [101(3)(b) TFEU]) but which is not relevant to the question whether an agreement is capable of improving the production or distribution of goods.

CoJ 8 June 1982 (Nungesser and Eisele v. Commission, 258/78) [1982] ECR 2015, para. 75.

In that regard, it must be stated [...] that the increase in the degree of concentration on **4.241** the market is a factor to be taken into consideration in examining an application for the renewal of an exemption under Article [101(3) TFEU], if such an increase affects the structure of competition on the relevant market. Such an effect does not always occur where [...], the trend towards concentration is at the level of production and the agreements to be examined by the Commission concern the distribution of products. However, such an effect may arise, in particular if the trend towards concentration helps to eliminate price competition or to oust other channels of distribution.

CoJ 22 October 1986 (Metro v. Commission (II), 75/84) [1986] ECR 3021, para. 88.

Before examining the various objections to the Commission's view raised by the **4.242** applicants [...], it should be noted that the possibility of eliminating competition in respect of a substantial part of the services in question must be assessed as a whole, taking into account in particular the specific characteristics of the relevant market, the restrictions of competition brought about by the agreement, the market shares of the parties to that agreement and the extent and intensity of external competition, both actual and potential. In the context of this comprehensive approach, those different elements are closely interlinked or may balance each other out. Thus, the greater the restrictions of internal competition between the parties, the more necessary it is for external competition to be keen and substantial if the agreement is to qualify for exemption. Similarly, the larger the market shares of the parties to the agreement, the stronger the potential competition must be. [...]

At this stage of the examination, it must be noted that, in order to determine whether an agreement affords its signatory parties the possibility, in respect of a substantial part of the products in question, of eliminating competition within the meaning of Article [101(3)(b) TFEU], the Commission cannot, in principle, rely merely on the fact that the agreement in question eliminates competition between those parties and that they account for a substantial part of the relevant market. First, the prohibition on eliminating competition is a narrower concept than that of the existence or acquisition of a dominant position, so that an agreement could be regarded as not eliminating competition within the meaning of Article [101(3)(b) TFEU], and therefore qualify for exemption, even if it established a dominant position for the benefit of its members […]. Second, potential competition must be taken into consideration before concluding that an agreement eliminates competition for the purposes of Article [101(3) TFEU] […].

General Court 28 February 2002 (Atlantic Container Line and others v. Commission, T-395/94) [2002] ECR II-875, paras 300 and 330.

F. TYPES OF CONDUCT FALLING UNDER ARTICLE 101 TFEU

1. Horizontal agreements

(a) *Agreements concerning prices and other trading conditions*

4.243   The joint fixing of sales prices by the producers of virtually all the quinine and quinidine distributed within the common market is capable of affecting trade between Member States and seriously restricts competition within the common market.

CoJ 15 July 1970 (ACF Chemiefarma v. Commission) [1970] ECR 661, para. 133.

4.244   The fact that the increases were uniform and simultaneous has in particular served to maintain the status quo, ensuring that the undertakings would not lose custom, and has thus helped to keep the traditional national markets in those goods 'cemented' to the detriment of any real freedom of movement of the products in question in the common market.

CoJ 14 July 1972 (ICI v. Commission, 48/69) [1972] ECR 619, para. 123.

4.245   [T]he fixing of a price, even one which merely constitutes a target, affects competition because it enables all the participants [of the cartel] to predict with a reasonable degree of certainty what the pricing policy pursued by their competitors will be.

CoJ 17 October 1972 (Vereniging van Cementhandelaren v. Commission, 8/72) [1972] ECR 977, para. 21.

4.246   Article [101(1) TFEU] expressly identifies agreements which 'directly or indirectly fix purchase or selling prices or any other trading conditions' as incompatible with the common market.

If a system of fixed selling prices is clearly in conflict with that provision, a price-list system under which the announcement of rebates on these prices is prohibited is equally so. [...]

In consequence, the control of the market exercised by the Groupement characterized by its pricing and rebates policy, and supported by penalties in order to ensure strict compliance with the general conditions of sale, was intended to and did restrict or distort competition [...] within the common market.

CoJ 26 November 1975 (Groupement des fabricants des Papier Peints v. Commission, 73/74) [1975] ECR 1491, paras 9, 10 and 21.

It is apparent from the file on the case that, first, the applicants did not confine **4.247** themselves to submitting joint applications for price increases but also acted in concert regarding the apportionment of the authorized increases as between the various products and the best time at which to put them into effect. The common price list was supplemented by measures concerning the discount rates to be granted. The adoption of the common price list was thus intended to restrict price competition.

CoJ 11 July 1989 (Belasco and others v. Commission, 246/86) [1989] ECR 2117, para. 12.

It follows from the foregoing that the Commission was right to consider that the **4.248** price-increase system constitutes fixing of part of the price, restricts competition between contractors regarding calculation costs and leads to an increase of prices which, in the case of the UPR rules, is larger if a contract awarder wishes to obtain competitive bids from a larger number of contractors. [...]

Such price manipulations undeniably constitute concerted price fixing within the meaning of Article [101(1)(a) TFEU] since, as the applicants have repeatedly stated, it remains possible for the contract awarder to award the contract to a contractor other than the lowest bidder. [...]

The system of protecting the entitled undertaking is intended to grant the contractor who has submitted the lowest blank figure at the meeting (that is to say the lowest price tender from which the price increases have been subtracted) protection of his tender as regards its content and price against negotiations which might take place between the contract awarder and other members of the SPO, both those who took part in the meeting and those who did not, the former being precluded from negotiating their tenders whilst the latter must obtain the consent of the entitled undertaking or an arbitration committee in order to be able to tender. To that end, the contractors taking part in the meeting start by agreeing between themselves the terms on which they will compete. Thus, they determine what should be the content of the various tenders so that they can provide equivalent alternatives for the contract awarder, from which a choice must be made thereafter only on the basis of the price.

It must be emphasized that, even if, at the meeting, the judgment as to the comparability of the tenders is as objective as possible, it is unacceptable for contractors unilaterally to substitute their judgment for that of the party awarding the contract, which must legitimately be entitled to bring to bear subjective preferences, such as the reputation of the contractor, his availability and his proximity, and to make a judgment itself, as future user, as to the equivalence, from its own point of view, of the various tenders.

General Court 21 February 1995 (VSPOB v. Commission, T-29/92) [1995] ECR II-289, paras 156, 158, 182 and 183.

4.249   The fact that the undertakings actually announced the agreed price increases and that the prices so announced served as a basis for fixing individual transaction prices suffices in itself for a finding that the collusion on prices had both as its object and its effect a serious restriction of competition.
General Court 14 May 1998 (Cascades v. Commission, T-308/94) [1998] ECR II-931, para. 194.

4.250   Examination of the facts shows that the infringement complained of consisted, in particular, in the joint fixing of prices and sales volumes on the PVC market. The aim of such an infringement, which is expressly mentioned by way of example in Article [101(1) TFEU], is anti-competitive.
General Court 20 April 1999 (Limburgse Vinyl Maatschappij and others v. Commission, Joined Cases T-305–307, 313–316, 318, 325, 328, 329 and 335/94) [1999] ECR II-931, para. 739.

4.251   An agreement such as that in the present case which prohibits the applicants from granting their customers discounts on the published rates of charges and surcharges has as its object the restriction of competition by indirectly fixing prices within the meaning of Article [101(1)(a) TFEU] [...] since, by means of that agreement, the FETTCSA parties have mutually deprived themselves of the freedom to grant their customers discounts on the published tariffs [...].
General Court 19 March 2003 (CMA CMG v. Commission, T-213/00) [2003] ECR II-913, para. 175.

4.252   As regards, first of all, the applicant's claim that it did not implement the price agreements, the Commission observed [...] that the agreements in question related to price objectives (or 'target prices'). Consequently, their implementation implies not that prices corresponding to the agreed price objective be applied, but that the parties endeavour to approach their price objectives. The Commission also indicated that '[f]rom the information in its possession it [was] clear that, in the present case, after most of the price agreements, the parties fixed their prices in accordance with their agreements'.
General Court 9 July 2003 (Cheil Jedang v. Commission, T-220/00) [2003] ECR II-2473, para. 193.

(b)   Sharing of markets

4.253   The sharing out of domestic markets has as its object the restriction of competition and trade within the Common Market.
CoJ 15 July 1970 (ACF Chemiefarma v. Commission, 41/69) [1970] ECR 661, para. 128.

Concerning more particularly cartels which, like this one, consist of market-sharing, it **4.254** should be noted at the outset that, according to the Guidelines, 'very serious' infringements essentially consist of horizontal restrictions such as price cartels and market-sharing quotas, or other practices which jeopardise the proper functioning of the single market, and that they also appear amongst the examples of agreements, decisions or concerted practices expressly declared incompatible with the common market in Article [101(1)(c) TFEU]. Apart from the serious distortion of competition which they entail, such agreements, by obliging the parties to respect distinct markets, often delimited by national frontiers, cause the isolation of those markets, thereby counteracting the [TFEU]'s main objective of integrating the Community market. Also, infringements of this type, especially where horizontal cartels are concerned, are classified by the case-law as 'particularly serious' or 'obvious infringements' [...].

General Court 18 July 2005 (Scandinavian Airlines System v. Commission, T-241/ 01) [2005] ECR II-2917, para. 85.

[...] In that regard, the [General Court] observed that it had already held [...] that **4.255** agreements which involve respecting domestic markets in themselves pursue an object restrictive of competition and fall within a category of agreements expressly prohibited by Article [101(1) TFEU] and that that object cannot be justified by an analysis of the economic context of the anti-competitive conduct concerned.

CoJ 25 January 2007 (Sumitomo and Nippon Steel v. Commission, Joined Cases C-403, 404/04P) [2007] ECR I-729, para. 43.

[T]he number of persons actually affected by the agreements to share clients at issue in **4.256** the main proceedings is irrelevant for the purpose of determining whether there is such a restriction of competition.

Indeed, [...], a finding that an agreement to share clients has an anti-competitive object – in particular a finding that the agreement may have a negative impact on the market – does not depend on the actual number of clients who are in fact shared out but simply on the terms and the objective aims of the agreement, considered in the light of the economic and legal context in which the agreement was concluded.

CoJ 16 July 2015 (ING Pensii Societate de Administrare a unui Fond de Pensii Administrat Privat SA, C-172/14), ECLI:EU:C:2015:484, paras 54 and 55.

In respect of such agreements, the analysis of the economic and legal context of which **4.257** the practice forms part may thus be limited to what is strictly necessary in order to establish the existence of a restriction of competition by object.

CoJ 20 January 2016 (Toshiba Corporation v. Commission, C-373/14), ECLI: EU:C:2016:26, para. 29.

(c) Certification systems and standards

It follows from the foregoing considerations that the Commission did not commit an **4.258** error of appraisal in finding [...] that SCK's certification system was not completely open [...] and did not allow equivalent guarantees offered by other systems to be accepted. Accordingly, the prohibition on hiring which reinforced the non-open nature of the certification system and had the effect of raising a substantial obstacle to access by third parties to the Netherlands market, and in particular firms established in another Member State [...] in fact constitutes a restriction of competition within the meaning of Article [101(1) TFEU]. That conclusion would be no different if the applicants could show that the clause is necessary in order to preserve the coherence of SCK's certification system. The fact that the system is not open and equivalent guarantees offered by other systems are not accepted means that the system itself is incompatible with Article [101(1) TFEU] even if it were proved, as the applicants claim, that it gave added value compared with the Netherlands legislation. A specific clause in such a system, such as the clause prohibiting hirings from uncertified firms, does not become compatible with Article [101(1) TFEU] because it is needed to preserve the coherence of that system, since the latter is by definition incompatible with Article [101(1) TFEU].

General Court 22 October 1997 (SCK and FNK v. Commission, Joined Cases T-213 and 218/96) [1997] ECR II-1739, para. 149.

4.259   [I]n the present case, the Commission examined the complaint in application of the [previous Guidelines on the applicability of Article 101 TFEU to horizontal cooperation agreements], to which the applicant had, moreover, referred in its complaint. In particular, the Commission examined the Standard in the light of paragraphs 162 and 163 of the Guidelines. According to those paragraphs [...] standards adopted by standards bodies recognised under Directive 98/34 in accordance with a non-discriminatory, open and transparent procedure, and compliance with which is not mandatory, do not, in principle, restrict competition and do not fall under Article [101 TFEU].

General Court 12 May 2010 (EMC Development v. Commission, T-432/05) [2010] ECR II-1629, para. 61.

(d)   Exchange of information

4.260   The first table shows that the producers exchanged their monthly sales figures. Combined with the comparisons made between those figures and those achieved in 1980 (comparisons which are made in the two other tables covering the same period) such an exchange of information which an independent operator would keep strictly secret as confidential business information corroborates the conclusions reached in the Decision [i.e. that Article 101 TFEU had been violated].

General Court 17 December 1991 (Hercules v. Commission, T-7/89) [1991] ECR II-1711, para. 217.

4.261   The [General Court] observes that [...] the Decision is the first in which the Commission has prohibited an information exchange system concerning sufficiently homogeneous products which does not directly concern the prices of those products, but which does not underpin any other anti-competitive arrangement either. As the applicant correctly argues, on a truly competitive market transparency between traders is in principle likely to lead to the intensification of competition between suppliers, since in such a situation, the fact that a trader takes into account information made available to him in order to adjust his conduct on the market is not likely, having regard to the atomized nature of the supply, to reduce or remove for the other traders any uncertainty about the foreseeable nature of its competitors' conduct. On the other hand, the [General Court] considers that, as the Commission argues this time, general use, as between main suppliers and, contrary to the applicant's contention, to their sole benefit and consequently to the exclusion of the other suppliers and of consumers, of exchanges of precise information at short intervals, identifying registered vehicles and the place of their registration is, on a highly concentrated oligopolistic market such as the market in question and on which competition is as a result already greatly reduced and exchange of information facilitated, likely to impair substantially the competition which exists between traders […]. In such circumstances, the sharing, on a regular and frequent basis, of information concerning the operation of the market has the effect of periodically revealing to all the competitors the market positions and strategies of the various individual competitors.

General Court 27 October 1994 (John Deere v. Commission, T-35/92) [1994] ECR II-957, para. 51.

As the Fides information exchange system was considered contrary to Article [101(1) TFEU] only because it supported the cartel found, the fact that the applicant did not supply information to that system is not, in itself, relevant. On the other hand, it is necessary to examine whether the applicant took part in discussions concerning the Fides statistics, as a means of supporting the anti-competitive activities in which it is shown to have participated. **4.262**

General Court 14 May 1998 (Buchmann v. Commission, T-295/94) [1998] ECR II-813, para. 128.

Such a prohibition exceeds what is necessary in order to bring the conduct in question into line with what is lawful because it seeks to prevent the exchange of purely statistical information which is not in, or capable of being put into, the form of individual information on the ground that the information exchanged might be used for anti-competitive purposes. First, it is not apparent from the Decision that the Commission considered the exchange of statistical data to be in itself an infringement of Article [101 (1) TFEU]. Second, the mere fact that a system for the exchange of statistical information might be used for anti-competitive purposes does not make it contrary to Article [101(1) TFEU], since in such circumstances it is necessary to establish its actual anti-competitive effect. **4.263**

General Court 14 May 1998 (Gruber + Weber v. Commission, T-310/94) [1998] ECR II-1043, para. 178.

In view of that reasoning, the [General Court] must be considered to have concluded correctly that the information exchange system reduces or removes the degree of uncertainty as to the operation of the market and that the system is therefore liable to have an adverse influence on competition between manufacturers. **4.264**

CoJ 28 May 1998 (John Deere v. Commission, C-7/95P) [1998] ECR I-3111, para. 90.

4.265 As is apparent both from the case-law and the practice followed by the Commission in adopting decisions, information exchange agreements are not generally prohibited automatically but only if they have certain characteristics relating, in particular, to the sensitive and accurate nature of recent data exchanged at short intervals. [...]

[I]f the Commission had taken account of the real scope of the notified agreement, which is limited to data on the sales of the participating undertakings alone, without distinguishing between the different consumer sectors, and which allows market shares to be calculated only approximately, it is not inconceivable that its evaluation would have been different and that it would have considered that the agreement was not contrary to Article 65(1) of the ECSC Treaty.

General Court 5 April 2001 (Wirtschaftsvereinigung Stahl and others v. Commission, T-16/98) [2001] ECR II-1207, paras 44 and 45.

4.266 Contrary to what the appellant claims, an information exchange system may constitute a breach of competition rules even where the relevant market is not a highly concentrated oligopolistic market. It is true that, in its judgment in Case T-35/92 *John Deere*, [...] which was upheld in this regard by the Court's judgment in *John Deere*, the [General Court] concluded that the tractors market was such a market. However, those judgments take into consideration a number of criteria in that regard, the only general principle applied in relation to the market structure being that supply must not be atomised.

CoJ 2 October 2003 (Thyssen Stahl v. Commission, C-194/99) [2003] ECR I-10821, para. 86.

4.267 [A]rticle [101(1) TFEU] must be interpreted as meaning that a system for the exchange of information on credit between financial institutions, such as the register, does not, in principle, have as its effect the restriction of competition within the meaning of that provision, provided that the relevant market or markets are not highly concentrated, that that system does not permit lenders to be identified and that the conditions of access and use by financial institutions are not discriminatory, in law or in fact. In the event that a system for the exchange of information on credit, such as that register, restricts competition within the meaning of Article [101(1) TFEU], the applicability of the exemption provided for in Article [101(3) TFEU] is subject to the four cumulative conditions laid down in that provision. It is for the national court to determine whether those conditions are satisfied. In order for the condition that consumers be allowed a fair share of the benefit to be satisfied, it is not necessary, in principle, for each consumer individually to derive a benefit from an agreement, a decision or a concerted practice. However, the overall effect on consumers in the relevant markets must be favourable.

CoJ 23 November 2006 (Asnef-Equifax and others, C-238/05) [2006] ECR I-11125, para. 72.

4.268 As regards the applicant's claim that the price information which was transmitted was known by the customers of the undertaking concerned before it was transmitted to the competitors and that, therefore, the information disclosed could already have been collected on the market by those competitors, it should be recalled that the mere fact of receiving information concerning competitors, which an independent operator preserves as business secrets, is sufficient to demonstrate the existence of an anti-competitive intention [...].

The applicant's claim that the price information was known by customers before it was transmitted to the competitors and, therefore, could be collected on the market must be rejected. That fact, if proved, does not mean that, at the time that the price lists were sent to the competitors, those prices already constituted objective market data that were readily accessible. The fact that those price lists were sent directly allowed the competitors to become aware of that information more simply, rapidly and directly than they would via the market. Further, that prior notification allowed them to create a climate of mutual certainty as to their future pricing policies.

In those circumstances, the [General Court] considers that [...] the Commission was right to find that the information exchange system set up between BPB, Knauf, Lafarge and Gyproc on price rises on the German market constituted a concerted practice which is contrary to Article [101(1) TFEU].

General Court 8 July 2008 (BPB v. Commission, T-53/03) [2008] ECR II-1333, paras 235–237.

(e) Non-competition clauses

See also the Commission Notice on restrictions directly related and necessary to concentrations (OJ 2005 C 56/24).

It should be stated at the outset that the Commission has rightly submitted [...] that **4.269** the fact that non-competition clauses are included in an agreement for the sale of an undertaking is not of itself sufficient to remove such clauses from the scope of Article [101 (1) TFEU].

In order to determine whether or not such clauses come within the prohibition in Article [101 (1) TFEU], it is necessary to examine what would be the state of competition if those clauses did not exist.

If that were the case, and should the vendor and the purchaser remain competitors after the transfer, it is clear that the agreement for the transfer of the undertaking could not be given effect. The vendor, with his particularly detailed knowledge of the transferred undertaking, would still be in a position to win back his former customers immediately after the transfer and thereby drive the undertaking out of business. Against that background non-competition clauses incorporated in an agreement for the transfer of an undertaking in principle have the merit of ensuring that the transfer has the effect intended. By virtue of that very fact they contribute to the promotion of competition because they lead to an increase in the number of undertakings in the market in question.

Nevertheless, in order to have that beneficial effect on competition, such clauses must be necessary to the transfer of the undertaking concerned and their duration and scope must be strictly limited to that purpose. [...].

CoJ 11 July 1985 (Remia v. Commission, C-42/84) [1985] ECR 2545, paras 17–20.

4.270   It must be borne in mind that the concept of an 'ancillary restriction' covers any restriction which is directly related and necessary to the implementation of a main operation [...].

A restriction 'directly related' to implementation of a main operation must be understood to be any restriction which is subordinate to the implementation of that operation and which has an evident link with it [...].

The condition that a restriction be necessary implies a two-fold examination. It is necessary to establish, first, whether the restriction is objectively necessary for the implementation of the main operation and, second, whether it is proportionate to it [...].

As regards the objective necessity of a restriction, it must be observed that inasmuch as the existence of a rule of reason in Community competition law cannot be upheld, it would be wrong, when classifying ancillary restrictions, to interpret the requirement for objective necessity as implying a need to weigh the pro and anti-competitive effects of an agreement [...].

That approach is justified not merely so as to preserve the effectiveness of Article [101(3) TFEU], but also on grounds of consistency. As Article [101 TFEU] does not require an analysis of the positive and negative effects on competition of a principal restriction, the same finding is necessary with regard to the analysis of accompanying restrictions [...].

Consequently, examination of the objective necessity of a restriction in relation to the main operation cannot but be relatively abstract. It is not a question of analysing whether, in the light of the competitive situation on the relevant market, the restriction is indispensable to the commercial success of the main operation but of determining whether, in the specific context of the main operation, the restriction is necessary to implement that operation. If, without the restriction, the main operation is difficult, or even impossible, to implement, the restriction may be regarded as objectively necessary for its implementation [...].

Where a restriction is objectively necessary to implement a main operation, it is still necessary to verify whether its duration and its material and geographic scope do not exceed what is necessary to implement that operation. If the duration or the scope of the restriction exceeds what is necessary in order to implement the operation, it must be assessed separately under Article [101(3) TFEU] [...].

It must be observed that, inasmuch as the assessment of the ancillary nature of a particular agreement in relation to a main operation entails complex economic assessments by the Commission, judicial review of that assessment is limited to verifying whether the relevant procedural rules have been complied with, whether the statement of the reasons for the decision is adequate, whether the facts have been accurately stated and whether there has been a manifest error of appraisal or misuse of powers [...].

If it is established that a restriction is directly related and necessary to achieving a main operation, the compatibility of that restriction with the competition rules must be examined with that of the main operation. Thus, if the main operation does not fall within the scope of the prohibition laid down in Article [101(1) TFEU], the same holds for the restrictions directly related and necessary for that operation. If, on the other hand, the main operation is a restriction within the meaning of Article [101(1) TFEU] but benefits from an exemption under Article [101(3) TFEU], that exemption also covers those ancillary restrictions [...].

General Court 29 June 2012 (E. ON Ruhrgas and others v. Commission, T–360/09), ECLI:EU:T:2012:332, paras 62–70.

Where it is a matter of determining whether an anti-competitive restriction can escape the prohibition laid down in Article [101 TFEU] because it is ancillary to a main operation that is not anti-competitive in nature, it is necessary to inquire whether that operation would be impossible to carry out in the absence of the restriction in question. Contrary to what the appellants claim, the fact that that operation is simply more difficult to implement or even less profitable without the restriction concerned cannot be deemed to give that restriction the 'objective necessity' required in order for it to be classified as ancillary. Such an interpretation would effectively extend that concept to restrictions which are not strictly indispensable to the implementation of the main operation. Such an outcome would undermine the effectiveness of the prohibition laid down in Article [101(1) TFEU]. **4.271**

However, that interpretation does not mean that there has been an amalgamation of, on the one hand, the conditions laid down by the case-law for the classification – for the purposes of the application of Article [101(1) TFEU] – if a restriction as ancillary, and, on the other hand, the criterion of the indispensability required under Article [101(3) TFEU] in order for a prohibited restriction to be exempted.

In that regard, suffice it to note that those two provisions have different objectives and that the latter criterion relates to the issue whether coordination between undertakings that is liable to have an appreciable adverse impact on the parameters of competition, such as the price, the quantity and quality of the goods or services, which is therefore covered by the prohibition rule laid down in Article [101(1) TFEU], can none the less, in the context of Article [101(3) TFEU], be considered indispensable to the improvement of production or distribution or to the promotion of technical or economic progress, while allowing consumers a fair share of the resulting benefits. By contrast, […] the objective necessity test referred to in those paragraphs concerns the question whether, in the absence of a given restriction of commercial autonomy, a main operation or activity which is not caught by the prohibition laid down in Article [101(1) TFEU] and to which that restriction is secondary, is likely not to be implemented or not to proceed.

In ruling […] that '[o]nly those restrictions which are necessary in order for the main operation to be able to function in any event may be regarded as falling within the scope of the theory of ancillary restrictions', and in concluding […] that 'the fact that the absence of the MIF may have adverse consequences for the functioning of the MasterCard system does not, in itself, mean that the MIF must be regarded as being objectively necessary, if it is apparent from an examination of the MasterCard system in its economic and legal context that it is still capable of functioning without it', the General Court did not, therefore, err in law.

CoJ 11 September 2014 (MasterCard Inc. and others v. Commission, C–382/12), ECLI:EU:C:2014:2201, paras 91–94.

(f) Pay-for-delay

It must also be observed that potential competition includes inter alia the activities of generic undertakings seeking to obtain the necessary [marketing authorisations], as **4.272** well as all the administrative and commercial steps required in order to prepare for entry to the market [...]. That potential competition is protected by Article 101 TFEU. If it were possible, without infringing competition law, to pay undertakings taking the necessary steps to prepare for the launch of a generic medicinal product [...] and which have made significant investments to that end, to cease or merely slow that process, effective competition would never take place, or would suffer significant delays, at the expense of consumers, that is to say, in the present case, patients or national health insurance schemes.

[T]he Commission considered, in the contested decision, that the fact that the restrictions contained in the agreements at issue had been obtained through significant reverse payments was decisive for the legal assessment of those agreements [...].

The contested decision nevertheless acknowledges that the existence of a reverse payment in the context of a patent settlement is not always problematic, particularly when (i) that payment is linked to the strength of the patent, as perceived by each of the parties, (ii) it is necessary in order to find an acceptable and legitimate solution in the eyes of the two parties and (iii) it is not accompanied by restrictions intended to delay the market entry of generics. [...]

However, where a reverse payment is combined with an exclusion of competitors from the market or a limitation of the incentives to seek market entry, the Commission rightly took the view that it was possible to consider that such a limitation did not arise exclusively from the parties' assessments of the strength of the patents but rather was obtained by means of that payment [...], constituting, therefore, a buying-off of competition.

The size of a reverse payment may constitute an indicator of the strength or weakness of a patent, as perceived by the parties to the agreements at the time they were concluded, and of the fact that originator undertaking was not initially convinced of its chances of succeeding in the event of litigation. Similarly, the Supreme Court of the United States has also held that the presence of a significant reverse payment in a patent settlement agreement can provide a workable surrogate for the weakness of a patent, without a court having to carry out a detailed analysis of the validity of that patent (judgment of the Supreme Court of the United States of 17 June 2013 in *Federal Trade Commission v. Actavis*, 570 U.S. (2013), 'the *Actavis* judgment'). Moreover, the applicants, [...], seem to acknowledge that, the higher the originator undertaking estimates the chances of its patent being found invalid or not infringed, and the higher the damage to the originator undertaking resulting from successful generic entry, the more money it will be willing to pay the generic undertakings to avoid that risk.

It must be noted, in that respect, that the Commission did not find, in the contested decision, that all patent settlement agreements containing reverse payments were contrary to Article 101(1) TFEU; it found only that the disproportionate nature of such payments, combined with several other factors—such as the fact that the amounts of those payments seemed to correspond at least to the profit anticipated by the generic undertakings if they had entered the market, the absence of provisions allowing the generic undertakings to launch their product on the market upon the expiry of the agreement without having to fear infringement actions brought by Lundbeck, or the presence, in those agreements, of restrictions going beyond the scope of Lundbeck's patents – led to the conclusion that the agreements at issue had as their object the restriction of competition, within the meaning of Article 101(1) TFEU, in the present case [...].

General Court 8 September 2016 (H. Lundbeck A/S and others v. Commission, T-472/13), ECLI:EU:T:2016:449, paras 171, 349–350 and 352–354.

2. Vertical agreements

(a) General

It is settled case-law that a call by a motor vehicle manufacturer to its authorised dealers is not a unilateral act which falls outside the scope of Article [101(1)] of the Treaty but is an agreement within the meaning of that provision if it forms part of a set of continuous business relations governed by a general agreement drawn up in advance [...]. [...] **4.273**

In this regard, it is clear [...] that the appellant implemented a policy of imposing supply quotas on Italian dealers with the express aim of blocking re-exports from Italy and thus of partitioning the Italian market. It is also clear [...] that this policy was able to be imposed by virtue of the dealership contract.

[T]he dealership contract provided for the possibility of limiting supplies to Italian dealers and [...] this limitation was imposed with the express aim of blocking re-exportation from Italy of the vehicles delivered to those dealers.

It follows that, by accepting the dealership contract, the Italian dealers consented to a measure which was subsequently used for the purpose of blocking re-exports from Italy and thus of restricting competition within the Community. [...]

It follows that [...] the limitation on re-exports, which was the objective pursued by the appellant, also resulted from the business conduct of the Italian dealers and that this conduct was influenced by the appellant, it being, furthermore, common ground that the means employed for that purpose, in particular the restricted supply of vehicles, resulted from clauses in the dealership contract and had thus received the agreement of the dealers.

CoJ 18 September 2003 (Volkswagen AG I v. Commission, C-338/00P) [2003] ECR I-9189, paras 60, 63–65 and 67.

[T]he case-law [...] does not imply that any call by a motor vehicle manufacturer to dealers constitutes an agreement within the meaning of Article [101(1) TFEU] and does not relieve the Commission of its obligation to prove that there was a concurrence of wills on the part of the parties to the dealership agreement in each specific case. **4.274**

[I]n order to constitute an agreement within the meaning of Article [101(1) TFEU], it is sufficient that an act or conduct which is apparently unilateral be the expression of the concurrence of wills of at least two parties, the form in which that concurrence is expressed not being by itself decisive.

[T]o find otherwise would have the effect of reversing the burden of proof of the existence of a breach of the competition rules and contravening the principle of presumption of innocence.

The will of the parties may result from both the clauses of the dealership agreement in question and from the conduct of the parties, and in particular from the possibility of there being tacit acquiescence by the dealers in a call from the manufacturer [...]. [...]

[The] Court notes that its case-law does not indicate that the compliance or non-compliance of the contractual clauses in question with the competition rules is necessarily decisive in that examination. [...]

The possibility that a call which is contrary to the competition rules may be regarded as being authorised by seemingly neutral clauses of a dealership agreement cannot be automatically excluded.

Consequently, the [General Court] could not, without making an error of law, refrain from examining the clauses of the dealership agreement individually, taking account, where applicable, of all other relevant factors, such as the aims pursued by that agreement in the light of the economic and legal context in which it was signed.

CoJ 13 July 2006 (Commission v. Volkswagen AG, C-74/04 P) [2006] ECR I-6585, paras 36–39 and 43–45.

4.275   Article 101(1) TFEU must be interpreted as meaning that agreements whereby car insurance companies come to bilateral arrangements, either with car dealers acting as car repair shops or with an association representing those dealers, concerning the hourly charge to be paid by the insurance company for repairs to vehicles insured by it, stipulating that that charge depends, inter alia, on the number and percentage of insurance contracts that the dealer has sold as intermediary for that company, can be considered to be a restriction of competition 'by object' within the meaning of that provision, where, following a concrete and individual examination of the wording and aim of those agreements and of the economic and legal context of which they form a part, it is apparent that they are, by their very nature, injurious to the proper functioning of normal competition on one of the two markets concerned.

CoJ 14 March 2013 (Allianz Hungária Biztosító Zrt v. Gazdasági Versenyhivatal, C-32/11), ECLI:EU:C:2013:160, para. 51.

(b) Agency

See also the Commission Notice – Guidelines on Vertical Restraints (OJ 2010 C 130/1), paras 12–21.

4.276   [A] travel agent of the kind referred to by the national court must be regarded as an independent agent who provides services on an entirely independent basis. He sells travel organized by a large number of different tour operators and a tour operator sells travel through a very large number of agents. Contrary to the Belgian Government's submissions, a travel agent cannot be treated as an auxiliary organ forming an integral part of a tour operator's undertaking.

CoJ 1 October 1987 (Vereniging van Vlaamse Reisbureaus, C-311/85) [1987] ECR 3801, para. 20.

4.277   Representatives can lose their character as independent traders only if they do not bear any of the risks resulting from the contracts negotiated on behalf of the principal and they operate as auxiliary organs forming an integral part of the principal's undertaking […]. However, the German VAG dealers assume, at least in part, the financial risks linked to the transactions concluded on behalf of VAG Leasing, in so far as they repurchase the vehicles from it upon the expiry of the leasing contracts. Furthermore, their principal business of sales and after-sales services is carried on, largely independently, in their own name and for their own account.

CoJ 24 October 1995 (Bundeskartellamt v. Volkswagen and VAG Leasing, C-266/93) [1995] ECR I-3477, para. 19.

4.278 [W]here an agent, although having separate legal personality, does not independently determine his own conduct on the market, but carries out the instructions given to him by his principal, the prohibitions laid down under Article [101(1) TFEU] do not apply to the relationship between the agent and the principal with which he forms an economic unit.

General Court 15 September 2005 (DaimlerChrysler AG v. Commission, T-325/01) [2005] ECR II-3319, para. 88.

4.279 [I]t is Mercedes-Benz, and not its German agents, which determines the conditions applying to all car sales, in particular the sale price, and which bears the principal risks associated with that activity, as the German agent is prevented by the terms of the agency agreement from purchasing and holding stocks of vehicles for sale. In those circumstances, it must be held that the relationship between the agents and the applicant is such that the former sell Mercedes-Benz vehicles in all material respects under the direction of the applicant, with the result that they should be treated in the same way as employees and considered as integrated in that undertaking and thus forming an economic unit with it. […]

It follows that the categorisation of the status of the German Mercedes-Benz agent under Article [101(1) TFEU] set out […] not undermined by the fact that the German Mercedes-Benz agents are required to undertake certain activities and assume certain financial obligations under the agency agreement. It should also be noted that the activities are carried out on markets other than the market at issue in the present case. Even if it must be recognised that those obligations expose the agent to certain limited risks, they do not of themselves operate to affect the relationship between the applicant and its agents under competition law as regards the market at issue in these proceedings.

General Court 15 September 2005 (DaimlerChrysler AG v. Commission, T-325/01) [2005] ECR II-3319, paras 102 and 113.

4.280 Article [101(1) TFEU] applies to an agreement for the exclusive distribution of motor-vehicle and other fuels, such as that at issue in the main proceedings, concluded between a supplier and a service-station operator where that operator assumes, to a non-negligible extent, one or more financial and commercial risks linked to the sale to third parties.

CoJ 14 December 2006 (Confederación Espaæola de Empresarios de Estaciones de Servicio v. Compaæía Espaæola de Petróleos SA, C-217/05) [2006] ECR I-11987, para. 65.

4.281   In the light of the foregoing considerations, the answer to Question 1(a) and 2(a) must be that an exclusive supply contract for petroleum products is capable of falling within the scope of Article [101(1) TFEU] where the service-station operator assumes, in a non-negligible proportion, one or more financial and commercial risks linked to the sale of those products to third parties and where that contract contains clauses capable of infringing competition, such as that relating to the fixing of the retail price. If the service-station operator does not assume such risks or assumes only a negligible share of them, only the obligations imposed on the operator in the context of services as an intermediary offered by the operator to the principal, such as the exclusivity and non-competition clauses, are capable of falling within the scope of that provision. It is for the referring court to ascertain, moreover, whether the contract at issue in the main proceedings has the effect of preventing, restricting or distorting competition within the meaning of Article [101 TFEU].

CoJ 11 September 2008 (CEPSA Estaciones de Servicio SA v. LV Tobar e Hijos SL, C-279/06) [2008] ECR I-6681, para. 44.

(c)   Block exemption regulations

See regarding the application of Art. 101 TFEU on vertical agreements Chapter 15 on Regulation No 330/2010 and the Commission Notice – Guidelines on Vertical Restraints (OJ 2010 C 130/1).

See regarding the application of Art. 101 TFEU on vertical distribution agreements in the automotive sector Chapter 16 on Regulation No 461/2010 in conjunction with Regulation No 330/2010 and the Commission notice – Supplementary guidelines on vertical restraints in agreements for the sale and repair of motor vehicles and for the distribution of spare parts for motor vehicles (OJ 2010 C 138/16).

(d)   Resale price restrictions

See regarding resale price restrictions Chapter 15 on Regulation No 330/2010 and the Commission Notice – Guidelines on Vertical Restraints (OJ 2010 C 130/1), paras 223–229.

(e)   Selective distribution

See regarding selective distribution Chapter 15 on Regulation No 330/2010 and the Commission Notice – Guidelines on Vertical Restraints (OJ 2010 C 130/1), paras 174–188.

(i)   General

4.282   Any marketing system based upon the selection of outlets necessarily entails the obligation on wholesalers forming part of the network to supply only appointed resellers and, accordingly, the right of the relevant producer to check that that obligation is fulfilled. In so far as the obligations undertaken in conne[ct]ion with verification are intended to ensure respect for the conditions of appointment regarding the criteria as to technical qualifications, they do not in themselves constitute a restriction on competition but are the corollary of the principal obligation and contribute to its fulfilment. However, in so far as they guarantee the fulfilment of more stringent obligations, they fall within the terms of the prohibition contained in Article [101(1) TFEU], unless they, together with the principal obligation to which they are related, are exempted, where appropriate, pursuant to Article [101(3) TFEU].

CoJ 25 October 1977 (Metro I, 26/76) [1977] ECR 1875, para. 7.

[T]he Commission was justified in recognizing that selective distribution systems **4.283** constituted, together with others, an aspect of competition which accords with Article [101(1) TFEU], provided that resellers are chosen on the basis of objective criteria of a qualitative nature relating to the technical qualifications of the reseller and his staff and the suitability of his trading premises and that such conditions are laid down uniformly for all potential resellers and are not applied in a discriminatory fashion.

CoJ 25 October 1977 (Metro I, 26/76) [1977] ECR 1875, para. 20.

See also CoJ 10 July 1980 (Lancôme v. Etos and Albert Heijn, 99/70) [1980] ECR 2511.

The mere fact at a certain time traders applying for admission to a distribution network **4.284** or who have already been admitted are not engaged in intra-community trade cannot suffice to exclude the possibility that restrictions on their freedom of action may impede intra-community trade, since the situation may change from one year to another in terms of alterations in the conditions or composition of the market both in the common market as a whole and in the individual national markets.

CoJ 25 October 1983 (AEG-Telefunken, 107/82) [1983] ECR 3151, para. 60.

See also CoJ 1 February 1978 (Miller International Schallplatten, 19/77) [1978] ECR 131.

It must be observed [...] that agreements which constitute a selective distribution **4.285** system and which [...] seek to maintain a specialized trade capable of providing specific services for high technology products are normally concluded in order to govern the distribution of those products for a certain number of years, because technological developments are not always foreseeable over such a period of time, those agreements necessarily have to leave certain matters to be decided later by the manufacturer. [I]t is precisely such later decisions that were provided for in [...] Ford AG's main dealer agreement as far as the models to be delivered under the terms of that agreement are concerned.

Such a decision on the part of the manufacturer does not constitute, on the part of the undertaking, a unilateral act which [...] would be exempt from prohibition contained in Article [101(1)] of the Treaty. On the contrary, it forms part of the contractual relations between the undertaking and its dealers, indeed, admission to the Ford AG dealer network implies acceptance by the contracting parties of the policy pursued by Ford with regard to the models to be delivered to the German market.

CoJ 17 September 1985 (Ford-Werke AG and Ford Europe Inc. v. Commission, Joined Cases 25 and 26/84) [1985] ECR 2725, paras 20 and 21.

4.286   [A]lthough the Court had held in previous decisions that 'simple' selective distribution systems are capable of constituting an aspect of competition compatible with Article [101(1) TFEU], there may nevertheless be a restriction or elimination of competition where the existence of a certain number of such systems does not leave any room for other forms of distribution based on a different type of competition policy or results in a rigidity in price structure which is not counterbalanced by other aspects of competition between products of the same brand and by the existence of effective competition between different brands.

   Consequently, the existence of a large number of selective distribution systems for a particular product does not in itself permit the conclusion that competition is restricted or distorted. Nor is the existence of such systems decisive as regards the granting or refusal of an exemption under Article [101(3)], since the only factor to be taken into consideration in that regard is the effect which such systems actually have on the competitive situation. Therefore the coverage ratio of selective distribution systems for colour television sets, to which metro refers, cannot in itself be regarded as a factor preventing an exemption from being granted.

CoJ 22 October 1986 (Metro II, 75/84) [1986] ECR 3021, paras 40 and 41.

4.287   A selective distribution system [...] falls outside the scope of Article [101(1) TFEU] only if it is objectively justified, account being also taken of the interests of consumers [...].

General Court 12 December 1996 (Galec, T-88/92) [1996] ECR II-1961, para. 112.

(ii)   Nature of the products

4.288   The nature and intensiveness of competition may vary to an extent dictated by the products or services in question and the economic structure of the relevant market sectors. In the sector covering the production of high quality and technically advanced consumer durables, where a relatively small number of large- and medium-scale producers offer a varied range of items which, or so consumers may consider, are readily interchangeable, the structure of the market does not preclude the existence of a variety of channels of distribution adapted to the peculiar characteristics of the various producers and to the requirements of the various categories of consumers.

CoJ 25 October 1977 (Metro I, 26/76) [1977] ECR 1875, para. 20.

4.289   In order to determine the exact nature of such 'qualitative' criteria for the selection of resellers, it is also necessary to consider whether the characteristics of the product in question necessitate a selective distribution system in order to preserve its quality and ensure its proper use, and whether those objectives are not already satisfied by national rules governing admission to the re-sale trade or the conditions of sale of the product in question. Finally, inquiry should be made as to whether the criteria laid down do not go beyond what is necessary. [...].

CoJ 11 December 1980 (L'Oréal, 31/80) [1980] ECR 3775, para. 16.

Such a system may be established for the distribution of newspapers and periodicals, **4.290** without infringing the prohibition contained in Article [101(1) TFEU], given the special nature of those products as regards their distribution. As AMP rightly pointed out, newspapers and periodicals can, as a general rule, only be sold by retailers during an extremely limited period of time whereas the public expects each distributor to be able to offer a representative selection of press publications, in particular those of the national press. For their part, publishers undertake to take back unsold copies and this gives rise to a continuous exchange of those products between publishers and distributors.

CoJ 3 July 1985 (Binon v. AMP, 243/83) [1985] ECR 2015, para. 32.

It is in the interests of consumers seeking to purchase luxury cosmetics that such **4.291** products are appropriately presented in retail outlets. Since they are high-quality products whose luxury image is appreciated by consumers, criteria which seek only to ensure that they are presented in an enhancing manner pursue an objective which improves competition by preserving that luxury image and thus counterbalances the restriction of competition inherent in selective distribution systems. [...]

That conclusion is not invalidated by the fact, established in the course of these proceedings, that in certain Member States, in particular the Netherlands but also the United Kingdom and France, a greater or lesser proportion of sales is by unauthorized distributors who obtain their supplies on the parallel market. It cannot be ruled out that consumers' interest in such sales has resulted in part from the luxury image whose preservation is due at least partly to selective distribution.

General Court 12 December 1996 (Galec, T-88/92) [1996] ECR II-1961, paras 113 and 115.

(iii) Selection criteria

The obligation on non-specialist wholesalers to open a special department is designed **4.292** to guarantee the sale of the products concerned under appropriate conditions and accordingly does not constitute a restriction on competition within the meaning of Article [101(1) TFEU].

CoJ 25 October 1977 (Metro I, 26/76) [1977] ECR 1875.

[...] A manufacturer who has introduced a selective distribution system cannot **4.293** therefore absolve himself, on the basis of an *a priori* evaluation of the characteristics of the various forms of distribution, from the duty of checking in each case whether a candidate for admission satisfies the specialist trade conditions. [...].

CoJ 25 October 1983 (AEG-Telefunken, 107/82) [1983] ECR 3151.

Furthermore, the applicant does not dispute that the number of authorized dealers is **4.294** restricted. In the letter which accompanied the notification of the dealer agreement, it was stated that the applicant was prepared to grant dealerships to any qualified dealer subject, however, to the condition that if in a small area there were already a large number of dealers, it reserved the right not to appoint a new dealer in order to avoid a situation in which standards of quality could no longer be maintained by dealers. The applicant claims that the reason for that restriction is that a dealer is required to keep a given number of cameras in stock and that if a large number of dealers were appointed as authorized dealers, the sales prospects of some would be such that their business profits would not justify the maintenance of the required stock. It does not challenge the statement of the decision to the effect that it was not prepared to appoint a dealer who effected parallel imports.

The Commission was justified in concluding from this that the applicant's selection of dealers was based not only on qualitative but also on quantitative criteria, the more so as it is common ground that of the 2,000 dealers in photographic equipment in the United Kingdom only approximately 100 are authorized dealers. Clause 28 of the dealer agreement allowed the applicant in fact to restrict the freedom of dealers, even authorized dealers, to establish their business in a location in which the applicant their presence capable of influencing competition between dealers.

The Commission was therefore right in finding that clauses 22 and 27 of the dealer agreement in force before 1 January 1979, clauses 6, 23 and 28 of the dealer agreement as amended on 1 January 1979 and the criteria for the selection of dealers constitute infringements of Article [101(1) TFEU].

CoJ 21 February 1984 (Hasselblad 86/82) [1984] ECR 883, paras 50–52.

4.295   [A] selective distribution system for newspapers and periodicals which affects trade between Member States is prohibited by Article [101(1)] of the Treaty if re-sellers are chosen on the basis of quantitative criteria. However, the Commission may, within the framework of an application for exemption under Article [101(3)], examine whether, in a particular case, criteria of that kind may be justified. [...]

[A] selective distribution system for newspapers and periodicals which affects trade between Member States is prohibited by Article [101(1)] if the criteria determining the choice of re-sellers are applied less strictly in relation to undertakings [which are part of a particular group of undertakings] than in relation to other retailers. [...]

[T]he requirement, in the framework of a selective distribution system for newspapers and periodicals which affects trade between Member States, that fixed prices must be respected renders that system incompatible with Article [101(1)] of the Treaty. However, the Commission may, in considering an application for exemption under Article [101(3)], examine whether, in a particular case, such an element of a distribution system may be justified.

CoJ 3 July 1985 (Binon v. AMP, 243/83) [1985] ECR 2015, paras 35, 38 and 47.

4.296   [...] A selective distribution system which resulted in the exclusion of certain forms of marketing capable of being used to sell products in enhancing conditions, for example in a space or area adapted for that purpose, would simply protect existing forms of trading from competition from new operators and would therefore be inconsistent with Article [101(1)] of the Treaty [...].

General Court 12 December 1996 (Galec, T-88/92) [1996] ECR II-1961, para. 116.

[...] It is not for this Court to rule on the application of those criteria [of a selective **4.297** distribution system] in specific cases.

[T]he application of those criteria in specific cases is not solely a matter for the manufacturer's discretion but must be determined objectively. For the Givenchy network to be lawful under Article [101(1) TFEU], an essential element is thus the possibility of obtaining independent and effective review of the application of those criteria in specific cases.

It is settled law that national courts are competent to apply Article [101(1)] of the Treaty because it has direct effect [...]. An applicant refused admission to the network who considers that the criteria at issue have been applied to him in a manner inconsistent with Article [101(1)], in particular in a discriminatory or disproportionate fashion, may therefore bring a case before the competent national courts. Such a case may also be brought, where appropriate, before the national authorities responsible for the application of Article [101(1)].

It is accordingly for the competent national courts or authorities to which such a case is referred to decide, in the light of the case-law of the Court of Justice and this Court where relevant, whether in a specific case Givenchy's selection criteria have been applied in a discriminatory or disproportionate fashion, thus infringing Article [101(1)]. Those national courts or authorities are responsible in particular for ensuring that the criteria at issue are not used to prevent new operators capable of selling the products in question in conditions which do not detract from their image from gaining admission to the network.

General Court 12 December 1996 (Galec, T-88/92) [1996] ECR II-1961, paras 120–123.

The term 'specified criteria', referred to in Article 1(1)(f) of Commission Regulation **4.298** (EC) No 1400/2002 of 31 July 2002 on the application of Article [101(3) TFEU] to categories of vertical agreements and concerted practices in the motor vehicle sector [now Regulation (EU) No 461/2010 in conjunction with Regulation (EU) No 330/2010], means, with respect to a quantitative selective distribution system within the meaning of that regulation, criteria the precise content of which may be verified. In order to benefit from the exemption provided for by that regulation, it is not necessary for such a system to be based on criteria that are objectively justified and applied in a uniform and non-differentiated manner in respect of all applicants for authorisation.

CoJ 14 June 2012 (Auto 24 SARL v. Jaguar Land Rover France SAS, C-158/11), ECLI:EU:C:2012:351, para. 39.

(iv) Other conditions

A restriction of price competition must [...] be regarded as being inherent in any **4.299** selective distribution system in view of the fact that prices charged by specialist traders necessarily remain within a much narrower span than that which might be envisaged in the case of competition between specialist and non-specialist traders. That restriction is counterbalanced by competition as regards the quality of the services supplied to customers, which would not normally be possible in the absence of an appropriate profit margin making it possible to support the higher expenses connected with those services. The maintenance of a certain level of prices is therefore lawful, but only to the extent to which it is strictly justified by the requirements of a system within which competition must continue to perform the functions assigned to it by the Treaty. In fact the object of such a system is solely the improvement of competition in so far as it relates to factors other than prices and not the guarantee of a high profit margin for approved re-sellers.

AEG was therefore not justified in taking the view that the acceptance of an undertaking to charge prices making possible a sufficiently high profit margin constituted a lawful condition for admission to a selective distribution system. By the very fact that it was authorized not to admit to and not to keep in its distribution network traders who were not, or were no longer, in a position to provide services typical of the specialist trade, it had at its disposal all the means necessary to enable it to ensure the effective application of the system. In such circumstances the existence of a price undertaking constitutes a condition which is manifestly foreign to the requirements of a selective distribution system and thus also affects freedom of competition.

CoJ 25 October 1983 (AEG-Telefunken, 107/82) [1983] ECR 3151, paras 42 and 43.

4.300 [T]he power [...] to require a dealer to stop publishing announcements in the press, to cease other advertising activities and to refrain from repeating them is tantamount to a right of retroactive censorship which enables the applicant to prohibit dealers who are particularly active in the field of competition and prices, and more particularly those who import otherwise than through Victor Hasselblad's sole distributors, from advertising their activities [and infringes Art. 101(1) TFEU].

CoJ 21 February 1984 (Hasselblad, 86/82) [1984] ECR 883, para. 43.

4.301 [A] prohibition of sales between authorized dealers constitutes a restriction of their economic freedom and, consequently, a restriction of competition.

CoJ 21 February 1984 (Hasselblad, 86/82) [1984] ECR 883, para. 46.

4.302 [As soon as] a selective distribution system satisfies the criteria for validity laid down in Article [101] of the Treaty, as defined by the Court in its case-law [...], the restriction of the manufacturer's guarantee to products covered by the contract which are obtained from authorized dealers must also be regarded as valid.

CoJ 13 January 1994 (Metro v. Cartier, C-376/92) [1994] ECR I-15, para. 34.

4.303 [T]o make the validity of a selective distribution system under Article [101(1)] of the Treaty conditional on its 'imperviousness' would lead to the paradoxical result that the most inflexible and most tightly sealed distribution systems would be treated more favourably under Article [101(1)] of the Treaty than distribution systems that are more flexible and more open to parallel transactions.

[T]he recognition of the validity of a selective distribution network in the common market cannot depend on the manufacturer's ability to ensure that the network is 'impervious' everywhere, given that the legislation of certain Member States may hinder or even prevent the achievement of that objective.

It follows from those observations that the 'imperviousness' of a selective distribution system is not a condition of its validity under Community law.

CoJ 13 January 1994 (Metro v. Cartier, C-376/92) [1994] ECR I-15, paras 26–28.

[A] selective distribution system which is not impervious and cannot therefore, under **4.304** national case-law on unfair competition, be enforced against third parties may be valid under Article [101(1) TFEU].

CoJ 5 June 1997 (VAG Händlerbeirat, C-41/96) [1997] ECR I-3123, para. 13.

As regards agreements constituting a selective distribution system, the Court has **4.305** already stated that such agreements necessarily affect competition in the common market [...]. Such agreements are to be considered, in the absence of objective justification, as 'restrictions by object'. [...]

[A]rticle 101(1) TFEU must be interpreted as meaning that, in the context of a selective distribution system, a contractual clause requiring sales of cosmetics and personal care products to be made in a physical space where a qualified pharmacist must be present, resulting in a ban on the use of the internet for those sales, amounts to a restriction by object within the meaning of that provision where, following an individual and specific examination of the content and objective of that contractual clause and the legal and economic context of which it forms a part, it is apparent that, having regard to the properties of the products at issue, that clause is not objectively justified.

CoJ 13 October 2011 (Pierre Fabre Dermo-Cosmétique SAS v. Président de l'Autorité de la concurrence and Ministre de l'Économie, de l'Industrie et de l'Emploi, C-439/09) [2011] ECR I-09419, paras 39 and 47.

(f) Exclusive distribution

See regarding exclusive distribution Chapter 15 on Regulation No 330/2010 and the Commission Notice – Guidelines on Vertical Restraints (OJ 2010 C 130/1), paras 151–173.

[A]n agreement whereby a producer entrusts the sale of his products in a given area to a **4.306** sole distributor cannot automatically fall under the prohibition in Article [101(1) TFEU]. But such an agreement may contain the elements set out in that provision, by reason of a particular factual situation or of the severity of the clauses protecting the exclusive dealership.

CoJ 30 June 1966 (LTM v. MBU, 56/65) [1966] ECR 235, para 2.

An exclusive dealing agreement falls within the prohibition of Article [101 TFEU] when **4.307** it impedes, in law or in fact, the importation of the products in question from other Member States into the protected territory by persons other than the exclusive importer.

More particularly, an exclusive dealing agreement may adversely affect trade between Member States and can have the effect of hindering competition if the concessionaire is able to prevent parallel imports from other Member States into the territory covered by the concession by means of the combined effects of the agreement and a national law requiring the exclusive use of a certain means of proof of authenticity. [...]

However, the fact that an agreement merely authorizes the concessionaire to exploit such a national rule or does not prohibit him from doing so, does not suffice, in itself, to render the agreement null and void.
CoJ 11 July 1974 (Dassonville, 8/74) [1974] ECR 837, paras 11, 12 and 15.

4.308   [T]he clauses of an exclusive licence agreement concluded between a holder of intellectual property rights and a broadcaster constitute a restriction on competition prohibited by Article 101 TFEU where they oblige the broadcaster not to supply decoding devices enabling access to that right holder's protected subject-matter with a view to their use outside the territory covered by that licence agreement.
CoJ 4 October 2011 (Football Association Premier League Ltd and others v QC Leisure and others, C-403/08 and C-429/08) [2011] ECR I-09083, para. 146.

4.309   Au vu des considérations qui précèdent, il y a lieu de répondre à la première question qu'un contrat, tel que celui en cause au principal, prévoyant la constitution d'un droit de superficie, en faveur d'un fournisseur de produits pétroliers afin qu'il construise une station-service et la donne en location au propriétaire du sol, et qui est assorti d'une obligation d'achat exclusif de longue durée, n'a pas, en principe, pour effet de restreindre sensiblement la concurrence et ne relève dès lors pas de l'interdiction prévue à l'article [101(1) TFEU], pour autant que, d'une part, la part de marché de ce fournisseur ne dépasse pas 3 %, alors que la part de marché cumulée de trois autres fournisseurs s'élève à environ 70 %, et, d'autre part, la durée dudit contrat n'est pas manifestement excessive par rapport à la durée moyenne des contrats généralement conclus sur le marché en cause, ce qu'il appartient à la juridiction de renvoi de vérifier.
CoJ 4 December 2014 (Estación de Servicio Pozuelo 4 SL, C-384/13), ECLI: EU:C:2014:2425, para. 42.

(g)   Single branding

See regarding single branding Chapter 15 on Regulation No 330/2010 and the Commission Notice – Guidelines on Vertical Restraints (OJ 2010 C 130/1), paras 129–150.

(i)   General

4.310   Agreements whereby an undertaking agrees to obtain its supplies from one undertaking to the exclusion of all others do not by their very nature necessarily include all the elements constituting incompatibility with the common market as referred to in Article [101(1) TFEU]. Such agreements may, however, exhibit such elements where, taken either in isolation or together with others, and in the economic and legal context in which they are made on the basis of a set of objective factors of law or of fact, they may affect trade between Member States and where they have either as their object or effect the prevention, restriction or distortion of competition.
CoJ 12 December 1967 (Brasserie De Haecht, 23/67) [1967] ECR 407, para. 3.

(ii) Beer supply agreements

[A] beer supply agreement is prohibited by Article [101(1) TFEU], if two cumulative **4.311** conditions are met. The first is that, having regard to the economic and legal context of the agreement at issue, it is difficult for competitors who could enter the market or increase their market share to gain access to the national market for the distribution of beer in premises for the sale and consumption of drinks. The fact that, in that market, the agreement at issue is one of a number of similar agreements having a cumulative effect on competition constitutes only one factor amongst others in assessing whether access to that market is indeed difficult. The second condition is that the agreement in question must make a significant contribution to the sealing-off effect brought about by the totality of those agreements in their economic and legal context. The extent of the contribution made by the individual agreement depends on the position of the contracting parties in the relevant market and on the duration of the agreement. [...]

    [A] beer supply agreement which permits the reseller to buy beer from other Member States is not such as to affect trade between States provided that the permission corresponds to a real possibility for a national or foreign supplier to supply the reseller with beers from other Member States.

CoJ 28 February 1991 (Delimitis, C-234/89) [1991] ECR I-935, paras 27 and 33.

(h) Franchising

See regarding franchising Chapter 15 on Regulation No 330/2010 and the Commission Notice – Guidelines on Vertical Restraints (OJ 2010 C 130/1), paras 189–191.

The compatibility of franchise agreements for the distribution of goods with Article **4.312** [101(1) TFEU] cannot be assessed *in abstracto* but depends on the provisions contained in such agreements. [...]

    In a system of distribution franchises of that kind an undertaking which has established itself as a distributor on a given market and thus developed certain business methods grants independent traders, for a fee, the right to establish themselves in other markets using its business name and the business methods which have made it successful. Rather than a method of distribution, it is a way for an undertaking to derive financial benefit from its expertise without investing its own capital. Moreover, the system gives traders who do not have the necessary experience access to methods which they could not have learned without considerable effort and allows them to benefit from the reputation of the franchisor's business name. Franchise agreements for the distribution of goods differ in that regard from dealerships or contracts which incorporate approved retailers into a selective distribution system, which do not involve the use of a single business name, the application of uniform business methods or the payment of royalties in return for the benefits granted. Such a system, which allows the franchisor to profit from his success, does not in itself interfere with competition. In order for the system to work two conditions must be met.

First, the franchisor must be able to communicate his know-how to the franchisees and provide them with the necessary assistance in order to enable them to apply his methods, without running the risk that that know-how and assistance might benefit competitors, even indirectly. It follows that provisions which are essential in order to avoid that risk do not constitute restrictions on competition for the purposes of Article [101(1)]. That is also true of a clause prohibiting the franchisee, during the period of validity of the contract and for a reasonable period after its expiry, from opening a shop of the same or a similar nature in an area where he may compete with a member of the network. The same may be said of the franchisee's obligation not to transfer his shop to another party without the prior approval of the franchisor; that provision is intended to prevent competitors from indirectly benefiting from the know-how and assistance provided.

Secondly, the franchisor must be able to take the measures necessary for maintaining the identity and reputation of the network bearing his business name or symbol. It follows that provisions which establish the means of control necessary for that purpose do not constitute restrictions on competition for the purposes of Article [101(1)].

CoJ 28 January 1986 (Pronuptia, 161/84) [1986] ECR 353, paras 14–17.

4.313   The compatibility of franchise agreements for the distribution of goods with Article [101(1) TFEU] depends on the provisions contained therein and on their economic context. Provisions which are strictly necessary in order to ensure that the know-how and assistance provided by the franchisor do not benefit competitors do not constitute restrictions of competition for the purposes of Article [101(1)]. Provisions which establish the control strictly necessary for maintaining the identity and reputation of the network identified by the common name or symbol do not constitute restrictions of competition for the purposes of Article [101(1)]. Provisions which share markets between the franchisor and the franchisees or between franchisees constitute restrictions of competition for the purposes of Article [101(1)].

The fact that the franchisor makes price recommendations to the franchisee does not constitute a restriction of competition, so long as there is no concerted practice between the franchisor and the franchisees or between the franchisees themselves for the actual application of such prices.

Franchise agreements for the distribution of goods which contain provisions sharing markets between the franchisor and the franchisees or between franchisees are capable of affecting trade between Member States.

CoJ 28 January 1986 (Pronuptia, 161/84) [1986] ECR 353, para. 27.

5

ARTICLE 102 TFEU*

ABUSE OF DOMINANCE

Any abuse by one or more undertakings of a dominant position within the internal market or in a substantial part of it shall be prohibited as incompatible with the internal market in so far as it may affect trade between Member States.

Such abuse may, in particular, consist in:

(a) directly or indirectly imposing unfair purchase or selling prices or other unfair trading conditions;

(b) limiting production, markets or technical development to the prejudice of consumers;

(c) applying dissimilar conditions to equivalent transactions with other trading parties, thereby placing them at a competitive disadvantage;

(d) making the conclusion of contracts subject to acceptance by the other parties of supplementary obligations which, by their nature or according to commercial usage, have no connection with the subject of such contracts.

OVERVIEW

A. GENERAL	5.01	
1. Direct effect	5.01	
2. *Ratione personae*	5.02	
3. *Ratione materiae*	5.02	
4. *Ratione loci* (Territorial jurisdiction)	5.04	
B. DOMINANCE	5.07	
1. General	5.07	
2. Market definition	5.12	
3. Market power	5.27	
4. Collective dominance	5.49	
C. SUBSTANTIAL PART OF THE INTERNAL MARKET	5.57	
D. ABUSE	5.60	

1. The objective concept of abuse	5.60
2. Capability of restricting competition	5.66
3. Categories of abuses	5.70
4. Abuse on secondary markets	5.134
5. Abuse of collective dominance	5.136
6. Justification	5.137
E. EFFECT ON TRADE BETWEEN MEMBER STATES	5.150
F. RELATION TO ARTICLES 101 AND 106 TFEU	5.152
1. Article 101 TFEU	5.152
2. Article 106 TFEU	5.157

---

* This chapter was written by Alvaro Pliego Selie.

A. GENERAL

See also the Communication from the Commission regarding Guidance on the Commission's enforcement priorities in applying Article [102 TFEU] to abusive exclusionary conduct by dominant undertakings (OJ 2009 C 45/2).

1. Direct effect

5.01   [T]he prohibitions of Articles [101](1) and [102 TFEU] tend by their very nature to produce direct effects in relations between individuals, these articles create direct rights in respect of the individuals concerned which the national courts must safeguard.
CoJ 30 January 1974 (SABAM, C-127/73) [1974] ECR 51, para. 16.

5.02   [E]ven within the framework of Article [106] the provision of Article [102] has direct effect.
CoJ 10 December 1991 (Porto di Genova, C-179/90) [1991] ECR I-5889, para. 23.

2. *Ratione personae*

(a)   Undertaking
See the case extracts in Section A.6(b) of Chapter 4 on Art. 101 TFEU.

(b)   Economic activity
See the case extracts in Section A.6(b)(i) of Chapter 4 on Art. 101 TFEU.

3. *Ratione materiae*

(a)   Agriculture
See Art. 175 Regulation No 1234/2007 for the agricultural markets within the meaning of Art. 1 of that Regulation. See Regulation No 1184/2006 for other products than referred to in Annex I to the TFEU.

(b)   Transport
See Regulations No 1419/2006, 246/2009 and 906/2009 and the Guidelines on the application of Article [101 TFEU] to maritime transport services.

5.03   [A]rticle [102 TFEU] is fully applicable to the whole of the air transport sector.
CoJ 11 April 1989 (Saeed Flugreisen, 66/86) [1989] ECR 803, para. 33.

4. *Ratione loci* (Territorial jurisdiction)

Community law is applicable to such an acquisition, which influences market condi- **5.04**
tions within the Community. The circumstance that Continental does not have its
registered office within the territory of one of the Member States is not sufficient to
exclude it from the application of Community law.
CoJ 21 February 1973 (Continental Can, 6/72) [1973] ECR 215, para. 16.

When an undertaking in a dominant position with the common market abuses its **5.05**
position in such a way that a competitor in the common market is likely to be
eliminated, it does not matter whether the conduct relates to the latter's exports or its
trade within the common market, once it has been established that this elimination will
have repercussions on the competitive structure within the common market.
*CoJ 6 March 1974 (Commercial Solvents, Joined Cases 6 and 7/73) [1974]
ECR 223, para. 33.*

[I]f the occupier of a dominant position, established in the common market, aims at **5.06**
eliminating a competitor who is also established in the common market, it is immaterial
whether this behaviour relates to trade between Member States once it has been shown
that such elimination will have repercussions on the patterns of competition in the
common market.
*CoJ 14 February 1978 (United Brands v. Commission, 27/76) [1978] ECR 207,
para. 201.*

B. DOMINANCE

1. General

The dominant position referred to in [Article 102 TFEU] relates to a position of **5.07**
economic strength enjoyed by an undertaking which enables it to prevent effective
competition being maintained on the relevant market by giving it the power to behave
to an appreciable extent independently of its competitors, customers and ultimately of
its consumers.

In general a dominant position derives from a combination of several factors which,
taken separately, are not necessarily determinative. […]

An undertaking's economic strength is not measured by its profitability; a reduced
profit margin or even losses for a time are not incompatible with a dominant position,
just as large profits may be compatible with a situation where there is effective
competition.

The fact that UBC's profitability is for a time moderate or non-existent must be
considered in the light of the whole of its operations.

The finding that, whatever losses UBC may make, the customers continue to buy more goods from UBC which is the dearest vendor, is more significant and this fact is a particular feature of the dominant position and its verification is determinative in this case.

CoJ 14 February 1978 (United Brands v. Commission, 27/76) [1978] ECR 207, paras 65, 66 and 126–128.

5.08   [A dominant position] does not preclude some competition, which it does where there is a monopoly or a quasi-monopoly, but enables the undertaking which profits by it, if not to determine, at least to have an appreciable influence on the conditions under which that competition will develop, and in any case to act largely in disregard of it so long as such conduct does not operate to its detriment. The existence of a dominant position may derive from several factors which, taken separately, are not necessarily determinative but among these factors a highly important one is the existence of very large market shares. [...]

On the other hand the relationship between the market shares of the undertaking concerned and of its competitors, especially those of the next largest, the technological lead of an undertaking over its competitors, the existence of a highly developed sales network and the absence of potential competition are relevant factors [for a dominant position], the first because it enables the competitive strength of the undertaking in question to be assessed, the second and third because they represent in themselves technical and commercial advantages and the fourth because it is the consequence of the existence of obstacles preventing new competitors from having access to the market.

CoJ 13 February 1979 (Hoffmann-La Roche, 85/76) [1979] ECR 461, paras 39 and 48.

5.09   [T]he Commission did not base its analysis solely on Cewal's market share. [O]ther factors were taken into account, namely the significant difference between Cewal's market share and that of its principal competitor, the benefits derived from the contract with Ogefrem giving Cewal exclusivity, the large size of its network, its capacities and the frequency of its services and, lastly, the experience acquired by Cewal over several decades on the market concerned. In light of those factors, the Court considers that the Commission was entitled to conclude that there was a dominant position.

General Court 8 October 1996 (Cewal, Joined Cases T-24–26/93 and T-28/93) [1996] ECR II-1201, paras 78 and 79.

5.10   Moreover, in the course of any decision applying Article [102 TFEU], the Commission must define the relevant market again and make a fresh analysis of the conditions of competition which will not necessarily be based on the same considerations as those underlying the previous finding of a dominant position.

General Court 22 March 2000 (Coca-Cola v. Commission, Joined Cases T-125/97 and T-127/97) [2000] ECR II-1733, para. 82.

5.11   [...] Article [102 TFEU] applies both to undertakings whose possible dominant position is established, as in this case, in relation to their suppliers and to those which are capable of being in the same position in relation to their customers.

General Court 17 December 2003 (British Airways v. Commission, T-219/99)
[2003] ECR II-5917, para. 101.

2. Market definition

See also the case extracts on Art. 2 Regulation No 139/2004 in Chapter 14 and the
Commission notice on the definition of the relevant market for the purposes of
Community competition law (OJ 1997 C 372/5).

In examining whether an undertaking holds a dominant position within the meaning of **5.12**
the first paragraph of Article [102 TFEU], it is of fundamental importance to define the
market in question and to define the substantial part of the common market in which
the undertaking may be able to engage in abuses which hinder effective competition
[…].

CoJ 11 December 2008 (Kanal 5 Ltd and TV 4 AB v. STIM, C-52/07) [2008]
ECR I-9275, para 19.

(a) Relevant product market

(i) General

For the appraisal of SLW's dominant position and the consequences of the disputed **5.13**
merger, the definition of the relevant market is of essential significance, for the
possibilities of competition can only be judged in relation to those characteristics of the
products in question by virtue of which those products are particularly apt to satisfy an
inelastic need and are only to a limited extent interchangeable with other products.

[…] In order to be regarded as constituting a distinct market, the products in
question must be individualized, not only by the mere fact that they are used for packing
certain products, but by particular characteristics of production which make them
specifically suitable for this purpose. Consequently, a dominant position on the market
for light metal containers for meat and fish cannot be decisive, as long as it has not been
proved that competitors from other sectors of the market for light metal containers are
not in a position to enter this market, by a simple adaptation, with sufficient strength to
create a serious counterweight.

CoJ 21 February 1973 (Continental Can, 6/72) [1973] ECR 215, paras 32 and 33.

In the decision it is primarily the organic peroxides market (including the benzoyl **5.14**
peroxide used in the plastics industry) that is held to be the relevant market, [in the
alternative] the flour additives market […] in the United Kingdom and Ireland […].
[…]

AKZO disputes this definition in view of the subject-matter of the decision, which
relates solely to its allegedly unlawful behaviour in the flour additives sector. […]

Secondly, it should be pointed out that before 1979 ECS operated solely in the flour
additives sector. It was only in the course of that year that it decided to extend its

activities to the plastics sector. Consequently, when the dispute arose, ECS had only an extremely small market share in that sector.

Moreover, it is not disputed that the plastics sector was more important to AKZO than the flour additives sector, since it had a much higher turnover in that sector.

AKZO therefore applied price reductions in a sector (that of flour additives) which was vital to ECS but only of limited importance to itself.

Furthermore, AKZO was able to set off any losses that it incurred in the flour additives sector against profits from its activity in the plastics sector, a possibility not available to ECS.

Finally, according to statements made by a manager of AKZO [...], AKZO did not adopt its behaviour in order to strengthen its position in the flour additives sector, but to preserve its position in the plastics sector by preventing ECS from extending its activities to that sector.

The Commission was in those circumstances justified in regarding the organic peroxides market as the relevant market, even though the abusive behaviour alleged was intended to damage ECS's main business activity in a different market.

CoJ 3 July 1991 (AKZO Chemie v. Commission, C-62/86) [1991] ECR I-3359, paras 35, 37 and 40–45.

(ii)   Input market

(1)   Raw materials

5.15   [I]t is in fact possible to distinguish the market in raw material necessary for the manufacture of a product from the market on which the product is sold. An abuse of a dominant position on the market in raw materials may thus have effects restricting competition in the market on which the derivatives of the raw material are sold and these effects must be taken into account in considering the effects of an infringement, even if the market for the derivative does not constitute a self-contained market.

CoJ 6 March 1974 (Commercial Solvents, Joined Cases 6 and 7/73) [1974] ECR 223, para. 22.

(2)   Approval services

5.16   The applicant maintains [that] the activity involved in applications for vehicle approval and the issue of certificates of conformity could not constitute a dominant position within the meaning of Article [102].

Far from constituting a market in itself, this activity is merely ancillary to the market in motor cars, the open and highly competitive nature of which is undesirable, [and] in which the applicant does not hold a dominant position.

The approval procedure in the context of which the impositions in question were made is, by nature, a duty governed by public law which is so delegated by the Belgian state that, for each make of motor car the performance of this duty is reserved exclusively to the manufacturer or its sole authorized agent, appointed by the public authority.

However, although it entrusted this task of inspection to private undertakings the state took no measures to fix or limit the charge imposed for the service rendered.

This legal monopoly, combined with the freedom of the manufacturer or sole authorized agent to fix the price for its service, leads to the creation of a dominant position within the meaning of Article [102] as, for any given make, the approval procedure can only be carried out in Belgium by the manufacturer or officially appointed authorized agent under conditions fixed unilaterally by that party.

CoJ 13 November 1975 (General Motors Continental, 26/75) [1975] ECR 1367, paras 4–9.

See also CoJ 11 November 1986 (British Leyland, 226/84) [1986] ECR 3263, paras 3–10; General Court 21 October 1997 (Deutsche Bahn, T-229/94) [1997] ECR II-1689), para. 57.

(3) Spare parts

[A]ccount must be taken of the fact that the conduct alleged against Hugin consists in **5.17** the refusal to supply spare parts to Liptons and, generally, to any independent undertaking outside its distribution network. The question is, therefore, whether the supply of spare parts constitutes a specific market or whether it forms part of a wider market. To answer that question it is necessary to determine the category of clients who require such parts. [...]

Consequently the market thus constituted by Hugin spare parts required by independent undertakings must be regarded as the relevant market [...]. It is in fact the market on which the alleged abuse was committed.

CoJ 31 May 1979 (Hugin v. Commission, 22/78) [1979] ECR 1869, paras 5 and 8.

(iii) Differentiated market

(1) Products belonging to different markets

If a product could be used for different purposes and if these different uses are in **5.18** accordance with economic needs, which are themselves also different, there are good grounds for accepting that this product may, according to the circumstances, belong to separate markets which may present specific features which differ from the standpoint both of the structure and of the conditions of competition. However this finding does not justify the conclusion that such a product together with all the other products which can replace it as far as concerns the various uses to which it may be put and with which it may compete, forms one single market.

The concept of the relevant market in fact implies that there can be effective competition between the products which form part of it and this presupposes that there is a sufficient degree of interchangeability between all the products forming part of the same market in so far as a specific use of such products is concerned.

CoJ 13 February 1979 (Hoffmann-La Roche, 85/76) [1979] ECR 461, para. 28.

(2) Differentiated products

5.19   [F]or the purposes of investigating the possibly dominant position of an undertaking on a given market, the possibilities of competition must be judged in the context of the market comprising the totality of the products which, with respect to their characteristics, are particularly suitable for satisfying constant needs and are only to a limited extent interchangeable with other products. [...]

On the other hand, in deciding whether a dominant position exists, neither the absence of elasticity of supply between different types and dimensions of tyres for heavy vehicles, which is due to differences in the conditions of production, nor the absence of interchangeability and elasticity of demand between those types and dimensions of tyre from the point of view of the specific needs of the user allow a number of smaller markets, reflecting those types and dimensions, to be distinguished, as Michelin NV suggests. Those differences between different types and dimensions of tyre are not vitally important for dealers, who must meet demand from customers for the whole range of heavy-vehicle tyres. Furthermore, in the absence of any specialization on the part of the undertakings concerned, such differences in the type and dimensions of a product are not a crucial factor in the assessment of an undertaking's market position because in view of their similarity and the manner in which they complement one another at the technical level, the conditions of competition on the market are the same for all the types and dimensions of the product.

CoJ 9 November 1983 (Michelin v. Commission, C-322/81) [1983] ECR 3461, paras 37 and 44.

5.20   [The applicant considers] that the relevant products are not solely the weekly programme listings and television magazines in which those listings are published. On the contrary, they include 'all advance programme information supplied to the public on a weekly or daily basis, since there exists a high degree of substitutability between the various forms of programme information'. In that respect, the applicant relies on a market survey indicating that only 19 per cent of television viewers use the RTE Guide – most viewers mainly consult the daily press to find out about television programmes. This shows that the information on daily schedules is, as far as viewers are concerned, substitutable for information on the weekly television schedules. [...]

As regards the definition of the relevant product market [...] the [General Court] finds that [...] the products thus defined represent specific markets which cannot be identified with the market for information on television programmes in general.

[...] That limited substitutability of weekly programme information is evidenced in particular by the success enjoyed, at the material time, by the specialized television magazines which were all that was available on the market in weekly guides in the United Kingdom and Ireland and, in the rest of the Community, by the comprehensive television guides available on the market in the other Member States. That clearly demonstrates the existence of a specific, constant and regular potential demand on the part of viewers, in this case in Ireland and Northern Ireland, for television magazines containing comprehensive television programme listings for the week ahead, irrespective of any other sources of programme information available on the market.

General Court 10 July 1991 (RTE v. Commission, T-69/89) [1991] ECR II-485, paras 30, 61 and 62.

See also the judgments on the same date in Case T-70/89 (BBC v. Commission) [1991] ECR II-535 and Case T-76/89 (ITP v. Commission) [1991] ECR II-575.

(iv)   SSNIP-test

[Influence of regulatory framework on health care pricing] In accordance with the **5.21** theoretical framework [i.e. paragraphs 15–19 of the Notice on market definition] with which the Commission aims to assess the available items of evidence in order to assess whether an existing product exercises a significant competitive constraint over a new product, it is necessary to consider whether, account being taken at the same time of the gradual growth in sales of the new product, a small increase in the price of the new product would lead to a shift in demand towards the existing product in such a way that that price increase would not be profitable, in view of the income which would have been generated had that increase not taken place. It should be pointed out that the gradual nature of the growth in sales of the new product would not necessarily disappear if that price increase were profitable and, consequently, if it were concluded that the existing product does not exercise a significant competitive constraint over the new product.

Consequently, the [General Court] finds that the Commission was entitled to take the view that, in principle, the gradual nature of the increase in sales of a new product substituting for an existing product cannot, in itself, suffice to conclude that the existing product exercises a significant competitive constraint over the new one. [...]

[A]lthough the national regulatory systems to a certain extent prevented normal competitive interaction on prices between pharmaceutical products, the fact remains that they were capable of significantly influencing the income of the pharmaceutical undertakings by setting prices or reimbursement levels by reference to the prices of generic products and by promoting or imposing the substitution of original PPIs by their generic versions at the dispensing stage in pharmacies.

The fact that, in the present case, the regulatory systems did not influence the prices or the amount of sales of PPIs by reference to the lower prices of H2 blockers leads to the conclusion that the reimbursement levels granted to PPIs to a large extent prevented the lower prices of H2 blockers from exercising a competitive constraint over them. It should be recalled in this respect that the purpose of defining the relevant market is to determine the competitive constraints on the product on the basis of which the market is defined. The fact that the absence or insignificance of those competitive constraints is due to the regulatory framework which determines the conditions under, and the extent to, which competitive interactions between products take place does not affect the relevance, in the context of market definition, of the finding that those competitive constraints are non-existent or insignificant.

Where it is established that a group of products is not subject to a significant extent to competitive constraints from other products, so that that group may be considered to form a relevant product market, the type or nature of the factors that shield that group of products from any significant competitive constraint is of only limited relevance, since the finding of an absence of such competitive constraints leads to the conclusion that an undertaking in a dominant position on the market thus defined would be able to affect the interests of consumers on that market by preventing, through abusive behaviour, the maintenance of effective competition.

Consequently, the Commission did not commit a manifest error of assessment in finding [...] that the initial setting and maintenance of the price of a new category of products at a level significantly higher than that of other products used within the same therapeutic area reflects a low degree of competitive pressure from those other products. [...]

[T]he Commission cannot maintain [...] that, in principle, the ability of an undertaking to maintain its prices above the reimbursement level, where demand tends to be more elastic, constitutes in itself evidence of an absence of any significant competitive constraint, without examining the extent to which the price of other potentially substitutable products is reimbursed by the national health insurance system. The Commission has failed to establish, in the present case, that the non-reimbursed portion of the price borne by patients when purchasing H2 blockers was lower than that of PPIs. Nevertheless [...] that error does not affect the soundness of the conclusions of the Commission, which took the view that, where prices exceeded reimbursement levels, the fact that absolute prices of PPIs were higher than those of H2 blockers showed that H2 blockers did not exercise any significant competitive con-straint over PPIs.

General Court 1 July 2010 (AstraZeneca v. Commission, T-321/05) [2010] ECR II-02805, paras 89–90, 173–176 and 182.

Confirmed in CoJ 6 December 2012 (AstraZeneca v. Commission, C-457/10 P), ECLI:EU:C:2012:770.

(b)   Relevant geographic market

(i)   General

5.22   Article [102 TFEU] clearly refers in each case to the position occupied by the undertaking concerned on the common market at the time when the latter acted in a way which is alleged to amount to an abuse.

CoJ 16 December 1975 (Suiker Unie, Joined Cases 40–48, 50, 54–56, 111, 113 and 114/73) [1975] ECR 1663, para. 450.

5.23   The opportunities for competition under Article [102 TFEU] must be considered having regard to the particular features of the product in question and with reference to a clearly defined geographic area in which it is marketed and where the conditions of competition are sufficiently homogeneous for the effect of the economic power of the undertaking concerned to be able to be evaluated.

CoJ 14 February 1978 (United Brands v. Commission, 27/76) [1978] ECR 207, para. 11.

[C]ontractual practices, even if abusive ones, on the part of an undertaking supplying **5.24**
telephone installations which has a large share of a regional market in a Member State
do not fall within the prohibition in Article [102 TFEU] where that undertaking does
not occupy a dominant position on the relevant market, in this case the domestic market
in telephone installations.

CoJ 5 October 1988 (Alsatel, 247/86) [1988] ECR 5987, para. 23.

(ii) Transport costs

The documents before the [General Court] show that there are large price differences **5.25**
for Hilti products between the Member States and that transport costs for nails are low.
Those two factors make parallel trading highly likely between the national markets of
the Community. It must therefore be concluded that the Commission was right in
taking the view that the relevant geographic market in this case is the Community as a
whole.

*General Court 12 December 1991 (Hilti, T-30/89) [1991] ECR II-1439,
para. 81.*

(c) Temporal markets

There is no unavoidable seasonal substitution since the consumer can obtain this fruit **5.26**
all the year round.

Since the banana is a fruit which is always available in sufficient quantities the
question whether it can be replaced by other fruits must be determined over the whole
of the year for the purpose of ascertaining the degree of competition between it and
other fresh fruit.

The studies of the banana market on the court's file show that on the latter market
there is no significant long-term cross-elasticity anymore than − as has been mentioned
− there is any seasonal substitutability in general between the banana and all the
seasonal fruits, as this only exists between the banana and two fruits (peaches and table
grapes) in one of the countries (West Germany) of the relevant geographic market.

As far as concerns the two fruits available throughout the year (oranges and apples)
the first are not interchangeable and in the case of the second there is only a relative
degree of substitutability.

This small degree of substitutability is accounted for by the specific features of the
banana and all the factors which influence consumer choice.

*CoJ 14 February 1978 (United Brands v. Commission, 27/76) [1978] ECR 207,
paras 26−30.*

3. Market power

*See paras 9–18 of the Communication from the Commission regarding Guidance on
the Commission's enforcement priorities in applying Article [102 TFEU] to abusive
exclusionary conduct by dominant undertakings (OJ 2009 C 45/2).*

(a) Market share

5.27 [Insignificant market shares rule out dominance] Whilst the share of the market occupied by an undertaking does not necessarily constitute the sole criterion for the existence of a dominant position it is however proper to conclude that in a market in highly technical products which nevertheless appear to the majority of consumers to be readily interchangeable, shares of the market as insignificant as that held by SABA rule out the existence of a dominant position unless exceptional circumstances obtain.
CoJ 25 October 1977 (Metro I, 26/76) [1977] ECR 1875, para. 17.

5.28 [Market share of 40–45 per cent does not automatically lead to dominance] A trader can only be in a dominant position on the market for a product if he has succeeded in winning a large part of this market.[…]
[I]t can be considered to be an established fact that UBC's share of the relevant market is always more than 40 per cent and nearly 45 per cent.
This percentage does not however permit the conclusion that UBC automatically controls the market.
It must be determined having regard to the strength and number of the competitors. […]
However an undertaking does not have to have eliminated all opportunity for competition in order to be in a dominant position.
CoJ 14 February 1978 (United Brands v. Commission, 27/76) [1978] ECR 207, paras 107–110 and 113.

5.29 [A] dominant position may derive from several factors which, taken separately, are not necessarily determinative but among these factors a highly important one is the existence of very large market shares.
A substantial market share as evidence of the existence of a dominant position is not a constant factor and its importance varies from market to market according to the structure of these markets, especially as far as production, supply and demand are concerned. […]
CoJ 13 February 1979 (Hofmann-La Roche, 85/76) [1979] ECR 461, paras 39 and 40.

5.30 [Market share of over 50 per cent] [V]ery large shares are in themselves, and save in exceptional circumstances, evidence of the existence of a dominant position […]. That is the situation where there is a market share of 50 per cent such as that found to exist in this case.
CoJ 3 July 1991 (AKZO Chemie v. Commission, C-62/86) [1991] ECR I-3359, para. 60.

5.31 [Market share of 32–36 per cent does not constitute conclusive evidence of dominance] According to the national court, at the time when DLG amended its statutes in 1988, it held around 36 per cent of the Danish fertilizer market and 32 per cent of the Danish market in plant protection products. While an undertaking which holds market shares of that size may, depending on the strength and number of its competitors, be considered to be in a dominant position, those market shares cannot on their own constitute conclusive evidence of the existence of a dominant position.

CoJ 15 December 1994 (Göttrup-Klim v. DLG, C-250/92) [1994] ECR I-5641, para. 48

[Declining market share does not rule out dominance] It follows that, throughout the **5.32** period concerned, Cewal's market shares remained high, despite their steady erosion. The [General Court] considers that, whilst retention of market share may show that a dominant position has been retained [...], a decline in market shares which are still very large cannot in itself constitute proof of the absence of a dominant position.

General Court 8 October 1996 (Cewal, Joined Cases T-24–26/93 and T-28/93) [1996] ECR II-1201, para. 77.

[Declining market share does not rule out dominance] The applicant cannot base an **5.33** argument on the fact that its market shares and prices fell during the period in question. When an undertaking actually implements practices with the aim of restricting competition, the fact that the result sought is not achieved is not enough to avoid the application of Article [102 TFEU] [...]. In any event, it is very probable that the fall in the applicant's market shares [...] and in its sales prices [...] would have been greater if the practices criticised in the contested decision had not been applied.

General Court 30 September 2003 (Michelin, T-203/01) [2003] ECR II-4071, para. 245.

(b) Barriers to entry

(i) General

The particular barriers to competitors entering the market are the exceptionally large **5.34** capital investments required for the creation and running of banana plantations, the need to increase sources of supply in order to avoid the effects of fruit diseases and bad weather (hurricanes, floods), the introduction of an essential system of logistics which the distribution of a very perishable product makes necessary, economies of scale from which newcomers to the market cannot derive any immediate benefit and the actual cost of entry made up inter alia of all the general expenses incurred in penetrating the market such as the setting up of an adequate commercial network, the mounting of very large-scale advertising campaigns, all those financial risks, the costs of which are irrecoverable if the attempt fails.

[A]lthough it is true that competitors are able to use the same methods of production and distribution as the applicant, they come up against almost insuperable practical and financial obstacles.

That is another factor peculiar to a dominant position.

CoJ 14 February 1978 (United Brands v. Commission, 27/76) [1978] ECR 207, paras 122–124.

(ii)   State intervention and exclusive rights

See also the case extracts in Chapter 9 on Article 106 TFEU.

5.35   [T]he fact that the absence of competition or its restriction on the relevant market is brought about or encouraged by provisions laid down by law in no way precludes the application of Article [102 TFEU].
CoJ 3 October 1985 (CBEM v. CLT and IPB, 311/84) [1985] ECR 3261, para. 16.

5.36   A Member State creates a situation in which the provision of a service is limited when the undertaking to which it grants an exclusive right extending to executive recruitment activities is manifestly not in a position to satisfy the demand prevailing on the market for activities of that kind and when the effective pursuit of such activities by private companies is rendered impossible by the maintenance in force of a statutory provision under which such activities are prohibited and non-observance of that prohibition renders the contracts concerned void.
CoJ 23 April 1991 (Höfner and Elser v. Macroton, C-41/90) [1990] ECR I-1979, para. 31.

5.37   [I]t appears from the circumstances described by the national court and discussed before the Court of Justice that the undertakings enjoying exclusive rights in accordance with the procedures laid down by the national rules in question are, as a result, induced either to demand payment for services which have not been requested, to charge disproportionate prices, to refuse to have recourse to modern technology, which involves an increase in the cost of the operations and a prolongation of the time required for their performance, or to grant price reductions to certain consumers and at the same time to offset such reductions by an increase in the charges to other consumers.
        In these circumstances it must be held that a Member State creates a situation contrary to Article [102 TFEU] where it adopts rules of such a kind as those at issue before the national court, which are capable of affecting trade between Member States [...].
CoJ 10 December 1991 (Porto di Genova, C-179/90) [1991] ECR I-5889, paras 19 and 20.

5.38   [I]t should be recalled that although merely creating a dominant position by granting exclusive rights within the meaning of Article [106(1) TFEU] is not in itself incompatible with Article [102], a Member State is in breach of the prohibitions contained in those two provisions if the undertaking in question, merely by exercising the exclusive rights granted to it, is led to abuse its dominant position or when such rights are liable to create a situation in which that undertaking is led to commit such abuses [...].
CoJ 12 February 1998 (Criminal Proceedings against Silvano Raso and others, C-163/96) [1998] ECR I-533, para. 27.

[T]he [General Court] and the Commission considered that the abuse consisted in the fact that Cewal had repeatedly insisted that the Zairean authorities strictly observe its exclusive right. **5.39**

It should be remembered that the existence of a dominant position means that, irrespective of the reasons which have led to such a position, the dominant undertaking or undertakings have a special responsibility not to allow their conduct to impair genuine undistorted competition on the common market [...].

It is established, in the present case, that Cewal sought to rely on the contractual exclusivity provided for in the Ogefrem Agreement in order to remove its only competitor from the market. Such conduct was in no way required by that agreement, since, under the second paragraph of Article 1 thereof, express provision is made for possible derogations, so that the requirements of Article [102 TFEU] could be met.

CoJ 16 March 2000 (Compagnie Maritime Belge Transports and others v. Commission C-395/96 and C-396/96) [2000] ECR I-1365, paras 84–86.

[A]n undertaking can be put in [a dominant position] when it is granted special or exclusive rights enabling it to determine whether and, as the case may be, in what conditions, other undertakings may have access to the relevant market and engage in their activities on that market. **5.40**

CoJ 1 July 2008 (MOTOE v. Elliniko Dimosio, C-49/07) [2008] ECR I-4863, para. 38.

(iii)   Infrastructure

If that examination leads the national court to conclude that a separate market in home-delivery schemes does exist, and that there is an insufficient degree of inter-changeability between Mediaprint's nationwide scheme and other, regional, schemes, it must hold that Mediaprint, which according to the information in the order for reference operates the only nationwide home-delivery service in Austria, is de facto in a monopoly situation in the market thus defined, and thus holds a dominant position in it. **5.41**

CoJ 26 November 1998 (Oscar Bronner v. Mediaprint, C-7/97) [1998] ECR I-7791, para. 35.

See also the Commission Notice on the application of the competition rules to access agreements in the telecommunications sector – framework, relevant markets and principles (OJ 1998 C 265/2).

(iv)   Fixed costs

[G]ross margins essentially reflect the difference between sales and the variable cost of producing the relevant output, before fixed costs. A company with a large proportion of fixed costs thus needs to generate substantial gross margins to cover its fixed costs and remain profitable. **5.42**

The barriers to entry discussed [i.e. the nature and the size of sunk investment required combined with capacity constraints, and significant product differentiation, in particular through brands] result from sunk investment, which is associated with fixed costs for activities such as R&D, marketing and plant investment. In general, a high share of fixed costs is indicative of significant barriers to entry and expansion. These barriers to entry give rise to market power, which in turn enables a firm to set prices above marginal costs. In the presence of fixed costs, pricing above marginal cost is necessary for a firm to generate profits and thus remain viable. As long as barriers to entry remain moderate, new entrants could be expected to compete away any supra-competitive profits, leading to more or less comparable levels of net profits across companies (after accounting for risk). The higher the proportion of fixed costs in a given industry, the more concentrated it is likely to be, because higher mark-ups are necessary for firms to remain profitable.

Commission 13 May 2009 (Intel, COMP/C-3 /37.990), paras 876 and 877.

(v) Standardization

5.43   There are substantial barriers to entry on the market, primarily due to the fact that the industry is locked in to JEDEC standards. Firstly, the initial costs and efforts relating to standards development are substantial. Furthermore, there are significant costs associated with switching from a standard once it has been adopted.

Commission 9 December 2009 (Rambus, COMP/38.636), para. 22.

(c) Vertical integration

5.44   [...] After examination, the Commission concluded, firstly, that Filtrona was not dependent on Tabacalera for its sales of cigarette filters, since Filtrona exports its filters to other markets and can change its production from ordinary filters to special filters and, secondly, that Tabacalera's decision to produce all the ordinary filters it needed was not an abuse of a dominant position, since a company's production of its own requirements is not in itself an abnormal act of competition. Production by cigarette manufacturers of their own filters is common practice in the industry. In addition, Tabacalera justified its vertical integration on economic grounds: production of all its filter requirements allows it to achieve economies of scale and generally to reduce its production costs. There were no special circumstances suggesting that Tabacalera's decision was part of an abusive behaviour or strategy.

Filtrona v. Tabacalera, Nineteenth Report on Competition Policy (1989), para. 61.

(d) Unavoidable trading partner

5.45   [...] An undertaking which has a very large market share and holds it for some time, by means of the volume of production and the scale of the supply which it stands for – without those having much smaller market shares being able to meet rapidly the demand from those who would like to break away from the undertaking which has the largest market share – is by virtue of that share in a position of strength which makes it an unavoidable trading partner and which, already because of this secures for it, at the very least during relatively long periods, that freedom of action which is the special feature of a dominant position.

CoJ 13 February 1979 (Hoffmann–La Roche, 85/76) [1979] ECR 461, para. 41.

The argument that the merchants were entitled to discontinue their contractual **5.46** relations with BG at any time has no force since the right to terminate a contract in no way prevents its actual application until such time as the right to terminate it has been exercised. It should be observed that an undertaking in a dominant position is powerful enough to require its customers not only to enter into such contracts but also to maintain them, with the result that the legal possibility of termination is in fact rendered illusory.

General Court 1 April 1993 (BPB Industries and British Gypsum, T-65/89) [1993] ECR II-389, para. 73.

In the present case, ADP, as the owner of the airport facilities, is alone in being able to **5.47** authorise access. [...] ADP indisputably enjoys a legal monopoly [...] to manage the airports concerned and is alone able to grant authorisation to carry out ground handling activities there and to determine the terms on which those activities are carried out.

In those circumstances, the [General Court] could properly conclude [...] that ADP wields economic power which enables it to prevent effective competition from being maintained in the relevant market by giving it the opportunity to act independently.

CoJ 24 October 2002 (Aeroports de Paris, C-82/01) [2002] ECR I-9297, paras 106 and 107.

[...] Intel's brand equity resulting from its investment in product differentiation and its **5.48** installed base have given it 'must stock' status at the OEM level, in other words, it is an unavoidable trading partner for OEMs. All the main OEMs offer predominantly or exclusively Intel-based products. Intel's must-stock status provides it with significant leverage over its OEM customers because a switch to an all- or majority-AMD product line-up would be unrealistic for them.

Commission 13 May 2009 (Intel, COMP/C-3 /37.990), para. 870.

(e)   Countervailing buyer power

See para. 18 of the Communication from the Commission regarding Guidance on the Commission's enforcement priorities in applying Article [102 TFEU] to abusive exclusionary conduct by dominant undertakings (OJ 2009 C 45/2).

4.   Collective dominance

[T]here is no legal or economic reason to suppose that the term 'undertaking' in Article **5.49** [102] has a different meaning from the one given to it in the context of Article [101]. There is nothing, in principle, to prevent two or more independent economic entities from being, on a specific market, united by such economic links that, by virtue of that fact, together they hold a dominant position vis-à-vis the other operators on the same market. This could be the case, for example, where two or more independent undertakings jointly have, through agreements or licences, a technological lead affording them the power to behave to an appreciable extent independently of their competitors, their customers and ultimately of their consumers [...].

General Court 10 March 1992 (SIV and others v. Commission, T-68/89, T-77/89 and T-78/89) [1992] ECR II-1403, para. 358.

5.50   Although the conclusion cannot automatically be drawn that a dominant position is held in a substantial part of the common market by an undertaking which, like IJM, has a non-exclusive concession covering only part of the territory of a Member State, a different assessment must apply where that undertaking belongs to a group of under-takings which collectively occupy a dominant position.

However, in order for such a collective dominant position to exist, the undertakings in the group must be linked in such a way that they adopt the same conduct on the market [...].

It is for the national court to consider whether there exist between the regional electricity distributors in the Netherlands links which are sufficiently strong for there to be a collective dominant position in a substantial part of the common market.

CoJ 27 April 1994 (Municipality of Almelo and others v. NV Energiebedrijf IJsselmij, C-393/92) [1994] ECR I-1477, paras 41–43.

5.51   In the case of an alleged collective dominant position, the Commission is therefore obliged to assess, using a prospective analysis of the reference market, whether the concentration which has been referred to it leads to a situation in which effective competition in the relevant market is significantly impeded by the undertakings involved in the concentration and one or more other undertakings which together, in particular because of correlative factors which exist between them, are able to adopt a common policy on the market and act to a considerable extent independently of their competitors, their customers, and also of consumers.

Such an approach warrants close examination in particular of the circumstances which, in each individual case, are relevant for assessing the effects of the concentration on competition in the reference market.

CoJ 31 March 1998 (Kali & Salz, C-68/94 and C-30/95) [1998] ECR I-1375, paras 221 and 222.

5.52   In [*General Court 10 March 1992 (SIV and others v. Commission, T-68/89, T-77/89 and T-78/89), [1992] ECR II-1403*], the [General Court] referred to links of a structural nature only by way of example and did not lay down that such links must exist in order for a finding of collective dominance to be made. [...]

Nor can it be deduced from the same judgment that the Court has restricted the notion of economic links to the notion of structural links referred to by the applicant.

Furthermore, there is no reason whatsoever in legal or economic terms to exclude from the notion of economic links the relationship of interdependence existing between the parties to a tight oligopoly within which, in a market with the appropriate characteristics, in particular in terms of market concentration, transparency and product homogeneity, those parties are in a position to anticipate one another's behaviour and are therefore strongly encouraged to align their conduct in the market, in particular in such a way as to maximise their joint profits by restricting production with a view to increasing prices. In such a context, each trader is aware that highly competitive action on its part designed to increase its market share (for example a price cut) would provoke identical action by the others, so that it would derive no benefit from its initiative. All the traders would thus be affected by the reduction in price levels.

That conclusion is all the more pertinent with regard to the control of concentrations, whose objective is to prevent anti-competitive market structures from arising or being strengthened. Those structures may result from the existence of economic links in the strict sense argued by the applicant or from market structures of an oligopolistic kind where each undertaking may become aware of common interests and, in particular, cause prices to increase without having to enter into an agreement or resort to a concerted practice.

General Court 25 March 1999 (Gencor v. Commission, T-102/96) [1999] ECR II-753, paras 273 and 275–277.

In order to establish the existence of a collective entity as defined above, it is necessary **5.53** to examine the economic links or factors which give rise to a connection between the undertakings concerned […].

In particular, it must be ascertained whether economic links exist between the undertakings concerned which enable them to act together independently of their competitors, their customers and consumers […].

The mere fact that two or more undertakings are linked by an agreement, a decision of associations of undertakings or a concerted practice within the meaning of Article [101(1) TFEU] does not, of itself, constitute a sufficient basis for such a finding.

On the other hand, an agreement, decision or concerted practice (whether or not covered by an exemption under Article [101(3) TFEU]) may undoubtedly, where it is implemented, result in the undertakings concerned being so linked as to their conduct on a particular market that they present themselves on that market as a collective entity vis-à-vis their competitors, their trading partners and consumers.

The existence of a collective dominant position may therefore flow from the nature and terms of an agreement, from the way in which it is implemented and, consequently, from the links or factors which give rise to a connection between undertakings which result from it. Nevertheless, the existence of an agreement or of other links in law is not indispensable to a finding of a collective dominant position; such a finding may be based on other connecting factors and would depend on an economic assessment and, in particular, on an assessment of the structure of the market in question.

CoJ 16 March 2000 (Compagnie Maritime Belge Transports and others v. Commission, Joined Cases C-395/96 and C-396/96) [2000] ECR I-1365, paras 41–45.

[T]hree conditions are necessary for a finding of collective dominance as defined: **5.54**

[i] first, each member of the dominant oligopoly must have the ability to know how the other members are behaving in order to monitor whether or not they are adopting the common policy. As the Commission specifically acknowledges, it is not enough for each member of the dominant oligopoly to be aware that interdependent market conduct is profitable for all of them but each member must also have a means of knowing whether the other operators are adopting the same strategy and whether they are maintaining it. There must, therefore, be sufficient market transparency for all

members of the dominant oligopoly to be aware, sufficiently precisely and quickly, of the way in which the other members' market conduct is evolving;

[ii] second, the situation of tacit coordination must be sustainable over time, that is to say, there must be an incentive not to depart from the common policy on the market. As the Commission observes, it is only if all the members of the dominant oligopoly maintain the parallel conduct that all can benefit. The notion of retaliation in respect of conduct deviating from the common policy is thus inherent in this condition. In that context, the Commission must not necessarily prove that there is a specific retaliation mechanism involving a degree of severity, but it must none the less establish that deterrents exist, which are such that it is not worth the while of any member of the dominant oligopoly to depart from the common course of conduct to the detriment of the other oligopolists. In this instance, the parties concur that, for a situation of collective dominance to be viable, there must be adequate deterrents to ensure that there is a long-term incentive in not departing from the common policy, which means that each member of the dominant oligopoly must be aware that highly competitive action on its part designed to increase its market share would provoke identical action by the others, so that it would derive no benefit from its initiative [...];

[iii] third, to prove the existence of a collective dominant position to the requisite legal standard, the Commission must also establish that the foreseeable reaction of current and future competitors, as well as of consumers, would not jeopardise the results expected from the common policy.

General Court 6 June 2002 (Air Tours v. Commission, T-342/99) [2002] ECR II-2585, para. 62

5.55   [...] In the present case, the market affected by the rules in question is a market for the provision of services where the buyers are players and clubs and the sellers are agents. In this market FIFA can be regarded as acting on behalf of football clubs since [...] it constitutes an emanation of those clubs as a second-level association of undertakings formed by the clubs.

A decision like the FIFA Players' Agents Regulations may, where it is implemented, result in the undertakings operating on the market in question, namely the clubs, being so linked as to their conduct on a particular market that they present themselves on that market as a collective entity vis-à-vis their competitors, their trading partners and consumers [...].

Because the regulations are binding for national associations that are members of FIFA and the clubs forming them, these bodies appear to be linked in the long term as to their conduct by rules that they accept and that other actors (players and players' agents) cannot break on pain of sanctions that may lead to their exclusion from the market, in particular in the case of players' agents. [S]uch a situation therefore characterises a collective dominant position for clubs on the market for the provision of players' agents' services, since, through the rules to which they adhere, the clubs lay down the conditions under which the services in question are provided.

It seems unrealistic to claim that FIFA, which is recognised as holding supervisory powers over the sport-related activity of football and connected economic activities, such as the activity of players' agents in the present case, does not hold a collective dominant position on the market for players' agents' services on the ground that is not an actor on that market.

*General Court 26 January 2005 (Laurent Piau v. Commission, T-193/02) [2005]
ECR II-00209, paras 112–115.*

Such correlative factors [for collective dominance as referred to in [*CoJ 31 March 1998* **5.56**
(Kali & Salz, C-68/94 and C-30/95) [1998] ECR I-1375, para. 221] include, in
particular, the relationship of interdependence existing between the parties to a tight
oligopoly within which, on a market with the appropriate characteristics, in particular
in terms of market concentration, transparency and product homogeneity, those parties
are in a position to anticipate one another's behaviour and are therefore strongly
encouraged to align their conduct on the market in such a way as to maximise their joint
profits by increasing prices, reducing output, the choice or quality of goods and services,
diminishing innovation or otherwise influencing parameters of competition. In such a
context, each operator is aware that highly competitive action on its part would provoke
a reaction on the part of the others, so that it would derive no benefit from its initiative.
[...]

Such tacit coordination is more likely to emerge if competitors can easily arrive at a
common perception as to how the coordination should work, and, in particular, of the
parameters that lend themselves to being a focal point of the proposed coordination.
Unless they can form a shared tacit understanding of the terms of the coordination,
competitors might resort to practices that are prohibited by Article [101 TFEU] in
order to be able to adopt a common policy on the market. Moreover, having regard to
the temptation which may exist for each participant in a tacit coordination to depart
from it in order to increase its short-term profit, it is necessary to determine whether
such coordination is sustainable. In that regard, the coordinating undertakings must be
able to monitor to a sufficient degree whether the terms of the coordination are being
adhered to. There must therefore be sufficient market transparency for each undertaking concerned to be aware, sufficiently precisely and quickly, of the way in which the
market conduct of each of the other participants in the coordination is evolving.
Furthermore, discipline requires that there be some form of credible deterrent mechanism that can come into play if deviation is detected. In addition, the reactions of
outsiders, such as current or future competitors, and also the reactions of customers,
should not be such as to jeopardise the results expected from the coordination.

The conditions laid down by the [*General Court 6 June 2002 (Air Tours v. Commission,
T-342/99) [2002] ECR II-2585, para. 62*] are not incompatible with the criteria set out
in the preceding paragraph of this judgment.

In applying those criteria, it is necessary to avoid a mechanical approach involving
the separate verification of each of those criteria taken in isolation, while taking no
account of the overall economic mechanism of a hypothetical tacit coordination.

In that regard, the assessment of, for example, the transparency of a particular market
should not be undertaken in an isolated and abstract manner, but should be carried out
using the mechanism of a hypothetical tacit coordination as a basis. It is only if such a
hypothesis is taken into account that it is possible to ascertain whether any elements of
transparency that may exist on a market are, in fact, capable of facilitating the reaching
of a common understanding on the terms of coordination and/or of allowing the
competitors concerned to monitor sufficiently whether the terms of such a common
policy are being adhered to. In that last respect, it is necessary, in order to analyse the
sustainability of a purported tacit coordination, to take into account the monitoring

mechanisms that may be available to the participants in the alleged tacit coordination in order to ascertain whether, as a result of those mechanisms, they are in a position to be aware, sufficiently precisely and quickly, of the way in which the market conduct of each of the other participants in that coordination is evolving.

CoJ 10 July 2008 (Impala, C-413/06) [2008] ECR I-4951, paras 121 and 123–126.

See also the case extracts in Chapter 14 on Regulation No 139/2004.

C. SUBSTANTIAL PART OF THE INTERNAL MARKET

5.57   For the purpose of determining whether a specific territory is large enough to amount to 'a substantial part of the common market' within the meaning of Article [102 TFEU] the pattern and volume of the production and consumption of the said product as well as the habits and economic opportunities of vendors and purchasers must be considered.

So far as sugar in particular is concerned it is advisable to take into consideration in addition to the high freight rates in relation to the price of the product and the habits of the processing industries and consumers the fact that Community rules have consolidated most of the special features of the former national markets.

CoJ 16 December 1975 (Suiker Unie, Joined Cases 40–48, 50, 54–56, 111, 113 and 114/73) [1975] ECR 1663, paras 371 and 372.

5.58   Regard being had in particular to the volume of traffic in that port and its importance in relation to maritime import and export operations as a whole in the Member State concerned, that market may be regarded as constituting a substantial part of the common market.

CoJ 10 December 1991 (Porto di Genova, C-179/90) [1991] ECR I-5889, para. 15.

5.59   The market for airport management services taken into account in this case concerns the international airports of Orly and CDG. In terms of domestic and international traffic, they are the largest French airports. [...]

Passengers and goods leaving or arriving in the Paris region, which is one of the largest economic areas in the Community, use air transport services to and from Orly and CDG which serve all the main domestic and Community airports. In addition, Orly and CDG act as efficient hubs for the transfer of many passengers wishing to go from one French region to a region in another Member State or vice versa. Lastly, the major international airports outside the Community are served by air transport services from the two Paris airports.

Commission 11 June 1998 (Alpha Flight Services v. Aéroports de Paris, IV/35.613), OJ 1998 L 230/10, paras 77 and 79.

D. ABUSE

1. The objective concept of abuse

[No fault requirement] If it can, irrespective of any fault, be regarded as an abuse if an **5.60** undertaking holds a position so dominant that the objectives of the Treaty are circumvented by an alteration to the supply structure which seriously endangers the consumer's freedom of action in the market, such a case necessarily exists if practically all competition is eliminated. Such a narrow precondition as the elimination of all competition need not exist in all cases. But the Commission, basing its decision on such elimination of competition, had to state legally sufficient reasons or, at least, had to prove that competition was so essentially affected that the remaining competitors could no longer provide a sufficient counterweight.
CoJ 21 February 1973 (Continental Can, 6/72) [1973] ECR 215, para. 29.

[Purpose of certain behaviour may however add to abusive character] Although it is **5.61** true […] that the fact that an undertaking is in a dominant position cannot disentitle it from protecting its own commercial interests if they are attacked, and that such an undertaking must be conceded the right to take such reasonable steps as it deems appropriate to protect its said interests, such behaviour cannot be countenanced if its actual purpose is to strengthen this dominant position and abuse it.
CoJ 14 February 1978 (United Brands v. Commission, 27/76) [1978] ECR 207, para. 189.

[Abuse is objective concept] […] The concept of abuse is an objective concept relating **5.62** to the behaviour of an undertaking in a dominant position which is such as to influence the structure of a market where, as a result of the very presence of the undertaking in question, the degree of competition is weakened and which, through recourse to methods different from those which condition normal competition in products or services on the basis of the transactions of commercial operators, has the effect of hindering the maintenance of the degree of competition still existing in the market or the growth of that competition.
CoJ 13 February 1979 (Hoffmann–La Roche, 85/76) [1979] ECR 461, para. 91.

[I]n prohibiting any abuse of a dominant position on the market in so far as it may affect **5.63** trade between Member States Article [102] covers practices which are likely to affect the structure of a market where, as a direct result of the presence of the undertaking in question, competition has already been weakened and which, through recourse to methods different from those governing normal competition in products or services based on traders' performance, have the effect of hindering the maintenance or development of the level of competition still existing on the market.
CoJ 9 November 1983 (Michelin v. Commission, C-322/81) [1983] ECR 3461, para. 70.

5.64   [Knowledge of abusive nature of conduct is not a prerequisite for applying Art. 102 TFEU] The fact that the applicant knew only from 1999 that it was being accused of abuse of its dominant position is irrelevant to the fact that its conduct constituted an infringement from 1 January 1998. An 'abuse' within the meaning of Article [102 TFEU] is an objective concept [...]. The dominant undertaking's own knowledge of the abusive nature of its conduct is not, therefore, a prerequisite for the application of Article [102 TFEU].

General Court 10 April 2008 (Deutsche Telekom v. Commission, T-271/03) [2008] ECR II-477, para. 327.

Confirmed in CoJ 14 October 2010 (Deutsche Telekom v. Commission, C-280/08) [2010] ECR I-09555.

5.65   [Deliberate nature of conduct is not required for applying Art. 102 TFEU] It follows from the objective nature of the concept of abuse [that] proof of the deliberate nature of the conduct and of the bad faith of the undertaking in a dominant position is not required for the purposes of identifying an abuse of a dominant position.

General Court 1 July 2010 (AstraZeneca v. Commission, T-321/05) [2010] ECR II-02805, para. 356.

Confirmed in CoJ 6 December 2012 (AstraZeneca v. Commission, C-457/10 P), ECLI:EU:C:2012:770.

2. Capability of restricting competition

5.66   [W]hile it is true that neither that provision [Article 102(d) TFEU] nor, more generally, Article [102 TFEU] as a whole contains any reference to the anti-competitive effect of bundling, the fact remains that, in principle, conduct will be regarded as abusive only if it is capable of restricting competition.

General Court 17 September 2007 (Microsoft v. Commission, T-201/04) [2007] ECR II-3601, para. 867.

5.67   [I]n order to determine whether the undertaking in a dominant position has abused such a position by its pricing practices, it is necessary to consider all the circumstances and to investigate whether the practice tends to remove or restrict the buyer's freedom to choose his sources of supply, to bar competitors from access to the market, to apply dissimilar conditions to equivalent transactions with other trading parties, thereby placing them at a competitive disadvantage, or to strengthen the dominant position by distorting competition [...].

   [...] Article [102 TFEU] thus refers not only to practices which may cause damage to consumers directly, but also to those which are detrimental to them through their impact on competition [...].

   It follows from this that Article [102 TFEU] prohibits a dominant undertaking from, inter alia, adopting pricing practices which have an exclusionary effect on its equally efficient actual or potential competitors, that is to say practices which are capable of making market entry very difficult or impossible for such competitors, and of making it more difficult or impossible for its co-contractors to choose between various sources of supply or commercial partners, thereby strengthening its dominant position by using methods other than those which come within the scope of competition on the merits. From that point of view, therefore, not all competition by means of price can be regarded as legitimate [...].

CoJ 14 October 2010 (Deutsche Telekom v. Commission, C-280/08) [2010] I-09555, paras 175–177.

[Not] every exclusionary effect is necessarily detrimental to competition [...]. Com- **5.68** petition on the merits may, by definition, lead to the departure from the market or the marginalisation of competitors that are less efficient and so less attractive to consumers from the point of view of, among other things, price, choice, quality or innovation.

CoJ 27 March 2012 (Post Danmark v Konkurrencerådet, C-209/10), ECLI: EU:C:2012:172, para. 22.

[Contestable demand] [T]he fact that a rebate scheme, such as that at issue in the main **5.69** proceedings, covers the majority of customers on the market may constitute a useful indication as to the extent of that practice and its impact on the market, which may bear out the likelihood of an anticompetitive exclusionary effect. [...]

[T]he assessment of whether a rebate scheme is capable of restricting competition must be carried out in the light of all relevant circumstances, including the rules and criteria governing the grant of the rebates, the number of customers concerned and the characteristics of the market on which the dominant undertaking operates.

CoJ 6 October 2015 (Post Danmark A/S v. Konkurrencerådet, C-23/14), ECLI: EU:C:2015:651, paras 46 and 68.

3. Categories of abuses

(a) General

[T]he list of abusive practices set out in the second paragraph of Article [102 TFEU] is **5.70** not exhaustive.

CoJ 14 November 1996 (Tetra Pak, C-333/94P) [1996] ECR I-5951, para. 37.

(b) Exclusive dealing

See paras 32–46 of the Communication from the Commission regarding Guidance on the Commission's enforcement priorities in applying Article [102 TFEU] to abusive exclusionary conduct by dominant undertakings (OJ 2009 C-45/2).

(i) Exclusive purchasing

An undertaking which is in a dominant position on a market and ties purchasers – even **5.71** if it does so at their request – by an obligation or promise on their part to obtain all or most of their requirements exclusively from the said undertaking abuses its dominant position within the meaning of Article [102 TFEU], whether the obligation in question is stipulated without further qualification or whether it is undertaken in consideration of the grant of a rebate. The same applies if the said undertaking, without tying the purchasers by a formal obligation, applies, either under the terms of agreements concluded with these purchasers or unilaterally, a system of fidelity rebates, that is to say discounts conditional on the customer's obtaining all or most of its requirements – whether the quantity of its purchases be large or small – from the undertaking in a dominant position.

Obligations of this kind to obtain supplies exclusively from a particular undertaking, whether or not they are in consideration of rebates or of the granting of fidelity rebates intended to give the purchaser an incentive to obtain his supplies exclusively from the undertaking in a dominant position, are incompatible with the objective of undistorted competition within the common market, because – unless there are exceptional circumstances which may make an agreement between undertakings in the context of Article [101] and in particular of paragraph (3) of that article, permissible – they are not based on an economic transaction which justifies this burden or benefit but are designed to deprive the purchaser of or restrict his possible choices of sources of supply and to deny other producers access to the market. [...]

Furthermore the English clause does not remove the discrimination resulting from the fidelity rebates between purchasers in similar circumstances depending on whether or not they reserve their freedom to choose their suppliers.

It is particularly necessary to stress that, even in the most favourable circumstances, the English clause does not in fact remedy to a great extent the distortion of competition caused by the clauses obliging purchasers to obtain their requirements exclusively from Roche and by the fidelity rebates on a market where an undertaking in a dominant position is operating and where for this reason the structure of competition has already been weakened. [...]

CoJ 13 February 1979 (Hofmann–La Roche, 85/76) [1979] ECR 461, paras 89, 90, 106 and 107.

5.72   [A]ccording to settled case-law, an undertaking which is in a dominant position on a market and ties purchasers – even if it does so at their request – by an obligation or promise on their part to obtain all or most of their requirements exclusively from that undertaking abuses its dominant position within the meaning of Article [102 TFEU] [...]. Applied to a purchaser in a dominant position, that case-law means that for De Beers to reserve to itself the whole of Alrosa's production exported outside the CIS could, even if the latter consented, constitute an abuse in the context of their relations.

Prima facie, the most appropriate way of bringing an abuse of this kind to an end would therefore have been to prohibit the parties from entering into any agreement allowing De Beers to reserve to itself the whole, or even a material part, of Alrosa's production exported outside the CIS, in order for Alrosa to re-establish its independence on the market and for third-party access to an alternative source of supply to be guaranteed, without it being necessary to prohibit all purchases by De Beers of diamonds produced by Alrosa [...]. [...]

Furthermore, even if it were to be accepted that the sale to De Beers of a limited quantity of diamonds could have allowed the latter to maintain or to reinforce its

market-maker role, and hence its dominant position, an infringement of the competition rules would not necessarily be established. Since the object of Article [102 TFEU] is not to prohibit the holding of dominant positions but solely to put an end to their abuse, the Commission cannot require an undertaking in a dominant position to refrain from making purchases which allow it to maintain or to strengthen its position on the market, if that undertaking does not, in so doing, resort to methods which are incompatible with the competition rules. While special responsibilities are incumbent on an undertaking which occupies such a position [...] they cannot amount to a requirement that the very existence of the dominant position be called into question.
General Court 11 July 2007 (Alrosa v. Commission T-170/06) [2007] ECR II-2601, paras 127, 128 and 146.

Annulled by CoJ 29 June 2010 (Alrosa v. Commission C-441/07 P) [2010] ECR I-05949, on other grounds.

(ii)   Rebates

See also para. 5.71 above on Exclusive purchasing.

[Quantity rebate versus Loyalty rebate] [S]ZV submits that a rebate such as the one in **5.73** question is a normal price reduction, which is lawful having regard to the importance of rationalizing sales in a competitive economy.

This way of conceiving a rebate disregards the fact that the rebate at issue is not to be treated as a quantity rebate exclusively linked with the volume of purchases from the producer concerned but has rightly been classified by the Commission as a 'loyalty' rebate designed, through the grant of a financial advantage, to prevent customers obtaining their supplies from competing producers.
CoJ 16 December 1975 (Suiker Unie, Joined Cases 40–48, 50, 54–56, 111, 113 and 114/93) [1975] ECR 1663, paras 517 and 518.

[Situation of shortage of oil products] Having regard to the general shortage of **5.74** petroleum products during the period under review and the difficult position in which the whole of the Netherlands market was placed, the application to ABG [an occasional customer] by BP of a rate of reduction identical or very close to that applied to its traditional customers would have resulted in a considerable diminution of the deliveries which those customers expected.

A duty on the part of the supplier to apply a similar rate of reduction in deliveries to all its customers in a period of shortage without having regard to obligations contracted towards its traditional customers could only flow from measures adopted within the framework of the Treaty, in particular Article 103 [EEC], or, in default of that, by the national authorities. [...]

Hence, in view of these circumstances, it does not appear that BP in this case abused a dominant position in relation to ABG within the meaning of Article [102 TFEU].
CoJ 29 June 1978 (Benzine en Petroleum Handelsmaatschappij BV and others v. Commission, 77/77) [1978] ECR 1513, paras 33, 34 and 43.

5.75   [Reference period over which rebates are calculated] The discount system [...] was based on an annual reference period. However, any system under which discounts are granted according to the quantities sold during a relatively long reference period has the inherent effect, at the end of that period, of increasing pressure on the buyer to reach the purchase figure needed to obtain the discount or to avoid suffering the expected loss for the entire period. In this case the variations in the rate of discount over a year as a result of one last order, even a small one, affected the dealer's margin of profit on the whole year's sales of Michelin heavy-vehicle tyres. In such circumstances, even quite slight variations might put dealers under appreciable pressure.

That effect was accentuated still further by the wide divergence between Michelin NV's market share and those of its main competitors. If a competitor wished to offer a dealer a competitive inducement for placing an order, especially at the end of the year, it had to take into account the absolute value of Michelin NV's annual target discount and fix its own discount at a percentage which, when related to the dealer's lesser quantity of purchases from that competitor, was very high. Despite the apparently low percentage of Michelin NV's discount, it was therefore very difficult for its competitors to offset the benefits or losses resulting for dealers from attaining or failing to attain Michelin NV's targets, as the case might be.

Furthermore, the lack of transparency of Michelin NV's entire discount system, whose rules moreover changed on several occasions during the relevant period, together with the fact that neither the scale of discounts nor the sales targets or discounts relating to them were communicated in writing to dealers meant that they were left in uncertainty and on the whole could not predict with any confidence the effect of attaining their targets or failing to do so.

CoJ 9 November 1983 (Michelin, C-322/81) [1983] ECR 3461, paras 81–83.

5.76   [Rebates being conditional on exclusivity] The [General Court] points out, secondly, that, as the Court of Justice has held (in the judgment in *Michelin* [...]), the application by a supplier who is in a dominant position, and upon whom as a result the customer is more or less dependent, of any form of loyalty rebate through which the supplier endeavours, by means of financial advantages, to prevent its customers from obtaining supplies from competitors constitutes an abuse within the meaning of Article [102 TFEU]. In the present case, the rebates granted between June and December 1985 to Northern Irish builders' merchants were indeed intended to prevent them from obtaining products from competing suppliers, it being sufficiently proved that those rebates, being conditional on exclusivity, necessarily implied that the recipients were not to handle imported plasterboard. It is of little importance, in that regard, whether, as the applicants maintain, the exclusive supply arrangements on which the benefit of the discounts at issue was conditional merely constituted one of several conditions imposed on the merchants.

General Court 1 April 1993 (BPB Industries and British Gypsum, T-65/89) [1993] ECR II-389, para. 120.

5.77   [Meeting competition] Whilst there is no dispute between the parties that an undertaking holding a dominant position has a particular responsibility with regard to competition on its market [...] they differ as to whether or not special rebates to customers facing competition constitute a reaction that is compatible with that respons-ibility, in so far as the prices in question are not predatory within the meaning of the case-law [...]. Such a practice constitutes abuse of a dominant position [...].

General Court 7 October 1999 (Irish Sugar v. Commission, T-228/97) [1999] ECR II-2969, paras 182 et seq.

[Practical effect of the thresholds for discounts] [I]t is of the very essence of a system of **5.78** quantity discounts that larger purchasers [...] or users [...] enjoy lower average unit prices or which amounts to the same higher average reductions than those offered to smaller purchasers [...] or users [...]. The mere fact that the result of quantity discounts is that some customers enjoy in respect of specific quantities a proportionally higher average reduction than others in relation to the difference in their respective volumes of purchase is inherent in this type of system, but it cannot be inferred from that alone that the system is discriminatory.

None the less, where as a result of the thresholds of the various discount bands, and the levels of discount offered, discounts (or additional discounts) are enjoyed by only some trading parties, giving them an economic advantage which is not justified by the volume of business they bring or by any economies of scale they allow the supplier to make compared with their competitors, a system of quantity discounts leads to the application of dissimilar conditions to equivalent transactions.

CoJ 29 March 2001 (Portuguese Republic v. Commission, C-163/99) [2001] ECR I-02613, paras 51 and 52.

[All circumstances must be taken into account in determining effect of quantity **5.79** discount] Quantity rebate systems linked solely to the volume of purchases made from an undertaking occupying a dominant position are generally considered not to have the foreclosure effect prohibited by Article [102 TFEU] [...]. If increasing the quantity supplied results in lower costs for the supplier, the latter is entitled to pass on that reduction to the customer in the form of a more favourable tariff [...]. Quantity rebates are therefore deemed to reflect gains in efficiency and economies of scale made by the undertaking in a dominant position.

It follows that a rebate system in which the rate of the discount increases according to the volume purchased will not infringe Article [102 TFEU] unless the criteria and rules for granting the rebate reveal that the system is not based on an economically justified countervailing advantage but tends, following the example of a loyalty and target rebate, to prevent customers from obtaining their supplies from competitors [...].

In determining whether a quantity rebate system is abusive, it will therefore be necessary to consider all the circumstances, particularly the criteria and rules governing the grant of the rebate, and to investigate whether, in providing an advantage not based on any economic service justifying it, the rebates tend to remove or restrict the buyer's freedom to choose his sources of supply, to bar competitors from access to the market, to apply dissimilar conditions to equivalent transactions with other trading parties or to strengthen the dominant position by distorting competition [...].

General Court 30 September 2003 (Michelin, T-203/01) [2003] ECR II-4071, paras 58–60.

5.80   [All relevant circumstances must be taken into account; individualised targets] In [*CoJ 9 November 1983 (Michelin, C-322/81) [1983] ECR 3461* and *CoJ 13 February 1979 (Hofmann-La Roche, 85/76) [1979] ECR 461*] the Court of Justice found that certain discounts granted by two undertakings in a dominant position were abusive in character.

[…] In *Michelin*, unlike in *Hoffmann-La Roche*, Michelin's co-contractors were not obliged to obtain their supplies wholly or partially from Michelin. However, the variable annual discounts granted by that undertaking were linked to objectives in the sense that, in order to benefit from them, its co-contractors had to attain individualised sales results. In that case, the Court found a series of factors which led it to regard the discount system in question as an abuse of a dominant position. In particular, the system was based on a relatively long reference period, namely a year, its functioning was non-transparent for co-contractors, and the differences in market share between Michelin and its main competitors were significant (see, to that effect, *Michelin, paras 81–83*).

[…] *Michelin* is particularly relevant to the present case, since it concerns a discount system depending on the attainment of individual sales objectives which constituted neither discounts for quantity, linked exclusively to the volume of purchases, nor fidelity discounts within the meaning of the judgment in *Hoffmann-La Roche*, since the system established by Michelin did not contain any obligation on the part of resellers to obtain all or a given proportion of its supplies from the dominant undertaking. […]

In order to determine whether the undertaking in a dominant position has abused such a position by applying a [discount system depending on the attainment of individual sales objectives] the Court has held that it is necessary to consider all the circumstances, particularly the criteria and rules governing the grant of the discount, and to investigate whether, in providing an advantage not based on any economic service justifying it, the discount tends to remove or restrict the buyer's freedom to choose his sources of supply, to bar competitors from access to the market, to apply dissimilar conditions to equivalent transactions with other trading parties or to strengthen the dominant position by distorting competition (*Michelin, para. 73*).

It follows that in determining whether, on the part of an undertaking in a dominant position, a system of discounts or bonuses which constitute neither quantity discounts or bonuses nor fidelity discounts or bonuses within the meaning of the judgment in *Hoffmann-La Roche* constitutes an abuse, it first has to be determined whether those discounts or bonuses can produce an exclusionary effect, that is to say whether they are capable, first, of making market entry very difficult or impossible for competitors of the undertaking in a dominant position and, secondly, of making it more difficult or impossible for its co-contractors to choose between various sources of supply or commercial partners.

It then needs to be examined whether there is an objective economic justification for the discounts and bonuses granted. [A]n undertaking is at liberty to demonstrate that its bonus system producing an exclusionary effect is economically justified. […]

First, an exclusionary effect may arise from goal-related discounts or bonuses, that is to say those the granting of which is linked to the attainment of sales objectives defined individually (*Michelin, paras 70–86*) […]. […]

It is also apparent from the case-law that the commitment of co-contractors towards the undertaking in a dominant position and the pressure exerted upon them may be particularly strong where a discount or bonus does not relate solely to the growth in turnover in relation to purchases or sales of products of that undertaking made by those co-contractors during the period under consideration, but extends also to the whole of the turnover relating to those purchases or sales. In that way, relatively modest variations – whether upwards or downwards – in the turnover figures relating to the products of the dominant undertaking have disproportionate effects on co-contractors (see, to that effect, *Michelin, para.* 81) [...].

The [General Court] found that the bonus schemes at issue gave rise to a similar situation. Attainment of the sales progression objectives gave rise to an increase in the commission paid on all BA tickets sold by the travel agent concerned, and not just on those sold after those objectives had been attained [...]. The [General Court] [...] states that the progressive nature of the increased commission rates had a 'very noticeable effect at the margin' and emphasises the radical effects which a small reduction in sales of BA tickets could have on the rates of performance-related bonus [...].

Finally, the Court took the view that the pressure exerted on resellers by an undertaking in a dominant position which granted bonuses with those characteristics is further strengthened where that undertaking holds a very much larger market share than its competitors (see, to that effect, *Michelin, para. 82*). It held that, in those circumstances, it is particularly difficult for competitors of that undertaking to outbid it in the face of discounts or bonuses based on overall sales volume. By reason of its significantly higher market share, the undertaking in a dominant position generally constitutes an unavoidable business partner in the market. Most often, discounts or bonuses granted by such an undertaking on the basis of overall turnover largely take precedence in absolute terms, even over more generous offers of its competitors. In order to attract the co-contractors of the undertaking in a dominant position, or to receive a sufficient volume of orders from them, those competitors would have to offer them significantly higher rates of discount or bonus. [...]

Therefore, the [General Court] was right to examine [...] whether the bonus schemes at issue had a fidelity-building effect capable of producing an exclusionary effect.

CoJ 15 March 2007 (British Airways v. Commission, C-95/04) [2007] ECR I-2331, paras 61, 63, 65, 67–69, 71, 73–75 and 77.

[Individualised targets leaving margin of discretion to supplier] [T]he Commission **5.81** [...] correctly considered the individualised quantity commitments not only in a purely formal way from the legal point of view but also taking into account the specific economic context in which the agreements in question operated. That was the basis for the Commission's conclusion, in the contested decision, that the agreements concerned were capable of excluding competitors.

Individualised quantity commitments [...] which de facto tie and/or induce the purchaser to obtain all or most of its requirements from the dominant undertaking and which are not based on an economic transaction which justifies this burden or benefit but are designed to remove or restrict the purchaser's freedom to choose his sources of supply and to deny producers access to the market, – even if it is accepted that they do not bind the purchaser by a formal obligation – constitute an abuse of a dominant position within the meaning of Article [102 TFEU].

Even if a number of examples confirm that, as regards quantity commitments and rebates, the applicants allowed a degree of flexibility in relation to due observance of deadlines and targets, that flexibility, which was even applied to certain agreements that the applicants concede were 'binding', in no way diminishes the foreclosure caused by those practices. On the contrary, the Commission stated, rightly, in the contested decision that the exact volume of purchases was less important to the applicants than the customer's loyalty. Indeed, that flexibility helped to maintain the incentive to buy the applicants' RVMs, even with regard to customers which otherwise would not have reached the requisite thresholds [...].

Moreover, the great majority of quantity commitments which the applicants describe as non-binding are agreements in which they made price and commercial terms conditional upon the customer purchasing a certain volume. Those agreements generally included a discount which was expressly made conditional upon achievement of a target. The customer was not legally bound to reach the target but was required to achieve it in order to obtain or keep the discount. [...]. Those agreements are similar to a retroactive rebate. The risk of losing the discount retroactively is a strong incentive to the customer to reach the target. The fact that the applicants might ultimately have not required reimbursement of the discount is irrelevant, as is the absence of documented acceptance by the customer of an offer from the applicants. What matters are the expectations of the customer at the time when it placed the orders in conformity with the terms and conditions of the offer.

General Court 9 September 2010 (Tomra v. Commission, T-155/06) [2010] ECR II-04361, paras 297–300.

5.82   [Quantity rebate v. (quasi) exclusivity rebate v. loyalty / fidelity rebate] First, quantity rebate systems ('quantity rebates') linked solely to the volume of purchases made from an undertaking occupying a dominant position are generally considered not to have the foreclosure effect prohibited by Article [102 TFEU]. If increasing the quantity supplied results in lower costs for the supplier, the latter is entitled to pass on that reduction to the customer in the form of a more favourable tariff. Quantity rebates are therefore deemed to reflect gains in efficiency and economies of scale made by the undertaking in a dominant position.

Second, there are rebates the grant of which is conditional on the customer's obtaining all or most of its requirements from the undertaking in a dominant position. [...]

Such exclusivity rebates, when applied by an undertaking in a dominant position, are incompatible with the objective of undistorted competition within the common market, because they are not based — save in exceptional circumstances — on an economic transaction which justifies this burden or benefit but are designed to remove or restrict the purchaser's freedom to choose his sources of supply and to deny other producers access to the market. [...]

Third, there are other rebate systems where the grant of a financial incentive is not directly linked to a condition of exclusive or quasi-exclusive supply from the undertaking in a dominant position, but where the mechanism for granting the rebate may also have a fidelity-building effect [...]. In examining whether the application of such a rebate constitutes an abuse of dominant position, it is necessary to consider all the circumstances, particularly the criteria and rules governing the grant of the rebate, and to investigate whether, in providing an advantage not based on any economic service justifying it, that rebate tends to remove or restrict the buyer's freedom to choose his sources of supply, to bar competitors from access to the market, or to strengthen the dominant position by distorting competition. [...]

[I]t it is only in the case of [fidelity rebates] that it is necessary to assess all the circumstances, and not in the case of exclusivity rebates falling within the second category.

That approach can be justified by the fact that exclusivity rebates granted by an undertaking in a dominant position are by their very nature capable of restricting competition. [...]

[T]he [as efficient competitor] test carried out in the contested decision takes as a starting point the circumstance [...] that an as-efficient competitor, which seeks to obtain the contestable share of the orders hitherto satisfied by a dominant undertaking which is an unavoidable trading partner, must compensate the customer for the exclusivity rebate that it would lose if it purchased a smaller portion than that stipulated by the exclusivity or quasi-exclusivity condition. The [as efficient competitor] test is designed to determine whether the competitor which is as efficient as the undertaking in a dominant position, which faces the same costs as the latter, can still cover its costs in that case. [...]

[E]ven in the case of [fidelity rebates], for which an examination of the circumstances of the case is necessary, it is not essential to carry out an [as efficient competitor] test. [...]

[I]n order to find anti-competitive effects, it is not necessary that a rebate system force an as-efficient competitor to charge 'negative' prices, that is to say prices lower than the cost price. In order to establish a potential anti-competitive effect, it is sufficient to demonstrate the existence of a loyalty mechanism.

General Court 12 June 2014 (Intel Corp. v. European Commission, T-286/09), ECLI:EU:T:2014:547, paras 75–78, 84, 85, 141 and 145.

[As efficient competitor test under circumstances relevant][I]t is not possible to infer **5.83** from Article [102 TFEU] or the case-law of the Court that there is a legal obligation requiring a finding to the effect that a rebate scheme operated by a dominant undertaking is abusive to be based always on the as-efficient-competitor test.

Nevertheless, that conclusion ought not to have the effect of excluding, on principle, recourse to the as-efficient-competitor test in cases involving a rebate scheme for the purposes of examining its compatibility with Article [102 TFEU].

On the other hand, in a situation such as that in the main proceedings, characterised by the holding by the dominant undertaking of a very large market share and by structural advantages conferred, inter alia, by that undertaking's statutory monopoly, which applied to 70% of mail on the relevant market, applying the as-efficient-competitor test is of no relevance inasmuch as the structure of the market makes the emergence of an as-efficient competitor practically impossible.

Furthermore, in a market such as that at issue in the main proceedings, access to which is protected by high barriers, the presence of a less efficient competitor might contribute to intensifying the competitive pressure on that market and, therefore, to exerting a constraint on the conduct of the dominant undertaking.

The as-efficient-competitor test must thus be regarded as one tool amongst others for the purposes of assessing whether there is an abuse of a dominant position in the context of a rebate scheme.

CoJ 6 October 2015 (Post Danmark A/S v. Konkurrencerådet, C-23/14), ECLI: EU:C:2015:651, paras 57–61.

(c) Tying and bundling

See paras 47–62 of the Communication from the Commission regarding Guidance on the Commission's enforcement priorities in applying Article [102 TFEU] to abusive exclusionary conduct by dominant undertakings (OJ 2009 C 45/2).

(i) Tying sales of spare parts to maintenance and repair services

5.84   The Commission takes the view that Hugin abused its dominant position by refusing to supply spare parts to Liptons and, generally, to any independent undertaking outside its own distribution network. That practice, which results from Hugin's policy of restricting the maintenance and repair of Hugin cash registers to its own technical departments, is said to constitute an abuse in that its effect is to prevent users of Hugin machines from choosing freely the undertaking which is to service and repair those machines and in that it has the effect of excluding any competition, and in particular a substantial competitor, in the sector of the servicing, maintenance, repair, renting out and reconditioning of Hugin machines.

CoJ 31 May 1979 (Hugin v. Commission, C-22/78) [1979] ECR 1869, para. 11.

5.85   As regards Hilti's selective and discriminatory policies towards its competitors and their customers, it is quite clear from the documents cited by the Commission [...] that Hilti did indeed pursue such policies. The strategy employed by Hilti against its competitors and their customers is not a legitimate mode of competition on the part of an undertaking in a dominant position. A selective and discriminatory policy such as that operated by Hilti impairs competition in as much as it is liable to deter other undertakings from establishing themselves in the market. The inescapable conclusion is therefore that the Commission had good reason to hold that such behaviour on Hilti's part was improper.

General Court 12 December 1991 (Hilti, T-30/89) [1991] ECR II-1439, para. 100.

Confirmed in CoJ 2 March 1994 (Hilti, C-53/92) [1994] ECR I-667.

5.86   [E]ven where tied sales of two products are in accordance with commercial usage or there is a natural link between the two products in question, such sales may still constitute abuse within the meaning of Article [102] unless they are objectively justified.

CoJ 14 November 1996 (Tetra Pak, C-333/94P) [1996] ECR I-5951, para. 37.

(ii) Conditions for abusive bundling

The [General Court] considers that the Commission's analysis of the constituent **5.87**
elements of bundling is correct and that it is consistent both with Article [102 TFEU]
and with the case-law.

[T]he Commission was correct to rely on [the following factors: (i) the tying and tied
products are two separate products; (ii) the undertaking concerned is dominant in the
market for the tying product; (iii) the undertaking concerned does not give customers a
choice to obtain the tying product without the tied product; and (iv) the practice in
question forecloses competition] and on the fact that the tying was without objective
justification in deciding whether Microsoft's conduct constituted abusive tying. [...]

[B]undling by an undertaking in a dominant position may also infringe Article [102
TFEU] where it does not correspond to the example given in Article [102(d) TFEU].
Accordingly, in order to establish the existence of abusive bundling, the Commission
was correct to rely in the contested decision on Article [102 TFEU] in its entirety and
not exclusively on Article [102(d) TFEU]. [...]

[A]s regards Microsoft's argument that the integration of Windows Media Player
[the tied product] in the Windows operating system [the tying product] from May
1999 constitutes a normal and necessary step in the evolution of that system and is in
keeping with the constant improvement of its media functionality, it is sufficient to
observe that the fact that tying takes the form of the technical integration of one
product in another does not have the consequence that, for the purpose of assessing its
impact on the market, that integration cannot be qualified as the bundling of two
separate products. [...]

[M]icrosoft cannot rely on the fact that customers are not required to pay anything
extra for Windows Media Player. [...]

[It] does not follow from either Article [102(d) TFEU] or the case-law on bundling
that consumers must necessarily pay a certain price for the tied product in order for it to
be concluded that they are subject to supplementary obligations within the meaning of
that provision.

Nor [is it relevant] that consumers are not obliged to use the Windows Media Player
which they find pre-installed on their client PC and that they can install and use other
undertakings' media players on their PCs. [...]

The [General Court] observes that [...] first, OEMs are deterred from pre-installing
a second streaming media player on client PCs and, second, consumers have an
incentive to use Windows Media Player at the expense of competing media players,
notwithstanding that the latter players are of better quality. [...]

[T]he release of the bundled version of Windows and Windows Media Player as the
only version of the Windows operating system capable of being pre-installed by OEMs
on new client PCs had the direct and immediate consequence of depriving OEMs of
the possibility previously open to them of assembling the products which they deemed
most attractive for consumers and, more particularly, of preventing them from choosing
one of Windows Media Player's competitors as the only media player. [...]

Furthermore, even if developers of media players competing with Microsoft succeeded in reaching an agreement with OEMs for the pre-installation of their product,
they would still be in a disadvantageous competitive position by comparison with
Microsoft. [...] In particular, the bundling prevents developers of third-party media

players from competing with Microsoft for that purpose on the intrinsic merits of the products. Second, [...] developers of third-party media players compete with each other in order to have their products pre-installed, while, owing to the bundling, Microsoft evades that competition and the significant additional costs which it entails. [...]

[T]he bundling of Windows and Windows Media Player from May 1999 inevitably had significant consequences for the structure of competition. That practice allowed Microsoft to obtain an unparalleled advantage with respect to the distribution of its product and to ensure the ubiquity of Windows Media Player on client PCs throughout the world, thus providing a disincentive for users to make use of third-party media players and for OEMs to pre-install such players on client PCs.

General Court 17 September 2007 (Microsoft v. Commission, T-201/04) [2007] ECR II-3601, paras 858, 859, 861, 935, 967, 969–971, 1046–1047 and 1054.

(d) Predatory pricing

See paras 63–74 of the Communication from the Commission regarding Guidance on the Commission's enforcement priorities in applying Article [102 TFEU] to abusive exclusionary conduct by dominant undertakings (OJ 2009 C 45/2).

(i) Pricing below average variable cost or below average total cost

5.88   It follows that Article [102 TFEU] prohibits a dominant undertaking from eliminating a competitor and thereby strengthening its position by using methods other than those which come within the scope of competition on the basis of quality. From that point of view, however, not all competition by means of price can be regarded as legitimate.

Prices below average variable costs (that is to say, those which vary depending on the quantities produced) by means of which a dominant undertaking seeks to eliminate a competitor must be regarded as abusive. A dominant undertaking has no interest in applying such prices except that of eliminating competitors so as to enable it subsequently to raise its prices by taking advantage of its monopolistic position, since each sale generates a loss, namely the total amount of the fixed costs (that is to say, those which remain constant regardless of the quantities produced) and, at least, part of the variable costs relating to the unit produced.

Moreover, prices below average total costs, that is to say, fixed costs plus variable costs, but above average variable costs, must be regarded as abusive if they are determined as part of a plan for eliminating a competitor. Such prices can drive from the market undertakings which are perhaps as efficient as the dominant undertaking but which, because of their smaller financial resources, are incapable of withstanding the competition waged against them.

CoJ 3 July 1991 (AKZO Chemie v. Commission, C-62/86) [1991] ECR I-3359, paras 70–72.

(ii) Discriminatory predation

5.89   It follows that, where a liner conference in a dominant position selectively cuts its prices in order deliberately to match those of a competitor, it derives a dual benefit. First, it eliminates the principal, and possibly the only, means of competition open to the competing undertaking. Second, it can continue to require its users to pay higher prices for the services which are not threatened by that competition.

It is not necessary, in the present case, to rule generally on the circumstances in which a liner conference may legitimately, on a case-by-case basis, adopt lower prices than those of its advertised tariff in order to compete with a competitor who quotes lower prices, or to decide on the exact scope of the expression 'uniform or common freight rates' in Article 1(3)(b) of Regulation No 4056/86.

It is sufficient to recall that the conduct at issue here is that of a conference having a share of over 90 per cent of the market in question and only one competitor. The appellants have, moreover, never seriously disputed, and indeed admitted at the hearing, that the purpose of the conduct complained of was to eliminate G & C from the market.

CoJ 16 March 2000 (Compagnie Maritime Belge Transports and others v. Commission C-395/96 and C-396/96) [2000] ECR I-1365, paras 117–119.

(iii)   No requirement to show possibility of recoupment

Furthermore, it would not be appropriate, in the circumstances of the present case, to **5.90** require in addition proof that Tetra Pak had a realistic chance of recouping its losses. It must be possible to penalize predatory pricing whenever there is a risk that competitors will be eliminated. The [General Court] found [...] that there was such a risk in this case. The aim pursued, which is to maintain undistorted competition, rules out waiting until such a strategy leads to the actual elimination of competitors.

CoJ 14 November 1996 (Tetra Pak v. Commission, C-333/94) [1996] ECR I-5951, para. 44.

[I]t does not follow from the case-law of the Court that proof of the possibility of **5.91** recoupment of losses suffered by the application, by an undertaking in a dominant position, of prices lower than a certain level of costs constitutes a necessary precondition to establishing that such a pricing policy is abusive. In particular, the Court has taken the opportunity to dispense with such proof in circumstances where the eliminatory intent of the undertaking at issue could be presumed in view of that undertaking's application of prices lower than average variable costs [...].

That interpretation does not, of course, preclude the Commission from finding such a possibility of recoupment of losses to be a relevant factor in assessing whether or not the practice concerned is abusive, in that it may, for example where prices lower than average variable costs are applied, assist in excluding economic justifications other than the elimination of a competitor, or, where prices below average total costs but above average variable costs are applied, assist in establishing that a plan to eliminate a competitor exists.

Moreover, the lack of any possibility of recoupment of losses is not sufficient to prevent the undertaking concerned reinforcing its dominant position, in particular, following the withdrawal from the market of one or a number of its competitors, so that the degree of competition existing on the market, already weakened precisely because of the presence of the undertaking concerned, is further reduced and customers suffer loss as a result of the limitation of the choices available to them.

CoJ 2 April 2009 (France Télécom v. Commission, C-202/07) [2009] ECR I-2369, paras 110–112.

(e) Refusal to supply

(i) General

See also paras 75–90 of the Communication from the Commission regarding Guidance on the Commission's enforcement priorities in applying Article [102 TFEU] to abusive exclusionary conduct by dominant undertakings (OJ 2009 C 45/2).

5.92   [A]n undertaking which has a dominant position in the market in raw materials and which, with the object of reserving such raw material for manufacturing its own derivatives, refuses to supply a customer, which is itself a manufacturer of these derivatives, and therefore risks eliminating all competition on the part of this customer, is abusing its dominant position within the meaning of Article [102 TFEU]. In this context it does not matter that the undertaking ceased to supply in the spring of 1970 because of the cancellation of the purchases by Zoja, because it appears from the applicants' own statement that, when the supplies provided for in the contract had been completed, the sale of aminobutanol would have stopped in any case.

CoJ 6 March 1974 (Commercial Solvents, Joined Cases 6 and 7/73) [1974] ECR 223, para. 25.

5.93   An undertaking in a dominant position for the purpose of marketing a product – which cashes in on the reputation of a brand name known to and valued by the consumers – cannot stop supplying a long-standing customer who abides by regular commercial practice, if the orders placed by that customer are in no way out of the ordinary.

Such conduct is inconsistent with the objectives laid down in Article 3(f) [EEC, cf. Protocol (No 27) on the internal market and competition], which are set out in detail in Article [102], especially in paragraphs (b) and (c), since the refusal to sell would limit markets to the prejudice of consumers and would amount to discrimination which might in the end eliminate a trading party from the relevant market. [...]

Although it is true [...] that the fact that an undertaking is in a dominant position cannot disentitle it from protecting its own commercial interests if they are attacked, and that such an undertaking must be conceded the right to take such reasonable steps as it deems appropriate to protect its said interests, such behaviour cannot be countenanced if its actual purpose is to strengthen this dominant position and abuse it.

CoJ 14 February 1978 (United Brands v. Commission, 27/76) [1978] ECR 207, paras 182–183 and 189.

5.94   [T]he Commission was correct in finding that the period of time required to obtain access considerably exceeded that which could be considered as reasonable and justified, thus amounting to an abusive refusal to provide the service in question, capable of causing EB a competitive disadvantage on the relevant market. By way of comparison, CBL, a direct competitor of EB, had obtained access to Cascade RS in only four months. [...].

General Court 9 September 2009 (Clearstream v. Commission, T-301/04) [2009] ECR II-03155, para. 151.

(ii)   Access to 'essential facilities'

See also the Commission Notice on the application of the competition rules to access agreements in the telecommunications sector – framework, relevant markets and principles (OJ 1998 C 265/2).

Therefore, even if that case-law on the exercise of an intellectual property right were **5.95** applicable to the exercise of any property right whatever, it would still be necessary, for the *Magill* judgment to be effectively relied upon in order to plead the existence of an abuse within the meaning of Article [102 TFEU] in a situation such as that which forms the subject-matter of the first question, not only that the refusal of the service comprised in home delivery be likely to eliminate all competition in the daily newspaper market on the part of the person requesting the service and that such refusal be incapable of being objectively justified, but also that the service in itself be indispensable to carrying on that person's business, inasmuch as there is no actual or potential substitute in existence for that home-delivery scheme.

That is certainly not the case even if, as in the case which is the subject of the main proceedings, there is only one nationwide home-delivery scheme in the territory of a Member State and, moreover, the owner of that scheme holds a dominant position in the market for services constituted by that scheme or of which it forms part.

In the first place, it is undisputed that other methods of distributing daily newspapers, such as by post and through sale in shops and at kiosks, even though they may be less advantageous for the distribution of certain newspapers, exist and are used by the publishers of those daily newspapers.

Moreover, it does not appear that there are any technical, legal or even economic obstacles capable of making it impossible, or even unreasonably difficult, for any other publisher of daily newspapers to establish, alone or in cooperation with other publishers, its own nationwide home-delivery scheme and use it to distribute its own daily newspapers.

It should be emphasised in that respect that, in order to demonstrate that the creation of such a system is not a realistic potential alternative and that access to the existing system is therefore indispensable, it is not enough to argue that it is not economically viable by reason of the small circulation of the daily newspaper or newspapers to be distributed.

For such access to be capable of being regarded as indispensable, it would be necessary at the very least to establish, [...] that it is not economically viable to create a second home-delivery scheme for the distribution of daily newspapers with a circulation comparable to that of the daily newspapers distributed by the existing scheme.

CoJ 26 November 1998 (Oscar Bronner v. Mediaprint, C-7/97) [1998] ECR I-7791, paras 41–46.

[Refusal of access to energy transport network] In the Statement of Objections the **5.96** Commission considered that an undertaking occupying a dominant position in the provision and use of an essential facility (i.e. a facility or infrastructure, without access to which competitors cannot provide services to their customers), and refusing other companies access to that facility without objective justification or granting access to competitors only on terms less favourable than those granted to its own services, infringes Article 102 TFEU. [...]

The Statement of Objections took the view that ENI's transport infrastructures to import gas may be considered an indispensible infrastructure since access to ENI's system of transport was objectively necessary to import gas and compete in the gas supply markets in Italy.

The Commission has further considered that there are technical, legal and economic obstacles capable of making it impossible, or at least unreasonably difficult, for the would-be importer to duplicate ENI's system of transport infrastructure (i.e. to create an infrastructure system capable of providing an input on a volume comparable to ENI's system or, at the very least, of a volume sufficient to exert an effective competitive constraint on the latter), alone or in cooperation with other users.

In this respect, the Statement of Objections has identified concerns that ENI may have abused its dominant position on the relevant markets, thereby violating Article 102 TFEU, by implementing a refusal to supply strategy on its international transmission pipelines. Based on an assessment of ENI's management and operation of the TENP/Transitgas and TAG pipelines, the Commission took the preliminary view that ENI may have foreclosed its competitors by refusing to grant them access to capacity available on its transport networks (capacity hoarding [...]) by granting access in a less attractive manner (capacity degradation [...]) and by strategically limiting investment (strategic underinvestment [...]).

These practices are considered to have taken place despite very significant short- and long-term demand from third-party shippers, potentially weakening competition on the downstream Italian gas markets and harming consumers in Italy. [...]

[...] According to the Commission's Statement of Objections, ENI's behaviour are capable of affecting trade between Member States because ENI's practices were capable of limiting the access to gas coming from other Member States and therefore raising barriers to entry for competing gas undertakings, including undertakings from other Member States, with regard to the gas supply markets. In other words, ENI's practices are likely to have affected import flows by hindering and excluding competitors from effectively competing with ENI in the supply markets in Italy.

Commission 29 September 2010 (ENI Spa, COMP/39.315), paras 39, 41–44 and 62.

(iii)   Intellectual property rights

5.97   Since the existence of patent rights is at present a matter solely of national law, the use made of them can only come within the ambit of Community law where such use contributes to a dominant position, the abuse of which may affect trade between Member States. Although the sale price of the protected product may be regarded as a factor to be taken into account in determining the possible existence of an abuse, a higher price for the patented product as compared with the unpatented product does not necessarily constitute an abuse.

CoJ 29 February 1968 (Parke, Davis Co v. Probel, 24/67) [1968] ECR 81.

The proprietor of a trade-mark does not enjoy a 'dominant position' within the meaning of Article [102] merely because he is in a position to prevent third parties from putting into circulation, on the territory of a Member State, products bearing the same trade mark. [I]t is also necessary that the proprietor should have power to impede the maintenance of effective competition over a considerable part of the relevant market [...]. **5.98**

CoJ 18 February 1971 (Sirena v. Eda, 40/70) [1971] ECR 69, para. 16.

A manufacturer of sound recordings who holds a right related to copyright does not occupy a dominant position within the meaning of Article [102 TFEU] merely by exercising his exclusive right to distribute the protected articles. **5.99**

Since that article requires that the position to which it refers should extend to a 'substantial part' of the common market this further requires that the manufacturer, alone or jointly with other undertakings in the same group, should have the power to impede the maintenance of effective competition over a considerable part of the relevant market, having regard in particular to the existence of any producers marketing similar products and to their position on the market.

CoJ 8 June 1971 (Deutsche Grammophon, 78/70) [1971] ECR 487, paras 16 and 17.

If abusive practices are exposed, it is also for the Court to decide whether and to what extent they affect the interests of authors or third parties concerned, with a view to deciding the consequences with regard to the validity and effect of the contracts in dispute or certain of their provisions. **5.100**

[T]he fact that an undertaking entrusted with the exploitation of copyrights and occupying a dominant position within the meaning of Article [102] imposes on its members obligations which are not absolutely necessary for the attainment of its object and which thus encroach unfairly upon a member's freedom to exercise his copyright can constitute an abuse.

CoJ 27 March 1974 (SABAM, C-127/73) [1974] ECR 313, paras 14 and 15.

It is sufficient to observe that to the extent to which the exercise of a trade-mark right is lawful in accordance with the provisions of Article [36 TFEU], such exercise is not contrary to Article [102 TFEU] on the sole ground that it is the act of an undertaking occupying a dominant position on the market if the trade-mark right has not been used as an instrument for the abuse of such a position. **5.101**

CoJ 23 May 1978 (Hoffmann–La Roche v. Centrafarm, 102/77) [1978] ECR 1139, para. 16.

Where an association exploiting composers' copyrights is to be regarded as an undertaking abusing a dominant position within the common market or in a substantial part of it, the fact that such abuse, in certain cases, relates only to the performance in non-member countries of contracts entered into in the territory of a Member State by parties within the jurisdiction of that state does not preclude the application of Article [102 TFEU]. **5.102**

CoJ 25 October 1979 (SACEM, 22/79) [1979] ECR 3275, para. 13.

5.103   In those circumstances it was not permissible for GVL to limit its services, even in the absence of harmonization of copyright laws, to artists whose rights it knew were governed by the German law. It could not exclude the possibility that certain foreign artists not resident in the Federal Republic of Germany might be able to assert rights of secondary exploitation. Furthermore, it knew that by refusing to manage such rights it was in fact preventing those artists from being paid the royalties to which they were entitled. [...]

   Such a refusal by an undertaking having a de facto monopoly to provide its services for all those who may be in need of them but who do not come within a certain category of persons defined by the undertaking on the basis of nationality or residence must be regarded as an abuse of a dominant position within the meaning of the first paragraph of Article [102 TFEU].

CoJ 2 March 1983 (GVL v. Commission, 7/82) [1983] ECR 483, paras 54 and 56.

5.104   Exercise of the exclusive right may be prohibited by Article [102] if it gives rise to certain abusive conduct on the part of an undertaking occupying a dominant position such as an arbitrary refusal to deliver spare parts to independent repairers, the fixing of prices for spare parts at an unfair level or a decision no longer to produce spare parts for a particular model even though many cars of that model remain in circulation, provided that such conduct is liable to affect trade between Member States.

CoJ 5 October 1988 (Maxicar, 53/87) [1988] ECR 6039, para. 16.

5.105   It must therefore be stated in reply to the second question submitted by the national court that the refusal by the proprietor of a registered design in respect of body panels to grant to third parties, even in return for reasonable royalties, a licence for the supply of parts incorporating the design cannot in itself be regarded as an abuse of a dominant position within the meaning of Article [102].

CoJ 5 October 1988 (Volvo, 238/87) [1988] ECR 6211, para. 11.

5.106   [T]he applicant, by reserving the exclusive right to publish its weekly television programme listings, was preventing the emergence on the market of a new product, namely a general television magazine likely to compete with its own magazine, the RTE Guide. The applicant was thus using its copyright in the programme listings which it produced as part of its broadcasting activity in order to secure a monopoly in the derivative market of weekly television guides.

   The applicant's conduct cannot, therefore, be covered in Community law by the protection conferred by its copyright in the programme listings.

General Court 10 July 1991 (RTE v. Commission, T-69/89) [1991] ECR II-485, para. 73.

Confirmed in CoJ 6 April 1995 (RTE v. Commission, C241/91 P and C-242/91 P) [2005] ECR I-743.

5.107   [H]ilti was not prepared to grant licences on a voluntary basis and that during the proceedings for the grant of licences of right it demanded a fee approximately six times higher than the figure ultimately appointed by the Comptroller of Patents. A reasonable trader, as Hilti claims to have been, should at least have realized that by demanding such a large fee it was needlessly protracting the proceedings for the grant of licences of right, and such behaviour undeniably constitutes an abuse.

General Court 12 December 1991 (Hilti, T-30/89) [1991] ECR II-1439, para. 99.

The refusal to supply the applicant could not fall within the prohibition laid down by Article [102 TFEU] unless it concerned a product or service which was either essential for the exercise of the activity in question, in that there was no real or potential substitute, or was a new product whose introduction might be prevented, despite specific, constant and regular potential demand on the part of consumers [...].   **5.108**

[T]he televised broadcasting of horse races, although constituting an additional, and indeed suitable, service for bettors, it is not in itself indispensable for the exercise of bookmakers' main activity, namely the taking of bets, as is evidenced by the fact that the applicant is present on the Belgian betting market and occupies a significant position as regards bets on French races. Moreover, transmission is not indispensable, since it takes place after bets are placed, with the result that its absence does not in itself affect the choices made by bettors and, accordingly, cannot prevent bookmakers from pursuing their business.

General Court 12 June 1997 (Ladbroke v. Commission, T-504/93) [1997] ECR II-00923, paras 131 and 132.

[T]he refusal by an undertaking in a dominant position to allow access to a product protected by an intellectual property right, where that product is indispensable for operating on a secondary market, may be regarded as abusive only where the undertaking which requested the licence does not intend to limit itself essentially to duplicating the goods or services already offered on the secondary market by the owner of the intellectual property right, but intends to produce new goods or services not offered by the owner of the right and for which there is a potential consumer demand.   **5.109**

CoJ 29 April 2004 (IMS Health GmbH Co. OHG v. NDC Health GmbH Co. KG, C-418/01) [2004] ECR I-5039, para. 49.

[T]he refusal by an undertaking holding a dominant position to license a third party to use a product covered by an intellectual property right cannot in itself constitute an abuse of a dominant position within the meaning of Article [102 TFEU]. It is only in exceptional circumstances that the exercise of the exclusive right by the owner of the intellectual property right may give rise to such an abuse.   **5.110**

[T]he following circumstances, in particular, must be considered to be exceptional:

- in the first place, the refusal relates to a product or service indispensable to the exercise of a particular activity on a neighbouring market;
- in the second place, the refusal is of such a kind as to exclude any effective competition on that neighbouring market;
- in the third place, the refusal prevents the appearance of a new product for which there is potential consumer demand.

Once it is established that such circumstances are present, the refusal by the holder of a dominant position to grant a licence may infringe Article [102 TFEU] unless the refusal is objectively justified.

The [General Court] notes that the circumstance that the refusal prevents the appearance of a new product for which there is potential consumer demand is found only in the case-law on the exercise of an intellectual property right. [...]

The circumstance relating to the appearance of a new product [...] cannot be the only parameter which determines whether a refusal to license an intellectual property right is capable of causing prejudice to consumers within the meaning of Article [102(b) TFEU]. As that provision states, such prejudice may arise where there is a limitation not only of production or markets, but also of technical development.

It was on that last hypothesis that the Commission based its finding in the contested decision. Thus, the Commission considered that Microsoft's refusal to supply the relevant information limited technical development to the prejudice of consumers [...].

The [General Court] finds that the Commission's findings [...] are not manifestly incorrect.

General Court 17 September 2007 (Microsoft v. Commission, T-201/04) [2007] ECR II-3601, paras 331–334 and 647–649.

5.111   [Patent ambush] In the preliminary assessment, the Commission considered that Rambus may have engaged in intentional deceptive conduct in the context of the standard-setting process by not disclosing the existence of the patents and patent applications which it later claimed were relevant to the adopted standard. Such behaviour is known as a 'patent ambush.'

The Commission took the view that Rambus may have been abusing its dominant position by claiming royalties for the use of its patents from JEDEC-compliant DRAM manufacturers at a level which, absent its allegedly intentional deceptive conduct, it would not have been able to charge. In the preliminary assessment, the Commission provisionally claiming royalties for the use of its patents from JEDEC-compliant DRAM manufacturers at a level which, absent its allegedly intentional deceptive conduct, it would not have been able to charge. In the preliminary assessment, the Commission provisionally concluded that claiming such royalties was incompatible with Article 102 TFEU, in light of the specific circumstances of this case, including Rambus' intentional breach of JEDEC policy and the underlying duty of good faith in the context of standard-setting, which resulted in a deliberate frustration of the legitimate expectations of the other participants in the standard-setting process.

Furthermore, the Commission considered that such alleged behaviour by Rambus undermined confidence in the standard-setting process, given that an effective standard-setting process is, in the sector relevant to the present case, a precondition to technical development and the development of the market in general to the benefit of consumers.

Commission 9 December 2009 (Rambus, COMP/38.636), paras 27–29.

[Standard essential patents] [A]rticle 102 TFEU must be interpreted as meaning that **5.112** the proprietor of an SEP [standardisation body], which has given an irrevocable undertaking to a standardisation body to grant a licence to third parties on FRAND terms, does not abuse its dominant position, within the meaning of Article 102 TFEU, by bringing an action for infringement seeking an injunction prohibiting the infringement of its patent or seeking the recall of products for the manufacture of which that patent has been used, as long as:

- prior to bringing that action, the proprietor has, first, alerted the alleged infringer of the infringement complained about by designating that patent and specifying the way in which it has been infringed, and, secondly, after the alleged infringer has expressed its willingness to conclude a licensing agreement on FRAND terms, presented to that infringer a specific, written offer for a licence on such terms, specifying, in particular, the royalty and the way in which it is to be calculated, and
- where the alleged infringer continues to use the patent in question, the alleged infringer has not diligently responded to that offer, in accordance with recognised commercial practices in the field and in good faith, this being a matter which must be established on the basis of objective factors and which implies, in particular, that there are no delaying tactics.[...]

[...] Article 102 TFEU must be interpreted as prohibiting an undertaking in a dominant position and holding an SEP, which has given an undertaking to the standardisation body to grant licences for that patent on FRAND terms, from bringing an action for infringement against the alleged infringer of its SEP and seeking the rendering of accounts in relation to past acts of use of that SEP or an award of damages in respect of those acts of use.

CoJ 16 July 2015 (Huawei Technologies Co. Ltd v. ZTE Corp., ZTE Deutschland GmbH, C170/13), ECLI:EU:C:2015:477, paras 71 and 72.

(f) Margin squeeze

See also paras 75–90 of the Communication from the Commission regarding Guidance on the Commission's enforcement priorities in applying Article [102 TFEU] to abusive exclusionary conduct by dominant undertakings (OJ 2009 C 45/2).

In the present case, it must be noted that the appellant does not deny that [...] the **5.113** spread between [Deutsche Telekom's wholesale] prices and its retail prices for end-user access services is capable of having an exclusionary effect on its equally efficient actual or potential competitors, since their access to the relevant service markets is, at the very least, made more difficult as a result of the margin squeeze which such a spread can entail for them.

[T]he mere fact that the appellant would have to increase its retail prices for end-user access services in order to avoid the margin squeeze of its competitors who are as efficient as the appellant cannot in any way, in itself, render irrelevant the test which the [General Court] applied in the present case for the purpose of establishing an abuse under Article [102 TFEU].

By further reducing the degree of competition existing on a market – the end-user access services market – already weakened precisely because of the presence of the appellant, thereby strengthening its dominant position on that market, the margin squeeze also has the effect that consumers suffer detriment as a result of the limitation of the choices available to them and, therefore, of the prospect of a longer-term reduction of retail prices as a result of competition exerted by competitors who are at least as efficient in that market [...].

In those circumstances, in so far as the appellant has scope to reduce or end such a margin squeeze [...] by increasing its retail prices for end-user access services, the [General Court] correctly held [...] that that margin squeeze is capable, in itself, of constituting an abuse within the meaning of Article [102 TFEU] in view of the exclusionary effect that it can create for competitors who are at least as efficient as the appellant. The [General Court] was not, therefore, obliged to establish, additionally, that the wholesale prices for local loop access services or retail prices for end-user access services were in themselves abusive on account of their excessive or predatory nature, as the case may be.

[A]s the abusive nature of the pricing practices at issue in the judgment under appeal stems [...] from their exclusionary effect on the appellant's competitors, the [General Court] did not err in law when it held [...] that the Commission had been correct to analyse the abusive nature of the appellant's pricing practices solely on the basis of the appellant's charges and costs. [...]

Such an approach is particularly justified because [...] it is also consistent with the general principle of legal certainty in so far as the account taken of the costs of the dominant undertaking allows that undertaking, in the light of its special responsibility under Article [102 TFEU] to assess the lawfulness of its own conduct. While a dominant undertaking knows what its own costs and charges are, it does not, as a general rule, know what its competitors' costs and charges are.

Since the retail market for end-user access services constitutes a separate market, and wholesale local loop access services are indispensable to enabling competitors who are at least as efficient as the appellant to enter into effective competition on that market with an undertaking which, as in the appellant's case, has a dominant position largely as a result of the legal monopoly it enjoyed before the liberalisation of the telecommunications sector, the establishment of a system of undistorted competition requires that the dominant undertaking should not be able – by means of its pricing practices on that retail market – to impose on all its equally efficient competitors a competitive disadvantage such as to prevent or restrict their access to that market or the growth of their activities on it.

[A] pricing practice such as that at issue in the judgment under appeal [...] constitutes an abuse within the meaning of Article [102 TFEU] if it has an exclusionary effect on competitors who are at least as efficient as the dominant undertaking itself by squeezing their margins and is capable of making market entry more difficult or impossible for those competitors, and thus of strengthening its dominant position on that market to the detriment of consumers' interests.

CoJ 14 October 2010 (Deutsche Telekom v. Commission, C-280/08) [2010] ECR I-09555, paras 178, 181–183, 200, 202 and 234.

[W]hen assessing whether a pricing practice which causes a margin squeeze is abusive, **5.114** account should as a general rule be taken primarily of the prices and costs of the undertaking concerned on the retail services market. Only where it is not possible, in particular circumstances, to refer to those prices and costs should those of its competitors on the same market be examined.

[T]he absence of any regulatory obligation to supply the ADSL input services on the wholesale market has no effect on the question of whether the pricing practice at issue in the main proceedings [a margin squeeze, Ed.] is abusive.

[I]n order to establish whether such a practice is abusive, that practice must have an anti-competitive effect on the market, but the effect does not necessarily have to be concrete, and it is sufficient to demonstrate that there is an anti-competitive effect which may potentially exclude competitors who are at least as efficient as the dominant undertaking.

Where a dominant undertaking actually implements a pricing practice resulting in a margin squeeze on its equally efficient competitors, with the purpose of driving them from the relevant market, the fact that the desired result, namely the exclusion of those competitors, is not ultimately achieved does not alter its categorisation as abuse within the meaning of Article 102 TFEU.

However, in the absence of any effect on the competitive situation of competitors, a pricing practice such as that at issue in the main proceedings cannot be classified as an exclusionary practice where the penetration of those competitors in the market concerned is not made any more difficult by that practice [...].

[B]y reason simply of the fact that the wholesale product is not indispensable for the supply of the retail product, a pricing practice which causes margin squeeze may not be able to produce any anti-competitive effect, even potentially.

Secondly, it is necessary to determine the level of margin squeeze of competitors at least as efficient as the dominant undertaking. If the margin is negative [...] an effect which is at least potentially exclusionary is probable, taking into account the fact that, in such a situation, the competitors of the dominant undertaking, even if they are as efficient, or even more efficient, compared with it, would be compelled to sell at a loss.

If, on the other hand, such a margin remains positive, it must then be demonstrated that the application of that pricing practice was, by reason, for example, of reduced profitability, likely to have the consequence that it would be at least more difficult for the operators concerned to trade on the market concerned.

It must then be concluded that, in order to establish that a pricing practice resulting in margin squeeze is abusive, it is necessary to demonstrate that, taking into account, in particular, the fact that the wholesale product is indispensable, that practice produces, at least potentially, an anti-competitive effect on the retail market which is not in any way economically justified.

The question whether a pricing practice introduced by a vertically integrated dominant undertaking in the wholesale market for ADSL input services and resulting in the margin squeeze of competitors of that undertaking in the retail market for broadband connection services to end users is abusive does not depend on whether that undertaking is dominant in that retail market.

[W]hether the pricing practice at issue is liable to drive out from the market concerned existing clients of the dominant undertaking or rather new clients of that undertaking is not, as a general rule, relevant to the assessment of whether the practice is abusive.

[W]hether the dominant undertaking is able to recoup any losses suffered as a result of applying the pricing practice at issue has no relevance to the matter of establishing whether that pricing practice is abusive.

[T]he fact that the markets concerned are growing rapidly and involve new technology, requiring high levels of investment, is not, as a general rule, relevant to establishing whether the pricing practice at issue constitutes an abuse within the meaning of Article 102 TFEU.

CoJ 17 February 2011 (Konkurrensverket v. TeliaSonera Sverige AB, C-52/09) [2011] ECR I-00527, paras 46, 59, 64–66, 72–74, 77, 89, 96, 103 and 111.

5.115   Moreover, while the Kingdom of Spain claims that, if the margin between the national and regional wholesale products, on the one hand, and the retail product, on the other, was so close that it amounted to being negative, with the result that no other operator could use those wholesale products, the conduct under examination ought then to be analysed as a refusal of access which should then be regarded as abusive only by reference to the criteria stated in *Case C-7/97 Bronner [1998] ECR I-7791*, such an argument must also fail.

The Court of Justice has made it clear that it cannot be inferred from *Bronner* that the conditions to be met in order to establish that a refusal to supply is abusive must necessarily also apply when assessing the abusive nature of conduct which consists in supplying services or selling goods on conditions which are disadvantageous or on which there might be no purchaser. Such conduct may, in itself, constitute an independent form of abuse distinct from that of refusal to supply […].

If *Bronner* were to be interpreted otherwise, that would amount to a requirement that before any conduct of a dominant undertaking in relation to its terms of trade could be regarded as abusive the conditions to be met to establish that there was a refusal to supply would in every case have to be satisfied, and that would unduly reduce the effectiveness of Article [102 TFEU] […].

General Court 29 March 2012 (Spain v. Commission, T-398/07), ECLI: EU:T:2012:173, paras 73–75.

Confirmed in CoJ 10 July 2014 (Telefónica SA, Telefónica de España SAU v. European Commission, C-295/12P), ECLI:EU:C:2014:2062.

(g)   Unfair conditions

(i)   Excessive pricing

(1)   General
5.116   As regards the abuse of a dominant position, although the price level of the product may not of itself necessarily suffice to disclose such an abuse, it may, however, if unjustified by any objective criteria, and if it is particularly high, be a determining factor.

CoJ 18 February 1971 (Sirena v. Eda, 40/70) [1971] ECR 69, para. 17.

(2) Excessive in relation to economic value

[Excessive in relation to cost of production is indication] The imposition by an **5.117**
undertaking in a dominant position directly or indirectly of unfair purchase or selling
prices is an abuse to which exception can be taken under Article [102 TFEU]. […]

In this case charging a price which is excessive because it has no reasonable relation to
the economic value of the product supplied would be such an abuse.

This excess could, inter alia, be determined objectively if it were possible for it to be
calculated by making a comparison between the selling price of the product in question
and its cost of production, which would disclose the amount of the profit margin […].

The questions therefore to be determined are whether the difference between the
costs actually incurred and the price actually charged is excessive, and, i[f] the answer to
this question is in the affirmative, whether a price has been imposed which is either
unfair in itself or when compared to competing products.

CoJ 14 February 1978 (United Brands v. Commission, 27/76) [1978] ECR 207,
paras 248 and 250–252.

[A]n undertaking abuses its dominant position where it has an administrative monop- **5.118**
oly and charges for its services fees which are disproportionate to the economic value of
the service provided.

CoJ 11 November 1986 (British Leyland, 226/84) [1986] ECR 3263, para. 27.

[Economic value may also depend on non-cost-related factors] [A]n analysis of **5.119**
excessive or unfair pricing abuse must focus on the price charged, and its relation to the
economic value of the product. While a comparison of prices and costs, which reveals
the profit margin of a particular company may serve as a first step in such an analysis,
this in itself cannot be conclusive as regards the existence of an abuse.

In line with what the Court has stated in para. 252 of the *United Brands* judgment, a
distinction must be made between the assessment of the difference between the price
and the production costs – the profit margin – and the assessment of whether the price
is unfair.

[E]ven if it were to be assumed that the profit margin of [Port of Helsingborg] is
high or even 'excessive', this would not be sufficient to conclude that the price charged
bears no reasonable relation to the economic value of the services provided. […]

While the ECJ in *United Brands* stated that 'charging a price which is excessive
because it has no reasonable relation to the economic value of the product supplied'
would be such an abuse', it provided no further details on how to determine this
'economic value' of the product/service provided.

[E]ven if it were to be assumed that there is a positive difference between the price
and the production costs exceeding what Scandlines claims as being a reasonable
margin (whatever that may be), the conclusion should not necessarily be drawn that the
price is unfair, provided that this price has a reasonable relation to the economic value of
the product/service supplied. The assessment of the reasonable relation between the
price and the economic value of the product/service must also take into account the
relative weight of non-cost-related factors.

Commission 23 July 2004 (Scandlines Sverige AB v. Port of Helsingborg, COMP/
A.36.568), paras 214–216, 218 and 228.

5.120   [Economic value of royalties] It cannot be denied that, by collecting royalties with respect to remuneration paid for the television broadcast of musical works protected by copyright, STIM pursues a legitimate aim, namely, safeguarding the rights and interests of its members vis-à-vis users of their musical works [...].

Furthermore, those royalties, which represent the consideration paid for the use of musical works protected by copyright for the purposes of television broadcast, must, in particular, be analysed with respect to the value of that use in trade.

In that connection, in so far as such royalties are calculated on the basis of the revenue of the television broadcasting societies, they are, in principle, reasonable in relation to the economic value of the service provided by STIM. [...]

However, it is conceivable that, in certain circumstances, the application of such a remuneration model may amount to an abuse, in particular when another method exists which enables the use of those works and the audience to be identified and quantified more precisely and that method is capable of achieving the same legitimate aim, which is the protection of the interests of composers and music editors, without however leading to a disproportionate increase in the costs incurred for the management of the contracts and the supervision of the use of musical works protected by copyright.

CoJ 11 December 2008 (Kanal 5 Ltd and TV 4 AB v. STIM, C-52/07) [2008] ECR I-9275, paras 35–37 and 40.

(3)   Excessive in relation to fee levels charged in other Member States

5.121   When an undertaking holding a dominant position imposes scales of fees for its services which are appreciably higher than those charged in other Member States and where a comparison of the fee levels has been made on a consistent basis, that difference must be regarded as indicative of an abuse of a dominant position. In such a case it is for the undertaking in question to justify the difference by reference to objective dissimilarities between the situation in the Member State concerned and the situation prevailing in all the other Member States.

CoJ 13 July 1989 (Tournier, 395/87) [1989] ECR 2521, para. 38.

(ii)   Other unfair conditions

5.122   [T]he fact that a producer or an association of producers forbids its agents, who sell in its name and for its account, to act at the same time for competing producers without its consent, corresponds to the nature and spirit of a legal and economic relationship of the kind in question.

In fact, if such an agent works for the benefit of his principal he may in principle be treated as an auxiliary organ forming an integral part of the latter's undertaking, who must carry out his principal's instructions and thus, like a commercial employee, forms an economic unit with this undertaking.

In these circumstances the abuse is not due to the fact that the principal forbids such an auxiliary organ, without his consent, to trade in products which could compete with his own.

The position is different if the agreements entered into between the principal and his agents, whom the contracting parties call 'trade representatives', confer upon these agents or allow them to perform duties which from an economic point of view are approximately the same as those carried out by an independent dealer, because they

provide for the said agents accepting the financial risks of the sales or of the perform-ance of contracts entered into with third parties.
CoJ 16 December 1975 (Suiker Unie, Joined Cases 40–48, 50, 54–56, 111, 113 and 114/73) [1975] ECR 1663, paras 479–482.

In any event, that information cannot suffice to call into question the Commission's **5.123** assessment in the contested decision as regards the abusive nature, in the light of Article [102 TFEU], of the conduct of DSD in requiring payment of a fee for all packaging carrying the Der Grüne Punkt logo and put into circulation in Germany, even where it has been proved that some of that packaging has been taken back and recovered by another exemption system or self-management solution.

[S]ince the function of the Der Grüne Punkt logo is to identify the possibility of having the package at issue collected by the DSD system and since that logo [without adverse effect on the essential function of DSD's mark] may be affixed together with other signs of other mechanisms making it possible to identify another possibility for collection by a competitor self-management solution or exemption system, it cannot be claimed that the contested decision constitutes a disproportionate impairment of the trade mark right or, in any event, an impairment which is not justified by the need to prevent an abuse of a dominant position within the meaning of Article [102 TFEU].
General Court 24 May 2007 (DSD Der Grüne Punkt v. Commission, T-151/01) [2007] ECR II-1607, paras 148 and 157.

Confirmed in CoJ 16 July 2009 (DSD Der Grüne Punkt v. Commission, C-385/07 P) [2009] ECR I-06155.

(h)   Price discrimination

(i)   General

See also paras 5.73–5.83 above on Rebates.

In the present case, ADP does not apply any commercial fee system which fixes in **5.124** advance the rates for the commercial fee based on turnover. In exchange for the airport management services provided by ADP, the commercial fees vary individually accord-ing to supplier or user engaged in the same ground handling activity […]. The fee charged within the same airport thus varies from one supplier to another and from one user to another, thus having an appreciable effect on the cost of the services concerned and on the structure of the costs borne by the carriers. Such discrimination has anti-competitive effects on the market for air transport services.
Commission 11 June 1998 (Alpha Flight Services v. Aéroports de Paris, IV/35.613), OJ 1998 L 230/10, para. 125.

The specific prohibition of discrimination in subparagraph (c) of the second paragraph **5.125** of Article [102 TFEU] forms part of the system for ensuring, in accordance with Article 3(1)(g) EC [cf. Protocol (No 27) on the internal market and competition], that competition is not distorted in the internal market. The commercial behaviour of the undertaking in a dominant position may not distort competition on an upstream or a downstream market, in other words between suppliers or customers of that undertaking. Co-contractors of that undertaking must not be favoured or disfavoured in the area of the competition which they practise amongst themselves.

Therefore, in order for the conditions for applying subparagraph (c) of the second paragraph of Article [102 TFEU] to be met, there must be a finding not only that the behaviour of an undertaking in a dominant market position is discriminatory, but also that it tends to distort that competitive relationship, in other words to hinder the competitive position of some of the business partners of that undertaking in relation to the others [...].

In that respect, there is nothing to prevent discrimination between business partners who are in a relationship of competition from being regarded as being abusive as soon as the behaviour of the undertaking in a dominant position tends, having regard to the whole of the circumstances of the case, to lead to a distortion of competition between those business partners. In such a situation, it cannot be required in addition that proof be adduced of an actual quantifiable deterioration in the competitive position of the business partners taken individually.

CoJ 15 March 2007 (British Airways v. Commission, C-95/04) [2007] ECR I-2331, paras 143–145.

5.126   In the present case, the application to a trading partner of different prices for equivalent services continuously over a period of five years and by an undertaking having a de facto monopoly on the upstream market could not fail to cause that partner a competitive disadvantage.

General Court 9 September 2009 (Clearstream v. Commission, T-301/04) [2009] ECR II-03155, para. 194.

(ii)   Geographic price discrimination

5.127   [T]he difference between the controlled price and the price of the product reimported from another Member State does not necessarily suffice to disclose [...] abuse; it may however, if unjustified by any objective criteria and if it is particularly marked, be a determining factor in such abuse.

CoJ 8 June 1971 (Deutsche Grammophon, 78/70) [1971] ECR 487, para. 19.

5.128   [T]he policy of differing prices [between Member States] enabling UBC to apply dissimilar conditions to equivalent transactions with other trading parties, thereby placing them at a competitive disadvantage, was an abuse of a dominant position.

CoJ 14 February 1978 (United Brands v. Commission, 27/76) [1978] ECR 207, para. 234.

(i)   Limitations on trade between Member States

5.129   [E]ven clauses prohibiting competition imposed by an undertaking occupying a dominant position on trade representatives may constitute an abuse, if foreign competitors find that there are no independent operators who can market the product in question on a sufficiently large scale, and are in practice forced to apply to the said undertaking's trade representatives if they wish to sell this product in the latter's sales territory, or if the said undertaking enlarges the scope of the prohibition of competition to such an extent that it no longer corresponds to the nature of the legal and economic relationship in question.

CoJ 16 December 1975 (Suiker Unie, Joined Cases 40–48, 50, 54–56, 111, 113 and 114/93) [1975] ECR 1663, para. 486.

To impose on the ripener the obligation not to resell bananas so long as he has not had **5.130** them ripened and to cut down the operations of such a ripener to contacts only with retailers is a restriction of competition.

Although it is commendable and lawful to pursue a policy of quality, especially by choosing sellers according to objective criteria relating to the qualifications of the seller, his staff and his facilities, such a practice can only be justified if it does not raise obstacles, the effect of which goes beyond the objective to be attained.

In this case, although these conditions for selection have been laid down in a way which is objective and not discriminatory, the prohibition on resale imposed upon duly appointed Chiquita ripeners and the prohibition of the resale of unbranded bananas – even if the perishable nature of the banana in practice restricted the opportunities of reselling to the duration of a specific period of time – when without any doubt an abuse of the dominant position since they limit markets to the prejudice of consumers and affects trade between Member States, in particular by partitioning national markets.

CoJ 14 February 1978 (United Brands v. Commission, 27/76) [1978] ECR 207, paras 157–159.

[A] producer of pharmaceutical products must be in a position to protect its own **5.131** commercial interests if it is confronted with orders that are out of the ordinary in terms of quantity. Such could be the case, in a given Member State, if certain wholesalers order from that producer medicines in quantities which are out of all proportion to those previously sold by the same wholesalers to meet the needs of the market in that Member State.

In view of the foregoing [Article 102 TFEU] must be interpreted as meaning that an undertaking occupying a dominant position on the relevant market for medicinal products which, in order to put a stop to parallel exports carried out by certain wholesalers from one Member State to other Member States, refuses to meet ordinary orders from those wholesalers is abusing its dominant position. It is for the national court to ascertain whether the orders are ordinary in the light of both the size of those orders in relation to the requirements of the market in the first Member State and the previous business relations between that undertaking and the wholesalers concerned.

CoJ 16 September 2008 (Sot. Lélos kai Sia EE, Joined Cases C-468/06 to C-478/ 06) [2008] ECR I-07139, paras 76 and 77.

(j) Lack of transparency

In the present case, the [General Court] observes that the submission to the public **5.132** authorities of misleading information liable to lead them into error and therefore to make possible the grant of an exclusive right to which an undertaking is not entitled, or to which it is entitled for a shorter period, constitutes a practice falling outside the scope of competition on the merits which may be particularly restrictive of competition. Such conduct is not in keeping with the special responsibility of an undertaking in a dominant position not to impair, by conduct falling outside the scope of competition on the merits, genuine undistorted competition in the common market [...].

It follows from the objective nature of the concept of abuse [...] that the misleading nature of representations made to public authorities must be assessed on the basis of objective factors and that proof of the deliberate nature of the conduct and of the bad faith of the undertaking in a dominant position is not required for the purposes of identifying an abuse of a dominant position [...]. [...]

The [General Court] therefore finds that, in view of the context in which those representations to the patent attorneys and patent offices were made, [AstraZeneca] could not reasonably be unaware that, in the absence of an express disclosure of the interpretation that it intended to adopt of Regulation No 1768/92 which underlay the choice of the dates provided in relation to France and Luxembourg, the patent offices would be prompted to construe those representations as indicating that the first technical marketing authorisation in the Community had been issued in Luxembourg in 'March 1988'. Thus, there was no need for the Commission to demonstrate AZ's bad faith or positively fraudulent intent on its part, it being sufficient to note that such conduct, characterised by a manifest lack of transparency, is contrary to the special responsibility of an undertaking in a dominant position not to impair by its conduct genuine undistorted competition in the common market (see, to that effect, *Nederlandsche Banden-Industrie-Michelin v. Commission* [...], para. 57).

General Court 1 July 2010 (AstraZeneca v. Commission, T-321/05) [2010] ECR II-02805, paras 355, 356 and 493.

Confirmed in CoJ 6 December 2012 (AstraZeneca v. Commission, C-457/10 P), ECLI:EU:C:2012:770.

(k) 'Sham action'

5.133   [L]egal proceedings can be characterised as an abuse, within the meaning of Article [102 TFEU], only if they cannot reasonably be considered to be an attempt to assert the rights of the undertaking concerned and can therefore only serve to harass the opposing party. It is therefore the situation existing when the action in question is brought which must be taken into account in order to determine whether that criterion is satisfied.

Furthermore, when applying that criterion, it is not a question of determining whether the rights which the undertaking concerned was asserting when it brought its action actually existed or whether that action was well founded, but rather of determining whether such an action was intended to assert what that undertaking could, at that moment, reasonably consider to be its rights. According to the second part of that criterion, as worded, it is satisfied solely when the action did not have that aim, that being the sole case in which it may be assumed that such action could only serve to harass the opposing party.

General Court 17 July 1998 (ITT Promedia v. Commission, 111/96) [1998] ECR II-2937, paras 72 and 73.

4. Abuse on secondary markets

[A]n abuse within the meaning of Article [102] is committed where, without any **5.134** objective necessity, an undertaking holding a dominant position on a particular market reserves to itself or to an undertaking belonging to the same group an ancillary activity which might be carried out by another undertaking as part of its activities on a neighbouring but separate market, with the possibility of eliminating all competition from such undertaking.
CoJ 3 October 1985 (CBEM Telemarketing v. CLT and IPB, 311/84) [1985] ECR 3261, para. 27.

It is true that application of Article [102] presupposes a link between the dominant **5.135** position and the alleged abusive conduct, which is normally not present where conduct on a market distinct from the dominated market produces effects on that distinct market. In the case of distinct, but associated, markets, as in the present case, application of Article [102] to conduct found on the associated, non-dominated, market and having effects on that associated market can only be justified by special circumstances.
CoJ 14 November 1996 (Tetra Pak, C-333/94P) [1996] ECR I-5951, para. 27.

5. Abuse of collective dominance

Whilst the existence of a joint dominant position may be deduced from the position **5.136** which the economic entities concerned together hold on the market in question, the abuse does not necessarily have to be the action of all the undertakings in question. It only has to be capable of being identified as one of the manifestations of such a joint dominant position being held. Therefore, undertakings occupying a joint dominant position may engage in joint or individual abusive conduct. It is enough for that abusive conduct to relate to the exploitation of the joint dominant position which the undertakings hold in the market. [...].
General Court 7 October 1999 (Irish Sugar v. Commission, T-228/97) [1999] ECR II-2969, para. 66.

6. Justification

(a) General

[A]lthough the burden of proof of the existence of the circumstances that constitute an **5.137** infringement of Article [102 TFEU] is borne by the Commission, it is for the dominant undertaking concerned, and not for the Commission, before the end of the administrative procedure, to raise any plea of objective justification and to support it with arguments and evidence. It then falls to the Commission, where it proposes to make a finding of an abuse of a dominant position, to show that the arguments and evidence relied on by the undertaking cannot prevail and, accordingly, that the justification put forward cannot be accepted.

General Court 17 September 2007 (Microsoft v. Commission, T-201/04) [2007] ECR II-3601, para. 688.

5.138   [T]he applicants had every opportunity to put forward an objective economic justification of their practices which was not anti-competitive. They could have explained what efficiency gains they thought they might make from their exclusivity agreements, quantity commitments and individualised rebate schemes. However, the applicants do not maintain before the Court that their conduct gave rise to the least discernible efficiency gain, was otherwise justified or resulted in lower prices or any other benefits for consumers.

General Court 9 September 2010 (Tomra v. Commission, T-155/06) [2010] ECR II-04361, para. 224.

Confirmed in CoJ 19 April 2012 (Tomra, C- 549/10P), [2012] ECLI:EU: C:2012:221.

(b)   Objective necessity

5.139   As the Commission has established, there are laws in the United Kingdom attaching penalties to the sale of dangerous products and to the use of misleading claims as to the characteristics of any product. There are also authorities vested with powers to enforce those laws. In those circumstances it is clearly not the task of an undertaking in a dominant position to take steps on its own initiative to eliminate products which, rightly or wrongly, it regards as dangerous or at least as inferior in quality to its own products.

It must further be held in this connection that the effectiveness of the Community rules on competition would be jeopardized if the interpretation by an undertaking of the laws of the various Member States regarding product liability were to take precedence over those rules. Hilti's argument based on its alleged duty of care cannot therefore be upheld.

CoJ 12 December 1991 (Hilti v. Commission, T-30/89) [1991] ECR II-1439, paras 118 and 119.

5.140   Furthermore, the applicant's argument as to the requirements for the protection of public health and its interests and those of its customers cannot be accepted. It is not for the manufacturers of complete systems to decide that, in order to satisfy requirements in the public interest, consumable products such as cartons constitute, with the machines with which they are intended to be used, an inseparable integrated system. [...].

In those circumstances, whatever the complexity in this case of aseptic filling processes, the protection of public health may be guaranteed by other means, in particular by notifying machine users of the technical specifications with which cartons must comply in order to be compatible with those machines, without infringing manufacturers' intellectual property rights. Moreover, even on the assumption, shared by the applicant, that machinery and cartons from various sources cannot be used together without the characteristics of the system being affected thereby, the remedy must lie in appropriate legislation or regulations, and not in rules adopted unilaterally by manufacturers, which would amount to prohibiting independent manufacturers from conducting the essential part of their business.

General Court 6 October 1994 (Tetra Pak International v. Commission, T-83/91) [1994] ECR II-755, paras 83 and 84.

(c) Protecting commercial interests

The [General Court] considers that it is not appropriate for an undertaking in a **5.141** dominant position to take, on its own initiative, measures intended as retaliation against commercial practices which it considers unlawful or unfair. Accordingly, it is irrelevant whether the measures referred to in the Decision were adopted in response to 'appeal' prices applied by certain competitors or [...] to forestall 'appeal' prices which certain merchants intended applying to imported products.

General Court 1 April 1993 (BPB Industries and British Gypsum, T-65/89) [1993] ECR II-389, para. 118.

It must be pointed out first of all that the Commission is in no way disputing the right **5.142** of an operator to align its prices on those previously charged by a competitor. It states [...] that '[w]hilst it is true that the dominant operator is not strictly speaking prohibited from aligning its prices on those of competitors, this option is not open to it where it would result in its not recovering the costs of the service in question'. [...]

Even if alignment of prices by a dominant undertaking on those of its competitors is not in itself abusive or objectionable, it might become so where it is aimed not only at protecting its interests but also at strengthening and abusing its dominant position. [...]

The arguments advanced by WIN as to the economies of scale and learning effects in order to justify its pricing below cost are not such as to call into question the finding made by the [General Court]. An undertaking which charges predatory prices may enjoy economies of scale and learning effects on account of increased production precisely because of such pricing. The economies of scale and learning effects cannot therefore exempt that undertaking from liability under Article [102 TFEU].

General Court 30 January 2007 (France Télécom (Wanadoo) v. Commission, T-340/03) [2007] ECR II-107, paras 176, 187 and 217.

In that respect [...] it is sufficient to state that, in order to appraise whether the refusal **5.143** by a pharmaceuticals company to supply wholesalers involved in parallel exports constitutes a reasonable and proportionate measure in relation to the threat that those exports represent to its legitimate commercial interests, it must be ascertained whether the orders of the wholesalers are out of the ordinary [...].

Thus, although a pharmaceuticals company in a dominant position, in a Member State where prices are relatively low, cannot be allowed to cease to honour the ordinary orders of an existing customer for the sole reason that that customer, in addition to supplying the market in that Member State, exports part of the quantities ordered to other Member States with higher prices, it is none the less permissible for that company to counter in a reasonable and proportionate way the threat to its own commercial interests potentially posed by the activities of an undertaking which wishes to be supplied in the first Member State with significant quantities of products that are essentially destined for parallel export.

CoJ 16 September 2008 (Sot. Lélos kai Sia EE, Joined Cases C-468/06–478/06) [2008] ECR I-07139, paras 70 and 71.

5.144   It should be observed that the preparation by an undertaking, even in a dominant position, of a strategy whose object it is to minimise erosion of its sales and to enable it to deal with competition from generic products is legitimate and is part of the normal competitive process, provided that the conduct envisaged does not depart from practices coming within the scope of competition on the merits, which is such as to benefit consumers.

General Court 1 July 2010 (AstraZeneca v. Commission, T-321/05) para. 804.

Confirmed in CoJ 6 December 2012 (AstraZeneca v. Commission, C-457/10 P), ECLI:EU:C:2012:770.

(d)   Efficiencies

5.145   In deciding whether Michelin NV abused its dominant position in applying its discount system it is therefore necessary to consider all the circumstances, particularly the criteria and rules for the grant of the discount, and to investigate whether, in providing an advantage not based on any economic service justifying it, the discount tends to remove or restrict the buyer's freedom to choose his sources of supply, to bar competitors from access to the market, to apply dissimilar conditions to equivalent transactions with other trading parties or to strengthen the dominant position by distorting competition.

CoJ 9 November 1983 (Michelin v. Commission, 322/81) [1983] ECR 3461, para. 73.

5.146   Assessment of the economic justification for a system of discounts or bonuses established by an undertaking in a dominant position is to be made on the basis of the whole of the circumstances of the case [...]. It has to be determined whether the exclusionary effect arising from such a system, which is disadvantageous for competition, may be counterbalanced, or outweighed, by advantages in terms of efficiency which also benefit the consumer. If the exclusionary effect of that system bears no relation to advantages for the market and consumers, or if it goes beyond what is necessary in order to attain those advantages, that system must be regarded as an abuse.

CoJ 15 March 2007 (British Airways v. Commission, C-95/04) [2007] ECR I-2331, para. 86.

(e) Contestable market

[T]he foreclosure by a dominant undertaking of a substantial part of the market cannot **5.147**
be justified by showing that the contestable part of the market is still sufficient to
accommodate a limited number of competitors. First, the customers on the foreclosed
part of the market should have the opportunity to benefit from whatever degree of
competition is possible on the market and competitors should be able to compete on the
merits for the entire market and not just for a part of it. Second, it is not the role of the
dominant undertaking to dictate how many viable competitors will be allowed to
compete for the remaining contestable portion of demand.
General Court 9 September 2010 (Tomra v. Commission, T-155/06) [2010] ECR
II-04361, para. 241.

Confirmed in CoJ 19 April 2012 (Tomra, C-549/10P), ECLI:EU:C:2012:221.

(f) Intellectual property rights

[M]icrosoft relied as justification for its conduct solely on the fact that the technology **5.148**
concerned was covered by intellectual property rights. It made clear that if it were
required to grant third parties access to that technology, that 'would … eliminate future
incentives to invest in the creation of more intellectual property' […]. In the reply, the
applicant also relied on the fact that the technology was secret and valuable and that it
contained important innovations.

  The [General Court] considers that, even on the assumption that it is correct, the fact
that the communication protocols covered by the contested decision, or the specifications for those protocols, are covered by intellectual property rights cannot constitute
objective justification. […] Microsoft's argument is inconsistent with the raison d'être
of the exception which that case-law [*CoJ 6 April 1995 (RTE v. Commission, C-241/91
P and C-242/91 P) [1995] ECR I-743* and *CoJ 29 April 2004 (IMS Health, C-418/01)
[2004] ECR I-5039*] thus recognises in favour of free competition, since if the mere fact
of holding intellectual property rights could in itself constitute objective justification for
the refusal to grant a licence, the exception established by the case-law could never
apply. […].
General Court 17 September 2007 (Microsoft v. Commission, T-201/04) [2007]
ECR II-3601, paras 689 and 690.

(g) State action defence

According to the case-law of the Court of Justice, it is only if anti-competitive conduct **5.149**
is required of undertakings by national legislation, or if the latter creates a legal
framework which itself eliminates any possibility of competitive activity on their part,
that Articles [101 and 102 TFEU] do not apply. In such a situation, the restriction of
competition is not attributable, as those provisions implicitly require, to the autonomous conduct of the undertakings. Articles [101 and 102 TFEU] may apply, however, if
it is found that the national legislation leaves open the possibility of competition which

may be prevented, restricted or distorted by the autonomous conduct of undertakings
[...].

The possibility of excluding anti-competitive conduct from the scope of Articles
[101 and 102 TFEU] on the ground that it has been required of the undertakings in
question by existing national legislation or that the legislation has precluded all scope
for any competitive conduct on their part has thus been accepted only to a limited extent
by the Court of Justice [...].

Thus, the Court has held that if a national law merely encourages or makes it easier
for undertakings to engage in autonomous anti-competitive conduct, those undertakings remain subject to Articles [101 and 102 TFEU] [...].

*CoJ 14 October 2010 (Deutsche Telekom v. Commission, C-280/08) [2010] ECR
I-09555, paras 80–82.*

E. EFFECT ON TRADE BETWEEN MEMBER STATES

See also paras 4.183–4.200 in Chapter 4 on Art. 101 TFEU.

5.150   The interpretation and application of the condition relating to effects on trade between
Member States contained in Articles [101 and 102 TFEU] must be based on the
purpose of that condition which is to define, in the context of the law governing
competition, the boundary between the areas respectively covered by Community law
and the law of the Member States. Thus Community law covers any agreement or any
practice which is capable of constituting a threat to freedom of trade between Member
States in a manner which might harm the attainment of the objectives of a single
market between the Member States, in particular by partitioning the national markets
or by affecting the structure of competition within the common market. On the other
hand conduct the effects of which are confined to the territory of a single Member State
is governed by the national legal order.

CoJ 31 May 1979 (Hugin v. Commission, C-22/78) [1979] ECR 1869, para. 17.

5.151   [T]he question of the responsibility imposed on a Member State by virtue of Articles
[102 TFEU] and [106(1) TFEU] arises only if the abusive conduct on the part of the
placement agency concerned is liable to affect trade between Member States. That does
not mean that the abusive conduct in question must actually have affected such trade. It
is sufficient to establish that it is capable of having such an effect [...].

CoJ 11 December 1997 (Job-centre, C-55/96) [1997] ECR I-7119, para. 36.

F. RELATION TO ARTICLES 101 AND 106 TFEU

1. Article 101 TFEU

(a) Application of Art. 101(3) does not preclude applicability of Art. 102

[T]he fact that agreements of this kind might fall within Article [101 TFEU] and in **5.152** particular within paragraph (3) thereof does not preclude the application of Article [102 TFEU], since this latter article is expressly aimed in fact at situations which clearly originate in contractual relations so that in such cases the Commission is entitled, taking into account the nature of the reciprocal undertakings entered into and to the competitive position of the various contracting parties on the market or markets in which they operate to proceed on the basis of Article [101 TFEU] or Article [102 TFEU].

CoJ 13 February 1979 (Hoffmann–La Roche, 85/76) [1979] ECR 461, para. 116.

Those considerations do not exclude the case where an agreement between two or more **5.153** undertakings which simply constitutes the formal measure setting the seal on an economic reality characterized by the fact that an undertaking in a dominant position has succeeded in having the tariffs in question applied by other undertakings. In such a case, the possibility that Articles [101 and 102] may both be applicable cannot be ruled out.

CoJ 11 April 1989 (Saeed Flugreisen, 66/86) [1989] ECR 803, para. 37.

(b) Individual exemption under Art. 101(3) does not preclude applicability of Art. 102

[T]he grant of exemption, whether individual or block exemption, under Article **5.154** [101(3) TFEU] cannot be such as to render inapplicable the prohibition set out in Article [102].

[T]he question remains whether, in practice, findings made with a view to the grant of exemption under Article [102](3) preclude application of Article [101]. [...]

[...] Consequently, in applying Article [102], the Commission must take account, unless the factual and legal circumstances have altered, of the earlier findings made when exemption was granted under Article [101](3).

[...] The result is that, where agreements to which undertakings in a dominant position are parties fall within the scope of a block-exemption regulation (that is, where the regulation is unlimited in scope), the effects of block exemption on the applicability of Article [102] must be assessed solely in the context of the scheme of Article [102].

General Court 10 July 1990 (Tetra Pak, T-51/89) [1990] ECR II-309, paras 25, 26, 28 and 29.

(c) Simultaneous application of Arts 101 and 102 TFEU

5.155   It is clear from the very wording of Articles [101](1)(a), (b), (d) and (e) and [102](a) to (d) [TFEU] that the same practice may give rise to an infringement of both provisions. Simultaneous application of Articles [101 TFEU] and [102 TFEU] cannot therefore be ruled out a priori. However, the objectives pursued by each of those two provisions must be distinguished.

Article [101 TFEU] applies to agreements, decisions and concerted practices which may appreciably affect trade between Member States, regardless of the position on the market of the undertakings concerned. Article [102 TFEU], on the other hand, deals with the conduct of one or more economic operators consisting in the abuse of a position of economic strength which enables the operator concerned to hinder the maintenance of effective competition on the relevant market by allowing it to behave to an appreciable extent independently of its competitors, its customers and, ultimately, consumers [...].

CoJ 16 March 2000 (Compagnie Maritime Belge Transports and others v. Commission C-395/96 and C-396/96) [2000] ECR I-1365, paras 33 and 34.

5.156   [A]s far as the existence of a regulatory lacuna is concerned, it should be pointed out that, whilst a minority shareholding of the type in question cannot, prima facie, be regulated under the [Merger Control] Regulation, it might be envisaged that the [TFEU] provisions on competition, and in particular Article [101 TFEU] and Article [102 TFEU], can be applied by the Commission to the conduct of the undertakings involved following the acquisition of the minority shareholding. In this regard it should be recalled that under Article 7(1) of Council Regulation (EC) No 1/2003 of 16 December 2002, where it finds that an infringement of Article [101 TFEU] or of Article [102 TFEU] has taken place, the Commission has the power to impose 'any behavioural or structural remedies which are proportionate to the infringement committed and necessary to bring the infringement effectively to an end'.

Whilst Article [101 TFEU] might, prima facie, be difficult to apply in cases, such as the present, in which the infringement in question arises from the acquisition of shares on the market and, therefore, the necessary meeting of minds might be difficult to establish, the applicant may ask the Commission to initiate a procedure under Article [102 TFEU] if it believes that Ryanair enjoys a dominant position on one or more markets and is abusing that dominant position by interfering with a direct competitor's business strategy and/or by exploiting its minority shareholding in a direct competitor to weaken its position.

Pres. General Court 18 March 2008 (Aer Lingus v. Commission, T-411/07R) [2008] ECR II-411, paras 103 and 104.

2. Article 106 TFEU

[T]he interpretation of Articles [102 TFEU] and [106 TFEU] taken together leads to **5.157** the conclusion that the fact that an undertaking to which a Member State grants exclusive rights has a monopoly is not as such incompatible with Article [102 TFEU]. It is therefore the same as regards an [extension] of exclusive rights following a new intervention by this state.

Moreover, if certain Member States treat undertakings entrusted with the operation of television, even as regards their commercial activities, in particular advertising, as undertakings entrusted with the operation of services of general economic interest, the same prohibitions apply, as regards their behaviour within the market, by reason of Article [106(2) TFEU], so long as it is not shown that the said prohibitions are incompatible with the performance of their tasks.

CoJ 30 April 1974 (Sacchi, 155/73) [1974] ECR 409, paras 14 and 15.

However, Article [102 TFEU] applies only to anti-competitive conduct engaged in by **5.158** undertakings on their own initiative [...], not to measures adopted by States. As regards measures adopted by States, it is Article [106(1) TFEU] that applies.

[W]here the extension of the dominant position of a public undertaking or undertaking to which the State has granted special or exclusive rights results from a State measure, such a measure constitutes an infringement of Article [106 TFEU] in conjunction with Article [102 TFEU].

CoJ 13 December 1991 (RTT v. GB-Inno-BM, C-18/88) [1991] ECR I-5941, paras 20 and 21.

See also the case extracts in Chapter 9 on Art. 106 TFEU.

6

ARTICLE 103 TFEU*

REGULATION REGARDING THE APPLICATION OF ARTS 101 AND 102

1. The appropriate regulations or directives to give effect to the principles set out in Articles 101 and 102 shall be laid down by the Council, on a proposal from the Commission and after consulting the European Parliament.

2. The regulations or directives referred to in paragraph 1 shall be designed in particular:

    (a) to ensure compliance with the prohibitions laid down in Article 101(1) and in Article 102 by making provision for fines and periodic penalty payments;

    (b) to lay down detailed rules for the application of Article 101(3), taking into account the need to ensure effective supervision on the one hand, and to simplify administration to the greatest possible extent on the other;

    (c) to define, if need be, in the various branches of the economy, the scope of the provisions of Articles 101 and 102;

    (d) to define the respective functions of the Commission and of the Court of Justice of the European Union in applying the provisions laid down in this paragraph;

    (e) to determine the relationship between national laws and the provisions contained in this Section or adopted pursuant to this Article.

6.01   [Intrinsic link between provisions on fines and Articles 101 and 102] Community law has established a comprehensive system for monitoring cartels and abuses of dominant positions which sets out a principle of prohibition, contained in Articles [101 and 102 TFEU], and sanctions for its infringement, on the basis of Article [103 TFEU]. Those articles must be understood as forming part of a comprehensive set of provisions designed to prohibit and punish anti-competitive practices.

It is apparent from Article [103(2)(a) TFEU] that the fines and periodic penalty payments which may be imposed on undertakings in connection with the application of Community competition law are designed to 'ensure compliance with the prohibitions

---

*   This chapter was written by Berend Reuder and Weijer VerLoren van Themaat.

laid down in Article [101(1) and 102 TFEU]'. The purpose of Article [103 TFEU] is therefore inter alia to ensure the effective supervision of cartels and abuses of dominant positions.

The Commission's power to impose fines on undertakings which intentionally or negligently commit an infringement of Articles [101(1)TFEU] or [102 TFEU] is one of the means conferred on the Commission in order to enable it to carry out the task of supervision entrusted to it by Community law […].

To dissociate the principle of prohibition of anti-competitive practices from the penalties provided for where that principle has not been observed would therefore deprive of any effectiveness the action taken by the authorities responsible for monitoring compliance with that prohibition and punishing such practices. Thus, the provisions of Articles [101 and 102 TFEU] would be ineffective if they were not accompanied by enforcement measures provided for in Article [103(2)(a) TFEU. […] [T]here is an intrinsic link between the fines and the application of Articles [101 and 102 TFEU].

The effectiveness of the penalties imposed by the national or Community competition authorities on the basis of Article [103(2)(a) TFEU] is therefore a condition for the coherent application of Articles [101 and 102 TFEU].

In proceedings relating to the penalties in respect of anti-competitive practices provided for in Article [103(2)(a) TFEU], the decision that the court seised must give is capable of impairing the effectiveness of those penalties and therefore might compromise the coherent application of Articles [101 TFEU] or [102 TFEU].

CoJ 11 June 2009 (Inspecteur van de Belastingdienst v. X BV, C-429/07) [2009] ECR I-4833, paras 33–38.

[Article 103 TFEU is a] purely procedural [provision].   **6.02**
CoJ 1 July 2010 (Emanuela Sbarigia v. Azienda USL RM/A, Comune di Roma, Assiprofar – Associazione Sindacale Proprietari Farmacia, Ordine dei Farmacisti della Provincia di Roma, C-393/08) [2010] ECR I-06337, para. 30.

In accordance with the provisions of Article 103 TFEU, it is for the European Union to **6.03** lay down the regulations or directives to give effect to the principles in Articles 101 TFEU and 102 TFEU concerning the competition rules applicable to undertakings. That power aims, in particular, to ensure observance of the prohibitions referred to in those articles by the imposition of fines and periodic penalty payments and to define the Commission's role in the application of those provisions.
CoJ 14 September 2010 (Akzo Nobel Chemicals Ltd and Akcros Chemicals Ltd v European Commission, C-550/07 P) [2010] ECR I-08301, para. 117.

[The legislative framework for ex ante regulation of the telecommunications markets] **6.04** has no effect on the competence which the Commission derives directly from Article 3(1) of Council Regulation No 17 of 6 February 1962, First Regulation implementing Articles [81 EC] and [82 EC] (OJ 1962 13, p. 204), and, since 1 May 2004, Article 7(1) of Regulation No 1/2003, to find infringements of Articles [101 and 102 TFEU] […].

[T]he competition rules laid down by the [Treaty] supplement, by ex post review, the legislative framework adopted by the European Union legislature for ex ante regulation of the telecommunications markets […].

Since Telefónica had leeway in which to prevent the margin squeeze […], the conduct of Telefónica penalised in the contested decision was within the scope of Article [102 TFEU] […].

Further, that legislative framework cannot call into question, for the purposes of the application of Article [102 TFEU], the division of competences established at the level of primary law by Articles [103 and 105 TFEU] […].

General Court 29 March 2012 (Kingdom of Spain v. European Commission, T-398/07), ECLI:EU:T:2012:173, paras 109–112.

7

ARTICLE 104 TFEU*

COMPETENCE OF AUTHORITIES IN MEMBER STATES

Until the entry into force of the provisions adopted in pursuance of Article 103, the authorities in Member States shall rule on the admissibility of agreements, decisions and concerted practices and on abuse of a dominant position in the internal market in accordance with the law of their country and with the provisions of Article 101, in particular paragraph 3, and of Article 102.

The term 'authorities in Member States' in Article [104 TFEU] refers to either the **7.01** administrative authorities entrusted, in most Member States, with the task of applying domestic legislation on competition subject to the review of legality carried out by the competent courts, or else the courts to which, in other Member States, that task has been especially entrusted.

CoJ 30 April 1986 (Asjes, Joined Cases 209–213/84) [1986] ECR I-1425, para 55.

[T]he term 'authorities in Member States' within the meaning of Article [104 TFEU] **7.02** does not include the criminal courts whose task is to punish breaches of the law.

CoJ 30 April 1986 (Asjes, Joined Cases 209–213/84) [1986] ECR I-1425, para. 56.

---

* This chapter was written by Berend Reuder and Weijer VerLoren van Themaat.

8

ARTICLE 105 TFEU*

APPLICATION OF ARTS 101 AND 102 BY THE COMMISSION

1. Without prejudice to Article 104, the Commission shall ensure the application of the principles laid down in Articles 101 and 102. On application by a Member State or on its own initiative, and in cooperation with the competent authorities in the Member States, which shall give it their assistance, the Commission shall investigate cases of suspected infringement of these principles. If it finds that there has been an infringement, it shall propose appropriate measures to bring it to an end.
2. If the infringement is not brought to an end, the Commission shall record such infringement of the principles in a reasoned decision. The Commission may publish its decision and authorise Member States to take the measures, the conditions and details of which it shall determine, needed to remedy the situation.
3. The Commission may adopt regulations relating to the categories of agreement in respect of which the Council has adopted a regulation or a directive pursuant to Article 103(2)(b).

8.01   [Article 105 TFEU is a] purely procedural [provision].
CoJ 1 July 2010 (Emanuela Sbarigia v. Azienda USL RM/A, Comune di Roma, Assiprofar – Associazione Sindacale Proprietari Farmacia, Ordine dei Farmacisti della Provincia di Roma, C-393/08) [2010] ECR I-06337, para. 30.

8.02   [I]n accordance with the principle of national procedural autonomy, in the absence of European Union rules governing the matter, it is for the domestic legal system of each Member State to designate the courts and tribunals having jurisdiction and to lay down the detailed procedural rules governing actions for safeguarding rights which individuals derive from European Union law [...].

However, in the present case, the Court is called on to decide on the legality of a decision taken by an institution of the European Union on the basis of a regulation adopted at European Union level, which, moreover, does not refer back to national law.

The uniform interpretation and application of the principle of legal professional privilege at European Union level are essential in order that inspections by the

---

*   This chapter was written by Berend Reuder and Weijer VerLoren van Themaat.

Commission in anti-trust proceedings may be carried out under conditions in which the undertakings concerned are treated equally. If that were not the case, the use of rules or legal concepts in national law and deriving from the legislation of a Member State would adversely affect the unity of European Union law. Such an interpretation and application of that legal system cannot depend on the place of the inspection or any specific features of the national rules.

As far as concerns the principle of conferred powers, it must be stated that the rules of procedure with respect to competition law, as set out in Article 14 of Regulation No 17 and Article 20 of Regulation No 1/2003, are part of the provisions necessary for the functioning of the internal market whose adoption is part of the exclusive competence conferred on the Union by virtue of Article 3(1)(b) TFEU.

In accordance with the provisions of Article 103 TFEU, it is for the European Union to lay down the regulations or directives to give effect to the principles in Articles 101 TFEU and 102 TFEU concerning the competition rules applicable to undertakings. That power aims, in particular, to ensure observance of the prohibitions referred to in those articles by the imposition of fines and periodic penalty payments and to define the Commission's role in the application of those provisions.

In that connection, Article 105 TFEU provides that the Commission is to ensure the application of the principles laid down in Articles 101 TFEU and 102 TFEU and to investigate cases of suspected infringement.

As the Advocate General stated […], national law is applicable in the context of investigations conducted by the Commission as European competition authority only in so far as the authorities of the Member States lend their assistance, in particular with a view to overcoming opposition by the undertakings concerned through the use of coercive measures, in accordance with Article 14(6) of Regulation No 17 or Article 20(6) of Regulation No 1/2003. However, the question of which documents and business records the Commission may examine and copy as part of its inspections under antitrust legislation is determined exclusively in accordance with EU law.

Accordingly, neither the principle of national procedural autonomy nor the principle of conferred powers may be invoked against the powers enjoyed by the Commission in the area in question.

CoJ 14 September 2010 (Akzo Nobel Chemicals Ltd and Akcros Chemicals Ltd v. Commission, C-550/07 P) [2010] ECR I-08301, paras 113–120.

[T]he simple fact that the Commission investigates a cartel which is detrimental to the **8.03** European Union's financial interests and imposes penalties on its members does not mean that the Commission lacks objective impartiality. Otherwise, the mere possibility that the Commission, or indeed any other EU institution, might be the victim of anti-competitive conduct, as referred to in Article [101 TFEU], would have the effect […] of depriving it of its competence to investigate such conduct, which cannot be accepted. It should be noted in particular that under Article [105 TFEU] the tasks entrusted to the Commission by the Treaties include precisely that of ensuring the application of the principles laid down in Articles [101 and 102 TFEU].

CoJ 11 July 2013 (Ziegler SA v European Commission, C-439/11 P), ECLI: EU:C:2013:513, para. 157.

8.04   [If] the parent company and its subsidiary form a single undertaking, the Commission's obligation under Article 105(1) TFEU to ensure the application of the principles laid down in Article 101 TFEU, inter alia, when deciding whether or not to impose a fine applies in the same way, whichever of the two companies is concerned, the parent company or its subsidiary. As the Court has held, there is no 'order of priority' when the Commission is imposing a fine on one or other of those companies.

CoJ 18 July 2013 (The Dow Chemical Company, Dow Deutschland Inc., Dow Deutschland Anlagengesellschaft mbH, Dow Europe GmbH v. European Commission, C-499/11 P), ECLI:EU:C:2013:482, para. 49.

8.05   [T]he Commission, entrusted by Article 105(1) TFEU with the task of ensuring application of the principles laid down in Articles 101 TFEU and 102 TFEU, is responsible for defining and implementing the orientation of European Union competition policy. In order to perform that task effectively, it is entitled to give differing degrees of priority to the complaints brought before it and, for that purpose, it has discretionary power.

General Court 25 November 2014 (Orange v. European Commission, T-402/13), ECLI:EU:T:2014:991, para. 37.

See also General Court 11 July 2013 (Diamanthandel A. Spira BVBA v. European Commission, joined cases T-108/07 and T-354/08), ECLI:EU:T:2013:367, para. 97. and General Court 21 January 2015 (easyJet Airline Co. Ltd v. European Commission, T-335/13) ECLI:EU:T:2015:36, para. 17.

8.06   [T]he Commission would be failing to fulfil the general supervisory role entrusted to it by Article 105(1) TFEU if it were authorised to reject a complaint solely on the ground that a competition authority of a Member State had received a complaint or that it had taken up the complaint of its own initiative, without those acts in any way being followed up and the case in question dealt with.

General Court 17 December 2014 (Si.mobil telekomunikacijske storitve d.d. v. European Commission, T-201/11), ECLI:EU:T:2014:1096, para. 48.

9

ARTICLE 106 TFEU*

PUBLIC UNDERTAKINGS

1. In the case of public undertakings and undertakings to which Member States grant special or exclusive rights, Member States shall neither enact nor maintain in force any measure contrary to the rules contained in the Treaties, in particular to those rules provided for in Article 18 and Articles 101 to 109.
2. Undertakings entrusted with the operation of services of general economic interest or having the character of a revenue-producing monopoly shall be subject to the rules contained in the Treaties, in particular to the rules on competition, in so far as the application of such rules does not obstruct the performance, in law or in fact, of the particular tasks assigned to them. The development of trade must not be affected to such an extent as would be contrary to the interests of the Union.
3. The Commission shall ensure the application of the provisions of this Article and shall, where necessary, address appropriate directives or decisions to Member States. (TFEU 14, 37, 288; Protocol (No 26) on services of general interest).

OVERVIEW

A. ARTICLE 106(1): OBLIGATIONS OF MEMBER STATES REGARDING PUBLIC UNDERTAKINGS   9.01
  1. General   9.01
  2. Examples of (prohibited) measures   9.11

B. ARTICLE 106(2) TFEU: EXCEPTIONAL DEROGATION FROM TREATY RULES   9.26
  1. General   9.26
  2. Definition of 'undertakings entrusted with the operation of services of general economic interest'   9.31
  3. Proportionality test   9.36

C. ARTICLE 106(3) TFEU: COMMISSION POWERS   9.46

D. RELATION TO ARTICLE 107 TFEU   9.55

---

*   This chapter was written by Alvaro Pliego Selie.

A. ARTICLE 106(1): OBLIGATIONS OF MEMBER STATES REGARDING PUBLIC UNDERTAKINGS

See for a definition of 'special rights' and 'exclusive rights' also recital 6 of Commission Directive 94/46/EC of 13 October 1994 amending Directive 88/301/EEC and Directive 90/388/EEC in particular with regard to satellite communications (OJ 1994 L 268/15).

1. General

9.01   [...] The interpretation of Articles [102] and [106] taken together leads to the conclusion that the fact that an undertaking to which a Member State grants exclusive rights has a monopoly is not as such incompatible with Article [102]. It is therefore the same as regards an [e]xtension of exclusive rights following a new intervention by this State.

   Moreover, if certain Member States treat undertakings entrusted with the operation of television, even as regards their commercial activities, in particular advertising, as undertakings entrusted with the operation of services of general economic interest, the same prohibitions apply, as regards their behaviour within the market, by reason of Article [106(2)], so long as it is not shown that the said prohibitions are incompatible with the performance of their tasks.

CoJ 30 April 1974 (Sacchi, 155/73) [1974] ECR 409, paras 14 and 15.

9.02   [W]hile it is true that Article [102] is directed at undertakings, none the less it is also true that the Treaty imposes a duty on Member States not to adopt or maintain in force any measure which could deprive that provision of its effectiveness.

   Thus Article [106] provides that, in the case of public undertakings and undertakings to which Member States grant special or exclusive rights, Member States shall neither enact nor maintain in force any measure contrary inter alia to the rules provided for in Articles [101] to [109].

   Likewise, Member States may not enact measures enabling private undertakings to escape from the constraints imposed by Articles [101] to [109] of the Treaty.

CoJ 16 November 1977 (SA GB-INNO-B.M. v. ATAB, 13/77) [1977] ECR 2115, paras 31–33.

9.03   [E]ven if the approval granted by a Member State must be regarded as the grant of an exclusive right within the meaning of Article [106 TFEU], that would not exempt the Member State from the obligation to respect other provisions of Community law, particularly those relating to the free circulation of goods [...].

CoJ 10 March 1983 (Inter-Huiles, 172/82) [1983] ECR I-555, para. 15.

9.04   [E]ven though Article [106(1) TFEU] presupposes the existence of undertakings which have certain special or exclusive rights, it does not follow that all the special or exclusive rights are necessarily compatible with the Treaty. That depends on different rules, to which Article [106(1) TFEU] refers.

CoJ 19 March 1991 (French Republic v. Commission, C-202/88) [1991] ECR I-1223, para. 22.

[...] Article [102] applies only to anti-competitive conduct engaged in by undertakings on their own initiative [...] not to measures adopted by States. As regards measures adopted by States, it is Article [106(1) TFEU] that applies. Under that provision, Member States must not, by laws, regulations or administrative measures, put public undertakings and undertakings to which they grant special or exclusive rights in a position which the said undertakings could not themselves attain by their own conduct without infringing Article [102 TFEU]. **9.05**

Accordingly, where the extension of the dominant position of a public undertaking or undertaking to which the State has granted special or exclusive rights results from a State measure, such a measure constitutes an infringement of Article [106 TFEU] in conjunction with Article [102 TFEU].

CoJ 13 December 1991 (RTT v. GB-Inno-BM, C-18/88) [1991] ECR I-5941, paras 20 and 21.

[E]ven within the framework of Article [106 TFEU], Article [102 TFEU] of the Treaty has direct effect and confers on individuals rights which the national courts must protect [...]. **9.06**

CoJ 8 June 2000 (Carra and others, C-258/98) [2000] ECR I-4217, para. 17.

It follows from the clear terms of Article [106(1) TFEU] that it has no independent effect in the sense that it must be read in conjunction with the relevant rules of the Treaty. **9.07**

CoJ 19 April 2007 (Asociación Nacional de Empresas Forestales (Asemfo) v. Transformación Agraria SA (Tragsa) and Administración del Estado, C-295/05) [2007] ECR I-2999, para. 40.

In addition, Article [106(1) TFEU] precludes Member States, in the case of public undertakings and undertakings to which they grant special or exclusive rights, from maintaining in force national legislation contrary to Articles [49 and 56 TFEU]. **9.08**

CoJ 17 July 2008 (ASM Brescia SpA v. Comune di Rodengo Saiano, C-347/06) [2008] ECR I-5641, para. 61.

The [amendment of the law] constitutes a State measure within the meaning of Article [106(1) TFEU] as do the enforcement measures by the Slovak authorities against an alleged breach of the reserved area. The Postal Regulatory Office, notwithstanding the fact that it might enjoy independence with regard to the central government and administration of the Slovak Republic, is a public body under Slovak law, invested with public powers and is as such, as regards the application of the Treaty rules, to be regarded as bound by the rules incumbent on the Member States. Enforcement activities of the Postal Regulatory Office are state measures which must conform to the rules of the [EU Treaties]. **9.09**

Commission 7 October 2008 (Slovakian postal legislation, C(2008) 5912), para. 88.

9.10   [Preferential rights for the exploration and exploitation of lignite deposits] [I]nfringement of Article [106 TFEU] in conjunction with Article [102 TFEU] may be established irrespective of whether any abuse actually exists. All that is necessary is for the Commission to identify a potential or actual anti-competitive consequence liable to result from the State measure at issue. Such an infringement may thus be established where the State measures at issue affect the structure of the market by creating unequal conditions of competition between companies, by allowing the public undertaking or the undertaking which was granted special or exclusive rights to maintain (for example by hindering new entrants to the market), strengthen or extend its dominant position over another market, thereby restricting competition, without it being necessary to prove the existence of actual abuse. [...]

     [I]t is sufficient to show that that potential or actual anti-competitive consequence is liable to result from the State measure at issue; it is not necessary to identify an abuse other than that which results from the situation brought about by the State measure at issue. [...]

CoJ 17 July 2014 (Commission v. Dimosia Epicheirisi Ilektrismou AE (DEI), C-553/12P), ECLI:EU:C:2014:2083, paras 46 and 47.

2. Examples of (prohibited) measures

9.11   A national provision or an agreement between national [insurance] bureaux established in the context of the green card system which declares that the national bureau bears sole responsibility for the settlement of claims for damage caused in the territory of that Member State by vehicles insured by foreign insurance companies but which still allows the national bureau or its members to rely on undertakings whose business consists solely in the settlement of accident claims on behalf of insurers in the sense of the handling and investigation of claims, is not incompatible with Article [106(1) TFEU] in conjunction with Articles [101] and [102].

CoJ 9 June 1977 (Van Ameyde, 90/76) [1977] ECR I-1091, para. 22.

9.12   [Funeral Services] Article [106(1)] of the Treaty must be interpreted as precluding public authorities from imposing on undertakings to which they have granted exclusive rights, such as a monopoly in the provision of the 'external services' for funerals, any conditions as to price that are contrary to Articles [101] and [102].

CoJ 4 May 1988 (Bodson v. Pompes funèbres, 30/87) [1988] ECR 2479.

9.13   [Public employment agency including executive search] [a] public employment agency engaged in employment procurement activities is subject to the prohibition contained in Article [102 TFEU], so long as the application of that provision does not obstruct the performance of the particular task assigned to it. A Member State which has conferred an exclusive right to carry on that activity upon the public employment agency is in breach of Article [106(1) TFEU] where it creates a situation in which that agency cannot avoid infringing Article [102 TFEU]. That is the case, in particular, where the following conditions are satisfied:

- the exclusive right extends to executive recruitment activities;
- the public employment agency is manifestly incapable of satisfying demand prevailing on the market for such activities;
- the actual pursuit of those activities by private recruitment consultants is rendered impossible by the maintenance in force of a statutory provision under which such activities are prohibited and non-observance of that prohibition renders the contracts concerned void.

The activities in question may extend to the nationals or to the territory of other Member States.

CoJ 23 April 1991 (Höfner and Elser v. Macroton, C-41/90) [1991] ECR I-1979, para. 34.

See also CoJ 8 June 2000 (Giovanni Carra, C-258/98) [2000] ECR I-4217.

[TV Broadcast services] Article [106(1) TFEU] prohibits the granting of an exclusive **9.14** right to transmit and an exclusive right to retransmit television broadcasts to a single undertaking, where those rights are liable to create a situation in which that undertaking is led to infringe Article [102] by virtue of a discriminatory broadcasting policy which favours its own programmes, unless the application of Article [102] obstructs the performance of the particular tasks entrusted to it.

CoJ 18 June 1991 (ERT v. DEP, C-260/89) [1991] ECR I-2925, para. 38.

[...] Article [106(1) TFEU], in conjunction with Articles [34 TFEU], [45 TFEU] and **9.15** [102 TFEU], precludes rules of a Member State which confer on an undertaking established in that State the exclusive right to organize dock work and require it for that purpose to have recourse to a dock-work company formed exclusively of national workers; [...].

CoJ 10 December 1991 (Porto di Genova, C-179/90) [1991] ECR I-5889, para. 24.

[The mere exercise of the exclusive right necessarily leading to abuse] The mere **9.16** creation of such a dominant position by the granting of an exclusive right within the meaning of Article [106(1)] is not as such incompatible with Article [102 TFEU]. A Member State contravenes the prohibitions contained in those two provisions only if, in merely exercising the exclusive right granted to it, the undertaking in question cannot avoid abusing its dominant position [...].

The alleged abuse in the present case consists in the charging of exorbitant prices by the insemination centres.

The question to be examined is therefore whether such a practice constituting the alleged abuse is the direct consequence of the national law. It should be noted in this regard that the law merely allows insemination centres to require breeders who request the centres to provide them with semen from other production centres to pay the additional costs entailed by that choice.

CoJ 5 October 1994 (La Crespelle, C-323/93) [1994] ECR I-5077, paras 18–20.

See also CoJ 25 October 2001 (Ambulanz Glöckner, C-475/99) [2001] ECR I-8089, para. 39; CoJ 30 March 2006 (Servizi, C-451/03) [2006] ECR I-2941, paras 21–23.

9.17   [Type approval requirements for radio equipment] Article [106(1) TFEU], read in conjunction with Article [102 TFEU], does not preclude the application of national provisions which prohibit the possession of radio transmitters or receivers without ministerial authorization, or the sale or hire of such equipment without a model having been granted type-approval as complying with the technical requirements determined by the competent minister, even if the equipment has been approved in another Member State.

CoJ 27 October 1993 (Lagauche, Joined Cases C-46/90 and C-93/91) [1993] ECR I-5267, para. 51.

9.18   [Approving of tariffs that necessarily leads to abuse of dominance] The mere fact of creating a dominant position by granting exclusive rights within the meaning of Article [106(1) TFEU] is not in itself incompatible with Article [102 TFEU].

However, a Member State infringes the prohibitions in those two articles if, by approving the tariffs adopted by the undertaking, it induces it to abuse its dominant position inter alia by applying dissimilar conditions to equivalent transactions with its trading partners, within the meaning of Article [102(c) TFEU].

CoJ 17 May 1994 (Corsica Ferries, C-18/93) [1994] ECR I-1783, paras 42 and 43.

9.19   [E]xclusive or special rights referred to must generally be taken to be rights which are granted by the authorities of a Member State to an undertaking or a limited number of undertakings otherwise than according to objective, proportional and non-discriminatory criteria, and which substantially affect the ability of other undertakings to provide or operate telecommunications networks or to provide telecommunications services in the same geographical area under substantially equivalent conditions.

CoJ 12 December 1996 (British Telecommunications, C-302/94) [1996] ECR I-6417, para. 34.

9.20   [Public undertaking charging unreasonable port duties pursuant to national regulations] [W]here a public undertaking which owns and operates a commercial port occupies a dominant position in a substantial part of the common market, it is contrary to Article [106(1) TFEU] in conjunction with Article [102 TFEU] for that undertaking to levy port duties of an unreasonable amount pursuant to regulations adopted by the Member State to which it is answerable or for it to exempt from payment of those duties its own ferry services and, reciprocally, some of its trading partners' ferry services, in so far as such exemptions entail the application of dissimilar conditions to equivalent services.

CoJ 17 July 1997 (GT-Link v. De Danske Stadbaner, C-242/95) [1997] ECR I-4449, para. 46.

[I]t is clear that in so far as the scheme laid down by the 1994 Law does not merely **9.21** grant the former dock-work company now reconstituted the exclusive right to supply temporary labour to terminal concessionaires and to other undertakings authorised to operate in the port but also enables it [...] to compete with them on the market in dock services, such former dock-work company now reconstituted will have a conflict of interest.

That is because merely exercising its monopoly will enable it to distort in its favour the equal conditions of competition between the various operators on the market in dock-work services [...].

The result is that the company in question is led to abuse its monopoly by imposing on its competitors in the dock-work market unduly high costs for the supply of labour or by supplying them with labour less suited to the work to be done.

CoJ 12 February 1998 (Raso, C–163/96) [1998] ECR I–533, paras 28–30.

[National rules requires undertaking to deliver their waste to national undertaking] **9.22** Article [106 TFEU], in conjunction with Article [102 TFEU], precludes rules such as the Long-term Plan [for the disposal of dangerous waste], whereby a Member State requires undertakings to deliver their waste for recovery, such as oil filters, to a national undertaking on which it has conferred the exclusive right to incinerate dangerous waste unless the processing of their waste in another Member State is of a higher quality than that performed by that undertaking if, without any objective justification and without being necessary for the performance of a task in the general interest, those rules have the effect of favouring the national undertaking and increasing its dominant position.

CoJ 25 June 1998 (Dusseldorp, C–203/96) [1998] ECR I–4075, para. 68.

[Pension schemes] In the present case, it is important to note that the supplementary **9.23** pension scheme offered by the Fund is based on the present norm in the Netherlands, namely that every worker who has paid contributions to that scheme for the maximum period of affiliation receives a pension, including the State pension under the AOW, equal to 70 per cent of his final salary.

Doubtless, some undertakings in the sector might wish to provide their workers with a pension scheme superior to the one offered by the Fund. However, the fact that such undertakings are unable to entrust the management of such a pension scheme to a single insurer and the resulting restriction of competition derive directly from the exclusive right conferred on the sectoral pension fund.

CoJ 21 September 1999 (Albany, C–67/96) [1999] ECR I–5751, paras 96 and 97.

See also CoJ 21 September 1999 (Brentjens, C–115 and 117/97) [1999] ECR I–6025; CoJ 21 September 1999 (Drijvende Bokken, C–219/97) [1999] ECR I–6121.

In the latter case, the reservation of patient transport services to the medical aid **9.24** organisations entrusted with the public ambulance service is sufficient for that measure to be characterised as a special or exclusive right within the meaning of Article [106(1) TFEU], for protection is conferred by a legislative measure on a limited number of undertakings which may substantially affect the ability of other undertakings to exercise the economic activity in question in the same geographical area under substantially equivalent conditions.

CoJ 25 October 2001 (Ambulanz Glöckner, C-475/99) [2001] ECR I-8089, para. 24.

9.25   [A] legal person whose activities consist not only in taking part in administrative decisions authorising the organisation of motorcycling events, but also in organising such events itself and in entering, in that connection, into sponsorship, advertising and insurance contracts, falls within the scope of Articles [102 and 106 TFEU]. Those articles preclude a national rule which confers on a legal person, which organises motorcycling events and enters, in that connection, into sponsorship, advertising and insurance contracts, the power to give consent to applications for authorisation to organise such competitions, without that power being made subject to restrictions, obligations and review.

CoJ 1 July 2008 (Motosykletistiki Omospondia Ellados NPID (MOTOE) v. Elliniko Dimosio, C-49/07) [2008] ECR I-4863, para. 53.

B. ARTICLE 106(2) TFEU: EXCEPTIONAL DEROGATION FROM TREATY RULES

1. General

9.26   Private undertakings may come under [Art. 106(2)], but they must be entrusted with the operation of services of general economic interest by an act of the public authority.

CoJ 21 March 1974 (Belgische Radio en Televisie v. SV SABAM and NV Fonior, 127/73) [1974] ECR 313, para. 20.

9.27   Even within the framework of Article [106], the prohibitions of Article [102] have a direct effect and confer on interested parties rights which the national courts must safeguard.

CoJ 30 April 1974 (Sacchi, 155/73) [1974] ECR I-409, para. 9.

9.28   In allowing derogations to be made from the general rules of the Treaty on certain conditions, [Art. 106(2)] seeks to reconcile the Member States' interest in using certain undertakings, in particular in the public sector, as an instrument of economic or fiscal policy with the Community's interest in ensuring compliance with the rules on competition and the preservation of the unity of the Common Market.

CoJ 19 March 1991(French Republic v. Commission, C-202/88) [1991] ECR I-1223, para. 12.

9.29   [I]t is for the national court to determine whether the practices of such an undertaking are compatible with Article [102 TFEU] and to verify whether those practices, if they

are contrary to that provision, may be justified by the needs of the particular task with which the undertaking may have been entrusted.
CoJ 18 June 1991 (ERT v. DEP, C-260/89) [1991] ECR I-2925, para. 34.

[I]t follows from the combined effect of paragraphs 1 and 2 of Article [106] that **9.30** paragraph 2 may be relied upon to justify the grant by a Member State, to an undertaking entrusted with the operation of services of general economic interest, of exclusive rights which are contrary to, in particular, Article [102 TFEU], to the extent to which performance of the particular task assigned to that undertaking can be assured only through the grant of such rights and provided that the development of trade is not affected to such an extent as would be contrary to the interests of the Community [...].

The management of particular waste may properly be considered to be capable of forming the subject of a service of general economic interest, particularly where the service is designed to deal with an environmental problem [...].

[A]rticle [106 TFEU], read in conjunction with Article [102 TFEU], does not preclude the establishment of a local system, such as the system in issue in the main proceedings, under which, in order to resolve an environmental problem resulting from the absence of processing capacity for non-hazardous building waste destined for recovery, a limited number of specially selected undertakings may process such waste produced in the area concerned, thus making it possible to ensure a sufficiently large flow of such waste to those undertakings, which precludes other undertakings from processing that waste, even though they are qualified to do so.
CoJ 23 May 2000 (FFAD v. Københavns Kommune, C-209/98) [2000] ECR I-3743, paras 74, 75 and 83.

2. Definition of 'undertakings entrusted with the operation of services of general economic interest'

See for an overview of services of general interest the Communication from the Commission on services of general interest in Europe (COM(2007) 725 final).

An undertaking which enjoys certain privileges for the accomplishment of tasks **9.31** entrusted to it by law, maintaining for this purpose close links with the public authorities, and which is responsible for ensuring the navigability of the State's most important waterway, may fall under Article [106(2) TFEU].

The application of Article [106(2) TFEU] involves an appraisal of the requirements, on the one hand, of the particular task entrusted to the undertaking concerned and, on the other hand, the protection of the interests of the Community. This appraisal depends on the objectives of general economic policy pursued by the States under the supervision of the Commission. Consequently, and without prejudice to the exercise by the Commission of the powers conferred by Article [106(3) TFEU], Article [106(2) TFEU] cannot create individual rights which the national courts must protect.
CoJ 14 July 1971 (Port de Mertert, 10/71) [1971] ECR 723.

9.32   An undertaking to which the State has not assigned any task and which manages private interests, including intellectual property rights protected by law, is not covered by the provisions of Article [106(2) TFEU].

CoJ 27 March 1974 (SABAM, C-127/73) [1974] ECR 313.

9.33   An examination of the aforementioned law shows, however, that the German legislation does not confer the management of copyright and related rights on specific undertakings but defines in a general manner the rules applying to the activities of companies which intend to undertake the collective exploitation of such rights.

Even if it is true that the monitoring of the activities of such companies as provided for by that law goes further than the public supervision of many other undertakings, that is however not sufficient for those companies to be included in the category of undertakings referred to in Article [106(2) TFEU].

CoJ 2 March 1983 (GVL v. Commission, 7/82) [1983] ECR 483, paras 31 and 32.

9.34   Furthermore, it is not apparent either from the wording of Article [106(2) TFEU] or from the case-law on that provision that a general interest task may be entrusted to an operator only as a result of a tendering procedure.

General Court 15 June 2005 (Fred Olsen, T-17/02) [2005] ECR II-02031, para. 239.

9.35   As regards competence to determine the nature and scope of an SGEI [services in the general economic interest] mission within the meaning of the Treaty, and also the degree of control that the Community institutions must exercise in that context, it follows from paragraph 22 of the Communication on SGEIs [OJ 2001 C 17, p. 4] and from the case-law of the [General Court] that Member States have a wide discretion to define what they regard as SGEIs and that the definition of such services by a Member State can be questioned by the Commission only in the event of manifest error […].

That prerogative of the Member State concerning the definition of SGEIs is confirmed by the absence of any competence specially attributed to the Commission and by the absence of a precise and complete definition of the concept of SGEI in Community law. The determination of the nature and scope of an SGEI mission in specific spheres of action which either do not fall within the powers of the Community, within the meaning of the first paragraph of Article [5 TEU], or are based on only limited or shared Community competence, within the meaning of the second paragraph of that article, remains, in principle, within the competence of the Member States. As the defendant and Ireland maintain, the health sector falls almost exclusively within the competence of the Member States. In that sector, the Community can engage, under Article [168 TFEU] and [5 TEU], only in action which is not legally binding, while fully respecting the responsibilities of the Member States for the organisation and provision of health services and medical care. It follows that the determination of SGEI obligations in this context also falls primarily within the competence of the Member States. That division of powers is also reflected, generally, in Article [14 TFEU], which provides that, given the place occupied by SGEIs in the shared values of the Union as well as their role in promoting social and territorial cohesion, the Community and the Member States, each within their respective powers and within the scope of application of the Treaty, are to take care that such services operate on the basis of principles and conditions which enable them to fulfil their missions.

[T]he combination of the obligations of open enrolment, community rating, lifetime cover and minimum benefits is apt to guarantee that the Irish population has wide and simple access to PMI services [private medical insurance system], which entitles those services to be characterised as universal within the meaning of Community law. The applicants' argument that, notwithstanding the mutualisation of premiums resulting from the community rating, the PMI services are not universal because they are not available to all strata of the Irish population, cannot be accepted. First [...] the criterion of universality does not require that the entire population should have or be capable of having recourse to it in practice. Second, the fact that approximately 50 per cent of the Irish population has subscribed to PMI cover indicates that, in any event, the PMI services respond to a very significant demand on the Irish PMI market and that they make a substantial contribution to the proper functioning of the social security system, in the broad sense, in Ireland. Third, that argument does not take account of the fact that, as the applicants themselves acknowledge, the PMI services available on the Irish PMI market may be subdivided into different groups of cover, including in particular basic cover, average cover and 'luxury' cover, which are offered at different prices and which meet separate demand from insured persons.

In that context, the fact that the prices of PMI services are neither regulated nor subject to a ceiling does not affect their universal nature either. While it is true that, in the absence of regulations on premiums for PMI cover, the level of rates for such cover is in principle determined by market forces, the fact none the less remains that, owing to the community rating obligation, the rate fixed is made uniform and applicable to all PMI contracts offering the same cover, independently of the age, sex and state of health of the persons insured. Owing to that uniformity of rates and to competition on rates between the different PMI insurers subject to PMI obligations, to the advantage of all insured persons, the risk of an excessive rate, which would be economically unaffordable for certain groups of persons, in particular as regards basic PMI cover, seems to be very limited in practice. On the contrary, as Ireland submits, community rating permits a cross-subsidy of premiums to the advantage of the most vulnerable insured persons, in particular the elderly and the sick, and ensures that they have easier access to PMI services, whereas such access would potentially be impeded, or indeed excluded, in a market in which rates were risk-based.

Furthermore, the universality criterion does not require that the service in question be free of charge or that it be offered without consideration of economic profitability. The fact that certain potential users do not have the necessary financial resources to take advantage of all the PMI cover available on the market, in particular 'luxury' cover, does not undermine its universal nature provided that the service in question is offered at uniform and non-discriminatory rates and on similar quality conditions for all customers [...].

General Court 12 February 2008 (BUPA, T-289/03) [2008] ECR II-81, paras 166, 167 and 201–204.

3. Proportionality test

9.36   Article [106(2) TFEU] may be app[l]icable to air carriers who are obliged, by the public authorities, to operate on routes which are not commercially viable but which it is necessary to operate for reasons of the general interest. However, for it to be possible for the effect of the competition rules to be restricted pursuant to Article [106(2) TFEU] by needs arising from performance of a task of general interest, the national authorities responsible for the approval of tariffs and the courts to which disputes relating thereto are submitted must be able to determine the exact nature of the needs in question and their impact on the structure of the tariffs applied by the airlines in question.
CoJ 11 April 1989 (Saeed Flugreisen, 66/86) [1989] ECR 803.

9.37   The exclusion or the restriction of competition on the market in telephone equipment cannot be regarded as justified by a task of a public service of general economic interest within the meaning of Article [106(2) TFEU]. The production and sale of terminals, and in particular of telephones, is an activity that should be open to any undertaking. In order to ensure that the equipment meets the essential requirements of, in particular, the safety of users, the safety of those operating the network and the protection of public telecommunications networks against damage of any kind, it is sufficient to lay down specifications which the said equipment must meet and to establish a procedure for type-approval to check whether those specifications are met.
CoJ 13 December 1991 (RTT v. GB-Inno-BM, C-18/88) [1991] ECR I-5941, para. 22.

9.38   [Art. 106(1) TFEU] must be read in conjunction with Article [106(2)] which provides that undertakings entrusted with the operation of services of general economic interest are to be subject to the rules on competition in so far as the application of such rules does not obstruct the performance, in law or in fact, of the particular tasks assigned to them.

That latter provision thus permits the Member States to confer on undertakings to which they entrust the operation of services of general economic interest, exclusive rights which may hinder the application of the rules of the Treaty on competition in so far as restrictions on competition, or even the exclusion of all competition, by other economic operators are necessary to ensure the performance of the particular tasks assigned to the undertakings possessed of the exclusive rights.

As regards the services at issue in the main proceedings, it cannot be disputed that the Régie des Postes is entrusted with a service of general economic interest consisting in the obligation to collect, carry and distribute mail on behalf of all users throughout the territory of the Member State concerned, at uniform tariffs and on similar quality conditions, irrespective of the specific situations or the degree of economic profitability of each individual operation.

The question which falls to be considered is therefore the extent to which a restriction on competition or even the exclusion of all competition from other economic operators is necessary in order to allow the holder of the exclusive right to perform its task of general interest and in particular to have the benefit of economically acceptable conditions.

The starting-point of such an examination must be the premise that the obligation on the part of the undertaking entrusted with that task to perform its services in conditions of economic equilibrium presupposes that it will be possible to offset less profitable sectors against the profitable sectors and hence justifies a restriction of competition from individual undertakings where the economically profitable sectors are concerned.

Indeed, to authorize individual undertakings to compete with the holder of the exclusive rights in the sectors of their choice corresponding to those rights would make it possible for them to concentrate on the economically profitable operations and to offer more advantageous tariffs than those adopted by the holders of the exclusive rights since, unlike the latter, they are not bound for economic reasons to offset losses in the unprofitable sectors against profits in the more profitable sectors.

However, the exclusion of competition is not justified as regards specific services dissociable from the service of general interest which meet special needs of economic operators and which call for certain additional services not offered by the traditional postal service, such as collection from the senders' address, greater speed or reliability of distribution or the possibility of changing the destination in the course of transit, in so far as such specific services, by their nature and the conditions in which they are offered, such as the geographical area in which they are provided, do not compromise the economic equilibrium of the service of general economic interest performed by the holder of the exclusive right.

CoJ 19 May 1993 (Corbeau, C–320/91) [1993] ECR I–2533, paras 13–19.

See also CoJ 23 May 2000 (FFAD v. Københavns Kommune) [2000] ECR I–3743, paras 74 and 75.

Restrictions on competition from other economic operators must be allowed in so far as they are necessary in order to enable the undertaking entrusted with such a task of general interest to perform it. In that regard, it is necessary to take into consideration the economic conditions in which the undertaking operates, in particular the costs which it has to bear and the legislation, particularly concerning the environment, to which it is subject. **9.39**

It is for the national court to consider whether an exclusive purchasing clause prohibiting local distributors from importing electricity is necessary in order to enable the regional distributor to perform its task of general interest.

CoJ 27 April 1994 (Municipality of Almelo and others v. NV Energiebedrijf IJsselmij, C–393/92) [1994] ECR I–1477, paras 49 and 50.

Being a provision permitting derogation from the Treaty rules, Article [106(2)] must be interpreted strictly. **9.40**

The Member States [...] cannot be precluded, when defining the services of general economic interest which they entrust to certain undertakings, from taking account of objectives pertaining to their national policy or from endeavouring to attain them by means of obligations and constraints which they impose on such undertakings.

[F]or the Treaty rules not to be applicable to an undertaking entrusted with a service of general economic interest under Article [106(2) TFEU], it is sufficient that the application of those rules obstruct the performance, in law or in fact, of the special obligations incumbent upon that undertaking. It is not necessary that the survival of the undertaking itself be threatened.

It is true that it is incumbent upon a Member State which invokes Article [106(2)], as a derogation from the fundamental rules of the Treaty, to show that the conditions for application of that provision are fulfilled.

However, as the Court has held [...], contrary to the Commission's contention, it is not necessary, in order for the conditions for the application of Article [106(2) TFEU] to be fulfilled, that the financial balance or economic viability of the undertaking entrusted with the operation of a service of general economic interest should be threatened. It is sufficient that, in the absence of the rights at issue, it would not be possible for the undertaking to perform the particular tasks entrusted to it, defined by reference to the obligations and constraints to which it is subject.

Whilst it is true that it is incumbent upon a Member State which invokes Article [106(2)] to demonstrate that the conditions laid down by that provision are met, that burden of proof cannot be so extensive as to require the Member State, when setting out in detail the reasons for which, in the event of elimination of the contested measures, the performance, under economically acceptable conditions, of the tasks of general economic interest which it has entrusted to an undertaking would, in its view, be jeopardized, to go even further and prove, positively, that no other conceivable measure, which by definition would be hypothetical, could enable those tasks to be performed under the same conditions.

CoJ 23 October 1997 (Commission v. Kingdom of the Netherlands, C-157/94) [1997] ECR I-5699, paras 37, 40, 43, 51, 52 and 58.

See also CoJ 23 October 1997 (Commission v. French Republic, C-159/94) [1997] ECR I-2461, paras 51–59.

9.41   Even if the task conferred on that undertaking could constitute a task of general economic interest, however, it is for the Netherlands Government [...] to show to the satisfaction of the national court that that objective cannot be achieved equally well by other means. Article [106(2) TFEU] can thus apply only if it is shown that, without the contested measure, the undertaking in question would be unable to carry out the task assigned to it.

CoJ 25 June 1998 (Dusseldorp, C-203/96) [1998] ECR I-4075, para. 67.

9.42   The supplementary pension scheme at issue in the main proceedings fulfils an essential social function within the Netherlands pensions system by reason of the limited amount of the statutory pension, which is calculated on the basis of the minimum statutory wage. [...]

If the exclusive right of the fund to manage the supplementary pension scheme for all workers in a given sector were removed, undertakings with young employees in good health engaged in non-dangerous activities would seek more advantageous insurance terms from private insurers. The progressive departure of 'good' risks would leave the sectoral pension fund with responsibility for an increasing share of 'bad' risks, thereby increasing the cost of pensions for workers, particularly those in small- and medium-sized undertakings with older employees engaged in dangerous activities, to which the fund could no longer offer pensions at an acceptable cost.

Such a situation would arise particularly in a case where, as in the main proceedings, the supplementary pension scheme managed exclusively by the Fund displays a high level of solidarity resulting, in particular, from the fact that contributions do not reflect the risk, from the obligation to accept all workers without a prior medical examination, the continuing accrual of pension rights despite exemption from the payment of contributions in the event of incapacity for work, the discharge by the Fund of arrears of contributions due from an employer in the event of insolvency and the indexing of the amount of pensions in order to maintain their value.

Such constraints, which render the service provided by the Fund less competitive than a comparable service provided by insurance companies, go towards justifying the exclusive right of the Fund to manage the supplementary pension scheme.

It follows that the removal of the exclusive right conferred on the Fund might make it impossible for it to perform the tasks of general economic interest entrusted to it under economically acceptable conditions and threaten its financial equilibrium.

CoJ 21 September 1999 (Albany, C-67/96) [1999] ECR I-5751, paras 105 and 108–111.

See also CoJ 21 September 1999 (Brentjens, C-115 and 117/97) [1999] ECR I-6025; CoJ 21 September 1999 (Drijvende Bokken, C-219/97) [1999] ECR I-6121.

9.43 [I]n paragraph 19 of *Corbeau* [*CoJ 19 May 1993 (Corbeau, C-320/91) [1993] ECR I-2533*] the Court held that the exclusion of competition is not justified in certain cases involving specific services, severable from the service of general interest in question, if those services do not compromise the economic equilibrium of the service of general economic interest performed by the holder of the exclusive rights.

[F]irst, unlike the situation in *Corbeau* the two types of service in question, traditionally assumed by the medical aid organisations, are so closely linked that it is difficult to sever the non-emergency transport services from the task of general economic interest constituted by the provision of the public ambulance service, with which they also have characteristics in common.

Second, the extension of the medical aid organisations' exclusive rights to the non-emergency transport sector does indeed enable them to discharge their general-interest task of providing emergency transport in conditions of economic equilibrium. The possibility which would be open to private operators to concentrate, in the non-emergency sector, on more profitable journeys could affect the degree of economic viability of the service provided by the medical aid organisations and, consequently, jeopardise the quality and reliability of that service.

CoJ 25 October 2001 (Firma Ambulanz Glöckner v. Landkreis Südwestpfalz, C-474/99) [2001] ECR I-8089, paras 59–61.

9.44 Article 7(2) of Directive 97/67 allows Member States to continue to reserve cross-border mail to the universal service provider, within certain price and weight limits, '[t]o the extent necessary to ensure the maintenance of universal service'. The same condition applies, in addition, under paragraphs 1 and 2 of that article, to the option of reserving to the universal postal service provider, within certain limits of price and weight, the clearance, sorting, transport and delivery of items of domestic correspondence and direct mail. [...]

The grounds which led the Community legislature to provide for the possibility of such a reservation are explained in recital (16) in the preamble to Directive 97/67, which states that 'the maintenance of a range of those services that may be reserved, in compliance with the rules of the Treaty and without prejudice to the application of the rules on competition, appears justified on the grounds of ensuring the operation of the universal service under financially balanced conditions'. [...]

It is clear from the case-law relating to primary law [...] that the criterion of the financial balance of the universal postal service can validly be taken into account by a Member State when it decides to reserve cross-border mail and that that criterion must in principle [...] be applied, taking into account only services which constitute the universal postal service and not other activities which the universal service provider, where appropriate, may provide. It may be that the latter also carries out other economic activities which must be excluded from the benefit of cross-subsidies from the reserved sectors.

However, it is also clear from that case-law that the condition laid down in Article 7(2) of Directive 97/67 cannot be reduced to a single financial issue, inasmuch as it cannot be ruled out that there may be other reasons for which, in accordance with Article [106(2) TFEU], the Member States can decide to reserve cross-border mail in order to ensure that the universal postal service provider is not prevented from achieving its specific objective.

Considerations, such as expediency, relating to the overall situation in the postal sector, including that linked to the degree of liberalisation of the market at the time when a decision is taken as regards cross-border mail, are not enough to justify the reservation of cross-border mail, unless, in the absence of such a reservation, the achievement of a universal postal service would be prevented, or the reservation is necessary to ensure that the universal service can be provided under acceptable economic conditions.

CoJ 15 November 2007 (International Mail Spain SL v. Administración del Estado and Correos, C-162/06) [2007] ECR I-9911, paras 27, 29 and 39–41.

See regarding services not forming part of the universal postal CoJ 17 May 2001 (TNT Traco SpA v. Poste Italiane SpA and others, C-340/99) [2001] ECR I-4109, paras 52 and 53.

9.45   [I]f the transfer clause and, as a result, the exclusive right of AG2R to manage the scheme for supplementary reimbursement of healthcare costs for all undertakings in the French traditional bakery sector were to be set aside, that body, although required under Addendum No 83 to offer cover to the employees of those undertakings on the conditions laid down in that addendum, would run the risk of suffering the defection of low-risk insured parties, who would have recourse to undertakings offering them comparable or better cover in return for lower contributions. In those circumstances, the increasing share of 'bad risks' which AG2R would have to cover would bring about a rise in the cost of cover, with the result that that body would no longer be able to offer cover of the same quality at an acceptable price.

That would a fortiori be the position in the case of a scheme which, like that at issue in the main proceedings, is characterised by a high degree of solidarity by reason of, inter alia, the fixed nature of the contributions and the obligation to accept all risks.

Such constraints, which render the service provided by the body concerned less competitive than a comparable service provided by insurance companies not subject to those constraints, argue in justification of the exclusive right of that body to manage such a scheme, without there being any possibility of exemption from affiliation.

Consequently, the annulment of a transfer clause such as that laid down in Addendum No 83 could have the result of making it impossible for the body concerned to accomplish the tasks of general economic interest which have been assigned to it under economically acceptable conditions.

CoJ 3 March 2011 (AG2R Prévoyance v. Beaudout Père et Fils SARL, C-437/09) [2011] ECR I-00973, paras 77–80.

C. ARTICLE 106(3) TFEU: COMMISSION POWERS

See also Directive 2006/111/EC on the transparency of financial relations between Member States and public undertakings as well as on financial transparency within certain undertakings (OJ 2006 L 318/17).

[The power] which is conferred upon the Commission [b]y Article [106(3)] thus **9.46** operates in a specific field of application and under conditions defined by reference to the particular objective of that article. It follows that the Commission's power to issue the contested directive depends on the needs inherent in its duty of surveillance provided for in Article [106] and that the possibility that rules might be laid down by the Council, by virtue of its general power under Article [110], containing provisions impinging upon the specific sphere of aids granted to public undertakings does not preclude the exercise of that power by the commission.

CoJ 6 July 1982 (French Republic, Italian Republic and United Kingdom of Great Britain and Northern Ireland v. Commission, Joined Cases 188–190/80) [1982] ECR 2545, para. 14.

It must be held in that regard that Article [106(3) TFEU] empowers the Commission **9.47** to specify in general terms the obligations arising under Article [106(1) TFEU] by adopting directives. […]. In view of its very nature, such a power cannot be used to make a finding that a Member State has failed to fulfil a particular obligation under the Treaty.

CoJ 19 March 1991 (French Republic v. Commission, C-202/88) [1991] ECR I-1223, para. 17.

9.48   If the power to adopt decisions, conferred on the Commission by Article [106(3)], is not to be deprived of all practical effect, the Commission must be empowered to determine that a given State measure is incompatible with the rules of the Treaty and to indicate what measures the State to which the decision is addressed must adopt in order to comply with its obligations under Community law. [...]

Such a power of assessment on the one hand in no way encroaches upon the powers which Article [258 TFEU] confers upon the Court; on the other hand it does not prejudice the rights of the defence which that provision guarantees for Member States.

CoJ 12 February 1992 (Koninklijke PTT Nederland NV and PTT Post BV v. Commission, Joined Cases 48/90 and 66/90) [1992] ECR I-565, paras 28 and 35.

9.49   That principle [respect for the rights of the defence] requires that, before the decision under Article [106(3) TFEU] is adopted, the Member State in question must receive an exact and complete statement of the objections which the Commission intends to raise against it. [...]

In this case [...] the Commission simply raised in general terms the question of the incompatibility of the Postal Law with Article [106(1)] read in conjunction with Article [102 TFEU] without setting out the various features which constituted an infringement of that article as they were subsequently set out in the contested decision.

It must be added that the Kingdom of the Netherlands, after its letter of 16 January 1989, was not given a further hearing by the Commission and in particular had no opportunity to make known its standpoint on the consultations which the Commission had had with the messenger service trade organizations. However, the Commission itself admitted during the written procedure that those consultations had been necessary to allow it to form an opinion on the foreseeable effects of the Postal Law on the operations of the private messenger undertakings.

In these circumstances, it must be declared that the rights of the defence were infringed [...].

CoJ 12 February 1992 (Koninklijke PTT Nederland NV and PTT Post BV v. Commission, Joined Cases 48/90 and 66/90) [1992] ECR I-565, paras 45 and 47–49.

9.50   [A]n individual may not, by means of an action against the Commission's refusal to take a decision against a Member State under Article [106(1) and (3)], indirectly compel that Member State to adopt legislation of general application.

CoJ 20 February 1997 (Bundesverband der Bilanzbuchhalter e.V. v. Commission, C-107/95 P) [1997] ECR I-947, para. 28.

9.51   [T]he Commission's power of supervision vis-à-vis Member States liable for infringing the rules of the Treaty, and particularly those relating to competition, necessarily entails the exercise of a discretion on that institution's part.

That discretion is notably wider in relation to compliance by Member States with the competition rules because, in the first place, Article [106(2) TFEU] requires the Commission to take account, in exercising that discretion, of the demands inherent in the particular tasks of the undertakings concerned and, secondly, because the authorities of the Member States may in some instances have a sufficient degree of latitude in regulating certain matters, such as, in the present case, the organization of public services in the postal sector [...].

In the absence of Community rules governing the matter, the Commission is not entitled to rule on the basis of public service tasks assigned to the public operator, such as the level of costs linked to that service, or the expediency of the political choices made in this regard by the national authorities, or La Poste's economic efficiency in the sector reserved to it [...].

General Court 27 February 1997 (FFSA and others, T-106/95) [1997] ECR II-229, paras 98, 99 and 108.

The wide discretion which the Commission enjoys in implementing Article [106 **9.52** TFEU] cannot undo the protection afforded to individuals by the general principle of Community law that any person must be able to obtain effective judicial review of decisions which may infringe a right conferred by the Treaties. In that connection, the possibility cannot be ruled out that exceptional situations might exist where an individual has standing to bring proceedings against a refusal by the Commission to adopt a decision pursuant to its supervisory functions under Article [106(1) and (3) TFEU].

General Court 3 June 1999 (TF1, T-17/96) [1999] ECR II-1757.

Confirmed in CoJ 12 July 2001 (Commission v. TF1, C-302 and C-308/99 P) [2001] ECR I-5603.

In the first place, the Portuguese Republic's argument that a directive of this type was **9.53** the only way to bring about the simultaneous harmonisation of national systems of airport charges similar to the Portuguese system is immaterial. The effect of that argument is merely to deny that that Member State has an obligation to amend its system of landing charges to bring it into conformity with the Treaty whilst systems of a similar type remain in force in other Member States. It is settled law, however, that a Member State may not rely on the fact that other Member States have also failed to perform their obligations in order to justify its own failure to fulfil its obligations under the Treaty. In the Community legal order established by the Treaty, the implementation of Community law by the Member States cannot be made subject to a condition of reciprocity. Articles [258 and 259 TFEU] provide the appropriate remedies in such cases [...].

CoJ 29 March 2001 (Portuguese Republic v. Commission, C-163/99) [2001] ECR I-2613, para. 22.

See also CoJ 11 January 1990 (Blanguernon, C-38/89) [1990] ECR I-83, para. 7.

Article [106(3)TFEU] requires the Commission to ensure that the Member States **9.54** comply with the obligations imposed on them, in regard to the undertakings covered by Article [106(1) TFEU], and expressly confers on it the power to take action for that purpose by way of directives and decisions. The Commission is empowered to determine that a given State measure is incompatible with the rules of the Treaty and to indicate what measures the State to which a decision is addressed must adopt in order to comply with its obligations under Community law [...].

In the present case, max.mobil, the applicant at first instance, had requested the Commission to find that the Republic of Austria had infringed the combined provisions of Articles [102 and 106(1) TFEU]. It alleged in its complaint that, by not drawing a distinction between the fee charged to max.mobil and that charged to its competitor, Mobilkom, even though the latter company, in its capacity as a subsidiary, received the support of the PTA for the establishment and operation of its GSM network, the Austrian authorities had unlawfully conferred advantages on Mobilkom in the allocation of frequencies.

It follows from paragraph 24 of the judgment in *Bundesverband der Bilanzbuchhalter v. Commission* that individuals may, in certain circumstances, be entitled to bring an action for annulment against a decision which the Commission addresses to a Member State on the basis of Article [106(3) TFEU] if the conditions laid down in the fourth paragraph of Article [263 TFEU] are satisfied.

It follows, however, from the wording of Article [106(3) TFEU] and from the scheme of that article as a whole that the Commission is not obliged to bring proceedings within the terms of those provisions, as individuals cannot require the Commission to take a position in a specific sense.

The fact that max.mobil has a direct and individual interest in annulment of the Commission's decision to refuse to act on its complaint is not such as to confer on it a right to challenge that decision. The letter by which the Commission informed max.mobil that it was not intending to bring proceedings against the Republic of Austria cannot be regarded as producing binding legal effects, with the result that it is not a challengeable measure that is capable of being the subject of an action for annulment. [...]

That finding is not at variance with the principle of sound administration or with any other general principle of Community law. No general principle of Community law requires that an undertaking be recognised as having standing before the Community judicature to challenge a refusal by the Commission to bring proceedings against a Member State on the basis of Article [106(3) TFEU].

CoJ 22 February 2005 (Commission v. T-Mobile Austria GmbH, C-141/02 P) [2005] ECR I-1283, paras 66–70 and 72.

D. RELATION TO ARTICLE 107 TFEU

9.55   [C]ase-law on the application of Articles [101 TFEU] and [102 TFEU], can be applied, mutatis mutandis, to the field of State aid, so that the grant of State aid may, under Article [106(2) TFEU], escape the prohibition laid down in Article [107 TFEU] provided that the sole purpose of the aid in question is to offset the additional costs incurred in performing the particular task assigned to the undertaking entrusted with the operation of a service of general economic interest and that the grant of the aid is necessary in order for that undertaking to be able to perform its public service obligations under conditions of economic equilibrium [...]. Determining whether the aid is necessary entails a general assessment of the economic conditions in which the undertaking in question performs the activities in the reserved sector, without taking account of any benefits it may draw from the sectors open to competition.

General Court 27 February 1997 (FFSA and others, T-106/95) [1997] ECR II-229, para. 178.

[...] The grant of the derogation from the prohibition on State aid laid down in Article **9.56** [106(2) TFEU] requires [...] the fulfilment of three conditions: first, the service in question must be an SGEI and clearly defined as such by the Member State; second, the undertaking in question must have been explicitly entrusted by the Member State with the provision of that SGEI; thirdly, the application of the competition rules of the Treaty – in this case, the ban on State aid – must obstruct the performance of the particular tasks assigned to the undertaking and the exemption from such rules must not affect the development of trade to an extent that would be contrary to the interests of the Community.

General Court 26 June 2008 (SIC – Sociedade Independente de Comunicaço, SA v. Commission, T-442/03) [2008] ECR II-1161, para. 144.

10

ARTICLE 107 TFEU*

GENERAL RULE: PROHIBITION OF AID

1. Save as otherwise provided in the Treaties, any aid granted by a Member State or through State resources in any form whatsoever which distorts or threatens to distort competition by favouring certain undertakings or the production of certain goods shall, in so far as it affects trade between Member States, be incompatible with the internal market.

2. The following shall be compatible with the internal market:
    (a) aid having a social character, granted to individual consumers, provided that such aid is granted without discrimination related to the origin of the products concerned;
    (b) aid to make good the damage caused by natural disasters or exceptional occurrences;
    (c) aid granted to the economy of certain areas of the Federal Republic of Germany affected by the division of Germany, in so far as such aid is required in order to compensate for the economic disadvantages caused by that division. Five years after the entry into force of the Treaty of Lisbon, the Council, acting on a proposal from the Commission, may adopt a decision repealing this point.

3. The following may be considered to be compatible with the internal market:
    (a) aid to promote the economic development of areas where the standard of living is abnormally low or where there is serious underemployment, and of the regions referred to in Article 349, in view of their structural, economic and social situation;
    (b) aid to promote the execution of an important project of common European interest or to remedy a serious disturbance in the economy of a Member State;
    (c) aid to facilitate the development of certain economic activities or

---

* This chapter was updated by Jacques Derenne. (The assistance of Ciara Barbu O'Connor is gratefully acknowledged.) New cases have been inserted (and others removed) in the current structure and division of matters which have not been reviewed yet.

of certain economic areas, where such aid does not adversely affect trading conditions to an extent contrary to the common interest;

(d) aid to promote culture and heritage conservation where such aid does not affect trading conditions and competition in the Union to an extent that is contrary to the common interest;

(e) such other categories of aid as may be specified by decision of the Council on a proposal from the Commission.

OVERVIEW

A. CRITERIA: ARTICLE 107(1) 10.01
  1. Granted by a Member State or through State resources 10.01
  2. Advantage 10.19
  3. Selectivity 10.36
  4. Distortion of competition 10.54
  5. Effect on trade between Member States 10.58

B. DIRECT EFFECT 10.71

C. ARTICLE 107(1) IN RELATION TO OTHER TREATY PROVISIONS 10.75
  1. General 10.75
  2. Free movement of goods 10.80
  3. Competition rules 10.81
  4. Social measures 10.82

D. FORM IN WHICH THE AID IS PROVIDED 10.83
  1. Aim of the measure 10.83
  2. Margin of appreciation 10.85
  3. Concept of 'subsidy' 10.89
  4. Capital injections 10.91
  5. Debt arrangement 10.102

  6. Loans 10.103
  7. Guarantees 10.104
  8. Cross-subsidisation 10.105
  9. Operating aid 10.106
  10. Sale of land 10.107
  11. Privatisation 10.114
  12. Reductions and non-payment of social security 10.115
  13. Fiscal measures 10.116
  14. Non-financial regulatory measures 10.121
  15. Minimum retail prices 10.123
  16. Fixing of tariffs by Member State 10.124
  17. Compensation for damages 10.125

E. ARTICLE 107(2): 'SHALL BE COMPATIBLE WITH THE INTERNAL MARKET' 10.126

F. ARTICLE 107(3): 'MAY BE CONSIDERED TO BE COMPATIBLE WITH THE INTERNAL MARKET' 10.127
  1. Article 107(3)(a) 10.131
  2. Article 107(3)(b) 10.138
  3. Article 107(3)(c) 10.142
  4. Article 107(3)(d) 10.145

NOTICE ON THE NOTION OF STATE AID

The Commission Notice on the Notion of State aid as referred to in Article 107(1) of the Treaty on the Functioning of the European Union (OJ 2016 C 262/1) aims at providing further clarification on the key concepts relating to the notion of State aid as referred to in Article 107(1) TFEU. The European Commission wishes to contribute to a more transparent and more consistent application of this notion across the Union. This will serve as a guide to Member States and undertakings in order to determine whether a public support should be subject to the rules on the control of State aid. The

Notice codifies the case-law of the Court of Justice and of the General Court of the European Union and, in an unprecedented fashion, supplements those findings with the Commission's own findings where there are gaps in the case-law. As to the content of the Notice, there are three notable developments:

- *The chapter 5 on selectivity offers guidance on different aspects of selectively, namely, material selectivity; regional selectivity; fiscal selectivity and similar measures; and a section on specific issues concerning tax measures.*
- *Section 5.4.4. on tax rulings offers guidance as to the question of whether the tax ruling merely applies to the ordinary tax rules or does it misapply tax rules resulting in a lower amount of tax being paid by an undertaking or a category of undertakings.*
- *Chapter 7 on infrastructure addresses whether the construction and operation of infrastructure is an economic activity or not.*

A. CRITERIA: ARTICLE 107(1)

1. Granted by a Member State or through State resources

(a) State resources

10.01   The prohibition contained in Article [107(1)] covers all aid granted by a Member State or through state resources without its being necessary to make a distinction whether the aid is granted directly by the state or by public or private bodies established or appointed by it to administer the aid.

A measure adopted by the public authority and favouring certain undertakings or products does not lose the character of a gratuitous advantage by the fact that it is wholly or partially financed by contributions imposed by the public authority and levied on the undertakings concerned.

CoJ 22 March 1977 (Steinike and Weinlig, 78/76) [1977] ECR 595, paras 21 and 22.

See also CoJ 19 June 1973 (Capalongo, 77/72) [1973] ECR 611.

10.02   [...] The financial advantage which traders derive from receiving a share in a Community tariff quota is not granted through State resources but through Community resources because the levy which is waived is part of Community resources. [...]

Therefore any incorrect application of Community law, even if taking the form of an incorrect allocation of a tariff quota, may only be dealt with as a breach of the relevant provisions of Community law; it may not be regarded as state aid or aid granted through state resources.

CoJ 13 October 1982 (Norddeutsches Vieh-und Fleischkontor, Joined Cases C-213/18–C-215/18) [1982] ECR 3583, paras 22 and 23.

Article [107(1) TFEU] is directed at all aid financed from public resources. It follows **10.03** that aid granted by regional or local bodies of Member States, whatever their status and description, comes under the said provision.
CoJ 14 October 1987 (Federal Republic of Germany v. Commission, 248/84) [1987] ECR 4013, para. 17.

The application by a Member State to merchant vessels entered in its International **10.04** Shipping Register of a system enabling seafarers who are nationals of non-member countries and have no permanent abode or residence in that Member State to be subjected to working conditions and rates of pay which are not covered by the law of that Member State and are considerably less favourable than those applicable to seafarers who are nationals of that Member State does not constitute State aid within the meaning of Article [107(1) TFEU].

A system of that kind does not seek, through its object and general structure, to create an advantage financed from State resources, that is, one which would constitute an additional burden for the State or for public or private bodies designated or established by the State, since its only purpose is to alter, in favour of shipping undertakings, the framework within which contractual relations are formed between those undertakings and their employees. The consequences of this with regard to the basis for the calculation of social security contributions and tax revenue, determined on the basis of low rates of pay, are inherent in the system and are not a means of granting a particular advantage to the undertakings concerned.
CoJ 17 March 1993 (Sloman Neptun v. Bodo Ziesemer, Joined Cases C-72/91 and C-73/91) [1993] ECR I-887, paras 13 and 21.

Only advantages which are granted directly or indirectly through State resources are to **10.05** be regarded as State aid within the meaning of Article [107(1) TFEU]. The wording of this provision itself and the procedural rules laid down in Article [108 TFEU] show that advantages granted from resources other than those of the State do not fall within the scope of the provisions in question. The distinction between aid granted by the State and aid granted through State resources serves to bring within the definition of aid not only aid granted directly by the State, but also aid granted by public or private bodies designated or established by the State.
CoJ 17 March 1993 (Sloman Neptun v. Bodo Ziesemer, Joined Cases C-72/91 and C-73/91) [1993] ECR I-887, para. 19.

See also CoJ 13 March 2001 (PreussenElektra, C-379/98) [2001] ECR I-2099, para. 58, and General Court 11 February 2009 (Iride & Iride Energia v. Commission, T-25/07) [2009] ECR II-245, para. 23.

[Concerning the question whether exclusion of small businesses from a national system **10.06** of protection of workers against unfair dismissal, constitutes aid within the meaning of Article 107(1) TFEU] Only advantages granted directly or indirectly through State resources are to be considered as State aid within the meaning of Article [107(1)].

Such a measure does not entail any direct or indirect transfer of State resources to those businesses but derives solely from the legislature's intention to provide a specific legislative framework for working relationships between employers and employees in small businesses and to avoid imposing on those businesses financial constraints which might hinder their development.

CoJ 30 November 1993 (Kirsammer v. Sidal, C-189/91) [1993] ECR I-6185, paras 16 and 17.

10.07   The judgment in *Case T-358/94 Air France v. Commission*, provides very clear confirmation that Article [107(1) TFEU] covers all the financial means by which the public sector may actually support undertakings, irrespective of whether or not those means are permanent assets of the public sector. Consequently, even though the sums involved in the measure allowing the PMU access to unclaimed winnings are not permanently held by the Treasury, the fact that they constantly remain under public control, and therefore available to the competent national authorities, is sufficient for them to be categorised as State aid and for the measure to fall within Article [107(1) TFEU].

CoJ 16 May 2000 (France v. Ladbroke Racing and Commission, C-83/98 P) [2000] ECR I-3271, para. 50.

See also General Court 12 December 1996 (Air France II, T-358/94) [1996] ECR II-2109, para. 67.

See also General Court 11 February 2009 (Iride & Iride Energia v. Commission T-25/07) [2009] ECRII-245, para. 25, and General Court 10 May 2016 (Germany v. Commission, T-47/15), ECLI:EU:T:2016:281, paras 86–90.

10.08   [T]he case-law of the Court of Justice shows that only advantages granted directly or indirectly through State resources are to be regarded as aid within the meaning of Article 107(1) TFEU. The distinction made in that provision between 'aid granted by a Member State' and aid granted 'through State resources' does not signify that all advantages granted by a State, whether financed through State resources or not, constitute aid, but is intended merely to bring within that definition both advantages which are granted directly by the State and those granted by a public or private body designated or established by the State [...].

[A]s regards the concept of State resources, Article 107(1) TFEU covers all the financial means by which authorities may actually support undertakings, irrespective of whether or not those means are permanent assets of the State. [...]

General Court 15 January 2013 (Aiscat v. Commission, T-182/10), ECLI: EU:T:2013:9, paras 103 and 104.

10.09   With regard to the first of those conditions, the settled case-law of the Court shows that only advantages granted directly or indirectly through State resources are to be considered aid within the meaning of Article 107(1) TFEU. The distinction made in that provision between aid granted by a Member State and aid granted through State resources does not signify that all advantages granted by a State, whether financed through State resources or not, constitute aid but is intended merely to bring within that definition both advantages which are granted directly by the State and those granted by a public or private body designated or established by the State. Thus, the prohibition in Article 107(1) TFEU may also cover, in principle, aid granted by public or private bodies established or appointed by the State to administer aid.

CoJ 30 May 2013 (Doux Élevage and Coopérative agricole UKL-ARREE, C-677/ 11), ECLI:EU:C:2013:348, para. 26.

The undertakings subject to the obligation to purchase retain the charges received from **10.10** final consumers in so far as they do not cover the undertakings' own total additional costs, with the result that part of the funds is not channelled through the account of the Caisse des dépôts et consignations, is not sufficient to exclude there being an intervention through State resources.

CoJ 19 December 2013 (Association Vent De Colère! Fédération nationale, C-262–12), ECLI:EU:C:2013:851, para. 27.

[A]n advantage conferred through State resources is an advantage which, once granted, **10.11** has a negative effect on State resources.

The simplest form that that negative effect can take is a transfer of resources from the State to the party on whom the advantage is conferred. However, according to the settled case-law of the Court of Justice, it is not necessary to establish in every case that there has been a transfer of State resources for the advantage conferred on one or more undertakings to be capable of being regarded as State aid […].

General Court 24 September 2015 (TV2/Denmark v. Commission, T-674/11), ECLI:EU:T:2015:684, paras 195 and 196.

(b) Imputability

[Concerning a measure of a public authority, financed by the authority and subject of **10.12** approval by the government] That judgment is not to be interpreted as meaning that a finding of State aid always presupposes the existence of approval of the public authorities, even where the financial transaction in question was decided upon and financed by a body which is itself part of the public sector. Consequently, even if the investment made by the Caisse in this case was not the subject of approval by the French Government, the fact that the Caisse, belonging to the public sector, used for that investment funds which were at its disposal is sufficient, as explained above, to characterize the investment as State action which may constitute aid within the meaning of Article [107(1) TFEU].

General Court 12 December 1996 (Air France II, T-358/94) [1996] ECR II-2109, para. 68.

In the contested decision, the Commission inferred the imputability of the financial **10.13** assistance granted to Stardust by Altus and SBT to the State simply from the fact that those two companies, as subsidiaries of Crédit Lyonnais, were indirectly controlled by the State.

Such an interpretation of the condition that, for a measure to be capable of being classified as State aid it must be imputable to the State, which infers such imputability from the mere fact that that measure was taken by a public undertaking, cannot be accepted.

Even if the State is in a position to control a public undertaking and to exercise a dominant influence over its operations, actual exercise of that control in a particular case cannot be automatically presumed. A public undertaking may act with more or less independence, according to the degree of autonomy left to it by the State. That might be the situation in the case of public undertakings such as Altus and SBT. Therefore, the mere fact that a public undertaking is under State control is not sufficient for measures taken by that undertaking, such as the financial support measures in question here, to be imputed to the State. It is also necessary to examine whether the public authorities must be regarded as having been involved, in one way or another, in the adoption of those measures.

CoJ 16 May 2002 (France v. Commission (Stardust Marine), C-482/99) [2002] ECR I-4397, paras 50–52.

10.14   The imputability to the State of an aid measure taken by a public undertaking may be inferred from a set of indicators arising from the circumstances of the case and the context in which that measure was taken. In that respect, the Court has already taken into consideration the fact that the body in question could not take the contested decision without taking account of the requirements of the public authorities or the fact that, apart from factors of an organic nature which linked the public undertakings to the State, those undertakings, through the intermediary of which aid had been granted, had to take account of directives issued by a Comitato Interministeriale per la Programmazione Economica (CIPE).

Other indicators might, in certain circumstances, be relevant in concluding that an aid measure taken by a public undertaking is imputable to the State, such as, in particular, its integration into the structures of the public administration, the nature of its activities and the exercise of the latter on the market in normal conditions of competition with private operators, the legal status of the undertaking (in the sense of its being subject to public law or ordinary company law), the intensity of the supervision exercised by the public authorities over the management of the undertaking, or any other indicator showing, in the particular case, an involvement by the public authorities in the adoption of a measure or the unlikelihood of their not being involved, having regard also to the compass of the measure, its content or the conditions which it contains.

CoJ 16 May 2002 (France v. Commission (Stardust Marine), C-482/99) [2002] ECR I-4397, paras 55 and 56.

See also General Court 26 June 2008 (SIC v. Commission, T-442/03), ECR II-1161, paras 93–95.

10.15   In transposing the exemption into national law, Member States are only implementing Community provisions in accordance with their obligations stemming from the Treaty.

Therefore, the provision at issue is not imputable to the German State, but in actual fact stems from an act of the Community legislature.

General Court 5 April 2006 (Deutsche Bahn v. Commission, T-351/02) [2006] ECR II-1047, para. 102.

It is clear that the national authorities cannot actually use the resources resulting from **10.16** the contributions at issue in the main proceedings to support certain undertakings. It is the inter-trade organisation that decides how to use those resources, which are entirely dedicated to pursuing objectives determined by that organisation. Likewise, those resources are not constantly under public control and are not available to State authorities.

Any influence that the Member State may exercise over the functioning of the inter-trade organisation by means of its decision extending an inter-trade agreement to all traders in an industry is not capable of altering the findings made in […] this judgment.

CoJ 30 May 2013 (Doux Élevage and Coopérative agricole UKL-ARREE, C-677/11), ECLI:EU:C:2013:348, paras 36 and 37.

(c) Trade association governed by public law

[T]he mere fact that a system of subsidies which benefits certain traders in a specific **10.17** sector is financed by a parafiscal charge levied on every supply of national goods in that sector is not sufficient to divest the system of its character as aid granted by a Member State within the meaning of Article [107 TFEU]. […] When, as in this instance, the proceeds of the charge are used to finance investments in technologically advanced equipment intended to improve productivity and product quality so as to enable the sector in question to compete with imports more effectively, the system cannot be regarded as neutral in terms of trade.

CoJ 11 November 1987 (France v. Commission, 259/85) [1987] ECR 4393, para. 23.

Having regard to all the foregoing considerations, the answer to be given to the three **10.18** first questions must be that on a proper construction of Articles [107(1) and 108(3) TFEU], bye-laws adopted by a trade association governed by public law for the purpose of funding an advertising campaign organised for the benefit of its members and decided on by them, through resources levied from those members and compulsorily earmarked for the funding of that campaign, do not constitute an integral part of an aid measure within the meaning of those provisions and it was not necessary for prior notification of them to be given to the Commission since it has been established that that funding was carried out by means of resources which that trade association, governed by public law, never had the power to dispose of freely.

CoJ 15 July 2004 (Pearle, C-345/02) [2004] ECR I-7139, para. 41.

2. Advantage

(a) Market economy investor principle

(i) Notion

10.19   The Commission showed itself to be aware of the implications of the principle of equal treatment as between public and private undertakings in its communication to the Member States of 17 September 1984 on public authorities' holdings in company capital (published in the Bulletin of the European Communities, September 1984). In that statement it correctly observes that its action may neither penalize nor favour public authorities which provide companies with equity capital.

It follows from that principle of equal treatment that capital placed by the State, directly or indirectly, at the disposal of an undertaking in circumstances which correspond to normal market conditions cannot be regarded as State aid. In the present case it must therefore be determined whether, in similar circumstances, a private industrial group might also have made up the operating losses of the four subsidiaries between 1983 and 1987.

CoJ 21 March 1991 (Italian Republic v. Commission, C-303/88) [1991] ECR I-1433, paras 19 and 20.

10.20   In order to determine whether a measure constitutes State aid it is necessary to consider whether in similar circumstances a private investor of a size comparable to that of the bodies administering the public sector might have provided injections of capital of such an amount [...].

[A]lthough the conduct of a private investor, with which the intervention of a public investor pursuing economic policy aims must be compared, need not be conduct of an ordinary investor laying out capital with a view to realizing a profit in the relatively short term, it must at least be the conduct of private holding company or a private group of undertakings pursuing a structural policy—whether general or sectoral—guided by prospects of profitability in the long term [...].

CoJ 14 September 1994 (Spain v. Commission, C-42/93) [1994] ECR I-4175, paras 13 and 14.

See also General Court 17 December 2015 (SNCF v. Commission, T-242/12), ECLI:EU:T:2015:1003, paras 291 and 292.

10.21   According to settled case-law, the charging by a Member State, or an entity on which it exerts influence, of a tariff fixed at a level lower than that which would normally be chosen may be regarded as aid for the purposes of Article [107(1) TFEU]. In such circumstances, the State, or the entity on which it exerts influence, does not apply the preferential tariff as an ordinary economic agent but uses it to confer a financial advantage on certain undertakings by forgoing the profit which it would normally realize. On the other hand, a preferential tariff does not constitute aid if, in the context of the market in question, it is objectively justified by economic reasons such as the need to withstand competition on the same market.

Since a complex economic appraisal is involved here, it should also be noted that, according to the case-law, in reviewing an act of the Commission which has necessitated such an appraisal, the Court must confine itself to verifying whether the Commission complied with the relevant rules governing procedure and the statement of reasons, whether the facts on which the contested finding was based have been accurately stated and whether there has been any manifest error of assessment or a misuse of powers.

CoJ 29 February 1996 (Belgium v. Commission, C-56/93) [1996] ECR I-723, paras 10 and 11.

As regards the classification of the disputed measures by the public authorities – acting **10.22** as an economic operator or through the intermediary of an economic operator – in favour of an undertaking, it should be noted that the Commission is entitled to use the private-investor test, which consists in determining whether the undertaking which benefited from the measure in question could have obtained the same economic advantages from a private investor operating under market conditions.

General Court 29 June 2000 (DSG v. Commission, T-234/95) [2000] ECR II-2603, para. 119.

It must be remembered that the assessment by the Commission of whether an **10.23** investment satisfies the private-investor test involves a complex economic appraisal. When the Commission adopts a measure involving such an appraisal, it consequently enjoys a wide discretion and judicial review is limited to verifying whether the Commission complied with the relevant rules governing procedure and the statement of reasons, whether there was any error of law, whether the facts on which the contested finding was based have been accurately stated and whether there has been any manifest error of assessment of those facts or any misuse of powers. In particular, the General Court is not entitled to substitute its own economic assessment for that of the author of the decision.

General Court 17 December 2008 (Ryanair Ltd v. Commission, T-196/04) [2008] ECR II-3643, para. 41.

It is however necessary, when applying the private-investor test, to envisage the **10.24** commercial transaction as a whole in order to determine whether the public entity and the entity which is controlled by it, taken together, have acted as rational operators in a market economy. The Commission must, when assessing the measures at issue, examine all the relevant features of the measures and their context, including those relating to the situation of the authority or authorities responsible for granting the measures at issue.

General Court 17 December 2008 (Ryanair Ltd v. Commission, T-196/04) [2008] ECR II-3643, para. 59.

The mere fact that, in the present case, the Walloon Region has regulatory powers in **10.25** relation to fixing airport charges does not mean that a scheme reducing those charges ought not to be examined by reference to the private-investor principle, since such a scheme could have been put in place by a private operator.

General Court 17 December 2008 (Ryanair Ltd v. Commission, T-196/04) [2008] ECR II-3643, para. 101.

10.26   In order to determine whether measures taken by the State represent the exercise of State authority or whether they are the consequence of obligations that the State must assume as shareholder, it is important to look not at the form of those measures, but at their nature, their subject-matter and the rules to which they are subject, while taking into account the objective pursued […].

Accordingly, in the case of an undertaking whose share capital is owned by the public authorities it must be considered whether, in similar circumstances, a private investor of a stature comparable to that of the bodies administering the public sector would have provided contributions of capital of the same size, having regard to the foreseeability of obtaining a return and leaving aside all social, regional-policy and sectoral consider- ations […].

Finally, it must be pointed out that the fact that the actions of the State as shareholder are assessed by the yardstick of a prudent private investor, whereas the actions of any normal private investor are not, does not constitute a failure to treat the State and such a private investor equally, since the State as shareholder is not in the same situation as a private investor. Unlike a private investor, who can count only on his own resources in order to finance his investments, the State has access to financial resources flowing from the exercise of public power, in particular from taxation […].

Consequently, the mere fact that the State has access to financial resources accrued through the exercise of State authority is not in itself sufficient justification for regarding the State's actions as attributable to the exercise of State authority. If it were, application of the prudent private-investor test to the conduct of a State which is a shareholder could well be futile or, at least, of disproportionately limited value, since, as a State, it inevitably has recourse to financial resources accrued through the exercise of public power, in particular from taxation.

General Court 15 December 2009 (EDF v. Commission, T-156/04) [2009] ECR II-4503, paras 229–232.

See also CoJ 5 June 2012 (Commission v. EDF, C-124/10 P), ECLI:EU: C:2012:318; General Court 11 September 2012 (Corsica Ferries France v. Commis- sion, T-565/08), ECLI:EU:T:2012:415, paras 79 and 80; CoJ 4 September 2014 (SNCM & France v. Corsica Ferries France, C-533/12 P and C-536/12 P, ECLI:EU:C:2014:2142, paras 30–41.

(ii)   Behaviour of private investor in comparable circumstances (pari passu)

10.27   All investments made by the Scheme in Venture Capital Funds will be made *pari passu* with the other investors. The terms of investment of these other investors, in terms of the risks, rewards, fiscal treatment, etc. are unaffected by the Scheme. It can therefore be considered that the interventions made by the Scheme respect the market economy investor principle.

Commission 14 October 2000 (Ireland – Seed and Venture Capital Fund Scheme), N 172/2000, SG(2000) D/107/07595.

The [General Court] observes that the test based on the conduct of a private investor **10.28** operating in normal market-economy conditions ensues from the principle that the public and private sectors are to be treated equally, pursuant to which capital placed directly or indirectly at the disposal of an undertaking by the State in circumstances which correspond to normal market conditions cannot be regarded as State aid.

A capital contribution from public funds must therefore be regarded as satisfying the private-investor test and not constituting State aid if, inter alia, it was made at the same time as a significant capital contribution on the part of a private investor made in comparable circumstances.
General Court 12 December 2000 (Alitalia v. Commission, T-296/97) [2000] ECR II-3871, paras 80 and 81.

See also Press release, European Commission of 19 July 2005, IP/95/805.

A guarantee measure, which involves the obligation for State authorities, inter alia **10.29** regional ones, to intervene in the event of insolvency or liquidation of the credit institution in question. Under that guarantee, the creditors of the credit institutions can exercise a direct right against the public authority acting as guarantor in a situation where the credit institution is in liquidation or insolvent and the assets of that institution do not suffice to satisfy them. [...]

What is decisive when applying the private-operator test is whether the measures in question are those which a private operator in a market economy, who counts on making a profit in the shorter or longer term, could have granted. Thus, regardless of how the commitments at issue could have been classified, the fundamental question which arises is that of whether those commitments are among those which could have been entered into by a private operator in a market economy.
General Court 28 February 2012 (Land Burgenland and Austria v. Commission, T-268/08 and T-281/08), ECLI:EU:T:2012:90, paras 149 and 157.

(b) Services of general economic interest

Article [107(1) TFEU] does not distinguish between measures of State intervention by **10.30** reference to their causes or aims but defines them in relation to their effects [...]. It follows that the concept of aid is an objective one, the test being whether a State measure confers an advantage on one or more particular undertakings [...].

[T]he fact that a financial advantage is granted to an undertaking by the public authorities to offset the cost of public service obligations which that undertaking is claimed to have assumed has no bearing on the classification of that measure as aid, although that aspect may be taken into account when considering whether the aid in question is compatible with the common market [...].
General Court 10 May 2000 (SIC v. Commission, T-46/97) [2000] ECR II-2125, paras 83 and 84.

10.31   It follows from the case-law that, where a State measure must be regarded as compensation for the services provided by the recipient undertakings in order to discharge public service obligations, so that those undertakings do not enjoy a real financial advantage and the measure thus does not have the effect of putting them in a more favourable competitive position than the undertakings competing with them, such a measure is not caught by Article [107(1) TFEU].

CoJ 24 July 2003 (Altmark Trans, C-280/00) [2003] ECR I-7747, para. 87.

See also General Court 16 September 2004 (Valmont v. Commission T-274/01), ECR II-3145, para. 129.

10.32   However, for such compensation to escape classification as State aid in a particular case, a number of conditions must be satisfied.

First, the recipient undertaking must actually have public service obligations to discharge, and the obligations must be clearly defined. In the main proceedings, the national court will therefore have to examine whether the public service obligations which were imposed on Altmark Trans are clear from the national legislation and/or the licences at issue in the main proceedings.

Second, the parameters on the basis of which the compensation is calculated must be established in advance in an objective and transparent manner, to avoid it conferring an economic advantage which may favour the recipient undertaking over competing undertakings.

Payment by a Member State of compensation for the loss incurred by an undertaking without the parameters of such compensation having been established beforehand, where it turns out after the event that the operation of certain services in connection with the discharge of public service obligations was not economically viable, therefore constitutes a financial measure which falls within the concept of State aid within the meaning of Article [107(1) TFEU].

Third, the compensation cannot exceed what is necessary to cover all or part of the costs incurred in the discharge of public service obligations, taking into account the relevant receipts and a reasonable profit for discharging those obligations. Compliance with such a condition is essential to ensure that the recipient undertaking is not given any advantage which distorts or threatens to distort competition by strengthening that undertaking's competitive position.

Fourth, where the undertaking which is to discharge public service obligations, in a specific case, is not chosen pursuant to a public procurement procedure which would allow for the selection of the tenderer capable of providing those services at the least cost to the community, the level of compensation needed must be determined on the basis of an analysis of the costs which a typical undertaking, well run and adequately provided with means of transport so as to be able to meet the necessary public service requirements, would have incurred in discharging those obligations, taking into account the relevant receipts and a reasonable profit for discharging the obligations.

It follows from the above considerations that, where public subsidies granted to undertakings expressly required to discharge public service obligations in order to compensate for the costs incurred in discharging those obligations comply with the conditions set out in paragraphs 89 to 93 above, such subsidies do not fall within Article

[107(1)TFEU]. Conversely, a State measure which does not comply with one or more of those conditions must be regarded as State aid within the meaning of that provision.
CoJ 24 July 2003 (Altmark Trans, C-280/00) [2003] ECR I-7747, paras 88–94.

See also General Court 16 September 2004 (Valmont v. Commission T-274/01), ECR II-3145, para. 131; General Court 1 July 2008 (Deutsche Post v. Commission T-266/02), ECR II-1233, para. 73.

[I]f a measure concerning the allocation by a Member State of a significant proportion **10.33** of charges [...] to a public undertaking is not linked to clearly defined public-service duties and/or if other conditions, such as those laid down in *Altmark Trans* [...], are not complied with, that measure must be classified as State aid within the meaning of [Art. 107(1) TFEU] in so far as it affects trade between Member States.
CoJ 27 November 2003 (Enirisorse, Joined Cases C-34/01 to C-38/01) [2003] ECR I-14243, para. 40.

See also General Court 24 September 2015 (TV2/Denmark v. Commission, T-674/11), ECLI:EU:T:2015:684.

[T]he Member State has a wide discretion not only when defining an SGEI mission **10.34** but also when determining the compensation for the costs, which calls for an assessment of complex economic facts [...].
General Court 12 February 2008 (BUPA v. Commission, T-289/03) [2008] ECR II-81, para. 214.

According to the fourth criterion laid down by the *Altmark* judgment, where the **10.35** undertaking which is to discharge public service obligations, in a specific case, is not chosen pursuant to a public procurement procedure, the level of compensation needed must be determined on the basis of an analysis of the costs which a typical undertaking, well run and adequately provided so as to be able to meet the necessary public service requirements, would have incurred in discharging those obligations, taking into account the relevant receipts and a reasonable profit for discharging the obligations. [...]

[T]he fourth *Altmark* criterion is not taken into account for assessing the compatibility of aid measures under Article [106(2) TFEU], since the conditions for that compatibility are different from the criteria in the *Altmark* judgment, which were laid down in order to assess the existence of State aid [...].
General Court 7 November 2012 (CBI v. Commission, T-137/10), ECLI:EU:T: 2012:584, paras 289 and 292.

3. Selectivity

(a) General

10.36   It must also be noted that FNE intervention is not limited sectorially or territorially or by reference to a restricted category of undertakings.

However, as the Commission has rightly pointed out, the FNE enjoys a degree of latitude which enables it to adjust its financial assistance having regard to a number of considerations such as, in particular, the choice of beneficiaries, the amount of the financial assistance and the conditions under which it is provided. The French Government itself concedes that the administration may depart from its own guidelines where particular circumstances justify that course of action.

In those circumstances, it must be held that, by virtue of its aim and general scheme, the system under which the FNE contributes to measures accompanying social plans is liable to place certain undertakings in a more favourable situation than others and thus to meet the conditions for classification as aid within the meaning of Article [107(1) TFEU].

CoJ 26 September 1996 (France v. Commission, C-241/94) [1996] ECR I-4551, paras 22–24.

10.37   [M]easures of purely general application do not fall within the ambit of Article 92(1) of the Treaty. However, the case-law has already made it clear that even interventions which, prima facie, apply to undertakings in general may be to a certain extent selective and, accordingly, be regarded as measures designed to favour certain undertakings or the production of certain goods. That is the case, in particular, where the administration called upon to apply a general rule has a discretionary power so far as concerns the application of the measure [...].

General Court 6 March 2002 (Diputación Foral de Álava and Others v. Commission, T-127/99, T-129/99 and T-148/99) [2002] ECR II-1275, para. 149.

10.38   [D]iscrimination consists in particular in treating like cases differently, involving a disadvantage for some operators in relation to others, without that difference in treatment being justified by the existence of substantial objective differences [...].

CoJ 26 September 2002 (Spain v. Commission, C-351/98) [2002] ECR I-8031, para. 57.

10.39   Article [107(1) TFEU] requires it to be determined whether, under a particular statutory scheme, a State measure is such as to favour 'certain undertakings or the production of certain goods' in comparison with others which, in the light of the objective pursued by the system in question, are in a comparable legal and factual situation. If that is the case, the measure concerned satisfies the condition of selectivity which is a constituent of the concept of State aid under that provision.

CoJ 29 April 2004 (GIL Insurance and others, C-308/01) [2004] ECR I-4777, para. 68.

See also CoJ 8 November 2001 (Adria-Wien Pipeline, C-143/99) [2001] ECR I-8365, para. 41.

(b)   Regional selectivity

10.40 It is possible that an infra-State body enjoys a legal and factual status which makes it sufficiently autonomous in relation to the central government of a Member State, with the result that, by the measures it adopts, it is that body and not the central government which plays a fundamental role in the definition of the political and economic environment in which undertakings operate. In such a case it is the area in which the infra-State body responsible for the measure exercises its powers, and not the country as a whole, that constitutes the relevant context for the assessment of whether a measure adopted by such a body favours certain undertakings in comparison with others in a comparable legal and factual situation, having regard to the objective pursued by the measure or the legal system concerned. [...]

In order to determine the selectivity of a measure adopted by an infra-State body which, like the measure at issue, seeks to establish in one part of the territory of a Member State a tax rate which is lower than the rate in force in the rest of that State it is appropriate, as stated in paragraph 58 of this judgment, to examine whether that measure was adopted by that body in the exercise of powers sufficiently autonomous vis-à-vis the central power and, if appropriate, to examine whether that measure indeed applies to all the undertakings established in or all production of goods on the territory coming within the competence of that body.

CoJ 6 September 2006 (Portugal v. Commission, C-88/03) [2006] ECR I-7115, paras 58 and 62.

(c)   Selectivity in the context of taxation

10.41 According to the case-law of the Court, aid in the form of an aid programme may concern a whole economic sector and still be covered by Article [107(1) TFEU] and a measure designed to give the undertakings of a particular industrial sector a partial reduction of the financial charges arising from the normal application of the general social security system, without there being any justification for this exemption on the basis of the nature or general scheme of this system, must be regarded as aid.

CoJ 17 June 1999 (Belgium v. Commission, C-75/97) [1999] ECR I-03671, para. 33.

See also CoJ 2 July 1974 (Italy v. Commission, 173/73) [1974] ECR I-709, para. 33.

10.42   According to the case-law of the Court, a measure which, although conferring an advantage on its recipient, is justified by the nature or general scheme of the system of which it is part does not fulfil that condition of selectivity.

CoJ 8 November 2001 (Adria-Wien Pipeline, C-143/99) [2001] ECR I-8365, para 42.

10.43   It is true that the concept of aid has been interpreted by the Court as not encompassing differential treatment of undertakings in the application of charges, where that differential treatment flows from the nature and general scheme of the system of charges in question.

However, in the present case the charges in question arise as a result of the undertakings' need to replace their commercial vehicles and normally come out of those undertakings' budgets. Accordingly, the support given to certain undertakings in funding part of those charges is not a consequence of the nature or general scheme of the system of charges in question and must be considered to favour those undertakings. In those circumstances the reasons cited by the Spanish Government to explain why large undertakings are ineligible under the Plan can only be viewed as justifying the way in which the measure is targeted, not as enabling the measure to escape classification as aid.

CoJ 26 September 2002 (Spain v. Commission, C-351/98) [2002] ECR I-8031, paras 42 and 43.

10.44   As the Commission itself states in paragraph 16 of the notice relating to State aid in the field of direct business taxation, in order for it to classify a tax measure as selective, it must begin by identifying and examining the common or 'normal' regime under the tax system applicable in the geographical area constituting the relevant reference framework. It is in relation to this common or 'normal' tax regime that the Commission must, secondly, assess and determine whether any advantage granted by the tax measure at issue may be selective by demonstrating that the measure derogates from that common regime inasmuch as the measure differentiates between economic operators who, in light of the objective assigned to the tax system of the Member State concerned, are in a comparable factual and legal situation.

If the Commission, in the course of the first two stages of its assessment as referred to in paragraph 143 above, has demonstrated the existence of derogations from the common or 'normal' tax regime resulting in a differentiation between undertakings, it is clear from settled case-law that such a differentiation is none the less not selective when it arises from the nature or general scheme of the system of charges of which it forms part. In that situation, the Commission must determine, in a third stage, whether the State measure in question is not selective in nature even though it gives an advantage to the undertakings which are able to benefit from it. In that regard, given that the differentiations provided for vis-à-vis the common or 'normal' tax regime constitute derogations and are prima facie selective, it is for the Member State to show that those differentiations are justified by the nature and general scheme of its tax system in that they derive directly from the basic or guiding principles of that system. In that context, a distinction must be made between, on the one hand, the objectives attributed to a particular tax regime and which are extrinsic to it and, on the other, the mechanisms inherent in the tax system itself which are necessary for the achievement of such objectives.

It should be added that, if the Commission has failed to carry out the first two stages of the review of a measure's selectivity, it cannot embark upon the third and final stage of its assessment, as otherwise it will go beyond the limits of that review. Such an approach would be liable, first, to enable the Commission to assume the role of the Member State with regard to determination of that State's tax system and of the common or 'normal' regime under it, including in relation to the objectives, the tax system's inherent mechanisms for achieving those objectives and its bases of taxation, and second, thus to make it impossible for the Member State to justify the differentiations in question on the basis of the nature and of the general scheme of the tax system notified, since the Commission would not first either have identified the common or 'normal' regime under that system or have established that those differentiations constitute derogations from that regime.

General Court 18 December 2008 (Gibraltar v. Commission, T-211/04 and T-215/ 04) [2008] ECR II-3745, paras 143–145.

See also CoJ 15 November 2011 (Commission and Spain v. Government of Gibraltar and UK, C-106/09 P and C-107/09 P) [2011] ECR I-11113, paras 145 and 146.

In the light of the case-law, the unavoidable conclusion is that the General Court **10.45** disregarded Article [107(1) TFEU], as interpreted by the Court of Justice, by holding that Member States are free, in balancing the various interests involved, to set their priorities as regards the protection of the environment and, as a result, to determine which goods or services they decide to subject to an environmental levy, with the result that the fact that such a levy does not apply to all similar activities which have a comparable impact on the environment does not mean that similar activities, which are not subject to the levy, benefit from a selective advantage.

CoJ 22 December 2008 (British Aggregates v. Commission, C-487/06 P) [2008] ECR I-0505, para. 86.

Even if that system could be described as an exceptional fiscal burden on a narrowly **10.46** defined economic sector, that in itself does not mean that that fiscal burden falls outside the prohibition laid down in Article [107(1) TFEU], since the capacity of that system to differentiate within that sector may satisfy the criteria of advantage and selectivity for the purposes of the case-law referred to [...]. Furthermore, in accordance with the legal concept of aid, which must be interpreted on the basis of objective factors, the purpose of a State measure, such as, in this instance, the environmental objective or the 'ecotax' quality of a specific or sectoral tax system, is not sufficient to exclude that measure outright from classification as 'aid' for the purposes of that provision, since such a measure must be assessed in relation to its effects and regardless of its causes or objectives. Consequently, the concept of aid within the meaning of Article [107(1) TFEU] requires consideration to be given to whether a specific or sectoral tax system entails distinctions the effect of which is to favour 'certain undertakings or the

production of certain goods' within the sector covered by that system, which presupposes that the underlying 'normal' taxation is first determined
General Court 7 March 2012 (British Aggregates v. Commission, T-210/02), ECLI:EU:T:2012:110, para. 52.

10.47   It is for the Member State which has introduced such a differentiation between undertakings in relation to charges to show that it is actually justified by the nature and general scheme of the system in question.
CoJ 21 June 2012 (BNP Paribas and BNL v. Commission, C-452/10 P), ECLI: EU:C:2012:366, para. 121.

10.48   A tax regime such as that at issue in the main proceedings may satisfy the condition of selectivity as an element of the concept of 'State aid' within the meaning of Article 107(1) TFEU if it were to be established that the reference system, namely the 'normal' system, consists in a prohibition on the deduction of losses in the case of a change of ownership for the purposes of the first subparagraph of Paragraph 122 of the TVL, in relation to which the authorisation procedure provided for in the third subparagraph of Paragraph 122 would constitute an exception. Such a regime may be justified by the nature or general scheme of the system of which it forms part, but justification is not possible if the competent national authorities, so far as concerns authorisation to derogate from the prohibition on the deduction of losses, have a discretion which empowers them to base authorisation decisions on criteria unrelated to that tax regime.
CoJ 18 July 2013 (P Oy, C-6/12), ECLI:EU:C:2013:525, para. 32.

10.49   Afin d'apprécier la sélectivité d'une mesure, il convient d'examiner si, dans le cadre d'un régime juridique donné, cette mesure constitue un avantage pour certaines entreprises par rapport à d'autres se trouvant dans une situation factuelle et juridique comparable [...].
[L]a notion d'aide d'État ne vise pas les mesures étatiques introduisant une différenciation entre entreprises et, partant, a priori sélectives, lorsque cette différenciation résulte de la nature ou de l'économie du système dans lequel elles s'inscrivent [...].
[A]fin d'évaluer le caractère éventuellement sélectif à l'égard de certaines entreprises d'un barème tarifaire établi par une entité publique pour l'utilisation d'un bien ou d'un service spécifique dans un secteur donné, il convient, notamment, de se référer à l'ensemble des entreprises utilisant, ou pouvant utiliser, ce bien ou ce service déterminé et d'examiner si seulement certaines d'entre elles bénéficient, ou sont en mesure de bénéficier, d'un éventuel avantage. La situation des entreprises qui ne veulent pas, ou ne peuvent pas, utiliser le bien ou le service en cause n'est ainsi pas directement pertinente pour apprécier l'existence d'un avantage. En d'autres termes, le caractère sélectif d'une mesure consistant en un barème tarifaire établi par une entité publique pour l'utilisation d'un bien ou d'un service mis à disposition par cette entité ne peut être évalué qu'au regard des clients, actuels ou potentiels, de ladite entité et du bien ou du service spécifique en cause et non au regard, notamment, des clients d'autres entreprises du secteur mettant à disposition des biens et des services similaires. Au demeurant, s'il devait être considéré que tout barème tarifaire non discriminatoire appliqué par une entité publique en contrepartie d'un bien ou d'un service donné possède un caractère

sélectif, cela aboutirait, en substance, à élargir de manière excessive la notion d'aides « favorisant certaines entreprises ou certaines productions », figurant à l'article 107, paragraphe 1, TFUE. Aussi, pour qu'un éventuel avantage accordé par une entité publique, dans le cadre de la fourniture de biens ou de services spécifiques, favorise certaines entreprises, il est nécessaire que des entreprises utilisant, ou souhaitant utiliser, ce bien ou ce service ne bénéficient pas, ou ne puissent pas bénéficier, dudit avantage de la part de cette entité dans ce cadre spécifique.

General Court 9 September 2014 (Lübeck v. Commission, T-461/12), ECLI: EU:T:2014:758, paras 45, 46 and 53.

See also CoJ December 2016 (Lübeck, C-524/14 P) EU:C:2016:971.

10.50 [T]he fact that the advantages are granted on the basis of an investment [...] to the exclusion of [...] other types of investment, does not mean that they are selective vis-à-vis investors so far as the operation is available to any undertakings [...].

General Court 17 December 2015 (Spain v. Commission & Lico Leasing v. Commission, Joined Cases T-515/13 and T-719/13), ECLI:EU:T:2015:1004, para. 143.

10.51 As regards, in particular, national measures that confer a tax advantage, it must be recalled that a measure of that nature which, although not involving the transfer of State resources, places the recipients in a more favourable position than other taxpayers is capable of procuring a selective advantage for the recipients and, consequently, of constituting State aid, within the meaning of Article 107(1) TFEU. On the other hand, a tax advantage resulting from a general measure applicable without distinction to all economic operators does not constitute such aid [...].

CoJ 21 December 2016 (Commission v. World Duty Free group & Commission v. Banco Santander Santusa, C-20/15 P and C-21/15 P), ECLI:EU:C:2016:981, para. 56.

See also General Court 4 February 2016 (Heitkamp BauHolding v. Commission, T-287/11), ECLI:EU:T:2016:60, paras 91–93, 159.

10.52 In that context, in order to classify a national tax measure as 'selective', the Commission must begin by identifying the ordinary or 'normal' tax system applicable in the Member State concerned, and thereafter demonstrate that the tax measure at issue is a derogation from that ordinary system, in so far as it differentiates between operators who, in the light of the objective pursued by that ordinary tax system, are in a comparable factual and legal situation [...].

The concept of 'State aid' does not, however, cover measures that differentiate between undertakings which, in the light of the objective pursued by the legal regime concerned, are in a comparable factual and legal situation, and are, therefore, a priori selective, where the Member State concerned is able to demonstrate that that differentiation is justified since it flows from the nature or general structure of the system of which the measures form part [...].

[T]he fact that the number of undertakings able to claim entitlement under a national measure is very large, or that those undertakings belong to various economic sectors, is not sufficient to call into question the selective nature of that measure and, therefore, to rule out its classification as State aid [...].

CoJ 21 December 2016 (Commission v. World Duty Free group & Commission v. Banco Santander Santusa, C-20/15 P and C-21/15 P), ECLI:EU:C:2016:981, paras 57, 58 and 80.

10.53   [T]he selectivity of a tax measure can be established even if that measure does not constitute a derogation from an ordinary tax system, but is an integral part of that system, [...] it is sufficient, in order to establish the selectivity of a measure that derogates from an ordinary tax system, to demonstrate that that measure benefits certain operators and not others, although all those operators are in an objectively comparable situation in the light of the objective pursued by the ordinary tax system.

Indeed, while it is not always necessary that a tax measure, in order for it to be established that it is selective, should derogate from an ordinary tax system, the fact that it can be so characterised is highly relevant in that regard where the effect of that measure is that two categories of operators are distinguished and are subject, a priori, to different treatment, namely those who fall within the scope of the derogating measure and those who continue to fall within the scope of the ordinary tax system, although those two categories are in a comparable situation in the light of the objective pursued by that system.

CoJ 21 December 2016 (Commission v. World Duty Free group & Commission v. Banco Santander Santusa, C-20/15 P and C-21/15 P), ECLI:EU:C:2016:981, paras 76 and 77.

4. Distortion of competition

10.54   The Court of Justice and the [General Court] have held that operating aid, that is to say aid which, like the aid in question, is intended to relieve an undertaking of the expenses which it would normally have had to bear in its day-to-day management or its usual activities, in principle distorts competition [...]. [...]

Where a public authority favours an undertaking operating in a sector which is characterised by intense competition by granting it a benefit, there is a distortion of competition or a risk of such distortion. Where the benefit is limited, competition is distorted to a lesser extent, but it is still distorted. The prohibition in Article [107(1) TFEU] applies to any aid which distorts or threatens to distort competition, irrespective of the amount, in so far as it affects trade between Member States.

General Court 30 April 1998 (Vlaamse Gewest (Flemish Region) v. Commission, T-214/95) [1998] ECR II-717, paras 43 and 46.

See also General Court 29 September 2000 (CETM v. Commission, T-55/99) [2000] ECR II-3207, para. 83.

When applied to the classification of aid, that principle requires the Commission to **10.55** indicate the reasons why it considers that the aid in question falls within the scope of Article [107(1) TFEU]. In that respect, even in cases where it is clear from the circumstances in which the aid has been granted that it is liable to affect trade between Member States and to distort or threaten to distort competition, the Commission must at least set out those circumstances in the statement of reasons for its decision.

General Court 30 April 1998 (Vlaamse Gewest (Flemish Region) v. Commission, T-214/95) [1998] ECR II-717, para. 64.

See also General Court 29 September 2000 (CETM v. Commission, T-55/99) [2000] ECR II-3207, para. 83.

[A]id which is intended to relieve an undertaking of the expenses which it would **10.56** normally have had to bear in its day-to-day management or its usual activities in principle distorts competition [...].

General Court 16 December 2010 (Netherlands & NOS v. Commission, T-231/06 and T-237/06) [2010] ECR II-5993, para. 119.

See also 26 October 2016 (Orange v. Commission, C-211/15 P), ECLI:EU: C:2016:798, para. 66.

[T]he purpose of categorising a national measure as State aid, it is not necessary to **10.57** demonstrate that the aid has a real effect on trade between Member States and that competition is actually being distorted, but only to examine whether that aid is liable to affect such trade and distort competition [...].

General Court 14 July 2011 (Freistaat Sachsen v. Commission, T-357/02 RENV) [2011] ECR II-5415, para. 30.

See also General Court 17 July 2014 (Westfälisch-Lippischer Sparkassen- und Giroverband v. Commission, T-457/09), ECLI:EU:T:2014:683, paras 228–229, 235 and 240–259.

5. Effect on trade between Member States

(a) General

When State financial aid strengthens the position of an undertaking compared with **10.58** other undertakings competing in intra-Community trade the latter must be regarded as affected by that aid.

CoJ 17 September 1980 (Philip Morris, 730/79) [1980] ECR 2671, para. 11.

Since the undertaking concerned exported about 40 per cent of its output to other **10.59** Member States, excess production capacity existed in the market in question and, in those circumstances, the aid granted to the undertaking had the effect of reducing its financial costs by comparison with those of its competitors, the Commission was entitled to conclude, in the absence of any information to the contrary, that the aid in question affected trade between Member States and distorted, or threatened to distort, competition within the meaning of Article [107(1) TFEU].

CoJ 10 July 1986 (Belgium v. Commission, 234/84) [1986] ECR 2263, para. 22.

10.60   Aid to an undertaking may be such as to affect trade between the Member States and distort competition where that undertaking competes with products coming from other Member States, even if it does not itself export its products. Such a situation may exist even if there is no over-capacity in the sector at issue. Where a Member State grants aid to an undertaking, domestic production may for that reason be maintained or increased with the result that, in circumstances such as those found to exist by the Commission, undertakings established in other Member States have less chance of exporting their products to the market in that Member State. Such aid is therefore likely to affect trade between Member States and distort competition.

CoJ 13 July 1988 (France v. Commission, 102/87) [1988] ECR 4067, para. 19.

10.61   Having regard to the interdependence between the markets on which Community undertakings operate, it is possible that aid might distort competition within the Community, even if the undertaking receiving it exports almost all its production outside the Community.

CoJ 21 March 1990 (Belgium v. Commission, C-142/87) [1990] ECR I-959, para. 35.

10.62   In the present case the contested act contains no information whatever as to the situation on the market in question, KAE's share of that market or the position of competing undertakings. As to the trade flows between Member States in the products concerned, the Commission does no more than cite the Member States' imports of products falling under three tariff headings, without determining KAE's share of those imports.

Secondly, the Commission in any event restricted itself to examining the situation of KAE, without giving in its decision any reasons for this. Since BV was named as the recipient of the alleged aid, the Commission ought to have examined how the acquisition of 74.9 per cent of KAE strengthened its competitive position in the fields of shipbuilding and marine and defence electronics, having regard in particular to the fact that BV already owned STN, which operated in the same sector as KAE, and having regard to the situation of the markets in question and the competing under-takings.

CoJ 24 October 1996 (Germany v. Commission, Bremer Vulkan, Joined Cases C-329/93, C-62/95 and C-63/95) [1996] ECR I-5151, paras 53 and 54.

See also CoJ 17 June 1999 (Belgium v. Commission, Maribel, C-75/97) [1999] ECR I-3671, para. 47.

10.63   In this respect, it must be observed, first, that it is not impossible that a public subsidy granted to an undertaking which provides only local or regional transport services and does not provide any transport services outside its State of origin may none the less have an effect on trade between Member States.

Where a Member State grants a public subsidy to an undertaking, the supply of transport services by that undertaking may for that reason be maintained or increased with the result that undertakings established in other Member States have less chance of providing their transport services in the market in that Member State.

CoJ 24 July 2003 (Altmark Trans, C-280/00) [2003] ECR I-7747, paras 77 and 78.

[The General Court] rightly explained that it would suffice that the Commission show **10.64** correctly how the aid at issue was likely to affect trade between Member States and to distort or threaten to distort competition. The [General Court] notably stressed in that context that the Commission was not obliged to carry out an economic analysis of the actual situation of the relevant market or the patterns of the trade in question between Member States or to show the real effect of the aid at issue, in particular on the prices applied by Wam, or to examine Wam's sales on the United Kingdom market. [...]

[The General Court], without erring in law, held, that the reasoning of the Commission in the contested decision even in combination with the finding that the financial situation of Wam has improved, are not sufficient to permit an understanding of how the aid at issue is liable, in the present case, to affect trade between Member States and to distort or threaten to distort competition in that sector.

Contrary to the claim of the Commission in that respect, the mere fact that Wam took part in intra-Community trade by exporting an important part of its production within the EU cannot suffice, in the particular circumstances of the case recalled in paragraph 55 of this judgment, to demonstrate those effects. [...]

It follows from the above that the [General Court], when it held that the Commission should have carried out a more detailed analysis of the potential consequences of the aid at issue on intra-Community trade and on competition and should have given additional information, in the contested decision, concerning those effects, did not intend to depart from the case-law cited above but to take into account the specific circumstances of the case, and it cannot be accused of erring in law in this respect.

CoJ 30 April 2009 (Commission v. Italian Republic and Wam SpA, C-494/06 P) [2009] ECR I-3639, paras 58, 60–61 and 64.

(b) Amount of aid/de minimis

[W]hilst the Court has held that the relatively small amount of aid or the relatively **10.65** small size of the undertaking which receives it does not as such exclude the possibility that intra-Community trade might be affected [...], a small amount of aid to an undertaking over a given period does not affect trade between Member States in particular economic sectors.

The Commission was therefore entitled to reach the view, in the exercise of its discretion to assess the possible economic effects of aid, that, other than in certain sectors where competitive conditions are of a particular kind and except in respect of export aid, aid in amounts falling below those laid down in the Community guidelines on State aid for SMEs, and subsequently in its Notice on the de minimis rule for State aid, does not affect trade and is therefore not caught by Articles [107 and 108 TFEU]. The amounts laid down by the Commission have not hitherto been challenged.

[…] The Commission may not therefore refuse to apply the de minimis rule to aid granted to undertakings in sectors which the various applicable provisions do not exclude from application of the rule.

CoJ 26 September 2002 (Spain v. Commission, C-351/98) [2002] ECR I-08031, paras 51–53.

10.66   Finally, according to the Court's case-law, there is no threshold or percentage below which it may be considered that trade between Member States is not affected. The relatively small amount of aid or the relatively small size of the undertaking which receives it does not as such exclude the possibility that trade between Member States might be affected […].

CoJ 24 July 2003 (Altmark Trans, C-280/00) [2003] ECR I-7747, para. 81.

See also General Court 17 December 2015 (Spain a.o. v. Commission, T-515/13 and T-719/13), ECLI:EU:T:2015:1004, paras 192–207.

(c)   No effect on trade between Member States – examples

10.67   The town of Dorsten runs several public swimming pools at a loss. Faced with substantial costs for renovating them and building a new open-air pool, it decided to put the new investment and the running of the pools out to tender in a Community-wide procedure in order to find a private operator to keep the amenity open for the local population. The wide-ranging rights and obligations laid down in the contract between the town and the operator include the obligation on the operator to make the pool available for schools and swimming clubs free of charge and the obligation on the town to make an annual payment of DM 2 million.

Commission 12 January 2001 (Germany – Leisure pool Dorsten), State aid N 258/2000.

See also General Court 12 May 2016 (Hamr v. Commission, T-693/14), ECLI: EU:T:2016:292, paras 62–64.

10.68   The aim of the measure is to increase the investment in the construction, extension and refurbishment of much needed hospital buildings. The cost of the scheme derives from non-collected taxes from private individuals. Based on information concerning currently proposed projects, the tax cost to the state would be a total of EUR 47 over seven years.

Commission 27 February 2002 (Ireland – Capital allowances for hospitals), State aid N 543/01.

10.69   Therefore, the Commission can conclude that, even if some distortion of (local) competition is not excluded, the support (if any) has no effect on trade within the meaning of Article [107(1) TFEU]. In particular, in these cases, also due to the geographical location of the marinas, their relatively small size, and the relatively small amounts of public support involved (in comparison with the number of moorings offered in the marinas), it can not reasonably be expected that this support will lead ship owners from other Member States to use the marinas concerned for mooring (be it fixed or daily) rather than a marina in another Member State.

Commission 29 October 2003 (The Netherlands – in favour of non-profit harbours for recreational crafts), State aid, C10/2003, para. 55.

For state measures to fall under the provision of Article [107(1)], they also have to have **10.70** a real or potential effect on trade between Member States. With the exception of a few large and internationally renowned museums, citizens do not cross borders with the principle aim to visit them. The Commission has generally deemed that local museum projects of limited scale do not affect trade between Member States. Accordingly, considering the local nature of the activities to be supported by the notified scheme, their limited scale and the modest amount of financial assistance, the Commission considers that the measure does not have an impact on intra-community trade.

Commission 18 February 2004 (Italy – Local Museums – Region of Sardinia), State aid N 630/2003.

B. DIRECT EFFECT

The provisions of Article [107(1)] are intended to take effect in the legal systems of **10.71** Member States, so that they may be invoked before national courts, where they have been put in concrete form by acts having general application provided for by Article [109] or by decisions in particular cases envisaged by Article [108(2)].

CoJ 19 June 1973 (Capolongo, 77/72) [1973] ECR 611, para. 6.

The direct effect of the prohibition on the Member State concerned from putting its **10.72** proposed measures into effect extends to all aid which is granted without being notified and, in the event of notification, is granted during the preliminary period, and up to the final decision where the Commission sets in motion the contentious procedure. As regards the whole of this period it confers rights on the individual which the national courts are bound to safeguard.

CoJ 11 December 1973 (Lorenz v. Germany, 120/73) [1973] ECR 1471.

The parties concerned cannot therefore simply, on the basis of Article [107] alone, **10.73** challenge the compatibility of an aid with Community law before national courts or ask them to decide as to any incompatibility which may be the main issue in actions before them or may arise as a subsidiary issue.

CoJ 22 March 1977 (Iannelli and Volpi, 74/76) [1977] ECR 557, para. 12.

The parties concerned cannot therefore simply, on the basis of Article [107] alone, **10.74** challenge the compatibility of an aid with community law before national courts or ask them to decide as to any compatibility which may be the main issue in actions before them or may arise a subsidiary issue. There is this right however where the provisions of Article [107] have been applied by the general provisions provided for in Article [109] or by specific decisions under Article [108(2)].

CoJ 22 March 1977 (Steinike and Weinlig, 78/76) [1977] ECR 595, para. 10.

C. ARTICLE 107(1) IN RELATION TO OTHER TREATY PROVISIONS

1. General

10.75   The fact that an aspect of aid, which is not necessary for the attainment of its object for its proper functioning, is incompatible with a provision of the Treaty other than Articles [107] and [108] does not in fact invalidate the aid as a whole or for that reason vitiate by reason of illegality the system of financing the said aid.

CoJ 22 March 1977 (Iannelli and Volpi, 74/76) [1977] ECR 557, para. 17.

10.76   It follows from Article 21 of Regulation no 2759/75 of the Council on the common organization of the market in pig meat that although Articles [107 to 109 TFEU] on aids are fully applicable to the pig meat sector, their application nevertheless remains subordinate to the provisions governing the common organization of the market established by the Regulation. Recourse by a Member State to the provisions of Articles [107 to 109] cannot receive priority over the provisions of the regulation on the organization of that sector of the market.

CoJ 26 June 1979 (Pigs and Bacon Commission v. Redmond, 177/78) [1979] ECR 2161, para. 11.

10.77   It must be borne in mind in this regard that in pursuing the various aims laid down in Article [39 TFEU] the Community institutions must constantly reconcile any conflicts between those aims taken individually and, where necessary, give any one of them the temporary priority which the facts or circumstances, in view of which their decisions are made, require.

Consequently, the Council committed no manifest error of assessment when deciding, in giving particular attention to the aim of guaranteeing wine producers a fair income, that the aid in question was to be considered to be compatible with the common market since they had not thereby caused a real and lasting disturbance in the functioning of the common organization of the wine market. Moreover, in the final recital of the preamble to the two decisions, the Council considered that the aid was, by derogation, compatible with the common market to the extent and for the period strictly necessary for restoring the situation of imbalance found to exist.

CoJ 29 February 1996 (Commission v. Council, C-122/94) [1996] ECR I-881, paras 24 and 25.

See also CoJ 5 October 2000 (Germany v. Commission, C-288/96) [2000] ECR I-8237.

[T]he Commission, in exercising its powers under Articles [107 and 108 TFEU], could **10.78** adopt guidelines requiring compliance, not only with criteria pertaining exclusively to competition policy, but also with those applicable in relation to the common fisheries policy, even if the Council had not expressly authorized it to do so.

CoJ 15 October 1996 (IJssel-Vliet, C-311/94) [1996] ECR I-5023, para. 34.

Article [107 TFEU] is in itself sufficient to prohibit the conduct by States referred to **10.79** therein and Article 5 of the [EC]Treaty, the second paragraph of which [cf. Article 4(3) TEU] provides that Member States are to abstain from any measure which could jeopardise the attainment of the objectives of the Treaty, cannot be used to extend the scope of Article [107 TFEU] to conduct by States that does not fall within it.

CoJ 13 March 2001 (PreussenElektra, C-379/98) [2001] ECR I-2099, para. 65.

2. Free movement of goods

The Treaty provisions on aid may in no case be used to frustrate the Treaty rules on the **10.80** free movement of goods. They both pursue a common purpose, namely to ensure the free movement of goods between Member States under normal conditions of competition. The fact that a national measure might be regarded as aid within the meaning of Article [107] is therefore not a sufficient reason to exempt it from the prohibition contained in Article [34].

CoJ 20 March 1990 (Du Pont de Nemours, C-21/88) [1990] ECR I-889, para. 20.

See also CoJ 5 June 1986 (Commission v. Italy, 103/84) [1986] ECR 1759.

3. Competition rules

When adopting a decision on the compatibility of aid with the common market, the **10.81** Commission must be aware of the risk of individual traders undermining competition in the common market.

Nevertheless, the procedure under Article [101] et seq. and that under Article [107 TFEU] et seq. are independent procedures governed by specific rules.

Consequently, when taking a decision on the compatibility of State aid with the common market, the Commission is not obliged to await the outcome of a parallel procedure initiated under Regulation No 17 [now Regulation No 1/2003], once it has reached the conclusion, based on an economic analysis of the situation and without any manifest error in the assessment of the facts, that the recipient of the aid is not in breach of Articles [101 and 102 TFEU].

CoJ 15 June 1993 (Matra v. Commission, C-225/91) [1993] ECR I-3203, paras 43–45.

4. Social measures

10.82   Consequently, Article [153 TEU] does not encroach upon the Member States' powers in the social field in so far as the latter is not covered by other provisions of the Treaty [...].

The fact that, in Article 1 of the contested decision, the Commission finds that measures adopted by the Kingdom of Spain in favour of Tubacex and Acería de Álava contain aid elements which were granted illegally and which are incompatible with Article [107 TFEU] and with Decision No 3855/91 does not affect the competence of the Member States in the social field, since they are required in any event to comply with Community rules on competition.

CoJ 29 April 1999 (Spain v. Commission, C-342/96) [1999] ECR I-2459, paras 21 and 22.

D. FORM IN WHICH THE AID IS PROVIDED

1. Aim of the measure

10.83   Article [107] does not therefore distinguish between the measures of state intervention concerned by reference to their causes or their aims but defines them in relation to their effects, so that the alleged fiscal nature or social aim of a measure taken by a Member State cannot suffice to exclude it from the ambit of Article [107].

CoJ 2 July 1974 (Italy v. Commission, 173/73) [1974] ECR 709, para. 13.

10.84   According to settled case-law, Article [107(1)] does not distinguish between measures of State intervention by reference to their causes or aims but defines them in relation to their effects.

CoJ 26 September 1996 (France v. Commission, C-241/94) [1996] ECR I-4551, para. 20.

See also CoJ 12 October 2000 (Spain v. Commission, C-480/98) [2000] ECR I-8717, para. 16.

2. Margin of appreciation

10.85   [Art. 107(1) TFEU] does not distinguish between measures of State intervention by reference to their causes or aims but defines them in relation to their effects. It follows that the concept of aid is objective, the test being whether a State measure confers an advantage on one or more particular undertakings. The characterisation of a measure as State aid, which, according to the Treaty, is the responsibility of both the Commission and the national courts, cannot in principle justify the attribution of a broad discretion to the Commission, save for particular circumstances owing to the complex nature of the State intervention in question. The relevance of the causes or aims of State measures falls to be appraised only in the context of determining – pursuant to Article [107(3) TFEU] – whether such measures are compatible with the common market. It is only in cases where Article [107(3) TFEU] falls to be applied and where, accordingly, the Commission must rely on complex economic, social, regional and sectoral assessments, that a broad discretion is conferred on that institution.

General Court 27 January 1998 (Ladbroke v. Commission, T-67/94) [1998] ECR II-1, para. 52.

Confirmed in CoJ 16 May 2000 (France v. Ladbroke and Commission, C-83/98 P) [2000] ECR I-3271, para. 25.

The short answer to that is that State aid, as defined in the Treaty, is a legal concept **10.86** which must be interpreted on the basis of objective factors. For that reason, the Community courts must in principle, having regard both to the specific features of the case before them and to the technical or complex nature of the Commission's assessments, carry out a comprehensive review as to whether a measure falls within the scope of Article [107(1) TFEU]. The [General Court] therefore did not err in law so far as concerns the scope of judicial review of the Commission's assessments.

CoJ 16 May 2000 (France v. Ladbroke and Commission, C-83/98 P) [2000] ECR I-3271, para. 25.

[A]s regards the consequences of that error of law on the part of the Commission, it is **10.87** settled case-law that, in the application of Article [107 TFEU], the Commission has a wide discretion, the exercise of which involves complex economic and social assessments. The Court may not therefore substitute its own assessment for that of the Commission or decide whether aid is compatible with the internal market.

General Court 20 March 2013 (Jørgen Andersen v. Commission, T-92/11), ECLI: EU:T:2013:143, para. 58

S'agissant de la portée du contrôle juridictionnel de la décision attaquée au regard de **10.88** l'article [107(1) TFEU], il ressort de la jurisprudence que la notion d'aide d'État, telle qu'elle est définie dans cette disposition, présente un caractère juridique et doit être interprétée sur la base d'éléments objectifs. Pour cette raison, le juge de l'Union européenne doit, en principe et compte tenu tant des éléments concrets du litige qui lui est soumis que du caractère technique ou complexe des appréciations portées par la Commission, exercer un entier contrôle en ce qui concerne la question de savoir si une mesure entre dans le champ d'application de l'article [107(1) TFEU] […].

General Court 13 September 2013 (Poste Italiane SpA v. Commission, T-525/08), ECLI:EU:T:2013:481, para. 47.

3. Concept of 'subsidy'

The concept of aid is nevertheless wider than that of a subsidy because it embraces not **10.89** only positive benefits, such as subsidies themselves, but also interventions which, in various forms, mitigate the charges which are normally included in the budget of an undertaking and which, without, therefore, being subsidies in the strict meaning of the word, are similar in character and have the same effect.

CoJ 23 February 1961 (Steenkolenmijnen, 30/59) [1961] ECR 3.

10.90   As the Court has already held in the context of the ECSC Treaty (judgment in Case 30/59), the concept of aid is thus wider than that of a subsidy because it embraces not only positive benefits, such as subsidies themselves, but also interventions which, in various forms, mitigate the charges which are normally included in the budget of an undertaking and which, without therefore being subsidies in the strict meaning of the word, are similar in character and have the same effect.

CoJ 15 March 1994 (Banco Exterior de Espaæa, C-387/92) [1994] ECR I-877, para. 13.

4.   Capital injections

10.91   The Treaty applies to aid granted by a State or through State resources 'in any form whatsoever'. It follows that no distinction can be drawn between aid granted in the form of loans and aid granted in the form of a holding acquired in the capital of an undertaking. Aid taking either form falls within the prohibition laid down in Article [107] where the conditions set out in that provision are fulfilled.

CoJ 14 November 1984 (Intermills, 323/82) [1984] ECR 3809, para. 31.

10.92   An appropriate way of establishing whether a subscription of capital of an undertaking is a State aid is to determine to what extent the undertaking would be able to obtain the sums in question on the private capital markets. In the case of an undertaking whose capital is held by the public authorities, the test is, in particular, whether in similar circumstances a private shareholder, having regard to the foreseeability of obtaining a return and leaving aside all social, regional-policy and sectoral considerations, would have subscribed the capital in question.

CoJ 10 July 1986 (Belgium v. Commission, 234/84) [1986] ECR 2263, para. 14.

10.93   For the purpose of deciding whether financial assistance granted to an undertaking by a Member State constitutes State aid, it is appropriate to apply the criterion based on the opportunities open to the undertaking of acquiring the amounts in question on private capital markets.

CoJ 14 February 1990 (France v. Commission, C-301/87) [1990] ECR I-307, para. 39.

10.94   As the [General Court] held in its judgment, a private shareholder may reasonably subscribe the capital necessary to secure the survival of an undertaking which is experiencing temporary difficulties but is capable of becoming profitable again, possibly after a reorganization. It must therefore be accepted that a parent company may also, for a limited period, bear the losses of one of its subsidiaries in order to enable the latter to close down its operations under the best possible conditions. Such decisions may be motivated not solely by the likelihood of an indirect material profit but also by other considerations, such as a desire to protect the group's image or to redirect its activities.

However, when injections of capital by a public investor disregard any prospect of profitability, even in the long term, such provision of capital must be regarded as aid within the meaning of Article [107 TFEU], and its compatibility with the common market must be assessed on the basis solely of the criteria laid down in that provision.

CoJ 21 March 1991 (Italy v. Commission, C-303/88) [1991] ECR I-1433, paras 21 and 22.

[T]he fact that a financial contribution is intended for productive investment does not **10.95** by itself preclude such a contribution from constituting aid when, regard being had to the situation of the undertaking, it appears improbable that a private shareholder would have subscribed the capital in question.

It is apparent from the contested decision [...] that the undertakings in whose favour the measures in dispute operated had suffered during the period immediately preceding the measures in question, sustained and considerable losses [...]. [...].

Even on the supposition that [...] these results were already foreseeable at the time of the financing operations in question, it must be pointed out that such forecasts were not of such a nature as to induce a private investor to tie up such considerable sums [...].

CoJ 3 October 1991 (Italy v. Commission, C-261/89) [1991] ECR I-4437, paras 9–10 and 12.

Although the conduct of a private investor, with which the intervention of a public **10.96** investor pursuing economic policy aims must be compared, need not be the conduct of an ordinary investor laying out capital with a view to realizing a profit in the relatively short term, it must at least be the conduct of a private holding company or a private group of undertakings pursuing a structural policy[,] whether general or sectoral[,] and guided by prospects of profitability in the longer term.

CoJ 14 September 1994 (Spain v. Commission, C-42/93) [1994] ECR I-4175, para. 14.

A distinction must be drawn between the obligations which the State must assume as **10.97** owner of the share capital of a company and its obligations as a public authority. Since the three companies in question were constituted as limited companies, the Patrimonio del Estado, as owner of the share capital, would only have been liable for their debts up to the liquidation value of their assets. That means in the present case that the obligations arising from the cost of redundancies, payment of unemployment benefits and aid for the restructuring of the industrial infrastructure must not be taken into consideration for the purpose of applying the private-investor test.

CoJ 14 September 1994 (Spain v. Commission, Joined Cases C-278/92 to 280/92) [1994] ECR I-4103, para. 22.

A private investor pursuing a structural policy whether general or sectoral and guided by **10.98** prospects of viability in the long term could not reasonably allow itself, after years of continuous losses, to make a contribution of capital which, in economic terms, proves to be not only costlier than selling the assets, but is moreover linked to the sale of the undertaking, which removes any hope of profit, even in the longer term.

CoJ 14 September 1994 (Spain v. Commission, Joined Cases C-278/92 to 280/92) [1994] ECR I-4103, para. 26.

10.99   Whether the intervention at issue constitutes aid depends, first, on the answer to the question whether the total value of the new BV shares corresponded to the value of 74.9 per cent of the share capital of KAE which BV acquired. If the two values coincide, the intervention cannot be described as aid. If, on the other hand, the total value of the new BV shares was less than the value of 74.9 per cent of KAE, a second question then arises, according to the Court's case-law, namely how a private investor, pursuing a structural policy[,] whether general or sectorial[,] and guided by prospects of profitability in the longer term, would have behaved, having regard to all the circumstances and all the relevant factors [...]. [...]

As well as the stock market price of the BV shares, such factors might reasonably be the past movement of that price, the agreement of 12 July 1991, the intrinsic worth of BV as an undertaking, the additional value which may have been contributed by the block of 2.8 million shares, the synergy effects expected from the merger of KAE and STN in accordance with the situation of the market, the inside information the parties to the agreement had on the market in question and on the situation of the competing undertakings, and the forecasts of how the BV share price would develop, having regard in particular to the situation of the market on which the undertaking operates. [...]

Instead of assessing all those factors, the Commission, in the contested act, merely stated, without adequate explanation, that the stock market price is the sole determining factor in valuing shares.

CoJ 24 October 1996 (Germany v. Commission, Bremer Vulkan, Joined Cases C-329/93, C-62/95 and C-63/95) [1996] ECR I-5151, paras 23, 33 and 36.

10.100   In normal circumstances, a prudent private investor would not have taken a decision irrevocably obliging him to make an investment of the size in question or to underwrite it, until the details of that investment had been finally fixed. In the present case, he would not therefore have taken such a decision before 17 February 1993. In a situation such as that at issue in this case – where the subscription in April 1993 to the securities in question had been preceded by several months of negotiations between the issuer and the subscriber – a prudent private investor would also have taken steps during that period of negotiations to monitor closely the economic and financial situation of the undertaking which was the subject-matter of his proposed investment. If a major setback occurred, he would not have hesitated to withdraw from that plan, unless he was legally obliged to carry it out. Consequently, the Commission was entitled to regard the investment decision as having being taken in April 1993, or on 17 February 1993 at the earliest.

General Court 12 December 1996 (Air France II, T-358/94) [1996] ECR II-2109, para. 79.

10.101   In that regard, in view of the evidence before it and in the exercise of its discretion in the matter, the Commission could reasonably take the view that both the value of the securities to which the private investors actually subscribed and that of the securities to which they wished to subscribe were considerably less than the total value of securities to which the CDC-P, a public sector body, subscribed. It was therefore entitled to conclude, without committing a manifest error of appraisal, that the intentions displayed by the private investors in this case did not show that a prudent private investor of the same size as the CDC-P, that is to say of the same size as the Caisse, would have risked an investment of FF 1.5 billion in Air France.

General Court 12 December 1996 (Air France II, T-358/94) [1996] ECR II-2109, para. 149.

See also General Court 12 December 2000 (Alitalia, T-269/97) [2000] ECR II-3871; General Court 25 June 1998 (Air France, T-371/94 and T-394/94) [1998] ECR II-2405; General Court 2 March 2012 (Netherlands & ING-Group v. Commission, T-29/10 and T-33/10), ECLI:EU:T:2012:98, paras 100–109;.

5. Debt arrangement

[…] According to settled case-law, a public body which has granted a debt remission should be compared to a private creditor who is seeking to obtain payment of sums owed to it by a debtor in financial difficulties. The status of creditor should be distinguished from that of a private investor in a market economy pursuing a structural policy – whether general or sectoral – guided by the longer-term prospects of profitability of the capital invested […]. **10.102**

It should be borne in mind that, when a firm faced with a substantial deterioration of its financial situation proposes an agreement or series of agreements for debt arrangement to its creditors with a view to remedying the situation and avoiding liquidation, each creditor must make a decision having regard to the amount offered to it under the proposed agreement, on the one hand, and the amount it expects to be able to recover following possible liquidation of the firm, on the other. Its choice is influenced by a number of factors, such as the creditor's status as a secured, preferential or ordinary creditor, the nature and extent of any security it may hold, its assessment of the chances of the firm being restored to viability, as well as the amount it would receive in the event of liquidation […].

General Court 7 December 2010 (Frucona Košice v. Commission, T-11/07) [2010] ECR II-5453, paras 114 and 115.

6. Loans

The Court has held […] that, in order to determine whether a State measure constitutes aid for the purposes of Article [107] of the Treaty, it is necessary to establish whether the recipient undertaking receives an economic advantage which it would not have obtained under normal market conditions […]. **10.103**

It has also held that the same is true of loans at reduced rates of interest granted by public authorities to an undertaking which enable the latter to avoid having to bear

costs which would normally have had to be met out of the undertaking's own financial resources, thereby preventing market forces from having their normal effect [...].
CoJ 29 April 1999 (Spain v. Commission, C–342/96) [1999] ECR I-2459, paras 41 and 42.

See also General Court 30 April 1998 (Cityflier, T–214/95) [1998] ECR II-717.

7. Guarantees

10.104 In order to determine the extent to which the security in question is in the nature of State aid, the relevant criterion is that indicated in the Commission's decision, namely whether Jadekost could have obtained the amounts in question on the capital market without the security.

Thus where, owing to an undertaking's precarious financial circumstances, no credit institution would agree to lend to it without a State guarantee, the entire amount of the secured loan which it obtains must be regarded as aid.
CoJ 5 October 2000 (Germany v. Commission, C–288/96) [2000] ECR I-8237, paras 30 and 31.

8. Cross-subsidisation

10.105 The provision of logistical and commercial assistance by a public undertaking to its subsidiaries, which are governed by private law and carry on an activity open to free competition, is capable of constituting State aid if the remuneration received in return is less than that which would have been demanded under normal market conditions. As regards that last condition, it is for the national court to determine what is normal remuneration for the services in question, such a determination presupposing an economic analysis taking into account all the factors which an undertaking acting under normal market conditions should have taken into consideration when fixing the remuneration for the services provided.
CoJ 11 July 1996 (SFEI v. La Poste, C–39/94) [1996] ECR I-3547, paras 61 and 62.

See also General Court 14 December 2000 (Ufex v. Commission, T–613/97) [2000] ECR II-4055.

9. Operating aid

10.106 Furthermore, as the Commission rightly contends, operating aid, that is to say, aid intended to relieve an undertaking of the expenses which it would itself normally have had to bear in its day-to-day management or its usual activities, does not in principle fall within the scope of Article [107(3)] aforesaid, and cannot therefore be regarded as authorized by Decision 75/397 or by the letter of 25 May 1978. According to the relevant case-law, the effect of such aid is in principle to distort competition in the

sectors in which it is granted, whilst nevertheless being incapable, by its very nature, of achieving any of the objectives of the aforesaid exceptions.
General Court 8 June 1995 (Siemens v. Commission, T-459/93) [1995] ECR II-1675, para. 48.

See also General Court 27 September 2012 (FEDECOM v. Commission, T-243/09), ECLI:EU:T:2012:497, para. 86.

10. Sale of land

The Commission believes that the value of land had to take account of its use, i.e. the fact that the land in question was to be used to build a theme park. It would thus be inappropriate to assign it a price comparable to that of land intended for residential purposes. In the absence of any other information, the assessment method used by TINSA (capitalisation of expected income) seems entirely appropriate in this case. **10.107**
Commission 2 August 2002 (Spain – Parc 'Terra Mítica'), State Aid C-42/2001, para. 70.

Measures which, in various forms, mitigate the burdens which are normally included in the budget of an undertaking and which are thereby similar to subsidies constitute benefits for the purposes of Article [107(1) TFEU], such as, among others, the supply of goods or services on favourable terms. **10.108**

When applied to the sale of land to an undertaking by a public authority, the consequence of that principle is that it must be determined whether, in particular, the sale price could not have been obtained by the purchaser under normal market conditions. Where the Commission carries out an examination for that purpose of the experts' reports drawn up after the transaction in question, it is bound to compare the sale price actually paid to the price suggested in those various reports and to determine whether it deviates sufficiently to justify a finding that there is a benefit. That method makes it possible to take into account the uncertainty of such a determination, which is by nature retrospective, of such market prices.
General Court 16 September 2004 (Valmont v. Commission, T-274/01) [2004] ECR II-3145, paras 44 and 45.

See also General Court 6 March 2002 (Diputación Foral de Álava and others v. Commission, T-127/99, T-129/99 and T-148/99) [2002] ECR II-1275, para. 73.

[W]hen assessing the value of an aid in the form of a sale of property at an allegedly preferential price, the principle of the private investor operating in a market economy applies. Therefore, the value of the aid is equal to the difference between what the recipient in fact paid and what it would have had to pay in an arm's length transaction on the open market to buy an equivalent property from a vendor in the private sector at the time of the relevant transaction. **10.109**

General Court 29 March 2007 (Scott v. Commission, T-366/00) [2007] ECR II-797, para. 105.

10.110   [T]he Commission may not be faulted because its assessment is approximate. In the case of a non-notified aid, it may be that the circumstances of the case are such that the Commission has difficulty in determining the precise value of the aid, particularly where a significant period of time has elapsed since the sale of the property in question. Those circumstances must be borne in mind when reviewing the legality of the Commission decision and particularly the issue as to whether the Commission conducted the Article [108(2) TFEU] examination procedure in a diligent manner. Nevertheless, the essential issue as to the determination of the value of the aid is a point of fact upon which the Community Court must carry out a comprehensive review. The mere fact that the Commission may have to resort to an approximate evaluation because of the circumstances of the case, does not mean that it had a margin of appreciation with regard to the determination of the amount to be recovered.

General Court 29 March 2007 (Scott v. Commission, T-366/00) [2007] ECR II-797, para. 96.

10.111   [...] Where the national law establishes rules for calculating the market value of land for their sale by public authorities, the application of those rules must, in order to comply with Article [107 TFEU], lead in all cases to a price as close as possible to the market value. As that market value is theoretical, except in the case of sales accepting the highest bid, a margin for variation on the price obtained as compared with the theoretical price must be tolerated [...].

CoJ 16 December 2010 (Seydaland v. BVVG, C-239/09) [2010] ECR I-13083, para. 35.

10.112   [...] It must be stated that, while it is clear that the best bid or an expert report are likely to provide prices corresponding to actual market values, as the Commission states in Title II, points 1 and 2(a), of the Communication, it cannot be ruled out that other methods may also achieve the same result.

CoJ 16 December 2010 (Seydaland v. BVVG, C-239/09) [2010] ECR I-13083, para. 39.

10.113   À cet égard, il convient de rappeler que, aux termes de la jurisprudence de la Cour, pour vérifier si la vente d'un terrain par une autorité publique à une personne privée constitue une aide d'État, il y a lieu, pour la Commission, d'appliquer le critère de l'investisseur privé dans une économie de marché, afin de vérifier si le prix payé par le présumé bénéficiaire de l'aide correspond au prix qu'un investisseur privé, agissant dans des conditions de concurrence normales, aurait pu fixer [...].

En outre, dans le cadre de l'application de ce principe de l'opérateur privé en économie de marché, il convient de comparer le prix de vente en cause à celui qu'un vendeur privé hypothétique, se trouvant dans la mesure du possible, dans la même situation que le vendeur, aurait exigé pour cette opération [...].

En l'espèce, il convenait donc de comparer le prix de vente du terrain en cause à celui qu'un vendeur privé hypothétique se trouvant, dans la mesure du possible, dans la même situation que la commune d'Åre aurait exigé pour cette opération.

Dans ce cadre, il convient d'examiner, compte tenu du contexte précédemment exposé, si c'est à juste titre que la Commission a considéré [...] que l'application du principe de l'opérateur privé en économie de marché impliquait, en l'espèce, de considérer que l'offre de Lidl constituait le meilleur indicateur pour évaluer la valeur de marché réelle du terrain en cause.

General Court 13 December 2011 (Konsum Nord ekonomisk förening v. Commission, T-244/08) [2011] ECR II-00444, paras 61–64.

11. Privatisation

(a) General

See Commission 27 February 2008 (Romania – Privatisation of Automobile Craiova (former Daewoo)), C-46/2007, paras 14–23.

(b) Privatisation by tendering

[W]here a public authority proceeds to sell an undertaking belonging to it by way of an open, transparent and unconditional tender procedure, it can be presumed that the market price corresponds to the highest offer, provided that it is established, first, that that offer is binding and credible and, secondly, that the consideration of economic factors other than the price is not justified. **10.114**

CoJ 24 October 2013 (Land Burgenland, & Grazer Wechselseitige Versicherung AG v. Commission, Joined Cases C-214/12 P, C-215/12 P and C-223/12 P), ECLI: EU:C:2013:682, para. 94.

12. Reductions and non-payment of social security

Such an advantage may arise as a result of certain measures being taken or even, as the Commission submits, as a result of the relevant authorities not taking measures in a particular set of circumstances. **10.115**

It is apparent from the documents before the Court that, notwithstanding the Spanish Government's assertions that the authorities used all available legal remedies to secure payment of the debts owed by the undertakings in the Magefesa group, the undertakings in question were able for several years to continue trading without complying with their tax and social security obligations.

In those circumstances, the Commission was justified in deciding that, in the particular circumstances of the case, the non-payment of taxes and social security contributions by Indosa, Cunosa, Migsa and Gursa during the periods mentioned in the contested Decision, constituted illegal aid which was incompatible with the common market within the meaning of Article [107(1) TFEU].

CoJ 12 October 2000 (Spain v. Commission, C-480/98) [2000] ECR I-8717, paras 19–21.

13. Fiscal measures

10.116   A preferential rediscount rate for exports, granted by a State in favour only of national products exported and for the purpose of helping them to compete in other Member States with products originating in the latter, constitutes an aid within the meaning of Article [107] the observance of which it is the Commission's task to ensure.

Neither the fact that the preferential rate in question is applicable to all national products exported and only to them nor the fact that in establishing it the French Government may have resolved to approximate the rate to those applied in the other member countries can remove from the measure in question the character of an aid which is prohibited except in the cases and procedures provided for by the Treaty.

CoJ 10 December 1969 (Commission v. France, Joined Cases C-6/69 and C- 11/69) [1969] ECR 523, paras 20 and 21.

See also CoJ 29 January 1998 (Commission v. Italy, C-280/95) [1998] ECR I-259.

10.117   Article [108(2)], by taking into account the connection which may exist between the aid granted by a Member State and the method by which it is financed through the resources of that State, does not therefore allow the Commission to isolate the aid as such from the method by which it is financed and to disregard this method if, in conjunction with the aid in its narrow sense, it renders the whole incompatible with the Common Market. [...]

In order to determine whether an aid 'affects trade between Member States', 'distorts or threatens to distort competition by favouring certain undertakings or the production of certain goods' and 'adversely affects trading conditions to an extent contrary to the common interest', it is necessary to consider all the legal and factual circumstances surrounding that aid, in particular whether there is an imbalance between the charges imposed on the undertakings or producers concerned on the one hand and the benefits derived from the aid in question on the other.

CoJ 25 June 1970 (France v. Commission, 47/69) [1970] ECR 487, paras 4 and 7.

10.118   While a parafiscal charge may come within the scope of either Article [30] or Article [110 TFEU] the use of the revenue from that charge to benefit domestic products may none the less constitute State aid which may be incompatible with the common market if the conditions set out in Article [107 TFEU], as interpreted by the Court, are fulfilled.

CoJ 2 August 1993 (CELBI, C-266/91) [1993] ECR I-4337, para. 21.

10.119   A measure by which the public authorities grant to certain undertakings a tax exemption which, although not involving a transfer of State resources, places the persons to whom the tax exemption applies in a more favourable financial situation than other taxpayers constitutes State aid within the meaning of Article [107 TFEU].

CoJ 15 March 1994 (Banco de Crédito Industrial v. Ayuntamiento de Valencia, C-387/92) [1994] ECR I-877, para. 14.

Taxes do not fall within the scope of the provisions of the Treaty concerning State aid **10.120** unless they constitute the method of financing an aid measure, so that they form an integral part of that measure.

For a tax, or part of a tax, to be regarded as forming an integral part of an aid measure, it must be hypothecated to the aid measure under the relevant national rules, in the sense that the revenue from the tax is necessarily allocated for the financing of the aid. In the event of such hypothecation, the revenue from the tax has a direct impact on the amount of the aid and, consequently, on the assessment of the compatibility of the aid with the common market. The Court thus held that, where there is such a link between the aid measure and its financing, the notification of the aid must also cover the method of financing, so that the Commission may consider it on the basis of all the facts. If this requirement is not satisfied, it is possible that the Commission may declare that an aid measure is compatible when, if the Commission had been aware of its method of financing, it could not have been so declared [...].

CoJ 13 January 2005 (Streekgewest, C-174/02) [2005] ECR I-85, paras 25 and 26.

14. Non-financial regulatory measures

The system at issue does not seek, through its object and general structure, to create an **10.121** advantage which would constitute an additional burden for the State or the above-mentioned bodies, but only to alter in favour of shipping undertakings the framework within which contractual relations are formed between those undertakings and their employees. The consequences arising from this, in so far as they relate to the difference in the basis for the calculation of social security contributions, mentioned by the national court, and to the potential loss of tax revenue because of the low rates of pay, referred to by the Commission, are inherent in the system and are not a means of granting a particular advantage to the undertakings concerned.

CoJ 17 March 1993 (Sloman Neptun, C-72/91 and 73/91) [1993] ECR I-887, para. 21.

In this case, it must be observed that non-application of generally applicable legislation **10.122** concerning fixed-term employment contracts to a single undertaking does not involve any direct or indirect transfer of State resources to that undertaking.

It follows that a provision of the kind at issue in the main proceedings does not constitute a means of directly or indirectly granting an advantage through State resources.

CoJ 7 May 1998 (Viscido and others v. Ente Poste Italiane, Joined Cases C-52/97, C-53/97 and C-54/97) [1998] ECR I-2629, paras 14 and 15.

15. Minimum retail prices

10.123   The fixing by a public authority of minimum retail prices for a product at the exclusive expense of consumers does not constitute an aid granted by a State within the meaning of that article.
CoJ 24 January 1978 (Van Tiggele, 82/77) [1978] ECR 25, para. 26.

16. Fixing of tariffs by Member State

10.124   Considered as a whole, these factors demonstrate that Gasunie in no way enjoys full autonomy in the fixing of gas tariffs but acts under the control and on the instructions of the public authorities. It is thus clear that Gasunie could not fix the tariff without taking account of the requirements of the public authorities.

It may therefore be concluded that the fixing of the contested tariff is the result of action by the Netherlands State and thus falls within the meaning of the phrase 'aid granted by a Member State' under Article [107 TFEU].
CoJ 2 February 1988 (Van der Kooy, Joined Cases C-67/85, C-68/85 and C-70/85) [1988] ECR 219, paras 37 and 38.

17. Compensation for damages

10.125   Damages which the national authorities of a Member State may be ordered to pay to individuals in compensation for damage they have caused to those individuals do not constitute aid within the meaning of Articles [107 and 108 TFEU].
CoJ 27 September 1988 (Asteris, Joined Cases C-106/87 to C-120/87) [1988] ECR 5515, para. 24.

E. ARTICLE 107(2): 'SHALL BE COMPATIBLE WITH THE INTERNAL MARKET'

10.126   Far from being implicitly repealed following German reunification, that provision was retained by both the Maastricht Treaty concluded on 7 February 1992 and the Amsterdam Treaty concluded on 2 October 1997. Moreover, an identical provision was inserted into Article 61(2)(c) of the Agreement on the European Economic Area concluded on 2 May 1992 (OJ 1994 L 1, p. 3).

Having regard to the objective scope of the rules of Community law, the authority and effectiveness of which must be preserved, it cannot therefore be assumed that that provision has become devoid of purpose since the reunification of Germany, as the Commission maintained at the hearing, contradicting its own administrative practice (see, in particular, the *Daimler-Benz* and *Tettau* decisions).

[S]ince it is a derogation from the general principle laid down in Article [107(1) TFEU] that State aid is incompatible with the common market, Article [107(2)(c)] must be interpreted narrowly.
General Court 15 December 1999 (Volkswagen and others v. Commission, Joined Cases T-132/96 and T-143/96) [1999] ECR II-3663, paras 130–132.

Confirmed in CoJ 12 July 2001 (Commission v. TF1, C-302/99 P and C-308/99 P) [2001] ECR I-5603.

F. ARTICLE 107(3): 'MAY BE CONSIDERED TO BE COMPATIBLE WITH THE INTERNAL MARKET'

In the application of Article [107(3) TFEU] the Commission has a discretion the exercise of which involves economic and social assessments which must be made in a Community context.   **10.127**

That is the context in which the Commission has with good reason assessed the standard of living and serious under-employment in the Bergen-op-Zoom area, not with reference to the national average in the Netherlands but in relation to the Community level.

CoJ 17 September 1980 (Philip Morris, 730/79) [1980] ECR 2671, para. 25.

The Commission in no way exceeded the limits of its discretion by considering that the granting of aid for an investment which increases production capacity in a sector in which there is already considerable over-production is contrary to the common interest and that aid of that sort is not of such a nature as to promote the economic development of the area at issue.   **10.128**

CoJ 24 February 1987 (Deufil, 310/85) [1987] ECR 901, para. 18.

Furthermore, as the Commission rightly contends, operating aid, that is to say, aid intended to relieve an undertaking of the expenses which it would itself normally have had to bear in its day-to-day management or its usual activities, does not in principle fall within the scope of Article [107(3)] aforesaid, and cannot therefore be regarded as authorized by Decision 75/397 or by the letter of 25 May 1978. According to the relevant case-law, the effect of such aid is in principle to distort competition in the sectors in which it is granted, whilst nevertheless being incapable, by its very nature, of achieving any of the objectives of the aforesaid exceptions.   **10.129**

General Court 8 June 1995 (Siemens v. Commission, T-459/93) [1995] ECR II-1675, para. 48.

À titre liminaire, il convient de rappeler que, selon une jurisprudence constante, l'article [107(3) TFEU] accorde à la Commission un large pouvoir d'appréciation en vue d'admettre des aides par dérogation à l'interdiction générale du paragraphe 1 dudit article, dans la mesure où l'appréciation, dans ces cas, de la compatibilité ou de l'incompatibilité d'une aide d'État avec le marché commun soulève des problèmes impliquant la prise en considération et l'appréciation de faits et de circonstances économiques complexes. Le contrôle exercé par le juge doit donc, à cet égard, se limiter à la vérification du respect des règles de procédure et de motivation, ainsi que de l'exactitude matérielle des faits, de l'absence d'erreur manifeste d'appréciation et de détournement de pouvoir. Il n'appartient donc pas au Tribunal de substituer son appréciation économique à celle de la Commission [...].   **10.130**

General Court 18 January 2012 (Djebel – SGPS, Sa v. Commission, T-422/07), ECLI:EU:T:2012:11, para. 107.

1. Article 107(3)(a)

10.131   The use of the words 'abnormally' and 'serious' in the exemption contained in Article [107(3)(a) TFEU] shows that it concerns only areas where the economic situation is extremely unfavourable in relation to the Community as a whole.

The exemption contained in Article [107(3)(c)], on the other hand, is wider in scope and gives the Commission power to authorize aid intended to further the economic development of areas of a Member State which are disadvantaged in relation to the national average.

CoJ 14 October 1987 (Germany v. Commission, 248/84) [1987] ECR 4013, para. 19.

10.132   Consequently, when taking a decision on the compatibility of State aid with the common market, the Commission is not obliged to await the outcome of a parallel procedure initiated under Regulation No 17 [now Regulation No 1/2003], once it has reached the conclusion, based on an economic analysis of the situation and without any manifest error in the assessment of the facts, that the recipient of the aid is not in breach of Articles [101 and 102 TFEU].

CoJ 15 June 1993 (Matra v. Commission, C-225/91) [1993] ECR I-3203, para. 45.

10.133   In a communication of 3 February 1979 on regional aid systems (OJ 1979 C 31, p. 9), to which Decision 92/317 and 92/321 refer, the Commission indicated that regional specificity is fulfilled where regional aid awarded in the regions benefiting from the European Regional Development Fund in principle forms part of a regional development programme within the meaning of Article 6 of Regulation (EEC) No 724/75 establishing that fund (OJ 1975 L 73, p. 1).

On the basis of those provisions, which were applicable at the material time, the Commission was justified in considering that ad hoc aid, that is to say, aid which does not form part of a national programme of Community interest, does not in principle meet the criterion of regional specificity. That aid is not primarily intended to facilitate the development of certain economic regions, but is granted, as in the present case, in the form of aid for the operation of undertakings in difficulty. In those circumstances, it is for the Member State concerned to establish that the aid in question actually fulfils the regional specificity criterion. None the less, the Commission must first specify the criteria according to which it considers ad hoc aid, exceptionally, to be regional in character. The fact that the aid in question was granted on the basis of ad hoc decisions cannot therefore preclude them from being described in the present case as regional aid within the meaning of Article [107(3)(a) TFEU].

CoJ 14 September 1994 (Spain v. Commission, Joined Cases C-278/92 to C-280/92) [1994] ECR I-4103, paras 48 and 49.

The difference in wording between Article [107(3)(a) TFEU] and Article [107(3)(c) **10.134**
TFEU] cannot lead to the conclusion that the Commission should take no account of
the Community interest when applying Article [107(3)(a)] and that it must confine
itself to verifying the regional specificity of the measures involved, without assessing
their impact on the relevant market or markets in the Community as a whole
CoJ 14 January 1997 (Spain v. Commission, C-169/95) [1997] ECR I-135, para.
17.

Regional aid should not give rise to a sectoral overcapacity at Community level. It is **10.135**
clear, in that regard, that the second indent of the second paragraph of point I.6 of
Communication 88/C 212/02, to the effect that aid must 'be designed to promote a
durable and balanced development of economic activity' and not give rise at Community level to a 'sectoral problem [...] more serious than the initial regional problem',
may apply to any regional aid, whatever its nature. Such assessments are not incompatible with the aim pursued by Article [107(3)(a)]. To accept the contrary would
encourage the achievement of economically precarious initiatives which, because they
do no more than aggravate the imbalances affecting the markets concerned, are
ultimately not suited to provide an effective and lasting solution to development
problems in the areas concerned.
CoJ 14 January 1997 (Spain v. Commission, C-169/95) [1997] ECR I-135, para.
22.

When the Commission assesses the compatibility of State aid with the common market **10.136**
in the light of the derogation provided for in Article [107(3)(a) TFEU], it must take
into account the Community interest and may not refrain from assessing the impact of
those measures on the relevant market or markets in the EEA as a whole. In such cases
the Commission is bound not only to verify that the measures are such as to contribute
effectively to the economic development of the regions concerned, but also to evaluate
the impact of the aid on trade between Member States, and in particular to assess the
sectorial repercussions they may have at Community level.
General Court 10 July 2012 (Smurfit Kappa Group plc v. Commission, T-304/08),
ECLI:EU:T:2012:351, para 82.

[I]n the context of Article 107(3)(a) TFEU, in order to be compatible with the internal **10.137**
market, the planned aid must be necessary for the development of less favoured areas.
To that end, it must be shown that, without the planned aid, the investment intended to
support the development of the region in question would not take place. If, on the other
hand, it appears that that investment would take place even without the planned aid, the
conclusion must be that the aid serves merely to improve the situation of the recipient
undertakings, without however meeting the requirement in Article 107(3)(a) TFEU
that it be necessary for the development of less favoured areas.
General Court 10 July 2013 (HGA a.o. v. Commission, C-630/11 P to C-633/11
P), ECLI:EU:C:2013:387, para. 105.

2. Article 107(3)(b)

10.138   The Commission has based its policy with regard to aid on the view that a project may not be described as being of common European interest for the purposes of Article [107(3)(b)] unless it forms part of a transnational European programme supported jointly by a number of governments of the Member States, or arises from concerted action by a number of Member States to combat a common threat such as environmental pollution.

In adopting that policy and in taking the view that the investments envisaged in this case did not fulfil the requisite conditions, the Commission did not commit a manifest error of judgement.

CoJ 8 March 1988 (Waalse Gewestexecutive and Glaverbel, Joined Cases C-62/87 and C-72/87) [1988] ECR 1573, paras 22 and 23.

10.139   Moreover, the question whether German reunification has caused a serious disturbance in the economy of the Federal Republic of Germany involves complex assessments of an economic and social nature, to be made within a Community context, which fall within the exercise of the wide discretion which the Commission enjoys under Article [107(3) TFEU] (see, by analogy, *Case C-355/95 P TWD v. Commission [1997] ECR I-2549, para. 26*). In that context, judicial review must be limited to verifying whether the rules on procedure and the statement of reasons have been complied with, that the facts are materially accurate, and that there has been no manifest error of assessment and no misuse of powers. In particular, it is not for the Community judicature to substitute its economic assessment for that of the Commission [...].

General Court 15 December 1999 (Volkswagen and others v. Commission, Joined Cases T-132/96 and T-143/96) [1999] ECR II-3663, para. 169.

10.140   [L]a dérogation prévue à l'article 107, paragraphe 3, sous b), TFUE et, partant, la notion de « perturbation grave de l'économie d'un État membre » doivent recevoir une interprétation stricte. D'autre part, la Commission jouit d'un large pouvoir d'appréciation dans la mise en œuvre de cette disposition dont l'exercice implique des évaluations d'ordre économique et social qui doivent être effectuées dans un contexte communautaire. Le juge de l'Union, en contrôlant la légalité de l'exercice d'une telle liberté, ne saurait substituer son appréciation en la matière à celle de l'autorité compétente, mais doit se limiter à examiner si cette dernière appréciation est entachée d'erreur manifeste ou de détournement de pouvoir [...].

General Court 12 December 2014 (Banco Privado Português and Massa Insolvente do Banco Privado Português v. Commission, T-487/11), ECLI:EU:T:2014:1077, para. 83.

(a) Financial crisis

10.141   [A]s regards the assessment, in the light of Article 107(3)(b) TFEU, of State guarantees granted to financial institutions in the context of the global financial crisis [...].

[T]he temporal limitation of aid granted in the form of a State guarantee and the obligation to notify any subsequent extension of that guarantee, as well as the obligation resting on the beneficiary of that guarantee to submit a restructuring plan are not mere formal requirements, but rather necessary conditions for that aid to be declared compatible with the internal market and means of ensuring that the emergency aid granted to an undertaking in difficulty does not go beyond what is necessary to achieve the common-interest objective concerned, which consists, in the present case, in preventing a serious disturbance in the national economy.

CoJ 5 March 2015 (Banco Privado Português and Massa Insolvente do Banco Privado Português, C-677/13), ECLI:EU:C:2015:151, para. 69 and 74.

3. Article 107(3)(c)

[T]he Commission was entitled, without exceeding the limits of its discretionary power, to form the view that the aid granted to CBSF could not come within the exemption provided for in Article [107(3)(c) TFEU] in favour of aid designed to facilitate the development of certain economic activities or of certain economic areas, where such aid did not adversely affect trading conditions to an extent contrary to the common interest. The aid lowered CBSF's costs and thereby reduced the competitiveness of other manufacturers within the Community, at the risk of forcing them to withdraw from the market even though they had hitherto been able to continue their activities by virtue of restructuring and improvements in productivity and quality, financed by their own resources.

10.142

CoJ 14 February 1990 (France v. Commission, C-301/87) [1990] ECR I-307, para. 50.

See also General Court 15 December 1999 (Volkswagen and others v. Commission, Joined Cases T-132/96 and T-143/96) [1999] ECR II-3663.

The Commission is right in considering that, in order to be declared compatible with Article [107(3) (c) TFEU], aid to undertakings in difficulty must be bound to a restructuring programme designed to reduce or redirect their activities. Since, according to the plan presented at the time of Imepiel's privatization, the sole purpose of the aid in question was to allow the beneficiary to continue its activities on a larger scale, the Commission was justified in declaring inapplicable the derogation provided for in Article [107(3)(c) TFEU].

10.143

CoJ 14 September 1994 (Spain v. Commission, Joined Cases C-278/92 to C-280/92) [1994] ECR I-4103, para. 67.

À cet égard, il y a lieu de rappeler que, selon la jurisprudence, une décision de la Commission ne saurait constituer, à elle seule, une pratique décisionnelle liant la Commission [...]. De plus, c'est dans le seul cadre de l'article [107(3)(c) TFEU] que doit être appréciée la légalité d'une décision de la Commission constatant qu'une aide nouvelle ne répond pas aux conditions d'application de cette dérogation, et non au regard d'une pratique décisionnelle antérieure de la Commission, à supposer celle-ci établie [...].

10.144

General Court 13 September 2012 (Italy v. Commission, T-379/09), ECLI: EU:T:2012:422, para. 102.

4. Article 107(3)(d)

10.145   [...] Article [107(3)(d)] allows the Council, acting by a qualified majority on a proposal from the Commission, to extend the range of aids which may be considered to be compatible with the common market beyond the categories mentioned in subparagraphs (a), (b) and (c).

The Council made use of that facility when it adopted the said Directive 87/167, which is the sixth in a series of directives on aid to shipbuilding. [...]

As regards production aid for shipbuilding and ship conversion, the criterion chosen is that the aid does not exceed the common maximum ceiling provided for in Article 4(1) of the Directive. This ceiling constitutes what the Council regarded as the balance between the conflicting requirements of respect for the rules of the common market and the maintenance of a sufficient level of activity in European shipyards and also the survival of an efficient and competitive European shipbuilding industry [...].

Clearly, therefore, compliance with the ceiling at issue is the essential condition for aid to shipbuilding to be regarded as compatible with the common market and, where that ceiling is exceeded, the aid in question is automatically incompatible.

In this context, therefore, the Commission's role is limited to checking that that condition has been observed. If, as the Belgian Government contends, the Commission was further required to reassess the compatibility of the aids, case by case, in relation to the criteria set out in Article [107(1)], that would not only deprive the Directive of any effectiveness: it would also be illogical, since any system of derogations necessarily presupposes that the aids referred to are at the outset incompatible with the common market.

CoJ 18 May 1993 (Belgium v. Commission, Joined Cases C-356/90 and C-180/91) [1993] ECR I-2323, paras 26, 27 and 31-33.

11

ARTICLE 108 TFEU*

PROCEDURE BEFORE THE COMMISSION: NOTIFICATION OF AID

1. The Commission shall, in cooperation with Member States, keep under constant review all systems of aid existing in those States. It shall propose to the latter any appropriate measures required by the progressive development or by the functioning of the internal market.

2. If, after giving notice to the parties concerned to submit their comments, the Commission finds that aid granted by a State or through State resources is not compatible with the internal market having regard to Article 107, or that such aid is being misused, it shall decide that the State concerned shall abolish or alter such aid within a period of time to be determined by the Commission.

    If the State concerned does not comply with this decision within the prescribed time, the Commission or any other interested State may, in derogation from the provisions of Articles 258 and 259, refer the matter to the Court of Justice of the European Union direct.

    On application by a Member State, the Council may, acting unanimously, decide that aid which that State is granting or intends to grant shall be considered to be compatible with the internal market, in derogation from the provisions of Article 107 or from the regulations provided for in Article 109, if such a decision is justified by exceptional circumstances. If, as regards the aid in question, the Commission has already initiated the procedure provided for in the first subparagraph of this paragraph, the fact that the State concerned has made its application to the Council shall have the effect of suspending that procedure until the Council has made its attitude known.

    If, however, the Council has not made its attitude known within three months of the said application being made, the Commission shall give its decision on the case.

3. The Commission shall be informed, in sufficient time to enable it to submit its comments, of any plans to grant or alter aid. If it considers

---

*   This chapter was updated by Jacques Derenne. (The assistance of Ciara Barbu O'Connor is gratefully acknowledged.) New cases have been inserted (and others removed) in the current structure and division of matters which have not been reviewed yet.

that any such plan is not compatible with the internal market having regard to Article 107, it shall without delay initiate the procedure provided for in paragraph 2. The Member State concerned shall not put its proposed measures into effect until this procedure has resulted in a final decision.

4. The Commission may adopt regulations relating to the categories of State aid that the Council has, pursuant to Article 109, determined may be exempted from the procedure provided for by paragraph 3 of this Article.

OVERVIEW

A. ARTICLE 108(1): CONSTANT REVIEW AND APPROPRIATE MEASURES	11.01	2. Examination of unlawful aid	11.68
		3. Standstill obligation	11.70
1. New aid and existing aid	11.01	4. Direct applicability of Article 108(3) TFEU	11.74
2. 'Appropriate measures'	11.16	5. Preliminary examination	11.75
		6. The role of the national courts	11.77
B. ARTICLE 108(2): FORMAL INVESTIGATION	11.18		
1. Formal investigation procedure	11.18	D. OTHER SUBJECTS	11.91
2. Interested parties	11.39	1. Action for annulment (Art. 263 TFEU)	11.91
		2. Recovery of aid	11.100
C. ARTICLE 108(3): REQUIREMENT TO NOTIFY AND STANDSTILL OBLIGATION	11.52	3. Complaints received by the Commission	11.123
1. Notification	11.52		

A. ARTICLE 108(1): CONSTANT REVIEW AND APPROPRIATE MEASURES

1. New aid and existing aid

11.01   First, the EC Treaty establishes different procedures according to whether the aid is existing or new. Whereas new aid must, under Article [108(3) TFEU], be notified in advance to the Commission and cannot be implemented before the procedure has culminated in a final decision, existing aid may, under Article [108(1) TFEU], be duly implemented as long as the Commission has not found it to be incompatible. Existing aid may therefore only be the subject, should the situation arise, of a decision of incompatibility producing effects for the future.
General Court 9 September 2009 (Territorio Histórico de Álava – Diputación Foral de Álava and Others v. Commission, Cases T-227/01 to T-229/01, T-265/01, T-266/01 and T-270/01) [2009] ECR II-3029, para. 228.

11.02   The Treaty on the functioning of the EU establishes different procedures according to whether the aid is existing or new. Whereas new aid must, under Article 108(3), be notified in advance to the Commission and cannot be implemented before the

procedure has culminated in a final decision, existing aid may, under Article 108(1), be duly implemented as long as the Commission has not found it to be incompatible [...].
General Court 24 March 2011 (Freistaat Sachsen and Others v. Commission, T-443/08 and T-455/08) [2011] ECR II-1311, para. 187.

[T]he concept of aid, whether existing or new, corresponds to an objective situation and **11.03** cannot depend on the conduct or statements of the institutions.
CoJ 21 July 2011 (Alcoa Trasformazioni v. Commission, C-194/09 P) [2011] ECR I-6311, para. 125.

(a) Existing aid

Aid implemented, during the Commission's silence, after a period necessary for its **11.04** preliminary examination, is thus subject, as an existing aid, to the provisions of Article [108](1) and (2).
CoJ 11 December 1973 (Lorenz v. Germany, 120/73) [1973] ECR 1471, para. 5.

That power of the Commission also covers State aid granted to the undertakings **11.05** referred to in Article [106(2)], in particular those which the Member States have made responsible for the management of services of general economic interest.
   It follows that the distinction which Article [108 TFEU] draws between existing aid and new aid is equally applicable to State aid granted to the undertakings covered by Article [106(2)].
CoJ 15 March 1994 (Banco de Crédito Industrial v. Ayuntamiento de Valencia, C-387/92) [1994] ECR I-877, paras 18 and 19.

If following the examination thus circumscribed the Commission finds that the **11.06** individual aid is in conformity with its decision approving the scheme it must be regarded as authorized aid, and thus as existing aid. Therefore the Commission is not entitled to order the suspension thereof since Article [108(3) TFEU] empowers it to do so only in regard to new aid.
CoJ 5 October 1994 (Italy v. Commission (Italgrani), C-47/91) [1994] ECR I-4635.

Thus, even on the assumption that it is wholly attributable to the State, the decision **11.07** which entered into force on 1 February 1989 cannot be regarded as constituting the granting or alteration of aid within the meaning of Article [108(3) TFEU].
   To take the contrary view would in effect be tantamount to requiring the Member State concerned to notify to the Commission and submit for its preventive review not only new aid or alterations of aid properly so-called granted to an undertaking in receipt of existing aid but also all measures which affect the activity of the undertaking and which may have an impact on the functioning of the common market, on competition

or simply on the actual amount, over a specific period, of aid which is available in principle but which necessarily varies in amount according to the undertaking's turnover.

Such an interpretation, which does not correspond to either the letter or the purpose of Article [108(3)], nor to the division of responsibility between the Commission and the Member States for which it provides, would give rise to legal uncertainty for undertakings and Member States, which would thus be obliged to notify in advance widely differing measures, which could not then be put into effect despite doubts as to whether they could be classified as new aid.

CoJ 9 August 1994 (Nationale Delcrederedienst, C–44/93) [1994] ECR I–3829, paras 31–33.

11.08   As far as that question and the application of paragraphs (1) and (3) of Article [108] are concerned, the emergence of new aid or the alteration of existing aid cannot be assessed according to the scale of the aid or, in particular, its amount in financial terms at any moment in the life of the undertaking if the aid is provided under earlier statutory provisions which remain unaltered. Whether aid may be classified as new aid or as alteration of existing aid must be determined by reference to the provisions providing for it.

CoJ 9 August 1994 (Nationale Delcrederedienst, C–44/93) [1994] ECR I–3829, para. 28.

11.09   [W]hen the Commission has before it a specific grant of an aid alleged to be made in pursuance of a previously authorized scheme, it cannot at the outset examine it directly in relation to the Treaty. Prior to the initiation of any procedure, it must first examine whether the aid is covered by the general scheme and satisfies the conditions laid down in the decision approving it. If it did not do so, the Commission could, whenever it examined an individual aid, go back on its decision approving the aid scheme which already involved an examination in the light of Article [107 TFEU]. This would jeopardize the principles of the protection of legitimate expectations and legal certainty from the point of view of both the Member States and traders since individual aid in strict conformity with the decision approving the aid scheme could at any time be called in question by the Commission [...].

If the Commission has doubts as to the conformity of individual aids with its decision approving the general scheme, it is up to it to order the Member State concerned to supply to it, within such period as it may specify, all such documentation, information and data as are necessary in order that it may form a view on the compatibility of the aid in question with its decision approving the aids scheme.

Should the Member State fail, notwithstanding the Commission's injunction, to supply the information requested, the Commission may order the suspension thereof and directly assess compatibility with the Treaty as if it was a new aid.

CoJ 5 October 1994 (Italy v. Commission (Italgrani), C–47/91) [1994] ECR I–4635, paras 24, 34 and 35.

See also CoJ 14 February 1990 (France v. Commission, C–301/87) [1990] ECR I–307 (Boussac).

[I]t is clear from Article 1 of Regulation No 659/1999 that existing aid means all aid **11.10** which existed prior to the entry into force of the EC Treaty in the respective Member States and all aid which has been authorised by the Commission or by the Council and that any alterations to existing aid must be deemed to be new aid.

According to that unequivocal provision, it is not 'altered existing aid' that must be regarded as new aid, but only the alteration as such that is liable to be classified as new aid. Accordingly, it is only where the alteration affects the actual substance of the original scheme that the latter is transformed into a new aid scheme. [...]

There can be no question of such a substantive alteration where the new element is clearly severable from the initial scheme. Article 108(3) treats alterations to existing aid as new aid in order to prevent the Member States from circumventing the obligation to notify new aid by extending the scope of a scheme that is already in force in order to achieve the same result [...].

General Court 16 December 2010 (Netherlands & NOS v. Commission, T-231/06 and T-237/06) [2010] ECR II-05993, paras 176–178.

See also 30 April 2002 (Government of Gibraltar v. Commission, T-195/01 and T-207/01) [2002] ECR II-2309, paras 109 and 111.

As regards aid implemented in [a Member State] before it acceded to the European **11.11** Union, the specific Act of Accession provides for a monitoring mechanism. [...]

Under that mechanism, measures implemented before accession but which, firstly, are still applicable post-accession and, secondly, satisfy the cumulative requirements of Article 107(1) on the date of accession, are subject to the specific rules laid down in the Act of Accession [...].

CoJ 29 November 2012 (Kremikovtzi C-262/11), ECLI:EU:C:2012:760, paras 51 and 52.

(b) New aid

If following the examination thus circumscribed the Commission finds that the **11.12** individual aid is in conformity with its decision approving the scheme it must be regarded as authorized aid, and thus as existing aid.

Where such aid was not notified to it, the Commission has the power, after giving the Member State in question an opportunity to submit its comments on the matter, to issue an interim decision requiring it to suspend immediately the payment of such aid pending the outcome of the examination of the aid and to provide the Commission, within such period as it may specify, with all such documentation, information and data as are necessary in order that it may examine the compatibility of the aid with the common market.

CoJ 5 October 1994 (Italy v. Commission (Italgrani), C-47/91) [1994] ECR I-4635, paras 25 and 26.

11.13   [M]easures to grant or alter aid must be regarded as new aid [...], in particular, where the alteration affects the actual substance of the original scheme, the latter is transformed into a new aid scheme. [...]
General Court 20 September 2011 (Regione autonoma della Sardegna and Others v. Commission, T-394/08, T-408/08, T-453/08 and T-454/08) [2011] ECR II-6255, para. 176.

11.14   [U]nder Article 108(3) TFEU the Commission must be informed of any plan to grant new aid before it is implemented and that any new aid granted without the Commission's approval is unlawful.
        Moreover, under Article 1(c) and (b) of Council Regulation (EC) No 659/1999 of 22 March 1999 laying down detailed rules for the application of Article 108 TFEU, new aid means 'all aid, that is to say, aid schemes and individual aid, which is not existing aid, including alterations to existing aid' and existing aid means 'authorised aid, that is to say, aid schemes and individual aid which have been authorised by the Commission or by the Council of the European Union'.
General Court 8 October 2014 (Alouminion v. Commission, T-542/11), ECLI: EU:T:2014:859, paras 48 and 49.

11.15   [I]t is clear from the very definitions of 'existing aid' and 'new aid' that where an aid is granted to a new beneficiary, different from the beneficiaries of an existing aid, it can only be new aid in the case of that new recipient.
General Court 24 September 2015 (TV2/Denmark v. Commission, T-674/11), ECLI:EU:T:2015:684, para. 236.

2. 'Appropriate measures'

11.16   Article [108(1) TFEU] creates an obligation of regular, periodic cooperation on the part of the Commission and the Member States, from which neither the Commission nor a Member State can release itself for an indefinite period depending on the unilateral will of either of them.

CoJ 29 July 1995 (Spain v. Commission, C-135/93) [1995] ECR I-1651.

11.17   As a result of the obligation of cooperation laid down by Article [108(1) TFEU] and of its acceptance of the rules laid down in the Guidelines, a Member State, such as the Netherlands, must apply the Guidelines when deciding on an application for aid for the construction of a vessel intended for fishing.
CoJ 15 October 1996 (IJssel-Vliet, C-311/94) [1996] ECR I-5023, para. 44.

B. ARTICLE 108(2): FORMAL INVESTIGATION

1. Formal investigation procedure

(a) Obligation on Commission to initiate the formal investigation procedure

Although [...] the obligation to initiate the procedure under Article [108(3)] does not **11.18** depend on the circumstances in which the aid is notified or on the provision of Article [107 TFEU] which is applied, it is for the Commission to determine, subject to review by the Court, on the basis of the factual and legal circumstances of the case, whether the difficulties involved in assessing the compatibility of the aid warrant the initiation of that procedure [...].

It follows that, since the Commission sought to rely on the absence of overcapacity in the sub-sector in question, it should have initiated the procedure under Article [108(2) TFEU] in order to ascertain, after obtaining all the requisite opinions, whether its assessment[,] which gave rise to serious difficulties[,] was correct.

Since it was not preceded by that procedure, Decision NN 12/91 is illegal [...].
CoJ 19 May 1993 (Cook, C-198/91) [1993] ECR I-2487, paras 30, 38 and 39.

It also follows from that case-law that the Commission is required to initiate the **11.19** procedure provided for in Article [108(2) TFEU] if an initial examination does not enable it to resolve all the difficulties raised by the question whether a State measure submitted to it for review constitutes aid for the purposes of Article [107(1) TFEU], unless, in the course of that initial examination, the Commission is able to satisfy itself that the measure at issue is in any event compatible with the common market, even if it is aid. [...]

It should be remembered in that respect that the Commission cannot limit itself to the preliminary phase under Article [108(3) TFEU] and take a favourable decision on a State measure which has not been notified unless it is in a position to reach the firm view, following an initial investigation, that the State measure in question cannot be classified as aid within the meaning of Article [107(1) TFEU] or that the measure, whilst constituting aid, is compatible with the common market. [...]

Finally, it should be noted that, according to the case-law, the fact that the time spent on an initial examination under Article [108(3) TFEU] considerably exceeds the time usually taken may, with other factors, justify the conclusion that the Commission encountered serious difficulties of assessment necessitating initiation of the procedure under Article [108(2) TFEU].
General Court 10 May 2000 (SIC v. Commission, T-46/97) [2000] ECR II-2125, paras 72, 91 and 102.

It follows that it is sufficient if the Commission has at its disposal, during that **11.20** preliminary phase, all such information as will enable it to conclude, without any extensive review being called for, whether a given State measure is compatible with the Treaty or raises doubt as to its compatibility.

General Court 15 February 2001 (Austria v. Commission, C-99/98) [2001] ECR I-1101, para. 54.

11.21   It follows that the procedure under Article [108(2) TFEU], which gives other Member States and the parties concerned the assurance that they will be able to make their views known and enables the Commission to be fully informed of all the facts of the case before taking its decision, is essential whenever the Commission has serious difficulties in determining whether an aid is compatible with the common market. Therefore, when taking a decision in favour of an aid, the Commission may restrict itself to the preliminary phase provided for under Article [108(3)] only if it is able to satisfy itself after an initial examination that the aid is compatible with the Treaty. If, on the other hand, the initial examination leads the Commission to the opposite conclusion or if it does not enable it to overcome all the difficulties involved in determining whether the aid is compatible with the common market, the Commission is under a duty to carry out all the requisite consultations and, for that purpose, to initiate the procedure under Article [108(2) TFEU].

The preliminary stage provided for in Article [108(3) TFEU] is intended merely to allow the Commission a sufficient period of time for reflection and investigation so that it can form a prima facie opinion on the draft aid plans notified to it, thus enabling it either to conclude, without the need for detailed examination, that the aid is compatible with the common market or, by contrast, to make a finding that the content of those plans raises doubts as to that compatibility.

CoJ 3 May 2001 (Portugal v. Commission, C-204/97) [2001] ECR I-3175, paras 33 and 34.

See also CoJ 20 March 1984 (Germany v. Commission, 84/82) [1984] ECR 1451, para. 13; CoJ 15 March 2001 (Prayon-Rupel v. Commission, T-73/98) [2001] ECR II-867, para. 42.

11.22   [I]n the light of Article 10(1) of Regulation No 659/1999, [...] where the Commission has in its possession information from whatever source regarding alleged unlawful aid, it is to examine that information without delay. That provision must not be understood as referring to the conclusion of the preliminary examination stage, but rather as relating to the beginning of the preliminary examination. [...]

General Court 20 September 2011 (Regione autonoma della Sardegna and Others v. Commission, T-394/08, T-408/08, T-453/08 and T-454/08) [2011] ECR II-6255, para. 97.

See also General Court 27 September 2011 (3F v. Commission, T-30/03 RENV) [2011] ECR II-6651, paras 57 and 58, 70–72.

11.23   [T]he procedure under Article [108(2) TFEU] is essential whenever the Commission has serious difficulties in determining whether aid is compatible with the common market. The Commission may therefore restrict itself to the preliminary examination under Article [108(3) TFEU] when taking a decision in favour of aid only if it is able to satisfy itself after an initial examination that the aid is compatible with the common market.

CoJ 24 January 2013 (Falles Fagligt Forbund ((3F) v. Commission, C-646/11 P), ECLI:EU:2013:36, para. 28.

(b)   The concept of 'serious difficulties'

Firstly, under Article [108 TFEU] the Commission's power to find aid to be compatible   **11.24**
with the common market upon the conclusion of the preliminary procedure is restricted
to aid measures that raise no serious difficulties. That criterion is thus an exclusive one.
The Commission may not, therefore, decline to initiate the formal investigation
procedure in reliance upon other circumstances, such as third-party interests, considerations of economy of procedure or any other ground of administrative convenience.

Secondly, where it encounters serious difficulties, the Commission must initiate the
formal procedure, having no discretion in this regard. Whilst its powers are circumscribed as far as initiating the formal procedure is concerned, the Commission nevertheless enjoys a certain margin of discretion in identifying and evaluating the
circumstances of the case in order to determine whether or not they present serious
difficulties. In accordance with the objective of Article [108(3) TFEU] and its duty of
good administration, the Commission may, amongst other things, engage in talks with
the notifying State or with third parties in an endeavour to overcome, during the
preliminary procedure, any difficulties encountered.

General Court 15 March 2001 (Prayon-Rupel v. Commission, T-73/98) [2001] ECR II-867, paras 44 and 45.

Thus, there is a clear contradiction between the content of those documents and the   **11.25**
contested decision, according to which CWP meant to abandon the use of elemental
phosphorus and the thermal process as a result of the acquisition of a chemical processor
which would enable it both to resolve its supply difficulties and to increase its product
range. A contradiction of that kind at least leads to the conclusion that, at the time
when it adopted the contested decision, the Commission did not have sufficient
information to enable it to form the view that the issue of whether or not the
restructuring plant could return CWP to viability was one that did not raise serious
difficulties.

General Court 15 March 2001 (Prayon-Rupel v. Commission, T-73/98) [2001] ECR II-867, para. 78.

It is clear from that chronology of events that the assessment of the proposal of aid to   **11.26**
CWP was fraught with difficulty from notification onwards. During the course of the
eight months between notification and the contested decision, the Commission made
three separate official requests for information of the German Government and two
competitors made their concerns known. The German Government refrained from
sending the Commission information that would assist it in its assessment in spite of
repeated demands on the latter's part. In particular, it was not until seven months after
notification of the aid plan that the German Government sent the Commission the

restructuring plan which the aid was intended to finance. The Commission therefore departed from the recommended timetable it had set itself for examining notified aid proposals. For its part, the German Government replied to the Commission out of time. In view of those factors, it must be acknowledged that the procedure conducted by the Commission appreciably exceeded, in the present case, what is normally required for an initial examination under Article [108(3) TFEU]. That circumstance is cogent evidence of the existence of serious difficulties.

CoJ 15 March 2001 (Prayon-Rupel v. Commission, T-73/98) [2001] ECR II-867, para. 107.

11.27   It is apparent from Article 4(4) of Regulation No 659/1999 and the case-law that the Commission is required to open the procedure provided for in Article [108(2) TFEU] if an initial examination does not enable it to overcome all the difficulties raised by the question whether the State measure under scrutiny constitutes aid for the purposes of Article [107(1) TFEU], unless, in the course of that initial examination, the Commission is able to satisfy itself that the measure at issue would in any event be compatible with the common market, even if it were aid.

The fact that the time spent considerably exceeds the time usually required for a preliminary examination under Article [108(3) TFEU] may, with other factors, justify the conclusion that the Commission encountered serious difficulties of assessment necessitating initiation of the procedure under [108(2) TFEU].

General Court 12 December 2006 (Asociación de Estaciones de Servicio de Madrid and Federación Catalana de Estaciones de Servicio v. Commission, T-95/03) [2006] ECR II-4739, paras 134 and 135.

11.28   [I]t is for the Commission to decide, on the basis of the factual and legal circumstances of the case, whether the difficulties involved in assessing the compatibility of the aid require the initiation of that procedure. That decision must satisfy three requirements.

Firstly, under Article [108 TFEU] the Commission's power to find aid to be compatible with the common market upon the conclusion of the preliminary examination procedure is restricted to aid measures that raise no serious difficulties. That criterion is thus an exclusive one. The Commission may not, therefore, decline to initiate the formal investigation procedure in reliance upon other circumstances, such as third-party interests, considerations of economy of procedure or any other ground of administrative convenience.

Secondly, where it encounters serious difficulties, the Commission must initiate the formal procedure, having no discretion in this regard. Whilst its powers are circumscribed as far as initiating the formal procedure is concerned, the Commission nevertheless enjoys a certain margin of discretion in identifying and evaluating the circumstances of the case in order to determine whether or not they present serious difficulties. In accordance with the objective of Article [108(3) TFEU] and its duty of good administration, the Commission may, amongst other things, engage in talks with the notifying State or with third parties in an endeavour to overcome, during the preliminary procedure, any difficulties encountered.

Thirdly, the notion of 'serious difficulties' is an objective one. Whether or not such difficulties exist requires investigation of both the circumstances under which the contested measure was adopted and its content. That investigation must be conducted objectively, comparing the grounds of the decision with the information available to the Commission when it took a decision on the compatibility of the disputed aid with the common market.

General Court 18 November 2009 (Scheucher–Fleisch GmbH and Others v. Commission, T-375/04) [2009] ECR II-4155, paras 71–74.

See also General Court 10 February 2009 (Deutsche Post AG and DHL International v. Commission, T-388/03) [2009] ECR II-00199, and CoJ September 2011 (Belgium v. Deutsche Post AG and DHL International, C-148/09) [2011] ECR I-08573, paras 31–34.

[A]ccording to the case-law, the procedure under Article 108(2), which guarantees the **11.29** Member States and the sectors concerned an opportunity to make their views known and allows the Commission to be fully informed of all the facts of the case before taking its decision, is essential whenever the Commission has serious difficulties in determining whether a State measure is compatible with the common market [...].The Commission cannot therefore limit itself to the preliminary procedure under Article 108(3) and take a favourable decision on a State measure unless it is in a position to reach the firm view, following an initial examination, that the measure cannot be classified as aid within the meaning of Article 107(1) or that the measure, while constituting aid, is compatible with the common market [...].

General Court 3 March 2010 (Bundesverband deutscher Banken v. Commission, T-36/06) [2010] ECR II-537, para. 125.

[T]he notion of serious difficulties is an objective one. Whether or not such difficulties **11.30** exist requires investigation of both the circumstances under which the contested measure was adopted and its content. That investigation must be conducted objectively, comparing the grounds of the decision with the information available to the Commission when it took a decision on the compatibility of the disputed aid with the common market [...]. The applicant bears the burden of proving the existence of serious difficulties and may discharge that burden of proof by reference to a body of consistent evidence, concerning, first, the circumstances and the length of the preliminary examination procedure and, second, the content of the contested decision.

General Court 3 March 2010 (Bundesverband deutscher Banken v. Commission, T-36/06) [2010] ECR II-537, para. 127.

[T]he question whether the Commission misapplied the private investor test is not to **11.31** be confused with the question whether there are serious difficulties which require the formal investigation procedure to be initiated. Consideration of whether serious difficulties exist is not aimed at establishing whether the Commission applied Article 107 correctly, but whether, at the time of its adoption of the contested decision, there was sufficiently comprehensive information available to it to enable it to assess the compatibility of the disputed measure with the common market.

General Court 3 March 2010 (Bundesverband deutscher Banken v. Commission, T-36/06) [2010] ECR II-537, para. 129.

See also General Court 1 July 2010 (M6 & TF1 v. Commission, T-568/08 and T-573/08) [2010] ECR II-3397, paras 60–61; General Court 9 September 2010 (British Aggregates a.o. v. Commission, T-359/04) [2010] ECR II-4227, paras 55–58, 90, 94–98, 102.

(c) Procedure between the Commission and the Member State granting the aid

11.32   The Commission cannot rely on the existence in those documents of information covered by business confidentiality. In so far as the Member State concerned was not afforded an opportunity to comment on that information, the Commission may not use it in its decision with regard to that State.

CoJ 10 July 1986 (Belgium v. Commission, 234/84) [1986] ECR 2263, para. 29.

11.33   Of the interested parties, the recipient of the aid does not play a special role pursuant to any provision governing the procedure for the review of State aid. The procedure for the review of State aid is not a procedure initiated 'against' the recipient or recipients of aid by virtue of which it or they could rely on rights as extensive as the rights of the defence as such.

General Court 14 January 2004 (Fleuren Compost v. Commission, T-109/01) [2004] ECR II-127, para. 44.

11.34   The procedure provided for in Article [108(2) TFEU] takes place primarily between the Commission and the Member State concerned. It is initiated against that State and not against the beneficiaries.

CoJ 6 October 2005 (Scott v. Commission, C-276/03) [2005] ECR I-8437, para. 33.

(d) Decision to initiate the formal investigation procedure

11.35   It should also be borne in mind that, according to Article 6(1) of Regulation No 659/1999, 'the decision to initiate the formal investigation procedure shall summarise the relevant issues of fact and law, shall include a preliminary assessment of the Commission as to the aid character of the proposed measure and shall set out the doubts as to its compatibility with the common market'. That decision and the publication thereof in the Official Journal of the European Communities inform the Member State and other interested parties of the facts on which the Commission intends to base its decision. It follows that, if those parties believe that some of the facts contained in the decision to initiate the formal investigation procedure are incorrect, they must inform the Commission thereof during the administrative procedure or risk not being able to challenge those facts at the litigation stage […]. By contrast, in accordance with the principles laid down in the case-law, where there is no information to the contrary from interested parties, the Commission is empowered to base itself on the factual elements it has at the time it adopts its final decision, even if they are incorrect, provided that the factual elements in question were the subject of an information injunction issued by the Commission to the Member State to provide it with the necessary information. If, however, it fails to order the Member State to provide it with information on the facts on which it intends to rely, it cannot subsequently justify any errors of fact by stating that, at the time of adopting the decision ending the formal investigation procedure, it was entitled to rely only on the information it had at that time.

General Court 19 October 2005 (Freistaat Thüringen v. Commission, T-318/00) [2005] ECR II-4179, para. 88.

It should be recalled, as a preliminary point, that the Commission must initiate a formal **11.36** investigation procedure, informing the interested parties, when, following a preliminary investigation, it has serious doubts as to the compatibility of the financial measure in question with the common market. It follows that the Commission cannot be required to present a complete analysis on the aid in question in its notice of intention to initiate that procedure. The Commission must, however, define sufficiently the framework of its investigation so as not to render meaningless the right of interested parties to put forward their comments.

General Court 31 May 2006 (Kuwait Petroleum v. Commission, T-354/99) [2006] ECR II-1475, para. 85.

[The contested act is a letter in which Commission informed the appellant that in view **11.37** of the judgment in *Athinaïki Techniki v Commission*, it was withdrawing an earlier decision to take no further action, reopening the preliminary examination procedure and repeating its earlier request to Athinaïki Techniki to submit to it evidence proving the grant of State aid.]

If the Commission were entitled to withdraw an act such as the contested act in those circumstances, it could perpetuate a state of inaction during the preliminary examination stage, contrary to its obligations under Articles 13(1) and 20(2) of Regulation No 659/1999 and avoid any judicial review. As the Advocate General stated in [...] his Opinion, it would be sufficient for the Commission to decide to take no further action on a complaint lodged by an interested party and then, after that party brought an action, to reopen the preliminary examination stage and repeat those operations as many times as are necessary in order to avoid any judicial review of its actions.

CoJ 16 December 2010 (Athinaïki Techniki v. Commission, C-362/09 P) [2010] ECR I-13275, para. 68.

[I]t follows from Article 4(4) of Regulation No 659/1999 that if, following the **11.38** preliminary examination, it finds that the contested measure raises doubts as to its compatibility with the common market, the Commission is required to adopt a decision initiating the formal investigation procedure under Article 108(2) and Article 6(1) of that regulation [...].

With regard to, [...] the length and circumstances of the preliminary examination procedure, while it is true that a period exceeding the two-month period provided for in Article 4(5) of Regulation No 659/1999 and the number of requests for information addressed to the Belgian authorities do not of themselves support the conclusion that the Commission should have initiated the formal investigation procedure, those elements may none the less constitute evidence that the Commission may have had doubts regarding the compatibility of the aid at issue with the common market.

CoJ 22 September 2011 (Belgium v. Deutsche Post and DHL International, C-148/09 P) [2011] ECR I-8573, paras 77 and 81.

2. Interested parties

(a) The concept of 'interested party'

11.39 The parties concerned, within the meaning of Article [108(2) TFEU] [...] are those persons, undertakings or associations whose interests might be affected by the grant of the aid, in particular competing undertakings and trade associations [...]
See (among others) CoJ 27 May 1997 (Commission v. Sytraval, C-367/95 P) [1998] ECR I-1719, para. 41.

See also Article 1(h) of Regulation No 659/1999.

11.40 It must be noted that the 'parties concerned' referred to in [Art. 108(2) TFEU] are not only the undertaking or undertakings receiving aid but equally the persons, undertakings or associations whose interests might be affected by the grant of the aid, in particular competing undertakings and trade associations. In other words, there is an indeterminate group of persons to whom notice must be given.

It follows that Article [108(2)] does not require individual notice to be given to particular persons. Its sole purpose is to oblige the Commission to take steps to ensure that all persons who may be concerned are notified and given an opportunity of putting forward their arguments. Under those circumstances, the publication of a notice in the Official Journal is an appropriate means of informing all the parties concerned that a procedure has been initiated.
CoJ 14 November 1984 (Intermills, 323/82) [1984] ECR 3809, paras 16 and 17.

11.41 The status of 'party concerned' is not therefore restricted to undertakings that are substantially affected by the grant of aid.
General Court 10 May 2006 (Air One SpA v. Commission, T-395/04) [2006] ECR II-1343, para. 36.

11.42 It is not excluded that a trade union may be regarded as 'concerned' within the meaning of Article [108(2) TFEU] if it shows that its interests or those of its members might be affected by the granting of aid. The trade union must, however, show to the requisite legal standard that the aid is likely to have a real effect on its situation or that of the seafarers it represents.
CoJ 9 July 2009 (3F v. Commission, C-319/07 P) [2009] ECR I-5963, para. 33.

11.43 As a consequence, that provision does not rule out the possibility that an undertaking which is not a direct competitor of the beneficiary of the aid, but which requires the same raw material for its production process, can be categorised as an interested party, provided that that undertaking demonstrates that its interests could be adversely affected by the grant of the aid.

For that purpose, it is necessary for that undertaking to establish, to the requisite legal standard, that the aid is likely to have a specific effect on its situation (see, to that effect, *3F v Commission, para. 33*).

CoJ 24 May 2011 (Commission v. Kronoply, C-83/09 P) [2011] ECR I-4441, paras 64 and 65.

(b)   The rights of interested parties

If a case necessitates initiating the procedure provided for in Article [108(2)], the **11.44** Commission must give the parties concerned notice to submit their comments. However, the sole aim of this is to obtain from persons concerned all information required for the guidance of the Commission with regard to its future action [...]. In its judgment in *Case 84/82 Germany v. Commission* the Court of Justice held (in paragraph 13) that the procedure provided for in that article 'guarantees the other Member States and the sectors concerned an opportunity to make their views known and allows the Commission to be fully informed of all the facts of the case before taking its decision'.

General Court 22 October 1996 (Skibsværftsforeningen and others v. Commission, T-266/94) [1996] ECR II-1399, para. 256.

However, by letter of 24 July 2001, the Commission replied to the letter from EURL *Le* **11.45** *Levant* 114 by noting that the one-month period from the date of publication of the decision to open the procedure allowed for the lodging of comments by the interested parties had 'long since lapsed', without adopting a position on the request for an extension of that period made by EURL *Le Levant* 114. That refusal is all the more deplorable because the decision to open the procedure did not identify the private investors as beneficiaries of the aid to be recovered but, on the contrary, gave the impression that the beneficiary was CIL, which had been named as the operator and ultimate owner of the vessel.

Accordingly, by refusing to allow an extension of the period as requested and thereby failing to give EURL *Le Levant* 114 an opportunity to submit its comments on the decision to open the procedure, without even giving reasons why the request of 19 July 2001 was not 'duly justified', the Commission infringed the third sentence of Article 6(1) of Regulation No 659/1999.

General Court 22 February 2006 (Le Levant 001 and others v. Commission, T-34/02) [2006] ECR II-267, paras 93 and 94.

In that procedure for reviewing State aid, interested parties other than the Member **11.46** State responsible for granting the aid, therefore, cannot themselves claim a right to debate the issues with the Commission in the same way as may that Member State. They have, effectively, the role of a source of information for the Commission.

In that regard, the procedure for review of State aid accords no special role to the recipient of State aid as compared with all interested parties. It is clear, moreover, that the procedure for reviewing State aid is not a procedure initiated 'against' the recipient of aid giving rise to rights on which it could rely which are as extensive as rights of defence as such. Nevertheless, even though the recipient of aid does not have the status of a party to the procedure, the case-law has granted it certain procedural rights which are designed to enable it to provide information to the Commission and to put forward its arguments.

In the present case, it is common ground that Scott was invited to submit its observations during the formal examination procedure under Article [108(2) TFEU] and under Article 6(1) of Regulation No 659/ 1999 and that Scott availed itself of that opportunity to submit detailed observations to the Commission on 23 November 1998.

However, it does not follow from the case-law that the Commission is therefore entitled to ignore all other observations made by the recipient of aid after the expiry of the deadline laid down by the decision to open the procedure. It is clear from the case-law that the Commission must conduct a diligent and impartial examination of the case under Article [108 TFEU]. It follows that the Commission might be obliged, in certain circumstances, to take into account the observations of the recipient of aid after the expiry of the time laid down by the decision to open the procedure.

It is worth noting that no provision of Regulation No 659/1999, including its Article 6, prevents the Commission from accepting such observations. Indeed, that latter article permits the Commission to extend the deadline for the submission for observations of interested parties in duly justified cases.

General Court 29 March 2007 (Scott v. Commission, T-366/00) [2007] ECR II-797, paras 53–57.

11.47   The reasonableness of the length of the procedure for review of State aid, whether that relates to the preliminary examination or the formal investigation procedure, must be appraised in the light of the circumstances specific to each case and, in particular, its context, the various procedural stages followed by the Commission, the conduct of the parties in the course of the procedure, the complexity of the case and its importance for the various parties involved.

General Court 9 September 2009 (Territorio Histórico de Álava – Diputación Foral de Álava and Others v. Commission, T-227/01 to T-229/01, T-265/01, T-266/01 and T-270/01) [2009] ECR II-3029, para. 336.

(c)   Limited role of interested parties

11.48   With regard to the examination by the Commission of plans to grant aid, that principle requires the Member State in question to be placed in a position in which it may effectively make known its views on the observations submitted by interested third parties under Article [108(2) TFEU] and on which the Commission proposes to base its decision. In so far as that Member State has not been afforded the opportunity to comment on such observations, the Commission may not incorporate them in its decision against that State without infringing the right to be heard.

However, in order for such an infringement to result in annulment, it is necessary to establish that, had it not been for such an irregularity, the outcome of the procedure might have been different.

CoJ 14 February 1990 (France v. Commission, C-301/87) [1990] ECR I-307, paras 30 and 31.

This case-law confers on the parties concerned the role of information sources for the **11.49** Commission in the administrative procedure instituted under Article [108(2) TFEU]. It follows that, far from enjoying the same rights of defence as those which individuals against whom a procedure has been instituted are recognised as having, the parties concerned have only the right to be involved in the administrative procedure to the extent appropriate in the light of the circumstances of the case.

General Court 6 March 2003 (Westdeutsche Landesbank Girozentrale v. Commission, T-228/99 and T-233/99) [2003] ECR II-435, para. 125.

It is true that case-law has granted the beneficiary of aid certain procedural rights. **11.50** However, those rights are designed to enable the beneficiary to provide information to the Commission and to put forward its arguments, but do not confer on it the status of a party to the procedure.

CoJ 6 October 2005 (Scott v. Commission, C-276/03) [2005] ECR I-8437, para. 34.

(d) Obligation of Commission to address complaints parties

The limited nature of the abovementioned rights to participate and to be informed, in **11.51** so far as they relate solely to the administrative procedure, is not at variance with the Commission's duty under Article [296 TFEU] to provide, in its final decision authorising planned aid, sufficient reasons which must address all the essential complaints which parties directly and individually concerned by that decision have made either on their own initiative or as a result of information supplied by the Commission. Thus, even on the assumption that the Commission may, in a particular case, validly prefer to use other sources of information and thereby reduce the significance of the participation of interested parties, it is not thereby released from its obligation to include an adequate statement of reasons in its decision.

General Court 25 June 1998 (British Airways and others v. Commission, T-371/94 and T-394/94) [1998] ECR II-2405, para. 64.

C. ARTICLE 108(3): REQUIREMENT TO NOTIFY AND STANDSTILL OBLIGATION

1. Notification

(a) Only in case of State aid

That Member States need not notify those measures which do not fulfil all the criteria **11.52** laid down in Article [107(1) TFEU]. That is now spelt out by Articles 2(1) and 1(a) of Council Regulation (EC) No 659/ 1999 of 22 March 1999 laying down detailed rules for the application of Article [108 TFEU].

Opinion of AG Jacobs 13 December 2001 (France v. Commission, C-482/99) [2002] ECR I-4397, para. 49.

11.53   It must also be pointed out that, according to settled case-law, classification as aid requires that all the conditions set out in that provision should be fulfilled.
CoJ 15 July 2004 (Pearle, C-345/02) [2004] ECR I-7139, para. 32.

11.54   On the other hand, only State aid within the meaning of Article [107(1) TFEU] is subject to the notification procedure laid down in Article [108(3) TFEU]. Pursuant to Article [107(1) TFEU], for a measure to be classified as State aid it must, inter alia, be liable to affect trade between Member States [...].
CoJ 21 July 2005 (Xunta de Galicia, C-71/04) [2005] ECR I-7419, para. 32.

(b)   In case of alterations to existing aid

11.55   Under Article 1(c) of the regulation on State aid procedure, alterations to existing aid are to be regarded as new aid. According to that unequivocal provision, it is not altered existing aid that must be regarded as new aid, but only the alteration as such that is liable to be classified as new aid.

That analysis is confirmed by *Case C-44/93 Namur-Les assurances du crédit*, where the Court of Justice held that measures to [...] alter aid must be regarded as new aid and that plans to [...] alter aid cannot be put into effect before the procedure has resulted in a final Commission decision.

Accordingly, it is only where the alteration affects the actual substance of the original scheme that the latter is transformed into a new aid scheme. There can be no question of such a substantive alteration where the new element is clearly severable from the initial scheme.
General Court 30 April 2002 (Gibraltar v. Commission, T-195/01) [2002] ECR II-2309, paras 109–111.

(c)   Notification of aid and the method of financing the aid (taxes)

11.56   [T]he method by which an aid is financed may render the entire aid scheme incompatible with the common market. Therefore, the aid cannot be considered separately from the effects of its method of financing. Quite to the contrary, consideration of an aid measure by the Commission must necessarily also take into account the method of financing the aid in a case where that method forms an integral part of the measure.

In such a case, the notification of the aid provided for in Article [108(3) TFEU] must also cover the method of financing, so that the Commission may consider it on the basis of all the facts. If this requirement is not satisfied, it is possible that the Commission may declare that an aid measure is compatible, when, if the Commission had been aware of its method of financing, it could not have been so declared. [...]

Since the obligation to notify also covers the method of financing the aid, the consequences of a failure by the national authorities to comply with the last sentence of Article [108(3) TFEU] must apply also to that aspect of the aid.

In that regard it must be observed, first, that it is for the national courts to uphold the rights of the persons concerned in the event of a possible breach by national authorities of the prohibition of putting aid into effect, to which the last sentence of Article [108(3)

TFEU] refers and which has direct effect and, second, that the Member State is in principle required to repay charges levied in breach of Community law.

It follows that where an aid measure of which the method of financing is an integral part has been implemented in breach of the obligation to notify, national courts must in principle order reimbursement of charges or contributions levied specifically for the purpose of financing that aid.

CoJ 21 October 2003 (Van Calster and Cleeren, C-261/01 and C-262/01) [2003] ECR I-12249, paras 49, 50 and 52–54.

Taxes do not fall within the scope of the provisions of the Treaty concerning State aid **11.57** unless they constitute the method of financing an aid measure, so that they form an integral part of that measure.

For a tax, or part of a tax, to be regarded as forming an integral part of an aid measure, it must be hypothecated to the aid measure under the relevant national rules, in the sense that the revenue from the tax is necessarily allocated for the financing of the aid. In the event of such hypothecation, the revenue from the tax has a direct impact on the amount of the aid and, consequently, on the assessment of the compatibility of the aid with the common market.

CoJ 13 January 2005 (Streekgewest Westelijk Noord-Brabant, C-174/02) [2005] ECR I-85, paras 25 and 26.

The documents in the file submitted to the Court do not suggest that the levy imposed **11.58** by the Meststoffenwet is hypothecated to the aid for the transport of manure introduced on the basis of Article 9(4) of that law. Under the Meststoffenwet, the competent authorities may exercise discretion in allocating the revenue from the levy to the various purposes, including that provided for in Article 9(4). The revenue from the levy therefore has no direct impact on the amount of aid as it may be used to finance other measures provided for in that law which do not have all the features of aid within the meaning of Article [107(1) TFEU].

CoJ 13 January 2005 (Pape, C-175/02) [2005] ECR I-127, para. 16.

According to consistent case-law, taxes do not fall within the scope of the [TFEU's] **11.59** provisions concerning State aid unless they constitute the method of financing an aid measure, so that they form an integral part of that measure.

If a tax effectively constitutes an integral part of an aid measure within the meaning of Article [107(1) TFEU], disregard on the part of the national authorities of the obligations arising from Article [108(3) TFEU] affects not only the lawfulness of the aid measure but also that of the tax which constitutes the method of financing it.

CoJ 27 October 2005 (Nazairdis SAS, now Distribution Casino France SAS and others, C-266/04, C-270/04, C-276/04, C-321/04 to C-325/04) [2005] ECR I-9481, paras 34 and 35.

(d)   Obligation of the Member State

11.60   The obligation provided for in the first sentence of Article [108(3)] to inform the Commission of plans to grant or alter aid does not apply solely to the initial plan, but also covers subsequent alterations to that plan; such information may be supplied to the Commission in the course of the consultations which take place following the initial notification.

CoJ 9 October 1984 (Heineken, Joined Cases 91/83 and 127/83) [1984] ECR 3435, para. 18.

11.61   It is apparent from the actual structure of Article [108(3) TFEU], which establishes a bilateral relationship between the Commission and the Member State, that only the Member States are under the obligation to notify. That obligation can thus not be regarded as satisfied by notification by the undertaking receiving the aid. As has already been held by the Court, the machinery for reviewing and examining State aid established by Article [108 TFEU] does not impose any specific obligation on the recipient of aid. First, the notification requirement and the prior prohibition on implementing planned aid are directed to the Member State. Second, the Member State is also the addressee of the decision by which the Commission finds that aid is incompatible with the common market and requests the Member State to abolish the aid within the period determined by the Commission.

CoJ 1 June 2006 (Vizcaya v. Commission (P & O European Ferries), C-442/03 P and C-471/03 P) [2006] ECR I-4845, para. 103.

(e)   When to notify

11.62   Article [108(3) TFEU] requires notification of 'any plans to grant or alter aid'. The aid measures must therefore be notified to the Commission while they are still at the draft stage, that is to say before they are implemented and while they are still capable of being adjusted in the light of any observations the Commission may have. Since Article [108(3) TFEU] does not contain any formal criterion, it is for each Member State to determine at what stage of the legislative procedure it decides to submit the aid plan for examination by the Commission, provided always that the plan is not implemented before the Commission has declared the aid compatible with the common market.

General Court 16 September 1998 (Waterleidingmaatschappij Noord-West Brabant v. Commission, T-188/95) [1998] ECR II-3713, para. 118.

See also CoJ March 2012 (Cantiere navale De Poli v. Commission, C-167/11 P), ECLI:EU:C:2012:164, paras 31 and 32.

(f)   Notification after the implementation of the aid measure

11.63   It must be stated in this regard that the Commission's final decision does not have the effect of regularizing ex post facto the implementing measures which were invalid because they had been taken in breach of the prohibition laid down by the last sentence of Article [108(3) TFEU], since otherwise the direct effect of that prohibition would be impaired and the interests of individuals, which, as stated above, are to be protected by national courts, would be disregarded. Any other interpretation would have the effect of according a favourable outcome to the non-observance by the Member State concerned of the last sentence of Article [108(3)] and would deprive that provision of its effectiveness.

CoJ 21 November 1991 (Fédération nationale du commerce extérieur des produits alimentaires, C-354/90) [1991] ECR I-5505, para. 16.

11.64 Moreover, the illegality of an aid measure, or of part of that measure, owing to infringement of the obligation to notify prior to its implementation is not affected by the fact that the measure has been held to be compatible with the common market by a final decision of the Commission.

The Court has already held that the Commission's final decision does not have the effect of regularising ex post facto implementing measures which were invalid because they had been taken in breach of the prohibition laid down by the last sentence of Article [108(3) TFEU], since otherwise the direct effect of that prohibition would be impaired and the interests of individuals, which are to be protected by national courts, would be disregarded. Any other interpretation would have the effect of according a favourable outcome to the non-observance of that provision by the Member State concerned and would deprive it of its effectiveness.

Furthermore, it is for the national courts to uphold the rights of the persons concerned in the event of any breach by the national authorities of the prohibition on putting aid into effect, which is referred to in the last sentence of Article [108(3) TFEU] and has direct effect. Where such a breach is invoked by individuals entitled to rely on it and is established by the national courts, the latter must take all the consequential measures under national law as regards both the validity of decisions giving effect to the aid measures concerned and the recovery of the financial support granted.

CoJ 21 October 2003 (Van Calster and Cleeren, C-261/01) [2003] ECR I-12249, paras 62–64.

11.65 Indeed, as the Advocate General pointed out in paragraph 50 of his Opinion, if, for any particular aid plan, whether compatible with the common market or not, failure to comply with Article [108(3) TFEU] carried no greater risk or penalty than compliance, the incentive for Member States to notify and await a decision on compatibility would be greatly diminished – as would, consequently, the scope of the Commission's control.

CoJ 5 October 2006 (Transalpine Ölleitung, C-368/04) [2006] ECR I-9957, para. 42.

11.66 It follows that it is of little consequence whether an application is made before or after adoption of the decision declaring the aid compatible with the common market, since that application relates to the unlawful situation resulting from the lack of notification.

Depending on what is possible under national law and the remedies available thereunder, the national court may thus, according to the case, be called upon to order recovery of unlawful aid from its recipients, even if that aid has subsequently been declared compatible with the common market by the Commission. In the same way, a national court may be required to rule on an application for compensation for the damage caused by reason of the unlawful nature of the aid.

CoJ 5 October 2006 (Transalpine Ölleitung, C–368/04) [2006] ECR I–9957, paras 55 and 56.

11.67   The reply to the first question referred must therefore be that the last sentence of Article [108(3) TFEU] is to be interpreted as meaning that the national court is not bound to order the recovery of aid implemented contrary to that provision, where the Commission has adopted a final decision declaring that aid to be compatible with the common market, within the meaning of Article [107 TFEU]. Applying Community law, the national court must order the aid recipient to pay interest in respect of the period of unlawfulness. Within the framework of its domestic law, it may, if appropriate, also order the recovery of the unlawful aid, without prejudice to the Member State's right to re-implement it, subsequently. It may also be required to uphold claims for compensation for damage caused by reason of the unlawful nature of the aid.

CoJ 12 February 2008 (CELF, C–199/06) [2008] ECR I–469, para. 55.

2.   Examination of unlawful aid

11.68   By contrast with Article [108(3)] which involves the power of the Commission to take immediate interim measures, where necessary, decisions taken under Article [108(2)] only take full effect on condition that the Commission indicates to the Member State concerned the aspects of the aid regarded as incompatible with the Treaty and therefore subject to abolition or alteration.

CoJ 12 July 1973 (Commission v. Germany, 70/72) [1973] ECR 813, para. 20.

11.69   If aid has been granted by a Member State without having been notified to the Commission at the planning stage, the decision finding that such aid is not compatible with the common market does not have to be based on grounds of establishing the real effect that such aid has had on competition or trade between Member States.

CoJ 14 February 1990 (France v. Commission, C–301/87) [1990] ECR I–307.

3.   Standstill obligation

(a)   Only in case of State aid

11.70   It must also be pointed out that, according to settled case-law, classification as aid requires that all the conditions set out in that provision should be fulfilled.

CoJ 15 July 2004 (Pearle, C–345/02) [2004] ECR I–7139, para. 32

11.71   The obligation to notify and the prohibition of implementation laid down in Article 108(3) TFEU apply to plans which may be classified as State aid within the meaning of Article 107(1) TFEU. Therefore, before drawing the appropriate conclusions from a possible infringement of the last sentence of Article 108(3) TFEU, national courts must first decide whether or not the measures in question constitute State aid.

CoJ 21 November 2013 (Deutsche Lufthansa AG v. Flughafen Frankfurt-Hahn GmbH, C-284/12), ECLI:EU:2013:755, para 35.

(b) Scope of the standstill obligation

The prohibition on the putting into effect of aid measures which is laid down in the last **11.72** sentence of Article [108(3) TFEU] applies to the proposed aid programme in its entirety and in the final version adopted by the national authorities. If the plan initially notified has in the meantime undergone alterations of which the Commission has not been informed, the prohibition applies to the plan as altered, unless the alteration in question is in actual fact a separate aid measure which should be assessed separately and which is therefore not such as to influence the assessment which the Commission has already made of the initial plan; in that case, the prohibition applies only to the aid measure introduced by the alteration.

CoJ 9 October 1984 (Heineken, Joined Cases 91/83 and 127/83) [1984] ECR 3435.

(c) Injunction to suspend

Once it has established that aid has been granted or altered without notification, the **11.73** Commission has a power to issue orders. It may, after giving the Member State in question an opportunity to submit its comments, issue an interim decision requiring it to suspend immediately the payment of such aid pending the outcome of the examination of the aid and to provide the Commission, within such period as the latter may specify, with all such documentation, information and data as are necessary in order that it may examine the compatibility of the aid with the common market. The Commission has the same power in cases where it has been notified of aid and the Member State in question has not awaited the outcome of the procedure provided for under Article [108(2) and (3) TFEU], but has instead proceeded to put the aid into effect, contrary to the prohibition contained in [108(3) TFEU].

Where the Member State complies in full with the Commission's order to provide the information requested, the Commission is obliged to examine the compatibility of the aid with the common market, in accordance with the procedure laid down in Article [108(2) and (3) TFEU]. However, if the Member State, notwithstanding the Commission's order, fails to provide that information, the Commission is empowered to terminate the procedure and makes its decision, on the basis of the information available to it, on the question whether or not the aid is compatible with the common market. If appropriate, such a decision may call for the recovery of the amount of aid which has already been paid.

If the Member State fails to suspend payment of the aid, notwithstanding the Commission's order, the latter is entitled, while carrying out the substantive examination of the aid, to bring the matter directly before the Court by applying for a declaration that such payment amounts to an infringement of the Treaty. Such a referral is justified in respect of urgency because there has been a decision embodying an order, taken after the Member State in question has been given notice to submit its comments, and thus after the conclusion of a preliminary procedure in which it has been enabled to put its case, as in the case of the means of redress provided under the second subparagraph of Article [108(2) TFEU], which is no more than a variant of the action for a declaration of failure to fulfil obligations, specifically adapted to the special problems which State aid poses for competition within the common market.

CoJ 14 February 1990 (France v. Commission, C-301/87) [1990] ECR I-307, paras 19–23.

See also CoJ 9 August 1994 (Nationale Delcrederedienst, C-44/93) [1994] ECR I-3829.

4. Direct applicability of Article 108(3) TFEU

11.74   Creates no individual rights except in the case of the final provision of Article [108(3)].
CoJ 15 July 1964 (Costa v. ENEL, 6/64) [1964] ECR 585.

5. Preliminary examination

(a) Request for information

11.75   It is only when the Commission considers that it does not have sufficient information to adopt a final decision that it enjoins a Member State to provide information.
General Court 5 August 2003 (Vizcaya v. Commission (P & O European Ferries), T-116/01 and T-118/01) [2003] ECR II-2957, para. 177.

(b) Assessment of the aid measure

11.76   In the case of an aid scheme, the Commission may confine itself to examining the general characteristics of the scheme in question without being required to examine each particular case in which it applies.
CoJ 15 December 2005 (Italy v. Commission, C-66/02) [2005] ECR I-10901, para. 91.

6. The role of the national courts

11.77   While the direct effect of the last sentence of Article [108] requires national courts to apply this provision without any possibility of its being excluded by rules of national law of any kind whatsoever, it is for the internal legal system of every Member State to determine the legal procedure leading to this result.
CoJ 11 December 1973 (Lorenz v. Germany, 120/73) [1973] ECR 1471, para. 9.

11.78   The provisions of Article [108] do not preclude a national court from referring a question on the interpretation of Article [107 TFEU] to the Court of Justice if it considers that a decision thereon is necessary to enable it to give judgment; in the

absence of implementing provisions within the meaning of Article [109] however a national court does not have jurisdiction to decide an action for a declaration that existing aid which has not been the subject of a decision by the Commission requiring the Member State concerned to abolish or alter it or a new aid which has been introduced in accordance with Article [108(3)] is incompatible with the Treaty.
CoJ 22 March 1977 (Steinike and Weinlig, 78/76) [1977] ECR 595, para. 15.

The possibility of bringing a direct action under the second paragraph of Article [263 **11.79** TFEU] against a decision adopted by a Community institution does not preclude the possibility of bringing an action in a national court against a measure adopted by a national authority for the implementation of that decision on the ground that the latter decision is unlawful.
CoJ 21 May 1987 (Rau, Joined Cases 133/85 to 136/85) [1987] ECR 2289.

In this respect it should be noted that the principal and exclusive role conferred on the **11.80** Commission by Articles [107] and [108] of the Treaty, which is to hold aid to be incompatible with the common market where this is appropriate, is fundamentally different from the role of national courts in safeguarding rights which individuals enjoy as a result of the direct effect of the prohibition laid down in the last sentence of Article [108](3) of the Treaty. Whilst the Commission must examine the compatibility of the proposed aid with the common market, even where the Member State has acted in breach of the prohibition on giving effect to aid, national courts do no more than preserve, until the final decision of the Commission, the rights of individuals faced with a possible breach by State authorities of the prohibition laid down by the last sentence of Article [108](3) of the Treaty. When those courts make a ruling in such a matter, they do not thereby decide on the compatibility of the aid with the common market, the final determination on that matter being the exclusive responsibility of the Commission, subject to the supervision of the Court of Justice.
CoJ 21 November 1991 (Fédération nationale du commerce extérieur des produits alimentaires, C-354/90) [1991] ECR I-5505, para. 14.

A national court, seised of a request that it should draw the appropriate conclusions **11.81** from an infringement of the last sentence of Article [108(3) TFEU], where the matter has also been referred to the Commission, which has not yet given a final decision as to whether the State measures constitute State aid, is not required to declare that it lacks jurisdiction or to stay proceedings until such time as the Commission has adopted a position on how the measures in question are to be categorized.
CoJ 11 July 1996 (SFEI and others v. La Poste and others, C-39/94) [1996] ECR I-3547, para. 53.

A national court requested to order the repayment of aid must grant that application if **11.82** it finds that the aid was not notified to the Commission, unless by reason of exceptional circumstances repayment is inappropriate.
CoJ 11 July 1996 (SFEI v. La Poste, C-39/94) [1996] ECR I-3547, para. 71.

11.83   It is for the national courts to interpret and apply the concept of State aid contained in Article [107(1) TFEU] in order to determine whether a State measure introduced without observance of the preliminary examination procedure provided for in Article [108(3)] ought to have been subject to that procedure.

CoJ 21 July 2005 (Administración del Estado v. Xunta de Galicia, C-71/04) [2005] ECR I-7419, para. 33.

11.84   [A]rticle 108(3) entrusts the national courts with the task of preserving, until the final decision of the Commission, the rights of individuals faced with a possible breach by State authorities of the prohibition laid down by that provision [...].

The objective of the national courts' tasks is therefore to pronounce measures appropriate to remedy the unlawfulness of the implementation of the aid, in order that the aid does not remain at the free disposal of the recipient during the period remaining until the Commission makes its decision.

A decision to stay proceedings would, *de facto*, have the same effect as a decision to refuse the application for safeguard measures. It would have the effect that no decision on the merits of that application would be taken before the Commission's decision. [...]

CoJ 11 March 2010 (CELF and Ministre de la Culture et de la Communication, C-1/09) [2010] ECR I-2099, paras 26, 30 and 31.

11.85   The purpose of Article 108(3) is clearly prompted by the consideration that, until a new decision has been adopted by the Commission, it cannot be presumed that that decision will be positive in its content.

There is an obligation to adopt safeguard measures only if the conditions justifying such measures are satisfied, namely, that there is no doubt regarding the classification as State aid, that the aid is about to be, or has been, implemented, and that no exceptional circumstances have been found which would make recovery inappropriate. [...]

CoJ 11 March 2010 (CELF and Ministre de la Culture et de la Communication, C-1/09) [2010] ECR I-2099, paras 34 and 36.

11.86   Under that system of supervision, the Commission and the national courts have different powers and responsibilities [...].

Proceedings may be commenced before national courts requiring those courts to interpret and apply the concept of aid contained in Article 107(1) TFEU, in particular in order to determine whether State aid introduced without observance of the preliminary examination procedure provided for in Article 108(3) TFEU ought to have been subject to this procedure. On the other hand, national courts do not have jurisdiction to give a decision on whether State aid is compatible with the internal market.

Whilst the Commission must examine the compatibility of the proposed aid with the internal market, even where the Member State has acted in breach of the prohibition on giving effect to aid contained in the final sentence of Article 108(3) TFEU, national courts, in such a situation, do no more than preserve, until the final decision of the Commission, the rights of individuals faced with a possible breach by State authorities of that prohibition.

CoJ 18 July 2013 (P Oy, C-6/12), ECLI:EU:C:2013:525, paras 37–39.

The initiation by the Commission of the formal examination procedure under Article **11.87** 108(2) TFEU cannot therefore release national courts from their duty to safeguard the rights of individuals faced with a possible breach of Article 108(3) TFEU [...].

However, the scope of that obligation may vary, depending on whether or not the Commission has initiated the formal examination procedure with regard to the measure at issue in the proceedings before the national court.

In a situation where the Commission has not yet initiated the formal examination procedure and has therefore not yet given a decision as to whether the measures under consideration are capable of constituting State aid, the national courts, seised of a request that they should draw the appropriate conclusions from a possible infringement of the last sentence of Article 108(3) TFEU, may have cause to interpret and apply the concept of aid with a view to determining whether those measures should have been notified to the Commission. Thus it is for those courts to verify, inter alia, whether the measure at issue constitutes an advantage and whether it is selective, that is to say whether it favours certain undertakings or certain producers within the meaning of Article 107(1) TFEU [...]. [...]

In a situation where the Commission has already initiated the formal examination procedure under Article 108(2) TFEU, it is necessary to consider which measures have to be taken by the national courts.

While the assessments carried out in the decision to initiate the formal examination procedure are indeed preliminary in nature, that does not mean that the decision lacks legal effect.

It must be pointed out in that regard that, if national courts were able to hold that a measure does not constitute aid within the meaning of Article 107(1) TFEU and, therefore, not to suspend its implementation, even though the Commission had just stated in its decision to initiate the formal examination procedure that that measure was capable of presenting aid elements, the effectiveness of Article 108(3) TFEU would be frustrated.

On the one hand, if the preliminary assessment in the decision to initiate the formal examination procedure is that the measure at issue constitutes aid and that assessment is subsequently confirmed in the final decision of the Commission, the national courts would have failed to observe their obligation under Article 108(3) TFEU and Article 3 of Regulation No 659/1999 to suspend the implementation of any aid proposal until the adoption of the Commission's decision on the compatibility of that proposal with the internal market.

On the other hand, even if in its final decision the Commission were to conclude that there were no aid elements, the preventive aim of the State aid control system established by the TFEU [...] requires that, following the doubt raised in the decision to initiate the formal examination procedure as to the aid character of that measure and its compatibility with the internal market, its implementation should be deferred until that doubt is resolved by the Commission's final decision.

CoJ 21 November 2013 (Deutsche Lufthansa AG v. Flughafen Frankfurt–Hahn GmbH, C-284/12), ECLI:EU:2013:755, paras 32–34 and 36–40.

[T]he rules implementing the principle of *res judicata* are a matter for the national legal **11.88** order, in accordance with the principle of the procedural autonomy of the Member States. However, such procedural rules must not be less favourable than those governing similar domestic situations (principle of equivalence) and must not be framed in such a way as to make it in practice impossible or excessively difficult to exercise the rights conferred by EU law (principle of effectiveness) [...].

CoJ 11 November 2015 (Klausner Holz Niedersachsen, C-505/14), ECLI: EU:C:2015:742, para 40.

(a) No ruling on the compatibility of the aid

11.89   Whilst the Commission must examine the compatibility of the proposed aid with the common market, even where the Member State has acted in breach of the prohibition on giving effect to aid, national courts do no more than preserve, until the final decision of the Commission, the rights of individuals faced with a possible breach by State authorities of the prohibition laid down by the last sentence of Article [108(3) TFEU]. When those courts make a ruling in such a matter, they do not thereby decide on the compatibility of the aid with the common market, the final determination on that matter being the exclusive responsibility of the Commission, subject to the supervision of the Court of Justice.

CoJ 21 November 1991 (Fédération nationale du commerce extérieur des produits alimentaires, C-354/90) [1991] ECR I-5505, para. 14.

(b) Deggendorf-doctrine

11.90   The national court is bound by a Commission decision adopted under Article [108(2) TFEU] where, in view of the implementation of that decision by the national authorities, the recipient of the aid to which the implementation measures are addressed brings before it an action in which it pleads the unlawfulness of the Commission's decision and where that recipient of aid, although informed in writing by the Member State of the Commission's decision, did not bring an action against that decision under the second paragraph of Article [263 TFEU], or did not do so within the period prescribed.

CoJ 9 March 1994 (Textilwerke Deggendorf, C-188/92) [1994] ECR I-833, para. 26.

D. OTHER SUBJECTS

1. Action for annulment (Art. 263 TFEU)

(a) Admissibility

11.91   Under the fourth paragraph of Article [263 TFEU], a natural or legal person may institute proceedings against a decision addressed to another person only if it is of direct and individual concern to the former.

According to settled case-law, persons other than those to whom a decision is addressed may claim to be individually concerned only if that decision affects them by reason of certain attributes which are peculiar to them or by reason of circumstances in which they are differentiated from all other persons and by virtue of those factors distinguishes them individually just as in the case of the person addressed.

In the case of a Commission decision on State aid, it must be borne in mind that, in the context of the procedure for reviewing State aid provided for in Article [108 TFEU], the preliminary stage of the procedure for reviewing aid under Article [108(3) TFEU], which is intended merely to allow the Commission to form a prima facie opinion on the partial or complete conformity of the aid in question, must be distinguished from the examination under Article [108(2) TFEU]. It is only in connection with the latter examination, which is designed to enable the Commission to be fully informed of all the facts of the case, that the [TFEU] imposes an obligation on the Commission to give the parties concerned notice to submit their comments.

Where, without initiating the formal review procedure under Article [108(2) TFEU], the Commission finds, on the basis of Article [108(3) TFEU], that aid is compatible with the common market, the persons intended to benefit from those procedural guarantees may secure compliance therewith only if they are able to challenge that decision before the Community judicature [...]. For those reasons, the Court declares to be admissible an action for the annulment of such a decision brought by a person who is concerned within the meaning of Article [108(2) TFEU] where he seeks, by instituting proceedings, to safeguard the procedural rights available to him under the latter provision.

The parties concerned, within the meaning of Article [108(2) TFEU], who are thus entitled under the fourth paragraph of Article [263 TFEU] to institute proceedings for annulment are those persons, undertakings or associations whose interests might be affected by the grant of the aid, in particular competing undertakings and trade associations [...].

On the other hand, if the applicant calls in question the merits of the decision appraising the aid as such, the mere fact that it may be regarded as concerned within the meaning of Article [108(2)] cannot suffice to render the action admissible. It must then demonstrate that it has a particular status within the meaning of the *Plaumann v. Commission* case-law. That applies in particular where the applicant's market position is substantially affected by the aid to which the decision at issue relates.

CoJ 13 December 2005 (Aktionsgemeinschaft Recht und Eigentum eV (ARE), C-78/03) [2005] ECR I-10737, paras 32–37.

See also CoJ 28 January 1986 (Cofaz and others v. Commission, C-169/84) [1986] ECR 391; CoJ 15 June 1993 (Matra v. Commission, C-225/91) [1993] ECR I-3203, paras 16–20; CoJ 19 May 1993 (Cook v. Commission, C-198/91) [1993] ECR I-2487, paras 23–26.

It must be pointed out that, with regard to the determination of a 'significant effect on **11.92** the position' of the appellant on the market in question, the Court has had occasion to clarify that the mere fact that a measure may exercise an influence on the competitive relationships existing on the relevant market and that the undertaking concerned was in a competitive relationship with the addressee of that measure cannot in any event suffice for that undertaking to be regarded as being individually concerned by that measure.

Therefore, an undertaking cannot rely solely on its status as a competitor of the undertaking in receipt of aid but must additionally show that its circumstances distinguish it in a similar way to the undertaking in receipt of the aid. [...]

Contrary to what the Commission asserts, it does not follow from the Court's case-law that a special status of this kind, which distinguishes a 'person other than the persons addressed', within the meaning of *Plaumann v. Commission*, from any other economic operator, must necessarily be inferred from factors such as a significant decline in turnover, appreciable financial losses or a significant reduction in market share following the grant of the aid in question. The grant of State aid can have an adverse effect on the competitive situation of an operator in other ways too, in particular by causing the loss of an opportunity to make a profit or a less favourable development than would have been the case without such aid. Similarly, the seriousness of such an effect may vary according to a large number of factors such as, in particular, the structure of the market concerned or the nature of the aid in question. Demonstrating a substantial adverse effect on a competitor's position on the market cannot, therefore, simply be a matter of the existence of certain factors indicating a decline in its commercial or financial performance [...]. [...]

If an effect of that kind is established, the fact that an undefined number of other competitors may, in appropriate circumstances, allege that they have suffered similar harm does not constitute an obstacle to the admissibility of the action brought by the appellant undertaking. [...]

CoJ 22 December 2008 (British Aggregates v. Commission, C-487/06 P) [2008] ECR I-10505, paras 47, 48, 53 and 56.

11.93   It is true that, as appears from Article 4(3) of Regulation No 659/1999, a decision of the Commission not to raise objections is taken where the Commission finds that the notified measure does not raise doubts as to its compatibility with the common market. If an applicant seeks the annulment of such a decision, he is essentially challenging the fact that the decision on the aid was adopted without the Commission initiating the formal review procedure, thereby infringing his procedural rights. For his action to be successful, the applicant may attempt to show that the compatibility of the measure in question should have given rise to doubts. The use of such arguments cannot, however, have the consequence of changing the subject-matter of the application or altering the conditions of its admissibility.

CoJ 9 July 2009 (3F v. Commission, C-319/07 P) [2009] ECR I-5963, para. 35.

11.94   In that regard, the Court has repeatedly held that an action for annulment for the purposes of Article [263 TFEU] must be available against all acts adopted by the institutions, whatever their nature or form, which are intended to have legal effects capable of affecting the interests of the applicant by bringing about a distinct change in his legal position [...].

It follows also from settled case-law concerning the admissibility of actions for annulment that it is necessary to look to the actual substance of the acts challenged in order to classify them [...].

By contrast, the form in which an act or decision is adopted is in principle irrelevant to the right to challenge such acts or decisions by way of an action for annulment. It is therefore, in principle, irrelevant for the classification of the act in question whether or not it satisfies certain formal requirements, namely in particular, that it is duly identified by its author and that it mentions the provisions providing the legal basis for it. It is therefore irrelevant that the act may not be described as a 'decision' or that it does not refer to Article 4(2), (3) or (4) of Regulation No 659/1999. It is also of no importance that the Member State concerned was not notified of the act at issue by the Commission, infringing Article 25 of that regulation, as such an error is not capable of altering the substance of that act […].

Furthermore, it is in principle those measures which definitively determine the position of the Commission upon the conclusion of an administrative procedure, and which are intended to have legal effects capable of affecting the interests of the complainant, that constitute acts open to challenge for the purposes of Article [263 TFEU], and not intermediate measures whose purpose is to prepare for the final decision, which do not have those effects […]. […]

Where the Commission finds, following examination of a complaint, that the investigation has revealed no grounds for concluding that there is State aid within the meaning of Article [107 TFEU], it refuses by implication to initiate the procedure provided for by Article [108(2) TFEU] […]. […]

Such a decision refusing to initiate the procedure provided for by Article [108(2) TFEU] is definitive and cannot be characterised as a mere provisional measure […]. […]

In such a situation, the persons intended to benefit from the procedural guarantees afforded by that provision may secure compliance therewith only if they are able to challenge the decision in question before the European Union judicature under the fourth paragraph of Article [263 TFEU]. That principle applies equally, whether the ground on which the decision is taken is that the Commission regards the aid as compatible with the common market or that, in its view, the very existence of aid must be discounted or where it considers that there is existing aid […].

CoJ 18 November 2010 (NDSHT v. Commission, C-322/09 P) [2010] ECR I-11911, paras 45–48, 51, 53 and 54.

Under the fourth paragraph of Article 263 TFEU, natural or legal persons may institute proceedings against an act which is not addressed to them and entails implementing measures only if that act is of direct and individual concern to them. **11.95**

As regards the second of those conditions, that is to say, being individually concerned by the act in question, it is settled case-law that persons other than those to whom a decision is addressed may claim to be individually concerned only if that decision affects them by reason of certain attributes which are peculiar to them or by reason of circumstances in which they are differentiated from all other persons and by virtue of these factors distinguishes them individually just as in the case of the person addressed.

It is also clear from settled case-law that the possibility of determining more or less precisely the number, or even the identity, of the persons to whom a measure applies by no means implies that it must be regarded as being of individual concern to them as long as that measure is applied by virtue of an objective legal or factual situation defined by it.

CoJ 19 December 2013 (Telefónica SA v. Commission, C-274/12 P), ECLI:EU:2013:852, paras 45–47.

(b) Assessment by the Union courts

11.96   By the second subparagraph of Article [108(2)] 'if the State [...] does not comply with this decision within the prescribed time, the Commission [...] may refer the matter to the Court of Justice direct'.

The head of submissions in question requests the Court to find that the defendant, by its failure to require the repayment by the recipients of the aid wrongly received, has not fulfilled an obligation incumbent upon it by virtue of the decision of 17 February 1971.

Such a request is admissible since the Commission is competent, when it has found that aid is incompatible with the common market, to decide that the State concerned must abolish or alter it. To be of practical effect, this abolition or modification may include an obligation to require repayment of aid granted in breach of the Treaty, so that in the absence of measures for recovery, the Commission may bring the matter before the Court. Moreover an application from the Commission, within the scope of the procedure under Articles [258 to 260], for a declaration that in omitting to take specific measures, a Member State has failed to fulfil an obligation under the Treaty, is equally admissible. Since the aim of the Treaty is to achieve the practical elimination of infringements and the consequences thereof, past and future, it is a matter for the Community authorities whose task it is to ensure that the requirements of the Treaty are observed to determine the extent to which the obligation of the Member State concerned may be specified in the reasoned opinions or decisions delivered under Articles [258] and [108(2)] respectively and in applications addressed to the Court.

CoJ 12 July 1973 (Commission v. Germany, 70/72) [1973] ECR 813, paras 11–13.

11.97   To allow a Member State to which a decision adopted under the first subparagraph of Article [108(2)] has been addressed a further opportunity to call in question the validity of that decision on the occasion of an application referred to in the second subparagraph of that article, in spite of the expiry of the period laid down in the third paragraph of Article [263 TFEU], would be impossible to reconcile with the principles governing the legal remedies established by the Treaty and would jeopardize the stability of that system and the principle of legal certainty upon which it is based.

CoJ 15 November 1983 (Commission v. France, 52/83) [1983] ECR 3707, para. 10.

11.98   Although the Commission is correct in arguing that the review of the compatibility of State aids with the common market under Articles [107] and [108] depends on the rule that any national measure granting aid may not be put into effect until the Commission has given a decision, it is also true that even if a Member State has infringed the provisions of Article [108] it may not be deprived of the right to challenge before the court, by means of Article [263] et seq. in particular, the legality of a Commission decision adversely affecting it and consequently it must be entitled to apply for the suspension of the operation of that decision in accordance with Article [279 TFEU]. That conclusion does not affect the Commission's right to apply to the Court for a declaration that the Kingdom of the Netherlands has infringed the last sentence of Article [108(3) TFEU].

CoJ 3 May 1985 (Van der Kooy, Joined Cases 67/85, 68/85 and 70/85) [1985] ECR 1315.

The Kingdom of Spain cannot rely on that element since it was put forward for the first **11.99** time in the application to the Court rather than in the course of the pre-litigation procedure laid down in Article [108 TFEU].

CoJ 14 September 1994 (Spain v. Commission, Joined Cases C-278/92, C-279/92 and C-280/92) [1994] ECR I-4103, para. 31.

2. Recovery of aid

Such a request is admissible since the Commission is competent, when it has found that **11.100** aid is incompatible with the common market, to decide that the State concerned must abolish or alter it. To be of practical effect, this abolition or modification may include an obligation to require repayment of aid granted in breach of the Treaty, so that in the absence of measures for recovery, the Commission may bring the matter before the Court.

CoJ 12 July 1973 (Commission v. Germany, 70/72) [1973] ECR 813, para. 13.

With regard to the alleged uncertainty of the identity of the addressees of the order for **11.101** recovery, it is clear from the contested decision that the aid was to be recovered from the undertakings which actually benefited from it, that is to say the four subsidiaries.

CoJ 21 March 1991 (Italy v. Commission, C-303/88) [1991] ECR I-1433, para. 57.

Consequently, Community law requires the competent authority to revoke a decision **11.102** granting unlawful aid, in accordance with a final decision of the Commission declaring the aid incompatible with the common market and ordering recovery, even if national law excludes recovery because the gain no longer exists, in the absence of bad faith on the part of the recipient of the aid.

CoJ 20 March 1997 (Alcan Deutschland, C-24/95) [1997] ECR I-1591, para. 54.

In that regard, it should be observed that no provision of Community law requires the **11.103** Commission, when ordering the recovery of aid declared incompatible with the common market, to fix the exact amount of the aid to be recovered. It is sufficient for the Commission's decision to include information enabling the recipient to work out himself, without overmuch difficulty, that amount [...].

CoJ 12 October 2000 (Spain v. Commission, C-480/98) [2000] ECR I-8717, para. 25.

See also 8 December 2011 (France Télécom v. Commission, C-81/10 P) [2011] ECR II-12899, para. 102.

11.104   The recovery of unlawful aid is the logical consequence of a finding that it is unlawful […] and seeks to re-establish the previously existing situation […].
CoJ 8 May 2003 (Italy and SIM 2 Multimedia v. Commission, C–328/99) [2003] ECR I–4035, para. 66.

11.105   The Court has consistently held that, in the matter of State aid, where, contrary to the provisions of Article 108(3), the aid has already been granted, the Commission, which has the power to require the national authorities to order repayment, is not obliged to provide specific reasons in order to justify the exercise of that. Article 14(1) of Regulation No 659/1999 states that 'where negative decisions are taken in cases of unlawful aid, the Commission shall decide that the Member State concerned shall take all necessary measures to recover the aid from the beneficiary'. The decision to recover the aid is therefore the more or less automatic consequence where that aid is held to be unlawful and incompatible, subject to the sole condition – which stems from the second sentence of that provision – that an order for recovery is not contrary to a general principle of Community law. […]
General Court 20 September 2011 (Regione autonoma della Sardegna and Others v. Commission, T–394/08, T–408/08, T–453/08 and T–454/08) [2011] ECR II–6255, para. 152.

11.106   [A]rticle 15(1) of Regulation No 659/1999 provides that the powers of the Commission to recover aid are to be subject to a limitation period of 10 years. It is apparent from Article 15(2) of the regulation that the limitation period does not begin to run until on the day on which the unlawful aid is awarded to the beneficiary. Consequently, the decisive factor in determining the starting point of the limitation period referred to in Article 15 is when the aid was in fact granted.
It is apparent from Article 15(2) of Regulation No 659/1999 that, for the purpose of determining the date on which the limitation period starts to run, that provision refers to the grant of aid to a beneficiary, not the date on which an aid scheme was adopted.
CoJ 8 December 2011 (France Télécom v. Commission, C–81/10 P) [2011] ECR I–12899, paras 80 and 81.

11.107   À titre liminaire, il convient de rappeler que l'État membre destinataire d'une décision l'obligeant à récupérer des aides illégales est tenu, en vertu de l'article 288 TFUE, de prendre toutes les mesures propres à assurer l'exécution de cette décision. Il doit parvenir à une récupération effective des sommes dues […].
En cas de décision constatant le caractère illégal et incompatible d'une aide, la récupération de celle-ci, ordonnée par la Commission, a lieu dans les conditions prévues à l'article 14, paragraphe 3, du règlement n° 659/1999 […].
En vertu de ladite disposition, la récupération d'une telle aide doit, ainsi qu'il ressort également du considérant 13 dudit règlement, s'effectuer sans délai et conformément aux procédures prévues par le droit national de l'État membre concerné, pour autant que ces dernières permettent l'exécution immédiate et effective de la décision de la Commission […].
En l'occurrence, conformément à l'article 3, paragraphe 1, de la décision C(2011) 1006 final, la République hellénique était tenue d'assurer la récupération 'immédiate' et

'effective' de l'aide illégale en cause. Cet État membre disposait à cette fin, en vertu de l'article 3, paragraphe 2, de cette décision, d'un délai de quatre mois à compter de la notification de ladite décision.

CoJ 17 October 2013 (Hellenic Republic v. Commission, C-263/12), ECLI:EU: 2013:673, paras 24–27.

(a) Objective of recovery

That objective is attained once the aid in question, increased where appropriate by **11.108** default interest, has been repaid by the recipient, in this case SNAM SpA, to ENI, the public body responsible for managing State holdings. By repaying the aid, the recipient forfeits the advantage which it had enjoyed over its competitors on the market, and the situation prior to payment of the aid is restored.

CoJ 4 April 1995 (Commission v. Italy, C-350/93) [1995] ECR I-699, para. 22.

The Court has consistently held that the obligation on a State to abolish aid regarded by **11.109** the Commission as being incompatible with the common market has as its purpose to re-establish the previously existing situation […].

That objective is attained once the aid in question, increased where appropriate by default interest, has been repaid by the recipient, in this case Finmeccanica, to IRI, the public body responsible for managing State holdings. By repaying the aid, the recipient forfeits the advantage which it had enjoyed over its competitors on the market, and the situation prior to payment of the aid is restored. […]

However, while it cannot be ruled out that the allocation of funds by the State to a public body such as IRI may constitute State aid within the meaning of Article [107 TFEU], the Commission, contrary to its submissions, did not find in the decision, on completion of the procedure laid down in the Treaty, that the fact that funds were made available by the State to IRI also constitutes aid incompatible with the common market.

CoJ 4 April 1995 (Commission v. Italy, C-348/93) [1995] ECR I-673, paras 26, 27 and 29.

See also CoJ 4 April 1995 (Commission v. Italy, C-350/93) [1995] ECR I-699.

(b) Recovery in accordance with national law

In principle the recovery of aid must take place in accordance with the relevant **11.110** procedural provisions of national law, subject however to the proviso that those provisions are to be applied in such a way that the recovery required by Community law is not rendered practically impossible. In particular, the interests of the Community must be taken fully into consideration in the application of a provision which requires the various interests involved to be weighed up before a defective administrative measure is withdrawn.

CoJ 20 March 1997 (Land Rheinland-Pfalz v. Alcan Deutschland GmbH, C-24/ 95) [1997] ECR I-1591, para. 24.

See also CoJ 21 March 1990 (Belgium v. Commission, C-142/87) [1990] ECR I-959, para. 61.

(c) Duty of genuine cooperation

11.111   If, in giving effect to a decision finding an aid to be incompatible with the common market and ordering its recovery, a Member State encounters unforeseen and unforeseeable difficulties or perceives consequences overlooked by the Commission, it may submit these problems for consideration by the Commission, together with proposals for suitable amendments to the decision in question. In such a case the Commission and the Member State must in accordance with the principle underlying Article [4(3) TEU], which imposes a duty of genuine cooperation on the Member States and Community institutions, work together in good faith with a view to overcoming the difficulties whilst fully observing the Treaty provisions, and in particular the provisions on aid.

In so far as the procedure laid down by national law is applicable to the recovery of an illegal aid, the relevant provisions of national law must be applied in such a way that the recovery required by Community law is not rendered practically impossible. Where a provision requires the various interests involved to be weighed up before a defective administrative measure is withdrawn, the interests of the Community must be taken fully into consideration.

CoJ 2 February 1989 (Commission v. Germany, 94/87) [1989] ECR 175, paras 9 and 12.

11.112   [A]lthough the statements of position by the Commission cannot bind the national court, to the extent that those statements of position are intended to facilitate the accomplishment of the task of the national authorities in the immediate and effective execution of the recovery decision and, having regard to the principle of cooperation in good faith, the national court must take them into account as a factor in the assessment of the dispute before it and must state reasons having regard to all the documents in the file submitted to it.

CoJ 13 February 2014 (Mediaset, C-69/13), ECLI:EU:C:2014:71, para. 31.

(d) Absolutely impossible

11.113   The fact that, on account of the undertaking's financial position, the Belgian authorities could not recover the sum paid does not constitute proof that implementation was impossible, because the Commission's objective was to abolish the aid, and, as the Belgian Government itself admits, that objective could be attained by proceedings for winding up the company, which the Belgian authorities could institute in their capacity as shareholder or creditor.

CoJ 15 January 1986 (Commission v. Belgium, 52/84) [1986] ECR 89, para. 14.

11.114   Where proceedings are brought against a Member State for failure to fulfil its obligations by not implementing a decision which was addressed to it under the first

subparagraph of Article [108(2)] requiring it to recover illegal aid and which it did not seek to have annulled, the only defence left to the Member State in those proceedings is to plead that it was absolutely impossible for it to implement the decision properly.
CoJ 2 February 1989 (Commission v. Germany, 94/87) [1989] ECR 175, para. 8.

The Court has also held that the only defence available to a Member State in opposing **11.115** an application by the Commission under Article [108(2) TFEU] for a declaration that it has failed to fulfil its Treaty obligations is to plead that it was absolutely impossible for it to implement the decision properly.
CoJ 22 March 2001 (Commission v. France, C-261/99) [2001] ECR I-2537, para. 23.

(e)   Legitimate expectations

Where, in the case of a State aid which is intended to meet the additional costs of an **11.116** operation previously the subject of an authorized aid and the examination of which did not call for deep research, the Commission did not take a decision declaring the said aid to be incompatible with the common market Article [107] and ordering its cancellation until 26 months after its notification, that delay is one which could establish on the part of the beneficiary of the aid a legitimate expectation of such a nature as to prevent the Commission from ordering the national authorities to order the refund of the aid.
CoJ 24 November 1987 (RSV, 223/85) [1987] ECR 4617.

In view of the mandatory nature of the supervision of State aid by the Commission **11.117** under Article [108 TFEU], undertakings to which an aid has been granted may not, in principle, entertain a legitimate expectation that the aid is lawful unless it has been granted in compliance with the procedure laid down in that article.

It is true that a recipient of illegally granted aid is not precluded from relying on exceptional circumstances on the basis of which it had legitimately assumed the aid to be lawful and thus declining to refund that aid. If such a case is brought before a national court, it is for that court to assess the material circumstances and, if necessary, seek a preliminary ruling on interpretation from the Court of Justice.

However, a Member State whose authorities have granted aid contrary to the procedural rules laid down in Article [108 TFEU] may not rely on the legitimate expectations of recipients in order to justify a failure to comply with the obligation to take the steps necessary to implement a Commission decision instructing it to recover the aid.
CoJ 20 September 1990 (Commission v. Germany, C-5/89) [1990] ECR I-3437, paras 14, 16 and 17.

The fact that the Commission initially decided not to raise any objections to the aid in **11.118** issue cannot be regarded as capable of having caused the recipient undertaking to entertain any legitimate expectation since that decision was challenged in due time before the Court, which annulled it. However regrettable it may be, the Commission's error cannot erase the consequences of the unlawful conduct of the Kingdom of Spain.

CoJ 14 January 1997 (Spain v. Commission, C-169/95) [1997] ECR I-135, para. 53.

11.119   Where State aid is found to be incompatible with the common market, the role of the national authorities is merely to give effect to the Commission's decision. The authorities do not, therefore, have any discretion as regards revocation of a decision granting aid. Thus, where the Commission, in a decision which has not been the subject of legal proceedings, orders the recovery of unduly paid sums, the national authorities are not entitled to reach any other finding.

Where the national authorities nevertheless allow the time-bar provided for in national law in respect of revocation of the decision granting the aid to come into effect, that situation cannot be treated in the same way as the situation where a trader does not know whether the competent administrative authorities are going to reach a decision, and where the principle of legal certainty requires that such uncertainty be brought to an end after a certain period has elapsed.

Since the national authorities have no discretion in the matter, the recipient of unlawfully granted aid ceases to be in a state of uncertainty once the Commission has adopted a decision finding the aid incompatible with the common market and requiring recovery.

The principle of legal certainty cannot therefore preclude repayment of the aid on the ground that the national authorities were late in complying with the decision requiring such repayment. If it could, recovery of unduly paid sums would be rendered practically impossible and the Community provisions concerning State aid deprived of effectiveness.

CoJ 20 March 1997 (Alcan Deutschland, C-24/95) [1997] ECR I-1591, paras 34–37.

11.120   The recipient's obligation to ensure that the procedure set out in Article [108(3) TFEU] has been complied with cannot, in fact, depend on the conduct of the State authorities, even if the latter were responsible for the illegality of the aid decision to such a degree that revocation appears to be a breach of good faith.

CoJ 20 March 1997 (Alcan Deutschland, C-24/95) [1997] ECR I-1591, para. 41.

(f)   Recovery and bankruptcy

11.121   [T]he main purpose of the repayment of unlawfully paid State aid is to eliminate the distortion of competition caused by the competitive advantage afforded by the unlawful aid. [...]

In the present case, the undertaking to which unlawful State aid was granted retains its legal personality and continues to carry out, for its own account, the activities subsidised by the State aid. Therefore, it is normally this undertaking that retains the competitive advantage connected with that aid and it is therefore this undertaking that must be required to repay an amount equal to that aid. The buyer cannot therefore be asked to repay such aid. [...]

In the light of the fact that in the present case SMI has been in liquidation since bankruptcy proceedings were opened on 1 July 1997, it should be pointed out that, as follows from the case-law on bankrupt undertakings that have received aid, the re-establishment of the previous situation and the elimination of the distortion of competition resulting from the unlawfully paid aid may, in principle, be achieved by registration of the liability relating to the repayment of the aid in question in the schedule of liabilities. In accordance with this case-law, such registration would be sufficient.

It is certainly possible that, in the event that hive-off companies are created in order to continue some of the activities of the undertaking that received the aid, where that undertaking has gone bankrupt, those companies may also, if necessary, be required to repay the aid in question, where it is established that they actually continue to benefit from the competitive advantage linked with the receipt of the aid. This could be the case, inter alia, where those hive-off companies acquire the assets of the company in liquidation without paying the market price in return or where it is established that the creation of such companies evades the obligation to repay that aid.

CoJ 29 April 2004 (Germany v. Commission (SMI), C-277/00) [2004] ECR I-3925, paras 76, 81, 85 and 86.

See also CoJ 20 September 2001 (Banks, C-390/98) [2001] ECR I-6117, paras 76–79; CoJ 8 May 2003 (Italy and SIM 2 Multimedia SpA v. Commission (Seleco), Joined Cases C-328/99 and C-399/00) [2003] ECR I-4035, paras 76, 77 and 83.

If the aid unlawfully paid has to be recovered from an undertaking which is insolvent or **11.122** subject to insolvency proceedings the purpose of which is to realise the assets and clear the liabilities, it is settled case-law that the fact that that undertaking is in difficulty or insolvent does not affect the obligation of recovery.

It is also settled case-law that the restoration of the previous situation and the elimination of the distortion of competition resulting from the unlawfully paid aid may in principle be achieved through registration of the liability relating to the repayment of the aid in question in the schedule of liabilities

CoJ 11 December 2012 (Spain v. Commission, C-610/10) ECLI:EU:C:2012:781, paras 71 and 72.

3. Complaints received by the Commission

[N]either the Treaty nor Community legislation lays down the procedural system for **11.123** dealing with complaints objecting to grants of State aid, that is also the position where such decisions concern State measures to which objection is taken in complaints on the ground that they constitute State aid contrary to the Treaty and the Commission refuses to initiate the procedure under Article [108(2) TFEU] because it considers either that the measures complained of do not constitute State aid within the meaning of Article [107 TFEU] or that they are compatible with the common market. Where the Commission adopts such a decision and proceeds, in accordance with its duty of sound administration, to inform the complainants of its decision, it is the decision addressed to the Member State which must form the subject-matter of any action for annulment which the complainant may bring, and not the letter to that complainant informing him of the decision.

CoJ 2 April 1998 (Sytraval, C–367/95 P) [1998] ECR I–1719, paras 44 and 45.

11.124   As regards [...] the proposition that the Commission is under an obligation in certain circumstances to conduct an exchange of views and arguments with the complainant, flowing, according to the contested judgment, from the Commission's obligation to state reasons for its decisions, it must be stated that there exists no basis for the imposition of such an obligation on the Commission [...].

[A]s regards the statement that the Commission is obliged to examine certain objections of its own motion, it must be stated, contrary to what was held by the [General Court], that the Commission is under no obligation to examine of its own motion objections which the complainant would certainly have raised had it been given the opportunity of taking cognisance of the information obtained by the Commission in the course of its investigation.

CoJ 2 April 1998 (Sytraval, C–367/95 P) [1998] ECR I–1719, paras 58 and 60.

12

ARTICLE 109 TFEU

DETERMINATION OF REGULATIONS REGARDING THE APPLICATION OF ARTS 107 AND 108

The Council, on a proposal from the Commission and after consulting the European Parliament, may make any appropriate regulations for the application of Articles 107 and 108 and may in particular determine the conditions in which Article 108(3) shall apply and the categories of aid exempted from this procedure.

Part 1

Section 3

REGULATIONS

13

REGULATION (EC) NO 1/2003 ON THE IMPLEMENTATION OF THE RULES ON COMPETITION*

COUNCIL REGULATION (EC) NO 1/2003 OF 16 DECEMBER 2002 ON THE IMPLEMENTATION OF THE RULES ON COMPETITION LAID DOWN IN ARTICLES 81 AND 82 OF THE TREATY (OJ 2003 L 1/1)

THE COUNCIL OF THE EUROPEAN UNION,

Having regard to the Treaty establishing the European Community, and in particular Article 83 thereof,

Having regard to the proposal from the Commission,[1]

Having regard to the opinion of the European Parliament,[2]

Having regard to the opinion of the European Economic and Social Committee,[3]

Whereas:

(1)   In order to establish a system which ensures that competition in the common market is not distorted, Articles 81 and 82 of the Treaty must be applied effectively and uniformly in the Community. Council Regulation No 17 of 6 February 1962, First Regulation implementing Articles 81 and 82[4] of the Treaty,[5] has allowed a Community competition policy to develop that has helped to disseminate a competition culture within the Community. In the light of experience, however, that Regulation should now be replaced by legislation designed to meet the challenges of an integrated market and a future enlargement of the Community.

---

*   This chapter was written by Mats Johnsson.
1   OJ C 365 E, 19.12.2000, p. 284.
2   OJ C 72 E, 21.3.2002, p. 305.
3   OJ C 155, 29.5.2001, p. 73.
4   The title of Regulation No 17 has been adjusted to take account of the renumbering of the Articles of the EC Treaty, in accordance with Article 12 of the Treaty of Amsterdam; the original reference was to Articles 85 and 86 of the Treaty.
5   OJ 13, 21.2.1962, p. 204/62. Regulation as last amended by Regulation (EC) No 1216/1999 (OJ L 148, 15.6.1999, p. 5).

(2) In particular, there is a need to rethink the arrangements for applying the exception from the prohibition on agreements, which restrict competition, laid down in Article 81(3) of the Treaty. Under Article 83(2)(b) of the Treaty, account must be taken in this regard of the need to ensure effective supervision, on the one hand, and to simplify administration to the greatest possible extent, on the other.

(3) The centralised scheme set up by Regulation No 17 no longer secures a balance between those two objectives. It hampers application of the Community competition rules by the courts and competition authorities of the Member States, and the system of notification it involves prevents the Commission from concentrating its resources on curbing the most serious infringements. It also imposes considerable costs on undertakings.

(4) The present system should therefore be replaced by a directly applicable exception system in which the competition authorities and courts of the Member States have the power to apply not only Article 81(1) and Article 82 of the Treaty, which have direct applicability by virtue of the case-law of the Court of Justice of the European Communities, but also Article 81(3) of the Treaty.

(5) In order to ensure an effective enforcement of the Community competition rules and at the same time the respect of fundamental rights of defence, this Regulation should regulate the burden of proof under Articles 81 and 82 of the Treaty. It should be for the party or the authority alleging an infringement of Article 81(1) and Article 82 of the Treaty to prove the existence thereof to the required legal standard. It should be for the undertaking or association of undertakings invoking the benefit of a defence against a finding of an infringement to demonstrate to the required legal standard that the conditions for applying such defence are satisfied. This Regulation affects neither national rules on the standard of proof nor obligations of competition authorities and courts of the Member States to ascertain the relevant facts of a case, provided that such rules and obligations are compatible with general principles of Community law.

(6) In order to ensure that the Community competition rules are applied effectively, the competition authorities of the Member States should be associated more closely with their application. To this end, they should be empowered to apply Community law.

(7) National courts have an essential part to play in applying the Community competition rules. When deciding disputes between private individuals, they protect the subjective rights under Community law, for example by awarding damages to the victims of infringements. The role of the national courts here complements that of the competition authorities of the Member States. They should therefore be allowed to apply Articles 81 and 82 of the Treaty in full.

(8) In order to ensure the effective enforcement of the Community competition rules and the proper functioning of the cooperation mechanisms contained in this Regulation, it is necessary to oblige the competition authorities and courts of the Member States to also apply Articles 81 and 82 of the Treaty where they apply national competition law to agreements and practices which may affect trade between Member States. In order to create a level playing field for agreements, decisions by associations of undertakings and concerted practices within the internal market, it is also necessary to determine pursuant to Article 83(2)(e) of the Treaty the relationship between national laws and Community competition law.

To that effect it is necessary to provide that the application of national competition laws to agreements, decisions or concerted practices within the meaning of Article 81(1) of the Treaty may not lead to the prohibition of such agreements, decisions and concerted practices if they are not also prohibited under Community competition law. The notions of agreements, decisions and concerted practices are autonomous concepts of Community competition law covering the coordination of behaviour of undertakings on the market as interpreted by the Community Courts. Member States should not under this Regulation be precluded from adopting and applying on their territory stricter national competition laws which prohibit or impose sanctions on unilateral conduct engaged in by undertakings. These stricter national laws may include provisions which prohibit or impose sanctions on abusive behaviour toward economically dependent undertakings. Furthermore, this Regulation does not apply to national laws which impose criminal sanctions on natural persons except to the extent that such sanctions are the means whereby competition rules applying to undertakings are enforced.

(9)   Articles 81 and 82 of the Treaty have as their objective the protection of competition on the market. This Regulation, which is adopted for the implementation of these Treaty provisions, does not preclude Member States from implementing on their territory national legislation, which protects other legitimate interests provided that such legislation is compatible with general principles and other provisions of Community law. In so far as such national legislation pursues predominantly an objective different from that of protecting competition on the market, the competition authorities and courts of the Member States may apply such legislation on their territory. Accordingly, Member States may under this Regulation implement on their territory national legislation that prohibits or imposes sanctions on acts of unfair trading practice, be they unilateral or contractual. Such legislation pursues a specific objective, irrespective of the actual or presumed effects of such acts on competition on the market. This is particularly the case of legislation which prohibits undertakings from imposing on their trading partners, obtaining or attempting to obtain from them terms and conditions that are unjustified, disproportionate or without consideration.

(10) Regulations such as 19/65/EEC,[6] (EEC) No 2821/71,[7] (EEC) No 3976/87,[8]

---

6   Council Regulation No 19/65/EEC of 2 March 1965 on the application of Article 81(3) (The titles of the Regulations have been adjusted to take account of the renumbering of the Articles of the EC Treaty, in accordance with Article 12 of the Treaty of Amsterdam; the original reference was to Article 85(3) of the Treaty) of the Treaty to certain categories of agreements and concerted practices (OJ 36, 6.3.1965, p. 533). Regulation as last amended by Regulation (EC) No 1215/1999 (OJ L 148, 15.6.1999, p. 1).

7   Council Regulation (EEC) No 2821/71 of 20 December 1971 on the application of Article 81(3) (The titles of the Regulations have been adjusted to take account of the renumbering of the Articles of the EC Treaty, in accordance with Article 12 of the Treaty of Amsterdam; the original reference was to Article 85(3) of the Treaty) of the Treaty to categories of agreements, decisions and concerted practices (OJ L 285, 29.12.1971, p. 46). Regulation as last amended by the Act of Accession of 1994.

8   Council Regulation (EEC) No 3976/87 of 14 December 1987 on the application of Article 81(3) (The titles of the Regulations have been adjusted to take account of the renumbering of the Articles of the EC Treaty, in accordance with Article 12 of the Treaty of Amsterdam; the original reference was to Article 85(3) of the Treaty) of the Treaty to certain categories of agreements and concerted practices in the air transport sector (OJ L 374, 31.12.1987, p. 9). Regulation as last amended by the Act of Accession of 1994.

325

(EEC) No 1534/91,[9] or (EEC) No 479/92[10] empower the Commission to apply Article 81(3) of the Treaty by Regulation to certain categories of agreements, decisions by associations of undertakings and concerted practices. In the areas defined by such Regulations, the Commission has adopted and may continue to adopt so called 'block' exemption Regulations by which it declares Article 81(1) of the Treaty inapplicable to categories of agreements, decisions and concerted practices. Where agreements, decisions and concerted practices to which such Regulations apply none the less have effects that are incompatible with Article 81(3) of the Treaty, the Commission and the competition authorities of the Member States should have the power to withdraw in a particular case the benefit of the block exemption Regulation.

(11) For it to ensure that the provisions of the Treaty are applied, the Commission should be able to address decisions to undertakings or associations of undertakings for the purpose of bringing to an end infringements of Articles 81 and 82 of the Treaty. Provided there is a legitimate interest in doing so, the Commission should also be able to adopt decisions which find that an infringement has been committed in the past even if it does not impose a fine. This Regulation should also make explicit provision for the Commission's power to adopt decisions ordering interim measures, which has been acknowledged by the Court of Justice.

(12) This Regulation should make explicit provision for the Commission's power to impose any remedy, whether behavioural or structural, which is necessary to bring the infringement effectively to an end, having regard to the principle of proportionality. Structural remedies should only be imposed either where there is no equally effective behavioural remedy or where any equally effective behavioural remedy would be more burdensome for the undertaking concerned than the structural remedy. Changes to the structure of an undertaking as it existed before the infringement was committed would only be proportionate where there is a substantial risk of a lasting or repeated infringement that derives from the very structure of the undertaking.

(13) Where, in the course of proceedings which might lead to an agreement or practice being prohibited, undertakings offer the Commission commitments such as to meet its concerns, the Commission should be able to adopt decisions which make those commitments binding on the undertakings concerned. Commitment decisions should find that there are no longer grounds for action by the Commission without concluding whether or not there has been or still is an infringement. Commitment decisions are without prejudice to the powers of competition authorities and courts of the Member States to make such a finding

---

9 Council Regulation (EEC) No 1534/91 of 31 May 1991 on the application of Article 81(3) (The titles of the Regulations have been adjusted to take account of the renumbering of the Articles of the EC Treaty, in accordance with Article 12 of the Treaty of Amsterdam; the original reference was to Article 85(3) of the Treaty) of the Treaty to certain categories of agreements, decisions and concerted practices in the insurance sector (OJ L 143, 7.6.1991, p. 1).

10 Council Regulation (EEC) No 479/92 of 25 February 1992 on the application of Article 81(3) (The titles of the Regulations have been adjusted to take account of the renumbering of the Articles of the EC Treaty, in accordance with Article 12 of the Treaty of Amsterdam; the original reference was to Article 85(3) of the Treaty) of the Treaty to certain categories of agreements, decisions and concerted practices between liner shipping companies (Consortia) (OJ L 55, 29.2.1992, p. 3). Regulation amended by the Act of Accession of 1994.

and decide upon the case. Commitment decisions are not appropriate in cases where the Commission intends to impose a fine.

(14) In exceptional cases where the public interest of the Community so requires, it may also be expedient for the Commission to adopt a decision of a declaratory nature finding that the prohibition in Article 81 or Article 82 of the Treaty does not apply, with a view to clarifying the law and ensuring its consistent application throughout the Community, in particular with regard to new types of agreements or practices that have not been settled in the existing case-law and administrative practice.

(15) The Commission and the competition authorities of the Member States should form together a network of public authorities applying the Community competition rules in close cooperation. For that purpose it is necessary to set up arrangements for information and consultation. Further modalities for the cooperation within the network will be laid down and revised by the Commission, in close cooperation with the Member States.

(16) Notwithstanding any national provision to the contrary, the exchange of information and the use of such information in evidence should be allowed between the members of the network even where the information is confidential. This information may be used for the application of Articles 81 and 82 of the Treaty as well as for the parallel application of national competition law, provided that the latter application relates to the same case and does not lead to a different outcome. When the information exchanged is used by the receiving authority to impose sanctions on undertakings, there should be no other limit to the use of the information than the obligation to use it for the purpose for which it was collected given the fact that the sanctions imposed on undertakings are of the same type in all systems. The rights of defence enjoyed by undertakings in the various systems can be considered as sufficiently equivalent. However, as regards natural persons, they may be subject to substantially different types of sanctions across the various systems. Where that is the case, it is necessary to ensure that information can only be used if it has been collected in a way which respects the same level of protection of the rights of defence of natural persons as provided for under the national rules of the receiving authority.

(17) If the competition rules are to be applied consistently and, at the same time, the network is to be managed in the best possible way, it is essential to retain the rule that the competition authorities of the Member States are automatically relieved of their competence if the Commission initiates its own proceedings. Where a competition authority of a Member State is already acting on a case and the Commission intends to initiate proceedings, it should endeavour to do so as soon as possible. Before initiating proceedings, the Commission should consult the national authority concerned.

(18) To ensure that cases are dealt with by the most appropriate authorities within the network, a general provision should be laid down allowing a competition authority to suspend or close a case on the ground that another authority is dealing with it or has already dealt with it, the objective being that each case should be handled by a single authority. This provision should not prevent the Commission from rejecting a complaint for lack of Community interest, as the case-law of the Court

of Justice has acknowledged it may do, even if no other competition authority has indicated its intention of dealing with the case.

(19) The Advisory Committee on Restrictive Practices and Dominant Positions set up by Regulation No 17 has functioned in a very satisfactory manner. It will fit well into the new system of decentralised application. It is necessary, therefore, to build upon the rules laid down by Regulation No 17, while improving the effectiveness of the organisational arrangements. To this end, it would be expedient to allow opinions to be delivered by written procedure. The Advisory Committee should also be able to act as a forum for discussing cases that are being handled by the competition authorities of the Member States, so as to help safeguard the consistent application of the Community competition rules.

(20) The Advisory Committee should be composed of representatives of the competition authorities of the Member States. For meetings in which general issues are being discussed, Member States should be able to appoint an additional representative. This is without prejudice to members of the Committee being assisted by other experts from the Member States.

(21) Consistency in the application of the competition rules also requires that arrangements be established for cooperation between the courts of the Member States and the Commission. This is relevant for all courts of the Member States that apply Articles 81 and 82 of the Treaty, whether applying these rules in lawsuits between private parties, acting as public enforcers or as review courts. In particular, national courts should be able to ask the Commission for information or for its opinion on points concerning the application of Community competition law. The Commission and the competition authorities of the Member States should also be able to submit written or oral observations to courts called upon to apply Article 81 or Article 82 of the Treaty. These observations should be submitted within the framework of national procedural rules and practices including those safeguarding the rights of the parties. Steps should therefore be taken to ensure that the Commission and the competition authorities of the Member States are kept sufficiently well informed of proceedings before national courts.

(22) In order to ensure compliance with the principles of legal certainty and the uniform application of the Community competition rules in a system of parallel powers, conflicting decisions must be avoided. It is therefore necessary to clarify, in accordance with the case-law of the Court of Justice, the effects of Commission decisions and proceedings on courts and competition authorities of the Member States. Commitment decisions adopted by the Commission do not affect the power of the courts and the competition authorities of the Member States to apply Articles 81 and 82 of the Treaty.

(23) The Commission should be empowered throughout the Community to require such information to be supplied as is necessary to detect any agreement, decision or concerted practice prohibited by Article 81 of the Treaty or any abuse of a dominant position prohibited by Article 82 of the Treaty. When complying with a decision of the Commission, undertakings cannot be forced to admit that they have committed an infringement, but they are in any event obliged to answer factual questions and to provide documents, even if this information may be used

to establish against them or against another undertaking the existence of an infringement.

(24) The Commission should also be empowered to undertake such inspections as are necessary to detect any agreement, decision or concerted practice prohibited by Article 81 of the Treaty or any abuse of a dominant position prohibited by Article 82 of the Treaty. The competition authorities of the Member States should cooperate actively in the exercise of these powers.

(25) The detection of infringements of the competition rules is growing ever more difficult, and, in order to protect competition effectively, the Commission's powers of investigation need to be supplemented. The Commission should in particular be empowered to interview any persons who may be in possession of useful information and to record the statements made. In the course of an inspection, officials authorised by the Commission should be empowered to affix seals for the period of time necessary for the inspection. Seals should normally not be affixed for more than 72 hours. Officials authorised by the Commission should also be empowered to ask for any information relevant to the subject matter and purpose of the inspection.

(26) Experience has shown that there are cases where business records are kept in the homes of directors or other people working for an undertaking. In order to safeguard the effectiveness of inspections, therefore, officials and other persons authorised by the Commission should be empowered to enter any premises where business records may be kept, including private homes. However, the exercise of this latter power should be subject to the authorisation of the judicial authority.

(27) Without prejudice to the case-law of the Court of Justice, it is useful to set out the scope of the control that the national judicial authority may carry out when it authorises, as foreseen by national law including as a precautionary measure, assistance from law enforcement authorities in order to overcome possible opposition on the part of the undertaking or the execution of the decision to carry out inspections in non-business premises. It results from the case-law that the national judicial authority may in particular ask the Commission for further information which it needs to carry out its control and in the absence of which it could refuse the authorisation. The case-law also confirms the competence of the national courts to control the application of national rules governing the implementation of coercive measures.

(28) In order to help the competition authorities of the Member States to apply Articles 81 and 82 of the Treaty effectively, it is expedient to enable them to assist one another by carrying out inspections and other fact-finding measures.

(29) Compliance with Articles 81 and 82 of the Treaty and the fulfilment of the obligations imposed on undertakings and associations of undertakings under this Regulation should be enforceable by means of fines and periodic penalty payments. To that end, appropriate levels of fine should also be laid down for infringements of the procedural rules.

(30) In order to ensure effective recovery of fines imposed on associations of undertakings for infringements that they have committed, it is necessary to lay down the conditions on which the Commission may require payment of the fine from the members of the association where the association is not solvent. In doing so, the Commission should have regard to the relative size of the undertakings

belonging to the association and in particular to the situation of small- and medium-sized enterprises. Payment of the fine by one or several members of an association is without prejudice to rules of national law that provide for recovery of the amount paid from other members of the association.

(31) The rules on periods of limitation for the imposition of fines and periodic penalty payments were laid down in Council Regulation (EEC) No 2988/74,[11] which also concerns penalties in the field of transport. In a system of parallel powers, the acts, which may interrupt a limitation period, should include procedural steps taken independently by the competition authority of a Member State. To clarify the legal framework, Regulation (EEC) No 2988/74 should therefore be amended to prevent it applying to matters covered by this Regulation, and this Regulation should include provisions on periods of limitation.

(32) The undertakings concerned should be accorded the right to be heard by the Commission, third parties whose interests may be affected by a decision should be given the opportunity of submitting their observations beforehand, and the decisions taken should be widely publicised. While ensuring the rights of defence of the undertakings concerned, in particular, the right of access to the file, it is essential that business secrets be protected. The confidentiality of information exchanged in the network should likewise be safeguarded.

(33) Since all decisions taken by the Commission under this Regulation are subject to review by the Court of Justice in accordance with the Treaty, the Court of Justice should, in accordance with Article 229 thereof be given unlimited jurisdiction in respect of decisions by which the Commission imposes fines or periodic penalty payments.

(34) The principles laid down in Articles 81 and 82 of the Treaty, as they have been applied by Regulation No 17, have given a central role to the Community bodies. This central role should be retained, whilst associating the Member States more closely with the application of the Community competition rules. In accordance with the principles of subsidiarity and proportionality as set out in Article 5 of the Treaty, this Regulation does not go beyond what is necessary in order to achieve its objective, which is to allow the Community competition rules to be applied effectively.

(35) In order to attain a proper enforcement of Community competition law, Member States should designate and empower authorities to apply Articles 81 and 82 of the Treaty as public enforcers. They should be able to designate administrative as well as judicial authorities to carry out the various functions conferred upon competition authorities in this Regulation. This Regulation recognises the wide variation which exists in the public enforcement systems of Member States. The effects of Article 11(6) of this Regulation should apply to all competition authorities. As an exception to this general rule, where a prosecuting authority brings a case before a separate judicial authority, Article 11(6) should apply to the prosecuting authority subject to the conditions in Article 35(4) of this Regulation. Where these conditions are not fulfilled, the general rule should apply. In

---

11   Council Regulation (EEC) No 2988/74 of 26 November 1974 concerning limitation periods in proceedings and the enforcement of sanctions under the rules of the European Economic Community relating to transport and competition (OJ L 319, 29.11.1974, p. 1).

any case, Article 11(6) should not apply to courts in so far as they are acting as review courts.

(36) As the case-law has made it clear that the competition rules apply to transport, that sector should be made subject to the procedural provisions of this Regulation. Council Regulation No 141 of 26 November 1962 exempting transport from the application of Regulation No 17[12] should therefore be repealed and Regulations (EEC) No 1017/68,[13] (EEC) No 4056/86[14] and (EEC) No 3975/87[15] should be amended in order to delete the specific procedural provisions they contain.

(37) This Regulation respects the fundamental rights and observes the principles recognised in particular by the Charter of Fundamental Rights of the European Union. Accordingly, this Regulation should be interpreted and applied with respect to those rights and principles.

(38) Legal certainty for undertakings operating under the Community competition rules contributes to the promotion of innovation and investment. Where cases give rise to genuine uncertainty because they present novel or unresolved questions for the application of these rules, individual undertakings may wish to seek informal guidance from the Commission. This Regulation is without prejudice to the ability of the Commission to issue such informal guidance.

HAS ADOPTED THIS REGULATION:

---

12 OJ 124, 28.11.1962, p. 2751/62; Regulation as last amended by Regulation No 1002/67/EEC (OJ 306, 16.12.1967, p. 1).

13 Council Regulation (EEC) No 1017/68 of 19 July 1968 applying rules of competition to transport by rail, road and inland waterway (OJ L 175, 23.7.1968, p. 1). Regulation as last amended by the Act of Accession of 1994.

14 Council Regulation (EEC) No 4056/86 of 22 December 1986 laying down detailed rules for the application of Articles 81 and 82 (The title of the Regulation has been adjusted to take account of the renumbering of the Articles of the EC Treaty, in accordance with Article 12 of the Treaty of Amsterdam; the original reference was to Articles 85 and 86 of the Treaty) of the Treaty to maritime transport (OJ L 378, 31.12.1986, p. 4). Regulation as last amended by the Act of Accession of 1994.

15 Council Regulation (EEC) No 3975/87 of 14 December 1987 laying down the procedure for the application of the rules on competition to undertakings in the air transport sector (OJ L 374, 31.12.1987, p. 1). Regulation as last amended by Regulation (EEC) No 2410/92 (OJ L 240, 24.8.1992, p. 18).

CHAPTER I

PRINCIPLES

ARTICLE 1 – APPLICATION OF ARTICLES 81 AND 82 OF THE TREATY

1. Agreements, decisions and concerted practices caught by Article 81(1) of the Treaty which do not satisfy the conditions of Article 81(3) of the Treaty shall be prohibited, no prior decision to that effect being required.
2. Agreements, decisions and concerted practices caught by Article 81(1) of the Treaty which satisfy the conditions of Article 81(3) of the Treaty shall not be prohibited, no prior decision to that effect being required.
3. The abuse of a dominant position referred to in Article 82 of the Treaty shall be prohibited, no prior decision to that effect being required.

ARTICLE 2 – BURDEN OF PROOF

In any national or Community proceedings for the application of Articles 81 and 82 of the Treaty, the burden of proving an infringement of Article 81(1) or of Article 82 of the Treaty shall rest on the party or the authority alleging the infringement. The undertaking or association of undertakings claiming the benefit of Article 81(3) of the Treaty shall bear the burden of proving that the conditions of that paragraph are fulfilled.

OVERVIEW

A. BURDEN AND STANDARD OF PROOF	13.01	C. SINGLE AND CONTINUOUS OR REPEATED INFRINGEMENT 13.16
1. General	13.01	
2. Undertaking publicly distancing itself from agreement or concerted practice	13.06	1. General 13.16
3. Limitation defence/duration	13.10	2. Continuous vs. repeated infringement 13.19
B. NATURE OF EVIDENCE	13.12	

A. BURDEN AND STANDARD OF PROOF

1. General

[T]he presumption of a causal connection [between the concerted practice and the market conduct of the undertakings participating in the practice] stems from Article [101(1) TFEU], as interpreted by the Court, and it consequently forms an integral part of applicable Community law.   **13.01**

[I]n examining whether there is a causal connection – a connection which must exist if it is to be established that there is concerted practice within the meaning of Article [101(1) TFEU] – the national court is required, subject to proof to the contrary, which it is for the undertakings concerned to adduce, to apply the presumption of a causal connection established in the Court's case-law, according to which, where they remain active on that market, such undertakings are presumed to take account of the information exchanged with their competitors.

CoJ 4 June 2009 (T-Mobile Netherlands B.V. and others v. RvB NMa, C-8/08) [2009] ECR I-4529, paras 52 and 53.

[I]t is not true that, as a matter of principle, the standard of proof required for the purposes of establishing the existence of an anti-competitive agreement in the framework of a vertical relationship is higher than that which is required in the framework of a horizontal relationship.   **13.02**

It is indeed true that factors which, in the context of a horizontal relationship, can sometimes suggest the existence of an anti-competitive agreement between competitors may prove inadequate for the purposes of establishing the existence of such an agreement in the framework of a vertical relationship between a manufacturer and a distributor, given that, in such a relationship, a certain measure of contact is lawful. However, the fact none the less remains that, for the purposes of assessing whether there is an illegal agreement, regard must be had to all the relevant factors, as well as to the economic and legal context specific to each case. The question whether it can be inferred from certain evidence that an agreement contrary to Article [101(1) TFEU] has been concluded cannot therefore be addressed in abstract terms, according to whether the relationship involved is vertical or horizontal, with that evidence being considered separately from the context and the other factors characterising the case.

CoJ 10 February 2011 (Activision Blizzard Germany, C-260/09 P) [2011] ECR I-419, paras 71 and 72.

13.03 [I]t is for the party or the authority alleging an infringement of the competition rules to prove its existence by establishing, to the requisite legal standard, the facts constituting an infringement, and it is for the undertaking invoking the benefit of a defence against a finding of an infringement to demonstrate that the conditions for applying such defence are satisfied, so that the authority will then have to resort to other evidence. The duration of the infringement is an intrinsic element of an infringement under Article [101(1) TFEU], the burden of proof of which is borne principally by the Commission [...].

That apportionment of the burden of proof may vary, however, inasmuch as the evidence on which a party relies may be of such a kind as to require the other party to provide an explanation or justification, failing which it is permissible to conclude that the burden of proof has been discharged [...].

General Court 12 July 2011 (Fuji Electric Co., T-132/07) [2011] ECR II-4091, paras 84 and 85.

See also CoJ 7 January 2004 (Aalborg Portland, C-204/00 P) [2004] ECR I-123, paras 78 and 79.

13.04 Admittedly, if the Commission finds that there has been an infringement of the competition rules on the basis that the established facts cannot be explained other than by the existence of anti-competitive behaviour, the Courts of the European Union will find it necessary to annul the decision in question where those undertakings put forward arguments which cast the facts established by the Commission in a different light and thus allow another plausible explanation of the facts to be substituted for the one adopted by the Commission in concluding that an infringement occurred. In such a case, it cannot be considered that the Commission has adduced proof of an infringement of competition law [...].

However, the Court has also held that, where the Commission has been able to establish that an undertaking had taken part in meetings between undertakings of a manifestly anti-competitive nature, the General Court was entitled to consider that it was for that undertaking to provide another explanation of the tenor of those meetings.

In so doing, the General Court had neither unduly reversed the burden of proof nor set aside the presumption of innocence [...].

Likewise, [...] when the Commission relies on evidence which is in principle sufficient to demonstrate the existence of the infringement, it is not sufficient for the undertaking concerned to raise the possibility that a circumstance arose which might affect the probative value of that evidence so that the Commission bears the burden of proving that that circumstance was not capable of affecting the probative value of that evidence. On the contrary, except in cases where such proof could not be provided by the undertaking concerned on account of the conduct of the Commission itself, it is for the undertaking concerned to prove to the requisite legal standard, on the one hand, the existence of the circumstance relied on by it and, on the other, that that circumstance calls in question the probative value of the evidence relied on by the Commission.

CoJ 22 November 2012 (E.ON Energie AG v. Commission, C-89/11 P), ECLI: EU:C:2012:738, paras 74–76.

[A]ccording to settled case-law, the Commission must prove the infringements found **13.05** by it and adduce evidence capable of demonstrating to the requisite legal standard the existence of circumstances constituting an infringement [...].

Any doubt in the mind of the Court must operate to the advantage of the undertaking to which the decision finding an infringement is addressed [...]. The Court cannot therefore conclude that the Commission has established the infringement at issue to the requisite legal standard if it still entertains any doubts on that point [...].

In the latter situation, account must be taken of the presumption of innocence, as it results in particular from Article 47 of the Charter of Fundamental Rights of the European Union [...], which Article 6(1) TEU recognises as having the same legal value as the Treaties [...]. Given the nature of the infringements in question and the nature and degree of severity of the ensuing penalties, the presumption of innocence applies in particular to the procedures relating to infringements of the competition rules applicable to undertakings which may result in the imposition of fines or periodic penalty payments [...].

The Commission must produce sufficiently precise and consistent evidence to support the firm conviction that the alleged infringement took place [...].

However, it is important to emphasise that it is not necessary for every item of evidence produced by the Commission to satisfy those criteria in relation to every aspect of the infringement. It is sufficient if the body of evidence relied on by the Commission, viewed as a whole, meets that requirement [...].

Moreover, as anti-competitive agreements are known to be prohibited, the Commission cannot be required to produce documents expressly attesting to contacts between the economic operators concerned. The fragmentary and sporadic items of evidence which may be available to the Commission must, in any event, be capable of being supplemented by inferences which allow the relevant circumstances to be reconstituted. The existence of an anti-competitive practice or agreement may therefore be inferred from a number of coincidences and indicia which, taken together, may, in the absence of another plausible explanation, constitute evidence of an infringement of the competition rules [...].

General Court 16 September 2013 (Wabco Europe and Others v. Commission, T-380/10), ECLI:EU:T:2013:449, paras 42 and 45–49.

See also CoJ 15 October 2002 (Limburgse Vinyl Maatschappij NV v. Commission, C-23/99 P) [2002] ECR I-8375, paras 513–523; General Court 25 October 2005 (Group Danone v. Commission, T-38/02) [2005] ECR II-4407, paras 217 and 218.

2. Undertaking publicly distancing itself from agreement or concerted practice

13.06   [I]n Anic Partecipazioni [...] the Court of Justice did not modify the principle that, where there is a dispute as to the existence of an infringement of the competition rules, it is for the Commission to prove the infringement which it has found and to adduce evidence capable of demonstrating to the requisite legal standard the existence of circumstances constituting an infringement.

In Anic Partecipazioni, it was established that an 'agreement', within the meaning of Article [101(1) TFEU], had been concluded at a meeting between various participants. The Court therefore held that an undertaking which had participated in that meeting had to bear the burden of proof if it subsequently wished to argue that it did not intend to participate in the implementation of the agreement thus established. It follows that the reversal of the burden of proof in that case took place after the existence of an agreement formed at a meeting between three undertakings had been established. Moreover, the possibility open to the undertaking concerned, which bore the burden of proof, was to withdraw from the agreement which had been established and not to deny its very existence.

CoJ 6 January 2004 (Bundesverband der Arzneimittel-Importeure eV and others v. Bayer AG, Joined Cases C-2/01 P and C-3/01 P) [2004] ECR I-23, paras 62 and 63.

See also General Court 27 September 2006 (Dresdner Bank AG and Others, Joined Cases T-44/02 OP, T-54/02 OP, T-56/02 OP, T-60/02 OP and T-61/02 OP) [2006] ECR II-3567.

13.07   It is for the Commission to prove the infringements which it finds by adducing, in the decisions in which it applies the competition rules, precise and coherent evidence demonstrating convincingly the existence of the facts constituting those infringements [...]

Where [...] the Commission has adduced evidence of the existence of an agreement, it is for an undertaking which has taken part in that agreement to adduce evidence that it distanced itself from that agreement, evidence which must demonstrate a clear intention, brought to the notice of the other participating undertakings, to withdraw from that agreement [...].

General Court 27 September 2006 (GlaxoSmithKline Services Unlimited v. Commission, T-168/01) [2006] ECR II-2969, paras 82 and 86.

[I]t is sufficient for the Commission to show that the undertaking concerned partici- **13.08**
pated in meetings at which anti-competitive agreements were concluded, without
manifestly opposing them, to prove to the requisite standard that the undertaking
participated in the cartel. Where participation in such meetings has been established, it
is for that undertaking to put forward evidence to establish that its participation in
those meetings was without any anti-competitive intention by demonstrating that it
had indicated to its competitors that it was participating in those meetings in a spirit
that was different from theirs [...].

    Nor is the fact that an undertaking does not act on the outcome of a meeting having
an anti-competitive object such as to relieve it of responsibility for the fact of its
participation in a cartel, unless it has publicly distanced itself from what was agreed in
the meeting [...].

    Furthermore, it has been held that the notion of publicly distancing oneself as a
means of excluding liability must be interpreted narrowly. In particular, silence by an
operator in a meeting during which the parties colluded unlawfully on a precise
question of pricing policy cannot be regarded an expression of firm and unambiguous
disapproval [...].

    It should also be noted, however, that the [...] case-law on tacit approval is based on
the premise that the undertaking concerned participated in meetings at which
anti-competitive agreements were concluded [...] or which were manifestly anti-
competitive [...]. Consequently, where the anti-competitive nature of a meeting has not
been established beyond doubt, that case-law does not apply [...]. [...]

    It should be borne in mind in that regard that the duration of the infringement is an
intrinsic element of an infringement under Article [101(1) TFEU], the burden of proof
of which is borne principally by the Commission. In this respect, according to the
case-law, if there is no evidence directly establishing the duration of an infringement,
the Commission should adduce at least evidence of facts sufficiently proximate in time
for it to be reasonable to accept that that infringement continued uninterruptedly
between two specific dates [...].

*General Court 30 November 2011 (Quinn Barlo Ltd and others, T-208/06) [2011]
ECR II-7953, paras 47, 49–51 and 155.*

*See also CoJ 8 July 1999 (Hüls v. Commission, C-199/92 P) ECR I-4287, para.
155, and Montecatini v. Commission, C-235/92 P) ECR I-4539, para. 181;
General Court 11 December 2003 (Adriatica di Navigazione, T-61/99) [2003]
ECR II-5349, para. 91.*

[W]hen it is established that an undertaking has participated in anti-competitive **13.09**
meetings between competing undertakings, it is for that undertaking to put forward
evidence to establish that its participation in those meeting was without any anti-
competitive intention by demonstrating that it had indicated to its competitors that it
was participating in those meetings in a spirit that was different from theirs. If an
undertaking's participation in such a meeting is not to be regarded as tacit approval of an

unlawful initiative or as subscribing to what is decided there, the undertaking must publicly distance itself from that initiative in such a way that the other participants will think that it is putting an end to its participation, or it must report the initiative to the administrative authorities [...].

CoJ 7 February 2013 (Protimonopolný úrad Slovenskej republiky v. Slovenská sporitel'ňa a.s. C-68/12), ECLI:EU:C:2013:71, para. 27.

3. Limitation defence/duration

13.10   In the present case, the general principle that the Commission is required to prove every constituent element of the infringement, including its duration, that is likely to have an effect on its definitive findings as to the gravity of that infringement, is not called into question by the fact that the applicant raised a defence of limitation, the burden of proof of which is in principle borne by the applicant. Not only does that defence not relate to the finding of an infringement, but it is clear that reliance on such a plea necessarily requires that the duration of the infringement and the date on which it came to an end be established. Those circumstances cannot alone provide justification for transferring the burden in this regard to the applicant. The duration of the infringement, which requires that the date on which it ended be known, is one of the essential elements of the infringement, which must be proved by the Commission, irrespective of the fact that the disputing of those elements also forms part of the defence of limitation [...].

General Court 16 November 2006 (Peróxidos Orgánicos, SA v. Commission, T-120/04) [2006] ECR II-4441, para. 52.

13.11   [W]here the Commission bases its decision solely on the conduct of the undertakings at issue on the market to conclude that there was an infringement, it is sufficient for those undertakings to prove the existence of circumstances which cast the facts established by the Commission in a different light and thus allow another, plausible explanation of those facts to be substituted for the one adopted by the Commission in concluding that the Community competition rules had been infringed [...].

[W]hen there is a dispute concerning the existence of an infringement, the requirement of legal certainty, on which economic operators are entitled to rely, means that the Commission, which bears the burden of proving infringements which it finds, must adduce evidence which will sufficiently establish the existence of the facts constituting the infringement. With specific regard to the alleged duration of an infringement, the same principle of legal certainty requires that, if there is no evidence directly establishing the duration of an infringement, the Commission should adduce at least evidence of facts sufficiently proximate in time for it to be reasonable to accept that that infringement continued uninterruptedly between two specific dates [...].

General Court 12 July 2011 (Mitsubishi Electric Corp, T-133/07) [2011] ECR II-4219, paras 72 and 241.

See also General Court 13 July 2011 (Trade-Stomil, T-53/07) [2011] ECR II-4657, para. 63.

B. NATURE OF EVIDENCE

[R]espect for fundamental rights is a condition of the lawfulness of European Union **13.12**
acts and that measures incompatible with respect for fundamental rights are not
acceptable in the European Union [...]. European Union law cannot therefore accept
evidence obtained in complete disregard of the procedure laid down for gathering it
[...]. The use of that procedure must, therefore, be regarded as an essential procedural
requirement within the meaning of the second paragraph of Article [263 TFEU]. [...]

It follows from this that any cartel participant may rely on the inadmissibility of
evidence of that cartel obtained by the Commission in disregard of the procedure laid
down for gathering it, such as the inspection procedure provided for in Article 20 of
Regulation No 1/2003, and it is not necessary to claim, much less prove, that
non-compliance with that procedure has resulted in harm to that person. Evidence
obtained outside the procedure laid down for that purpose cannot be regarded as
evidence that has been lawfully constituted and that may be used by the Commission in
its investigation.

General Court 12 December 2012 (Almamet GmbH v. European Commission,
T-410/09), ECLI:EU:T:2012:676, paras 39 and 40.

So far as concerns the types of evidence which may be relied on to establish an **13.13**
infringement of Article 101 TFEU and Article 53 of the EEA Agreement, the basic
principle in EU law is that evidence may be freely adduced [...].

Consequently, an absence of documentary evidence is relevant only in the overall
assessment of the probative value of the body of evidence relied on by the Commission.
It does not, in itself, however, enable the undertaking concerned to call the Commission's claims into question by presenting a different explanation of the facts. An
applicant may do so only where the evidence submitted by the Commission does not
enable the infringement to be established unequivocally and without the need for
interpretation [...].

In addition, no provision or general principle of EU law prohibits the Commission
from relying, as against an undertaking, on statements made by other incriminated
undertakings. If that were not the case, the burden of proving conduct contrary to
Article 101 TFEU and Article 53 of the EEA Agreement, which is borne by the
Commission, would be unsustainable and incompatible with its task of supervising the
proper application of those provisions [...].

However, an admission by one undertaking accused of having participated in a cartel,
the accuracy of which is contested by several other undertakings similarly accused,
cannot be regarded as constituting adequate proof of an infringement committed by the
latter undertakings unless it is supported by other evidence, given that the degree of
corroboration required may be lesser in view of the reliability of the statements at issue
[...].

As regards the probative value of the various items of evidence, the only relevant
criterion for the purpose of evaluating the evidence produced is its reliability [...].

According to the general rules relating to evidence, the credibility, and, thus, the
probative value, of a document depends on the person from whom it originates, the
circumstances in which it came into being, the person to whom it was addressed and
whether it appears sound and reliable [...].

General Court 16 September 2013 (Keramag Keramische Werke AG and Others v. Commission, T-379/10 and T-381/10), ECLI:EU:T:2013:457, paras 102–107.

13.14   With respect to the probative value of statements by leniency applicants, it is settled case-law that there is no general provision or principle of European Union law which prohibits the Commission from using statements against an undertaking which have been provided by other undertakings involved in the infringement. Statements made pursuant to the Leniency Notice cannot therefore be regarded as devoid of probative value on that ground alone [...].

Some caution as to the evidence provided voluntarily by the main participants in an unlawful agreement is however understandable, since they might tend to play down the importance of their contribution to the infringement and maximise that of others. None the less, given the inherent logic of the procedure provided for in the 2002 Leniency Notice, the fact of seeking to benefit from the application of that notice in order to obtain a reduction in the fine does not necessarily create an incentive for the other participants in the cartel in question to submit distorted evidence [...].

Indeed, any attempt to mislead the Commission could call into question the sincerity and the completeness of cooperation of the undertaking seeking to benefit, and thereby jeopardise its chances of benefiting fully under the Leniency Notice [...].

On that point, it should be borne in mind that the Commission may not compel an undertaking to provide it with answers which might involve an admission on its part of the existence of an infringement which it is incumbent upon the Commission to prove [...]. [...]

Thus, when a person admits that he committed an infringement and therefore admitted the existence of facts other than those whose existence could be directly inferred from the available information, that implies, a priori, in the absence of special circumstances indicating otherwise, that that person had resolved to tell the truth. Statements which run counter to the interests of the declarant must therefore in principle be regarded as particularly reliable evidence [...].

However, according to well-established case-law, an admission by one undertaking accused of having participated in a cartel, the accuracy of which is contested by several other undertakings similarly accused, cannot be regarded as constituting adequate proof of an infringement committed by the latter unless it is supported by other evidence [...].

For the purpose of examining the probative value of statements by leniency applicants, the Court takes into account inter alia the strength of consistent evidence supporting the relevance of those statements and the absence of evidence demonstrating that they have tended to play down the importance of their contribution to the infringement and maximise that of other undertakings [...].

General Court 16 September 2013 (Nynäs Petroleum and Nynas Petróleo v. Commission, T-482/07), ECLI:EU:T:2013:437, paras 189–192 and 195–197.

13.15   In that regard, it must be recalled that the principle which prevails in EU law is that the evidence may be freely adduced [...].

As a general rule, no provision or general principle of EU law prohibits the Commission from relying, as against an undertaking, on statements made by other incriminated undertakings. If that were not the case, the burden of proving conduct contrary to Articles 101 TFEU and 102 TFEU, which is borne by the Commission, would be unsustainable and incompatible with the task of supervising the proper application of those provisions which is entrusted to it by the FEU Treaty […].

However, the powers available to the Commission during the preliminary phases of investigation and collection of information must be reconciled with compliance with the fundamental rights and general principles of EU law, which apply in all procedures under the European Union competition rules.

General Court 29 February 2016 (Schenker Ltd v. European Commission, T-265/ 12), ECLI:EU:T:2016:111, paras 40–42.

C. SINGLE AND CONTINUOUS OR REPEATED INFRINGEMENT

1. General

The notion of a single infringement covers a situation in which several undertakings **13.16** participated in an infringement in which continuous conduct in pursuit of a single economic aim was intended to distort competition, and also individual infringements linked to one another by the same object (all the elements sharing the same purpose) and the same subjects (the same undertakings, who are aware that they are participating in the common object) […]. That interpretation cannot be challenged on the ground that one or several elements of that series of acts or continuous conduct could also constitute in themselves an infringement of Article [101 TFEU] […].

General Court 24 March 2011 (Aalberts Industries NV, T-385/06) [2011] ECR II-1223, para. 86.

[T]hree conditions must be met in order to establish participation in a single and **13.17** continuous infringement, namely the existence of an overall plan pursuing a common objective, the intentional contribution of the undertaking to that plan, and its awareness (proved or presumed) of the offending conduct of the other participants.

General Court 16 June 2011 (Team Relocations NV, T-204/08 and T-212/08) [2011] ECR II-3569, para. 37.

[A]n infringement of Article [101(1) TFEU] can result not only from an isolated act, **13.18** but also from a series of acts or from continuous conduct, even if one or more aspects of that series of acts or continuous conduct could also, in themselves and taken in isolation, constitute an infringement of that provision. Accordingly, if the different actions form part of an 'overall plan', because their identical object distorts competition within the common market, the Commission is entitled to impute responsibility for those actions on the basis of participation in the infringement considered as a whole […].

An undertaking which has participated in such a single and complex infringement through its own conduct, which fell within the definition of an agreement or a concerted practice having an anti-competitive object for the purposes of Article [101(1) TFEU] and was intended to help bring about the infringement as a whole, may accordingly be liable also in respect of the conduct of other undertakings in the context

of the same infringement throughout the period of its participation in the infringement. That is the position where it is shown that the undertaking intended, through its
own conduct, to contribute to the common objectives pursued by all the participants
and that it was aware of the offending conduct planned or put into effect by other
undertakings in pursuit of the same objectives or that it could reasonably have foreseen
it and was prepared to take the risk [...].

An undertaking may thus have participated directly in all the forms of anti-
competitive conduct comprising the single and continuous infringement, in which case
the Commission is entitled to attribute liability to it in relation to that conduct as a
whole and, therefore, in relation to the infringement as a whole. Equally, the undertaking may have participated directly in only some of the forms of anti-competitive
conduct comprising the single and continuous infringement, but have been aware of all
the other unlawful conduct planned or put into effect by the other participants in the
cartel in pursuit of the same objectives, or could reasonably have foreseen that conduct
and have been prepared to take the risk. In such cases, the Commission is also entitled
to attribute liability to that undertaking in relation to all the forms of anti-competitive
conduct comprising such an infringement and, accordingly, in relation to the infringement as a whole.

On the other hand, if an undertaking has directly taken part in one or more of the
forms of anti-competitive conduct comprising a single and continuous infringement,
but it has not been shown that that undertaking intended, through its own conduct, to
contribute to all the common objectives pursued by the other participants in the cartel
and that it was aware of all the other offending conduct planned or put into effect by
those other participants in pursuit of the same objectives, or that it could reasonably
have foreseen all that conduct and was prepared to take the risk, the Commission is
entitled to attribute to that undertaking liability only for the conduct in which it had
participated directly and for the conduct planned or put into effect by the other
participants, in pursuit of the same objectives as those pursued by the undertaking itself,
where it has been shown that the undertaking was aware of that conduct or was able
reasonably to foresee it and prepared to take the risk.

That cannot, however, relieve the undertaking of liability for conduct in which it has
undeniably taken part or for conduct for which it can undeniably be held responsible.
Nor is the fact that an undertaking did not take part in all aspects of an anti-competitive
arrangement or that it played only a minor role in the aspects in which it did participate
material for the purposes of establishing the existence of an infringement on its part,
given that those factors need to be taken into consideration only when the gravity of the
infringement is assessed and only if and when it comes to determining the fine [...].

*CoJ 6 December 2012 (Commission v. Verhuizingen Coppens NV, C-441/11 P),
ECLI:EU:C:2012:778, paras 41–45.*

2. Continuous vs. repeated infringement

13.19   [T]he notion of a single infringement covers a situation in which several undertakings
participated in an infringement in which continuous conduct in pursuit of a single
economic aim was intended to distort competition and also individual infringements
linked to one another by the same object and the same undertakings [...].

In other words, the way in which the infringement was committed determines whether it may be categorised as a single, continuing infringement or a single, repeated infringement.

Furthermore, it must be borne in mind, as regards a continuing infringement, that the notion of an overall plan means that the Commission may assume that an infringement has not been interrupted even if, in relation to a specific period, it has no evidence of the participation of the undertaking concerned in that infringement, provided that that undertaking participated in the infringement prior to and after that period and provided that there is no proof or indicia that the infringement was interrupted so far as concerns that undertaking. In that case, it will be able to impose a fine in respect of the whole of the period of infringement, including the period in respect of which it does not have evidence of the participation of the undertaking concerned [...].

By contrast, if the participation of an undertaking in the infringement may be regarded as having been interrupted and the undertaking may be regarded as having participated in the infringement prior to and after that interruption, that infringement may be categorised as repeated if – as in the case of a continuing infringement [...] – there is a single objective which it pursued both before and after the interruption, a circumstance which may be deduced from the identical nature of the objectives of the practices at issue, of the goods concerned, of the undertakings which participated in the collusion, of the main rules for its implementation, of the natural persons involved on behalf of the undertakings and, lastly, of the geographical scope of those practices. The infringement is then single and repeated and, although the Commission may impose a fine in respect of the whole of the period of the infringement, it may not do so for the period during which the infringement was interrupted.

Consequently, separate periods of infringement in which the same undertaking takes part, but in respect of which a common objective cannot be established, cannot be categorised as a single infringement – continuing or repeated – and constitute separate infringements.

General Court 17 May 2013 (Trelleborg Industrie SAS and Trelleborg AB v. Commission, T-147/09 and T-148/09), ECLI:EU:T:2013:259, paras 85–89.

As regards the lack of evidence of an agreement during certain specific periods or, at least, the lack of evidence of its implementation by an undertaking during a given period, it should be recalled that the fact that such evidence has not been produced in relation to certain specific periods does not preclude the infringement from being regarded as established during a longer overall period than those periods, provided that such a finding is supported by objective and consistent indicia. In the context of an infringement extending over a number of years, the fact that the agreement is shown to have applied during different periods, which may be separated by longer or shorter periods, has no effect on the existence of the agreement, provided that the various actions which form part of the infringement pursue a single purpose and fall within the framework of a single and continuous infringement [...]. **13.20**

In that regard, a number of criteria have been identified in the case-law as being relevant for the assessment of the single nature of an infringement, namely the identity of the objectives of the practices in question [...]; the identity of the goods and services concerned [...]; the identity of the undertakings that took part in the practices [...]; and the identity of the means of implementing it […]. Furthermore, the identity of the natural persons involved on behalf of the undertakings and the identity of the geographic scope of the practices at issue may also be taken into consideration for the purposes of that examination.

The case-law thus allows the Commission to presume that the infringement – or an undertaking's participation in the infringement – has not been interrupted, even where it does not have evidence of the infringement for certain specific periods, provided that the different actions forming part of the infringement pursue a single aim and may come within the framework of a single and continuous infringement; and such a finding must be supported by objective and consistent indicia that show the existence of an overall plan.

Where those conditions are satisfied, the concept of a continuous infringement thus allows the Commission to impose a fine for the whole of the infringement period taken into consideration and determines the date on which time begins to run for the purpose of limitation, that is to say, the date on which the continuous infringement ceased.

However, the undertakings accused of collusion may rebut that presumption, by putting forward indicia or evidence showing that, on the contrary, the infringement – or their participation therein – did not continue during those periods.

Furthermore, it is necessary to distinguish the concept of repeated infringement from the concept of continuous infringement […] that distinction being confirmed, moreover, by the use of the conjunction 'or' in Article 25(2) of Regulation No 1/2003.

Where it can be established that an undertaking's participation in the infringement was interrupted and that the infringement committed by the undertaking before and after that period has the same features, to be assessed, in particular, by reference to the identity of the objectives and practices at issue, the products concerned, the undertakings which took part in the collusion, the principal means of implementing it, the natural persons involved on behalf of the undertakings and, last, the geographic scope of those practices, the infringement in question must be characterised as a single infringement and as a repeated infringement.

In that case, the Commission cannot impose a fine in respect of the period during which the infringement was interrupted.

General Court 17 May 2013 (K Manuli Rubber Industries SpA v. Commission, T-154/09), ECLI:EU:T:2013:260, paras 193–200.

ARTICLE 3 – RELATIONSHIP BETWEEN ARTICLES 81 AND 82 OF THE TREATY AND NATIONAL COMPETITION LAWS

1. Where the competition authorities of the Member States or national courts apply national competition law to agreements, decisions by associations of undertakings or concerted practices within the meaning of Article 81(1) of the Treaty which may affect trade between Member States within the meaning of that provision, they shall also apply Article 81 of the Treaty to such agreements, decisions or concerted practices. Where the competition authorities of the Member States or national courts apply national competition law to any abuse prohibited by Article 82 of the Treaty, they shall also apply Article 82 of the Treaty.

2. The application of national competition law may not lead to the prohibition of agreements, decisions by associations of undertakings or concerted practices which may affect trade between Member States but which do not restrict competition within the meaning of Article 81(1) of the Treaty, or which fulfil the conditions of Article 81(3) of the Treaty or which are covered by a Regulation for the application of Article 81 (3) of the Treaty. Member States shall not under this Regulation be precluded from adopting and applying on their territory stricter national laws which prohibit or sanction unilateral conduct engaged in by undertakings.

3. Without prejudice to general principles and other provisions of Community law, paragraphs 1 and 2 do not apply when the competition authorities and the courts of the Member States apply national merger control laws nor do they preclude the application of provisions of national law that predominantly pursue an objective different from that pursued by Articles 81 and 82 of the Treaty.

Consequently, in order to determine whether or not a restriction of competition is **13.21** appreciable, the competition authority of a Member State may take into account the thresholds established in paragraph 7 of the *de minimis* notice but is not required to do so. Such thresholds are no more than factors among others that may enable that authority to determine whether or not a restriction is appreciable by reference to the actual circumstances of the agreement. [...]

In light of the above, the answer to the question referred is that Article 101(1) TFEU and Article 3(2) of Regulation No 1/2003 must be interpreted as not precluding a national competition authority from applying Article 101(1) TFEU to an agreement between undertakings that may affect trade between Member States, but that does not reach the thresholds specified by the Commission in its de minimis notice, provided that that agreement constitutes an appreciable restriction of competition within the meaning of that provision.

General Court 17 May 2013 (Expedia Inc. v. Autorité de la concurrence and Others, C-226/11), ECLI:EU:C:2012:795, paras 31 and 38.

13.22   In the light of all the foregoing considerations the answer to the first question is that European Union law, in particular the principle of effectiveness, precludes a provision of national law under which access to documents forming part of the file relating to national proceedings concerning the application of Article 101 TFEU, including access to documents made available under a leniency programme, by third parties who are not party to those proceedings with a view to bringing an action for damages against participants in an agreement or concerted practice is made subject solely to the consent of all the parties to those proceedings, without leaving any possibility for the national courts of weighing up the interests involved

CoJ 6 June 2013 (Bundeswettbewerbsbehörde v. Donau Chemie AG and Others, C-536/11), ECLI:EU:C:2013:404, para. 49.

CHAPTER II

POWERS

ARTICLE 4 – POWERS OF THE COMMISSION

For the purpose of applying Articles 81 and 82 of the Treaty, the Commission shall have the powers provided for by this Regulation.

ARTICLE 5 – POWERS OF THE COMPETITION AUTHORITIES OF THE MEMBER STATES

The competition authorities of the Member States shall have the power to apply Articles 81 and 82 of the Treaty in individual cases. For this purpose, acting on their own initiative or on a complaint, they may take the following decisions:

- **requiring that an infringement be brought to an end,**
- **ordering interim measures,**
- **accepting commitments,**
- **imposing fines, periodic penalty payments or any other penalty provided for in their national law.**

Where on the basis of the information in their possession the conditions for prohibition are not met they may likewise decide that there are no grounds for action on their part.

13.23   [A]rticle 5 of the Regulation must be interpreted as precluding a national competition authority, in the case where, in order to apply Article 102 TFEU, it examines whether the conditions for applying that article are satisfied and where, following that examination, it forms the view that there has been no abuse, from being able to take a decision stating that there has been no breach of that article. [...]

   [T]he second paragraph of Article 5 of the Regulation is directly applicable and precludes the application of a rule of national law which would require a procedure relating to the application of Article 102 TFEU to be brought to an end by a decision stating that there has been no breach of that article.

CoJ 3 May 2011 (Prezes Urzedu Ochrony Konkurencji i Konsumentów v Tele2 Polska, C-375/09) [2011] ECR I-3055, paras 30 and 35.

13.24   As for the national competition authorities, since they do not have the power to adopt a negative decision, that is to say, a decision concluding that there is no infringement of Article 101 TFEU [...], they cannot cause undertakings to entertain a legitimate expectation that their conduct does not infringe that provision. It appears, moreover, from the wording of the first question that the national competition authority examined the conduct of the undertakings at issue in the main proceedings on the basis of national competition law only. [...]

   [I]n order to ensure that Article 101 TFEU is applied effectively in the general interest [...], the national competition authorities must proceed by way of exception only not to impose a fine where an undertaking has infringed that provision intentionally or negligently.

   It should be noted, furthermore, that such a decision not to impose a fine can be made under a national leniency programme only in so far as the programme is implemented in such a way as not to undermine the requirement of effective and uniform application of Article 101 TFEU.

Thus, in the case of the Commission's power to reduce fines under its own leniency programme, it is apparent from the Court's case-law that a reduction of a fine for cooperation on the part of undertakings participating in infringements of European Union competition law is justified only if such cooperation makes it easier for the Commission to carry out its task of finding an infringement and, where relevant, of bringing it to an end, whilst the undertaking's conduct must also reveal a genuine spirit of cooperation […].

As regards immunity from or not imposing a fine, in order for such treatment – which is moreover at issue in the main proceedings – not to undermine the effective and uniform application of Article 101 TFEU, it can be accorded in strictly exceptional situations only, such as where an undertaking's cooperation has been decisive in detecting and actually suppressing the cartel.

CoJ 18 June 2013 (Bundeswettbewerbsbehörde and Bundeskartellanwalt v. Schenker & Co. AG and Others, C-681/11), ECLI:EU:C:2013:404, paras 42 and 46–49.

ARTICLE 6 – POWERS OF THE NATIONAL COURTS

National courts shall have the power to apply Articles 81 and 82 of the Treaty.

CHAPTER III

COMMISSION DECISIONS

ARTICLE 7 – FINDING AND TERMINATION OF INFRINGEMENT

1.   **Where the Commission, acting on a complaint or on its own initiative, finds that there is an infringement of Article 81 or of Article 82 of the Treaty, it may by decision require the undertakings and associations of undertakings concerned to bring such infringement to an end. For this purpose, it may impose on them any behavioural or structural remedies which are proportionate to the infringement committed and necessary to bring the infringement effectively to an end. Structural remedies can only be imposed either where there is no equally effective behavioural remedy or where any equally effective behavioural remedy would be more burdensome for the undertaking concerned than the structural remedy. If the Commission has a legitimate interest in doing so, it may also find that an infringement has been committed in the past.**

2.   **Those entitled to lodge a complaint for the purposes of paragraph 1 are natural or legal persons who can show a legitimate interest and Member States.**

[N]either Regulations No 17 and No 2842/98 nor Regulations No 1/2003 and No   **13.25**
773/2004 contain express provisions relating to the action to be taken concerning the substance of a complaint and any obligations on the part of the Commission to carry out an investigation. On that point, it must be borne in mind that the Commission is under no obligation to initiate procedures to establish possible infringements of Community law and that the rights conferred on complainants by those regulations do not include the right to obtain a final decision as to the existence or non-existence of the alleged infringement […].

It is on the basis of those principles that the case-law has recognised that, if the Commission is under no obligation to rule on the existence or non-existence of an infringement, it cannot be compelled to carry out an investigation, because such an investigation could have no purpose other than to seek evidence of the existence or non-existence of an infringement which it is not required to establish […].

However, although the Commission cannot be compelled to conduct an investigation, it is nevertheless obliged to examine carefully the factual and legal particulars brought to its notice by the complainant in order to decide whether they disclose conduct of such a kind as to distort competition in the common market and affect trade between the Member States […]. Furthermore, since the Commission's only obligation is to examine the factual and legal particulars brought to its notice by the complainant, it is not, contrary to the applicant's assertions, incumbent on the Commission to prove that it has adopted measures of investigation.

General Court 12 May 2010 (EMC Development v. Commission, T-432/05) [2010] ECR II-01629, paras 57–59.

ARTICLE 8 – INTERIM MEASURES

1. **In cases of urgency due to the risk of serious and irreparable damage to competition, the Commission, acting on its own initiative may by decision, on the basis of a prima facie finding of infringement, order interim measures.**
2. **A decision under paragraph 1 shall apply for a specified period of time and may be renewed in so far this is necessary and appropriate.**

OVERVIEW

A. PRIMA FACIE CASE	13.26	B. THREAT OF IRREPARABLE DAMAGE	13.27

A. PRIMA FACIE CASE

[I]n proceedings relating to the legality of a Commission decision concerning the **13.26** adoption of interim measures, the requirement of a finding of a prima facie infringement cannot be placed on the same footing as the requirement of certainty that a final decision must satisfied. In the present case the reasons adopted by the Commission for the decision at issue – confirmed, moreover, during the hearing – amount to requiring that, for a grant of interim measures to be possible, the existence of a clear and flagrant infringement must already be established at the stage of the mere prima facie appraisal which has to serve as the basis for the grant of such measures.
General Court 24 January 1992 (La Cinq v. Commission, T-44/90) [1992] ECR II-1, para. 61.

B. THREAT OF IRREPARABLE DAMAGE

In formulating the requirement embodied in its conception of irreparable damage, the **13.27** Commission went beyond what is required by the case-law of the Court of Justice, which merely refers to damage which could no longer be remedied by the decision to be adopted by the Commission upon the conclusion of the administrative procedure [...].
General Court 24 January 1992 (La Cinq v. Commission T-44/90) [1992] ECR II-1, para. 80.

Nevertheless, even though the possibility of IMS Health being unable to recover the **13.28** financial losses it may suffer as a result of the execution of the contested decision cannot be excluded, interim relief is generally not granted in respect of financial damage unless the applicant is in a position to adduce evidence that would justify a prima facie finding that, failing the relief sought, the losses alleged would be such as to threaten its survival.

Order General Court 10 August 2001 (IMS Health Inc. v. Commission, T-184/01R) [2001] ECR II–2349, para. 121.

See also Order CoJ 11 April 2002 (NDC Health GmbH Co. KG and NDC Health Corporation v. Commission and IMS Health Inc, C-481/01P(R)) [2002] ECR I-3401; Order General Court 18 March 2008 (Aer Lingus Group, T-411/07R) [2008] ECR II–411, para. 131.

ARTICLE 9 – COMMITMENTS

1. **Where the Commission intends to adopt a decision requiring that an infringement be brought to an end and the undertakings concerned offer commitments to meet the concerns expressed to them by the Commission in its preliminary assessment, the Commission may by decision make those commitments binding on the undertakings. Such a decision may be adopted for a specified period and shall conclude that there are no longer grounds for action by the Commission.**

2. **The Commission may, upon request or on its own initiative, reopen the proceedings:**
   (a) **where there has been a material change in any of the facts on which the decision was based;**
   (b) where the undertakings concerned act contrary to their commitments; or
   (c) **where the decision was based on incomplete, incorrect or misleading information provided by the parties.**

OVERVIEW

A. PERIOD OF VALIDITY OF COMMITMENT DECISIONS 13.29	B. PROPORTIONALITY 13.30

A. PERIOD OF VALIDITY OF COMMITMENT DECISIONS

As regards the period in which the decision-making commitments binding may remain in force, it should be noted that while Article 9(1) of Regulation No 1/2003 provides that such a decision may be adopted for a specified period, it does not, however, require this. The definitive wording of Article 9 of Regulation No 1/2003 falls to be distinguished in that regard, as the Commission rightly points out, from the wording which had been used at the stage of the Commission proposal for a Council Regulation on the implementation of the rules on competition laid down in Articles [101 and 102 TFEU] (COM(2000) 582 final), which provided that such a decision was 'to be adopted for a specified period'. There is, accordingly, no reason of principle which prohibits the Commission from making commitments for an indefinite period binding. **13.29**

General Court 11 July 2007 (Alrosa Company Ltd v. Commission, T-170/06) [2007] ECR II-2601, para. 91.

B. PROPORTIONALITY

13.30   [A]lthough Article 9, unlike Article 7 of Regulation No 1/2003, does not expressly refer to proportionality, the principle of proportionality, as a general principle of European Union law, is none the less a criterion for the lawfulness of any act of the institutions of the Union, including decisions taken by the Commission in its capacity of competition authority.

That being so, in the examination of acts of the Commission, whether in the context of Article 7 or of Article 9 of Regulation No 1/2003, the questions always arise, first, of the precise extent and limits of the obligations which flow from the observance of that principle and, second, of the limits of judicial review.

The specific characteristics of the mechanisms provided for in Articles 7 and 9 of Regulation No 1/2003 and the means of action available under each of those provisions are different, which means that the obligation on the Commission to ensure that the principle of proportionality is observed has a different extent and content, depending on whether it is considered in relation to the former or the latter article.

Article 7 of Regulation No 1/2003 expressly indicates the extent to which the principle of proportionality applies in situations covered by that article. In accordance with Article 7(1) of the regulation, the Commission may impose on the undertakings concerned any behavioural or structural remedies which are proportionate to the infringement committed and necessary to bring the infringement effectively to an end.

Article 9 of that regulation, by contrast, provides merely that in proceedings under that provision, as follows from recital 13 in the preamble to the regulation, the Commission is not required to make a finding of an infringement, its task being confined to examining, and possibly accepting, the commitments offered by the undertakings concerned in the light of the problems identified by it in its preliminary assessment and having regard to the aims pursued.

Application of the principle of proportionality by the Commission in the context of Article 9 of Regulation No 1/2003 is confined to verifying that the commitments in question address the concerns it expressed to the undertakings concerned and that they have not offered less onerous commitments that also address those concerns adequately. When carrying out that assessment, the Commission must, however, take into consideration the interests of third parties.

Judicial review for its part relates solely to whether the Commission's assessment is manifestly incorrect. [...]

There is therefore no reason why the measure which could possibly be imposed in the context of Article 7 of Regulation No 1/2003 should have to serve as a reference for the purpose of assessing the extent of the commitments accepted under Article 9 of the regulation, or why anything going beyond that measure should automatically be regarded as disproportionate. Even though decisions adopted under each of those provisions are in either case subject to the principle of proportionality, the application of that principle none the less differs according to which of those provisions is concerned.

Undertakings which offer commitments on the basis of Article 9 of Regulation No 1/2003 consciously accept that the concessions they make may go beyond what the Commission could itself impose on them in a decision adopted under Article 7 of the regulation after a thorough examination. On the other hand, the closure of the infringement proceedings brought against those undertakings allows them to avoid a finding of an infringement of competition law and a possible fine.

Moreover, the fact that the individual commitments offered by an undertaking have been made binding by the Commission does not mean that other undertakings are deprived of the possibility of protecting the rights they may have in connection with their relations with that undertaking.

CoJ 29 June 2010 (Commission v. Alrosa Company Ltd, C-441/07P) [2010] ECR I-5945, paras 36–42 and 47–49.

ARTICLE 10 – FINDING OF INAPPLICABILITY

Where the Community public interest relating to the application of Articles 81 and 82 of the Treaty so requires, the Commission, acting on its own initiative, may by decision find that Article 81 of the Treaty is not applicable to an agreement, a decision by an association of undertakings or a concerted practice, either because the conditions of Article 81(1) of the Treaty are not fulfilled, or because the conditions of Article 81(3) of the Treaty are satisfied.

The Commission may likewise make such a finding with reference to Article 82 of the Treaty.

CHAPTER IV

COOPERATION

ARTICLE 11 – COOPERATION BETWEEN THE COMMISSION AND THE
COMPETITION AUTHORITIES OF THE MEMBER STATES

1. The Commission and the competition authorities of the Member
    States shall apply the Community competition rules in close
    cooperation.
2. The Commission shall transmit to the competition authorities of the
    Member States copies of the most important documents it has col-
    lected with a view to applying Articles 7, 8, 9, 10 and Article 29 (1). At
    the request of the competition authority of a Member State, the Com-
    mission shall provide it with a copy of other existing documents neces-
    sary for the assessment of the case.
3. The competition authorities of the Member States shall, when acting
    under Article 81 or Article 82 of the Treaty, inform the Commission in
    writing before or without delay after commencing the first formal
    investigative measure. This information may also be made available to
    the competition authorities of the other Member States.
4. No later than 30 days before the adoption of a decision requiring that an
    infringement be brought to an end, accepting commitments or with-
    drawing the benefit of a block exemption Regulation, the competition
    authorities of the Member States shall inform the Commission. To
    that effect, they shall provide the Commission with a summary of the
    case, the envisaged decision or, in the absence thereof, any other docu-
    ment indicating the proposed course of action. This information may
    also be made available to the competition authorities of the other
    Member States. At the request of the Commission, the acting com-
    petition authority shall make available to the Commission other docu-
    ments it holds which are necessary for the assessment of the case. The
    information supplied to the Commission may be made available to the
    competition authorities of the other Member States. National com-
    petition authorities may also exchange between themselves infor-
    mation necessary for the assessment of a case that they are dealing with
    under Article 81 or Article 82 of the Treaty.
5. The competition authorities of the Member States may consult the
    Commission on any case involving the application of Community law.

6.   **The initiation by the Commission of proceedings for the adoption of a decision under Chapter III shall relieve the competition authorities of the Member States of their competence to apply Articles 81 and 82 of the Treaty. If a competition authority of a Member State is already acting on a case, the Commission shall only initiate proceedings after consulting with that national competition authority.**

See also the Commission Notice on cooperation within the Network of Competition Authorities (OJ 2004 C 101/43).

13.31   Lastly, it should be noted that a competition authority such as the Epitropi Antagonis-mou is required to work in close cooperation with the Commission of the European Communities and may, pursuant to Article 11(6) of Council Regulation (EC) No 1/2003 [...] be relieved of its competence by a decision of the Commission. It should moreover be noted in this context that Article 11(6) of Regulation No 1/2003 essentially maintains the rule in Article 9(3) of Council Regulation No 17 [...] that the competition authorities of the Member States are automatically relieved of their competence where the Commission initiates its own proceedings [...].

CoJ 31 May 2005 (Syfait and others v. GlaxoSmithKline, C-53/03) [2005] ECR I-4609, para. 34.

13.32   [A]rticle 11(1) of Regulation No 1/2003 does indeed lay down a general rule to the effect that the Commission and the national authorities are required to cooperate closely, but it does not require the Commission to refrain from making an inspection in a case which is being dealt with by a national competition authority in parallel.

General Court 8 March 2007 (France Télécom v. Commission, T-340/04) [2007] ECR II-573, para. 128.

ARTICLE 12 – EXCHANGE OF INFORMATION

1. For the purpose of applying Articles 81 and 82 of the Treaty the Commission and the competition authorities of the Member States shall have the power to provide one another with and use in evidence any matter of fact or of law, including confidential information.

2. Information exchanged shall only be used in evidence for the purpose of applying Article 81 or Article 82 of the Treaty and in respect of the subject-matter for which it was collected by the transmitting authority. However, where national competition law is applied in the same case and in parallel to Community competition law and does not lead to a different outcome, information exchanged under this Article may also be used for the application of national competition law.

3. Information exchanged pursuant to paragraph 1 can only be used in evidence to impose sanctions on natural persons where:
    the law of the transmitting authority foresees sanctions of a similar kind in relation to an infringement of Article 81 or Article 82 of the Treaty or, in the absence thereof,
    the information has been collected in a way which respects the same level of protection of the rights of defence of natural persons as provided for under the national rules of the receiving authority. However, in this case, the information exchanged cannot be used by the receiving authority to impose custodial sanctions.

13.33 [T]he provisions of European Union law on cartels, and in particular Regulation No 1/2003, must be interpreted as not precluding a person who has been adversely affected by an infringement of European Union competition law and is seeking to obtain damages from being granted access to documents relating to a leniency procedure involving the perpetrator of that infringement. It is, however, for the courts and tribunals of the Member States, on the basis of their national law, to determine the conditions under which such access must be permitted or refused by weighing the interests protected by European Union law.

CoJ 14 June 2011 (Pfleiderer, C-360/09) [2011] ECR I-5161, para. 32.

ARTICLE 13 – SUSPENSION OR TERMINATION OF PROCEEDINGS

1. **Where competition authorities of two or more Member States have received a complaint or are acting on their own initiative under Article 81 or Article 82 of the Treaty against the same agreement, decision of an association or practice, the fact that one authority is dealing with the case shall be sufficient grounds for the others to suspend the proceedings before them or to reject the complaint. The Commission may likewise reject a complaint on the ground that a competition authority of a Member State is dealing with the case.**

2. **Where a competition authority of a Member State or the Commission has received a complaint against an agreement, decision of an association or practice which has already been dealt with by another competition authority, it may reject it.**

See also the Commission Notice on cooperation within the Network of Competition Authorities (OJ 2004 C 101/43).

ARTICLE 14 – ADVISORY COMMITTEE

1. The Commission shall consult an Advisory Committee on Restrictive Practices and Dominant Positions prior to the taking of any decision under Articles 7, 8, 9, 10, 23, Article 24(2) and Article 29(1).

2. For the discussion of individual cases, the Advisory Committee shall be composed of representatives of the competition authorities of the Member States. For meetings in which issues other than individual cases are being discussed, an additional Member State representative competent in competition matters may be appointed. Representatives may, if unable to attend, be replaced by other representatives.

3. The consultation may take place at a meeting convened and chaired by the Commission, held not earlier than 14 days after dispatch of the notice convening it, together with a summary of the case, an indication of the most important documents and a preliminary draft decision. In respect of decisions pursuant to Article 8, the meeting may be held seven days after the dispatch of the operative part of a draft decision. Where the Commission dispatches a notice convening the meeting which gives a shorter period of notice than those specified above, the meeting may take place on the proposed date in the absence of an objection by any Member State. The Advisory Committee shall deliver a written opinion on the Commission's preliminary draft decision. It may deliver an opinion even if some members are absent and are not represented. At the request of one or several members, the positions stated in the opinion shall be reasoned.

4. Consultation may also take place by written procedure. However, if any Member State so requests, the Commission shall convene a meeting. In case of written procedure, the Commission shall determine a time-limit of not less than 14 days within which the Member States are to put forward their observations for circulation to all other Member States. In case of decisions to be taken pursuant to Article 8, the time-limit of 14 days is replaced by seven days. Where the Commission determines a time-limit for the written procedure which is shorter than those speci-fied above, the proposed time-limit shall be applicable in the absence of an objection by any Member State.

5. The Commission shall take the utmost account of the opinion deliv-ered by the Advisory Committee. It shall inform the Committee of the manner in which its opinion has been taken into account.

6. Where the Advisory Committee delivers a written opinion, this opin-ion shall be appended to the draft decision. If the Advisory Committee

recommends publication of the opinion, the Commission shall carry out such publication taking into account the legitimate interest of undertakings in the protection of their business secrets.

7.   At the request of a competition authority of a Member State, the Commission shall include on the agenda of the Advisory Committee cases that are being dealt with by a competition authority of a Member State under Article 81 or Article 82 of the Treaty. The Commission may also do so on its own initiative. In either case, the Commission shall inform the competition authority concerned.

A request may in particular be made by a competition authority of a Member State in respect of a case where the Commission intends to initiate proceedings with the effect of Article 11(6). The Advisory Committee shall not issue opinions on cases dealt with by competition authorities of the Member States. The Advisory Committee may also discuss general issues of Community competition law.

ARTICLE 15 – COOPERATION WITH NATIONAL COURTS

1. In proceedings for the application of Article 81 or Article 82 of the Treaty, courts of the Member States may ask the Commission to transmit to them information in its possession or its opinion on questions concerning the application of the Community competition rules.

2. Member States shall forward to the Commission a copy of any written judgment of national courts deciding on the application of Article 81 or Article 82 of the Treaty. Such copy shall be forwarded without delay after the full written judgment is notified to the parties.

3. Competition authorities of the Member States, acting on their own initiative, may submit written observations to the national courts of their Member State on issues relating to the application of Article 81 or Article 82 of the Treaty. With the permission of the court in question, they may also submit oral observations to the national courts of their Member State. Where the coherent application of Article 81 or Article 82 of the Treaty so requires, the Commission, acting on its own initiative, may submit written observations to courts of the Member States. With the permission of the court in question, it may also make oral observations. For the purpose of the preparation of their observations only, the competition authorities of the Member States and the Commission may request the relevant court of the Member State to transmit or ensure the transmission to them of any documents necessary for the assessment of the case.

4. This Article is without prejudice to wider powers to make observations before courts conferred on competition authorities of the Member States under the law of their Member State.

See also the Commission Notice on the cooperation between the Commission and the courts of the EU Member States in the application of Articles [101] and [102 TFEU] (OJ 2004 C 101/54) and the Commission Notice on cooperation within the Network of Competition Authorities (OJ 2004 C 101/43).

Thus, the first subparagraph of Article 15(3) of Regulation No 1/2003 refers to two **13.34** different types of intervention with separate fields of application: intervention by the national competition authorities before the national courts of their Member State on issues relating to the application of Articles [101 TFEU] or [102 TFEU]; and intervention by the Commission before courts of the Member States where the coherent application of Articles [101 TFEU] or [102 TFEU] so requires.

The four sentences of that subparagraph, and above all the fact that the second and fourth sentences are almost entirely identical, emphasises the fact that the Community legislature intended to draw a distinction between those two situations, despite the fact that they appear in the same subparagraph.

Consequently, a literal interpretation of the first subparagraph of Article 15(3) of Regulation No 1/2003 leads to the conclusion that the option for the Commission, acting on its own initiative, to submit written observations to courts of the Member States is subject to the sole condition that the coherent application of Articles [101 TFEU] or [102 TFEU] so requires. That condition may be fulfilled even if the proceedings concerned do not pertain to issues relating to the application of Article [101] or Article [102 TFEU].

CoJ 11 June 2009 (Inspecteur van de belastingdienst, C-429/07) [2009] ECR I-4833, paras 28–30.

13.35   [T]here is an intrinsic link between the fines and the application of Articles [101 and 102 TFEU].

The effectiveness of the penalties imposed by the national or Community competition authorities on the basis of Article [103(2)(a) TFEU] is therefore a condition for the coherent application of Articles [101 TFEU] and [102 TFEU].

In proceedings relating to the penalties in respect of anti-competitive practices provided for in Article [103(2)(a) TFEU], the decision that the court seised must give is capable of impairing the effectiveness of those penalties and therefore might compromise the coherent application of Articles [101 TFEU] or [102 TFEU]. [...]

It follows from all of the foregoing that the third sentence of the first subparagraph of Article 15(3) of Regulation No 1/2003 must be interpreted as meaning that it permits the Commission to submit on its own initiative written observations to a national court of a Member State in proceedings relating to the deductibility from taxable profits of the amount of a fine or a part thereof imposed by the Commission for infringement of Articles [101 TFEU] or [102 TFEU].

CoJ 11 June 2009 (Inspecteur van de belastingdienst, C-429/07) [2009] ECR I-4833, paras 36–38 and 40.

ARTICLE 16 – UNIFORM APPLICATION OF COMMUNITY COMPETITION LAW

1. **When national courts rule on agreements, decisions or practices under Article 81 or Article 82 of the Treaty which are already the subject of a Commission decision, they cannot take decisions running counter to the decision adopted by the Commission. They must also avoid giving decisions which would conflict with a decision contemplated by the Commission in proceedings it has initiated. To that effect, the national court may assess whether it is necessary to stay its proceedings. This obligation is without prejudice to the rights and obligations under Article 234 of the Treaty.**
2. **When competition authorities of the Member States rule on agreements, decisions or practices under Article 81 or Article 82 of the Treaty which are already the subject of a Commission decision, they cannot take decisions which would run counter to the decision adopted by the Commission.**

Indeed, even when the Commission has in its decision determined the precise effects of **13.36** the infringement, it still falls to the national court to determine individually the loss caused to each of the persons to have brought an action for damages. Such an assessment is not contrary to Article 16 of Regulation No 1/2003.
CoJ 6 November 2012 (Europese Gemeenschap v. Otis NV and Others, C-199/11), ECLI:EU:C:2012:684, para. 66.

See also the Commission Notice on the cooperation between the Commission and the courts of the EU Member States in the application of Articles [101] and [102 TFEU] (OJ 2004 C 101/54) and the Commission Notice on cooperation within the Network of Competition Authorities (OJ 2004 C 101/43).

It follows that the ECN, being intended to encourage discussion and cooperation in the **13.37** implementation of competition policy, does not have the power to adopt legally binding rules.

In that respect, the Court has already held that neither the Commission Notice on Cooperation, nor the Commission Notice on immunity from fines and reduction of fines in cartel cases [...] is binding on Member States [...].

Moreover, the Notice on Cooperation and the Leniency Notice, adopted in the context of the ECN, were published in 2004 and 2006, respectively, in the 'C' series of the Official Journal of the European Union, which, by contrast with the 'L' series of the Official Journal, is not intended for the publication of legally binding measures, but only of information, recommendations and opinions concerning the European Union.

It follows that those notices are not capable of creating obligations on Member States.

CoJ 20 January 2016 (DHL Express (Italy) Srl and DHL Global Forwarding (Italy) SpA v. Autorità Garante della Concorrenza e del Mercato, C–428/14), ECLI:EU:C:2016:27, paras 32–35.

CHAPTER V

POWERS OF INVESTIGATION

ARTICLE 17 – INVESTIGATIONS INTO SECTORS OF THE ECONOMY AND INTO TYPES OF AGREEMENTS

1. Where the trend of trade between Member States, the rigidity of prices or other circumstances suggest that competition may be restricted or distorted within the common market, the Commission may conduct its inquiry into a particular sector of the economy or into a particular type of agreements across various sectors. In the course of that inquiry, the Commission may request the undertakings or associations of undertakings concerned to supply the information necessary for giving effect to Articles 81 and 82 of the Treaty and may carry out any inspections necessary for that purpose.

    The Commission may in particular request the undertakings or associations of undertakings concerned to communicate to it all agreements, decisions and concerted practices. The Commission may publish a report on the results of its inquiry into particular sectors of the economy or particular types of agreements across various sectors and invite comments from interested parties.

2. Articles 14, 18, 19, 20, 22, 23 and 24 shall apply mutatis mutandis.

ARTICLE 18 – REQUESTS FOR INFORMATION

1. In order to carry out the duties assigned to it by this Regulation, the Commission may, by simple request or by decision, require undertakings and associations of undertakings to provide all necessary information.

2. When sending a simple request for information to an undertaking or association of undertakings, the Commission shall state the legal basis and the purpose of the request, specify what information is required and fix the time-limit within which the information is to be provided, and the penalties provided for in Article 23 for supplying incorrect or misleading information.

3. Where the Commission requires undertakings and associations of undertakings to supply information by decision, it shall state the legal basis and the purpose of the request, specify what information is required and fix the time-limit within which it is to be provided. It shall also indicate the penalties provided for in Article 23 and indicate or impose the penalties provided for in Article 24. It shall further indicate the right to have the decision reviewed by the Court of Justice.

4. The owners of the undertakings or their representatives and, in the case of legal persons, companies or firms, or associations having no legal personality, the persons authorised to represent them by law or by their constitution shall supply the information requested on behalf of the undertaking or the association of undertakings concerned. Lawyers duly authorised to act may supply the information on behalf of their clients. The latter shall remain fully responsible if the information supplied is incomplete, incorrect or misleading.

5. The Commission shall without delay forward a copy of the simple request or of the decision to the competition authority of the Member State in whose territory the seat of the undertaking or association of undertakings is situated and the competition authority of the Member State whose territory is affected.

6. At the request of the Commission the governments and competition authorities of the Member States shall provide the Commission with all necessary information to carry out the duties assigned to it by this Regulation.

OVERVIEW

A. GENERAL	13.38	C. PARAGRAPH 3: INFORMATION REQUEST BY DECISION	13.42
B. PARAGRAPH 1: POWERS OF THE COMMISSION TO REQUEST INFORMATION	13.39	D. PARAGRAPH 4: OBLIGATION TO COOPERATE	13.44

A. GENERAL

[A] response to a request for information must be taken to include not only the answers to the actual questions asked by the Commission, but also to information supplied which goes beyond the particular scope of those questions as well as information supplied by the undertaking on its own initiative which does not directly relate to any specific question asked by the Commission. **13.38**

Commission 17 November 1981 (CCI, IV/30.211), OJ 1981 L 27/31.

B. PARAGRAPH 1: POWERS OF THE COMMISSION TO REQUEST INFORMATION

It must be stated, with respect to the Commission's right to require the disclosure of documents in connection with a request for information, that [Articles 18 and 20 of Regulation No 1/2003] establish two entirely independent procedures. The fact that an investigation under Article [20] has already taken place cannot in any way diminish the powers of investigation available to the Commission under Article [18]. No consideration of a procedural nature inherent in Regulation No 17 thus prevents the Commission from requiring, for the purposes of a request for information, the disclosure of documents of which it was unable to take a copy or extract when carrying out a previous investigation. **13.39**

CoJ 18 October 1989 (Orkem v. Commission, 374/87) [1989] ECR 3283, para. 14.

It is in principle for the Commission to decide whether a particular item of information is necessary to enable it to bring to light an infringement of the competition rules and even if it already has some indicia, or indeed proof, of the existence of an infringement, the Commission may legitimately take the view that it is necessary to order further investigations enabling it to better define the scope of the infringement or to determine its duration [...]. **13.40**

General Court 8 March 2007 (France Télécom v. Commission, T-340/04) [2007] ECR II-573, para. 148.

See also General Court 12 July 2007 (Groupement des cartes bancaires (CB), T-266/03) [2007] ECR II-83, para. 63.

371

13.41   Regulation No 1/2003 [...] imposes no obligation on the Commission as regards the choice of the type of request for information (simple request or decision), the addressees of those requests, the actual time-limit for replying, the information requested – other than that such information must be necessary – or the analysis of the information provided. In addition, the applicant has adduced no evidence capable of establishing that those five aspects of the requests for information sent in the present case demonstrate a lack of care, seriousness and diligence on the part of the Commission in the investigations carried out.

General Court 11 July 2013 (Diamanthandel A. Spira BVBA v. Commission, T-108/07 and T-354/08), ECLI:EU:T:2013:367, para. 121.

C. PARAGRAPH 3: INFORMATION REQUEST BY DECISION

13.42   [T]he measures of inquiry adopted by the Commission during the preliminary investigation stage – in particular, the measures of investigation and requests for information under Articles 11 and 14 of Regulation No 17 [now Art. 18 and 20 Regulation No 1/2003] – suggest, by their very nature, that an infringement has been committed and may have a significant impact on the situation of the undertakings suspected.

Consequently, it is necessary to prevent the rights of the defence from being irremediably compromised during that stage of the administrative procedure since the measures of inquiry taken may be decisive in providing evidence of the unlawful nature of conduct engaged in by undertakings for which they may be liable [...].

As regards the scope of that duty to inform, it should be noted that, in a request for information – whether informal for the purposes of Article 11(2) of Regulation No 17 or in the form of a decision under Article 11(5) thereof – the Commission is required, under Article 11(3) and in order, inter alia, to respect the rights of defence of the undertakings concerned, to state the legal basis and the purpose of that request. Thus, the necessity, for the purposes of Article 11(1) of Regulation No 17, of the information requested by the Commission must be assessed by reference to the purpose of the inquiry, as compulsorily stated in the request for information itself. In that regard, the [General Court] has pointed out that the Commission is entitled to require only the disclosure of information which may enable it to investigate putative infringements which justify the investigation and which are set out in the request for information as such [...].

In that regard, it is apparent from the case-law that, although it is true that the Commission is not required to communicate to the addressee of a decision ordering investigation all the information at its disposal concerning the putative infringements or to make a precise legal analysis of those infringements, it must nevertheless clearly indicate the presumed facts which it intends to investigate [...].

The [General Court] considers that the requirements set out [...] above apply independently of the question whether the request for information, which is sent to an undertaking suspected of having committed an infringement, is a formal decision for the purposes of Article 11(5) of Regulation No 17, or an informal letter for the purposes of Article 11(2) thereof. In addition, in the context of the preliminary investigation stage, the opportunity for the undertaking concerned to prepare its defence effectively cannot vary depending on whether the Commission adopts a measure of inquiry under Article 11 or Article 14 of Regulation No 17, since all those measures suggest that an infringement has been committed and may have a significant impact on the situation of the undertakings suspected [...].

General Court 8 July 2008 (AC Treuhand AG, T-99/04) [2008] ECR II-1501, paras 50–55.

See also General Court 12 December 1991 (SEP v. Commission, T-39/90) [1991] ECR II-1497, para. 25; General Court 8 March 1995 (Société générale v. Commission, T-34/93) [1995] ECR II-545, paras 39, 40, 62 and 63.

[Article 18(3) of Regulation No 1/2003] provides that the Commission 'shall state the legal basis and the purpose of the request, specify what information is required and fix the time-limit within which it is to be provided'. Moreover, it states that the Commission 'shall also indicate the penalties provided for in Article 23', that it 'shall indicate or impose the penalties provided for in Article 24' and that it 'shall further indicate the right to have the decision reviewed by the Court of Justice'. **13.43**

That obligation to state specific reasons is a fundamental requirement, designed not merely to show that the request for information is justified but also to enable the undertakings concerned to assess the scope of their duty to cooperate whilst at the same time safeguarding their rights of defence [...].

With respect to the obligation to state the 'purpose of the request', this relates to the Commission's obligation to indicate the subject of its investigation in its request, and therefore to identify the alleged infringement of competition rules [...].

In that regard, the Commission is not required to communicate to the addressee of a decision requesting information all the information at its disposal concerning the presumed infringements, or to make a precise legal analysis of those infringements, providing it clearly indicates the suspicions which it intends to investigate [...]. [...]

As correctly noted by the General Court in paragraph 34 of the decision at issue, 'the Commission is entitled to require the disclosure only of information which may enable it to investigate presumed infringements which justify the conduct of the investigation and are set out in the request for information'.

Since the necessity of the information must be judged in relation to the purpose stated in the request for information, that purpose must be indicated with sufficient precision, otherwise it will be impossible to determine whether the information is necessary and the Court will be prevented from exercising judicial review [...]

However, an excessively succinct, vague and generic—and in some respects, ambiguous—statement of reasons does not fulfil the requirements of the obligation to state reasons laid down in Article 18(3) of Regulation No 1/2003 in order to justify a request for information which, as in the present case, occurred more than two years after the first inspections, and even though the Commission had already sent a number of requests for information to undertakings suspected of involvement in an infringement and several months after the decision to initiate proceedings. Given those factors, it must be stated that the decision at issue was adopted at a time when the Commission already had information that would have allowed it to present more precisely the suspicions of infringement by the companies involved.

CoJ 10 March 2016 (HeidelbergCement AG v. European Commission, C-247/14 P), ECLI:EU:C:2016:149, paras 18–21, 23–24 and 39.

D. PARAGRAPH 4: OBLIGATION TO COOPERATE

13.44   [R]egulation No 17 [now Regulation No 1/2003] does not give an undertaking under investigation any right to evade the investigation on the ground that the results thereof might provide evidence of an infringement by it of the competition rules. On the contrary, it imposes on the undertaking an obligation to cooperate actively, which implies that it must make available to the Commission all information relating to the subject-matter of the investigation.

In the absence of any right to remain silent expressly embodied in Regulation No 17, it is appropriate to consider whether and to what extent the general principles of Community law, of which fundamental rights form an integral part and in the light of which all Community legislation must be interpreted, require, as the applicant claims, recognition of the right not to supply information capable of being used in order to establish, against the person supplying it, the existence of an infringement of the competition rules.

In general, the laws of the Member States grant the right not to give evidence against oneself only to a natural person charged with an offence in criminal proceedings. A comparative analysis of national law does not therefore indicate the existence of such a principle, common to the laws of the Member States, which may be relied upon by legal persons in relation to infringements in the economic sphere, in particular infringements of competition law.

As far as Article 6 of the European Convention is concerned, although it may be relied upon by an undertaking subject to an investigation relating to competition law, it must be observed that neither the wording of that article nor the decisions of the European Court of Human Rights indicate that it upholds the right not to give evidence against oneself.

Article 14 of the International Covenant, which upholds, in addition to the presumption of innocence, the right (in paragraph 3(g)) not to give evidence against oneself or to confess guilt, relates only to persons accused of a criminal offence in court proceedings and thus has no bearing on investigations in the field of competition law. […]

In that connection, the Court observed recently, in its judgment of 21 September 1989 in *Joined Cases 46/87 and 227/88 Hoechst v. Commission* [1989] ECR 2859, paragraph 15, that whilst it is true that the rights of the defence must be observed in administrative procedures which may lead to the imposition of penalties, it is necessary to prevent those rights from being irremediably impaired during preliminary inquiry procedures which may be decisive in providing evidence of the unlawful nature of conduct engaged in by undertakings and for which they may be liable. Consequently, although certain rights of the defence relate only to contentious proceedings which follow the delivery of the statement of objections, other rights must be respected even during the preliminary inquiry.

Accordingly, whilst the Commission is entitled, in order to preserve the useful effect of Article 11(2) and (5) of Regulation No 17 [now Art. 18(2) and (5) Regulation No 1/2003], to compel an undertaking to provide all necessary information concerning such facts as may be known to it and to disclose to it, if necessary, such documents relating thereto as are in its possession, even if the latter may be used to establish, against it or another undertaking, the existence of anti-competitive conduct, it may not, by means of a decision calling for information, undermine the rights of defence of the undertaking concerned.

Thus, the Commission may not compel an undertaking to provide it with answers which might involve an admission on its part of the existence of an infringement which it is incumbent upon the Commission to prove.

CoJ 18 October 1989 (Orkem v. Commission, 374/87) [1989] ECR 3283, paras 27–31 and 33–35.

See also CoJ 29 June 2006 (Commission v. SGL Carbon AG) [2006] ECR I-5915, paras 39–42.

Thus, an undertaking in receipt of a request for information pursuant to Article 11(5) of **13.45** Regulation No 17 [now Art. 18(5) of Regulation No 1/2003] cannot be recognised as having an absolute right of silence. To acknowledge the existence of such a right would go beyond what is necessary in order to preserve the rights of defence of undertakings and would constitute an unjustified hindrance to the Commission's performance of its duty to ensure that the rules on competition within the common market are observed. A right of silence can be acknowledged only to the extent that the undertaking concerned would be compelled to provide answers which might involve an admission on its part of the existence of an infringement which it is incumbent upon the Commission to prove [...].

In order to ensure the effectiveness of Article 11 of Regulation No 17, the Commission is therefore entitled to compel the undertakings to provide all necessary information concerning such facts as may be known to them and to disclose to the Commission, if necessary, such documents relating thereto as are in their possession, even if the latter may be used to establish the existence of anti-competitive conduct. This power of the Commission to obtain information does not fall foul of either Article 6(1) and (2) of the ECHR or the case-law of the European Court of Human Rights [...].

In any event, the mere fact of being obliged to answer purely factual questions put by the Commission and to comply with its request for the production of documents already in existence cannot constitute a breach of the principle of respect for the rights of the defence or impair the right to fair legal process, which offer, in the specific field of competition law, protection equivalent to that guaranteed by Article 6 of the ECHR. There is nothing to prevent the addressee of a request for information from showing, whether later during the administrative procedure or in proceedings before the Community judicature, when exercising its rights of defence, that the facts set out in its replies or the documents produced by it have a different meaning from that ascribed to them by the Commission [...].

Lastly, where, in a request for information under Article 11 of Regulation No 17, the Commission, in addition to putting purely factual questions and requesting production of pre-existing documents, asks an undertaking to describe the object and course of a number of meetings in which it participated and also the results of or the conclusions reached in those meetings, when it is clear that the Commission suspects that the object of those meetings was to restrict competition, a request of that nature is of such a kind as to require the undertaking concerned to admit its participation in an infringement of the Community competition rules, so that the undertaking is not required to answer questions of that type. In such a situation, the fact that an undertaking none the less supplies information on those points must be regarded as spontaneous cooperation on the undertaking's part capable of justifying a reduction in the amount of the fine, in application of the Leniency Notice […]. It is also apparent from the case-law that, in the same situation, undertakings cannot claim that their right not to incriminate themselves has been infringed where they voluntarily replied to such a request […].

General Court 28 April 2010 (Amann & Söhne, T-446/05) [2010] ECR II-1255, paras 326–329.

ARTICLE 19 – POWER TO TAKE STATEMENTS

1. In order to carry out the duties assigned to it by this Regulation, the Commission may interview any natural or legal person who consents to be interviewed for the purpose of collecting information relating to the subject-matter of an investigation.

2. Where an interview pursuant to paragraph 1 is conducted in the premises of an undertaking, the Commission shall inform the competition authority of the Member State in whose territory the interview takes place. If so requested by the competition authority of that Member State, its officials may assist the officials and other accompanying persons authorised by the Commission to conduct the interview.

ARTICLE 20 – THE COMMISSION'S POWERS OF INSPECTION

1. In order to carry out the duties assigned to it by this Regulation, the Commission may conduct all necessary inspections of undertakings and associations of undertakings.

2. The officials and other accompanying persons authorised by the Commission to conduct an inspection are empowered:

    (a) to enter any premises, land and means of transport of undertakings and associations of undertakings;

    (b) to examine the books and other records related to the business, irrespective of the medium on which they are stored;

    (c) to take or obtain in any form copies of or extracts from such books or records;

    (d) to seal any business premises and books or records for the period and to the extent necessary for the inspection;

    (e) to ask any representative or member of staff of the undertaking or association of undertakings for explanations on facts or documents relating to the subject-matter and purpose of the inspection and to record the answers.

3. The officials and other accompanying persons authorised by the Commission to conduct an inspection shall exercise their powers upon production of a written authorisation specifying the subject matter and purpose of the inspection and the penalties provided for in Article 23 in case the production of the required books or other records related to the business is incomplete or where the answers to questions asked under paragraph 2 of the present Article are incorrect or misleading. In good time before the inspection, the Commission shall give notice of the inspection to the competition authority of the Member State in whose territory it is to be conducted.

4. Undertakings and associations of undertakings are required to submit to inspections ordered by decision of the Commission. The decision shall specify the subject matter and purpose of the inspection, appoint the date on which it is to begin and indicate the penalties provided for in Articles 23 and 24 and the right to have the decision reviewed by the Court of Justice. The Commission shall take such decisions after consulting the competition authority of the Member State in whose territory the inspection is to be conducted.

5. Officials of as well as those authorised or appointed by the competition authority of the Member State in whose territory the inspection is to be conducted shall, at the request of that authority or of the Commission, actively assist the officials and other accompanying persons authorised

by the Commission. To this end, they shall enjoy the powers specified in paragraph 2.

6. Where the officials and other accompanying persons authorised by the Commission find that an undertaking opposes an inspection ordered pursuant to this Article, the Member State concerned shall afford them the necessary assistance, requesting where appropriate the assistance of the police or of an equivalent enforcement authority, so as to enable them to conduct their inspection.

7. If the assistance provided for in paragraph 6 requires authorisation from a judicial authority according to national rules, such authorisation shall be applied for. Such authorisation may also be applied for as a precautionary measure.

8. Where authorisation as referred to in paragraph 7 is applied for, the national judicial authority shall control that the Commission decision is authentic and that the coercive measures envisaged are neither arbitrary nor excessive having regard to the subject matter of the inspection. In its control of the proportionality of the coercive measures, the national judicial authority may ask the Commission, directly or through the Member State competition authority, for detailed explanations in particular on the grounds the Commission has for suspecting infringement of Articles 81 and 82 of the Treaty, as well as on the seriousness of the suspected infringement and on the nature of the involvement of the undertaking concerned. However, the national judicial authority may not call into question the necessity for the inspection nor demand that it be provided with the information in the Commission's file. The lawfulness of the Commission decision shall be subject to review only by the Court of Justice.

OVERVIEW

A. GENERAL   13.46

B. PARAGRAPH 2: LEGAL PRIVILEGE   13.51
    1. General   13.51
    2. Documents other than privileged correspondence between lawyer and client   13.53
    3. Procedure protection confidentiality 13.55
    4. Limitation of legal privilege for in-house lawyers   13.57

C. PARAGRAPHS 3 AND 4: CHOICE BETWEEN INVESTIGATION BY AUTHORISATION AND INVESTIGATION ORDERED BY DECISION   13.58

D. PARAGRAPH 4: MOTIVATION INSPECTION DECISION   13.59

E. PARAGRAPHS 5 TO 8: GRANTING ASSISTANCE TO COMMISSION OFFICIALS   13.61

A. GENERAL

13.46   In accordance with the general principle of Community law affording protection against arbitrary or disproportionate intervention by public authorities in the sphere of the private activities of any person, whether natural or legal, a national court having jurisdiction under domestic law to authorise entry upon and seizures at the premises of undertakings suspected of having infringed the competition rules is required to verify that the coercive measures sought in pursuance of a request by the Commission for assistance under Article 14(6) of Regulation No 17 [now Art. 20(6) Regulation No 1/2003] are not arbitrary or disproportionate to the subject-matter of the investigation ordered. Without prejudice to any rules of domestic law governing the implementation of coercive measures, Community law precludes review by the national court of the justification of those measures beyond what is required by the foregoing general principle.

Community law requires the Commission to ensure that the national court in question has at its disposal all the information which it needs in order to carry out the review which it is required to undertake. In that regard, the information supplied by the Commission must in principle include:

- a description of the essential features of the suspected infringement, that is to say, at the very least, an indication of the market thought to be affected and of the nature of the suspected restrictions of competition;
- explanations concerning the manner in which the undertaking at which the coercive measures are aimed is thought to be involved in the infringement in question;
- detailed explanations showing that the Commission possesses solid factual information and evidence providing grounds for suspecting such infringement on the part of the undertaking concerned;
- as precise as possible an indication of the evidence sought, of the matters to which the investigation must relate and of the powers conferred on the Community investigators; and
- in the event that the assistance of the national authorities is requested by the Commission as a precautionary measure, in order to overcome any opposition on the part of the undertaking concerned, explanations enabling the national court to satisfy itself that, if authorisation for the coercive measures were not granted on precautionary grounds, it would be impossible, or very difficult, to establish the facts amounting to the infringement.]

On the other hand, the national court may not demand that it be provided with the evidence in the Commission's file on which the latter's suspicions are based.

Where the national court considers that the information communicated by the Commission does not fulfil the requirements set out above, it cannot, without violating Article 14(6) of Regulation No 17 and Article 5 [EEC Treaty, cf. Art. 4(3) TEU], simply dismiss the application brought before it. In such circumstances, it is required as rapidly as possible to inform the Commission, or the national authority which has brought the latter's request before it, of the difficulties encountered, where necessary by asking for any clarification which it may need in order to carry out the review which it is to undertake. Not until any such clarification is forthcoming, or the Commission fails to take any practical steps in response to its request, may the national court refuse to grant the assistance sought on the ground that, in the light of the information available to it, it is unable to hold that the coercive measures envisaged are not arbitrary or disproportionate to the subject-matter of those measures.

The information to be provided by the Commission to the national court may be contained either in the investigation decision itself or in the request made to the national authorities under Article 14(6) of Regulation No 17, or indeed in an answer – even given orally – to a question put by that court.

CoJ 22 October 2002 (Roquette Frères, C-94/00) [2002] ECR I-9011, para. 99.

However, in the context of the provisions of Article 14 of Regulation No 17 [now **13.47** Article 20 of Regulation 1/2003], it is necessary to ensure that observance of the rights of the defence does not impair the effectiveness of investigations to enable the Commission to carry out its role as guardian of the Treaty in competition matters [...]. The Court of Justice thus recognised that the powers to carry out investigations without previous notification did not constitute an infringement of the fundamental rights of undertakings, since the aim of the powers given to the Commission by Article 14 of Regulation No 17 was to enable it to carry out its duty under the [Treaty] of ensuring that the rules on competition were applied in the internal market, to prevent competition from being distorted to the detriment of the public interest, individual undertakings and consumers and to contribute to the maintenance of the system of competition intended by the Treaty which undertakings are absolutely bound to comply with [...].

That is why it is necessary to weigh the general principles of European Union law relating to the rights of the defence against the effectiveness of the Commission's powers of investigation and thus to prevent the possible destruction or concealment of relevant documents.

The Court therefore takes the view that the presence of an undertaking's external or in-house lawyer is possible when the Commission carries out an investigation, but that the presence of an external or in-house lawyer cannot determine the legality of the investigation. When an undertaking so desires, and in particular when it does not have a lawyer at the investigation site, it can thus request the advice of a lawyer by telephone and ask that lawyer to go there as soon as possible. In order to ensure that the exercise of that right to legal assistance does not impair the proper conduct of the investigation, the persons charged with carrying out the investigation must be able to enter all the undertaking's premises immediately, to notify it of the inspection decision and to occupy the offices of their choice, without waiting until the undertaking has consulted its lawyer. The persons charged with carrying out the investigation must also be put in a position to control the undertaking's telephone and computer communications in order, in particular, to prevent the undertaking from contacting other undertakings which are also the subject of an investigation decision. Moreover, the time which the Commission is required to grant an undertaking to enable it to contact its lawyer before the Commission starts consulting the books and other records, taking copies, affixing seals on premises or documents or asking any representative or member of staff of the undertaking for oral explanations depends on the particular circumstances of each individual case and, in any event, can be only extremely limited and reduced to a strict minimum. [...]

According to the case-law, undertakings are under an obligation to cooperate actively in the investigative measures in the course of the preliminary inquiry procedure [...]. [...]

The Courts of the European Union have also pointed out that the Commission may exercise its investigative powers on all the business premises of the undertaking which is the subject of the decision taken by it, while having regard to the rights of the defence [...] and to rights attaching to the protection of property [...]. Furthermore, it is for the Commission, and not for the undertaking concerned or a third party, to decide whether or not a document must be produced to it [...].

Consequently, the mere fact that the applicant's lawyers initially refused to grant the Commission access to the office of one of its directors is sufficient for the applicant to be considered to have refused to submit totally to the investigation decision, without there being any requirement for the Commission to show that the delay caused by that refusal may have led to the destruction or concealment of documents.

General Court 27 September 2012 (Koninklijke Wegenbouw Stevin BV v. Commission, T-357/06), ECLI:EU:T:2012:488, paras 230–232, 236, 238 and 239.

13.48 [W]hen the Commission carries out an inspection at the premises of an undertaking under Article 20(4) of Regulation No 1/2003, it is required to restrict its searches to the activities of that undertaking relating to the sectors indicated in the decision ordering the inspection and accordingly, once it has found, after examination, that a document or other item of information does not relate to those activities, to refrain from using that document or item of information for the purposes of its investigation. [...]

It must therefore be held that, in the present case, the Commission was under an obligation, in order to adopt the inspection decision, to have reasonable grounds to justify an inspection at the applicants' premises covering all the applicants' activities in relation to electric cables and the material associated with those cables. [...]

Accordingly, it must be found that the Commission has not demonstrated that it had reasonable grounds for ordering an inspection covering all electric cables and the material associated with those cables.

General Court 14 November 2012 (Nexans France SAS and Nexans SA v. Commission, T-135/09), ECLI:EU:T:2012:596, paras 64, 67 and 91.

13.49 [I]t cannot be concluded that the Commission is precluded from initiating an inquiry in order to verify or supplement information which it happened to obtain during a previous inspection if that information indicates the existence of conduct contrary to the competition rules [...]. In a new inquiry, the Commission is entitled to request fresh copies of the documents obtained during the first inquiry and then to use them as evidence in the case to which the second inquiry relates, without the rights of defence of the undertakings concerned being affected as a result [...].

General Court 12 December 2012 (Almamet GmbH v. European Commission, T-410/09), ECLI:EU:T:2012:676, para. 30.

13.50 Therefore, the inevitable conclusion to be drawn from the recent case-law of the ECtHR is that the lack of a prior judicial warrant is not capable, in itself, of rendering an interference within the meaning of Article 8 ECHR illegal. [...]

First, it has been held that, during an inspection, Commission officials have, inter alia, the power to have shown to them the documents they request, to enter such premises as they choose, and to have shown to them the contents of any piece of furniture which they indicate. On the other hand, they may not obtain access to premises or furniture by force or oblige the staff of the undertaking to give them such access, or carry out searches without the permission of the management of the undertaking [...]. [...]

If the assistance of the competent national authority has been requested, the Member State concerned must ensure that the Commission's action is effective and must respect the various general principles of EU law, in particular the protection of natural and legal persons against arbitrary and disproportionate interventions by public authorities in the private sphere [...]. [...]

The competent national body, whether judicial or non-judicial, must consider whether the coercive measures envisaged are arbitrary or excessive having regard to the subject-matter of the investigation. The Commission must make sure that the national body in question has all that it needs to perform that supervisory task and to ensure that, in the implementation of the coercive measures, the national rules are respected [...].

General Court 6 September 2013 (Deutsche Bahn AG and Others v. European Commission, T-289/11, T-290/11 and T-521/11), ECLI:EU:T:2013:404, paras 67, 86, 92 and 93.

B. PARAGRAPH 2: LEGAL PRIVILEGE

1. General

[T]here are to be found in the national laws of the Member States common criteria **13.51** inasmuch as those laws protect, in similar circumstances, the confidentiality of written communications between lawyer and client provided that, on the one hand, such communications are made for the purposes and in the interests of the client's rights of defence and, on the other hand, they emanate from independent lawyers, that is to say, lawyers who are not bound to the client by a relationship of employment.

Viewed in that context Regulation No 17 [now Regulation No 1/2003] must be interpreted as protecting, in its turn, the confidentiality of written communications between lawyer and client subject to those two conditions, and thus incorporating such elements of that protection as are common to the laws of the Member States.

As far as the first of those two conditions is concerned, in Regulation No 17 itself, in particular in the eleventh recital in its preamble and in the provisions contained in Article 19, care is taken to ensure that the rights of the defence may be exercised to the full, and the protection of the confidentiality of written communications between lawyer and client is an essential corollary to those rights. In those circumstances, such protection must, if it is to be effective, be recognized as covering all written communications exchanged after the initiation of the administrative procedure under Regulation No 17 which may lead to a decision on the application of Articles [101 and 102 TFEU] or to a decision imposing a pecuniary sanction on the undertaking. It must also be possible to extend it to earlier written communications which have a relationship to the subject-matter of that procedure.

As regards the second condition, it should be stated that the requirement as to the position and status as an independent lawyer, which must be fulfilled by the legal adviser from whom the written communications which may be protected emanate, is based on a conception of the lawyer's role as collaborating in the administration of justice by the courts and as being required to provide, in full independence, and in the overriding interests of that cause, such legal assistance as the client needs. The counterpart of that protection lies in the rules of professional ethics and discipline which are laid down and enforced in the general interest by institutions endowed with the requisite powers for that purpose. Such a conception reflects the legal traditions common to the Member States and is also to be found in legal order of the Community, as is demonstrated by Article 17 of the protocols on the statutes of the Court of Justice of the [EU] and the EAEC [...].

Having regard to the principles of the Treaty concerning freedom of establishment and the freedom to provide services the protection thus afforded by Community law, in particular in the context of Regulation No 17, to written communications between lawyer and client must apply without distinction to any lawyer entitled to practise his profession in one of the Member States, regardless of the Member State in which the client lives.

Such protection may not be extended beyond those limits, which are determined by the scope of the common rules on the exercise of the legal profession as laid down in Council Directive 77/249/EEC [...], which is based in its turn on the mutual recognition by all the Member States of the national legal concepts of each of them on this subject.

In view of all these factors it must therefore be concluded that although Regulation No 17, and in particular Article 14 thereof, interpreted in the light of its wording, structure and aims, and having regard to the laws of the Member States, empowers the Commission to require, in the course of an investigation within the meaning of that article, production of the business documents the disclosure of which it considers necessary, including written communications between lawyer and client, for proceedings in respect of any infringements of Articles [101 and 102 TFEU], that power is, however, subject to a restriction imposed by the need to protect confidentiality, on the conditions defined above, and provided that the communications in question are exchanged between an independent lawyer, that is to say one who is not bound to his client by a relationship of employment, and his client.

CoJ 18 May 1982 (AM&S Europe Ltd v. Commission, C-155/79) [1982] ECR 1575, paras 21–27.

13.52   Having regard to the particular nature of the principle of LPP, the purpose of which is both to guarantee the full exercise of individuals' rights of defence and to safeguard the requirement that any person must be able, without constraint, to consult his lawyer [...], the [General Court] considers that the fact that the Commission reads the content of a confidential document is in itself a breach of this principle. Contrary to what the Commission seems to submit, the protection of LPP therefore goes beyond the requirement that information provided by an undertaking to its lawyer or the content of the advice given by that lawyer cannot be used against it in a decision which penalises a breach of the competition rules.

First, that protection seeks to safeguard the public interest in the proper administration of justice in ensuring that a client is free to consult his lawyer without fear that any confidences which he imparts may subsequently be disclosed. Secondly, its purpose is to avoid the harm which may be caused to the undertaking's rights of the defence as a result of the Commission reading the contents of a confidential document and improperly adding it to the investigation file. Therefore, even if that document is not used as evidence in a decision imposing a penalty under the competition rules, the undertaking may suffer harm which cannot be made good or can only be made good with great difficulty. Information covered by LPP might be used by the Commission, directly or indirectly, in order to obtain new information or new evidence without the undertaking in question always being able to identify or prevent such information or evidence from being used against it. Moreover, harm which the undertaking concerned would suffer as a result of disclosure to third parties of information covered by LPP could not be made good, for example if that information were used in a statement of objections in the course of the Commission's administrative procedure. The mere fact that the Commission cannot use privileged documents as evidence in a decision imposing a penalty is thus not sufficient to make good or eliminate the harm which resulted from the Commission's reading the content of the documents.

General Court 17 September 2007 (Akzo Nobel Chemicals Ltd and Akcros Chemicals Ltd v. Commission, Joined Cases T-125/03 and T-253/03) [2007] ECR II-3523, paras 86 and 87.

2. Documents other than privileged correspondence between lawyer and client

In this case it appears that that legal advice [received from independent legal advisers by way of written communication] was reported on in internal notes distributed within the undertaking so that it might be the subject of consideration by managerial staff. In such a case, and although the aforesaid legal advice was not received by way of correspondence, it must be held that the principle of the protection of written communications between lawyer and client may not be frustrated on the sole ground that the content of those communications and of that legal advice was reported in documents internal to the undertaking. Thus the principle of the protection of written communications between lawyer and client must, in view of its purpose, be regarded as extending also to the internal notes which are confined to reporting the text or the content of those communications. It follows that the request for confidential treatment made by the applicant must be allowed in so far as it refers to those documents.

13.53

Order General Court 4 April 1990 (Hilti v. Commission, T-30/89) [1990] ECR II-163, para. 18.

13.54   [P]reparatory documents [e.g. to collect information that is useful or indispensable to understand the context, nature and/or scope of the facts regarding which legal advice is sought], even if they were not exchanged with a lawyer or were not created for the purpose of being sent physically to a lawyer, may none the less be covered by LPP, provided that they were drawn up exclusively for the purpose of seeking legal advice from a lawyer in exercise of the rights of the defence. On the other hand, the mere fact that a document has been discussed with a lawyer is not sufficient to give it such protection.

It must be borne in mind that protection under LPP is an exception to the Commission's powers of investigation, which are essential to enable it to discover, bring to an end and penalise infringements of the competition rules. Such infringements are often carefully concealed and usually very harmful to the proper functioning of the common market. For this reason, the possibility of treating a preparatory document as covered by LPP must be construed restrictively. It is for the undertaking relying on this protection to prove that the documents in question were drawn up with the sole aim of seeking legal advice from a lawyer. This should be unambiguously clear from the content of the documents themselves or the context in which those documents were prepared and found.

General Court 17 September 2007 (Akzo Nobel Chemicals Ltd and Akcros Chemicals Ltd v. Commission, Joined Cases T-125/03 and T-253/03) [2007] ECR II-3523, paras 123 and 124.

3.   Procedure protection confidentiality

13.55   If an undertaking which is the subject of an investigation under Article 14 of Regulation No 17 [now Art. 20 Regulation No 1/2003] refuses, on the ground that it is entitled to protection of the confidentiality of information, to produce, among the business records demanded by the Commission, written communications between itself and its lawyer, it must nevertheless provide the Commission's authorized agents with relevant material of such a nature as to demonstrate that the communications fulfil the conditions for being granted legal protection [...], although it is not bound to reveal the contents of the communications in question.

Where the Commission is not satisfied that such evidence has been supplied, the appraisal of those conditions is not a matter which may be left to an arbitrator or to a national authority. Since this is a matter involving an appraisal and a decision which affect the conditions under which the Commission may act in a field as vital to the functioning of the Common Market as that of compliance with the rules on competition, the solution of disputes as to the application of the protection of the confidentiality of written communications between lawyer and client may be sought only at community level.

In that case it is for the Commission to order, pursuant to Article 14(3) of Regulation No 17, production of the communications in question and, if necessary, to impose on the undertaking fines or periodic penalty payments under that regulation as a penalty for the undertaking's refusal either to supply such additional evidence as the commission considers necessary or to produce the communications in question whose confidentiality, in the Commission's view, is not protected in law.

The fact that by virtue of Article [278 TFEU] any action brought by the undertaking concerned against such decisions does not have suspensory effect provides an answer to the Commission's concern as to the effect of the time taken by the procedure before the Court on the efficacy of the supervision which the Commission is called upon to exercise in regard to compliance with the treaty rules on competition, whilst on the other hand the interests of the undertaking concerned are safeguarded by the possibility which exists under Articles [278] and [279], as well as under Article 83 of the rules of procedure of the Court, of obtaining an order suspending the application of the decision which has been taken, or any other interim measure.

CoJ 18 May 1982 (AM&S Europe Ltd v. Commission, C-155/79) [1982] ECR 1575, paras 29–32.

[T]he mere fact that an undertaking claims that a document is protected by legal **13.56** professional privilege is not sufficient to prevent the Commission from reading that document if the undertaking produces no relevant material of such a kind as to prove that it is actually protected by LPP. The undertaking concerned may, in particular, inform the Commission of the author of the document and for whom it was intended, explain the respective duties and responsibilities of each, and refer to the objective and the context in which the document was drawn up. Similarly, it may also mention the context in which the document was found, the way in which it was filed and any related documents.

In a significant number of cases, a mere cursory look by the Commission officials at the general layout, heading, title or other superficial features of the document will enable them to confirm the accuracy of the reasons invoked by the undertaking and to determine whether the document at issue was confidential, when deciding whether to put it aside. Nevertheless, on certain occasions, there would be a risk that, even with a cursory look at the document, in spite of the superficial nature of their examination, the Commission officials would gain access to information covered by legal professional privilege. That may be so, in particular, if the confidentiality of the document in question is not clear from external indications.

[T]he undertaking concerned is not bound to reveal their contents when presenting the Commission officials with relevant material of such a nature as to demonstrate that the documents fulfil the conditions for being granted legal protection [...]. Accordingly, the [General Court] concludes that an undertaking subject to an investigation under Article 14(3) of Regulation No 17 [now Art. 20(4) Regulation No 1/2003] is entitled to refuse to allow the Commission officials to take even a cursory look at one or more specific documents which it claims to be covered by LPP, provided that the undertaking considers that such a cursory look is impossible without revealing the content of those documents and that it gives the Commission officials appropriate reasons for its view.

Where, in the course of an investigation under Article 14(3) of Regulation No 17, the Commission considers that the material presented by the undertaking is not of such a nature as to prove that the documents in question are confidential, in particular where that undertaking refuses to give the Commission officials a cursory look at a document, the Commission officials may place a copy of the document or documents in question in a sealed envelope and then remove it with a view to a subsequent resolution of the dispute. This procedure enables risks of a breach of legal professional privilege to be avoided while at the same time enabling the Commission to retain a certain control over the documents forming the subject-matter of the investigation and avoiding the risk that the documents will subsequently disappear or be manipulated.

Use of the sealed envelope procedure cannot, moreover, be considered to be at odds with the requirement [...] that, in the case of a dispute with the undertaking concerned as to whether a particular document is confidential, the Commission must adopt a decision ordering that document to be produced. The reason for such a requirement lies in the specific context of the judgment in *AM & S*, in particular the fact that the initial decision ordering an inspection at the premises of the undertaking in question was not a formal decision under Article 14(3) of Regulation No 17 [...] and the undertaking in question was therefore entitled, as it in fact did, to refuse to produce the documents requested by the Commission.

In any event, the [General Court] would point out that where the Commission is not satisfied with the material and explanations provided by the representatives of the undertaking for the purposes of proving that the document concerned is covered by LPP, the Commission must not read the contents of the document before it has adopted a decision allowing the undertaking concerned to refer the matter to the [General Court], and, if appropriate, to make an application for interim relief [...].

General Court 17 September 2007 (Akzo Nobel Chemicals Ltd and Akcros Chemicals Ltd v. Commission, Joined Cases T-125/03 and T-253/03) [2007] ECR II-3523, paras 80–85.

4. Limitation of legal privilege for in-house lawyers

13.57   As regards, first of all, the applicants' principal argument, it must be pointed out that in its judgment in *AM & S* , the General Court expressly held that the protection accorded to LPP under Community law, in the application of Regulation No 17 [now Regulation No 1/2003], only applies to the extent that the lawyer is independent, that is to say, not bound to his client by a relationship of employment (paragraphs 21, 22 and 27 of the judgment). The requirement as to the position and status as an independent lawyer, which must be met by the legal adviser from whom the written communications which may be protected emanate, is based on a concept of the lawyer's role as collaborating in the administration of justice by the courts and as being required to provide, in full independence, and in the overriding interests of the administration of justice, such legal assistance as the client needs [...].

It follows that the Court expressly excluded communications with in-house lawyers, that is, legal advisers bound to their clients by a relationship of employment, from protection under LPP. It must also be pointed out that the Court reached a conscious decision on that exception, given that the issue had been debated at length during the proceeding and that Advocate General Sir Gordon Slynn had expressly proposed in his Opinion for that judgment that where a lawyer bound by an employment contract remains a member of the profession and subject to its discipline and ethics, he should be treated in the same way as independent lawyers [...].

General Court 17 September 2007 (Akzo Nobel Chemicals Ltd and Akcros Chemicals Ltd v. Commission, Joined Cases T-125/03 and T-253/03) [2007] ECR II-3523, paras 166 and 167.

C. PARAGRAPHS 3 AND 4: CHOICE BETWEEN INVESTIGATION BY AUTHORISATION AND INVESTIGATION ORDERED BY DECISION

[A]s regards the need to verify that the coercive measures are proportionate to the **13.58** subject-matter of the investigation ordered by the Commission, it should be noted that this involves establishing that such measures are appropriate to ensure that the investigation can be carried out. [...]

In addition, review of the proportionality of the coercive measures envisaged to the subject-matter of the investigation involves establishing that such measures do not constitute, in relation to the aim pursued by the investigation in question, a disproportionate and intolerable interference [...].

In that regard, it should certainly be kept in view that, in relation to the proportionality of the investigation measure itself, the Court has held that the Commission's choice between an investigation by straightforward authorisation and an investigation ordered by a decision does not depend on matters such as the particular seriousness of the situation, extreme urgency or the need for absolute discretion, but rather on the need for an appropriate inquiry, having regard to the special features of the case. The Court has concluded in that regard that, where an investigation decision is solely intended to enable the Commission to gather the information needed to assess whether the Treaty has been infringed, such a decision is not contrary to the principle of proportionality [...].

CoJ 22 October 2002 (Roquette Frères, C-94/00) [2002] ECR I-9011, paras 71, 76 and 77.

See also CoJ 26 June 1980 (National Panasonic v. Commission, 136/79) [1980] ECR 2033, paras 28 and 30; General Court 8 March 2007 (France Télécom, T-340/04) [2007] ECR II-573, para. 147.

D. PARAGRAPH 4: MOTIVATION INSPECTION DECISION

Next, it should be noted that the Commission is required to point out in a decision **13.59** ordering investigation, under Article 14(3) of Regulation No 17 [now Art. 20(4) Regulation No 1/2003], the subject-matter and purpose of that investigation. That requirement constitutes a fundamental guarantee of the rights of defence of the undertakings concerned, with the result that the scope of the obligation to state the reasons on which decisions ordering investigations are based cannot be restricted on the basis of considerations concerning the effectiveness of the investigation.

General Court 8 July 2008 (AC Treuhand AG, T-99/04) [2008] ECR II-1501, para. 54.

[I]t is open to undertakings that have undergone an inspection to challenge before the **13.60** EU Courts the lawfulness of the inspection decision and [...] such judicial proceedings can be initiated immediately after the company has been notified of the Commission decision, meaning that there is no need to wait until the Commission has adopted the final decision on the suspected infringement of the EU competition rules in order to bring an action for annulment before the European Union Courts.

[I]f the Community judicature annuls the inspection decision or holds that there has been an irregularity in the conduct of the investigation, the Commission will be prevented from using, for the purposes of infringement proceedings, any documents or evidence which it might have obtained in the course of that investigation [...]. [...]

The Court stated in that regard that such a requirement is aimed at preserving, in addition to business secrecy, expressly referred to in Article 28, undertakings' rights of defence, which Article 20(4) is intended to safeguard. Those rights would be seriously endangered if the Commission were able to rely on evidence against undertakings which was obtained during an investigation but was not related to the subject-matter or purpose thereof [...].

On the other hand, it cannot be concluded therefrom that the Commission is barred from initiating an inquiry in order to verify or supplement information which it happened to obtain during a previous investigation if that information indicates the existence of conduct contrary to the competition rules in the Treaty. Such a bar would go beyond what is required to safeguard professional secrecy and the rights of the defence and would thus constitute an unjustified hindrance to the Commission in the accomplishment of its task of ensuring compliance with the competition rules in the common market and identifying infringements of Articles 101 TFEU and 102 TFEU [...].

It follows from the foregoing that, on the one hand, the Commission is required to state reasons for its decision ordering an inspection. On the other hand, if the statement of reasons for that decision circumscribes the powers conferred on the Commission's agents, a search may be made only for those documents coming within the scope of the subject-matter of the inspection. [...]

In the present case, it is apparent from both paragraph 162 of the judgment under appeal and the Commission's statements at the hearing that it informed its agents immediately, before the first inspection was conducted, that there was another complaint against Deutsche Bahn concerning its subsidiary DUSS. [...]

That prior information, which was not part of the general background information on the case but rather pertained to the existence of a separate complaint, is unrelated to the subject-matter of the first inspection decision. Accordingly, the lack of reference to that complaint in the description of the subject-matter of that inspection decision infringes the obligation to state reasons and the rights of defence of the undertaking concerned. [...]

Therefore, the first inspection was vitiated by irregularity since the Commission's agents, being previously in possession of information unrelated to the subject-matter of that inspection, proceeded to seize documents falling outside the scope of the inspection as circumscribed by the first contested decision.

CoJ 18 June 2015 (Deutsche Bahn AG and Others v. European Commission, C-583/13 P), ECLI:EU:C:2015:404, paras 44, 45, 58–61, 64 and 66.

E. PARAGRAPHS 5 TO 8: GRANTING ASSISTANCE TO COMMISSION OFFICIALS

The Commission must make sure that the competent body under national law has all **13.61** that it needs to exercise its own supervisory powers. It should be pointed out that that body, whether judicial or otherwise, cannot in this respect substitute its own assessment of the need for the investigations ordered for that of the Commission, the lawfulness of whose assessments of fact and law is subject only to review by the Court of Justice. On the other hand, it is within the powers of the national body, after satisfying itself that the decision ordering the investigation is authentic, to consider whether the measures of constraint envisaged are arbitrary or excessive having regard to the subject-matter of the investigation and to ensure that the rules of national law are complied with in the application of those measures.

CoJ 21 September 1989 (Hoechst v. Commission, Joined Cases 46/87 and 227/99) [1989] ECR 2859, para. 35.

ARTICLE 21 – INSPECTION OF OTHER PREMISES

1. If a reasonable suspicion exists that books or other records related to the business and to the subject-matter of the inspection, which may be relevant to prove a serious violation of Article 81 or Article 82 of the Treaty, are being kept in any other premises, land and means of transport, including the homes of directors, managers and other members of staff of the undertakings and associations of undertakings concerned, the Commission can by decision order an inspection to be conducted in such other premises, land and means of transport.

2. The decision shall specify the subject matter and purpose of the inspection, appoint the date on which it is to begin and indicate the right to have the decision reviewed by the Court of Justice. It shall in particular state the reasons that have led the Commission to conclude that a suspicion in the sense of paragraph 1 exists. The Commission shall take such decisions after consulting the competition authority of the Member State in whose territory the inspection is to be conducted.

3. A decision adopted pursuant to paragraph 1 cannot be executed without prior authorisation from the national judicial authority of the Member State concerned. The national judicial authority shall control that the Commission decision is authentic and that the coercive measures envisaged are neither arbitrary nor excessive having regard in particular to the seriousness of the suspected infringement, to the importance of the evidence sought, to the involvement of the undertaking concerned and to the reasonable likelihood that business books and records relating to the subject matter of the inspection are kept in the premises for which the authorisation is requested. The national judicial authority may ask the Commission, directly or through the Member State competition authority, for detailed explanations on those elements which are necessary to allow its control of the proportionality of the coercive measures envisaged. However, the national judicial authority may not call into question the necessity for the inspection nor demand that it be provided with information in the Commission's file. The lawfulness of the Commission decision shall be subject to review only by the Court of Justice.

4. The officials and other accompanying persons authorised by the Commission to conduct an inspection ordered in accordance with paragraph 1 of this Article shall have the powers set out in Article 20 (2)(a), (b) and (c). Article 20(5) and (6) shall apply mutatis mutandis.

ARTICLE 22 – INVESTIGATIONS BY COMPETITION AUTHORITIES OF MEMBER STATES

1.   The competition authority of a Member State may in its own territory carry out any inspection or other fact-finding measure under its national law on behalf and for the account of the competition authority of another Member State in order to establish whether there has been an infringement of Article 81 or Article 82 of the Treaty. Any exchange and use of the information collected shall be carried out in accordance with Article 12.

2.   At the request of the Commission, the competition authorities of the Member States shall undertake the inspections which the Commission considers to be necessary under Article 20(1) or which it has ordered by decision pursuant to Article 20(4). The officials of the competition authorities of the Member States who are responsible for conducting these inspections as well as those authorised or appointed by them shall exercise their powers in accordance with their national law. If so requested by the Commission or by the competition authority of the Member State in whose territory the inspection is to be conducted, officials and other accompanying persons authorised by the Commission may assist the officials of the authority concerned.

CHAPTER VI

PENALTIES

ARTICLE 23 – FINES

1. The Commission may by decision impose on undertakings and associations of undertakings fines not exceeding 1per cent of the total turnover in the preceding business year where, intentionally or negligently:

  (a) they supply incorrect or misleading information in response to a request made pursuant to Article 17 or Article 18(2);

  (b) in response to a request made by decision adopted pursuant to Article 17 or Article 18(3), they supply incorrect, incomplete or misleading information or do not supply information within the required time-limit;

  (c) they produce the required books or other records related to the business in incomplete form during inspections under Article 20 or refuse to submit to inspections ordered by a decision adopted pursuant to Article 20(4);

  (d) in response to a question asked in accordance with Article 20(2)(e),

      – they give an incorrect or misleading answer,

      – they fail to rectify within a time-limit set by the Commission an incorrect, incomplete or misleading answer given by a member of staff, or

      – they fail or refuse to provide a complete answer on facts relating to the subject-matter and purpose of an inspection ordered by a decision adopted pursuant to Article 20(4);

  (e) seals affixed in accordance with Article 20(2)(d) by officials or other accompanying persons authorised by the Commission have been broken.

2. The Commission may by decision impose fines on undertakings and associations of undertakings where, either intentionally or negligently:

  (a) they infringe Article 81 or Article 82 of the Treaty; or

  (b) they contravene a decision ordering interim measures under Article 8; or

  (c) they fail to comply with a commitment made binding by a decision pursuant to Article 9.

  For each undertaking and association of undertakings participating in the infringement, the fine shall not exceed 10 per cent of its total turnover in the preceding business year. Where the infringement of an association relates to the activities of its members, the fine shall not exceed 10 per cent of the sum of the total turnover of each member active on the market affected by the infringement of the association.

3.   In fixing the amount of the fine, regard shall be had both to the gravity and to the duration of the infringement.

4.   When a fine is imposed on an association of undertakings taking account of the turnover of its members and the association is not solvent, the association is obliged to call for contributions from its members to cover the amount of the fine. Where such contributions have not been made to the association within a time-limit fixed by the Commission, the Commission may require payment of the fine directly by any of the undertakings whose representatives were members of the decision-making bodies concerned of the association. After the Commission has required payment under the second subparagraph, where necessary to ensure full payment of the fine, the Commission may require payment of the balance by any of the members of the association which were active on the market on which the infringement occurred. However, the Commission shall not require payment under the second or the third subparagraph from undertakings which show that they have not implemented the infringing decision of the association and either were not aware of its existence or have actively distanced themselves from it before the Commission started investigating the case. The financial liability of each undertaking in respect of the payment of the fine shall not exceed 10 per cent of its total turnover in the preceding business year.

5.   Decisions taken pursuant to paragraphs 1 and 2 shall not be of a criminal law nature.

OVERVIEW

A. GENERAL	13.62	5. Mitigating circumstances 13.123
		6. Aggravating circumstances 13.138
B. PARAGRAPH 1: FINES FOR INCORRECT		7. Principle of proportionality 13.146
OR MISLEADING INFORMATION ETC.	13.66	8. Equality of treatment 13.159
		9. *Ne bis in idem* 13.164
C. PARAGRAPH 3: FIXING THE AMOUNT		10. Leniency 13.171
OF THE FINE	13.68	11. Ability to pay 13.175
1. General	13.68	
2. Legal framework	13.71	D. PARAGRAPH 4: ASSOCIATIONS OF
3. Guidelines on the method for		UNDERTAKINGS 13.177
setting the fine	13.76	1. Calculation turnover associations of
4. Factors of assessment	13.82	undertakings 13.177

E.	LIABILITY	13.178	4.	Legal and economic links	13.194
	1. General	13.178	5.	Legal and economic continuity	13.197
	2. Imputability of infringement on		6.	Representation in administrative	
	parent company/companies	13.181		procedure	13.204
	3. Joint and several liability	13.189	7.	Vertical relation	13.206

A. GENERAL

See also the Guidelines on the method of setting fines imposed pursuant to Article 23(2)(a) of Regulation No 1/2003. See regarding the periods of limitation also recital 31.

13.62   The penalties provided for in Article 15 of Regulation No 17 [now Art. 23 Regulation No 1/2003] are not in the nature of periodic penalty payments. Their object is to suppress illegal activities and to prevent any recurrence. This object could not be adequately attained if the imposition of a penalty were to be restricted to current infringements alone. The Commission's power to impose penalties is in no way affected by the fact that the conduct constituting the infringement has ceased and that it can no longer have detrimental effects. For the purpose of fixing the amount of the fine, the gravity of the infringement is to be appraised by taking into account in particular the nature of the restrictions on competition, the number and size of the undertakings concerned, the respective proportions of the market controlled by them within the community and the situation of the market when the infringement was committed.
CoJ 15 July 1970 (Boehringer Mannheim, 45/69) [1970] ECR 769, para. 53.

13.63   The prior fixing of a maximum aggregate amount for the fine, fixed in relation to the seriousness of the danger which the agreement represented to competition and trade in the common market, is not incompatible with the individual fixing of the penalty. Consideration of the situation and of the individual conduct of each undertaking and of the importance of the role which it played in the agreement of the fine.
CoJ 15 July 1970 (Boehringer Mannheim, 45/69) [1970] ECR 769, para. 55.

13.64   The power to impose fines, which that regulation confers on the Commission, therefore stems from the provisions of the Treaty itself and is intended to facilitate the effective application of the prohibitions laid down in those articles.
General Court 5 April 2006 (Degussa, T-279/02) [2006] ECR II-897, para. 87.

13.65   It should be recalled in that regard that [...] Article 23(2) of Regulation No 1/2003 provide that, for each undertaking and association of undertakings participating in the infringement, the fine is not to exceed 10 per cent of its total turnover in the preceding business year. Those provisions do not refer to the sum of various fines imposed on a company. [...] Thus, as a rule, the characterisation of certain unlawful actions as constituting one and the same infringement or as constituting multiple infringements affects the penalty that may be imposed, since a finding that multiple infringements exist may entail the imposition of a number of distinct fines, each time within the limits laid down in [...] Article 23(2) of Regulation No 1/2003. [...]

It is true that, [...] the Commission may impose a single fine for multiple infringements [...].

However, that is merely a possibility of which the Commission has made use in certain circumstances, in particular where the infringements form part of a coherent overall strategy [...], or where the infringements constitute a single offence [...], or where the infringements ascertained in the Commission decision were concerned with the same type of conduct on different markets, in particular the fixing of prices and of quotas and exchange of information, and the undertakings involved in those infringements were, largely, the same [...].

General Court 28 April 2010 (Amann & Söhne, T-446/05) [2010] ECR II-1255, paras 150, 154 and 155.

B. PARAGRAPH 1: FINES FOR INCORRECT OR MISLEADING INFORMATION ETC.

Any statement is incorrect which gives a distorted picture of the true facts asked for, and which departs significantly from reality on major points.   **13.66**
Commission 25 November 1981 (Telos, IV/29.895), OJ 1981 L 58/19.

[T]he Commission rightly set out the reasons why the infringement of breaking a seal   **13.67**
was, as such, a particularly serious infringement, referring primarily to the purpose of seals, which is to prevent evidence from being lost during the inspection, and the need to ensure that the fine imposed has a sufficiently deterrent effect. In that regard, it is also important to point out that, on the one hand, as regards the infringement of breaking a seal, the legislature has, in Regulation No 1/2003, laid down more severe penalties than those which were provided for in the previous set of rules, in order to take into account the particularly serious nature of that infringement. On the other hand, it is clear from the case-law that, in setting the amount of fines, the Commission is justified in taking into consideration the need to ensure that they have a sufficiently deterrent effect [...], to which even greater importance attaches in the context of an infringement of breaking a seal, in order that undertakings should not be able to consider that it would pay them to break a seal in the course of an inspection [...].[...]

General Court 15 December 2010 (E.ON Energie AG, T-141/08) [2010] ECR II-5761, para. 288.

C. PARAGRAPH 3: FIXING THE AMOUNT OF THE FINE

1. General

The Commission states that many undertakings carry on conduct which they know to   **13.68**
be contrary to Community law because the profit which they derive from their unlawful

conduct exceeds the fines imposed hitherto. Conduct of that kind can only be deterred by fines which are heavier than in the past.

CoJ 7 June 1983 (SA Musique Diffusion Française v. Commission, Joined Cases 100–103/80) [1983] ECR 1825, para. 104.

13.69   [N]either Regulation No 1/2003 nor the Guidelines provide that the amount of fines must be determined in direct relation to the size of the affected market, that being only one relevant factor among others. That legal framework does not therefore expressly require the Commission to take account of the limited size of the product market.

General Court 28 April 2010 (Amann & Söhne, T-446/05) [2010] ECR II-1255, para. 174.

13.70   In any event, the applicants cannot complain that the Commission did not specify the starting amount imposed on each company for each of the abuses of a dominant position at issue. It should be borne in mind, in this respect, that the Commission is not bound to break down the amount of the fine between the various aspects of the abuse, or to state specifically how it took into account each of the components of the abuse for the purposes of setting the fine [...]. In addition, the Commission cannot divest itself of its own power of assessment by mechanical recourse to arithmetical formulas alone [...].

General Court 1 July 2010 (Astra Zeneca AB, T-321/05) [2010] ECR II-2805, para. 906.

2. Legal framework

13.71   [T]he Commission's power to impose fines on undertakings which intentionally or negligently commit an infringement of Article [101 TFEU] is one of the means conferred on the Commission in order to enable it to carry out the supervisory task conferred on it by Community law. That task certainly includes the duty to investigate and punish individual infringements, but it also encompasses the duty to pursue a general policy designed to apply, in competition matters, the principles laid down by the [TFEU] and to guide the conduct of undertakings in the light of those principles. It was for that reason that the Court of Justice held that in assessing the gravity of an infringement for the purpose of fixing the amount of the fine the Commission must take into consideration not only the particular circumstances of the case but also the context in which the infringement occurs and must ensure that its action has the necessary deterrent effect, especially as regards those types of infringement which are particularly harmful to the attainment of the objectives of the Community. The Court went on to state that it was open to the Commission to have regard to the fact that, although infringements of a specific type were established as being unlawful at the outset of Community competition policy, they were still relatively frequent on account of the profit that some of the undertakings concerned are able to derive from them and, consequently, it was open to the Commission to raise the level of fines so as to reinforce their deterrent effect. The Court concluded that the fact that in the past the Commission had imposed fines of a certain level for certain types of infringement did not mean that it was stopped from raising that level within the limits indicated in Regulation No 17 [now Regulation No 1/2003] if that was necessary to ensure the implementation of

Community competition policy (judgment in *Joined Cases 100 to 103/80 Pioneer* [...], paras 105–109).

General Court 10 March 1992 (Montedipe SpA, T-14/89) [1992] ECR II-1155, para. 346.

[...] The Commission's previous decision-making practice therefore does not in itself **13.72** serve as a legal framework for the fines imposed in competition matters, since that framework is defined solely in Regulation No 17 [now Regulation No 1/2003] and in those Guidelines [...].

General Court 30 September 2003 (Michelin, T-203/01) [2003] ECR II-4071, paras 254 and 298.

See also General Court 14 May 1998 (Mayr-Melnhof v. Commission, T-347/94) [1998] ECR II-1751, para. 368; General Court 20 March 2002 (LR AF 1998 v. Commission, T-23/99) [2002] ECR II-1705, paras 234 and 337.

[T]he Commission has a wide margin of discretion in fixing the amount of fines in **13.73** order to steer the conduct of undertakings towards compliance with the competition rules [...]. The [General Court] is, however, under a duty to verify whether the amount of the fine imposed is proportionate in relation to the gravity and duration of the infringement [...] and to weigh the gravity of the infringement and the circumstances invoked by the applicant [...].

General Court 21 October 2003 (General Motors Nederland B.V. and Opel Neder-land B.V. v. Commission, T-368/00) [2003] ECR II-4491, para. 189.

Confirmed: CoJ 6 April 2006 (General Motors, C-551/03P) [2006] ECR I-3173.

The Commission is not, moreover, bound to apply a precise mathematical formula, **13.74** either for the total amount of the fine or where it is broken down into different elements [...].

General Court 13 January 2004 (JCB, T-67/01) [2004] ECR II-49, para. 188.

See also General Court 14 May 1998 (Stora Kopparbergs Bergslags v. Commission, T-354/94) [1998] ECR II-2111, para. 119.

The Court notes, at the outset, that the Commission has a margin of discretion when **13.75** fixing the amount of fines, in order that it may direct the conduct of undertakings towards compliance with the competition rules [...].

The amount of the fine is set by the Commission according to the gravity of the infringement and, where appropriate, to its duration. The gravity of an infringement has to be determined by reference to criteria such as the particular circumstances of the case, its context and the dissuasive effect of the fines. Objective factors such as the content and duration of the anti-competitive conduct, the number of incidents and their intensity, the extent of the market affected and the damage to the economic public order must be taken into account. The analysis must also take into consideration the relative importance and market share of the undertakings responsible and also any repeated infringements [...].

However, each time the Commission decides to impose fines pursuant to competition law, it must observe general principles of law, which include the principle of equal treatment as interpreted by the Community Courts [...].

According to settled case-law, the principle of equal treatment or non-discrimination requires that comparable situations must not be treated differently and that different situations must not be treated in the same way unless such treatment is objectively justified [...].

To the extent to which reliance is to be placed on the turnover of undertakings involved in the same infringement for the purpose of determining the proportions between the fines to be imposed, the period to be taken into consideration must be ascertained in such a way that the resulting turnovers are as comparable as possible [...].

The principle of proportionality, for its part, requires that measures adopted by Community institutions do not exceed the limits of what is appropriate and necessary in order to attain the objectives legitimately pursued by the legislation in question; when there is a choice between several appropriate measures recourse must be had to the least onerous, and the disadvantages caused must not be disproportionate to the aims pursued [...].

General Court 12 July 2011 (Mitsubishi Electric Corp., T-133/07) [2011] ECR II-4219, paras 264–269.

3. Guidelines on the method for setting the fine

13.76   Although Article 15(4) of Regulation No 17 [now Art. 23(4) Regulation No 1/2003] provides that Commission decisions imposing fines for infringement of competition law are not of a criminal nature [...], the Commission is none the less required to observe the general principles of Community law, and in particular the principle of non-retroactivity, in any administrative procedure capable of leading to fines under the Treaty rules on competition [...].

General Court 9 July 2003 (Cheil Jedang, T-220/00) [2003] ECR II-2473, paras. 44.

13.77   [A]lthough the Commission has a margin of discretion in setting the amount of fines [...], it cannot depart from the rules which it has imposed on itself [...]. Thus, the Commission was required to take account of the terms of the Guidelines in calculating the fines, in particular of the mandatory provisions thereof.

General Court 8 July 2004 (Mannesmannröhren-Werke AG v. Commission T-44/00) [2004] ECR II-2223, para. 212.

The Guidelines cannot therefore be regarded as excessively and unlawfully limiting the Commission's discretion in fixing fines, but must rather be viewed as an instrument allowing undertakings to have a more precise idea of the competition policy which the Commission intends to follow in order to ensure the transparency and objectivity of its decisions on fines [...]. **13.78**

General Court 18 July 2005 (Scandinavian Airlines System, T-241/01) [2005] ECR II-2917, para. 75.

[T]he obligation to state reasons does not require the Commission to indicate in its decision the figures relating to the method of calculating the fines [...]. **13.79**

General Court 17 September 2007 (Microsoft, T-201/04) [2007] ECR II-3601, para. 1361.

Although the Guidelines may not be regarded as rules of law which the administration is always bound to observe, they nevertheless form rules of practice from which the administration may not depart in an individual case without giving reasons that are compatible with the principle of equal treatment [...]. The fact that, in the Guidelines, the Commission set out its approach to assessment of the gravity of an infringement does not prevent it from assessing that criterion as a whole by reference to all the relevant circumstances of the case, including factors that are not expressly mentioned in the Guidelines [...]. [...] **13.80**

The adoption of the Guidelines has not rendered irrelevant the previous case-law under which the Commission enjoys a discretion as to whether or not to take account of certain matters when setting the amount of the fines it intends imposing, by reference in particular to the circumstances of the case. Thus, in the absence of any binding indication in the Guidelines regarding the mitigating circumstances that may be taken into account, it must be concluded that the Commission has retained a degree of latitude in making an overall assessment of the extent to which a reduction of fines may be made in respect of mitigating circumstances [...].

General Court 8 September 2010 (Deltafina v Commission, T-29/05) [2010] ECR II-4077, paras 230 and 348.

It has been consistently held that, within the limits laid down in Regulation No 1/2003, the Commission enjoys a wide discretion when exercising its power to impose such fines [...]. That power is however limited; where the Commission adopts guidelines which are consistent with the Treaty and are designed to specify the criteria which it intends to apply in the exercise of its discretion, the Commission itself then limits that discretion in that it must comply with the guidelines which it has imposed upon itself [...]. The Commission may not depart from the Guidelines in an individual case without giving reasons that are compatible with the principle of equal treatment [...]. **13.81**

General Court 2 February 2012 (The Dow Chemical Company v. Commission, T-77/08), ECLI:EU:T:2012:47, para 139.

4. Factors of assessment

(a) General

13.82   In fixing the amount of the fines under Article 15(2) [now Art. 23(2) Regulation No 1/2003] regard shall be had both to the gravity and to the duration of the infringement so that the court has to take particular account of the legislative background and economic context of the conduct to which exception is taken, the nature of the restrictions of competition as well as the number and size of the undertakings concerned. [...]

Finally in the case of each of the undertakings in question the importance of the infringement or infringements upheld by the Court must be compared with the importance of all the infringements for which the Commission has blamed the applicants.

[I]n addition, in so far as an infringement upheld by the court has been committed by several applicants, it is appropriate to consider how seriously each of them participated in it.

CoJ 16 December 1975 (Suiker Unie, 40/73–48/73, 50/73, 54/73–56/73, 111/73, 113/73 and 114/73) [1975] ECR 1663, paras 612, 622 and 623.

13.83   [T]he gravity of the infringement [...] has to be determined by reference to criteria such as the particular circumstances of the case, its context and the dissuasive effect of the fines.

Objective factors such as the content and duration of the anti-competitive conduct, the number of incidents and their intensity, the extent of the market affected and the damage to the economic public order must be taken into account. The analysis must also take into consideration the relative importance and market share of the undertakings responsible and also any repeated infringements.

Where an infringement has been committed by a number of persons, the relative gravity of the participation of each of them will be examined.

CoJ 7 January 2004 (Aalborg Portland, Joined Cases C-204/00, 205/00, 213/00, 217/00, 219/00) [2004] ECR I-123, paras 90–92.

See also CoJ 7 June 1983 (SA Musique Diffusion Française v. Commission, Joined Cases 100–103/80) [1983] ECR 1825, paras 120 and 129; CoJ 17 July 1997 (Ferriere Nord SpA v. Commission, C-219/95) [1997] ECR I-4411, para. 33.

13.84   The Court of Justice has held that, in order to determine the amount of a fine, it is necessary to take account of the duration of the infringements and of all the factors capable of affecting the assessment of their gravity, such as the conduct of each of the undertakings, the role played by each of them in the establishment of the concerted practices, the profit which they were able to derive from those practices, their size, the value of the goods concerned and the threat that infringements of that type pose to the European Community [...].

The Court has also stated that objective factors such as the content and duration of the anti-competitive conduct, the number of incidents and their intensity, the extent of the market affected and the damage to the economic public order must be taken into account. The analysis must also take into consideration the relative importance and market share of the undertakings responsible and also any repeated infringements [...].
CoJ 8 December 2011 (KME Germany AG, KME France SAS and KME Italy SpA, C-272/09 P) [2011] ECR I-12789, paras 96 and 97.

(b) Repeat infringements

Moreover, there is nothing in the Guidelines to indicate that the indication that the repeat infringement in question must be a repeat infringement of the same under-taking(s) in an infringement of the same type must be understood as meaning that the Commission may not take into account, in order to establish repeat infringement under Article [101 TFEU], infringements found under the CS Treaty. On the contrary, the heading of the Guidelines shows that they apply both to the calculation of fines imposed under Article 15(2) of Regulation No 17 [now Art. 23(2) Regulation No 1/2003] and to those imposed pursuant to Article 65(5) CS. **13.85**
General Court 19 May 2010 (Outokumpu Oyj, T-20/05) [2010] ECR II-89, para. 63.

Moreover, the principle of proportionality requires that the time elapsed between the infringement in question and a previous breach of the competition rules be taken into account in assessing the undertaking's tendency to infringe those rules. For the purposes of judical review of the Commission's measures in matters of competition law, the General Court and, where appropriate, the Court of Justice may therefore be called upon to scrutinise whether the Commission has complied with that principle when it increased, for repeated infringement, the fine imposed, and, in particular, whether such increase was imposed in the light of, among other things, the time elapsed between the infringement in question and the previous breach of the competition rules. **13.86**

In the present case, the General Court observed, in paragraph 727 of the judgment under appeal, that the history of the infringements found against Lafarge shows [...] [that] it had already been the subject of Commission measures imposed previously under Decision 94/815, and since its subsidiary none the less continued to participate actively in the cartel in question until 1998, that is for four years after that decision had been notified to it. [...]

As regards the complaint alleging breach of a general principle common to the Member States that repeated infringement outside a maximum period cannot be taken into account, that complaint must be rejected as inoperative since, [...], European Union competition law does not authorise the Commission to take account of repeated infringement without any limitation in time.
CoJ 17 June 2010 (Lafarge SA, C-413/08 P) [2010] ECR I-5361, paras 70, 71 and 73.

[F]irst, the principle of respect for the rights of the defence precludes a competition decision in which the Commission imposes a fine on an undertaking without first **13.87** having informed it of the objections relied on against it from being held to be lawful and, second, given its importance, the statement of objections must specify unequivocally the legal person on whom fines may be imposed and be addressed to that person [...].

Thus, it cannot be accepted that the Commission is entitled to decide, when making a determination as to the aggravating circumstance of repeated infringement, that an undertaking should be held liable for a previous infringement in relation to which it was not penalised by a Commission decision and in the establishment of which it was not the addressee of a statement of objections, with the result that such an undertaking was not given an opportunity, in the procedure leading to the adoption of the decision establishing the previous infringement, to make representations with a view to disputing that it formed an economic unit with certain other undertakings.

General Court 13 July 2011 (ThyssenKrupp Liften Ascenseurs NV and others, T-144/07 and others) [2011] ECR II-5129, paras 318 and 319.

(c) Turnover

13.88   It follows that, on the one hand, it is permissible, for the purpose of fixing the fine, to have regard both to the total turnover of the undertaking, which gives an indication, albeit approximate and imperfect, of the size of the undertaking and its economic power, and to the proportion of that turnover accounted for by the goods in respect of which the infringement was committed, which gives an indication of the scale of the infringement. On the other hand, it follows that it is important not to confer on one or the other of those figures an importance disproportionate in relation to the other factors and, consequently, that the fixing of an appropriate fine cannot be the result of a simple calculation based on the total turnover. That is particularly the case where the goods concerned account for only a small part of that figure. It is appropriate for the Court to bear in mind those considerations in its assessment, by virtue of its powers of unlimited jurisdiction, of the gravity of the infringements in question.

CoJ 7 June 1983 (SA Musique Diffusion Française, Joined Cases 100–103/80) [1983] ECR 1825, para. 121.

13.89   It should be borne in mind that in determining the fine account may be taken both of the overall turnover of the undertaking, which gives some indication, however approximate and imperfect it may be, of the size and economic strength of that undertaking, and of the part of that turnover represented by the goods concerned in the infringement which therefore serves to provide an indication of the extent of that infringement. Consequently, neither one or the other of those figures should be given too much weight compared with the other factors relevant to an assessment and the determination of an appropriate fine cannot be the result of a simple calculation on the basis of overall turnover. The Court must take account of those considerations in assessing, in the exercise of its unlimited jurisdiction, the seriousness of the infringements at issue.

CoJ 12 November 1985 (Krupp, C-183/83) [1985] ECR 3609, para. 37.

13.90   Article 15(2) of Regulation No 17 [now Art. 23(2) Regulation No 1/2003] contains no territorial limit in regard to the turnover of undertakings which have infringed the competition rules which is to be taken into account in determining the amount of the fine to be imposed on them, so that the Commission cannot be required to take account only of the total turnover realized on the market in which the infringement was committed.

CoJ 8 February 1990 (Tipp-Ex, C-279/87) [1990] ECR I-261, para. 39.

[T]he Commission, which took account not of the total turnover achieved by the **13.91** applicant but only of the turnover in welded steel mesh in the Community of Six and did not exceed the 10 per cent ceiling, did not therefore, having regard to the gravity and duration of the infringement, infringe Article 15 of Regulation No 17 [now Art. 23 Regulation No 1/2003].

General Court 6 April 1995 (Tréfilunion, T-148/89) [1995] ECR II-1063, para. 140.

See also, in respect of the application of the 10 per cent rule, General Court 14 July 2016 (Parker Hannifin Manufacturing Srl, formerly Parker ITR Srl and Parker-Hannifin Corp. v. European Commission, T-146/09 RENV), ECLI:EU:T: 2016:411, paras 154–164.

The Commission also acted correctly in taking the turnover in the reference year (1990) **13.92** and converting that figure into ECUs on the basis of the average exchange rates for that same year. In the first case, the taking into account of the turnover achieved by each undertaking during the reference year, that is to say, the last complete year of the period of infringement found, enabled the Commission to assess the size and economic power of each undertaking and the scale of the infringement committed by each of them, those aspects being relevant for an assessment of the gravity of the infringement committed by each undertaking [...]. In the second place, taking into account, in order to convert the turnover figures in question into ECUs, the average exchange rates for the reference year adopted, enabled the Commission to prevent any monetary fluctuations occurring after the cessation of the infringement from affecting the assessment of the undertakings' relative size and economic power and the scale of the infringement committed by each of them and, accordingly, its assessment of the gravity of that infringement. The assessment of the gravity of an infringement must have regard to the economic reality as revealed at the time when that infringement was committed.

General Court 14 May 1998 (Enso Española v. Commission, T-348/94) [1998] ECR II-1875, para. 339.

See also General Court 19 March 2003 (CMA CGM and others v. Commission, T-213/00) [2003] ECR II-913, para. 460; General Court 11 March 1999 (Aristrain v. Commission, T-156/94) [1999] ECR II-645, paras 663 and 664.

Now, for the purposes of assessing the 'effective capacity of the undertakings concerned **13.93** to cause significant damage to the lysine market in the EEA' (para. 304 of the decision), which implies an assessment of the real importance of the undertakings on the market affected by their unlawful conduct, that is to say their influence on that market, total turnover is an imprecise guide. It is of course possible for a powerful undertaking with a multitude of different business activities to have only a very limited presence in certain specific markets, such as the lysine market. Similarly, an undertaking with a strong position in a geographical market outside the Community may have only a weak position in the Community or EEA market. In such cases, the mere fact that the undertaking in question has a high total turnover does not necessarily mean that it has a decisive influence in the market affected by the infringement. That is why the Court emphasised in paragraph 139 of its judgment in *Case C-185/95 P Baustahlgewebe v Commission* [1998] ECR I-8417 that although an undertaking's market shares cannot be a decisive factor in concluding that an undertaking belongs to a powerful economic entity, they are nevertheless relevant in determining the influence which it may exert on the market.

General Court 9 July 2003 (Cheil Jedang, T-220/00) [2003] ECR II-2473, para. 88.

13.94   To the extent that the Commission assessed the relative size of the applicant by reference to its total turnover and did not merely refer to the turnover in respect of the service covered by the cartel sanctioned, it erred in its application to the applicant of the 'relative size' factor […] as the relevant factor in the present case for imposing fines on the undertakings. It therefore erred in assessing the 'weight and importance of the undertakings in the relevant market and, therefore, the real impact of the offending conduct of each undertaking on competition'.

General Court 11 December 2003 (Adriatica, T-61/99) [2003] ECR II-5349, para. 196.

Confirmed in CoJ 16 February 2006 (Adriatica, C-111/04P) [2006] ECR I-22.

13.95   In analysing the 'effective economic capacity of the offenders to cause significant damage to competition', which involves an assessment of the actual importance of those undertakings in the market affected, that is to say, their influence on the market, their total turnover gives only an incomplete picture. The possibility cannot be ruled out that a powerful undertaking with many different activities may have only a limited presence in a specific product market. Similarly, the possibility cannot be ruled out that an undertaking occupying an important position in a geographical market outside the Community occupies only a weak position in the Community or EEA market. In such circumstances, the mere fact that the undertaking concerned has a high total turnover does not necessarily mean that it has a decisive influence on the market affected.

General Court 29 November 2005 (SNCZ, T-52/02) [2005] ECR II-5005, para. 65.

13.96   [T]he Commission may, when assessing the gravity of the infringement and setting the starting amount of the fine, base its assessment of the effective economic capacity of offenders to cause significant damage to other operators on data relating to turnover and market share in the market concerned, unless there are particular circumstances, such as the characteristics of that market, which are such as appreciably to diminish the significance of those data and to require, for the assessment of the influence of the undertakings on the market, other relevant factors to be taken into account.

General Court 15 March 2006 (Daiichi Pharmaceutical, T-26/02) [2006] ECR II-713, para. 61.

[T]he proportion of turnover derived from the goods in respect of which the infringement was committed is likely to give a fair indication of the scale of the infringement on the relevant market [...]. That turnover figure is likely to give a fair indication of the liability of each undertaking on those markets, since it constitutes an objective criterion which gives a proper measure of the harm which the offending conduct represents for normal competition and it is therefore a good indicator of the capacity of each undertaking to cause damage. **13.97**

In the light of those considerations, the Commission did not act in breach of the principle of proportionality by giving priority, when setting the starting amounts for the calculation of the fines to be imposed on Amann and Cousin, to the turnovers achieved on the relevant markets and for the products concerned.

General Court 28 April 2010 (Amann & Söhne, T-446/05) [2010] ECR II-1255, paras 188 and 189.

Thus, it has previously been held that, by relying exclusively on the worldwide turnover of the undertaking concerned and by not taking into account, therefore, the market shares in terms of volume of the undertakings in question on the market affected or even their turnover on that market, the Commission failed to apply the fourth and sixth paragraphs of Section 1A of the Guidelines. An assessment of the specific weight, that is to say, of the actual impact of the infringement committed by each of the undertakings, in fact involves establishing the scale of the infringement committed by each of them, rather than the importance of the undertaking in question in terms of its size or economic power. The proportion of turnover derived from the goods in respect of which the infringement was committed is likely to give a fair indication of the scale of the infringement on the relevant market [...]. **13.98**

General Court 28 April 2010 (Okley Threads Ltd v. Commission, T-448/05) [2010] ECR II-69, para. 66.

It should be borne in mind that, since the Commission is under no obligation to calculate the fine on the basis of amounts determined by reference to the overall turnover of the undertakings concerned, it is also under no obligation to ensure, where fines are imposed on a number of undertakings involved in the same infringement, that the final amounts of the fines resulting from its calculations for the undertakings concerned reflect every difference between those undertakings in terms of their overall turnover or their turnover on the relevant product market [...]. **13.99**

In that regard, it should be pointed out that, likewise, neither Article 15(2) of Regulation No 17 nor Article 23(3) of Council Regulation (EC) No 1/2003 of 16 December 2002 on the implementation of the rules on competition laid down in Articles [101 TFEU] and [102 TFEU] [...]; 'Regulation No 1/2003') requires that, where fines are imposed on a number of undertakings involved in the same infringement, the fine imposed on an undertaking which is small- or medium-sized must be no higher, as a percentage of turnover, than the fines imposed on the larger undertakings. It is clear from those provisions that, both for small- or medium-sized undertakings and for larger undertakings, account must be taken, in determining the amount of the fine, of the gravity and duration of the infringement. Where the Commission imposes on undertakings involved in a single infringement fines which are justified, for each of them, by reference to the gravity and duration of the infringement, it cannot be criticised on the ground that, for some of the undertakings, the fine is higher in relation to its turnover than that imposed on the others [...].

General Court 28 April 2010 (Okley Threads Ltd v. Commission, T-448/05) [2010] ECR II-69, paras 70 and 71.

13.100   [T]here is no valid reason to require that the turnover of a relevant market be calculated excluding certain production costs. As the Commission has rightly pointed out, there are in all industries costs inherent in the final product which the manufacturer cannot control but which nevertheless constitute an essential element of its business as a whole and which, therefore, cannot be excluded from its turnover when fixing the starting amount of the fine [...]. The fact that the price of copper constitutes an important part of the final price of plumbing tubes or that the risk of fluctuations of copper prices is far higher than for other raw materials does not invalidate that conclusion.

General Court 19 May 2010 (Outokumpu Oyj, T-20/05) [2010] ECR II-89, para. 77.

13.101   It has consistently been held that, in assessing the gravity of an infringement, regard must be had to a large number of factors, the nature and importance of which vary according to the type of infringement in question and the particular circumstances of the case. Those factors may, depending on the circumstances, include the volume and value of the goods in respect of which the infringement was committed and the size and economic power of the undertaking and, consequently, the influence which the undertaking was able to exert on the market [...].

While the Court of Justice has concluded from this that it is permissible, for the determination of the fine, to take into account both the undertaking's overall turnover, which is an indication of the size of the undertaking and its economic strength, and that part of the turnover which derives from the goods which are the subject of the infringement and which therefore is capable of giving an indication of the scale of the infringement, it has nevertheless recognised that the overall turnover of an undertaking gives only an approximate and imperfect indication of the size of that undertaking [...].

It has also pointed out on a number of occasions that it is important not to confer on one or the other of those figures an importance which is disproportionate in relation to the other factors to be assessed in relation to the gravity of the infringement [...].

The General Court did not, therefore, err in law or, in particular, infringe either the principle of proportionality or that of non-discrimination when it observed in paragraph 100 of the judgment under appeal that turnover, although vague and imperfect, is an adequate criterion for assessing the size and economic power of the undertakings concerned.

CoJ 8 December 2011 (KME Germany AG, KME France SAS and KME Italy SpA, C-389/10 P) [2011] ECR II-13125, paras 58–61.

Il s'ensuit que, même si la Commission ne devait pas évaluer la concurrence potentielle **13.102**
au regard de chacun des services invoqués par la requérante aux fins de la constatation de
l'infraction [...] elle aurait néanmoins dû examiner si la requérante était fondée à
soutenir que la valeur des ventes des services en cause devait être exclue du calcul de
l'amende en raison de l'absence de concurrence potentielle des parties au regard de ces
services.

À cet égard, il y a lieu de rappeler que, ainsi que la Cour l'a déjà jugé, la Commission
doit apprécier, dans chaque cas d'espèce et au vu de son contexte ainsi que des objectifs
poursuivis par le régime de sanctions établi par le règlement n° 1/2003, l'impact
recherché sur l'entreprise concernée, notamment en tenant compte d'un chiffre
d'affaires qui reflète la situation économique réelle de celle-ci durant la période au cours
de laquelle l'infraction a été commise [...].

Il est loisible, en vue de la détermination du montant de l'amende, de tenir compte
aussi bien du chiffre d'affaires global de l'entreprise qui constitue une indication, fût-elle
approximative et imparfaite, de la taille de celle-ci et de sa puissance économique que de
la part de ce chiffre qui provient des produits faisant l'objet de l'infraction et qui est donc
de nature à donner une indication de l'ampleur de celle-ci.

General Court 28 June 2016 (Portugal Telecom SGPS, SA v. European Commission,
T-208/13), ECLI:EU:T:2016:368, paras 230–232.

(d) Market share

Although an undertaking's market shares cannot be a decisive factor in concluding that **13.103**
an undertaking belongs to a powerful economic entity, they are nevertheless relevant in
determining the influence which it may exert on the market.

CoJ 17 December 1998 (Baustahlgewebe v. Commission, C-185/95 P) [1998] ECR
I-8417, para. 139.

However [...] it cannot be inferred from the case-law mentioned [*Judgment Baustahl-* **13.104**
gewebe v. Commission] that, in order to assess the influence of an undertaking on the
market or, to follow the wording used in the Guidelines, its effective economic capacity
to cause significant damage to other operators, that capacity must be measured by
requiring the Commission first to define the market and to assess its size, taking into
account the volume of that undertaking's turnover.

CoJ 3 September 2009 (William Prym GmbH Co. KG, Prym Consumer GmbH Co.
KG v. Commission, C-534/07P) [2009] ECR I-7415, para. 63.

(e) Size of the geographic market

[T]he size of the geographic market is not an autonomous criterion in the sense that **13.105**
only infringements affecting most of the Member States would be classifiable as 'very
serious'. Neither the EC Treaty [now Treaty on the functioning of the EU], nor
Regulation No 17 [now Regulation No 1/2003], nor the Guidelines, nor the case-law
support the conclusion that only geographically very extensive restrictions may be
classified as such [...].

Accordingly, the small size of the relevant geographic market does not preclude the infringement established in the present case being classified as 'very serious'.

General Court 8 September 2010 (Deltafina v. Commission, T-29/05) [2010] ECR II-4077, paras 240 and 241.

13.106 Admittedly, for the purpose of the application of Article [101(1) TFEU], the Commission is not required to show the actual anti-competitive effects of agreements or practices which have as their object the prevention, restriction or distortion of competition […].

Nevertheless, in accordance with settled case-law, Article [101(1) TFEU] is not applicable if the effect of a restrictive practice on intra-Community trade or on competition is not 'appreciable'. An agreement escapes the prohibition laid down in Article [101(1) TFEU] if it restricts competition or affects trade between Member States only insignificantly […].

Consequently, there is an obligation on the Commission to define the market in a decision applying Article [101 TFEU] where it is impossible, without such a definition, to determine whether the agreement or concerted practice at issue is liable to affect trade between Member States and has as its object or effect the prevention, restriction or distortion of competition […].

General Court 16 June 2011 (Ziegler SA, T-199/08) [2011] ECR II-3508, paras 43–45.

(f) Gravity of the infringement

13.107 In fixing the amount of the fines regard must be had to the duration of the infringements established and to all the factors capable of affecting the assessment of the gravity of the infringements, such as the conduct of each of the undertakings, the role played by each of them in the establishment of the concerted practices, the profit which they were able to derive from those practices, their size, the value of the goods concerned and the threat that infringements of that type pose to the objectives of the Community.

CoJ 7 June 1983 (SA Musique Diffusion Française, Joined Cases 100–103/80) [1983] ECR 1825, para 129.

13.108 Quite apart from the inherently very serious nature of any market-sharing or price-fixing agreement, the following factors are relevant to the Commission's assessment of the gravity of the infringement:

(a) The illegality of the quota agreement was compounded by the adoption of a fraudulent scheme of collusive bidding. The majority of business in this industry is accounted for by tendering procedures which envisage competitive bidding between the participants. The public authorities and contractors which commissioned the tendering procedure were entitled to expect that the bids submitted were not the result of secret collusion between the participants. In supply contracts over ECU 400 000, a statutory scheme of competitive bidding is prescribed by Community law in the public interest: the producers combined unlawfully to defeat the intention of the community legislature.

(b)   The unlawful scheme was aggressively pursued and implemented, not only with regard to ensuring the compliance of its members but also with a view to eliminating the only competitor of any importance outside the cartel, namely Powerpipe.

The Commission therefore considers that the present infringement constituted a very serious infringement of Article [101(1)] for which the likely fines would be at least ECU 20 million.

Commission 21 October 1998 (Pre-Insulated Pipe Cartel, IV/35.691), OJ 1999 L 24/1, para. 165.

[F]or the purposes of applying Article [101(1) TFEU], it is sufficient that the aim of an **13.109** agreement should be to restrict, prevent or distort competition, irrespective of the actual effects of that agreement.

Consequently, in the case of agreements reached at meetings of competing undertakings:

- that provision is infringed where those meetings have such an aim and are thus intended to organise artificially the operation of the market;
- the liability of a particular undertaking in respect of the infringement is properly established where it participated in those meetings with knowledge of their aim, even if it did not proceed to implement any of the measures agreed at those meetings.

The greater or lesser degree of regular participation by the undertaking in the meetings and of completeness of its implementation of the measures agreed is relevant not to the establishment of its liability but rather to the extent of that liability and thus to the severity of the penalty.

CoJ 15 October 2002 (Limburgse Vinyl Maatschappij and others. v. Commission, C-238/99P, C-244/99P, C-245/99P, C-247/99P, C-250/99P–C-252/99P and C-254/99P) [2002] ECR I-8375, paras 508–510.

See also CoJ 28 June 2005 (Dansk Rørindustrie and others v. Commission, Joined Cases C-189, 202, 205–208 and 213/02P) [2005] ECR I-5425, para. 145.

[T]he effect which an anti-competitive practice has is therefore not a conclusive **13.110** criterion for assessing the proper amount of a fine. Factors relating to the intentional aspect may be more significant than those relating to the effects, particularly where they relate to infringements which are intrinsically serious, such as price-fixing and market-sharing, factors which are present in this case.

CoJ 2 October 2003 (Thyssen Stahl v. Commission, C-194/99P) [2003] ECR I-10821, para. 118.

[I]n the Guidelines the Commission indicates that very serious infringements are **13.111** 'generally … horizontal restrictions such as price cartels and market-sharing quotas, or other practices which jeopardise the proper functioning of the single market, such as the partitioning of national markets' […]. It follows from this indicative description that agreements or concerted practices involving in particular, as in the present case, the parcelling out of clienteles on the one hand and the partitioning of the common market on the other may warrant being classified as very serious solely on the basis of their nature, without it being necessary for such conduct to cover a particular geographical area or have a particular impact. That conclusion is corroborated by the fact that [...] the indicative description of serious infringements mentions that 'these will more often than not be horizontal or vertical restrictions ... but more rigorously applied, with a wider market impact, and with effects in extensive areas of the common market', that of very serious infringements does not mention any requirement as to the actual market impact or the effects produced in a particular geographical area.

General Court 27 July 2005 (Brasserie Nationale SA, T-49/02–T-51/02) [2005] ECR II-3033, para. 178.

13.112   Article 23(3) of Regulation No 1/2003 provides that, in fixing the amount of the fine for infringements of Article 81(1) EC, regard is to be had both to the gravity and to the duration of the infringement.

It has consistently been held that the gravity of infringements of competition law must be assessed in the light of numerous factors, such as, inter alia, the particular circumstances of the case, its context and the dissuasive effect of fines, although no binding or exhaustive list of the criteria to be applied has been drawn up [...].

It has been acknowledged in case-law that, in order to determine the amount of a fine, it is necessary to take account of the duration of the infringements and of all the factors capable of affecting the assessment of their gravity, such as the conduct of each of the undertakings, the role played by each of them in the establishment of the concerted practices, the profit which they were able to derive from those practices, their size, the value of the goods concerned and the threat that infringements of that type pose to the European Union [...].

It has also been held that objective factors such as the content and duration of the anti-competitive conduct, the number of incidents and their intensity, the extent of the market affected and the damage to the economic public order must be taken into account. The analysis must also take into consideration the relative importance and market share of the undertakings responsible and also any repeated infringements [...].

This large number of factors requires that the Commission carry out a thorough examination of the circumstances of the infringement [...].

General Court 18 June 2013 (Fluorsid SpA and Minmet Financing Co. v. Commission, T-404/08) ECLI:EU:T:2013:321, paras 143–147.

(g)   Duration of the infringement

13.113   As regards the lack of evidence that there was an agreement during certain specific periods or, at least, the lack of evidence of its implementation by an undertaking during a given period, it should be recalled that the fact that such evidence has not been produced in relation to certain specific periods does not preclude the infringement from being regarded as established during a longer overall period than those periods, provided that such a finding is supported by objective and consistent indicia. In the context of an infringement extending over a number of years, the fact that the agreement is shown to have applied during different periods, which may be separated by longer or shorter periods, has no effect on the existence of the agreement, provided that the various actions which form part of the infringement pursue a single purpose and fall within the framework of a single and continuous infringement [...].

It is also apparent from the case-law that a party which tacitly approves of an unlawful initiative, without publicly distancing itself from the content of that initiative or reporting it to the administrative authorities, effectively encourages the continuation of the infringement and compromises its discovery. That complicity constitutes a passive mode of participation in the infringement which is capable of rendering the undertaking concerned liable [...].

CoJ 6 December 2012 (Commission v. Verhuizingen Coppens NV, C-441/11 P), ECLI:EU:C:2012:778, paras 72 and 73.

[T]he system of competition established by Articles 101 TFEU and 102 TFEU is **13.114** concerned with the economic consequences of agreements, or of any comparable form of concertation or coordination, rather than with their legal form. Consequently, in the case of agreements which have ceased to be in force, it is sufficient, in order for Article 101 TFEU to apply, that they produce their effects beyond the date on which the unlawful contacts formally come to an end. It follows that the duration of an infringement may be assessed by reference to the period during which the undertakings concerned engaged in conduct prohibited by that article [...]. In other words, the General Court could in theory have found there to be an infringement, for example, throughout the whole period in which the unlawful prices were applied, which would have led, in the present case, to a result objectively less favourable to the appellants' interests.

CoJ 30 May 2013 (Quinn Barlo Ltd and Others v. Commission, C-70/12 P), ECLI:EU:C:2013:351, para. 40.

In that regard, it should be observed that [...] the only way in which it can be concluded **13.115** that an undertaking has definitively ceased to belong to a cartel is if it has publicly distanced itself from the content of the cartel.

In addition, the Court of Justice has held that it is indeed the understanding which the other participants in a cartel have of the undertaking concerned that is of critical importance when assessing whether that undertaking had sought to distance itself from the unlawful agreement.

General Court 13 September 2013 (Total Raffinage Marketing v. Commission, T-566/08), ECLI:EU:T:2013:423, paras 372 and 373.

(h)   Consequences of the infringement

With regard to the first part, it must be observed next that the second subparagraph of **13.116** Article 15(2) [now Art. 23(2) Regulation No 1/2003] does not require (or indeed allow) any reference to the initial conditions in the first subparagraph, or indeed to the case-law of the Court of Justice on determination of the amount of the fines. It is apparent from that case-law that the gravity of infringements must be determined by reference to numerous factors such as, in particular, the particular circumstances of the case, its context and the dissuasive element of fines; moreover, no binding or exhaustive list of the criteria which must be applied has been drawn up.

CoJ 25 March 1996 (SPO and others v. Commission, C-137/95P) [1996] ECR I-1611, para. 54.

13.117   It came to reduce the gravity of the infringement after observing that 'the infringement had a limited actual impact on the market' and that, 'during the period of the infringement, the Greek Government encouraged the undertakings to keep fare increases within the inflation rates' and that consequently 'fares were kept at one of the lowest levels within the common market for maritime transport from one Member State to the other' […]. Furthermore, the Commission took account of the fact that the infringement 'produced its effect within a limited part of the common market, namely three of the Adriatic sea routes', a market that is small compared to other markets within the Community […].

General Court 11 December 2003 (Minoan Lines SA, T-66/99) [2003] ECR II-5515, para. 281.

13.118   It must be observed that, in line with the settled case-law, the gravity of an infringement is assessed in the light of numerous factors, such as the particular circumstances of the case, its context and the dissuasive effect of fines, in respect of which the Commission has a margin of discretion […].

In that context, when determining the gravity of the infringement, the Commission was legitimately able to take into consideration the fact that the undertakings took many precautions to prevent the cartel from being exposed and also the harm incurred by the general public. Those two factors do not, strictly speaking, constitute 'aggravating circumstances' as claimed by the applicants.

General Court 8 October 2008 (Schunk, T-69/04) [2008] ECR II-2567, paras 152 and 154.

13.119   Determination of the actual impact of a cartel on the market requires a comparison of the market situation resulting from the cartel with that which would have resulted from free competition. Such a comparison necessarily involves recourse to assumptions, given the multiplicity of variables capable of having an impact on the market.

In recital 629 of the decision at issue, the Commission emphasised the impossibility of determining what the evolution of prices during the period of the infringement would have been in the absence of the cartel. Having refuted the appellants' arguments, it provided evidence from which it concluded, in recital 673 of that decision, that the anti-competitive scheme had overall had an impact on the market, although it was not possible to quantify it precisely.

[…] In paragraphs 87 and 90 of its judgment [the General Court] checked, moreover, that the Commission had demonstrated to the requisite legal standard the actual impact of the cartel on the relevant market. However, it did so for the sake of completeness, as indicated in paragraph 84 of that judgment, and after correctly observing, in paragraph 82, that the actual impact of cartels on the market is not a decisive factor for determining the level of fines. […]

CoJ 8 December 2011 (KME Germany AG, KME France SAS and KME Italy SpA, C-389/10 P) [2011] ECR I-13125, paras 39–40 and 42.

(i) Deterrence

[I]t is in any event permissible for the Commission to increase the level of fines in order **13.120** to reinforce their deterrent effect.

General Court 30 September 2003 (Michelin, T-203/01) [2003] ECR II-4071, para. 254.

The Court has consistently held that the purpose of the multiplier for deterrence and of **13.121** taking into consideration, in that context, the size and global resources of the undertaking in question resides in the desired impact on that undertaking, and the penalty must not be negligible in the light, particularly, of the financial capacity of that undertaking [...]. The Court has also had occasion to state that disproportionate importance must not be attributed to turnover [...].

CoJ 18 July 2013 (The Dow Chemical Company and others v. Commission, case C-499/11 P), ECLI:EU:C:2013:482, para. 86.

In that regard, it must be recalled that 'deterrence' is one of the factors to be taken into **13.122** account in calculating the amount of the fine. In accordance with settled case-law, fines imposed for infringements of Article [101 TFEU], as laid down in Article 23(2) of Regulation No 1/2003, are designed to penalise the unlawful acts of the undertakings concerned and to deter both the undertakings in question and other economic operators from infringing, in future, the rules of European Union competition law. The link between, on the one hand, the size and overall resources of undertakings and, on the other, the need to ensure that the fine has a deterrent effect cannot be disputed [...].

It is the impact sought on the undertaking concerned which justifies the size and overall resources of that undertaking being taken into consideration in order to ensure that the fine has sufficient deterrent effect, and the penalty must not be negligible in the light, particularly, of the financial capacity of that undertaking [...].

It follows that, in order to impose a fine of an amount likely to deter the undertakings concerned from infringing, in future, the rules of European Union competition law, it is necessary to take into consideration the size and overall resources of those undertakings at the time when the contested decision is adopted [...].

CoJ 26 September 2013 (Alliance One International Inc. v. Commission, C-679/11 P), ECLI:EU:C:2013:606, paras 73–75.

5. Mitigating circumstances

Secondly, whilst it is indeed important that the applicant took steps to prevent fresh **13.123** infringements of Community competition law from being committed by members of its staff in the future, that circumstance does not alter the fact that an infringement has been found to have been committed in the present case. Faced with that fact, the [General Court] would point out that it has already held that the criteria set out in point

108 of the decision justify the general level of the fines imposed and that the criteria for achieving a fair balance between the amount of the fines imposed on the various undertakings concerned, set forth in point 109 of the decision, are sufficient and well founded. It must be added in this regard that, here again, the fact that in a previous case the Commission considered that, having regard to the factual circumstances, account should be taken of the steps taken by the undertaking in question to prevent fresh infringements of Community competition law from occurring in the future cannot oblige it to take account in the same way of similar measures in the present case, since the Commission emphasised in the decision (point 108) that the infringement of Article [101(1) TFEU] was particularly serious and had been committed intentionally and in conditions of great secrecy.

General Court 17 December 1991 (Hercules Chemicals v. Commission, T-7/89) [1991] ECR II-1711, para. 357.

See also General Court 12 December 2007 (BASF, T-101/05 and T-11/05) [2007] ECR II-4949, para. 52; General Court 15 March 2006 (BASF v. Commission, T-15/02) [2006] ECR II-497, paras 266 and 267.

13.124   Consequently, although the implementation of a compliance programme demonstrates the intention of the undertaking in question to prevent future infringements and thus better enables the Commission to accomplish its task of applying the principles laid down by the Treaty in competition matters and of influencing undertakings in that direction, the mere fact that in certain of its previous decisions the Commission took the implementation of a compliance programme into consideration as a mitigating factor does not mean that it is obliged to act in the same manner in this case.

General Court 14 May 1998 (Mo och Domsjö v. Commission, T-352/94) [1998] ECR II-1989, para. 417.

13.125   However, it is implicit that to benefit from this opportunity for a reduction, an undertaking must act in good faith and not attempt to deceive the Commission on a important aspect of the case [...].

Commission 21 October 1998 (Pre-Insulated Pipe Cartel, 35.691), OJ 1999 L 24/1, para. 180.

13.126   [O]ne circumstance that may indicate the adoption by an undertaking of a passive role within a cartel is where the undertaking's participation in cartel meetings is significantly more sporadic than that of the 'ordinary' members of the cartel [...]; another is where it enters the market affected by the infringement late, regardless of the length of its involvement in the infringement [...]; another is where a representative of another undertaking which has participated in the infringement makes an express declaration to such effect [...].

General Court 9 July 2003 (Cheil Jedang, T-220/00) [2003] ECR II-2473, para. 168.

[T]he mere fact that an undertaking which has cooperated with the Commission and **13.127** which for that reason has been given a reduction in the amount of its fine has successfully challenged the decision before the Community judicature cannot justify a fresh review of the size of the reduction granted to it.

General Court 11 December 2003 (Minoan Lines SA, T-66/99) [2003] ECR II-5515, para. 358.

Confirmed in CoJ 17 November 2005 (Minoan Lines, C-121/04 P), not published.

Marlines, Adriatica, Anek and Ventouris [had] played an exclusively 'follow-my-leader' **13.128** role in the infringement. These considerations [justified] a reduction of the fines by 15 per cent for those undertakings.

General Court 11 December 2003 (Ventouris SA, T-59/99) [2003] ECR II-5257, para. 212.

[T]he Commission is responsible for the excessive duration of the procedure. Although **13.129** that finding has no consequence regarding the legality of the contested decision, the fact remains that, [...], the [General Court] may consider whether a reduction of the fine imposed is justified.

General Court 16 December 2003 (FEG, T-5/00) [2003] ECR II-5761, para. 436.

The [General Court] did not err in law in holding [...] that although it was important **13.130** that LR A/S had taken measures to prevent future infringements of Community competition law by its personnel, that fact did not alter the reality of the infringement found in the present case. The [General Court] was correct to hold that that fact did not in itself mean that the Commission was obliged to reduce the appellant's fine on account of an attenuating circumstance.

CoJ 28 June 2005 (Dansk Rørindustrie and others v. Commission, Joined Cases C-189, 202, 205–208 and 213/02P) [2005] ECR I-5425, para. 373.

In support of its claim, the applicant argues that there was no difference in the **13.131** willingness of the parties to the cartel to cooperate and that it fully cooperated with the Commission.

That circumstance, supposing it to be established, is, however, irrelevant. The mere willingness of an undertaking to cooperate is of no significance. Section D.2, first indent, of the Leniency Notice provides for a reduction only in favour of an undertaking which 'provides the Commission with information, documents or other evidence which contribute to establishing the infringement' and not in favour of an undertaking which is merely willing to cooperate, or limits itself to cooperating, with the Commission.

Similarly, according to consistent case-law, a reduction in the fine on account of cooperation during the administrative procedure is justified only if the conduct of the undertaking enabled the Commission to establish the existence of an infringement with less difficulty, and, where appropriate, bring it to an end [...].

CoJ 18 July 2005 (Scandinavian Airlines System, T-241/01) [2005] ECR II-2917, paras 211–213.

13.132   Although, under its Guidelines [...], the Commission may, in respect of aggravating circumstances, increase a fine in order to exceed the amount of gains improperly made as a result of the infringement, that possibility does not mean that the Commission is then under an obligation to establish in every case, for the purpose of determining the amount of the fine, the financial advantage linked to the infringement found to have been committed [...]. In other words, the absence of such an advantage cannot be regarded as an attenuating circumstance.

General Court 29 November 2005 (SNCZ, T-52/02) [2005] ECR II-5005, para. 91.

13.133   [T]he Guidelines, which have since then expressly contemplated that non-implementation in practice of an offending agreement should be taken into account as an attenuating circumstance. [T]he Commission may not depart from the rules which it has imposed on itself. Moreover, the greater or lesser degree of implementation by a member of the cartel of the measures agreed with the other members, although not relevant to the establishment of its liability, may have a bearing on the extent of that liability and thus on the severity of the penalty.

   Therefore, in holding that it was not required to take into account, as an attenuating circumstance, the breach of the obligations assumed by the applicant in the [...] cartel, the Commission infringed the Guidelines.

General Court 15 March 2006 (Daiichi Pharmaceutical, T-26/02) [2006] ECR II-713, paras 105 and 106.

13.134   [I]n view of the fact that the actual effects of the infringement have been only partly demonstrated, the [General Court] considers that the amount of the fine determined according to the gravity of the infringement must be reduced from EUR 35 million to EUR 30 million.

General Court 5 April 2006 (Degussa, T-279/02) [2006] ECR II-897, para. 254.

13.135   In order to benefit from a reduction on grounds of cooperation, the conduct of the undertaking concerned must facilitate the Commission's task of finding and bringing to an end infringements of the Community competition rules [...].

   The applicant's assertion that 'the undisputed facts constituted an infringement of Article 65(1) CS' was, in the circumstances of the case [...], of no assistance to the Commission.

   Moreover, it follows from the case-law of the Court of Justice that a reduction under the Leniency Notice can be justified only where the information provided and, more generally, the conduct of the undertaking concerned might be considered to demonstrate a genuine spirit of cooperation on its part [...].

   In its reply to the 2006 statement of objections, the applicant initially vigorously challenged the possibility that the Commission could apply Article 65(1) CS in the present case and impute liability for the infringement of that article to the applicant, denying – for the first time since the commencement of the initial procedure – any validity of the statement of 23 July 1997, and then added at the end a statement which was supposed to demonstrate its cooperation but which, in reality, is intrinsically ambiguous and misleading.

The applicant's conduct, which reflects a strategy of seeking to reconcile contradictory aims, cannot be considered to demonstrate a genuine spirit of cooperation on its part.

General Court 1 July 2009 (ThyssenKrupp Stainless AG v. Commission, T-24/07) [2009] ECR II-2309, paras 309–313.

Section 3 of the Guidelines provides for a reduction in the basic amount where there are **13.136** 'particular mitigating circumstances', such as an exclusively passive or 'follow-my-leader' role in the infringement, non-implementation in practice of the collusive agreements or practices, termination of the infringement as soon as the Commission intervenes or other circumstances which are not referred to explicitly.

[W]ith regard to [...] the purported non-implementation of the agreements reached at the meetings, it must be considered whether the arguments put forward by BST are capable of showing that, during the period in which BST was party to the unlawful agreements, it actually avoided implementing those agreements by adopting competitive conduct on the market or, at the very least, that it clearly and substantially breached the obligations relating to the implementation of the cartel to the point of disrupting its very operation [...]. [...]

It should be recalled that a passive role implies that the undertaking adopted a 'low profile', that is to say, that it did not actively participate in the creation of any anti-competitive agreements [...].

[O]ne circumstance that may be taken into account as indicating the adoption by an undertaking of a passive role within a cartel is where the undertaking's attendance at cartel meetings is significantly more sporadic than that of the 'ordinary' cartel members; another is where it enters the market affected by the infringement late, regardless of the length of its involvement in the infringement; yet another is where express statements to that effect are made by representatives of other undertakings which participated in the infringement [...].

General Court 28 April 2010 (Belgian Sewing Thread (BST) v. Commission, T-452/05) [2010] ECR II-1373, paras 104, 111, 119 and 120.

[T]he Commission is not required to recognise the existence of an attenuating **13.137** circumstance consisting of non-implementation of a restrictive agreement unless the undertaking relying on that circumstance is able to show that it clearly and substantially opposed the implementation of the agreement, to the point of disrupting the very functioning of it, and that it did not give the appearance of adhering to the agreement and thereby incite other undertakings to implement the agreement in question. It would be too easy for undertakings to reduce the risk of being required to pay a heavy fine if they were able to take advantage of an unlawful agreement and then benefit from a reduction in the fine on the ground that they had played only a limited role in implementing the infringement, when their attitude encouraged other undertakings to act in a way that was more harmful to competition [...]. [...]

The termination of the infringement can, logically, constitute an attenuating circumstance only if there are reasons to suppose that the undertakings concerned were encouraged to cease their anti-competitive conduct by the interventions in question, the situation in which the infringement has already come to an end before the date on which the Commission first intervenes not being covered by that provision in the Guidelines [...].

General Court 8 September 2010 (Deltafina v Commission, T-29/05) [2010] ECR II-4077, paras 350 and 355.

6. Aggravating circumstances

13.138   [...] Section 2 of the Guidelines sets out a non-exhaustive list of aggravating circumstances which may lead to an increase in the basic amount of the fine. Among them is the 'role of leader in, or instigator of, the infringement'.

In the present case, it is clear from the decision that the Commission took three essential factors into consideration before concluding that ADM had acted as ringleader in the infringement: the sales at low prices which it made until June 1992 and again at the beginning of 1993, the threats which it made on a number of occasions to smaller producers and lastly its attendance at several bilateral meetings with Ajinomoto the purpose of which was to discuss the strategic direction of the cartel and to have the other producers agree to price and quota initiatives. In addition, it has been asserted that ADM was the inspiration behind the structure of the cartel, drawing on its past experience in another cartel concerning citric acid. Those factors must be assessed in the particular context of the present case and especially in light of the market position enjoyed by the undertakings and the resources at their disposal.

General Court 9 July 2003 (Archer Daniels Midland, T-224/00) [2003] ECR II-2597, paras 240 and 241.

13.139   [A]n increase in the fine by reference to the duration of the infringement is not limited to a situation in which there is a direct relation between the duration and serious harm caused to the Community objectives referred to in the competition rules.

General Court 30 September 2003 (Michelin, T-203/01) [2003] ECR II-4071, para. 278.

13.140   [T]he Commission may impose a heavier fine on an undertaking which occupies a decisive position within the market and where the impact of its actions on the market is more significant than that of the actions of other undertakings committing the same infringement, without violating the principle of equal treatment by so doing.

General Court 11 December 2003 (Minoan Lines SA, T-66/99) [2003] ECR II-5515, para. 284.

13.141   The Guidelines provide that account must be taken, as an aggravating circumstance, of the need to increase the penalty in order to exceed the amount of gains improperly made as a result of the infringement, when it is objectively possible to estimate that amount. As the Commission maintained, it follows that where that aggravating circumstance is found to exist the basic amount will be increased where on an objective estimate of such improper gains it can be established that the level of the basic amount is insufficient to neutralise the profit which an undertaking derives from the infringement.

In those circumstances, the Guidelines do not entail the inherent risk that the profit will be taken into account twice.

CoJ 28 June 2005 (Dansk Rørindustrie and others v. Commission, Joined Cases C–189, 202, 205–208 and 213/02P) [2005] ECR I-5425, paras 294 and 295.

Furthermore, as regards the Commission's claims regarding the possibility that under-   **13.142**
takings may abuse the above procedure by making requests, merely as delaying tactics, for protection under LPP which are clearly unfounded, or by opposing, without objective justification, any cursory look at the documents during an investigation, the Court would point out that the Commission has the means, where appropriate, to discourage and penalise such conduct. In fact, such conduct may be penalised under Article 23(1) of Regulation No 1/2003 (and previously under Article 15(1) of Regulation No 17) or be taken into account as aggravating circumstances when calculating any fine imposed in the context of a decision imposing a penalty under the competition rules.

General Court 17 September 2007 (Akzo Nobel Chemicals Ltd., T-125/03 and T-253/03) [2007] ECR II-3523, para. 89.

It should be pointed out, at this stage, that the [...] challenges [...] have been rejected   **13.143**
pursuant to the case-law under which facts which an undertaking has expressly acknowledged during the administrative procedure are to be regarded as established, that undertaking being barred from putting forward pleas disputing those facts in proceedings before the [General Court] [...].

That being so, there are no grounds for cancelling the minimum reduction of 10 per cent allowed to Schunk under the second indent of paragraph 2 of Section D of the Leniency Notice and the Commission's counterclaim must therefore be rejected [...].

In its pleadings, the Commission refers to *Tokai I*[...], in which the [General Court] upheld a claim that the Commission's fine should be increased, even though the applicant's arguments did not call into question the facts which had expressly been accepted. The [General Court] stated that the Commission, contrary to any expectation which it might reasonably have based on the applicant's objective cooperation in the administrative procedure, had to draw up and submit a defence to the [General Court] dealing with a challenge concerning illegal acts which it was entitled to consider that the applicant would no longer call in question. [...]

The fact that the Commission was constrained to draw up a defence dealing with a challenge to facts which it was entitled to consider that the applicant would no longer call in question is not such as to justify, in the light of the two exclusive criteria for determining the amount of the fine, an increase of that fine. In other words, the expenses incurred by the Commission as a result of the proceedings before the [General Court] are not a criterion for determining the amount of the fine and must only be taken into account when applying the provisions of the Rules of Procedure relating to costs.

General Court 8 October 2008 (Schunk, T-69/04) [2008] ECR II-2567, paras 258–260 and 262.

13.144 [T]he Commission may, in determining the amount of the increase for repeat infringement, take account of evidence tending to confirm the propensity of the undertaking concerned to ignore the competition rules, including the time which has elapsed between the infringements in question.
General Court 19 May 2010 (Outokumpu Oyj, T-20/05) [2010] ECR II-89, para. 68.

13.145 While the evidence relied on by the Commission [...] demonstrates that Deltafina played an active and direct role in the processors' cartel, it does not suffice to establish that that company represented a significant driving force in the cartel or even that its role was more important than that of any of the Spanish processors. It should be noted in particular that, even though the Commission was entitled [...] to attribute the whole of the infringement in question to Deltafina, the fact nevertheless remains that, during a period of infringement lasting over five years, Deltafina was present at only a very limited number of meetings of the processors' cartel at which the unlawful agreements were concluded – at most, four meetings out of a total of almost 30 – and that its participation in exchanges of correspondence and information between the members of the cartel was relatively limited.

Moreover, there is nothing in the file to show that Deltafina took any initiatives to create the cartel or that it was instrumental in securing the participation of any of the Spanish processors. [...].
General Court 8 September 2010 (Deltafina v. Commission, T-29/05) [2010] ECR II-4077, paras 333 and 334.

See also General Court 14 July 2016 (Parker Hannifin Manufacturing Srl, formerly Parker ITR Srl and Parker-Hannifin Corp v. European Commission, T-146/09 RENV) ECLI:EU:T:2016:411, paras 151–154 (increase for aggravating circumstances to relate to period during which infringing activity under investigated company's control).

7. Principle of proportionality

(a) Profit derived from (illegal) practices

13.146 Nor, second, can the applicant plead infringement of the principle of proportionality on the ground that the Commission did not calculate its fine according to the profit it had made on the relevant market.
General Court 20 March 2002 (LR AF 1998 A/S, formerly Løgstør Rør A/S v. Commission, T-23/99) [2002] ECR II-1705, para. 307.

[W]ith regard to […] this plea, alleging that the Commission infringed the principle of **13.147** proportionality by not taking account of the fact that the applicant earned almost no profit from the product in question and that it had even, in some years, incurred losses in that segment of the market, it must be borne in mind that, although the amount of the fine imposed must be proportionate to the duration of the infringement and the other factors capable of affecting the assessment of the gravity of the infringement, such as the profit that the undertaking was able to derive from its practices […], the fact that an undertaking did not benefit from the infringement cannot, according to the case-law, preclude the imposition of a fine, since otherwise it would cease to have a deterrent effect […].

It follows that the Commission is not required, in order to fix fines, to take into consideration any lack of benefit from the infringement […].

General Court 29 November 2005 (Heubach, T-64/02) [2005] ECR II-5137, paras 184 and 185.

(b)   Assessment conduct undertaking in relation to gravity infringement

In fixing the amount of the fines regard must be had to the duration of the infringe- **13.148** ments established and to all factors capable of affecting the assessment of the gravity of the infringements, such as the conduct of each of the undertakings, the role played by each of them in the establishment of the concerted practices, the profit which they were able to derive from those practices, their size, the value of the goods concerned and the threat that infringements of that type pose to the objectives of the Community.

CoJ 7 June 1983 (SA Musique Diffusion Française v. Commission, Joined Cases 100/80–103/80) [1983] ECR 1825, para. 129.

[T]he Court observes, first, that it has held that where an infringement has been **13.149** committed by several undertakings, the relative gravity of the participation of each of them must be examined […]. However, the [General Court] found […] that the Commission had correctly established the role played by Anic in the infringement during the period of its participation and that it took proper account of that role in determining the amount of the fine to be imposed on it.

CoJ 8 July 1999 (Commission v. Anic, C-49/92 P) [1999] ECR I-4125, para. 150.

[W]here an infringement has been committed by several undertakings, the Commis- **13.150** sion must take account of the role played by each of the undertakings in the infringe- ment […] and must, therefore, examine the relative gravity of the participation of each of them […]. In particular, the fact that an undertaking has not taken part in all aspects of an anti-competitive scheme or that it has played only a minor role in the aspects in which it did participate must be taken into consideration when the gravity of the infringement is assessed and if and when it comes to determining the fine […]. […]

In this case, it is clear from the Decision that the Commission concluded that the infringement was a serious breach of Community competition rules […] after recognis- ing […] that the infringement had a limited actual impact on the market and thus after accepting the undertakings' argument that they had not applied in full all the specific price agreements and that they had engaged, during the period of the infringement, in price competition through discounting. The Commission also expressly acknowledged that the Greek Government, during the period of the infringement, had encouraged the undertakings to keep fare increases within the inflation rates and that fares had consequently been kept at one of the lowest levels within the common market for maritime transport from one Member State to the other. The Commission also agreed [...] that the infringement had produced effects within a limited part of the common market, namely three of the Adriatic Sea routes, at the same time emphasising that, even if all Greece-Italy routes were taken into account, the market was still small compared to other markets within the European Union. Lastly, the Commission took account [...] of the figures for the number of passengers, cars and trailers transported during 1996 in this market by comparison with the other shipping routes of the European Union. [...]

The Commission therefore punished in like manner the undertakings which participated in two infringements and those which participated in only one of them, in disregard of the principle of proportionality. However, for reasons of equity and proportionality, it is important that the companies whose involvement is limited to a single cartel are punished less severely than the companies which participated in all the agreements in issue. The Commission cannot punish with the same degree of severity the companies which the decision charges with two infringements and those which, like the applicant, are charged with only one of them.

General Court 11 December 2003 (Ventouris SA, T-59/99) [2003] ECR II-5257, paras 200, 206 and 219.

See also CoJ 7 June 1983 (SA Musique Diffusion Française v. Commission, Joined Cases 100/80–103/80) [1983] ECR 1825, paras 120 and 129; General Court 17 December 1991 (Hercules Chemicals v. Commission, T-7/89) [1991] ECR II-1711, para. 110; General Court 8 July 2008 (AC-Treuhand AG, T-99/04) [2008] ECR II-1501, para. 132.

13.151   [I]t is clear from the use of the expression 'in some cases' and the term 'in particular' in the Guidelines that weighting according to the individual size of undertakings is not a systematic stage in the calculation which the Commission has imposed on itself but falls within the scope of the flexibility which it has granted itself in cases where it is called for. It is appropriate in this context to refer to the case-law according to which the Commission enjoys a discretion enabling it to take account or not take account of certain factors when determining the amount of the fines which it intends imposing, having regard in particular to the circumstances of the case [...].

General Court 8 July 2004 (JFE Engineering, T-67/00) [2004] ECR II-2501, para. 553.

13.152   Furthermore, in assessing the cooperation given by members of a cartel, only a manifest error of assessment on the part of the Commission is open to censure, since the Commission enjoys a broad discretion in assessing the quality and usefulness of the cooperation provided by an undertaking, especially in comparison with the contributions made by other undertakings [...]. In exercising that discretion, however, the Commission cannot disregard the principle of equal treatment. [...]

It must be held that, in the light of the additional efforts made by BST, it was rewarded with a reduction in its fine which was only 5 per cent higher than the reduction granted to Amann, Gütermann and Zwicky, even though they did not make any such efforts during the administrative procedure. The difference between the reduction granted to BST and the reduction granted to Amann, Gütermann and Zwicky is unreasonably narrow.

For all of those reasons, it must be held that the 20 per cent reduction granted to BST for its cooperation is insufficient and that, accordingly, the Commission made a manifest error of assessment.

General Court 28 April 2010 (Belgian Sewing Thread (BST) v. Commission, T-452/05) [2010] ECR II-1373, paras 142, 150 and 151.

[A]ccording to the Guidelines, agreements or concerted practices involving in particu- **13.153** lar, as in the present case, price-fixing and customer-sharing may be classified as 'very serious' on the basis of their nature alone, without it being necessary for such conduct to have a particular impact or cover a particular geographic area. That conclusion is supported by the fact that, whilst the description of 'serious' infringements expressly mentions market impact and effects over extensive areas of the common market, the description of 'very serious' infringements makes no mention of a requirement that there be an impact or that there be effects in a particular geographic area […].

General Court 19 May 2010 (KME Germany AG v. Commission, T-25/05) [2010] ECR II-91, para. 83.

(c) Relation fine undertakings involved in the same infringement

As the Commission is not obliged to calculate the fine by reference to amounts based on **13.154** the turnover of the undertakings concerned, it is likewise not required to ensure, where fines are imposed on several undertakings involved in the same infringement, that the final amount of the fines produced by the calculation for the undertakings concerned, reflects any distinction between them regarding their total turnover or their turnover in the relevant product market […].

In that connection, it must be pointed out that Article 15(2) of Regulation No 17 [now Art. 23(2) of Regulation 1/2003] likewise does not require that, where fines are imposed on several undertakings involved in the same infringement, the fine imposed on a small- or medium-sized undertaking must not be greater, as a percentage of turnover, than those imposed on the larger undertakings. It is clear from that provision that, both for small- or medium-sized undertakings and for larger undertakings, account must be taken, in determining the amount of the fine, of the gravity and duration of the infringement.

General Court 29 November 2005 (SNCZ, T-52/02) [2005] ECR II-5005, paras 73 and 74.

See also General Court 20 March 2002 (Dansk Rørindustri v. Commission, T-21/99) [2002] ECR II-1681, para. 202; CoJ 28 June 2005 (Dansk Rørindustrie and others v. Commission, Joined Cases C-189, 202, 205–208 and 213/02P) [2005] ECR I-5425, para. 312.

13.155   [W]here an infringement has been committed by several undertakings, the relative gravity of the participation of each of them must be examined [...] in order to determine whether there are any aggravating or attenuating circumstances relating to them.

That conclusion follows logically from the principle that penalties must fit the offence, so that an undertaking may be penalised only for acts imputed to it individually, a principle applying in any administrative procedure that may lead to the imposition of sanctions under Community competition law [...].

General Court 29 November 2005 (Union Pigments, T-62/02) [2005] ECR II-5057, paras 118 and 119.

13.156   The final amount of the fine is not, in principle, an appropriate factor in assessing the possible lack of proportionality of the fine as regards the importance of the participants in the cartel. That final amount is set, inter alia, on the basis of various factors linked to the individual conduct of the undertaking in question, such as the duration of the infringement, the existence of aggravating or attenuating circumstances and the degree to which that undertaking cooperated, but not to its market share or turnover.

Conversely, the starting amount of the fine is, in the instant case, a relevant factor in assessing the possible lack of proportionality of the fine as regards the importance of the participants in the cartel.

General Court 4 July 2006 (Hoek Loos v. Commission, T-304/02) [2006] ECR II-1887, paras 85 and 86.

See also General Court 29 April 2004 (Tokai Carbon and others, T-236/01 and others) [2004] ECR II-1181, paras 244–249.

13.157   An undertaking whose liability is established in relation to several branches of a cartel contributes more to the effectiveness and the seriousness of the cartel than an offender involved in only one branch of it. Thus, the first undertaking commits a more serious infringement than the second.

In this respect, it must be emphasised that, in accordance with the principle of individual liability and that penalties should fit the individual offender, the Commission is required to take into account, when assessing the relative seriousness of the participation of each offender in a cartel, the fact that certain offenders may not be held liable, [...], for all the branches of that cartel.

With regard to the application of the Guidelines, that assessment necessarily has to be made at the stage when a specific starting amount is set, since the taking into account of attenuating circumstances only allows the basic amount of the fine to be adjusted by reference to the arrangements for the offender's implementation of the cartel. An offender who is not held responsible for certain branches of that cartel cannot have been involved in the implementation of those aspects. The infringement of the rules of competition law is, owing to the limited scope of the infringement established in respect of that offender, less serious than that attributed to offenders who participated in all aspects of the infringement.

General Court 19 May 2010 (IMI v. Commission, T-18/05) [2010] ECR II-1769, paras 162–164.

See also General Court 19 May 2010 (Chalkor AE v. Commission, T-21/05) [2010] ECR II-1895, paras 99–101.

(d) New calculation method for fine

The Court finds that it cannot be inferred that the fine imposed by the contested **13.158** decision is disproportionate merely because, if the new method for calculating fines – as set out in those guidelines, which are not applicable to the facts of the present case – were applied, the fine would be lower.

That finding merely reflects the margin of discretion enjoyed by the Commission for the purposes of establishing, in compliance with the requirements set out in Regulation No 17 and Regulation No 1/2003, the method which it intends to apply in order to calculate the fines and thus to give practical effect to the competition policy for which it is responsible.

General Court 28 April 2010 (Gütermann AG and Zwicky & Co., T-456/05 and T-457/05) [2010] ECR II-1443, paras 285 and 286.

8. Equality of treatment

In order to take account of the difference in size of the undertakings which took part in **13.159** the infringement, the Commission divided the undertakings into four categories according to their relative importance in the market in the Community, subject to adjustment where appropriate to take account of the need to ensure effective deterrence [...].

As regards the determination of the starting-points for each category, the Commission stated, following a question put by the Court, that these amounts reflect the importance of each undertaking in the pre-insulated pipe sector, having regard to its size and weight compared with ABB and in the context of the cartel. For that purpose, the Commission took into account not only their turnover on the relevant market but also the relative importance which the members of the cartel ascribed to each of them, as evidenced by the quotas allocated within the cartel [...], and by the results obtained and forecast in 1995 [...].

In addition, the Commission made a further upward adjustment of the starting point for the calculation of the fine to be imposed on ABB, to ECU 50 million, to take account of its position as one of Europe's largest industrial combines [...].

In that context, it must be held, having regard to all the relevant factors taken into consideration in fixing the specific starting points, that the difference between the starting point chosen for the applicant and that chosen for ABB is objectively justified. Since the Commission is not required to ensure that the final amounts of the fines for the undertakings concerned to which its calculations lead reflect every difference between them in terms of turnover, the applicant cannot criticise the Commission because the starting point taken for it resulted in a fine higher, in percentage of total turnover, than the fine imposed on ABB.

Furthermore, the General Court has already held that the Commission, in so far as, in determining the amount of the fines, it relied in the present case on the turnover of an undertaking on the relevant market, is not obliged to take into account, in assessing the gravity of the infringement, the relationship between the total turnover of an undertaking and the turnover produced by the goods which are the subject-matter of the infringement [...]. A fortiori, therefore, the Commission is not obliged to set the fines according to the total turnover of the undertakings concerned in a situation such as the present case, where it chose to take a series of relevant factors into account in assessing the gravity and duration of the infringement and, in particular, in determining the starting points for the calculation of the fines.

General Court 20 March 2002 (LR AF 1998 A/S, formerly Løgstør Rør A/S v. Commission, T-23/99) [2002] ECR II-1705, paras 295–299.

13.160   [W]here an undertaking has acted in breach of Article [101(1) TFEU], it cannot escape being penalised altogether on the ground that other traders have not been fined, even where, as in this case, those traders' circumstances are not the subject of proceedings before the Court [...].

General Court 16 December 2003 (FEG, T-5/00) [2003] ECR II-5761, para. 430.

See also CoJ 31 March 1993 (Ahlström Osakeyhtiö and others v. Commission, C-89/85, C-104/85, C-114/85, C-116/85, C-117/85, C-125/85 and C-129/85) [1993] ECR I-1307, para. 197.

13.161   As regards the division of the members of the cartel into several categories [...] although such an approach by the Commission ignores the differences in size between undertakings in the same category, it cannot in principle be condemned. The Commission is not required, when determining fines, to ensure, where fines are imposed on a number of undertakings involved in the same infringement, that the final amounts of the fines resulting from its calculations for the undertakings concerned reflect any distinction between the undertakings concerned in terms of their overall turnover [...].

The Commission did not therefore err in fact or in law in dividing the applicants into categories when determining the gravity of the infringement.

The fact none the less remains that such a division by categories must comply with the principle of equal treatment, according to which it is prohibited to treat similar situations differently and different situations in the same way, unless such treatment is objectively justified [...]. Likewise, the Guidelines provide in point 1.A, sixth indent, that a 'considerable' disparity between the sizes of the undertakings committing infringements of the same type may justify a differentiation for the purposes of the assessment of the gravity of the infringement. Furthermore, according to the case-law, the amount of the fine must at least be proportionate in relation to the factors taken into account in the assessment of the gravity of the infringement [...].

Consequently, where the Commission divides the undertakings concerned into categories for the purpose of setting the amount of the fines, the thresholds for each of the categories thus identified must be coherent and objectively justified [...].

In that regard, the Commission, in stating in the introduction to the Guidelines that the margin of discretion which it enjoys when setting the amount of fines must follow 'a coherent and non-discriminatory policy which is consistent with the objectives pursued in penalising infringements of the competition rules', undertook to be guided by those principles when it determines the amount of fines imposed for infringements of the competition rules.

General Court 29 April 2004 (Tokai Carbon and others, Cases T-236/01 and others) [2004] ECR II-1181, paras 217–221.

13.162

Secondly, [...], although it is true that the Commission is not required, when determining the amounts of fines, to ensure, where fines are imposed on a number of undertakings involved in the same infringement, that the final amounts of the fines reflect any distinction between the undertakings concerned in terms of their overall turnover [...], the fact remains that the classification of undertakings by category, in accordance with the principle of equal treatment, must be objectively justified, since that requirement has to be interpreted more strictly where that classification is designed, not to determine the specific weight of the offending conduct of each undertaking, but to set the rate of increase in the amount of the fine determined according to the gravity of the infringement in order to ensure that the fine has a sufficient deterrent effect, an operation which serves a different and separate purpose and is based on an objective assessment of the undertakings' capacity to mobilise the funds necessary for the payment of the fine.

Consequently, the General Court considers it necessary, in the exercise of its unlimited jurisdiction, to reduce the rate of increase in the amount of the fine determined according to the gravity of the infringement applied to Degussa, so that that rate reflects the significant difference in size between Degussa and Aventis (see, to that effect, *Tokai Carbon and others v. Commission* [...]).

General Court 5 April 2006 (Degussa, T-279/02) [2006] ECR II-897, paras 338 and 339.

13.163

[W]here, in a case concerning an infringement involving several different undertakings, the Commission adopts, within the framework laid down by the case-law, a certain method for determining whether it is appropriate to attribute liability both to the subsidiaries which materially committed that infringement and to their parent companies, it must – save in specific circumstances – rely for such determination on the same criteria in the case of all those undertakings. The Commission is bound by the principle of equal treatment, which, according to settled case-law, requires that comparable situations must not be treated differently, and different situations must not be treated in the same way, unless such treatment is objectively justified [...].

General Court 12 October 2011 (Alliance One International, Inc., T-41/05) [2011] ECR II-7101, para. 123.

See also CoJ 18 July 2013 (The Dow Chemical Company and Others v. Commission, case C-499/11 P), ECLI:EU:C:2013:482, para. 86.

9. *Ne bis in idem*

13.164   The possibility of concurrent sanctions need not mean that the possibility of two parallel proceedings pursuing different ends is unacceptable. [...] the acceptability of a dual procedure of this kind follows in fact from the special system of the sharing of jurisdiction between the Community and the Member States with regard to cartels. If, however, the possibility of two procedures being conducted separately were to lead to the imposition of consecutive sanctions, a general requirement of natural justice, such as that expressed at the end of the second paragraph of Article 90 of the ECSC Treaty, demands that any previous punitive decision must be taken into account in determining any sanction which is to be imposed. In any case, so long as no regulation has been issued under Article [103(2)(e) TFEU], no means of avoiding such a possibility is to be found in the general principles of Community law [...].

CoJ 13 February 1969 (Walt Wilhelm, 14/68) [1969] ECR 1, para. 11.

13.165   The [General Court] cannot therefore uphold the applicants' argument that, by imposing a fine on them for their involvement in a cartel already sanctioned by the American and Canadian authorities, the Commission infringed the principle of *non bis in idem*, according to which a second penalty may not be imposed on the same person in respect of the same infringement.

   In this connection, suffice it to recall that the Community judicature has held that an undertaking may be made the defendant to two parallel sets of proceedings concerning the same infringement and, thus, incur concurrent sanctions, one imposed by the competent authority of the Member State in question, the other a Community sanction. That possibility is justified where the two sets of proceedings pursue different ends [...].

General Court 9 July 2003 (Archer Daniels Midland, T-224/00) [2003] ECR II-2597, paras 88 and 89.

13.166   In so far as the [General Court] found that the judgments in the United States and Canada applied to a larger group of agreements and concerted practices, it cannot be found that that Court distorted the evidence. The reference in paragraph 102 of the judgment under appeal to 'judgments delivered in the United States and Canada [which] related to a larger group of agreements and concerted practices' must be read in the light of paragraph 5 of *Boehringer Mannheim v. Commission* which refers to a 'wider body of facts' and to which the General Court referred in the preceding paragraph. It must therefore be understood as meaning that those judgments also apply to the cartel in respect of citric acid, which is not in issue in the contested decision.

CoJ 18 May 2006 (Archer, C-397/03P) [2006] ECR I-4429, para. 57.

13.167   More specifically, the Court of Justice recalled that the application of the principle *non bis in idem* was subject to a threefold condition of identity of the facts, unity of the offender and unity of the protected legal interest. That principle therefore precludes a penalty being imposed on the same person more than once for the same unlawful conduct for the purpose of protecting the same legal asset [...].

General Court 18 June 2008 (Hoechst GmbH v. Commission, T-410/03) [2008] ECR II-881, para. 600.

See also CoJ 7 January 2004 (Aalborg Portland, C-204/00P) [2004] ECR I-123, para. 338; General Court 17 May 2011 (Arkema France, T-343/08) [2011] ECR II-2287, para. 81.

Finally, on the basis of its case-law that taking into account the turnover of the members **13.168** of an association of undertakings in determining the 10 per cent limit does not mean that a fine has been imposed on them or even that the association in question has an obligation to recover the amount of the fine from its members [...], the [General Court] concluded, [...], that, since the individual farmers who were indirect members of the appellant federations were not penalised in the contested decision, the fact that the basic members of FNB, FNPL and JA were also members of FNSEA did not prevent the Commission from penalising each of those federations individually.

Therefore, the [General Court] could conclude, correctly, in paragraph 344 of the judgment under appeal, that the principle *non bis in idem* was not infringed, since the infringers were not identical, nor was the principle of proportionality, since the appellant federations' members, whether direct or indirect, were not fined twice for one and the same infringement.

CoJ 18 December 2008 (Coop de France bétail et viande, C-101/07P and C-110/07P) [2008] ECR I-10193, paras 129 and 130.

It must be borne in mind that the principle *non bis in idem* does not in itself preclude the **13.169** resumption of proceedings in respect of the same anti-competitive conduct where the first decision was annulled for procedural reasons without any ruling having been given on the substance of the facts alleged, since the annulment decision cannot in such circumstances be regarded as an 'acquittal' within the meaning given to that expression in penal matters. In such a case, the penalties imposed by the new decision are not added to those imposed by the annulled decision but replace them [...].

General Court 1 July 2009 (ThyssenKrupp Stainless AG v. Commission, T-24/07) [2009] ECR II-2309, para. 190.

[T]he *ne bis in idem* principle does not preclude penalties which the national com- **13.170** petition authority of the Member State concerned imposes on undertakings participating in a cartel on account of the anti-competitive effects to which the cartel gave rise in the territory of that Member State prior to its accession to the European Union, where the fines imposed on the same cartel members by a Commission decision taken before the decision of the said national competition authority was adopted were not designed to penalise the said effects.

CoJ 14 February 2012 (Toshiba Corporation and Others v. Úřad pro ochranu hospodářské soutěže, C-17/10), ECLI:EU:C:2012:72, para. 103.

10. Leniency

13.171   It follows that, in the present case [imposition of penalties for the infringement in the UK was time-barred], the provision of information concerning the UK market cannot be covered by Section D2 of the Leniency Notice. Indeed, the fact that an undertaking has placed before the Commission information relating to acts for which that undertaking has not had to pay a fine pursuant to Regulation No 17 or Regulation No 1/2003 does not amount to cooperation falling within the scope of the Leniency Notice [...].
General Court 28 April 2010 (Okley Threads Ltd v. Commission, T-448/05) [2010] ECR II-69, para. 125.

13.172   In the present case, it is important first to make it clear that, although Section D2 of the Leniency Notice does not contemplate the possibility of new information and evidence being provided after notification of the statement of objections, that in no way rules out the possibility that such a circumstance might lead to a reduction in the fine on the basis of that provision. The list of circumstances set out in Section D2 of the Leniency Notice is merely illustrative, as is confirmed by the use of the words 'may include'.
General Court 28 April 2010 (Gütermann AG and Zwicky & Co., T-456/05 and T-457/05) [2010] ECR II-1443, para. 223.

13.173   Moreover, it is inherent in the logic of immunity from fines that only one of the cartel members can have the benefit, given that the effect being sought is to create a climate of uncertainty within cartels by encouraging their denunciation to the Commission. That uncertainty results precisely from the fact that the cartel participants know that only one of them can benefit from immunity from being fined by denouncing the other participants in the infringement, thereby exposing them to the risk that they face more severe fines.

In a situation such as that in this case, in which the Commission knows that a cartel exists but does not have certain essential information capable of establishing the total duration of that infringement, it is particularly desirable to have recourse to such a mechanism, particularly in order to prevent the offenders from coming to an agreement to hide that information.

Such a situation is distinct from that in which the Commission is already aware of evidence, but is seeking to complement it. In that latter case, the granting of a fine reduction to the offenders rather than immunity from a fine to a single undertaking, is justified by the fact that the aim is no longer to reveal a fact likely to lead to an increase in the fine imposed, but to assemble as much evidence as possible in order to reinforce the Commission's ability to establish the facts in question.
General Court 19 May 2010 (KME Germany AG v. Commission, T-25/05) [2010] ECR II-91, paras 137–139.

13.174   The Court recalls that Article 23(2) of Regulation No 1/2003, which is the legal basis for imposing fines in the event of infringement of the EU competition rules, confers on the Commission a margin of assessment in setting fines [...]. That was the context in which, in order to ensure the transparency and objectivity of its fining decisions, the

Commission adopted and published the 2002 Leniency Notice [now the 2006 Leniency Notice]. The notice constitutes an instrument intended to define, while complying with higher-ranking law, the criteria which the Commission proposes to apply in the exercise of its discretion, which is thus subject to a self-imposed limitation [...], in so far as the Commission must comply with self-imposed guidelines [...].

The limitation which the Commission has imposed on its discretion by adopting the 2002 Leniency Notice is not, however, incompatible with the retention of a considerable margin of assessment [...].

The 2002 Leniency Notice displays flexibility in a number of ways, enabling the Commission to exercise its discretion in accordance with Article 23 of Regulation No 1/2003, as interpreted by the Court of Justice [...].

Thus, the Commission enjoys a broad margin of assessment when it is required to determine whether the evidence provided by an undertaking that has stated that it wishes to benefit from the 2002 Leniency Notice represents significant added value for the purposes of point 21 [now point 24] of the notice [...]. As regards point 8(a) and (b) [now refers to point 8] of the notice, it is clear that that considerable margin of assessment results from the actual wording of that provision, which expressly refers to the provision of evidence which, 'in the Commission's view', either enables it to adopt a decision to carry out an investigation or enables it to find an infringement [...].

General Court 13 July 2011 (Kone Oyj, Kone GmbH and Kone BV, T-151/07) [2011] ECR II-5313, paras 80–83.

11. Ability to pay

Furthermore, Disem-Andries maintains that the Commission made a mistake in its assessment inasmuch as, in calculating the amount of the fine imposed on it, it did not take account of its adverse financial situation. **13.175**

That argument cannot be accepted either. As the Commission has rightly observed, recognition of such an obligation would be tantamount to conferring an unjustified competitive advantage on undertakings least well adapted to the conditions of the market.

CoJ 8 November 1983 (IAZ and others v. Commission, Joined Cases 96/82–102/82, 104/82, 105/82, 108/82 and 110/82) [1983] ECR 3369, paras 54 and 55.

See also General Court 20 March 2002 (LR AF 1998 A/S, formerly Løgstør Rør A/S v. Commission, T-23/99) [2002] ECR II-1705, para. 308; General Court 14 May 1998 (Fiskeby Board v. Commission, T-319/94) [1998] ECR II-1331, paras 75 and 76; General Court 14 May 1998 (Enso Espaœola v. Commission, T-348/94) [1998] ECR II-1875, para. 316.

As regards the complaint that Section 5(b) of the Guidelines has been misapplied, it must be pointed out that, according to settled case-law, the Commission is not required when determining the fine to take account of an undertaking's financial losses since recognition of such an obligation would have the effect of conferring an unfair **13.176** competitive advantage on the undertakings least well adapted to the conditions of the market [...].

That case-law is not called into question by Section 5(b) of the Guidelines, which states that an undertaking's real ability to pay must be taken into consideration. That ability applies only in a 'specific social context' consisting of the consequences which payment of the fine would have, in particular, by leading to an increase in unemployment or deterioration in the economic sectors upstream and downstream of the undertaking concerned [...].

Furthermore, the fact that a measure adopted by a Community authority brings about the insolvency or liquidation of a given undertaking is not, as such, prohibited. Although the liquidation of an undertaking in its existing legal form may adversely affect the financial interests of the owners, investors or shareholders, it does not mean that the personal, tangible and intangible elements represented by the undertaking would also lose their value [...].

General Court 19 May 2010 (KME Germany AG v. Commission, T-25/05) [2010] ECR II-91, paras 165–167.

D. PARAGRAPH 4: ASSOCIATIONS OF UNDERTAKINGS

See also recital 30.

1. Calculation turnover associations of undertakings

13.177   The [General Court] considers that the use of the general term 'infringement' in Article 15(2) of Regulation No 17 [now Art. 23 Regulation 1/2003], inasmuch as it covers without distinction agreements, concerted practices and decisions of associations of undertakings, suggests that the ceilings specified by that provision apply in the same manner to agreements and concerted practices, and also to decisions of associations of undertakings. It follows that the ceiling of 10 per cent of turnover must be calculated by reference to the turnover of each of the undertakings which were parties to those agreements and concerted practices or of the undertakings, as a whole, which were members of the said associations of undertakings, at least where, by virtue of its internal rules, the association is able to bind its members.

The soundness of this analysis is borne out by the fact that, in fixing the amount of fines, account may be taken, inter alia, of the influence which the undertaking was able to exert on the market, in particular by reason of its size and economic power of which the undertaking's turnover gives an indication [...] and by reason of the dissuasive effect which those fines must have [...]. The influence which an association of undertakings has been able to exert on the market does not depend on its own 'turnover', which discloses neither its size nor its economic power, but on the turnover of its members, which constitutes an indication of its size and economic power.

General Court 23 February 1994 (CB and Europay, Joined Cases T-39/92 and T-40/92) [1994] ECR II-49, paras 136 and 137.

E. LIABILITY

1. General

For the application of the competition rules of the [TFEU] to undertakings, this raises **13.178** the question whether an undertaking existing after restructuring can be held liable for the involvement of a predecessor in the restrictive agreements.

The term 'undertaking' is not defined in the Treaty. It may refer to any entity engaged in commercial activities, and in the case of a large industrial group it may be appropriate (according to the circumstances) to apply the term to a parent or to a subsidiary company or to the economic unit formed by the parent and subsidiaries together.

Commission 2 August 1989 (Welded steel mesh, 31.553), OJ 1989, L 260, para. 194.

[I]n prohibiting undertakings inter alia from entering into agreements or participating **13.179** in concerted practices which may affect trade between Member States and have as their object or effect the prevention, restriction or distortion of competition within the common market, Article [101(1) TFEU] is aimed at economic units which consist of a unitary organization of personal, tangible and intangible elements which pursues a specific economic aim on a long-term basis and can contribute to the commission of an infringement of the kind referred to in that provision.

General Court 10 March 1992 (Shell, T-11/89) [1992] ECR II-757, para. 311.

It must be observed in that connection that [...] Community competition law is based **13.180** on the principle of the personal responsibility of the economic entity which has committed the infringement. If the parent company is part of that economic unit, which [...] may consist of several legal persons, the parent company is regarded as jointly and severally liable with the other legal persons making up that unit for infringements of competition law. Even if the parent company does not participate directly in the infringement, it exercises, in such a case, a decisive influence over the subsidiaries which have participated in it. It follows that, in that context, the liability of the parent company cannot be regarded as strict liability.

CoJ 10 September 2009 (Akzo Nobel NV and Others v. Commission of the European Communities, C-97/08 P) [2009] ECR I-8237, para. 77.

2. Imputability of infringement on parent company/companies

[I]t must be concluded that [...] the competent personnel, and in particular the **13.181** management of Akzo Nobel, play a significant role in several essential aspects of the strategy of the subsidiaries in question and reserve the power of final decision with respect to a range of matters that define their course of conduct on the market.

The argument that decisions relating to pricing and price increases are in principle taken by the marketing managers for the products concerned, who act within their respective subsidiaries, and in particular by the choline chloride marketing manager [...], cannot refute that conclusion. The same applies to the arguments based on the two-level structure of the Akzo Nobel group, which is claimed to have the objective of removing commercial policy in the strict sense from the control of Akzo Nobel [...]. [a]ttribution of an infringement by a subsidiary to the parent company does not require proof that the parent company influences its subsidiary's policy in the specific area in which the infringement occurred, in the present case distribution and pricing. On the other hand, the economic and legal organisational links between the parent company and its subsidiary may establish that the parent exercises influence over the subsidiary's strategy and therefore that they can be viewed as a single economic entity.

The argument based on the fact that each subsidiary has its own management board [...] lacks conviction. Every incorporated company has a management board appointed by its shareholders, in this case by Akzo Nobel.

Therefore, even on the assumption that the applicants' reasoning [in the first paragraph of this citation] in respect of the burden of proof [...] is correct, the fact remains that they have not succeeded in rebutting the presumption that Akzo Nobel, the parent company owning 100 per cent of the capital of the subsidiaries to which the decision was addressed, exercised decisive influence over its subsidiaries' policies. It must therefore be concluded that Akzo Nobel, together with those subsidiaries, constitutes an undertaking for the purposes of Article [101 TFEU], without there being any need to ascertain whether Akzo Nobel exercised influence over the conduct at issue. Consequently, the first plea must be rejected.

General Court 17 September 2007 (Akzo Nobel Chemicals Ltd and Akcros Chemicals Ltd v. Commission, T-1125/05) [2007] ECR II-5049, paras 37 and 82–85.

Confirmed in CoJ 10 September 2009 (Akzo Nobel Chemicals Ltd and Akcros Chemicals Ltd v. Commission, C-97/08P) [2009] ECR I-8237, paras 60–65.

See also General Court 9 September 2009 (Clearstream Banking AG, Clearstream International v. Commission, T-301/04) [2009] ECR II-3155, paras 201 and 202.

13.182   [T]he conduct of the subsidiary on the market cannot be the only factor which enables the liability of the parent company to be established, but is only one of the signs of the existence of an economic unit.

[I]n order to ascertain whether a subsidiary determines its conduct on the market independently, account must be taken not only of [price policy, the production and distribution activities, the sales targets, the gross margins, the sales costs, the cash flow, stock and marketing], but also of all the relevant factors relating to economic, organisational and legal links which tie the subsidiary to the parent company, which may vary from case to case and cannot therefore be set out in an exhaustive list. [...]

CoJ 10 September 2009 (Akzo Nobel Chemicals Ltd and Akcros Chemicals Ltd v. Commission, C-97/08P) [2009] ECR I-8237, paras 73 and 74.

13.183   [I]n order to rebut the presumption that a parent company which holds 100 per cent of the capital of its subsidiary actually exercises a decisive influence over that subsidiary, it is for the parent company to put before the EU judicature any evidence relating to the organisational, economic and legal links between its subsidiary and itself which are apt to demonstrate that they do not constitute a single economic entity [...].

It should also be pointed out that, contrary to what the appellants claim, given its rebuttable nature, that presumption, which may be rebutted in an individual case by relying on the series of factors referred to by the General Court, does not lead to the automatic attribution of liability to the parent company holding 100 per cent of the capital of its subsidiary, which would be contrary to the principle of personal responsibility on which EU competition law is based. [...]

CoJ 20 January 2011 (General Química SA, C-90/09 P) [2011] ECR I-0001, paras 51 and 52.

See also General Court 13 July 2011 (The Dow Chemical Company and others, T-42/07) [2011] ECR II-4531, paras 58 and 59.

In the present case, for the entire duration of the infringement in question, Eni held, directly or indirectly, at least 99.97 per cent of the capital in the companies which were directly active within its group in the BR and ESBR sectors, namely EniChem Elastomeri, EniChem SpA and Versalis, which Eni does not dispute. In consequence, the presumption [of imputation of liability] is applicable to Eni. [...] **13.184**

[The facts adduced by Eni] would be such as to demonstrate that Versalis enjoyed a certain autonomy as regards its chemical activities. However, that fact is not sufficient alone to establish that Eni, and, in particular, Versalis, did not form a single undertaking for the purpose of Article 101 TFEU. In addition, the fact that Eni was 'merely' a technical and financial coordinator or that it provided those undertakings with financial and investment assistance, as it has submitted, shows that it did not refrain from exercising a decisive influence over its subsidiaries. [...]

That conclusion cannot be called into question by the fact that Eni had never operated directly in the chemical sector or that there had never been any management overlap between the parent company and the subsidiaries. The fact that the parent company did not participate directly in that infringement or encourage it to be committed is not such as to show that those two companies did not constitute a single economic unit [...]. In addition, Eni does not dispute that it was possible for it to coordinate investments within the group even in the absence of such an overlap or its direct participation in the operational management of its subsidiaries.

Nor can Eni's other arguments put forward in that context succeed, namely that it did not have information on the strategic and commercial plans or on their implementation and was not involved in the decision-making processes to define strategic and commercial plans or annual sales volumes and prices, in so far as they relate only to the operational activities in the chemical sector.

[T]he presumption of decisive influence rests on the fact that it is precisely the prerogatives of a parent company which wholly or almost wholly owns its subsidiary which enables that parent company, except in exceptional circumstances, to exercise decisive influence over the conduct of its subsidiary [...], and that, accordingly, proof of the absence of such a decisive influence is to be adduced not by the Commission but by the parent company itself.

[...] The fact that it is difficult to prove the opposite in order to rebut a presumption does not imply, of itself, that it is in fact irrebuttable [...]. More specifically, to rebut the presumption in question, Eni would have had to show that Versalis could act with complete autonomy not only at the operational level but also at the financial level, which it failed to do.

CoJ 8 May 2013 (ENI SpA v. Commission, C-508/11 P), ECLI:EU:C:2013:289, paras 49 and 64–68.

13.185   [The case-law regarding the presumption that the parent company exercises decisive influence over the conduct of its subsidiary if it has a 100 per cent shareholding in that subsidiary] does not imply that the Commission is bound to rely exclusively on that presumption. There is nothing to prevent the Commission from establishing that a parent company actually exercises decisive influence over its subsidiary by means of other evidence or by a combination of such evidence and that presumption […].

CoJ 26 September 2013 (Alliance One International v. Commission, C-679/11 P), ECLI:EU:C:2013:606, para. 40.

13.186   The Court of Justice has stipulated that [when assessing whether the conduct of a subsidiary may be imputed to the parent company] account must be taken of all the relevant factors relating to the economic, organisational and legal links which tie the subsidiary to the parent company, which may vary from case to case and cannot therefore be set out in an exhaustive list […]. […]

It should be noted in that regard that the principle that it is necessary to check whether the parent company actually exercised decisive influence over its subsidiary applies only where the subsidiary is not wholly owned by its parent company. According to settled case-law of the Court of Justice, where the entire capital of the subsidiary is owned, there is no longer any requirement to carry out such a check since, in those circumstances, there is a presumption of decisive influence on the part of the parent company which has the burden of rebutting that presumption […].

CoJ 26 September 2013 (The Dow Chemical Company v. Commission, C-179/12 P), ECLI:EU:C:2013:605, paras 54 and 56.

13.187   At the outset, it must be recalled, from the Court of Justice's settled case-law, that responsibility for the conduct of a subsidiary may be imputed to the parent company in particular where, although having a separate legal personality, that subsidiary does not decide independently upon its own conduct on the market, but carries out, in all material respects, the instructions given to it by the parent company, having regard in particular to the economic, organisational and legal links between those two legal entities. In such a situation, since the parent company and its subsidiary are part of the same economic unit and therefore form a single undertaking for the purposes of [Article 101 TFEU], the Commission may address a decision imposing fines to the parent company, without having to establish the personal involvement of the latter in the infringement […].

It also follows from the Court of Justice's settled case-law that, in the particular case in which a parent company holds, directly or indirectly, all or almost all of the capital in a subsidiary which has committed an infringement of the EU competition rules, there is a rebuttable presumption that that parent company actually exercises a decisive influence over its subsidiary […].

In such a situation, it is sufficient for the Commission to prove that all or almost all of the capital in the subsidiary is held, directly or indirectly, by the parent company in order to take the view that that presumption is fulfilled. Accordingly, the Commission will then be able to regard the parent company as responsible for its subsidiary's conduct and as jointly and severally liable for the payment of the fine imposed on that subsidiary, unless the parent company, which has the burden of rebutting that presumption, adduces sufficient evidence to show that its subsidiary acts independently on the market [...].

Therefore, when that presumption is established, as is not disputed by the appellants in this case, such a presumption implies, unless it is rebutted, that the actual exercise of decisive influence by the parent company over its subsidiary is considered established and gives grounds for the Commission to hold the former company responsible for the conduct of the latter, without having to produce any further evidence.

CoJ 16 June 2016 (Evonik Degussa GmbH and AlzChem AG, formerly AlzChem Trostberg GmbH, formerly AlzChem Hart GmbH v. European Commission, C-155/14 P), ECLI:EU:C:2016:446, paras 27–30.

Once the presumption of actual exercise of decisive influence is established, it is solely **13.188** for the parent company holding all or almost all of the capital of its subsidiary to rebut it.

In order to rebut that presumption, a parent company must, in the context of the actions against a Commission decision, put before the EU judicature any evidence relating to the organisational, economic and legal links between its subsidiary and itself which are such as to demonstrate that they do not constitute a single economic entity [...].

In order to assess whether that subsidiary decides independently upon its own conduct on the market or carries out, in all material respects, the instructions given to it by its parent company [...] the EU judicature must take into consideration all relevant factors, which may vary from case to case and therefore cannot be set out in an exhaustive list [...].

As part of that review, it is for the General Court to carry out an assessment of the facts which are contemporaneous with the period of the infringement, but without prejudice to the possibility of relying on elements relating to a prior period, in so far as it is able to establish the relevance of those elements to the period of the infringement and it does not automatically apply to the period of the infringement the conclusions stemming from the assessment of elements prior to that period.[...]

As part of this overall assessment, although the existence of an express instruction given by a parent company to its subsidiary not to participate in any anticompetitive practices in a given market can be a strong indication of the actual exercise of decisive influence by the parent over the subsidiary, the fact that the subsidiary did not comply with this instruction cannot be regarded by the General Court [...] as a strong indication of actual exercise of such influence.

However, the fact that a subsidiary does not comply with an instruction given by its parent company is not sufficient, by itself, to establish the absence of actual exercise of decisive influence by the parent over the subsidiary, given that the Court of Justice has already stated that it is not necessary for the subsidiary to carry out all the parent company's instructions to demonstrate decisive influence, as long as the failure to carry out those instructions is not the norm […]. […]

In that regard, the Court has already held that the fact that it is difficult to adduce the evidence necessary to rebut a presumption of actual exercise of decisive influence does not in itself mean that that presumption is in fact irrebuttable, especially where the entities against which the presumption operates are those best placed to seek that evidence within their own sphere of activity.

CoJ 16 June 2016 (Evonik Degussa GmbH and AlzChem AG, formerly AlzChem Trostberg GmbH, formerly AlzChem Hart GmbH v. European Commission, C-155/14 P), ECLI:EU:C:2016:446, paras 31–34, 40–41 and 44.

3. Joint and several liability

13.189 [The Commission decision did not specify the extent of liability on the jointly and severally liable parties] Since the applicant has never formed a single economic unit with FLS Plast and FLSmidth, the principle that penalties should be specific to the offender and to the offence requires that the amount actually paid by the applicant does not exceed its share of the joint and several liability. That share corresponds to the proportion of the amount ascribed to the applicant in relation to the total of the limits up to which the successive parent companies are jointly and severally liable for payment of the fine imposed on Trioplast Wittenheim. It is important to note, in this connection, that the principle that penalties should be specific to the offender and to the offence, in accordance with which an economic unit may be penalised only for acts imputed to it individually, applies in any administrative procedure that may lead to the imposition of sanctions under competition law […].

Article 2, first paragraph, point (f), of the contested decision fails to indicate the share which falls to the applicant, whilst at the same time allowing the Commission full discretion in calling on the respective joint and several liabilities of the successive parent companies which never together formed an economic unit. That provision is therefore inconsistent with the obligation which rests upon the Commission, in accordance with the principle of legal certainty, to enable the applicant to know for certain the exact amount of the fine which it must pay in respect of the period for which it is held jointly and severally liable with Trioplast Wittenheim for the infringement. The contested decision thus breaches both the principle of legal certainty and the principle that penalties should be specific to the offender and to the offence.

General Court 13 September 2010 (Trioplast v. Commission, T-40/06) [2010] ECR II-4893, paras 169 and 170.

13.190 [W]here several persons may be held personally liable for the participation in an infringement of one and the same undertaking for the purposes of competition law, they must be regarded as jointly and severally liable for that infringement […].

[…] The joint and several liability for the payment of fines imposed for an infringement of Article [101 TFEU] and Article 53 of the EEA Agreement, inasmuch as it contributes to the effective recovery of those fines, is part of the objective of deterrence which is pursued generally by competition law […] and respects the principle of *non bis in idem*, a fundamental principle of European Union law, also laid down in Article 4 of Protocol No 7 of the ECHR, which precludes penalising more than once, for the same infringement of competition law, the same conduct of the undertaking on the market through the persons which may be held personally liable for it [...].

The fact that the personal liabilities incurred by several companies due to the participation of the same undertaking in an infringement is not identical does not prevent them from being fined jointly and severally, since the joint and several liability for payment of a fine covers only the period of the infringement during which they formed an economic unit and thus constituted an undertaking for the purposes of competition law.

In that regard, contrary to what the Commission claims in its argument [...], it is not free to determine the sums to be paid jointly and severally. It follows from the principle that penalties must be specific to the offender and to the offence concerned, [...], that each company must be able to discern from the decision imposing a fine on it to be paid jointly and severally with one or more other companies the amount which it is required to bear in relation to the other joint and several debtors, once payment has been made to the Commission. To that end, the Commission must, inter alia, specify the periods during which the companies concerned were jointly liable for the unlawful conduct of the undertakings which participated in the cartel and, where necessary, the degree of liability of those companies for that conduct.

General Court 3 March 2011 (Siemens AG Österreich and Others, Joined Cases T-122/07–T-124/07) [2011] ECR II-793, paras 150–153.

13.191
According to settled case-law, joint and several liability may be imputed to undertakings even if the legal entities constituting the undertaking during the infringement no longer belong to the same group [...].

It follows from this that, contrary to the applicant's assertion, the separation – after the infringement of Article [101 TFEU] had ceased, but before the adoption of the contested decision – of the two legal entities Pegler and Tomkins, which belonged to the infringing undertaking, does not preclude the applicant's liability.

General Court 24 March 2011 (Pegler Ltd, T-386/06) [2011] ECR I-1267, paras 101 and 102.

13.192
[T]he applicant could not be held liable for the infringement on the part of Agroexpansión in respect of the period prior to 18 November 1997, since it is only from that date onwards that it formed an economic unit with Agroexpansión and thus an undertaking within the meaning of Article [101 TFEU]. Since the joint and several liability for payment of a fine can cover only the period of the infringement during which the parent company and the subsidiary constituted such an undertaking, the Commission was not justified in requiring the applicant to pay jointly and severally, with Agroexpansión, the total amount imposed on Agroexpansión, that is EUR 2 592 000, namely an amount which relates to the entire infringement period. [...]

General Court 12 October 2011 (Alliance One International, Inc., T-41/05) [2011] ECR II-7101, para. 202.

See also in this respect, General Court 14 July 2016 (Parker Hannifin Manufacturing Srl, formerly Parker ITR Srl and Parker-Hannifin Corp. v. European Commission, T-146/09 RENV), ECLI:EU:T:2016:411, paras 153–154.

13.193   Where two parent companies each have a 50 per cent shareholding in the joint venture which committed an infringement of the rules of competition law, it is only for the purposes of establishing liability for participation in the infringement of that law and only in so far as the Commission has demonstrated, on the basis of factual evidence, that both parent companies did in fact exercise decisive influence over the joint venture, that those three entities can be considered to form a single economic unit and therefore form a single undertaking for the purposes of Article [101 TFEU].

CoJ 26 September 2013 (EI du Pont de Nemours and Company v. Commission, C-172/12 P), ECLI:EU:C:2013:601, para. 47.

4.   Legal and economic links

13.194   In reply to the arguments put forward by the Commission, the applicants add that Finnboard pays its operating costs itself out of the income from commission received and that, contrary to the Commission's claims, those costs are not covered by the member companies.

The member companies were able to control the activities of Finnboard with the result that it was not able to determine its conduct on the market in an autonomous manner. As well as issuing instructions concerning the marketing of their products, the member companies also sent their own representative to Finnboard's Board of Directors. It is, moreover, inconceivable that the applicants would place their products in the hands of an organisation over which they had no control, and which could have fixed prices and conditions of sale as it wished without having to take account of their instructions. Furthermore, Finnboard's running costs were paid by the member companies.

General Court 14 May 1998 (Metsä–Serla and Others v. Commission, Joined Cases T-339/94 and T-342/ 94) [1998] ECR II-1727, paras 27 and 34.

13.195   Moreover, it is not disputed that a member of the applicant's management board participated in, and even presided over, the meetings of the PWG until 1988. According to the decision, the main discussions with an anti-competitive object took place in the PWG and that finding is not disputed by the applicant.

In those circumstances, the Commission has proved that through the involvement of the member of its management board the applicant was actively implicated in the anti-competitive conduct of KNP Vouwkarton. In involving itself in that way in the participation of one of its subsidiaries in the cartel, the applicant was aware, and must also have approved of, Badische's participation in the infringement in which KNP Vouwkarton took part.

The applicant's responsibility is not affected by the fact that the attendance of the member of its management board at meetings of the bodies of the PG Paperboard ceased in 1988. It was for the applicant, as parent company, to adopt in regard to its subsidiaries any measure necessary to prevent the continuation of an infringement of which it was aware. Furthermore, the applicant has not disputed that it did not even attempt to prevent the continuation of the infringement.

General Court 14 May 1998 (KNP v. Commission, T-309/94) [1998] ECR II-1007, paras 47–49.

[S]ince it is settled case-law that the anti-competitive conduct of an undertaking can be attributed to another undertaking where it has not decided independently upon its own conduct on the market, but carried out, in all material respects, the instructions given to it by that other undertaking, having regard in particular to the economic and legal links between them […]. **13.196**

[I]t is clear from […] this judgment that the appellants were held individually liable for an infringement which they are deemed to have committed themselves on account of their legal and economic links with Finnboard and by which they were able to determine Finnboard's conduct on the market.

CoJ 16 November 2000 (Metsä–Serla and others v. Commission, C-294/98P) [2000] ECR I-10065, paras 27 and 34.

5. Legal and economic continuity

As the applicant assumed all the rights and liabilities of the four cooperatives of the old association, it must be treated as the economic successor both of the old association and of its members, which indeed is what those members intended. **13.197**

The applicant moreover does not deny that the name 'Suiker Unie' always covered the same undertakings, which were run for the most part by the same persons and had their registered offices at the same address.

It does not even claim that its conduct on the sugar market differed from that of the former association.

In these circumstances, so far as the sugar market is concerned, the main feature of the conduct of the applicant and its predecessor was its obvious continuity, which means that the whole of this behaviour must be attributed to the applicant.

CoJ 16 December 1975 (Suiker Unie, Joined Cases 40–48, 50, 54, 56, 111, 113, and 114/73) [1975] ECR 1663, paras 84–87.

For the purposes of Article [101 TFEU], a change in the legal form and name of an undertaking does not create a new undertaking free of liability for the anti-competitive behaviour of its predecessor, when, from an economic point of view, the two are identical. **13.198**

CoJ 28 March 1984 (CRAM and Rheinzink, Joined Cases 29 and 30/83) [1984] ECR 1679, para. 9.

However, where between the commission of the infringement and the time when the undertaking in question must answer for it the person responsible for the operation of that undertaking has ceased to exist in law, it is necessary, first, to find the combination of physical and human elements which contributed to the commission of the infringement and then to identify the person who has become responsible for their operation, so **13.199** as to avoid the result that because of the disappearance of the person responsible for its operation when the infringement was committed the undertaking may fail to answer for it.

General Court 17 December 1991 (Anic v. Commission, T-6/89) [1991] ECR II-1623, para. 237.

13.200   Although the appellant was rightly held liable for the conduct of the two subsidiaries in question with effect from their acquisition, it had not been proved that it could validly be held liable for their infringements prior to that date.

It falls, in principle, to the legal or natural person managing the undertaking in question when the infringement was committed to answer for that infringement, even if, when the decision finding the infringement was adopted, another person had assumed responsibility for operating the undertaking.

CoJ 16 November 2000 (Cascades v. Commission, C-279/98 P) [2000] ECR I-9693, paras 77 and 78.

See also in this respect, General Court 14 July 2016 (Parker Hannifin Manufacturing Srl, formerly Parker ITR Srl and Parker-Hannifin Corp v. European Commission, T-146/09 RENV) ECLI:EU:T:2016:411, paras 153 and 154 .

13.201   The [General Court] attributed to the appellant the infringements committed by Feldmühle and CBC [...].

It should be noted that it falls, in principle, to the legal or natural person managing the undertaking in question when the infringement was committed to answer for that infringement, even if, at the time of the decision finding the infringement, another person had assumed responsibility for operating the undertaking.

In the present case there is no dispute that Feldmühle and CBC continued to exist after control of them had been acquired by the appellant in September 1990, so that responsibility for their actions had to be attributed to the legal person that directed the operation of their businesses in the period preceding their acquisition by the appellant.

The fact that the appellant could not have been unaware during that period that Feldmühle and CBC were participating in the cartel, because it had itself been participating in it since January 1987 through its subsidiary Kopparfors, cannot [...] suffice to impute to it responsibility for the infringements committed by those companies prior to their acquisition.

CoJ 16 November 2000 (Stora v. Commission, C-286/98) [2000] ECR I-9925, paras 36–39.

13.202   When the [General Court] concluded [...] that Aalborg and Aktieselskabet Aalborg Portland-Cement Fabrik constituted the same economic entity for the purposes of applying Article [101(1) TFEU], that finding must be taken to mean that the undertaking run by Aalborg from 1990 is the same as that previously run by Aktieselskabet Aalborg Portland-Cement Fabrik [...].

The fact that Aktieselskabet Aalborg Portland-Cement Fabrik still exists as a legal entity does not invalidate that finding and did not therefore in itself constitute a ground for annulling the cement decision in respect of Aalborg.

In that regard, it is true that in *Commission v. Anic* [...] the Court held that there can be economic continuity only where the legal person responsible for running the undertaking has ceased to exist in law after the infringement has been committed. However, that case concerned two existing and functioning undertakings one of which had simply transferred part of its activities to the other and where there was no structural link between them. As is apparent from [...] this judgment, that is not the position in this case.

CoJ 7 January 2004 (Aalborg Portland A/S, C-204/00P, Irish Cement Ltd, C-205/ 00P, Ciments français SA, C-211/00P, Italcementi – Fabbriche Riunite Cemento SpA, C-213/00P, Buzzi Unicem SpA, C-217/00P and Cementir – Cementerie del Tirreno SpA, C-219/00P v. Commission, Joined Cases C-204/00P, C-205/00P, C-211/ 00P, C-213/00P, C-217/00P and C-219/00P) [2004] ECR I-123, paras 357–359.

As to the circumstances in which an entity that is not responsible for the infringement **13.203** can nevertheless be penalised for that infringement, it must be held first that this situation arises if the entity that has committed the infringement has ceased to exist, either in law [...] or economically. With regard to the latter, it is worth noting that a penalty imposed on an undertaking that continues to exist in law, but has ceased economic activity, is likely to have no deterrent effect.

Next, it must be noted that if no possibility of imposing a penalty on an entity other than the one which committed the infringement were foreseen, undertakings could escape penalties by simply changing their identity through restructurings, sales or other legal or organisational changes. This would jeopardise the objective of suppressing conduct that infringes the competition rules and preventing its reoccurrence by means of deterrent penalties [...].

Consequently, as the Court has already held, when an entity that has committed an infringement of the competition rules is subject to a legal or organisational change, this change does not necessarily create a new undertaking free of liability for the conduct of its predecessor that infringed the competition rules, when, from an economic point of view, the two are identical [...].

[T]he legal forms of the entity that committed the infringement and the entity that succeeded it are irrelevant. Imposing a penalty for the infringement on the successor can therefore not be excluded simply because, as in the main proceedings, the successor has a different legal status and is operated differently from the entity that it succeeded.

CoJ 11 December 2007 (ETI and others, C-280/06) [2007] ECR I-10893, paras 40–43.

6. Representation in administrative procedure

As that subsidiary was wholly owned, the [General Court] could legitimately assume **13.204** [...] that the parent company in fact exercised decisive influence over its subsidiary's conduct, particularly since it had found [...] that during the administrative procedure the appellant had presented itself as being, as regards companies in the Stora Group, the Commission's sole interlocutor concerning the infringement in question. In those circumstances, it was for the appellant to reverse that presumption by adducing sufficient evidence.

CoJ 16 November 2000 (Stora, C-286/98) [2000] ECR I-9925, para. 29.

13.205   Given the fact that the whole of the share capital of the subsidiary was held, the Commission is entitled to assume that the parent company exerted a decisive influence on the conduct of its subsidiary, particularly where the parent company had put itself forward in the administrative procedure as being the sole representative of the companies in the group.

In those circumstances, it is for the parent company to rebut that presumption by sufficient evidence.

General Court 15 September 2005 (DaimlerChrysler AG v. Commission, T-325/01) [2005] ECR II-3319, paras 219 and 220.

7. Vertical relation

13.206   In the case of companies having a vertical relationship, such as a principal and its agent or intermediary, two factors have been taken to be the main parameters for determining whether there is a single economic unit: first, whether the intermediary takes on any economic risk and, secondly, whether the services provided by the intermediary are exclusive. [...]

In so far as concerns the question whether the services provided by the agent are exclusive, the Court has held that it tends not to suggest economic unity if, at the same time as it conducts business for the account of its principal, an agent undertakes, as an independent dealer, a very considerable amount of business for its own account on the market for the product or service in question [...].

General Court 11 December 2003 (Minoan Lines SA v. Commission, T-66/99) [2003] ECR II-5515, paras 126 and 128.

ARTICLE 24 – PERIODIC PENALTY PAYMENTS

1.   The Commission may, by decision, impose on undertakings or associations of undertakings periodic penalty payments not exceeding 5% of the average daily turnover in the preceding business year per day and calculated from the date appointed by the decision, in order to compel them:

   (a)   to put an end to an infringement of Article 81 or Article 82 of the Treaty, in accordance with a decision taken pursuant to Article 7;

   (b)   to comply with a decision ordering interim measures taken pursuant to Article 8;

   (c)   to comply with a commitment made binding by a decision pursuant to Article 9;

   (d)   to supply complete and correct information which it has requested by decision taken pursuant to Article 17 or Article 18(3);

   (e)   to submit to an inspection which it has ordered by decision taken pursuant to Article 20(4).

2.   Where the undertakings or associations of undertakings have satisfied the obligation which the periodic penalty payment was intended to enforce, the Commission may fix the definitive amount of the periodic penalty payment at a figure lower than that which would arise under the original decision. Article 23(4) shall apply correspondingly.

See also General Court 17 September 2007 (Microsoft, T-201/04) [2007] ECR II-3601, paras 1254–1259.

CHAPTER VII

LIMITATION PERIODS

ARTICLE 25 – LIMITATION PERIODS FOR THE IMPOSITION OF PENALTIES

1. The powers conferred on the Commission by Articles 23 and 24 shall be subject to the following limitation periods:
    (a) three years in the case of infringements of provisions concerning requests for information or the conduct of inspections;
    (b) five years in the case of all other infringements.
2. Time shall begin to run on the day on which the infringement is committed. However, in the case of continuing or repeated infringements, time shall begin to run on the day on which the infringement ceases.
3. Any action taken by the Commission or by the competition authority of a Member State for the purpose of the investigation or proceedings in respect of an infringement shall interrupt the limitation period for the imposition of fines or periodic penalty payments. The limitation period shall be interrupted with effect from the date on which the action is notified to at least one undertaking or association of undertakings which has participated in the infringement. Actions which interrupt the running of the period shall include in particular the following:
    (a) written requests for information by the Commission or by the competition authority of a Member State;
    (b) written authorisations to conduct inspections issued to its officials by the Commission or by the competition authority of a Member State;
    (c) the initiation of proceedings by the Commission or by the competition authority of a Member State;
    (d) notification of the statement of objections of the Commission or of the competition authority of a Member State.
4. The interruption of the limitation period shall apply for all the undertakings or associations of undertakings which have participated in the infringement.
5. Each interruption shall start time running afresh. However, the limitation period shall expire at the latest on the day on which a period equal to twice the limitation period has elapsed without the Commission having imposed a fine or a periodic penalty payment. That period shall

be extended by the time during which limitation is suspended pursuant to paragraph 6.

6. The limitation period for the imposition of fines or periodic penalty payments shall be suspended for as long as the decision of the Commission is the subject of proceedings pending before the Court of Justice.

OVERVIEW

A. APPLICABLE LIMITATION PERIODS	13.207	D. PARAGRAPH 3: INTERRUPTION OF LIMITATION PERIOD	13.215
B. PRINCIPLE OF LEGAL CERTAINTY	13.211		
		E. PARAGRAPH 6: PROCEEDINGS PENDING BEFORE THE COURT OF	
C. BURDEN OF PROOF: SINGLE AND CONTINUOUS INFRINGEMENT	13.213	JUSTICE	13.217

A. APPLICABLE LIMITATION PERIODS

13.207 In order to fulfil their function, limitation periods must be fixed in advance, and the fixing of their duration and the detailed rules for their application comes within the powers of the Community legislature […].

CoJ 2 October 2003 (International Power and others/NALOO, C-172/01P, C-175/01P, C-176/01P and C-180/01P) [2003] ECR I-11421, para. 106.

See also CoJ 24 September 2002 (Falck and Acciaierie di Bolzano v. Commission, C-74/00P and C-75/00P) [2002] ECR I-7869, para. 139.

13.208 It must be emphasised that the finding and the appraisal of the specific characteristics of a repeated infringement come within the Commission's discretion and that the Commission cannot be bound by any limitation period when making such a finding.

[R]epeated infringement is an important factor which the Commission must appraise, since the purpose of taking repeated infringement into account is to induce undertakings which have demonstrated a tendency towards infringing the competition rules to change their conduct. The Commission may therefore, in each individual case, take into consideration the indicia which confirm such a tendency, including, for example, the time that has elapsed between the infringements in question.

CoJ 8 February 2007 (Groupe Danone, C-3/06P) [2007] ECR I-1331, paras 38 and 39.

13.209 Nevertheless […] those acts must be regarded as giving notice of enforcement of a decision taken previously, that is to say the Welded steel mesh decision. As such, whether they occur before or after any time-bar, those acts cannot be regarded as having produced legal effects binding on, and capable of affecting the interests of, Ferriere

Nord. In reality, they merely constitute acts purely preparatory to enforcement. Neither the former nor the latter acts constitute acts open to challenge [...].

CoJ 6 December 2007 (Ferriere Nord SpA, C-516/06P) [2007] ECR I-10685, para. 29.

13.210   Under Article 25(2) of Regulation No 1/2003, time is to begin to run on the day on which the infringement is committed. However, in the case of continuing or repeated infringements, time is to begin to run on the day on which the infringement ceases.

General Court 17 May 2013 (Manuli Rubber Industries SpA (MRI) v. Commission, T-154/09), ECLI:EU:T:2013:260, para. 190.

B. PRINCIPLE OF LEGAL CERTAINTY

13.211   The second recital in the preamble to Regulation No 2988/74 states that the limitation period was introduced to ensure legal certainty. According to that recital, 'for the matter to be covered fully, it is necessary that provision for limitation be made not only as regards the power to impose fines or penalties, but also as regards the power to enforce decisions imposing fines, penalties or periodic penalty payments; [...] such provisions should specify the length of limitation periods, the date on which time starts to run and the events which have the effect of interrupting or suspending the limitation period; [...] in this respect the interests of undertakings and associations of undertakings on the one hand, and the requirements imposed by administrative practice, on the other hand, should be taken into account'.

General Court 19 March 2003 (CMA CGM and others v. Commission, T-213/00) [2003] ECR II-913, para. 322.

See also General Court 8 July 2008 (Compagnie Maritime Belge, T-276/04) [2008] ECR II-1277, para. 43.

13.212   For so long as the limitation period provided for by Regulation No 2988/74 has not expired, any undertaking or association of undertakings which is the subject of a competition policy investigation under Regulation No 17 [now Art. 23 Regulation No 1/2003] remains in a position of uncertainty as to the outcome of that procedure and the possible imposition of penalties or fines. Thus, the prolongation of the uncertainty alleged by the applicants concerning the action to be taken regarding them and the adverse effects on their reputation is inherent in the procedures for the application of Regulation No 17 [now Art. 23 Regulation No 1/2003] and does not in itself constitute any impairment of the rights of the defence.

General Court 16 December 2003 (Nederlandse Federatieve Vereniging voor de Groothandel op Elektrotechnisch Gebied en Technische Unie v. Commission, T-5/00 and T-6/00) [2003] ECR II-5761, para. 91.

C. BURDEN OF PROOF: SINGLE AND CONTINUOUS INFRINGEMENT

As a preliminary point, the requirement of legal certainty, on which economic operators **13.213** are entitled to rely, entails that when there is a dispute concerning the existence of an infringement of competition law the Commission, which bears the burden of proving infringements which it finds, must adduce evidence which will sufficiently establish the existence of the facts constituting the infringement. With specific regard to the alleged duration of an infringement, the same principle of legal certainty requires that, if there is no evidence directly establishing the duration of an infringement, the Commission should adduce at least evidence of facts sufficiently proximate in time for it to be reasonable to accept that that infringement continued uninterruptedly between two specific dates.

General Court 7 July 1994 (Dunlop Slazenger v. Commission, T-43/92) [1994] ECR II-441, para. 79.

In the present case, the general principle that the Commission is required to prove every **13.214** constituent element of the infringement, including its duration, that is likely to have an effect on its definitive findings as to the gravity of that infringement, is not called into question by the fact that the applicant raised a defence of limitation, the burden of proof of which is in principle borne by the applicant. Not only does that defence not relate to the finding of an infringement, but it is clear that reliance on such a plea necessarily requires that the duration of the infringement and the date on which it came to an end be established. Those circumstances cannot alone provide justification for transferring the burden in this regard to the applicant. The duration of the infringement, which requires that the date on which it ended be known, is one of the essential elements of the infringement, which must be proved by the Commission, irrespective of the fact that the disputing of those elements also forms part of the defence of limitation [...]. That conclusion is also justified in light of the fact that the non-limitation of a Commission proceeding under the regulation on limitation is the application of an objective legal criterion, pursuant to the principle of legal certainty [...], confirmed by the second recital in the preamble to that regulation, and, thus, is a condition for the validity of any decision imposing a penalty. The Commission is required to comply with this condition even if the undertaking concerned has raised no defence in this regard.

That apportionment of the burden of proof is likely to vary, however, inasmuch as the evidence on which a party relies may be of such a kind as to require the other party to provide an explanation or justification, failing which it is permissible to conclude that the burden of proof has been discharged [...].

General Court 16 November 2006 (Peróxidos Orgánicos, T-120/04) [2006] ECR II-4441, paras 52 and 53.

See also CoJ 7 January 2004 (Aalborg Portland and others v. Commission, C-204/ 00P, C-205/00P, C-211/00P, C-213/00P, C-217/00P and C-219/00P) [2004] ECR I-123, para. 79.

D. PARAGRAPH 3: INTERRUPTION OF LIMITATION PERIOD

13.215   Although a request for information may interrupt the limitation period for fines where its purpose is to enable the Commission to comply with its obligations in fixing the fine, therefore, the Commission cannot, for instance, make requests for information the sole purpose of which is to prolong the limitation period artificially so as to preserve the power to impose a fine [...]. Requests for information solely for that purpose cannot be necessary for infringement proceedings. Furthermore, if the Commission were able to interrupt the limitation period by sending requests for information not necessary for the proceedings it would be able systematically to prolong the limitation period up to the ten-year maximum laid down by Article 2(3) of Regulation No 2988/74, thereby subverting the five-year limitation period laid down by Article 1(1) of that regulation and converting it into a ten-year one.
General Court 19 March 2003 (CMA CGM v. Commission, T-213/00) [2003] ECR II-913, para. 488.

13.216   As regards limitation under Article 1(1)(b) and (2) of the regulation on limitation, the [General Court] points out that in the case of continuing or repeated infringements, for the Commission's power to impose fines to be time-barred, five years must have elapsed from the day on which the infringement ceased. Under Article 2(1), that period may be interrupted by any action taken by the Commission to investigate the infringement, in particular written requests for information, that interruption taking effect from the date on which that request is notified to the addressee and with the consequence, under Article 2(3), that time starts running afresh from that date.
General Court 16 November 2006 (Peróxidos Orgánicos, T-120/04) [2006] ECR II-4441, para. 46.

E. PARAGRAPH 6: PROCEEDINGS PENDING BEFORE THE COURT OF JUSTICE

13.217   According to the case-law, it is the very fact that an action is pending before the General Court or the Court of Justice that justifies the suspension of the limitation period [...].
The Court has also held that, if an addressee of a decision decides to bring an action for annulment, the matter to be tried by the European Union judicature relates only to those aspects of the decision which concern that addressee. Unchallenged aspects concerning other addressees, on the other hand, do not form part of the matter to be tried by the Union judicature [...]. [...]
It follows, first, that, with respect to undertakings which have not brought actions against a final decision of the Commission imposing a fine on them under Article 65 CS or Article 23 of Regulation No 1/2003, that decision becomes final and, secondly, that that finality starts time running against them for the enforcement of the decision, as laid down by Article 4 of Decision No 715/78 and Article 26 of Regulation No 1/2003.
Consequently, with respect to those undertakings, an action brought by another undertaking against the same final decision cannot have any suspensive effect. [...]

Since Article 3 of Decision No 715/78 and Article 25(6) of Regulation No 1/2003 do not therefore draw any distinctions as regards decisions to which suspensive effect is attached, contrary to the Commission's claims, erga omnes effect need not be attached to actions brought against the acts referred to in Article 2 of Decision No 715/78 and Article 25(3) of Regulation No 1/2003 against which actions lie.

Having regard to the foregoing, it must be concluded that the General Court did not err in law in holding that the suspension of the limitation period which Article 3 of Decision No 715/78 and Article 25(6) of Decision No 1/2003 attach to judicial proceedings takes effect only inter partes.

CoJ 29 March 2011 (ArcelorMittal Luxembourg SA v. Commission, C-201/09 P and C-216/09 P) [2011] ECR I-2239, paras 141, 142, 144, 145, 147 and 148.

ARTICLE 26 – LIMITATION PERIOD FOR THE ENFORCEMENT OF PENALTIES

1. The power of the Commission to enforce decisions taken pursuant to Articles 23 and 24 shall be subject to a limitation period of five years.
2. Time shall begin to run on the day on which the decision becomes final.
3. The limitation period for the enforcement of penalties shall be interrupted:
    (a) by notification of a decision varying the original amount of the fine or periodic penalty payment or refusing an application for variation;
    (b) by any action of the Commission or of a Member State, acting at the request of the Commission, designed to enforce payment of the fine or periodic penalty payment.
4. Each interruption shall start time running afresh.
5. The limitation period for the enforcement of penalties shall be suspended for so long as:
    (a) time to pay is allowed;
    (b) enforcement of payment is suspended pursuant to a decision of the Court of Justice.

13.218   The provisions governing the Commission's power to impose fines for infringement of the rules on competition do not lay down any period of limitation.

In order to fulfil their function, limitation periods must be fixed in advance.

The fixing of their duration and the detailed rules for their application come within the powers of the Community legislature.

Although, in the absence of any provisions on this matter, the fundamental requirement of legal certainty has the effect of preventing the Commission from indefinitely delaying the exercise of its power to impose fines, its conduct in the present case cannot be regarded as constituting a bar to the exercise of that power as regards participation in the concerted practices of 1964 and 1965.

CoJ 14 July 1972 (ICI v. Commission, 48/69) [1972] ECR 619, paras 46–49.

See also CoJ 14 July 1972 (Geigy v. Commission 52/69) [1972] ECR 787, paras 20–22.

13.219   Therefore, contrary to what the appellants maintain, it is not only preparatory acts which fall outside the scope of the judicial review provided for in Article [263 TFEU] but any act not producing legal effects which are binding on and capable of affecting the interests of the individual, such as confirmatory measures and implementing measures […].

CoJ 12 September 2006 (Reynolds Tobacco and others v. Commission, C-131/03P) [2006] ECR I-7795, para. 55.

See also CoJ 1 December 2005 (United Kingdom v. Commission, C-46/03) [2005] ECR I-10167, para. 25.

With regard to the Commission's argument that the mere existence of the bank **13.220** guarantee excludes any application to the relationship between the applicant and the Commission of Regulation No 2988/74 [now Art. 26 Regulation No 1/2003], it is appropriate to point out that the existence of that contractual relationship between the Banco di Roma and the Commission cannot prevent the possibility of the Commission's power to enforce the Welded steel mesh decision on expiry of the time-limit laid down in Article 4 of that regulation being time-barred. Regulation No 2988/74 established a complete system of rules covering in detail the periods within which the Commission is entitled, without undermining the fundamental requirement of legal certainty, to enforce decisions imposing fines on undertakings which are the subject of proceedings under the Community competition rules [...].

General Court 27 September 2006 (Ferriére Nord, T-153/04) [2006] ECR II-3889, para. 45.

CHAPTER VIII

HEARINGS AND PROFESSIONAL SECRECY

ARTICLE 27 – HEARING OF THE PARTIES, COMPLAINANTS AND OTHERS

1. Before taking decisions as provided for in Articles 7, 8, 23 and Article 24(2), the Commission shall give the undertakings or associations of undertakings which are the subject of the proceedings conducted by the Commission the opportunity of being heard on the matters to which the Commission has taken objection. The Commission shall base its decisions only on objections on which the parties concerned have been able to comment. Complainants shall be associated closely with the proceedings.

2. The rights of defence of the parties concerned shall be fully respected in the proceedings. They shall be entitled to have access to the Commission's file, subject to the legitimate interest of undertakings in the protection of their business secrets. The right of access to the file shall not extend to confidential information and internal documents of the Commission or the competition authorities of the Member States. In particular, the right of access shall not extend to correspondence between the Commission and the competition authorities of the Member States, or between the latter, including documents drawn up pursuant to Articles 11 and 14. Nothing in this paragraph shall prevent the Commission from disclosing and using information necessary to prove an infringement.

3. If the Commission considers it necessary, it may also hear other natural or legal persons. Applications to be heard on the part of such persons shall, where they show a sufficient interest, be granted. The competition authorities of the Member States may also ask the Commission to hear other natural or legal persons.

4. Where the Commission intends to adopt a decision pursuant to Article 9 or Article 10, it shall publish a concise summary of the case and the main content of the commitments or of the proposed course of action. Interested third parties may submit their observations within a time limit which is fixed by the Commission in its publication and which may not be less than one month. Publication shall have regard to the legitimate interest of undertakings in the protection of their business secrets.

The statement of objections must set forth the essential facts upon which the Commission is relying at that stage of the procedure and the assessments set out by the Commission in that document are therefore purely provisional in character. Subsequently, the administrative procedure gives the undertakings an opportunity to explain themselves and, where appropriate, to bring the agreements or practices complained of into line with the rules of the Treaty. The Commission must take into account the factors emerging from the administrative procedure in order either to abandon such objections as have been shown to be unfounded or to amend and supplement its arguments, both in fact and in law, in support of the objections which it maintains. **13.221**

Order CoJ 18 June 1986 (British American Tobacco Company Ltd v. Commission, Joined Cases 142 and 156/ 84) [1986] ECR 1899, para. 13.

See also CoJ 3 September 2009 (William Prym GmbH Co. KG, Prym Consumer GmbH Co. KG v. Commission, C-534/07 P) [2009] ECR I-7415, para. 28.

[...] Furthermore it is settled case-law that that obligation is satisfied if the decision does not allege that the persons concerned have committed infringements other than those referred to in the notice of complaints and only takes into consideration facts on which the persons concerned have had the opportunity of making known their views. **13.222**

General Court 28 February 2002 (Compagnie générale maritime and others v. Commission, T-86/95) [1995] ECR II-1011, para. 205.

See also CoJ 15 July 1970 (ACF Chemiefarma v. Commission, 41/69) [1970] ECR 661, paras 26 and 94.

In examining the complaint of breach of the rights of the defence it should be noted at the outset that according to settled case-law, the statement of objections must be couched in terms that, even if succinct, are sufficiently clear to enable the parties concerned properly to identify the conduct complained of by the Commission. It is only on that basis that the statement of objections can fulfil its function under the Community regulations of giving undertakings all the information necessary to enable them properly to defend themselves, before the Commission adopts a final decision [...]. **13.223**

General Court 28 February 2002 (Compagnie générale maritime and others v. Commission, T-86/95) [1995] ECR II-1011, para. 205.

See also General Court 14 May 1998 (Mo och Domsjö v. Commission, T-352/94) [1998] ECR II-1989, para. 63; General Court 14 May 1998 (Enso Espaæola v. Commission, T-348/94) [1998] ECR II-1875, para. 83; General Court 14 May 1998 (Cascades v. Commission, T-308/94) [1998] ECR II-925, para. 42; General Court 22 October 2002 (Schneider Electric v. Commission, T-310/01) [2002] ECR II-4071, para. 438; General Court 30 January 2007 (France Télécom, T-340/03) [2007] ECR II-107, para. 18.

13.224   The final decision of the Commission is not, however, necessarily required to be a replica of the statement of objections [...]. It is in light of those principles that the present complaint of breach of the applicants' rights of defence falls to be assessed.
General Court 28 February 2002 (Compagnie générale maritime and others v. Commission, T-86/95) [1995] ECR II-1011, para. 205.

See also General Court 8 October 1996 (Compagnie Maritime Belge Transports and others v. Commission, T-24/93–T-26/93 and T-28/93) [1996] ECR II-1201, para. 113; General Court 7 June 1983 (SA Musique Diffusion Française v. Commission, Joined Cases 100–103/80) [1983] ECR 1825, para. 14; CoJ 15 July 1970 (ACF Chemiefarma v. Commission, 41/69) ECR 661, para. 91.

13.225   [I]t is permissible to supplement the statement of objections in the light of the parties' response, whose arguments show that they have actually been able to exercise their rights of defence. The Commission may also, in the light of the administrative procedure, revise or supplement its arguments of fact or law in support of its objections [...].
General Court 22 October 2002 (Schneider Electric v. Commission, T-310/01) [2002] ECR II-4071, para. 438.

See also General Court 30 January 2007 (France Télécom, T-340/03) [2007] ECR II-107, para. 18.

13.226   However, it is necessary in a case of this kind, if the right to be heard is to be complied with, first, that the undertakings which proposed those commitments be informed of the essential factual elements on the basis of which the Commission required new commitments and, secondly, that those undertakings can express their views on the matter. In the present case, the applicant was provided only with a summary of the conclusions which the Commission drew from the third-party observations. At the meeting of 27 October 2005, the Commission merely informed it of the fact that the third-party comments had principally referred to the risk of partitioning of the market and the risk of a cartel between De Beers and Alrosa, and that the Commissioner for Competition had requested the team responsible for the case not to accept the joint commitments in the circumstances. At the same time, Alrosa received a summary of the third-party observations and was informed of the nature of the commitments which the Commission expected the parties to give following the negative result of the consultation with third parties: cessation of all relations with effect from 2009 and a new offer of commitments, on that basis, before the end of November 2005.
General Court 11 July 2007 (Alrosa Company Ltd v. Commission, T-170/06) [2007] ECR II-2601, para. 196.

13.227   Given its importance, the statement of objections must specify unequivocally the legal person on whom fines may be imposed and be addressed to that person [...]. [...]
      The [General Court] was thus correct in holding [...] that the statement of objections had not enabled Bolloré to acquaint itself with the objection based on that

involvement or even with the facts established by the Commission in the decision in support of that objection, so that Bolloré had been unable properly to defend itself during the administrative procedure vis-à-vis the objection and the facts in question.

However [...] the [General Court] held that the defect would entail the annulment of the contested decision only if the allegations concerned could not be substantiated to the requisite legal standard on the basis of other evidence in the decision on which the undertakings concerned had been given the opportunity to comment. It added that if it were to transpire, upon examination of the substance, that the Commission had been correct to hold Bolloré liable for the participation of its subsidiary Copigraph in the cartel, the fact that the Commission had erred in law would not be sufficient to justify annulment of the decision because the error could not have had a decisive effect on the operative part thereof.

Those considerations led the [General Court], following its examination of the substance, to hold [...] that Bolloré was liable for the infringement of its subsidiary Copigraph irrespective of the direct involvement of the parent company and to uphold, in that judgment, the contested decision in so far as it ordered Bolloré to pay the fine imposed by the Commission, even though, on one essential point, Bolloré's rights of defence had been infringed.

However, the fact that in the contested decision Bolloré was held liable on the ground that it was involved in its capacity as Copigraph's parent company, as well as on the ground of its direct involvement, does not preclude the decision possibly having been based on conduct in respect of which Bolloré was not able to defend itself.

The [General Court] thus erred in law in failing to draw any legal conclusion from its finding that Bolloré's rights of defence had not been observed. Bolloré's first ground of appeal must therefore be declared well founded.

CoJ 3 September 2009 (Papierfabrik August Koehler AG, Bolloré, Distibuidora Vizcaína de Papeles SL v. Commission, Joined Cases C-322/07 P, C-327/07 P and C-338/07 P) [2009] ECR I-07191, paras 38, 41–45.

The right to be heard extends to all the matters of fact and of law which form the basis **13.228** for the decision-making act but not the final position which the administration intends to adopt [...].

In this case, the applicants [...] indicate that, in reaction to their reply to the statement of objections, the Commission adopted a new reasoning to justify the finding that they had participated in the cartel between 1994 and 1996.

The applicants' argument amounts to claiming that, before adopting the contested decision, the Commission should have heard their observations on the reasoning by which it intended to refute the arguments put forward in their reply to the statement of objections. Such a requirement finds no support in the case-law, and cannot be imposed on the Commission.

[...] The legal classification of the facts made in the statement of objections is, by definition, only provisional, and a subsequent Commission decision cannot be annulled on the sole ground that the definitive conclusions drawn from those facts do not correspond precisely with that intermediate classification [...].

General Court 19 May 2010 (IMI v. Commission, T-18/05) [2010] ECR II-1769, paras 109–112.

13.229   It follows that Alrosa could have had the status of 'undertaking concerned' only in the context of the proceedings brought under Article [101 TFEU], in which no decision was taken. In that context, Alrosa could not therefore claim the procedural rights reserved to the parties to the proceedings concerning the individual commitments, since those commitments were offered by De Beers in the administrative proceedings relating to the application of Article [102 TFEU] under reference COMP/E-2/38.381, which were terminated by the contested decision.

[…], only if it transpired that the Commission without an objective reason made a single factual situation the subject of two separate sets of proceedings would Alrosa have to be accorded the rights enjoyed by an undertaking concerned in relation to the proceedings brought under Article [102 TFEU]. However, the General Court did not find that the Commission misused its powers in that way in the present case, nor indeed was there any evidence in support of that view. It was objectively justified for the Commission to conduct two separate sets of administrative proceedings in view of their different material legal bases, Article [101 TFEU] on the one hand and Article [102 TFEU] on the other. With regard to the proceedings under Article [102 TFEU], only De Beers as the presumed dominant undertaking could be the addressee of the statement of objections and the Commission's final decision in those proceedings.

That being so, it is permissible for a third-party undertaking which considers itself to be affected by a decision taken under Article 7 or Article 9 of Regulation No 1/2003 to protect its rights by bringing an action against that decision. It does not follow, however, that such an undertaking, in the present case Alrosa, acquires the status of a 'party concerned' within the meaning of Article 27(2) of Regulation No 1/2003.

CoJ 29 June 2010 (Commission v. Alrosa Company Ltd, C-441/07P) [2010] ECR I-5945, paras 88–90.

13.230   According to settled case-law, provided that the Commission indicates expressly in the statement of objections that it will consider whether it is appropriate to impose fines on the undertakings concerned and that it sets out the principal elements of fact and of law that may give rise to a fine, such as the gravity and the duration of the alleged infringement and the fact that it has been committed 'intentionally or negligently', it fulfils its obligation to respect the right of the undertakings concerned to be heard. In doing so, it provides them with the necessary elements to defend themselves not only against a finding of infringement but also against the fact of being fined […].

Moreover, it is apparent from the case-law that to oblige the Commission to give to undertakings under investigation specific indications of the level of the contemplated fines at the stage of the statement of objections would in effect require it inappropriately to anticipate its final decision […]. […]

It is true that the Commission did not indicate in the statement of objections that Deltafina could be characterised as the leader of the cartel. It should be noted that such a characterisation has important consequences as to the amount of the fine to be imposed on the undertaking concerned. Thus, in accordance with Section 2 of the Guidelines, it is an aggravating circumstance which results in a significant increase in the amount of the fine. Similarly, in accordance with Section B(e) of the Leniency Notice, such characterisation automatically rules out the benefit of a very significant reduction of the fine, even if the undertaking classified as leader meets all the conditions laid down for obtaining such a reduction. It is therefore for the Commission to set out in the statement of objections the evidence which it considers relevant for the purpose of enabling the undertaking which may be characterised as the leader of the cartel to reply to such a claim. However, in the light of the fact that that statement is but a step in the adoption of the final decision and does not therefore constitute the Commission's definitive position, the Commission cannot be required, already at that stage, to carry out a legal classification of the evidence on which it relies in its final decision in characterising an undertaking as the leader of the cartel.

General Court 8 September 2010 (Deltafina v. Commission, T-29/05) [2010] ECR II-4077, paras 324, 325 and 327.

In that regard, it must be recalled that the competition rules cannot be interpreted as meaning that the person concerned in an administrative procedure is under an obligation to reply to the statement of objections sent to him by the Commission. Neither the rules setting out the rights and duties of undertakings within the administrative procedure provided for by competition law nor any general principle of law oblige those undertakings to do any more than supply the Commission with such information as it has requested from them under Article 18 of Regulation No 1/2003. Such a duty would, in the absence of any legal basis, be difficult to reconcile with the principle of respecting the rights of the defence, since it would create difficulties for a person who, having failed for whatever reason to reply to a statement of objections, wished to bring legal proceedings [...]. Thus, while the legality of the Commission decision finding that a person has infringed competition law and consequently imposing a fine on that person can be assessed only in relation to the facts and points of law pertaining at the date when the decision was adopted [...], it does not follow that the person concerned is under an obligation to supply to the Commission, at the stage of the administrative procedure, all the material on which it may wish to rely in support of an action for annulment, brought before the Courts of the European Union, of the decision adopted at the conclusion of the administrative procedure. **13.231**

General Court 12 July 2011 (Fuji Electric Co. Ltd, T-132/07) [2011] ECR II-4091, para. 124.

ARTICLE 28 – PROFESSIONAL SECRECY

1. **Without prejudice to Articles 12 and 15, information collected pursuant to Articles 17 to 22 shall be used only for the purpose for which it was acquired.**

2. **Without prejudice to the exchange and to the use of information foreseen in Articles 11, 12, 14, 15 and 27, the Commission and the competition authorities of the Member States, their officials, servants and other persons working under the supervision of these authorities as well as officials and civil servants of other authorities of the Member States shall not disclose information acquired or exchanged by them pursuant to this Regulation and of the kind covered by the obligation of professional secrecy. This obligation also applies to all representatives and experts of Member States attending meetings of the Advisory Committee pursuant to Article 14.**

13.232   The sphere of information covered by the obligation of professional secrecy extends beyond business secrets of undertakings (Opinion of Advocate General Lenz in *Case 53/85 AKZO Chemie v. Commission* [1986] ECR 1965, at 1977). A distinction should be drawn, in this respect, between the protection that must be afforded to information covered by the obligation of professional secrecy in relation to persons, undertakings or associations of undertakings having a right to be heard in the context of proceedings applying the competition rules, and that which should be afforded to such information in relation to the general public. The obligation on officials and other servants of the institutions not to disclose information in their possession covered by the obligation of professional secrecy, laid down in Article [339 TFEU] and implemented, in the field of competition rules applicable to undertakings, by Article 20(2) of Regulation No 17 [now Article 28(2) Regulation No 1/2003], is mitigated in regard to persons on whom Article 19(2) [now Article 27 Regulation No 1/2003] confers the right to be heard. The Commission may communicate to such persons certain information covered by the obligation of professional secrecy in so far as it is necessary to do so for the proper conduct of the investigation. However, that power does not apply to business secrets, which are afforded very special protection (see, to that effect, *AKZO Chemie v. Commission*, paras 26–28). Conversely, information covered by the obligation of professional secrecy cannot be disclosed to the general public, irrespective of whether business secrets or other confidential information are involved.

General Court 30 May 2006 (Bank Austria Creditanstalt AG v. Commission, T-198/03) [2006] ECR II-01429, para. 29.

See also General Court 12 October 2007 (Pergan Hilffstoffe für industrielle Prozesse, T-474/04) [2007] ECR II-4225, paras 59–66.

The [General Court] would point out that the interest of an undertaking which the **13.233** Commission has fined for breach of competition law in the non-disclosure to the public of details of the offending conduct of which it is accused does not merit any particular protection, given, first, the public interest in knowing as fully as possible the reasons for any Commission action, the interest of economic operators in knowing the sort of behaviour for which they are liable to be penalised and the interest of persons harmed by the infringement in being informed of the details thereof so that they may, where appropriate, assert their rights against the undertakings punished, and, second, the fined undertaking's ability to seek judicial review of such a decision [...]. [...]

The [General Court] considers, further, that, since the Commission's findings relating to an infringement committed by an undertaking are capable of infringing the principle of the presumption of innocence, those findings must, in principle, be regarded as confidential as regards the public, and therefore as being of the kind covered by the obligation of professional secrecy. This principle stems, inter alia, from the need to respect the reputation and dignity of the person concerned as that person has not been finally found guilty of an infringement [...]. The confidentiality of such information is confirmed by Article 4(1)(b) of Regulation No 1049/2001, which provides that information, whose disclosure would harm the protection of privacy and the integrity of the individual, is to be protected. Finally, the confidentiality of that information cannot depend on whether, and to what extent, it is of probative value for the purpose of proceedings at national level.

General Court 12 October 2007 (Pergan Hilffstoffe für industrielle Prozesse, T-474/04) [2007] ECR II-4225, paras 72 and 78.

CHAPTER IX

EXEMPTION REGULATIONS

ARTICLE 29 – WITHDRAWAL IN INDIVIDUAL CASES

1. Where the Commission, empowered by a Council Regulation, such as Regulations 19/65/EEC, (EEC) No 2821/71, (EEC) No 3976/87, (EEC) No 1534/91 or (EEC) No 479/ 92, to apply Article 81 (3) of the Treaty by regulation, has declared Article 81(1) of the Treaty inapplicable to certain categories of agreements, decisions by associations of undertakings or concerted practices, it may, acting on its own initiative or on a complaint, withdraw the benefit of such an exemption Regulation when it finds that in any particular case an agreement, decision or concerted practice to which the exemption Regulation applies has certain effects which are incompatible with Article 81(3) of the Treaty.

2. Where, in any particular case, agreements, decisions by associations of undertakings or concerted practices to which a Commission Regulation referred to in paragraph 1 applies have effects which are incompatible with Article 81(3) of the Treaty in the territory of a Member State, or in a part thereof, which has all the characteristics of a distinct geographic market, the competition authority of that Member State may withdraw the benefit of the Regulation in question in respect of that territory.

CHAPTER X

GENERAL PROVISIONS

ARTICLE 30 – PUBLICATION OF DECISIONS

1. **The Commission shall publish the decisions, which it takes pursuant to Articles 7 to 10, 23 and 24.**
2. **The publication shall state the names of the parties and the main content of the decision, including any penalties imposed. It shall have regard to the legitimate interest of undertakings in the protection of their business secrets.**

However, that power does not apply to all documents of the kind covered by the obligation of professional secrecy. Article 19(3) which provides for the publication of notices prior to the granting of negative clearance or exemptions, and Article 21 which provides for the publication of certain decisions, both require the Commission to have regard to the legitimate interest of undertakings in the protection of their business secrets. Business secrets are thus afforded very special protection. Although they deal with particular situations, those provisions must be regarded as the expression of a general principle which applies during the course of the administrative procedure. It follows that a third party who has submitted a complaint may not in any circumstances be given access to documents containing business secrets. Any other solution would lead to the unacceptable consequence that an undertaking might be inspired to lodge a complaint with the Commission solely in order to gain access to its competitors' business secrets. **13.234**

It is undoubtedly for the Commission to assess whether or not a particular document contains business secrets. After giving an undertaking an opportunity to state its views, the Commission is required to adopt a decision in that connection which contains an adequate statement of the reasons on which it is based and which must be notified to the undertaking concerned. Having regard to the extremely serious damage which could result from improper communication of documents to a competitor, the Commission must, before implementing its decision, give the undertaking an opportunity to bring an action before the court with a view to having the assessments made reviewed by it and to preventing disclosure of the documents in question.
CoJ 24 June 1986 (AKZO Chemie v. Commission, 53/85) [1986] ECR 1965, paras 28 and 29.

The information covered by professional secrecy may be both confidential information and business secrets. Article [339 TFEU] applies to 'information of the kind covered by professional secrecy'. It applies in particular to 'information about undertakings, their business relations or their cost components'. It thus expressly refers to information which, in principle, falls, by reason of its content, within the category of business secrets, as defined by the Court of Justice [...]. **13.235**

General Court 18 September 1996 (Postbank v. Commission, T-353/94) [1996] ECR II-921, para. 86.

13.236   The [General Court] has jurisdiction in two respects over actions contesting Commission decisions imposing fines on undertakings for infringement of the competition rules.

First, under Article [263 TFEU] it has the task of reviewing the legality of those decisions. In that context, it must in particular review compliance with the duty to state reasons laid down in Article [296 TFEU], infringement of which renders a decision liable to annulment.

Second, the [General Court] has power to assess, in the context of the unlimited jurisdiction accorded to it by Article [261 TFEU] and Article 17 of Regulation No 17 [now Article 23 Regulation No 1/2003], the appropriateness of the amounts of fines. That assessment may justify the production and taking into account of additional information which is not as such required, by virtue of the duty to state reasons under Article [296 TFEU], to be set out in the decision.

CoJ 16 November 2000 (KNP BT v. Commission, C-248/98 P) [2000] ECR I-9641, paras 38–40.

See also General Court 9 July 2003 (Cheil Jedang Corp. v. Commission, T-220/00) [2003] ECR II-2473, para. 44.

13.237   It follows that, when the hearing officer takes a decision under the third paragraph of Article 9 of Decision 2001/462, he must not merely examine whether the version of a decision taken under Regulation No 17 and intended for publication contains business secrets or other information enjoying similar protection. He must also check whether that version contains other information which cannot be disclosed to the public either on the basis of rules of Community law affording such information specific protection or because it is information of the kind covered by the obligation of professional secrecy. Accordingly, the hearing officer's decision does produce legal effects inasmuch as it determines whether a text for publication contains such information.

This interpretation of the third paragraph of Article 9 of Decision 2001/462 is consistent with Article 21(2) of Regulation No 17 [now Article 30(2) Regulation No 1/2003], which provides that 'the publication ... shall have regard to the legitimate interest of undertakings in the protection of their business secrets'. That provision, which underlines the particular protection required for business secrets, cannot be construed as limiting the protection afforded by other rules of Community law, such as Article [339 TFEU], Article 20(2) of Regulation No 17 and Regulation No 45/2001, to other information covered by the obligation of professional secrecy. [...]

In order that information be of the kind to fall within the ambit of the obligation of professional secrecy, it is necessary, first of all, that it be known only to a limited number of persons. It must then be information whose disclosure is liable to cause serious harm to the person who has provided it or to third parties. Finally, the interests liable to be harmed by disclosure must, objectively, be worthy of protection. The assessment as to the confidentiality of a piece of information thus requires the legitimate interests opposing disclosure of the information to be weighed against the public interest that the activities of the Community institutions take place as openly as possible.

General Court 30 May 2006 (Bank Austria Creditanstalt v. Commission, T-198/03) [2006] ECR II-1429, paras 34, 35 and 71.

It cannot, however, be inferred from the principle of lawfulness that publication of **13.238** measures adopted by the institutions is prohibited where it is not explicitly prescribed by the Treaties or by another act of general application. As Community law currently stands, such a prohibition would be incompatible with Article 1 EU, according to which, within the European Union, 'decisions are taken as openly as possible'. This principle is reflected in Article [15 TFEU], which, subject to certain conditions, grants citizens a right of access to documents of the institutions. It is also expressed, inter alia, in Article [297 TFEU], which makes the entry into force of certain acts of the institutions subject to publication, and in numerous provisions of Community law which, like Article 21(1) of Regulation No 17 [now Article 30(1) Regulation No 1/2003], require the institutions to provide the public with an account of their activities. In accordance with this principle, and in the absence of provisions explicitly ordering or prohibiting publication, the power of the institutions to make acts which they adopt public is the rule, to which there are exceptions in so far as Community law, in particular through provisions ensuring compliance with the obligation of professional secrecy, prevents disclosure of such acts or of certain information contained therein. [...]

Thus, the aim of Article 21(2) of Regulation No 17 is not to limit the Commission's freedom to publish, of its own volition, a version of its decision that is fuller than the minimum necessary and also to include information whose publication is not required, in so far as the disclosure of that information is not inconsistent with the protection of professional secrecy.

General Court 30 May 2006 (Bank Austria Creditanstalt v. Commission, T-198/03) [2006] ECR II-1429, paras 69 and 79.

In addition, the [General Court] would point out that the second part of Article **13.239** [30(2)], like [Article 28 of Regulation No 1/2003], is only the expression in secondary Community legislation of the protection of professional secrecy laid down in Article [339 TFEU] [...].

The [General Court] would point out, next, that neither Article [339 TFEU] nor Regulation No 17 [now Regulation No 1/2003] state explicitly what information, apart from business secrets, is covered by the obligation of professional secrecy. It is apparent, however, from the open wording of Article [339 TFEU] (which prohibits disclosure of 'information of the kind covered by the obligation of professional secrecy, in particular information about undertakings, their business relations or their cost components'), from Article 13(1) of Regulation No 2842/98 [now Article 16(1) Regulation No 773/2004] and from the case-law, that the concept of 'information covered by the obligation of professional secrecy' also includes confidential information other than business secrets [...].

It follows from this wider understanding of the concept of 'information covered by the obligation of professional secrecy' that Article 21 of Regulation No 17 [now Article 30 Regulation No 1/2003] and Article 9 of Decision 2001/462 must be interpreted as meaning that they apply, in the same way as Article 13(1) of Regulation No 2842/98 [now Article 16(1) Regulation No 773/2004], both to business secrets and to other confidential information. In addition, the confidentiality of information, for which professional secrecy requires that it be protected under Article [339 TFEU], may also stem from other provisions of primary or secondary Community law, such as Article 4 of Regulation No 1049/2001 [...] or from Article [16 TFEU] and Regulation (EC) No 45/2001 of the European Parliament and of the Council of 18 December 2000 on the protection of individuals with regard to the processing of personal data by the Community institutions and bodies and on the free movement of such data (OJ 2001 L 8, p. 1) [...].

As regards, generally, the nature of business secrets or other information covered by the obligation of professional secrecy, it is necessary, first of all, that such business secrets or confidential information be known only to a limited number of persons. Next, it must be information whose disclosure is liable to cause serious harm to the person who has provided it or to third parties ([...] see also Commission Notice 2005/C 325/07 on the rules for access to the Commission file in cases pursuant to Articles 81 [EC] and 82 [EC] (OJ 2005 C 325, p. 7), paragraphs 3.2.1 and 3.2.2). Finally, the interests liable to be harmed by disclosure must be worthy of protection. The assessment as to the confidentiality of a piece of information requires, in this regard, the individual legitimate interests opposing disclosure of the information to be weighed against the public interest that the activities of the Community institutions take place as openly as possible [...].

General Court 12 October 2007 (Pergan Hilffstoffe für industrielle Prozesse, T-474/ 04) [2007] ECR II-4225, paras 62–65.

ARTICLE 31 – REVIEW BY THE COURT OF JUSTICE

The Court of Justice shall have unlimited jurisdiction to review decisions whereby the Commission has fixed a fine or periodic penalty payment. It may cancel, reduce or increase the fine or periodic penalty payment imposed.

OVERVIEW

A. GENERAL	13.240	C. NO UNLIMITED JURISDICTION IN APPEAL	13.249
B. EXERCISE OF UNLIMITED JURISDICTION	13.247		

A. GENERAL

13.240 The [General Court] has jurisdiction in two respects over actions contesting Commission decisions imposing fines on undertakings for infringement of the competition rules. First, under Article [263 TFEU], it has the task of reviewing the legality of those decisions. In that context, it must in particular review compliance with the duty to state reasons laid down in Article [296 TFEU], infringement of which renders a decision liable to annulment. Secondly, the [General Court] has power to assess, in the exercise of the unlimited jurisdiction accorded to it by Article [261 TFEU] and Article 17 of Regulation No 17 [now Article 31 Regulation No 1/2003], the appropriateness of the amounts of fines. That assessment may justify the production and taking into account of additional information which the duty to state reasons does not as such require to be set out in the decision [...].
General Court 9 July 2003 (Cheil Jedang Corp. v. Commission, T-220/00) [2003] ECR II-2473, para. 215.

13.241 [T]he Community judicature is empowered to exercise its unlimited jurisdiction where the question of the amount of the fine is before it and that that jurisdiction may be exercised to reduce that amount as well as to increase it.
CoJ 8 February 2007 (Groupe Danone v. Commission, C-3/06) [2007] ECR I-1331, para. 62.

13.242 The review of legality is supplemented by the unlimited jurisdiction which the Courts of the European Union were afforded by Article 17 of Regulation No 17 and which is now recognised by Article 31 of Regulation No 1/2003, in accordance with Article 261 TFEU. That jurisdiction empowers the Courts, in addition to carrying out a mere review of the lawfulness of the penalty, to substitute their own appraisal for the Commission's and, consequently, to cancel, reduce or increase the fine or penalty payment imposed [...].

It must, however, be pointed out that the exercise of unlimited jurisdiction does not amount to a review of the Court's own motion, and that proceedings before the Courts of the European Union are inter partes. With the exception of pleas involving matters of public policy which the Courts are required to raise of their own motion, such as the failure to state reasons for a contested decision, it is for the applicant to raise pleas in law against that decision and to adduce evidence in support of those pleas.

CoJ 8 December 2011 (Chalkor AE Epexergasias Metallon, C-386/10 P) [2011] ECR I-13085, paras 63 and 64.

13.243   As regards the review of legality, the Court of Justice has held that whilst, in areas giving rise to complex economic assessments, the Commission has a margin of discretion with regard to economic matters, that does not mean that the Courts of the European Union must refrain from reviewing the Commission's interpretation of information of an economic nature. Not only must those Courts establish, among other things, whether the evidence relied on is factually accurate, reliable and consistent but also whether that evidence contains all the information which must be taken into account in order to assess a complex situation and whether it is capable of substantiating the conclusions drawn from it [...].

CoJ 8 December 2011 (KME Germany AG, KME France SAS and KME Italy SpA, C-272/09 P) [2011] ECR I-12789, para. 94.

13.244   Ruling on the principle of effective judicial protection, a general principle of EU law to which expression is now given by Article 47 of the Charter, the Court of Justice has held that, in addition to the review of legality provided for by the FEU Treaty, the European Union judicature has the unlimited jurisdiction which it is afforded by Article 31 of Regulation No 1/2003, in accordance with Article 261 TFEU, and which empowers it to substitute its own appraisal for the Commission's and, consequently, to cancel, reduce or increase the fine or periodic penalty payment imposed [...].

As regards the review of legality, the Court has pointed out that the European Union judicature must carry it out on the basis of the evidence adduced by the applicant in support of the pleas in law put forward and that it cannot use the Commission's margin of discretion – either as regards the choice of factors taken into account in the application of the 2002 Leniency Notice or as regards the assessment of those factors – as a basis for dispensing with the conduct of an in-depth review of the law and of the facts [...].

As the review provided for by the Treaties involves review by the European Union judicature of both the law and the facts, and means that it has the power to assess the evidence, to annul the decision at issue and to alter the amount of a fine, the Court has concluded that the review of legality provided for under Article 263 TFEU, supplemented by the unlimited jurisdiction in respect of the amount of the fine, provided for under Article 31 of Regulation No 1/2003, is not contrary to the requirements of the principle of effective judicial protection which is currently set out in Article 47 of the Charter [...].

CoJ 24 October 2013 (Kone Oyj and Others v. Commission, C-510/11 P), ECLI: EU:C:2013:696, paras 23–25.

It should also be noted that the system of judicial review of Commission decisions **13.245** relating to proceedings under Articles 101 TFEU and 102 TFEU consists in a review of the legality of the acts of the institutions for which provision is made in Article 263 TFEU, which may be supplemented, pursuant to Article 261 TFEU and at the request of applicants, by the General Court's exercise of unlimited jurisdiction with regard to the penalties imposed in that regard by the Commission […].

In that regard, as the Court has stated on many occasions, the scope of judicial review provided for in Article 263 TFEU extends to all the elements of Commission decisions relating to proceedings applying Articles 101 TFEU and 102 TFEU which are subject to in-depth review by the General Court, in law and in fact, in the light of the pleas raised by the appellants and taking into account all the elements submitted by the latter, whether those elements pre-date or post-date the contested decision, whether they were submitted previously in the context of the administrative procedure or, for the first time, in the context of the proceedings before the General Court, in so far as those elements are relevant to the review of the legality of the Commission decision […].

It should be noted, however, that the EU Courts cannot, in the context of the review of legality referred to in Article 263 TFEU, substitute their own reasoning for that of the author of the contested act […]. […]

Therefore, when they exercise their unlimited jurisdiction provided for in Article 261 TFEU and Article 31 of Regulation No 1/2003, the EU Courts are empowered, in addition to the mere review of the legality of the penalty, to substitute their own assessment in relation to the determination of the amount of that penalty for that of the Commission, which adopted the measure in which that amount was initially fixed.

By contrast, the scope of that unlimited jurisdiction is strictly limited, unlike the review of legality provided for in Article 263 TFEU, to determining the amount of the fine.

It follows from this that the unlimited jurisdiction enjoyed by the General Court on the basis of Article 31 of Regulation No 1/2003 concerns solely the assessment by that Court of the fine imposed by the Commission, to the exclusion of any alteration of the constituent elements of the infringement lawfully determined by the Commission in the decision under examination by the General Court.

CoJ 21 January 2016 (Galp Energía España SA and Others v. European Commission, C-603/13 P), ECLI:EU:C:2016:38, paras 71–73 and 75–77.

As to the remainder, it must be borne in mind that, with regard to judicial review of **13.246** decisions whereby the Commission imposes a fine or periodic penalty payment for infringement of the competition rules, in addition to the review of legality provided for in Article 263 TFEU, the European Union judicature has the unlimited jurisdiction which it is afforded by Article 31 of Regulation No 1/2003, in accordance with Article 261 TFEU, and which empowers it to substitute its own appraisal for the Commission's and, consequently, to cancel, reduce or increase the fine or periodic penalty payment imposed.

However, it is important to note that the exercise of powers of unlimited jurisdiction provided for in Article 261 TFEU and in Article 31 of Regulation No 1/2003 does not amount to a review of the Court's own motion and that proceedings before the Courts of the European Union are inter partes. With the exception of pleas involving matters of public policy, which the Courts are required to raise of their own motion, it is therefore for the applicant to raise pleas in law against the decision at issue and to adduce evidence in support of those pleas.

On the other hand, in order to satisfy the requirements of the principle of effective judicial protection enshrined in the first paragraph of Article 47 of the Charter of Fundamental Rights of the European Union ('the Charter') and bearing in mind that Article 23(3) of Regulation No 1/2003 provides that the amount of the fine must be fixed by reference to the gravity and duration of the infringement, the General Court is bound, in the exercise of the powers conferred by Articles 261 and 263 TFEU, to examine all complaints based on issues of fact and law which seek to show that the amount of the fine is not commensurate with the gravity or the duration of the infringement.

CoJ 9 June 2016 (Repsol Lubricantes y Especialidades, SA and Others v. European Commission, C-617/13 P), ECLI:EU:C:2016:416, paras 84–86.

B. EXERCISE OF UNLIMITED JURISDICTION

13.247   [T]he Guidelines are without prejudice to the assessment of the fine by the Community judicature when it exercises that unlimited jurisdiction [...].

It is therefore appropriate for the [General Court] to exercise its unlimited jurisdiction, as BASF has requested it to examine the question of the amount of the fine imposed.

General Court 12 December 2007 (BASF and UCB, T-101/05 en T-111/05) [2007] ECR II-4949, paras 213 and 214.

See also General Court 8 October 2008 (Schunk GmbH, Schunk Kohlenstoff-Technik GmbH, T-69/04) [2008] ECR II-2567, paras 242 and 243.

13.248   [G]iven that the Commission merely imposed on the applicant a fine of a minimal amount of EUR 1 000 and that that amount as such has not been called into question by the applicant, the [General Court] is not required to give a ruling on the exact extent of the applicant's participation for the purposes of its effect on the lawfulness of the level of the fine imposed.

General Court 8 July 2008 (AC-Treuhand AG, T-99/04) [2008] ECR II-1501, para. 155.

C. NO UNLIMITED JURISDICTION IN APPEAL

13.249   The Court cannot therefore, at the appeal stage, examine whether the amount of the fine fixed by the [General Court], in the exercise of its unlimited jurisdiction, is proportionate in relation to the gravity and duration of the infringement as established by the [General Court] on completion of its appraisal of the facts [...].

CoJ 18 September 2003 (Volkswagen, C-338/00) [2003] ECR I-9189, para. 151.

As regards the allegedly disproportionate nature of the fine, on the other hand, it must **13.250** be borne in mind that it is not for the Court of Justice, when ruling on questions of law in the context of an appeal, to substitute, on grounds of fairness, its own assessment for that of the [General Court] exercising its unlimited jurisdiction to rule on the amount of fines imposed for infringements of Community law […].

CoJ 28 June 2005 (Dansk Rørindustrie and Others v. Commission, Joined Cases C-189, 202, 205–208 and 213/02P) [2005] ECR I-5425, para. 245.

ARTICLE 32

(Repealed.)

Repealed by Regulation (EC) 1419/2006 of 25 September 2006 (OJ 2006 L 269/1, entry into force 18 October 2006)

ARTICLE 33 – IMPLEMENTING PROVISIONS

1. The Commission shall be authorised to take such measures as may be appropriate in order to apply this Regulation. The measures may concern, inter alia:

    (a) the form, content and other details of complaints lodged pursuant to Article 7 and the procedure for rejecting complaints;

    (b) the practical arrangements for the exchange of information and consultations provided for in Article 11;

    (c) the practical arrangements for the hearings provided for in Article 27.

2. Before the adoption of any measures pursuant to paragraph 1, the Commission shall publish a draft thereof and invite all interested parties to submit their comments within the time-limit it lays down, which may not be less than one month. Before publishing a draft measure and before adopting it, the Commission shall consult the Advisory Committee on Restrictive Practices and Dominant Positions.

    See Commission Regulation (EC) No 773/2004 of 7 April 2004 relating to the conduct of proceedings by the Commission pursuant to Articles 81 and 82 of the EC Treaty (OJ 2004 L 123/18) and Commission Regulation (EC) No 622/2008 of 30 June 2008 amending Regulation (EC) No 773/2004, as regards the conduct of settlement procedures in cartel cases (OJ 2008 L 171/3).

CHAPTER XI

TRANSITIONAL, AMENDING AND FINAL PROVISIONS

ARTICLE 34 – TRANSITIONAL PROVISIONS

1. **Applications made to the Commission under Article 2 of Regulation No 17, notifications made under Articles 4 and 5 of that Regulation and the corresponding applications and notifications made under Regulations (EEC) No 1017/68, (EEC) No 4056/86 and (EEC) No 3975/87 shall lapse as from the date of application of this Regulation.**

2. **Procedural steps taken under Regulation No 17 and Regulations (EEC) No 1017/68, (EEC) No 4056/86 and (EEC) No 3975/87 shall continue to have effect for the purposes of applying this Regulation.**

13.251   [...] The fact that Regulation No 1/2003, which now governs the implementation of the rules on competition laid down in Articles [101 TFEU] and [102 TFEU] put an end to the notification procedure which previously existed therefore has no effect on the enforcement of a judgment granting the applicant's application for annulment [of a Commission decision concluding that an agreement on site-sharing falls within the scope of Art. 101(1) TFEU].

General Court 2 May 2006 (O2 (Germany) v. Commission), T-328/03) [2006] ECR I-1231, para. 48.

ARTICLE 35 – DESIGNATION OF COMPETITION AUTHORITIES OF MEMBER STATES

1. **The Member States shall designate the competition authority or authorities responsible for the application of Articles 81 and 82 of the Treaty in such a way that the provisions of this regulation are effectively complied with. The measures necessary to empower those authorities to apply those Articles shall be taken before 1 May 2004. The authorities designated may include courts.**

2. **When enforcement of Community competition law is entrusted to national administrative and judicial authorities, the Member States may allocate different powers and functions to those different national authorities, whether administrative or judicial.**

3. **The effects of Article 11(6) apply to the authorities designated by the Member States including courts that exercise functions regarding the preparation and the adoption of the types of decisions foreseen in Article 5. The effects of Article 11(6) do not extend to courts in so far as they act as review courts in respect of the types of decisions foreseen in Article 5.**

4. **Notwithstanding paragraph 3, in the Member States where, for the adoption of certain types of decisions foreseen in Article 5, an authority brings an action before a judicial authority that is separate and different from the prosecuting authority and provided that the terms of this paragraph are complied with, the effects of Article 11(6) shall be limited to the authority prosecuting the case which shall withdraw its claim before the judicial authority when the Commission opens proceedings and this withdrawal shall bring the national proceedings effectively to an end.**

Although Article 35(1) of the Regulation leaves it to the domestic legal order of each **13.252** Member State to determine the detailed procedural rules for legal proceedings brought against decisions of the competition authorities designated thereunder, such rules must not jeopardise the attainment of the objective of the regulation, which is to ensure that Articles 101 TFEU and 102 TFEU are applied effectively by those authorities. [...]

[...] Article 35 of [Regulation 1/2003] must be interpreted as precluding national rules which do not allow a national competition authority to participate, as a defendant or respondent, in judicial proceedings brought against a decision that the authority itself has taken. It is for the national competition authorities to gauge the extent to which their intervention is necessary and useful having regard to the effective application of EU competition law. However, if the national competition authority consistently fails to enter an appearance in such judicial proceedings, the effectiveness of Articles 101 TFEU and 102 TFEU is jeopardised. [...]

CoJ 7 December 2010 (Vlaamse federatie van verenigingen van Brood-en Banketbakkers, Ijsbereiders en Chocoladebewerkers (VEBIC), C-439/08) [2010] ECR I-12471, paras 57 and 64.

ARTICLE 36 – AMENDMENT OF REGULATION (EEC) NO 1017/68

Regulation (EEC) No 1017/68 is amended as follows:

1. **Article 2 is repealed;**
2. **in Article 3(1), the words 'The prohibition laid down in Article 2' are replaced by the words 'The prohibition in Article 81(1) of the Treaty';**
3. **Article 4 is amended as follows:**

    (a) **In paragraph 1, the words 'The agreements, decisions and concerted practices referred to in Article 2' are replaced by the words 'Agreements, decisions and concerted practices pursuant to Article 81(1) of the Treaty';**

    (b) **Paragraph 2 is replaced by the following:**

    '2. If the implementation of any agreement, decision or concerted practice covered by paragraph 1 has, in a given case, effects which are incompatible with the requirements of Article 81(3) of the Treaty, undertakings or associations of undertakings may be required to make such effects cease.'

4. **Articles 5 to 29 are repealed with the exception of Article 13(3) which continues to apply to decisions adopted pursuant to Article 5 of Regulation (EEC) No 1017/68 prior to the date of application of this Regulation until the date of expiration of those decisions;**
5. **in Article 30, paragraphs 2, 3 and 4 are deleted.**

ARTICLE 37 – AMENDMENT OF REGULATION (EEC) NO 2988/74

In Regulation (EEC) No 2988/74, the following Article is inserted:
'Article 7a
Exclusion
This Regulation shall not apply to measures taken under Council Regulation (EC) No 1/2003 of 16 December 2002 on the implementation of the rules on competition laid down in Articles 81 and 82 of the Treaty.'[16]

---

16   OJ L 1, 4.1.2003, p. 1.

ARTICLE 38 – AMENDMENT OF REGULATION (EEC) NO 4056/86

Regulation (EEC) No 4056/86 is amended as follows:

1. Article 7 is amended as follows:

    (a) Paragraph 1 is replaced by the following:

    '1. Breach of an obligation

    Where the persons concerned are in breach of an obligation which, pursuant to Article 5, attaches to the exemption provided for in Article 3, the Commission may, in order to put an end to such breach and under the conditions laid down in Council Regulation (EC) No 1/2003 of 16 December 2002 on the implementation of the rules on competition laid down in Articles 81 and 82 of the Treaty[17] adopt a decision that either prohibits them from carrying out or requires them to perform certain specific acts, or withdraws the benefit of the block exemption which they enjoyed.'

    (b) Paragraph 2 is amended as follows:

    (i) In point (a), the words 'under the conditions laid down in Section II' are replaced by the words 'under the conditions laid down in Regulation (EC) No 1/2003';

    (ii) The second sentence of the second subparagraph of point (c)(i) is replaced by the following:

    'At the same time it shall decide, in accordance with Article 9 of Regulation (EC) No 1/2003, whether to accept commitments offered by the undertakings concerned with a view, inter alia, to obtaining access to the market for non conference lines.'

2. Article 8 is amended as follows:

    (a) Paragraph 1 is deleted.

    (b) In paragraph 2 the words 'pursuant to Article 10' are replaced by the words 'pursuant to Regulation (EC) No 1/2003'.

    (c) Paragraph 3 is deleted;

3. Article 9 is amended as follows:

    (a) In paragraph 1, the words 'Advisory Committee referred to in Article 15' are replaced by the words 'Advisory Committee referred to in Article 14 of Regulation (EC) No 1/2003';

    (b) In paragraph 2, the words 'Advisory Committee as referred to in Article 15' are replaced by the words 'Advisory Committee referred to in Article 14 of Regulation (EC) No 1/2003';

4. Articles 10 to 25 are repealed with the exception of Article 13(3) which continues to apply to decisions adopted pursuant to Article 81(3) of the

---

17   OJ L 1, 4.1.2003, p. 1.

Treaty prior to the date of application of this Regulation until the date of expiration of those decisions;

5.   in Article 26, the words 'the form, content and other details of complaints pursuant to Article 10, applications pursuant to Article 12 and the hearings provided for in Article 23(1) and (2)' are deleted.

ARTICLE 39 – AMENDMENT OF REGULATION (EEC) NO 3975/87

Articles 3 to 19 of Regulation (EEC) No 3975/87 are repealed with the exception of Article 6(3) which continues to apply to decisions adopted pursuant to Article 81(3) of the Treaty prior to the date of application of this Regulation until the date of expiration of those decisions.

ARTICLE 40 – AMENDMENT OF REGULATIONS NO 19/65/EEC, (EEC) NO 2821/71 AND (EEC) NO 1534/91

Article 7 of Regulation No 19/65/EEC, Article 7 of Regulation (EEC) No 2821/71 and Article 7 of Regulation (EEC) No 1534/91 are repealed.

ARTICLE 41 – AMENDMENT OF REGULATION (EEC) NO 3976/87

Regulation (EEC) No 3976/87 is amended as follows:

1. Article 6 is replaced by the following:
    'Article 6
    The Commission shall consult the Advisory Committee referred to in Article 14 of Council Regulation (EC) No 1/2003 of 16 December 2002 on the implementation of the rules on competition laid down in Articles 81 and 82 of the Treaty[18] before publishing a draft Regulation and before adopting a Regulation.'
2. Article 7 is repealed.

---

18   OJ L 1, 4.1.2003, p. 1.

ARTICLE 42 – AMENDMENT OF REGULATION (EEC) NO 479/92

Regulation (EEC) No 479/92 is amended as follows:

1. **Article 5 is replaced by the following:**
   'Article 5
   Before publishing the draft Regulation and before adopting the Regulation, the Commission shall consult the Advisory Committee referred to in Article 14 of Council Regulation (EC) No 1/2003 of 16 December 2002 on the implementation of the rules on competition laid down in Articles 81 and 82 of the Treaty'.[19]
2. **Article 6 is repealed.**

---

[19]   OJ L 1, 4.1.2003, p. 1.

ARTICLE 43 – REPEAL OF REGULATIONS NO 17 AND NO 141

1.   Regulation No 17 is repealed with the exception of Article 8(3) which continues to apply to decisions adopted pursuant to Article 81(3) of the Treaty prior to the date of application of this Regulation until the date of expiration of those decisions.
2.   Regulation No 141 is repealed.
3.   References to the repealed Regulations shall be construed as references to this Regulation.

ARTICLE 44 – REPORT ON THE APPLICATION
OF THE PRESENT REGULATION

Five years from the date of application of this Regulation, the Commission shall report to the European Parliament and the Council on the functioning of this Regulation, in particular on the application of Article 11(6) and Article 17.

On the basis of this report, the Commission shall assess whether it is appropriate to propose to the Council a revision of this Regulation.

ARTICLE 45 – ENTRY INTO FORCE

This Regulation shall enter into force on the 20th day following that of its publication in the Official Journal of the European Communities. It shall apply from 1 May 2004.

This Regulation shall be binding in its entirety and directly applicable in all Member States.

14

REGULATION (EC) NO 139/2004 ON THE CONTROL OF CONCENTRATIONS BETWEEN UNDERTAKINGS*

COUNCIL REGULATION (EC) NO 139/2004 OF 20 JANUARY 2004 ON THE CONTROL OF CONCENTRATIONS BETWEEN UNDERTAKINGS (OJ 2004 L 24/1)

THE COUNCIL OF THE EUROPEAN UNION,

Having regard to the Treaty establishing the European Community, and in particular Articles 83 and 308 thereof,

Having regard to the proposal from the Commission,[1]

Having regard to the opinion of the European Parliament,[2]

Having regard to the opinion of the European Economic and Social Committee,[3]

Whereas:

(1) Council Regulation (EEC) No 4064/89 of 21 December 1989 on the control of concentrations between undertakings[4] has been substantially amended. Since further amendments are to be made, it should be recast in the interest of clarity.

(2) For the achievement of the aims of the Treaty, Article 3(1)(g) gives the Community the objective of instituting a system ensuring that competition in the internal market is not distorted. Article 4(1) of the Treaty provides that the activities of the Member States and the Community are to be conducted in accordance with the principle of an open market economy with free competition. These principles are essential for the further development of the internal market.

(3) The completion of the internal market and of economic and monetary union, the enlargement of the European Union and the lowering of international barriers to

---

* This chapter was written by Karsten Metzlaff and Peter Stauber.

1   OJ C 20, 28.1.2003, p. 4.
2   Opinion delivered on 9.10.2003 (not yet published in the Official Journal).
3   Opinion delivered on 24.10.2003 (not yet published in the Official Journal).
4   OJ L 395, 30.12.1989, p. 1. Corrected version in OJ L 257, 21.9.1990, p. 13. Regulation as last amended by Regulation (EC) No 1310/97 (OJ L 180, 9.7.1997, p. 1). Corrigendum in OJ L 40, 13.2.1998, p. 17.

trade and investment will continue to result in major corporate reorganisations, particularly in the form of concentrations.

(4) Such reorganisations are to be welcomed to the extent that they are in line with the requirements of dynamic competition and capable of increasing the competitiveness of European industry, improving the conditions of growth and raising the standard of living in the Community.

(5) However, it should be ensured that the process of reorganisation does not result in lasting damage to competition; Community law must therefore include provisions governing those concentrations which may significantly impede effective competition in the common market or in a substantial part of it.

(6) A specific legal instrument is therefore necessary to permit effective control of all concentrations in terms of their effect on the structure of competition in the Community and to be the only instrument applicable to such concentrations. Regulation (EEC) No 4064/89 has allowed a Community policy to develop in this field. In the light of experience, however, that Regulation should now be recast into legislation designed to meet the challenges of a more integrated market and the future enlargement of the European Union. In accordance with the principles of subsidiarity and of proportionality as set out in Article 5 of the Treaty, this Regulation does not go beyond what is necessary in order to achieve the objective of ensuring that competition in the common market is not distorted, in accordance with the principle of an open market economy with free competition.

(7) Articles 81 and 82, while applicable, according to the case-law of the Court of Justice, to certain concentrations, are not sufficient to control all operations which may prove to be incompatible with the system of undistorted competition envisaged in the Treaty. This Regulation should therefore be based not only on Article 83 but, principally, on Article 308 of the Treaty, under which the Community may give itself the additional powers of action necessary for the attainment of its objectives, and also powers of action with regard to concentrations on the markets for agricultural products listed in Annex I to the Treaty.

(8) The provisions to be adopted in this Regulation should apply to significant structural changes, the impact of which on the market goes beyond the national borders of any one Member State. Such concentrations should, as a general rule, be reviewed exclusively at Community level, in application of a "one-stop shop" system and in compliance with the principle of subsidiarity. Concentrations not covered by this Regulation come, in principle, within the jurisdiction of the Member States.

(9) The scope of application of this Regulation should be defined according to the geographical area of activity of the undertakings concerned and be limited by quantitative thresholds in order to cover those concentrations which have a Community dimension. The Commission should report to the Council on the implementation of the applicable thresholds and criteria so that the Council, acting in accordance with Article 202 of the Treaty, is in a position to review them regularly, as well as the rules regarding pre-notification referral, in the light of the experience gained; this requires statistical data to be provided by the Member States to the Commission to enable it to prepare such reports and possible

proposals for amendments. The Commission's reports and proposals should be based on relevant information regularly provided by the Member States.

(10) A concentration with a Community dimension should be deemed to exist where the aggregate turnover of the undertakings concerned exceeds given thresholds; that is the case irrespective of whether or not the undertakings effecting the concentration have their seat or their principal fields of activity in the Community, provided they have substantial operations there.

(11) The rules governing the referral of concentrations from the Commission to Member States and from Member States to the Commission should operate as an effective corrective mechanism in the light of the principle of subsidiarity; these rules protect the competition interests of the Member States in an adequate manner and take due account of legal certainty and the 'one-stop shop' principle.

(12) Concentrations may qualify for examination under a number of national merger control systems if they fall below the turnover thresholds referred to in this Regulation. Multiple notification of the same transaction increases legal uncertainty, effort and cost for undertakings and may lead to conflicting assessments. The system whereby concentrations may be referred to the Commission by the Member States concerned should therefore be further developed.

(13) The Commission should act in close and constant liaison with the competent authorities of the Member States from which it obtains comments and information.

(14) The Commission and the competent authorities of the Member States should together form a network of public authorities, applying their respective competences in close cooperation, using efficient arrangements for information-sharing and consultation, with a view to ensuring that a case is dealt with by the most appropriate authority, in the light of the principle of subsidiarity and with a view to ensuring that multiple notifications of a given concentration are avoided to the greatest extent possible. Referrals of concentrations from the Commission to Member States and from Member States to the Commission should be made in an efficient manner avoiding, to the greatest extent possible, situations where a concentration is subject to a referral both before and after its notification.

(15) The Commission should be able to refer to a Member State notified concentrations with a Community dimension which threaten significantly to affect competition in a market within that Member State presenting all the characteristics of a distinct market. Where the concentration affects competition on such a market, which does not constitute a substantial part of the common market, the Commission should be obliged, upon request, to refer the whole or part of the case to the Member State concerned. A Member State should be able to refer to the Commission a concentration which does not have a Community dimension but which affects trade between Member States and threatens to significantly affect competition within its territory. Other Member States which are also competent to review the concentration should be able to join the request. In such a situation, in order to ensure the efficiency and predictability of the system, national time limits should be suspended until a decision has been reached as to the referral of the case. The Commission should have the power to examine and deal with a concentration on behalf of a requesting Member State or requesting Member States.

(16) The undertakings concerned should be granted the possibility of requesting referrals to or from the Commission before a concentration is notified so as to further improve the efficiency of the system for the control of concentrations within the Community. In such situations, the Commission and national competition authorities should decide within short, clearly defined time limits whether a referral to or from the Commission ought to be made, thereby ensuring the efficiency of the system. Upon request by the undertakings concerned, the Commission should be able to refer to a Member State a concentration with a Community dimension which may significantly affect competition in a market within that Member State presenting all the characteristics of a distinct market; the undertakings concerned should not, however, be required to demonstrate that the effects of the concentration would be detrimental to competition. A concentration should not be referred from the Commission to a Member State which has expressed its disagreement to such a referral. Before notification to national authorities, the undertakings concerned should also be able to request that a concentration without a Community dimension which is capable of being reviewed under the national competition laws of at least three Member States be referred to the Commission. Such requests for pre-notification referrals to the Commission would be particularly pertinent in situations where the concentration would affect competition beyond the territory of one Member State. Where a concentration capable of being reviewed under the competition laws of three or more Member States is referred to the Commission prior to any national notification, and no Member State competent to review the case expresses its disagreement, the Commission should acquire exclusive competence to review the concentration and such a concentration should be deemed to have a Community dimension. Such pre-notification referrals from Member States to the Commission should not, however, be made where at least one Member State competent to review the case has expressed its disagreement with such a referral.

(17) The Commission should be given exclusive competence to apply this Regulation, subject to review by the Court of Justice.

(18) The Member States should not be permitted to apply their national legislation on competition to concentrations with a Community dimension, unless this Regulation makes provision therefor. The relevant powers of national authorities should be limited to cases where, failing intervention by the Commission, effective competition is likely to be significantly impeded within the territory of a Member State and where the competition interests of that Member State cannot be sufficiently protected otherwise by this Regulation. The Member States concerned must act promptly in such cases; this Regulation cannot, because of the diversity of national law, fix a single time limit for the adoption of final decisions under national law.

(19) Furthermore, the exclusive application of this Regulation to concentrations with a Community dimension is without prejudice to Article 296 of the Treaty, and does not prevent the Member States from taking appropriate measures to protect legitimate interests other than those pursued by this Regulation, provided that such measures are compatible with the general principles and other provisions of Community law.

(20) It is expedient to define the concept of concentration in such a manner as to cover operations bringing about a lasting change in the control of the undertakings concerned and therefore in the structure of the market. It is therefore appropriate to include, within the scope of this Regulation, all joint ventures performing on a lasting basis all the functions of an autonomous economic entity. It is moreover appropriate to treat as a single concentration transactions that are closely connected in that they are linked by condition or take the form of a series of transactions in securities taking place within a reasonably short period of time.

(21) This Regulation should also apply where the undertakings concerned accept restrictions directly related to, and necessary for, the implementation of the concentration. Commission decisions declaring concentrations compatible with the common market in application of this Regulation should automatically cover such restrictions, without the Commission having to assess such restrictions in individual cases. At the request of the undertakings concerned, however, the Commission should, in cases presenting novel or unresolved questions giving rise to genuine uncertainty, expressly assess whether or not any restriction is directly related to, and necessary for, the implementation of the concentration. A case presents a novel or unresolved question giving rise to genuine uncertainty if the question is not covered by the relevant Commission notice in force or a published Commission decision.

(22) The arrangements to be introduced for the control of concentrations should, without prejudice to Article 86(2) of the Treaty, respect the principle of non-discrimination between the public and the private sectors. In the public sector, calculation of the turnover of an undertaking concerned in a concentration needs, therefore, to take account of undertakings making up an economic unit with an independent power of decision, irrespective of the way in which their capital is held or of the rules of administrative supervision applicable to them.

(23) It is necessary to establish whether or not concentrations with a Community dimension are compatible with the common market in terms of the need to maintain and develop effective competition in the common market. In so doing, the Commission must place its appraisal within the general framework of the achievement of the fundamental objectives referred to in Article 2 of the Treaty establishing the European Community and Article 2 of the Treaty on European Union.

(24) In order to ensure a system of undistorted competition in the common market, in furtherance of a policy conducted in accordance with the principle of an open market economy with free competition, this Regulation must permit effective control of all concentrations from the point of view of their effect on competition in the Community. Accordingly, Regulation (EEC) No 4064/89 established the principle that a concentration with a Community dimension which creates or strengthens a dominant position as a result of which effective competition in the common market or in a substantial part of it would be significantly impeded should be declared incompatible with the common market.

(25) In view of the consequences that concentrations in oligopolistic market structures may have, it is all the more necessary to maintain effective competition in such markets. Many oligopolistic markets exhibit a healthy degree of competition. However, under certain circumstances, concentrations involving the elimination

of important competitive constraints that the merging parties had exerted upon each other, as well as a reduction of competitive pressure on the remaining competitors, may, even in the absence of a likelihood of coordination between the members of the oligopoly, result in a significant impediment to effective competition. The Community courts have, however, not to date expressly interpreted Regulation (EEC) No 4064/89 as requiring concentrations giving rise to such non-coordinated effects to be declared incompatible with the common market. Therefore, in the interests of legal certainty, it should be made clear that this Regulation permits effective control of all such concentrations by providing that any concentration which would significantly impede effective competition, in the common market or in a substantial part of it, should be declared incompatible with the common market. The notion of "significant impediment to effective competition" in Article 2(2) and (3) should be interpreted as extending, beyond the concept of dominance, only to the anti-competitive effects of a concentration resulting from the non-coordinated behaviour of undertakings which would not have a dominant position on the market concerned.

(26) A significant impediment to effective competition generally results from the creation or strengthening of a dominant position. With a view to preserving the guidance that may be drawn from past judgments of the European courts and Commission decisions pursuant to Regulation (EEC) No 4064/89, while at the same time maintaining consistency with the standards of competitive harm which have been applied by the Commission and the Community courts regarding the compatibility of a concentration with the common market, this Regulation should accordingly establish the principle that a concentration with a Community dimension which would significantly impede effective competition, in the common market or in a substantial part thereof, in particular as a result of the creation or strengthening of a dominant position, is to be declared incompatible with the common market.

(27) In addition, the criteria of Article 81(1) and (3) of the Treaty should be applied to joint ventures performing, on a lasting basis, all the functions of autonomous economic entities, to the extent that their creation has as its consequence an appreciable restriction of competition between undertakings that remain independent.

(28) In order to clarify and explain the Commission's appraisal of concentrations under this Regulation, it is appropriate for the Commission to publish guidance which should provide a sound economic framework for the assessment of concentrations with a view to determining whether or not they may be declared compatible with the common market.

(29) In order to determine the impact of a concentration on competition in the common market, it is appropriate to take account of any substantiated and likely efficiencies put forward by the undertakings concerned. It is possible that the efficiencies brought about by the concentration counteract the effects on competition, and in particular the potential harm to consumers, that it might otherwise have and that, as a consequence, the concentration would not significantly impede effective competition, in the common market or in a substantial part of it, in particular as a result of the creation or strengthening of a dominant

position. The Commission should publish guidance on the conditions under which it may take efficiencies into account in the assessment of a concentration.

(30) Where the undertakings concerned modify a notified concentration, in particular by offering commitments with a view to rendering the concentration compatible with the common market, the Commission should be able to declare the concentration, as modified, compatible with the common market. Such commitments should be proportionate to the competition problem and entirely eliminate it. It is also appropriate to accept commitments before the initiation of proceedings where the competition problem is readily identifiable and can easily be remedied. It should be expressly provided that the Commission may attach to its decision conditions and obligations in order to ensure that the undertakings concerned comply with their commitments in a timely and effective manner so as to render the concentration compatible with the common market. Transparency and effective consultation of Member States as well as of interested third parties should be ensured throughout the procedure.

(31) The Commission should have at its disposal appropriate instruments to ensure the enforcement of commitments and to deal with situations where they are not fulfilled. In cases of failure to fulfil a condition attached to the decision declaring a concentration compatible with the common market, the situation rendering the concentration compatible with the common market does not materialise and the concentration, as implemented, is therefore not authorised by the Commission. As a consequence, if the concentration is implemented, it should be treated in the same way as a non-notified concentration implemented without authorisation. Furthermore, where the Commission has already found that, in the absence of the condition, the concentration would be incompatible with the common market, it should have the power to directly order the dissolution of the concentration, so as to restore the situation prevailing prior to the implementation of the concentration. Where an obligation attached to a decision declaring the concentration compatible with the common market is not fulfilled, the Commission should be able to revoke its decision. Moreover, the Commission should be able to impose appropriate financial sanctions where conditions or obligations are not fulfilled.

(32) Concentrations which, by reason of the limited market share of the undertakings concerned, are not liable to impede effective competition may be presumed to be compatible with the common market. Without prejudice to Articles 81 and 82 of the Treaty, an indication to this effect exists, in particular, where the market share of the undertakings concerned does not exceed 25% either in the common market or in a substantial part of it.

(33) The Commission should have the task of taking all the decisions necessary to establish whether or not concentrations with a Community dimension are compatible with the common market, as well as decisions designed to restore the situation prevailing prior to the implementation of a concentration which has been declared incompatible with the common market.

(34) To ensure effective control, undertakings should be obliged to give prior notification of concentrations with a Community dimension following the conclusion of the agreement, the announcement of the public bid or the acquisition of a controlling interest. Notification should also be possible where the undertakings concerned satisfy the Commission of their intention to enter into an agreement

for a proposed concentration and demonstrate to the Commission that their plan for that proposed concentration is sufficiently concrete, for example on the basis of an agreement in principle, a memorandum of understanding, or a letter of intent signed by all undertakings concerned, or, in the case of a public bid, where they have publicly announced an intention to make such a bid, provided that the intended agreement or bid would result in a concentration with a Community dimension. The implementation of concentrations should be suspended until a final decision of the Commission has been taken. However, it should be possible to derogate from this suspension at the request of the undertakings concerned, where appropriate. In deciding whether or not to grant a derogation, the Commission should take account of all pertinent factors, such as the nature and gravity of damage to the undertakings concerned or to third parties, and the threat to competition posed by the concentration. In the interest of legal certainty, the validity of transactions must nevertheless be protected as much as necessary.

(35) A period within which the Commission must initiate proceedings in respect of a notified concentration and a period within which it must take a final decision on the compatibility or incompatibility with the common market of that concentration should be laid down. These periods should be extended whenever the undertakings concerned offer commitments with a view to rendering the concentration compatible with the common market, in order to allow for sufficient time for the analysis and market testing of such commitment offers and for the consultation of Member States as well as interested third parties. A limited extension of the period within which the Commission must take a final decision should also be possible in order to allow sufficient time for the investigation of the case and the verification of the facts and arguments submitted to the Commission.

(36) The Community respects the fundamental rights and observes the principles recognised in particular by the Charter of Fundamental Rights of the European Union.[5] Accordingly, this Regulation should be interpreted and applied with respect to those rights and principles.

(37) The undertakings concerned must be afforded the right to be heard by the Commission when proceedings have been initiated; the members of the management and supervisory bodies and the recognised representatives of the employees of the undertakings concerned, and interested third parties, must also be given the opportunity to be heard.

(38) In order properly to appraise concentrations, the Commission should have the right to request all necessary information and to conduct all necessary inspections throughout the Community. To that end, and with a view to protecting competition effectively, the Commission's powers of investigation need to be expanded. The Commission should, in particular, have the right to interview any persons who may be in possession of useful information and to record the statements made.

(39) In the course of an inspection, officials authorised by the Commission should have the right to ask for any information relevant to the subject matter and purpose of the inspection; they should also have the right to affix seals during

---

5   OJ C 364, 18.12.2000, p. 1.

inspections, particularly in circumstances where there are reasonable grounds to suspect that a concentration has been implemented without being notified; that incorrect, incomplete or misleading information has been supplied to the Commission; or that the undertakings or persons concerned have failed to comply with a condition or obligation imposed by decision of the Commission. In any event, seals should only be used in exceptional circumstances, for the period of time strictly necessary for the inspection, normally not for more than 48 hours.

(40) Without prejudice to the case-law of the Court of Justice, it is also useful to set out the scope of the control that the national judicial authority may exercise when it authorises, as provided by national law and as a precautionary measure, assistance from law enforcement authorities in order to overcome possible opposition on the part of the undertaking against an inspection, including the affixing of seals, ordered by Commission decision. It results from the case-law that the national judicial authority may in particular ask of the Commission further information which it needs to carry out its control and in the absence of which it could refuse the authorisation. The case-law also confirms the competence of the national courts to control the application of national rules governing the implementation of coercive measures. The competent authorities of the Member States should cooperate actively in the exercise of the Commission's investigative powers.

(41) When complying with decisions of the Commission, the undertakings and persons concerned cannot be forced to admit that they have committed infringements, but they are in any event obliged to answer factual questions and to provide documents, even if this information may be used to establish against themselves or against others the existence of such infringements.

(42) For the sake of transparency, all decisions of the Commission which are not of a merely procedural nature should be widely publicised. While ensuring preservation of the rights of defence of the undertakings concerned, in particular the right of access to the file, it is essential that business secrets be protected. The confidentiality of information exchanged in the network and with the competent authorities of third countries should likewise be safeguarded.

(43) Compliance with this Regulation should be enforceable, as appropriate, by means of fines and periodic penalty payments. The Court of Justice should be given unlimited jurisdiction in that regard pursuant to Article 229 of the Treaty.

(44) The conditions in which concentrations, involving undertakings having their seat or their principal fields of activity in the Community, are carried out in third countries should be observed, and provision should be made for the possibility of the Council giving the Commission an appropriate mandate for negotiation with a view to obtaining non-discriminatory treatment for such undertakings.

(45) This Regulation in no way detracts from the collective rights of employees, as recognised in the undertakings concerned, notably with regard to any obligation to inform or consult their recognised representatives under Community and national law.

(46) The Commission should be able to lay down detailed rules concerning the implementation of this Regulation in accordance with the procedures for the exercise of implementing powers conferred on the Commission. For the adoption of such implementing provisions, the Commission should be assisted by an

Advisory Committee composed of the representatives of the Member States as specified in Article 23,

HAS ADOPTED THIS REGULATION:

ARTICLE 1 – SCOPE

1. Without prejudice to Article 4(5) and Article 22, this Regulation shall apply to all concentrations with a Community dimension as defined in this Article.

2. A concentration has a Community dimension where:
    (a) the combined aggregate worldwide turnover of all the under-takings concerned is more than EUR 5000 million; and
    (b) the aggregate Community-wide turnover of each of at least two of the undertakings concerned is more than EUR 250 million, unless each of the undertakings concerned achieves more than two-thirds of its aggregate Community-wide turnover within one and the same Member State.

3. A concentration that does not meet the thresholds laid down in para-graph 2 has a Community dimension where:
    (a) the combined aggregate worldwide turnover of all the under-takings concerned is more than EUR 2500 million;
    (b) in each of at least three Member States, the combined aggregate turnover of all the undertakings concerned is more than EUR 100 million;
    (c) in each of at least three Member States included for the purpose of point (b), the aggregate turnover of each of at least two of the undertakings concerned is more than EUR 25 million; and
    (d) the aggregate Community-wide turnover of each of at least two of the undertakings concerned is more than EUR 100 million, unless each of the undertakings concerned achieves more than two-thirds of its aggregate Community-wide turnover within one and the same Member State.

4. On the basis of statistical data that may be regularly provided by the Member States, the Commission shall report to the Council on the operation of the thresholds and criteria set out in paragraphs 2 and 3 by 1 July 2009 and may present proposals pursuant to paragraph 5.

5. Following the report referred to in paragraph 4 and on a proposal from the Commission, the Council, acting by a qualified majority, may revise the thresholds and criteria mentioned in paragraph 3.

OVERVIEW

A. GENERAL	(p.501)	C.	COMPETENCE OF THE EUROPEAN COMMISSION IN CASE OF AN AMENDMENT OF THE PROPOSED CONCENTRATION	14.02
B. EXTRATERRITORIAL APPLICATION	14.01			
		D.	NOTION OF 'UNDERTAKINGS CONCERNED'	14.03

A. GENERAL

See also the Commission Consolidated Jurisdictional Notice; recitals 9, 10 and 12; Article 5.

B. EXTRATERRITORIAL APPLICATION

Application of the Regulation is justified under public international law when it is foreseeable that a proposed concentration will have an immediate and substantial effect in the Community.   **14.01**
General Court 25 March 1999 (Gencor v. Commission, T-102/96) [1999] ECR II-753, para. 90.

C. COMPETENCE OF THE EUROPEAN COMMISSION IN CASE OF AN AMENDMENT OF THE PROPOSED CONCENTRATION

[It] goes without saying that the Commission loses its competence to examine a   **14.02**
concentration where the undertakings concerned completely abandon the proposed concentration.

However, the position is otherwise where the parties do no more than propose partial amendments to the draft. Proposals of that kind could not have the effect of requiring the Commission to re-examine its competence, without allowing the undertakings concerned significantly to disturb the course of the proceedings and the effectiveness of the control which the legislature sought to put in place, by obliging the Commission to verify its competence on a regular basis to the detriment of the examination of the substance of the case. [...]

In particular [...], it is necessary, when reviewing the proportionality of conditions or obligations which the Commission may, by virtue of Article 8(2) of Regulation No 4064/89 [now Regulation No 139/ 2004] impose on the parties to a concentration, not to determine whether the concentration still has a Community dimension after those conditions or obligations have been complied with, but to be satisfied that those conditions and those obligations are proportionate to and would entirely eliminate the competition problem that has been identified.

CoJ 18 December 2007 (Cementbouw v. Commission, C-202/06 P) [2007] ECR I-12129, paras 40, 41 and 54.

D. NOTION OF 'UNDERTAKINGS CONCERNED'

14.03   The TDA Group comprises, directly or indirectly, approximately [...] natural persons who are legally bound to always exercise collectively and jointly (as opposed to individually) their respective individual voting rights in Maxam. According to the Commission's Consolidated Jurisdictional Notice (paragraphs 151 and 152), natural persons cannot be considered as 'undertakings concerned' in the sense of the Merger Regulation if they do not carry out further economic activities or control one or more other economic undertakings. The TDA Group includes Maxam's current managers, technical experts, other employees and individual co-investors who do not currently hold control of any other economic undertaking. The TDA Group cannot therefore be considered as an undertaking concerned in the sense of the Jurisdictional Notice.

As a result of the above, post-transaction Advent and the TDA Group will acquire joint control of Maxam. However, only Advent can be considered an undertaking concerned in the sense of the Jurisdictional Notice and be therefore viewed as notifying party.

Commission 6 February 2012 (Advent/Maxam, M.6411), paras 6 and 7.

ARTICLE 2 – APPRAISAL OF CONCENTRATIONS

1.   Concentrations within the scope of this Regulation shall be appraised in accordance with the objectives of this Regulation and the following provisions with a view to establishing whether or not they are compatible with the common market.

In making this appraisal, the Commission shall take into account:

(a)   the need to maintain and develop effective competition within the common market in view of, among other things, the structure of all the markets concerned and the actual or potential competition from undertakings located either within or outwith the Community;

(b)   the market position of the undertakings concerned and their economic and financial power, the alternatives available to suppliers and users, their access to supplies or markets, any legal or other barriers to entry, supply and demand trends for the relevant goods and services, the interests of the intermediate and ultimate consumers, and the development of technical and economic progress provided that it is to consumers' advantage and does not form an obstacle to competition.

2.   A concentration which would not significantly impede effective competition in the common market or in a substantial part of it, in particular as a result of the creation or strengthening of a dominant position, shall be declared compatible with the common market.

3.   A concentration which would significantly impede effective competition, in the common market or in a substantial part of it, in particular as a result of the creation or strengthening of a dominant position, shall be declared incompatible with the common market.

4.   To the extent that the creation of a joint venture constituting a concentration pursuant to Article 3 has as its object or effect the coordination of the competitive behaviour of undertakings that remain independent, such coordination shall be appraised in accordance with the criteria of Article 81(1) and (3) of the Treaty, with a view to establishing whether or not the operation is compatible with the common market.

5.   In making this appraisal, the Commission shall take into account in particular:

–   whether two or more parent companies retain, to a significant extent, activities in the same market as the joint venture or in a market which is downstream or upstream from that of the joint venture or in a neighbouring market closely related to this market,

 – whether the coordination which is the direct consequence of the creation of the joint venture affords the undertakings concerned the possibility of eliminating competition in respect of a substantial part of the products or services in question.

OVERVIEW

A. GENERAL (p.504)

B. GENERAL CONSIDERATIONS FOR
APPRAISAL OF CONCENTRATIONS 14.04
 1. Standard of proof 14.04
 2. Parallel notifications 14.08
 3. Counterfactual in case of change
 from joint to sole control 14.11

C. PARAGRAPHS 2 AND 3: SUBSTANTIVE
ANALYSIS 14.14
 1. Relevant market 14.14

 2. Horizontal mergers 14.29
 3. Non-horizontal mergers 14.62
 4. Failing firm defence 14.70
 5. Efficiency defence 14.74

D. PARAGRAPHS 4 AND 5: ASSESSMENT
OF COORDINATED EFFECTS JV 14.78

E. PROCEDURAL ASPECTS 14.79
 1. Liability of the European Commission
 in case of annulment of a decision 14.79

A. GENERAL

See recitals 23–29 and 32.

B. GENERAL CONSIDERATIONS FOR APPRAISAL OF CONCENTRATIONS

1. Standard of proof

14.04 [Prospective analysis] A prospective analysis of the kind necessary in merger control must be carried out with great care since it does not entail the examination of past events – for which often many items of evidence are available which make it possible to understand the causes – or of current events, but rather a prediction of events which are more or less likely to occur in future if a decision prohibiting the planned concentration or laying down the conditions for it is not adopted.

 Thus, the prospective analysis consists of an examination of how a concentration might alter the factors determining the state of competition on a given market in order to establish whether it would give rise to a serious impediment to effective competition. Such an analysis makes it necessary to envisage various chains of cause and effect with a view to ascertaining which of them are the most likely.

CoJ 15 February 2005 (Commission v. Tetra Laval, C-12/03 P) [2008] ECR I-987, paras 42 and 43.

[I]t follows from Article 2(3) [...] that, in relation to concentrations, if a notified **14.05** transaction creates or strengthens a dominant position, on just one market, as a result of which effective competition would be significantly impeded in the common market, the Commission must, in principle, prohibit it, even if the transaction does not give rise to any other impediment to competition [...]. [...]

[W]here the Commission finds that a dominant position will be created or strengthened on a single market for various separate and independent reasons, it must be held in principle, and absent any indication to the contrary in the relevant grounds of the decision adopted by the Commission, that each of the reasons put forward would, of itself, have caused the Commission to make that finding.

[...] Accordingly, a prohibition decision should not be annulled on the ground that the applicant has shown that the analysis adopted in relation to one or more markets is vitiated by one or more errors, if it is nevertheless apparent from the prohibition decision that the notified merger satisfied those criteria in relation to one or more other markets [...] [and these were not contested in the application].

General Court 14 December 2005 (Honeywell v. Commission, T-209/01) [2005]
ECR II-5527, paras 79, 81 and 96.

[Same standard of proof for decision approving a concentration and for decision **14.06** prohibiting concentration] [T]here is nothing in Article 2(2) or (3) of the Regulation which states that it imposes different standards of proof in relation to decisions approving a concentration, on the one hand, and decisions prohibiting a concentration, on the other.

Thus, as the Court has, in substance, already held, the prospective analysis called for in relation to the control of concentrations, which consists of an examination of how a concentration might alter the factors determining the state of competition on a given market in order to establish whether it would give rise to a significant impediment to effective competition, makes it necessary to envisage various chains of cause and effect with a view to ascertaining which of them is the most likely [...]. [...]

Furthermore, it is true that, as is apparent from the Court's case-law, the decisions of the Commission as to the compatibility of concentrations with the common market must be supported by a sufficiently cogent and consistent body of evidence [...] and that in the context of the analysis of a 'conglomerate-type' concentration the quality of the evidence produced by the Commission in order to establish that it is necessary to adopt a decision declaring the concentration incompatible with the common market is particularly important [...].

However, it cannot be deduced from that that the Commission must, particularly where it pursues a theory of collective dominance, comply with a higher standard of proof in relation to decisions prohibiting concentrations than in relation to decisions approving them. That case-law merely reflects the essential function of evidence, which is to establish convincingly the merits of an argument or, as in the case of the control of concentrations, to support the conclusions underpinning the Commission's decisions [...]. Furthermore, the fact that an issue of collective dominance does, or does not, arise, cannot of itself have an impact on the standard of proof which applies. In that regard, the inherent complexity of a theory of competitive harm put forward in relation to a notified concentration is a factor which must be taken into account when assessing the plausibility of the various consequences such a concentration may have, in order to identify those which are most likely to arise, but such complexity does not, of itself, have an impact on the standard of proof which is required.

It follows that, where it has been notified of a proposed concentration pursuant to the Regulation, the Commission is, in principle, required to adopt a position, either in the sense of approving or of prohibiting the concentration, in accordance with its assessment of the economic outcome attributable to the concentration which is most likely to ensue.

CoJ 10 July 2008 (Impala, C-413/06 P) [2008] ECR I-4951, paras 46, 47 and 50–52.

14.07   As regards the standard of proof, [...] the Commission is, in principle, required to adopt a position, either in the sense of approving or of prohibiting the concentration notified to it, based on its assessment of the economic outcome attributable to the concentration which is the most likely to ensue. An assessment of probabilities is therefore involved, as the Commission contends, and not, as the applicants submit, an obligation on the Commission to show beyond any reasonable doubt that a concentration does not give rise to any competition concerns.

General Court 11 December 2013 (Cisco Systems and Messagenet v. Commission, T-79/12), ECLI:EU:T:2013:635, para. 47.

See also *CoJ 10 July 2008 (Bertelsmann and Sony Corporation of America v. Impala, C-413/06 P) [2008] ECR I-4951, paras 50–54.*

2. Parallel notifications

14.08   [Simultaneous analysis] On 10 July 2001 Shell and DEA notified the Commission of their agreement whereby Shell will acquire control over DEA (case *COMP/M.2389 . Shell/DEA*). This transaction will equally affect the market for ethylene on the ARG+. A single analysis of this market was carried out for the two cases, which leads to the present decision as well as to a parallel decision in case M.2389 – Shell/DEA, adopted simultaneously.

Commission 20 December 2001 (BP/E.ON, M.2533), OJ 2002 C 276/31, para. 18.

See also *Commission 20 December 2001 (Shell/Dea, M. 2389), OJ 2003 L 15/35, para. 21.*

14.09   [First notification prevails over second notification] Following the notification of the present concentration, the Commission received on 4 April 2007 a notification of a subsequent transaction [*Case M 4600 TUI/First Choice*]. This second transaction partly covers the same markets (i.e. tour operating business in UK and Ireland) as the markets on which Thomas Cook and MyTravel are active.

The Commission will assess the impact of these two transactions in light of the competitive situation that prevailed at the time of the respective notification. In view of the dates of notification, this implies that the present transaction will be assessed independently from the second transaction. Any further consolidation in the tour operating business brought about by the TUI/First Choice merger will be analysed taking into account the competitive circumstances prevailing at the time of the second notification.

In this respect, the Commission observes that it is inherent in the system of the Merger Regulation that a party that is the first to notify a concentration that, assessed on its own merits, would not significantly impede effective competition in the common market or in a substantial part thereof, is entitled to have its operation declared compatible with the common market within the applicable time limits. It is settled case-law that the relevant counter-factual for assessing a merger is, in principle, the competitive situation that prevails at the time of its notification. While it is true that the Commission is required to carry out a prospective analysis that takes account of future events and market developments, the administrative authorisation of future mergers in the same market with a Community dimension is under the control of the Commission.

Commission 4 May 2007 (KarstadtQuelle/MyTravel, M. 4601), paras 48–50.

See also Commission 4 June 2007 (Tui/First Choice, M.4600), paras 66–68.

[First notification prevails over second notification] On 14 May 2008, the Commission **14.10** authorised the acquisition without commitments by TomTom of Tele Atlas, the competitor of NAVTEQ in the supply of navigable digital map databases. The acquisition of NAVTEQ by Nokia was notified to the Commission after the notification of the acquisition of Tele Atlas by TomTom. The Commission therefore conducted, before the 14 May 2008, its assessment of the merger between Nokia and NAVTEQ on the hypothesis that TomTom and Tele Atlas were vertically integrated.

Commission 2 July 2008 (Nokia/Navteq, M.4942), para. 260.

See also Commission 14 May 2008 (TomTom/Tele Atlas, M. 4854), paras 187 and 188.

3. Counterfactual in case of change from joint to sole control

Also given that DPAG already had control over SOH, jointly with Securicor, prior to **14.11** this transaction and that the present transaction involves DPAGs acquisition of sole control from Securicor there is no evidence to suggest that this acquisition of sole control will of itself lead to any discernible change in the competitive conditions on this market.

Commission 19 June 2003 (Deutsche Post/Securicor, M.3155), OJ 2003 C 222/4, para. 14.

The proposed operation will have only a minor impact on the competitive situation in **14.12** liner shipping services because it will only result in a change from joint to sole control by Royal Nedlloyd over PONL and will therefore not significantly alter the competitive situation as it is today. Royal Nedlloyd already controls PONL since 1996 when it transferred all of its respective containerised liner shipping activities to the joint venture and does not have any containerised liner shipping activities outside its respective 50 per cent stake in PONL.

Commission 29 March 2004 (PO/Royal Nedlloyd/Po Nedlloyd, M.3379), para 11.

14.13   In the present case, in order to properly assess the impact of KLM's acquisition of Maersks 50 per cent shareholding in Martinair, and the effects of the resulting move from joint to sole control by KLM, it is first necessary to analyse the extent to which KLM and Martinair have constrained each other pre-merger. To this end, the Commission must consider the organisation and corporate governance of Martinair as well as the extent and nature of the competitive interaction between the parties on the markets where their activities overlap.

[T]he parties have confirmed that KLM has no influence on Martinair's decisions on entering a particular route, business cases with respect to individual routes, increasing or decreasing capacity or frequencies on individual routes or allocating aircraft to such routes. All these decisions are taken independently by internal decision-making bodies within Martinair. [...]

[...] The proposed change from joint to sole control would remove Martinair's current operational independence from KLM and eliminate the existing degree of competition between the two airlines as described in this section, in particular as regards the routes where Air France-KLM and Martinair are currently competing. However, the fact that KLM already has control of Martinair pre-merger clearly reduces the likely anti-competitive effects of the merger.

Commission 17 December 2008 (KLM-Martinair, M.5141), paras 16, 18 and 22.

C. PARAGRAPHS 2 AND 3: SUBSTANTIVE ANALYSIS

1. Relevant market

See also the Commission notice on the definition of the Relevant Market; Annex (Form CO) to Regulation No 802/2004; the case extracts under Art. 102 TFEU.

14.14   [New product markets] As preliminary remark, the Commission considers that a concentration may not only affect competition in existing markets, but also competition in innovation and new product markets. This may be the case when a concentration concerns entities currently developing new products or technologies which either may one day replace existing ones or which are being developed for a new intended use and will therefore not replace existing products but create a completely new demand. In principle, the effects of a concentration on competition in innovation in this type of situation may not be sufficiently assessed by restricting the assessment to actual or potential competition in existing product markets.

Commission 28 January 2015 (Novartis/Glaxosmithkline Oncology Business, M.7275), para. 89.

For the determination of the relevant geographic market, the following elements can be of relevance.

(a) Trade patterns

It is common ground that all Member States apart from Germany import substantial **14.15** quantities of potash from other Member States, and sometimes from non-member countries. [...]

Moreover, it may be seen from data provided by the United Nations Food and Agriculture Organisation that in the period from 1987 to 1989 potash prices in each Member State apart from Germany did not differ significantly, whereas German prices were 20 per cent higher than those in other Member States. [...]

Furthermore, as the Commission observes, transport costs do not appear to constitute a barrier to trade flows within the Community apart from Germany. That view is supported by the fact that trade flows exist between non-contiguous States such as the United Kingdom and Spain, Spain and Ireland, Spain and Italy, Spain and Belgium/Luxembourg, Germany and Ireland, Germany and Portugal, Germany and Italy, and France and the Netherlands. [...]

In those circumstances and in the absence of evidence to the contrary, the Commission's economic assessment that the Community apart from Germany constitutes a unit which is sufficiently homogeneous to be regarded overall as a separate geographical market appears sufficiently well founded [...].

CoJ 31 March 1998 (Kali + Salz, C-68/94 and C-30/95) [1998] ECR I-1375, paras 144, 148, 149 and 151.

The market investigation has confirmed that suppliers and traders of copper scrap offer **14.16** their scrap on a world-wide basis, and that many EEA-based buyers of scrap also purchase from sources outside the EEA.

Commission 23 January 2008 (Norddeutsche Affinerie/Cumerio, M.4781), para. 26.

(b) Price differences

[...] Even if the present price level in the Western European market was to increase by a **14.17** small but significant percentage, e.g. 5 per cent, it could not be expected that such an increase in price would bring about imports by the larger stockists from Japan, as the difference in price level between Japan and Western Europe, taking into account the 10 per cent import duty and transport costs, would still be substantial. If prices in Western Europe were to increase, for example by 5 per cent, reimports of SST exported by Western European or Japanese producers to North America would also not be possible given the higher price level in North America, the 10 per cent import duty and transport costs. Reimports would only become attractive with a stronger price increase in Western Europe.

Commission 31 January 1994 (Mannesmann/Vallourec/Ilva, M.315), OJ 1994 L 102/15, para. 25.

(c)   (National) preferences

14.18   The relevant geographic market for tv broadcasting is in the present case limited to the Netherlands. The relevant factors to be taken into account include the applicable regulatory regime, the existing language barriers, cultural factors and other conditions of competition prevailing in this market (eg the structure of the market for cable networks), on the basis of these elements there is a clear distinction to be made between the Netherlands and other countries.

Commission 20 September 1995 (RTL/Veronica/Endemol, M.553), OJ 1996 L 134/32, para. 25.

See also Commission 5 May 1995 (Kirch/Richemont/MultiChoice/Telepiu, M.584), OJ 1995 C 82/5, para. 17.

14.19   Although the chains operated by Blokker are active in other Member States (Bart Smit and Blokker in Belgium, Intertoys in Germany) and the Toys 'R' Us formula is operated in large parts of Europe, the geographic market cannot be defined on a basis wider than a national market. Consumer preferences and habits differ from one Member State to another.

Commission 26 June 1997 (Blokker/Toys 'R' Us, M.890), OJ 1998 L 316/1, para. 42.

(d)   Transportation costs and distances

14.20   [T]he overwhelming majority of customers in those Member States source their raw particle board from plants located within 500 km of their own facilities.

In such a market, national market shares are imperfect indicators of post-merger market power, as national boundaries do not necessarily reflect the competitive inter-action between plants (for example, two plants located on each side of a border would be closer substitutes than two plants in the same country but located far from each other). What ultimately matters for the competitive assessment is the change in the set of alternative suppliers that customers will be able to economically source from after the merger. [...]

Consequently, the geographic area where the originally intended transaction may have affected the conditions of competition lies within a radius of about 500 km around the original Targets production facilities (hereinafter referred to as 'the affected area'). Customers inside this area that have identical sets of realistic supply alternatives are likely to belong to the same relevant geographic market because they are likely to face homogeneous conditions of competition. In applying this approach, the Commission considers that transportation distances for raw particle board can be used as a first proxy to determine whether or not a particular production plant belongs to a set of realistic supply alternatives for a given customer.

For the purpose of this analysis, it is not necessary to give a precise, general definition of the relevant geographic market, since the competitive analysis will in any event have to focus on the affected area. For customers in that area, potential alternative suppliers will be identified in order to determine to what extent their choices would be affected by the proposed merger.

Commission 19 September 2007 (Kronospan/Constantia, M.4525), paras 26, 27, 29 and 30.

Indications were given that the transports costs are insignificant in relation to the total value of the copper scrap (less than 1 per cent). The high copper price has further limited the importance of transport costs in sourcing copper scrap world-wide. **14.21**

Commission 23 January 2008 (Norddeutsche Affinerie/Cumerio, M.4781), para. 26.

Although packaging products are commodities with a high degree of standardization throughout Europe, transport costs for (empty) industrial packaging products generally limit the distance across which these products can be sold. In that sense, the parties have submitted information confirming that large plastic drums and IBCs could be transported at least 600–700 km far away from their production plant, meanwhile small plastic drums, jerrycans and fassets could be transported beyond that distance. Therefore, the relevant geographic market for plastic drums and IBCs could be considered to be regional in scope, encompassing at least a radius of 600–700 km around every production plant. **14.22**

Commission 21 January 2009 (Mauser Holding International/Reyde/JV, M.5394), para. 23.

[The relevant geographic market defined according to delivery distances] [T]he Commission takes the view that the geographic scope of the market for plastic front and rear bumpers is regional in scope, encompassing a catchment area of 250 km around each of the OEMs' production plants. This is so for the following reasons. **14.23**

First, the information provided by the Notifying Party indicates that the vast majority of plastic front and rear bumpers are delivered within 250 km from where they are produced. [...] Longer delivery distances, especially those above 500 km are possible, but the analysis of the actual supply streams provided by the Notifying Party indicates that these are exceptional.

Supply distances are important because of three elements: (i) the risk of scratching the paint of the bumper, (ii) the need to deliver the finished bumper on the customers' production line within a very precise time frame, and (iii) the price of the bumper since transport costs can increase with the distance and therefore lead to less attractive prices. [...]

[Further], the analysis of tender information gathered during the market investigation indicates that distance is an important parameter to determine the competitiveness of the suppliers.

Commission 11 July 2016 (Plastic Omnium/Faurecia Exterior Automotive Business, M.7893), paras 59–61 and 67.

(e) Regulatory differences and other trade barriers

14.24   Although insurance markets may become more open to intra-community competition in the foreseeable future, geographic markets seem at present to be mostly national in view of differences of national regulatory systems.
Commission 15 November 1993 (Fortis/CGER, M.342), OJ 1993 C 23, para. 25.

14.25   The Sugar Regime was reformed in 2006 in order to increase the competitiveness of the EU sugar industry and to improve the market orientation of the sector by removing some of the regulatory barriers. Apart from a decrease in guaranteed prices and elimination of export subsidies for surplus sugar, the reform will result in a significant reduction of the sugar beet quota which is assigned for production in the EU. Member States with a less competitive industry like Portugal or Ireland do no longer have beet sugar industries or have significantly reduced their sugar producing capacities (as for example Spain, Italy, Greece, or Finland). This beet quota reduction is gradual and will continue until 2010/2011. As a result of the reform, the EU is expected to become a net importer of sugar (or sugar raws which is the input material for sugar refined in the EU) mainly from LDCs and ACP countries. This change on the demand side is comple-mented by liberalisation of imports as of 1 October 2009 removing the import quotas for established refiners. [...]

As a result, the relevant geographic market for the procurement of sugar cane raws covers at least the ACP and LDC countries who are allowed to have quota-free and duty-free access to the EEA. [...]
Commission 30 March 2009 (ABF/Azucarera, M.5449), paras 46 and 51.

14.26   [T]he respondents consider that there are also different market conditions for the provision of mail delivery services in the respective Nordic countries, mainly due to regulatory differences (e.g. with respect to VAT exemptions, reserved areas, taxation and licensing) leading to different levels of competition in these countries. While the mail markets in Sweden and Finland have been fully liberalised, Denmark and Norway have still retained reserved areas. These differences, and also differences in the geo-graphy of these countries have influence on the level of competition, of the provided services and their pricing in each of the Nordic countries.
Commission 21 April 2009 (Posten AB/Post Danmark A/S, M.5152), para. 23.

(f) Chain of substitution

14.27   Although a significant volume of raw float glass is transported across international borders, raw float glass is a bulky, heavy product. As a result, it is expensive to transport over great distances, for example, the cost of transportation by lorry amounts to between 7.5 and 10 per cent of the selling price at a distance of 500 km.

[...] Consequently, the natural geographical area of supply from a given float-glass production plant can be represented by concentric circles with a length of radius determined by the relative transport cost. Based on the information submitted by the parties, 80–90 per cent of a plants production is sold within a radius of 500 km, although of course some float glass is transported beyond this distance. In this light, the various supply areas can be seen as a series of overlapping circles with their centres at the float-glass plant. There are in total float-glass plants in the Community, with the further seven plants in Eastern Europe and Scandinavia. Within the Community there is a relative concentration in UK/Benelux/Northern France and Germany on the one hand and in Northern Spain/Northern Italy on the other hand. To a certain extent the argument could be made that there is a Northern European and Southern European market. However, given the dispersion of the individual float plants and the varying degrees of overlap for the natural supply areas, so that effects can be transmitted from one circle to another, it seems appropriate to consider that the geographical reference market is the Community as a whole. This would seem to be confirmed by the available price data. Based on the price information submitted by the parties for Belgium, France, Italy, Germany and the United Kingdom, prices for the benchmark 4 mm clear float class, cross-over and track one another typically within a narrow band. Although the float glass producers tend to have their highest market shares in the Member States where their float glass production is located, the market share data submitted by the parties demonstrates that there is a substantial degree of interpenetration at the national level. Therefore the Commission considers that the conditions of competition are sufficiently homogenous to allow the geographical reference market to be taken as the Community as a whole.

Commission 21 December 1993 (Pilkington/SIV, M.358), OJ 1994 L 15/24, para. 16.

[...] The parties' data on delivery confirm that most of their sales are delivered within a **14.28** radius of 1 000 km, but a smaller percentage also above 1 500 km and outside the EEA. However, in view of the dispersion of suppliers of copper rod in Europe there are overlapping geographical circles around production sites which influence each others' competitive situation, leading to the conclusion that the geographic market is to be defined as EEA-wide.

Commission 23 January 2008 (Norddeutsche Affinerie/Cumerio, M.4781), para. 49.

2. Horizontal mergers

See also recitals 24–26; the Guidelines on the assessment of horizontal mergers; Sections 6 and 7 of Annex I (Form CO) to Regulation No 802/2004.

(a) Non-coordinated effects

[T]he actual intentions of the new entity to reduce or increase its production capacity **14.29** are not decisive for the competitive assessment of this case. What counts is, in the Commission's view, the mere fact that the new entity will have the economic power to implement different strategic options, thus demonstrating its ability to act independently of its competitors and customers.

Commission 17 October 2001 (CVC/Lenzing, M.2187), OJ 2004 L 82/20, para. 167.

14.30   The Horizontal Merger Guidelines distinguish between two main ways in which mergers between actual or potential competitors on the same relevant market may significantly impede effective competition, namely non-coordinated and coordinated effects. Non-coordinated effects may significantly impede effective competition by eliminating important competitive constraints on one or more firms, which consequently would have increased market power, without resorting to coordinated behaviour. In that regard, the Horizontal Merger Guidelines consider not only the direct loss of competition between the merging firms, but also the reduction in competitive pressure on non-merging firms in the same market that could be brought about by the merger.

The Horizontal Merger Guidelines list a number of factors which may influence whether or not significant non-coordinated effects are likely to result from a merger, such as the large market shares of the merging firms, the fact that the merging firms are close competitors, the limited possibilities for customers to switch suppliers, or the fact that the merger would eliminate an important competitive force. These factors apply equally when determining whether a merger would create or strengthen a dominant position, or would otherwise significantly impede effective competition due to non-coordinated effects. Furthermore, not all of these factors need to be present to make significant non-coordinated effects likely and this is not an exhaustive list.

Commission 28 May 2015 (Hutchison 3G UK/Telefonica Ireland, M.6992), paras 189 and 190.

(i)   High market shares

14.31   [High market share, but small increment and dependence on one customer] On the overall market for transport liability insurance the parties combined market shares is estimated at [60–70 per cent] in Sweden. The increment through the operation will be relatively small and will not, in any event, be as great as it seems at first sight. [...] Moreover, [a large share] of If P&C's business in this market can be attributed to one large Swedish customer, [...] which is a multinational corporation. If P&C were to lose this customer, its market share would drop significantly. It has to be noted that contracts in transport liability are usually short term and are awarded as the result of a competitive bidding process where If P&C will face competition from other large providers [...]. [Therefore no serious doubt with regard to the creation or strengthening of a dominant position.]

Commission 18 December 2001 (Sampo/Varma Samp/IF Holding, M. 2676), OJ 2002 C 145/8, para. 26.

14.32   [High market shares neutralised by immature market without significant expansion barriers] It is clear that the operation will create a combined entity that has a relatively high market share in the market for oceanic cruises in the UK. However, this alone does not confer dominance and there are several specific characteristics of the oceanic cruises market in the UK which have led the Commission to conclude that the proposed operation will not create competition concerns.

The UK market is relatively immature and is forecast to grow rapidly in the next few years. This growth will provide opportunities for existing players to expand their operations and for new players to enter the market. The ability for new entry and expansion has been proven by recent history in the market. [...]

There are no significant barriers to expansion for international operators. In the short term (within a year), these operators can expand by increasing the proportion of UK customers on their ships and the threat of such expansion will be a significant competitive restraint on the combined entity. In the medium term (in one and a half to two years), they could further enhance their position in the UK by dedicating ships to the UK market.

The Commission therefore concludes that the operation will not create or strengthen a dominant position on the UK market for the provision of oceanic cruises as a result of which effective competition would be significantly impeded in the common market and the EEA.

Commission 24 July 2002 (Carnival Corporation/P&O Princess, M.2706), OJ 2005 C 318/6, para. 62.

[Market share of 50 per cent +] Furthermore, although the importance of market shares **14.33** may vary from one market to another, very large shares are in themselves, and save in exceptional circumstances, evidence of the existence of a dominant position [...]. The Court of Justice held in its judgment in *Case C-62/86 AKZO v Commission* [1991] ECR I-3359, paragraph 60, that that was so in the case of a 50 per cent market share.

General Court 14 December 2005 (General Electric v. Commission, T-210/01) [2005] ECR II-5575, para. 115.

[Combined market share of 70–80 per cent, with negligible variations over past three **14.34** years] Based on the notifying parties' own submission [...] their combined market shares in the upstream market was just below [70–80] per cent with only negligible variations over the past three years. Such high market shares suggest that the merged entity is likely to enjoy significant market power in the absence of any mitigating factors. Furthermore it is worth noting that the overlap between the notifying parties is also significant with Campina holding a [40–50] per cent market share pre-merger and Friesland Foods a [20–30] per cent share. This is indicative of strong non-coordinated effects in the form of higher prices or reduced quality and choice. [...]

In addition to pointing to high market shares [the parties would be the closest competitors; supermarket chains do not have the possibility to switch to an alternative brand with the required level of recognition to compete with those of the notifying parties; it is unlikely that competitors would significantly increase supply in the case of a price increase, customers of the notifying parties will not be in a position to exert countervailing buyer power to a sufficient degree so as to offset or mitigate the non-coordinated effects of the merger; and foreign competitors did not assert an immediate entry in case of a 5–10 per cent price increase in the Netherlands, Ed.]

Commission 17 December 2008 (Friesland Foods/Campina, M. 5046), paras 240 and 242.

[Relevance of market shares] The Commission considers, that in line with its Horizon- **14.35** tal Merger Guidelines, market shares and concentration levels provide useful first indications of the market structure and of the competitive importance of both the merging parties in this case and their competitors. In that respect, whether a market share is above or below a certain level is ultimately not determinative in the analysis of the effects of the proposed concentration. What matters is the context in which these market shares need to be interpreted, notably whether they provide good indications of Universal's market size post-merger and its relative position as compared to its competitors. [...]

Post-merger, the merged entity will be the undisputed market leader by a large margin. The existence of very large market shares and the relationship between the market shares of the undertakings involved in the concentration and their competitors, especially those of the next largest, is on its own indicative of the creation of a dominant position post-merger.

Commission 21 September 2012 (Universal Music Group/EMI, M.6458), paras 362 and 372.

14.36   [High market shares not indicative of market power in case of short innovation cycles and free products] With respect to the very high market share on the narrow market, it is apparent from paragraph 17 of the Guidelines on horizontal mergers and from the case-law to which that paragraph refers that market shares of 50 per cent or more are liable to constitute serious evidence of the existence of a dominant position. However, it should be made clear that market shares may only be used as indicia of competition concerns to the extent that the market to which those shares relate has been defined beforehand. The same is true of the HHI to which the applicants also refer. [...]

Moreover, and above all, as highlighted by the Commission in the contested decision and in the defence as well as by the intervener, the consumer communications sector is a recent and fast-growing sector which is characterised by short innovation cycles in which large market shares may turn out to be ephemeral. In such a dynamic context, high market shares are not necessarily indicative of market power and, therefore, of lasting damage to competition which Regulation No 139/2004 seeks to prevent.

General Court 11 December 2013 (Cisco Systems and Messagenet v. Commission, T-79/12), ECLI:EU:T:2013:635, paras 65 and 69.

(ii)   Closeness of competition

(1)   Bidding markets

14.37   As ISTs are procured through bidding procedures, market shares (either calculated on the basis of sales or installed base) only reflect previous wins and may be an unreliable proxy for the competitive strength of the players in the market. [...]

Commission 10 July 2003 (Siemens/Alstom Gas and Steam Turbines, M.3148), OJ 2003 C 207/25, para. 35.

14.38   In a tender market, sufficient competition can exist even with relatively few suppliers and market shares alone do not constitute an adequate basis on which to analyse the competitive situation. [...]

As part of the Phase II market investigation the Commission therefore analysed more closely those tenders and projects in which both AEE and Lentjes had taken part as bidders. [...]

In conclusion it can be said that, according to the in-depth analysis of tenders, even after the parties planned merger, both in the complete plant segment and in the plant part segment there would be a sufficient number of competitors capable of participating in tenders. The projects in which Lentjes and AEE simultaneously took part did not possess any special features that conferred a comparative advantage on the parties, nor was there any evidence to suggest that Lentjes might have been a constraining competitive factor for AEE.

Commission 5 December 2007 (AEE/Lentjes, M. 4647), paras 57, 59 and 70.

[Analysis closeness of substitution] As market shares may not be an exact indicator of **14.39** market power in the present case, the potential anti-competitive effects of the merger have primarily been assessed on the basis of an analysis of closeness of substitution.

Closeness of substitution can be assessed by analysing and drawing conclusions from the selection of the group of products which a customer considers prior to a procurement decision. All products which are considered by the customer in the procurement process are potential 'close substitutes' to the product eventually selected. However, the inclusion of a particular Modelling or Requirements Management tool on a long list or short list does not necessarily mean that it is a close substitute to all other tools listed, or to the tool eventually selected by the customer. [...] The customer will often only know whether the long- and even the short-listed products were realistic substitutes to the tool eventually chosen by the end of the procurement process. [...]

In the context of the in-depth investigation, a qualitative analysis has been made of the closeness of substitution issue. This analysis has been supplemented by a quantitative analysis, to the extent that the quality of the underlying data allowed such an analysis. [...]

The subsequent quantitative analysis was based on an analysis of win/loss data.

'Win/loss' data describe instances where each Party won a new contract (e.g. contract with a firm that was not yet a customer, new project of an existing customer) as well as instances where each Party lost a potential contract (e.g. renewal of an already existing contract, extension of an already existing contract, new potential business opportunity). The purpose of such a quantitative analysis is to assist in the assessment of closeness of substitution between each Party's products, e.g. by measuring 'meeting' frequencies of each Party's products in customers' procurement processes and by measuring whether the presence of each Party's offering has an influence on the outcome of customers' procurement processes.

Commission 5 March 2008 (IBM/Telelogic, M. 4747), paras 152, 154, 155 and 186.

See also Commission 13 November 2006 (Nokia/Siemens, M.4297), paras 83–87.

In a sealed-bid first price auction framework, mergers can generate non-coordinated **14.40** effects in a similar way as in ordinary markets with differentiated goods. Assuming that both products continue to be offered post-merger, the extent of the effect will depend on the degree of closeness of competition between the merging parties' products, as well as on their respective margins. The only difference with ordinary markets with differentiated goods is that the diversion of sales between competing firms should be understood in terms of the expected sales (i.e. the probability of winning the tender) rather than actual sales. That is, each firm knows that if it bids less aggressively, its probability of winning the tender will decrease, and the probability of winning the tender enjoyed by each of its competitors in that tender will increase. The diversion ratio between Firm A and Firm B is therefore determined by the fraction of the reduction in Firm A's winning probability that is captured by Firm B (and vice versa for the diversion ratio from Firm B to Firm A). A merger between Firm A and Firm B will induce each firm to bid less aggressively since a higher bid by Firm A will increase the probability of winning of Firm B, and thus increase its profits (in proportion to its pre-merger margin).

Commission 29 June 2015 (Siemens/Dresser-Rand, M.7429), para. 224.

(2) Product differentiation

14.41   [Parties' products are close substitutes] The overlap in the parties' activities occurs in the crisp bread segment, where Barilla owns the leading 'Wasa' brand and Kamps is active with its 'LiekenUrkorn' brand. Both brands are priced at a significant premium ([>>100 per cent]) to private labels of comparable quality. [...]

The market investigation indicates that Wasa is by far the largest supplier of bread substitutes. In addition, LiekenUrkorn is the closest substitute to Wasa, and vice versa, both in a tentative crisp bread market and also in a wider bread substitutes market. The parties' market shares do therefore not fully reflect Barilla/Kamps' combined market power. According to estimates submitted by retail chains and competitors, consumers are significantly more likely to switch from Wasa to LiekenUrkorn, and vice versa, in response to a price increase than to any other bread substitute product. As a result, Wasa's pricing power is to a significant degree restrained by the fact that consumers would switch to LiekenUrkorn in response to a price increase, whereas LiekenUrkorn would lose a significant number of customers to Wasa (but to a much lesser degree to other bread substitutes) if it attempted to raise prices above current levels.

Commission 25 June 2002 (Barilla/BPL/Kamps, M.2817), OJ 2002 C 198/4, paras 31 and 34.

14.42   [Product differentiation used as one of the arguments to rebut high market shares] [T]he parties have submitted and the market investigation has confirmed that – besides price – the competition in the markets of alpine skis and alpine bindings is also driven by product differentiation and brand positioning. In addition to the large number of different types of skis and bindings offered at several price levels and quality standards (e.g. cross-carver, slalom-carver, all-mountain skis, racing-skis, freestyle), each supplier endeavours to assign to its products a specific brand image. According to the parties, the products of Amer and Salomon provide quite different brand images – Atomic a strong 'racing' image, Salomon a 'lifestyle' image.

Commission 12 May 2005 (Amer/Salomon, M.3765), para. 62.

14.43   [Parties' products are differentiated] [O]n a product market including espresso machines and pad machines, the parties would hold a very high market share ([60–70] per cent) far ahead of their nearest competitors [...].

The main reason for these higher market shares in a wider market lies in the fact that Philips Senseo machines represent the overwhelming majority of all pad machines sold in Belgium and that in Belgium pad machines are very popular compared to espresso machines. [...]

[Respondents] indicated that [Saeco's] closest competitor with respect to espresso machines are De Longhi or Magimix as those companies produce similar types of espresso machines that have globally the same positioning. With respect to Philips' closest competitor, several respondents mentioned Seb with its brand Krups. Whilst several respondents acknowledge that Philips is a very strong brand, they do not consider that this applies to espresso machines but rather to traditional drip and pad machines.

The fact that Senseo machines and espresso machines are remote competitors is further documented by the price level differences of the most widely sold Philips and SIG products in Belgium. [...]

In the light of these price differences, it can therefore be expected that if Philips were to attempt to increase the price for SIG's espresso machines, customers would rather switch to competing espresso machines providers (such as De Longhi or Magimix), which are much closer substitutes in terms of price ranges and functionalities.

Similarly, if post merger Philips were to attempt to increase the price of Senseo machines, these machines' potential customers would not in all likelihood migrate to full automatic espresso machines in the light of the already existing price differences.

Commission 17 July 2009 (Koninklijke Philips Electronics/Saeco International Group, M.5547), paras 68, 69 and 72–75.

[Parties are close competitors] Post transaction, the market share of the merged entity **14.44** will be [60–70] per cent with a substantial increment (Cadbury [20–30] per cent) and competitors are significantly smaller than the new entity (Jutrzenka below [5–10] per cent, Ferrero [0–5] per cent and Nestlé [0–5] per cent).

While according to well-established case law, very large market shares – 50 per cent or more – may in themselves be evidence of the existence of a dominant market position, it is also important to note that several additional elements indicate that the acquisition of Cadbury by Kraft may significantly impede effective competition by removing important competitive constraints exercised from the market on the new merged entity.

The Parties are perceived by a majority of competitors and customers as being the closest competitors in terms of brand positioning and brand recognition which is the most important selection aspect for chocolate tablets. Both Kraft and Cadbury own some very strong brands, often regarded by Polish customers as 'must have brands'. Kraft is active with its two main tablet brands, Milka and Alpen Gold and Cadbury with its iconic Polish brand Wedel. Kraft's Milka and Alpen Gold enjoy very strong brand recognition amongst Polish customers. Similarly, Cadbury's Wedel brand is the best-known brand in Poland that customers associate with tradition, good quality and reliability. The large majority of the respondents to the market investigation regard the Parties' respective brands are the three most important, 'best selling' chocolate tablets brand in Poland. Accordingly, the transaction will lead to a consolidation of several very important brands, often qualified by customers as 'must have' brands. [...]

The market investigation also indicates that Cadbury is the closest competitor to Kraft with respect to price, shelf presence, innovation, promotion and product range.

[...] There are also indications that there is a very close correlation between Cadbury's Wedel and Kraft's Milka brands in terms of price (index) and market share. [...]

Commission 6 January 2010 (Kraft Foods/Cadbury, M.5644), paras 111–113 and 115.

(iii)   Elimination of a strong competitive force ('maverick')

See also recital 25.

14.45   [Elimination of maverick in mergers from four to three players] [T-Mobile Austria (23 per cent) acquired competitor Tele.ring (12 per cent). Both companies provide mobile telephony services in Austria. In Austria, only three other mobile network operators are present in these markets, namely Mobilkom (42 per cent), ONE (18 per cent) and H3G (5 per cent)] Tele.ring is currently one of the most active companies in the market for end consumers in terms of price competition. The removal of this active competitor through the proposed transaction and the creation of a market structure with two similarly large network providers, Mobilkom (42 per cent) and T-Mobile (35 per cent), raise concerns that the planned transaction could harm the Austrian consumer through possible price increases. The Commission found that the proposed acquisition of Tele.ring by T-Mobile, in its original form, would have removed from the Austrian mobile telephony market the operator which has offered consumers the most advantageous prices in recent years. On the basis of price comparisons and an analysis of the switching behaviour of customers, the Commission concluded that Tele.ring has exerted considerable competitive pressure, in particular on the two largest operators, namely Mobilkom and T-Mobile Austria. Following the proposed transaction, in its original form, although T-Mobile would not have become the market leader in Austria, the concentration would have significantly impeded effective competition on the Austrian market for the provision of mobile telephony services to final consumers.

Commission 26 April 2006 (T-Mobile Austria – Tele.ring, M. 3916) (Press release IP/06/535; IP/06/1417).

14.46   It is likely that after the transaction, Linde will not compete to the same extent as it would have done absent the merger.

After the transaction, Linde will not anymore have the role of a newcomer who has to gain market shares from the large established wholesalers in order to achieve an own significant position. [...]

The market structure after the merger is therefore likely to result in less intensive competition, higher prices and a smaller total quantity if compared to a market structure with a newcomer who is ready to accept a lower price in order to enter the market. Generally, a price decrease resulting from an increase in total supply often does not affect the newcomer in the same way as the large incumbents. Any company bringing new quantities into the market has to take into account the losses that occur due to the resulting decrease in price affecting not only the new sales made on the basis of the additional quantities but also (maybe after some delay) the already existing supply relationships. With a higher existing market share, this trade-off is likely to occur at a smaller additional quantity than with a lower market share. This is all the more true against the background that the newcomer might be ready to 'invest' into lower margins in order to establish a stronger market position.

Commission 6 June 2006 (Linde/BOC, M.4141), paras 164–166.

[Elimination of maverick in mergers from four to three players] Currently there are four **14.47** large banks in the Netherlands ABN AMRO, ING, Rabobank and, with some distance from the big three, Fortis. Having a small(er) customer base, by nature Fortis has had the incentive to break into existing customer relations and compete on price and non-price parameters in order to increase its customer base. [...]

Post merger this competitive force would be removed as the incentives of the merged entity would change to become those of market leader rather than of a market challenger to those of a market leader. The new likely strategy would rather be to leverage the Dutch market leadership on the international network and exploiting value added skills on the existing customer base, rather than to gain more customers through an aggressive market strategy.

Commission 3 October 2007 (Fortis/ABN AMRO Assets, M.4844), paras 105 and 109.

[Extending the scope of 'important competitive force'] In particular, the Notifying **14.48** Party claims that while previously the Commission has 'typically' relied on showing dominance and closeness of competition to establish non-coordinated effects, in this case it is not seeking to establish either. Instead, the Commission's analysis focuses (albeit together with factors such as market share and concentration levels, the likely incentives of competitors to increase prices and the low likelihood of entry) on the qualification of Three as an important competitive force. In the Notifying Party's view this is problematic, as the Commission typically relies on a finding that a firm is an important competitive force as 'an aggravating factor' in situations where the merged entity would achieve a dominant position or where the Parties are particularly close competitors.

The Notifying Party submits that, in the absence of dominance and/or a finding that Three and O2 are each other's closest competitors, the condition under recital 25 of the Merger Regulation and paragraph 25 of the Horizontal Merger Guidelines that they exert 'important competitive constraints' on each other is unlikely to be met. The Notifying Party suggests that if the Commission were to find non-coordinated effects in the absence of dominance or the parties being the closest competitors, for instance because Three would be an important competitive force, it would have to meet a different and higher standard of proof. This standard would be 'very demanding' and would require 'particularly strong and unambiguous evidence'. [...]

[C]ontrary to the Notifying Party's claims, the Commission is not required, for the purposes of finding non-coordinated effects in the absence of dominance, to show that Three and O2 are each other's closest competitors on the relevant markets. The Horizontal Merger Guidelines refer to merging firms being 'close competitors' as opposed to being each other's closest competitors as suggested by the Notifying Party. Moreover, closeness of competition is only one of the factors listed in the Horizontal Merger Guidelines as potentially influencing whether significant non-coordinated effects are likely to result from a merger. The qualification of a firm as an important competitive force can be equally relevant. [...]

Commission 28 May 2015 (Hutchison 3G UK/Telefonica Ireland, M.6992), paras 194, 195 and 200.

(iv) Elimination of a potential competitor

14.49   Telia and Telenor represent the strongest potential entrants in each other's national markets. Once they are merged, this competitive pressure would be lost. This would be true irrespective of whether or not they were, prior to the merger, actual competitors. [...]

[...] Within the Nordic region, Telia and Telenor had, prior to the merger, been uniquely well placed not only to use the advantages outlined above in terms of financial capacity, expertise, brand image, etc. but also to 'trade' access to each other's networks.

[T]he heightened potential for entry by the two merging parties also arises from geographical adjacency. It has been observed elsewhere in Europe that operators in neighbouring territories are often the first entrant into each other's markets; [...]. There are also various further factors at work here, including higher brand recognition of a nearby operator, and relatively greater business, linguistic and cultural ties, as well as greater knowledge of close-by markets, and the proximity of their networks (which allows them, inter alia, to by-pass some of the access prices).

Commission 13 October 1999 (Telia/Telenor, M.1439), OJ 2001 L 40/01, paras 148, 150 and 151.

14.50   Prior to the proposed concentration as notified, BOC had entered the bulk and cylinder markets for certain atmospheric gases in Belgium and the Netherlands [...].

In so far as Belgium is a market distinct from France, namely for those gases that can be transported less economically over large distances, Air Liquide would strengthen its dominant position in France by eliminating potential competition in the French market and actual competition in an adjacent market. Firstly, BOC must be seen to be a potential competitor in France, having demonstrated that it can establish a bulk and cylinder gases business in continental Europe. Secondly, the elimination of BOC's position in continental Europe would relieve Air Liquide of the competitive pressure arising from BOC's presence in a market adjacent to its home base. Thirdly, by removing a competitor in the Belgium market and acquiring that competitor's additional market share, Air Liquide would become an even stronger player in Belgium, where it has already captured a large part of the market. Air Liquide would thus be able to counter other potential entrants into its home market more effectively in a neighbouring country from which entry into the French market could easily be attempted, for instance by supplying the industrial regions of Northern France. [...]

The present transaction would strengthen Air Liquide's dominant position in France because it would eliminate BOC as an actual and potential competitor in France. It is this permanent and structural change in the market, and not a business decision by one competitor, that raises the competition concern.

Commission 18 January 2001 (Air Liquide/BOC, M.1630), OJ 2002 L 92/16, paras 196, 198 and 200.

The in-depth investigation sought to clarify whether the removal of STX as a potential **14.51** competitor would have significant anti-competitive effects on the market. According to the Commission's Horizontal Guidelines for a merger with a potential competitor to have significant anti-competitive effects, two basic conditions must be fulfilled. First, the potential competitor must already exert a significant constraining influence or there is a significant likelihood that it would grow into an effective competitive force. Second, there must not be a sufficient number of other potential competitors, which could maintain sufficient competitive pressure after the merger.

[…] During the market investigation no plans or specific evidence was found indicating a likely and timely entry by STX in the market in a significant way. The market participants associate STX with the cruise ship market mainly due to the recent isolated instance of bidding for Saga Lines. Although STX admits its intention to enter the market in the long-term, it has clearly not invested enough efforts into preparing a significant entry into the market for cruise ships. It should therefore be concluded that STX does not currently exert a significant constraining influence on builders of cruise ships and that there is no significant likelihood that it will grow into an effective competitive force in the short term. [...]

[O]ther Far-East shipbuilders are more advanced than STX in their steps towards entering into the cruise ship market. In any event, there is nothing to suggest that STX would be more advanced than these companies in preparing a significant entry into the market. [...]

To conclude, the merger would not have significant anti-competitive effects as a result of the elimination of STX as a potential competitor of the three current large builders of cruise ships.

Commission 5 May 2008 (STX/Aker Yards, M.4956), paras 49, 55, 62 and 69.

See also Commission 21 April 2009 (Posten AB/Post Danmark A/S, M.5152), paras 35–48.

[A]fter the proposed merger a dominant position on the German market for agricul- **14.52** tural potash will be strengthened. However, it has also concluded that K + S's dominant position would be reinforced even in the absence of the merger, because MdK would withdraw from the market in the foreseeable future if it was not acquired by another undertaking and its market share would then accrue to K + S; it can be practically ruled out that an undertaking other than K + S would acquire all or a substantial part of MdK. The merger is not therefore the cause of the reinforcement of a dominant position on the German market. [...]

Commission 14 December 1993 (Kali-Salz/MdK/Treuhand, M.308), OJ 1994 L 186/38, para. 95.

(v)   GUPPI (gross upward pricing pressure index) test

UPP makes it possible to estimate to what extent the merged firm would have the **14.53** incentive to raise prices post merger given in particular prices, margins and diversion ratios observed in the market. This section analyses what it would be profitable for the merged entity to do. Its ability to act on those incentives depends on the existence or otherwise of countervailing factors which could frustrate a price increase and is analysed elsewhere in this decision [...]. In the absence of such countervailing factors, the Parties may be considered to have the ability to act in keeping with the economic incentives which they face.

It is possible to compute the likely price increases which the Proposed Transaction would create the incentive to bring about based on the UPP together with an assumption on the cost pass-through rate (namely that resulting from linear demand). The predicted price increase is likely to be less precise than a full merger simulation since it ignores the feedback effects between the two products and between the other rivals (these factors typically increase the magnitude of the predicted price increases further) and does not take any merger-specific efficiencies into account. However, these assumptions make it possible to go beyond the general UPP result directionality and to quantify the unilateral incentive for the merged entity to increase prices as a result of the merger.

Key inputs to the UPP analysis are the diversion ratios between the Parties. For the post-paid segment, these ratios are estimated on the basis of the data available in the national MNP data.

Competition takes place for 'contestable' users. As unit prices decrease in the industry and the functionality of handsets increases, the value of existing tariff plans and of the investment in a handset decreases over time, meaning that at some point there is always an incentive to switch. Therefore having the option to remain on an existing contract is not an effective constraint on current pricing behaviour. [...]

In the Commission's view, the use of ARPU is justified as a single measure of price in order to estimate the predicted price increase, in particular given limitations in the available data and the intractability of more complex models, by the following considerations. ARPU allows the use of a single value to conceptually represent the price of the 'typical' phone bundle offered by each firm, which is demanded in unit quantities. Evidence provided by the Parties shows that only 10–15 per cent of revenues from phone users are out-of-bundle and that this figure continues to decline. It is also appropriate to work with the simplifying assumption that usage needs are exogenous and that customers choose between brands, that is to say, they choose the provider with the most interesting offer given these exogenous needs.

Upward pricing pressure arises because, post merger, the new entity would not lose all switchers after a unilateral price increase of one of its brands, but rather would retain a significant number and therefore internalise part of the losses which a price increase would otherwise bring about. For instance, if the merged entity were to increase the prices for Orange services relative to what Orange would have done in the absence of the merger, it would internalize the effect that some customers would switch to H3G's own brand. This would make a price increase of Orange tariffs profitable for the merged entity where it would not have been for Orange in the standalone scenario. A similar reasoning would apply to an even greater extent to H3G plans. Upward pricing pressure is to be understood relative to the direction which prices would have taken in the absence of the merger. To the extent that decreasing prices would be expected in the absence of the merger, upward pricing pressure does not necessarily mean that prices would increase as a result of the merger in absolute terms. The possibility to increase prices may also imply pursuit by the merged entity of fewer improvements in functionality of the services available than would have applied in the absence of the merger, resulting in consumer welfare losses by mechanisms other than price. Reduction of handset subsidies may also be a way to realise a price increase. In the Commission's analysis, upward pricing pressure is taken to encompass all mechanisms by which the merged entity could increase its margins relative to the pre-merger situation.

It is important also to stress that the UPP methodology does not take into consideration the feedback effects of unilateral price increases by the merged entity on the two remaining rivals. Since an increase in prices by the merged entity would provide an incentive to TA and T-Mobile to follow suit, the expected consequence of the UPP on the Parties as a result of the merger is likely to be an overall increase in prices relative to the situation in the absence the merger. The UPP therefore underestimates the effect of the merger on the prices which the merged entity would adopt, and also does not quantify the extent to which the prices of competitors would be expected to rise in response. The UPP predicted for the Parties, in the short run, applies to new business and therefore on its own to about 40–45 per cent of the contestable market. [...]

The UPP approach has been widely used, including in the mobile telecommunications industry in the recent AT&T/T-Mobile case in the USA. The Parties have no suggestion as to an alternative, better methodology which would have been available to the Commission in the context of this case.

It is therefore clear that there exists no generally agreed and tested, robust alternative approach which could have been used to underpin the Commission's findings. The Commission has therefore done what was feasible given the available data. GUPPI is a generally accepted component of a merger analysis.
Commission 12 December 2012 (Hutchison 3G Austria/Orange Austria, M.6437), paras 310–313, 315–317, 346 and 347.

(vi) Effects on consumers and cultural diversity

In line with this framework, the Commission's assessment of the effects of the proposed **14.54** concentration has focussed on all consumer benefits from effective competition and all relevant competitive parameters on recorded music markets. In particular, the Commission has assessed whether, due to the increase in the post-merger size of Universal and its market power, the proposed concentration is likely to lead to the following:

(a) More disadvantageous commercial terms for digital customers (including higher wholesale prices and licensing fees), likely resulting in higher prices for end users of digital music services; and

(b) A reduction of consumer choice and innovation with respect to digital music services.

The Commission considers that if that were the case, the proposed concentration would also have a negative impact on cultural diversity. Article 167 (4) of the TFEU requires the Union to take cultural diversity aspects into account in its actions under the other provisions of the Treaties, including Union competition rules. Moreover, the UNESCO Convention on the protection and the promotion of the diversity of cultural expressions to which the Union is a Party sets out a comprehensive set of guiding principles relating to the diversity of cultural expressions. The case-law has confirmed that other Treaty objectives may be taken into account in the context of the assessment of a concentration. [...]

During the Commission's investigation, the Notifying Party submitted that the Commission did not compare the terms obtained by Universal with the terms obtained by all of its competitors. [...]

Confidentiality restraints preclude the Commission from including the terms and conditions of all of Universal's competitors in the comparison and from disclosing those details to the Notifying Party. In any event, as the market investigation and the quantitative analysis undertaken by the Commission demonstrates that the correlation between the size of record companies and favourable commercial terms for digital platforms is not limited to Universal and EMI but instead applies across the whole recorded music industry, there is no need to analyse the commercial terms and conditions of the competitors that create these discrepancies. The Commission therefore assesses the implications of the competitive position of the other competitors to Universal on the basis of that evidence. [...]

Commission 21 September 2012 (Universal Music Group/EMI, M.6458), paras 442, 443, 513 and 514.

(vii) Network effects

14.55   Network effects arise when the value of a product/service to its users increases with the number of other users of the product/service.

The Commission notes that, in the present case, both Parties have large networks of users: WhatsApp had close to 600 million users and Facebook Messenger had close to [250–350] million users in July 2014 worldwide.

Respondents to the market investigation indicated that the size of the user base and the number of a user's friends/relatives on the same consumer communications app is of important or critical value to customers of consumer communications apps. These parameters increase the utility of the service for a user since they increase the number of people he or she can reach. Therefore, the Commission considers that in the present case network effects exist in the market for consumer communications apps.

The existence of network effects as such does not a priori indicate a competition problem in the market affected by a merger. Such effects may however raise competition concerns in particular if they allow the merged entity to foreclose competitors and make more difficult for competing providers to expand their customer base. Network effects have to be assessed on a case-by-case basis.

Commission 3 October 2014 (Facebook/Whatsapp, M.7217), paras 127–130.

(b) Coordinated effects

14.56   [Three conditions for collective dominance] As the applicant has argued and as the Commission has accepted in its pleadings, three conditions are necessary for a finding of collective dominance as defined:

- first, each member of the dominant oligopoly must have the ability to know how the other members are behaving in order to monitor whether or not they are adopting the common policy. As the Commission specifically acknowledges, it is not enough for each member of the dominant oligopoly to be aware that interdependent market conduct is profitable for all of them but each member must also have a means of knowing whether the other operators are adopting the same strategy and whether they are maintaining it. There must, therefore, be sufficient market transparency for all members of the dominant oligopoly to be aware, sufficiently precisely and quickly, of the way in which the other members' market conduct is evolving;

- second, the situation of tacit coordination must be sustainable over time, that is to say, there must be an incentive not to depart from the common policy on the market. As the Commission observes, it is only if all the members of the dominant oligopoly maintain the parallel conduct that all can benefit. The notion of retaliation in respect of conduct deviating from the common policy is thus inherent in this condition. In this instance, the parties concur that, for a situation of collective dominance to be viable, there must be adequate deterrents to ensure that there is a long-term incentive in not departing from the common policy, which means that each member of the dominant oligopoly must be aware that highly competitive action on its part designed to increase its market share would provoke identical action by the others, so that it would derive no benefit from its initiative [...].

- third, to prove the existence of a collective dominant position to the requisite legal standard, the Commission must also establish that the foreseeable reaction of current and future competitors, as well as of consumers, would not jeopardise the results expected from the common policy. [...]

In that context, the Commission must not necessarily prove that there is a specific retaliation mechanism involving a degree of severity, but it must none the less establish that deterrents exist, which are such that it is not worth the while of any member of the dominant oligopoly to depart from the common course of conduct to the detriment of the other oligopolists.

General Court 6 June 2002 (Airtours v. Commission, T-342/99) [2002] ECR II-2585, paras 62 and 195.

[Conditions may be established indirectly] It follows that, in the context of the **14.57** assessment of the existence of a collective dominant position, although the three conditions defined by the [General Court] in *Airtours v Commission* [...], which were inferred from a theoretical analysis of the concept of a collective dominant position, are indeed also necessary, they may, however, in the appropriate circumstances, be established indirectly on the basis of what may be a very mixed series of indicia and items of evidence relating to the signs, manifestations and phenomena inherent in the presence of a collective dominant position.

Thus, in particular, close alignment of prices over a long period, especially if they are above a competitive level, together with other factors typical of a collective dominant position, might, in the absence of an alternative reasonable explanation, suffice to demonstrate the existence of a collective dominant position, even where there is no firm direct evidence of strong market transparency, as such transparency may be presumed in such circumstances.

General Court 13 July 2006 (Impala v. Commission T-464/04) [2006] ECR II-02289, paras 251 and 252.

14.58   [Collective dominance as a result of participation in a competitor] The Commission has further investigated whether the fact that A-TEC, the main competitor of the parties on the EEA market for copper shapes, which is also an important minority shareholder in both NA and Cumerio, could give rise to coordinated effects on this market. [...]

The Commission currently has no indications that A-TEC and the new entity would have the intention to cooperate after the transaction, nor that they would coordinate their market behaviour on the market for copper shapes. However, A-TECs minority shareholdings might slightly increase the economic incentive to reach a common understanding to coordinate their business strategies on the market for copper shapes. The existence of the minority shareholding would also entail a minimum flow of information about the activities of the new entity to A-TEC which might facilitate reaching an understanding on the terms of coordination.

Commission 23 January 2008 (Norddeutsche Affinerie/Cumerio, M.4781), paras 183 and 185.

14.59   In applying those [Airtours-]criteria, it is necessary to avoid a mechanical approach involving the separate verification of each of those criteria taken in isolation, while taking no account of the overall economic mechanism of a hypothetical tacit coordination.

CoJ 10 July 2008 (Impala, Case C-413/06 P) [2008] ECR I-4951, para. 125.

14.60   [Coordinated effects] By its very nature, tacit coordination can be difficult to prove. Price-fixing or market sharing agreements in violation of Article [101 TFEU] can generally be proven by way of hard evidence (generally written documents). In contrast, tacit coordination, as indicated by the Court of Justice, *'is likely to emerge if competitors can easily arrive at a common perception as to how the coordination should work'*. Tacit coordination can thus only be inferred indirectly from observing and adequately interpreting the actual conduct of market players in light of existing market conditions, affecting their ability and incentives to tacitly coordinate their actions. [...]

It follows from all of the above that the assessment of the coordinated effects of the proposed merger can be structured into three parts: (a) Assessment of the presence of market conditions conducive to tacit coordination (b) Identification of a likely mechanism for tacit coordination and the resulting degree of tacit coordination that can be expected in the absence of the merger (c) Assessment of the extent to which the merger significantly impedes effective competition by making the existing degree of tacit coordination easier, more stable or more effective for the three firms concerned either by making such coordination more robust or by permitting firms attain even higher prices.

Commission 23 September 2008 (ABF/GBI Business, M.4980), paras 140 and 144.

(c)   Countervailing buyer power

14.61   The Transaction leads to a further concentration on already highly concentrated markets. It reinforces the leading market position of the Target by removing an important and close competitor on the markets for plastic front and rear bumpers. Switching, barriers to entry and expansion as well as countervailing buyer power of the customers are not a sufficient competitive constraint on the combined entity. [...]

The Commission takes the view that any countervailing buyer power of the OEMs will likely not be sufficient to counter the increase in market power that the merger is likely to create.[…]

Firstly, with regard to the argument that all manufacturers can satisfy the technical requirement specified by the OEMs and therefore compete for RFQs, the market investigation indicated that this is not necessarily true. [...] Therefore the Commission takes the view that not all suppliers are necessarily interchangeable.

Countervailing buyer power may exist if a customer could credibly threaten to resort, within a reasonable timeframe, to alternative sources of supply. [...]

With regard to the threat to switch to alternative suppliers the Commission considers that any possibility of switching which existed pre-merger will be eliminated or significantly reduced as a result of the merger in a number of geographic markets. [...]

With regard to the argument of near-perfect visibility of the OEMs on the suppliers' cost structure, the information provided by the Notifying Party [...] indicates that PO's average margin for plastic front and rear bumpers is between [...]% and [...]%. According to that submission, those margins take into account most of the costs, i.e. the cost of raw material (including the cost of subcontracted components and inbound transport costs), the cost of direct and indirect labour related to the production of the program, the cost of production (including outbound transport costs) and the depreciation of fixed assets directly linked to the program.

This evidence contradicts the Notifying Party's claim that OEMs have near perfect visibility of the cost structure of the suppliers and exploit that information to their advantage in negotiations. If that were the case, bumper manufacturers would be limited to significantly lower profit margins as a result of the negotiations with OEMs. Hence, either OEMs do not have good visibility on the suppliers' cost structure or they do not exploit that information in the negotiation process.

Commission 11 July 2016 (Plastic Omnium/Faurecia Exterior Automotive Business, M.7893), paras 85, 175–178, 193 and 194.

3. Non-horizontal mergers

See also the Guidelines on the assessment of non-horizontal mergers.

(a) Vertical mergers

(i) Foreclosure

For anti-competitive foreclosure to arise, a number of conditions must be present as **14.62** some of the strategies that the new entity might put in place can also have pro-competitive effects [...]. As indicated in paragraph 94 of the Non-Horizontal Merger Guidelines, the (i) ability to foreclose; (ii) the incentives to foreclose; and (iii) the overall impact on effective competition need to be assessed.

Commission 11 March 2008 (Google/DoubleClick, M.4731), para. 293.

See for detailed application of these criteria for instance the following decisions: Commission 11 March 2008 (Google/DoubleClick, M.4731), paras 287–366; Commission 14 May 2008 (TomTom/Tele Atlas, M.4854), paras 190–251; Commission 2 July 2008 (Nokia/Navteq, M.4942), paras 264–379; Commission 4 August 2008 (Itema/Barcovision, M.4874), paras 37–92.

(ii)   Coordinated effects as a result of a vertical merger

14.63   [T]here is no clear evidence that the vertical integration of TomTom and Tele Atlas would increase the scope for coordination between map database producers. Unlike horizontal mergers, the proposed operation does not facilitate the achievement of terms of coordination by removing one player in the market. The proposed operation neither increases price transparency, nor does it eliminate a pricing maverick that would prevent coordination from taking place. [...]
Commission 14 May 2008 (TomTom/Tele Atlas, M.4854), para. 281.

See also Commission 2 July 2008 (Nokia/Navteq, M.4942), paras 390–408.

(b)   Conglomerate mergers

(i)   General

14.64   The Commission's analysis of a merger producing a conglomerate effect is conditioned by requirements similar to those defined by the [General Court] with regard to the creation of a situation of collective dominance [...]. Thus the Commission's analysis of a merger transaction which is expected to have an anti-competitive conglomerate effect calls for a particularly close examination of the circumstances which are relevant for an assessment of that effect on the conditions of competition in the reference market. As the Court has already held, where the Commission takes the view that a merger should be prohibited because it will create or strengthen a dominant position within a foreseeable period, it is incumbent upon it to produce convincing evidence thereof (*Air Tours v Commission*, para. 63). Since the effects of a conglomerate-type merger are generally considered to be neutral, or even beneficial, for competition on the markets concerned, as is recognised in the present case by the economic writings cited in the analyses annexed to the parties' written pleadings, the proof of anti-competitive conglomerate effects of such a merger calls for a precise examination, supported by convincing evidence, of the circumstances which allegedly produce those effects (see, by analogy, *Air Tours v Commission*, para. 63).
General Court 25 October 2002 (Tetra Laval v. Commission, T-5/02) [2002] ECR II-4381, para. 155.

14.65   As regards proof of such conglomerate effects, the case-law has established that the quality of the evidence produced by the Commission in order to establish that it is necessary for it to adopt a decision declaring a concentration incompatible with the internal market is particularly important. The assessment of a conglomerate-type concentration is based on a prospective analysis in which, first, the consideration of a lengthy period of time in the future and, second, the leveraging necessary to give rise to a significant impediment to effective competition mean that the chains of cause and effect are dimly discernible, uncertain and difficult to establish [...].

It should be borne in mind that the Commission may declare a concentration incompatible with the internal market only if the significant impediment to competition is the direct and immediate effect of the concentration. Such an impediment, which would stem from future decisions by the merged entity, may be regarded as a direct and immediate effect of the concentration, if that future conduct is made possible and economically rational by the alteration of the characteristics and the structure of the market caused by the concentration [...].

General Court 11 December 2013 (Cisco Systems and Messagenet v. Commission, T-79/12) ECLI:EU:T:2013:635, paras 117 and 118.

See also: CoJ 10 July 2008 (Bertelsmann and Sony Corporation of America v. Impala, C-413/06 P) [2008] ECR I-4951, paras 50–54; CoJ 6 June 2002 (Airtours v. Commission, T-342/99) [2002] ECR II-2585, para. 58.

(ii) 'Bundling': Leverage a strong position from one market to another

It is also necessary to distinguish [...] between three distinct practices: pure bundling **14.66** (where sales are tied by means of a purely commercial obligation to purchase two or more products as a bundle); technical bundling (where sales are tied by means of the technical integration of the products); and mixed bundling (where a number of products are sold as a package on more favourable terms than if the products are purchased separately). [...]

[Pure bundling:] Given the extreme nature, from a commercial perspective, of the behaviour described above, which would have been necessary in this instance for the merged entity to implement a strategy based on pure bundling, it was incumbent on the Commission to take into account the effect which the Community-law prohibition on abuses of a dominant position might have had on the merged entities incentive to implement such practices. [...]

[Technical bundling: In relation to the future development of the market, the Commission must show] a detailed analysis of the technical integration which might be achieved [...] and of the likely influence of such integration on the way the different markets concerned might evolve. It is not enough for the Commission to put forward a series of logical but hypothetical developments which, were they to materialise, it fears would have harmful effects for competition on a number of different markets. Rather, the onus is on it to carry out a specific analysis of the likely evolution of each market on which it seeks to show that a dominant position would be created or strengthened as a result of the merger and to produce convincing evidence to bear out that conclusion. [...]

[Mixed bundling: To offer lower prices for a range of products subject to the requirement that all the products were selected] will have economic effects on the market only in so far as customers accept it and, in particular, do not demand that the offer is unbundled product by product. The onus was thus on the Commission to show that the merged entity would have been able to insist that the package it was offering its customers was not unbundled. Furthermore, as has been held above, the Commission was required to establish that there was a likelihood of the merged entity actually exploiting the possibility of engaging in mixed bundling.

General Court 14 December 2005 (General Electric v. Commission, T-210/01) [2005] ECR II-5575, paras 406, 425, 429 and 432.

(iii) Relation assessment of conglomerate mergers and Art. 102 TFEU

14.67   However, the use, by an undertaking with a dominant position like Tetra's on the aseptic carton markets, of pressure in the form of tied sales or incentives such as predatory pricing or loyalty rebates that are not objectively justified, would usually constitute an abuse of that position. As [the General Court] has already held, the possible recourse to such strategies cannot be presumed by the Commission, as it has done in the contested decision, in order to justify a decision prohibiting a merger transaction which has been notified to it in accordance with the Regulation [...]. It follows that the leveraging practices which may be taken into consideration by the [General Court] are limited to those which, at least probably, do not constitute an abuse of a dominant position on the aseptic carton markets.

General Court 25 October 2002 (Tetra Laval v. Commission, T-5/02) [2002] ECR II-4381, para. 218.

14.68   Since the view is taken [...] that adoption of the conduct [...] is an essential step in leveraging, the [General Court] was right to hold that the likelihood of its adoption must be examined comprehensively, that is to say, taking account, [...] both of the incentives to adopt such conduct and the factors liable to reduce, or even eliminate, those incentives, including the possibility that the conduct is unlawful.

However, it would run counter to the Regulation's purpose of prevention to require the Commission [...] to examine, for each proposed merger, the extent to which the incentives to adopt anti-competitive conduct would be reduced, or even eliminated, as a result of the unlawfulness of the conduct in question, the likelihood of its detection, the action taken by the competent authorities, both at Community and national level, and the financial penalties which could ensue.

An assessment such as that required by the [General Court] would make it necessary to carry out an exhaustive and detailed examination of the rules of the various legal orders which might be applicable and of the enforcement policy practised in them. Moreover, if it is to be relevant, such an assessment calls for a high probability of the occurrence of the acts envisaged as capable of giving rise to objections on the ground that they are part of anti-competitive conduct.

It follows that, at the stage of assessing a proposed merger, an assessment intended to establish whether an infringement of Article [102 TFEU] is likely and to ascertain that it will be penalised in several legal orders would be too speculative and would not allow the Commission to base its assessment on all of the relevant facts with a view to establishing whether they support an economic scenario in which a development such as leveraging will occur.

Consequently, the [General Court] erred in law in rejecting the Commission's conclusions as to the adoption by the merged entity of anti-competitive conduct capable of resulting in leveraging on the sole ground that the Commission had, when assessing the likelihood that such conduct might be adopted, failed to take account of the unlawfulness of that conduct and, consequently, of the likelihood of its detection, of action by the competent authorities, both at Community and national level, and of the financial penalties which might ensue.

CoJ 15 February 2005 (Commission v. Tetra Laval, C-12/03 P) [2005] ECR I-987, paras 74–78.

See also General Court 14 December 2005 (General Electric v. Commission, T-210/01) [2005] ECR II-5575, paras 71–73.

The combination of Strålfors and PDK, competitors argue, could enable Strålfors to price below costs for a limited period of time in an attempt to squeeze competitors out of the market for mail preparation services. However, it would constitute an infringement to Art. [102 TFEU], if, by way of pricing, market dominance in one market (mail distribution) is used to extend market power into another market (printing and enveloping). Given the fact that Strålfors is a separate legal entity with separate accounts, and that PDK's prices are regulated and publicly available, the Danish Competition Authority could take appropriate action to ensure that reasonably efficient competitors can profitably replicate the price structure of the merged entity. **14.69**

Commission 21 April 2009 (Posten AB/Post Danmark A/S, M.5152), para. 162.

4. Failing firm defence

[A concentration can be regarded as a rescue merger if] the competitive structure resulting from the concentration would deteriorate in similar fashion even if the concentration did not proceed. **14.70**

CoJ 31 March 1998 (France v. Commission, Kali + Salz, Joined Cases C-68/94 and C-30/95) [1998] ECR I-1375, para. 115.

The approach taken by the Court of Justice is wider than the criteria set out in the Commission's decision in *Kali + Salz*. According to the Court of Justice, a merger can be regarded as a rescue merger if the competitive structure resulting from the concentration would deteriorate in similar fashion even if the concentration did not proceed, that is to say, even if the concentration was prohibited. **14.71**

In general terms, the concept of the 'rescue merger' requires that the undertakings to be acquired can be regarded as 'failing firms' and that the merger is not the cause of the deterioration of the competitive structure. Thus, for the application of the rescue merger, two conditions must be satisfied:

(a) the acquired undertaking would in the near future be forced out of the market if not taken over by another undertaking; and

(b) there is no less anti-competitive alternative purchase.

However, the application of these two criteria does not completely rule out the possibility of a takeover by third parties of the assets of the undertakings concerned in the event of their bankruptcy. If such assets were taken over by competitors in the course of bankruptcy proceedings, the economic effects would be similar to a takeover of the failing firms themselves by an alternative purchaser. Thus it needs to be established in addition to the first two criteria, that the assets to be purchased would inevitably disappear from the market in the absence of the merger.

Given this general framework, the Commission regards the following criteria as relevant for the application of the concept of the 'rescue merger':

(a) the acquired undertaking would in the near future be forced out of the market if not taken over by another undertaking;

(b) there is no less anti-competitive alternative purchase; and

(c) the assets to be acquired would inevitably exit the market if not taken over by another undertaking.

In any event, the application of the concept of the 'rescue merger' requires that the deterioration of the competitive structure through the merger is at least no worse than in the absence of the merger.

Commission 11 July 2001 (BASF/Eurodiol/Pantochim, M.2314), OJ 2001 L 132/45, paras 139–143.

See also Commission 2 April 2003 (Newscorp/Telepiù, M.2876), OJ 2004 L 110/73; Commission 14 February 2002 (Danish Crown/Steff Houlberg, M.2662), OJ 2002 C 114/22; Commission 5 September 2002 (Ernst & Young France/ Andersen France, M.2816), OJ 2002 C 232/6; Commission 1 July 2002 (Deloitte Touche/Andersen (UK), M.2810), OJ 2002 C 200/8.

14.72   [The failing firm defence is justified if no alternative possible purchaser exists] The Commission considers that Nynas is most likely the only undertaking that is seriously interested in taking over the Harburg refinery assets. No other undertaking is likely to have the ability and incentive to take over the Harburg refinery assets in the absence of the notified transaction. In particular, Ergon is unlikely to purchase the Harburg refinery assets. Therefore there is no prospect of a less anti-competitive alternative purchase of the Harburg refinery assets.

[T]he most likely outcome that can reasonably be predicted is that Shell will close the Harburg refinery assets. Rebuilding the Harburg refinery assets elsewhere would be prohibitively expensive and would take a very long time. Thus, in the absence of the notified transaction, the Harburg refinery assets would most likely exit the market.

Commission 2 September 2013 (Nynas/Shell/Harburg Refinery, M.6360), paras 360 and 361.

14.73   [If the failing firm is part of a group company] [I]t does not also have to be established that Olympic would endanger the viability of the whole Marfin Group. Such an approach would not correspond to the *rationale* underlying the failing firm analysis, namely that because of the failure of the acquired company (and not necessarily of its parent) the competitive situation post-merger would not be worse than absent the merger.

Nevertheless, even if the non-viability of the whole Marfin group does not have to be proven as such, it becomes apparent that Marfin's ability and incentive to support Olympic is conditioned by its own financial situation, and thus the latter must be taken into account when assessing the first criterion of the failing firm analysis.

[…] Olympic's financial results must be assessed by applying cost allocation rules that reflect Olympic's true economic costs and cannot be attributed to intra-group arrangements that would present Olympic more loss-making than it would be as an independent company. Finally, Marfin's decision to let Olympic "fail" must make sense for the group as a whole, namely Olympic's negative financial results need not be economically justified for Marfin by other benefits (if any) possibly brought by Olympic to the group.

Commission 9 October 2013 (Aegean/ Olympic II, M.6796), paras 688–690.

5. Efficiency defence

See also recital 29.

According to the Merger Regulation and the Commission's Horizontal Guidelines, it is **14.74** possible that efficiencies brought about by a merger counteract the effects on competition and in particular the potential harm to consumers that it might otherwise have. Parties to a concentration may thus detail the efficiency gains generated by the concentration that are likely to enhance the ability and the incentive of the merged entity to act pro-competitively for the benefit of consumers. Typical examples of such efficiencies include cost savings, new product introduction and service or product improvement. Efficiency claims need to be reasoned, quantified and supported by internal studies and documents if necessary. The parties have to demonstrate that such efficiencies are likely to benefit directly customers in the relevant markets where competition concerns have been identified and could not have been achieved to a similar extent by means that are less anti-competitive than the proposed concentration. […]

In conclusion, the parties have failed to demonstrate that the efficiencies brought about by the proposed transaction are not attainable by a less anti-competitive alternative and would directly benefit end customers in the three relevant product markets where competition concerns have been identified. For these reasons, the Commission considers that the efficiencies presented by the parties cannot be considered to offset the adverse effect of the proposed transaction on competition.

Commission 4 July 2006 (Inco/Falconbridge, M.4000), paras 530 and 550.

The overall impact of the transaction however will also be affected by the likely **14.75** efficiencies that are brought about by the merger and substantiated by the parties. While there is a lack of anti-competitive effects irrespective of efficiencies, these efficiencies form a part of the overall competitive assessment.

As set out in the Non-Horizontal Merger Guidelines, 'a vertical merger allows the merged entity to internalise any pre-existing double mark-ups resulting from both parties setting their prices independently pre-merger'. In this case, the problem of double mark-ups cannot be discarded since the marginal cost of map databases [is close to zero and consequently gross margins on map databases are high]. [...]

When assessing whether efficiencies generated by the elimination of double mark-ups are merger specific, the Commission examined whether vertical cooperation or vertical agreements may, short of a merger, achieve similar benefits. [...] In particular, the Commission reviewed TeleAtlas's and NAVTEQ's contracts with PND manufacturers, and found that, while volume discounts are common in the industry, these discounts are too limited to substantially eliminate double mark-ups. [...]

In addition to the elimination of the double marginalisation, the proposed operation is likely to create other efficiencies. The fact that vertical integration may lead to such efficiencies is explicitly referred to in the Non-Horizontal Merger Guidelines, which indicate that vertical mergers 'may align the incentives of the parties with regard to investments in new products, new production processes and in the marketing of products'. [...]

Specifically, the parties argue that the transaction will bring significant efficiencies due to the integration of TomTom's [...] data to improve Tele Atlas's map databases. [...]

Although end-customers would certainly benefit from the more frequent and comprehensive map database updates made possible by the merger, these efficiencies are difficult to quantify and the estimates provided by the parties are not particularly convincing. [...]

The Commission also examined whether these efficiencies should be considered merger specific. Although part of the efficiencies put forward by the parties could potentially be achieved through contract, both parties are unlikely to pursue investments of the same order of magnitude as the integrated company. Such investments are risky for the non-integrated company since they are very specific to the particular relationship and hence subject to a so-called hold-up problem. Such a situation arises when a party refrains from cooperating with another due to the concern that it would become captive of its partner, for instance, because of specific investments that are only valuable if used with this partner and therefore loses all bargaining power. In addition, the difficulty in specifying all the required investments upfront and the uncertainty about the future environment in which the parties will operate makes it impossible to provide full protection to a non-integrated company through a long-term contract. It must therefore be concluded that the proposed transaction will be likely to bring 'better maps – faster', as the parties suggested, than what could be achieved through contractual means in the absence of the merger, and hence that they are, at least in part, merger specific.

Commission 14 May 2008 (TomTom/Tele Atlas, M.4854), paras 238, 239, 241, 244, 246, 248 and 249.

See also Commission 2 July 2008 (Nokia/Navteq, M.4942), paras 364–376.

14.76   In the present case, the parties have submitted a study which provides indications on the type and the size of supply-side efficiencies which would arise if the parties merge.

According to the study, supply-side efficiencies would consist mainly of joint purchasing benefits, overhead reductions, rationalisation of frontline operations, systems integration and network efficiencies. At least some of these cost savings appear relevant and the study provides an order of magnitude of total annual cost savings (EUR 16.4 million). However, for the purpose of this merger investigation, amongst other issues, it would be necessary to examine to what extent such efficiencies would be passed on to consumers. As the study does not distinguish between efficiencies affecting parties fixed cost and efficiencies affecting variable cost, it is difficult to infer from it the expected reduction of the parties' operating cost (and a possible pass-on to consumers).

The study also identifies a number of demand-side efficiencies which would arise as a consequence of the merger. These would consist of the elimination of the double marginalisation effect for feeder passengers, an increase in flight bundles available to passengers, a reduced risk of delay, frequent flyer benefits and improved check-in facilities. Even if these efficiencies are likely to exist to some extent, however, they are very difficult to be quantified and the study's attempt to do so relies on rather strong assumptions. [...]

Commission 17 December 2008 (KLM–Martinair, M.5141), paras 409 and 410.

In the first place, the Court rejects the argument that the 2004 Guidelines require only **14.77** that efficiencies must be shown to benefit customers and not that they can be clawed back. [...] [T]he Commission stated, whilst referring to points 79, 80 and 84 of those guidelines, that, even if cost savings accrued on the side of the customers, if they were clawed back by the merged entity, they could not be taken into account as efficiency. First, no part of those guidelines states that the Commission could not take into account the fact that the efficiency gains stemming from the merger can, in whole or in part, be clawed back. Secondly, it can be inferred from those guidelines that those gains may be passed on only partially and therefore that they can be clawed back by the parties to the concentration, given that point 84 of the guidelines in question states that the Commission has to be sure that the efficiencies will be passed on 'to a sufficient degree' to the consumer, without making a distinction on the basis of the nature or the form of those gains. Moreover, contrary to what the applicant claims, it is not only when the efficiencies in question take the form of cost savings by the merged entity that those parties must demonstrate that they will be passed on to customers, rather than retained by the parties. That is not explicitly stated in the guidelines and, in any event, the Commission must check the overall effect of the concentration and, in particular, that some gains consisting of cost reductions for customers cannot be clawed back. It is necessary, on the same grounds, to reject the argument, put forward at the stage of the reply, that passing on is relevant only in cases where a merged entity is in possession of a thing that can be transferred to a customer.

General Court 9 March 2015 (Deutsche Börse v. Commission, T-175/12) ECLI: EU:T:2015:148, para. 273.

See also Commission 21 January 2010 (Oracle/Sun Microsystems, M.5529), paras 164–167.

D. PARAGRAPHS 4 AND 5: ASSESSMENT OF COORDINATED EFFECTS JV

See recital 27.

14.78   Both Mubadala (through its subsidiaries ADAT and SR Technics) and Rolls-Royce are active in the supply of MRO services for LCA engines.

However, the notifying parties perform these activities mostly in the EEA while JVCO will not be active in this geographic area. Besides, considering a worldwide market for the supply of MRO services for LCA engines, as explained above, the position of Mubadala is limited and most of its sales ([90–100] per cent) come from SR Technics, over which Mubadala only exerts joint control.

For these reasons, the coordination between Mubadala and Rolls-Royce resulting from the operation of the joint venture is unlikely to allow them to affect competition on the market for MRO services for LCA engines.

Commission 16 February 2009 (Mubadala/Rolls Royce/JV, M.5399), paras 37–39.

E. PROCEDURAL ASPECTS

1. Liability of the European Commission in case of annulment of a decision

14.79   [Conditions for non-contractual liability] It must first be borne in mind that it is settled case-law that, in order for the Community to incur non-contractual liability under the second paragraph of Article [340(2) TFEU] for unlawful conduct of its institutions, a number of conditions must be satisfied: the institution's conduct must be unlawful, actual damage must have been suffered and there must be a causal link between the conduct and the damage pleaded [...].

Where, as in this case, a legal measure is relied on as a basis for an action for damages, that measure, in order to be capable of causing the Community to incur non-contractual liability, must constitute a sufficiently serious breach of a rule of law intended to confer rights on individuals.

The decisive criterion in that regard is whether the Community institution concerned manifestly and gravely disregarded the limits on its discretion [...].

The system of rules which the Court of Justice has worked out in relation to the non-contractual liability of the Community takes into account, inter alia, the complexity of the situations to be regulated, difficulties in the application or interpretation of the legislation and, more particularly, the margin of discretion available to the author of the act in question [...].

Where the institution criticised has only considerably reduced, or even no, discretion, the mere infringement of Community law may be sufficient to establish the existence of a sufficiently serious breach of Community law [...]. [...]

Moreover, it is for the party seeking to establish the Community's liability to adduce conclusive proof as to the existence or extent of the damage he alleges and to establish a sufficiently direct causal link between that damage and the conduct complained of on the part of the Community institution [...].

[A] sufficiently serious breach of Community law, for the purposes of establishing the non-contractual liability of the Community, cannot be constituted by failure to fulfil a legal obligation, which [...] can be explained by the objective constraints to which the institution and its officials are subject as a result of the provisions governing the control of concentrations.

On the other hand, the right to compensation for damage resulting from the conduct of the institution becomes available where such conduct takes the form of action manifestly contrary to the rule of law and seriously detrimental to the interests of persons outside the institution and cannot be justified or accounted for by the particular constraints to which the staff of the institution, operating normally, is objectively subject.

General Court 11 July 2007 (Schneider Electric v. Commission, T-351/03) [2007] ECR II-2237, paras 113–117, 119, 123 and 124.

[Liability in case of breach of an undertaking's right of defence] It must be borne in mind that, before adopting a decision finding that a concentration is incompatible with the common market, the Commission is required, under Article 18(1) of the Regulation, to give the notifying undertakings an opportunity, at every stage of the procedure up to consultation of the Advisory Committee, of making known their views on the objections against them. [...] **14.80**

In this case, a manifest and serious breach of Article 18(1) and (3) of the Regulation stems from the fact of the Commission's drafting a statement of objections in such a way that, as is apparent from the *Schneider I* judgment, the applicant could not ascertain that, if it did not submit corrective measures conducive to reducing or eliminating the support between its positions and those of Legrand in the French sectoral markets, it had no chance of securing a declaration that the transaction was compatible with the common market. [...]

That breach of the rights of the defence is neither justified nor accounted for by the particular constraints to which Commission staff are objectively subject. The fault at issue, the existence and extent of which are not contested by the Commission, therefore imposes upon the Community a duty to make good the harmful consequences.

The defendant's argument as to the difficulty inherent in undertaking a complex market analysis under a very rigid time constraint is irrelevant, since the fact giving rise to the damage under consideration here is not the analysis of the relevant markets contained in the statement of objections or the incompatibility decision but the omission from the statement of objections of a reference which was of the essence as regards its consequences and from the operative part of the incompatibility decision [...].

It follows that the breach of Schneider's rights of defence is to be regarded in this case as a manifest and serious disregard by the Commission of the limits to which it is subject and, as such, constitutes a sufficiently serious breach of a rule of law intended to confer rights on individuals.

The breach of Schneider's rights of defence therefore constitutes a fault on the part of the Commission such as to cause the Community to incur non-contractual liability, provided that it is established in addition that there was real and certain damage and a sufficiently direct causal link between that damage and the sufficiently serious breach of Community law constituting a fault.

General Court 11 July 2007 (Schneider Electric v. Commission, T-351/03) [2007] ECR II-2237, paras 145, 152 and 154–157.

See also in appeal CoJ 16 July 2009 (Commission v. Schneider Electric, C-440/07 P) [2009] ECR I-6413.

14.81   [No liability Commission in case of an incorrect substantive assessment] However, for such a finding to be made, it is necessary to bear in mind that the economic analyses necessary for the characterisation in competition law, of a given situation or transaction involve generally, as regards both the facts and the reasoning based on the recital of the facts, complex and difficult intellectual exercises, which may inadvertently contain some inadequacies, such as approximations, inconsistencies, or indeed certain omissions. That applies all the more in the control of concentrations, in view in particular of the time constraints to which the institution is subject. [...]

Such inadequacies in the economic analysis are all the more likely to occur where, as in the case of the control of concentrations, the analysis has a prospective element. The gravity of a documentary or logical inadequacy may, in such circumstances, not always constitute a sufficient circumstance to cause the Community to incur liability. In the present case, the [General Court] considers that the difficulty which is inherent in the prospective aspect of the analysis of the effects of the concentration on competition, after it has been put into effect, is added to by the fact that the economic situation in question was especially complex, inasmuch as the Commission was required to assess the possible creation of a collective dominant position of an oligopolistic rather than a merely duopolistic nature on a market for a product which combines a sale through a travel agency, with air transport and a stay in a hotel and on which competition is practised more in relation to capacity than prices. [...]

[...] It is in that context that the administration's discretion, within the meaning of the case-law resulting from Bergaderm, must be interpreted. Such an exercise is by its nature more demanding than that which is required in an action for annulment, where the [General Court] need only, within the limits of the pleas in law put forward by the applicant, examine the lawfulness of the contested decision in order to satisfy itself that the Commission has correctly appraised the different elements which enable it to declare the notified concentration incompatible with the common market for the purposes of Article 2(1) and (3) of Regulation No 4064/89 [now Regulation No 139/2004]. Accordingly, contrary to what the applicant claims, mere errors of assessment and the failure to put forward relevant evidence in the context of *Airtours v Commission* cannot of themselves be sufficient to give rise to a manifest and grave infringement of the limits imposed on the Commission's discretion in the control of concentrations and in the presence of a complex oligopoly situation.

General Court 9 September 2008 (MyTravel Group v. Commission, T-212/03) [2008] ECR II-1967, paras 81, 82 and 85.

ARTICLE 3 – DEFINITION OF CONCENTRATION

1. A concentration shall be deemed to arise where a change of control on a lasting basis results from:

    (a)   the merger of two or more previously independent undertakings or parts of undertakings, or

    (b)   the acquisition, by one or more persons already controlling at least one undertaking, or by one or more undertakings, whether by purchase of securities or assets, by contract or by any other means, of direct or indirect control of the whole or parts of one or more other undertakings.

2. Control shall be constituted by rights, contracts or any other means which, either separately or in combination and having regard to the considerations of fact or law involved, confer the possibility of exercising decisive influence on an undertaking, in particular by:

    (a)   ownership or the right to use all or part of the assets of an undertaking;

    (b)   rights or contracts which confer decisive influence on the composition, voting or decisions of the organs of an undertaking.

3. Control is acquired by persons or undertakings which:

    (a)   are holders of the rights or entitled to rights under the contracts concerned; or

    (b)   while not being holders of such rights or entitled to rights under such contracts, have the power to exercise the rights deriving therefrom.

4. The creation of a joint venture performing on a lasting basis all the functions of an autonomous economic entity shall constitute a concentration within the meaning of paragraph 1(b).

5. A concentration shall not be deemed to arise where:

    (a)   credit institutions or other financial institutions or insurance companies, the normal activities of which include transactions and dealing in securities for their own account or for the account of others, hold on a temporary basis securities which they have acquired in an undertaking with a view to reselling them, provided that they do not exercise voting rights in respect of those securities with a view to determining the competitive behaviour of that undertaking or provided that they exercise such voting rights only with a view to preparing the disposal of all or part of that undertaking or of its assets or the disposal of those securities and that any such disposal takes place within one year of the date of acquisition; that period may be extended by the Commission on

request where such institutions or companies can show that the disposal was not reasonably possible within the period set;

(b) control is acquired by an office-holder according to the law of a Member State relating to liquidation, winding up, insolvency, cessation of payments, compositions or analogous proceedings;

(c) the operations referred to in paragraph 1(b) are carried out by the financial holding companies referred to in Article 5(3) of Fourth Council Directive 78/660/EEC of 25 July 1978 based on Article 54(3)(g) of the Treaty on the annual accounts of certain types of companies[6] provided however that the voting rights in respect of the holding are exercised, in particular in relation to the appointment of members of the management and supervisory bodies of the undertakings in which they have holdings, only to maintain the full value of those investments and not to determine directly or indirectly the competitive conduct of those undertakings.

OVERVIEW

A. GENERAL   (p.542)

B. PARAGRAPHS 1 AND 2: CONCENTRATION AS A RESULT OF A STRUCTURAL CHANGE IN CONTROL   14.82
  1. De facto control   14.82
  2. Sole control   14.88
  3. Joint control   14.95
  4. Interrelated transactions   14.99
  5. Acquisition of control by the State 14.109

6. Scope of 'undertakings concerned' in case of acquisition of control by state-owned enterprises (SOE)   14.111
7. No control/concentration   14.113
8. Lasting structural change   14.120

C. PARAGRAPH 4: THE CREATION OF A JOINT VENTURE   14.121

D. PARAGRAPH 5: CREDIT INSTITUTIONS, FINANCIAL INSTITUTIONS OR INSURANCE COMPANIES   14.127

A. GENERAL

See also the Commission Consolidated Jurisdictional Notice; recital 20.

---

6   OJ L 222, 14. 8. 1978, p. 11. Directive as last amended by Directive 2003/51/EC of the European Parliament and of the Council (OJ L 178, 17.7.2003, p. 16).

B. PARAGRAPHS 1 AND 2: CONCENTRATION AS A RESULT OF A STRUCTURAL CHANGE IN CONTROL

1. De facto control

[Acquisition of de jure control in case of existing de facto control] […] Ford offers to **14.82** purchase from Commerzbank 5 per cent of the share capital of The Hertz Corporation (Hertz). Following the notified operation Ford will hold 54 per cent of the shares of Hertz. […]

Before the present operation, Ford was already the single major shareholder of Hertz, holding 49 per cent of the voting rights and having the power to appoint four directors out of a total of nine members of Hertz's Board whose decisions were taken by simple majority. Ford was also granted substantial veto rights on matters which should be viewed as primarily aimed to protect Ford's financial investment in Hertz. These matters included inter alia the issuance of shares, changes to the company statutes, acquisitions or divestitures and vehicle supply agreements. Ford's voting and veto rights in Hertz described above, although important, did not confer upon it a 'de jure' right of control of Hertz since, on the one hand, Ford did not have the majority of the votes on the Board, and on the other, the veto rights which were granted to Ford did not include essential matters related to the conduct of Hertz's businesses such as the establishment of the business plan and the budget and decisions regarding major capital expenditure.

However, in addition to these rights […] Ford was also granted by the 1989 Stockholders Agreement between Ford and all other shareholders in Hertz the power to convert, at its sole discretion and at any time, part of its class C shares into class B shares, and by this operation to increase its representation on Hertz's Board to an absolute majority with the addition of two other directors. Ford's conversion rights could be exercised in a matter of hours and did not require any further cash disbursement.

For instance, should the Hertz's other stockholders decide to support a Board decision against Ford's will, in a matter of days or even hours Ford would have the possibility of converting a minimum of 200 class C shares into 200 class B shares, so becoming entitled, according to the Stockholders Agreement, to appoint two additional directors and thus take control of the Board. The new Board, controlled by Ford, would then be able to vote again on the contested matters and take a new decision in accordance with Ford's proposals.

Ford's unconditional right to obtain a majority on the Hertz Board at any time can therefore be viewed as conferring upon them 'de facto' sole control of Hertz. […]

For the foregoing reasons, taking into account that the notified operation – although allowing Ford to obtain a 'de jure' control of Hertz by acquiring a majority of the voting rights and of the Board representation – does not imply a change in the quality and degree of decisive influence already exercised by Ford on the conduct of the business of Hertz, the proposed operation does not satisfy the conditions of Article 3(1) of the Merger Regulation and therefore does not fall within its scope.

Commission 7 March 1994 (Ford/Hertz, M.397), OJ 1994 C 121/00, paras 1, 5–10.

14.83   [De facto control without de jure control] Despite the fact that RTL has not acquired any additional shares in M6, the divestment of Suez's shares will lead to passive acquisition of sole control by RTL for the following reasons. [...]

In the present case, RTL [has limited] voting rights to 34 per cent, even though RTL owns 48.39 per cent of M6 shares. M6 itself holds 0.91 per cent of its shares without any voting rights. The remaining 50.7 per cent of shares and votes are widely dispersed among a large number of small shareholders.

Under such circumstances, it is almost certain that RTL will achieve a majority of votes cast at future shareholders' meetings. It is indeed very unlikely that enough small shareholders will participate in these meetings to account for the majority of the votes cast. The Commission found that in the years 2001, 2002 and 2003, only a limited proportion of the small shareholders were represented. [...] Moreover, the incentives of small shareholders to participate in future shareholders' meetings and to coalesce will be reduced following Suez divestment. Indeed, under the previous shareholding structure – where Suez and RTL both had 34 per cent of the votes – a coalition of a limited number of small shareholders could possibly have an influence on the balance between the two main shareholders, while, under the new shareholding structure, virtually all minority shareholders should coalesce to achieve a majority.

Following Suez's divestment, RTL will be able to determine the strategic and commercial behaviour of M6 [...].

Based on the above, it can be concluded that the notified transaction results in Bertelsmann acquiring via RTL sole control of M6 within the meaning of Article 3(1)(b) of the Merger Regulation.

Commission 12 March 2004 (RTL/M6, M.3330), OJ 2004 C 95/35, paras 7, 9–12.

14.84   [Passive acquisition of de facto control] [...] on 16 May 2011 IF P&C increased its shareholding in TopDK from 14.74 per cent to 21.24 per cent (including treasury shares), which resulted in an increase of its voting rights from 16.44 per cent to 22.75 per cent (as per TopDK's Annual General Meeting (GM) of 12 April 2011).

Even if the absolute number of shares held by IF P&C has not increased since then, TopDK has accelerated, over the course of 2011–2013, an on-going Share Buyback Programme it launched in 1998. Due to this programme and the ensuing cancellation of shares, IF P&C's shareholding and voting rights gradually increased over time. As per 18 June 2013, IF P&C's shareholding in TopDK increased to 25.18 per cent (including treasury shares) and its voting rights to 26.51 per cent. [...]

As to past voting patterns, the Commission's analysis revealed that IF P&C already achieved a simple majority of the votes present at three recent GMs [...].

The Commission's prospective analysis revealed that a shareholder with 26.51 per cent of the voting rights would have achieved a simple majority at each of the seven most recent GMs. The conclusion would be the same if one of the methods proposed by IF P&C, consisting in adjustments for the effect of the variance in its shareholdings on the number of voting shares attending each GM, is applied.

Moreover, TopDK's shareholder structure is quite dispersed with only IF P&C holding more than 5 per cent of the shares. IF P&C is also the only industrial shareholder among TopDK's top 20 shareholders. Also, based on the evidence in the file, there are no indications of a possible community of interest – or other incentives –

among the remaining shareholders for them to align their position so as to countervail IF P&C's voting rights.

Given that a simple majority at GMs allows IF P&C to adopt alone a number of important decisions, such as the appointment of the members of the Board of Directors, and indirectly to influence, namely by having the possibility to veto, other strategic decisions, such as budget, finances, business policies and the appointment of the Executive Board, the Commission concludes that IF P&C passively acquired de facto sole control over TopDK.

Commission 12 March 2004 (IF P&C/TopDanmark, M.6957), paras 4, 5, 8–11.

[Shareholder attendance rates] During 2007 and 2008 Renova Industries acquired 31.1 **14.85** per cent of Sulzer's capital from different sellers. Until end of May 2009, when the agreement expired, Renova Industries was prevented from fully exercising its voting rights by a 'Stand-Still Agreement' it concluded in October 2007 with Sulzer. Until 31 May 2009, the agreement prevented Renova Industries from exercising de facto control over Sulzer.

As the stand-still agreement was soon to expire, Renova Industries notified the acquisition of control over Sulzer on 8 May 2009.

The assessment of de facto control needs to consider shareholders' attendance at annual shareholders' meetings. Over the last years, the presence rate at the Annual General Meeting was with one exception close or below 40 per cent [...]. The parties explain that there is only one other large shareholder, Fidelity International, with 4.88 per cent of Sulzer's capital while the rest of Sulzer's capital is widely dispersed. With 31.1 per cent Renova Industries will thus likely have a majority in the shareholders' meeting (now that it exercises full rights after the expiry of the Stand-Still Agreement) and will have the ability to appoint the majority of the Board, which is the strategic decision-making body of the company. Therefore, it can be concluded that Renova Industries has de facto control over Sulzer following the expiry of the stand still obligation.

Commission 17 June 2009 (Renova Industries/Sulzer, M.5469), paras 4 and 5.

[No de facto control due to lack of stable majority at meetings] PepsiCo already owns **14.86** approximately 43 per cent of the voting rights in PAS. However, PepsiCo does not have de facto control over PAS given that it does not have a stable majority of votes at PAS's last three Annual General Meetings. Furthermore, PepsiCo does not have: (a) any special or significant veto rights that would give it decisive influence in PAS; (b) any special rights to board representation or nomination of persons to management positions in PAS. As a shareholder, PepsiCo can nominate directors to the board of PAS, if it disagrees with the directors proposed by the board. Any nominations proposed by PepsiCo are subject to a majority vote of shareholders at a shareholder meeting. However PepsiCo does not have the ability to either positively endorse or veto any shareholder meeting decisions; (c) any other agreement or arrangement with any other shareholder in PAS that could give rise to collective voting or any suggestion of commonality of interests between the shareholders. Furthermore PAS is not controlled by any single shareholder.

Commission 26 October 2009 (Pepsico/Pepsi Americas, M.5632), para. 6.

See also Commission 22 September 1997 (KLM/Air UK, M.967), OJ 1997 C 372/20, paras 5–17; Commission 10 June 2009 (Electrabel/Compagnie Nationale du Rhone, M.4994); Commission 30 November 2009 (ArcelorMittal/Miglani/JV, M.5643.), para. 5.

14.87   [De facto control due to the intent to acquire control by a shareholder] Acquiring the majority of votes in the general meeting would also enable KB Holding to decide on the members of the board and influence the decisions of the board members because of the possibility of revoking their appointment.

Moreover, the clear intent of Mr Thiele, who indirectly controls KB Holding, is to acquire control. This is evidenced by the attempt to do so through the public bid and following the failure to acquire control through that bid, the current proposed share acquisition.

In light of the above and based on the evidence available to it, the Commission concludes that it is highly likely that KB Holding will acquire a stable majority in the future general meetings of Vossloh following the implementation of the proposed transaction. KB Holding thus acquires de facto sole control of Vossloh.

Commission 14 September 2015 (Knorr Bremse/Vossloh, M.7538), paras 13–15.

2. Sole control

(a) General

14.88   [...] As a result of the transaction, Thomas Gook will hold [more than 50] per cent of the ordinary shares of NewCo (and hence Gold Medal). The remaining shares will be held by Kenneth Townsley.

Thomas Cook alone will exercise decisive influence over strategic commercial decisions of NewCo (and hence Gold Medal). Thomas Cook and Kenneth Townsley each appoint three members of NewCo's Board of Directors. Thomas Cook, as the majority shareholder, will be entitled to appoint the Chairman of the Board who holds the casting vote at Board meetings and therefore has decisive influence at Board level and at shareholder meetings. In view of the above, the operation constitutes a concentration pursuant to Article 3(1) (b) of the EC Merger Regulation.

Commission 30 March 2009 (Thomas Cook Group/Gold Medal International, M.5462), paras 2 and 3.

14.89   [Acquisition of sole control by acquisition of brand (rights)] The present transaction does not relate to an acquisition of an undertaking by way of a share deal but to the acquisition of specific assets. According to Article 3(1)(b) of the Merger Regulation, also the acquisition of certain assets of an undertaking may constitute the object of control for the purposes of the Merger Regulation. In particular, paragraph 24 of the Commission's Consolidated Jurisdictional Notice further specifies that assets such as brands, without additional assets may constitute a business with a market presence, to which a market turnover can be clearly attributed.

Privileg is a well-recognised and long-established trademark in Germany and Austria. The market investigation has shown that brand names/good reputation play a significant role in the competitive process in the markets concerned. The market investigation has also confirmed that customers are likely to demand Privileg-branded products even without a transfer of customer lists, sales organisations or similar assets to Whirlpool. Furthermore, the fact that Quelle did not have its own production assets for Privileg-branded domestic appliances (but used third-party suppliers) underlines that in the case at hand production assets do not appear essential for a market presence and that the use of the Privileg brand would suffice to achieve such presence. It is therefore likely that, in this particular and very specific case, the transfer of the Privileg trademark will be sufficient to transfer the market presence of Privileg in the markets concerned.

As the rights to the Privileg brand thus constitute a business with a market presence, to which a market turnover can be clearly attributed, the acquisition of these rights by Whirlpool constitutes an acquisition of control within the meaning of Article 3(1)(b) of the Merger Regulation.

Commission 7 July 2010 (Whirlpool/Privileg Rights, M.5859), paras 6–8.

14.90 [Acquisition of sole control not excluded by certain special rights for minority shareholder] Comcast will acquire sole control of Navy:

– As regards shareholder decisions, a majority of the equity present will be required to pass a resolution. Prior written consent by GE is only required for certain decisions that are limited to minority shareholder redemption rights and so long as GE's direct and indirect equity interest is more than 20 per cent.

– GE has the right to appoint two directors out of five in the board so long as GE's direct and indirect equity interest is more than 20 per cent and one director so long as GE's direct and indirect equity interest is equal to 10 per cent. Comcast has the right to appoint the remaining directors. A majority of the board directors, with a majority of those present being Comcast directors and, so long as GE's direct and indirect equity interest is higher than 10 per cent, one GE director being present, will be required to pass a resolution. GE will however not have a right of veto over board decisions since a board meeting can be reconvened within 24 hours of a meeting adjourned because a GE director was not present.

– Although prior written consent of GE is needed for the appointment of a CEO in the first three and a half years, the approval is no longer required if GE has failed to approve two candidates suggested by the board.

Commission 13 July 2010 (Comcast/NBC Universal, M.5779), para. 7.

14.91 [Acquisition of control by contractual veto rights] Anglo Irish Bank and RBS (the banks) intend to restructure Arnotts' existing debt in return for (i) a warrant and a call option concerning the entire issued share capital of Arnotts, and (ii) associated control rights.

According to the Shareholders Agreement, a so-called 'Lender Consent' of each bank is required in relation to [...], as well as a number of other matters likely to impact upon the day-to-day operation of the business of Arnotts. Once Lender Consent is given in respect of any matter, Arnotts and its shareholders are required to implement such matters. Furthermore, both banks have by way of 'Lender Consent' an effective veto right over the exercise of the voting rights attached to the shares held by Art Holdings Ltd.

Upon completion of the present transaction, the two banks will, on a contractual basis, each have important veto rights concerning key strategic decisions [...] of Arnotts' commercial behaviour. Conversely, Art Holdings Ltd will not be in a position to exercise decisive influence on Arnotts, given that the two banks' consent is required for the exercise by Art Holdings Ltd of its voting rights in Arnotts in respect of each of these key strategic decisions and given that Art Holdings Ltd can no longer decide on Arnotts' board composition. The above will therefore result in joint control by the Anglo Irish Bank and RBS over Arnotts.

Commission 9 August 2010 (Anglo Irish Bank/RBS/Arnotts, M.5826), paras 5–7.

(b) Negative sole control

14.92   On 25 June 2009 MTN, Belgacom and Swisscom entered into a Shareholders' Agreement in order to regulate the rights and obligations of the respective shareholders in relation to BICS, as well as the activities, governance and organisation of BICS. In terms of the Shareholders' Agreement, the board of directors of BICS will be composed of nine members. Five of these members will be appointed by Belgacom. Swisscom and MTN will appoint two directors each. Whereas the Shareholders' Agreement provides that decisions of the board of directors normally require a simple majority of votes cast, the said agreement also stipulates that as of from 1 January 2010, any action or decision in connection with the Board Reserved Matters (including the adoption of the business plan, the approval or amendment of the annual budget and major investments), shall only be validly taken if the approval of either (i) at least one Belgacom director and one Swisscom director or (ii) at least one Belgacom director and one MTN director has first been obtained.

Therefore, as of 1 January 2010 Belgacom will acquire negative sole control of BICS since only Belgacom will be able to veto the strategic board decisions in BICS (including the adoption of the business plan, the approval or amendment of the annual budget and major investments). By contrast, neither of the two minority shareholders, Swisscom and MTN, will similarly be in a position to veto such decisions. They will therefore not enjoy the same level of influence in BICS. It is therefore concluded that Belgacom will acquire sole control, within the meaning of the EC Merger Regulation, over the enlarged activities of BICS.

Commission 26 October 2009 (Belgacom/BICS/MTN, M.5584), paras 10 and 11.

14.93   [...] whilst Deutsche Bank does not have the power to on its own to impose decisions regarding the commercial strategy of Actavis, it has the power to appoint three out of seven members of the Board and to block the appointment of the chairman, a power that is not enjoyed by any other shareholder. DB may thus be considered to hold negative sole control over Actavis under the terms and conditions set out under paragraph 54 of the Jurisdictional Notice.

Commission 22 September 2010 (Deutsche Bank/Actavis, M.5949), para. 9.

The Commission finds that in addition Mubadala would enjoy sole control over Mubadala Sub. The Commission reaches this conclusion in view of Mubadala's right to determine the majority of the members of the board and its ability to forge changing alliances either with GSO or Jynwell, depending on its interest. In contrast to the situation of joint negative control, sole negative control can exist if no other shareholders enjoy the same level of influence as the shareholder that is always needed to forge a majority. The shareholder enjoying negative sole control does not necessarily have to cooperate with specific other shareholders in determining the strategic behaviour of the controlled undertaking. [...]

14.94

Commission 19 April 2012 (Sony/Mubadala/EMI Music Publishing, M.6459), para. 16.

3. Joint control

Ballin KG will be jointly controlled by Kühne and HGV. They will each have the ability to appoint one managing director of the General Partner of Ballin KG [...]. Furthermore, the Articles of Association of Ballin KG confer Kühne and HGV veto rights that go beyond the rights normally attributed to a minority shareholder. In particular, the Articles of Association allow Kühne and HGV to block resolutions regarding strategic decisions at the level of Ballin JV. On the basis of these rights Kühne and HGV have the possibility of exercising decisive influence on the commercial behaviour of HL AG.

14.95

As regards the rights of TUI, Ballin KG and TUI have agreed that a qualified majority of 75 per cent of the votes is required at the level of Ballin JV also with respect to certain resolutions related to the operational business. The qualified majority of 75 per cent is required, among others, for the adoption of the budget, certain investments and certain rights with regard to the appointment of the board. The veto rights of TUI therefore exceed the normal veto rights of a minority shareholder and therefore confer TUI control over HL AG.

Commission 6 February 2009 (Kühne/HGV/TUI/Hapag-Lloyd, M.5450), paras 9 and 10.

Mubadala and Rolls-Royce (together, the notifying parties) will have joint control over JVCO. Indeed, each notifying party will appoint two directors. Decisions requiring the approval of the Board of Directors (affirmative vote of 75 per cent of the directors present with at least one director from each notifying party) will include: the adoption of JVCO's budget and business plan, the appointment of senior management and the appointment of the Chief Executive Officer. Hence, each notifying party will have a veto right over these decisions. In particular, Rolls-Royce's veto rights go beyond the veto rights normally accorded to minority shareholders in order to protect their financial interests as investors in the joint venture.

14.96

Commission 16 February 2009 (Mubadala/Rolls Royce/JV, M.5399), para. 6.

The envisaged operation involves the acquisition by Mytilineos of 65 per cent stake in Corinthos Power through a special purpose vehicle, namely, ARGYRITIS GH AVEE, while the remaining 35 per cent will be retained by MOH. [...]

14.97

MOH will be entitled to appoint the Chairman of the Board of Directors while Mytilineos will nominate the CEO. In addition, although Mytilineos will have the majority of voting rights within the Board of Directors, MOH will enjoy veto rights with respect to some strategic decisions of the joint venture including the approval of the annual budget and the business plan. Therefore, both parties will jointly control Corinthos Power.

Commission 30 March 2009 (Mytilineos/Motor Oil/Corinthos Power, M.5445), paras 5 and 6.

14.98   [Acquisition of indirect joint control] The board of Virgin Active Group will have as voting members four directors – two appointed by CVC and two appointed by Virgin Group Holdings. Virgin Active Group board's decisions will require simple majority, and although CVC's appointed director will enjoy a casting vote on a number of matters, Virgin Group Holdings will retain a veto right to certain reserved matters [...]. Therefore, CVC and Virgin Group Holdings will acquire indirect joint control of Virgin Active Group. The proposed transaction therefore constitutes a concentration within the meaning of Article 3(1)(b) of the Merger Regulation.

Commission 14 October 2011 (CVC/Virgin Group Holdings/Virgin Active Group, M.6354), para. 6.

4. Interrelated transactions

14.99   The proposed operation consists of two transactions. In one transaction, RA will transfer its flexible automation systems business dedicated to the design and integration of body work and sheet metal work (automotive body in white (BIW) activities) into a newly created 100 per cent subsidiary, the so-called Newco; ABB will acquire a 50 per cent participation in Newco through ABB France. In the other, ABB, through ABB Robotique, will purchase the assets of the robotics business which is organised in RA's ACMA robotics business division.

These two operations constitute two different concentrations because the nature of the control exercised by the undertakings concerned is different for the two operations. Furthermore, the two products concerned belong to separate markets which are not in the same sector, notwithstanding the fact that robots are one of the components of transfer line systems.

Commission 9 March 1993 (ABB/Renault Automation, M.409), OJ 1994 C 80/0, para. 4.

14.100   Kingfisher will acquire a 60 per cent controlling share of Wegert through its subsidiary Eijsvogel, under the condition that Wegert acquires 100 per cent of ProMarkt.

This operation includes several transactions which constitute one concentration within the meaning of Article 3(1)(b) of the Regulation. Although this set of transactions entails more than one change of control, it must be regarded as a single operation since the different elements are mutually interdependent: both the acquisition of ProMarkt by Wegert and the acquisition of a controlling interest in the latter by Kingfisher are conditioned to each other so that one cannot proceed without the other. Kingfisher provides the capital for the entire operation and all transactions will be carried out simultaneously. Kingfisher is not interested in acquiring one of the main businesses without the other. [...]

Commission 18 June 1998 (Kingfisher/Wegert/Promart, M.1188), OJ 1998 C 342/3, paras 6 and 7.

The parties notified two transactions. In one transaction, Dana will acquire GKN's **14.101** medium and heavy propeller shaft businesses (MHP shafts). In the other transaction, Dana and GKN will create a joint venture for light propeller shafts (LP shafts). [...]

These two operations constitute two different concentrations because the nature of the control exercised by the undertakings concerned is different for Danas acquisition of GKN's MHP shafts business and for the joint venture created by Dana and GKN. The operation involves thus the acquisition of joint control of one part of an undertaking and sole control of another part, which is in principle regarded as constituting two separate concentrations under the Merger Regulation. No specific circumstances justify a deviation from this principle.

Commission 4 November 1999 (Dana/GKN, M.1587), OJ 2000 C 9/10, paras 5 and 6.

The parties notified three transactions [...]. **14.102**

The notified transactions are part of an agreement between the parties, to restructure their global business activities. The third operation constitutes a concentration separate from the first two transactions, because the nature of control acquired by the undertaking concerned is different on the one hand for the joint ventures JointCo and EC JointCo and on the other hand for the acquisition of Bosch's air conditioning business by Valeo. The operation thus involves the acquisition of joint control of one part of an undertaking and sole control of another part, which is in principle regarded as constituting two separate concentrations under the Merger Regulation.

Commission 28 July 2000 (Valeo/Robert Bosch/JV, M.2046), OJ 2001 C 270/6, paras 6 and 7.

The notifications refer to three changes in the quality of control. In principle each **14.103** change of control constitutes a separate transaction, unless the different acquisitions of control are interdependent. In the present case it appears that the operations involve the same buyer and the same seller, they have been concluded simultaneously, and the economic rationale of the transaction is the acquisition of all the relevant parts of TXU Europe. They can therefore be treated for the purpose of the present decision as a single operation. [...]

Commission 20 December 2001 (EDF/TXU Europe/Westburton Power Station and EDF/TXU Europe/24, M.2679), OJ 2002 C 43/21, para 4.

That general and teleological definition of a concentration – the result being control of **14.104** one or more undertakings – implies that it makes no difference whether the direct or indirect acquisition of control was acquired in one, two or more stages by means of one, two or more transactions, provided that the end result constitutes a single concentration.

Nor does it matter whether, when they notify a concentration to the Commission, the parties propose to conclude two or more transactions or whether they have already concluded them before notifying them. It is for the Commission, in each case, to ascertain whether those transactions are unitary in nature, so that they constitute a single concentration for the purposes of Article 3 of Regulation No 4064/89 [now Regulation No 139/2004].

Such an approach seeks to identify, in accordance with the circumstances of fact and of law specific to each case and with a concern to ascertain the economic reality underlying the transactions, the economic aim pursued by the parties, by examining, when faced with a number of legally distinct transactions, whether the undertakings concerned would have been inclined to conclude each transaction taken in isolation or whether, on the contrary, each transaction constitutes only an element of a more complex operation, without which it would not have been concluded by the parties.

In other words, in order to determine the unitary nature of the transactions in question, it is necessary, in each individual case, to ascertain whether those transactions are interdependent, in such a way that one transaction would not have been carried out without the other. [...]

It follows that a concentration within the meaning of Article 3(1) of Regulation No 4064/89 may be deemed to arise even in the case of a number of formally distinct legal transactions, provided that those transactions are interdependent in such a way that none of them would be carried out without the others and that the result consists in conferring on one or more undertakings direct or indirect economic control over the activities of one or more other undertakings.

General Court 23 February 2006 (Cementbouw Handel Industrie v. Commission, T-282/02) [2006] ECR II-319, paras 104–107 and 109.

14.105   On 22 May 2008 the parties entered into a Share Purchase Agreement outlining the terms of the acquisition of TP Haluco. According to this agreement, Total produce will control 60 per cent of the shares in TP Haluco whilst Haluco will hold the remaining 40 per cent. According to a Shareholders Agreement entered into between Total produce and Haluco, the day-to-day management of TP Haluco will be performed by the Management Board and a number of strategic decisions, such as approval of business plans and change of strategy of the group, will require the agreement of the majority of the members of the Supervisory Board. Furthermore, Haluco as a minority shareholder is granted veto rights [...].

Against this background, it can be concluded that the transaction constitutes an acquisition of joint control of TP Haluco. This conclusion is not modified by the notifying parties' argument to the effect that this acquisition constitutes a first transitory phase of an overall concentration giving Total Produce sole control and that it should therefore not be considered a separate change of control on a lasting basis. In fact, the Commission considers that the joint control period can be considered not to have a distinct impact on the market structure only if this period does not exceed one year. In the present case, as the acquisition of joint control will last for a period exceeding two years, the transaction should be considered an acquisition of joint control by Total Produce and Haluco.

Commission 11 August 2006 (Total Produce/Haluco/JV, M. 5201), paras 8 and 9.

Mauser and Reyde intend to establish a jointly controlled, 50/50, full-function joint **14.106** venture in Spain – Mauser Reyde Ibérica, S.L. – (the 'JV'), for the production and sale of IBCs within the Iberian Peninsula and the South of France.

The transaction is a result of Mauser's intention to close its production site in Coursan in the South of France. This site mainly supplies customers in Spain. It produces plastic IBCs and other rigid industrial packaging products (plastic drums). Whereas the IBC activities will be contributed to the JV, the remaining Coursan business (the production of plastic drums) will be sold to Reyde. [...]

The JV transaction and the asset transfer are contained in separate agreements. However, the two transactions are economically linked, both being a consequence of the intended closing of the Coursan site, as well as de jure linked. Therefore, the transactions are interdependent and should be treated as a single concentration.
Commission 21 January 2009 (Mauser Holding International/Reyde/JV, M.5394), paras 4–6.

The Agreement giving effect to the transaction also states that at a later stage all **14.107** Mytilineos shares in Corinthos Power may be transferred to Endesa Hellas, a joint venture between Mytilineos and Endesa S.A. However, there is no exact timeframe foreseen for this future change of control [...]. Finally, under the current transaction, the joint venture can operate [...] before Endesa Hellas acquires any rights on shares in Corinthos Power. Therefore, any possible future transfer of shares from Mytilineos to Endesa Hellas does not form part of the present transaction.
Commission 30 March 2009 (Mytilineos/Motor Oil/Corinthos Power, M.5445), para. 7.

[Treatment of several transactions as single concentration] Recital 39 of the Commis- **14.108** sion Consolidated Jurisdictional Notice under Council Regulation (EC) No 139/2004 on the control of concentrations between undertakings (the Jurisdictional Notice) states that it is appropriate to treat as a single concentration transactions that are closely connected in that they are linked by condition. Furthermore, recital 42 of the Jurisdictional Notice states that transactions involving the acquisition of joint control of one part of an undertaking and sole control of another part constitute only one concentration if they are interdependent and if the undertaking acquiring sole control is also acquiring joint control.

The Commission considers that Tech Data Corporation has sole control over Tech Data Europe, which will acquire sole control of the Triade Holding. As a result, Tech Data Corporation will acquire sole control of the Triade Holding. Tech Data Corporation also has joint control of Brightstar Europe, which will acquire sole control over two subsidiaries of the Triade Holding. As a result, Tech Data Corporation will acquire joint control of the two subsidiaries of the Triade Holding sold to Brightstar Europe.

Given that the two transactions are subject to one SPA and that the SPA does not provide for the possibility that only one of the two acquisitions is completed and the other is not, it can be concluded that the two transactions are interdependent. It can also be concluded that Tech Data Corporation acquires sole control over the Triade Holding and joint control over the two subsidiaries of the Triade Holding sold to Brightstar Europe. The two transactions can therefore be considered as one concentration within the meaning of Article 3, paragraph 1(b) of the Merger Regulation.

Commission 22 September 2010 (Tech Data Europe/Brightstar Europe/Triade Holding, M.5903), paras 10–12.

5. Acquisition of control by the State

14.109   IVO-Neste is a holding company specially established to implement the merger between the two state-owned companies [IVO and Neste]. [...]

The Merger Regulation is, in principle, applicable to concentrations between public companies. The decisive criteria is whether each of the state-owned companies constitutes an economic unit with an independent power of decision see recital 12 of the Merger Regulation [now recital 22 Regulation No 139/2004]. The companies can be considered to be independent undertakings in the meaning of Article 3 of the Merger Regulation if they are given the power to implement independently their respective commercial conduct on the market and their commercial policy.

On the basis of the investigation carried out by the Commission, it can be concluded that both Neste and IVO act independently on the market. Both companies' operative matters are run independently by the respective operative managements. The state exercises its ownership control only in questions relating to the shareholding of the state, such as sales of shares, listings etc. There are no indications that the commercial conduct of Neste and IVO has been coordinated in the past. Subsequently, the Merger Regulation is applicable to the present operation.

Commission 2 June 1998 (Neste/IVO, M.931), OJ 1998 C 218/4, paras 4, 7 and 8.

14.110   [SoFFin, a Market Stabilisation Fund controlled by the Federal Republic of Germany, acquires control of the whole of the undertaking Hypo Real Estate Holding AG (HRE, Germany)]

In the present case the Commission follows a two-step approach for determining whether or not the acquisition by the German Federal State (further referred to as 'Bund') via SoFFin of control of HRE is notifiable under the Merger Regulation. This approach consists (i) in establishing whether HRE will post-transaction make up an economic unit that retains an independent power of decision [see recital 22 Regulation No 139/2004]; (ii) if this is not clearly the case, establishing which is the ultimate acquiring entity (SoFFin or an entity ultimately controlling SoFFin if SoFFin itself cannot be considered having an independent power of decision) and, which other undertakings controlled by this ultimate acquiring entity need to be considered for the purpose of calculating relevant turnover. [...]

[...] HRE will post-transaction be subject to coordination of commercial conduct and will not constitute an economic unit with an independent power of decision within the meaning of the Merger Regulation.

As HRE will not retain an independent power of decision post-transaction, the Commission needs to identify the ultimate acquiring entity and whether there are other undertakings controlled (directly or indirectly, solely or jointly) by this entity. Other undertakings controlled by the same ultimate acquiring entity within the meaning of the Merger Regulation may be subject to coordination with HRE and will therefore need to be considered for the purpose of calculating relevant turnover. [...]

[SoFFin is controlled by the Federal Ministry of Finance (BMF). BMF supervises, amongst others, Kreditanstalt für Wiederaufbau (KfW)] On the basis of the far-reaching supervisory powers exercised by BMF KfW cannot be considered an entity constituting an economic unit with an independent power of decision. [...]

For the purpose of assessing jurisdiction over the present case, it is already sufficient to include the turnover of KfW at the level of BMF in order to meet the turnover thresholds and to conclude that the transaction has a Community dimension. [...]

Commission 14 May 2009 (SoFFin/Hypo Real Estate, M.5508), paras 5, 6, 24 and 25.

6. Scope of 'undertakings concerned' in case of acquisition of control by state-owned enterprises (SOE)

[Independent power of decision from State] ChemChina is owned by the Chinese **14.111** State. For the purpose of the competitive assessment in the chemical markets in question, it is relevant to assess whether ChemChina is an independent economic entity, or whether it belongs to a wider economic entity including more enterprises owned by the Chinese State active in the same markets.

As regards state-owned enterprises, Recital 22 of the Merger Regulation states however that, in order to respect the principle of non-discrimination between the public and private sectors, account has to be taken of undertakings making up an economic unit with independent power of decision, irrespective of the way in which their capital is held or of the rules of administrative supervision applicable to them.

The Commission has in the past considered several concentrations involving undertakings owned by Member States. In those cases, the Commission assessed to what extent the companies concerned had an independent power of decision from the State.

In those cases, the overall assessment of whether the state-owned companies constitute units with independent decision-making power was guided by the possible power of the State to influence the companies' commercial strategy and the likelihood for the State to actually coordinate their commercial conduct, either by imposing or facilitating such coordination.

In order to assess whether the State has the power to coordinate the commercial conduct of companies, the Commission has previously taken into account factors such as the degree of interlocking directorships between entities owned by the same entity or the existence of adequate safeguards ensuring that commercially sensitive information is not shared between such undertakings.

When assessing the chain of control of state-owned companies, the approach is, first, to establish whether it has an independent power of decision, and, second, if this is not the case, to determine which is the ultimate State entity and which other undertakings owned by this entity need to be considered as one economic entity.

In the present case, ChemChina is owned by the Chinese State. The ownership of Chinese State owned enterprises (SOEs) lies either with the central government (under the State Council) or regional/municipal governments.

ChemChina is one of the approximately 125 large SOEs financed and owned by the central government. As an undertaking under central government ownership, Chem-China is reporting to the SASAC established on the central-level government under the State Council (Central SASAC or just SASAC). The SOEs owned by provincial and regional/municipal authorities are reporting to a large number of regional-level SASACs (Regional SASACs).

The Parties argue that ChemChina has independent power of decision from Central SASAC. They also argue that Local SASACs are independent from the Central SASAC and that as a result SOEs owned by regional/municipal governments are independent from SOEs owned by the central government. The Parties submit that the level of State intervention in China in the industry sectors relevant to this transaction is very minor.

As a preliminary point it should be noted that in China the chemical industry in which Bluestar and ChemChina operate, and more specifically the silicon industry in which Bluestar has most overlapping activities with Elkem, is characterised by relatively limited public ownership and a fragmented market structure.

In order to assess a potential coordination by the state of the behaviour of several SOEs active on a relevant market the following sections look closer into the power of the Central and Regional SASACs to exercise decisive influence on Chinese SOEs.

ChemChina's and Bluestar's independence from Central SASAC and other undertakings reporting to Central SASAC

As regards ChemChina's and Bluestar's independence from Central SASAC, the parties explain that SASAC essentially exercises the basic ownership functions on behalf of the State as a non-managerial trustee. Apart from nominating the top management in the Company, SASAC's key functions are, according to the Parties, to review the end-year results of the company and ensure that the company is operating within the permitted business licence.

According to the Parties, SASAC does not interfere with the strategic decision-making of ChemChina, such as approval of the business plan or budget. The Parties explain that SASAC should respect, in accordance with the law, the independent operation of the SOEs in question and cannot interfere in their production and operational activities apart from performing the responsibilities of an investor.

The Parties also state that SASAC has to date not requested commercial information from ChemChina or in other way influenced the commercial operations of the company. They conclude that ChemChina enjoys independent power of decision from SASAC.

According to the information gathered via the Parties, the Central SASAC employs around 800 people. Generally, it is either Central SASAC or the central political organs who appoint senior management of the SOEs. Dividend policy is not established by SASAC on a company-by-company basis, but across the board for all SOEs reporting to it, similarly to a tax. Also, management remuneration is done according to a point system which takes different factors into account.

However, in this case it is not necessary to conclude on whether ChemChina is independent from Central SASAC, as the market position of the companies under Central SASAC is limited in the markets concerned. Accordingly, the proposed transaction would not lead to any competition concerns even if all other SOEs in the markets concerned under Central SASAC were to be regarded as one economic entity.

ChemChina's and Bluestar's independence from Regional SASACs and undertakings reporting to Regional SASACs

According to the Parties and the studies and submissions provided by them, central SASAC has no operational control over local SASACs or undertakings under local SASACs' control.

First, it is submitted that the fundamental role both of central and local SASACs is to exercise separate ownership control. SOEs under Regional SASACs are owned by regional governments. Regional SASACs are therefore supposed to act primarily in their own interest and, apparently, not in the interest of the central government.

Secondly, managerial appointment authority for Regional SASACs seems to reside exclusively with local government and local political organs, not with Central SASAC.

Thirdly, it is submitted that there is no direct command-relationship between central SASAC and Regional SASACs. Central SASAC apparently cannot issue instructions to individual local SASACs, cannot replace managers and has no influence over Regional SASAC's assets and revenues. Central SASAC can establish general procedures and principles that local asset management should rely on as they execute their mission.

Fourthly, Central and Regional SASACs are said to pursue different strategies and objectives. Regional SASACs do not hold the same type of firms as the strategically important firms under the responsibility of the Central SASAC.

Fifthly, it is submitted that there are significant regional differences between the strategies and processes of different Regional SASACs, which shows that Central SASAC does not exercise strong authority over Regional SASACs and undertakings under their resposibility.

As regards the silicon industry, as already said at the centrally owned level there is only Bluestar/ChemChina. To the extent that other State-owned enterprises have a presence in the industry their ownership is dispersed among the more than 100 Regional SASACs.

According to the parties, in light of the foregoing considerations, it can be excluded that Central SASAC through the channel of professional and regulatory oversight over Regional SASACs would be able to align the market behaviour of firms under the authority of Regional SASACs.

From the Commission's analysis it would appear that in the silicon and carbon industry sector relevant for this transaction, there is indeed no indication that Regional SASACs and the SOEs under their supervision would form one economic entity with Central SASAC and affiliated companies.

Commission 31 March 2011 (China National Bluestar/Elkem, M.6082), paras 7–31.

14.112 [Power to coordinate commercial conduct] In order to assess whether the State has the power to coordinate the commercial conduct of companies, the Commission has previously taken into account factors such as the degree of interlocking directorships between entities owned by the same entity or the existence of adequate safeguards ensuring that commercially sensitive information is not shared between such undertakings.

When assessing the chain of control of state-owned companies, the approach is, first, to establish whether the company has an independent power of decision, and, second, if this is not the case, to determine which is the ultimate State entity and which other undertakings owned by this entity need to be considered as one economic entity.

In the present case, the ownership of Chinese SOEs lies either with the central government, with regional/municipal governments, or occasionally with other public entities. Sinochem is one of the 129 mostly large SOEs financed and owned by the central government. As an undertaking under central government ownership, Sinochem reports to Central SASAC.

The Parties submit that Sinochem is an economic unit that has an independent power of decision from the Chinese State. They argue that SASAC's limited statutory powers such as various provisions of the Law of the People's Republic of China on State-Owned Assets of Enterprises or Interim Regulations on Supervision and Management of Stateowned Assets of Enterprises prevent it from exercising a decisive influence over Sinochem and that SASAC does not intervene in the strategic decision-making process (e.g. by approving business plans or budget). They emphasise provisions regarding a separation of ownership from management, operational autonomy of SOEs and a purely supportive role of SASAC which does not interfere in SOEs' production and operation activities, apart from performing the responsibilities of investor. Sinochem submits that SASAC's rights are limited to approving the scope of Sinochem's business activities. Furthermore, Sinochem states that there are no interlocking directorships between Sinochem and other Central or local SASAC owned companies.

None the less, the core legislation itself and the associated information outlined on SASAC's website contain a number of provisions which can be read as suggesting that SASAC does in practice have certain powers to involve itself in Sinochem's commercial behaviour in a strategic manner, among others the right to approve mergers or of strategic investment decisions. At the same time, a number of external sources suggest that commercial decisions of SOEs could be influenced by the Chinese state. It appears from such sources that influence may be exercised through formal channels such as SASAC, but also in less formal ways. Sinochem's and SASAC's own official statements provide certain indications in this regard. For example, Sinochem's Annual Report shows that there is at least a very close cooperation between Sinochem and the Chinese Government.

In light of the above, in the absence of representations by the Chinese State and accompanying evidence, it is not possible to conclude whether or not Sinochem enjoys an independent power of decision in the sense of the Merger Regulation. [...]

Commission 19 May 2011 (DSM/Sinochem/JV, M.6113), paras 11–16.

7. No control/concentration

14.113   [Call option insufficient to create control] BA will acquire a 49.9 per cent interest in TAT E.A., the remaining 50.1 per cent will continue to be held by TAT. By virtue of the Acquisition Agreement BA is also granted an option to purchase the outstanding shares at any time up to 1 April 1997 and TAT is granted an option to require BA to do so on 1 April 1997. Since it is not certain whether these options will be exercised, the possible second transaction will not be taken into account for the assessment of the operation that is currently taking place.

Commission 27 November 1992 (British Airways/TAT, M.259), OJ 1992 C 326, para 5.

[Veto rights over issuance of fresh equity and substantial acquisitions insufficient to create control] Under the terms of an investment agreement BT is to purchase 20 per cent of the outstanding shares of common stock of MCI. It will be entitled to three out of 15 seats on MCI's board and will hold a veto over certain decisions such as the issuance of fresh equity, substantial acquisitions or disposals and borrowings taking the company over a certain gearing threshold. These are normal minority shareholder protection rights and do not constitute a power of veto over competitive behaviour and commercial strategy.

14.114

Commission 13 September 1993 (British Telecom/MCI, M.353), OJ 1993 C 253/0, para. 15.

[Voting in concert] The notifying parties state that NEC and Bull will acquire joint control over PBN which, in their opinion, is currently solely controlled by the founders. After the transaction, NEC will have the power to appoint three members of the Board; Bull two members; and the founders the remaining four. According to the parties, NEC and Bull, both having long-term common interests as external investors in PBN, should be treated for the purposes of this notification as voting in concert on the Board of Directors and also as shareholders in General Meetings. However, the concerted voting in the future by NEC and Bull is a pure assumption by the notifying parties which is not sufficient, in the absence of stronger legal or factual elements, to prove the existence of a situation of joint control within PBN.

14.115

Commission 6 February 1998 (NEC/BULL/PBN, M. 1095), OJ 1998 C 53/07, para. 5.

[No acquisition of control in case of minority shareholdings] Thus, any transaction or group of transactions which brings about 'a change of control on a lasting basis' by conferring 'the possibility of exercising decisive influence on the undertaking concerned' is a concentration which is deemed to have arisen for the purposes of the Merger Regulation. Such concentrations have the following characteristics in common: where before the operation there were two distinct undertakings for a given economic activity, there will only be one after it. Unlike in the case of a merger in which one of the two undertakings concerned ceases to exist, the Commission thus has to determine whether the result of the implementation of the concentration is to confer on one of the undertakings the power to control the other, that is to say a power which it did not previously hold. That power to control is the possibility of exercising decisive influence on an undertaking, in particular where the undertaking with that power is able to impose choices on the other in relation to its strategic decisions.

14.116

It is apparent from the above that the acquisition of a shareholding which does not, as such, confer control as defined in Article 3 of the merger regulation does not constitute a concentration which is deemed to have arisen for the purposes of that regulation. On that point, European Union law differs from the law of some of the Member States, in which the national authorities are authorised under provisions of national law on the control of concentrations to take action in connection with minority shareholdings in the broader sense [...].

Contrary to the applicant's claims, the concept of concentration cannot be extended to cases in which control has not been obtained and the shareholding at issue does not, as such, confer the power of exercising decisive influence on the other undertaking, but forms part, in a broader sense, of a notified concentration examined by the Commission and declared incompatible with the common market following that examination, without there having been any change of control within the above meaning. [...]

The bounds of the powers invested in the Commission for the purposes of merger control would be exceeded if it were accepted that the Commission may order the divestment of a minority shareholding on the sole ground that it represents a theoretical economic risk when there is a duopoly, or a disadvantage for the attractiveness of the shares of one of the undertakings making up that duopoly.

General Court 6 July 2010 (Aer Lingus Group v. Commission, T-411/07) [2010] ECR II-03691, paras 63–65 and 76.

14.117   [Meetings between minority shareholder and management insufficient to create control] Thus, in so far as concerns the claim that Ryanair used its shareholding to seek access to Aer Lingus's confidential strategic plans and business secrets, the only evidence provided in support of that claim is a letter in which Ryanair requests, in general terms, a meeting to be held with the management of Aer Lingus. The application does not contain any evidence that confidential information was actually exchanged during such a meeting. In any event, such an exchange of information would not be a direct consequence of the minority shareholding, but would constitute subsequent conduct on the part of the two companies which could potentially be examined under Article 81 EC [now Article 101 TFEU].

General Court 6 July 2010 (Aer Lingus Group v. Commission, T-411/07) [2010] ECR II-03691, para. 70.

14.118   [Voting against shareholders' resolutions (issue of shares) insufficient to create control] Similarly, as regards the claim that Ryanair voted against a special resolution that would have allowed the Board of Directors to issue shares without having first to offer them to existing shareholders, as is generally required under company law, it is apparent from the comments of Aer Lingus's CEO, reported in *The Irish Times* of 7 July 2007 in an article entitled 'Ryanair blocks Aer Lingus bid to reduce holding' and cited by the Commission without being disputed by the applicant, that the failure of that resolution did not have a significant impact on the company.

General Court 6 July 2010 (Aer Lingus Group v. Commission, T-411/07) [2010] ECR II-03691, para. 71.

14.119   [Request for extraordinary general meetings insufficient to create control] In so far as concerns the claim that Ryanair requisitioned two extraordinary general meetings in order to reverse strategic decisions adopted by Aer Lingus, the Commission states, without being contradicted by the applicant, that the Board of Directors of Aer Lingus rejected those two requests and that the planned decisions were implemented in spite of Ryanair's opposition. That example illustrates the fact that, contrary to the applicant's claims, Ryanair is not in a position to be able to impose its will.

General Court 6 July 2010 (Aer Lingus Group v. Commission, T-411/07) [2010] ECR II-03691, para. 72.

8. Lasting structural change

[Minimum time period for lasting change in structure of undertakings] AXA PE will **14.120** enjoy veto rights over certain strategic business decisions concerning G6 Rete Gas: a) for a five-year period, AXA PE will be able to veto any material change to G6 Rete Gas's Initial Business Plan as updated/revised on an annual basis; b) for a five-year period, AXA PE will be able to veto G6 Rete Gas's annual budget, should the latter materially differ from what was agreed in the Initial Business Plan as revised on a rolling basis, unless such difference is due to external factors (such as general market conditions) which are out of the parties' control/course of action and could not be foreseen at the time of the adoption/amendment of the relevant business plan; and c) AXA PE will also be able to veto decisions concerning G6 Rete Gas's strategic investments.

After the initial five-year period if certain financial criteria have not been met (rate of return, dividend) AXA PE will have a veto right over any new business plans and budgets designed to rectify the situation.

Based on the above, F2i and AXA PE will exercise joint control over G6 Rete Gas for a period long enough to bring about a lasting change in the structure of the undertakings concerned. [...]

Commission 24 August 2011 (F2i/AXA Funds/G6 Rete Gas, M.6302), paras 8–10.

C. PARAGRAPH 4: THE CREATION OF A JOINT VENTURE

[Not full function] The transaction, involving the establishment of Compass, is not a **14.121** concentration within the meaning [...] of the Merger Regulation since Compass will not be a full-function joint venture. The joint venture does not have access to sufficient resources including finance, staff, and assets in order to conduct on a lasting basis its business activities. In particular, Compass will have limited financial autonomy. [...]

Another element suggesting that the joint venture will lack autonomy from the parents is that its staff (initially three people and over the next five years approximately 7–10 people) will be mainly seconded from the parents. In addition, pursuant to the shareholders' agreement, the parties will provide or secure the provision of a number of services to the joint venture, such as marketing, tendering, information technology, metering and financial support. In connection with the last point, the parties have expressly agreed that if parental support is requested by trading counterparties those counterparties may seek the parents' guarantees to support Compass's payment obligations.

Commission 15 October 1998 (ENW/Eastern, M.1315), OJ 1998 C 344/7, paras 7 and 9.

[Full function] The JV will be full-functional as, it will perform capacity auctioning **14.122** activities on a long-lasting and autonomous basis. The JV is founded for indefinite period of time. The clients of the JV will be the shareholders on the one hand and any traders willing to sell or buy the transmission rights on the secondary market on the other hand. Once in operation, it will finance itself through cost-based service fees to be paid by its customers. The business plan of the parties foresees that around [20–40] per cent of the JV's revenue will be derived from third parties, mainly from fees linked to the secondary capacity trading.

In the long run, CASC aims to provide other related services, such as intra-day capacity trading, which would further increase the share of the revenue obtained from third parties. [...]

Commission 14 August 2008 (CASC/JV, M. 5154), paras 13 and 14.

14.123   [Full function] JVCO fulfils the full-functionality criteria laid out in the Commission Consolidated Jurisdictional Notice. First, JVCO will have sufficient resources to operate independently on a market as it will be managed by a dedicated team to perform its activities, will have access to requisite staff (through secondments from the notifying parties or direct employment), will have its own business premises and will acquire its own equipment. Second, JVCO's activities will go beyond one specific function of the parents as it will have the ability to make sales of certain services directly to third parties and without relying on the parents' functional entities. Third, according to JVCO's business plan, it is expected that more than [...] per cent of JVCO's turnover will be made with third parties after the first year of operation. Last, JVCO will operate on a lasting basis, the JV agreement being concluded for an indefinite duration subject to limited rights of termination and with a clause precluding the parents from selling their shares in JVCO before three years.

Commission 16 February 2009 (Mubadala/Rolls Royce/JV, M.5399), para. 7.

14.124   [Full function] Corinthos Power will be a full-function joint venture given that it will perform on a lasting basis all the functions of an autonomous economic unit and will have an indefinite duration. Moreover, according to the Joint Venture Agreement, Corinthos Power has the right to use the necessary land for the construction of the power plant by virtue of a [...] years' lease agreement. In operational respects, it will be autonomous from its parents with regard to its management as it will have its own board of directors and CEO dedicated to the company's affairs. Furthermore, it is intended to carry out its business for its own benefit in accordance with its own business plan and annual budget. Finally, according to the Joint Venture Agreement, it is foreseen that Corinthos Power will have sufficient financial resources to operate independently on the market.

Commission 30 March 2009 (Mytilineos/Motor Oil/Corinthos Power, M.5445), para. 8.

14.125   [Full function joint venture] Bei dem Zusammenschluss handelt es sich um die Gründung eines Vollfunktionsgemeinschaftsunternehmens im Sinne von Art. 3 Abs. 4 FKVO. EMS, IP, 71m und TFP sollen die gemeinsame Kontrolle an NewCo erlangen. Jeder Gesellschafter wird 25% der Anteile halten. Bei dem Abschluss, der Änderung und der Beendigung von Verträgen mit Geschäftsführern und bei der Verabschiedung der Geschäftsordnung für die Geschäftsführer ist Einstimmigkeit erforderlich. In anderen für die Kontrolle rechtlich relevanten Angelegenheiten ist eine qualifizierte Mehrheit (75% der Stimmen) erforderlich, nämlich bei der Genehmigung des Business Plans und des Budgets.

Nach dem Entwurf des Business-Plans, werden das Inventar und die Marketing-Informationen für die Online-Werbung in der Anfangsphase überwiegend von den Gesellschaftern an NewCo zur Verfügung gestellt. Dieses Inventar wird allerdings von NewCo nur in Kombination mit den neu entwickelten Produkten zur Zielgruppenansprache vermarktet. NewCo wird seine Produkte ausschließlich an Dritte verkaufen.

Darüber hinaus ist NewCo für die Vermarktung seines Produktes in den Angeboten Dritter offen. Nach dem Entwurf des Business Plans sollen im dritten Jahr [20–30%] des von NewCo vermarkteten Inventars von Dritten (also Nicht-Gesellschaftern) stammen. Der Anteil des von Dritten stammenden Inventars soll auch danach kontinuierlich ausgebaut werden.

Obwohl NewCo in der Anlaufphase stark von den Muttergesellschaften abhängig sein wird, ist es aus folgenden Gründen als ein Vollfunktionsgemeinschaftsunternehmen anzusehen:

Erstens soll NewCo von Beginn an als plattformübergreifende Marke positioniert werden, die selbständig und von ihren Gesellschaftern unabhängig ist. Sie soll auch die gemeinsam abgestimmten Kennzeichnungsrechte, insbesondere Marken, Werktitel, Unternehmenskennzeichen und Domains, selbst halten. Das GU wird über ein sich dem Tagesgeschäft widmendes Management und ausreichende Ressourcen wie finanzielle Mittel, Personal sowie materielle und immaterielle Vermögenswerte verfügen.

Zweitens wird das NewCo von Gesellschaftern gegründet, um erhebliche Größenvorteilen zu erzielen. Wichtig ist, dass die Gesellschafter dieses Produkt allein nicht anbieten können, da gerade die Bündelung der Reichweiten der Gesellschafter sowie von Dritten seine Entwicklung ermöglicht und dadurch einen 'Mehrwert' generiert. Die Entwicklung solcher Produkte entspricht einem Marktbedürfnis, welches jeder einzelne Vermarkter alleine nicht realisieren kann. Das kommerzielle Ziel wird sein, das Netz der angeschlossenen Online-Verlage zu vergrößern. Das folgt aus der Tatsache, dass die Qualität des Produktes (zielgruppengenaue Online-Werbung) mit steigender Anzahl der Websites im Netzwerk deutlich zunimmt.

Drittens wird das NewCo mit seinen Muttergesellschaften marktübliche Beziehungen auf der Grundlage der üblichen Geschäftsbedingungen unterhalten. Im Hinblick auf den kommerziellen Charakter der Beziehung, haben die Parteien bestätigt, dass das Online-Inventar an das GU zu marktüblichen Bedingungen zur Verfugung gestellt wird. Das GU wird seine Muttergesellschaften geschäftlich genauso behandeln wie Dritte. Es wird einen festen Prozentsatz der durch die angezeigte Werbung erzielten Einnahmen an die Online-Verlage zahlen.

Viertens wird NewCo ein neues, hochwertiges Produkt im Bereich der Zielgruppen-Online-Werbung entwickeln und im deutschsprachigen Raum vermarkten. Es geht darum, mit Hilfe des NewCo-Produktes ein neues Produkt-und Preissegment zu erschließen. Mit dem Inventar, das bislang von den Gesellschaftern vor allem im Niedrigpreissegment ('run-of-network') verkauft wird, soll durch das von NewCo entwickelte Produkt ein im Durchschnitt doppelt so hoher Preis erzielt werden. Über das NewCo-Produkt soll also eine beträchtliche Wertschöpfung erzielt werden.

Commission 21 January 2010 (SevenOne Media/G+J Electronic Media Sales/ Tomorrow Focus Portal/IP Deutschland/JV, M.5676), paras 15–22.

[Full functionality does not exclude assumption of 'single undertaking' for the purposes **14.126** of Article 101 TFEU] Third, as regards the applicants' argument based on the fact that

DDE was a full-function joint venture, the Court would point out that, although a full-function joint venture, for the purposes of Regulation No 4064/89, is deemed to perform on a lasting basis all the functions of an autonomous economic entity, and is, therefore, economically autonomous from an operational viewpoint, that autonomy does not mean, as the Commission made clear in paragraph 93 of its Consolidated Jurisdictional Notice under Regulation No 139/2004 [...], that the joint venture enjoys autonomy as regards the adoption of its strategic decisions and that it is not therefore under the decisive influence exercised by its parent companies for the purposes of the application of Article 81 EC [now Article 101 TFEU]. In the present case, [...] the Members' Committee held the power to take decisions determining DDE's business strategy and did in fact exercise that power.

General Court 2 February 2012 (DuPont v Commission, T-76/08), ECLI:EU:T: 2012:46, para. 78.

See also General Court 2 February 2012 (The Dow Chemical Company v Commission, T-77/08) ECLI:EC:T:2012:47, para. 93.

D. PARAGRAPH 5: CREDIT INSTITUTIONS, FINANCIAL INSTITUTIONS OR INSURANCE COMPANIES

14.127   [Criteria Financial holding company] CDCH has submitted that as Porterbrook is to be acquired by 'financial holding companies', within the meaning of Article 3(5)(c) of the Merger Regulation, the transaction is not notifiable.

It is the view of the Commission that this interpretation of Article 3(5)(c) is inappropriate. 'Financial holding companies' are defined in Article 5(3) of the Fourth Council Directive (78/660/EEC) of 1978 concerning the annual accounts of certain types of companies as being: 'those companies the sole object of which is to acquire holdings in other undertakings, and to manage such holdings and to turn them to profit, without involving themselves directly or indirectly in the management of such undertakings [...]. limitations imposed on the activities of these companies must be such that compliance [...] can be supervised by an [...] authority'.

CDCH has submitted its Memorandum and Articles of Association to the Commission to support its assertion that it is a 'financial holding company' and quotes clause 3(1), which states that one of CDCH's objects is 'to carry on the business of an investment company'. However CDCH's Memorandum of Association also shows, through 39 other clauses, that it may acquire shares or securities (clauses 2 and 3), lend money (clause 6), constitute trusts (clause 7), guarantee, support or secure (clause 9), manage, supervise or control businesses (clause 19), develop land (clause 22), effect insurance (clause 25) etc. Clearly therefore its sole object is not simply to acquire holdings in other undertakings and to manage such holdings and to turn them to profit as required by the Article 5(3) definition set out above. For these reasons it is not considered that CDCH forms a 'financial holding company' within the meaning of the Fourth Directive and, therefore, the Merger Regulation. [...]

The second test of Article 3(5)(c) is to ascertain whether the 'financial holding company' manages its investments simply 'to maintain the full value of those investments' or whether it 'determine[s] directly or indirectly the competitive conduct of those undertakings.' In this respect it should be recalled that the Charterhouse Group will control [...] of the shareholding of Porterbrook; in addition, it may appoint [...] 'special directors' to Porterbrook Leasing Company MEBO Ltd, one of whose consent is necessary to permit this company to undertake certain transactions. [...]

It could be argued that a number of the above consents are necessary to safeguard the full value of CDCH's investment. However the far more probable interpretation is that these restrictions can be employed in managing directly, or indirectly, the day-to-day business of Porterhouse.

For these reasons the Commission does not consider that the exemption foreseen by Article 3(5)(c) is appropriate in this case and that therefore the transaction is subject to the Merger Regulation.

Commission 11 December 1995 (Charterhouse/Porterbrook, M.669), OJ 1995 C 350/18, paras 6–8 and 10–13.

ARTICLE 4 – PRIOR NOTIFICATION OF CONCENTRATIONS AND
PRE-NOTIFICATION REFERRAL AT THE REQUEST OF THE NOTIFYING
PARTIES

1. Concentrations with a Community dimension defined in this Regu-
    lation shall be notified to the Commission prior to their implementa-
    tion and following the conclusion of the agreement, the announcement
    of the public bid, or the acquisition of a controlling interest.

    Notification may also be made where the undertakings concerned
    demonstrate to the Commission a good faith intention to conclude an
    agreement or, in the case of a public bid, where they have publicly
    announced an intention to make such a bid, provided that the intended
    agreement or bid would result in a concentration with a Community
    dimension.

    For the purposes of this Regulation, the term "notified concentra-
    tion" shall also cover intended concentrations notified pursuant to the
    second subparagraph. For the purposes of paragraphs 4 and 5 of this
    Article, the term "concentration" includes intended concentrations
    within the meaning of the second subparagraph.

2. A concentration which consists of a merger within the meaning of
    Article 3(1)(a) or in the acquisition of joint control within the meaning
    of Article 3(1)(b) shall be notified jointly by the parties to the merger or
    by those acquiring joint control as the case may be. In all other cases,
    the notification shall be effected by the person or undertaking acquir-
    ing control of the whole or parts of one or more undertakings.

3. Where the Commission finds that a notified concentration falls within
    the scope of this Regulation, it shall publish the fact of the notification,
    at the same time indicating the names of the undertakings concerned,
    their country of origin, the nature of the concentration and the eco-
    nomic sectors involved. The Commission shall take account of the
    legitimate interest of undertakings in the protection of their business
    secrets.

4. Prior to the notification of a concentration within the meaning of
    paragraph 1, the persons or undertakings referred to in paragraph 2
    may inform the Commission, by means of a reasoned submission, that
    the concentration may significantly affect competition in a market
    within a Member State which presents all the characteristics of a dis-
    tinct market and should therefore be examined, in whole or in part, by
    that Member State.

    The Commission shall transmit this submission to all Member
    States without delay. The Member State referred to in the reasoned
    submission shall, within 15 working days of receiving the submission,

express its agreement or disagreement as regards the request to refer the case. Where that Member State takes no such decision within this period, it shall be deemed to have agreed.

Unless that Member State disagrees, the Commission, where it considers that such a distinct market exists, and that competition in that market may be significantly affected by the concentration, may decide to refer the whole or part of the case to the competent authorities of that Member State with a view to the application of that State's national competition law.

The decision whether or not to refer the case in accordance with the third subparagraph shall be taken within 25 working days starting from the receipt of the reasoned submission by the Commission. The Commission shall inform the other Member States and the persons or undertakings concerned of its decision. If the Commission does not take a decision within this period, it shall be deemed to have adopted a decision to refer the case in accordance with the submission made by the persons or undertakings concerned.

If the Commission decides, or is deemed to have decided, pursuant to the third and fourth subparagraphs, to refer the whole of the case, no notification shall be made pursuant to paragraph 1 and national competition law shall apply. Article 9(6) to (9) shall apply mutatis mutandis.

5.   With regard to a concentration as defined in Article 3 which does not have a Community dimension within the meaning of Article 1 and which is capable of being reviewed under the national competition laws of at least three Member States, the persons or undertakings referred to in paragraph 2 may, before any notification to the competent authorities, inform the Commission by means of a reasoned submission that the concentration should be examined by the Commission.

The Commission shall transmit this submission to all Member States without delay.

Any Member State competent to examine the concentration under its national competition law may, within 15 working days of receiving the reasoned submission, express its disagreement as regards the request to refer the case.

Where at least one such Member State has expressed its disagreement in accordance with the third subparagraph within the period of 15 working days, the case shall not be referred. The Commission shall, without delay, inform all Member States and the persons or undertakings concerned of any such expression of disagreement.

Where no Member State has expressed its disagreement in accordance with the third subparagraph within the period of 15 working days, the concentration shall be deemed to have a Community dimension and shall be notified to the Commission in accordance with paragraphs 1 and 2. In such situations, no Member State shall apply its national competition law to the concentration.

6.   The Commission shall report to the Council on the operation of paragraphs 4 and 5 by 1 July 2009. Following this report and on a proposal from the Commission, the Council, acting by a qualified majority, may revise paragraphs 4 and 5.

OVERVIEW

A. GENERAL	(p.568)	C. PARAGRAPH 2: GOOD FAITH INTENTION TO CONCLUDE
B. PARAGRAPH 1: 'SUSPENSIVE EFFECT' AND 'GUN JUMPING'	14.128	AGREEMENT 14.129

A. GENERAL

See also Annexes (Form CO and Form RS) to Regulation No 802/2004; Commission Notice on a simplified procedure for treatment of certain concentrations under Council Regulation (EC) No 139/2004 (OJ 2013 C 366/5); Commission Notice on Case Referral in respect of concentrations (OJ 2005 C 56/2); recitals 11, 12, 14–16 and 34.

B. PARAGRAPH 1: 'SUSPENSIVE EFFECT' AND 'GUN JUMPING'

14.128   [Bertelsmann and Kirch intend to merge their digital TV activity. According to recent press reports in Germany, Bertelsmann and Kirch would have started to broadcast their respective digital TV programmes Premiere and DF1.] No formal notification has been filed with the Commission as yet. Such notification is required by the Merger Regulation. The Commission can only start dealing with the case once it is provided with a complete notification.

[The Commissioner for Competition recalls] a basic principle of the Merger Regulation, i.e. that no merger can be put into force, unless the Commission gives its formal approval. He therefore expressed his dissatisfaction with the fact that apparently part of the operation is already being implemented. The Commissioner announced that he requested his services to investigate further this question and collect the information necessary in view of possible action to be taken by the Commission for a full assessment of this matter. Should it be established that the parties have violated the suspensive effect of the Merger Regulation, Mr Van Miert made it clear that the parties would be well advised to stop such a violation immediately, otherwise the Commission could impose fines of up to 10 per cent of the parties' aggregate turnover.

Press release IP/97/953. Commission 27 May 1998 (Bertelsmann/Kirch/Premiere, M.993), OJ 1999 L 53/1.

C. PARAGRAPH 2: GOOD FAITH INTENTION TO CONCLUDE AGREEMENT

On 15 June 2010, News Corp announced pursuant to Rule 2.4 of the UK Takeover **14.129** Code, that it had approached the Board of Directors of BSkyB and, proposed to make an offer to acquire the entire issued and to be issued share capital of BSkyB not already owned by News Corp. News Corp and BSkyB have so far been unable to reach a mutually agreeable price. However, both parties entered into a Cooperation Agreement on 15 June 2010 agreeing to proceed with the regulatory process to facilitate the transaction.

The announcement made by News Corp on 15 June 2010 along with the Cooperation Agreement concluded between News Corp and BSkyB on 15 June 2010 are sufficient to meet the relevant legal standard to constitute a notifiable concentration within the meaning of Article 4(1) of the Merger Regulation.

Commission 21 December 2010 (News Corp/BSkyB, M.5932), paras 5 and 6.

ARTICLE 5 – CALCULATION OF TURNOVER

1. Aggregate turnover within the meaning of this Regulation shall comprise the amounts derived by the undertakings concerned in the preceding financial year from the sale of products and the provision of services falling within the undertakings' ordinary activities after deduction of sales rebates and of value added tax and other taxes directly related to turnover. The aggregate turnover of an undertaking concerned shall not include the sale of products or the provision of services between any of the undertakings referred to in paragraph 4.

    Turnover, in the Community or in a Member State, shall comprise products sold and services provided to undertakings or consumers, in the Community or in that Member State as the case may be.

2. By way of derogation from paragraph 1, where the concentration consists of the acquisition of parts, whether or not constituted as legal entities, of one or more undertakings, only the turnover relating to the parts which are the subject of the concentration shall be taken into account with regard to the seller or sellers.

    However, two or more transactions within the meaning of the first subparagraph which take place within a two-year period between the same persons or undertakings shall be treated as one and the same concentration arising on the date of the last transaction.

3. In place of turnover the following shall be used:
    (a) for credit institutions and other financial institutions, the sum of the following income items as defined in Council Directive 86/635/EEC,[7] after deduction of value added tax and other taxes directly related to those items, where appropriate:
    (i) interest income and similar income;
    (ii) income from securities:
        - income from shares and other variable yield securities,
        - income from participating interests,
        - income from shares in affiliated undertakings;
    (iii) commissions receivable;
    (iv) net profit on financial operations;
    (v) other operating income.
    The turnover of a credit or financial institution in the Community or in a Member State shall comprise the income items, as defined above, which are received by the branch or division of that

---

7   OJ L 372, 31. 12. 1986, p. 1. Directive as last amended by Directive 2003/51/EC of the European Parliament and of the Council.

institution established in the Community or in the Member State in question, as the case may be;

(b) for insurance undertakings, the value of gross premiums written which shall comprise all amounts received and receivable in respect of insurance contracts issued by or on behalf of the insurance undertakings, including also outgoing reinsurance premiums, and after deduction of taxes and parafiscal contributions or levies charged by reference to the amounts of individual premiums or the total volume of premiums; as regards Article 1(2)(b) and (3)(b), (c) and (d) and the final part of Article 1(2) and (3), gross premiums received from Community residents and from residents of one Member State respectively shall be taken into account.

4. Without prejudice to paragraph 2, the aggregate turnover of an undertaking concerned within the meaning of this Regulation shall be calculated by adding together the respective turnovers of the following:

(a) the undertaking concerned;

(b) those undertakings in which the undertaking concerned, directly or indirectly:

   (i) owns more than half the capital or business assets, or

   (ii) has the power to exercise more than half the voting rights, or

   (iii) has the power to appoint more than half the members of the supervisory board, the administrative board or bodies legally representing the undertakings, or

   (iv) has the right to manage the undertakings' affairs;

(c) those undertakings which have in the undertaking concerned the rights or powers listed in (b);

(d) those undertakings in which an undertaking as referred to in (c) has the rights or powers listed in (b);

(e) those undertakings in which two or more undertakings as referred to in (a) to (d) jointly have the rights or powers listed in (b).

5. Where undertakings concerned by the concentration jointly have the rights or powers listed in paragraph 4(b), in calculating the aggregate turnover of the undertakings concerned for the purposes of this Regulation:

(a) no account shall be taken of the turnover resulting from the sale of products or the provision of services between the joint undertaking and each of the undertakings concerned or any other undertaking connected with any one of them, as set out in paragraph 4(b) to (e);

(b) **account shall be taken of the turnover resulting from the sale of products and the provision of services between the joint undertaking and any third undertakings. This turnover shall be apportioned equally amongst the undertakings concerned.**

OVERVIEW

A. GENERAL	(p.572)	C. PARAGRAPH 2: CONSECUTIVE ACQUISITIONS	14.132
B. GEOGRAPHIC ALLOCATION OF TURNOVER	14.130	D. PARAGRAPH 4: ATTRIBUTION OF TURNOVER	14.136

A. GENERAL

See also Commission Consolidated Jurisdictional Notice; recitals 9, 10 and 22.

B. GEOGRAPHIC ALLOCATION OF TURNOVER

14.130   Given that ICO is registered in the Cayman Islands but is actually managed in London, whether ICO should be seen as a Community company is decisive in determining whether or not the proposed transaction has a Community dimension. [...]

[...] It appears that ICO was formed as a result of a project established by Inmarsat (an international organisation based in London, which has now become a UK-listed company) to offer world-wide data and voice communication services through the use of a satellite-based telecommunication network. For that purpose, ICO was incorporated in 1994 in England and Wales. This company was subsequently liquidated and the assets were transferred to a Cayman Islands company, which itself was changed into a Bermuda Company. However, these changes, which seem to have primarily been made for tax purposes, have not altered the management structure of the company. As ICO has formally stated, its principal place of business is in London, where all ICO's day-to-day management is carried out and where 73 per cent of ICO's personnel is located, the remainder being spread in several locations around the world. In the light of the foregoing, it appears that, formally speaking, the parties are correct in claiming that ICO is a Cayman Islands (or more precisely a Bermuda Islands) registered company but that, economically speaking, ICO is still clearly a United Kingdom based company.

In the calculation of turnover for the purposes of the Merger Regulation, it is the economic reality of a situation that should be taken into account. Indeed, [...] 'the set of rules [concerning the calculation of turnover] are designed to ensure that the resulting figures are a true representation of economic reality'. In this case, therefore, HSC's turnover with ICO should be allocated to the United Kingdom.

Furthermore, it appears that, although the satellite contract between HSC and ICO is formally placed with the Cayman Islands company, it was finally negotiated by ICO's

London staff, and that any important modifications to this contract would be negotiated in London. If account is also taken of the place where the transaction was in reality carried out, and therefore where competition between HSC and other satellite prime contractors took place, it clearly points to the United Kingdom.

[...] HSC's turnover with ICO should therefore be allocated to the United Kingdom and included in its EEA turnover.

Commission 29 September 2000 (Boeing/Hughes, M.1879), OJ 2004 L 63/53, paras 11–15.

In previous airline cases, the Commission identified the following three possibilities for geographical allocation of turnover: (1) to allocate revenue from individual routes to the country of destination (this option was specifically mentioned in some cases for transatlantic routes and was abandoned in the later decisions not involving transatlantic routes [...]); (2) to allocate the turnover in a 50/50 ratio to the country of origin and the country of final destination so as to take into account the cross-border character of the service provided ('50/50 method'); (3) to allocate the turnover to the country where the ticket sale occurred (referred to also as 'point of sale method'). **14.131**

Commission 27 June 2007 (Ryanair/Aer Lingus, M.4439), para. 18.

C. PARAGRAPH 2: CONSECUTIVE ACQUISITIONS

The notified concentration does not meet the turnover thresholds of Article 1(2) and 1(3) of the Merger Regulation [...]. **14.132**

This concentration has however a Community dimension, and therefore falls under the Commission's jurisdiction, because of the criterion laid down by Article 5(2) of the Merger Regulation.

According to this provision on the calculation of the turnover, when two or more transactions for the acquisition of different parts of an undertaking take place in a two years period between the same parties, these transactions shall be treated as one concentration. For the calculation of the turnover, the notified operation should therefore be considered together with the operation by which, in 2004, Repsol YPF (the ultimate parent company of the Repsol Group) acquired all assets and activities of Shell Petroleum in Portugal apart from its LPG business (see case COMP/M.3516). Considering that the latter concentration had Community dimension, as the turnover thresholds of Article 1(2) of the Merger Regulation were met, also the present concentration shall be deemed of Community dimension.

Commission 2 March 2005 (Repsol Butano/Shell Gas (LPG), M.3664), paras 6–8.

[Global assessment also includes the interpretation of the second subparagraph of Article 5(2)], so where the acquisition of parts of one or more undertakings takes place in a number of transactions within a two-year period between the same persons or undertakings, the turnover must relate to the acquired parts considered together. **14.133**

The underlying reason for the insertion of the second subparagraph of Article 5(2) [...] is to ensure that the same undertakings or the same persons do not artificially break a transaction down into a number of partial sales of assets, over a period of time, with the aim of avoiding the thresholds laid down in Regulation No 4064/89 [now Regulation No 139/2004] which determine the Commission's competence in application of that regulation.

General Court 23 February 2006 (Cementbouw Handel Industrie v. Commission, T-282/02) [2006] ECR II-319, paras 117 and 118.

14.134   On 3 February 2010, Faurecia entered into a sales and purchase agreement with the insolvency administrator of Plastal Germany to acquire the business and all operating assets of Plastal Germany from the Plastal Group. The transaction was cleared by the Commission on 24 March 2010 (COMP/M.5799).

In addition, Faurecia entered into an Option Agreement with the Plastal Group regarding all shares in Plastal Spain and in Plastal S.A.S. (Plastal France) which were held by Plastal Germany. Faurecia exercised the call option for Plastal Spain on 29 June 2010.

According to Article 5(2) second subparagraph of the Merger Regulation, two or more transactions which take place within a two-year period between the same persons or undertakings shall be treated as one and the same concentration arising on the date of the last transaction. The acquisition of Plastal Germany and of Plastal Spain by Faurecia falls under this provision.

Commission 30 September 2010 (Faurecia/Plastal, M.5977), paras 4–6.

14.135   The Ebony transaction on its own does not meet the thresholds of Article 1(2) and (3) of the Merger Regulation as the target business does not derive any turnover outside of the PRC. However, as the Ebony transaction takes place between the same undertakings as the Meridian transaction within a two-year period, Article 5(2) second subparagraph of the Merger Regulation requires both transactions to be treated as one and the same concentration arising on the date of the last transaction.

Commission 9 November 2010 (TPV/Philips monitors and colour TVs, M.5964), para. 9.

D. PARAGRAPH 4: ATTRIBUTION OF TURNOVER

14.136   [The] first argument is based on the 'ownership' by Mister Minit of 'more than half the business assets' of the franchisee's business in accordance with the first indent of Article 5.4(b) of the Merger Regulation in relation to the calculation of turnover. However, the said indent cannot be interpreted to cover a situation in which the undertaking which owns the assets is paid by another undertaking for the use of those assets in carrying out its own business activities for the duration of a given contractual period. The object and consequence of the said counter-payment by the other undertaking is that it acquires control over the assets concerned for the purposes of their exploitation in its own business during that period. Such is the situation in the present case where the franchisee pays [...] rent to the franchisor for the use of the equipment and fixtures owned by this latter undertaking. Thus, the Commission considers that Mister Minit, the franchisor, does not control the assets concerned and, consequently, cannot be said to effectively 'own' them for the purposes of interpreting Article 5.4(b) of the Merger

Regulation. Therefore, the Commission considers that the said Article 5.4(b), first indent, cannot be invoked to justify including the turnover of the franchised businesses in the aggregate turnover of Mister Minit.

Commission 9 July 1997 (UBS/Mister Minit, M.940), OJ 1997 C 232/5, para. 14.

[T]he risks assigned by the party to the franchisor, on the one hand, and to the **14.137** franchisee, on the other hand, are considered by the Commission to correspond to risks in relation to two separate businesses, i.e., those of the franchisor, in relation to his franchisor business (i.e. the franchising of know-how, trade mark use, goodwill etc., the leasing/renting of the related premises, equipment etc. and the provision and negotiation of supplies) and those of the franchisee, in relation to the franchisee business (i.e. the provision of shoe repair and key-cutting services etc.).

Furthermore, the 'de facto control/economic dependence' arguments of the party discussed above do not demonstrate (nor does the party so claim) that Mister Minit has 'the right to manage' the franchisee's affairs, in accordance with the last indent of Article 5.4(b) of the Merger Regulation. Consequently, the Commission likewise considers that the said arguments do not justify the party including the turnover of the franchised businesses in the aggregate turnover of Mister Minit.

Commission 9 July 1997 (UBS/Mister Minit, M.940), OJ 1997 C 232/5, paras 16 and 17.

The above shows that the UK Trustee holds (in numbers) a little bit more than half of **14.138** the shares. However, the relevant criterion for Article 5(4)(b)(i) of the Merger Regulation is not the number of shares, but the capital they represent (i.e. the nominal value of the shares). The aggregate nominal value of the shares held by IAG represents far more than half of the capital of BA. [...]

[T]he criteria of Article 5(4)(b)(iii) of the Merger Regulation are satisfied and the turnover of Iberia should be added to that of IAG because IAG has the power to appoint more than half of the directors of Iberia. It is immaterial at which level of IAG the ultimate decision is taken, or how the voting rights of IAG's shareholders are weighted in case of a vote, what matters is that IAG has the power to appoint seven of the eleven directors.

Commission 30 March 2012 (IAG/BMI, M.6447), paras 10 and 15.

ARTICLE 6 – EXAMINATION OF THE NOTIFICATION AND INITIATION OF PROCEEDINGS

1. The Commission shall examine the notification as soon as it is received.

    (a) Where it concludes that the concentration notified does not fall within the scope of this Regulation, it shall record that finding by means of a decision.

    (b) Where it finds that the concentration notified, although falling within the scope of this Regulation, does not raise serious doubts as to its compatibility with the common market, it shall decide not to oppose it and shall declare that it is compatible with the common market.

    A decision declaring a concentration compatible shall be deemed to cover restrictions directly related and necessary to the implementation of the concentration.

    (c) Without prejudice to paragraph 2, where the Commission finds that the concentration notified falls within the scope of this Regulation and raises serious doubts as to its compatibility with the common market, it shall decide to initiate proceedings. Without prejudice to Article 9, such proceedings shall be closed by means of a decision as provided for in Article 8(1) to (4), unless the undertakings concerned have demonstrated to the satisfaction of the Commission that they have abandoned the concentration.

2. Where the Commission finds that, following modification by the undertakings concerned, a notified concentration no longer raises serious doubts within the meaning of paragraph 1(c), it shall declare the concentration compatible with the common market pursuant to paragraph 1(b).

    The Commission may attach to its decision under paragraph 1(b) conditions and obligations intended to ensure that the undertakings concerned comply with the commitments they have entered into vis-à-vis the Commission with a view to rendering the concentration compatible with the common market.

3. The Commission may revoke the decision it took pursuant to paragraph 1(a) or (b) where:

    (a) the decision is based on incorrect information for which one of the undertakings is responsible or where it has been obtained by deceit, or

    (b) the undertakings concerned commit a breach of an obligation attached to the decision.

4.	In the cases referred to in paragraph 3, the Commission may take a decision under paragraph 1, without being bound by the time limits referred to in Article 10(1).

5.	The Commission shall notify its decision to the undertakings concerned and the competent authorities of the Member States without delay.

OVERVIEW

A. GENERAL	(p.577)	C. COMMITMENTS	14.141
B. PARAGRAPH 1: INVESTIGATION BY THE COMMISSION	14.139	D. ANCILLARY RESTRAINTS	(p.581)

A. GENERAL

See also recitals 21, 33 and 35, and Arts 10 and 21.

B. PARAGRAPH 1: INVESTIGATION BY THE COMMISSION

See also DG Competition Information note on Art. 6 (1)c 2nd sentence of Regulation 139/2004 (abandonment of concentrations).

Although the Commission has no discretion as regards the initiation of the Phase II procedure where it encounters serious doubts with respect to the compatibility of a concentration with the common market, Article 6(1)(c) of the Regulation providing that, in that case, the Commission 'shall decide to initiate proceedings', it nevertheless enjoys a certain margin of discretion in identifying and evaluating the circumstances of the case in order to determine whether or not they present serious doubts or, where commitments have been proposed, whether they continue to present them […]. **14.139**
General Court 3 April 2003 (Philips v. Commission, T-119/02) [2003] ECR II–1433, para. 77.

[T]he parties to a merger agreement cannot deprive the Commission of its competence by withdrawing their notification, the Commission must still, when exercising that competence, rule on a real merger transaction and not, following withdrawal of the notification and abandonment of the transaction in the form initially envisaged, on vague intentions of the parties to merge their activities in a modified form in the future, as it has done in the present case. **14.140**

Furthermore, the Commission cannot, without running the risk of making errors of assessment liable to have a substantial impact on its evaluation of the merger transaction actually in issue, conduct its assessment in relation to the provisions of an agreement whose implementation the parties have formally stated that they are abandoning.

General Court 28 September 2004 (MCI v. Commission, T-310/00) [2004] ECR II-3253, paras 96 and 97.

C. COMMITMENTS

14.141   [...] An 'up-front buyer' commitment implies that the parties may not complete the notified operation before having entered into a binding agreement with a purchaser for the business, approved by the Commission. A 'fix-it-first' commitment is a solution whereby the parties identify a purchaser for the business to be divested and already conclude a binding agreement during the Commission's review of the notified operation. The main difference between the two options is that in the case of an up-front buyer, the identity of the purchaser is not known to the Commission prior to the authorisation decision. A clearance of a merger on such terms therefore leaves the Notifying party exposed to the commercial risks consequent on being unable to find a suitable buyer for the business to be divested.

Commission 30 January 2013 (UPS/TNT Express, M.6570), para. 2001.

14.142   When a concentration raises competition concerns because it could significantly impede effective competition, in particular as a result of the creation or strengthening of a dominant position, the parties may seek to modify the concentration in order to resolve the competition concerns and thereby gain clearance of their merger. The commitments have to eliminate the competition concerns entirely and have to be comprehensive and effective in all respects. In assessing whether proposed commitments are likely to eliminate the competition concerns identified, the Commission will consider all relevant factors including inter alia the type, scale and scope of the proposed commitments, judged by reference to the structure and particular characteristics of the market in which the competition concerns arise, including the position of the parties and other participants on the market. [...]

The Commission has to be able to conclude with the requisite degree of certainty that it will be possible to implement the commitments and that it is likely that the new commercial structures resulting from them will be sufficiently workable and lasting to ensure that the significant impediment to effective competition will not materialize. [...]

Commitments must be put forward by the Parties and the Commission has the power to accept only such commitments as are capable of rendering the Transaction compatible with the internal market. [...]

The Commission welcomes fix-it-first remedies in particular where the identity of the purchaser is crucial for the effectiveness of the proposed remedy because the purchaser needs to have specific characteristics in order for the remedy to solve the competition concerns. If the parties choose to enter into a binding agreement with a suitable purchaser during the procedure by way of a fix-it-first solution, the Commission can in those circumstances conclude with certainty that the commitments will be implemented with a sale to a suitable purchaser. This can resolve the Commission's concerns particularly in cases where, given the circumstances, only very few potential purchasers can be considered suitable.

A clearance decision which is combined with a fix-it-first remedy is appropriate in cases in which there is a sufficient degree of likelihood that the entrant would eliminate all identified competition concerns and that the remedy would be workable and implementable.

Commission 27 February 2013 (Ryanair/Aer Lingus III, M.6663), paras 1672, 1673, 1676, 1679 and 1680.

[Acceptance of other commitments than divestitures] If *'divestitures are the benchmark for other remedies in terms of effectiveness and efficiency'*, the Commission *'may accept other types of commitments but only in circumstances where the other remedy proposed is at least equivalent in its effects to a divestiture'*. Often, a sufficient reduction of entry barriers is not achieved by individual measures, but by a package comprising a combination of divestiture remedies and access commitments or a commitments package with the overall aim of facilitating entry of competitors. If the commitments offered actually make entry by sufficient competitors timely and likely, they can be considered to have a similar effect on competition in the market as a divestiture. If it cannot be concluded that the lowering of the entry barriers by the proposed commitments is likely to lead to the entry of new competitors, such as to eliminate any significant impediment to effective competition in the market, the Commission will reject such remedy package. The notice on remedies points out specifically that, in air transport mergers, a mere reduction of barriers to entry by a commitment of the parties to offer slots on specific airports may not always be sufficient to ensure the entry of new competitors on those routes where competition problems arise and to render the remedy equivalent in its effects to a divestiture. **14.143**

Commission 27 February 2013 (Ryanair/Aer Lingus III, M.6663), para. 1686.

[Case-by-case analysis] The Commission points out that whether a remedy is suitable to eliminate the competition concerns identified can only be examined on a case-by-case basis. The mere fact that certain remedies have been accepted in previous airline cases cannot be a decisive factor and justify accepting such remedies in the present case. The Commission has to assess the proposed commitments taking into account the specificities of the transaction under review. **14.144**

Commission 27 February 2013 (Ryanair/Aer Lingus III, M.6663), para. 1694.

[Commitments involving pre-existing contractual rights of a third party] A competitor raised some doubts as regards the viability and effectiveness of the final Commitments. In particular, it questioned how the Commission would ensure that Array would enter into cooperation agreements with the Suitable Partner. Second, it stated that the final Commitments should have expressly indicated the terms and conditions of the cooperation agreement between Array and the Suitable Partner. [...] **14.145**

The final Commitments do not detail the terms and conditions of the cooperation agreement to be entered into Array and the Suitable Partner because the Commission considered not appropriate to let Novartis and Array solely decide on those elements. However, the final Commitments envision the overarching goal of these agreements

[...]. The Commission will assess the suitability of the Suitable Partner also against this important requirement, in a separate decision.

Commission 28 January 2015 (Novartis/Glaxosmithkline Oncology Business, M.7275), paras 305 and 308.

14.146   [The scope of divestitures beyond the geographical markets in which a competitive concern would arise] However, the overwhelming majority of respondents expressed their concerns about the viability of the divestiture in so far as it is limited only to Denmark and Sweden. Indeed the market test indicated that in order to ensure that effective competition is maintained in Denmark and Sweden, the scope of the proposed divestiture would need to be extended to cover at least the EEA.

This restriction of the Divestment Business to Denmark and Sweden appears to give rise to serious viability issues for the proposed Divestment Business, throughout the value chain, from R&D to manufacturing as well as marketing and sales. A purchaser would not be able to develop economies of scale and rely on its ability to sell the Vanguard on an international scale.

Manufacturing the Vanguard for only Denmark and Sweden would disproportion- ately increase the cost of production for the relatively small volumes [...] and would render the business uncompetitive. The respondents to the market investigation clearly indicated that it would not be feasible to produce an implant to be sold in only Denmark and Sweden and that the purchaser of the Vanguard Divestment Business would not have the incentives to develop the product line only for two countries. In this regard, the market test indicated that the expected unit volumes in Denmark and Sweden will not generate enough sales to compensate for the fixed costs and the investments making it difficult to establish a profitable business. Moreover, according to the respondents to the market investigation 'the geographic limitation also excludes the opportunity to really grow or develop the Vanguard into other and more interesting [geographic] markets'. [...]

The Commission took the view that the Commitments [...] as drafted only to include Denmark and Sweden in the scope of the Vanguard Divestment business, were not sufficient. [...]

The Divestment Businesses consist of: [...] the divestiture of the Vanguard Knee Divestment Business [...] in Denmark and Sweden and, in order to ensure the viability of the Vanguard Knee Divestment Business in Denmark and Sweden, an EEA-wide licence to the rights and know-how which are currently used and are needed for the manufacturing of an exact copy of the Vanguard Knee Product Line, under a different brand name, for the EEA and for the development of the pipeline projects as defined at the time of the transfer of the legal title to the respective purchaser ('Closing') (the 'Vanguard Knee EEA Licence'). [...]

On this basis, the Commission concludes that the Final Commitments are suitable to remove the significant impediment to effective competition that would have been likely to result from the proposed merger, and adequately address all the comments of the respondents to the market test.

Commission 30 March 2015 (Zimmer/Biomet, M.7265), paras 1874–1877, 1898 and 1952.

[Commitments in pre-notifying phase (fix-first-remedy)] In order to remove the **14.147** competition concerns arising from the proposed transaction [...], the Notifying Party submitted commitments as a fix-it-first solution (that is to say that the Notifying Party identified and entered into a legally binding agreement with a buyer outlining the essential of the purchase during the Commission procedure) on the same day of formal notification of the proposed transaction (the 'First Commitments'). [...]
Commission 17 September 2015 (NXP Semiconductors/Freescale Semiconductor, M.7585), para. 198.

D. ANCILLARY RESTRAINTS

See Commission Notice on restrictions directly related and necessary to concentrations (OJ 2005 C 56/24); Para. 9 Annex (Form CO) to Regulation No 802/2004; recital 21; Commission 25 March 2011 (Atos Origin/Siemens IT Solutions & Services, M.6127), paras 8, 10 and 11 (cf. below in relation to Article 8(1) Merger Regulation).

ARTICLE 7 – SUSPENSION OF CONCENTRATIONS

1. A concentration with a Community dimension as defined in Article 1, or which is to be examined by the Commission pursuant to Article 4(5), shall not be implemented either before its notification or until it has been declared compatible with the common market pursuant to a decision under Articles 6(1)(b), 8(1) or 8(2), or on the basis of a presumption according to Article 10(6).

2. Paragraph 1 shall not prevent the implementation of a public bid or of a series of transactions in securities including those convertible into other securities admitted to trading on a market such as a stock exchange, by which control within the meaning of Article 3 is acquired from various sellers, provided that:

    (a) the concentration is notified to the Commission pursuant to Article 4 without delay; and

    (b) the acquirer does not exercise the voting rights attached to the securities in question or does so only to maintain the full value of its investments based on a derogation granted by the Commission under paragraph 3.

3. The Commission may, on request, grant a derogation from the obligations imposed in paragraphs 1 or 2. The request to grant a derogation must be reasoned. In deciding on the request, the Commission shall take into account inter alia the effects of the suspension on one or more undertakings concerned by the concentration or on a third party and the threat to competition posed by the concentration. Such a derogation may be made subject to conditions and obligations in order to ensure conditions of effective competition. A derogation may be applied for and granted at any time, be it before notification or after the transaction.

4. The validity of any transaction carried out in contravention of paragraph 1 shall be dependent on a decision pursuant to Article 6(1)(b) or Article 8(1), (2) or (3) or on a presumption pursuant to Article 10(6).

    This Article shall, however, have no effect on the validity of transactions in securities including those convertible into other securities admitted to trading on a market such as a stock exchange, unless the buyer and seller knew or ought to have known that the transaction was carried out in contravention of paragraph 1.

OVERVIEW

A. GENERAL	14.148	B. DEROGATION	14.149

A. GENERAL

See also recital 34.

[Obligation to suspend implementation of a concentration applies also to acquisition of **14.148** minority shareholding which does not confer control] In that regard, the acquisition of a shareholding which does not, as such, confer control for the purposes of Article 3 of the Merger Regulation may fall within the scope of Article 7. The Commission's approach must be understood as using the concept of 'single concentration' to limit the risk of finding itself in a situation in which a decision finding incompatibility would need to be supplemented by a decision to dissolve in order to put an end to control acquired even before the Commission has taken a decision on its effects on competition. When the Commission requested Ryanair not to exercise its voting rights, whereby it was also pointed out that those voting rights did not grant Ryanair control of Aer Lingus […], it merely asked Ryanair to avoid putting itself in a situation in which it would be implementing a concentration liable to give rise to a measure adopted on the basis of Article 8(4) and (5) if found to be incompatible with the common market.
General Court 6 July 2010 (Aer Lingus Group v. Commission, T-411/07) [2010] ECR II-03691, para. 83.

B. DEROGATION

[…] OPI was created by OSR and PI with the purpose of submitting a joint bid for the **14.149** second cellular mobile GSM (Global System for Mobile Communications) licence in Italy to be awarded by the Ministry of Post and Telecommunications.

[T]he Commission has granted to OPI a derogation from the obligation to suspend the concentration, imposed by Article 7(1) of the Merger Regulation. This was necessary for OPI to be in a position to meet the deadlines established by the licence and to operate in competition with Telecom Italia, which has already built its GSM network and has a significant presence in the market for analogue mobile telephony in Italy. At this purpose OPI has already undertaken some activities which are preliminary to the start up of its cellular service (such as the award of contracts for the construction of the network, the funding agreements, construction and installation of sites).
Commission 27 March 1995 (Omnitel, M.538), OJ 1995 C96/3, paras 3 and 6.

The Commission granted a derogation, on the basis of Article 7(4), on 6 March 1995 **14.150** whereby the suspensive effect of the Merger Regulation, on concentrations with a community dimension, was waived in relation to this operation. This was necessary given the need to effect a rapid completion of the operation in order to prevent serious damage to Barings and third parties.

Commission 11 April 1995 (ING v. Barings, M. 573), OJ 1995 C114/6, para. 7.

14.151   On an application from SEB, the Commission on 27 September 2001 granted a derogation from suspension, as provided for by Article 7(3) of the Merger Regulation. The basic reason for this decision was that the receivers had insisted that any offer to buy should be unconditional. The derogation granted by the Commission was limited to the management of the purchased assets and ran until the authorising decision was adopted. It did not, however, authorise SEB to carry out the operation immediately, since the business was to be transferred only after the Commission's authorisation had been given.

Commission 27 September 2001 (SEB/Moulinex, M. 2621), OJ 2005 L 138/18, para. 11.

14.152   [T]he Commission, based on a reasoned request from Powergen, adopted a decision pursuant to Article 7(3) of the Merger Regulation granting Powergen a derogation from the obligation [...] to suspend the implementation of a concentration until it has been declared compatible with the common market [...]. This decision enabled Powergen to make an unconditional offer for the United Kingdom assets of TXU Europe. [...]

Commission 15 November 2002 (E.ON/TXU-Europe Group plc, M.3007), OJ 2003 C 14/8, para. 2.

See also Commission 14 October 1994 (Matra Marconi Space/Satcomms, M.497), OJ 1994 C 307/3, para. 1; Commission 22 November 1999 (BP/JV Dissolution, M. 1820), OJ 2000 C 98/9, para. 2; Commission 6 January 1999 (Philips/Lucent Technologies (II), M.1358), OJ 1999 C 39/13, para. 7; Commission 23 June 2003 (WPP v. Cordiant, M. 3209), OJ 2003 C 212/9, para 6.

ARTICLE 8 – POWERS OF DECISION OF THE COMMISSION

1.   Where the Commission finds that a notified concentration fulfils the criterion laid down in Article 2(2) and, in the cases referred to in Article 2(4), the criteria laid down in Article 81(3) of the Treaty, it shall issue a decision declaring the concentration compatible with the common market.

    A decision declaring a concentration compatible shall be deemed to cover restrictions directly related and necessary to the implementation of the concentration.

2.   Where the Commission finds that, following modification by the undertakings concerned, a notified concentration fulfils the criterion laid down in Article 2(2) and, in the cases referred to in Article 2(4), the criteria laid down in Article 81(3) of the Treaty, it shall issue a decision declaring the concentration compatible with the common market.

    The Commission may attach to its decision conditions and obligations intended to ensure that the undertakings concerned comply with the commitments they have entered into vis-à-vis the Commission with a view to rendering the concentration compatible with the common market.

    A decision declaring a concentration compatible shall be deemed to cover restrictions directly related and necessary to the implementation of the concentration.

3.   Where the Commission finds that a concentration fulfils the criterion defined in Article 2(3) or, in the cases referred to in Article 2(4), does not fulfil the criteria laid down in Article 81(3) of the Treaty, it shall issue a decision declaring that the concentration is incompatible with the common market.

4.   Where the Commission finds that a concentration:

    (a)   has already been implemented and that concentration has been declared incompatible with the common market, or

    (b)   has been implemented in contravention of a condition attached to a decision taken under paragraph 2, which has found that, in the absence of the condition, the concentration would fulfil the criterion laid down in Article 2(3) or, in the cases referred to in Article 2(4), would not fulfil the criteria laid down in Article 81(3) of the Treaty, the Commission may:

        –   require the undertakings concerned to dissolve the concentration, in particular through the dissolution of the merger or the disposal of all the shares or assets acquired, so as to restore the situation prevailing prior to the implementation of the concentration; in circumstances where restoration of the situation prevailing before the implementation of the concentration is not possible through dissolution of the concentration, the Commission may take any other measure appropriate to achieve such restoration as far as possible,

–   order any other appropriate measure to ensure that the undertakings concerned dissolve the concentration or take other restorative measures as required in its decision.

In cases falling within point (a) of the first subparagraph, the measures referred to in that subparagraph may be imposed either in a decision pursuant to paragraph 3 or by separate decision.

5.   The Commission may take interim measures appropriate to restore or maintain conditions of effective competition where a concentration:

   (a)   has been implemented in contravention of Article 7, and a decision as to the compatibility of the concentration with the common market has not yet been taken;

   (b)   has been implemented in contravention of a condition attached to a decision under Article 6(1)(b) or paragraph 2 of this Article;

   (c)   has already been implemented and is declared incompatible with the common market.

6.   The Commission may revoke the decision it has taken pursuant to paragraphs 1 or 2 where:

   (a)   the declaration of compatibility is based on incorrect information for which one of the undertakings is responsible or where it has been obtained by deceit; or

   (b)   the undertakings concerned commit a breach of an obligation attached to the decision.

7.   The Commission may take a decision pursuant to paragraphs 1 to 3 without being bound by the time limits referred to in Article 10(3), in cases where:

   (a)   it finds that a concentration has been implemented

      (i)   in contravention of a condition attached to a decision under Article 6(1)(b), or

      (ii)   in contravention of a condition attached to a decision taken under paragraph 2 and in accordance with Article 10(2), which has found that, in the absence of the condition, the concentration would raise serious doubts as to its compatibility with the common market; or

   (b)   a decision has been revoked pursuant to paragraph 6.

8.   The Commission shall notify its decision to the undertakings concerned and the competent authorities of the Member States without delay.

OVERVIEW

A. GENERAL	14.153	D. PARAGRAPHS 4 AND 5: RESTORATIVE MEASURES	14.156
B. ARTICLE 102 TFEU VERSUS REMEDIES	14.154	1. General	14.156
		2. Meaning of 'Implementation'	14.160
C. PARAGRAPH 1: ASSESSMENT OF ANCILLARY RESTRAINTS	14.155		

A. GENERAL

See also recitals 30, 31 and 33 and Articles 10 and 16–21; Commission Notice on remedies.

[Unnecessary or insufficient commitments which are proposed by the parties to a **14.153** concentration do not have binding effect for Commission] Le Tribunal relève que ces dispositions concernent, pour l'essentiel, des situations dans lesquelles les parties notifiantes ne respecteraient pas les conditions et charges dont serait assortie une décision d'autorisation. Or, force est de constater qu'en l'espèce la décision d'autorisation a été adoptée au titre de l'article 8, paragraphe 1, du règlement n° 139/2004 et ne comporte ni condition ni charge. Par conséquent, la Commission n'a pas violé le règlement n° 139/2004 en ne faisant pas respecter des conditions ou des charges qui, à ce stade du dossier, étaient devenues caduques. [...]

En l'espèce, il suffit de relever que la requérante n'a jamais reçu aucune assurance de la part de la Commission selon laquelle cette dernière acceptait les engagements proposés par Blackstone et Celanese. Ceci ressort clairement de la décision d'autorisation, qui ne mentionne les engagements proposés que pour indiquer qu'ils n'ont pas été considérés suffisants pour lever les doutes sérieux identifiés en première phase. En tout état de cause, il est clair que la Commission ne s'est pas engagée à faire respecter des engagements qu'elle n'a jamais acceptés.

General Court 1 September 2011 (Communauté de communes de Lacq v. Commission, T-132/10) [2011] ECR II-00254, paras 30 and 33.

B. ARTICLE 102 TFEU VERSUS REMEDIES

In the general monitoring of abuses of dominant positions under Article [102 TFEU], **14.154** proof of a dominant position in the market in question and abuse [...] must be adduced by the Commission and by third parties. Conversely, the commitments imposed as preconditions of a decision approving a concentration have the effect of transferring the burden of proof of compliance to the undertakings concerned by the operation in question. To that extent, the commitments already go beyond the general monitoring provided for in Article [102 TFEU].

In addition, if there were no commitments, it would be necessary to introduce a national or Community procedure under Article [102 TFEU], the outcome of which would be uncertain and, in any event, more difficult to impose. [...] Commitments, on the other hand, impose detailed obligations to be met within short periods of time, compliance with which is ensured by an effective, binding arbitration procedure which reverses the burden of proof and places it on the Kirch group. Commitments thus offer far greater legal certainty than Article [102 TFEU].

General Court 30 September 2003 (ARD v. Commission, T-158/00) [2003] ECR II-3825, paras 202 and 203.

C. PARAGRAPH 1: ASSESSMENT OF ANCILLARY RESTRAINTS

14.155   In addition to this concentration, AO and Siemens have also agreed to develop a partnership (i) with respect to IT services, through the execution of a customer relationship agreement whereby Siemens will commit for a seven-year period to a certain volume of IT services in connection with the operation of Siemens' IT infrastructure and applications worldwide and (ii) with respect to the joint development of new IT services and solutions, through the execution of a global alliance agreement, a common investment agreement, a collaboration agreement, a Siemens One agreement and a HTTS Agreement, all of which governing the future operational collaboration between AO and Siemens in order to provide AO with development opportunities in hi-tech transactional services and growing sectors such as healthcare, energy, transport or manufacturing. [...]

According to the Commission Notice on restrictions directly related and necessary to concentrations, the Commission is not obliged to assess and individually address ancillary restraints.

The Commission, in this decision, does not take a position whether all of these agreements between AO and Siemens are directly related to and necessary for the implementation of the concentration. This decision under the Merger Regulation is therefore without prejudice to a potential assessment of the additional agreements between AO and Siemens under EU or Member States' competition law.

Commission 25 March 2011 (Atos Origin/Siemens IT Solutions & Services, M.6127), paras 8, 10 and 11.

D. PARAGRAPHS 4 AND 5: RESTORATIVE MEASURES

1. General

14.156   Restoration of conditions of effective competition is the primary concern in proceedings pursuant to Article 8(4) of the Merger Regulation. Both the text and the scheme of the Merger Regulation indicate that this requires the removal of any residual structural impediments to effective competition on the relevant markets arising from the prohibited concentration. Article 8(4) envisages that, in situations where concentrations prohibited by the Commission have already been implemented, the restoration of effective competition must, in principle, be effected by means of a separation of the undertakings or assets brought together through the prohibited transaction.

In applying Article 8(4) of the Merger Regulation the Commission has regard to the principle of proportionality. This principle dictates that, when the Commission is faced with different possible options, such as divestiture structures, which could restore conditions of effective competition as required by Article 8(4), the Commission should allow a choice or should adopt the least restrictive option.

Having regard to proportionality, the Commission considers the legitimate interests of the undertakings concerned, when pursuing the primary Community interest of restoring conditions of effective competition by giving effect to its prohibition decision. This should include not only the interests of the acquiring undertaking, Tetra, which naturally wants to preserve as much of the value of its investment as possible, but also of the acquired undertaking, Sidel, which wants to minimise the period of uncertainty it faces and to continue its operations as an independent entity without the imposition of unduly disruptive or onerous measures.

Commission 30 January 2002 (Tetra Laval/Sidel, M.2416), OJ 2004 L 038/01, paras 11–13.

The [General Court] finds [...], that the scheme of the Regulation [...], show that the **14.157** objective of Article 8(4) is to allow the Commission to adopt all the decisions necessary for the restoration of conditions of effective competition. When, as in the present case, the concentration has been implemented pursuant to Article 7[2] of the Regulation, the separation of the undertakings involved in the concentration is the logical consequence of the decision declaring the concentration incompatible with the common market.

However, the adoption of a divestiture decision subsequent to the adoption of a decision declaring a concentration incompatible with the common market presupposes that the latter decision is valid. Since the object of a divestiture decision adopted pursuant to Article 8(4) of the Regulation is to restore conditions of effective competition which have been impeded by the prohibited concentration, it is obvious that its validity is contingent on that of the decision prohibiting the concentration and that, accordingly, annulment of the latter decision completely deprives the divestiture decision of any legal basis.

General Court 25 October 2002 (Tetra Laval/Commission, T-80/02) [2002] ECR II-4519, paras 36 and 37.

['Implementation' – Relevant point in time] In order to assess the lawfulness of the **14.158** contested decision in the light of the power invested in the Commission to require an undertaking to dissolve a concentration, in particular through the disposal of all the shares acquired in another undertaking, the reference point must be the relevant moment established by Article 8(4) of the Merger Regulation, which envisages a 'concentration' which 'has already been implemented' and which 'has been declared incompatible with the common market' [...].

In that regard, the contested decision was indeed adopted at a time when the Commission had declared that the concentration notified by Ryanair was incompatible with the common market. Since the Commission did not address the issue of Ryanair's minority shareholding in Aer Lingus in the Ryanair decision, which found the notified concentration to be incompatible under Article 8(3) of the Merger Regulation, it could still do so in a separate decision adopted on the basis of the final sentence of Article 8(4) of that regulation.

General Court 6 July 2010 (Aer Lingus Group v. Commission, T-411/07) [2010] ECR II-03691, paras 59 and 60.

14.159   [Commission is not entitled to require dissolution without prior acquisition of control] [...] According to the actual terms used in Article 8(4) of the regulation, the power to require the disposal of all the shares acquired by an undertaking in another undertaking exists only 'to restore the situation prevailing prior to the implementation of the concentration'. If control has not been acquired, the Commission does not have the power to dissolve the concentration. If the legislature had wished to grant the Commission broader powers than those laid down in the Merger Regulation, it would have enacted a provision to that effect.

General Court 6 July 2010 (Aer Lingus Group v. Commission, T-411/07) [2010] ECR II-03691, para. 66.

2. Meaning of 'Implementation'

14.160   The way in which the expression 'implemented' is set out in the sample of other official languages analysed above indicates that, prima facie, the definition of 'implementation' envisaged under Article 8(4) and 8(5) encompasses full consummation of the concentration. [...]

Under the applicant's first claim, namely that Ryanair's shareholding in Aer Lingus gives rise to serious competition concerns, the applicant argued that the refusal of the Commission to adopt measures under Article 8(4) to request disposal of Ryanair's minority shareholding is contrary to previous Commission decisions, and referred in particular to the Commission's decisions in *Tetra Laval/ Sidel* and *Schneider/Legrand*. In this respect, for the sake of completeness, it should be pointed out that this evidence also cannot reverse the conclusions reached above. In particular, the fact that in *Tetra Laval/Sidel* and *Schneider/Legrand* the Commission found that the retention of a minority shareholding in the target in the notified transaction which had been prohibited under the Regulation would impede the restoration of effective competition, and therefore ordered the disposal of all the shares acquired, is irrelevant for the purposes of the present proceedings. Indeed, it is consistent with the above conclusions that the Commission's powers in those cases had been triggered by the 'implementation' of the transaction, in other words, by a change of control. Once the powers of the Commission had been triggered, the Commission was entitled, as specifically provided for under Article 8(4), to 'require the undertakings concerned to dissolve the concentration, in particular through the dissolution of the merger or the disposal of all the shares or assets acquired, so as to restore the situation prevailing prior to the implementation of the concentration'.

Pres. General Court 18 March 2008 (Aer Lingus v. Commission, T-411/07R) [2008] ECR II-411, paras 90 and 97.

ARTICLE 9 – REFERRAL TO THE COMPETENT AUTHORITIES OF THE MEMBER STATES

1. The Commission may, by means of a decision notified without delay to the undertakings concerned and the competent authorities of the other Member States, refer a notified concentration to the competent authorities of the Member State concerned in the following circumstances.

2. Within 15 working days of the date of receipt of the copy of the notification, a Member State, on its own initiative or upon the invitation of the Commission, may inform the Commission, which shall inform the undertakings concerned, that:

   (a) a concentration threatens to affect significantly competition in a market within that Member State, which presents all the characteristics of a distinct market, or

   (b) a concentration affects competition in a market within that Member State, which presents all the characteristics of a distinct market and which does not constitute a substantial part of the common market.

3. If the Commission considers that, having regard to the market for the products or services in question and the geographical reference market within the meaning of paragraph 7, there is such a distinct market and that such a threat exists, either:

   (a) it shall itself deal with the case in accordance with this Regulation; or

   (b) it shall refer the whole or part of the case to the competent authorities of the Member State concerned with a view to the application of that State's national competition law.

   If, however, the Commission considers that such a distinct market or threat does not exist, it shall adopt a decision to that effect which it shall address to the Member State concerned, and shall itself deal with the case in accordance with this Regulation.

   In cases where a Member State informs the Commission pursuant to paragraph 2(b) that a concentration affects competition in a distinct market within its territory that does not form a substantial part of the common market, the Commission shall refer the whole or part of the case relating to the distinct market concerned, if it considers that such a distinct market is affected.

4. A decision to refer or not to refer pursuant to paragraph 3 shall be taken:

(a)   as a general rule within the period provided for in Article 10(1), second subparagraph, where the Commission, pursuant to Article 6(1)(b), has not initiated proceedings; or

(b)   within 65 working days at most of the notification of the concentration concerned where the Commission has initiated proceedings under Article 6(1)(c), without taking the preparatory steps in order to adopt the necessary measures under Article 8(2), (3) or (4) to maintain or restore effective competition on the market concerned.

5.   If within the 65 working days referred to in paragraph 4(b) the Commission, despite a reminder from the Member State concerned, has not taken a decision on referral in accordance with paragraph 3 nor has taken the preparatory steps referred to in paragraph 4(b), it shall be deemed to have taken a decision to refer the case to the Member State concerned in accordance with paragraph 3(b).

6.   The competent authority of the Member State concerned shall decide upon the case without undue delay.

Within 45 working days after the Commission's referral, the competent authority of the Member State concerned shall inform the undertakings concerned of the result of the preliminary competition assessment and what further action, if any, it proposes to take. The Member State concerned may exceptionally suspend this time limit where necessary information has not been provided to it by the undertakings concerned as provided for by its national competition law.

Where a notification is requested under national law, the period of 45 working days shall begin on the working day following that of the receipt of a complete notification by the competent authority of that Member State.

7.   The geographical reference market shall consist of the area in which the undertakings concerned are involved in the supply and demand of products or services, in which the conditions of competition are sufficiently homogeneous and which can be distinguished from neighbouring areas because, in particular, conditions of competition are appreciably different in those areas. This assessment should take account in particular of the nature and characteristics of the products or services concerned, of the existence of entry barriers or of consumer preferences, of appreciable differences of the undertakings' market shares between the area concerned and neighbouring areas or of substantial price differences.

8.   In applying the provisions of this Article, the Member State concerned may take only the measures strictly necessary to safeguard or restore effective competition on the market concerned.

9.   In accordance with the relevant provisions of the Treaty, any Member State may appeal to the Court of Justice, and in particular request the application of Article 243 of the Treaty, for the purpose of applying its national competition law.

OVERVIEW

A. GENERAL   14.161

B. PARAGRAPH 2: SIGNIFICANT EFFECT
    WITHIN A MEMBER STATE   14.162

C. PARAGRAPH 3: COMMISSION
    DECISION REGARDING REQUEST
    FOR REFERRAL   14.163

A. GENERAL

See recitals 11, 12, 14 and 15.

[Appeal by third party possible] Consequently, since the effect of the Referral Decision   **14.161**
is to deprive the applicant of the application of Regulation [No 139/2004] and the procedural rights under it for third parties and of the judicial protection provided for by the Treaty, it must be held that the Referral Decision is capable of affecting the legal situation of the applicant. [...]

   Since the Referral Decision deprives the applicant of the opportunity to challenge before the [General Court] assessments which it would have been entitled to challenge had the referral not been made, it must be held that the Referral Decision individually affects the applicant in the same way as it would have been affected by the Approval Decision had the referral not been made [...].

General Court 3 April 2003 (Philips v. Commission, T-119/02) [2003] ECR II-1433, paras 286 and 297.

B. PARAGRAPH 2: SIGNIFICANT EFFECT WITHIN A MEMBER STATE

[Comprehensive review] For that reason, the Community judicature must, having   **14.162**
regard both to the specific features of the case before it and the technical or complex nature of the Commission's assessments, carry out a comprehensive review as to whether a concentration falls within the scope of Article 9(2)(a).

General Court 3 April 2003 (Philips v. Commission, T-119/02) [2003] ECR II-1433, para. 326.

C. PARAGRAPH 3: COMMISSION DECISION REGARDING REQUEST FOR REFERRAL

14.163   Pursuant to Article 9(3) of the Merger Regulation, the Commission assesses whether, having regard to the market for the products or services in question and the geographical reference market, there is such a distinct market within the Member State seeking the referral and that such a threat to competition exists. The Commission has then the possibility to either itself deal with the case or refer whole or part of the case to the competent authorities of the Member State concerned with a view to the application of that State's national competition law.

Commission 14 February 2002 (Danish Crown/Steff-Houlberg, M.2662), para. 17.

14.164   [Limited review] It is apparent from the wording of the first subparagraph of Article 9(3) that the Commission has broad discretion as regards that decision. However, as the Commission itself conceded in its defence, that discretion is not unlimited. [...]

It follows [...] that, although Regulation [139/2004] confers on the Commission broad discretion as to whether or not to refer a concentration, it cannot decide to make such a referral if, when the Member State's request for a referral is examined, it is clear, on the basis of a body of precise and coherent evidence, that such a referral cannot safeguard or restore effective competition on the relevant markets.

Review by the Community judicature of the question whether the Commission has properly exercised its discretion in deciding whether or not to refer a concentration is therefore a limited review which, in the light of Regulation [139/2004] must be restricted to establishing whether the Commission was entitled, without committing a manifest error of assessment, to consider that the referral to the national competition authorities would enable them to safeguard or restore effective competition on the relevant market so that it was unnecessary to deal with the case itself.

General Court 3 April 2003 (Philips v. Commission, T-119/02) [2003] ECR II-1433, paras 342–344.

14.165   [Transfer of exclusive competence] By adopting the Referral Decision, the Commission terminated the procedure applying Regulation No 4064/89 [now Regulation 139/2004] to those aspects of the concentration which are the subject of the referral and transferred exclusive competence to assess those aspects to the French competition authorities ruling on the basis of their national law; it thereby lost any power to deal with those aspects. It cannot therefore be permitted to intervene in the decision-making process of the French competition authorities.

General Court 3 April 2003 (Philips v. Commission, T-119/02) [2003] ECR II-1433, para. 372.

14.166   [T]he French authorities asked for part of the case to be referred to them under Article 9 of the regulation. [...] The French authorities argued that each of [the mentioned relevant markets] had a national dimension.

By decision of 23 July 2003, the Commission rejected the French authorities' request [...].

For the market for sales of school textbooks by publishers to dealers, the Commission considered that all the conditions imposed by Article 9(2)(a) of the regulation were satisfied. For the market for sales of educational supporting materials by publishers to dealers, the Commission, at the time when it took its decision under Article 9 of the regulation, was not able to determine whether the geographic dimension was national or supranational, though the other conditions imposed by Article 9(2)(a) of the regulation were satisfied. For these two markets, even if the market for educational supporting materials had a national geographic dimension, the Commission decided to analyse the effects of the merger itself, in accordance with point (a) in the first subparagraph of Article 9(3) of the regulation, in view of the close links between these two markets and the remainder of the book business.

Commission 7 January 2004 (Lagardere/Natexis/VUP, M.2978), OJ 2004 L 125/54, paras 11, 12 and 14.

Decision in which the Commission rejected request for referral (French language): Commission 23 July 2003 (Lagardere/Natexis/VUP aux autorités nationales compétentes de la France, M.2978).

[Non-referral decision by Commission may not be contested by third parties for reason of wider procedural rights under national procedural laws of Member State to which merger has not been referred] So far as concerns the applicant's argument that the non-referral decision modifies the conditions of assessment of the merger at issue, it must be borne in mind that Article 9(9) of Regulation No 139/2004 allows only the Member State concerned the possibility to appeal for the purpose of applying its national competition law. By contrast, there is nothing in the system for the control of concentrations with a Community dimension, as provided in that regulation, to indicate that the applicant is entitled to challenge the non-referral decision on the ground that that decision precludes the investigation of the merger at issue and the avenues of legal redress against the decision conducting that investigation from being determined by the law of a Member State, and not by EU law. **14.167**

It should also be noted that the admissibility of an action against the non-referral decision cannot result from the fact that the national law in question may confer on the applicant more extensive procedural rights and/or judicial protection than provided for under EU law. Legal certainty precludes the admissibility of an action brought before the EU Courts from being dependent on whether the legal system of the Member State whose national competition authority unsuccessfully requested the referral of the merger investigation confers on interested third parties more extensive procedural rights and/or judicial protection than provided for under EU law. In that regard, it must be noted that the scope of those procedural rights and of judicial protection depends on a range of factors which are, firstly, difficult to compare and, secondly, subject to developments in legislation and case-law that are difficult to monitor.

Furthermore, the very purpose of an action for annulment before the EU Courts is to ensure compliance with EU law, irrespective of the scope of the procedural rights and judicial protection that it confers, and not to claim the more extensive protection that may be provided for under national law.

General Court 12 October 2011 (Association Belge des Consommateurs test-chats ASBL v. Commission, T-224/10) [2011] ECR II-07177, paras 82–84.

14.168   [Explicit rejection of a Referral Request] On 20 November 2013, Germany, via the Bundeskartellamt ('BKartA') requested, on the basis of Article 9(2)(a) of the Merger Regulation, a referral of the proposed transaction from the Commission to the BKartA (the 'Referral Request').

In the Referral Request, Germany considers that the proposed transaction threatens to significantly affect competition in the German retail market for mobile telecommunications services, as well as in the German wholesale market for access and call origination, both of which present all the characteristics of distinct markets in accordance with Article 9(2)(a) of the Merger Regulation. Moreover, Germany considers that it is best placed to deal with the proposed transaction.

As the Commission decided to initiate proceedings, it was unnecessary for it to pronounce on the Referral Request in phase I of its investigation.

On 2 January 2014 Germany, via the BKartA submitted a reminder of their Referral Request under Article 9(2)(a) of the Merger Regulation, pursuant to Article 9(5) of that regulation.

By letter dated 10 January 2014, the Commission informed of its intention to reject the Referral Request. By letter dated 17 January 2014, Germany stated that it disagrees with the Commission's view that there are no grounds for a referral of the case.

On 30 January 2014 the Commission adopted a decision rejecting Germany's referral request. The Commission considers that the criteria for a referral provided for in Article 9(2)(a) of the Merger Regulation are fulfilled with regard to the proposed transaction. However, in exercising its discretion the Commission did not consider it appropriate to refer the proposed transaction to the BKartA for a number of reasons, including the need to ensure a coherent and consistent approach when assessing mergers in the telecom sector in different Member States falling into the Commission's competence and the fact that the Commission has developed significant expertise in markets for mobile telecommunications services within its jurisdiction over the last years.

Commission 2 July 2015 (Telefónica Deutschland/E-Plus, M.7018), paras 18–23.

ARTICLE 10 – TIME LIMITS FOR INITIATING PROCEEDINGS AND FOR DECISIONS

1. Without prejudice to Article 6(4), the decisions referred to in Article 6(1) shall be taken within 25 working days at most. That period shall begin on the working day following that of the receipt of a notification or, if the information to be supplied with the notification is incomplete, on the working day following that of the receipt of the complete information.

    That period shall be increased to 35 working days where the Commission receives a request from a Member State in accordance with Article 9(2) or where, the undertakings concerned offer commitments pursuant to Article 6(2) with a view to rendering the concentration compatible with the common market.

2. Decisions pursuant to Article 8(1) or (2) concerning notified concentrations shall be taken as soon as it appears that the serious doubts referred to in Article 6(1)(c) have been removed, particularly as a result of modifications made by the undertakings concerned, and at the latest by the time limit laid down in paragraph 3.

3. Without prejudice to Article 8(7), decisions pursuant to Article 8(1) to (3) concerning notified concentrations shall be taken within not more than 90 working days of the date on which the proceedings are initiated. That period shall be increased to 105 working days where the undertakings concerned offer commitments pursuant to Article 8(2), second subparagraph, with a view to rendering the concentration compatible with the common market, unless these commitments have been offered less than 55 working days after the initiation of proceedings.

    The periods set by the first subparagraph shall likewise be extended if the notifying parties make a request to that effect not later than 15 working days after the initiation of proceedings pursuant to Article 6(1)(c). The notifying parties may make only one such request. Likewise, at any time following the initiation of proceedings, the periods set by the first subparagraph may be extended by the Commission with the agreement of the notifying parties. The total duration of any extension or extensions effected pursuant to this subparagraph shall not exceed 20 working days.

4. The periods set by paragraphs 1 and 3 shall exceptionally be suspended where, owing to circumstances for which one of the undertakings involved in the concentration is responsible, the Commission has had to request information by decision pursuant to Article 11 or to order an inspection by decision pursuant to Article 13.

The first subparagraph shall also apply to the period referred to in Article 9(4)(b).

5.   Where the Court of Justice gives a judgment which annuls the whole or part of a Commission decision which is subject to a time limit set by this Article, the concentration shall be re-examined by the Commission with a view to adopting a decision pursuant to Article 6(1).

The concentration shall be re-examined in the light of current market conditions.

The notifying parties shall submit a new notification or supplement the original notification, without delay, where the original notification becomes incomplete by reason of intervening changes in market conditions or in the information provided. Where there are no such changes, the parties shall certify this fact without delay.

The periods laid down in paragraph 1 shall start on the working day following that of the receipt of complete information in a new notification, a supplemented notification, or a certification within the meaning of the third subparagraph.

The second and third subparagraphs shall also apply in the cases referred to in Article 6(4) and Article 8(7).

6.   Where the Commission has not taken a decision in accordance with Article 6(1)(b), (c), 8(1), (2) or (3) within the time limits set in paragraphs 1 and 3 respectively, the concentration shall be deemed to have been declared compatible with the common market, without prejudice to Article 9.

OVERVIEW

A. GENERAL	(p.598)	C. PARAGRAPH 4: EXCEPTIONAL CIRCUMSTANCES FOR SUSPENSION 14.170
B. PARAGRAPH 2: TIME-LIMIT FOR CLEARANCE DECISION	14.169	

A. GENERAL

See also recital 35 and Articles 6, 8 and 9.

B. PARAGRAPH 2: TIME-LIMIT FOR CLEARANCE DECISION

14.169 Pursuant to Article 10(2) of the Merger Regulation, the Commission has to take a clearance decision as soon as the serious doubts referred to in Article 6(1)(c) of the Merger Regulation are removed as a result of commitments submitted by the parties. This rule applies to commitments proposed in phase II-proceedings before the Commission issues a statement of objections. The Commission may decide not to carry out a market test if it is clear from the information already at its disposal that the proposed remedies cannot be accepted.

Commission 27 February 2013 (Ryanair/Aer Lingus III, M.6663), para. 1702.

C. PARAGRAPH 4: EXCEPTIONAL CIRCUMSTANCES FOR SUSPENSION

14.170 Where a decision requiring information has been properly sent by the Commission to a notifying undertaking, the fact that the term 'exceptionally' is used does not preclude that decision from automatically suspending the four-month period from the date on which it is found that the necessary information has not been provided until the date on which it is provided.

General Court 22 October 2002 (Schneider Electric v. Commission, T-310/01) [2002] ECR II-4071, para. 106.

ARTICLE 11 – REQUESTS FOR INFORMATION

1. In order to carry out the duties assigned to it by this Regulation, the Commission may, by simple request or by decision, require the persons referred to in Article 3(1)(b), as well as undertakings and associations of undertakings, to provide all necessary information.

2. When sending a simple request for information to a person, an undertaking or an association of undertakings, the Commission shall state the legal basis and the purpose of the request, specify what information is required and fix the time limit within which the information is to be provided, as well as the penalties provided for in Article 14 for supplying incorrect or misleading information.

3. Where the Commission requires a person, an undertaking or an association of undertakings to supply information by decision, it shall state the legal basis and the purpose of the request, specify what information is required and fix the time limit within which it is to be provided. It shall also indicate the penalties provided for in Article 14 and indicate or impose the penalties provided for in Article 15. It shall further indicate the right to have the decision reviewed by the Court of Justice.

4. The owners of the undertakings or their representatives and, in the case of legal persons, companies or firms, or associations having no legal personality, the persons authorised to represent them by law or by their constitution, shall supply the information requested on behalf of the undertaking concerned. Persons duly authorised to act may supply the information on behalf of their clients. The latter shall remain fully responsible if the information supplied is incomplete, incorrect or misleading.

5. The Commission shall without delay forward a copy of any decision taken pursuant to paragraph 3 to the competent authorities of the Member State in whose territory the residence of the person or the seat of the undertaking or association of undertakings is situated, and to the competent authority of the Member State whose territory is affected. At the specific request of the competent authority of a Member State, the Commission shall also forward to that authority copies of simple requests for information relating to a notified concentration.

6. At the request of the Commission, the governments and competent authorities of the Member States shall provide the Commission with all necessary information to carry out the duties assigned to it by this Regulation.

7. In order to carry out the duties assigned to it by this Regulation, the Commission may interview any natural or legal person who consents to be interviewed for the purpose of collecting information relating to the

subject matter of an investigation. At the beginning of the interview, which may be conducted by telephone or other electronic means, the Commission shall state the legal basis and the purpose of the interview. Where an interview is not conducted on the premises of the Commission or by telephone or other electronic means, the Commission shall inform in advance the competent authority of the Member State in whose territory the interview takes place. If the competent authority of that Member State so requests, officials of that authority may assist the officials and other persons authorised by the Commission to conduct the interview.

See recital 38.

It follows from the case-law that the Commission may exercise the powers conferred on it by Article 11 of Regulation No 139/2004 only to the extent that it considers that it is not in possession of all the information necessary to enable it to decide on the compatibility of the concentration concerned with the common market [...]. [...]

   [T]he need for the information covered by a request under Article 11 of Regulation No 139/2004 must be assessed by reference to the view that the Commission could reasonably have held, at the time the request in question was made, of the extent of the information necessary to examine the concentration. Accordingly, that assessment cannot be based on the actual need for the information in the subsequent procedure before the Commission; that need is dependent on many factors and cannot therefore be determined with certainty at the time the request for information is made.

General Court 4 February 2009 (Omya v. Commission, T-145/06) [2009] ECR II-145, paras 28 and 30.

14.171

[Relevance of market tests] In particular as regards the questionnaires, it is important to note that the market investigation is by no means an opinion poll. For instance, the fact that the majority of third parties provide a similar opinion in reply to a specific question, can only be an indication for the Commission's own investigation, not a foregone conclusion. Likewise, it would not be appropriate to assume that the answers to the questionnaires can always be considered to be fully informed and objective. The specific level of knowledge of respondents might vary, the questions might have been misunderstood, the replies might be more or less representative, and the opinion provided might be biased to influence the Commission's decision-making process in a certain way.

Commission 27 February 2013 (Ryanair/Aer Lingus III, M.6663), para. 1702.

14.172

ARTICLE 12 – INSPECTIONS BY THE AUTHORITIES OF THE MEMBER STATES

1. At the request of the Commission, the competent authorities of the Member States shall undertake the inspections which the Commission considers to be necessary under Article 13(1), or which it has ordered by decision pursuant to Article 13(4). The officials of the competent authorities of the Member States who are responsible for conducting these inspections as well as those authorised or appointed by them shall exercise their powers in accordance with their national law.

2. If so requested by the Commission or by the competent authority of the Member State within whose territory the inspection is to be conducted, officials and other accompanying persons authorised by the Commission may assist the officials of the authority concerned.

See also recitals 13 and 40.

ARTICLE 13 – THE COMMISSION'S POWERS OF INSPECTION

1. In order to carry out the duties assigned to it by this Regulation, the Commission may conduct all necessary inspections of undertakings and associations of undertakings.

2. The officials and other accompanying persons authorised by the Commission to conduct an inspection shall have the power:

    (a) to enter any premises, land and means of transport of undertakings and associations of undertakings;

    (b) to examine the books and other records related to the business, irrespective of the medium on which they are stored;

    (c) to take or obtain in any form copies of or extracts from such books or records;

    (d) to seal any business premises and books or records for the period and to the extent necessary for the inspection;

    (e) to ask any representative or member of staff of the undertaking or association of undertakings for explanations on facts or documents relating to the subject matter and purpose of the inspection and to record the answers.

3. Officials and other accompanying persons authorised by the Commission to conduct an inspection shall exercise their powers upon production of a written authorisation specifying the subject matter and purpose of the inspection and the penalties provided for in Article 14, in the production of the required books or other records related to the business which is incomplete or where answers to questions asked under paragraph 2 of this Article are incorrect or misleading. In good time before the inspection, the Commission shall give notice of the inspection to the competent authority of the Member State in whose territory the inspection is to be conducted.

4. Undertakings and associations of undertakings are required to submit to inspections ordered by decision of the Commission. The decision shall specify the subject matter and purpose of the inspection, appoint the date on which it is to begin and indicate the penalties provided for in Articles 14 and 15 and the right to have the decision reviewed by the Court of Justice. The Commission shall take such decisions after consulting the competent authority of the Member State in whose territory the inspection is to be conducted.

5. Officials of, and those authorised or appointed by, the competent authority of the Member State in whose territory the inspection is to be conducted shall, at the request of that authority or of the Commission, actively assist the officials and other accompanying persons authorised

by the Commission. To this end, they shall enjoy the powers specified in paragraph 2.

6.   Where the officials and other accompanying persons authorised by the Commission find that an undertaking opposes an inspection, including the sealing of business premises, books or records, ordered pursuant to this Article, the Member State concerned shall afford them the necessary assistance, requesting where appropriate the assistance of the police or of an equivalent enforcement authority, so as to enable them to conduct their inspection.

7.   If the assistance provided for in paragraph 6 requires authorisation from a judicial authority according to national rules, such authorisation shall be applied for. Such authorisation may also be applied for as a precautionary measure.

8.   Where authorisation as referred to in paragraph 7 is applied for, the national judicial authority shall ensure that the Commission decision is authentic and that the coercive measures envisaged are neither arbitrary nor excessive having regard to the subject matter of the inspection. In its control of proportionality of the coercive measures, the national judicial authority may ask the Commission, directly or through the competent authority of that Member State, for detailed explanations relating to the subject matter of the inspection. However, the national judicial authority may not call into question the necessity for the inspection nor demand that it be provided with the information in the Commission's file. The lawfulness of the Commission's decision shall be subject to review only by the Court of Justice.

Investigative powers Commission see the case extracts under Regulation No 1/2003, Articles 18–22; see recitals 38–41.

ARTICLE 14 – FINES

1. The Commission may by decision impose on the persons referred to in Article 3(1)b, undertakings or associations of undertakings, fines not exceeding 1 per cent of the aggregate turnover of the undertaking or association of undertakings concerned within the meaning of Article 5 where, intentionally or negligently:

    (a) they supply incorrect or misleading information in a submission, certification, notification or supplement thereto, pursuant to Article 4, Article 10(5) or Article 22(3);

    (b) they supply incorrect or misleading information in response to a request made pursuant to Article 11(2);

    (c) in response to a request made by decision adopted pursuant to Article 11(3), they supply incorrect, incomplete or misleading information or do not supply information within the required time limit;

    (d) they produce the required books or other records related to the business in incomplete form during inspections under Article 13, or refuse to submit to an inspection ordered by decision taken pursuant to Article 13(4);

    (e) in response to a question asked in accordance with Article 13(2)(e),
        – they give an incorrect or misleading answer,
        – they fail to rectify within a time limit set by the Commission an incorrect, incomplete or misleading answer given by a member of staff, or
        – they fail or refuse to provide a complete answer on facts relating to the subject matter and purpose of an inspection ordered by a decision adopted pursuant to Article 13(4);

    (f) seals affixed by officials or other accompanying persons authorised by the Commission in accordance with Article 13(2)(d) have been broken.

2. The Commission may by decision impose fines not exceeding 10 per cent of the aggregate turnover of the undertaking concerned within the meaning of Article 5 on the persons referred to in Article 3(1)b or the undertakings concerned where, either intentionally or negligently, they:

    (a) fail to notify a concentration in accordance with Articles 4 or 22(3) prior to its implementation, unless they are expressly authorised to do so by Article 7(2) or by a decision taken pursuant to Article 7(3);

    (b) implement a concentration in breach of Article 7;

(c) implement a concentration declared incompatible with the common market by decision pursuant to Article 8(3) or do not comply with any measure ordered by decision pursuant to Article 8(4) or (5);

(d) fail to comply with a condition or an obligation imposed by decision pursuant to Articles 6(1)(b), Article 7(3) or Article 8(2), second subparagraph.

3. In fixing the amount of the fine, regard shall be had to the nature, gravity and duration of the infringement.

4. Decisions taken pursuant to paragraphs 1, 2 and 3 shall not be of a criminal law nature.

OVERVIEW

A. GENERAL	(p.606)	C. PARAGRAPH 2: FAILURE TO NOTIFY A CONCENTRATION	14.176
B. PARAGRAPH 1: PROVIDING INCORRECT OR MISLEADING INFORMATION	14.173		

A. GENERAL

See also recitals 31 and 43.

B. PARAGRAPH 1: PROVIDING INCORRECT OR MISLEADING INFORMATION

14.173   [...] KLM explains that in providing the information it based itself on the in-flight magazine published by Transavia. [...]

The supply of that incorrect information was grossly negligent. Even if the parties' explanation concerning the use of Transavia's in-flight magazine is accepted, then a high degree of negligence is involved. An in-flight magazine is a marketing or promotional brochure where accuracy is not necessarily guaranteed. The parties should have used a more reliable source of information, such as internal statistics of Transavia or the Transavia timetable which was later sent to the Commission. As Transavia is a fully controlled subsidiary that information was readily available to KLM.

Accordingly, KLM's failure to supply correct information on this point constitutes an infringement for which a fine may be imposed under Article 14(1)(a) of the Merger Regulation.

Commission 14 December 1999 (KLM/Martinair III, M.1608), OJ 2005 L 50/10, paras 24, 36 and 37.

The infringement committed by Mitsubishi took the form of failure to provide **14.174** information within the period fixed by a Commission decision pursuant to [...] the Merger Regulation. [...]

[T]he Commission had no alternative but to estimate the overall size of the market and the market shares of the market participants partly on information obtained from other market operators and customers. This increased significantly the Commission's workload and led to estimates which cannot be considered to be as reliable as first-hand information from Mitsubishi itself.

The information requested from Mitsubishi had a material impact on the assessment of the substance of the case. [...] [T]he Commission could not verify the parties' claim concerning the size of the refurbishment market nor establish Mitsubishi's position there. Accordingly, the conclusion must be that Mitsubishi's failure to supply the information requested constitutes a very serious infringement.

Mitsubishi claimed [...] that it had provided all the information that could be provided. However, Mitsubishi is a large industrial conglomerate, active world-wide in several business sectors. It is therefore reasonable to conclude that Mitsubishi has detailed knowledge of the activities which it carries on. Accordingly, given the size of the company, it is reasonable to assume that Mitsubishi has modern reporting systems that would have enabled it to provide the information requested. [...]

Commission 14 July 2000 (Mitsubishi Heavy Industries, M.1634), OJ 2001 L 4/31, paras 12 and 15–17.

[Notification was incorrect and misleading] [...] The notification is the basis and the **14.175** starting-point of the Commission's investigation of a merger case. It determines to a large extent the approach of the Commission towards the case and the areas and focal points of its investigation. Incorrect and misleading information creates the risk that important aspects relevant for the competitive assessment of the transaction are neither investigated nor analysed by the Commission, and its final decision consequently is based on incorrect information. In assessing mergers, the Commission is subject to extremely tight deadlines. In this framework it is essential for the Commission's work that it can focus its investigation on the relevant issues from the very beginning of the procedure, based on comprehensive and correct information provided in the notification.

[...] The absence of intention [...] has to be taken into account in adjusting the amount of a fine. The Commission agrees that there was no intention on Deutsche BP's side, but takes the view that Deutsche BP acted negligently in a considerable degree.

The fact that the omitted information did not form the basis for competition concerns which resulted in a need for remedies cannot be taken into account as a mitigating factor. The information requirements set out in the Form CO, which [...] the Merger Regulation serves to protect and enforce, do not differentiate according to the likely outcome of the competition analysis. [...] The fact that at the end of the Commission's assessment, taking into account the information that initially was missing, the transaction did not lead to competition concerns, does not reduce the gravity of the omission. This gravity depends on the relevance of the information for the investigation and assessment, but not on the final outcome of this assessment.

Commission 19 June 2002 (BP/Erdölchemie, M.2624), OJ 2004 L 91/48, paras 49–51.

See also Commission 28 July 1999 (Sanofi/Synthélabo, M.1543); Commission 7 July 2004 (Tetra Laval/Sidel, M.3255).

C. PARAGRAPH 2: FAILURE TO NOTIFY A CONCENTRATION

14.176   It must be borne in mind that by its nature the infringement at issue breaches the most basic principle of the Community system of merger control, which is *ex ante* control. Unlike Articles [101 and 102 TFEU] themselves, the Community legislature has expressly conferred on the Commission the sole power to assess concentrations with a Community dimension. To protect this basic principle the legislature has laid down heavy penalties (up to 10 per cent of the turnover of the undertakings concerned) in case of infringement.

   The Commission takes the view that the presence of damage to competition would indeed render the infringement more serious, and that the absence of any such damage in the present case is an important factor to be taken into account in determining the amount of the fine. However, the fact that the transaction does not raise competition concerns does not take away from the seriousness of the infringement.

Commission 10 June 2009 (Electrabel/Compagnie Natiale du Rhone, M.4994), paras 193 and 194.

14.177   [Relation between failure to notify and implementation prior to clearance] In the applicant's submission, that recital clearly reveals that the Commission takes issue with it for failure to notify or, at least, for being late in notifying the transaction, in contradiction to Article 1 of the operative part, which refers to the infringement consisting in putting into effect a concentration before it was notified. As the Commission correctly submits, however, the fact that it stated at that recital to the contested decision that the applicant ought to have contacted it earlier does not mean that the breach of the obligation to notify the concentration is at the basis of the infringement found, for which a fine was imposed, since a breach of the obligation to suspend the concentration may exist, as is apparent from the words of Article 7(1) of Regulation No 4064/89 [Article 7(1) Regulation No 139/2004], whether or not the concentration was notified.

General Court 12 December 2012 (Electrabel v. Commission, T-332/09), para. 185.

ARTICLE 15 – PERIODIC PENALTY PAYMENTS

1. The Commission may by decision impose on the persons referred to in Article 3(1)b, undertakings or associations of undertakings, periodic penalty payments not exceeding 5 per cent of the average daily aggregate turnover of the undertaking or association of undertakings concerned within the meaning of Article 5 for each working day of delay, calculated from the date set in the decision, in order to compel them:

    (a) to supply complete and correct information which it has requested by decision taken pursuant to Article 11(3);

    (b) to submit to an inspection which it has ordered by decision taken pursuant to Article 13(4);

    (c) to comply with an obligation imposed by decision pursuant to Article 6(1)(b), Article 7(3) or Article 8(2), second subparagraph; or;

    (d) to comply with any measures ordered by decision pursuant to Article 8(4) or (5).

2. Where the persons referred to in Article 3(1)(b), undertakings or associations of undertakings have satisfied the obligation which the periodic penalty payment was intended to enforce, the Commission may fix the definitive amount of the periodic penalty payments at a figure lower than that which would arise under the original decision.

See also recitals 31 and 43.

ARTICLE 16 – REVIEW BY THE COURT OF JUSTICE

The Court of Justice shall have unlimited jurisdiction within the meaning of Article 229 of the Treaty to review decisions whereby the Commission has fixed a fine or periodic penalty payments; it may cancel, reduce or increase the fine or periodic penalty payment imposed.

14.178   [Regarding the scope of judicial review by the Court of Justice] The applicants submit that, unlike decisions taken under Article 8 of Regulation No 139/2004, the Commission does not have any discretion when taking decisions pursuant to Article 6(1)(b) of that regulation. The review of legality that the Court is called upon to carry out for decisions taken under Article 6(1)(b) does not involve ascertaining whether or not the concentration in question significantly impedes competition in the internal market, but rather whether the concentration objectively gives rise to serious doubts requiring further investigation. [...]

It is true that the applicants observe, also correctly, that Article 6(1)(c) of Regulation No 139/2004 does not confer on the Commission any discretion as regards the initiation of an additional, second phase of investigation where it encounters serious doubts with respect to the compatibility of a concentration with the internal market. Indeed, where the Commission has serious doubts as to the compatibility with the internal market of a concentration, it is obliged to initiate a second phase of investigation. However, even if the notion of 'serious doubts' is an objective one, the Commission correctly observes that the fact remains that, before adopting a decision under Article 6(1)(c) of Regulation No 139/2004, it must carry out complex economic assessments and that it enjoys, for that purpose, a certain margin of discretion of which the Court must take account [...].

Consequently, irrespective of whether decisions are adopted under Article 6 or on the basis of Article 8 of Regulation No 139/2004, the case law provides for an identical standard of judicial review. In both cases, as the Commission submits, the review by the European Union judicature of complex economic assessments made by the Commission is limited to checking compliance with the rules governing procedure and the statement of reasons, the substantive accuracy of the facts as well as the absence of manifest errors of assessment or misuse of powers. In that respect, it should be borne in mind that the European Union judicature must not only ascertain whether the evidence relied on is factually accurate, reliable and consistent but also whether that evidence contains all the information which must be taken into account in order to assess a complex situation and whether it is capable of substantiating the conclusions drawn from it [...].

General Court 11 December 2013 (Cisco Systems and Messagenet v. Commission, T-79/12), ECLI:EU:T:2013:635, paras 43, 49 and 50.

See also General Court 13 May 2015 (Niki Luftfahrt v. Commission, T-162/10), ECLI:EU:T:2015:283, para. 86; General Court 3 April 2003 (Royal Philips Electronics v. Commission, T-119/02) [2003] ECR II-1433, para. 77.

See also in respect of decision adopted under Art. 8: CoJ 15 February 2005 (Commission v. Tetra Laval, C-12/03 P) [2005] ECR I-00987, para. 39 and in respect of decisions adopted under Art. 6 General Court 9 July 2007 (Sun Chemical Group and Others v. Commission, T-282/06) [2007] ECR II-02149, para. 60.

[…] With regard to assessment of the implementation of the commitments, the judicial **14.179** review is the same as that on the compatibility of a concentration with the common market or on the need to obtain commitments in order to authorise a concentration […].

General Court 5 September 2014 (Éditions Odile Jacob v. Commission, T-471/11), ECLI:EU:T:2014:739, para. 137.

See also General Court 3 April 2003 (Petrolessence and SG2R v. Commission, T-342/00), ECLI:EU:T:2003:97, paras 101–103.

ARTICLE 17 – PROFESSIONAL SECRECY

1. **Information acquired as a result of the application of this Regulation shall be used only for the purposes of the relevant request, investigation or hearing.**

2. **Without prejudice to Article 4(3), Articles 18 and 20, the Commission and the competent authorities of the Member States, their officials and other servants and other persons working under the supervision of these authorities as well as officials and civil servants of other authorities of the Member States shall not disclose information they have acquired through the application of this Regulation of the kind covered by the obligation of professional secrecy.**

3. **Paragraphs 1 and 2 shall not prevent publication of general information or of surveys which do not contain information relating to particular undertakings or associations of undertakings.**

See also recital 42.

OVERVIEW

A. PARAGRAPH 1: USE OF INCIDENTALLY GAINED INFORMATION	14.180	B. PARAGRAPH 2: SCOPE OF NON-DISCLOSURE OBLIGATION	14.181

A. PARAGRAPH 1: USE OF INCIDENTALLY GAINED INFORMATION

14.180   [Paragraph 1] This provision prohibited in principle the Commission from using, in the context of the State aid procedure, the information that had been submitted to it in connection with the merger procedure.

However, the applicant submits that the case-law of the Court has reduced the scope of Article 17 of the Merger Regulation inasmuch as, when the Commission incidentally gains knowledge of certain information in a procedure under competition law, and if this information indicates the existence of an infringement of other competition rules, it may then open a second procedure to verify the accuracy of the information or to supplement it, in particular by asking for the same documents and using them for purposes of evidence.

It should be noted, in that regard, that, even if the information gathered under the Merger Regulation may not be directly used as evidence in a procedure not governed by that regulation, they nevertheless amount to factors that may, where appropriate, be taken into account to justify the opening of a procedure under another legal basis [...].

General Court 1 March 2016 (Secop v. Commission, T-79/14), ECLI:EU:T: 2016:118, paras 80–82.

B. PARAGRAPH 2: SCOPE OF NON-DISCLOSURE OBLIGATION

[Paragraph 2: Scope of non-disclosure obligation in case of request for access to documents pursuant to Regulation No 1049/2001] It must be borne in mind, in that regard, that only certain information is covered by business secrets. Similarly, the obligation of professional secrecy does not have such a scope that it can justify a general and abstract refusal of access to documents submitted in connection with notification of a merger. It is true that neither Article 287 EC [now Article 339 TFEU] nor the Merger Regulation states exhaustively what information, by its very nature, is covered by professional secrecy. Nevertheless, it is apparent from the wording of Article 17(2) of the Merger Regulation, which provides that information acquired through the application of the Regulation of the kind covered by professional secrecy is not to be disclosed, that not all information thus acquired is necessarily covered by professional secrecy. Accordingly, the assessment as to the confidentiality of an item of information requires, on the one hand, that the individual legitimate interests opposing disclosure of the information be weighed against, on the other, the public interest in ensuring that the activities of the Community institutions take place as openly as possible [...].

14.181

By undertaking a concrete, individual assessment of the documents requested, in accordance with the first indent of Article 4(2) of Regulation No 1049/2001, the Commission is thus in a position to ensure that the provisions applicable to mergers retain their effectiveness, in full compliance with Regulation No 1049/2001. It follows that the obligation of professional secrecy and the protection of business secrets, which follow from Article 287 EC [now Article 339 TFEU] and from Article 17 of the Merger Regulation, are not such as to release the Commission from undertaking a concrete examination of each document concerned, as required by Article 4(2) of Regulation No 1049/2001. [...]

Finally, in any event, the fact that the parties involved in merger investigation proceedings regard the documents which they send as confidential cannot release the Commission, when in receipt of a request under Regulation No 1049/2001, from the obligation to carry out a concrete, effective examination of the documents requested with a view to possible application of the exceptions laid down in Article 4 of that regulation.

General Court 7 July 2010 (Agrofert Holding v. Commission, T-111/07) [2010] ECR II-00128, paras 69, 70 and 86.

See also General Court 30 May 2006 (Bank Austria Creditanstalt v. Commission, T-198/03) [2006] ECR II-1429, para. 71; General Court 12 October 2007 (Pergan Hilfsstoffe für industrielle Prozesse v. Commission, T-474/04) [2007] ECR II-4225, paras 63–66.

ARTICLE 18 – HEARING OF THE PARTIES AND OF THIRD PERSONS

1. Before taking any decision provided for in Article 6(3), Article 7(3), Article 8(2) to (6), and Articles 14 and 15, the Commission shall give the persons, undertakings and associations of undertakings concerned the opportunity, at every stage of the procedure up to the consultation of the Advisory Committee, of making known their views on the objections against them.

2. By way of derogation from paragraph 1, a decision pursuant to Articles 7(3) and 8 (5) may be taken provisionally, without the persons, undertakings or associations of undertakings concerned being given the opportunity to make known their views beforehand, provided that the Commission gives them that opportunity as soon as possible after having taken its decision.

3. The Commission shall base its decision only on objections on which the parties have been able to submit their observations. The rights of the defence shall be fully respected in the proceedings. Access to the file shall be open at least to the parties directly involved, subject to the legitimate interest of undertakings in the protection of their business secrets.

4. In so far as the Commission or the competent authorities of the Member States deem it necessary, they may also hear other natural or legal persons. Natural or legal persons showing a sufficient interest and especially members of the administrative or management bodies of the undertakings concerned or the recognised representatives of their employees shall be entitled, upon application, to be heard.

See also recitals 36, 37 and 42.

OVERVIEW

A. STATEMENT OF OBJECTIONS	14.182	C. ACCESS TO FILES	14.189
B. RIGHT TO BE HEARD	14.187		

A. STATEMENT OF OBJECTIONS

14.182   [Statement of objections must be sufficiently clear] [T]he statement of objections must be couched in terms that, even if succinct, are sufficiently clear to enable the parties concerned properly to identify the conduct complained of by the Commission. It is only on that basis that the statement of objections can fulfil its function under the Community regulations of giving undertakings all the information necessary to enable them properly to defend themselves, before the Commission adopts a final decision […].

General Court 28 February 2002 (Compagnie générale maritime and others v. Commission, T-86/95) [2002] ECR II-1011, para. 442.

[Functions and requirement of statement of objections] According to well-established **14.183** case-law, the Decision need not necessarily replicate the statement of objections. Thus, it is permissible to supplement the statement of objections in the light of the parties' response, whose arguments show that they have actually been able to exercise their rights of defence. The Commission may also, in the light of the administrative procedure, revise or supplement its arguments of fact or law in support of its objections […].

As the Commission contended at the hearing, it is clearly open to it to finalise its assessment of the compatibility of a concentration with the common market in the light of the corrective measures proposed by the notifying parties, since, by definition, those measures could not be envisaged before the statement of objections was drawn up.

None the less the statement of objections must contain an account of the objections cast in sufficiently clear terms to achieve the objective ascribed to it by the Community regulations, namely to provide all the information the undertakings need to defend themselves properly before the Commission adopts a final decision.

That is particularly so in this case, where what the Commission did was not to take proceedings under Articles [101 and 102 TFEU] in respect of anti-competitive practices which had already taken place and of which the undertakings concerned could not have failed to be aware: what it found to be incompatible with the common market was a concentration affecting the structure of competition in the national sectoral markets […].

In addition, in the procedures for reviewing concentrations, the statement of objections is not solely intended to spell out the complaints and give the undertaking to which it is addressed the opportunity to submit comments in response. It is also intended to give the notifying parties the chance to suggest corrective measures and, in particular, proposals for divestiture and sufficient time, given the requirement for speed which characterises the general scheme of Regulation No 4064/89 [now Regulation 139/ 2004], to ascertain the extent to which divestiture is necessary with a view to rendering the transaction compatible with the common market in good time.

General Court 22 October 2002 (Schneider Electric v. Commission, T-310/01) [2002] ECR II-4071, paras 438–442.

[Statement of objections delimits scope of the administrative procedure] It is apparent **14.184** from the Court's case-law that the right to a fair hearing, which is a fundamental principle of Community law and forms, in particular, part of the rights of the defence, requires that the undertaking concerned must have been afforded the opportunity, during the administrative procedure, to make known its views on the truth and relevance of the facts and circumstances alleged and on the documents used by the Commission to support its claim that there has been an infringement of the [TFEU] […]. […]

It follows, by analogy with the case-law on Articles [101 TFEU] and [102 TFEU], that the statement of objections is a procedural and preparatory document which, in order to ensure that the rights of the defence may be exercised effectively, delimits the scope of the administrative procedure initiated by the Commission, thereby preventing the latter from relying on other objections in its decision terminating the procedure in question [...].

It follows that the Commission is not obliged to maintain the factual or legal assessments set forth in that document. On the contrary, it must give as reasons for its ultimate decision its final assessments based on the situation existing at the time the formal proceedings are closed [...].

Furthermore, the Commission is not obliged to explain any differences with respect to its provisional assessments set out in the statement of objections [...].

CoJ 10 July 2008 (Bertelsmann and Sony Corporation of America v. Impala, C-413/06 P) [2008] ECR I-04951, paras 61 and 63–65.

14.185   [Arguments put forward by parties after the statement of objections] [T]he notifying parties cannot, as a rule, be criticised for putting forward certain – potentially decisive – arguments, facts or evidence only in their arguments in reply to the statement of objections. It is only with that statement that the parties to the concentration can obtain detailed indications as to the reservations of the Commission in relation to their proposed concentration and as to the arguments and evidence on which it relies in that regard. As is apparent [...], it flows from the notifying undertakings' rights of defence laid down in the second sentence of Article 18(3) of the Regulation and in Article 13(2) of the Implementing Regulation that those undertakings have the right to submit in their written and oral hearing following receipt of the statement of objections all material which they consider capable of refuting the Commission's objections and of leading it to approve their proposed concentration. Contrary to what the [General Court] suggests, in particular in paragraph 414 of the judgment under appeal, a line of argument put forward in reply to the statement of objections forms part of the investigation to be undertaken in the formal proceedings. Such a line of argument is not submitted out of time, but at the time laid down for that purpose in the procedure for the control of concentrations.

CoJ 10 July 2008 (Bertelsmann and Sony Corporation of America v. Impala, C-413/06 P) [2008] ECR I-4951, para. 89.

14.186   [Competition problems not mentioned in statement of objections] In order to ensure that the rights of the defence may be exercised effectively, the statement of objections delimits the scope of the administrative procedure initiated by the Commission, thereby preventing the latter from relying on other objections in its decision terminating the procedure [...].

For that purpose, Art. 18(3) of the Regulation implies that, when the Commission finds during the in-depth investigation, following the statement of objections, that a competition problem which may give rise to a declaration of incompatibility has not been mentioned, or has been inadequately formulated, in the statement of objections, it must either abandon the objection concerned at the stage of its final decision or put the undertakings concerned in a position to submit, before the final decision, all observations on the substantive issues and proposals for relevant corrective measures.

CoJ 16 July 2009 (Commission v. Schneider Electric, C–440/07 P) [2009] ECR I–6413, paras 164 and 165.

B. RIGHT TO BE HEARD

['Sufficient interest' in case of consumer protection associations when concentration **14.187** has only secondary (indirect) effects on consumers] As regards the first condition [...], it should be noted that, while it provides that consumer associations are entitled to be heard only where the proposed concentration concerns products or services used by final consumers, Article 11(c), second indent, of Regulation No 802/2004 none the less does not impose the obligation that the purpose of the proposed concentration must relate immediately to those products or services. [...]

It does, admittedly, follow from the clearance decision that the Commission took the view that the merger at issue gave rise only to secondary effects on consumers. [...] [T]he Commission acknowledged that the merger at issue was likely to affect various Belgian retail markets, but took the view that this related to secondary effects that did not raise serious doubts as to the compatibility of the merger at issue with the common market. The existence of those secondary effects is also mentioned in recital 207 of the clearance decision.

However, the fact that those effects may be secondary in nature does not deprive the applicant of its right to be heard. The Commission cannot interpret Article 11(c), second indent, of Regulation No 802/2004 in restrictive terms which limit the application of that provision, in essence, to cases in which a merger has direct effects on markets concerning ultimate consumers. That is, a fortiori, the case since, first, point (b) of the second subparagraph of Article 2(1) of Regulation No 139/2004 provides that, as regards appraisal of concentrations, the Commission must take into account, inter alia, the interests of the intermediate and ultimate consumers. Second, under Article 153(2) EC, which essentially has the same wording as Article 12 TFEU, consumer-protection requirements must be taken into account in defining and implementing other EU policies and activities. Furthermore, Article 38 of the Charter of Fundamental Rights of the European Union (OJ 2007 C 303, p. 1) provides that EU policies must ensure a high level of consumer protection.

Lastly, the Commission cannot reject the claim of a consumer association which seeks to be heard as a third party demonstrating a sufficient interest in a merger without providing that association with an opportunity to show in what respect consumers may be concerned by the merger at issue [...].

General Court 12 October 2011 (Association Belge des Consommateurs test-chats ASBL v. Commission, T-224/10) [2011] ECR II-07177, paras 40 and 42–44.

See also General Court 27 January 2000 (BEUC v. Commission, T-256/97) [2000] ECR II-101, para. 77.

[Request to be heard might be made only after concentration has been notified to **14.188** Commission] Since the Commission is to take a decision under Article 6 of Regulation No 139/2004 only with regard to 'notified concentrations', it is consistent with the logic of the EU legislation on merger control to take the view that the steps which third parties are required to undertake in order to be involved in the procedure must be taken following the formal notification of a concentration.

Furthermore, it must be taken into account that, very frequently, information relating to possible transactions liable to come within the scope of Regulation No 139/2004 is circulating within the sectors concerned, and even in the press, long before those transactions are at all notified to the Commission as mergers.

In that regard, first, the fact that a request to be heard under Article 18(4) of Regulation No 139/2004 and Article 16(1) of Regulation No 802/2004 must be made following notification of the transaction to which it relates makes it possible, in the interest of third parties, to avoid such requests being made by them without the Commission having determined the purpose of the merger control procedure, as that determination is made only at the time of notification of the transaction at issue. Second, this means that the Commission does not have to separate systematically, from amongst the requests received, those which concern transactions attributable only to abstract hypotheses, or even to mere hearsay, from those which concern transactions resulting in a notification.

The opposite scenario would lead to an unnecessarily heavier burden being placed on the Commission by the EU legislation on merger control. Indeed, the need for third parties wishing to exercise their right to be heard to make their request to that end following notification of the merger at issue is consistent with the need for speed which, according to the case-law, characterises the general scheme of the EU rules on merger control and which requires the Commission to comply with strict time-limits for the adoption of its final decision (see Case *C-202/06 P Cementbouw Handel & Industrie v Commission* [2007] ECR I-12129, para. 39, and *Case C-413/06 P Bertelsmann and Sony Corporation of America v Impala* [2008] ECR I-4951, para. 49). Consequently, in view of those strict time-limits, the Commission cannot be required to investigate, for each notified concentration, whether, prior to notification, third parties had already expressed an interest.

General Court 12 October 2011 (Association Belge des Consommateurs test-chats ASBL v. Commission, T-224/10) [2011] ECR II-07177, paras 53–56.

C. ACCESS TO FILES

14.189   [Access to files for parties other than the involved in the merger] In accordance with well-established case-law, in order to justify refusal of access to a document the disclosure of which has been requested, it is not sufficient, in principle, for that document to be covered by an activity mentioned in Article 4(2) and (3) of Regulation No 1049/2001. The institution concerned must also provide explanations as to how access to that document could specifically and actually undermine the interest protected by an exception laid down in that article [...].

However, the Court has acknowledged that it is open to the EU institution concerned to base its decisions in that regard on general presumptions which apply to certain categories of documents, as considerations of a generally similar kind are likely to apply to requests for disclosure relating to documents of the same nature [...].

Accordingly, the Court has already acknowledged the existence of such presumptions in four particular cases, namely with regard to [...] the documents exchanged between the Commission and notifying parties or third parties in the course of merger control proceedings [...].

CoJ 27 February 2014 (Commission v. EnBW, C-365/12 P), ECLI:EU:C: 2014:112, paras 64–66.

See also CoJ 28 June 2012 (Commission v. Éditions Odile Jacob, C-404/10 P), ECLI:EU:C:2012:393, paras 123–128; CoJ 29 June 2010 (Commission v Technische Glaswerke I!menau, C-139/07 P) [2010] ECR I-05885, para. 61.

ARTICLE 19 – LIAISON WITH THE AUTHORITIES OF THE MEMBER STATES

1. The Commission shall transmit to the competent authorities of the Member States copies of notifications within three working days and, as soon as possible, copies of the most important documents lodged with or issued by the Commission pursuant to this Regulation. Such documents shall include commitments offered by the undertakings concerned vis-à-vis the Commission with a view to rendering the concentration compatible with the common market pursuant to Article 6(2) or Article 8(2), second subparagraph.

2. The Commission shall carry out the procedures set out in this Regulation in close and constant liaison with the competent authorities of the Member States, which may express their views upon those procedures. For the purposes of Article 9 it shall obtain information from the competent authority of the Member State as referred to in paragraph 2 of that Article and give it the opportunity to make known its views at every stage of the procedure up to the adoption of a decision pursuant to paragraph 3 of that Article; to that end it shall give it access to the file.

3. An Advisory Committee on concentrations shall be consulted before any decision is taken pursuant to Article 8(1) to (6), Articles 14 or 15 with the exception of provisional decisions taken in accordance with Article 18(2).

4. The Advisory Committee shall consist of representatives of the competent authorities of the Member States. Each Member State shall appoint one or two representatives; if unable to attend, they may be replaced by other representatives. At least one of the representatives of a Member State shall be competent in matters of restrictive practices and dominant positions.

5. Consultation shall take place at a joint meeting convened at the invitation of and chaired by the Commission. A summary of the case, together with an indication of the most important documents and a preliminary draft of the decision to be taken for each case considered, shall be sent with the invitation. The meeting shall take place not less than 10 working days after the invitation has been sent. The Commission may in exceptional cases shorten that period as appropriate in order to avoid serious harm to one or more of the undertakings concerned by a concentration.

6. The Advisory Committee shall deliver an opinion on the Commission's draft decision, if necessary by taking a vote. The Advisory Committee may deliver an opinion even if some members are absent and unrepresented. The opinion shall be delivered in writing and appended

to the draft decision. The Commission shall take the utmost account of the opinion delivered by the Committee. It shall inform the Committee of the manner in which its opinion has been taken into account.

7.   The Commission shall communicate the opinion of the Advisory Committee, together with the decision, to the addressees of the decision. It shall make the opinion public together with the decision, having regard to the legitimate interest of undertakings in the protection of their business secrets.

See also recital 13.

ARTICLE 20 – PUBLICATION OF DECISIONS

1.   The Commission shall publish the decisions which it takes pursuant to Article 8(1) to (6), Articles 14 and 15 with the exception of provisional decisions taken in accordance with Article 18(2) together with the opinion of the Advisory Committee in the Official Journal of the European Union.

2.   The publication shall state the names of the parties and the main content of the decision; it shall have regard to the legitimate interest of undertakings in the protection of their business secrets.

See also recital 42.

ARTICLE 21 – APPLICATION OF THE REGULATION AND JURISDICTION

1. This Regulation alone shall apply to concentrations as defined in Article 3, and Council Regulations (EC) No 1/2003,[8] (EEC) No 1017/68,[9] (EEC) No 4056/86[10] and (EEC) No 3975/87[11] shall not apply, except in relation to joint ventures that do not have a Community dimension and which have as their object or effect the coordination of the competitive behaviour of undertakings that remain independent.

2. Subject to review by the Court of Justice, the Commission shall have sole jurisdiction to take the decisions provided for in this Regulation.

3. No Member State shall apply its national legislation on competition to any concentration that has a Community dimension.

    The first subparagraph shall be without prejudice to any Member State's power to carry out any enquiries necessary for the application of Articles 4(4), 9(2) or after referral, pursuant to Article 9(3), first subparagraph, indent (b), or Article 9(5), to take the measures strictly necessary for the application of Article 9(8).

4. Notwithstanding paragraphs 2 and 3, Member States may take appropriate measures to protect legitimate interests other than those taken into consideration by this Regulation and compatible with the general principles and other provisions of Community law.

    Public security, plurality of the media and prudential rules shall be regarded as legitimate interests within the meaning of the first subparagraph.

    Any other public interest must be communicated to the Commission by the Member State concerned and shall be recognised by the Commission after an assessment of its compatibility with the general principles and other provisions of Community law before the measures referred to above may be taken. The Commission shall inform the Member State concerned of its decision within 25 working days of that communication.

---

8   OJ L 1, 4.1.2003, p. 1.
9   OJ L 175, 23. 7. 1968, p. 1. Regulation as last amended by Regulation (EC) No 1/2003 (OJ L 1, 4.1.2003, p. 1).
10 OJ L 378, 31. 12. 1986, p. 4. Regulation as last amended by Regulation (EC) No 1/2003.
11 OJ L 374. 31. 12. 1987, p. 1. Regulation as last amended by Regulation (EC) No 1/2003.

OVERVIEW

A. GENERAL   (p.624)

B. PARAGRAPH 1: EXCLUSIVE
   COMPETENCE FOR THE COMMISSION   14.190
   1. General   14.190
   2. European merger control without
      prejudice to separate assessment
      under State aid rules   14.191

C. PARAGRAPH 3: APPLICABILITY OF
   NATIONAL COMPETITION LAW   14.192

D. PARAGRAPH 4: COMPETENCES OF
   COMMISSION V. MEMBER STATES   14.193

A. GENERAL

See also recitals 8 and 18.

B. PARAGRAPH 1: EXCLUSIVE COMPETENCE FOR THE COMMISSION

1. General

14.190 First, the Commission cannot refrain from taking account of complaints from undertakings which are not party to a concentration capable of having a Community dimension. Indeed, the implementation of such a transaction for the benefit of undertakings in competition with the complainants is likely to bring about an immediate change in the complainants' situation on the market or markets concerned. That is why Article 18 of the Merger Regulation provides that interested third parties are entitled to be heard by the Commission [...].

Furthermore, the Commission cannot validly maintain that it is not required to take a decision on the very principle of its competence as supervising authority, when it is solely responsible, under Article 21 of the Merger Regulation, for taking, subject to review by the Court of Justice, the decisions provided for by that regulation. If the Commission refused to adjudicate formally, at the request of third-party undertakings, on the question whether or not a concentration which has not been notified to it falls within the scope of the regulation, it would make it impossible for such undertakings to take advantage of the procedural guarantees which the Community legislation accords them. The Commission would, at the same time, deprive itself of a means of checking that undertakings which are parties to a concentration with a Community dimension comply properly with their obligation to notify. Moreover, the complainant undertakings could not challenge, by means of an action for annulment, a refusal by the Commission to act which, as was stated in the previous paragraph, is likely to do them harm.

Finally, nothing justifies the Commission in avoiding its obligation to undertake, in the interests of sound administration, a thorough and impartial examination of the complaints which are made to it. [...]

CoJ 25 September 2003 (Schlüsselverlag J.S. Moser and others v. Commission, C-170/02) [2003] ECR I-9889, paras 27–29.

2. European merger control without prejudice to separate assessment under State aid rules

The present decision is without prejudice to any eventual assessment or decision that **14.191** the European Commission may undertake or adopt in the field of State aids affecting the undertakings which are parties to the proposed transaction.
Commission 1 July 2010 (Geely/Daqiing/Volvo Cars, M.5789), para. 4.

C. PARAGRAPH 3: APPLICABILITY OF NATIONAL COMPETITION LAW

Like the Commission, the Court points out that Article 21(3) of the Merger Regu- **14.192** lation states that '[n]o Member State shall apply its national legislation on competition to any concentration that has a Community dimension' and that it thus does not confer the power on the Commission to adopt a measure producing binding legal effects of such a kind as to affect Aer Lingus's interests. [...]

[...] Where there is no concentration with a Community dimension, the Member States remain free to apply their national competition law to Ryanair's shareholding in Aer Lingus in accordance with the rules in place to that effect.
General Court 6 July 2010 (Aer Lingus Group v. Commission, T-411/07) [2010] ECR II-03691, paras 90 and 91.

D. PARAGRAPH 4: COMPETENCES OF *COMMISSION V. MEMBER STATES*

It is clear from the first subparagraph of Article 21(4) of Regulation No 139/2004 that **14.193** the sole jurisdiction of the Commission, as laid down in Article 21(2), concerns the protection only of the interests to which the regulation refers, namely interests relating to the protection of competition. In relation to those interests, the Commission has power to take a decision declaring a concentration compatible with the common market pursuant to Article 8(1) to (3) of Regulation No 139/2004.

On the other hand, that exclusive competence of the Commission does not prevent the Member States from taking appropriate measures to protect legitimate interests other than those pursued by Regulation No 139/2004, as stated by recital 19 of the preamble to the regulation. However, in that respect the Commission has, under the third subparagraph of Article 21(4) of Regulation No 139/2004, power to monitor compliance by the Member State with the general principles and other provisions of Community law in order to ensure that its decision under Article 8 of the regulation is effective.
Order General Court 2 September 2010 (Schemaventotto v. Commission, T-58/09) [2010] ECR II-03863, paras 108 and 109.

14.194   [No competence of Commission for decision after abandonment of merger] Consequently, as the proposed merger was abandoned by Autostrade and the intervener on 13 December 2006 and as the scrutiny of the interests referred to in Article 21(4) of Regulation No 139/2004 aims to ensure the effectiveness of Commission decisions under Article 8 of Regulation No 139/2004, the Commission was no longer competent to terminate the procedure pursuant to Article 21(4) by a decision relating to the recognition of a public interest protected by the national measures at issue.

That conclusion is not called into question by the fact that the procedure under Article 21(4) has not only an objective function, but also a subjective function, namely to protect the interests of the undertakings concerned relating to the proposed merger from the viewpoint of ensuring the legal certainty and the speed of that procedure. On that point it must be observed that, because the proposed merger was abandoned by the undertakings concerned, the subjective function had ceased to be relevant. As the proposed merger had been abandoned, it was no longer necessary to protect the interests of the undertakings concerned in relation to it.

Also by reason of the abandonment of the proposed merger the Commission's termination of the procedure in question cannot be equivalent to a Commission decision declaring a concentration incompatible with the common market by virtue of Article 8(3) of Regulation No 139/2004, which concerns only cases where the proposed merger is not abandoned by the undertakings concerned [...].

It must therefore be concluded that the Commission was no longer competent to terminate the procedure initiated pursuant to Article 21(4) of Regulation No 139/2004 by a decision relating to the recognition of a public interest protected by the national measures at issue. In that respect, it must be observed that there is nothing to indicate that in the present case the Commission took a decision exceeding its powers. The decision of 13 August 2008 therefore produced no binding legal effects capable of affecting the applicant's interests by bringing about a distinct change in its legal position. The Commission could only take the formal decision to take no further action in the procedure. The decision of 13 August 2008 to discontinue the procedure had no other effect and therefore it cannot constitute a challengeable act.

Order General Court 2 September 2010 (Schemaventotto v. Commission, T-58/09) [2010] ECR II-03863, paras 117–120.

14.195   [Transformation of procedure pursuant to Art. 21(4) ECMR into infringement procedure] By continuing the Article 21(4) procedure after the abandonment of the proposed merger, the Commission therefore no longer envisaged taking a decision on the recognition of a public interest protected by the national measures in question, but rather a decision declaring that Italy had infringed Article 21. In doing so, therefore, the Commission in effect left the framework of the Article 21(4) procedure by continuing it as an infringement action such as that provided for by Article 226 EC [now Article 258 TFEU] or Article 86(3) EC [now Article 106(3) TFEU]. [...]

Consequently, the decision contained in the letter of 13 August 2008 does not constitute a challengeable act by reason also of the fact that, after the proposed merger was abandoned, the procedure actually initiated by the Commission under Article 21(4) of Regulation No 139/2004 acquired the character of an infringement action. [...]

With regard to the argument of the applicant and the intervener that, if the action is inadmissible, the applicant would be deprived of the right to effective judicial protection, it must be observed that the provisions which may be infringed by the national measures in question, namely Articles 43 EC [now Article 49 TFEU] and 56 EC [now Article 63 TFEU], have direct effect and individuals may bring an action on the ground of their infringement before a national court.

Order General Court 2 September 2010 (Schemaventotto v. Commission, T-58/09) [2010] ECR II-03863, paras 124, 126 and 129.

ARTICLE 22 – REFERRAL TO THE COMMISSION

1.   One or more Member States may request the Commission to examine any concentration as defined in Article 3 that does not have a Community dimension within the meaning of Article 1 but affects trade between Member States and threatens to significantly affect competition within the territory of the Member State or States making the request.

   Such a request shall be made at most within 15 working days of the date on which the concentration was notified, or if no notification is required, otherwise made known to the Member State concerned.

2.   The Commission shall inform the competent authorities of the Member States and the undertakings concerned of any request received pursuant to paragraph 1 without delay.

   Any other Member State shall have the right to join the initial request within a period of 15 working days of being informed by the Commission of the initial request.

   All national time limits relating to the concentration shall be suspended until, in accordance with the procedure set out in this Article, it has been decided where the concentration shall be examined. As soon as a Member State has informed the Commission and the undertakings concerned that it does not wish to join the request, the suspension of its national time limits shall end.

3.   The Commission may, at the latest 10 working days after the expiry of the period set in paragraph 2, decide to examine, the concentration where it considers that it affects trade between Member States and threatens to significantly affect competition within the territory of the Member State or States making the request. If the Commission does not take a decision within this period, it shall be deemed to have adopted a decision to examine the concentration in accordance with the request.

   The Commission shall inform all Member States and the undertakings concerned of its decision. It may request the submission of a notification pursuant to Article 4.

   The Member State or States having made the request shall no longer apply their national legislation on competition to the concentration.

4.   Article 2, Article 4(2) to (3), Articles 5, 6, and 8 to 21 shall apply where the Commission examines a concentration pursuant to paragraph 3. Article 7 shall apply to the extent that the concentration has not been implemented on the date on which the Commission informs the undertakings concerned that a request has been made.

Where a notification pursuant to Article 4 is not required, the period set in Article 10(1) within which proceedings may be initiated shall begin on the working day following that on which the Commission informs the undertakings concerned that it has decided to examine the concentration pursuant to paragraph 3.

5. **The Commission may inform one or several Member States that it considers a concentration fulfils the criteria in paragraph 1. In such cases, the Commission may invite that Member State or those Member States to make a request pursuant to paragraph 1.**

OVERVIEW

A. GENERAL	14.196	B. PARAGRAPH 1: INFLUENCE OF TRADE BETWEEN MEMBER STATES	14.197

A. GENERAL

See also recitals 11, 12, 14 and 15.

Moreover, taking into account that the proposed transaction was notified in Spain and would be notifiable in the UK and that both Member States made a request under Article 22, an assessment of the proposed transaction by the Commission increases administrative efficiency, avoids duplication and fragmentation of enforcement effort, as well as potentially incoherent treatment (regarding investigation, assessment and possible remedies) by multiple authorities, pursuant to the one-shop-stop principle laid down in paragraph 11 of the Referral Notice. **14.196**

Finally, the Commission is the more appropriate authority to deal with the proposed transaction. It is better positioned to gather information from other operators in the two relevant markets, many of which are established outside Spain. Also, the CNMC may have difficulties to design and implement effective remedies in the case at hand given that the assets of the merged entity will be located outside Spain.

Commission 14 August 2014 (Dolby/Doremi, M.7297), C(2014) 5984 final, paras 35 and 36.

B. PARAGRAPH 1: INFLUENCE OF TRADE BETWEEN MEMBER STATES

According to Article 22(1), the Commission can only intervene 'in so far as the concentration affects trade between Member States'. The Commission considers that this condition is met since the operation has effects on air transport between Belgium and the United Kingdom. **14.197**

Commission 17 February 1993 (British Airways/Dan Air, M.278), OJ 1996 L 134/32, para. 7.

14.198 [T]he Commission received a request from the Dutch Government pursuant to Article 22 of Council Regulation (EC) No.4064/89 (Merger Regulation) [now Regulation 139/2004] to examine the proposed joint venture Holland Media Groep SA (HMG) between RTL4 SA (RTL), Vereniging Veronica Omroeporganisatie (Veronica) and Endemol Entertainment Holding BV (Endemol). [...]

 The concentration affects trade between Member States within the meaning of Article 22(1) of the Merger Regulation. The creation of the joint venture will influence the conditions for new entrants on the Dutch TV broadcasting market and the TV advertising market, including broadcasters from outside the Netherlands. It will also have an impact on the market for the acquisition of foreign (in particular English) language programmes within the Netherlands. In addition, the joint venture, HMG, is itself a company based in Luxembourg and at least the two channels RTL4 and RTL5 are broadcast under the licence ('concession') conferred by the Grand Duchy of Luxembourg. Moreover, Dutch public TV channels are fed in through cable networks in Belgium. A change in the structure of the Dutch TV market will therefore have at least an indirect impact on the TV markets in Belgium. Furthermore, if the legal situation in Belgium with regard to VTM is changed so as to result in increased competition from foreign channels on this market, such competition would be likely, in particular, from Dutch commercial channels, including the HMG channels.

Commission 20 September 1995 (RTL/Veronica/Endemol, M.553), OJ 1993 C 68/05, paras 1 and 16.

14.199 The Commission considered that, on balance the requirements for a referral are met and the case should be best assessed at a Community level. The relevant markets are very likely to be wider than national in geographic scope. [...] The parties' market shares would be important and from the comments the OFT received in its procedure, at this stage, it cannot be excluded that competitors may have difficulties to effectively compete with the parties post merger.

 Furthermore, it cannot be excluded that parallel investigations by the BKartA and the OFT would lead to divergent results which in the presence of EEA-wide markets should be avoided. The referral enables the Commission to ensure a coherent treatment of the case.

 Therefore, given the EEA impact of the transaction and to ensure consistency of the investigation and analysis of its impact on competition, the Commission considers to be the best placed authority to assess this concentration, and that the present case is appropriate for a referral to the Commission pursuant to Article 22 of the EC Merger Regulation.

Referral Decision Commission 17 April 2008 (Danisco/Abitec, M.5109), paras 30–32.

ARTICLE 23 – IMPLEMENTING PROVISIONS

1. The Commission shall have the power to lay down in accordance with the procedure referred to in paragraph 2:
    (a) implementing provisions concerning the form, content and other details of notifications and submissions pursuant to Article 4;
    (b) implementing provisions concerning time limits pursuant to Article 4(4), (5) Articles 7, 9, 10 and 22;
    (c) the procedure and time limits for the submission and implementation of commitments pursuant to Article 6(2) and Article 8(2);
    (d) implementing provisions concerning hearings pursuant to Article 18.

2. The Commission shall be assisted by an Advisory Committee, composed of representatives of the Member States.
    (a) Before publishing draft implementing provisions and before adopting such provisions, the Commission shall consult the Advisory Committee.
    (b) Consultation shall take place at a meeting convened at the invitation of and chaired by the Commission. A draft of the implementing provisions to be taken shall be sent with the invitation. The meeting shall take place not less than 10 working days after the invitation has been sent.
    (c) The Advisory Committee shall deliver an opinion on the draft implementing provisions, if necessary by taking a vote. The Commission shall take the utmost account of the opinion delivered by the Committee.

ARTICLE 24 – RELATIONS WITH THIRD COUNTRIES

1.   **The Member States shall inform the Commission of any general difficulties encountered by their undertakings with concentrations as defined in Article 3 in a third country.**

2.   **Initially not more than one year after the entry into force of this Regulation and, thereafter periodically, the Commission shall draw up a report examining the treatment accorded to undertakings having their seat or their principal fields of activity in the Community, in the terms referred to in paragraphs 3 and 4, as regards concentrations in third countries. The Commission shall submit those reports to the Council, together with any recommendations.**

3.   **Whenever it appears to the Commission, either on the basis of the reports referred to in paragraph 2 or on the basis of other information, that a third country does not grant undertakings having their seat or their principal fields of activity in the Community, treatment comparable to that granted by the Community to undertakings from that country, the Commission may submit proposals to the Council for an appropriate mandate for negotiation with a view to obtaining comparable treatment for undertakings having their seat or their principal fields of activity in the Community.**

4.   **Measures taken under this Article shall comply with the obligations of the Community or of the Member States, without prejudice to Article 307 of the Treaty, under international agreements, whether bilateral or multilateral.**

See also recital 44; Agreement between the Government of the United States of America and the Commission of the European Communities regarding the application of their competition laws (OJ 1995 L 95/47).

14.200   Pursuant to Article VI of the Agreement, the European Commission has sought an appropriate way to take account of important national interests of the United States, particularly those stemming from the consolidation of the US defence industry. [...] The Commission took the above concerns into consideration to the extent consistent with Community law.

Commission 30 July 1997 (Boeing/McDonnell Douglas, M.877), OJ 1997 L 336/16.

ARTICLE 25 – REPEAL

1. Without prejudice to Article 26(2), Regulations (EEC) No 4064/89 and (EC) No 1310/97 shall be repealed with effect from 1 May 2004.
2. References to the repealed Regulations shall be construed as references to this Regulation and shall be read in accordance with the correlation table in the Annex.

ARTICLE 26 – ENTRY INTO FORCE AND TRANSITIONAL PROVISIONS

1. This Regulation shall enter into force on the 20th day following that of its publication in the Official Journal of the European Union.
   It shall apply from 1 May 2004.

2. Regulation (EEC) No 4064/89 shall continue to apply to any concentration which was the subject of an agreement or announcement or where control was acquired within the meaning of Article 4(1) of that Regulation before the date of application of this Regulation, subject, in particular, to the provisions governing applicability set out in Article 25(2) and (3) of Regulation (EEC) No 4064/89 and Article 2 of Regulation (EEC) No 1310/97.

3. As regards concentrations to which this Regulation applies by virtue of accession, the date of accession shall be substituted for the date of application of this Regulation.

ANNEX

Table 14A.1   Correlation Table

Regulation (EEC) No 4064/89	This Regulation
Article 1(1), (2) and (3)	Article 1(1), (2) and (3)
Article 1(4)	Article 1(4)
Article 1(5)	Article 1(5)
Article 2(1)	Article 2(1)
–	Article 2(2)
Article 2(2)	Article 2(3)
Article 2(3)	Article 2(4)
Article 2(4)	Article 2(5)
Article 3(1)	Article 3(1)
Article 3(2)	Article 3(4)
Article 3(3)	Article 3(2)
Article 3(4)	Article 3(3)
–	Article 3(4)
Article 3(5)	Article 3(5)
Article 4(1) first sentence	Article 4(1) first subparagraph
Article 4(1) second sentence	–
–	Article 4(1) second and third subparagraphs
Article 4(2) and (3)	Article 4(2) and (3)
–	Article 4(4) to (6)
Article 5(1) to (3)	Article 5(1) to (3)
Article 5(4), introductory words	Article 5(4), introductory words
Article 5(4) point (a)	Article 5(4) point (a)
Article 5(4) point (b), introductory words	Article 5(4) point (b), introductory words
Article 5(4) point (b), first indent	Article 5(4) point (b)(i)
Article 5(4) point (b), second indent	Article 5(4) point (b)(ii)
Article 5(4) point (b), third indent	Article 5(4) point (b)(iii)
Article 5(4) point (b), fourth indent	Article 5(4) point (b)(iv)
Article 5(4) points (c), (d) and (e)	Article 5(4) points (c), (d) and (e)
Article 5(5)	Article 5(5)
Article 6(1), introductory words	Article 6(1), introductory words
Article 6(1) points (a) and (b)	Article 6(1) points (a) and (b)
Article 6(1) point (c)	Article 6(1) point (c), first sentence
Article 6(2) to (5)	Article 6(2) to (5)
Article 7(1)	Article 7(1)
Article 7(3)	Article 7(2)

Regulation (EEC) No 4064/89	This Regulation
Article 7(4)	Article 7(3)
Article 7(5)	Article 7(4)
Article 8(1)	Article 6(1) point (c), second sentence
Article 8(2)	Article 8(1) and (2)
Article 8(3)	Article 8(3)
Article 8(4)	Article 8(4)
–	Article 8(5)
Article 8(5)	Article 8(6)
Article 8(6)	Article 8(7)
–	Article 8(8)
Article 9(1) to (9)	Article 9(1) to (9)
Article 9(10)	–
Article 10(1) and (2)	Article 10(1) and (2)
Article 10(3)	Article 10(3) first subparagraph, first sentence
–	Article 10(3) first subparagraph, second sentence
–	Article 10(3) second subparagraph
Article 10(4)	Article 10(4) first subparagraph
–	Article 10(4), second subparagraph
Article 10(5)	Article 10(5), first and fourth subparagraphs
–	Article 10(5), second, third and fifth subparagraphs
Article 10(6)	Article 10(6)
Article 11(1)	Article 11(1)
Article 11(2)	–
Article 11(3)	Article 11(2)
Article 11(4)	Article 11(4) first sentence
–	Article 11(4) second and third sentences
Article 11(5) first sentence	–
Article 11(5) second sentence	Article 11(3)
Article 11(6)	Article 11(5)
–	Article 11(6) and (7)
Article 12	Article 12
Article 13(1) first subparagraph	Article 13(1)
Article 13(1) second subparagraph, introductory words	Article 13(2) introductory words
Article 13(1) second subparagraph, point (a)	Article 13(2) point (b)

Regulation (EEC) No 4064/89	This Regulation
Article 13(1) second subparagraph, point (b)	Article 13(2) point (c)
Article 13(1) second subparagraph, point (c)	Article 13(2) point (e)
Article 13(1) second subparagraph, point (d)	Article 13(2) point (a)
–	Article 13(2) point (d)
Article 13(2)	Article 13(3)
Article 13(3)	Article 13(4) first and second sentences
Article 13(4)	Article 13(4) third sentence
Article 13(5)	Article 13(5), first sentence
–	Article 13(5), second sentence
Article 13(6) first sentence	Article 13(6)
Article 13(6) second sentence	–
–	Article 13(7) and (8)
Article 14(1) introductory words	Article 14(1) introductory words
Article 14(1) point (a)	Article 14(2) point (a)
Article 14(1) point (b)	Article 14(1) point (a)
Article 14(1) point (c)	Article 14(1) points (b) and (c)
Article 14(1) point (d)	Article 14(1) point (d)
–	Article 14(1) points (e) and (f)
Article 14(2) introductory words	Article 14(2) introductory words
Article 14(2) point (a)	Article 14(2) point (d)
Article 14(2) points (b) and (c)	Article 14(2) points (b) and (c)
Article 14(3)	Article 14(3)
Article 14(4)	Article 14(4)
Article 15(1) introductory words	Article 15(1) introductory words
Article 15(1) points (a) and (b)	Article 15(1) points (a) and (b)
Article 15(2) introductory words	Article 15(1) introductory words
Article 15(2) point (a)	Article 15(1) point (c)
Article 15(2) point (b)	Article 15(1) point (d)
Article 15(3)	Article 15(2)
Articles 16 to 20	Articles 16 to 20
Article 21(1)	Article 21(2)
Article 21(2)	Article 21(3)
Article 21(3)	Article 21(4)
Article 22(1)	Article 21(1)
Article 22(3)	–
–	Article 22(1) to (3)
Article 22(4)	Article 22(4)

Regulation (EEC) No 4064/89	This Regulation
Article 22(5)	–
–	Article 22(5)
Article 23	Article 23(1)
–	Article 23(2)
Article 24	Article 24
–	Article 25
Article 25(1)	Article 26(1), first subparagraph
–	Article 26(1), second subparagraph
Article 25(2)	Article 26(2)
Article 25(3)	Article 26(3)
–	Annex

15

REGULATION (EU) NO 330/2010 ON VERTICAL AGREEMENTS*

COMMISSION REGULATION (EU) NO 330/2010 OF 20 APRIL 2010 ON THE APPLICATION OF ARTICLE 101(3) OF THE TREATY ON THE FUNCTIONING OF THE EUROPEAN UNION TO CATEGORIES OF VERTICAL AGREEMENTS AND CONCERTED PRACTICES (OJ 2010 L 102/1)

THE EUROPEAN COMMISSION

Having regard to the Treaty on the Functioning of the European Union,

Having regard to Regulation No 19/65/EEC of the Council of 2 March 1965 on the application of Article 85(3) of the Treaty to certain categories of agreements and concerted practices,[1] and in particular Article 1 thereof,

Having published a draft of this Regulation,

After consulting the Advisory Committee on Restrictive Practices and Dominant Positions,

Whereas:

(1) Regulation No 19/65/EEC empowers the Commission to apply Article 101(3) of the Treaty on the Functioning of the European Union[2] by regulation to certain categories of vertical agreements and corresponding concerted practices falling within Article 101(1) of the Treaty.

(2) Commission Regulation (EC) No 2790/1999 of 22 December 1999 on the application of Article 81(3) of the Treaty to categories of vertical agreements and concerted practices[3] defines a category of vertical agreements which the Commission regarded as normally satisfying the conditions laid down in Article

---

* This chapter was written by Edmon Oude Elferink.
1   OJ 36, 6.3.1965, p. 533.
2   With effect from 1 December 2009, Article 81 of the EC Treaty has become Article 101 of the Treaty on the Functioning of the European Union. The two Articles are, in substance, identical. For the purposes of this Regulation, references to Article 101 of the Treaty on the Functioning of the European Union should be understood as references to Article 81 of the EC Treaty where appropriate.
3   OJ L 336, 29.12.1999, p. 21.

101(3) of the Treaty. In view of the overall positive experience with the application of that Regulation, which expires on 31 May 2010, and taking into account further experience acquired since its adoption, it is appropriate to adopt a new block exemption regulation.

(3)   The category of agreements which can be regarded as normally satisfying the conditions laid down in Article 101(3) of the Treaty includes vertical agreements for the purchase or sale of goods or services where those agreements are concluded between non-competing undertakings, between certain competitors or by certain associations of retailers of goods. It also includes vertical agreements containing ancillary provisions on the assignment or use of intellectual property rights. The term 'vertical agreements' should include the corresponding concerted practices.

(4)   For the application of Article 101(3) of the Treaty by regulation, it is not necessary to define those vertical agreements which are capable of falling within Article 101(1) of the Treaty. In the individual assessment of agreements under Article 101(1) of the Treaty, account has to be taken of several factors, and in particular the market structure on the supply and purchase side.

(5)   The benefit of the block exemption established by this Regulation should be limited to vertical agreements for which it can be assumed with sufficient certainty that they satisfy the conditions of Article 101(3) of the Treaty.

(6)   Certain types of vertical agreements can improve economic efficiency within a chain of production or distribution by facilitating better coordination between the participating undertakings. In particular, they can lead to a reduction in the transaction and distribution costs of the parties and to an optimisation of their sales and investment levels.

(7)   The likelihood that such efficiency-enhancing effects will outweigh any anti-competitive effects due to restrictions contained in vertical agreements depends on the degree of market power of the parties to the agreement and, therefore, on the extent to which those undertakings face competition from other suppliers of goods or services regarded by their customers as interchangeable or substitutable for one another, by reason of the products' characteristics, their prices and their intended use.

(8)   It can be presumed that, where the market share held by each of the undertakings party to the agreement on the relevant market does not exceed 30 per cent, vertical agreements which do not contain certain types of severe restrictions of competition generally lead to an improvement in production or distribution and allow consumers a fair share of the resulting benefits.

(9)   Above the market share threshold of 30 per cent, there can be no presumption that vertical agreements falling within the scope of Article 101(1) of the Treaty will usually give rise to objective advantages of such a character and size as to compensate for the disadvantages which they create for competition. At the same time, there is no presumption that those vertical agreements are either caught by Article 101(1) of the Treaty or that they fail to satisfy the conditions of Article 101(3) of the Treaty.

(10)   This Regulation should not exempt vertical agreements containing restrictions which are likely to restrict competition and harm consumers or which are not indispensable to the attainment of the efficiency-enhancing effects. In particular,

vertical agreements containing certain types of severe restrictions of competition such as minimum and fixed resale-prices, as well as certain types of territorial protection, should be excluded from the benefit of the block exemption established by this Regulation irrespective of the market share of the undertakings concerned.

(11) In order to ensure access to or to prevent collusion on the relevant market, certain conditions should be attached to the block exemption. To this end, the exemption of non-compete obligations should be limited to obligations which do not exceed a defined duration. For the same reasons, any direct or indirect obligation causing the members of a selective distribution system not to sell the brands of particular competing suppliers should be excluded from the benefit of this Regulation.

(12) The market-share limitation, the non-exemption of certain vertical agreements and the conditions provided for in this Regulation normally ensure that the agreements to which the block exemption applies do not enable the participating undertakings to eliminate competition in respect of a substantial part of the products in question.

(13) The Commission may withdraw the benefit of this Regulation, pursuant to Article 29(1) of Council Regulation (EC) No 1/2003 of 16 December 2002 on the implementation of the rules on competition laid down in Articles 81 and 82 of the Treaty,[4] where it finds in a particular case that an agreement to which the exemption provided for in this Regulation applies nevertheless has effects which are incompatible with Article 101(3) of the Treaty.

(14) The competition authority of a Member State may withdraw the benefit of this Regulation pursuant to Article 29(2) of Regulation (EC) No 1/2003 in respect of the territory of that Member State, or a part thereof where, in a particular case, an agreement to which the exemption provided for in this Regulation applies nevertheless has effects which are incompatible with Article 101(3) of the Treaty in the territory of that Member State, or in a part thereof, and where such territory has all the characteristics of a distinct geographic market.

(15) In determining whether the benefit of this Regulation should be withdrawn pursuant to Article 29 of Regulation (EC) No 1/2003, the anti-competitive effects that may derive from the existence of parallel networks of vertical agreements that have similar effects which significantly restrict access to a relevant market or competition therein are of particular importance. Such cumulative effects may for example arise in the case of selective distribution or non-compete obligations.

(16) In order to strengthen supervision of parallel networks of vertical agreements which have similar anti-competitive effects and which cover more than 50 per cent of a given market, the Commission may by regulation declare this Regulation inapplicable to vertical agreements containing specific restraints relating to the market concerned, thereby restoring the full application of Article 101 of the Treaty to such agreements,

HAS ADOPTED THIS REGULATION:

---

4   OJ L 1, 4.1.2003, p. 1.

ARTICLE 1 – DEFINITIONS

1. For the purposes of this Regulation, the following definitions shall apply:

    (a) 'vertical agreement' means an agreement or concerted practice entered into between two or more undertakings each of which operates, for the purposes of the agreement or the concerted practice, at a different level of the production or distribution chain, and relating to the conditions under which the parties may purchase, sell or resell certain goods or services:

    (b) 'vertical restraint' means a restriction of competition in a vertical agreement falling within the scope of Article 101(1) of the Treaty:

    (c) 'competing undertaking' means an actual or potential competitor: 'actual competitor' means an undertaking that is active on the same relevant market: 'potential competitor' means an undertaking that, in the absence of the vertical agreement, would, on realistic grounds and not just as a mere theoretical possibility, in case of a small but permanent increase in relative prices be likely to undertake, within a short period of time, the necessary additional investments or other necessary switching costs to enter the relevant market:

    (d) 'non-compete obligation' means any direct or indirect obligation causing the buyer not to manufacture, purchase, sell or resell goods or services which compete with the contract goods or services, or any direct or indirect obligation on the buyer to purchase from the supplier or from another undertaking designated by the supplier more than 80 per cent of the buyer's total purchases of the contract goods or services and their substitutes on the relevant market, calculated on the basis of the value or, where such is standard industry practice, the volume of its purchases in the preceding calendar year:

    (e) 'selective distribution system' means a distribution system where the supplier undertakes to sell the contract goods or services, either directly or indirectly, only to distributors selected on the basis of specified criteria and where these distributors undertake not to sell such goods or services to unauthorised distributors within the territory reserved by the supplier to operate that system:

    (f) 'intellectual property rights' includes industrial property rights, know how, copyright and neighbouring rights:

    (g) 'know-how' means a package of non-patented practical information, resulting from experience and testing by the supplier,

which is secret, substantial and identified: in this context, 'secret' means that the know-how is not generally known or easily accessible: 'substantial' means that the know-how is significant and useful to the buyer for the use, sale or resale of the contract goods or services: 'identified' means that the know-how is described in a sufficiently comprehensive manner so as to make it possible to verify that it fulfils the criteria of secrecy and substantiality:

(h) 'buyer' includes an undertaking which, under an agreement falling within Article 101(1) of the Treaty, sells goods or services on behalf of another undertaking:

    (i) 'customer of the buyer' means an undertaking not party to the agreement which purchases the contract goods or services from a buyer which is party to the agreement.

2. For the purposes of this Regulation, the terms 'undertaking', 'supplier' and 'buyer' shall include their respective connected undertakings. 'Connected undertakings' means:

(a) undertakings in which a party to the agreement, directly or indirectly:

    (i) has the power to exercise more than half the voting rights, or

    (ii) has the power to appoint more than half the members of the supervisory board, board of management or bodies legally representing the undertaking, or

    (iii) has the right to manage the undertaking's affairs:

(b) undertakings which directly or indirectly have, over a party to the agreement, the rights or powers listed in point (a):

(c) undertakings in which an undertaking referred to in point (b) has, directly or indirectly, the rights or powers listed in point (a):

(d) undertakings in which a party to the agreement together with one or more of the undertakings referred to in points (a), (b) or (c), or in which two or more of the latter undertakings, jointly have the rights or powers listed in point (a):

(e) undertakings in which the rights or the powers listed in point (a) are jointly held by:

    (i) parties to the agreement or their respective connected undertakings referred to in points (a) to (d), or

    (ii) one or more of the parties to the agreement or one or more of their connected undertakings referred to in points (a) to (d) and one or more third parties.

The term 'specified criteria', referred to in Article 1(1)(f) of Commission Regulation **15.01** (EC) No 1400/2002 of 31 July 2002 on the application of Article [101(3) TFEU] to categories of vertical agreements and concerted practices in the motor vehicle sector [now Regulation (EU) No 461/2010 in conjunction with Regulation (EU) No 330/2010], means, with respect to a quantitative selective distribution system within the meaning of that regulation, criteria the precise content of which may be verified. In order to benefit from the exemption provided for by that regulation, it is not necessary for such a system to be based on criteria that are objectively justified and applied in a uniform and non-differentiated manner in respect of all applicants for authorisation.

CoJ 14 June 2012 (Auto 24 SARL v. Jaguar Land Rover France SAS, C-158/11), ECLI:EU:C:2012:351, para. 39.

ARTICLE 2 – EXEMPTION

1. Pursuant to Article 101(3) of the Treaty and subject to the provisions of this Regulation, it is hereby declared that Article 101(1) of the Treaty shall not apply to vertical agreements.

    This exemption shall apply to the extent that such agreements contain vertical restraints.

2. The exemption provided for in paragraph 1 shall apply to vertical agreements entered into between an association of undertakings and its members, or between such an association and its suppliers, only if all its members are retailers of goods and if no individual member of the association, together with its connected undertakings, has a total annual turnover exceeding EUR 50 million. Vertical agreements entered into by such associations shall be covered by this Regulation without prejudice to the application of Article 101 of the Treaty to horizontal agreements concluded between the members of the association or decisions adopted by the association.

3. The exemption provided for in paragraph 1 shall apply to vertical agreements containing provisions which relate to the assignment to the buyer or use by the buyer of intellectual property rights, provided that those provisions do not constitute the primary object of such agreements and are directly related to the use, sale or resale of goods or services by the buyer or its customers. The exemption applies on condition that, in relation to the contract goods or services, those provisions do not contain restrictions of competition having the same object as vertical restraints which are not exempted under this Regulation.

4. The exemption provided for in paragraph 1 shall not apply to vertical agreements entered into between competing undertakings. However, it shall apply where competing undertakings enter into a non-reciprocal vertical agreement and:

    (a) the supplier is a manufacturer and a distributor of goods, while the buyer is a distributor and not a competing undertaking at the manufacturing level: or

    (b) the supplier is a provider of services at several levels of trade, while the buyer provides its goods or services at the retail level and is not a competing undertaking at the level of trade where it purchases the contract services.

5. This Regulation shall not apply to vertical agreements the subject matter of which falls within the scope of any other block exemption regulation, unless otherwise provided for in such a regulation.

See also the Commission Notice – Guidelines on Vertical Restraints (OJ 2010 C 130/1).

15.02 [System] [A Block Exemption Regulation] is limited to providing economic agents […] with certain possibilities enabling them to remove their distribution and servicing agreements from the scope of the prohibition contained in Article [101(1) TFEU] despite the inclusion in those agreements of certain types of exclusivity and no-competition clauses. However, the provisions of [such a] Regulation […] do not compel economic agents to make use of those possibilities. Nor do those provisions have the effect of amending the content of such an agreement or of rendering it void where all the conditions laid down in the Regulation are not satisfied.

Where an agreement does not satisfy all the conditions laid down by [such a] Regulation […] the parties may either request the Commission to adopt an individual decision declaring Article [101(1) TFEU] inapplicable [this possibility has come to an end pursuant to the implementation of Regulation No 1/2003] or contend that the conditions laid down in another regulation providing exemption in respect of other categories of agreements are satisfied, or even establish that the agreement in question is on some other ground not incompatible with the prohibition contained in Article [101(1) TFEU].

CoJ 18 December 1986 (VAG France v. Magne, C-10/86) [1986] ECR 4071, paras 12 and 13.

ARTICLE 3 – MARKET SHARE THRESHOLD

1. **The exemption provided for in Article 2 shall apply on condition that the market share held by the supplier does not exceed 30 per cent of the relevant market on which it sells the contract goods or services and the market share held by the buyer does not exceed 30 per cent of the relevant market on which it purchases the contract goods or services.**

2. **For the purposes of paragraph 1, where in a multi party agreement an undertaking buys the contract goods or services from one undertaking party to the agreement and sells the contract goods or services to another undertaking party to the agreement, the market share of the first undertaking must respect the market share threshold provided for in that paragraph both as a buyer and a supplier in order for the exemption provided for in Article 2 to apply.**

[Definition of secondary markets] [T]he applicant submits that the practice of selective **15.03** distribution of spare parts – entailing the refusal to provide those parts to independent watch makers and the prohibition on undertakings within the network from providing those parts to operators outside the network – is a practice which is contrary to Article [101 TFEU] and cannot qualify for the block exemption provided for in Regulation No 2790/1999 [currently Regulation No 330/2010].

Article 2(1) of that regulation provides as follows: 'Pursuant to Article [101(3) TFEU] and subject to the provisions of this Regulation, it is hereby declared that Article [101(1) TFEU] shall not apply to agreements or concerted practices entered into between two or more undertakings each of which operates, for the purposes of the agreement, at a different level of the production or distribution chain, and relating to the conditions under which the parties may purchase, sell or resell certain goods or services ('vertical agreements'). This exemption shall apply to the extent that such agreements contain restrictions of competition falling within the scope of Article [101](1) ('vertical restraints').'

According to Article 3 of that regulation, 'the exemption provided for in Article 2 shall apply on condition that the market share held by the supplier does not exceed 30 per cent of the relevant market on which it sells the contract goods or services.'

In addition, according to point 94 of the guidelines on vertical restraints (OJ 2000 C 291, p. 1) [currently OJ 2010 C 130, p. 1]: 'Where a supplier produces both original equipment and the repair or replacement parts for this equipment, the supplier will often be the only or the major supplier on the after-market for the repair and replacement parts … The relevant market for application of … Regulation [No 2790/1999] [currently No 330/2010] may be the original equipment market including the spare parts or a separate original equipment market and after-market depending on the circumstances of the case, such as the effects of the restrictions involved, the lifetime of the equipment and importance of the repair or replacement costs.'

The Commission concluded as follows, in point 33 of the contested decision, in that regard: '… As explained before, the analysis made by the Commission for the purpose of current proceedings has led to the conclusion that the spare parts aftermarket is not to be viewed as a market distinct from the primary market. Consequently, an overall market power of a particular watch manufacturer must be assessed, and in particular its position and strength on the primary market is to be taken into consideration. Therefore, taking into account that none of the watch manufacturer[s] being subject to the complaint appears to have either a dominant position on the primary market, or its market share exceeds 30 per cent, it seems that they could benefit from the Block Exemption Regulation.'

It cannot be ruled out that, had the Commission not committed the manifest error of assessment [...] [the Commission had not shown that a moderate price increase for spare parts by a particular producer would cause a shift in demand to watches from another producer, rendering such an increase unprofitable, and thus, made a manifest error of assessment in examining them together as forming part of a single relevant market, Ed.], it might well have concluded that the spare parts specific to individual brands constituted separate relevant markets, depending on their substitutability.

However, the contested decision does not show that the market share of the Swiss watch manufacturers is also less than 30 per cent on the markets for brand-specific spare parts.

Accordingly, in those circumstances it cannot be ruled out that, had the manifest error of assessment [...] not taken place, and if the Commission had included in the contested decision its finding in the provisional position document that the manufacturers of luxury/prestige watches were the only suppliers of the specific ranges of spare parts for their own brands, it would have concluded that the exemption provided for in Regulation No 2790/1999 [currently Regulation No 330/2012] was inapplicable, in the light of Article 3 thereof.

General Court 15 December 2010 (Confédération européenne des associations d'horlogers-réparateurs (CEAHR) v. Commission, T-427/08) [2010] ECR II-05865, paras 133–140.

ARTICLE 4 – RESTRICTIONS THAT REMOVE THE BENEFIT OF THE BLOCK EXEMPTION – HARDCORE RESTRICTIONS

The exemption provided for in Article 2 shall not apply to vertical agreements which, directly or indirectly, in isolation or in combination with other factors under the control of the parties, have as their object:

(a) the restriction of the buyer's ability to determine its sale price, without prejudice to the possibility of the supplier to impose a maximum sale price or recommend a sale price, provided that they do not amount to a fixed or minimum sale price as a result of pressure from, or incentives offered by, any of the parties:

(b) the restriction of the territory into which, or of the customers to whom, a buyer party to the agreement, without prejudice to a restriction on its place of establishment, may sell the contract goods or services, except:

    (i) the restriction of active sales into the exclusive territory or to an exclusive customer group reserved to the supplier or allocated by the supplier to another buyer, where such a restriction does not limit sales by the customers of the buyer,

    (ii) the restriction of sales to end users by a buyer operating at the wholesale level of trade,

    (iii) the restriction of sales by the members of a selective distribution system to unauthorised distributors within the territory reserved by the supplier to operate that system, and

    (iv) the restriction of the buyer's ability to sell components, supplied for the purposes of incorporation, to customers who would use them to manufacture the same type of goods as those produced by the supplier:

(c) the restriction of active or passive sales to end users by members of a selective distribution system operating at the retail level of trade, without prejudice to the possibility of prohibiting a member of the system from operating out of an unauthorised place of establishment:

(d) the restriction of cross-supplies between distributors within a selective distribution system, including between distributors operating at different level of trade:

(e) the restriction, agreed between a supplier of components and a buyer who incorporates those components, of the supplier's ability to sell the components as spare parts to end-users or to repairers or other service providers not entrusted by the buyer with the repair or servicing of its goods.

OVERVIEW

A. GENERAL	(p.650)	D. DE FACTO PROHIBITION ON SALES VIA INTERNET IN SELECTIVE DISTRIBUTION	
B. RESALE PRICE CLAUSES	15.04	AGREEMENTS	15.06
		1. General	15.06
C. RESALE PRICE CLAUSES IN VERTICAL		2. Integrity of selective distribution	
AGREEMENTS FOR PETROLEUM		system	15.07
PRODUCTS	15.05	3. Territorial restrictions	15.08

A. GENERAL

See also Section F.2 of Chapter 4 on Article 101 TFEU.

B. RESALE PRICE CLAUSES

15.04   [C]ontractual clauses relating to the retail price of goods, […], are eligible for the block exemption under Regulation No 1984/83, as amended by Regulation No 1582/97, and Regulation No 2790/1999 [currently Regulation No 330/2010] when the supplier does no more than impose a maximum sale price or recommend a sale price and when, therefore, it is genuinely possible for the reseller to determine that retail price. On the other hand, such clauses are ineligible for those exemptions where they lead, directly or by indirect or concealed means, to the fixing of a retail price or the imposition of a minimum sale price by the supplier. It is for the national court to determine whether such obligations constrain the reseller, taking account of all of the contractual obligations in their economic and legal context, and of the conduct of the parties to the main proceedings.
CoJ 2 April 2009 (Pedro IV Servicios SL v. Total Espaæa SA, C-260/07) [2009] ECR I-2437, para. 84.

C. RESALE PRICE CLAUSES IN VERTICAL AGREEMENTS FOR PETROLEUM PRODUCTS

15.05   Since the Court is not in a position to assess the discretion that Tobar had to determine the retail price of the petroleum products, following the authorisation granted to that company by CEPSA's letter of 2 November 2001, it is for the referring court to examine whether that authorisation made it genuinely possible for the reseller to lower that sale price, taking account of the actual effect of all the clauses of the contract at issue in the main proceedings in their economic and legal context. In particular, it is necessary to ascertain whether such a retail price is not, in reality, fixed by indirect or concealed means, such as the fixing of the margin of the service station operator, threats, intimidation, warnings, penalties or incentives.

If the referring court were to conclude that Tobar was, in reality, required to charge the fixed or minimum sale price imposed by CEPSA, that contract could not qualify for the block exemption established by Regulation No 2790/1999 [currently Regulation No 330/2010]. However, where an agreement does not satisfy all the conditions provided for by an exempting regulation, it will be caught by the prohibition provided for in Article [101(1) TFEU] only if its object or effect is to restrict appreciably competition within the common market and it is capable of affecting trade between Member States [...]. In that latter case, and in the absence of individual exemption pursuant to Article [101(3) TFEU], the price agreement would be automatically void under Article [101(2) TFEU].

By contrast, if the unilateral amendment of the contract at issue in the main proceedings meant that the clause relating to the retail price of the petroleum products was to be brought into line with the competition rules, that contract would then qualify for the block exemption, subject to its satisfying all the conditions laid down in Regulation No 2790/1999 [currently Regulation No 330/2010]. However, [...] such an amendment cannot result in the retroactive validity of that contract from the point of view of the block exemption under Regulation No 1984/83.

It follows from settled case-law that, once the conditions for the application of Article [101(1) TFEU] are met and so long as the agreement concerned does not justify the grant of an exemption under Article [101(3) TFEU], the nullity referred to in Article [101(2) TFEU] can be relied on by anyone. Since that nullity is absolute, it is capable of having a bearing on all the effects, either past or future, of the agreement concerned (*Joined Cases C 295/04–C 298/04 Manfredi* and others [2006] ECR I 6619, para. 57 [...]). [...]

It follows that [...] Articles 10 to 13 of Regulation No 1984/83 must be interpreted as precluding the application of the block exemption to an exclusive supply contract which provides for the fixing of the retail price by the supplier. It is for the referring court to ascertain whether, under national law, the contractual clause relating to that sale price can be amended by unilateral authorisation of the supplier, such as that at issue in the main proceedings, and whether a contract which is automatically void may become valid following an amendment of that contractual clause which has the effect of bringing that clause into line with Article [101(1) TFEU].

CoJ 11 September 2008 (CEPSA Estaciones de Servicio SA v. LV Tobar e Hijos SL, C-279/06) [2008] ECR I-6681, paras 71–74 and 76.

D. DE FACTO PROHIBITION ON SALES VIA INTERNET IN SELECTIVE DISTRIBUTION AGREEMENTS

1. General

Article 4(c) of Regulation No 2790/1999 [currently Regulation No 330/2010] must be **15.06** interpreted as meaning that the block exemption provided for in Article 2 of that regulation does not apply to a selective distribution contract which contains a clause prohibiting de facto the internet as a method of marketing the contractual products.

However, such a contract may benefit, on an individual basis, from the exception provided for in Article 101(3) TFEU where the conditions of that provision are met.
CoJ 13 October 2011 (Pierre Fabre Dermo-Cosmétique SAS v. Président de l'Autorité de la concurrence and Ministre de l'Économie, de l'Industrie et de l'Emploi, C-439/09) [2011] ECR I-09419, para. 59.

2. Integrity of selective distribution system

15.07   The definition of the term '[unauthorised distributors]' in Article [4(b)(iii) of Regulation No 330/2010] shows that a supplier may prohibit dealers from supplying natural or legal persons deemed to be 'resellers' only where the latter dispose of [products] in a new condition. The purpose of putting leasing contracts on the same footing as resales is to allow the supplier to guarantee the integrity of the distribution network by avoiding a leasing contract which includes a transfer of ownership or an option to purchase before the expiry of the contract being used to facilitate the acquisition outside the [selective] distribution network of the ownership of a [product] when it is still in a new condition.
General Court 15 September 2005 (DaimlerChrysler v. Commission, T-325/01) [2005] ECR II-3319, para. 153.

3. Territorial restrictions

15.08   BMW Belgium and the members of the advisory committee, authors of the circular of 29 September 1975, intentionally addressed those circulars to the Belgian dealers, thereby inviting them to subscribe to an agreement whereby they undertook not to re-export the products in question. In so doing, BMW Belgium and the members of the advisory committee thus committed the said infringement intentionally.

As for the participation in that infringement of the Belgian dealers who signed the circular of 29 September 1975 from BMW Belgium, although it is true that the bonds of economic dependence existing between them and BMW Belgium were liable to affect their freedom of initiative and decision, the existence of those bonds did not make it impossible to refuse to consent to the agreement which was proposed to them, as is shown by the considerable number of dealers who refrained from doing so.

Having regard to the terms of the dealership agreement concluded with BMW Belgium, it cannot be accepted that the BMW Belgium dealers did not understand that the circular from BMW Belgium of 29 September 1975, considered according to its text and in the light of the warning contained in the circular of the same date from the advisory committee, as requiring the cessation of all sales abroad, or that they were unaware of the fact that by giving their consent in writing to the proposal of BMW Belgium they were agreeing to an export prohibition which went beyond the selective distribution conditions of BMW Munich.
CoJ 12 July 1979 (BMW Belgium and others v. Commission, Joined Cases 32/78 and 36–82/78) [1979] ECR 2435, paras 35–37.

15.09   With regard to the Commission's refusal to grant an exemption under Article [101(3)], it must be emphasized that the Commission was entitled to consider that, when examining the main dealer agreement with a view to deciding whether or not to grant an exemption, it was obliged to take account of all the circumstances surrounding the application of that agreement and that it was thus entitled to take the view that the mere refusal to supply German dealers with right-hand-drive cars suitable for export was a key element in partitioning the common market artificially [...]. The decision adds that in balancing the improvement in distribution of cars resulting from the agreement against the disadvantages, in regard to competition which flowed from the fact that it was impossible to buy right-hand-drive cars in Germany at German prices and that competitive pressure in the United Kingdom was thus significantly reduced [...], the Commission arrived at the conclusion that the first two conditions in Article [101(3)] were not satisfied.

CoJ 17 September 1985 (Ford-Werke AG and Ford Europe Inc. v. Commission, Joined Cases 25 and 26/85) [1985] ECR 2725, para. 33.

Article [101(1) TFEU] must be interpreted as meaning that it precludes a motor **15.10** vehicle manufacturer which sells its vehicles through a selective distribution system from agreeing with its authorized dealers that they are not to deliver vehicles to independent leasing companies where, without granting an option to purchase, those companies make them available to lessees whose residence or seat is outside the contract territory of the dealer in question, or from calling on such dealers to act in that manner. [...]

Accordingly, although Regulation No 123/85 [now Regulation 461/2010 in conjunction with Regulation 330/2010] provides manufacturers with substantial means of protecting their distribution systems, it does not authorize them to partition their markets. In the present case, the object and effect of the call contained in the circular are to confine the distribution of vehicles of the BMW mark by the German dealers within the system to their own contract territories and to impose that prohibition also on those dealers' customers engaging in leasing outside the BMW system. That call cannot, therefore, be exempted under Article [101(3)] of the Treaty by virtue of Regulation No 123/85 [now Regulation 461/2010 in conjunction with Regulation 330/2010].

CoJ 24 October 1995 (Bayerische Motorenwerke AG v. ALD Auto-Leasing D GmbH, C-70/93) [1995] ECR I-3439, paras 22 and 37.

[A] measure which is liable to partition the market between Member States cannot **15.11** come under those provisions of Regulation No 123/85 [now Regulation 461/2010 in conjunction with Regulation 330/2010] that deal with the obligations which a distributor may lawfully assume under a dealership contract. The [General Court] properly held [...] that, although that regulation provided manufacturers with substantial means by which to protect their distribution systems, it did not authorise them to adopt measures which contributed to a partitioning of the market [...].

CoJ 18 September 2003 (Volkswagen AG I v. Commission, C-338/00P) [2003] ECR I-9189, para. 49.

[A]n agreement concerning distribution has a restrictive object for the purposes of **15.12** Article [101 TFEU] if it clearly manifests the will to treat export sales less favourably than national sales and thus leads to a partitioning of the market in question [...].

[S]uch an objective can be achieved not only by direct restrictions on exports but also through indirect measures, such as [the implementation by a motor manufacturer in its dealership contracts of a measure excluding export sales from the system of bonuses granted to dealers], since they influence the economic conditions of such transactions. [...]

[I]n order to determine whether an agreement is to be considered to be prohibited by reason of the distortion of competition which is its effect, the competition in question should be assessed within the actual context in which it would occur in the absence of the agreement in dispute [...].

[I]t was necessary in situations such as that in this case to examine what the conduct of Netherlands dealers and the competitive situation in the market in question would have been, if export sales had not been excluded from the bonus policy.

CoJ 6 April 2006 (General Motors Nederland B.V. and Opel Nederland B.V. v. Commission, C-551/03 P) [2006] ECR I-3173, paras 67, 68, 72 and 73.

ARTICLE 5 – EXCLUDED RESTRICTIONS

1. The exemption provided for in Article 2 shall not apply to the following obligations contained in vertical agreements:
    (a) any direct or indirect non-compete obligation, the duration of which is indefinite or exceeds five years:
    (b) any direct or indirect obligation causing the buyer, after termination of the agreement, not to manufacture, purchase, sell or resell goods or services:
    (c) any direct or indirect obligation causing the members of a selective distribution system not to sell the brands of particular competing suppliers.
    For the purposes of point (a) of the first subparagraph, a non-compete obligation which is tacitly renewable beyond a period of five years shall be deemed to have been concluded for an indefinite duration.
2. By way of derogation from paragraph 1(a), the time limitation of five years shall not apply where the contract goods or services are sold by the buyer from premises and land owned by the supplier or leased by the supplier from third parties not connected with the buyer, provided that the duration of the non-compete obligation does not exceed the period of occupancy of the premises and land by the buyer.
3. By way of derogation from paragraph 1(b), the exemption provided for in Article 2 shall apply to any direct or indirect obligation causing the buyer, after termination of the agreement, not to manufacture, purchase, sell or resell goods or services where the following conditions are fulfilled:
    (a) the obligation relates to goods or services which compete with the contract goods or services:
    (b) the obligation is limited to the premises and land from which the buyer has operated during the contract period:
    (c) the obligation is indispensable to protect know-how transferred by the supplier to the buyer:
    (d) the duration of the obligation is limited to a period of one year after termination of the agreement.
    Paragraph 1(b) is without prejudice to the possibility of imposing a restriction which is unlimited in time on the use and disclosure of know-how which has not entered the public domain.

OVERVIEW

| A. GENERAL | 15.13 | B. NON-COMPETE AND EXCLUSIVITY CLAUSES IN VERTICAL AGREEMENTS FOR PETROLEUM PRODUCTS | 15.14 |

A. GENERAL

15.13 [T]he contractual restrictions on retailers must be examined not just in a purely formal manner from the legal point of view but also by taking into account the specific economic context in which those agreements operate.

Accordingly, […], since the possibility of terminating the distribution agreements does not in any way preclude the effective enforcement of those agreements during the period in which that option is not used, it is necessary to take into account the actual duration of those agreements in assessing their effects on the relevant market. […]

The effects of an agreement on competition must be assessed in the context in which it occurs and where it might combine with others to have a cumulative effect on competition ([…]).

In order to assess whether a number of contracts impede access to the market in question, it is necessary to define the nature and extent of all similar contracts tying a large number of outlets to a number of national producers. The effect of those networks of contracts on access to the market depends specifically on the number of outlets thus tied to producers in relation to those which are not so tied, the duration of the commitments entered into and the quantities of goods to which those commitments relate.

Order CoJ 28 September 2006 (Unilever Bestfoods (Ireland) Ltd v. Commission, C-552/03 P) [2006] ECR I-9091, paras 54, 55, 84 and 85.

B. NON-COMPETE AND EXCLUSIVITY CLAUSES IN VERTICAL AGREEMENTS FOR PETROLEUM PRODUCTS

15.14 [T]he prohibition laid down by Article [101(1)] of the Treaty does not apply to an exclusive purchasing agreement entered into by a motor-fuels supplier which the retailer may terminate upon one year's notice at any time where all that supplier's exclusive purchasing agreements, whether considered separately or as a whole, taken together with the network of similar agreements made by the totality of suppliers, have an appreciable effect on the closing-off of the market but where the agreements of the same kind as the agreement at issue in the main proceedings by reason of their duration represent only a very small proportion of the totality of one supplier's exclusive purchasing agreements, of which the majority are fixed term contracts entered into for more than one year.

CoJ 7 December 2000 (Neste Markkinionti Oy v. Yötuuli Ky e.a., C-214/99) [2000] ECR I-11121, para. 39.

[A]n exclusive supply contract, such as that at issue in the main proceedings, is capable **15.15** of benefiting from a block exemption provided for in Regulation No 1984/83 if it complies with the maximum duration of 10 years referred to in Article 12(1)(c) of that regulation and if the supplier grants the service station operator, in return for exclusivity, substantial commercial advantages which contribute to an improvement in distribution, facilitate the establishment or modernisation of the service station and lower the distribution costs. It is for the referring court to assess whether those conditions are satisfied in the case in the main proceedings.

CoJ 11 September 2008 (CEPSA Estaciones de Servicio SA v. LV Tobar e Hijos SL, C-279/06) [2008] ECR I-6681, para. 62.

Article 12(2) of Regulation No 1984/83 must be interpreted as meaning that, for the **15.16** purposes of applying the exception which it laid down, that provision did not require the supplier to be the owner of the land on which he had built the service station which he let to the reseller.

CoJ 2 April 2009 (Pedro IV Servicios SL v. Total Espaæa SA, C-260/07) [2009] ECR I-2437, para. 60.

Article 5(a) of Regulation No 2790/1999 [currently Regulation No 330/2010] must be **15.17** interpreted as meaning that, for the purposes of applying the exception which it lays down, that provision requires that the supplier is the owner both of the service station which he lets to the reseller and of the land on which it is built, or, if he is not the owner, that he leases the land and service station from third parties not connected to the reseller.

CoJ 2 April 2009 (Pedro IV Servicios SL v. Total Espaæa SA, C-260/07) [2009] ECR I-2437, para. 69.

Article 5(a) of Regulation No 2790/1999 [currently Regulation No 330/2010] must be **15.18** interpreted as precluding, for the purposes of the implementation of the derogation set out therein, the duration of an exclusive rights agreement from exceeding the time limitations laid down in that regulation, when the owner of a plot of land has granted to a supplier a surface right for a period of 25 years and the latter is required to build a service station to be let to the owner of the land so that he can operate that service station for the same period as the duration of that right.

CoJ 3 September 2009 (Lubricantes y Carburantes Galaicos SL v. GALP Energía Espaæa SAU, C-506/07) [2009] ECR I-00134, para. 47.

ARTICLE 6 – NON-APPLICATION OF THIS REGULATION

Pursuant to Article 1a of Regulation No 19/65/EEC, the Commission may by regulation declare that, where parallel networks of similar vertical restraints cover more than 50 per cent of a relevant market, this Regulation shall not apply to vertical agreements containing specific restraints relating to that market.

ARTICLE 7 – APPLICATION OF THE MARKET SHARE THRESHOLD

For the purposes of applying the market share thresholds provided for in Article 3 the following rules shall apply:

(a) the market share of the supplier shall be calculated on the basis of market sales value data and the market share of the buyer shall be calculated on the basis of market purchase value data. If market sales value or market purchase value data are not available, estimates based on other reliable market information, including market sales and purchase volumes, may be used to establish the market share of the undertaking concerned:

(b) the market shares shall be calculated on the basis of data relating to the preceding calendar year:

(c) the market share of the supplier shall include any goods or services supplied to vertically integrated distributors for the purposes of sale:

(d) if a market share is initially not more than 30 per cent but subsequently rises above that level without exceeding 35 per cent, the exemption provided for in Article 2 shall continue to apply for a period of two consecutive calendar years following the year in which the 30 per cent market share threshold was first exceeded:

(e) if a market share is initially not more than 30 per cent but subsequently rises above 35 per cent, the exemption provided for in Article 2 shall continue to apply for one calendar year following the year in which the level of 35 per cent was first exceeded:

(f) the benefit of points (d) and (e) may not be combined so as to exceed a period of two calendar years:

(g) the market share held by the undertakings referred to in point (e) of the second subparagraph of Article 1(2) shall be apportioned equally to each undertaking having the rights or the powers listed in point (a) of the second subparagraph of Article 1(2).

ARTICLE 8 – APPLICATION OF THE TURNOVER THRESHOLD

1. For the purpose of calculating total annual turnover within the meaning of Article 2(2), the turnover achieved during the previous financial year by the relevant party to the vertical agreement and the turnover achieved by its connected undertakings in respect of all goods and services, excluding all taxes and other duties, shall be added together. For this purpose, no account shall be taken of dealings between the party to the vertical agreement and its connected undertakings or between its connected undertakings.

2. The exemption provided for in Article 2 shall remain applicable where, for any period of two consecutive financial years, the total annual turnover threshold is exceeded by no more than 10 per cent.

ARTICLE 9 – TRANSITIONAL PERIOD

The prohibition laid down in Article 101(1) of the Treaty shall not apply during the period from 1 June 2010 to 31 May 2011 in respect of agreements already in force on 31 May 2010 which do not satisfy the conditions for exemption provided for in this Regulation but which, on 31 May 2010, satisfied the conditions for exemption provided for in Regulation (EC) No 2790/1999.

[Conditions for the transitional period] [O]n a proper construction of Article [...] of **15.19** [the Block Exemption Regulation], once the transitional period provided for by Article [...] of that regulation has expired, the block exemption under that regulation did not apply to contracts satisfying the conditions for block exemption under [the former Block Exemption Regulation] which had as their object at least one of the hardcore restrictions listed in Article [...], with the result that all the contractual terms restrictive of competition contained in such contracts were liable to be caught by the prohibition laid down in Article [101(1) TFEU], if the conditions for exemption under Article [101(3) TFEU] were not satisfied.
CoJ 30 November 2006 (A. Brünsteiner GmbH, Autohaus Hilgert GmbH v. Bayerische Motorenwerke AG (BMW), Joined Cases C-376/05 and C-377/05) [2006] ECR I-11383, para. 51.

Eu égard à l'ensemble des considérations qui précèdent, il convient de répondre à la **15.20** seconde question que l'article 12, paragraphe 2, du règlement n° 2790/1999 doit être interprété en ce sens qu'un contrat en vigueur au 31 mai 2000 incluant une clause de non-concurrence et satisfaisant aux conditions d'exemption prévues par le règlement n° 1984/83, sans toutefois satisfaire à celles prévues par le règlement n° 2790/1999, est exempté de l'interdiction énoncée à l'article [101 TFUE] jusqu'au 31 décembre 2001.
CoJ 4 December 2014 (Estación de Servicio Pozuelo 4 SL, C-384/13), ECLI: EU:C:2014:2425, para. 48.

ARTICLE 10 – PERIOD OF VALIDITY

This Regulation shall enter into force on 1 June 2010.

It shall expire on 31 May 2022.

16

REGULATION (EU) NO 461/2010 ON VERTICAL AGREEMENTS IN THE MOTOR VEHICLES SECTOR*

COMMISSION REGULATION (EU) NO 461/2010 OF 27 MAY 2010 ON THE APPLICATION OF ARTICLE 101(3) OF THE TREATY ON THE FUNCTIONING OF THE EUROPEAN UNION TO CATEGORIES OF VERTICAL AGREEMENTS AND CONCERTED PRACTICES IN THE MOTOR VEHICLE SECTOR
(OJ 2010 L 129/52)

THE EUROPEAN COMMISSION,

Having regard to the Treaty on the Functioning of the European Union,

Having regard to Regulation No 19/65/EEC of the Council of 2 March 1965 on the application of Article 85(3) of the Treaty to certain categories of agreements and concerted practices,[1] and in particular Article 1 thereof,

Having published a draft of this Regulation,

After consulting the Advisory Committee on Restrictive Practices and Dominant Positions,

Whereas:

(1)   Regulation No 19/65/EEC empowers the Commission to apply Article 101(3) of the Treaty on the Functioning of the European Union[2] by regulation to certain categories of vertical agreements and corresponding concerted practices falling within Article 101(1) of the Treaty. Block exemption regulations apply to vertical agreements which fulfil certain conditions and may be general or sector-specific.

(2)   The Commission has defined a category of vertical agreements which it regards

---

*   This chapter was written by Edmon Oude Elferink.
1   OJ 36, 6.3.1965, p. 533/65.
2   With effect from 1 December 2009, Article 81 of the EC Treaty has become Article 101 of the Treaty on the Functioning of the European Union. The two Articles are, in substance, identical. For the purposes of this Regulation, references to Article 101 of the Treaty on the Functioning of the European Union should be understood as references to Article 81 of the EC Treaty where appropriate.

as normally satisfying the conditions laid down in Article 101(3) of the Treaty and to this end has adopted Commission Regulation (EU) No 330/2010 of 20 April 2010 on the application of Article 101(3) of the Treaty on the Functioning of the European Union to categories of vertical agreements and concerted practices,[3] which replaces Commission Regulation (EC) No 2790/1999.[4]

(3) The motor vehicle sector, which includes both passenger cars and commercial vehicles, has been subject to specific block exemption regulations since 1985, the most recent being Commission Regulation (EC) No 1400/2002 of 31 July 2002 on the application of Article 81(3) of the Treaty to categories of vertical agreements and concerted practices in the motor vehicle sector.[5] Regulation (EC) No 2790/1999 expressly stated that it did not apply to vertical agreements the subject matter of which fell within the scope of any other block exemption regulation. The motor vehicle sector therefore fell outside the scope of that Regulation.

(4) Regulation (EC) No 1400/2002 expires on 31 May 2010. However, the motor vehicle sector should continue to benefit from a block exemption in order to simplify administration and reduce compliance costs for the undertakings concerned, while ensuring effective supervision of markets in accordance with Article 103(2)(b) of the Treaty.

(5) Experience acquired since 2002 regarding the distribution of new motor vehicles, the distribution of spare parts and the provision of repair and maintenance services for motor vehicles, makes it possible to define a category of vertical agreements in the motor vehicle sector which can be regarded as normally satisfying the conditions laid down in Article 101(3) of the Treaty.

(6) This category includes vertical agreements for the purchase, sale or resale of new motor vehicles, vertical agreements for the purchase, sale or resale of spare parts for motor vehicles and vertical agreements for the provision of repair and maintenance services for such vehicles, where those agreements are concluded between non-competing undertakings, between certain competitors, or by certain associations of retailers or repairers. It also includes vertical agreements containing ancillary provisions on the assignment or use of intellectual property rights. The term 'vertical agreements' should be defined accordingly to include both such agreements and the corresponding concerted practices.

(7) Certain types of vertical agreements can improve economic efficiency within a chain of production or distribution by facilitating better coordination between the participating undertakings. In particular, they can lead to a reduction in the transaction and distribution costs of the parties and to an optimisation of their sales and investment levels.

(8) The likelihood that such efficiency-enhancing effects will outweigh any anti-competitive effects due to restrictions contained in vertical agreements depends on the degree of market power of the parties to the agreement and, therefore, on the extent to which those undertakings face competition from other suppliers of goods or services regarded by their customers as interchangeable or substitutable

---

3   OJ L 102, 23.4.2010, p. 1.
4   OJ L 336, 29.12.1999, p. 21.
5   OJ L 203, 1.8.2002, p. 30.

for one another, by reason of the products' characteristics, their prices and their intended use. Vertical agreements containing restrictions which are likely to restrict competition and harm consumers, or which are not indispensable to the attainment of the efficiency-enhancing effects, should be excluded from the benefit of the block exemption.

(9)   In order to define the appropriate scope of a block exemption regulation, the Commission must take into account the competitive conditions in the relevant sector. In this respect, the conclusions of the in-depth monitoring of the motor vehicle sector set out in the Evaluation Report on the operation of Commission Regulation (EC) No 1400/2002 of 28 May 2008[6] and in the Commission Communication on The Future Competition Law Framework applicable to the Motor Vehicle sector of 22 July 2009[7] have shown that a distinction should be drawn between agreements for the distribution of new motor vehicles and agreements for the provision of repair and maintenance services and distribution of spare parts.

(10)   As regards the distribution of new motor vehicles, there do not appear to be any significant competition shortcomings which would distinguish this sector from other economic sectors and which could require the application of rules different from and stricter than those set out in Regulation (EU) No 330/2010. The market-share threshold, the non-exemption of certain vertical agreements and the other conditions laid down in that Regulation normally ensure that vertical agreements for the distribution of new motor vehicles comply with the require-ments of Article 101(3) of the Treaty. Therefore, such agreements should benefit from the exemption granted by Regulation (EU) No 330/2010, subject to all the conditions laid down therein.

(11)   As regards agreements for the distribution of spare parts and for the provision of repair and maintenance services, certain specific characteristics of the motor vehicle aftermarket should be taken into account. In particular, the experience acquired by the Commission in applying Regulation (EC) No 1400/2002 shows that price increases for individual repair jobs are only partially reflected in increased reliability of modern cars and lengthening of service intervals. These latter trends are linked to technological evolution and to the increasing complex-ity and reliability of automotive components that the vehicle manufacturers purchase from original equipment suppliers. Such suppliers sell their products as spare parts in the aftermarket both through the vehicle manufacturers' authorised repair networks and through independent channels, thereby representing an important competitive force in the motor vehicle aftermarket. The costs borne on average by consumers in the Union for motor vehicle repair and maintenance services represent a very high proportion of total consumer expenditure on motor vehicles.

(12)   Competitive conditions in the motor vehicle aftermarket also have a direct bearing on public safety, in that vehicles may be driven in an unsafe manner if

6   SEC (2008) 1946.
7   COM (2009) 388.

they have been repaired incorrectly, as well as on public health and the environment, as emissions of carbon dioxide and other air pollutants may be higher from vehicles which have not undergone regular maintenance work.

(13) In so far as a separate aftermarket can be defined, effective competition on the markets for the purchase and sale of spare parts, as well as for the provision of repair and maintenance services for motor vehicles, depends on the degree of competitive interaction between authorised repairers, that is to say those operating within repair networks established directly or indirectly by vehicle manufacturers, as well as between authorised and independent operators, including independent spare parts suppliers and repairers. The latter's ability to compete depends on unrestricted access to essential inputs such as spare parts and technical information.

(14) Having regard to those specificities, the rules in Regulation (EU) No 330/2010, including the uniform market share threshold of 30 per cent, are necessary but are not sufficient to ensure that the benefit of the block exemption is reserved only to those vertical agreements for the distribution of spare parts and for the provision of repair and maintenance services for which it can be assumed with sufficient certainty that the conditions of Article 101(3) of the Treaty are satisfied.

(15) Therefore, vertical agreements for the distribution of spare parts and for the provision of repair and maintenance services should benefit from the block exemption only if, in addition to the conditions for exemption set out in Regulation (EU) No 330/2010, they comply with stricter requirements concerning certain types of severe restrictions of competition that may limit the supply and use of spare parts in the motor vehicle aftermarket.

(16) In particular, the benefit of the block exemption should not be granted to agreements that restrict the sale of spare parts by members of the selective distribution system of a vehicle manufacturer to independent repairers, which use them for the provision of repair or maintenance services. Without access to such spare parts, independent repairers would not be able to compete effectively with authorised repairers, since they could not provide consumers with good quality services which contribute to the safe and reliable functioning of motor vehicles.

(17) Moreover, in order to ensure effective competition on the repair and maintenance markets and to allow repairers to offer end users competing spare parts, the block exemption should not cover vertical agreements which, although they comply with Regulation (EU) No 330/2010, none the less restrict the ability of a producer of spare parts to sell such parts to authorised repairers within the distribution system of a vehicle manufacturer, independent distributors of spare parts, independent repairers or end users. This does not affect the liability of producers of spare parts under civil law, or the ability of vehicle manufacturers to require the authorized repairers within their distribution system to only use spare parts that match the quality of the components used for the assembly of a certain motor vehicle. Moreover, in view of the vehicle manufacturers' direct contractual involvement in repairs under warranty, free servicing, and recall operations, agreements containing obligations on authorised repairers to use only spare parts supplied by the vehicle manufacturer for those repairs should be covered by the exemption.

(18) Finally, in order to allow authorised and independent repairers and end users to

identify the manufacturer of motor vehicle components or of spare parts and to choose between alternative parts, the block exemption should not cover agreements by which a manufacturer of motor vehicles limits the ability of a manufacturer of components or original spare parts to place its trade mark or logo on those parts effectively and in a visible manner.

(19) In order to allow all operators time to adapt to this Regulation, it is appropriate to extend the period of application of the provisions of Regulation (EC) No 1400/2002 relating to vertical agreements for the purchase, sale and resale of new motor vehicles until 31 May 2013. As regards vertical agreements for the distribution of spare parts and for the provision of repair and maintenance services, this Regulation should apply from 1 June 2010 so as to continue to ensure adequate protection of competition on the motor vehicle aftermarkets.

(20) The Commission will, on a continuous basis, monitor developments in the motor vehicle sector and will take appropriate remedial action if competition shortcomings arise which may lead to consumer harm on the market for the distribution of new motor vehicles or the supply of spare parts or after-sales services for motor vehicles.

(21) The Commission may withdraw the benefit of this Regulation, pursuant to Article 29(1) of Council Regulation (EC) No 1/2003 of 16 December 2002 on the implementation of the rules on competition laid down in Articles 81 and 82 of the Treaty,[8] where it finds in a particular case that an agreement to which the exemption provided for in this Regulation applies nevertheless has effects which are incompatible with Article 101(3) of the Treaty.

(22) The competition authority of a Member State may withdraw the benefit of this Regulation pursuant to Article 29(2) of Regulation (EC) No 1/2003 in respect of the territory of that Member State, or a part thereof where, in a particular case, an agreement to which the exemption provided for in this Regulation applies nevertheless has effects which are incompatible with Article 101(3) of the Treaty in the territory of that Member State, or in a part thereof, and where such territory has all the characteristics of a distinct geographic market.

(23) In determining whether the benefit of this Regulation should be withdrawn pursuant to Article 29 of Regulation (EC) No 1/2003, the anti-competitive effects that may derive from the existence of parallel networks of vertical agreements that have similar effects which significantly restrict access to a relevant market or competition therein are of particular importance. Such cumulative effects may, for example, arise in the case of selective distribution or non-compete obligations.

(24) In order to strengthen supervision of parallel networks of vertical agreements which have similar anti-competitive effects and which cover more than 50 per cent of a given market, the Commission may by regulation declare this Regulation inapplicable to vertical agreements containing specific restraints relating to the market concerned, thereby restoring the full application of Article 101 of the Treaty to such agreements.

(25) In order to assess the effects of this Regulation on competition in motor vehicle retailing, in the supply of spare parts and in after sales servicing for motor vehicles

---

8   OJ L 1, 4.1.2003, p. 1.

in the internal market, it is appropriate to draw up an evaluation report on the operation of this Regulation,

HAS ADOPTED THIS REGULATION:

CHAPTER I

COMMON PROVISIONS

ARTICLE 1 – DEFINITIONS

1. For the purposes of this Regulation, the following definitions shall apply:

    (a) 'vertical agreement' means an agreement or concerted practice entered into between two or more undertakings each of which operates, for the purposes of the agreement or the concerted practice, at a different level of the production or distribution chain, and relating to the conditions under which the parties may purchase, sell or resell certain goods or services;

    (b) 'vertical restraint' means a restriction of competition in a vertical agreement falling within the scope of Article 101(1) of the Treaty;

    (c) 'authorised repairer' means a provider of repair and maintenance services for motor vehicles operating within the distribution system set up by a supplier of motor vehicles;

    (d) 'authorised distributor' means a distributor of spare parts for motor vehicles operating within the distribution system set up by a supplier of motor vehicles;

    (e) 'independent repairer' means:

        (i) a provider of repair and maintenance services for motor vehicles not operating within the distribution system set up by the supplier of the motor vehicles for which it provides repair or maintenance;

        (ii) an authorised repairer within the distribution system of a given supplier, to the extent that it provides repair or maintenance services for motor vehicles in respect of which it is not a member of the respective supplier's distribution system;

    (f) 'independent distributor' means:

        (i) a distributor of spare parts for motor vehicles not operating within the distribution system set up by the supplier of the motor vehicles for which it distributes spare parts;

        (ii) an authorised distributor within the distribution system of a given supplier, to the extent that it distributes spare parts for motor vehicles in respect of which it is not a member of the respective supplier's distribution system;

    (g) 'motor vehicle' means a self-propelled vehicle intended for use on public roads and having three or more road wheels;

(h)   'spare parts' means goods which are to be installed in or upon a motor vehicle so as to replace components of that vehicle, including goods such as lubricants which are necessary for the use of a motor vehicle, with the exception of fuel;

(i)   'selective distribution system' means a distribution system where the supplier undertakes to sell the contract goods or services, either directly or indirectly, only to distributors selected on the basis of specified criteria and where these distributors undertake not to sell such goods or services to unauthorised distributors within the territory reserved by the supplier to operate that system. For the purposes of this Regulation, the terms 'undertaking', 'supplier', 'manufacturer' and 'buyer' shall include their respective connected undertakings.

'Connected undertakings' means:

(a)   undertakings in which a party to the agreement, directly or indirectly:

(i)   has the power to exercise more than half the voting rights; or

(ii)   has the power to appoint more than half the members of the supervisory board, board of management or bodies legally representing the undertaking; or

(iii)   has the right to manage the undertaking's affairs;

(b)   undertakings which directly or indirectly have, over a party to the agreement, the rights or powers listed in point (a);

(c)   undertakings in which an undertaking referred to in point (b) has, directly or indirectly, the rights or powers listed in point (a);

(d)   undertakings in which a party to the agreement together with one or more of the undertakings referred to in points (a), (b) or (c), or in which two or more of the latter undertakings, jointly have the rights or powers listed in point (a);

(e)   undertakings in which the rights or the powers listed in point (a) are jointly held by:

(i)   parties to the agreement or their respective connected undertakings referred to in points (a) to (d); or

(ii)   one or more of the parties to the agreement or one or more of their connected undertakings referred to in points (a) to (d) and one or more third parties.

16.01   The term 'specified criteria', referred to in Article 1(1)(f) of Commission Regulation (EC) No 1400/2002 of 31 July 2002 on the application of Article [101(3) TFEU] to categories of vertical agreements and concerted practices in the motor vehicle sector [now Regulation (EU) No 461/2010 in conjunction with Regulation (EU) No 330/ 2010], means, with respect to a quantitative selective distribution system within the meaning of that regulation, criteria the precise content of which may be verified. In

order to benefit from the exemption provided for by that regulation, it is not necessary for such a system to be based on criteria that are objectively justified and applied in a uniform and non-differentiated manner in respect of all applicants for authorisation.
CoJ 14 June 2012 (Auto 24 SARL v. Jaguar Land Rover France SAS, C-158/11), ECLI:EU:C:2012:351, para. 39.

CHAPTER II

VERTICAL AGREEMENTS RELATING TO THE PURCHASE, SALE OR RESALE OF NEW MOTOR VEHICLES

ARTICLE 2 – APPLICATION OF REGULATION (EC) NO 1400/2002

Pursuant to Article 101(3) of the Treaty, from 1 June 2010 until 31 May 2013, Article 101(1) of the Treaty shall not apply to vertical agreements relating to the conditions under which the parties may purchase, sell or resell new motor vehicles, which fulfil the requirements for an exemption under Regulation (EC) No 1400/2002 that relate specifically to vertical agreements for the purchase, sale or resale of new motor vehicles.

See Regulation (EC) No 1400/2002 (OJ 2002 L 203/30) and Explanatory Brochure for Regulation (EC) No 1400/2002 (together with the relevant case law).

Cases and references relating to conditions for exemption under Regulation (EC) No 1400/2002:

- *Termination for reorganisation*
  - o *CoJ 7 September 2006 (VW–Audi Forhandlerforeningen, acting on behalf of Vulcan Silkeborg A/S/ Skandinavisk Motor Co. A/S v. Skandinavisk Motor Co. A/S, C-125/05) [2006] ECR I-7637.*
  - o *CoJ 30 November 2006 (A. Brünsteiner GmbH, Autohaus Hilgert GmbH/Bayerische Motorenwerke AG (BMW), Joined Cases C-376/05 and C-377/05) [2006] ECR I-11383.*
  - o *Order CoJ 26 January 2007 (Auto Peter Petschenig GmbH v. Toyota Frey Austria GmbH, C-273/06) [2007] ECR I-14.*
- *Termination with immediate effect*
  - o *CoJ 18 January 2007 (City Motors Groep NV v. Citroën Benelux NV, C-421/05) [2007] ECR I-653.*
- *Intermediaries*
  - o *General Court 12 July 1991 (Automobiles Peugeot SA and Peugeot SA v. Commission, T-23/90) [1991] ECR II-653.*
  - o *Order General Court 22 April 1993 (Automobiles Peugeot SA and Peugeot SA v. Commission, T-9/92) [1993] ECR II-493.*
  - o *CoJ 16 June 1994 (Automobiles Peugeot SA and Peugeot SA v. Commission, C-322/93P) [1994] ECR I-2727.*

- *Access to technical information*
  - o *See also Regulations 715/2007 (OJ 2007 L 171/1), 692/2008 (OJ 2008 L 199/1) and 595/2009 (OJ 2009 L 188/1).*
- *Leasing restrictions*
  - o *CoJ 24 October 1995 (Bundeskartellamt v. Volkswagen and VAG Leasing, C-226/93) [1995] ECR I-3477.*
- *Multi-branding and sales targets*
  - o *CoJ 30 April 1998 (Cabour and others v. Arnor, C-230/96) [1998] ECR I-2055.*

ARTICLE 3 – APPLICATION OF REGULATION (EU) NO 330/2010

With effect from 1 June 2013, Regulation (EU) No 330/2010 shall apply to vertical agreements relating to the purchase, sale or resale of new motor vehicles.

See Chapter 15 on Regulation (EU) No 330/2010 and the Commission Notice – Guidelines on Vertical Restraints (OJ 2010 C 130/1).

CHAPTER III

VERTICAL AGREEMENTS RELATING TO THE MOTOR VEHICLE AFTERMARKET

ARTICLE 4 – EXEMPTION

Pursuant to Article 101(3) of the Treaty and subject to the provisions of this Regulation Article 101(1) of the Treaty shall not apply to vertical agreements relating to the conditions under which the parties may purchase, sell or resell spare parts for motor vehicles or provide repair and maintenance services for motor vehicles, which fulfil the requirements for an exemption under Regulation (EU) No 330/2010 and do not contain any of the hardcore clauses listed in Article 5 of this Regulation.

This exemption shall apply to the extent that such agreements contain vertical restraints.

[…] Commission Regulation No 123/85 [now Regulation (EU) No 461/2010 in **16.02** conjunction with Regulation (EU) No 330/2010] […] does not lay down any mandatory provisions directly affecting the validity or the content of contractual provisions or oblige the contracting parties to adapt the contents of their agreement but merely lays down conditions which, if they are satisfied, exclude certain contractual provisions from the prohibition and consequently from the automatic nullity provided for in Article [101(1) and (2) TFEU] and […] it is for the national court, in the event that certain contractual provisions are void, to determine the consequences thereof in accordance with relevant national law.

CoJ 18 December 1986 (VAG France SA v. Établissements Magne SA, C-10/86) [1986] ECR 4071, para. 16.

Regulation No 123/85 [now Regulation No 461/2010 in conjunction with Regulation **16.03** 330/2010] […] is limited to providing economic agents in the motor-vehicle industry with certain possibilities enabling them to remove their distribution and servicing agreements from the scope of the prohibition contained in Article [101(1) TFEU] despite the inclusion in those agreements of certain types of exclusivity and no-competition clauses.

It follows that, […], it cannot be said, in general terms, that motor-vehicle distribution has been exempted from the application of Article [101(1)]

Order of the President of the General Court 21 May 1990 (Automobiles Peugeot SA and Peugeot SA v. Commission, T-23/90 R) [1990] ECR II-00195, paras 20 and 21.

16.04   Article [101(1)] prohibits certain anti-competitive agreements or practices. Among the consequences which an infringement of that prohibition may have in civil law, only one is expressly provided for in Article [101(2) TFEU], namely the nullity of the agreement. The other consequences attaching to an infringement of Article [101] of the Treaty, such as the obligation to make good the damage caused to a third party or a possible obligation to enter into a contract [...] are to be determined under national law. Consequently, it is the national courts which, where appropriate, may, in accordance with the rules of national law, order one trader to enter into a contract with another.

     As freedom of contract must remain the rule, the Commission cannot in principle be considered to have, among the powers to issue orders which are available to it for the purpose of bringing to an end infringements of Article [101(1)], the power to order a party to enter into contractual relations, since in general the Commission has suitable remedies at its disposal for the purpose of requiring an undertaking to terminate an infringement.

     In particular, there cannot be held to be any justification for such a restriction on freedom of contract where several remedies exist for bringing an infringement to an end. This is true of infringements of Article [101(1)] arising out of the application of a distribution system. Such infringements can also be eliminated by the abandonment or amendment of the distribution system. Consequently, the Commission undoubtedly has the power to find that an infringement exists and to order the parties concerned to bring it to an end, but it is not for the Commission to impose upon the parties its own choice from among all the various potential courses of action which are in conformity with the Treaty.

General Court 18 September 1992 (Automec v. Commission, T-24/90) [1992] ECR II-2223, paras 50–52.

16.05   Regulation No 123/85 85 [now Regulation No 461/2010 in conjunction with Regulation 330/2010], in accordance with the function thus assigned to it in relation to the application of Article [101] of the Treaty, concerns only contractual relations between suppliers and their approved distributors and specifies the conditions under which certain agreements between them are lawful having regard to the competition rules of the Treaty.

     It is thus concerned only with the content of agreements which parties tied to a distribution network for a specified product may lawfully conclude having regard to the rules of the Treaty prohibiting restrictions affecting normal competition within the common market.

     Since, therefore, it confines itself to stating what the parties to such agreements may or may not undertake to do in relations with third parties, that regulation does not, in contrast, serve to regulate the activities of such third parties, who may operate in the market outside the framework of distribution agreements. [...]

     Regulation No 123/85 [now Regulation No 461/2010 in conjunction with Regulation 330/2010] must be interpreted as not preventing a trader who is neither an approved reseller in the distribution network of a manufacturer of a particular make of motor vehicle nor an authorized intermediary within the meaning of [...] that regulation from undertaking parallel imports and operating as an independent reseller of new vehicles of that make. Nor does that regulation prevent an independent trader from carrying on at the same time the business of authorized intermediary and that of non-approved reseller of vehicles acquired by way of parallel imports.

CoJ 15 February 1996 (Nissan v. Dupasquier, C-309/94) [1996] ECR I-677, paras 16–18 and 23.

[T]he imperviousness of a selective distribution system is not a condition for its validity **16.06** under Community law. [I]n order to appraise the lawfulness of an agreement under Article [101] of the Treaty, it is not necessary to enquire whether the conditions are fulfilled for that agreement to be capable of being enforced against third parties by means of an action for unfair competition [...].

It follows that a selective distribution system which is not impervious and cannot therefore, under national case-law on unfair competition, be enforced against third parties may be valid under Article [101] of the Treaty.

[N]either Article [101(3)] of the Treaty nor Regulation No 123/85 [now Regulation No 461/2010 in conjunction with Regulation 330/2010] is to be interpreted as precluding the application of national case-law on unfair competition under which a selective distribution system, even if enjoying exemption under those provisions, is not enforceable against third parties unless it is impervious

CoJ 5 June 1997 (VAG–Händlerbeirat eV v. SYD Consult, C-41/96) [1997] ECR I-3123, paras 12, 13 and 19.

[T]he prohibition set out in Article [101(1)] of the Treaty applies to clauses in a motor **16.07** vehicle dealership contract which are not covered by the block exemption if, having regard to the economic and legal context, their object or effect is perceptibly to restrict competition within the common market and they are capable of affecting trade between Member States.

CoJ 30 April 1998 (Cabour and others v. Arnor, C-230/96) [1998] ECR I-2055, para. 52.

The old regulation [No 123/85, now Regulation No 461/2010 in conjunction with **16.08** Regulation 330/2010] does not lay down mandatory provisions directly affecting the validity of the clauses of a contract or obliging the parties to adapt their terms or likewise have the effect of rendering a contract void where all the conditions laid down in the old regulation are not satisfied [...].

In such a situation, the contract in question will be caught by the prohibition laid down in Article [101(1)] only if its object or effect is perceptibly to restrict competition within the common market and it is capable of appreciably affecting trade between Member States.

General Court 21 January 1999 (Riviera Auto Service v. Commission, T-185/96, T-189/96 and T-190/96) [1999] ECR II-93, paras 30 and 31.

See also the Commission notice – supplementary guidelines on vertical restraints in agreements for the sale and repair of motor vehicles and for the distribution of spare parts for motor vehicles (OJ 2010 C 138/16).

ARTICLE 5 – RESTRICTIONS THAT REMOVE THE BENEFIT OF THE BLOCK EXEMPTION – HARDCORE RESTRICTIONS

The exemption provided for in Article 4 shall not apply to vertical agreements which, directly or indirectly, in isolation or in combination with other factors under the control of the parties, have as their object:

(a)　the restriction of the sales of spare parts for motor vehicles by members of a selective distribution system to independent repairers which use those parts for the repair and maintenance of a motor vehicle;

(b)　the restriction, agreed between a supplier of spare parts, repair tools or diagnostic or other equipment and a manufacturer of motor vehicles, of the supplier's ability to sell those goods to authorised or independent distributors or to authorised or independent repairers or end users;

(c)　the restriction, agreed between a manufacturer of motor vehicles which uses components for the initial assembly of motor vehicles and the supplier of such components, of the supplier's ability to place its trade mark or logo effectively and in an easily visible manner on the components supplied or on spare parts.

See also the supplementary guidelines on vertical restraints in agreements for the sale and repair of motor vehicles and for the distribution of spare parts for motor vehicles (OJ 2010 C 138/16).

16.09　The right of a proprietor of a protected design to prevent third parties from manufacturing and selling or importing, without his consent, products incorporating the design constitutes the very subject-matter of his exclusive right. It follows that an obligation imposed upon the proprietor of a protected design to grant to third parties, even in return for a reasonable royalty, a licence for the supply of products incorporating the design would lead to the proprietor thereof being deprived of the substance of his exclusive right, and that a refusal to grant such a licence cannot in itself constitute an abuse of a dominant position.

[T]he exercise of such an exclusive right by the proprietor of a registered design in respect of car body panels may be prohibited by Article [102 TFEU] if it involves, on the part of an undertaking holding a dominant position, certain abusive conduct such as the arbitrary refusal to supply spare parts to independent repairers, the fixing of prices for spare parts at an unfair level or a decision no longer to produce spare parts for a particular model even though many cars of that model are still in circulation, provided that such conduct is liable to affect trade between Member States.

CoJ 5 October 1988 (Volvo v. Veng, 238/87) [1988] ECR 6211, paras 8 and 9.

CHAPTER IV

FINAL PROVISIONS

ARTICLE 6 – NON-APPLICATION OF THIS REGULATION

Pursuant to Article 1a of Regulation No 19/65/EEC, the Commission may by regulation declare that, where parallel networks of similar vertical restraints cover more than 50% of a relevant market, this Regulation shall not apply to vertical agreements containing specific restraints relating to that market.

ARTICLE 7 – MONITORING AND EVALUATION REPORT

The Commission will monitor the operation of this Regulation and draw up a report on its operation by 31 May 2021 at the latest, having regard in particular to the conditions set out in Article 101(3) of the Treaty.

ARTICLE 8 – PERIOD OF VALIDITY

This Regulation shall enter into force on 1 June 2010.

It shall expire on 31 May 2023.

17

REGULATION (EU) NO 1308/2013 ESTABLISHING A COMMON ORGANISATION OF THE MARKETS IN AGRICULTURAL PRODUCTS AND REPEALING COUNCIL REGULATIONS*

REGULATION (EU) No 1308/2013 OF THE EUROPEAN PARLIA-MENT AND OF THE COUNCIL OF 17 DECEMBER 2013 ESTAB-LISHING A COMMON ORGANISATION OF THE MARKETS IN AGRICULTURAL PRODUCTS AND REPEALING COUNCIL REGULATIONS (EEC) NO 922/72, (EEC) NO 234/79, (EC) NO 1037/2001 AND (EC) NO 1234/2007 (OJ L 347, 20.12.2013, P. 671)

THE EUROPEAN PARLIAMENT AND THE COUNCIL OF THE EUROPEAN UNION,

Having regard to the Treaty on the Functioning of the European Union, and in particular the first subparagraph of Article 42 and Article 43(2) thereof,

Having regard to the proposal from the European Commission,

After transmission of the draft legislative act to the national parliaments,

Having regard to the opinion of the Court of Auditors,

Having regard to the opinions of the European Economic and Social Commit-tee,

Having regard to the opinion of the Committee of the Regions,

Acting in accordance with the ordinary legislative procedure,

Whereas: [...]

(171) In accordance with Article 42 TFEU, the provisions of the TFEU concerning competition apply to the production of and trade in agricultural products only to the extent determined by Union legislation within the

---

* This chapter was written by Greetje van Heezik.

framework of Article 43(2) TFEU and in accordance with the procedure laid down therein.

(172) In view of the specific characteristics of the agricultural sector and its reliance on the good functioning of the entire food supply chain, including the effective application of competition rules in all related sectors throughout the whole food chain, which can be highly concentrated, special attention should be paid to the application of the competition rules laid down in Article 42 TFEU. To that end, there is a need for close cooperation between the Commission and the competition authorities of Member States. Moreover, guidelines adopted, where appropriate, by the Commission are a suitable instrument to provide guidance to undertakings and other stakeholders concerned.

(173) It should be provided that the rules on competition relating to the agreements, decisions and practices referred to in Article 101 TFEU and to abuse of a dominant position apply to the production of, and the trade in, agricultural products, provided that their application does not jeopardise the attainment of the objectives of the CAP.

(174) A special approach should be allowed in the case of farmers' or producer organisations or their associations, the objective of which is the joint production or marketing of agricultural products or the use of joint facilities, unless such joint action excludes competition or jeopardises the attainment of the objectives of Article 39 TFEU.

(175) Without prejudice to the regulation of supply for certain products, such as cheese and ham benefitting from a protected designation of origin or a protected geographic indication, or wine, which is governed by a specific set of rules, a special approach should be taken as regards certain activities of interbranch organisations on the condition that they do not lead to the partitioning of markets, affect the sound operation of the CMO, distort or eliminate competition, entail the fixing of prices or quotas, or create discrimination. [...]

(191) In order to respond to periods of severe market imbalance, specific categories of collective actions by private operators may be appropriate, as exceptional measures, in order to stabilise the sectors concerned, subject to precise safeguards, limits and conditions. Where such actions could fall under the scope of Article 101(1) TFEU, the Commission should be able to provide a derogation for a limited period. These actions should however complement Union action in the framework of public intervention and private storage or exceptional measures envisaged by this Regulation, and should not impair the functioning of the internal market.

ARTICLE 206

COMMISSION GUIDELINES ON THE APPLICATION OF COMPETITION RULES TO AGRICULTURE

Save as otherwise provided in this Regulation, and in accordance with Article 42 TFEU, Articles 101 to 106 TFEU and the implementing provisions thereto shall, subject to Articles 207 to 210 of this Regulation, apply to all agreements, decisions and practices referred to in Article 101(1) and Article 102 TFEU which relate to the production of, or trade in, agricultural products.

In order to ensure the functioning of the internal market and the uniform application of Union competition rules, the Commission and the competition authorities of the Member States shall apply the Union competition rules in close cooperation.

In addition, the Commission shall, where appropriate, publish guidelines to assist the national competition authorities, as well as undertakings.

ARTICLE 1 REGULATION NO 1184/2006[1]

This Regulation lays down rules concerning the applicability of Articles 101 to 106 and of Article 108(1) and (3) of the Treaty on the functioning of the European Union (TFEU) in relation to production of, or trade in, the products listed in Annex I to the TFEU with the exception of the products covered by Council Regulation (EC) No 1234/20074 and Regulation (EU) No 1379/2013 of the European Parliament and of the Council.

ARTICLE 1A REGULATION NO 1184/2006

Articles 81 to 86 of the Treaty and provisions made for their implementation shall, subject to Article 2 of this Regulation, apply to all agreements, decisions and practices referred to in Articles 81(1) and 82 of the Treaty which relate to the production of, or trade in, the products referred to in Article 1.

---

1   Council Regulation (EC) No 1184/2006 of 24 July 2006 applying certain rules of competition to the production of, and trade in, agricultural products (OJ L 214, 4.8.2006, p. 7)

OVERVIEW

A. SCOPE OF REGULATION NO 1184/2006 VS. REGULATION NO 1308/2013 AND REGULATION NO 1379/2013	17.01	B. SCOPE OF ARTICLES 206 AND 209 17.03 1. General 17.03 2. Article 1A Regulation No 1184/2006 17.04

A. SCOPE OF REGULATION NO 1184/2006 VS. REGULATION NO 1308/2013 AND REGULATION NO 1379/2013

See Regulation (EU) No 1379/2013 of the European Parliament and of the Council of 11 December 2013 on the common organisation of the markets in fishery and aquaculture products, amending Council Regulations (EC) No 1184/2006 and (EC) No 1224/2009 and repealing Council Regulation (EC) No 104/2000, recital 25: 'It is appropriate to lay down competition rules applicable to the production and marketing of fishery and aquaculture products, taking into account the specific characteristics of the fishery and aquaculture sector, including fragmentation of the sector, the fact that fish are a shared resource and the large extent of imports, which should be subject to the same rules as Union fishery and aquaculture products. In the interests of simplification, the relevant provisions of Council Regulation No 1184/ 2006 should be incorporated into this Regulation. Regulation (EC) No 1184/2006 should, therefore, no longer be applicable to fishery and aquaculture products.'

[I]n applying the rules of competition law the national competition authorities have to observe the value [of] judgments and requirements of Community agricultural law. Where Community competition law is applied (Articles [101 and 102 TFEU]), agricultural policy takes precedence over the competition law chapter of the [TFEU under Article [39](2)], read in conjunction with Article [43](1) TFEU]. If, conversely, national competition law is applied, the principle of the primacy of Community law will result in the considerations underlying the common agricultural policy taking priority. **17.01**

Accordingly, if it were to be inferred from the agricultural law of the Community that private storage is always permissible without further conditions, at any rate to avert serious disturbance of the market, such a requirement would also have to be taken into consideration in the context of the application of the competition rules by the competition authorities. [...]

If a national competition authority were to refuse to apply the relevant provisions of competition law to a privately agreed and financed scheme for the storage of olive oil, or to apply them only in diluted form, there would be a risk that the common Agricultural policy would be jeopardised. Under Regulation No [1184/2006, and Articles 206 and 209 of Regulation No 1308/2013], an essential part of that policy is the application of the rules on competition to the production of agricultural products and trade in them. Not least, that is a specific expression of the aim of the common agricultural policy to ensure that supplies reach consumers at reasonable prices (Article [39](1)(e) TFEU).

Opinion AG Kokott 12 February 2009 (Compañía Española de Comercialización de Aceite SA, C-505/07) [2009] ECR I-08963, paras 96, 97 and 100.

See also CoJ 26 June 1979 (Pigs and Bacon Commission v. Redmond, 177/78) [1979] ECR 2161, para. 11.

17.02   On the basis that the objectives pursued by the CAP are not necessarily the same as those intended to be promoted by competition policy, and that there may therefore be a tension in the implementation of those policies, Article 42 TFEU, the wording of which essentially corresponds to Article 36 of the EC Treaty, although establishing the precedence of the CAP over the competition objectives set out in the Treaty, lays down a general rule for reconciling the two. […]

It is therefore in fact for the Council of the European Union to define whether and how far the EU competition rules apply to the agriculture sector, although that application must not compromise the attainment of the objectives of the CAP. […]

It therefore follows from Article 42 TFEU, which lays down both the precedence of the CAP over competition policy and, at the same time, the possibility for the Council to decide to what extent the rules on competition must be applied in the agricultural sector, that certain behaviour of players in the agricultural markets may automatically escape the competition rules and in particular those on anticompetitive agreements. That exclusion must, however, be strictly circumscribed, since that is required by the secondary legislation to which the primary law refers. In the end, therefore, it is all about finding a balance between pursuit of the objectives of the CAP and the need to maintain effective competition on agricultural markets.

Opinion AG Wahl 6 April 2017 (APVE e.o., C-671/15), ECLI:EU:C:2017:281, paras 35, 37 and 43.

B. SCOPE OF ARTICLES 206 AND 209

1.   General

17.03   [T]he scope of [the Articles 206 and 209 of Regulation No 1308/ 2013] and of [Regulation No 1184/2006], applying certain rules of competition to production of and trade in agricultural products was restricted by Article 1 thereof to the production of and trade in the products listed in annex [I] to the Treaty. That Regulation may not therefore be applied to the manufacture of a product which does not come under annex [I] even if it is a substance ancillary to the production of another product which itself comes under that annex. In order for the regulation to be applicable to rennet that product must therefore itself come under annex II to the Treaty.

CoJ 25 March 1981 (Coöperatieve Stremsel-en Kleurselfabriek, 61/80) [1981] ECR 851, para. 21.

See also the Commission Notice – Guidelines on the application of the specific rules set out in Articles 169, 170 and 171 of the CMO Regulation for the olive oil, beef and veal and arable crops sectors (OJ 2015 C 431/01), paras 13, 14 and 18.

See also CoJ 30 January 1985 (BNIC v. Clair, 123/83) [1985] ECR 391, para. 15; General Court 2 July 1992 (Dansk Pelsdyravlerforening, T-61/89) [1992] ECR II-1931, paras 36 and 37; CoJ 15 December 1994 (Gottrup-Klim and others v.DLG, C-250/92) [1994] ECR I-5641.

See also the publication of DG COMP 'An overview of European competition rules applying in the agricultural sector' (June 2016, published on the website of DG Comp).

2.   Article 1A Regulation No 1184/2006

It thus follows from the scheme intended by the authors of the Treaties that a measure **17.04** may escape the application of the competition rules where those measures are necessary to the POs and APOs in order to carry out one or more of the tasks assigned to them.

That finding is echoed by Article 175 of Regulation No 1234/2007, which succeeded Article 1 of Regulation No 26 and Article 1a of Regulation No 1184/2006, and which provides that the competition rules apply 'save as otherwise provided for in this Regulation'. That is particularly true of regulations establishing CMOs which frame certain responsibilities and certain methods of intervention in agricultural markets. Those regulations assign to entities active in the production of and trade in agricultural products—the POs and the APOs—certain specific tasks and responsibilities which may lead them to adopt certain forms of coordination. [...]

Consequently, where, in the regulations governing the CMOs and the regulations introducing implementing rules for them, the Council makes provision for certain concertation measures, it thereby precludes the application of the competition rules and, in particular, the prohibition of anticompetitive agreements under Article 101(1) TFEU. In other words, agreements, decisions and concerted practices of POs and APOs which comply with those regulations necessarily escape the application of Article 101(1) TFEU.

Opinion AG Wahl 6 April 2017 (APVE e.o., Case C-671/15), ECLI:EU:C: 2017:281, paras 66, 67 and 71.

ARTICLE 209

EXCEPTIONS FOR THE OBJECTIVES OF THE CAP AND FARM-ERS AND THEIR ASSOCIATIONS

1. Article 101(1) TFEU shall not apply to the agreements, decisions and practices referred to in Article 206 of this Regulation necessary for the attainment of the objectives set out in Article 39 TFEU.

    Article 101(1) TFEU shall not apply to agreements, decisions and concerted practices of farmers, farmers' associations, or associations of such associations, or producer organisations recognised under Article 152 of this Regulation, or associations of producer organisations rec-ognised under Article 156 of this Regulation, which concern the pro-duction or sale of agricultural products or the use of joint facilities for the storage, treatment or processing of agricultural products, unless the objectives of Article 39 TFEU are jeopardised.

    This paragraph shall not apply to agreements, decisions and con-certed practices which entail an obligation to charge an identical price or by which competition is excluded.

2. Agreements, decisions and concerted practices which fulfil the condi-tions referred to in paragraph 1 of this Article shall not be prohibited, no prior decision to that effect being required.

    In any national or Union proceedings for the application of Article 101 TFEU, the burden of proving an infringement of Article 101(1) TFEU shall rest on the party or the authority alleging the infringement. The party claiming the benefit of the exemptions provided in paragraph 1 of this Article shall bear the burden of proving that the conditions of that paragraph are fulfilled.

ARTICLE 2 REGULATION NO 1184/2006

1. Article 81(1) of the Treaty shall not apply to those agreements, deci-sions and practices referred to in Article 1a of this Regulation which form an integral part of a national market organisation or are necessary for attainment of the objectives set out in Article 33 of the Treaty.

    In particular, it shall not apply to agreements, decisions and prac-tices of farmers, farmers' associations, or associations of such associa-tions belonging to a single Member State which concern the production or sale of agricultural products or the use of joint facilities for the storage, treatment or processing of agricultural products, and under which there is no obligation to charge identical prices, unless the

Commission finds that competition is thereby excluded or that the objectives of Article 33 of the Treaty are jeopardised.

2. After consulting the Member States and hearing the undertakings or associations of undertakings concerned and any other natural or legal person that it considers should be heard, the Commission shall have sole power, subject to review by the Court of Justice, to determine, by decision which shall be published, which agreements, decisions and practices fulfil the conditions specified in paragraph 1.

    The Commission shall so determine either on its own initiative or at the request of a competent authority of a Member State or of an interested undertaking or association of undertakings.

3. The publication shall state the names of the parties and the main content of the decision. It shall have regard to the legitimate interest of undertakings in the protection of their business secrets.

OVERVIEW

A. PARAGRAPH 1: FARMERS, FARMERS'		B. DIVISION OF COMPETENCE IN ARTICLE 2(2) OF
ASSOCIATIONS	17.05	REGULATION NO 1184/2006 17.14

A. PARAGRAPH 1: FARMERS, FARMERS' ASSOCIATIONS

Article 39 TFEU:

The objectives of the common agricultural policy shall be:

(a) to increase agricultural productivity by promoting technical progress and by ensuring the rational development of agricultural production and the optimum utilisation of the factors of production, in particular labour;
(b) thus to ensure a fair standard of living for the agricultural community, in particular by increasing the individual earnings of persons engaged in agriculture;
(c) to stabilise markets;
(d) to assure the availability of supplies;
(e) to ensure that supplies reach consumers at reasonable prices.[...]

The conditions for the admission of dealers are imposed either by agreements between **17.05** growers and dealers, such as the exclusive buying obligation and obligation to have a packing centre, or by decisions of the Syndicat des Expéditeurs de Saint-Malo, in respect of the requirement for a majority vote on the Board of Directors and the obligation on dealers only to buy and dispatch on their own account. They do not form part of agreements between farmers or decisions of farmers' associations within the meaning of the [first] sentence of Article [209](1) of Regulation No [1308/2013], so that the exemption provided for therein does not apply in this case.

Commission 2 December 1977 (Cauliflowers, IV/28.948), OJ 1978 L 21/23, para. III. 3.

17.06 The association formed by the German Farmers' Union and German Raiffeisen Association and their respective Land Associations and the Central Association of Private Dairies to administer the MFF is an association of trade associations serving the common economic interests of its members. It is not, however, an association of farmers' associations within the meaning of the [first] sentence of Article [209](1) which, like farmers' cooperatives, carry on on behalf of their members common commercial activities in the field of the production or sale of agricultural products or the use of joint facilities for the storage, treatment or processing of agricultural products.

Commission 7 December 1984 (Milchförderungsfonds, IV/28.930), OJ 1985 L 35/35.

17.07 Since ML is a private company and not an association of farmers, it cannot be maintained that the Meldoc agreement is covered by the exception provided for in the [first] sentence of Article [209](1).

Commission 26 November 1986 (Meldoc, IV/31.204), OJ 1986 L 348/50.

17.08 Campina therefore informed the Commission that its members would in future be able to resign at three different times of the year (1 April, 1 September or at the end of the financial year) without having to pay a fee, provided they gave two years' notice. Members would, however, be free to by-pass this procedure by giving shorter notice of three months. In that event, there would be only one date of departure (1 April) and a resignation fee of 4 per cent, applicable from 1 January 1991, would be payable. Campina's undertaking will have the effect of strengthening competition between Campina and other dairies with regard to milk produced by Campina members, thus giving the latter greater freedom of action without adversely affecting the economic and financial stability of Campina.

   Although the Commission considers that the exclusive supply obligation and the new resignation clauses still comprise restrictions of competition, it believes that they are acceptable in view of the structure of the milk market concerned and Campina's position on that market. In those circumstances, it concluded that the restrictions of competition which resulted from an exclusivity obligation lasting for a maximum of two years and benefi[t]ting a cooperative which is not in a dominant position on the relevant market, are covered by the special exemption provisions contained in Council Regulation [Reg.No. 1308/2013 of 17 December 2013].

XXIst report on competition policy (1991) (Campina), para. 84.

See also XXIInd report on competition policy (1992) (Milk Marketing Board), paras 161–167.

It is apparent, first of all, from the genesis of that regulation that, by adding that second **17.09** sentence[,] which did not appear in the Commission's original proposal for a regulation[,] at the behest of the European Parliament, the legislature sought to introduce an exception applying in favour of agreements, decisions and practices of farmers where they fulfil the criteria laid down in it, unless the Commission finds that competition is thereby excluded or that the objectives of Article 39 of the Treaty are jeopardised.

Next, that desire to protect agricultural cooperatives is apparent from the reasons given for the regulation, and in particular from the fourth recital in the preamble to Regulation No [1184/2006 and the 175th recital of Regulation No 1308/2013], which states that special attention is warranted in the case of farmers' organisations.

To interpret the second sentence as having no independent meaning would run squarely counter to the wishes of the legislature, inasmuch as it would result in more stringent conditions being applied to agreements which are to be made more flexible, since they would have to fulfil the conditions laid down in both the first and second sentences. Moreover, the Commission could scarcely find that an agreement jeopardised the objectives of Article 39 of the Treaty if, by virtue of the derogation set out in the first sentence, it had already been established that that agreement or decision was necessary for the attainment of those objectives.

CoJ 12 December 1995 (Dijkstra and others v. Friesland Frico Domo, C-319/93, Van Roessel and others v. Campina Melkunie, C-40/94, De Bie and others v. Campina Melkunie, C-224/94) [1995] ECR I-4471, paras 18–20.

The [second] derogation [i.e. the second sentence] is subject to three cumulative **17.10** conditions. For that derogation to be applicable, it must be confirmed, firstly, that the agreements in question concern cooperative associations belonging to a single Member State, secondly that they do not cover prices but concern rather the production or sale of agricultural products or the use of joint facilities for the storage, treatment or processing of such products, and thirdly that they do not exclude competition or jeopardize the objectives of the common agricultural policy.

With regard to the third condition, it cannot be ruled out that the cumulative effect of clauses in statutes tying the members to the association for long periods and thereby depriving them of the possibility of approaching competitors jeopardizes one of the objectives of the common agricultural policy, namely [...] that of increasing individual earnings in the agricultural sector, in so far as those active in that sector will not be able to benefit from competition in purchase prices for raw materials paid by different processors.

CoJ 12 December 1995 (Oude Luttikhuis v. Coberco, C-399/93) [1995] ECR I-4515, paras 27 and 28.

In addition, [Article 209 of Regulation No 1308/2013 and Article 2 of Regulation No **17.11** 1184/2006] must be interpreted as to requiring that any restriction of competition through measures which were to be justified under its terms be proportionate to the objective sought, that is to say that no other less restrictive measures would allow the objectives pursued to be attained. In the present case, the producers. Representatives have failed to give any reason as to why price fixing arrangements should be considered proportionate. Moreover, by their very nature, restrictions on competition in the form of price fixing arrangements could be found to be necessary and proportionate to the objectives sought by Article [39 TFEU] only in very exceptional circumstances. As the Court of Justice recently recalled that '*the maintenance of effective competition on the market for agricultural products is one of the objectives of the common agricultural policy*' and that '*the common organisations of the markets in agricultural products are not [...] a competition-free zone*'.

Commission 20 October 2004 (Raw Tobacco Spain, COMP/C.38.238/B.2), para. 345.

17.12   The exception at (c) [at the second sub paragraph of Article 209(1)] is also ruled out where the two infringements at issue are concerned. First, the restrictive practice engaged in by the processors involves parties other than farmers and is designed, among other things, to fix prices (the average prices, the price brackets and other minor price aspects). Second, the restrictive practice engaged in by the producer representatives is also designed to fix prices (the price brackets but also the average minimum price per producer and the average minimum price per group). Accordingly, the exception at (c) cannot apply to any of the infringements at issue.

Commission 20 October 2004 (Raw Tobacco Spain, COMP/C.38.238/B.2), para. 346.

17.13   The exception at [paragraph 1, second sentence] is excluded as well since practices described [...] involve parties other than farmers.

Commission 15 October 2008 (Bananas, COMP/39188), para. 346.

See also the Commission Notice – Guidelines on the application of the specific rules set out in Articles 169, 170 and 171 of the CMO Regulation for the olive oil, beef and veal and arable crops sectors (OJ 2015 C 431/01), paras 30 and 31.

B. DIVISION OF COMPETENCE IN ARTICLE 2(2) OF REGULATION NO 1184/2006

17.14   To require the Commission to consult the Member States even in cases where it is in no doubt that the exceptions provided for under Regulation No [1184/2006] cannot apply would oblige the Commission to fulfil unnecessary formalities and needlessly delay enquiries into the matters concerned.

CoJ 15 May 1975 (Frubo, 71/74) [1975] ECR 563, para. 11.

17.15   The fact that, in accordance with the provisions of Regulation (EEC) No 1516/74, the Belgian authorities approved, by Ministerial Decree of 14 October 1987, the inter-trade agreements in question cannot in any way be taken to mean that the agreements comply with the provisions of Regulation No [1184/2006] or with the competition rules laid down in the [TFEU]. As stipulated in Article 2 (2) of Regulation No [1184/2006], [...]

the Commission has sole power to determine by decision which agreements, decisions and practices fulfil the conditions specified in Article 2 (1) of Regulation No [1184/2006].

Commission 19 December 1989 (Sugar beet, 32.414), OJ 1990 L 31/32.

As regards the division of powers between the Commission and the national courts for **17.16** the purposes of applying Article 2(1) of Regulation No [1184/2006], it should first of all be pointed out that, by virtue of Article 2(2) and (3), the Commission has exclusive competence, subject to review by the Court, to determine whether an agreement fulfils the conditions specified in Article 2(1).

On the other hand, the Commission does not have exclusive competence to apply Article [101(1)] [...] the Commission shares that competence with the national courts. [...] Article [101](1) produces direct effects in relations between individuals and creates direct rights in respect of the individuals concerned which those national courts must safeguard. [...]

[A] national court before which a party pleads the nullity of a clause in the statutes of an agricultural cooperative on the ground that it infringes Article [101(1) TFEU], and before which the cooperative seeks to rely on Article 2(1) of Regulation No [1184/2006], may continue the proceedings and adjudicate on the dispute if it is clear that the criteria for the application of Article [101(1)] are not fulfilled, or may declare the clause void under Article [101(2)] if it is certain that that provision does not fulfil the conditions for application of the exception laid down in Article 2(1) of Regulation No [1184/2006] and does not qualify for exemption under Article [101(3)]. Where there is any doubt, the national court may, if it is appropriate and consistent with the national rules of procedure, obtain additional information from the Commission or allow the parties to seek a decision from the Commission.

CoJ 12 December 1995 (Dijkstra and others v. Friesland Frico Domo, C-319/93, Van Roessel and others v. Campina Melkunie, C-40/93, De Bie and others v. Campina Melkunie, C-224/94) [1995] ECR I-4471, paras 25, 26 and 36.

Article 2(2) of Regulation [No 1184/2006] seeks only to establish the competent **17.17** authority to apply Community competition law.

It must, however, be borne in mind that where the national competition authorities act in the area governed by the common organisation of the market for the sector in question, they are under an obligation to refrain from adopting any measure which might undermine or create exceptions to that common organisation [...].

Moreover, as regards cases coming within the scope *ratione materiae* not only of Article [101(1) TFEU], but also of national competition law, the national authorities cannot take decisions which conflict with those of the Commission, or create the risk of such a conflict [...].

Accordingly, it must be held that, [...], the national competition authorities are empowered to control – and, therefore, to prohibit – a mechanism for the storage of olive oil which is agreed and financed outside the scope of Article [31(1) sub b] of Regulation No [1308/2013], and which is likely to affect the Community market.

[T]o the extent that the national competition authorities refrain from taking any measure which might undermine or create exceptions to the common organisation of the market in olive oil and from taking decisions which conflict with those of the Commission or create the risk of such conflict, they can apply national competition law to an agreement which is likely to affect the market in olive oil at Community level.

CoJ 1 October 2009 (Compañía Española de Comercialización de Aceite SA, C-505/07) [2009] ECR I-08963, paras 54–58.

See also CoJ 9 September 2003 (Milk Marque and National Farmers' Union, C-137/ 00) [2003] ECR I-7975, para. 94; CoJ 14 December 2000 (Masterfoods and HB, C-344/98) [2000] ECR I-11369, paras 51 and 52.

ARTICLE 210

AGREEMENTS AND CONCERTED PRACTICES OF RECOG-
NISED INTERBRANCH ORGANISATIONS

1. Article 101(1) TFEU shall not apply to agreements, decisions and
    concerted practices of interbranch organisations recognised under
    Article 157 of this Regulation with the object of carrying out the
    activities listed in point (c) of Article 157(1) and, for the milk and milk
    products sector, in point (c) of Article 157(3) of this Regulation, and,
    for the olive oil and table olives and tobacco sectors, in Article 162 of
    this Regulation.

2. Paragraph 1 shall apply provided that:
    (a) the agreements, decisions and concerted practices referred to
           therein have been notified to the Commission; and
    (b) within two months of receipt of all the details required the Com-
           mission has not found that those agreements, decisions or con-
           certed practices are incompatible with Union rules.
    Where the Commission finds that the agreements, decisions or con-
    certed practices referred to in paragraph 1 are incompatible with Union
    rules, it shall set out its finding without applying the procedure referred
    to in Article 229(2) or (3).

3. The agreements, decisions and concerted practices referred to in para-
    graph 1 may not be put into effect before the lapse of the two- month
    period referred to in point (b) of the first subparagraph of paragraph 2.

4. Agreements, decisions and concerted practices shall in any case be
    declared incompatible with Union rules if they:
    (a) may lead to the partitioning of markets within the Union in any
           form;
    (b) may affect the sound operation of the market organisation;
    (c) may create distortions of competition which are not essential to
           achieving the objectives of the CAP pursued by the interbranch
           organisation activity;
    (d) entail the fixing of prices or the fixing of quotas;
    (e) may create discrimination or eliminate competition in respect of a
           substantial proportion of the products in question.

5. If, following the expiry of the two-month period referred to in point (b)
    of the first subparagraph of paragraph 2, the Commission finds that the
    conditions for applying paragraph 1 have not been met, it shall, without
    applying the procedure referred to in Article 229(2) or (3), take a
    decision declaring that Article 101(1) TFEU applies to the agreement,
    decision or concerted practice in question.

That Commission decision shall not apply earlier than the date of its notification to the interbranch organisation concerned, unless that interbranch organisation has given incorrect information or abused the exemption provided for in paragraph 1.

6.   In the case of multiannual agreements, the notification for the first year shall be valid for the subsequent years of the agreement. However, in that event, the Commission may, on its own initiative or at the request of another Member State, issue a finding of incompatibility at any time.

7.   The Commission may adopt implementing acts laying down the measures necessary for the uniform application of this Article. Those implementing acts shall be adopted in accordance with the examination procedure referred to in Article 229(2). […]

SECTION 4

AGREEMENTS AND DECISONS DURING PERIODS OF SEVERE IMBALANCE IN MARKETS

ARTICLE 222

APPLICATION OF ARTICLE 101(1) TFEU

1. During periods of severe imbalance in markets, the Commission may adopt implementing acts to the effect that Article 101(1) TFEU is not to apply to agreements and decisions of recognised producer organisations, their associations and recognised interbranch organisations in any of the sectors referred to in Article 1(2) of this Regulation, provided that such agreements and decisions do not undermine the proper functioning of the internal market, strictly aim to stabilise the sector concerned and fall under one or more of the following categories:
    (a) market withdrawal or free distribution of their products;
    (b) transformation and processing;
    (c) storage by private operators;
    (d) joint promotion measures;
    (e) agreements on quality requirements;
    (f) joint purchasing of inputs necessary to combat the spread of pests and diseases in animals and plants in the Union or of inputs necessary to address the effects of natural disasters in the Union;
    (g) temporary planning of production taking into account the specific nature of the production cycle.
    The Commission shall specify in implementing acts the substantive and geographic scope of this derogation and, subject to paragraph 3, the period for which the derogation applies.
    Those implementing acts shall be adopted in accordance with the examination procedure referred to in Article 229(2).
2. Paragraph 1 shall apply only if the Commission has already adopted one of the measures referred to in this Chapter, if products have been bought in under public intervention or if aid for private storage referred to in Chapter I of Title I of Part II has been granted.
3. The agreements and decisions referred to in paragraph 1 shall only be valid for a period of up to six months.

However, the Commission may adopt implementing acts authorising such agreements and decisions for a further period of up to six- months. Those implementing acts shall be adopted in accordance with the examination procedure referred to in Article 229(2).

Part 2

EUROPEAN CONVENTION ON HUMAN RIGHTS (ECHR) AND CHARTER OF FUNDAMENTAL RIGHTS OF THE EUROPEAN UNION (CHARTER)

Section 1

EUROPEAN CONVENTION ON HUMAN RIGHTS

ARTICLE 1 ECHR*

OBLIGATION TO RESPECT HUMAN RIGHTS

The High Contracting Parties shall secure to everyone within their jurisdiction the rights and freedoms defined in Section I of this Convention.

OVERVIEW

A.	GENERAL (p.703)	D.	NO DIRECT BINDING EFFECT VIS-À-VIS THE EU PRIOR TO ACCESSION 18.15
B.	THE ECHR: A SUPRA-NATIONAL HUMAN RIGHTS TREATY 18.01		1. No binding effect vis-à-vis the EU as such 18.15
C.	METHODS OF INTERPRETATION 18.02		2. No binding effect vis-à-vis the EU as holder of powers which have been deferred to it by the Member
	1. General 18.02		States 18.16
	2. The ECHR as a living instrument 18.04		
	3. The Vienna Treaty on the Law of Treaties, Sens Clair and Purposive Construction 18.06	E.	EU MEMBER STATE RESPONSIBILITY WHEN DEFERRING POWERS TO THE EU 18.17
	4. Member State practice 18.12		1. General 18.17
	5. Other sources of International Law 18.13		2. Equivalent guarantees 18.21

A. GENERAL

In relation to the ECHR, this part only contains case extracts on Article 1, outlining the ECHR's scope of application and methods of interpretation. The ECHR's substantive provisions and the case extracts regarding those provisions can be found under the relevant provisions of the Charter. The Annex provides a table showing the relevant Charter provisions in their order of appearance in the ECHR.

---

* This chapter was written by Herman Speyart.

B. THE ECHR: A SUPRA-NATIONAL HUMAN RIGHTS TREATY

18.01   Unlike international treaties of the classic kind, the [EHR] Convention comprises more than mere reciprocal engagements between Contracting States. It creates, over and above a network of mutual, bilateral undertakings, objective obligations which, in the words of the Preamble benefit from a 'collective enforcement'.

Eur. Court H.R. 18 January 1978 (Ireland v. the United Kingdom), Series A no 25, p. 90, para. 239.

C. METHODS OF INTERPRETATION

1.   General

18.02   In interpreting [EHR] Convention provisions, [the Court] must have regard to the special character of the Convention as a treaty for the collective enforcement of human rights and fundamental freedoms.

[In applying the EHR Convention], the Court must bear in mind the special character of the Convention as an instrument of European public order (*ordre public*) for the protection of individual human beings and its mission, as set out in Article 19, 'to ensure the observance of the engagements undertaken by the High Contracting Parties'.

Eur. Court H.R. (Grand Chamber) 23 March 1995 (Loizidou v. Turkey, no 15318/89), Series A no 310, paras 71 and 93.

18.03   The Court has emphasised that, as an international treaty, the Convention must be interpreted in the light of the rules of interpretation provided for in Articles 31 to 33 of the Vienna Convention of 23 May 1969 on the Law of Treaties [...].

Thus, in accordance with the Vienna Convention, the Court is required to ascertain the ordinary meaning to be given to the words in their context and in the light of the object and purpose of the provision from which they are drawn [...].

Regard must also be had to the fact that the context of the provision is a treaty for the effective protection of individual human rights and that the Convention must also be read as a whole, and interpreted in such a way as to promote internal consistency and harmony between its various provisions [...].

The Court emphasises that the object and purpose of the Convention, as an instrument for the protection of human rights, requires that its provisions must be interpreted and applied in a manner which renders its rights practical and effective, not theoretical and illusory [...].

Furthermore the Convention comprises more than mere reciprocal engagements between Contracting States [...].

Account must also be taken of any relevant rules and principles of international law applicable in relations between the Contracting Parties [...]; the Convention cannot be interpreted in a vacuum and should so far as possible be interpreted in harmony with other rules of international law of which it forms part [...].

Being made up of a set of rules and principles that are accepted by the vast majority of States, the common international or domestic-law standards of European States reflect a reality that the Court cannot disregard when it is called upon to clarify the scope of a Convention provision [...]. The consensus emerging from specialised international instruments and from the practice of Contracting States may constitute a relevant consideration for the Court when it interprets the provisions of the Convention in specific cases [...].

Finally, recourse may also be had to supplementary means of interpretation, including the preparatory work (travaux préparatoires) of the treaty, either to confirm a meaning determined in accordance with the above steps, or to establish the meaning where it would otherwise be ambiguous, obscure, or manifestly absurd or unreasonable [...]. It can be seen from the case-law that the travaux préparatoires are not delimiting for the question whether a right may be considered to fall within the scope of an Article of the Convention if the existence of such a right was supported by the growing measure of common ground that had emerged in the given area [...].

Eur. Court H.R. (Grand Chamber) 8 November 2016 (Magyar Helsinki Bizottság v. Hungary, no. 18030/11), unreported, paras 118–125.

2. The ECHR as a living instrument

The [EHR] Convention is a living instrument which must be interpreted in the light of **18.04** present-day conditions.
Eur. Court H.R. 25 April 1978 (Tyrer v. the United Kingdom), Series A no 26, p. 15, para. 31.

See also Eur. Court H.R. 27 September 1990 (Cossey v. the United Kingdom), Series A no 184, p. 14, para. 35; Eur. Court H.R. 16 April 2002 (Colas Est v. France, no 37971/97), ECHR 2002-III, paras 41 and 42.

It follows that these provisions cannot be interpreted solely in accordance with the **18.05** intentions of their authors as expressed more than forty years ago.
Eur. Court H.R. (Grand Chamber) 23 March 1995 (Loizidou v. Turkey, no 15318/89), Series A no 310, para. 71.

3. The Vienna Treaty on the Law of Treaties, Sens Clair and Purposive Construction

[...] The Court is prepared to consider, as do the Government and the Commission, **18.06** that it should be guided by Articles 31 to 33 of the Vienna Convention of 23 May 1969 on the Law of Treaties. [I]ts Articles 31 to 33 enunciate in essence generally accepted principles of international law to which the Court has already referred on occasion. In this respect, for the interpretation of the European Convention account is to be taken of those Articles subject, where appropriate, to 'any relevant rules of the organization' – the Council of Europe – within which it has been adopted (Article 5 of the Vienna Convention).

In the way in which it is presented in the 'general rule' in Article 31 of the Vienna Convention, the process of interpretation of a treaty is a unity, a single combined operation; this rule, closely integrated, places on the same footing the various elements enumerated in the four paragraphs of the Article.

As stated in Article 31 para. 2 of the Vienna Convention, the preamble to a treaty forms an integral part of the context. Furthermore, the preamble is generally very useful for the determination of the 'object' and 'purpose' of the instrument to be construed. [...]

Eur. Court H.R. (Plenary) 21 February 1975 (Golder v. the United Kingdom, no. 445/70), Series A no. 18, paras 29, 30 and 34.

18.07   The Convention is intended to guarantee not rights that are theoretical or illusory but rights that are practical and effective.

Eur. Court H.R. 9 October 1979 (Airey v. Ireland, no 6289/73), Series A no 32, p. 12, para. 24.

See also Eur. Court H.R. 13 May 1980 (Artico v. Italy, no 6694/74), Series A no 37, p. 16, para. 33; Eur. Court H.R. 27 November 2008 (Salduz v. Turkey, no 36391/ 02), para. 50.

18.08   The prominent place held in a democratic society by the right to a fair trial [...] prompts the Court to prefer a 'substantive', rather than a 'formal', conception of the 'charge' contemplated by Article 6 para. 1. The Court is compelled to look behind the appearances and investigate the realities of the procedure in question.

Eur. Court H.R. 27 February 1980 (Deweer v. Belgium, no 6903/75), Series A no 35, p. 30, para. 44.

18.09   [To interpret the provisions of the EHR Convention], the Court will seek to ascertain the ordinary meaning to be given to the terms of this provision in their context and in the light of its object and purpose.

Eur. Court H.R. (Plenary) 18 December 1986 (Johnston a.o. v. Ireland, no. 9697/82) Series A no. 112, para. 51.

18.10   In addition, the object and purpose of the [EHR] Convention as an instrument for the protection of individual human beings requires that its provisions be interpreted and applied so as to make its safeguards practical and effective.

Eur. Court H.R. 7 July 1989 (Soering v. the United Kingdom), Series A no 161, p. 35, para. 87.

18.11   [...] The Court must have regard to the fact that the context of the provision is a treaty for the effective protection of individual human rights and that the Convention must be read as a whole, and interpreted in such a way as to promote internal consistency and harmony between its various provisions [...]. Recourse may also be had to supplementary means of interpretation, including the preparatory works to the Convention, either to confirm a meaning determined in accordance with the above steps, or to establish the meaning where it would otherwise be ambiguous, obscure or manifestly absurd or unreasonable.

Eur. Court H.R. (Grand Chamber) 29 January 2008 (Saadi v. the United Kingdom, no. 13229/03), ECHR 2008, para. 62.

4. Member State practice

[The Court] shall also take into account, together with the context, 'any subsequent **18.12** practice in the application of the treaty which establishes the agreement of the parties regarding its interpretation' (see Article 31(3)(b) of the Vienna Convention of 23 May 1969 on the Law of Treaties).

Eur. Court H.R. (Grand Chamber) 23 March 1995 (Loizidou v. Turkey, no 15318/89), Series A no 310, para. 70.

5. Other sources of International Law

Article 31 paragraph 3(c) of the Vienna Convention indicates that account is to be **18.13** taken, together with the context, of 'any relevant rules of international law applicable in the relations between the parties'. Among those rules are general principles of law and especially 'general principles of law recognized by civilized nations' (Art. 38 para. 1 (c) of the Statute of the International Court of Justice). Incidentally, the Legal Committee of the Consultative Assembly of the Council of Europe foresaw in August 1950 that 'the Commission and the Court must necessarily apply such principles' in the execution of their duties and thus considered it to be 'unnecessary' to insert a specific clause to this effect in the Convention (Documents of the Consultative Assembly, working papers of the 1950 session, Vol. III, no. 93, p. 982, para. 5). [...]

Eur. Court H.R. (Plenary) 21 February 1975 (Golder v. the United Kingdom, no. 445/70), Series A no. 18, para. 35.

The Convention [...] cannot be interpreted in a vacuum. [...] The Court must be **18.14** mindful of the Convention's special character as a human rights treaty, and it must also take the relevant rules of international law into account [...]. The Convention should so far as possible be interpreted in harmony with other rules of international law of which it forms part.

Eur. Court H.R. (Grand Chamber) 21 November 2001 (Al-Adsani v. the United Kingdom, no. 35763/97), ECHR 2001–XI, para. 55.

D. NO DIRECT BINDING EFFECT VIS-À-VIS THE EU PRIOR TO ACCESSION

1. No binding effect vis-à-vis the EU as such

The European Community has separate legal personality as an international inter- **18.15** governmental organisation (see Article [281 EC, cf Art. 47 TEU]). At present, the

European Community is not a party to the [EHR] Convention [...]. The application is therefore incompatible with the provisions of the Convention ratione personae within the meaning of Article 35§3 of the [EHR] Convention in so far as the applicant associations complaints must be understood as directed against the European Community itself and must be rejected pursuant to Article 35§4.

Eur. Commission H.R. 10 July 1978 (CFDT v. European Communities, no 8030/77), DR 13, p. 231.

See also Eur. Court H.R. 20 January 2009 (Coöperatieve Producentenorganisatie van de Nederlandse Kokkelvisserij U.A. v. The Netherlands, no 13645/05), unreported, para. B.2.

2. No binding effect vis-à-vis the EU as holder of powers which have been deferred to it by the Member States

18.16   Moreover, even as the holder of [...] sovereign power [transferred to it by the EU Member States], [the European Community] is not itself held responsible under the [EHR] Convention for proceedings before, or decisions of, its organs as long as it is not a Contracting Party.

Eur. Commission H.R. 10 July 1978 (CFDT v. European Communities, no 8030/77), DR 13, p. 235.

See also Eur. Court H.R. 20 January 2009 (Coöperatieve Producentenorganisatie van de Nederlandse Kokkelvisserij U.A. v. The Netherlands, no 13645/05), unreported, para. B.2.

E. EU MEMBER STATE RESPONSIBILITY WHEN DEFERRING POWERS TO THE EU

1. General

18.17   The [EHR] Convention does not, on the one hand, prohibit Contracting Parties from transferring sovereign power to an international (including a supranational) organisation in order to pursue cooperation in certain fields of activity.

Eur. Commission H.R. 9 February 1990 (M&Co v. Germany, no 13258/87), DR 64, p. 138.

See also Eur. Court H.R. (Grand Chamber) 30 June 2005 (Bosphorus Hava Yollari v. Ireland, no 45036/ 98), ECHR Reports 2005–VI, para. 152.

18.18   On the other hand, it has also been accepted that a Contracting Party is responsible under Article 1 of the [EHR] Convention for all acts and omissions of its organs regardless of whether the act or omission in question was a consequence of domestic law or of the necessity to comply with international legal obligations. Article 1 makes no distinction as to the type of rule or measure concerned and does not exclude any part of a Contracting Party's 'jurisdiction' from scrutiny under the Convention.

Eur. Court H.R. 30 January 1998 (United Communist Party of Turkey and others v. Turkey, no 133/1996), ECHR Reports 1998-I, pp. 17–18, para. 29.

See also Eur. Court H.R. (Grand Chamber) 30 June 2005 (Bosphorus Hava Yollari v. Ireland, no 45036/ 98), ECHR Reports 2005-VI, para. 153.

In reconciling both these positions and thereby establishing the extent to which a **18.19** State's action can be justified by its compliance with obligations flowing from its membership of an international organisation to which it has transferred part of its sovereignty, the Court has recognised that absolving Contracting States completely from their [EHR] Convention responsibility in the areas covered by such a transfer would be incompatible with the purpose and object of the Convention; the guarantees of the Convention could be limited or excluded at will, thereby depriving it of its peremptory character and undermining the practical and effective nature of its safeguards.

Eur. Commission H.R. 9 February 1990 (M&Co v. Germany, no 13258/87), DR 64, p. 145.

See also Eur. Court H.R. (Grand Chamber) 30 June 2005 (Bosphorus Hava Yollari v. Ireland, no 45036/ 98), ECHR Reports 2005-VI, para. 154.

The State is considered to retain [EHR] Convention liability in respect of treaty **18.20** commitments subsequent to the entry into force of the Convention [...].

Eur. Court H.R. (Grand Chamber) 30 June 2005 (Bosphorus Hava Yollari v. Ireland, no 45036/98), ECHR Reports 2005-VI, para. 154.

See also Eur. Court H.R. (Grand Chamber) 18 February 1999 (Matthews v. the United Kingdom, no 24833/94), ECHR Reports 1999-I, paras 29 and 32–34.

2. Equivalent guarantees

(a) General

In the Court's view, State action taken in compliance with such legal obligations is **18.21** justified as long as the relevant organisation is considered to protect fundamental rights, as regards both the substantive guarantees offered and the mechanisms controlling their observance, in a manner which can be considered at least equivalent to that for which the [EHR] Convention provides. By 'equivalent' the Court means 'comparable'; any requirement that the organisation's protection be 'identical' could run counter to the interest of international cooperation pursued.

Eur. Commission H.R. 9 February 1990 (M&Co v. Germany, no 13258/87), DR 64, p. 145.

See also Eur. Court H.R. (Grand Chamber) 30 June 2005 (Bosphorus Hava Yollari v. Ireland, no 45036/98), ECHR Reports 2005-VI, para. 155.

(b)   Two-step test: general level and protection in the individual case concerned

18.22   If such equivalent protection is considered to be provided by the organisation, the presumption will be that a State has not departed from the requirements of the [EHR] Convention when it does no more than implement legal obligations flowing from its membership of the organisation. However, any such presumption can be rebutted if, in the circumstances of a particular case, it is considered that the protection of Convention rights was manifestly deficient. In such cases, the interest of international cooperation would be outweighed by the Convention's role as a 'constitutional instrument of European public order' in the field of human rights.

Eur. Court H.R. (Grand Chamber) 30 June 2005 (Bosphorus Hava Yollari v. Ireland, no 45036/98), ECHR Reports 2005-VI, para. 156.

(c)   Finding of equivalence

18.23   [After an analysis of the system of protection of fundamental rights in the Community] In such circumstances, the Court finds that the protection of fundamental rights by Community law can be considered to be, and to have been at the relevant time, 'equivalent' [...] to that of the [EHR] Convention system. Consequently, the presumption arises that Ireland did not depart from the requirements of the Convention when it implemented legal obligations flowing from its membership of the European Community.

Eur. Court H.R. (Grand Chamber) 30 June 2005 (Bosphorus Hava Yollari v. Ireland, no 45036/98), ECHR Reports 2005-VI, para. 165.

(d)   In relation to the grant of an exequatur for a Commission Decision imposing a fine

18.24   By granting executory power to a judgment of the European Court of Justice the competent German authorities did not act quasi as Community organs and are not to that extent beyond the scope of control exercised by the [EHR] Convention organs. Under Article 1 of the Convention the Member States are responsible for all acts and omissions of their domestic organs allegedly violating the Convention regardless of whether the act or omission in question is a consequence of domestic law or regulations or of the necessity to comply with international obligations.

Eur. Commission H.R. 9 February 1990 (M&Co v. Germany, no 13258/87), DR 64, p. 138.

(e)   In relation to the preliminary reference procedure

The nexus between a preliminary ruling by the ECJ under Article [267 TFEU] and the **18.25** domestic proceedings which give rise to it is obvious. It is the domestic court which, finding itself faced with a question of Community law to which it requires an answer in order to decide a case pending before it, seeks the ECJ's assistance in terms of its own choosing; the interpretation which the ECJ then gives of Community law is authoritative and cannot be ignored by the domestic court.

Eur. Court H.R. 20 January 2009 (Coöperatieve Producentenorganisatie van de Nederlandse Kokkelvisserij U.A. v. the Netherlands, no 13645/05), unreported, para. B.3.

Part 2

Section 2

CHARTER OF FUNDAMENTAL RIGHTS OF THE EUROPEAN UNION

19

ARTICLE 7 CHARTER[*]

RESPECT FOR PRIVATE AND FAMILY LIFE

Everyone has the right to respect for his or her private and family life, home and communications.

ARTICLE 8 ECHR – RIGHT TO RESPECT FOR PRIVATE AND FAMILY LIFE

1. **Everyone has the right to respect for his private and family life, his home and his correspondence.**
2. **There shall be no interference by a public authority with the exercise of this right except such as is in accordance with the law and is necessary in a democratic society in the interests of national security, public safety or the economic well-being of the country, for the prevention of disorder or crime, for the protection of health or morals, or for the protection of the rights and freedoms of others.**

OVERVIEW

A. EXPLANATION RELATING TO
   ARTICLE 7 CHARTER (p.716)

B. SCOPE OF APPLICATION 19.01
   1. Respect for the home 19.01
   2. Respect for correspondence 19.09
   3. Respect for privacy of telephone calls 19.11

C. INTERFERENCE 19.12

D. JUSTIFICATION FOR THE INTERFERENCE 19.14

   1. General 19.14
   2. In accordance with the law 19.17
   3. Legitimate aim 19.29
   4. Necessary in a democratic society 19.31
   5. Assessment of the EU System 19.53

E. LEGAL PRIVILEGE 19.56
   1. Eur. Court H.R. 19.56
   2. EU Courts 19.57

F. EXCLUSIONARY RULE (p.754)

---

[*] This chapter was written by Herman Speyart.

A. EXPLANATION RELATING TO ARTICLE 7 CHARTER

The rights guaranteed in Article 7 correspond to those guaranteed by Article 8 of the ECHR. To take account of developments in technology the word 'correspondence' has been replaced by 'communications'.

In accordance with Article 52(3), the meaning and scope of this right are the same as those of the corresponding article of the ECHR. Consequently, the limitations which may legitimately be imposed on this right are the same as those allowed by Article 8 of the ECHR.

B. SCOPE OF APPLICATION

1. Respect for the home

(a) Eur. Court H.R.

19.01   As regards the word 'home', appearing in the English text of Article 8, the Court observes that in certain Contracting States, notably Germany [...], it has been accepted as extending to business premises. Such an interpretation is, moreover, fully consonant with the French text, since the word 'domicile' has a broader connotation than the word 'home' and may extend, for example, to a professional person's office. In this context also, it may not always be possible to draw precise distinctions, since activities which are related to a profession or business may well be conducted from a person's private residence and activities which are not so related may well be carried on in an office or commercial premises. A narrow interpretation of the words 'home' and 'domicile' could therefore give rise to the same risk of inequality of treatment as a narrow interpretation of the notion of 'private life' [...].

More generally, to interpret the words 'private life' and 'home' as including certain professional or business activities or premises would be consonant with the essential object and purpose of Article 8, namely to protect the individual against arbitrary interference by the public authorities [...]. Such an interpretation would not unduly hamper the Contracting States, for they would retain their entitlement to 'interfere' to the extent permitted by para. 2 of Article 8; that entitlement might well be more far-reaching where professional or business activities or premises were involved than would otherwise be the case.

Eur. Court H.R. 16 December 1992 (Niemietz v. Germany, no 13710/88), Series A No. 251–B, paras 30 and 31.

19.02   As regards the rights secured to companies by the Convention, it should be pointed out that the Court has already recognised a company's right under Article 41 to compensation for non-pecuniary damage sustained as a result of a violation of Article 6 §1 of the Convention [...]. Building on its dynamic interpretation of the Convention, the

Court considers that the time has come to hold that in certain circumstances the rights guaranteed by Article 8 of the Convention may be construed as including the right to respect for a company's registered office, branches or other business premises [...].

Eur. Court H.R. 16 April 2002 (Colas Est v. France no 37971/97), ECHR Reports 2002-III, para. 41.

The Court recalls that it has repeatedly held that the notion of 'home' in Article 8 §1 **19.03** encompasses not only a private individual's home but may also extend, for example, to a person's office used for professional purposes. Consequently, 'home' is to be construed as including also the registered office of a company run by a private individual, as well as a legal person's registered office, branches and other business premises.

Eur. Court H.R. 15 February 2011 (Heino v. Finland, no 56720/09), ECHR Reports 2011, para. 33.

The Court first reiterates that, as interpreted in its case-law, the word "home", **19.04** appearing in the English text of Article 8, – the word 'domicile' in the French text has a broader connotation – covers residential premises and may extend also to certain professional or business premises [...]. It includes not only the registered office of a company owned and run by a private individual [...] but also that of a legal person and its branches and other business premises [...]. Such an interpretation would not unduly hamper the Contracting States, for they would retain their entitlement to 'interfere' to the extent permitted by paragraph 2 of Article 8; that entitlement might well be more far-reaching where professional or business activities or premises were involved than would otherwise be the case [...].

The Court further reiterates that in certain previous cases concerning complaints under Article 8 related to the search of business premises and the search and seizure of electronic data, the Court found an interference with 'the right to respect for home' [...] and 'correspondence' [...]. On the other hand, it did not find it necessary to examine whether there had also been an interference with the right to respect for 'private life' [...].

Eur. Court H.R. 14 March 2013 (Bernh Larsen Holding AS a.o. v. Norway, no. 24117/08), unreported, paras 104 and 105.

(b) EU Courts

[Now out-dated case-law of the CoJ] Since the applicant has also relied on the **19.05** requirements stemming from the fundamental right to the inviolability of the home, it should be observed that, although the existence of such a right must be recognized in the Community legal order as a principle common to the laws of the Member States in regard to the private dwellings of natural persons, the same is not true in regard to undertakings, because there are not inconsiderable divergences between the legal systems of the Member States in regard to the nature and degree of protection afforded to business premises against intervention by the public authorities.

No other inference is to be drawn from Article 8(1) of the European Convention on Human Rights which provides that: 'Everyone has the right to respect for his private and family life, his home and his correspondence.' The protective scope of that article is concerned with the development of man's personal freedom and may not therefore be extended to business premises. Furthermore, it should be noted that there is no case-law of the European Court of Human Rights on that subject.

None the less, in all the legal systems of the Member States, any intervention by the public authorities in the sphere of private activities of any person, whether natural or legal, must have a legal basis and be justified on the grounds laid down by law, and, consequently, those systems provide, albeit in different forms, protection against arbitrary or disproportionate intervention. The need for such protection must be recognized as a general principle of Community law. In that regard, it should be pointed out that the Court has held that it has the power to determine whether measures of investigation taken by the Commission under the ECSC Treaty are excessive […].

CoJ 21 September 1989 (Hoechst v. Commission, Joined Cases 46/87 and 227/88) [1989] ECR 2859, paras 17–19.

See also CoJ 17 October 1989 (Dow Chemical Ibérica a.o. v. Commission, Joined Cases 97/87–99/87) [1989] ECR 3165, paras 14–16.

19.06   [New case-law CoJ] For the purposes of determining the scope of that principle [of protection from any arbitrary or unreasonable international sphere of private activities of a person, whether natural or legal] in relation to the protection of business premises, regard must be had to the case-law of the European Court of Human Rights subsequent to the judgment in *Hoechst*. According to that case-law, first, the protection of the home provided for in Article 8 of the ECHR may in certain circumstances be extended to cover such premises (see, in particular, the judgment of 16 April 2002 in *Colas Est and others v. France*, […] § 41) and, second, the right of interference established by Article 8(2) of the ECHR 'might well be more far-reaching where professional or business activities or premises were involved than would otherwise be the case' (*Niemietz v. Germany*, […], § 31).

CoJ 22 October 2002 (Roquette Frères, C-94/00) [2002] ECR I-9011, para. 29.

19.07   [I]l y a lieu de relever que l'exigence d'une protection contre des interventions de la puissance publique dans la sphère d'activité privée d'une personne, qu'elle soit physique ou morale, qui seraient arbitraires ou disproportionnées constitue un principe général du droit de l'Union […]. Ce principe a été consacré à l'article 7 de la charte des droits fondamentaux de l'Union européenne, proclamée à Nice le 7 décembre 2000 (JO C 364, p. 1), aux termes duquel '[t]oute personne a droit au respect de sa vie privée et familiale, de son domicile et de ses communications'.

General Court 14 November 2012 (Prysmian v. Commission, T-140/09), ECLI: EU:T:2012:597, para. 35.

19.08   It should be noted in that regard that the fundamental right to the inviolability of the home is a general principle of EU law […], as now expressed in Article 7 of the Charter, which corresponds to Article 8 of the ECHR.

Furthermore, although it is apparent from the case-law of the ECtHR that the protection provided for in Article 8 of the ECHR may extend to certain commercial premises, the fact remains that that court did hold that interference by a public authority could go further for professional or commercial premises or activities than in other cases [...].

CoJ 18 June 2015 (Deutsche Bahn a.o. v. Commission, C-583/13 P), ECLI: EU:C:2013:404, paras 19 and 20.

2. Respect for correspondence

In [...] connection [with the question whether the search operations have covered **19.09** 'correspondence' and materials that can properly be regarded as such for the purposes of Article 8], it is sufficient to note that that provision does not use, as it does for the word 'life', any adjective to qualify the word 'correspondence'. And, indeed, the Court has already held that, in the context of correspondence in the form of telephone calls, no such qualification is to be made [...]. Again, in a number of cases relating to correspondence with a lawyer [...], the Court did not even advert to the possibility that Article 8 might be inapplicable on the ground that the correspondence was of a professional nature.

Eur. Court H.R. 16 December 1992 (Niemietz v. Germany, no 13710/88), Series A No. 251-B, para. 32.

Having regard to its above-cited case-law extending the notion of 'home' to a company's **19.10** business premises, the Court sees no reason to distinguish between [Wieser], who is a natural person, and [Bicos], which is a legal person, as regards the notion of 'correspondence'.

Eur. Court H.R. 16 October 2007 (Wieser and Bicos v. Austria, no 74336/01), unreported, para. 45.

3. Respect for privacy of telephone calls

Although telephone conversations are not expressly mentioned in paragraph 1 of **19.11** Article 8, the Court considers [...] that such conversations are covered by the notions of 'private life' and 'correspondence' referred to by this provision.

Eur. Court H.R. (Plenary) 6 September 1978 (Klass and others v. Germany, no 5029/71), Series A no. 28, para. 41.

C. INTERFERENCE

It suffices for the Court to find that [...] the search of the room occupied by the **19.12** applicant amounted to an interference, within the meaning of Article 8, with his right to respect for his home.

Eur. Court H.R. 16 December 1997 (Camenzind v. Switzerland, no 136/96), ECHR Reports 1997-VIII, para. 35.

19.13   In the instant case, the Court observes that during a large-scale administrative investigation, officials from the DGCCRF went to the applicant companies' head offices and branches in order to seize several thousand documents. It notes that the Government did not dispute that there had been interference with the applicant companies' right to respect for their home [...], although they argued that the companies could not claim a right to the protection of their business premises 'with as much force as an individual could in relation to his professional or business address' [...] and that, consequently, the entitlement to interfere 'might well be more far-reaching'.

Eur. Court H.R. 16 April 2002 (Colas Est v. France, no 37971/97), ECHR Reports 2002-III, para. 42.

D. JUSTIFICATION FOR THE INTERFERENCE

1. General

19.14   The exceptions provided for in paragraph 2 of Article 8, since they provide for an exception to a right guaranteed by the Convention, are to be interpreted narrowly, and the need for them in a given case must be convincingly established.

Eur. Court H.R. (Plenary) 6 September 1978 (Klass and others v. Germany, no 5029/71), Series A no 28, p. 21, para. 42.

See also Eur. Court H.R. 25 February 1993 (Funke v. France, no 10828/84), Series A no 256-A, p. 24–25, para. 55.

19.15   [The Contracting States] entitlement [to 'interfere' to the extent permitted by para. 2 of Art. 8] might well be more far-reaching where professional or business activities or premises were involved than would otherwise be the case.

Eur. Court H.R. 16 December 1992 (Niemietz v. Germany, no 13710/88), Series A No. 251-B, para. 31.

19.16   [In determining] whether [an] interference was justified under paragraph 2 of Article 8 [it must be determined] whether it [i] was 'in accordance with the law', [ii] pursued one or more of the legitimate aims set out in that paragraph and [iii] was 'necessary in a democratic society' to achieve the aim or aims in question.

Eur. Court H.R. 16 December 1997 (Camenzind v. Switzerland, no 136/96), ECHR Reports 1997-VIII, para. 35, subdivision added.

2. In accordance with the law

(a) General

19.17   The expression 'in accordance with the law', within the meaning of Article 8 §2 requires [i] firstly that the impugned measure should have some basis in domestic law; it also refers to the quality of the law in question, requiring that [ii] it should be accessible to the person concerned, who must moreover be able to foresee its consequences for him, and [iii] compatible with the rule of law.

Eur. Court H.R. 24 April 1990 (Kruslin v. France, no 11801/85), Series A no 176-A, p. 21, para. 27, subdivision added.

[T]he expression 'in accordance with the law', within the meaning of Article 8 § 2 **19.18** requires firstly that the impugned measure should have some basis in domestic law. Second, the domestic law must be accessible to the person concerned. Third, the person affected must be able, if need be with appropriate legal advice, to foresee the consequences of the domestic law for him, and fourth, the domestic law must be compatible with the rule of law [...].

Eur. Court H.R. 15 February 2011 (Heino v. Finland, no 56720/09), ECHR Reports 2011, para. 36.

(b) In accordance with national laws

An interference cannot be regarded as 'in accordance with the law' unless, first of all, it **19.19** has some basis in domestic law.

Eur. Court H.R. 26 March 1987 (Leander v. Sweden, no 9248/81), Series A no 116, p. 23, para. 50.

[Common law:] The English courts have indeed referred in this context to their **19.20** inherent jurisdiction, particularly as regards the ex parte nature of Anton Piller orders; in other respects their making appears to be founded on the general statutory power of the courts to grant injunctions and on the Rules of the Supreme Court [...]. In any event, even if the applicant's view were to be adopted, there would in the Court's opinion still have been a sufficient legal basis for the interference complained of, since 'law' includes unwritten or common law.

Eur. Court H.R. 30 March 1989 (Chappell v. UK, no 10461/83), Series A no 152-A, p. 26, para. 52.

[Written law:] In relation to paragraph 2 of Article 8 of the Convention and other **19.21** similar clauses, the Court has always understood the term 'law' in its 'substantive' sense, not its 'formal' one; it has included both enactments of lower rank than statutes and unwritten law. It cannot disregard settled case-law. [...] In a sphere covered by the written law, the 'law' is the enactment in force as the competent courts have interpreted it in the light, if necessary, of any new practical developments.

Eur. Court H.R. 24 April 1990 (Kruslin v. France, no 11801/85), Series A no 176-A, para. 29.

See also Eur. Court H.R. 16 April 2002 (Colas Est v. France, no 37971/97), ECHR Reports 2002-III, para. 43.

(c) Accessible

19.22   The relevant texts and case-law were all published, so clearly no problem arises concerning the law's 'accessibility', as that expression is understood in the Court's earlier judgments.

Eur. Court H.R. 30 March 1989 (Chappell v. UK, no 10461/83), Series A no 152-A, p. 26, para. 56.

(d) Foreseeable

19.23   As regards 'foreseeability', as likewise understood, the applicant maintained that the granting of Anton Piller orders and, in particular, their terms were largely matters of discretionary practice and that the state of the law was too 'amorphous' for it to constitute 'law' for the purposes of paragraph 2 of Article 8. The Court does not share this view. Since 1974 a substantial body of case-law has restated and refined the principles followed by the English courts as regards Anton Piller orders [...]. It is true that some variations may occur as between the content of individual orders. Nevertheless, the basic terms and conditions for the grant of this relief were, at the relevant time, laid down with sufficient precision for the 'foreseeability' criterion to be regarded as satisfied.

Eur. Court H.R. 30 March 1989 (Chappell v. UK, no 10461/83), Series A no 152-A, p. 26, para. 56.

(e) Compatible with the rule of law

19.24   [Test] [Article 8 § 2 of the Convention] does not merely refer back to domestic law but also relates to the quality of the law, requiring it to be compatible with the rule of law [...]. [It] thus implies [...] that there must be a measure of legal protection in domestic law against arbitrary interferences by public authorities with the rights safeguarded by paragraph 1.

[I]t would be contrary to the rule of law for the legal discretion granted to the executive to be expressed in terms of an unfettered power. Consequently, the law must indicate the scope of any such discretion conferred on the competent authorities and the manner of its exercise with sufficient clarity [...] to give the individual adequate protection against arbitrary interference.

Eur. Court H.R. 2 August 1984 (Malone v. the United Kingdom, no 8691/79), Series A no 82, p. 32, paras 67 and 68.

19.25   Article 8 § 2 requires the law in question to be 'compatible with the rule of law'. In the context of searches and seizures, the domestic law must provide some protection to the individual against arbitrary interference with Article 8 rights. Thus, the domestic law must be sufficiently clear in its terms to give citizens an adequate indication as to the circumstances in and conditions on which public authorities are empowered to resort to any such measures.

Eur. Court H.R. 25 March 1998 (Kopp v. Switzerland, no 13/1997), ECHR Reports 1998-II, p. 541, para. 64.

See also Eur. Court H.R. 13 January 2009 (Sorvisto v. Finland, no 19348/04), ECHR Reports 2009, para. 112.

The Court would emphasise that search and seizure represent a serious interference **19.26** with private life, home and correspondence and must accordingly be based on a 'law' that is particularly precise. It is essential to have clear, detailed rules on the subject.

In that connection, the Court notes that the relationship between the Coercive Measures Act, the Code of Judicial Procedure and the Advocates Act (read together) was somewhat unclear and gave rise to diverging views on the extent of the protection afforded to privileged material in searches and seizures, a situation which was identified also by the Deputy Chancellor of Justice of Finland.

The applicant was thus deprived of the minimum degree of protection to which he was entitled under the rule of law in a democratic society.

Eur. Court H.R. 27 September 2005 (Petri Sallinen and others v. Finland, no 50882/99), ECHR Reports 2005-VIII, paras 90–92.

[Non-compliant Finnish system] The Court must examine the 'quality' of the legal **19.27** rules applicable to the applicant in the instant case. It notes in the first place that under the Coercive Measures Act, Chapter 4, section 2, subsection 2, a document shall not be seized for evidential purposes if it may be presumed to contain information in regard to which a person is not allowed to give evidence. Under the Code of Judicial Procedure, Chapter 17, Article 23, counsel may not testify in respect of what a client has told him or her for the purpose of pleading a case.

On the face of the above-mentioned provision of the Code of Judicial Procedure, the Court finds the text unclear as far as it concerns confidentiality. The above-mentioned domestic law does not state with the requisite clarity whether the notion of 'pleading a case' covers only the relationship between a lawyer and his or her clients in a particular case or their relationship generally. The Court refers to a lawyer's general obligation of professional secrecy and confidentiality. In this respect the Court refers to the Recommendation Rec(2000)21 of the Committee of Ministers, according to which States should take all necessary measures to ensure the respect of the confidentiality of the client-lawyer relationship.

The Government sought to resolve this by noting that, in the applicant's case, the question of foreseeability must be solved on the basis of Chapter 4, section 2 of the Coercive Measures Act and Chapter 17, Article 23 of the Code of Judicial Procedure and that since the precedent decisions of the Supreme Court, the expression 'pleading a case' has been given a precise meaning.

The Court, however, is not convinced by these arguments. The precedent decisions of the Supreme Court were given only in December 2003 whereas the seizure in the present case took place on 17 May 1999. Even if the Supreme Court decisions were capable of clarifying the provisions in question, this does not change the fact that at the time of the seizure, the applicant could not benefit from this new interpretation.

Moreover, as the Court already found in the *Sallinen* case [...], there was no independent or judicial supervision when granting the search warrant as the decision to authorise the order was taken by the police themselves [...].

The Court would emphasise in this connection that search and seizure represent a serious interference with Article 8 rights, in the instant case correspondence, and must accordingly be based on a law that is particularly precise. It is essential to have clear, detailed rules on the subject, setting out safeguards against possible abuse or arbitrariness.

In that connection, the Court reiterates that the relationship between the Coercive Measures Act and the Code of Judicial Procedure (read together) was somewhat unclear and gave rise to diverging views on the extent of the protection afforded to privileged material in search and seizure, a situation which was identified also by the Deputy Chancellor of Justice of Finland (valtioneuvoston apulaisoikeuskansleri, justitiekansleradjointen i statsrådet) in the context of the *Sallinen* case [...].

The Court concludes that, even if there could be said to be a general legal basis for the measures provided for in Finnish law, that law does not indicate with sufficient clarity the circumstances in which privileged material could be subject to search and seizure. The applicant was thus deprived of the minimum degree of protection to which he was entitled under the rule of law in a democratic society [...]. The Court has thus no reason to reach a different conclusion in the present case than in the *Sallinen* case.

Eur. Court H.R. 13 January 2009 (Sorvisto v. Finland, no 19348/04), ECHR Reports 2009, paras 113–120.

19.28   [Non-compliant Finnish system] The Court must [...] examine the 'quality' of the legal rules applicable to the applicant in the instant case. It notes in the first place that under Chapter 5 of the Coercive Measures Act, a search may be conducted, inter alia, if there is reason to suspect that an offence has been committed and provided the maximum sentence applicable exceeds six months' imprisonment. The search warrant is issued by the investigative organs themselves. A search may be carried out even without a warrant in urgent cases.

With regard to the safeguards against abuse existing in the Finnish legislation, the Court observes that, in the absence of a requirement for prior judicial authorisation, the investigation authorities had unfettered discretion to assess the expediency and scope of the search and seizure. Moreover, in cases of urgency, a search could be carried out even without a warrant. The Court notes that in such cases the officer conducting the search was thus competent to assess alone whether or not to conduct the search and to what extent.

The Court would emphasise in this connection that search and seizure represent a serious interference with Article 8 rights, in the instant case a lawyer's office and her correspondence, and must accordingly be based on a law that is particularly precise. It is essential to have clear, detailed rules on the subject, setting out safeguards against possible abuse or arbitrariness [...]. Moreover, the Court has repeatedly held that since persecution and harassment of members of the legal profession strikes at the very heart of the Convention system, the searching of lawyers' premises should be subject to especially strict scrutiny [...].

Turning to the present case, the Court reiterates that it has already found in the *Sallinen and Others case* [...], that there was no independent or judicial supervision when granting the search warrant as the decision to authorise the order was taken by the police themselves [...].

The Court notes that the absence of a prior judicial warrant may be counterbalanced by the availability of an ex post factum judicial review [...]. However, in the present case the applicant did not have any effective access, a posteriori, to a court to have both the lawfulness of, and justification for, the search warrant reviewed. The applicant's right to respect for her home was thus violated by the fact that there was no prior judicial warrant and no possibility to obtain an effective judicial review a posteriori of either the decision to order the search or the manner in which it was conducted [...]. The situation was aggravated by the fact that the search took place in an attorney's office.

The Court therefore concludes that, even if there could be said to be a general legal basis for the impugned measures in Finnish law, that law does not provide sufficient judicial safeguards either before the granting of a search warrant or after the search. The applicant was thus deprived of the minimum degree of protection to which she was entitled under the rule of law in a democratic society.

Eur. Court H.R. 15 February 2011 (Heino v. Finland, no 56720/09), ECHR Reports 2011, paras 41–46.

See also Eur. Court H.R. 15 February 2011 (Harju v. Finland, no. 56716/09), para. 40 et seq.

3. Legitimate aim

The purpose of the interference with the applicant companies' right to respect for their premises was to obtain evidence of unlawful agreements between public-works contractors in the award of roadworks contracts. The interference was manifestly in the interests of both 'the economic well-being of the country' and 'the prevention of crime'. **19.29**

Eur. Court H.R. 16 April 2002 (Colas Est v. France, no 37971/97), ECHR Reports 2002-III, para. 44.

[L]'ingérence dans le domicile et le secret des correspondances des requérantes tendait à la recherche d'indices et de preuves de l'existence d'ententes illicites. Elle poursuivait donc à la fois le « bien-être économique du pays » et « la prévention des infractions pénales » au sens de l'article 8 § 2 de la Convention. **19.30**

Eur. Court H.R. 2 April 2015 (Vinci Construction and GTM Génie Civil et Services v. France, nos. 63629/10 and 60567/10), available only in French, unreported, para. 72.

See also Eur. Court H.R. 2 October 2014 (Delta Pekárny v. Czech Republic, no. 97/11), unreported, available in French and Czech only, para. 81.

4.   Necessary in a democratic society

(a)   General

19.31   The Contracting States have a certain margin of appreciation in assessing the need for an interference, but it goes hand in hand with European supervision.

Eur. Court H.R. (Plenary) 6 September 1978 (Klass and others v. Germany, no 5029/71), Series A no 28, p. 21, para. 42.

See also Eur. Court H.R. 25 February 1993 (Funke v. France, no 10828/84), Series A no. 256-A, pp. 24–25, para. 55; Eur. Court H.R. 16 December 1997 (Camenzind v. Switzerland, no 136/96), ECHR Reports 1997-VIII, para. 44.

19.32   The notion of 'necessity' implies that the interference corresponds to a pressing social need and, in particular, that it is proportionate to the legitimate aim pursued.

Eur. Court H.R. (Plenary) 24 March 1988 (Olsson v. Sweden, no 10465/83), Series A no 130, p. 31, para. 67.

(b)   Adequate safeguards

19.33   The Court [...] recognises that [national authorities] may consider it necessary to have recourse to measures such as house searches and seizures in order to obtain physical evidence of [...] offences and, where appropriate, to prosecute those responsible. Nevertheless, the relevant legislation and practice must afford adequate and effective safeguards against abuse and arbitrariness.

Eur. Court H.R. (Plenary) 6 September 1978 (Klass and others v. Germany, no 5029/71), Series A no 28, p. 21, para. 42.

See also Eur. Court H.R. 25 February 1993 (Funke v. France, no 10828/84), Series A no. 256-A, p. 24–25, para. 56.

19.34   Elements taken into consideration are, in particular, whether the search was based on a warrant issued by a judge and based on reasonable suspicion, whether the scope of the warrant was reasonably limited and – where the search of a lawyer's office was concerned – whether the search was carried out in the presence of an independent observer in order to ensure that materials subject to professional secrecy were not removed [...].

Eur. Court H.R. 16 October 2007 (Wieser and Bicos v. Austria, no 74336/01), unreported, para. 57.

(c)   Two-step test

19.35   As regards the [proportionality test], the Court must [i] firstly ensure that the relevant legislation and practice afford individuals 'adequate and effective safeguards against abuse' [...]. If individuals are to be protected from arbitrary interference by the authorities with the rights guaranteed under Article 8, a legal framework and very strict limits on such powers are called for. Secondly, the Court must consider [ii] the particular circumstances of each case in order to determine whether, in the concrete case, the interference in question was proportionate to the aim pursued.

Eur. Court H.R. 16 December 1997 (Camenzind v. Switzerland, no 136/96), ECHR Reports 1997-VIII, para. 45, subdivision added.

The criteria the Court has taken into consideration in determining this latter issue have **19.36** been, among others, the circumstances in which the search order had been issued, in particular further evidence available at that time, the content and scope of the warrant, the manner in which the search was carried out, including the presence of independent observers during the search, and the extent of possible repercussions on the work and reputation of the person affected by the search.

Eur. Court H.R. 7 June 2007 (Smirnov v. Russia, no 71362/01), para. 44.

(d) Importance of prior judicial authorisation

Notwithstanding the margin of appreciation which the Court recognises the Contract- **19.37** ing States have in this sphere, it must be particularly vigilant where [...] the authorities are empowered under national law to order and effect searches without a judicial warrant.

Eur. Court H.R. 16 December 1997 (Camenzind v. Switzerland, no 136/96), ECHR Reports 1997-VIII, para. 45.

In the present case, the Court notes that the search was carried out under a warrant **19.38** issued by a judge, who was required by law to be satisfied that there was reasonable ground for suspecting that the commission of a tax fraud had occurred and that evidence might be found at the premises to be searched. While the applicant complains that the granting of the warrant was obtained in an ex parte procedure, whereas in other statutory contexts inter partes procedures are provided for, the Court would note that there may be good reason not to give forewarning of a proposed search. The scrutiny given by a judge, even in an ex parte procedure, is none the less an important safeguard against abuse [...]. It does not consider any strong objection arises from the fact that it was a circuit judge in this case, rather than a more senior judge. It would note that in domestic law it is often a magistrate who provides the police with warrants for criminal investigations.

Eur. Court H.R. 19 September 2002 (Tamosius v. the United Kingdom, no 62002/00), ECHR Reports 2002-VIII, p. 9 et seq.

(e) Disproportionate national systems

[German judicial searches] [The Court] has formed the opinion that [...] the measure **19.39** complained of was not proportionate to [the] aims [pursued]. It is true that the offence in connection with which the search was effected, involving as it did not only an insult to but also an attempt to bring pressure on a judge, cannot be classified as no more than minor. On the other hand, the warrant was drawn in broad terms, in that it ordered a search for and seizure of 'documents', without any limitation, revealing the identity of the author of the offensive letter; this point is of special significance where, as in Germany, the search of a lawyer's office is not accompanied by any special procedural safeguards, such as the presence of an independent observer. More importantly, having regard to the materials that were in fact inspected, the search impinged on professional secrecy to an extent that appears disproportionate in the circumstances; it has, in this connection, to be recalled that, where a lawyer is involved, an encroachment on professional secrecy may have repercussions on the proper administration of justice and hence on the rights guaranteed by Article 6 of the Convention. In addition, the attendant publicity must have been capable of affecting adversely the applicant's professional reputation, in the eyes both of his existing clients and of the public at large.

Eur. Court H.R. 16 December 1992 (Niemietz v. Germany, no 13710/88), Series A No. 251-B, para. 35.

19.40 [French customs searches] The relevant legislation and practice did not afford adequate and effective safeguards against abuse in the instant case. At the material time […] the customs authorities had very wide powers; in particular, they had exclusive competence to assess the expediency, number, length and scale of inspections. Above all, in the absence of any requirement of a judicial warrant the restrictions and conditions provided for in law, which were emphasised by the Government […], appear too lax and full of loopholes for the interferences with the applicants' rights to have been strictly proportionate to the legitimate aim pursued.

Eur. Court H.R. 25 February 1993 (Funke v. France, no 10828/84), Series A no 256-A, pp. 24–25, para. 55.

19.41 [French competition searches according to former legislation] The Court observes […] that [the relevant legislation and practice did not afford adequate and effective safeguards against abuse] in the instant case. At the material time […] the relevant authorities had very wide powers which, pursuant to the 1945 ordinance, gave them exclusive competence to determine the expediency, number, length and scale of inspections. Moreover, the inspections in issue took place without any prior warrant being issued by a judge and without a senior police officer being present […]. That being so, even supposing that the entitlement to interfere may be more far-reaching where the business premises of a juristic person are concerned […], the Court considers, having regard to the manner of proceeding outlined above, that the impugned operations in the competition field cannot be regarded as strictly proportionate to the legitimate aims pursued […].

Eur. Court H.R. 16 April 2002 (Colas Est v. France, no 37971/97), ECHR Reports 2002-III, para. 50.

19.42 [Belgian judicial searches] La Cour note que les perquisitions opérées en l'espèce se sont accompagnées de certaines garanties de procédure. Elles ont été ordonnées par le conseiller instructeur, qui certes na pas procédé lui-même aux perquisitions mais a délégué cette tâche au commissaire général aux délégations judiciaires. Quant aux conditions dans lesquelles les perquisitions se déroulèrent, il y a lieu de relever quelles ont été opérées, à chaque fois, en présence des requérants ou d'un de leurs proches, par un officier de police judiciaire assisté par plusieurs inspecteurs et, au cours de certaines perquisitions, par deux experts, qui effectuèrent pour leur part une copie des contenus des systèmes informatiques. La durée des perquisitions varia entre une demi-heure et trois heures. A la fin de celles-ci, des procès-verbaux furent dressés.

En revanche, la Cour, rappelant qu'aucune infraction n'était reprochée aux requérants, se doit de constater que les différents mandats de perquisition étaient rédigés en termes larges […]. En effet, le conseiller instructeur ordonna, le 23 juin 1995, la série des perquisitions 'à l'effet d'y rechercher et d'y saisir tous documents et objets utiles à l'instruction' […], sans aucune limitation. Ces mandats de perquisition, qui ne donnaient aucune information sur l'instruction en cause, sur les lieux précis à visiter et sur les objets à saisir, octroyaient ainsi de larges pouvoirs aux enquêteurs […]. Un grand nombre d'objets, dont des disquettes informatiques et des disques durs des ordinateurs des requérants, furent effectivement saisis; le contenu de certains documents et supports magnétiques fut copié. En outre, le Gouvernement admet que les requérants ne reçurent pas d'information sur les poursuites qui ont rendu l'opération nécessaire. Ils ont ainsi été laissés dans l'ignorance quant aux motifs concrets des perquisitions effectuées chez eux.

Eur. Court H.R. 15 July 2003 (Ernst and others v. Belgium, no 33400/96), unreported, paras 115 and 116.

[Russian judicial searches] With regard to the safeguards against abuse existing in the **19.43** Russian legislation the Court observes that, in the absence of a requirement for prior judicial authorisation, the investigation authorities had unfettered discretion to assess the expediency and scope of the search and seizure. In the cases of *Funke, Crémieux and Miailhe v. France* the Court found that owing, above all, to the lack of a judicial warrant, 'the restrictions and conditions provided for in law... appear[ed] too lax and full of loopholes for the interferences with the applicant's rights to have been strictly proportionate to the legitimate aim pursued' and held that there had been a violation of Article 8 of the Convention […]. In the present case, however, the absence of a prior judicial warrant was, to a certain extent, counterbalanced by the availability of an ex post factum judicial review. The applicant could, and did, make a complaint to a court which was called upon to review both the lawfulness of, and justification for, the search warrant. The efficiency of the actual review carried out by the domestic courts will be taken into account in the following analysis of the necessity of the interference.

The Court observes that the applicant himself was not charged with, or suspected of, any criminal offence or unlawful activities. On the other hand, the applicant submitted documents showing that he had represented, at different times, four persons in criminal case no 7806, in connection with which the search had been ordered. In these circumstances, it is of particular concern for the Court that, when the search of the applicant's flat was ordered, no provision for safeguarding the privileged materials protected by professional secrecy was made.

The search order was drafted in extremely broad terms, referring indiscriminately to 'any objects and documents that [were] of interest for the investigation of criminal case [no 7806]', without any limitation. The order did not contain any information about the ongoing investigation, the purpose of the search or the reasons why it was believed that the search at the applicant's flat would enable evidence of any offence to be obtained

[…]. Only after the police had penetrated into the applicant's flat was he invited to hand over 'documents relating to the public company T. and the federal industrial group R'. However, neither the order nor the oral statements by the police indicated why documents concerning business matters of two private companies – in which the applicant did not hold any position – should have been found on the applicant's premises […]. The ex post factum judicial review did nothing to fill the lacunae in the deficient justification of the search order. The Oktyabrskiy Court confined its finding that the order had been justified, to a reference to four named documents and other unidentified materials, without describing the contents of any of them […]. The court did not give any indication as to the relevance of the materials it referred to and, moreover, two out of the four documents appeared after the search had been carried out. The Court finds that the domestic authorities failed in their duty to give 'relevant and sufficient' reasons for issuing the search warrant.

As regards the manner in which the search was conducted, the Court further observes that the excessively broad terms of the search order gave the police unrestricted discretion in determining which documents were 'of interest' for the criminal investigation; this resulted in an extensive search and seizure. The seized materials were not limited to those relating to business matters of two private companies. In addition, the police took away the applicant's personal notebook, the central unit of his computer and other materials, including his client's authority form issued in unrelated civil proceedings and a draft memorandum in another case. As noted above, there was no safeguard in place against interference with professional secrecy, such as, for example, a prohibition on removing documents covered by lawyer-client privilege or supervision of the search by an independent observer capable of identifying, independently of the investigation team, which documents were covered by legal professional privilege […]. Having regard to the materials that were inspected and seized, the Court finds that the search impinged on professional secrecy to an extent that was disproportionate to whatever legitimate aim was pursued. The Court reiterates in this connection that, where a lawyer is involved, an encroachment on professional secrecy may have repercussions on the proper administration of justice and hence on the rights guaranteed by Article 6 of the Convention […].

In sum, the Court considers that the search carried out, without relevant and sufficient grounds and in the absence of safeguards against interference with professional secrecy, at the flat of the applicant, who was not suspected of any criminal offence but was representing defendants in the same criminal case, was not 'necessary in a democratic society'. There has therefore been a violation of Article 8 of the Convention.

Eur. Court H.R. 7 June 2007 (Smirnov v. Russia, no 71362/01), paras 45–49.

19.44   [Austrian judicial searches] In the present case, the search of the applicant's computer facilities was based on a warrant issued by the investigating judge in the context of legal assistance for the Italian authorities which were conducting criminal proceedings for illegal trade in medicaments against a number of companies and individuals. It relied on the fact that invoices addressed to Novamed, 100 per cent owned by the applicant company, had been found. In these circumstances, the Court is satisfied that the search warrant was based on reasonable suspicion.

The Court also finds that the search warrant limited the documents or data to be looked for in a reasonable manner, by describing them as any business documents revealing contacts with the suspects in the Italian proceedings. The search remained within these limits, since the officers searched for documents or data containing either the word Novamed or Bicos or the name of any of the suspects.

Moreover, the Code of Criminal Procedure provides further procedural safeguards as regards the seizure of documents and electronic data. The Court notes the following provisions of the Code:

a. The occupant of premises searched shall be present;
b. A report is to be drawn up at the end of the search and items seized are to be listed;
c. If the owner objects to the seizure of documents or data carriers they are to be sealed and put before the judge for a decision as to whether or not they are to be used for the investigation; and
d. In addition, as far as the search of a lawyer's office is concerned, the presence of a representative of the Bar Association is required. [...]

What is striking in the present case is that the same safeguards were not observed as regards the electronic data. A number of factors show that the exercise of the applicant's rights in this respect was restricted. Firstly, the member of the Bar Association, though temporarily present during the search of the computer facilities, was mainly busy supervising the seizure of documents and could therefore not properly exercise his supervisory function as regards the electronic data. Secondly, the report setting out which search criteria had been applied and which files had been copied and seized was not drawn up at the end of the search but only later the same day. Moreover, the officers apparently left once they had finished their task without informing the first applicant or the representative of the Bar Association of the results of the search.

Eur. Court H.R. 16 October 2007 (Wieser and Bicos v. Austria, no 74336/01), unreported, paras 58–60 and 63.

[Romanian Judicial Searches] [L]a Cour constate que la perquisition a été effectuée le **19.45** matin du 19 décembre 2000 par le procureur F.M., qui avait ouvert le même jour une enquête pénale concernant la première requérante. Si, dans un domaine tel que la lutte contre le trafic d'influence, les autorités peuvent estimer nécessaire de recourir à certaines mesures, comme les visites domiciliaires et les saisies, pour établir la preuve matérielle de délits et en poursuivre le cas échéant les auteurs, encore faut-il que la législation et la pratique en la matière offrent des garanties adéquates et suffisantes contre les abus [...].

Or il n'en allait pas ainsi en l'occurrence. A l'époque des faits [...] les procureurs disposaient de pouvoirs fort larges, ayant notamment compétence pour apprécier seuls l'opportunité, le nombre, la durée et l'ampleur des perquisitions et des saisies. Conformément au droit interne en vigueur à l'époque des faits, le procureur décida en l'espèce de procéder à la perquisition domiciliaire et l'effectua sans bénéficier d'un mandat, et d'autant moins d'un mandat judiciaire. Le seul document écrit précisant de manière succincte le but de la perquisition et les motifs ayant conduit le procureur à la mener fut le procès-verbal de perquisition rédigé à la fin de la visite domiciliaire. La Cour observe qu'il s'agissait d'une atteinte grave au droit des deux premiers requérants au respect de leur domicile, laissée à la discrétion du procureur qui, comme elle l'a déjà jugé, en tant que magistrat du ministère public, ne remplissait pas l'exigence d'indépendance à l'égard de l'exécutif […].

Par ailleurs, si en l'absence de mandat judiciaire préalable, la perquisition en cause n'a été soumise à aucun contrôle a priori, la Cour observe qu'à l'époque des faits les deux premiers requérants ne bénéficiaient non plus d'une voie de recours effective pour faire contrôler a posteriori, par un juge, la légalité et le bien-fondé de la perquisition en question […]. De ce fait, effectuée en l'absence de mandat et, ainsi qu'il ressort du procès-verbal, de témoins assistants, la perquisition réalisée par le procureur n'a pas respecté les garanties minimales que les dispositions légales imposaient aux autorités chargées de l'enquête pénale et n'a pas non plus été soumise au contrôle des autorités judiciaires […].

Eu égard aux dispositions légales lâches et lacunaires régissant la perquisition domiciliaire à l'époque des faits, et notamment aux pouvoirs fort larges du procureur en la matière, la Cour considère que les deux premiers requérants n'ont pas joui du degré minimal de protection contre l'arbitraire voulu par l'article 8 de la Convention.

Eur. Court H.R. 1 April 2008 (Varga v. Romania, no 73957/01), paras 71–74.

19.46   [Disproportionate Czech Competition Authority Searches] Dans la présente affaire, l'inspection dans les locaux commerciaux de la société requérante situés à Prague a eu lieu le 19 novembre 2003, à savoir le jour même de l'ouverture d'une procédure administrative à son encontre, motivée par des soupçons d'un comportement anti-concurrentiel. Si, dans un domaine tel que la protection de la compétition économique, les autorités peuvent estimer nécessaire de recourir à certaines mesures, comme les perquisitions ou inspections, pour éviter la disparition ou la dissimulation des éléments de preuve, établir la preuve matérielle de pratiques anticoncurrentielles et en poursuivre le cas échéant les auteurs, encore faut-il que la législation et la pratique en la matière prévoient suffisamment de garanties pour éviter que les autorités ne puissent prendre des mesures arbitraires portant atteinte au droit des requérants au respect de leur domicile […].

En l'espèce, la société requérante a été informée de l'ouverture de cette procédure par une notification signée par le directeur supérieur de l'Autorité et remise à ses représent-ants au début de l'inspection, qui mentionnait comme objet de la procédure une possible violation de l'article 3 § 1 de la loi no 143/2001 sur la protection de la concurrence économique consistant en une entente présumée sur les prix de vente de produits boulangers. La notification a été accompagnée d'une autorisation à effectuer l'inspection, établie par l'Autorité, laquelle comportait selon la requérante les noms des agents chargés de l'inspection. Force est donc de constater que cette notification ne mentionne que très sommairement l'objet de la procédure administrative et ne détaille ni les faits ni les pièces sur lesquels reposent les présomptions de pratiques anticoncur-rentielles […].

Conformément au droit interne, le seul fait d'avoir ouvert une procédure administra-tive à l'encontre de la société requérante donnait à l'Autorité de la concurrence le droit de procéder à l'inspection. Celle-ci n'a donc pas fait l'objet d'une autorisation préalable par un juge, qui aurait pu la circonscrire ou contrôler son déroulement […], ni n'a été ordonnée par une décision susceptible de réexamen judiciaire. L'article 21 § 4 de la loi no 143/2001 laisse en effet une large marge de manœuvre à l'Autorité quant à l'appréciation de la nécessité et de l'ampleur des perquisitions […]. Le seul document écrit précisant de manière succincte le but de l'inspection et les motifs ayant conduit l'Autorité à la mener a été le procès-verbal d'inspection rédigé à la fin de celle-ci […].

Néanmoins, la Cour a déjà eu l'occasion d'affirmer que, dans de telles situations, l'absence d'un mandat de perquisition peut être contrecarrée par un contrôle judiciaire ex post facto sur la légalité et la nécessité de cette mesure d'instruction […]. Encore faut-il que ce contrôle soit efficace dans les circonstances particulières de l'affaire en cause […]. En pratique, cela implique que les personnes concernées puissent obtenir un contrôle juridictionnel effectif, en fait comme en droit, de la mesure litigieuse et de son déroulement ; lorsqu'une opération jugée irrégulière a déjà eu lieu, le ou les recours disponibles doivent permettre de fournir à l'intéressé un redressement approprié […].

En l'espèce, le contrôle effectif de la légalité et de la nécessité de l'inspection en cause était d'autant plus nécessaire qu'à aucun moment avant celle-ci il n'avait été précisé quels étaient concrètement les documents liés à la procédure administrative que l'Autorité s'attendait à découvrir dans les locaux de la société requérante […].

Il existe en l'occurrence une controverse entre les parties quant à la question de savoir si ce contrôle a été dispensé dans les deux procédures menées en l'espèce sur le fondement de l'article 65 du code de justice administrative, à savoir celle portant sur la violation des règles matérielles de la concurrence et celle relative à l'amende infligée à la société requérante. En revanche, les deux parties semblent admettre qu'il n'y avait pas lieu pour la requérante d'engager une action contre une ingérence illégale au sens de l'article 82 du code de justice administrative, qui semble être pourtant le mécanisme de protection le plus adéquat dans ces situations […]. En effet, dans les circonstances de la cause, cette action était vouée à l'échec, soit parce qu'elle ne remplirait pas la condition de viser une ingérence en cours ou susceptible de se répéter (condition abrogée au 1er janvier 2012, voir paragraphe 43 ci-dessus), soit parce qu'elle revêt un caractère subsidiaire à celle prévue par l'article 65 dudit code, que la requérante a engagée pour contester la décision sur l'amende […]).

La société requérante allègue que la procédure relative à l'amende infligée en vertu de l'article 22 de la loi no 143/2011 portait uniquement sur son comportement et sur le montant de l'amende, alors que la procédure sur le fond engagée le 19 novembre 2003 se concentrait sur la question de savoir s'il y a eu violation des règles matérielles de la concurrence. Selon la société requérante, les tribunaux se sont donc en l'espèce limités à examiner la légalité de l'inspection mais n'ont jamais examiné la conduite de l'Autorité, les motifs, le but et l'ampleur de l'inspection, ni son caractère nécessaire et proportionné […].

La Cour constate en effet qu'aucune de ces deux procédures ne visait directement la régularité de l'inspection même et qu'aucun recours en contestation du déroulement de l'inspection n'était prévu. Même si notamment la Cour suprême administrative s'est livrée, dans son arrêt du 29 mai 2009 […], à une analyse des questions relatives à la base légale, au but légitime et à la proportionnalité, elle s'est concentrée essentiellement sur l'étendue des pouvoirs que la loi conférait aux agents de l'autorité une fois qu'il a été décidé d'effectuer une inspection, et sur le respect de ces pouvoirs par les agents. Tout en notant que les arguments de la société requérante relatifs à l'étendue du contrôle judiciaire revêtent un caractère plutôt théorique et tout en reconnaissant que les décisions des juridictions nationales sont très bien élaborées et s'appuient sur la jurisprudence de la Cour, la Cour se doit de constater que les tribunaux saisis en l'espèce ne se sont pas penchés sur les éléments de fait ayant conduit l'Autorité à effectuer l'inspection [...]. En conséquence, l'exercice par l'Autorité de son pouvoir d'apprécier l'opportunité, la durée et l'ampleur de l'inspection n'a pas fait l'objet d'un examen judiciaire. A ce titre, ne saurait être considéré comme suffisant le constat du tribunal régional selon lequel l'ingérence dans la sphère du compétiteur concerné était justifiée dès le moment où l'Autorité avait des soupçons qu'un certain comportement sur le marché résultait d'un contact entre les compétiteurs, contact qui ne pouvait être démontré que par les preuves obtenues lors de l'inspection [...].

Il s'ensuit que, par ce biais, la requérante n'aurait pas pu prétendre à un redressement approprié dans l'hypothèse où l'inspection aurait été jugée irrégulière. Sur ce point, la Cour observe que la possibilité de se prévaloir dans ces circonstances de la loi no 82/1998 pour demander une indemnisation semble avoir été pour la première fois évoquée dans l'arrêt de la Cour administrative suprême du 13 février 2014 [...], et que le Gouvernement ne mentionne pas ce moyen.

Il est vrai que l'inspection litigieuse s'est déroulée en présence de représentants de la société requérante [...], que l'Autorité n'avait pas le droit de saisir des documents et s'est vu remettre seulement des copies [...] et que ses agents étaient tenus par l'obligation de confidentialité [...]. Toutefois, la Cour considère qu'en l'absence d'une autorisation préalable d'un juge, d'un contrôle effectif a posteriori de la nécessité de la mesure contestée et d'une réglementation relative à une éventuelle destruction des copies obtenues [...], ces garanties procédurales n'étaient pas suffisantes pour prévenir le risque d'abus de pouvoir de la part de l'Autorité de la concurrence [...].

Ces éléments suffisent à la Cour pour conclure que, tel qu'effectué en l'espèce, le contrôle judiciaire ex post facto n'a pas offert à la société requérante suffisamment de garanties contre l'arbitraire, de sorte que l'ingérence dans ses droits ne peut pas être considérée comme étant étroitement proportionnée au but légitime recherché.

Eur. Court H.R. 2 October 2014 (Delta Pekárny v. Czech Republic, no. 97/11), unreported, available in French and Czech only, paras 84–93.

19.47   [Disproportionate French Competition Authority Searches] À l'instar de ce qu'elle avait fait dans l'arrêt Société Canal Plus et autres (précité, § 55), la Cour relève d'emblée que les visites domiciliaires effectuées dans les locaux des requérantes avaient pour objectif la recherche de preuves de pratiques anticoncurrentielles possiblement imputables à ces dernières et n'apparaissent pas dès lors, en elles-mêmes, disproportionnées aux regards des exigences de l'article 8 de la Convention. La Cour réitère également son constat selon lequel la procédure interne en cause prévoyait un certain nombre de garanties et renvoie sur ce point à ce qu'elle avait dit dans l'arrêt Société Canal Plus et autres [...].

Il reste que la question plus spécifiquement posée par la présente affaire est celle de savoir si ces garanties ont été appliquées de manière concrète et effective, et non pas théorique et illusoire, notamment au regard du grand nombre de documents informatiques et messages électroniques saisis, ainsi que de l'exigence renforcée du respect de la confidentialité qui s'attache aux correspondances échangées entre un avocat et son client.

En l'espèce, la Cour considère, avec le Gouvernement, que les enquêteurs se sont efforcés de circonscrire leurs fouilles et de ne procéder qu'à des saisies en rapport avec l'objet de leur enquête. De plus, la Cour ne souscrit pas à l'argumentation des requérantes selon laquelle elles n'auraient pas été mises en mesure d'identifier les documents saisis à l'issue des opérations en cause. Elle relève à ce titre qu'un inventaire suffisamment précis, indiquant le nom des fichiers, leur extension, leur provenance et leur empreinte numérique avait été dressé et leur avait été remis, ainsi qu'une copie des documents saisis. Partant, la Cour estime que les saisies pratiquées ne pouvaient être qualifiées de « massives et indifférenciées ».

En revanche, la Cour constate que les saisies ont porté sur de nombreux documents informatiques, incluant l'intégralité des messageries électroniques professionnelles de certains employés des sociétés requérantes. Or, il n'est pas contesté que ces documents et messageries comportaient un certain nombre de fichiers et informations relevant de la confidentialité attachée aux relations entre un avocat et son client. Elle note à ce titre que la DGCCRF avait expressément indiqué dans ses conclusions en défense devant le JLD ne pas s'opposer à la restitution des pièces couvertes ainsi par le secret professionnel.

La Cour relève ensuite que, pendant le déroulement des opérations en cause, les requérantes n'ont pu ni prendre connaissance du contenu des documents saisis, ni discuter de l'opportunité de leur saisie. Or, de l'avis de la Cour, à défaut de pouvoir prévenir la saisie de documents étrangers à l'objet de l'enquête et a fortiori de ceux relevant de la confidentialité qui s'attache aux relations entre un avocat et son client, les requérantes devaient pouvoir faire apprécier a posteriori et de manière concrète et effective leur régularité. Un recours, tel que celui ouvert par l'article L.450–4 du code de commerce, devait leur permettre d'obtenir, le cas échéant, la restitution des documents concernés ou l'assurance de leur parfait effacement, s'agissant de copies de fichiers informatiques.

À cet effet, la Cour estime qu'il appartient au juge, saisi d'allégations motivées selon lesquelles des documents précisément identifiés ont été appréhendés alors qu'ils étaient sans lien avec l'enquête ou qu'ils relevaient de la confidentialité qui s'attache aux relations entre un avocat et son client, de statuer sur leur sort au terme d'un contrôle concret de proportionnalité et d'ordonner, le cas échéant, leur restitution. Or, la Cour constate qu'en l'espèce, si les requérantes ont exercé le recours que la loi leur ménageait devant le JLD, ce dernier, tout en envisageant la présence d'une correspondance émanant d'un avocat parmi les documents retenus par les enquêteurs, s'est contenté d'apprécier la régularité du cadre formel des saisies litigieuses, sans procéder à l'examen concret qui s'imposait.

Compte tenu de ce qui précède, la Cour juge que les saisies effectuées aux domiciles des requérantes étaient, dans les circonstances de l'espèce, disproportionnées par rapport au but visé.

Eur. Court H.R. 2 April 2015 (Vinci Construction and GTM Génie Civil et Services v. France, nos. 63629/10 and 60567/10), available only in French, unreported, paras 74–80.

(f) Proportionate national systems

[UK Anton Piller Order]   **19.48**
A.   The grant and terms of the order, as such
The order made against Mr Chappell and his company was granted only after Mr Justice Whitford had been supplied with evidence establishing that the requisite conditions were met [...]. Bearing in mind the nature and scope of the applicant's

business [...], the Court – quite apart from any question of the United Kingdom's margin of appreciation – entertains no doubt that the actual grant of the order was a necessary step in the effective pursuit by the plaintiffs of their copyright action.

It has also to be noted that the order itself incorporated significant limitations on its scope. Thus, the relief afforded was granted for a short period only; restrictions were placed on the times at which and the number of persons by whom the plaintiffs' search could be effected; and any materials seized could be used only for a specified purpose [...]. In this way, the measure was accompanied by safeguards calculated to keep its impact within reasonable bounds. Furthermore, these safeguards were buttressed by a series of undertakings given by the plaintiffs or their solicitors, and a variety of remedies was available to the applicant in the event that he considered the order to have been improperly executed [...].

On the subject of safeguards, the applicant submitted that if the arrangements between the plaintiffs and the police had been more fully disclosed to the High Court at the outset, further conditions would have been imposed. Their result, he said, would have been to preclude the two searches of his premises being conducted simultaneously. Whilst this may be so, the Court does not consider that on this account the order, in substance, was not 'necessary'. At most, this point may go to the question, which the Court examines below, whether the actual execution of the order was proportionate to the legitimate aim pursued.

Mr Chappell further maintained – and in this he was supported by a minority of the Commission – that the High Court was unable to supervise implementation of the Anton Piller order to a sufficient degree. In his view, its execution should, rather than being left to the plaintiffs' solicitors, have been entrusted to or supervised by an independent court official.

The Court is not persuaded by this argument. It is true that a solicitor executing such an order may find himself faced with a conflict between his obligations to his client and his duty to the court, as one of its officers. However, a solicitor who fails to abide by an undertaking of his incorporated in the order lays himself open to heavy penalties, even to the point in *some circumstances of putting his professional career in jeopardy* ([...]).

B.   The execution of the order

There remains the question whether the actual execution of the order can be regarded as 'necessary' and, in particular, as proportionate to the legitimate aim pursued. [...]

Of more consequence are the remaining factors relied on, namely the manner in which the plaintiffs gained entry to the applicant's premises and the fact that the latter were searched, simultaneously, by 16 or 17 people. The Court would agree with the criticisms of these aspects of the case made by the Court of Appeal, which described what happened as 'disturbing' and 'unfortunate and regrettable' [...].

Mr Chappell was admittedly not afforded a proper opportunity to refuse the plaintiff's entry to his premises at the door, since members of their party entered together with Detective Chief Inspector A [...].

However, the applicant subsequently raised no objection on this score. Indeed, rather than exercising his right of asking the plaintiffs to leave, he acquiesced, after receiving legal advice, in their search operations. Moreover, it was not until such advice had been tendered that those operations were put in hand [...].

Manifestly the simultaneous searches by the police and the plaintiffs must have been distracting for Mr Chappell and must have created difficulties for him, as regards supervision and as regards taking advice from and giving instructions to his solicitor. Indeed, Mr Justice Warner recognised that this circumstance made the execution of the Anton Piller order 'more oppressive than it should have been' [...].

Against this have to be weighed the following factors. Firstly, it is clear that the two searches concerned at least partly the same materials. Secondly, the applicant made no request for one of the searches to be deferred until the other had been completed. Thirdly, the domestic courts – after hearing first-hand evidence – found that in fact Mr Chappell was able to look after his interests whilst the order was being implemented [...]. Finally, Mr Justice Warner found that 'there was nothing inherently wrong with the mode of execution' of the order and the Court of Appeal concluded that it was not necessary to set the order aside for the purpose of doing justice to Mr Chappell [...].

In the light of the above, the Court is of the opinion that the shortcomings in the procedure followed – which, by its very nature, was bound to cause some difficulties for the applicant – were not so serious that the execution of the order can, in the circumstances of the case, be regarded as disproportionate to the legitimate aim pursued.

Eur. Court H.R. 30 March 1989 (Chappell v. UK, no 10461/83), Series A no 152-A, p. 26, paras 59–66.

[Swiss searches under telecommunications legislation] [...] With regard to the safe-guards provided by Swiss law, the Court notes that under the Federal Administrative Criminal Law Act of 22 March 1974 [...], a search may, subject to exceptions, only be effected under a written warrant issued by a limited number of designated senior public servants (section 48) and carried out by officials specially trained for the purpose (section 20); they each have an obligation to stand down if circumstances exist which could affect their impartiality (section 29). Searches can only be carried out in 'dwellings and other premises [...] if it is likely that a suspect is in hiding there or if objects or valuables liable to seizure or evidence of the commission of an offence are to be found there' (section 48); they cannot be conducted on Sundays, public holidays or at night 'except in important cases or where there is imminent danger' (section 49). At the beginning of a search the investigating official must produce evidence of identity and inform the occupier of the premises of the purpose of the search. That person or, if he is absent, a relative or a member of the household must be asked to attend. In principle, there will also be a public officer present to ensure that '[the search] does not deviate from its purpose'. A record of the search is drawn up immediately in the presence of the persons who attended; if they so request, they must be provided with a copy of the search warrant and of the record (section 49). Furthermore, searches for documents are subject to special restrictions (section 50). In addition, suspects are entitled, whatever the circumstances, to representation (section 32); anyone affected by an 'investigative measure' who has 'an interest worthy of protection in having the measure [...] quashed or varied' may complain to the Indictment Division of the Federal Court (sections 26 and 28). Lastly, a 'suspect' who is found to have no case to answer may seek compensation for the losses he has sustained (sections 99–100). As regards the manner in which the search was conducted, the Court notes that it was at Mr Camenzind's request that it was carried out by a single official [...]. It took place in the applicant's

19.49

presence after he had been allowed to consult the file on his case and telephone a lawyer [...]. Admittedly, it lasted almost two hours and covered the entire house, but the investigating official did no more than check the telephones and television sets; he did not search in any furniture, examine any documents or seize anything [...].

[Proportionality accepted.]

Eur. Court H.R. 16 December 1997 (Camenzind v. Switzerland, no 136/96), ECHR Reports 1997–VIII, para. 46.

19.50 [British judicial searches (see above para. 19.43 regarding warrants)] The applicant has also complained about the breadth of the warrant granted, in particular that it did not give specific detail of the articles or persons which were the subject of the search. The Court recalls that the first warrant related to any items relating to serious tax fraud. However, a second warrant was issued, which included a schedule of 35 companies and individuals listed as being under investigation. It was this warrant that was executed, although the domestic courts gave the opinion that both were equally lawful. The Court is not persuaded that in these circumstances the applicant was denied sufficient indication of the purpose of the search to enable him to assess whether the investigation team acted unlawfully or exceeded their powers.

The Court also recalls that the search was carried out under the supervision of counsel, whose task was to identify which documents were covered by legal professional privilege and should not be removed. Though the applicant has denied that this provided any substantial safeguard, the Court notes that the counsel, nominated by the Attorney General, was under instructions to act independently from the investigation team and to give independent advice. The applicant has not claimed, in any domestic proceedings, that the counsel erred in the exercise of his judgment. The Court sees nothing sinister in the inclusion in counsel's instructions of a reference to consulting the investigation team where necessary to clarify the alleged relevance of an item to the investigation. It would appear only logical that the investigation team be required to justify why they wish to remove certain items.

[proportionality accepted].

Eur. Court H.R. 19 September 2002 (Tamosius v. the United Kingdom, no 62002/00), ECHR Reports 2002–VIII, p. 9 et seq.

19.51 [T]he Court observes that the domestic law in force at the material time permitted an investigator to penetrate into a home against the will of those living there for the purpose of carrying out an inspection of a crime scene. The domestic law defined the scope of the inspection as 'finding and securing the traces of the crime and other physical evidence, clarifying the crime scene and other relevant circumstances'. The inspection of a crime scene was supplemented by a power of seizure and did not require prior judicial approval. The criminal proceedings could be opened either before the inspection or shortly afterwards [...]. The domestic law further provided that the inspection was to be conducted in the presence of attesting witnesses. Whether it was necessary for an accused, a suspect, a victim, a witness or an expert to take part was left to the discretion of the investigator. A record of the inspection had to be drawn up [...]. A person could ex post facto challenge the lawfulness of the investigator's actions before a court [...]. The Court is satisfied that the above restrictions and conditions of the domestic law were sufficient to exclude arbitrary intrusions into people's homes.

Turning to the circumstances of the present case the Court observes that the inspection of the applicant's home implied a certain urgency and for that reason was carried out prior to institution of the criminal proceedings against the applicant. The Court further observes that the investigator did not overstep the scope of the inspection as defined in the domestic law. The inspection was conducted in the presence of two attesting witnesses. The record of the inspection was drawn up thereafter. Shortly afterwards, within a matter of a few days, criminal proceedings were instituted against the applicant on suspicion of forgery of official documents. The applicant used his right to challenge the lawfulness of the applied investigative measure.

Regard being had to the above, the Court considers that the interference with the applicant's right to respect for his home had been proportionate to the legitimate aim pursued.

Eur. Court H.R. 14 January 2010 (Mastepan v. Russia, no 3708/03), paras 43–45.

[Proportionate French Competition Authority Searches] Si, pour se prononcer sur la **19.52** « nécessité » d'une ingérence « dans une société démocratique », la Cour doit tenir compte de la marge d'appréciation laissée aux Etats contractants, elle ne se borne toutefois pas à se demander si l'Etat défendeur a usé de son pouvoir d'appréciation de bonne foi, avec soin et de manière sensée. Dans l'exercice de son contrôle, il lui faut considérer les décisions critiquées à la lumière de l'ensemble de l'affaire et déterminer si les motifs invoqués à l'appui des ingérences en cause sont « pertinents et suffisants ». Par ailleurs, s'agissant en particulier des visites domiciliaires et des saisies, la Cour a déjà eu l'occasion de souligner que, si les Etats peuvent estimer nécessaire de recourir à de telles mesures pour établir la preuve matérielle des délits et en poursuivre le cas échéant les auteurs, il faut que leur législation et leur pratique en la matière offrent des garanties suffisantes contre les abus […].

En l'espèce, la Cour constate que l'ordonnance du juge des libertés et de la détention du 8 février 2005 détaille les faits et pièces sur lesquels reposent les présomptions de pratiques anticoncurrentielles prohibées par les articles 420–1 et 420–2 du code de commerce pesant sur plusieurs entreprises et organisations professionnelles, au nombre desquelles se trouvent les requérantes, et qu'il autorise « à procéder ou à faire procéder, dans les locaux » de CANAL PLUS « aux visites et aux saisies de tous documents nécessaires à la recherche de la preuve des agissements qui entrent dans le champ des pratiques prohibées par les points 1 et 2 de l'article L. 420–1 du code de commerce et de l'article 81 du traité de Rome et/ou par les articles L. 420–2 alinéa 1 du code de commerce et 82 du traité de Rome relevés dans le secteur de la gestion des droits dans le football professionnel et celui de la publicité dans les stades de football ainsi que toute manifestation de ces agissements prohibés ». Il est donc incontestable que les visites domiciliaires effectuées dans les locaux des requérantes avaient pour objectif la recherche de preuves de pratiques anticoncurrentielles possiblement imputables à ces dernières. Dans ces circonstances et eu égard à la marge d'appréciation dont dispose l'autorité judiciaire en la matière, la Cour estime qu'elle était fondée à considérer les visites domiciliaires comme nécessaires à cette fin, et voit dans la saisie de documents relatifs auxdits agissements un motif pertinent et suffisant.

Par ailleurs, comme l'article L. 16 B du livre des procédures fiscales, l'article L. 450–4 du code de commerce énonce un certain nombre de garanties : d'une part, il prévoit une autorisation judiciaire préalable du juge qui vérifie si la demande d'autorisation est fondée ; d'autre part, les opérations de visite et saisie s'effectuent sous l'autorité et le contrôle de ce même juge, qui désigne un ou plusieurs officiers de police judiciaire chargés d'assister à ces opérations et de le tenir informé, qui peut à tout moment décider de la suspension ou l'arrêt de la visite, et qui peut se rendre dans les locaux pendant l'intervention. En outre, il prévoit un recours en contestation du déroulement des opérations de visite et saisie auprès du juge les ayant autorisées dans un délai de deux mois.

Il ne ressort pas du dossier que la procédure n'ait pas été respectée en l'espèce. La Cour relève que, dans son ordonnance, le juge a circonscrit la visite et désigné nommément neuf officiers de police judiciaire chargés de le tenir informé du déroulement des opérations. Il a également précisé les conditions de désignation des enquêteurs habilités à procéder aux visites. L'ordonnance du juge informait également les personnes concernées des voies des recours pour contester la régularité des opérations. Enfin, la Cour relève que les requérantes ont pu soumettre les opérations de visite et saisie au contrôle des autorités judiciaires qui ont vérifié leur régularité par des décisions dument motivées.

Le fait qu'en violation de l'article 6 § 1 de la Convention, les requérantes n'aient pas bénéficié d'un contrôle juridictionnel effectif pour contester l'ordonnance d'autorisation du juge au sens de cette disposition (paragraphes 44 et 45 ci-dessus) ne met pas en cause la pertinence de ces garanties; cela ressort d'ailleurs clairement des motifs de l'arrêt Ravon et autres [...].

Compte tenu de ce qui précède, la Cour estime que, dans les circonstances de l'espèce, les visites domiciliaires et saisies dont les requérantes ont fait l'objet n'ont pas été disproportionnées.

Eur. Court H.R. 21 December 2010 (Société Canal Plus a.o. v. France, no. 29408/08), only available in French, unreported, paras 54–59.

5. Assessment of the EU System

See also Chapter 24 Section C.2. on the requirements that apply under Article 47 Charter and Article 6(1) ECHR to the judicial review of inspections.

19.53   [C]ommunity law provides a range of guarantees.

First of all, the coercive measures for which application may be made to national authorities in the implementation of Article 14(6) of Regulation No 17 [now Art. 20(6) Regulation No 1/2003] are intended solely to enable Commission officials to exercise the investigatory powers vested in that institution. Those powers, which are listed in Article 14(1) [now Art. 20(2) Regulation No 1/2003] of that regulation, are themselves clearly circumscribed.

Thus, the scope of the Commission's investigatory powers does not extend to cover, in particular, documents of a non-business nature, that is to say, documents not relating to the market activities of the undertaking [...].

Next, without prejudice to the guarantees under domestic law governing the implementation of coercive measures, undertakings under investigation are protected by various Community guarantees, including, in particular, the right to legal representation and the privileged nature of correspondence between lawyer and client [...].

Lastly, Article 14(3) of Regulation No 17 [now Art. 20(4) Regulation No 1/2003] requires the Commission to state reasons for the decision ordering an investigation by specifying its subject-matter and purpose. As the Court has held, this is a fundamental requirement, designed not merely to show that the proposed entry onto the premises of the undertakings concerned is justified but also to enable those undertakings to assess the scope of their duty to cooperate whilst at the same time safeguarding their rights of defence [...].

The Commission is likewise obliged to state in that decision, as precisely as possible, what it is looking for and the matters to which the investigation must relate [...]. As the Court has held, that requirement is intended to protect the rights of defence of the undertakings concerned, which would be seriously compromised if the Commission could rely on evidence against undertakings which was obtained during an investigation but was not related to the subject-matter or purpose thereof [...].

Third, an undertaking against which the Commission has ordered an investigation may bring an action against that decision before the Community judicature under the fourth paragraph of Article [263 TFEU]. If the decision in question were annulled by the Community judicature, the Commission would in that event be prevented from using, for the purposes of proceeding in respect of an infringement of the Community competition rules, any documents or evidence which it might have obtained in the course of that investigation, as otherwise the decision on the infringement might, in so far as it was based on such evidence, be annulled by the Community judicature [...].

Clearly, the existence of the power of judicial review so conferred on the Community judicature and the detailed rules, particularly those referred to in paragraphs 43 to 48 above, governing the exercise by the Commission of its investigatory powers, help to protect undertakings against arbitrary measures and to keep such measures within the limits of what is necessary in order to pursue the legitimate interests specified in paragraph 42 of this judgment.

Fourth, as emerges from paragraphs 35 and 39 of this judgment, the competent national court is required to ensure that the Commission's action is effective and to refrain from substituting its own assessment of the need for the investigations ordered for that of the Commission, the lawfulness of whose assessments of fact and law may be reviewed only by the Community judicature.

Although the national court with jurisdiction to authorise coercive measures must take into account the particular context in which its jurisdiction has been invoked, as well as the considerations set out in paragraphs 42 to 51 above, those requirements cannot prevent or absolve it from performing its obligation to ensure, in the specific circumstances of each individual case, that the coercive measure envisaged is not arbitrary or disproportionate to the subject-matter of the investigation ordered [...].

CoJ 22 October 2002 (Roquette Frères, C-94/00) [2002] ECR I-9011, paras 43–52.

19.54   [Reasonable suspicion requirement] À cet égard, en premier lieu, il y a lieu de relever que les facultés d'enquête de la Commission seraient dépourvues d'utilité si elle devait se limiter à demander la production de documents qu'elle serait à même d'identifier au préalable de façon précise. Un tel droit implique, au contraire, la faculté de rechercher des éléments d'information divers qui ne sont pas encore connus ou pleinement identifiés. Sans une telle faculté, il serait impossible à la Commission de recueillir les éléments d'information nécessaires à l'inspection au cas où elle se heurterait à un refus de collaboration ou encore à une attitude d'obstruction de la part des entreprises concernées [...].

En second lieu, l'exercice de cette faculté de rechercher des éléments d'information divers qui ne sont pas encore connus ou pleinement identifiés permet à la Commission d'examiner certains documents de nature professionnelle de l'entreprise destinataire d'une décision prise au titre de l'article 20, paragraphe 4, du règlement n° 1/2003, alors même qu'elle ignore s'ils relèvent des activités visées par cette décision, afin de vérifier si tel est le cas et d'éviter que l'entreprise en cause ne cache à la Commission des éléments de preuve pertinents pour l'enquête sous prétexte qu'ils ne sont pas couverts par l'objet de celle-ci.

Néanmoins, en dépit de ce qui précède, lorsqu'elle effectue une inspection dans les locaux d'une entreprise en vertu de l'article 20, paragraphe 4, du règlement n° 1/2003, la Commission est tenue de limiter ses recherches aux activités de cette entreprise relatives aux secteurs indiqués dans la décision ordonnant l'inspection et, donc, une fois qu'elle a constaté, après examen, qu'un document ou une information ne relevait pas de ces activités, de s'abstenir de l'utiliser aux fins de son enquête.

En effet, si la Commission n'était pas soumise à cette limitation, tout d'abord, elle aurait en pratique la possibilité, à chaque fois qu'elle est en possession d'un indice lui permettant de soupçonner qu'une entreprise a commis une infraction aux règles de la concurrence dans un domaine précis de ses activités, d'effectuer une inspection portant sur l'ensemble de celles-ci et ayant pour but ultime de déceler l'existence de toute infraction auxdites règles ayant pu être commise par cette entreprise, ce qui est incompatible avec la protection de la sphère d'activité privée des personnes juridiques garantie en tant que droit fondamental dans une société démocratique.

Ensuite, l'obligation de la Commission d'indiquer le but et l'objet de l'inspection dans les décisions prises au titre de l'article 20, paragraphe 4, du règlement n° 1/2003 aurait une finalité purement formelle si elle était définie de la manière suggérée par la Commission. La jurisprudence selon laquelle cette obligation a notamment pour but de permettre aux entreprises concernées de saisir la portée de leur devoir de collaboration serait méconnue, dans la mesure où cette obligation s'étendrait systématiquement à l'ensemble des activités des entreprises en cause.

Il convient donc de considérer que, en l'espèce, la Commission était dans l'obligation de disposer d'indices suffisamment sérieux justifiant la réalisation d'une inspection dans les locaux des requérantes et portant sur l'ensemble des activités de celles-ci relatives aux câbles électriques et au matériel associé à ces câbles pour adopter la décision d'inspection.

General Court 14 November 2012 (Prysmian v. Commission, T-140/09), ECLI: EU:T:2012:597, paras 60–65.

[On whether the absence of a prior judicial search authorisation is sufficiently compen- **19.55** sated by other safeguards] It must be noted that the exercise of the powers of inspection conferred on the Commission by Article 20(4) of Regulation No 1/2003 vis-à-vis an undertaking constitutes a clear interference with the latter's right to respect for its privacy, private premises and correspondence. That is not disputed by the Commission or by the interveners in these proceedings. The question at issue in this instance is therefore whether the lack of a prior judicial warrant automatically renders the administrative interference illegal and, as the case may be, whether the system established by Regulation No 1/2003 offers sufficient safeguards in the absence of prior judicial authorisation.

In its recent decisions [*Harju v. Finland* and *Heino v. Finland*], the ECtHR drew attention to the importance of conducting a particularly rigorous review in cases where inspections can take place without prior judicial authorisation. It also clearly laid down the principle that the absence of prior judicial authorisation may be counterbalanced by a comprehensive post-inspection review.

Therefore, the inevitable conclusion to be drawn from the recent case-law of the ECtHR is that the lack of a prior judicial warrant is not capable, in itself, of rendering an interference within the meaning of Article 8 ECHR illegal.

The arguments of the applicants seeking to limit the scope of the ECtHR's judgments in *Heino v. Finland* and *Harju v. Finland*, [...] do not call that conclusion into question.

According to the applicants, those judgments show that only a situation of imminent danger, with a view to preventing the commission of a crime, could justify the absence of prior judicial authorisation.

It should be noted, as the Commission did, that, first, paragraph 31 of the ECtHR's judgment in *Harju v. Finland*, [...] on which the applicants rely to illustrate the importance of the existence of imminent danger, is found in the section of the judgment summarising the defendant's submissions and not in the section containing the ECtHR's assessment. Second, in contrast to the applicants' contentions, it is clear that the assessment of the ECtHR is not in any way based on the existence of imminent danger. Indeed, the existence of imminent danger is no longer a decisive factor in the judgments of the ECtHR, *Mastepan v. Russia* [...] and *Varga v. Romania* [...]. Finally, as the Commission correctly points out, the fact that the ECtHR's judgments in *Harju v. Finland* and *Heino v. Finland*, [...] fall within the area of criminal law increases their relevance to these proceedings.

The arguments of the applicants seeking to prove that the approach adopted in the ECtHR's judgment in *Société Colas Est and Others v. France*, [...] applies in its entirety to the present case cannot succeed either.

It is evident from that judgment, notably paragraph 49 thereof, that the absence of a prior warrant is only one of the factors borne in mind by the ECtHR when deciding whether Article 8 of the ECHR has been infringed. In particular, the ECtHR took into account the extent of the powers held by the competent authority, the circumstances of the interference and the fact that the system in place at the material time provided for only a limited number of safeguards. This differs from the situation under EU law [...].

Even if the lack of a prior judicial warrant is not capable, in itself, of rendering an interference illegal—in contrast to the assertions of the applicants—it is necessary to examine whether the system established by Regulation No 1/2003, particularly Article

20(4) thereof, and the way in which that article was applied by the adoption of the three inspection decisions, offered appropriate and sufficient safeguards so as to restrict sufficiently the powers of the Commission. The ECtHR has consistently pointed out that an acceptable level of protection against interferences with rights under Article 8 of the ECHR entails a legal framework and strict limits (*Harju v. Finland*, [...] paragraph 39; *Heino v. Finland*, [...] paragraph 40; *Varga v. Romania*, [...] paragraph 70; and *Société Canal Plus and Others v. France*, [...] paragraph 54).

In that connection, it should be noted that there are five categories of safeguards. These relate to, first, the statement of reasons on which inspection decisions are based, second, the limits imposed on the Commission during the conduct of inspections, third, the impossibility for the Commission to carry out an inspection by force, fourth, the intervention of national authorities and, fifth, the existence of ex post facto remedies.

[Safeguard 1: Statement of reasons]

In the first place, it has been held that the purpose of the statement of reasons on which an inspection decision is based is to show that the operation carried out on the premises of the undertakings concerned is justified (see *France Télécom v Commission*, [...] paragraph 57 and the case-law cited). That decision also has to comply with the requirements set forth in Article 20(4) of Regulation No 1/2003. The decision must therefore specify the subject-matter and purpose of the inspection, appoint the date on which it is to begin and indicate the penalties provided for in Articles 23 and 24 of that regulation, as well as the right to have the decision reviewed by the Court of Justice. According to the case-law, the statement of reasons must also state the suppositions and presumptions that the Commission wishes to investigate [...].

[Safeguard 2: Limits imposed on the Commission during the conduct of an inspection]

In the second place, limits are imposed on the Commission during the conduct of an inspection.

First, documents of a non-business nature, that is to say documents not relating to the activities of the undertaking on the market, are excluded from the scope of the Commission's investigatory powers [...].

Second, undertakings subject to an inspection ordered pursuant to an inspection decision are entitled to receive legal assistance or even to preserve the confidentiality of lawyer-client correspondence, although the latter safeguard does not apply to information exchanged between the undertaking concerned and a lawyer bound to it by a relationship of employment [...].

Third, although Regulation No 1/2003 imposes an obligation of active cooperation on an undertaking subject to inspection, the Commission may not compel the undertaking concerned to provide it with answers which might involve an admission on its part of the existence of an infringement which it is incumbent upon the Commission to prove [...]. This principle, developed in the context of the implementation of Article 11 of Council Regulation No 17 of 6 February 1962, the first regulation implementing Articles [81 EC] and [82 EC] (OJ English Special Edition, Series I, 1959–1962, p. 87), also applies to questions that the inspectors may ask in the course of an inspection carried out under Article 20(4) of Regulation No 1/2003.

Fourth, mention must be made of the existence of the explanatory notes notified to undertakings together with inspection decisions. These explanatory notes describe the methodology that the Commission has bound itself to apply when conducting an inspection. They usefully define the content of the principle of respect for defence rights and the principle of good administration, as they are perceived by the Commission.

[Safeguard 3: The impossibility for the Commission to carry out an inspection by force]

In the third place, the Commission does not have excessive coercive measures at its disposal which would invalidate the possibility, in practice, of opposing the inspection under Article 20(6) of Regulation No 1/2003, in contrast to the applicants' assertions.

[Safeguard 4: The intervention of national authorities]

In the fourth place, as regards the safeguards offered by the opposition procedure provided for in Article 20(6) of Regulation No 1/2003, the Commission is under the obligation to seek assistance from the national authorities of the Member State where the inspection is to be carried out. That procedure triggers the application of the review mechanisms specific to the Member State concerned, mechanisms which may be of a judicial nature.

[Safeguard 5: The existence of ex post facto remedies]

In the fifth place, the limits on the interference constituted by an inspection are also founded on the ex post facto review, by the European Union Courts, of the legality of the decision ordering the inspection.

[Conclusion]

The Court considers that all five categories of safeguards mentioned above were guaranteed in the present case. In particular, the three inspection decisions include the information provided for in Article 20(4) of Regulation No 1/2003. The Commission took care to state the names of the recipients of the decisions, the reasons which led it to suspect the existence of unlawful practices, the type of suspected practices thought to be anti-competitive, the affected market for goods and services, the geographical market where the alleged practices applied, the relationship between those practices and the conduct of the undertaking in receipt of the decisions, the officials authorised to carry out the inspection, the means at their disposal and the obligations incumbent on the competent staff of the undertaking, the date and places of the inspection, the penalties risked in the event of obstruction, and the possibility of and prerequisites for raising legal action. It follows from the consideration of the fourth plea in law that such information was properly included in the three inspection decisions [...].

As regards the conduct of the first inspection and the applicants' contention that a Commission official threatened to close their IT system if they did not release the e-mail account passwords of certain staff members, it must be stated—besides the fact that the Commission objected to that contention—that the applicants' lawyers did not formally record the alleged incident, with the result that no evidence is available to prove that it occurred. Furthermore, the applicants did not dispute the Commission's account set out in its defence, according to which, despite its directions, the applicants blocked access to computers and e-mail accounts for a particularly long period, until day two of the inspection, without the Commission calling on the national authorities to implement coercive measures. As regards the *Sanofi Aventis* case, it is evident from the material in the case file, particularly the Commission document bearing the reference MEMO/08/357 of 2 June 2008, that the Commission intended to penalise not the fact that the undertaking opposed an inspection, in general terms, but the fact that it opposed, in this specific case, the copying of documents by the Commission. The proceedings were also closed.

In the light of the considerations set out in paragraphs 65 to 101 above, the first plea in law and the plea of illegality, in so far as it concerns Article 20(4) of Regulation No 1/2003, must be rejected as unfounded.

General Court 6 September 2013 (Deutsche Bahn a.o. v. Commission, Joined Cases T-289/11, T-290/11 and T-521/11), ECLI:EU:T:2013:404, paras 65–75, 79–83, 85, 91, 95 and 100–102, upheld in CoJ 18 June 2015 (Deutsche Bahn a.o. v. Commission, C-583/13 P), ECLI:EU:C:2013:404, paras 19–36.

E. LEGAL PRIVILEGE

1. Eur. Court H.R.

19.56   It is clearly in the general interest that any person who wishes to consult a lawyer should be free to do so under conditions which favour full and uninhibited discussion. It is for this reason that the lawyer-client relationship is, in principle, privileged. Indeed, in its *S. v. Switzerland* judgment of 28 November 1991 the Court stressed the importance of a prisoner's right to communicate with counsel out of earshot of the prison authorities. It was considered, in the context of Article 6, that if a lawyer were unable to confer with his client without such surveillance and receive confidential instructions from him his assistance would lose much of its usefulness, whereas the Convention is intended to guarantee rights that are practical and effective (Series A no 220, pp. 15–16, para. 48; see also, in this context, the *Campbell and Fell v. the United Kingdom* judgment of 28 June 1984, Series A no 80, p. 49, paras. 111–113).

In the Court's view, similar considerations apply to a prisoner's correspondence with a lawyer concerning contemplated or pending proceedings where the need for confidentiality is equally pressing, particularly where such correspondence relates, as in the present case, to claims and complaints against the prison authorities. That such correspondence be susceptible to routine scrutiny, particularly by individuals or authorities who may have a direct interest in the subject-matter contained therein, is not in keeping with the principles of confidentiality and professional privilege attaching to relations between a lawyer and his client.

Admittedly, as the Government pointed out, the borderline between mail concerning contemplated litigation and that of a general nature is especially difficult to draw and correspondence with a lawyer may concern matters which have little or nothing to do with litigation. Nevertheless, the Court sees no reason to distinguish between the different categories of correspondence with lawyers which, whatever their purpose, concern matters of a private and confidential character. In principle, such letters are privileged under Article 8.

Eur. Court H.R. 25 March 1992 (Campbell v. the United Kingdom, no 13590/88), Series A no 233, paras 46–48.

2. EU Courts

See also the case extracts in Chapter 13 on Art. 20 of Regulation No. 1/2003.

However, the rules [of Regulation No 17, now Regulation No 1/2003] do not exclude **19.57** the possibility of recognizing, subject to certain conditions, that certain business records are of a confidential nature. Community law, which derives from not only the economic but also the legal interpenetration of the Member States, must take into account the principles and concepts common to the laws of those states concerning the observance of confidentiality, in particular, as regards certain communications between lawyer and client. That confidentiality serves the requirements, the importance of which is recognized in all of the Member States, that any person must be able, without constraint, to consult a lawyer whose profession entails the giving of independent legal advice to all those in need of it.

As far as the protection of written communications between lawyer and client is concerned, it is apparent from the legal systems of the Member States that, although the principle of such protection is generally recognized, its scope and the criteria for applying it vary, as has, indeed, been conceded both by the applicant and by the parties who have intervened in support of its conclusions. [...]

Apart from these differences, however, there are to be found in the national laws of the Member States common criteria inasmuch as those laws protect, in similar circumstances, the confidentiality of written communications between lawyer and client provided that, on the one hand, such communications are made for the purposes and in the interests of the client's rights of defence and, on the other hand, they emanate from independent lawyers, that is to say, lawyers who are not bound to the client by a relationship of employment.

Viewed in that context Regulation No 17 must be interpreted as protecting, in its turn, the confidentiality of written communications between lawyer and client subject to those two conditions, and thus incorporating such elements of that protection as are common to the laws of the Member States.

As far as the first of those two conditions is concerned, in Regulation No 17 itself, in particular in the eleventh recital in its preamble and in the provisions contained in Article 19, care is taken to ensure that the rights of the defence may be exercised to the full, and the protection of the confidentiality of written communications between lawyer and client is an essential corollary to those rights. In those circumstances, such protection must, if it is to be effective, be recognized as covering all written communications exchanged after the initiation of the administrative procedure under Regulation No 17 which may lead to a decision on the application of Articles [101 and 102 TFEU] or to a decision imposing a pecuniary sanction on the undertaking. It must also be possible to extend it to earlier written communications which have a relationship to the subject-matter of that procedure.

As regards the second condition, it should be stated that the requirement as to the position and status as an independent lawyer, which must be fulfilled by the legal adviser from whom the written communications which may be protected emanate, is based on a conception of the lawyer's role as collaborating in the administration of justice by the courts and as being required to provide, in full independence, and in the overriding interests of that cause, such legal assistance as the client needs. The counterpart of that protection lies in the rules of professional ethics and discipline which are laid down and enforced in the general interest by institutions endowed with the requisite powers for that purpose. Such a conception reflects the legal traditions common to the Member States and is also to be found in legal order of the Community, as is demonstrated by Article 17 of the protocols on the [CoJ's statutes].

Having regard to the principles of the Treaty concerning freedom of establishment and the freedom to provide services the protection thus afforded by Community law, in particular in the context of Regulation No 17, to written communications between lawyer and client must apply without distinction to any lawyer entitled to practise his profession in one of the Member States, regardless of the Member State in which the client lives.

Such protection may not be extended beyond those limits, which are determined by the scope of the common rules on the exercise of the legal profession as laid down in Council Directive 77/249/EEC [...], which is based in its turn on the mutual recognition by all the Member States of the national legal concepts of each of them on this subject.

In view of all these factors it must therefore be concluded that although Regulation No 17, and in particular Article 14 thereof, interpreted in the light of its wording, structure and aims, and having regard to the laws of the Member States, empowers the Commission to require, in the course of an investigation within the meaning of that article, production of the business documents the disclosure of which it considers necessary, including written communications between lawyer and client, for proceedings in respect of any infringements of Articles [101 and 102 TFEU], that power is, however, subject to a restriction imposed by the need to protect confidentiality, on the conditions defined above, and provided that the communications in question are exchanged between an independent lawyer, that is to say one who is not bound to his client by a relationship of employment, and his client.

Finally, it should be remarked that the principle of confidentiality does not prevent a lawyer's client from disclosing the written communications between them if he considers that it is in his interests to do so. [...]

If an undertaking which is the subject of an investigation under Article 14 of Regulation No 17 refuses, on the ground that it is entitled to protection of the confidentiality of information, to produce, among the business records demanded by the Commission, written communications between itself and its lawyer, it must nevertheless provide the Commission's authorized agents with relevant material of such a nature as to demonstrate that the communications fulfil the conditions for being granted legal protection as defined above, although it is not bound to reveal the contents of the communications in question.

Where the Commission is not satisfied that such evidence has been supplied, the appraisal of those conditions is not a matter which may be left to an arbitrator or to a national authority. Since this is a matter involving an appraisal and a decision which affect the conditions under which the Commission may act in a field as vital to the functioning of the Common Market as that of compliance with the rules on competition, the solution of disputes as to the application of the protection of the confidentiality of written communications between lawyer and client may be sought only at community level.

In that case it is for the Commission to order, pursuant to Article 14(3) of Regulation No 17, production of the communications in question and, if necessary, to impose on the undertaking fines or periodic penalty payments under that regulation as a penalty for the undertaking's refusal either to supply such additional evidence as the Commission considers necessary or to produce the communications in question whose confidentiality, in the Commission's view, is not protected in law.

The fact that by virtue of Article [278 TFEU] any action brought by the undertaking concerned against such decisions does not have suspensory effect provides an answer to the Commission's concern as to the effect of the time taken by the procedure before the Court on the efficacy of the supervision which the Commission is called upon to exercise in regard to compliance with the treaty rules on competition, whilst on the other hand the interests of the undertaking concerned are safeguarded by the possibility which exists under Articles [278 en 279 TFEU], as well as under Article 83 of the rules of procedure of the Court, of obtaining an order suspending the application of the decision which has been taken, or any other interim measure.

CoJ 18 May 1982 (AM&S Europe Ltd v. Commission, 155/79) [1982] ECR 1575, paras 18, 19 and 21–32.

An examination of the aforesaid documents shows that they are, essentially, notes **19.58** internal to the undertaking reporting the content of advice received from independent, and thus external, legal advisers.

Such legal advice would be covered by the principle of the protection of confidentiality laid down by the Court of Justice if it had been received from independent legal advisers by way of written communication.

In this case it appears that that legal advice was reported on in internal notes distributed within the undertaking so that it might be the subject of consideration by managerial staff. In such a case, and although the aforesaid legal advice was not received by way of correspondence, it must be held that the principle of the protection of written communications between lawyer and client may not be frustrated on the sole ground that the content of those communications and of that legal advice was reported in documents internal to the undertaking. Thus the principle of the protection of written communications between lawyer and client must, in view of its purpose, be regarded as extending also to the internal notes which are confined to reporting the text or the content of those communications. It follows that the request for confidential treatment made by the applicant must be allowed in so far as it refers to those documents.

General Court 4 April 1990 (Hilti v. Commission, T-30/89) [1990] ECR II-163, paras 16–18.

It is apparent, therefore, that the mere fact that an undertaking claims that a document **19.59** is protected by legal professional privilege is not sufficient to prevent the Commission from reading that document if the undertaking produces no relevant material of such a kind as to prove that it is actually protected by LPP. The undertaking concerned may, in particular, inform the Commission of the author of the document and for whom it was intended, explain the respective duties and responsibilities of each, and refer to the objective and the context in which the document was drawn up. Similarly, it may also mention the context in which the document was found, the way in which it was filed and any related documents.

In a significant number of cases, a mere cursory look by the Commission officials at the general layout, heading, title or other superficial features of the document will enable them to confirm the accuracy of the reasons invoked by the undertaking and to determine whether the document at issue was confidential, when deciding whether to put it aside. Nevertheless, on certain occasions, there would be a risk that, even with a cursory look at the document, in spite of the superficial nature of their examination, the Commission officials would gain access to information covered by legal professional privilege. That may be so, in particular, if the confidentiality of the document in question is not clear from external indications.

As stated [...], it is clear from *AM & S* that the undertaking concerned is not bound to reveal their contents when presenting the Commission officials with relevant material of such a nature as to demonstrate that the documents fulfil the conditions for being granted legal protection (paragraph 29 of the judgment). Accordingly, the [General Court] concludes that an undertaking subject to an investigation under Article 14(3) of Regulation No 17 [now Art. 20(4) Regulation No 1/2003] is entitled to refuse to allow the Commission officials to take even a cursory look at one or more specific documents which it claims to be covered by LPP, provided that the undertaking considers that such a cursory look is impossible without revealing the content of those documents and that it gives the Commission officials appropriate reasons for its view.

Where, in the course of an investigation under Article 14(3) of Regulation No 17, the Commission considers that the material presented by the undertaking is not of such a nature as to prove that the documents in question are confidential, in particular where that undertaking refuses to give the Commission officials a cursory look at a document, the Commission officials may place a copy of the document or documents in question in a sealed envelope and then remove it with a view to a subsequent resolution of the dispute. This procedure enables risks of a breach of legal professional privilege to be avoided while at the same time enabling the Commission to retain a certain control over the documents forming the subject-matter of the investigation and avoiding the risk that the documents will subsequently disappear or be manipulated.

Use of the sealed envelope procedure cannot, moreover, be considered to be at odds with the requirement set out in paragraph 31 of *AM&S* that, in the case of a dispute with the undertaking concerned as to whether a particular document is confidential, the Commission must adopt a decision ordering that document to be produced. The reason for such a requirement lies in the specific context of the judgment in *AM&S*, in particular the fact that the initial decision ordering an inspection at the premises of the undertaking in question was not a formal decision under Article 14(3) of Regulation No 17 (Opinion of Advocate General Warner in *AM&S*, p. 1624) and the undertaking in question was therefore entitled, as it in fact did, to refuse to produce the documents requested by the Commission.

In any event, the [General Court] would point out that where the Commission is not satisfied with the material and explanations provided by the representatives of the undertaking for the purposes of proving that the document concerned is covered by LPP, the Commission must not read the contents of the document before it has adopted a decision allowing the undertaking concerned to refer the matter to the [General Court], and, if appropriate, to make an application for interim relief (see, to that effect, *AM&S*, para. 32).

Having regard to the particular nature of the principle of LPP, the purpose of which is both to guarantee the full exercise of individuals' rights of defence and to safeguard the requirement that any person must be able, without constraint, to consult his lawyer ([...]), the [General Court] considers that the fact that the Commission reads the content of a confidential document is in itself a breach of this principle. Contrary to what the Commission seems to submit, the protection of LPP therefore goes beyond the requirement that information provided by an undertaking to its lawyer or the content of the advice given by that lawyer cannot be used against it in a decision which penalises a breach of the competition rules.

First, that protection seeks to safeguard the public interest in the proper administration of justice in ensuring that a client is free to consult his lawyer without fear that any confidences which he imparts may subsequently be disclosed. Secondly, its purpose is to avoid the harm which may be caused to the undertaking's rights of the defence as a result of the Commission reading the contents of a confidential document and improperly adding it to the investigation file. Therefore, even if that document is not used as evidence in a decision imposing a penalty under the competition rules, the undertaking may suffer harm which cannot be made good or can only be made good with great difficulty. Information covered by LPP might be used by the Commission, directly or indirectly, in order to obtain new information or new evidence without the undertaking in question always being able to identify or prevent such information or evidence from being used against it. Moreover, harm which the undertaking concerned would suffer as a result of disclosure to third parties of information covered by LPP could not be made good, for example if that information were used in a statement of objections in the course of the Commission's administrative procedure. The mere fact that the Commission cannot use privileged documents as evidence in a decision imposing a penalty is thus not sufficient to make good or eliminate the harm which resulted from the Commission's reading the content of the documents.

Protection under LPP also requires the Commission, once it has adopted its decision rejecting a request under that head, not to read the content of the documents in question until it has given the undertaking concerned the opportunity to refer the matter to the [General Court]. In that regard, the Commission is bound to wait until the time-limit for bringing an action against the rejection decision has expired before reading the contents of those documents. In any event, to the extent that such an action does not have suspensory effect, it is for the undertaking concerned to bring an application for interim relief seeking suspension of operation of the decision rejecting the request for LPP (see, to that effect, *AM & S*, para. 32). [...]

In the present case, the [General Court] finds that the Set A documents do not by themselves constitute written communications with an independent lawyer or an internal note reporting the content of a communication with such a lawyer. Nor do the applicants submit that those documents were prepared in order to be sent physically to an independent lawyer. Accordingly, it must be held that those documents do not formally come within the categories of documents expressly identified in the above-mentioned case-law.

751

The applicants claim, nevertheless, that those documents must be recognised as being covered by LPP, since, in their view, they were prepared in order to seek legal advice. According to the applicants, those documents were drawn up, for the particular purpose of a conference call with a lawyer with the aim of obtaining legal advice.

In that regard, it must be pointed out that the principle of the protection of the confidentiality of written communications between lawyer and client is an essential corollary to the effective exercise of the rights of the defence (*AM&S*, para. 23) ([…]). According to settled case-law, observance of the right to be heard is, in all proceedings in which sanctions, in particular fines or penalty payments, may be imposed, a fundamental principle of Community law which must be respected even if the proceedings in question are administrative proceedings (*Case 85/76 Hoffman-La Roche v. Commission* [1979] ECR 461, para. 9, and *Case T-308/94 Cascades v. Commission* [1998] ECR II-925, para. 39). Therefore, it is necessary to prevent those rights from being irremediably impaired during preliminary inquiry procedures, including, in particular, investigations which may be decisive in providing evidence of the unlawful nature of conduct engaged in by undertakings for which they may be liable (*Joined Cases 46/87 and 227/88 Hoechst v. Commission* [1989] ECR 2859, para. 15).

Similarly, it must be pointed out that LPP meets the need to ensure that every person must be able, without constraint, to consult a lawyer whose profession entails the giving of independent legal advice to all those in need of it (*AM&S*, para. 18). That principle is thus closely linked to the concept of the lawyer's role as collaborating in the administration of justice by the courts (*AM&S*, para. 24) ([…]).

However, so that a person may be able effectively to consult a lawyer without constraint, and so that the latter may effectively perform his role as collaborating in the administration of justice by the courts and providing legal assistance for the purpose of the effective exercise of the rights of the defence, it may be necessary, in certain circumstances, for the client to prepare working documents or summaries, in particular as a means of gathering information which will be useful, or essential, to that lawyer for an understanding of the context, nature and scope of the facts for which his assistance is sought. Preparation of such documents may be particularly necessary in matters involving a large amount of complex information, as is often the case with procedures imposing penalties for breaches of Articles [101 and 102 TFEU]. In those circumstances, the [General Court] holds that the fact that the Commission reads such documents during an investigation may well prejudice the rights of the defence of the undertaking under investigation and the public interest in ensuring that every client is able to consult his lawyer without constraint.

Accordingly, the [General Court] concludes that such preparatory documents, even if they were not exchanged with a lawyer or were not created for the purpose of being sent physically to a lawyer, may none the less be covered by LPP, provided that they were drawn up exclusively for the purpose of seeking legal advice from a lawyer in exercise of the rights of the defence. On the other hand, the mere fact that a document has been discussed with a lawyer is not sufficient to give it such protection. […]

The Set B documents contain, in addition to the manuscript notes already examined, e-mail correspondence of May and June 2000 exchanged between the General Manager of Akcros Chemicals and Mr S., an Advocate on the roll of the Netherlands Bar, who at the material time was a member of the legal department of Akzo Nobel, in which capacity he coordinated competition-law matters.

As regards, first of all, the applicants' principal argument, it must be pointed out that in its judgment in *AM&S*, the Court of Justice expressly held that the protection accorded to LPP under Community law, in the application of Regulation No 17, only applies to the extent that the lawyer is independent, that is to say, not bound to his client by a relationship of employment (paras 21, 22 and 27 of the judgment). The requirement as to the position and status as an independent lawyer, which must be met by the legal adviser from whom the written communications which may be protected emanate, is based on a concept of the lawyer's role as collaborating in the administration of justice by the courts and as being required to provide, in full independence, and in the overriding interests of the administration of justice, such legal assistance as the client needs (*AM&S*, para. 24).

It follows that the Court expressly excluded communications with in-house lawyers, that is, legal advisers bound to their clients by a relationship of employment, from protection under LPP. It must also be pointed out that the Court reached a conscious decision on that exception, given that the issue had been debated at length during the proceeding and that Advocate General Sir Gordon Slynn had expressly proposed in his Opinion for that judgment that where a lawyer bound by an employment contract remains a member of the profession and subject to its discipline and ethics, he should be treated in the same way as independent lawyers (Opinion of Advocate General Sir Gordon Slynn in *AM & S*, p. 1655).

The [General Court] therefore concludes that, contrary to what the applicants and certain interveners submit, the Court in its judgment in *AM & S* defined the concept of independent lawyer in negative terms in that it stipulated that such a lawyer should not be bound to his client by a relationship of employment ([…]), rather than positively, on the basis of membership of a Bar or Law Society or being subject to professional discipline and ethics. The Court thus laid down the test of legal advice provided 'in full independence' (*AM&S*, para. 24), which it identifies as that provided by a lawyer who, structurally, hierarchically and functionally, is a third party in relation to the undertaking receiving that advice.

Accordingly, [the General Court] rejects the applicants' principal argument and holds that the correspondence exchanged between a lawyer bound to Akzo Nobel by a relationship of employment and a manager of a company belonging to that group is not covered by LPP, as defined in *AM & S*.

General Court 17 September 2007 (Akzo Nobel Chemicals Ltd and Akcros Chemicals Ltd v. Commission, Joined Cases T-125/03 and T-253/03) [2007] ECR II-3523, paras 80–88, 118–123 and 165–169.

Confirmed in CoJ 14 September 2010 (C-550/07 P) [2010] ECR I- 08301.

F. EXCLUSIONARY RULE

Please refer to Section H.6. of Chapter 24 on Article 47 Charter.

20

ARTICLE 16 CHARTER[*]

FREEDOM TO CONDUCT A BUSINESS

The freedom to conduct a business in accordance with Union law and national laws and practices is recognised.

OVERVIEW

A. EXPLANATION RELATING TO ARTICLE 16 CHARTER (p.755)	B. GENERAL	20.01

A. EXPLANATION RELATING TO ARTICLE 16 CHARTER

This Article is based on Court of Justice case-law which has recognised freedom to exercise an economic or commercial activity (see judgments of 14 May 1974, Case 4/73 Nold [1974] ECR 491, para. 14 of the grounds, and of 27 September 1979, Case 230–78 SpA Eridiana and others [1979] ECR 2749, paras 20 and 31 of the grounds) and freedom of contract (see inter alia Sukkerfabriken Nykøbing judgment, Case 151/78 [1979] ECR 1, para. 19 of the grounds, and judgment of 5 October 1999, C-240/97 Spain v. Commission [1999] ECR I-6571, para. 99 of the grounds) and Article 119(1) and (3) of the Treaty on the Functioning of the European Union, which recognises free competition. Of course, this right is to be exercised with respect for Union law and national legislation. It may be subject to the limitations provided for in Article 52(1) of the Charter.

B. GENERAL

20.01 The protection afforded by Article 16 of the Charter covers the freedom to exercise an economic or commercial activity, the freedom of contract and free competition, as is apparent from the explanations relating to that article, which, in accordance with the

---

[*] This chapter was written by Herman Speyart.

third subparagraph of Article 6(1) TEU and Article 52(7) of the Charter, have to be taken into consideration for the interpretation of the Charter [...].

In addition, the freedom of contract includes, in particular, the freedom to choose with whom to do business [...] and the freedom to determine the price of a service [...].

[I]n accordance with the Court's case-law, the freedom to conduct a business is not absolute, but must be viewed in relation to its social function [...].

On the basis of that case-law and in the light of the wording of Article 16 of the Charter, which differs from the wording of the other fundamental freedoms laid down in Title II thereof, yet is similar to that of certain provisions of Title IV of the Charter, the freedom to conduct a business may be subject to a broad range of interventions on the part of public authorities which may limit the exercise of economic activity in the public interest.

That circumstance is reflected, inter alia, in the way in which Article 52(1) of the Charter requires the principle of proportionality to be implemented.

CoJ 22 January 2013 (Sky Österreich, C-283/11), ECLI:EU:2013:28, paras 42, 43 and 45–47.

21

ARTICLE 17(1) CHARTER*

RIGHT TO PROPERTY

Everyone has the right to own, use, dispose of and bequeath his or her lawfully acquired possessions. No one may be deprived of his or her possessions, except in the public interest and in the cases and under the conditions provided for by law, subject to fair compensation being paid in good time for their loss. The use of property may be regulated by law in so far as is necessary for the general interest.

ARTICLE 1 PROTOCOL 1 EHRC

Every natural or legal person is entitled to the peaceful enjoyment of his possessions. No one shall be deprived of his possessions except in the public interest and subject to the conditions provided for by law and by the general principles of international law.

 The preceding provisions shall not, however, in any way impair the right of a State to enforce such laws as it deems necessary to control the use of property in accordance with the general interest or to secure the payment of taxes or other contributions or penalties.

OVERVIEW

A. EXPLANATION RELATING TO ARTICLE 17(1) CHARTER	(p.757)	B. GENERAL	21.01

A. EXPLANATION RELATING TO ARTICLE 17(1) CHARTER

This Article is based on Article 1 of the Protocol to the ECHR: [...]

---

*   This chapter was written by Herman Speyart.

This is a fundamental right common to all national constitutions. It has been recognised on numerous occasions by the case-law of the Court of Justice, initially in the Hauer judgment (13 December 1979, [1979] ECR 3727). The wording has been updated but, in accordance with Article 52(3), the meaning and scope of the right are the same as those of the right guaranteed by the ECHR and the limitations may not exceed those provided for there.

B. GENERAL

21.01   [T]he appellants complain that the General Court did not carry out the review of proportionality in the light of the case-law of the European Court of Human Rights, in particular its judgment in *Mamidakis v. Greece*, but referred solely to its own case-law and that of the Court of Justice.

[I]n so far as the appellants plead infringement of the Charter, they can establish an error of law in the review carried out by the General Court only by demonstrating that it did not give the right to property the same meaning and scope as those laid down by the ECHR.

So far as concerns the taking into account of Schindler Holding and its subsidiaries as an economic entity, suffice it to state that this is not an incorrect premiss in the General Court's reasoning, but involves a fundamental principle of competition law that is covered by settled case-law, as has just been pointed out in paragraphs 101 to 103 of the present judgment in response to the seventh plea. The perpetrator of an infringement of competition law is indeed defined by reference to economic entities even if in law those entities consist of several natural or legal persons.

CoJ 18 July 2013 (Schindler v. Commission, C-501/11 P), ECLI:EU:C:2013:522, paras 125, 128 and 129.

22

ARTICLE 20 CHARTER*

EQUALITY BEFORE THE LAW

Everyone is equal before the law.

OVERVIEW

A. EXPLANATION RELATING TO
ARTICLE 20 CHARTER   (p.759)

B. GENERAL   22.01

C. IN RELATION TO THE FINDING OF AN
INFRINGEMENT   22.02

D. IN RELATION TO A LENIENCY REBATE   22.03

E. IN RELATION TO THE CALCULATION
OF A FINE BY THE EUROPEAN
COMMISSION   22.04

F. IN RELATION TO THE REVIEW OF A
FINE BY THE EU COURTS   22.05

A. EXPLANATION RELATING TO ARTICLE 20 CHARTER

This Article corresponds to a general principle of law which is included in all European constitutions and has also been recognised by the Court of Justice as a basic principle of Community law (judgment of 13 November 1984, Case 283/83 Racke [1984] ECR 3791; judgment of 17 April 1997, Case C-15/95 EARL [1997] ECR I-1961; and judgment of 13 April 2000, Case C-292/97 Karlsson [2000] ECR 2737).

B. GENERAL

The principle of equal treatment, as a general principle of EU law, requires that **22.01** comparable situations must not be treated differently and that different situations must not be treated in the same way, unless such treatment is objectively justified.
CoJ 13 November 1984 (Racke, 283/83) [1984] ECR 3791, para. 7.

---

* This chapter was written by Herman Speyart.

C. IN RELATION TO THE FINDING OF AN INFRINGEMENT

22.02   The fact that a trader who was in a position similar to that of an applicant was not found by the Commission to have committed any infringement cannot [...] constitute a ground for setting aside the finding of an infringement by that applicant, provided it was properly established.
CoJ 31 March 1993 (Ahlströ, Osakeyhtiö, Joined Cases C-89/85, C-104/85, C-114/85, C-116/85, C-117/85, C-125/85, C-126/85, C-127/85, C-128/85 and C-129/85) [1993] ECR I-1307, para. 146.

D. IN RELATION TO A LENIENCY REBATE

22.03   [T]he General Court stated that [...] the situation of the Kone Group and Thyssen-Krupp Group were not comparable for reasons [...] which concerned, in particular, the added value represented by the evidence provided in those two situations.
        Thus, given that the General Court had concluded that the situations in question were not comparable, it was fully entitled to find [...] that the Commission had not breached the principle of equal treatment.
CoJ 24 October 2013 (Kone v. Commission, C-510/11 P), ECLI:EU:C:2013:696, paras 101 and 102.

E. IN RELATION TO THE CALCULATION OF A FINE BY THE EUROPEAN COMMISSION

22.04   [T]he Commission is not required, when assessing fines in accordance with the gravity and duration of the infringement in question, to ensure, where fines are imposed on a number of undertakings involved in the same infringement, that the final amounts of the fines resulting from its calculations for the undertakings concerned reflect any distinction between them in terms of their overall turnover or their relevant turnover.
CoJ 28 June 2005 (Dansk Rørindustrie A/S and others v. Commission, Joined Cases C-189/02 P, C-202/02 P, C-205/02 P–C-208/02 P and C-213/02 P) [2005] ECR I-05425, para. 312.

F. IN RELATION TO THE REVIEW OF A FINE BY THE EU COURTS

22.05   [W]hen the amount of the fine to be imposed on [undertakings for infringements of Community law] is determined, the exercise of unlimited jurisdiction cannot result in discrimination between [them].
        In the present case, there is no dispute that the fines were fixed by the Commission, in regard to all the undertakings involved in the infringement, using a method of calculation which was not called in question by the [General Court]. If the [General

Court] intended, in the case of the appellant, to depart specifically from that method or from some of the figures adopted by the Commission, it should have given reasons for doing so in the contested judgment.

CoJ 16 November 2000 (Sarrió v. Commission, C-291/98 P) [2000] ECR I-9991, paras 97 and 98.

[W]hen the amount of fines is being decided, the exercise of unlimited jurisdiction **22.06** cannot result in discrimination between undertakings which have participated in an agreement contrary to Article [101(1) TFEU] and […] if the [General Court] intended, in the case of one of those undertakings, to depart specifically from the method followed by the Commission, which it had not called in question, it should have given reasons for doing so in the judgment under appeal.

CoJ 15 October 2002 (Limburgse Vinyl Maatschappij a.o. v. Commission, Joined Cases C-238/99 P, C-244/99 P, C-245/99 P, C-247/99 P, C-250/99 P to C-252/99 P and C-254/99 P) [2002] ECR I-8375, para. 617; and CoJ 18 September 2003 (Volkswagen v Commission, C-338/00 P) [2003] ECR I-9189, para. 146.

See also CoJ 28 June 2005 (Dansk Rørindustrie A/S and others v. Commission, Joined Cases C-189/02 P, C-202/02 P, C-205/02 P–C-208/02 P and C-213/02 P) [2005] ECR I-05425, para. 337.

[A]lthough it is for the Court, in the exercise of its unlimited jurisdiction in this regard, **22.07** to assess for itself the circumstances of the case and the nature of the infringement in question in order to determine the amount of the fine (*Case 322/81 Michelin v Commission* [1983] ECR 3461, para. 111), the exercise of unlimited jurisdiction cannot result, when the amount of the fines to be imposed is determined, in discrimination between undertakings which have participated in an agreement or concerted practice, contrary to Article [101(1) TFEU]. Accordingly, the guidance which can be drawn from the Guidelines is, as a general rule, capable of guiding the Courts of the European Union in their exercise of that jurisdiction where the Commission has applied those guidelines for the purposes of calculating the fines imposed on the other undertakings penalised by the decision which those Courts are asked to examine […].

CoJ 6 December 2012 (Commission v. Verhuizingen Coppens, C-441/11 P), ECLI: EU:C:2012:778, para. 80.

23

ARTICLE 41 CHARTER*

RIGHT TO GOOD ADMINISTRATION

1. Every person has the right to have his or her affairs handled impartially, fairly and within a reasonable time by the institutions, bodies, offices and agencies of the Union.
2. This right includes:
   (a) the right of every person to be heard, before any individual measure which would affect him or her adversely is taken;
   (b) the right of every person to have access to his or her file, while respecting the legitimate interests of confidentiality and of professional and business secrecy;
   (c) the obligation of the administration to give reasons for its decisions.
3. Every person has the right to have the Union make good any damage caused by its institutions or by its servants in the performance of their duties, in accordance with the general principles common to the laws of the Member States.
4. Every person may write to the institutions of the Union in one of the languages of the Treaties and must have an answer in the same language.

OVERVIEW

A. EXPLANATION RELATING TO ARTICLE 41 CHARTER	(p.763)	C. RIGHTS OF THE DEFENCE	23.10
		1. Applicability to preliminary inquiries	23.13
B. REASONABLE PERIOD	23.01	2. Right to be heard	23.14
1. General	23.01	3. Statement of objections	23.16
2. Test	23.02	4. Access to the file	23.25
3. Assessment in respect of administrative proceedings	23.07		
4. Consequences of a failure to adopt a decision within a reasonable period	23.09		

---

* This chapter was written by Herman Speyart.

A. EXPLANATION RELATING TO ARTICLE 41 CHARTER

Article 41 is based on the existence of the Union as subject to the rule of law whose characteristics were developed in the case-law which enshrined inter alia good administration as a general principle of law (see inter alia Court of Justice judgment of 31 March 1992 in Case C-255/90 P Burban [1992] ECR I-2253, and [General Court] judgments of 18 September 1995 in Case T-167/94 Nölle [1995] ECR II-2589, and 9 July 1999 in Case T-231/97 New Europe Consulting and others [1999] ECR II-2403). The wording for that right in the first two paragraphs results from the case-law (Court of Justice judgment of 15 October 1987 in Case 222/86 Heylens [1987] ECR 4097, para. 15 of the grounds, judgment of 18 October 1989 in Case 374/87 Orkem [1989] ECR 3283, judgment of 21 November 1991 in Case C-269/90 TU München [1991] ECR I-5469, and [General Court] judgments of 6 December 1994 in Case T-450/93 Lisrestal [1994] ECR II-1177, 18 September 1995 in Case T-167/94 Nölle [1995] ECR II-2589) and the wording regarding the obligation to give reasons comes from Article 296 of the Treaty on the Functioning of the European Union (cf. also the legal base in Article 298 of the Treaty on the Functioning of the European Union for the adoption of legislation in the interest of an open, efficient and independent European administration).

Paragraph 3 reproduces the right now guaranteed by Article 340 of the Treaty on the Functioning of the European Union. Paragraph 4 reproduces the right now guaranteed by Article 20(2)(d) and Article 25 of the Treaty on the Functioning of the European Union. In accordance with Article 52(2) of the Charter, those rights are to be applied under the conditions and within the limits defined by the Treaties.

The right to an effective remedy, which is an important aspect of this question, is guaranteed in Article 47 of this Charter.

B. REASONABLE PERIOD

1. General

Please also refer to Section I of Chapter 24 on Article 47 Charter.

Compliance with the reasonable time requirement in the conduct of administrative **23.01** procedures relating to competition policy constitutes a general principle of Community law whose observance the Community judicature ensures […]. […]

The excessive duration of the first phase of the administrative procedure may have an effect on the future ability of the undertakings concerned to defend themselves, in particular by reducing the effectiveness of the rights of the defence in the second phase of the procedure.

[T]he more time that elapses between a measure of investigation such as, in the present case, the sending of the warning letter and the notification of the statement of objections, the more unlikely it becomes that exculpatory evidence relating to the infringements set out in the statement of objections can be obtained [...]. For that reason, examination of any interference with the exercise of the rights of the defence must not be confined to the actual phase in which those rights are fully effective, that is to say, the second phase of the administrative procedure. The assessment of the source of any undermining of the effectiveness of the rights of the defence must extend to the entire procedure and be carried out by reference to its total duration.

CoJ 21 September 2006 (Nederlandse Federatieve Vereniging voor de Groothandel op Elektrotechnisch Gebied v. Commission, C-105/04 P) [2006] ECR I-8725, paras 35, 49 and 50.

2. Test

Please also refer to Section I of Chapter 24 on Article 47 Charter.

23.02   [T]he reasonableness of [the duration of proceedings] must be appraised in the light of the circumstances specific to each case and, in particular, the importance of the case for the person concerned, its complexity and the conduct of the applicant and of the competent authorities [...].

CoJ 17 December 1998 (Baustahlgewebe v. Commission, C-185/95 P) [1998] ECR I-8417, para. 29.

See also CoJ 15 October 2002 (Limburgse Vinyl Maatschappij a.o. v. Commission, Joined Cases C-238/99 P, C-244/99 P, C-245/99 P, C-247/99 P, C-250/99 P–C-252/99 P and C-254/99 P) [2002] ECR I-8375, para. 187; CoJ of 16 July 2009 (Der Grüne Punkt, C-385/07 P) [2009] ECR I-6155, para. 181; CoJ (Grand Chamber) 26 November 2013 (Kendrion v. Commission, C-50/12 P), ECLI:EU:C:2013:771, para. 96; CoJ (Grand Chamber) 26 November 2013 (Gascogne Sack Deutschland v. Commission, C-40/12 P), ECLI:EU:C:2013:768, para. 91.

23.03   As regards the importance of the proceedings to the appellant, it must be emphasised that its economic survival was not directly endangered by the proceedings. The fact nevertheless remains that, in the case of proceedings concerning infringement of competition rules, the fundamental requirement of legal certainty on which economic operators must be able to rely and the aim of ensuring that competition is not distorted in the internal market are of considerable importance not only for an applicant himself and his competitors but also for third parties in view of the large number of persons concerned and the financial interests involved.

CoJ 17 December 1998 (Baustahlgewebe v. Commission, C-185/95 P) [1998] ECR I-8417, para. 30.

See also CoJ 16 July 2009 (Der Grüne Punkt, C-385/07 P) [2009] ECR I-6155, para. 186; CoJ (Grand Chamber) 26 November 2013 (Kendrion v. Commission,

C-50/12 P), ECLI:EU:C:2013:771, para. 98; CoJ (Grand Chamber) 26 November 2013 (Gascogne Sack Deutschland v. Commission, C-40/12 P), ECLI: EU:C:2013:768, para. 93.

[A]n administrative procedure may involve an examination in two successive stages.   **23.04**

The first stage, covering the period up to notification of the statement of objections, begins on the date on which the Commission, exercising the powers conferred on it by Articles 11 and 14 of Regulation No 17 [now Art. 18 and 20 Regulation No 1/2003] in the context of a preliminary investigation, takes measures involving a complaint that an infringement has been committed and having a significant impact on the situation of the suspected undertakings [...]. This stage must enable the Commission, after investigation, to adopt a position on the course which the procedure is to follow.

The second stage covers the period from notification of the statement of objections to adoption of the final decision. It must enable the Commission to reach a final decision on the alleged infringement.

Since each of those two stages has its own internal logic, the complaint must be rejected [...].

The [General Court] was therefore not obliged to assess the reasonableness of the time taken in the light of all of the criteria referred to by LVM and DSM, since, in paragraphs 124 to 133 of the contested judgment, it considered that the duration of the first procedural stage, namely four years and four months, was justified by the complexity of the case and that the second, lasting ten months, could not even be considered excessive.

CoJ 15 October 2002 (Limburgse Vinyl Maatschappij a.o. v. Commission, Joined Cases C-238/99 P, C-244/99 P, C-245/99 P, C-247/99 P, C-250/99 P–C-252/99 P and C-254/99 P) [2002] ECR I-8375, paras 181–184 and 189.

See also CoJ 21 September 2006 (Technische Unie v. Commission, C-113/04 P) [2006] ECR I-8831, paras 42 and 43.

However, that list of criteria is not exhaustive and the assessment of the reasonableness   **23.05**
of the period in question does not require a systematic examination of the circumstances of the case in the light of each of them where the duration of the proceedings appears justified in the light of one of them. The purpose of those criteria is to determine whether the time taken in the handling of a case is justified. Thus, the complexity of the case or the dilatory conduct of the applicant may be deemed to justify a duration which is prima facie too long. Conversely, the time taken may be regarded as longer than is reasonable in the light of just one criterion, in particular where its duration is the result of the conduct of the competent authorities. Where appropriate, the duration of a procedural stage may be regarded as reasonable from the outset if it appears to be consistent with the average time taken in handling a case of its type.

CoJ 15 October 2002 (Limburgse Vinyl Maatschappij a.o. v. Commission, Joined Cases C-238/99 P, C-244/99 P, C-245/99 P, C-247/99 P, C-250/99 P–C-252/99 P and C-254/99 P) [2002] ECR I-8375, para. 188.

See also CoJ 16 July 2009 (Der Grüne Punkt, C-385/07 P) [2009] ECR I-6155, para. 92; CoJ (Grand Chamber) 26 November 2013 (Kendrion v. Commission, C-50/12 P), ECLI:EU:C:2013:771, para. 97; CoJ (Grand Chamber) 26 November 2013 (Gascogne Sack Deutschland v. Commission, C-40/12 P), ECLI: EU:C:2013:768, para. 92.

23.06   A proper examination of the length of the proceedings requires assessing each individual stage of the proceedings separately. If any stage of the proceedings was excessively long, this fact alone justifies the finding that there has been an infringement of the right to have a matter adjudicated upon within a reasonable time. None the less, also the overall duration of the administrative and judicial proceedings must satisfy the requirement that proceedings are dealt with within reasonable time (compare the Opinion of Advocate General Kokott in *Case C-110/10 P Solvay v Commission*, judgment of 25 October 2011, [[2011] ECR I-10439], points 81 to 83).

EFTA Court 18 April 2012 (Posten Norge AS v. EFTA Surveillance Authority, E-15/10) [2012] EFTACR 246, para. 277.

3. Assessment in respect of administrative proceedings

Please refer to Section I of Chapter 24 on Article 47 Charter for the assessment in respect of judicial proceedings

23.07   [I]l y a lieu d'observer que, en ce qui concerne la première phase de la procédure administrative, c'est-à-dire celle qui s'étend de la signification aux requérantes de la décision d'inspection en mars 2000 jusqu'à la réception de la communication des griefs en août 2005, un laps de temps de 65 mois s'est écoulé.

Les inspections au cours de l'enquête ayant été effectuées aux mois de mars et d'avril 2000, la durée d'ensemble de cette phase de la procédure administrative ne saurait être justifiée par le seul fait que la Commission a adressé aux parties une série de demandes de renseignements entre 2001 et 2005.

Ainsi, en l'absence d'information ou de justification complémentaire de la part de la Commission quant aux actes d'enquêtes diligentés au cours de cette période, la durée de la première phase de la procédure doit être considérée comme excessive […].

La seconde phase de la procédure administrative, s'étendant de la réception de la communication des griefs à l'adoption de la décision attaquée en avril 2007, a duré 20 mois, excédant ainsi, en l'absence de justification complémentaire, le délai normalement nécessaire à l'adoption de la décision.

Par conséquent, il y a lieu de constater que la durée de la procédure administrative en cause a été excessive et résultait d'une inaction imputable à la Commission, conduisant à une violation du principe du délai raisonnable.

General Court 16 June 2011 (Heineken v. Commission, T-240/07) [2011] ECR II-3355, paras 290–294.

See also General Court 16 December 2003 (Nederlandse Federatieve Vereniging voor de Groothandel op Elektrotechnisch Gebied en Technische Unie v. Commission, T-5/00 and T-6/00) [2003] ECR II-5761.

In the case at hand, ESA itself acknowledged in the contested decision, at recital 851, **23.08** that the duration of the administrative procedure was considerable. While it did not consider itself legally bound to do so, ESA found it appropriate, in the exercise of its discretion in fixing the fines, to reduce the amount of the fine by EUR 1 million.

Indeed, between the date when Norway Post was first affected by the present proceedings and the date of the adoption of the contested *decision*, that is, between 2 May 2003, when the first request for information was sent to Norway Post, and 14 July 2010, when the contested decision was adopted, more than seven years and two months, or 86 months, elapsed. That duration appears already prima facie to be too long.

Having regard more specifically to the investigation period, which was concluded when ESA notified the Statement of Objections to Norway Post on 17 December 2008, the Court notes that it amounted to more than five years and eight months, or 68 months, which must be considered prima facie as too long. Contrary to what ESA asserts, the Court cannot see that this duration was justified by any particular difficulties of the case which go beyond what is normal for competition law cases. On the contrary, it would seem that both the definition of the relevant market and the question whether Norway Post entertained a dominant position on that market were rather straightforward. Norway Post did not dispute the existence or content of the agreements with its partners. Under those circumstances, it is unjustifiable, for example, that the questionnaires to the distance selling companies were sent only in October and November 2007. Indeed, between the end of 2005 and October 2007, it appears that ESA pursued no serious activity in investigating the infringement.

Under these circumstances, it must be held that the duration of ESA's investigation was excessive.

In addition, the Court notes that it took ESA 17 months to adopt the contested decision after it had sent Norway Post, at its request, a Norwegian translation of the Statement of Objections on 6 February 2009. Also the duration of this period appears prima facie too long. In particular, the Court notes that, although it had already drawn up its Statement of Objections, it took ESA one year to draft the final decision after Norway Post made its last submissions on 13 July 2009. Also the duration of this period must thus be considered excessive.

ESA reduced the basic amount of the fine by EUR 1 million, which corresponds to a discount of circa 7.2 per cent. Having regard to the important delays encountered in the pursuit of the proceedings, the Court agrees with the applicant's plea that the fine must be further reduced.

EFTA Court 18 April 2012 (Posten Norge AS v. EFTA Surveillance Authority, E-15/10) [2012] EFTACR 246, paras 278–284.

4. Consequences of a failure to adopt a decision within a reasonable period

(a)   EU Courts

Please refer to Section I.5 of Chapter 24 on Article 47 Charter.

(b)   EFTA Court

23.09   Under Article 13 ECHR, the infringement of a fundamental right through failure to adjudicate in reasonable time requires an effective remedy. A reduction of a sentence may be an appropriate redress of such a violation, if it is done in an express and measurable manner (compare, for example, *European Court of Human Rights Scordino v. Italy (no 1) [GC], no 36813/97, § 186, Reports of Judgments and Decisions 2006-V*). When reducing the sentence, in the case at hand the fine, regard must be had to all the circumstances; in particular, on the one hand, the seriousness of the infringement committed by Norway Post and, on the other hand, the seriousness of the infringement of the applicant's right under Article 6 ECHR to have the proceedings against it concluded within reasonable time (compare also the Opinion of Advocate General Kokott in *Solvay v Commission*, [[2011] ECR I-1377], point 196).

In exercising its unlimited jurisdiction in reviewing the fine, having regard to all the circumstances of the case, the Court considers it appropriate to reduce the basic amount of the fine by 20 per cent. An effective remedy requires a substantial reduction of the fine and well beyond ESA's assumption.

As regards, finally, the alleged less serious nature of the infringement, the Court notes that the applicant has raised this plea only in the reply. Accordingly, it must be dismissed as inadmissible pursuant to Article 37(2) of the Rules of Procedure.

It follows from all of the foregoing that the amount of the fine imposed on the applicant must be amended by reducing the fine from EUR 12.89 million to EUR 11.112 million.

EFTA Court 18 April 2012 (Posten Norge AS v. EFTA Surveillance Authority, E-15/10) [2012] EFTACR 246, paras 285–288.

C. RIGHTS OF THE DEFENCE

Please refer to the case extracts in Chapter 13 on Article 27 of Regulation 1/2003 (paras 13.221–13.231).

23.10   The necessity to have regard to the rights of the defence is a fundamental principle of Community law which the Commission must observe in administrative procedures which may lead to the imposition of penalties under the rules of competition laid down in the Treaty.

CoJ 9 November 1983 (Michelin v. Commission, 322/81) [1983] ECR 3466, para. 7.

[R]espect for the rights of the defence is, in all proceedings initiated against a person **23.11** which are liable to culminate in a measure adversely affecting that person, a fundamental principle of Community law which must be guaranteed even in the absence of any rules governing the proceedings in question.

CoJ 24 October 1996 (Commission v. Lisrestal, C-32/95 P) [1996] ECR I-5387, para. 21.

The rights of the defence are fundamental rights forming an integral part of the general **23.12** principles of law, whose observance the Court ensures […], drawing inspiration for that purpose from the constitutional traditions common to the Member States and from the guidelines supplied by international treaties for the protection of human rights on which the Member States have collaborated or to which they are signatories, such as the [ECHR].

CoJ 7 January 2004 (Aalborg Portland and others v. Commission, C-204/00 P, C-205/00 P, C-211/00 P, C-213/00 P, C-217/00 P and C-219/00 P) [2004] ECR I-123, para. 64.

See also CoJ 25 October 2011 (Solvay v. Commission, C-110/10 P) [2013] ECR I-10439, para. 47.

1. Applicability to preliminary inquiries

In [its judgment of 9 November 1983 in *Case 322/81 Michelin v. Commission*, [1983] **23.13** ECR 3461, para. 7], the Court pointed out that the rights of the defence must be observed in administrative procedures which may lead to the imposition of penalties. But it is also necessary to prevent those rights from being irremediably impaired during preliminary inquiry procedures including, in particular, investigations which may be decisive in providing evidence of the unlawful nature of conduct engaged in by undertakings for which they may be liable.

Consequently, although certain rights of the defence relate only to the contentious proceedings which follow the delivery of the statement of objections, other rights, such as the right to legal representation and the privileged nature of correspondence between lawyer and client (recognised by the Court in the judgment of 18 May 1982 in *Case 155/79 AM&S v Commission* ([1982] ECR 1575)) must be respected as from the preliminary inquiry stage.

CoJ 21 September 1989 (Hoechst v. Commission, Joined Cases 46/87 and 227/88) [1989] ECR 2859, paras 15 and 16.

See also CoJ 17 October 1989 (Dow Chemical Ibérica a.o. v. Commission, Joined Cases 97/87–99/87) [1989] ECR 3165, paras 12 and 13.

2. Right to be heard

Observance of the right to be heard is in all proceedings in which sanctions, in **23.14** particular fines or penalty payments, may be imposed a fundamental principle of

Community law which must be respected even if the proceedings in question are administrative proceedings.

[I]n order to respect the principle of the right to be heard the undertakings concerned must have been afforded the opportunity during the administrative procedure to make known their views on the truth and relevance of the facts and circumstances alleged and on the documents used by the Commission to support its claim that there has been an infringement of Article [102 TFEU].

CoJ 13 February 1979 (Hoffmann–La Roche v. Commission, 85/76) [1979] ECR 461, paras 9 and 11.

See also CoJ 7 June 1983 (SA Musique Diffusion Française v. Commission, Joined Cases 100–103/80) [1983] ECR 1825, para. 10; CoJ 9 November 1983 (Michelin v. Commission, 322/81) [1983] ECR 3466, para. 7; CoJ 6 April 1995 (BPB Industries and British Gypsum v. Commission, C-310/93 P) [1995] ECR I-865, para. 21; CoJ 7 January 2004 (Aalborg Portland and others v. Commission, C-204/00 P, C-205/00 P, C-211/00 P, C-213/00 P, C-217/00 P and C-219/00 P) [2004] ECR I-123, para. 66; CoJ 25 October 2011 (Solvay v. Commission, C-110/10 P) [2011] ECR I-10439, para. 48.

23.15 [O]bservance of the right to be heard is, in all proceedings initiated against a person which are liable to culminate in a measure adversely affecting that person, a fundamental principle of Community law which must be guaranteed even in the absence of any rules governing the proceedings in question […].

[Observance of that right] requires that any person on whom a penalty may be imposed must be placed in a position in which he can effectively make known his view of the matters on the basis of which the Commission imposes the penalty.

CoJ 29 June 1994 (Fiskano v. Commission, C-135/92) [1994] ECR I-2899, paras 39 and 40.

3. Statement of objections

23.16 That principle [of the rights of defence] requires, in particular, that the statement of objections which the Commission sends to an undertaking on which it envisages imposing a penalty for an infringement of the competition rules contain the essential elements used against it, such as the facts, the characterisation of those facts and the evidence on which the Commission relies, so that the undertaking may submit its arguments effectively in the administrative procedure brought against it […].

CoJ 15 July 1970 (ACF Chemiefarma v. Commission, 41/69) [1970] ECR 661, para. 26.

23.17 [I]n order to respect the principle of the right to be heard the undertakings concerned must have been afforded the opportunity during the administrative procedure to make known their views on the truth and relevance of the facts and circumstances alleged and on the documents used by the Commission to support its claim that there has been an infringement of Article [102 TFEU].

CoJ 13 February 1979 (Hoffmann-La Roche v. Commission, 85/76) [1979] ECR 461, para. 11

See also CoJ 23 October 1974 (Transocean Marine Paint Association v. Commission, 17/74) [1974] ECR 1063, para. 15; CoJ 7 June 1983 (SA Musique Diffusion Française v. Commission, Joint Cases 100–103/80) [1983] ECR 1825, para. 10.

[A]rticle 19(1) of Regulation no 17 requires the Commission, before taking a decision, to give the parties concerned the opportunity of being heard on the matters to which the Commission has taken objection and the Commission, in its Regulation No 99/63 of 25 July 1963 on the hearings provided for in Article 19(1) and (2) of Regulation No 17, instituted a procedure of an adversary nature. Under that procedure the Commission must notify its objections to the undertakings concerned, which may then reply in writing within a stated period. Where appropriate, and particularly in cases where the Commission proposes to impose fines, the undertakings may be afforded an oral hearing. Under the terms of Article 4 of Regulation No 99/63 the Commission may, in its decisions, deal only with those objections raised against undertakings in respect of which they have been afforded the opportunity of making known their views. **23.18**

As the Court recalled in its judgment of 13 February 1979 in *Case 85/76* (*Hoffmann-La Roche v. Commission* [1979] ECR 461), the above-mentioned provisions are an application of the fundamental principle of Community law which requires the right to a fair hearing to be observed in all proceedings, even those of an administrative nature, and lays down in particular that the undertaking concerned must have been afforded the opportunity, during the administrative procedure, to make known its views on the truth and relevance of the facts and circumstances alleged and on the documents used by the Commission to support its claim that there has been an infringement of the Treaty. [...]

It is clear from previous decisions of the Court that the statement of objections must set forth clearly all the essential facts upon which the Commission is relying at that stage of the procedure. That may be done summarily and the decision is not necessarily required to be a replica of the Commission's statement of objections. The Commission must take into account the factors emerging from the administrative procedure in order either to abandon such objections as have been shown to be unfounded or to amend and supplement its arguments, both in fact and in law, in support of the objections which it maintains, provided however that it relies only on facts on which the parties concerned have had an opportunity to make known their views and provided that, in the course of the administrative procedure, it has made available to the undertakings concerned the information necessary for their defence.

CoJ 7 June 1983 (SA Musique Diffusion Française v. Commission, Joined Cases 100–103/80) [1983] ECR 1825, paras 9, 10 and 14.

To give indications as regards the level of the fines envisaged, before the undertakings have been invited to submit their observations on the allegations against them, would be to anticipate the Commission's decision and would thus be inappropriate. **23.19**

CoJ 7 June 1983 (SA Musique Diffusion Française and others v. Commission, Joined Cases 100–103/80) [1983] ECR 1825, para 21.

23.20   [T]he Commission is required to specify unequivocally, in the statement of objections, the persons on whom fines may be imposed. [...]
It follows that the [General Court] erred in law when it confirmed that the Commission was entitled to impose on members of Cewal individual fines, fixed in accordance with an assessment of their participation in the conduct in question, when the statement of objections was addressed only to Cewal.

CoJ 16 March 2000 (Compagnie Maritime Belge Transports and others. v. Commission, Joined Cases C-395/96 P and C-396/96 P) [2000] ECR I-1365, paras 143 and 146.

23.21   [A]ccording to a consistent line of decisions of the Court of Justice, provided that the Commission indicates expressly in the statement of objections that it will consider whether it is appropriate to impose fines on the undertakings concerned and that it sets out the principal elements of fact and of law that may give rise to a fine, such as the gravity and the duration of the alleged infringement and the fact that it has been committed 'intentionally or negligently', it fulfils its obligation to respect the undertakings' right to be heard. The [General Court] also correctly held that, in doing so, it provides them with the necessary elements to defend themselves not only against a finding of infringement but also against the fact of being fined.

CoJ 28 June 2005 (Dansk Rørindustrie A/S and others v. Commission, Joined Cases C-189/02 P, C-202/02 P, C-205/02 P–C-208/02 P and C-213/02 P) [2005] ECR I-05425, para. 428.

23.22   In this respect, classification as leader of a cartel has significant consequences regarding the amount of the fine to be imposed on an undertaking described as such. Thus, under Section 2 of the Guidelines, it constitutes an aggravating circumstance which leads to a significant increase in the basic amount of the fine. Similarly, under Section B(e) of the Leniency Notice, such a classification automatically excludes the granting of a very substantial reduction of the fine, even if an undertaking classified as a leader fulfils all the conditions set out in that provision to qualify for such a reduction.
Accordingly, it is for the Commission to set out in the statement of objections the evidence which it considers relevant to enable an undertaking under investigation which may be classified as a leader of the cartel to respond to such an objection. However, in light of the fact that that statement remains a step in the adoption of the final decision and does not therefore constitute the Commission's definitive position, the Commission cannot be required, already at that stage, to carry out a legal classification of the evidence on which it relies in its final decision in classifying an undertaking as leader of the cartel.

CoJ 9 July 2009 (Archer Daniels Midlands v. Commission, C-511/06 P) [2009] ECR I-5843, paras 70 and 71.

23.23   However, it must be stated that, in the circumstances of the present case, the mere fact that the documents containing the facts used as a basis for classifying ADM as a leader of the cartel were annexed to the statement of objections is not sufficient to satisfy the above-mentioned requirements, since that statement did not enable ADM to dispute those facts and, consequently, to exercise its rights effectively.

It should be noted that the items of evidence which are the source of the facts used as a basis for classifying ADM as a leader of the cartel in the contested decision necessarily, by their nature, have a subjective aspect, since they consist of testimonies of persons involved in the infringement procedure initiated by the Commission or other national competition authorities.

Thus, the FBI Report is the result of the interview with a former ADM representative who enjoyed immunity in the procedure conducted by the United States antitrust authorities.

The second item of evidence consists of an unsolicited statement by Cerestar, a competitor of ADM on the citric acid market, which itself participated in the cartel in question.

The mere fact that those documents were annexed to the statement of objections did not enable the appellant to assess the credence which the Commission gave to each of the items of evidence set out in those documents.

Accordingly, in the circumstances of the present case, it cannot be considered that the Commission, by merely annexing to the statement of objections the documents and items of evidence from which it took the facts on which it relied in the contested decision in order to classify the appellant as a leader in the cartel but without referring to those facts expressly in the wording itself of that statement, afforded ADM the opportunity to exercise its rights.

CoJ 9 July 2009 (Archer Daniels Midland Co. v. Commission, C-511/06 P) [2009] ECR I-5843, paras 89–94.

The [General Court] thus erred in law in failing to draw any legal conclusion from its **23.24** finding that Bolloré's rights of defence had not been observed. [...]

[T]he contested decision must be annulled in so far as it concerns Bolloré.

CoJ 3 September 2009 (Koehler and others v. Commission, Joined Cases C-322/07 P, C-327/07 P and C-328/07 P) [2009] ECR I-7191, paras 45 and 48.

4. Access to the file

[I]n order to respect the principle of the right to be heard the undertakings concerned **23.25** must have been afforded the opportunity during the administrative procedure to make known their views on the truth and relevance of the facts and circumstances alleged and on the documents used by the Commission to support its claim that there has been an infringement of Article [102 TFEU].

CoJ 13 February 1979 (Hoffmann–La Roche v. Commission, 85/76) [1979] ECR 461, para. 11.

See also CoJ 7 June 1983 (SA Musique Diffusion Française v. Commission, Joined Cases 100–103/80) [1983] ECR 1825, para. 10; CoJ 9 November 1983 (Michelin v. Commission, 322/81) [1983] ECR 3466, para. 7; CoJ 6 April 1995 (BPB Industries and British Gypsum v. Commission, C-310/93 P) [1995] ECR I-865, para. 21; CoJ 25 October 2011 (Solvay v. Commission, C-110/10 P) [2011] ECR I-10439, para. 48.

23.26   [A]ccess to the file in competition cases is intended in particular to enable the addressees of statements of objections to acquaint themselves with the evidence in the Commission's file so that on the basis of that evidence they can express their views effectively on the conclusions reached by the Commission in its statement of objections [...].

CoJ 17 December1998 (Baustahlgewebe v. Commission, C-185/95 P) [1998] ECR I-8417, para. 89.

See also CoJ 8 July 1999 (Hercules Chemicals v. Commission, C-51/92 P) [1999] ECR I-4235, para. 75; CoJ 15 October 2002 (Limburgse Vinyl Maatschappij a.o. v. Commission, Joined Cases C-238/99 P, C-244/99 P, C-245/99 P, C-247/99 P, C-250/99 P–C-252/99 P and C-254/99 P) [2002] ECR I-8375, para. 315; CoJ 2 October 2003 (Corus UK v. Commission, C-199/99 P) [2003] ECR I-11177, para. 125.

23.27   Thus the general principles of Community law governing the right of access to the Commission's file are designed to ensure effective exercise of the rights of the defence, including the right to be heard.

CoJ 8 July 1999 (Hercules Chemicals v. Commission, C-51/92 P) [1999] ECR I-4235, para. 76.

See also CoJ 15 October 2002 (Limburgse Vinyl Maatschappij a.o. v. Commission, Joined Cases C-238/99 P, C-244/99 P, C-245/99 P, C-247/99 P, C-250/99 P–C-252/99 P and C-254/99 P), [2002] ECR I-8375, para. 316; CoJ 2 October 2003 (Corus UK v. Commission, C-199/99 P) [2003] ECR I-11177, para. 125.

23.28   In the case of a decision concerning infringement of the competition rules applicable to undertakings and imposing fines or penalty payments, breach of those general principles of Community law in the procedure prior to the adoption of the decision can, in principle, cause the decision to be annulled if the rights of defence of the undertaking concerned have been infringed.

In such a case, the infringement committed is not remedied by the mere fact that access was made possible at a later stage, in particular during the judicial proceedings relating to an action in which annulment of the contested decision is sought.

Although belated disclosure of documents in the file allows the undertaking that has brought an action against a Commission decision to derive from them pleas and arguments in support of the forms of order it is seeking, it does not put the undertaking back into the situation it would have been in if it had been able to rely on those documents in presenting its written and oral observations to the Commission. It is not therefore an adequate remedy for the infringement of the rights of the defence that occurred before the decision was adopted.

CoJ 8 July 1999 (Hercules Chemicals v. Commission, C-51/92 P) [1999] ECR I-4235, paras 77–79.

See also CoJ 15 October 2002 (Limburgse Vinyl Maatschappij a.o. v. Commission, Joined Cases C-238/99 P, C-244/99 P, C-245/99 P, C-247/99 P, C-250/99 P–C-252/99 P and C-254/99 P) [2002] ECR I-8375, paras 317–318; CoJ 25 October 2011 (Solvay v. Commission, C-110/10 P) [2011] ECR I-10439, paras 50 and 51.

A corollary of the principle of respect for the rights of the defence, the right of access to **23.29** the file means that the Commission must give the undertaking concerned the opportunity to examine all the documents in the investigation file which may be relevant for its defence [...]. Those documents include both incriminating evidence and exculpatory evidence, save where the business secrets of other undertakings, the internal documents of the Commission or other confidential information are involved [...].

It may be that the undertaking draws the Commission's attention to documents capable of providing a different economic explanation for the overall economic assessment carried out by the Commission, in particular those describing the relevant market and the importance and the conduct of the undertakings acting on that market.

The [Eur. Court H.R.] has none the less held that, just like observance of the other procedural safeguards enshrined in Article 6(1) of the ECHR, compliance with the adversarial principle relates only to judicial proceedings before a 'tribunal' and that there is no general, abstract principle that the parties must in all instances have the opportunity to attend the interviews carried out or to receive copies of all the documents taken into account in the case of other persons [...].

The failure to communicate a document constitutes a breach of the rights of the defence only if the undertaking concerned shows, first, that the Commission relied on that document to support its objection concerning the existence of an infringement [...] and, second, that the objection could be proved only by reference to that document [...].

If there were other documentary evidence of which the parties were aware during the administrative procedure that specifically supported the Commission's findings, the fact that an incriminating document not communicated to the person concerned was inadmissible as evidence would not affect the validity of the objections upheld in the contested decision [...].

It is thus for the undertaking concerned to show that the result at which the Commission arrived in its decision would have been different if a document which was not communicated to that undertaking and on which the Commission relied to make a finding of infringement against it had to be disallowed as evidence.

On the other hand, where an exculpatory document has not been communicated, the undertaking concerned must only establish that its non-disclosure was able to influence, to its disadvantage, the course of the proceedings and the content of the decision of the Commission [...].

It is sufficient for the undertaking to show that it would have been able to use the exculpatory documents in its defence [...], in the sense that, had it been able to rely on them during the administrative procedure, it would have been able to put forward evidence which did not agree with the findings made by the Commission at that stage and would therefore have been able to have some influence on the Commission's assessment in any decision it adopted, at least as regards the gravity and duration of the conduct of which it was accused and, accordingly, the level of the fine.

The possibility that a document which was not disclosed might have influenced the course of the proceedings and the content of the Commission's decision can be established only if a provisional examination of certain evidence shows that the documents not disclosed might – in the light of that evidence – have had a significance which ought not to have been disregarded [...].

CoJ 7 January 2004 (Aalborg Portland and others v. Commission, C-204/00 P) [2004] ECR I-123, paras 68–76.

See also CoJ 25 October 2011 (Solvay v. Commission, C-110/10 P) [2011] ECR I-10439, para. 49.

23.30   As th[e] examination [by the General Court] is limited to a judicial review of the pleas in law, it has neither the object nor the effect of replacing a full investigation of the case in the context of an administrative procedure [...]. It is common ground that belated disclosure of documents in the file does not put the undertaking which has brought the action against the Commission decision back into the situation it would have been in if it had been able to rely on those documents in presenting its written and oral observations to the Commission.

CoJ 7 January 2004 (Aalborg Portland and others v. Commission, C-204/00 P) [2004] ECR I-123, para. 103.

See also CoJ 25 October 2011 (Solvay v. Commission, C-110/10 P) [2011] ECR I-10439, para. 51.

24

ARTICLE 47 CHARTER

RIGHT TO AN EFFECTIVE REMEDY AND TO AN IMPARTIAL TRIBUNAL

Everyone whose rights and freedoms guaranteed by the law of the Union are violated has the right to an effective remedy before a tribunal in compliance with the conditions laid down in this Article.

Everyone is entitled to a fair and public hearing within a reasonable time by an independent and impartial tribunal previously established by law. Everyone shall have the possibility of being advised, defended and represented.

Legal aid shall be made available to those who lack sufficient resources in so far as such aid is necessary to ensure effective access to justice.

ARTICLE 6(1) AND (3)(C) ECHR – RIGHT TO A FAIR TRIAL AND LEGAL REPRESENTATION AND AID

1. In the determination of his civil rights and obligations or of any criminal charge against him, everyone is entitled to a fair and public hearing within a reasonable time by an independent and impartial tribunal established by law. Judgment shall be pronounced publicly but the press and public may be excluded from all or part of the trial in the interests of morals, public order or national security in a democratic society, where the interests of juveniles or the protection of the private life of the parties so require, or to the extent strictly necessary in the opinion of the court in special circumstances where publicity would prejudice the interests of justice.

3. Everyone charged with a criminal offence has the following minimum rights:
    (c) to defend himself in person or through legal assistance of his own choosing or, if he has not sufficient means to pay for legal assistance, to be given it free when the interests of justice so require

ARTICLE 13 ECHR – EFFECTIVE REMEDY

Everyone whose rights and freedoms as set forth in this Convention are violated shall have an effective remedy before a national authority notwithstanding that the violation has been committed by persons acting in an official capacity.

OVERVIEW

A. EXPLANATION RELATING TO ARTICLE 47
CHARTER (p.778)

B. GENERAL 24.01
  1. Relationship between the principles of effective remedy (para. 1) and fair trial (para. 2) 24.01
  2. General principles 24.02

C. SCOPE OF APPLICATION OF ARTICLES 47 CHARTER AND ARTICLES 6 AND 13 ECHR 24.07
  1. General applicability of Article 47 Charter 24.07
  2. Civil rights and obligations within the meaning of Article 6 ECHR 24.08
  3. Criminal charge within the meaning of Article 6 ECHR 24.14

D. INDEPENDENT AND IMPARTIAL TRIBUNAL 24.28
  1. Concept of 'Tribunal' 24.28
  2. Independence 24.35
  3. Impartiality 24.37

E. FULL JURISDICTION 24.43
  1. Legal standard 24.43
  2. Assessment 24.46

F. ACCESS 24.57
  1. General 24.57
  2. Effet utile 24.58
  3. Restrictions 24.60

G. EFFECTIVE REMEDY 24.62
  1. Legal standard 24.62
  2. In relation to dawn raids 24.63

H. FAIR TRIAL 24.66
  1. Applicability to pre-trial proceedings 24.66
  2. Imposition of fines by an administrative body 24.69
  3. Principle of adversarial proceedings 24.76
  4. Equality of arms 24.88
  5. Access to the file in criminal proceedings 24.92
  6. Exclusionary rule 24.95
  7. Obligation to state the grounds of a judgment 24.97
  8. Waiver of rights 24.100

I. REASONABLE PERIOD 24.102
  1. General 24.102
  2. Relevant period 24.104
  3. Legal standard 24.108
  4. Assessment 24.110
  5. Consequences of a failure to adjudicate within a reasonable period 24.113

J. PUBLIC HEARING 24.118

K. ACCESS TO A LAWYER 24.119
  1. General 24.119
  2. During an interrogation 24.121
  3. Legal privilege (p.837)

L. LEGAL AID 24.126
  1. Scope 24.126
  2. Assistance by a lawyer and dispensation of the cost of proceedings 24.127
  3. Grant procedure 24.128
  4. Availability to a legal person 24.129

A. EXPLANATION RELATING TO ARTICLE 47 CHARTER

The first paragraph is based on Article 13 of the ECHR: [...].
However, in Union law the protection is more extensive since it guarantees the

right to an effective remedy before a court. The Court of Justice enshrined that right in its judgment of 15 May 1986 as a general principle of Union law (Case 222/84 Johnston [1986] ECR 1651; see also judgment of 15 October 1987, Case 222/86 Heylens [1987] ECR 4097 and judgment of 3 December 1992, Case C-97/91 Borelli [1992] ECR I-6313). According to the Court, that general principle of Union law also applies to the Member States when they are implementing Union law. The inclusion of this precedent in the Charter has not been intended to change the system of judicial review laid down by the Treaties, and particularly the rules relating to admissibility for direct actions before the Court of Justice of the European Union. The European Convention has considered the Union's system of judicial review including the rules on admissibility, and confirmed them while amending them as to certain aspects, as reflected in Articles 251 to 281 of the Treaty on the Functioning of the European Union, and in particular in the fourth paragraph of Article 263. Article 47 applies to the institutions of the Union and of Member States when they are implementing Union law and does so for all rights guaranteed by Union law.

The second paragraph corresponds to Article 6(1) of the ECHR which reads as follows: […].

In Union law, the right to a fair hearing is not confined to disputes relating to civil law rights and obligations. That is one of the consequences of the fact that the Union is a community based on the rule of law as stated by the Court in Case 294/83, 'Les Verts' v. European Parliament (judgment of 23 April 1986, [1986] ECR 1339). Nevertheless, in all respects other than their scope, the guarantees afforded by the ECHR apply in a similar way to the Union.

With regard to the third paragraph, it should be noted that in accordance with the case-law of the European Court of Human Rights, provision should be made for legal aid where the absence of such aid would make it impossible to ensure an effective remedy (ECHR judgment of 9 October 1979, Airey, Series A, Volume 32, p. 11). There is also a system of legal assistance for cases before the Court of Justice of the European Union.

B. GENERAL

1. Relationship between the principles of effective remedy (para. 1) and fair trial (para. 2)

In many previous cases in which the Court has found a violation of Article 6(1) it did **24.01** not consider it necessary also to rule on an accompanying complaint made under Article 13. More often than not this was because in the circumstances Article 6(1) was deemed to constitute a lex specialis in relation to Article 13.

Thus, where the Convention right asserted by the individual is a 'civil right' recognised under domestic law – such as the right of property – the protection afforded by Article 6(1) will also be available […]. In such circumstances the safeguards of

Article 6(1), implying the full panoply of a judicial procedure, are stricter than, and absorb, those of Article 13 [...].

The Court has applied a similar logic in cases where the applicant's grievance has been directed at the adequacy of an existing appellate or cassation procedure coming within the ambit of both Article 6(1) under its 'criminal' head and Article 13 [...].

In such cases there is no legal interest in re-examining the same subject matter of complaint under the less stringent requirements of Article 13.

Eur. Court H.R. (Grand Chamber) 26 October 2000 (Kudla v. Poland, no. 30210/96), ECHR Reports 2000–XI, para. 146.

2. General principles

(a) European Court of Human Rights (Eur. Court H.R.)

24.02   The Contracting States enjoy considerable freedom in the choice of the means of ensuring that their legal system satisfies the requirements of Article 6. [The Court's] task is to determine whether the method chosen by them in this connection leads to results which, in the cases which come before it, are consistent with the requirements of the Convention.

Eur. Court H.R. 24 May 1991 (Quaranta v. Switzerland, no. 12744/87), Series A no. 205, p. 16, para. 30.

(b) European Union (EU) Courts

24.03   The requirement of judicial control [...] reflects a general principle of law which underlies the constitutional traditions common to the Member States. That principle has also been laid down in Articles 6 and 13 [ECHR].

[By virtue of that principle], all persons have the right to obtain an effective remedy in a competent court against measures which they consider to be contrary to [EU law].

CoJ 15 May 1986 (Johnston, 222/84) [1986] ECR 1651, paras 18 and 19.

See also CoJ 15 October 1987 (Heylens, 222/86) [1987] ECR 4097, para. 14, and CoJ 3 December 1992 (Oleifici Borelli, C-97/91) [1992] ECR I-6313, para. 14.

24.04   The requirement for effective judicial review of any Commission decision that finds and punishes an infringement of those Community competition rules is a general principle of Community law which follows from the common constitutional traditions of the Member States.

General Court 14 May 1998 (Enso Española v. Commission, T-384/94) [1998] ECR II-1875, para. 60.

24.05   It should be noted that Article 6(1) of the EHRC provides that in the determination of his civil rights and obligations or of any criminal charge against him, everyone is entitled to a fair and public hearing within a reasonable time by an independent and impartial tribunal established by law.

The general principle of Community law that everyone is entitled to fair legal process, which is inspired by those fundamental rights [...], and in particular the right to legal process within a reasonable period, is applicable in the context of proceedings brought against a Commission decision imposing fines on an undertaking for infringement of competition law.

CoJ 17 December 1998 (Baustahlgewebe v. Commission, C-185/95 P) [1998] ECR 1–8417, paras 20 and 21.

[T]he right to a fair trial, which derives inter alia from Article 6 of the ECHR, **24.06** constitutes a fundamental right which the European Union respects as a general principle under Article 6(2) EU [old].

CoJ 26 June 2007 (Ordre des barreaux francophones et germanophone and others, C-305/05) [2007] ECR I-5305, para. 29.

C. SCOPE OF APPLICATION OF ARTICLES 47 CHARTER AND ARTICLES 6 AND 13 ECHR

1. General applicability of Article 47 Charter

The appellant took the view at the hearing that the argument that competition **24.07** proceedings are criminal in nature (within the meaning of Article 6 of the ECHR) is not relevant to the Court's review, since that review has to satisfy the same criteria whether the proceedings are regarded as forming part of the hard core of criminal law within the meaning of the case-law of the European Court of Human Rights or are covered by administrative law.

Moreover, as the appellant noted in its appeal, Article 47 of the Charter implements in European Union law the protection afforded by Article 6(1) of the ECHR. It is necessary, therefore, to refer only to Article 47.

CoJ 8 December 2011 (Chalkor v. Commission, C-386/10 P) [2011] ECR I-13085, paras 50 and 51.

See also CoJ 6 November 2012 (EC v. Otis a.o., C-199/11), ECLI:EU:C: 2012:684, para. 47.

2. Civil rights and obligations within the meaning of Article 6 ECHR

For Article 6, paragraph (1), [in its civil rights and obligations limb] to be applicable to **24.08** a case it is not necessary that both parties to the proceedings should be private persons [...]. The wording of Article 6, paragraph (1), is far wider; the French expression 'contestations sur (des) droits et obligations de caractère civil' covers all proceedings the result of which is decisive for private rights and obligations, [even if the proceedings concern a dispute between an individual and a public authority acting in its sovereign capacity]. The English text 'determination of ... civil rights and obligations', confirms this interpretation. The character of the legislation which governs how the matter is to be determined (civil, commercial, administrative law, etc.) and that of the authority which is invested with jurisdiction in the matter (ordinary court, administrative body, etc.) are therefore of little consequence.

Eur. Court H.R. 16 July 1971 (Ringeisen v. Austria, no. 2614/65), Series A, no. 13, para. 94.

24.09   Both the Commission and the Government agree that the concept of 'civil rights and obligations' cannot be interpreted solely by reference to the domestic law of the respondent State.

The problem of the 'autonomy' of the meaning of the expressions used in the Convention, compared with their meaning in domestic law, has already been raised before the Court on several occasions. [T]he Court has already acknowledged, implicitly, that the concept of 'civil rights and obligations' is autonomous [...].

The Court confirms this case-law on the present occasion. Hence, it considers that the same principle of autonomy applies to the concept in question; any other solution might lead to results incompatible with the object and purpose of the Convention [...].

Whilst the Court thus concludes that the concept of 'civil rights and obligations' is autonomous, it nevertheless does not consider that, in this context, the legislation of the State concerned is without importance. Whether or not a right is to be regarded as civil within the meaning of this expression in the Convention must be determined by reference to the substantive content and effects of the right – and not its legal classification – under the domestic law of the State concerned. In the exercise of its supervisory functions, the Court must also take account of the object and purpose of the Convention and of the national legal systems of the other Contracting State [...].

Eur. Court H.R. 28 June 1978 (König v. Germany, no. 6232/73), Series A no. 27, p. 29, paras 88 and 89.

24.10   It will however apply to disputes of a 'genuine and serious nature' concerning the actual existence of the right as well as to the scope or manner in which it is exercised.

Eur. Court H.R. 23 October 1985 (Benthem v. the Netherlands, no. 8848/80), Series A no. 97, p. 14, para. 32.

24.11   [...] Article 6(1) extends only to 'contestations' (disputes) over (civil) 'rights and obligations' which can be said, at least on arguable grounds, to be recognised under domestic law; it does not itself guarantee any particular content for (civil) 'rights and obligations' in the substantive law of the Contracting States.[...]

Eur. Court H.R. 21 February 1986 (James and others v. the United Kingdom, no. 8793/79), Series A no. 98, p. 46, para. 81.

24.12   The Court considers that tax matters still form part of the hard core of public-authority prerogatives, with the public nature of the relationship between the taxpayer and the community remaining predominant. Bearing in mind that the Convention and its Protocols must be interpreted as a whole, the Court also observes that Article 1 of Protocol No. 1, which concerns the protection of property, reserves the right of States to enact such laws as they deem necessary for the purpose of securing the payment of taxes

[…]. Although the Court does not attach decisive importance to that factor, it does take it into account. It considers that tax disputes fall outside the scope of civil rights and obligations, despite the pecuniary effects which they necessarily produce for the taxpayer.

Eur. Court H.R. (Grand Chamber) 12 July 2001 (Ferrazzini v. Italy, no. 44759/ 98), only available in French, ECHR 2001-VII, para. 29.

Il s'agit en l'espèce de vérifier si la procédure à laquelle les requérants revendiquent **24.13** l'accès vise à voir trancher une « contestation » – réelle et sérieuse – sur un « droit » de « nature civile » que l'on peut prétendre, au moins de manière défendable, reconnu en droit interne […], étant entendu que l'article 6 § 1 n'assure par lui-même aux « droits et obligations de caractère civil » aucun contenu déterminé ni ne vise à créer de nouveaux droits matériels dénués de base juridique dans l'Etat concerné […].

Eur. Court H.R. 21 February 2008 (Ravon v. France, no. 18497/03), only available in French, para. 24.

3. Criminal charge within the meaning of Article 6 ECHR

(a) Concept

(i) European Court of Human Rights

[…] In the Neumeister judgment of 27 June 1968, the Court has already held that the **24.14** word 'charge' must be understood 'within the meaning of the Convention' […].

The question of the 'autonomy' of the concept of 'criminal' does not call for exactly the same reply.

The Convention without any doubt allows the States, in the performance of their function as guardians of the public interest, to maintain or establish a distinction between criminal law and disciplinary law, and to draw the dividing line, but only subject to certain conditions. The Convention leaves the States free to designate as a criminal offence an act or omission not constituting the normal exercise of one of the rights that it protects. This is made especially clear by Article 7. Such a choice, which has the effect of rendering applicable Articles 6 and 7, in principle escapes supervision by the Court.

The converse choice, for its part, is subject to stricter rules. If the Contracting States were able at their discretion to classify an offence as disciplinary instead of criminal, or to prosecute the author of a 'mixed' offence on the disciplinary rather than on the criminal plane, the operation of the fundamental clauses of Articles 6 and 7 would be subordinated to their sovereign will. A latitude extending thus far might lead to results incompatible with the purpose and object of the Convention. The Court therefore has jurisdiction, under Article 6 and even without reference to Articles 17 and 18, to satisfy itself that the disciplinary does not improperly encroach upon the criminal.

In short, the 'autonomy' of the concept of 'criminal' operates, as it were, one way only.

Hence, the Court must specify [...] whether a given 'charge' [...] counts as 'criminal' within the meaning of Article 6.

In this connection, it is first necessary to know whether the provision(s) defining the offence charged belong, according to the legal system of the respondent State, to criminal law, disciplinary law or both concurrently. This however provides no more than a starting point. The indications so afforded have only a formal and relative value and must be examined in the light of the common denominator of the respective legislation of the various Contracting States.

The very nature of the offence is a factor of greater import. When a serviceman finds himself accused of an act or omission allegedly contravening a legal rule governing the operation of the armed forces, the State may in principle employ against him disciplinary law rather than criminal law. In this respect, the Court expresses its agreement with the Government.

However, supervision by the Court does not stop there. Such supervision would generally prove to be illusory if it did not also take into consideration the degree of severity of the penalty that the person concerned risks incurring. In a society subscribing to the rule of law, there belong to the 'criminal' sphere deprivations of liberty liable to be imposed as a punishment, except those which by their nature, duration or manner of execution cannot be appreciably detrimental. The seriousness of what is at stake, the traditions of the Contracting States and the importance attached by the Convention to respect for the physical liberty of the person all require that this should be so.

Eur. Court H.R. 8 June 1976 (Engel and others v. the Netherlands, nos. 5100/71, 5101/71, 5102/71, 5354/72 and 5370/72), Series A no. 22–1, p. 647, paras 81 and 82.

See also Eur. Court H.R. (Grand Chamber) 9 November 2003 (Ezeh and Connors v. the United Kingdom, nos. 39665/98 and 40086/98), ECHR Reports 2003-X, paras 82–86; Eur. Court H.R. (Grand Chamber) 23 November 2006 (Jussila v. Finland, no. 73053/01), ECHR Reports 2006-XIV, paras 30 and, 31.

24.15   [...] The concept embodied in the French expression 'accusation en matière pénale' is [...] 'autonomous'; it has to be understood 'within the meaning of the Convention' [...], more especially since the English text of Article 6 paragraph 1 – like that of Article 5 paragraph 2 – employs the term 'charge' which is very wide in scope. [...]

[T]he prominent place held in a democratic society by the right to a fair trial [...] prompts the Court to prefer a 'substantive', rather than a 'formal', conception of the 'charge' contemplated by Article 6 paragraph 1. The Court is compelled to look behind the appearances and investigate the realities of the procedure in question.

Eur. Court H.R. 27 February 1980 (Deweer v. Belgium, no. 6903/75), Series A no. 35, p. 30, paras 42 and 44.

24.16   [Regarding fines for the infringement of road traffic rules] The Convention is not opposed to States, in the performance of their task as guardians of the public interest, both creating or maintaining a distinction between different categories of offences for the purposes of their domestic law and drawing the dividing line, but it does not follow that the classification thus made by the States is decisive for the purposes of the Convention.

By removing certain forms of conduct from the category of criminal offences under domestic law, the law-maker may be able to serve the interests of the individual [...] as well as the needs of the proper administration of justice, in particular in so far as the judicial authorities are thereby relieved of the task of prosecuting and punishing contraventions – which are numerous but of minor importance – of road traffic rules. The Convention is not opposed to the moves towards 'decriminalisation' which are taking place – in extremely varied forms – in the member States of the Council of Europe. The Government quite rightly insisted on this point. Nevertheless, if the Contracting States were able at their discretion, by classifying an offence as 'regulatory' instead of criminal, to exclude the operation of the fundamental clauses of Articles 6 and 7, the application of these provisions would be subordinated to their sovereign will. A latitude extending thus far might lead to results incompatible with the object and purpose of the Convention.

[...] The first matter to be ascertained is whether or not the text defining the offence in issue belongs, according to the legal system of the respondent State, to criminal law; next, the nature of the offence and, finally, the nature and degree of severity of the penalty that the person concerned risked incurring must be examined, having regard to the object and purpose of Article 6, to the ordinary meaning of the terms of that Article and to the laws of the Contracting States.

[T]he indications furnished by the domestic law of the respondent State have only a relative value. The second criterion stated above – the very nature of the offence, considered also in relation to the nature of the corresponding penalty – represents a factor of appreciation of greater weight. [...]

Eur. Court H.R. 21 February 1984 (Öztürk v. Germany, no. 8544/79), Series A no. 73, p. 18, paras 49, 50 and 52.

[Regarding fines for the infringement of road traffic rules] The Court points out that **24.17** the second and third criteria adopted in the judgments in the *Engel* and others case and the *Öztürk* case are alternative and not cumulative ones: for Article 6 to apply in virtue of the words 'criminal charge', it suffices that the offence in question should by its nature be 'criminal' from the point of view of the Convention, as in the instant case, or should have made the person concerned liable to a sanction which, in its nature and degree of severity, belongs in general to the 'criminal' sphere (see also the *Campbell and Fell* judgment of 28 June 1984, Series A no. 80, pp. 35–38, §§ 69–73).

Eur. Court H.R. 25 August 1987(Lutz v. Germany, no. 9912/82) Series A no. 123, para. 55.

[Regarding fines for the infringement of tax rules] As regards the nature and severity of **24.18** the penalty risked, the fines were, in the Court's opinion, not inconsiderable: they amounted to CHF 3,875.85 for the fiscal year 1981/82 and CHF 2,882.90 for 1983/84 [...]. Moreover, in setting these figures, the authorities took the applicants cooperative attitude into account; the fines might in fact have been four times as large [...].

As regards the nature of the offence, it is noted that tax legislation lays down certain requirements, to which it attaches penalties in the event of non-compliance. The penalties, which in the present case take the form of fines, are not intended as pecuniary compensation for damage but are essentially punitive and deterrent in nature [...]. As regards the classification of the proceedings under national law, the Court attaches weight to the finding of the highest court in the land, the Federal Court, in its judgment in the present case, that the fine in question was 'penal' in character and depended on the 'guilt' of the offending taxpayer [...].

Having regard to the above features, the Court considers that Article 6 is applicable under its criminal head.

Eur. Court H.R. 29 August 1997 (A.P., M.P. and T.P. v. Switzerland, no. 41545/98), ECHR Reports 1997-V, paras 40–44.

See also Eur. Court H.R. 3 May 2001 (J.B. v. Switzerland, no. 31827/96), ECHR Reports 2001-VI, paras 48 and 49.

24.19 [C]riminal penalties have been customarily recognised as comprising the twin objectives of punishment and deterrence (see *Öztürk*, *Bendenoun* and *Lauko*, [...], pp. 20–21, § 53, p. 20, § 47, and p. 2505, § 58, respectively).

It is [...] true that the extreme gravity of the offence may be indicative of its criminal nature, as indicated in *Campbell and Fell* [...]. However, that does not conversely mean that the minor nature of an offence can, of itself, take it outside the ambit of Article 6, as there is nothing in the Convention to suggest that the criminal nature of an offence, within the meaning of the second of the Engel criteria, necessarily requires a certain degree of seriousness (see *Öztürk*, [...], pp. 20–21, § 53).

The nature and severity of the penalty which was 'liable to be imposed' on the applicants (see *Engel and Others*, [...], pp. 34–35, § 82) are determined by reference to the maximum potential penalty for which the relevant law provides (see *Campbell and Fell*, [...], pp. 37–38, § 72; *Weber v. Switzerland*, judgment of 22 May 1990, Series A no. 177, p. 18, § 34; *Demicoli v. Malta*, judgment of 27 August 1991, Series A no. 210, p. 17, § 34; *Benham*, [...], p. 756, § 56; and *Garyfallou AEBE*, [...], p. 1810, §§ 33–34).

The actual penalty imposed is relevant to the determination (see *Campbell and Fell*, [...], p. 38, § 73, and *Bendenoun*, [...], p. 20, § 47) but it cannot diminish the importance of what was initially at stake (see *Engel and Others*, [...], p. 36, § 85, together with *Demicoli*, *Garyfallou AEBE* and *Weber*, [...]).

Eur. Court H.R. (Grand Chamber) 9 November 2003 (Ezeh and Connors v. the United Kingdom, nos. 39665/98 and 40086/98), ECHR Reports 2003-X, paras 104, 105 and 120.

24.20 La Cour constate d'abord que les pratiques anticoncurrentielles reprochées en l'espèce à la société requérante ne constituent pas une infraction pénale au sens du droit italien. Les comportements anticoncurrentiels y sont en effet sanctionnés non pas sur le fondement du droit pénal, mais sur celui de la loi no 287 du 10 octobre 1990 sur la concurrence et les pratiques commerciales loyales. Cela n'est toutefois pas décisif aux fins de l'applicabilité de l'article 6 de la Convention, les indications que fournit le droit interne n'ayant qu'une valeur relative (*Öztürk c. Allemagne*, 21 février 1984, § 52, série A n° 73).

Quant à la nature de l'infraction, il apparaît que les dispositions dont la violation a été reprochée à la société requérante visaient à préserver la libre concurrence sur le marché. La Cour rappelle que l'AGCM, autorité administrative indépendante, a comme but d'exercer une surveillance sur les accords restrictifs de la concurrence ainsi que sur les abus de position dominante. Elle affecte donc les intérêts généraux de la société normalement protégés par le droit pénal (Stenuit c. France, précité, § 62). En outre, il convient de noter que l'amende infligée visait pour l'essentiel à punir pour empêcher la réitération des agissements incriminés. On peut dès lors en conclure que l'amende infligée était fondée sur des normes poursuivant un but à la fois préventif et répressif (mutatis mutandis, *Jussila*, précité, § 38).

Quant à la nature et à la sévérité de la sanction «susceptible d'être infligée» à la requérante (*Ezeh et Connors c. Royaume-Uni* [GC], nos 39665/98 et 40086/98, § 120, CEDH 2003-X), la Cour constate que l'amende en question ne pouvait pas être remplacée par une peine privative de liberté en cas de non-paiement (a contrario, *Anghel c. Roumanie*, n° 28183/03, § 52, 4 octobre 2007). Cependant, elle note que l'AGCM a prononcé en l'espèce une sanction pécuniaire de six millions d'euros, sanction qui présentait un caractère répressif puisqu'elle visait à sanctionner une irrégularité, et préventif, le but poursuivi étant de dissuader la société intéressée de recommencer. En outre, la Cour note que la requérante souligne que le caractère punitif de ce type d'infraction ressort aussi de la jurisprudence du Conseil d'Etat.

A la lumière de ce qui précède et compte tenu du montant élevé de l'amende infligée, la Cour estime que la sanction relève, par sa sévérité, de la matière pénale (*Öztürk* précité, § 54, et, a contrario, *Inocêncio c. Portugal* (déc.), no 43862/98, CEDH 2001-I).

Au demeurant, la Cour rappelle également qu'à propos de certaines autorités administratives françaises compétentes en droit économique et financier et disposant de pouvoirs de sanction, elle a jugé que l'article 6, sous son volet pénal, s'appliquait notamment à propos du Conseil de la concurrence (*Lilly c. France* (déc.), no 53892/00, 3 décembre 2002), du Conseil des marchés financiers (*Didier c. France* (déc.), no 58188/00, 27 août 2002) et de la Commission bancaire (*Dubus S.A. c. France*, no 5242/04, § 36, 11 juin 2009).

Eur. Court H.R. 27 September 2011 (A. Menarini Diagnostics v. Italy, no 43509/08), unreported, paras 39–43.

(ii) EU Courts

24.21 It must also be accepted that, given the nature of the infringements in question and the nature and degree of severity of the ensuing penalties, the principle of the presumption of innocence applies to the procedures relating to infringements of the competition rules applicable to undertakings that may result in the imposition of fines or periodic penalty payments.

CoJ 8 July 1999 (Hüls v. Commission, C-199/92 P) [1999] ECR 1–4287, para. 150 and CoJ 8 July 1999 (Montecatini v. Commission, C-235/92 P) [1999] ECR I-4539, para. 176.

(b) Distinction between hard core criminal law and other criminal charges

24.22 While it may be noted that the above-mentioned cases in which an oral hearing was not considered necessary concerned proceedings falling under the civil head of Article 6(1) and that the requirements of a fair hearing are the most strict in the sphere of criminal law, the Court would not exclude that in the criminal sphere the nature of the issues to be dealt with before the tribunal or court may not require an oral hearing. Notwithstanding the consideration that a certain gravity attaches to criminal proceedings, which are concerned with the allocation of criminal responsibility and the imposition of a punitive and deterrent sanction, it is self-evident that there are criminal cases which do not carry any significant degree of stigma. There are clearly 'criminal charges' of differing weight. What is more, the autonomous interpretation adopted by the Convention institutions of the notion of a 'criminal charge' by applying the *Engel* criteria have underpinned a gradual broadening of the criminal head to cases not strictly belonging to the traditional categories of the criminal law, for example administrative penalties (*Öztürk*, [...]), prison disciplinary proceedings (*Campbell and Fell v. the United Kingdom*, 28 June 1984, Series A no. 80), customs law (*Salabiaku v. France*, 7 October 1988, Series A no. 141-A), competition law (*Société Stenuit v. France*, 27 February 1992, Series A no. 232-A), and penalties imposed by a court with jurisdiction in financial matters (*Guisset v. France*, no. 33933/96, ECHR Reports 2000-IX). Tax surcharges differ from the hard core of criminal law; consequently, the criminal-head guarantees will not necessarily apply with their full stringency (see *Bendenoun and Janosevic*, § 46 and § 81 respectively, where it was found compatible with Article 6(1) for criminal penalties to be imposed, in the first instance, by an administrative or non-judicial body, and, a contrario, *Findlay*, [...]).

Eur. Court H.R. (Grand Chamber) 23 November 2006 (Jussila v. Finland, no. 73053/01), ECHR Reports 2006-XIV, para. 43.

(c)   Moment when the charge is brought

24.23   The period to be taken into consideration for verifying whether [Article 6(1)] has been observed necessarily begins with the day on which a person is charged, for otherwise it would not be possible to determine the charge, as this word is understood within the meaning of the Convention.

Eur. Court H.R. 27 June 1968 (Neumeister v. Austria, no. 1936/6), Series A no. 87, p. 26, para. 18.

24.24   As regards the beginning of the period to be taken into consideration, the Court is of opinion that it must run from 9 November 1961, the date on which the first charges were levelled against Wemhoff and his arrest was ordered.

It was on that date that his right to a hearing within a reasonable time came into being so that the criminal charges could be determined.

Eur. Court H.R. 27 June 1968 (Wemhoff v. Germany, no. 2122/64), Series A no. 7, p. 26, para. 19.

24.25   [...] The 'reasonable time' may on occasion 'start to run from a date prior to the seisin of the trial court, of the 'tribunal' competent for the 'determination ... of [the] criminal charge" [...]. The *Wemhoff* and *Neumeister* judgments of 27 June 1968 and then the *Ringeisen* judgment of 16 July 1971 took as the starting-point the moment of arrest, the moment when the person was officially notified that he would be prosecuted and the moment when preliminary investigations were opened, respectively.

[…] The 'charge' could, for the purposes of Article 6 par. 1, be defined as the official notification given to an individual by the competent authority of an allegation that he has committed a criminal offence. In several decisions and opinions the Commission has adopted a test that appears to be fairly closely related, namely whether 'the situation of the [suspect] has been substantially affected'. […]

Eur. Court H.R. 27 February 1980 (Deweer v. Belgium, no. 6903/75), Series A no. 35, p. 30, paras 42 and 46.

[T]his may have occurred on a date prior to the case coming before the trial court […], **24.26** such as the date of arrest, the date when the person concerned was officially notified that he would be prosecuted or the date when the preliminary investigations were opened […]. [The 'charge'] may in some instances take the form of other measures which carry the implication of such an allegation and which likewise substantially affect the situation of the suspect […].

Eur. Court H.R. 10 December 1982 (Corigliano v. Italy, no. 8304/78), Series A, no. 57, p. 13, para. 34.

['C]harge', for the purposes of Article 6, may in general be defined as 'the official **24.27** notification given to an individual by the competent authority of an allegation that he has committed a criminal offence', although 'it may in some instances take the form of other measures which carry the implication of such an allegation and which likewise substantially affect the situation of the suspect' […].

Eur. Court H.R. 21 February 1984 (Öztürk v. Germany, no. 8544/79), Series A no. 73, p. 18, para. 55.

D. INDEPENDENT AND IMPARTIAL TRIBUNAL

1. Concept of 'Tribunal'

(a) European Court of Human Rights

[T]he Court observes that the Regional Commission is a 'tribunal' within the meaning **24.28** of Article 6, paragraph (1), of the Convention as it is independent of the executive and also of the parties, its members are appointed for a term of five years and the proceedings before it afford the necessary guarantees.

Eur. Court H.R. 16 July 1971 (Ringeisen v. Austria, no. 2614/65), Series A no. 13, para. 95.

According to the Court's case-law […], use of the term 'tribunal' is warranted only for **24.29** an organ which satisfies a series of further requirements – independence of the executive and of the parties to the case, duration of its members' term of office, guarantees afforded by its procedure – several of which appear in the text of Article 6 paragraph 1 itself.

Eur. Court H.R. (Grand Chamber) 23 June 1981 (Le Compte and others v. Belgium, no. 6878/75 and 7238/ 75) Series A no. 43, para. 51.

24.30   La Cour rappelle [...] que seul mérite l'appellation de «tribunal» un organe répondant à une série de critères – telle l'indépendance à l'égard de l'exécutif et des parties – et jouissant de la plénitude de juridiction, et que, pour qu'un tel «tribunal» puisse décider d'une contestation sur des droits et obligations de caractère civil en conformité avec cette disposition, il faut qu'il ait compétence pour se pencher sur toutes les questions de fait ou de droit pertinentes pour le litige dont il se trouve saisi.

Eur. Court H.R. 21 February 2008 (Ravon v. France, no. 18497/03), ECHR Reports 2008, para. 27.

24.31   The Court reiterates that for the purposes of Article 6(1) of the Convention a tribunal need not be a court of law integrated with the standard judicial machinery (see *Rolf Gustafson v. Sweden*, 1 July 1997, § 45, Reports of Judgments and Decisions 1997-IV) since a tribunal, within the meaning of Article 6(1), is characterised in the substantive sense of the term by its judicial function, that is to say, the determining of matters within its competence on the basis of rules of law and after proceedings conducted in a prescribed manner (see *Philis*, [...], § 50). It must also satisfy a series of requirements – independence, in particular of the executive, impartiality and guarantees afforded by its procedure – several of which appear in the text of Article 6(1) itself (see *Zlinsat, spol. s.r.o., v. Bulgaria*, no. 57785/00, § 75, 15 June 2006).

Eur. Court H.R. 5 February 2009 (Olujic v. Croatia, no. 22330/05), ECHR Reports 2009, par. 37.

(b)   European Union Courts

(i)   In relation to the Commission

24.32   The Commission [...] cannot [...] be classed as a tribunal within the meaning of Article 6 of the European Convention for the Protection of Human Rights, under which everyone is entitled to a fair hearing by an independent and impartial tribunal.

CoJ 29 October 1980 (Landewyck and others v. Commission, Joined Cases 209–215 and 218/78) [1980] ECR 3125.

Reiterated in General Court 26 April 2007 (Bolloré v. Commission, T-109/02) [2007] ECR II-947, para. 86.

(ii)   In relation to the General Court

24.33   First, the [General Court] is an independent and impartial court, established by Council Decision 88/ 591/ECSC, EEC, Euratom of 24 October 1988 (OJ 1988 L 319, p. 1, corrected version in OJ 1989 L 241, p. 4). As is apparent from the third recital in the preamble to that decision, the Court was established in order particularly to improve the judicial protection of individual interests in respect of actions requiring close examination of complex facts.

Second, by virtue of Article 3(1)(c) of that decision, the [General Court] is required to exercise the jurisdiction conferred on the Court of Justice by the Treaties establishing the Communities and by the acts adopted in implementation thereof, inter alia, 'in actions brought against an institution of the Communities by natural or legal persons pursuant to the second paragraph of Article 173 of the EEC Treaty relating to the implementation of the competition rules applicable to undertakings'. In the context of actions based on Article 173 of the [EEC] Treaty [now Art. 236 TFEU], the review of the legality of a Commission decision finding an infringement of the competition rules and imposing a fine in that respect on the natural or legal person concerned must be regarded as effective judicial review of the measure in question. The pleas on which the natural or legal person concerned may rely in support of his application for annulment are of such a nature as to allow the Court to assess the correctness in law and in fact of any accusation made by the Commission in competition proceedings.

General Court 14 May 1998 (Enso Española v. Commission, T-384/94) [1998] ECR II-1875, paras 62 and 63.

[T]he action for annulment available under Article 230 EC [now art. 236 TFEU] **24.34** against Commission decisions adopted under Article 8(3) and (4) of the [EC merger] regulation is a remedy incorporating the safeguards required by Article 6(1) of the Convention.

General Court 11 July 2007 (Schneider Electric, T-351/03) [2007] ECR II-2237, para. 184

2. Independence

(a) European Court of Human Rights

In order to establish whether a body can be considered independent, regard must be **24.35** had, inter alia, to the manner of appointment of its members and to their term of office, to the existence of guarantees against outside pressures and to the question whether the body presents an appearance of independence (see, inter alia, *Langborger v. Sweden*, 22 June 1989, § 32, Series A no. 155, and *Bryan v. the United Kingdom*, 22 November 1995, § 37, Series A no. 335-A).

Eur. Court H.R. 5 February 2009 (Olujic v. Croatia, no. 22330/05), para. 38.

(b) European Union Courts

With regard, in particular, to the right of access to a tribunal, it must be made clear that, **24.36** for a 'tribunal' to be able to determine a dispute concerning rights and obligations arising under EU law in accordance with Article 47 of the Charter, it must have power to consider all the questions of fact and law that are relevant to the case before it.

It is true in that respect that, according to the Court's case-law [...], which is now given legislative expression in Article 16 of Regulation No 1/2003, when national courts rule on agreements, decisions or practices under, inter alia, Article 101 TFEU which are already the subject of a Commission decision, they cannot take decisions running counter to the decision adopted by the Commission.

That rule also applies when national courts are hearing an action for damages for loss sustained as a result of an agreement or practice which has been found by a decision of the Commission to infringe Article 101 TFEU.

An application of the EU competition rules is thus based on an obligation of sincere cooperation between the national courts, on the one hand, and the Commission and the EU Courts, on the other, in the context of which each acts on the basis of the role assigned to it by the Treaty [...].

It must be borne in mind in that regard that it is the EU Courts – not the courts of the Member States – which have exclusive jurisdiction to review the legality of the acts of the EU institutions. National courts do not have power to declare such acts invalid [...].

The rule that national courts may not take decisions running counter to a Commission decision relating to a proceeding under Article 101 TFEU is thus a specific expression of the division of powers, within the EU, between, on the one hand, national courts and, on the other, the Commission and the EU Courts.

That rule does not mean, however, that the defendants in the main proceedings are denied their right of access to a tribunal, as referred to in Article 47 of the Charter.

Indeed, EU law provides for a system of judicial review of Commission decisions relating to proceedings under Article 101 TFEU which affords all the safeguards required by Article 47 of the Charter.

In this connection, it must be stated that the legality of a Commission decision may be reviewed by the EU Courts under Article 263 TFEU. In this case, the defendants in the main proceedings, to whom the decision had been addressed, did in fact bring actions for the annulment of that decision, as has been recalled in paragraphs 20 to 22 of this judgment.

Those defendants maintain, however, that the review of legality carried out by the EU Courts under Article 263 TFEU in the sphere of competition law is insufficient because of, inter alia, the margin of discretion which those Courts allow the Commission in economic matters.

The Court of Justice has stated in this connection that, whilst, in areas giving rise to complex economic assessments, the Commission has a margin of discretion with regard to economic matters, that does not mean that the EU Courts must refrain from reviewing the Commission's interpretation of information of an economic nature. Those Courts must, among other things, not only establish whether the evidence relied on is factually accurate, reliable and consistent but also ascertain whether that evidence contains all the information which must be taken into account in order to assess a complex situation and whether it is capable of substantiating the conclusions drawn from it [...].

The EU Courts must also establish of their own motion that the Commission has stated reasons for its decision and, among other things, that it has explained the weighting and assessment of the factors taken into account [...].

The EU Courts must also carry out the review of legality incumbent upon them on the basis of the evidence adduced by the applicant in support of the pleas in law put forward. In carrying out such a review, the Courts cannot use the Commission's margin of discretion – either as regards the choice of factors taken into account in the application of the criteria mentioned in the Commission notice entitled 'Guidelines on the method of setting fines imposed pursuant to Article 23(2)(a) of Regulation (EC) No 1/2003' […] or as regards the assessment of those factors – as a basis for dispensing with the conduct of an in-depth review of the law and of the facts […].

Finally, the review of legality is supplemented by the unlimited jurisdiction which the EU Courts were afforded by Article 17 of Council Regulation No 17 of 6 February 1962, First Regulation implementing Articles [81] and [82] of the Treaty […] and which is now recognised by Article 31 of Regulation No 1/2003, in accordance with Article 261 TFEU. That jurisdiction empowers the Courts, in addition to carrying out a mere review of the lawfulness of the penalty, to substitute their own appraisal for the Commission's and, consequently, to cancel, reduce or increase the fine or penalty payment imposed […].

The review provided for by the Treaties thus involves review by the EU Courts of both the law and the facts, and means that they have the power to assess the evidence, to annul the contested decision and to alter the amount of a fine. The review of legality provided for in Article 263 TFEU, supplemented by the unlimited jurisdiction in respect of the amount of the fine, provided for in Article 31 of Regulation No 1/2003, therefore meets the requirements of the principle of effective judicial protection in Article 47 of the Charter […].

As to the objection raised by the defendants in the main proceedings that the power of review is conferred on the Court of Justice, whose independence they claim is undermined on the ground that the Court is itself an EU institution, suffice it to state that it is wholly unfounded in the light of all the safeguards laid down in the Treaties, which ensure the independence and impartiality of the Court of Justice, and the fact that all judicial bodies necessarily form part of the State or supranational organisation to which they belong, a fact which on its own is not capable of entailing an infringement of Article 47 of the Charter or Article 6 of the ECHR.

Finally, a civil action for damages, such as the action before the referring court, requires, as can be seen from the order for reference, not only that a harmful event be found to have occurred, but also that loss and a direct link between the loss and that harmful event be established. Whilst it is true that, because of its obligation not to take decisions running counter to a Commission decision finding an infringement of Article 101 TFEU, the national court is required to accept that a prohibited agreement or practice exists, the existence of loss and of a direct causal link between the loss and the agreement or practice in question remains, by contrast, a matter to be assessed by the national court.

Indeed, even when the Commission has in its decision determined the precise effects of the infringement, it still falls to the national court to determine individually the loss caused to each of the persons to have brought an action for damages. Such an assessment is not contrary to Article 16 of Regulation No 1/2003.

In view of all the foregoing considerations, the Commission cannot be regarded as judge and party in its own cause in the context of a dispute such as that in the main proceedings.

CoJ 6 November 2012 (EC v. Otis a.o., C-199/11), ECLI:EU:C: 2012:684, paras 49–67.

3. Impartiality

(a) General

24.37   The Court considers that Article 6 paragraph 1 of the Convention imposes an obligation on every national court to check whether, as constituted, it is 'an impartial tribunal' within the meaning of that provision (Art. 6(1)) where, as in the instant case, this is disputed on a ground that does not immediately appear to be manifestly devoid of merit.
Eur. Court H.R. 23 April 1996 (Remli v. France, no. 16839/90), ECHR Reports 1996, p. 574, para 48.

(b) Objective and subjective test

24.38   [I]t is of fundamental importance in a democratic society that the courts inspire confidence in the public and above all, as far as criminal proceedings are concerned, in the accused [...]. To that end Article 6 requires a tribunal falling within its scope to be impartial. Impartiality normally denotes absence of prejudice or bias and its existence can be tested in various ways. The Court has thus distinguished between a subjective approach, that is endeavouring to ascertain the personal conviction or interest of a given judge in a particular case, and an objective approach, that is determining whether he or she offered sufficient guarantees to exclude any legitimate doubt in this respect.
Eur. Court H.R. 5 February 2009 (Olujic v. Croatia, no. 22330/05), para. 57.

See also Eur. Court H.R. 1 October 1982 (Piersack v. Belgium), Series A no. 53, para. 30; Eur. Court H.R. 24 February 1993 (Fey v. Austria), Series A no. 255-A, p. 12, para. 28; Eur. Court H.R. 26 February 1993 (Padovani v. Italy), Series A no. 257-B, para. 27; Eur. Court H.R. 25 February 1997 (Findlay v. United Kingdom), Reports 1997-I, p. 281, para. 73; Eur. Court H.R. (Grand Chamber) 16 December 2003 (Grieves v. the United Kingdom, no. 57067/00), Reports 2003-XII, para. 69.

24.39   In applying the subjective test the Court has consistently held that the personal impartiality of a judge must be presumed until there is proof to the contrary [...]. As regards the type of proof required, the Court has, for example, sought to ascertain whether a judge has displayed hostility or ill-will or has arranged to have a case assigned to himself for personal reasons [...]. The principle that a tribunal shall be presumed to be free of personal prejudice or partiality is long established in the case-law of the Court [...]. Although in some cases it may be difficult to procure evidence with which to rebut the presumption, it must be remembered that the requirement of objective impartiality provides a further important guarantee [...]. In other words, the Court has recognised the difficulty of establishing a breach of Article 6 on account of subjective partiality and for this reason has in the vast majority of cases raising impartiality issues focused on the objective test. However, there is no watertight division between the two notions, since the conduct of a judge may not only prompt objectively held misgivings as to impartiality from the point of view of the external observer (objective test), but may also go to the issue of his or her personal conviction (subjective test) [...].

The Court has held for instance that the judicial authorities are required to exercise maximum discretion with regard to the cases with which they deal in order to preserve their image as impartial judges. That discretion should dissuade them from making use of the press, even when provoked. It is the higher demands of justice and the elevated nature of judicial office which impose that duty [...]. Thus, where a court president publicly used expressions which implied that he had already formed an unfavourable view of the applicant's case before presiding over the court that had to decide it, his statements were such as to justify objectively the accused's fears as to his impartiality [...]. On the other hand, in another case, where a judge engaged in public criticism of the defence and publicly expressed surprise that the accused had pleaded not guilty, the Court approached the matter on the basis of the subjective test [...].

In applying the objective test the Court also gives importance to situations of a personal character and considers the conduct of the judges in a given case. In terms of the objective test, such conduct may be sufficient to ground legitimate and objectively justified apprehensions as in the above- mentioned *Buscemi* case, but it may also be of such a nature as to raise an issue under the subjective test (as, for example, in the *Lavents* case, [...]) and even disclose personal bias. In this context, therefore, whether a case falls to be dealt with under one test or the other, or both, will depend on the particular facts of the contested conduct.

Eur. Court H.R. 5 February 2009 (Olujic v. Croatia, no. 22330/05), paras 58–60.

(c) Following remandment

(i) European Court of Human Rights

[I]t cannot be stated as a general rule resulting from the obligation to be impartial that a **24.40** superior court which sets aside an administrative or judicial decision is bound to send the case back to a different jurisdictional authority or to a differently composed branch of that authority.
Eur. Court H.R. 16 July 1971 (Ringeisen v. Austria, no. 2614/65), Series A no. 13, para. 97.

[N]o ground for legitimate suspicion can be discerned in the fact that three of the seven **24.41** members of the disciplinary section [hearing the case on remand from the Cour de Cassation] had taken part in the first decision [annulled by the Cour de Cassation].
Eur. Court H.R. 26 September 1995 (Diennet v. France, 25/1994), Series A no. 325 A, para. 38.

(ii) EU Courts

Furthermore, the fact that the same judge sits in two Chambers hearing and deter- **24.42** mining the same case in succession, cannot, by itself, give rise to doubt as to the impartiality of the [General Court] in the absence of any other objective evidence.

In that respect, it is not apparent that the referral of the case back to a Chamber with an entirely different composition from that which first heard and determined the case must, or can, under Community law, be regarded as a general obligation.

Moreover, the Court of Human Rights considered that it cannot be stated as a general rule resulting from the obligation to be impartial that a court quashing an administrative or judicial decision is bound to send the case back to a different judicial authority or to a differently composed branch of that authority [...].

It must also be observed that, under Article 27(3) of the ECHR, when a case is referred to the Grand Chamber of the Court of Human Rights, on a referral following a Chamber's judgment, no judge from the Chamber which rendered the judgment is to sit in the Grand Chamber, with the exception of the President of the Chamber and the judge who sat in respect of the State Party concerned. The ECHR thus accepts that judges who heard and determined the case initially may sit in another formation hearing and determining the same case again, and that that is not in itself incompatible with the requirements of a fair trial.

In those circumstances, it has not been established in the present case that the composition of the Chamber which delivered the judgment under appeal was unlawful merely as a result of the presence in that Chamber of a member of the [General Court] who had already sat in the Chamber which previously heard and determined the case.

CoJ 1 July 2008 (Chronopost SA and La Poste, Joined cases C-341/06 P and C-342/06 P) [2008] ECR I-4777, paras 56–60.

E. FULL JURISDICTION

1. Legal standard

24.43   For civil cases, just as for criminal charges [...], Article 6 paragraph 1 draws no distinction between questions of fact and questions of law. Both categories of question are equally crucial for the outcome of proceedings relating to 'civil rights and obligations'. Hence, the 'right to a court' [...] and the right to a judicial determination of the dispute [....] cover questions of fact just as much as questions of law.

Eur. Court H.R. (Grand Chamber) 23 June 1981 (Le Compte, Van Leuven and De Meyere v. Belgium, no. 6878/75 and 7238/75), Series A no. 43, para. 51.

24.44   [T]he tribunal in question must have jurisdiction to examine all questions of fact and law relevant to the dispute before it.

Eur. Court H.R. 17 December 1996 (Terra Woningen B.V. v. the Netherlands), ECHR Reports 1996-VI, pp. 2122–23, para. 52.

See also Eur. Court H.R. (Grand Chamber) 13 February 2003 (Chevrol v. France, no. 49636/99), ECHR Reports 2003-III, para. 77.

24.45   Parmi les caractéristiques d'un organe judiciaire de pleine juridiction figure le pouvoir de réformer en tous points, en fait comme en droit, la décision entreprise, rendue par

l'organe inférieur. Il doit notamment avoir compétence pour se pencher sur toutes les questions de fait et de droit pertinentes pour le litige dont il se trouve saisi.
Eur. Court H.R. 4 March 2003 (Silvester's Horeca Service v. Belgium, no, 47650/ 99), para. 27.

See also Eur. Court H.R. 27 September 2011 (A. Menarini Diagnostics v. Italy, no 43509/08), para. 61.

2. Assessment

(a) Insufficiency of a pure constitutionality review

[T]he Austrian Constitutional Court does not have the requisite jurisdiction. Its review **24.46** is confined to ascertaining whether the administrative decision is in conformity with the Constitution. It may even refuse to consider the merits of a complaint where 'it cannot be expected that the judgment will clarify an issue of constitutional law'. It accordingly lacked the powers required under Article 6 paragraph 1.
Eur. Court H.R. 21 September 1993 (Zumtobel v. Austria), Series A no. 268-A, p. 13, para. 30.

See also Eur. Court H.R. 25 November 1994 (Ortenberg v. Austria), Series A no. 295-B, pp. 49–50, para. 32; Eur. Court H.R. 26 April 1995 (Fischer v. Austria), Series A no. 312, p. 17, para. 29; Eur. Court H.R. 23 October 1995 (Gradinger v. Austria, no. 15963/90), Series A no. 328-C, paras 42–44.

(b) Insufficiency of a review restricted to points of law

[T]he Court of Cassation does not have jurisdiction to rectify factual errors or to **24.47** examine whether the sanction is proportionate to the fault [...]. It follows that Article 6 par. 1 was not satisfied unless its requirements were met by the Appeals Council itself.
Eur. Court H.R. (Plenary) 23 June 1981 (Le Compte, Van Leuven and De Meyere v. Belgium, no. 6878/75 and 7238/75) Series A no. 43, para. 51.

The Court of Cassation does not take cognisance of the merits of the case, which means **24.48** that many aspects of 'contestations' (disputes) concerning 'civil rights and obligations', including review of the facts and assessment of the proportionality between the fault and the sanction, fall outside its jurisdiction.
Eur. Court H.R. (Plenary) 10 February 1983 (Albert and Le Compte v. Belgium), Series A no. 58, p. 16, para. 36.

(c) Insufficiency in case of deference of the court to decisions of the executive

24.49   [T]here was uncertainty at the relevant time as to whether district courts should themselves decide whether the 'further inspection under the Soil Cleaning (Temporary Provisions) Act' justified the conclusion that 'pollution of the soil' was 'such as to cause serious danger to public health or the environment', or in the alternative accept without question or examination of their own the determination by the competent authorities that soil-cleaning measures were required. However, the Schiedam District Court, in its judgment in the present case, held that such risk was 'necessarily implied' by the Provincial Executive's decision.

In so doing the Schiedam District Court, a 'tribunal' satisfying the requirements of Article 6 paragraph 1, deprived itself of jurisdiction to examine facts which were crucial for the determination of the dispute.

In these circumstances the applicant company cannot be considered to have had access to a tribunal invested with sufficient jurisdiction to decide the case before it. There has accordingly been a violation of Article 6 paragraph 1.

Eur. Court H.R. 17 December 1996 (Terra Woningen B.V. v. the Netherlands), ECHR Reports 1996-VI, pp. 2122–23, paras 53–55.

24.50   The Court observes that the Conseil d'Etat's practice of referring preliminary questions for interpretation means that, when the administrative court is called upon to give a ruling on the conditions governing the application of the reciprocity clause in Article 55 of the French Constitution, it is obliged to ask the Minister for Foreign Affairs to clarify whether the treaty in issue has been applied on a reciprocal basis and to draw the necessary consequences, and it must then abide by his interpretation in all circumstances. The Government conceded this.

It observes that although, following a change in the case-law, that practice is no longer employed in the interpretation of international treaties [...], it is still used where the reciprocity clause is concerned.

The Court accepts that the application to the instant case of its conclusion in Beaumartin, as called for by the applicant, is by no means automatic, since the assessment of the applicability of treaties is different from the interpretation of treaties, being, in particular, more of a factual than a purely legal nature. The Court considers it beyond doubt that, in order to determine whether or not, in a particular case, the treaty has been applied by the other contracting State, the courts may be required to consult the Ministry of Foreign Affairs, which, by its very nature, will be likely to possess information about that State's application of the treaty.

However, the Court notes that in the instant case the Conseil d'Etat, in accordance with its own case-law, relied entirely on a representative of the executive for a solution to the problem before it, concerning the applicability of treaties. It dismissed the applicant's application purely on the ground that the Minister for Foreign Affairs had stated that Article 5 of the 1962 Government Declaration could not be regarded as having been in force on the relevant date, as it had not been applied by Algeria. However, even if consultation of the Minister by the Conseil d'Etat may appear necessary in order to assess whether the reciprocity requirement has been satisfied, that court's current practice of referring a preliminary question for interpretation, as in the instant case, obliges it to abide by the opinion of the Minister – an external authority who is also a representative of the executive – without subjecting that opinion to any criticism or discussion by the parties.

The Court observes, in addition, that the Minister's involvement, which was decisive for the outcome of the legal proceedings, was not open to challenge by the applicant, who was, moreover, not afforded any opportunity to give her opinion on the use of the referral procedure or the wording of the question, or to have the basis of her own reply to the question examined, or to submit a reply to the Minister, which might have been helpful or even decisive in the eyes of the court. In fact, when the applicant was apprised of the Minister for Foreign Affairs' observations, she produced to the Conseil d'Etat several pieces of factual evidence to show that the 1962 Government Declaration had indeed been applied by the Algerian government. These included statements from Algerian Ministries certifying that medical qualifications obtained in France were recognised as being equivalent in Algeria. However, the Conseil d'Etat did not even consider that evidence and was therefore unwilling to assess whether it was well-founded. That is clear from the judgment delivered on 9 April 1999, in which the Conseil d'Etat held that it was not its task to assess whether Algeria had implemented the 1962 Government Declaration or to draw its own inferences in the event that the declaration had not been applied; it based its decision solely on the opinion of the Minister for Foreign Affairs. In so doing, the Conseil d'Etat considered itself to be bound by the opinion, thereby voluntarily depriving itself of the power to examine and take into account factual evidence that could have been crucial for the practical resolution of the dispute before it.

That being so, the applicant cannot be considered to have had access to a tribunal which had, or had accepted, sufficient jurisdiction to examine all the factual and legal issues relevant to the determination of the dispute […].

Eur. Court H.R. (Grand Chamber) 13 February 2003 (Chevrol v. France, no. 49636/99), ECHR Reports 2003-III, paras 78–83.

(d) Full review of sanctions by an administrative court

(i) European Court of Human Rights

As to the applicant's arguments concerning the Administrative Court's limited powers **24.51** to examine questions of fact and to take new evidence, there is nothing before the Court to suggest that any such limitations were in issue in his case. As is evident from the extensive reasoning in its judgment (see paragraph 13 above), the Administrative Court considered all the applicant's submissions on their merits, point by point, without ever having to decline jurisdiction in replying to them or in ascertaining facts.

Regard being had to the nature of Mr Fischer's concrete complaints as well as to the scope of review necessitated by such complaints, the Administrative Court's review of the decision being challenged fulfilled the requirements of Article 6 paragraph 1.

Eur. Court H.R. 26 April 1995 (Fischer v. Austria), Series A no. 312, p. 17, para. 29.

The powers of the Administrative Court must be assessed in the light of the fact that **24.52** the court in this case was sitting in proceedings that were of a criminal nature for the purposes of the Convention. It follows that when the compatibility of those powers with Article 6 paragraph 1 is being gauged, regard must be had to the complaints raised in that court by the applicant as well as to the defining characteristics of a 'judicial body that has full jurisdiction'. These include the power to quash in all respects, on questions of fact and law, the decision of the body below. As the Administrative Court lacks that power, it cannot be regarded as a 'tribunal' within the meaning of the Convention. [...]

Eur. Court H.R. 23 October 1995 (Gradinger v. Austria, no. 15963/90), Series A no. 328-C, para. 44

24.53 La Cour doit constater qu'en l'espèce, la société requérante n'eut pas la possibilité de soumettre la décision prise à son encontre à un tel contrôle de pleine juridiction. Dans son arrêt rendu le 3 octobre 1996 suite à l'opposition à contrainte formée par la société requérante, la cour d'appel de Bruxelles estima en effet qu'elle était uniquement appelée à examiner la réalité des infractions au code de la TVA et à contrôler la légalité des amendes fiscales réclamées, sans être compétente pour apprécier l'opportunité ou accorder une remise complète ou partielle de celles-ci. Cette interprétation fut confirmée en son temps par la Cour de cassation qui rejeta, le 5 février 1999, le pourvoi formé contre cet arrêt aux motifs que le droit de contrôle exercé par le juge saisi d'une opposition à contrainte n'impliquait pas que ce juge puisse « exonérer le redevable des obligations qui lui sont légalement imposées par les autorités, uniquement pour des motifs d'opportunité ou d'équité ».

Eur. Court H.R. 4 March 2003 (Silvester's Horeca Service v. Belgium, no. 47650/99), para. 28.

24.54 En l'espèce, la société requérante a pu attaquer la sanction administrative litigieuse devant le TAR de Rome, et interjeter appel contre la décision de ce dernier devant le Conseil d'Etat. Selon la jurisprudence de la Cour, ces organes satisfont aux exigences d'indépendance et d'impartialité qu'un «tribunal» doit posséder au sens de l'article 6 de la Convention [...].

La Cour rappelle, tout d'abord, que seul mérite l'appellation de «tribunal» au sens de l'article 6 § 1 un organe jouissant de la plénitude de juridiction et répondant à une série d'exigences telles que l'indépendance à l'égard de l'exécutif comme des parties en cause [...].

Par ailleurs, la Cour rappelle que la nature d'une procédure administrative peut différer, sous plusieurs aspects, de la nature d'une procédure pénale au sens strict du terme. Si ces différences ne sauraient exonérer les Etats contractants de leur obligation de respecter toutes les garanties offertes par le volet pénal de l'article 6, elles peuvent néanmoins influencer les modalités de leur application [...].

La Cour note que dans le cas d'espèce, les juridictions administratives se sont penchées sur les différentes allégations de fait et de droit de la société requérante. Elles ont dès lors examiné les éléments de preuve recueillis par l'AGCM. De plus, le Conseil d'Etat a rappelé que lorsque l'administration dispose d'un pouvoir discrétionnaire, même si le juge administratif n'a pas le pouvoir de se substituer à l'autorité administrative indépendante, il peut toutefois vérifier si l'administration a fait un usage approprié de ses pouvoirs.

De ce fait, la Cour note que la compétence des juridictions administratives n'était pas limitée à un simple contrôle de légalité. Les juridictions administratives ont pu vérifier si, par rapport aux circonstances particulières de l'affaire, l'AGCM avait fait un usage approprié de ses pouvoirs. Elles ont pu examiner le bien-fondé et la proportionnalité des choix de l'AGCM et même vérifier ses évaluations d'ordre technique.

De plus, le contrôle effectué sur la sanction a été de pleine juridiction dans la mesure où le TAR et le Conseil d'Etat ont pu vérifier l'adéquation de la sanction à l'infraction commise et le cas échéant auraient pu remplacer la sanction [...].

En particulier, le Conseil d'Etat, en allant au delà d'un contrôle «externe» sur la cohérence logique de la motivation de l'AGCM, s'est livré à une analyse détaillée de l'adéquation de la sanction par rapport aux paramètres pertinents, y compris la proportionnalité de la sanction même.

La décision de l'AGCM ayant été soumise au contrôle ultérieur d'organes judiciaires de pleine juridiction, aucune violation de l'article 6 § 1 de la Convention ne saurait être décelée en l'espèce.

Eur. Court H.R. 27 September 2011 (A. Menarini Diagnostics v. Italy, no 43509/08), paras 58–67.

(ii) EU Courts

The judicial review of the decisions of the institutions was arranged by the founding **24.55** Treaties. In addition to the review of legality, now provided for under Article 263 TFEU, a review with unlimited jurisdiction was envisaged in regard to the penalties laid down by regulations.

As regards the review of legality, the Court of Justice has held that whilst, in areas giving rise to complex economic assessments, the Commission has a margin of discretion with regard to economic matters, that does not mean that the Courts of the European Union must refrain from reviewing the Commission's interpretation of information of an economic nature. Not only must those Courts establish, among other things, whether the evidence relied on is factually accurate, reliable and consistent but also whether that evidence contains all the information which must be taken into account in order to assess a complex situation and whether it is capable of substantiating the conclusions drawn from it [...].

With regard to the penalties for infringements of competition law, the second subparagraph of Article 15(2) of Regulation No 17 provides that in fixing the amount of the fine, regard is to be had both to the gravity and to the duration of the infringement. The same wording appears in Article 23(3) of Regulation No 1/2003.

The Court of Justice has held that, in order to determine the amount of a fine, it is necessary to take account of the duration of the infringements and of all the factors capable of affecting the assessment of their gravity, such as the conduct of each of the undertakings, the role played by each of them in the establishment of the concerted practices, the profit which they were able to derive from those practices, their size, the value of the goods concerned and the threat that infringements of that type pose to the European Community [...].

The Court has also stated that objective factors such as the content and duration of the anti-competitive conduct, the number of incidents and their intensity, the extent of the market affected and the damage to the economic public order must be taken into account. The analysis must also take into consideration the relative importance and market share of the undertakings responsible and also any repeated infringements [...].

This large number of factors requires that the Commission carry out a thorough examination of the circumstances of the infringement.

In the interests of transparency the Commission adopted the Guidelines, in which it indicates the basis on which it will take account of one or other aspect of the infringement and what this will imply as regards the amount of the fine.

The Guidelines, which, the Court has held, form rules of practice from which the administration may not depart in an individual case without giving reasons compatible with the principle of equal treatment [...], merely describe the method used by the Commission to examine infringements and the criteria that the Commission requires to be taken into account in setting the amount of a fine.

It is important to bear in mind the obligation to state reasons for acts of the European Union. That is a particularly important obligation in the present case. It is for the Commission to state the reasons for its decision and, in particular, to explain the weighting and assessment of the factors taken into account [...]. The Courts must establish of their own motion that there is a statement of reasons.

Furthermore, the Courts must carry out the review of legality incumbent upon them on the basis of the evidence adduced by the applicant in support of the pleas in law put forward. In carrying out such a review, the Courts cannot use the Commission's margin of discretion – either as regards the choice of factors taken into account in the application of the criteria mentioned in the Guidelines or as regards the assessment of those factors – as a basis for dispensing with the conduct of an in-depth review of the law and of the facts.

The review of legality is supplemented by the unlimited jurisdiction which the Courts of the European Union were afforded by Article 17 of Regulation No 17 and which is now recognised by Article 31 of Regulation No 1/2003, in accordance with Article 261 TFEU. That jurisdiction empowers the Courts, in addition to carrying out a mere review of the lawfulness of the penalty, to substitute their own appraisal for the Commission's and, consequently, to cancel, reduce or increase the fine or penalty payment imposed [...].

It must, however, be pointed out that the exercise of unlimited jurisdiction does not amount to a review of the Court's own motion, and that proceedings before the Courts of the European Union are inter partes. With the exception of pleas involving matters of public policy which the Courts are required to raise of their own motion, such as the failure to state reasons for a contested decision, it is for the applicant to raise pleas in law against that decision and to adduce evidence in support of those pleas.

That requirement, which is procedural in nature, does not conflict with the rule that, in regard to infringements of the competition rules, it is for the Commission to prove the infringements found by it and to adduce evidence capable of demonstrating to the requisite legal standard the existence of the circumstances constituting an infringement. What the applicant is required to do in the context of a legal challenge is to identify the impugned elements of the contested decision, to formulate grounds of challenge in that regard and to adduce evidence – direct or circumstantial – to demonstrate that its objections are well founded.

The review provided for by the Treaties thus involves review by the Courts of the European Union of both the law and the facts, and means that they have the power to assess the evidence, to annul the contested decision and to alter the amount of a fine. The review of legality provided for under Article 263 TFEU, supplemented by the unlimited jurisdiction in respect of the amount of the fine, provided for under Article 31 of Regulation No 1/2003, is not therefore contrary to the requirements of the principle of effective judicial protection in Article 47 of the Charter.

CoJ 8 December 2011 (KME v. Commission, C-389/10 P) [2011] ECR I-13125, paras 120–133.

[T]he analysis by the European Union judicature of the pleas in law raised in an action **24.56** for annulment has neither the object nor the effect of replacing a full investigation of the case in the context of an administrative procedure. As such a limitation of judicial review is, however, inherent in the notion of the review of legality, it cannot be understood as unduly limiting the review of legality which the European Union judicature is authorised to carry out [...]

CoJ 24 October 2013 (Kone v. Commission, C-510/11 P), ECLI:EU:C:2013:696, para. 26.

See also CoJ 2 september 2010 (Commission v. Deutsche Post, C-399/08 P) [2010] ECR I-7831, para. 84.

F. ACCESS

1. General

Article 6 paragraph 1 does not state a right of access to the courts or tribunals in express **24.57** terms. It enunciates rights which are distinct but stem from the same basic idea and which, taken together, make up a single right not specifically defined in the narrower sense of the term. It is the duty of the Court to ascertain, by means of interpretation, whether access to the courts constitutes one factor or aspect of this right. [...]

The terms of Article 6 paragraph 1 of the European Convention, taken in their context, provide reason to think that this right is included among the guarantees set forth. [...]

[T]he right of access constitutes an element which is inherent in the right stated by Article 6 paragraph 1. This is not an extensive interpretation forcing new obligations on the Contracting States: it is based on the very terms of the first sentence of Article 6 paragraph 1 read in its context and having regard to the object and purpose of the Convention, a lawmaking treaty [...], and to general principles of law. The Court thus reaches the conclusion [...] that Article 6 paragraph 1 secures to everyone the right to have any claim relating to his civil rights and obligations brought before a court or tribunal. In this way the Article embodies the 'right to a court', of which the right of access, that is the right to institute proceedings before courts in civil matters, constitutes one aspect only. To this are added the guarantees laid down by Article 6 paragraph 1 (Art. 6(1)) as regards both the organisation and composition of the court, and the conduct of the proceedings. In sum, the whole makes up the right to a fair hearing. [...]

Eur. Court H.R. (Plenary) 21 February 1975 (Golder v. the United Kingdom, no. 4451/70), Series A no. 18, p. 13, paras 28, 31 and 36.

2. Effet utile

24.58   The applicant did have access to the High Court and then to the Court of Appeal, only to be told that his actions were barred by operation of law […]. To this extent, he thus had access to the remedies that existed within the domestic system.

   This of itself does not necessarily exhaust the requirements of Article 6 paragraph 1 (Art. 6(1)). It must still be established that the degree of access afforded under the national legislation was sufficient to secure the individual's 'right to a court', having regard to the rule of law in a democratic society. […]

Eur. Court H.R. 28 May 1985 (Ashingdane v. the United Kingdom, no. 8225/78) Series A no. 93, p. 24, paras 56 and 57.

24.59   [a] l'instar des autres droits garantis par la Convention, le droit d'accès aux tribunaux doit être concret et effectif.

Eur. Court H.R. 21 February 2008 (Ravon v. France, no. 18497/03), only available in French, para. 27.

3. Restrictions

24.60   The Court considers […] that the right of access to the courts is not absolute. As this is a right which the Convention sets forth (see Articles 13, 14, 17 and 25) without, in the narrower sense of the term, defining, there is room, apart from the bounds delimiting the very content of any right, for limitations permitted by implication. […]

   In its judgment of 23 July 1968 on the merits of the case relating to certain aspects of the laws on the use of languages in education in Belgium, the Court ruled that:

   'The right to education … by its very nature calls for regulation by the State, regulation which may vary in time and place according to the needs and resources of the community and of individuals. It goes without saying that such regulation must never injure the substance of the right to education nor conflict with other rights enshrined in the Convention.' […]

   These considerations are all the more valid in regard to a right which, unlike the right to education, is not mentioned in express terms.

Eur. Court H.R. 21 February 1975 (Golder v. the United Kingdom, no. 4451/70), Series A no. 18, p. 13, para. 38.

24.61   […] Certainly, the right of access to the courts is not absolute but may be subject to limitations; these are permitted by implication since the right of access 'by its very nature calls for regulation by the State, regulation which may vary in time and in place according to the needs and resources of the community and of individuals' […]. In laying down such regulation, the Contracting States enjoy a certain margin of appreciation. Whilst the final decision as to observance of the Convention's requirements rests with the Court, it is no part of the Court's function to substitute for the assessment of the national authorities any other assessment of what might be the best policy in this field […].

Nonetheless, the limitations applied must not restrict or reduce the access left to the individual in such a way or to such an extent that the very essence of the right is impaired [...]. Furthermore, a limitation will not be compatible with Article 6 paragraph 1 if it does not pursue a legitimate aim and if there is not a reasonable relationship of proportionality between the means employed and the aim sought to be achieved. In this respect, the Contracting States enjoy a certain margin of appreciation, although the final decision as to the observance of the Convention's requirements rests with the Court. It must be satisfied that the limitations applied do not restrict or reduce the access left to the individual in such a way or to such an extent that the very essence of the right is impaired. Furthermore, a limitation will not be compatible with Article 6 paragraph 1 if it does not pursue a legitimate aim and if there is not a reasonable relationship of proportionality between the means employed and the aim sought to be achieved.

Eur. Court H.R. 28 May 1985 (Ashingdane v. the United Kingdom, no. 8225/78) Series A no. 93, p. 24, para. 57.

See also Eur. Court H.R. 22 October 1996 (Stubbings and others v. the United Kingdom), ECHR 1996-IV, p. 1502, paras 51–52; Eur. Court H.R. 13 July 1995 (Tolstoy Miloslavsky v. the United Kingdom), Series A no. 316-B, p. 80, paras 62–67; Eur. Court H.R. (Grand Chamber) 18 February 1999 (Waite and Kennedy v. Germany, no. 26083/94), ECHR Reports 1999-I, para. 59 and Eur. Court H.R. 10 May 2001 (T.P. and K.M. v. the United Kingdom, no. 28945/95), p. 28, para. 98.

G. EFFECTIVE REMEDY

1. Legal standard

The principles that emerge from the Court's jurisprudence on the interpretation of **24.62** Article 13 (Art. 13) include the following:

    (a)   where an individual has an arguable claim to be the victim of a violation of the rights set forth in the Convention, he should have a remedy before a national authority in order both to have his claim decided and, if appropriate, to obtain redress (see the above-mentioned *Klass and others* judgment, Series A no. 28, p. 29, § 64);

    (b)   the authority referred to in Article 13 (Art. 13) may not necessarily be a judicial authority but, if it is not, its powers and the guarantees which it affords are relevant in determining whether the remedy before it is effective (ibid., p. 30, § 67);

    (c)   although no single remedy may itself entirely satisfy the requirements of Article 13 (Art. 13), the aggregate of remedies provided for under domestic law may do so (see, mutatis mutandis, the above-mentioned *X v. the United Kingdom* judgment, Series A no. 46, p. 26, § 60, and the *Van Droogenbroeck* judgment of 24 June 1982, Series A no. 50, p. 32, § 56);

(d)   neither Article 13 (Art. 13) nor the Convention in general lays down for the Contracting States any given manner for ensuring within their internal law the effective implementation of any of the provisions of the Convention – for example, by incorporating the Convention into domestic law (see the *Swedish Engine Drivers' Union* judgment of 6 February 1976, Series A no. 2O, p. 18, § 50).

It follows from the last-mentioned principle that the application of Article 13 (art. 13) in a given case will depend upon the manner in which the Contracting State concerned has chosen to discharge its obligation under Article 1 (Art. 1) directly to secure to anyone within its jurisdiction the rights and freedoms set out in section I (see the above-mentioned *Ireland v. the United Kingdom* judgment, Series A no. 25, p. 91, § 239).

Eur. Court H.R. (Grand Chamber) 25 March 1983 (Silver a.o. v. the United Kingdom, no. 5947/72), Series A, no. 61, para. 113.

2. In relation to dawn raids

(a) European Court of Human Rights

24.63   Selon la Cour, [le droit a l'accès effectif a un tribunal] implique en matière de visite domiciliaire que les personnes concernées puissent obtenir un contrôle juridictionnel effectif, en fait comme en droit, de la régularité de la décision prescrivant la visite ainsi que, le cas échéant, des mesures prises sur son fondement; le ou les recours disponibles doivent permettre, en cas de constat d'irrégularité, soit de prévenir la survenance de l'opération, soit, dans l'hypothèse oø une opération jugée irrégulière a déjà eu lieu, de fournir à l'intéressé un redressement approprié.

[La Cour] considère qu'à elle seule, la possibilité de se pourvoir en cassation – dont les requérants ont d'ailleurs usé – ne répond pas aux exigences de l'article 6 § 1 dès lors qu'un tel recours devant la Cour de cassation, juge du droit, ne permet pas un examen des éléments de fait fondant les autorisations litigieuses.

La circonstance que l'autorisation de procéder à des visites domiciliaires est délivrée par un juge – de sorte qu'à première vue, un contrôle juridictionnel incluant un examen de cette nature se trouve incorporé dans le processus décisionnel lui-même – ne suffit pas à combler cette lacune. En effet, si, comme la Cour l'a jugé sur le terrain de l'article 8 de la Convention dans l'affaire Keslassy à laquelle le Gouvernement se réfère, cela contribue à garantir la préservation du droit au respect de la vie privée et du domicile, l'on ne saurait considérer que l'instance au cours de laquelle le juge examine la demande d'autorisation est conforme à l'article 6 § 1 alors que la personne visée par la perquisition projetée – qui ignore à ce stade l'existence d'une procédure intentée à son encontre – ne peut se faire entendre.

Certes, l'article L. 16 B prévoit en outre que les opérations s'effectuent sous le contrôle du juge qui les a ordonnées, de sorte que, pendant leur déroulement, les personnes dont les locaux sont concernés ont la possibilité de le saisir en vue notamment d'une suspension ou de l'arrêt de la visite. Cependant, s'il s'agit là aussi d'une garantie que la Cour prend en compte dans le contexte de l'article 8 de la Convention (ibidem) et dans laquelle on peut voir une modalité propre à assurer un contrôle de la régularité des mesures prises sur le fondement de l'autorisation délivrée par ledit juge, cela ne permet pas un contrôle indépendant de la régularité de l'autorisation elle-même. Par ailleurs, l'accès des personnes concernées à ce juge apparaît plus théorique qu'effectif. En effet – cela ressort de la jurisprudence de la Cour de cassation – les agents qui procèdent à la visite n'ont pas l'obligation légale de faire connaître aux intéressés leur droit de soumettre toute difficulté au juge (et ils ne l'ont pas fait en l'espèce), lequel n'est tenu de mentionner dans l'ordonnance d'autorisation ni la possibilité ni les modalités de sa saisine en vue de la suspension ou de l'arrêt de la visite; la présence des intéressés n'est d'ailleurs pas requise (il suffit que deux témoins tiers soient présents) et la loi ne prévoit pas la possibilité pour ceux-ci de faire appel à un avocat ou d'avoir des contacts avec l'extérieur; en outre, en l'espèce en tout cas, les coordonnées du juge compétent ne figuraient pas sur les ordonnances d'autorisation et n'ont pas été fournies aux requérants par les agents qui ont procédé aux visites. De surcroît, en raison d'un revirement de la jurisprudence de la Cour de cassation, les intéressés n'ont plus la faculté de saisir le juge qui a autorisé les opérations après l'achèvement de celles-ci: il ne peut plus connaître a posteriori d'une éventuelle irrégularité entachant ces opérations, une telle contestation relevant, selon la Cour de cassation, du contentieux dont peuvent être saisies les juridictions appelées à statuer sur les poursuites éventuellement engagées sur le fondement des documents appréhendés.

Eur. Court H.R. 21 February 2008 (Ravon v. France, no. 18497/03), only available in French, unreported, paras 28–31.

[Assessment of a remedy introduced by the French legislature following the *Ravon* **24.64** judgment quoted under the preceding point] [I]l y a lieu de relever qu'après l'introduction de la requête, une réforme du système de contrôle des opérations de visite et de saisie prévu à l'article L. 450–4 du code de commerce a été effectuée, afin d'offrir de nouvelles voies de recours […].

La Cour constate que les autorités, souhaitant tirer les conséquences de l'arrêt Ravon et autres dans le domaine du droit de la concurrence, ont modifié le droit interne par une ordonnance du 13 novembre 2008, afin de permettre aux personnes ayant fait l'objet de visite domiciliaire d'interjeter appel de l'ordonnance d'autorisation du juge des libertés et de la détention devant le premier président de la cour d'appel […].

Cette ordonnance contient également des dispositions transitoires rétroactives pour les opérations de visite et saisie effectuées avant son adoption. Son article 5, alinéa IV, prévoit notamment que si l'autorisation de visite et saisie a fait l'objet d'un pourvoi en cassation ayant donné lieu à un arrêt de rejet de la Cour de cassation, un recours en contestation de l'autorisation est ouvert devant la cour d'appel de Paris saisie dans le cadre de l'article L. 464–8 du code de commerce […]. La Cour relève que les requérantes seraient susceptibles d'être concernées par ces dispositions transitoires, comme le soutient le Gouvernement, puisque l'instruction menée par l'Autorité de la concurrence est toujours en cours […].

Cependant, elle constate que cette action ne pourra être exercée que si un recours au fond est formé contre la décision de l'Autorité de la concurrence, ce qui rend nécessairement l'accessibilité de cette voie de recours incertaine, compte tenu de l'exigence préalable à la fois d'une décision au fond et d'un recours contre celle-ci. Par ailleurs, la décision au fond de l'Autorité de la concurrence, qui n'est toujours pas rendue à ce jour, n'interviendra donc que plusieurs années après les décisions de 2005. Or, la Cour rappelle qu'en plus d'un contrôle en fait et en droit de la régularité et du bien-fondé de la décision ayant prescrit la visite, le recours doit également fournir un redressement approprié, ce qui implique nécessairement la certitude, en pratique, d'obtenir un contrôle juridictionnel effectif de la mesure litigieuse et ce, dans un délai raisonnable.

Compte tenu de ce qui précède, la Cour estime que le recours en contestation prévu par l'ordonnance du 13 novembre 2008 ne répond pas, en l'espèce, aux exigences de l'article 6 § 1 de la Convention.

Eur. Court H.R. 21 December 2010 (Société Canal Plus a.o. v. France, no. 29408/08), only available in French, unreported, paras 38–41.

See also Eur. Court H.R. 21 December 2010 (Compagnie des Gaz de Pétrole Primagaz v. France, no. 29613/08), only available in French, unreported, paras 26–29. and Eur. Court H.R. 5 May 2011 (Socitété Métallurgique Liotard Frères v. France, no. 29598/0890), paras 18–23.

(b)   European Union Courts

24.65   [...] This plea in law must be interpreted as meaning that the adoption of an inspection decision has to be conditional on the Commission obtaining a prior judicial warrant following a comprehensive review, covering matters of both fact and law, as provided for in Article 6(1) of the ECHR. [...]

As regards the arguments of the applicants in this respect, it should be noted, in the first place, that they have misinterpreted the ECtHR's judgments in *Société Métallurgique Liotard Frères v. France* and *Société Canal Plus and Others v. France* [...].

Indeed, as the Commission has noted, it is apparent from these judgments that the key issue is the intensity of the review and not the point in time when it was carried out. That review must cover all matters of fact and law and provide an appropriate remedy if an activity found to be unlawful has already taken place (*Société Canal Plus and Others v. France* [...], para. 36).

In the second place, an inspection decision may be challenged under Article 263 TFEU. Consequently, in contrast to the applicants' contentions, the lack of a comprehensive review conducted ex ante by a national authority charged with issuing a warrant is, on any view, irrelevant. Article 20(4) of Regulation No 1/2003 provides for such a review by the European Union Courts and requires it to be mentioned in the decision ordering the inspection at the undertaking's premises. The Commission met this procedural requirement when it adopted the first, second and third inspection decisions and the applicants knew that they were able to bring an action enabling them to challenge the need for the inspection, as these cases show.

In the third place, it cannot seriously be argued that the General Court is not in a position to conduct a review of the facts and operates solely as a 'court of cassation', as the applicants contend. Indeed, the European Union Courts, ruling on an action for annulment brought under Article 263 TFEU against an inspection decision, conducts both a legal and factual review and has the power to evaluate the evidence and annul the contested decision. It has been held that, when carrying out their review of inspection decisions, the European Union Courts may find it necessary to satisfy themselves that there exist reasonable grounds for suspecting an infringement of the competition rules by the undertakings concerned [...]. It also follows from these considerations that the applicants' second argument (see paragraph 105 above)—according to which the supposed absence of a comprehensive judicial review of the inspection decisions after the inspections had begun infringed Article 6(1) of the ECHR—must be rejected.

In the fourth place, it should be noted, as the Commission correctly points out, that the annulment of the inspection decision, or even the finding of an irregularity in the course of measures implemented by authorised officials, precludes the institution from using the information gathered during the contested activities for the purpose of infringement proceedings [...].

Accordingly, the second plea in law must be rejected in its entirety as unfounded.

General Court 6 September 2013 (Deutsche Bahn a.o. v. Commission, Joined Cases T-289/11, T-290/11 and T-521/11), EU:T:2013:404, paras 108–114, upheld in CoJ 18 June 2015 (Deutsche Bahn a.o. v. Commission, C-583/13 P), EU:C:2013:404, paras 19–36.

H. FAIR TRIAL

1. Applicability to pre-trial proceedings

(a) European Court of Human Rights

Whilst Article 6 paragraph 1 embodies the 'right to a court' [...], it nevertheless does **24.66** not oblige the Contracting States to submit 'contestations' (disputes) over 'civil rights and obligations' to a procedure conducted at each of its stages before 'tribunals' meeting the Articles various requirements. Demands of flexibility and efficiency, which are fully compatible with the protection of human rights, may justify the prior intervention of administrative or professional bodies and, a fortiori, of judicial bodies which do not satisfy the said requirements in every respect.

Eur. Court H.R. (Grand Chamber) 23 June 1981 (Le Compte and others v. Belgium, no. 6878/75 and 7238/ 75), Series A no. 43, para. 51.

[...] Certainly the primary purpose of Article 6 as far as criminal matters are concerned **24.67** is to ensure a fair trial by a 'tribunal' competent to determine 'any criminal charge', but it does not follow that the Article has no application to pre-trial proceedings. [...] Other requirements of Article 6 (Art. 6) – especially of paragraph 3 (Art. 6(3)) – may also be relevant before a case is sent for trial if and in so far as the fairness of the trial is likely to be seriously prejudiced by an initial failure to comply with them. [...]

[T]he manner in which Article 6 paragraphs 1 and 3 (c) is to be applied during the preliminary investigation depends on the special features of the proceedings involved and on the circumstances of the case; in order to determine whether the aim of Article 6 – a fair trial – has been achieved, regard must be had to the entirety of the domestic proceedings conducted in the case [...].

Eur. Court H.R. 24 November 1993 (Imbrioscia v. Switzerland, no. 13972/88), Series A no. 275, p. 13, paras 36 and 38.

See also Eur. Court H.R. (Grand Chamber) 27 November 2008 (Salduz v. Turkey, no. 36391/02), unreported, para. 50.

24.68   [T]he functions performed by the inspectors, in practice as well as in theory, essentially investigative [...]. The Inspectors did not adjudicate, either in form or in substance. They themselves said in their report that their findings would not be dispositive of anything [...]. They did not make a legal determination as to criminal or civil liability concerning the Fayed brothers, and in particular concerning the latter's civil right to honour and reputation. The purpose of their inquiry was to ascertain and record facts which might subsequently be used as the basis for action by other competent authorities – prosecuting, regulatory, disciplinary or even legislative. [...]

Acceptance of the applicants' argument would entail that a body carrying out preparatory investigations at the instance of regulatory or other authorities should always be subject to the guarantees of a judicial procedure set forth in Article 6 para. 1 (art. 6–1) by reason of the fact that publication of its findings is liable to damage the reputation of the individuals whose conduct is being investigated. Such an interpretation of Article 6 para. 1 (art. 6–1) would in practice unduly hamper the effective regulation in the public interest of complex financial and commercial activities [....].

Eur. Court H.R. 21 September 1994 (Fayed v. United Kingdom, no. 17101/90), Series A no. 294–B, p. 47, paras 61 and 62.

(b)   European Union Courts

Please refer to the case extracts under Article 41(2) Charter, Chapter 23 Section C.

2.   Imposition of fines by an administrative body

(a)   An administrative body may impose a sanction, provided that such sanction is open to appeal

Please also refer to Section E. above on Full jurisdiction.

(i)   European Court of Human Rights

24.69   In many Member States of the Council of Europe, the duty of adjudicating on disciplinary offences is conferred on jurisdictional organs of professional associations. Even in instances where Article 6 paragraph 1 is applicable, conferring powers in this manner does not in itself infringe the Convention. [...] Nonetheless, in such circumstances the Convention calls at least for one of the two following systems: either the jurisdictional organs themselves comply with the requirements of Article 6 paragraph 1, or they do not so comply but are subject to subsequent control by a judicial body that has full jurisdiction – that is to say, which has the competence to furnish 'a [judicial] determination ... of the matters in dispute, both for questions of fact and for questions of law' – 'and does provide the guarantees of Article 6 paragraph 1.

Eur. Court H.R. (Plenary) 10 February 1983 (Albert and Le Compte v. Belgium, no. 7299/75 and 7496/76), Series A no. 58, p. 16, para. 29.

Article 6(3) (e) [ECHR] was thus applicable in the instant case. It in no wise follows **24.70** from this, the Court would want to make clear, that the very principle of the system adopted in the matter by the German legislature is being put in question. Having regard to the large number of minor offences, notably in the sphere of road traffic, a Contracting State may have good cause for relieving its courts of the task of their prosecution and punishment. Conferring the prosecution and punishment of minor offences on administrative authorities is not inconsistent with the Convention provided that the person concerned is enabled to take any decision thus made against him before a tribunal that does offer the guarantees of Article 6 [EHRC].

Eur. Court H.R. 21 February 1984 (Öztürk v. Germany, no. 8544/79), Series A no. 73, p. 18, para. 56.

See also Eur. Court H.R. 24 February 1994 (Bendenoun v. France), Series A no. 284, para. 46; Eur. Court H.R. 23 October 1995 (Gradinger v. Austria, no. 15963/90), Series A no. 328-C, para. 42; Eur. Court H.R. 4 March 2003 (Silvester's Horeca Service v. Belgium, no 47650/99), paras 25–26.

En l'espèce, la sanction litigieuse n'a pas été infligée par un juge à l'issue d'une procédure **24.71** judiciaire contradictoire, mais par l'AGCM. Si confier à des autorités administratives la tâche de poursuivre et de réprimer les contraventions n'est pas incompatible avec la Convention, il faut souligner cependant que l'intéressé doit pouvoir saisir de toute décision ainsi prise à son encontre un tribunal offrant les garanties de l'article 6 […].

Le respect de l'article 6 de la Convention n'exclut donc pas que dans une procédure de nature administrative, une «peine» soit imposée d'abord par une autorité administrative. Il suppose cependant que la décision d'une autorité administrative ne remplissant pas elle-même les conditions de l'article 6 § 1 subisse le contrôle ultérieur d'un organe judiciaire de pleine juridiction […].

Eur. Court H.R. 27 September 2011 (A. Menarini Diagnostics v. Italy, no 43509/ 08), paras 58 and 59

(ii)   EU Courts

[T]he fact that decisions imposing fines in competition matters are adopted by the **24.72** Commission is not in itself contrary to Article 6 of the ECHR as interpreted by the European Court of Human Rights. It is to be noted in this connection that, in its judgment in *A. Menarini Diagnostics v. Italy*, relating to a penalty imposed by the Italian competition authority for anti-competitive practices similar to those of which the appellants were accused, the European Court of Human Rights considered that, given that the fine imposed was high, the penalty, because of its severity, fell within the criminal sphere.

It pointed out, however, in paragraph 58 of that judgment, that, entrusting the prosecution and punishment of breaches of the competition rules to administrative authorities is not inconsistent with the ECHR in so far as the person concerned has an opportunity to challenge any decision made against him before a tribunal that offers the guarantees provided for in Article 6 of the ECHR.

In paragraph 59 of its judgment in *A. Menarini Diagnostics v. Italy*, the European Court of Human Rights explained that, in administrative proceedings, the obligation to comply with Article 6 of the ECHR does not preclude a 'penalty' from being imposed by an administrative authority in the first instance. For this to be possible, however, decisions taken by administrative authorities which do not themselves satisfy the requirements laid down in Article 6(1) of the ECHR must be subject to subsequent review by a judicial body that has full jurisdiction. The characteristics of such a body include the power to quash in all respects, on questions of fact and law, the decision of the body below. The judicial body must in particular have jurisdiction to examine all questions of fact and law relevant to the dispute before it.

Ruling on the principle of effective judicial protection, a general principle of European Union law to which expression is now given by Article 47 of the Charter and which corresponds, in European Union law, to Article 6(1) of the ECHR, the Court of Justice has held that, in addition to the review of legality provided for by the FEU Treaty, the European Union judicature has the unlimited jurisdiction which it is afforded by Article 31 of Regulation No 1/2003, in accordance with Article 261 TFEU, and which empowers it to substitute its own appraisal for the Commission's and, consequently, to cancel, reduce or increase the fine or periodic penalty payment imposed (*Chalkor v. Commission*, para. 63).

As regards the review of legality, the Court has pointed out that the European Union judicature must carry it out on the basis of the evidence adduced by the applicant in support of the pleas in law put forward and that it cannot use the Commission's margin of discretion – either as regards the choice of factors taken into account in the application of the criteria mentioned in the 1998 Guidelines or as regards the assessment of those factors – as a basis for dispensing with the conduct of an in-depth review of the law and of the facts (*Chalkor v. Commission*, para. 62).

As the review provided for by the Treaties involves review by the European Union judicature of both the law and the facts, and means that it has the power to assess the evidence, to annul the contested decision and to alter the amount of a fine, the Court has concluded that the review of legality provided for under Article 263 TFEU, supplemented by the unlimited jurisdiction in respect of the amount of the fine, provided for under Article 31 of Regulation No 1/2003, is not contrary to the requirements of the principle of effective judicial protection which is currently set out in Article 47 of the Charter (*Chalkor v. Commission*, para. 67).

CoJ 18 July 2013 (Schindler v. Commission, C-501/11 P), ECLI:EU:C:2013:522, paras 33–38.

(b) Except in relation to serious charges

24.73 [T]he defects referred to above [could not] be corrected by any subsequent review proceedings. Since the applicant's hearing was concerned with serious charges classified as 'criminal' under both domestic and Convention law, he was entitled to a first-instance tribunal which fully met the requirements of Article 6 paragraph 1.

Eur. Court H.R. 25 February 1997 (Findlay v. the United Kingdom, no. 22107/ 93), ECHR Reports 1997-I, para. 79, quoting Eur. Court H.R. 26 October 1984 (De Cubber v. Belgium), Series A no. 86, pp. 16–18, paras 31 and 32.

(c)   Lawfulness of having one and the same body investigate and fine

It is also settled law that the Commission cannot be described as a 'tribunal' within the   **24.74**
meaning of Article 6 of the ECHR [...]. The applicant's argument that the Decision is
unlawful simply because it was adopted under a system in which the Commission
carries out both investigatory and decision-making functions is therefore irrelevant.
The Court emphasises, however, that the Commission is required, during the administrative procedure before it, to observe the procedural guarantees provided for by
Community law.
General Court 14 May 1998 (Enso Española v. Commission, T-384/94) [1998]
ECR II-1875, para. 56.

(d)   No obligation to remand to a different body following annulment

[T]here is no rule of law or principle which prevents the Commission from entrusting   **24.75**
to the same officials re-examination of a concentration in compliance with a judgment
annulling a decision declaring that concentration to be incompatible with the common
market. [Reference to the cases *Ringeisen* and *Diennet* of the Eur. Court H.R.].
   It follows that the fact that the teams of officials responsible for the various stages of
investigation of the transaction were composed wholly or partly of the same members
does not constitute a sufficiently serious breach by the Commission of a rule of law
intended to confer rights on individuals.
General Court 11 July 2007 (Schneider Electric, T-351/03) [2007] ECR
II-2237, paras 185 and 188.

3.   Principle of adversarial proceedings

(a)   General

(i)   European Court of Human Rights

The right to an adversarial trial means, in a criminal case, that both prosecution and   **24.76**
defence must be given the opportunity to have knowledge of and comment on the
observations filed and the evidence adduced by the other party. Various ways are
conceivable in which national law may secure that this requirement is met. However,
whatever method is chosen, it should ensure that the other party will be aware that
observations have been filed and will get a real opportunity to comment thereon. [...]
Eur. Court. H.R. 28 August 1991 (Brandstetter v. Austria, no. 11170/84,
12876/87 and 13468/87), Series A no. 211, pp. 22–23, para. 67.

[T]he hearing [...] before the Court of Cassation concluded with the avocat général's   **24.77**
submissions to the effect that Mr Borger's appeal should not be allowed. At no time
could the latter reply to those submissions: before hearing them, he was unaware of their
contents because they had not been communicated to him in advance; thereafter he was
prevented from doing so by statute. Article 1107 of the Judicial Code prohibits even the

lodging of written notes following the intervention of the member of the procureur général's department.

The Court cannot see the justification for such restrictions on the rights of the defence. Once the avocat général had made submissions unfavourable to the applicant, the latter had a clear interest in being able to submit his observations on them before argument was closed. The fact that the Court of Cassation's jurisdiction is confined to questions of law makes no difference in this respect.

Further and above all, the inequality was increased even more by the avocat général's participation, in an advisory capacity, in the Court's deliberations. Assistance of this nature, given with total objectivity, may be of some use in drafting judgments, although this task falls in the first place to the Court of Cassation itself. It is however hard to see how such assistance can remain limited to stylistic considerations, which are in any case often indissociable from substantive matters, if it is in addition intended, as the Government also affirmed, to contribute towards maintaining the consistency of the case-law. Even if such assistance was so limited in the present case, it could reasonably be thought that the deliberations afforded the avocat général an additional opportunity to promote, without fear of contradiction by the applicant, his submissions to the effect that the appeal should be dismissed.

Eur. Court H.R. 30 October 1991 (Borgers v. Belgium, no. 12005/86), paras 27 and 28.

See also Eur. Court H.R. 20 February 1996 (Vermeulen v. Belgium), ECHR Reports 1996-I, p. 234, para. 33.

24.78   [T]he concept of fair trial [...] means in principle the opportunity for the parties to a criminal or civil trial to have knowledge of and comment on all evidence adduced or observations filed [...] with a view to influencing the court's decision [...].
Eur. Court H.R. 20 February 1996 (Lobo Machado v. Portugal, no. 15764/89), ECHR Reports 1996-I, p. 206, para. 31.

See also Eur. Court H.R. 18 February 1997 (Nideröst-Huber v. Switzerland, no. 18990/91), ECHR Reports 1997-I, p. 6, para. 24.

24.79   Regard being had [...] to what was at stake for the applicant in the proceedings in the Court of Cassation and to the nature of the submissions made by [...] the avocat general, the fact that it was impossible for Mr Vermeulen to reply to them before the end of the hearing infringed his right to adversarial proceedings. [...]
Eur. Court H.R. 20 February 1996 (Vermeulen v. Belgium), ECHR Reports 1996-I, p. 234, para. 41.

24.80   [...] The right to an adversarial trial means, in a criminal case, that both prosecution and defence must be given the opportunity to have knowledge of and comment on the observations filed and the evidence adduced by the other party [...].
Eur. Court H.R. 16 February 2000 (Rowe and Davis v. the United Kingdom, no. 28901/95), ECHR Reports 2000-II, para. 60.

Ce principe vaut pour les observations et pièces présentées par les parties [...], mais **24.81** aussi par un magistrat indépendant tel que le commissaire du Gouvernement [...], par une administration [...] ou par la juridiction auteur du jugement entrepris [...].

Eur. Court H.R. 16 February 2006 (Prikyan and Angelova v. Bulgaria, no. 44624/99), para. 42.

(ii)   EU Courts

It would infringe a basic principle of law to base a judicial decision on facts and **24.82** documents of which the parties, or one of them, have not been able to take cognizance and in relation to which they have not therefore been able to formulate an opinion.

CoJ 22 March 1961 (S.N.U.P.A.T. v. High Authority, 42/59 and 49/59) [1961] ECR 103, para. 158.

See also CoJ 10 January 2002. (Plant and others v. Commission Case C–480/99 P) [2002] ECR I– 265, para. 24; CoJ 2 October 2003 (Corus UK v. Commission, C–199/99) [2003] ECR I–11177, para. 19.

The Community Courts ensure that the rule that the parties should be heard is **24.83** respected in proceedings before them and that they themselves respect that rule.

CoJ 2 December 2009 (Commission v. Ireland and others, Aluminiumoxide excise duties, C–89/08) [2009] ECR I–11245, para. 51.

(b)   Applicability when the court applies grounds of its own motion

(i)   European Court of Human Rights

Le juge doit respecter lui-même le principe du contradictoire, en particulier lorsqu'il **24.84** prononce la déchéance d'un pourvoi en cassation pour un motif d'irrecevabilité retenu d'office [...].

Eur. Court H.R. 13 October 2005 (Clinique des Acacias and others v. France, 65399/01, 65406/ 01, 65405/01 and 65407/01), para. 38.

See also Eur. Court H.R. 18 December 2003 (Skondrianos v. Greece, 63000/00, 74291/01 and 74292/01), paras 29 and 30.

(ii)   EU Courts

The European Court of Human Rights has consistently held that the adversarial nature **24.85** of proceedings is one of the factors which enables their fairness to be assessed, but it may be balanced against other rights and interests.

The adversarial principle means, as a rule, that the parties have a right to a process of inspecting and commenting on the evidence and observations submitted to the court. However, in some cases it may be necessary for certain information to be withheld from the parties in order to preserve the fundamental rights of a third party or to safeguard an important public interest [...].

CoJ 14 February 2008 (Varec SA v. Belgian State, C-450/06) [2008] ECR I-581, paras 46 and 47.

24.86   The rule that the parties should be heard must benefit all parties to proceedings before the Community judicature, irrespective of their legal status. The Community institutions may also, therefore, avail themselves of that principle when they are parties to such proceedings.

A court must itself observe the rule that the parties should be heard, in particular, when it decides a dispute on a ground it has identified of its own motion [references to the Eur. Court H.R. judgments in *Skondrianos, Clinique des Acacias and Prikyan and Angelova*].

As the Advocate General stated at points 93 to 107 of his Opinion, the principle that the parties should be heard does not, as a rule, merely confer on each party to proceedings the right to be apprised of the documents produced and observations made to the Community Courts by the other party and to discuss them, and does not merely prevent the Community Courts from basing their decision on facts and documents which the parties, or one of them, have not had an opportunity to examine and on which they have therefore been unable to comment. It also, as a rule, implies a right for the parties to be apprised of pleas in law raised by those Courts of their own motion, on which they intend basing their decisions, and to discuss them.

In order to satisfy the requirements associated with the right to a fair hearing, it is important for the parties to be apprised of, and to be able to debate and be heard on, the matters of fact and of law which will determine the outcome of the proceedings.

Accordingly, except in particular cases such as, inter alia, those provided for by the rules of procedure of the Community Courts, those Courts cannot base their decisions on a plea raised of their own motion, even one involving a matter of public policy and – as in the present case – based on the absence of a statement of reasons for the decision at issue, without first having invited the parties to submit their observations on that plea.

Moreover, in the analogous context of Article 6 of the ECHR, the Court of Justice has held that it is precisely in deference to that article and to the very purpose of every individual's right to adversarial proceedings and to a fair hearing within the meaning of that provision that the Court may of its own motion, on a proposal from the Advocate General or at the request of the parties, order that the oral procedure be reopened, in accordance with Article 61 of its Rules of Procedure, if it considers that it lacks sufficient information, or that the case must be dealt with on the basis of an argument which has not been debated between the parties (see the order of 4 February 2000 in Case C-17/98 *Emesa Sugar* [2000] ECR I-665, paragraphs 8, 9 and 18, and Joined Cases C-270/97 and C-271/97 *Deutsche Post* [2000] ECR I-929, paragraph 30).

CoJ 2 December 2009 (Commission v. Ireland and others, Aluminiumoxide excise duties, C-89/08) [2009] ECR I-11245, paras 53–58.

(c) Exceptions

The European Court of Human Rights has consistently held that the adversarial nature **24.87** of proceedings is one of the factors which enables their fairness to be assessed, but it may be balanced against other rights and interests.

The adversarial principle means, as a rule, that the parties have a right to a process of inspecting and commenting on the evidence and observations submitted to the court. However, in some cases it may be necessary for certain information to be withheld from the parties in order to preserve the fundamental rights of a third party or to safeguard an important public interest [...].

CoJ 14 February 2008 (Varec SA v. Belgian State, C-450/06) [2008] ECR I-581, paras 46 and 47.

4. Equality of arms

(a) General

(i) European Court of Human Rights

[...] '[E]quality of arms' implies that each party must be afforded a reasonable **24.88** opportunity to present his case – including his evidence – under conditions that do not place him at a substantial disadvantage vis-à-vis his opponent. [...]

Eur. Court H.R. 27 October 1993 (Dombo Beheer v. the Netherlands, no. 14448/88), Series A no. 274, para. 33.

See also Eur. Court H.R. 23 October 1996 (Ankerl v. Switzerland), ECHR Reports 1996-V, p. 1567, para. 38 ; and Eur. Court H.R. 18 February 1997 (Nideröst-Huber v. Switzerland, no. 18990/91), ECHR Reports 1997-I, p. 6, para. 23.

[On the intervention of a Government Commissioner in French expropriation pro- **24.89** ceedings] As noted above, the Government Commissioner's tasks are entrusted to the Director of Revenue (Property) of the département in which the Expropriations Division is based or delegated to another official from this administrative authority. In that basis, he, like the expropriating authority, has access to the land charges register, which lists all property transfers. Expropriated parties have only limited access to this register, which is not open for free consultation by individuals: they may receive information and extracts subject to the condition of strictly limiting the references searched for (Article 39 of Decree no. 55–1350 of 14 October 1955). Thus, even at this stage, the expropriated party is at a disadvantage vis-à-vis his opponents.

Furthermore, at first instance, no text requires the Government Commissioner, unlike the other parties (Articles R. 13–22 and R. 13–23 of the Expropriations Code), to give notice of his pleadings; it is enough if he files them with the registry, and he is not even obliged to inform the other parties that this has been done. In addition, he is the last to speak, both at first instance and on appeal (Articles R. 13–31 and R. 13–32 of the Expropriations Code).

Finally and above all, both at first instance and on appeal (Article R. 15–53 of the Expropriations Code), the Government Commissioner's submissions assume particular significance where they tend towards a lower valuation than that proposed by the expropriating authority.

It follows from Article R. 13–35 of the Expropriations Code that 'the judge rules within the limits of the parties' submissions ... and of the Government Commissioner's submissions where the latter proposes a valuation that is lower than that of the expropriating authority'; Article R. 13–36 of the same Code adds that, in such a situation, 'where the judgment rejects the Government Commissioner's submissions ..., it must specifically state the reasons for such a rejection'.

The Court understands the spirit of this rule and the logic on which it is based: the duties of Government Commissioner are entrusted to the Director of Revenue (Property), who, by virtue of his powers in the administrative, tax and property fields, is well versed in the techniques of property valuation and expert analysis, and has access to the most relevant information in this field; thus, he appears to be the party best placed to advise the court on the value of the expropriated assets, and addresses it in what might be described as a task of 'expert analysis'.

Nevertheless, this rule has the effect of binding the judge to a considerable extent; the judge does not necessarily have the same experience in property valuation as the Director of the Revenue Department, may not appoint another expert at first instance (Article R. 13–28 of the Expropriations Code) and may ask for another expert opinion on appeal only '[e]xceptionally ... on the basis of a reasoned order' (Article R. 13–52 of the Expropriations Code). Admittedly, the expropriated party has the option of producing his own expert opinion at his own expense, but the court is not obliged to take it into account in the same way as the Government Commissioner's submissions.

It should be added that this rule necessarily works against the expropriated party, since the court is not obliged to provide any particular explanation when rejecting the Government Commissioner's submissions where these contain a valuation that is higher than that proposed by the expropriating authority.

In sum, the expropriated party in compensation proceedings is faced not only by the expropriating authority but also by the Government Commissioner; the Government Commissioner and the expropriating authority (which, in certain cases, is represented by an official from the same administrative entity as the Government Commissioner) enjoy significant advantages as regards access to relevant information; in addition, the Government Commissioner, who is simultaneously both an expert and a party to the proceedings, occupies a dominant position in the proceedings and wields considerable influence with regard to the court's assessment (see, mutatis mutandis, Bönisch v. Austria, judgment of 6 May 1985, Series A no. 92). In the Court's opinion, all this creates an imbalance detrimental to the expropriated party that is incompatible with the principle of equality of arms. Consequently, it concludes that in this case there has been a breach of this principle and a violation of Article 6 § 1 of the Convention.

Eur. Court H.R. 24 April 2003 (Yvon v. France, no. 44962/98), unreported, paras 34–37.

24.90 La Cour rappelle que, selon sa jurisprudence, le principe de l'égalité des armes – l'un des éléments de la notion plus large de procès équitable – requiert que chaque partie se voie offrir une possibilité raisonnable de présenter sa cause dans des conditions qui ne la placent pas dans une situation de net désavantage par rapport à son adversaire (voir, parmi d'autres, *De Haes et Gijsels c. Belgique*, 24 février 1997, § 53, Recueil des arrêts et décisions 1997-I, et *Gacon c. France*, no 1092/04, § 31, 22 mai 2008).

La Cour relève, en l'espèce, que les observations écrites du ministre de l'Economie ont été déposées le 28 avril 2006, celles du Conseil de la concurrence le 2 mai 2006 et que la requérante a produit un mémoire en duplique le 25 août 2006. En outre, la requérante a été mise en mesure de répliquer aux observations orales du ministère public à l'audience. La Cour estime donc que le fait que le Conseil de la concurrence, le ministre de l'Economie et le ministère public aient fait part de leurs observations à la cour d'appel de Paris n'a pas empêché la requérante d'en prendre connaissance et de répliquer à ces observations, bénéficiant ainsi d'une procédure contradictoire.

Cependant, dans l'appréciation de ce grief, la théorie des apparences doit aussi entrer en jeu, en particulier du fait que la requérante considère avoir dû faire face à trois représentants de l'administration poursuivante dans son procès devant la cour d'appel. Ce faisant, la Cour n'entend pas se prononcer sur la question de savoir si le Conseil de la concurrence, autorité administrative indépendante, et le ministère public peuvent être considérés comme des représentants de l'administration poursuivante. Seul lui importe, à cet égard, le sentiment de la requérante d'avoir fait face à trois adversaires l'accusant de pratiques anticoncurrentielles.

La Cour a déjà souligné en maintes occasions l'importance des apparences en matière d'administration de la justice (*Kress c. France* [GC], no 39594/98, § 82, CEDH 2001-VI ; *Borgers c. Belgique*, 30 octobre 1991, § 24, série A no 214-B) mais non sans préciser que l'optique des intéressés ne joue pas à elle seule un rôle décisif : il faut de surcroît que les appréhensions des justiciables, par exemple quant au caractère équitable de la procédure, puissent passer pour objectivement justifiées (voir, notamment, *Kraska c. Suisse*, 19 avril 1993, § 32, série A no 254-B, et la décision *Lilly France* précitée).

En l'espèce, la Cour constate que la requérante n'établit pas en quoi les représentants du Conseil de la concurrence, du ministre de l'Economie et du ministère public auraient été privilégiés de quelque façon que ce soit au cours de la procédure en raison de leur qualité (mutatis mutandis *Association de défense des actionnaires minoritaires c. France* (déc.), no 60151/09, 25 mai 2010). A ce titre, la requérante n'invoque aucune limitation pénalisante, par rapport aux autres parties ou intervenants, tant du délai pour présenter ses observations écrites que du temps de parole qui lui a été accordé à l'audience. La requérante ne prétend pas non plus que les représentants du Conseil de la concurrence, du ministre de l'Economie et du ministère public aient disposé d'une occasion supplémentaire d'appuyer leurs conclusions auprès des juges, à l'abri de la contradiction (voir, a contrario, *Borgers*, précité, § 28). Comme la Cour l'a constaté supra, la requérante a pu répondre aux observations de chacun de ces représentants et ce, tout au long de la procédure. La Cour estime donc qu'aucune atteinte n'a été portée, même en apparence, au principe de l'égalité des armes.

Quant au grief tenant en particulier à l'intervention du Conseil de la concurrence dans le débat ouvert par le recours contre sa propre décision juridictionnelle, la Cour s'en tient à la même conclusion, à savoir que la faculté pour le Conseil de présenter des observations écrites à la cour d'appel ne porte pas atteinte au principe de l'égalité des armes dès lors que la requérante a été mise en mesure de répliquer à ces observations. La Cour est consciente de l'autorité particulière qui s'attache à l'opinion du Conseil de la concurrence. Elle souligne toutefois qu'il entre dans l'office du juge d'apprécier la pertinence des observations de cet organisme en prenant en compte tant la compétence technique de celui-ci que sa volonté ne pas être déjugé.

Eu égard à ce qui précède, la Cour ne saurait déceler, en l'espèce, aucune atteinte au principe de l'égalité des armes devant la cour d'appel de Paris.

Eur. Court H.R. (Admissability Decision) 13 March 2012 (Société Bouygues Télécom, no. 2324/08), para. 62–68.

(ii) EU Courts

24.91   The referring court asks, in the second place, whether, in a civil action such as the one before it, there is a breach of the principle of equality of arms because the Commission itself conducted the investigation relating to the infringement in question.

The defendants in the main proceedings contend that the Commission is, on that account, in a privileged position compared with them, which has enabled it to gather and use information – including information that is confidential and thus protected by business secrecy – which is not available to all the defendants.

The Commission's response, in the context of the present reference, is that, when preparing the action in the main proceedings, it made use only of information in the public version of the decision of 27 February 2007. The Commission also explains that the departments responsible for the main proceedings, namely the Offices for 'Infrastructure and Logistics' in Brussels and Luxembourg, do not have a right of privileged access to the confidential file of the Directorate-General for Competition. For that reason, the Commission is, it submits, on an equal footing with every other litigant.

The principle of equality of arms, which is a corollary of the very concept of a fair hearing (Joined Cases C-514/07 P, C-528/07 P and C-532/07 P *Sweden and Others v API and Commission* [2010] ECR I-8533, para. 88), implies that each party must be afforded a reasonable opportunity to present his case, including his evidence, under conditions that do not place him at a substantial disadvantage vis-à-vis his opponent.

As the Advocate General has observed in point 58 of his Opinion, the aim of equality of arms is to ensure a balance between the parties to proceedings, guaranteeing that any document submitted to the court may be examined and challenged by any party to the proceedings. Conversely, the harm which a lack of balance will be likely to cause must, as a rule, be proved by the person who has suffered it.

It emerges from the order for reference that the information to which the defendants in the main proceedings refer has not been provided to the national court by the Commission, the latter having also explained that it has relied only on the information available in the non-confidential version of the decision finding an infringement of Article 81 EC. In such circumstances a breach of the principle of equality of arms is therefore precluded.

The defendants in the main proceedings argue that the balance between the parties has been jeopardised because the Commission conducted the investigation into the infringement of Article 101 TFEU with the aim of subsequently claiming compensation for the loss sustained as a result of that infringement. That argument is belied by the prohibition, set out in Article 28(1) of Regulation No 1/2003, on using information gathered in the course of the investigation for purposes other than those of the investigation.

Nor does the fact that both the decision of 27 February 2007 and the decision to bring the action for damages in the main proceedings were taken by the College of Commissioners call the foregoing considerations in question, since EU law contains a sufficient number of safeguards to ensure that the principle of equality of arms is observed in such an action – for example, the safeguards deriving from Article 339 TFEU, Article 28 of Regulation No 1/2003 and point 26 of the Commission Notice on the co-operation between the Commission and the courts of the EU Member States in the application of Articles 81 and 82 EC.

Finally, nor can the Court accept the arguments which the defendants in the main proceedings base on the judgment in *Yvon v France*, No 44962/98, ECHR 2003-V. The factors which led the European Court of Human Rights to make a finding of infringement of Article 6 ECHR – which include, inter alia, the considerable impact of the Government Commissioner's submissions on the assessment of the court dealing with expropriation cases and the rules concerning the Government Commissioner's access to, and use of, relevant information – were not accompanied, unlike the factors characterising the case in the main proceedings here, by judicial review or safeguards comparable or equivalent to those mentioned in paragraphs 63 and 75 of this judgment.

CoJ 6 November 2012 (EC v. Otis a.o., C-199/11), ECLI:EU:C:2012:684, paras 68–76.

5. Access to the file in criminal proceedings

[...] In addition Article 6(1) requires [...] that the prosecution authorities disclose to the defence all material evidence in their possession for or against the accused. **24.92**

Eur. Court H.R. (Grand Chamber) 16 February 2000 (Rowe and Davis v. the United Kingdom, no. 28901/95), ECHR Reports 2000-II, para. 60.

However, [...] the entitlement to disclosure of relevant evidence is not an absolute right. In any criminal proceedings there may be competing interests, such as national security or the need to protect witnesses at risk of reprisals or keep secret police methods of investigation of crime, which must be weighed against the rights of the accused [...]. In some cases it may be necessary to withhold certain evidence from the defence so as to preserve the fundamental rights of another individual or to safeguard an important public interest. However, only such measures restricting the rights of the defence which are strictly necessary are permissible under Article 6(1) [...]. Moreover, in order to ensure that the accused receives a fair trial, any difficulties caused to the defence by a limitation on its rights must be sufficiently counterbalanced by the procedures followed by the judicial authorities [...]. **24.93**

Eur. Court H.R. 16 February 2000 (Rowe and Davis v. the United Kingdom, no. 28901/95), ECHR Reports 2000-II, para. 61.

See also Eur. Court H.R. 26 March 1996 (Doorson v. the Netherlands, no. 20524/92), ECHR Reports 1996-II, paras 69 and 70.

24.94   During the applicants' trial at first instance the prosecution decided, without notifying the judge, to withhold certain relevant evidence on grounds of public interest. Such a procedure, whereby the prosecution itself attempts to assess the importance of concealed information to the defence and weigh this against the public interest in keeping the information secret, cannot comply with the above- mentioned requirements of Article 6(1). [...]

Eur. Court H.R. 16 February 2000 (Rowe and Davis v. the United Kingdom, no. 28901/95), ECHR Reports 2000-II, para. 63.

See also Eur. Court H.R. 24 April 2007 (V. v. Finland, 40412/98), unreported, para. 75.

6. Exclusionary rule

24.95   While Article 6 of the Convention guarantees the right to a fair trial, it does not lay down any rules on the admissibility of evidence as such, which is therefore primarily a matter for regulation under national law. The Court therefore cannot exclude as a matter of principle and in the abstract that unlawfully obtained evidence of the present kind may be admissible. It has only to ascertain whether Mr. Schenks trial as a whole was fair.

[I]t notes first of all that the rights of the defence were not disregarded. The applicant was not unaware that the recording complained of was unlawful because it had not been ordered by the competent judge. He had the opportunity – which he took – of challenging its authenticity and opposing its use, having initially agreed that it should be heard [...]. The fact that his attempts were unsuccessful makes no difference. [...]

The Court also attaches weight to the fact that the recording of the telephone conversation was not the only evidence on which the conviction was based. [...]

In conclusion, the use of the disputed recording in evidence did not deprive the applicant of a fair trial and therefore did not contravene Article 6 paragraph 1 (Art. 6(1)).

Eur. Court H.R. (Plenary) 12 July 1988 (Schenk v. Switzerland, no. 10862/84), Series A no. 140, paras 46–49.

See also Eur. Court H.R. 12 May 2000 (Khan v. the United Kingdom, no. 35394/97), ECHR Reports 2000, for a case in which the conviction, other than in Schenk v. Switzerland, was solely based on inadmissible evidence.

24.96   [After repeating *Schenk* and *Khan*] [...] The question which must be answered is whether the proceedings as a whole, including the way in which the evidence was obtained, were fair. This involves an examination of the unlawfulness in question and, where the violation of another Convention right is concerned, the nature of the violation found.

In determining whether the proceedings as a whole were fair, regard must also be had as to whether the rights of the defence have been respected. In particular, it must be examined whether the applicant was given an opportunity to challenge the authenticity of the evidence and to oppose its use. In addition, the quality of the evidence must be taken into consideration, as must the circumstances in which it was obtained and whether these circumstances cast doubts on its reliability or accuracy. While no problem of fairness necessarily arises where the evidence obtained was unsupported by other material, it may be noted that where the evidence is very strong and there is no risk of its being unreliable, the need for supporting evidence is correspondingly weaker […]. In this connection, the Court further attaches weight to whether the evidence in question was or was not decisive for the outcome of the proceedings.

As to the examination of the nature of the Convention violation found, the Court reiterates that the question whether the use as evidence of information obtained in violation of Article 8 rendered a trial as a whole unfair contrary to Article 6 has to be determined with regard to all the circumstances of the case, including, respect for the applicant's defence rights and the quality and importance of the evidence in question.

Eur. Court H.R. (Grand Chamber) 1 June 2010 (Gäfgen v. Germany, no. 22978/ 05), paras 164 and 165.

7. Obligation to state the grounds of a judgment

[T]he duty on the [General Court] under Article 36 and the first paragraph of Article **24.97** 53 of the Statute of the Court of Justice to state reasons for its judgments does not require the [General Court] to provide an account that follows exhaustively and one by one all the arguments articulated by the parties to the case. The reasoning may therefore be implicit on condition that it enables the persons concerned to know why the measures in question were taken and provides the Court of Justice with sufficient material for it to exercise its power of judicial review.

CoJ 7 January 2004 (Aalborg Portland and Others v. Commission Joined Cases C-204/00 P, C-205/00 P, C-211/00 P, C-213/00 P, C-217/00 P and C-219/00 P) [2004] ECR I-123, para. 372.

The European Court of Human Rights […] held […] that the defendant's lack of **24.98** awareness of the grounds of the judgment of an appeal court within the period allowed for bringing an appeal against that judgment before the court of cassation constituted an infringement of the combined provisions of Article 6(1) and (3) of the ECHR, because the person concerned had been unable to bring an appropriate and effective appeal .

CoJ 14 December 2006 (ASML, C-283/05) [2006] ECR I-12041, para. 28, quoting Eur. Court H.R. 16 December 1992 (Hadjianastassiou v. Greece), Series A. No 252, paras 29–37.

The Court has held that the observance of the right to a fair trial requires that all **24.99** judgments be reasoned to enable the defendant to see why judgment has been pronounced against him and to bring an appropriate and effective appeal against it.

CoJ 6 September 2012 (Trade Agency v. Seramico, C-619/10), ECLI:EU:C: 2012:531, para. 53.

8. Waiver of rights

24.100
[N]either the letter nor the spirit of Article 6 of the Convention prevents a person from waiving of his own free will, either expressly or tacitly, the entitlement to the guarantees of a fair trial [...]. However, if it is to be effective for Convention purposes, a waiver of the right to take part in the trial must be established in an unequivocal manner and be attended by minimum safeguards commensurate to its importance [...].

Eur. Court H.R. (Grand Chamber) 27 November 2008 (Salduz v. Turkey, no. 36391/02), para. 59.

24.101
Regarding the scope of the right to an effective judicial remedy and to a fair trial provided for in Article 47 of the Charter, and the rights of the defence guaranteed by Article 48(2) thereof, it should be observed that, although the right of the accused to appear in person at his trial is an essential component of the right to a fair trial, that right is not absolute [...]. The accused may waive that right of his own free will, either expressly or tacitly, provided that the waiver is established in an unequivocal manner, is attended by minimum safeguards commensurate to its importance and does not run counter to any important public interest. In particular, violation of the right to a fair trial has not been established, even where the accused did not appear in person, if he was informed of the date and place of the trial or was defended by a legal counsellor to whom he had given a mandate to do so.

CoJ (Grand Chamber) 26 February 2013 (Melloni, C-399/11), ECLI:EU:C: 2013:107, para. 49, quoting Eur. Court H.R. 14 June 2001 (Medenica v. Switzerland, no. 20491/92), ECHR Reports 2001-VI, paras 56–59; Eur. Court H.R. (Grand Chamber) 1 March 2006 (Sejdovic v. Italy, no. 56581/00), ECHR Reports 2006-II, paras 84, 86 and 98; and Eur. Court H.R. 24 April 2012 (Haralampiev v. Bulgaria, no. 29648/03), paras 32 and 33.

I. REASONABLE PERIOD

1. General

(a) European Court of Human Rights

24.102
The Court is of opinion that the precise aim of this provision in criminal matters is to ensure that accused persons do not have to lie under a charge for too long and that the charge is determined. [...]

Eur. Court H.R. 27 June 1968 (Wemhoff v. Germany, no. 2122/64), Series A no. 7, p. 26, para. 18.

(b) European Union Courts

It should be noted that Article 6(1) of the EHRC provides that in the determination of **24.103**
his civil rights and obligations or of any criminal charge against him, everyone is
entitled to a fair and public hearing within a reasonable time by an independent and
impartial tribunal established by law.

The general principle of Community law that everyone is entitled to fair legal
process, which is inspired by those fundamental rights […], and in particular the right
to legal process within a reasonable period, is applicable in the context of proceedings
brought against a Commission decision imposing fines on an undertaking for infringement of competition law.

CoJ 17 December 1998 (Baustahlgewebe v. Commission, C–185/95 P) [1998] ECR
I–8417, paras 20 and 21.

2. Relevant period

(a) Start

See extracts in Section C.3.(C) (Moment when the charge is brought).

(b) End

[…] There is […] no doubt that the period to be taken into consideration in applying **24.104**
this provision lasts at least until acquittal or conviction, even if this decision is reached
on appeal. There is furthermore no reason why the protection given to the persons
concerned against the delays of the court should end at the first hearing in a trial:
unwarranted adjournments or excessive delays on the part of trial courts are also to be
feared.

Eur. Court H.R. 27 June 1968 (Wemhoff v. Germany, no. 2122/64), Series A no. 7,
p. 26, para. 18.

Article 6 (1) […] indicates as the final point, the judgment determining the charge; this **24.105**
may be a decision given by an appeal court when such a court pronounces upon the
merits of the charge. […]

Eur. Court H.R. 27 June 1968 (Neumeister v. Austria, no. 1936/6), Series A no. 87,
p. 26, para. 19.

[T]he Court is called on to rule on the applicability of Article 6 to proceedings in **24.106**
cassation […].

The Government's arguments are based, essentially on the words 'bien-fondé de
toute accusation' ('in the determination of any criminal charge against him') which
delimit the scope of the application of Article 6 paragraph 1 in criminal cases. Article 95
of the Belgian Constitution provides that the Court of Cassation 'does not deal with the
merits of the cases submitted to it'. Accordingly, in the Government's view there is not,
strictly speaking, a prosecution or a defence before that Court: prosecution and defence

cease to exist the moment that the judges dealing with the merits give judgment in final instance, subject to the possibility of their being reborn in the event of the Court of Cassation referring a case back to a lower court after quashing the decision attacked. [...]

The Court cannot accept this view. Judicial decisions always affect persons. In criminal matters, especially, accused persons do not disappear from the scene when the decision of the judges at first instance or appeal gives rise to an appeal in cassation. [...]

Therefore, Article 6 paragraph 1 (Art. 6(1)) is indeed applicable to proceedings in cassation. [...]

Eur. Court H.R. 17 January 1970 (Delcourt v. Belgium, no. 2689/65), Series A no. 11, pp. 13–15, paras 23–26.

24.107   [...] As regards the period to which Article 6 (Art. 6) is applicable, the Court has held that in criminal matters this period covers the whole of the proceedings in question, including appeal proceedings [...]. The position [...] is no different in the case of disputes [...] over civil rights and obligations for which Article 6 paragraph 1 likewise requires that there be – at first instance, on appeal or in cassation – a determination.

Eur. Court H.R. 28 June 1978 (König v. Germany, no. 6232/73), Series A no. 27, p. 33, para. 98.

See also Eur. Court H.R. 15 July 1982 (Eckle v. Germany, no. 8130/78), para. 76.

3. Legal standard

Please also refer to Section B.2 of Chapter 23 on Article 41 Charter.

24.108   The reasonableness of the duration of proceedings covered by Article 6 paragraph 1 of the Convention must be assessed in each case according to its circumstances. When enquiring into the reasonableness of the duration of criminal proceedings, the Court has had regard, inter alia, to the complexity of the case, to the applicant's conduct and to the manner in which the matter was dealt with by the administrative and judicial authorities [...]. The Court [...] considers that the same criteria must serve in the present case as the basis for its examination of the question whether the duration of the proceedings before the administrative courts exceeded the reasonable time stipulated by Article 6 paragraph 1.

Eur. Court H.R. 28 June 1978 (König v. Germany, no. 6232/73), Series A no. 27, p. 33, para. 99.

24.109   The 'reasonableness' of the length of proceedings must be assessed in the light of the circumstances of the case and with reference to the following criteria: the complexity of the case, the conduct of the applicant and of the relevant authorities and what was at stake for the applicant in the dispute.

Eur. Court H.R. (Grand Chamber) 6 April 2000 (Comingersoll S.A. v. Portugal, no. 35382/97), ECHR Reports 2000-IV. para. 19.

4. Assessment

Please also refer to Section B.3. of Chapter 23 under Article 41 on Assessment in respect of administrative proceedings.

[T]he duration of the proceedings now being considered by the Court was about five **24.110** years and six months.

It must first be stated that such a duration is, at first sight, considerable. [...]

[Reference to the case law on the applicable test, see above.]

[What was at stake for the applicant in the dispute]

The appellant was exposed to the risk, under Article 15(2) of Regulation No 17 [now Art. 23(2) Regulation No 1/2003], of a fine of up to 10 per cent of its turnover in the preceding business year. In this case, under Articles 3 and 4 of the Decision, the Commission imposed on the applicant a fine of ECU 4.5 million payable within a period of three months following its notification, together with default interest at the rate of 12.5 per cent per annum after that period.

In that connection, Article [299 TFEU] provides, in particular, that Commission decisions which impose a pecuniary obligation on persons other than States are to be enforceable and that enforcement is to be governed by the rules of civil procedure in the State in the territory of which it is carried out. Under the combined provisions of Articles [278, 279 and 299 TFEU] and Article 4 of Decision 88/591, applications to the [General Court] do not have suspensory effect; the [General Court] may, if it considers that the circumstances so require, order that application of the contested act be suspended, prescribe any interim measures which may be necessary and, if appropriate, suspend enforcement.

In this case, it is clear from documents before the Court that no measure to recover the fine was taken in the course of the Court proceedings because the appellant furnished a bank guarantee, as required by the Commission. Such a fact cannot, however, deprive the appellant of its right to fair legal process within a reasonable period and in particular to a decision on the merits of the allegations of infringement of competition law made against it by the Commission and of the fines imposed on it in that regard.

In view of all those circumstances, it must be held that the procedure before the [General Court] was of genuine importance to the appellant.

[Complexity of the case:]

As regards the complexity of the case, it must be borne in mind that, in its decision, the Commission concluded that 14 manufacturers of welded steel mesh had infringed Article [101 TFEU] by a series of agreements or concerted practices concerning delivery quotas and the prices of that product. The appellant's application was one of 11, submitted in three different languages, which were formally joined for the purposes of the oral procedure.

In that regard, it is clear from the documents before the Court and from the contested judgment that the procedure concerning the appellant called for a detailed examination of relatively voluminous documents and points of fact and law of some complexity.

[Conduct of the applicant:]

As regards the conduct of the appellant before the [General Court], it appears from the file that the time-limit for submitting a rejoinder was, at its request, extended by about one month.

In that connection, the Commission's argument that the procedure before the [General Court] was delayed because the appellant's lawyer did not initially take part in the administrative procedure before the Commission and that he then focused the major part of his arguments, ill-advisedly, on the fine which the Commission had imposed on it for participating in the structural crisis cartel cannot be upheld.

An undertaking which is the subject of a Commission decision finding infringements of competition law and imposing fines on it must be able to contest by all means which it considers appropriate the merits of the charges made against it.

It has not thus been established that the appellant contributed, in any significant way, to the protraction of the proceedings.

[Conduct of the General Court:]

As regards the conduct of the competent authorities, it must be borne in mind that the purpose of attaching the [General Court] to the Court of Justice and of introducing two levels of jurisdiction was, first, to improve the judicial protection of individual interests, in particular in proceedings necessitating close examination of complex facts, and, second, to maintain the quality and effectiveness of judicial review in the Community legal order, by enabling the Court of Justice to concentrate on its essential task, namely to ensure that in the interpretation and application of Community law the law is observed.

That is why the structure of the Community judicial system justifies, in certain respects, the [General Court], which is responsible for establishing the facts and undertaking a substantive examination of the dispute, being allowed a relatively longer period to investigate actions calling for a close examination of complex facts. However, that task does not relieve the Community court established especially for that purpose from the obligation of observing reasonable time-limits in dealing with cases before it.

Account must also be taken of the constraints inherent in proceedings before the Community judicature, associated in particular with the use of languages provided for in Article 35 of the Rules of Procedure of the [General Court], and of the obligation, laid down in Article 30(2) of those rules, to publish judgments in the languages referred to in Article 1 of Regulation No 1 of the Council of 15 April 1958 determining the languages to be used by the European Economic Community […].

However, it must be held that the circumstances of this case are not such as to indicate that constraints of that kind can provide justification for the time which the proceedings took before the [General Court].

It must be emphasised, as far as the principle of a reasonable time is concerned, that two periods are of significance with respect to the proceedings before the [General Court]. Thus, about 32 months elapsed between the end of the written procedure and the decision to open the oral procedure. Admittedly, it was decided by order of 13 October 1992 to join the 11 cases for the purposes of the oral procedure. It must be pointed out, however, that, in that period, no other measure of organisation of procedure or of inquiry was adopted. In addition, 22 months elapsed between the close of the oral procedure and the delivery of the judgment of the [General Court].

Even if account is taken of the constraints inherent in proceedings before the Community judicature, investigation and deliberations of such a duration can be justified only by exceptional circumstances. Since there was no stay of the proceedings before the [General Court], under Articles 77 and 78 of its Rules of Procedure or otherwise, it must be concluded that no such circumstances exist in this case.

In the light of the foregoing considerations, it must be held, notwithstanding the relative complexity of the case, that the proceedings before the [General Court] did not satisfy the requirements concerning completion within a reasonable time.

CoJ 17 December 1998 (Baustahlgewebe v. Commission, C-185/95 P) [1998] ECR I-8417, paras 28, 31–47.

In the present case, it must be stated that the length of the proceedings before the [General Court], which amounted to approximately five years and ten months, cannot be justified by any of the particular circumstances of the case. **24.111**

It appears, in particular, that the period between the notification, in September 2002, of the end of the written procedure and the opening, in June 2006, of the oral procedure lasted for three years and nine months. The length of that period cannot be explained by the circumstances of the case, whether it be the complexity of the dispute, the conduct of the parties or by supervening procedural matters.

As regards, in particular, the complexity of the dispute, the proceedings brought by DSD against the decision at issue and Decision 2001/837, while requiring a detailed examination of the Packaging Ordinance, DSD's contractual links, the Commission decisions and the arguments relied on by DSD, were not of a difficulty or scope which prevented the [General Court] from scrutinising the documents in the case and preparing for the oral procedure within a period of less than three years and nine months.

Moreover, as the Court of Justice has already held, in the case of proceedings concerning infringement of competition rules, the fundamental requirement of legal certainty on which economic operators must be able to rely and the aim of ensuring that competition is not distorted in the internal market are of considerable importance not only for an applicant himself and his competitors but also for third parties, in view of the large number of persons concerned and the financial interests involved […]. In the present case, having regard to DSD's dominant position, the size of the market for services on which DSD and its competitors were carrying on business, the possible effects of the outcome of the dispute on the practice to be followed and the fees to be paid by manufacturers and distributors of packaged products and the questions raised by the dispute as regards the extremely widespread use of the DGP logo, the period of time between the end of the written procedure and the next phase of the procedure was excessive.

Furthermore […] that period of time was not interrupted either by the adoption by the [General Court] of measures of organisation of procedure or by procedural issues raised by the parties.

In the light of the above, it must be held that there was a failure, in the proceedings before the [General Court], to have regard to the requirement that the case be dealt with within a reasonable time.

CoJ 16 July 2009 (Der Grüne Punkt, C-385/07 P) [2009] ECR I-6155, paras 183–188.

24.112   [I]t must be stated that the length of the proceedings before the General Court, which amounted to approximately five years and nine months, cannot be justified by any of the particular circumstances of the present case.

It is apparent, in particular, that the period between the end of the written procedure, when the Commission's rejoinder was lodged in February 2007, and the opening, in December 2010, of the oral procedure lasted for approximately three years and ten months. The length of that period cannot be explained by the circumstances of the case, whether it be the complexity of the dispute, the conduct of the parties or supervening procedural matters.

As regards the complexity of the dispute, it is apparent from examining the action brought by the appellant, as summarised in paragraph 12 above, that, while requiring a detailed examination, the pleas relied on did not present any particular difficulties. Although it is true that around 15 addressees of the contested decision brought actions for its annulment before the General Court, that fact could not prevent it from scrutinising the documents in the case and preparing for the oral procedure within a period of less than three years and ten months.

As regards the conduct of the parties and supervening procedural matters, it must be noted that it was only after a period of three years and ten months that the General Court adopted, in December 2010, a measure of organisation of procedure, by inviting Kendrion to respond in writing to a question. The appellant responded on 12 January 2011 within the period prescribed, and its conduct did not therefore have any effect on the overall length of the proceedings.

In the light of the foregoing, it must be found that the procedure in the General Court breached the second paragraph of Article 47 of the Charter in that it failed to comply with the requirement that it adjudicate within a reasonable time, which constitutes a sufficiently serious breach of a rule of law that is intended to confer rights on individuals.

CoJ (Grand Chamber) 26 November 2013 (Kendrion v. Commission, C-50/12 P), ECLI:EU:C:2013:771, paras 102–106 and CoJ (Grand Chamber) 26 November 2013 (Gascogne Sack Deutschland v. Commission, C-40/12 P), ECLI:EU:C: 2013:768, paras 97–102.

5. Consequences of a failure to adjudicate within a reasonable period

(a) European Court of Human Rights

24.113   [...] The Court considers that the correct interpretation of Article 13 is that that provision guarantees an effective remedy before a national authority for an alleged breach of the requirement under Article 6(1) to hear a case within a reasonable time.

Eur. Court H.R. (Grand Chamber) 26 October 2000 (Kudla v. Poland, no. 30210/96), ECHR Reports 2000-XI, para. 156.

24.114   [In relation to a practice whereby Italy, which had systematically been found to infringe the reasonable time-requirement, introduced a special damage reparation system]

The Court reiterates that it falls first to the national authorities to redress any alleged violation of the Convention. [...] In so far as the parties appear to link the issue of victim status to the more general question of effectiveness of the remedy and seek guidelines on affording the most effective domestic remedies possible, the Court proposes to address the question in a wider context by giving certain indications as to the characteristics which such a domestic remedy should have, having regard to the fact that, in this type of case, the applicants ability to claim to be a victim will depend on the redress which the domestic remedy will have given him or her.

The best solution [in relation to domestic remedies against breaches of the Convention] in absolute terms is indisputably, as in many spheres, prevention. The Court recalls that it has stated on many occasions that Article 6(1) imposes on the Contracting States the duty to organise their judicial systems in such a way that their courts can meet each of its requirements, including the obligation to hear cases within a reasonable time [...]. Where the judicial system is deficient in this respect, a remedy designed to expedite the proceedings in order to prevent them from becoming excessively lengthy is the most effective solution. Such a remedy offers an undeniable advantage over a remedy affording only compensation since it also prevents a finding of successive violations in respect of the same set of proceedings and does not merely repair the breach a posteriori, as does a compensatory remedy of the type provided for under Italian law for example.

The Court has on many occasions acknowledged that this type of remedy is 'effective' in so far as it allows for an earlier decision by the court concerned [...].

It is also clear that for countries where length-of-proceedings violations already exist, a remedy designed only to expedite the proceedings – although desirable for the future – may not be adequate to redress a situation in which it is obvious that the proceedings have already been excessively long.

Different types of remedy may redress the violation appropriately. The Court has already affirmed this in respect of criminal proceedings, where it was satisfied that the length of proceedings had been taken into account when reducing the sentence in an express and measurable manner [...].

Moreover, some States, such as Austria, Croatia, Spain, Poland and the Slovak Republic, have understood the situation perfectly by choosing to combine two types of remedy, one designed to expedite the proceedings and the other to afford compensation [...].

However, States can also choose to introduce only a compensatory remedy, as Italy has done, without that remedy being regarded as ineffective [...].

Eur. Court H.R. (Grand Chamber) 29 March 2006 (Pizzati v. Italy, no. 62361/ 00), paras 69–77.

(b) European Union Courts

[Superseded case law providing for immediate redress] For reasons of economy of **24.115** procedure and in order to ensure an immediate and effective remedy regarding a procedural irregularity of that kind, it must be held that the plea alleging excessive duration of the proceedings is well founded for the purposes of setting aside the contested judgment in so far as it set the amount of the fine imposed on the appellant at ECU 3 million.

However, in the absence of any indication that the length of the proceedings affected their outcome in any way, that plea cannot result in the contested judgment being set aside in its entirety.

CoJ 17 December 1998 (Baustahlgewebe v. Commission, C-185/95 P) [1998] ECR I-8417, paras 48 and 49.

24.116 As regards the consequences that arise where proceedings before the [General Court] fail to be completed within a reasonable time, DSD invokes the rule laid down in the first paragraph of Article 61 of the Statute of the Court of Justice that where an appeal is well founded the Court is to quash the decision of the [General Court]. Since the present plea alleges that judgment was not delivered within a reasonable time and that the failure to do so constitutes a breach of procedure which adversely affects the interests of the appellant within the meaning of Article 58 of the Statute, a finding that such a breach occurred must necessarily lead, in DSD'S view, to the setting aside of the judgment under appeal, irrespective of whether that breach of procedure had an effect on the outcome of the dispute. Were the judgment not to be set aside, the Court of Justice would not be acting in compliance with Article 61 of the Statute.

By that argument, DSD proposes that the Court should reconsider its case-law, according to which failure to deliver judgment within a reasonable time will lead to the setting aside of the judgment under appeal only where there are indications that the excessive length of the proceedings affected their outcome (see, to that effect, *Baustahlgewebe v. Commission*, para. 49). In the present case, DSD has not established that such indications exist.

Admittedly, it is true, as DSD has pointed out, that failure to adjudicate within a reasonable time constitutes a procedural irregularity (see, to that effect, *Baustahlgewebe v. Commission*, para. 48).

It nonetheless remains the case that the first paragraph of Article 61 of the Statute of the Court of Justice should be interpreted and applied purposively.

In so far as there is nothing to suggest that the failure to adjudicate within a reasonable time may have had an effect on the outcome of the dispute, the setting aside of the judgment under appeal would not remedy the infringement of the principle of effective legal protection committed by the [General Court].

In addition, […] having regard to the need to ensure that Community competition law is complied with, the Court of Justice cannot allow an appellant to reopen the question of the existence of an infringement, on the sole ground that there was a failure to adjudicate within a reasonable time, where all of its pleas directed against the findings made by the [General Court] concerning that infringement and the administrative procedure relating to it have been rejected as unfounded.

Conversely, […] the failure on the part of the [General Court] to adjudicate within a reasonable time can give rise to a claim for damages brought against the Community under Article 235 EC and the second paragraph of Article 288 EC [now Art. 268 and Art. 340, second paragraph, TFEU].

CoJ 16 July 2009 (Der Grüne Punkt v. Commission C-385/07 P) [2009] ECR I-6155, paras 189–195.

24.117 [a] failure to adjudicate within a reasonable time must, as a procedural irregularity constituting the breach of a fundamental right, give rise to an entitlement of the party concerned to an effective remedy granting him appropriate relief.

Although the appellant seeks to have the judgment under appeal set aside and, in the alternative, a reduction of the fine imposed on it, the Court notes that it has held that, where there are no indications that the excessive length of the proceedings before the General Court affected their outcome, failure to deliver judgment within a reasonable time cannot lead to the setting aside of the judgment under appeal [...].

That case-law is based, in particular, on the consideration that, where the failure to adjudicate within a reasonable time has no effect on the outcome of the dispute, the setting aside of the judgment under appeal would not remedy the infringement of the principle of effective legal protection committed by the General Court [...].

In so far as the appellant complains that the General Court failed to draw the appropriate inferences from its failure to adjudicate within a reasonable time, it must be pointed out that the appellant does not claim to have provided any evidence to the General Court from which it could be inferred that the procedural irregularity in question could have affected the outcome of the dispute before it and, on that basis, could give grounds for annulling the contested decision.

In addition, it should be recalled that, having regard to the need to ensure that the competition rules of European Union law are complied with, the Court of Justice cannot allow an appellant to reopen the question of the validity or amount of a fine, on the sole ground that there was a failure to adjudicate within a reasonable time, where all of its pleas directed against the findings made by the General Court concerning the amount of that fine and the conduct that it penalises have been rejected [...].

It follows that the failure to adjudicate within a reasonable time in a legal action against a Commission decision imposing a fine on an undertaking for infringing the EU competition rules cannot lead to the annulment, in whole or in part, of the fine imposed by that decision.

In so far as the appellant requested, before the General Court, a reduction in the fine imposed on it in order to take into account the adverse consequences for the appellant of the excessive length of the proceedings before the General Court, it must be found that, first, the purpose of such a request is different from annulment proceedings, which are limited to reviewing the lawfulness of the contested measure and, second, the request entails the examination of facts different from those taken into consideration in a procedure for annulment. It follows that the General Court did not err in law in holding, in paragraph 18 of the judgment under appeal, that, in an action for annulment before it, the legality of the contested decision could be assessed only in the light of the facts and circumstances at the Commission's disposal as at the date on which it was adopted.

In those circumstances, the General Court was fully entitled to reject as ineffective Kendrion's complaint alleging a failure to have regard to the principle that judgment must be given within a reasonable time.

In so far as the appellant requests the Court of Justice, in the alterative, to reduce, for the same reasons as those relied on before the General Court, the fine which was imposed on it, it must be borne in mind that, when first faced with a similar situation, the Court of Justice granted such an application, for reasons of economy of procedure and in order to ensure an immediate and effective remedy regarding a procedural irregularity of that kind and, accordingly, reduced the amount of the fine [*Baustahl-gewebe*, quoted above].

In a later case concerning a Commission decision finding that there had been abuse of a dominant position yet not imposing a fine, the Court held that the failure on the part of the General Court to adjudicate within a reasonable time can give rise to a claim for damages [*Der Grüne Punkt*, quoted above].

Admittedly, the present case concerns a situation analogous to that giving rise to the judgment in *Baustahlgewebe v. Commission*. However, a claim for damages brought against the European Union pursuant to Article 268 TFEU and the second paragraph of Article 340 TFEU constitutes an effective remedy of general application for asserting and penalising such a breach, since such a claim can cover all the situations where a reasonable period of time has been exceeded in proceedings.

It is therefore appropriate for the Court of Justice to rule that the sanction for a breach, by a Court of the European Union, of its obligation under the second paragraph of Article 47 of the Charter to adjudicate on the cases before it within a reasonable time must be an action for damages brought before the General Court, since such an action constitutes an effective remedy.

It follows that a claim for compensation for the damage caused by the failure by the General Court to adjudicate within a reasonable time may not be made directly to the Court of Justice in the context of an appeal, but must be brought before the General Court itself.

It will [...] be for the General Court to assess both the actual existence of the harm alleged and the causal connection between that harm and the excessive length of the legal proceedings in dispute by examining the evidence submitted for that purpose.

In that regard, it should be noted that, in an action for damages based on a breach by the General Court of the second paragraph of Article 47 of the Charter, in so far as it failed to have regard to the requirement that the case be dealt with within a reasonable time, the General Court must, in accordance with the second paragraph of Article 340 TFEU, take into consideration the general principles applicable in the legal systems of the Member States for actions based on similar breaches. In that context, the General Court must, in particular, ascertain whether it is possible to identify, in addition to any material loss, any other type of harm sustained by the party affected by the excessive period, which should, where appropriate, be suitably compensated.

It is therefore for the General Court, which has jurisdiction under Article 256(1) TFEU, to determine such claims for damages, sitting in a different composition from that which heard the dispute giving rise to the procedure whose duration is criticised and applying the criteria set out in paragraphs 96 to 100 above.

CoJ (Grand Chamber) 26 November 2013 (Kendrion v. Commission, C-50/12 P), ECLI:C:EU:2013:771, paras 81–82 and 83, 86–96, 99–101 and CoJ (Grand Chamber) 26 November 2013 (Gascogne Sack Deutschland v. Commission, C-40/12 P), ECLI:EU:C:2013:768, paras 80 and 81 and 90 and 95–96.

J. PUBLIC HEARING

24.118   The Court reiterates that the public character of proceedings before the judicial bodies referred to in Article 6(1) protects litigants against the administration of justice in secret with no public scrutiny; it is also one of the means whereby confidence in the courts, superior and inferior, can be maintained. By rendering the administration of justice visible, publicity contributes to the achievement of the aim of Article 6(1), namely a fair trial, the guarantee of which is one of the fundamental principles of any democratic society, within the meaning of the Convention (see, among many other authorities, *Axen v. Germany*, 8 December 1983, § 25, Series A no. 72).

The right to a public hearing implies a public hearing before the relevant court (see, inter alia, mutatis mutandis, *Fredin v. Sweden* (no. 2), 23 February 1994, § 21, Series A no. 283A, and *Fischer v. Austria*, 26 April 1995, § 44, Series A no. 312). Article 6(1) does not, however, prohibit courts from deciding, in the light of the special features of the case submitted to them, to derogate from this principle: in accordance with the actual wording of this provision, 'the press and public may be excluded from all or part of the trial in the interests of morals, public order or national security in a democratic society, where the interests of juveniles or the protection of the private life of the parties so require, or to the extent strictly necessary in the opinion of the court in special circumstances where publicity would prejudice the interests of justice'; holding proceedings, whether wholly or partly, in camera must be strictly required by the circumstances of the case (see, for example, mutatis mutandis, *Diennet v. France*, 26 September 1995, § 34, Series A no. 325-A).

Moreover, the Court has held that exceptional circumstances relating to the nature of the issues to be decided by the court in the proceedings concerned (see, mutatis mutandis, *Miller v. Sweden*, no. 55853/00, § 29, 8 February 2005) may justify dispensing with a public hearing (see, in particular, *Göç v. Turkey* [GC], no. 36590/97, § 47, ECHR 2002-V). It thus considers, in particular, that social security proceedings, which are highly technical, are often better dealt with in writing than in oral submissions, and that, as systematically holding hearings may be an obstacle to the particular diligence required in social security cases, it is understandable that in this sphere the national authorities should have regard to the demands of efficiency and economy (see, for example, *Miller and Schuler-Zgraggen*, cited above). It should be pointed out, however, that in the majority of cases concerning proceedings before 'civil' courts ruling on the merits in which it has arrived at that conclusion the applicant had had the opportunity of requesting a public hearing.

The position is rather different where, both on appeal (if applicable) and at first instance, 'civil' proceedings on the merits are conducted in private in accordance with a general and absolute principle, without the litigant being able to request a public hearing on the ground that his case presents special features. Proceedings conducted in that way cannot in principle be regarded as compatible with Article 6(1) of the Convention (see, for example, *Diennet and Göç*, [...]): other than in wholly exceptional circumstances, litigants must at least have the opportunity of requesting a public hearing, though the court may refuse the request and hold the hearing in private on account of the circumstances of the case and for the aforementioned reasons.

Eur. Court H.R. (Grand Chamber) 12 April 2006 (Martinie v. France, no. 58675/00), paras 39–42.

K. ACCESS TO A LAWYER

1. General

24.119   [...] Although not absolute, the right of everyone charged with a criminal offence to be effectively defended by a lawyer, assigned officially if need be, is one of the fundamental features of fair trial.[...]
Eur. Court H.R. 23 November 1993 (Poitrimol v. France), Series A no. 277-A, para. 34.

See also Eur. Court H.R. 28 February 2008 (Demebukov v. Bulgaria, no. 68020/ 01), para. 50.

24.120   The right set out in paragraph 3(c) of Article 6 of the Convention is one element, amongst others, of the concept of a fair trial in criminal proceedings contained in paragraph 1 [...].
Eur. Court H.R. 24 November 1993 (Imbrioscia v. Switzerland, no. 13972/88), Series A no. 275, p. 13, para. 37.

2. During an interrogation

24.121   [...] To deny access to a lawyer for the first 48 hours of police questioning, in a situation where the rights of the defence may well be irretrievably prejudiced, is – whatever the justification for such denial – incompatible with the rights of the accused under Article 6.
Eur. Court H.R. 8 February 1996 (John Murray v. the United Kingdom), ECHR Reports 1996-I, para. 66.

24.122   National laws may attach consequences to the attitude of an accused at the initial stages of police interrogation which are decisive for the prospects of the defence in any subsequent criminal proceedings. In such circumstances, Article 6 will normally require that the accused be allowed to benefit from the assistance of a lawyer already at the initial stages of police interrogation. However, this right has so far been considered capable of being subject to restrictions for good cause. The question, in each case, has therefore been whether the restriction was justified and, if so, whether, in the light of the entirety of the proceedings, it has not deprived the accused of a fair hearing, for even a justified restriction is capable of doing so in certain circumstances.
Eur. Court H.R. 27 November 2008 (Salduz v. Turkey, no. 36391/02), para. 52.

See also Eur. Court H.R. 8 February 1996 (John Murray v. the United Kingdom), Reports 1996-I, paras 63 and 65.

24.123   [T]he Court finds that in order for the right to a fair trial to remain sufficiently 'practical and effective', [...] Article 6(1) requires that, as a rule, access to a lawyer should be provided as from the first interrogation of a suspect by the police, unless it is demonstrated in the light of the particular circumstances of each case that there are compelling reasons to restrict this right. Even where compelling reasons may exceptionally justify denial of access to a lawyer, such restriction – whatever its justification – must not unduly prejudice the rights of the accused under Article 6 […]. The rights of the defence will in principle be irretrievably prejudiced when incriminating statements made during police interrogation without access to a lawyer are used for a conviction.

Eur. Court H.R. 27 November 2008 (Salduz v. Turkey, no. 36391/02), para. 55.

Moreover, the Court observes that the present case is different from previous cases **24.124** concerning the right to legal assistance in pre-trial proceedings […] because the applicant was not formally arrested or interrogated in police custody. He was stopped for a road check. This check and the applicant's self-incriminating statements were both carried out and made in public in the presence of two attesting witnesses. […]

Although the applicant in the present case was not free to leave, the Court considers that the circumstances of the case as presented by the parties, and established by the Court, disclose no significant curtailment of the applicant's freedom of action, which could be sufficient for activating a requirement for legal assistance already at this stage of the proceedings.

Eur. Court H.R. 18 February 2010 (Zaichenko v. Russia, no. 39660/02), paras 47 and 48.

La Cour rappelle […] que la personne placée en garde à vue a le droit d'être assistée d'un **24.125** avocat dès le début de cette mesure ainsi que pendant les interrogatoires, et ce a fortiori lorsqu'elle n'a pas été informée par les autorités de son droit de se taire […].

Eur. Court H.R. 14 October 2010 (Brusco v. France, no. 1466/07), para. 45.

3. Legal privilege

Please refer to the same heading in Chapter 19 on Article 7 Charter.

L. LEGAL AID

1. Scope

[…] It is important [in the context of access to a court] for a litigant not to be denied the **24.126** opportunity to present his case effectively before the court (Eur. Court H.R., judgment in *Steel and Morris v. the United Kingdom* of 15 February 2005, ECHR 2005-II, § 59). The right of access to a court is not, however, absolute.

Ruling on legal aid in the form of assistance by a lawyer, the [Eur. Court H.R.] has held that the question whether the provision of legal aid is necessary for a fair hearing must be determined on the basis of the particular facts and circumstances of each case and will depend, inter alia, upon the importance of what is at stake for the applicant in the proceedings, the complexity of the relevant law and procedure and the applicant's capacity to represent himself effectively (Eur. Court H.R., judgments in *Airey v. Ireland*, § 26; *McVicar v. the United Kingdom*, §§ 48 and 49; *P., C. and S. v. the United Kingdom* of 16 July 2002, ECHR 2002-VI, § 91, and *Steel and Morris v. the United Kingdom*, § 61). Account may be taken, however, of the financial situation of the litigant or his prospects of success in the proceedings (Eur. Court H.R., judgment in *Steel and Morris v. the United Kingdom*, § 62).

CoJ 22 December 2010 (DEB, C-279/09) [2010] ECR I-13849, paras 45 and 46.

2. Assistance by a lawyer and dispensation of the cost of proceedings

24.127   As regards legal aid in the form of dispensation from payment of the costs of proceedings or from provision of security for costs before an action is brought, the European Court of Human Rights has similarly examined all the circumstances in order to determine whether the limitations applied to the right of access to the courts had undermined the very core of that right, whether those limitations pursued a legitimate aim and whether there was a reasonable relationship of proportionality between the means employed and the legitimate aim sought to be achieved (see, to that effect, Eur. Court H.R., judgments in *Tolstoy-Miloslavsky v. the United Kingdom* of 13 July 1995, Series A No 316-B, paras 59–67, and *Kreuz v. Poland* of 19 June 2001, ECHR 2001-VI, paras 54 and 55).

It is apparent from those decisions that legal aid may cover both assistance by a lawyer and dispensation from payment of the costs of proceedings.

CoJ 22 December 2010 (DEB, C-279/09) [2010] ECR I-13849, paras 47 and 48.

3. Grant procedure

24.128   The European Court of Human Rights has also held that, although a selection procedure for cases may be established in order to determine whether legal aid may be granted, that procedure must operate in a non-arbitrary manner (see, to that effect, Eur. Court H.R., judgment in *Del Sol v. France* of 26 February 2002, § 26; decision in *Puscasu v. Germany* of 29 September 2009, p. 6, last paragraph; judgment in *Pedro Ramos v. Switzerland* of 14 October 2010, § 49).

CoJ 22 December 2010 (DEB, C-279/09) [2010] ECR I-13849, para. 49.

4. Availability to a legal person

24.129   As regards in particular Article 47(3) of the Charter, the last paragraph of the Explanation relating to Article 47 mentions the judgment in *Airey v. Ireland* of 9 October 1979 (Eur. Court H.R., Series A, No 32, p. 11), according to which provision should be made for legal aid where the absence of such aid would make it impossible to ensure an effective remedy. No indication is given as to whether such aid must be granted to a legal person or of the nature of the costs covered by that aid.

That provision must be interpreted in its context, in the light of other provisions of EU law, the law of the Member States and the case-law of the European Court of Human Rights.

As the Commission of the European Communities observed in its written submissions, the word 'person' used in the first two paragraphs of Article 47 of the Charter may cover individuals, but, from a purely linguistic point of view, it does not exclude legal persons.

It should be noted in that connection that, although the explanations relating to the Charter do not provide any clarification in this regard, the use of the word 'Person', in the German language version of Article 47, as opposed to the word 'Mensch', which is used in numerous other provisions – for example, in Articles 1, 2, 3, 6, 29, 34 and 35 of the Charter – may be an indication that legal persons are not excluded from the scope of that article.

Moreover, the right to an effective remedy before a court, enshrined in Article 47 of the Charter, is to be found under Title VI of that Charter, relating to justice, in which other procedural principles are established which apply to both natural and legal persons.

Similarly, the inclusion of the provision relating to the grant of legal aid in the article of the Charter relating to the right to an effective remedy indicates that the assessment of the need to grant that aid must be made on the basis of the right of the actual person whose rights and freedoms as guaranteed by EU law have been violated, rather than on the basis of the public interest of society, even if that interest may be one of the criteria for assessing the need for the aid.

It is apparent from the examination of the case-law of the European Court of Human Rights that the grant of legal aid to legal persons is not in principle impossible, but must be assessed in the light of the applicable rules and the situation of the company concerned.

The subject-matter of the litigation may be taken into consideration, in particular its economic importance.

For the purposes of taking account of the financial capacity of an applicant, where that applicant is a legal person, consideration may be given inter alia to the form of the company (whether it is a capital company or a partnership, whether it is a limited liability company or otherwise); the financial capacity of its shareholders; the objects of the company; the manner in which it has been set up; and, more specifically, the relationship between the resources allocated to it and the intended activity.

In the light of all of the foregoing, the answer to the question referred must be that the principle of effective judicial protection, as enshrined in Article 47 of the Charter, must be interpreted as meaning that it is not impossible for legal persons to rely on that principle and that aid granted pursuant to that principle may cover, inter alia, dispensation from advance payment of the costs of proceedings and/or the assistance of a lawyer.

CoJ 22 December 2010 (DEB C-279/09) [2010] ECR I-13849, paras 36–40, 42, 52–54 and 59.

25

ARTICLE 48 CHARTER*

PRESUMPTION OF INNOCENCE AND RIGHTS OF THE DEFENCE

Everyone who has been charged shall be presumed innocent until proved guilty according to law.

Respect for the rights of the defence of anyone who has been charged shall be guaranteed.

ARTICLE 6(2) AND (3) ECHR

2. Everyone charged with a criminal offence shall be presumed innocent until proved guilty according to law.

3. Everyone charged with a criminal offence has the following minimum rights:

    (a) to be informed promptly, in a language which he understands and in detail, of the nature and cause of the accusation against him;

    (b) to have adequate time and facilities for the preparation of his defence;

    (c) to defend himself in person or through legal assistance of his own choosing or, if he has not sufficient means to pay for legal assistance, to be given it free when the interests of justice so require;

    (d) to examine or have examined witnesses against him and to obtain the attendance and examination of witnesses on his behalf under the same conditions as witnesses against him;

    (e) to have the free assistance of an interpreter if he cannot understand or speak the language used in court.

OVERVIEW

A. EXPLANATION RELATING TO ARTICLE 48 CHARTER	(p.841)	1. General	25.01
		2. In relation to parental liability	25.15
		3. In relation to the causal link in case	
B. PRESUMPTION OF INNOCENCE	25.01	of a concerted practice	25.18

---

* This chapter was written by Herman Speyart.

4. In relation to participation in a meeting with an anti-competitive character ... 25.21

C. RIGHTS OF THE DEFENCE – GENERAL ... 25.22

D. PRIVILEGE AGAINST SELF-INCRIMINATION AND RIGHT TO REMAIN SILENT ... 25.25
1. Intrinsic to the concept of 'fair trial' ... 25.25
2. Scope ... 25.28
3. Test ... 25.30
4. Right to remain silent *stricto sensu* ... 25.33

5. Order to submit information or documents ... 25.36
6. Inferences which may be drawn from the exercise of the right to remain silent ... 25.44

E. OBLIGATION TO MENTION THE PRIVILEGE AGAINST SELF-INCRIMINATION AND THE RIGHT TO REMAIN SILENT ... 25.46

F. ACCESS TO LEGAL ASSISTANCE AND LEGAL AID ... (p.856)

A. EXPLANATION RELATING TO ARTICLE 48 CHARTER

Article 48 is the same as Article 6(2) and (3) of the ECHR: [...].

B. PRESUMPTION OF INNOCENCE

1. General

(a) Eur. Court H.R.

The presumption of innocence enshrined in paragraph 2 of Article 6 is one of the **25.01** elements of the fair criminal trial that is required by paragraph 1.
Eur. Court H.R. 27 February 1980 (Deweer, no 6903/75), Series A no 35, p. 30, para. 56.

See also Eur. Court H.R. 25 March 1983 (Minelli v. Switzerland, no 8660/79), Series A no 62, para. 27; Eur. Court H.R. 10 February 1995 (Allenet de Ribemont v. France 15175/89), Series A no 308, para. 35.

In the Court's judgment, the presumption of innocence will be violated if, without the **25.02** accused's having previously been proved guilty according to law and, notably, without his having had the opportunity of exercising his rights of defence, a judicial decision concerning him reflects an opinion that he is guilty. This may be so even in the absence of any formal finding; it suffices that there is some reasoning suggesting that the court regards the accused as guilty.
Eur. Court H.R. 25 March 1983 (Minelli v. Switzerland, no 8660/79), Series A no 62, para. 27.

[Possibility of the use of reversible presumptions of fact or law] [...] Presumptions of **25.03** fact or of law operate in every legal system. Clearly, the Convention does not prohibit such presumptions in principle. It does, however, require the Contracting States to remain within certain limits in this respect as regards criminal law. [...] Article 6 paragraph 2 does not therefore regard presumptions of fact or of law provided for in the criminal law with indifference. It requires States to confine them within reasonable limits which take into account the importance of what is at stake and maintain the rights of the defence. [...]

Eur. Court H.R. 7 October 1988 (Salabiaku v. France, no 10519/83), Series A no 141-A, p. 15, para. 28.

See also Eur. Court H.R. 25 September 1992 (Pham Hoang v. France, no 13191/ 87), Series A no 243, paras 33–36.

25.04   Paragraph 2 embodies the principle of the presumption of innocence. It requires, inter alia, that when carrying out their duties, the members of a court should not start with the preconceived idea that the accused has committed the offence charged; the burden of proof is on the prosecution, and any doubt should benefit the accused.

Eur. Court H.R. 6 December 1988 (Barberà, Messegué and Jabardo v. Spain, no 10590/83), Series A no 146, p. 31, para. 77.

25.05   [The presumption of innocence] will be violated if a judicial decision concerning a person charged with a criminal offence reflects an opinion that he is guilty before he has been proved guilty according to law. It suffices, even in the absence of any formal finding, that there is some reasoning suggesting that the court regards the accused as guilty.

Eur. Court H.R. 10 February 1995 (Allenet de Ribemont v. France 15175/89), Series A no 308, para. 35.

25.06   The Court considers that the presumption of innocence may be infringed not only by a judge or court but also by other public authorities.

Eur. Court H.R. 10 February 1995 (Allenet de Ribemont v. France, no 15175/89), Series A no 308, para. 36.

25.07   Thus, the presumption of innocence will be infringed where the burden of proof is shifted from the prosecution to the defence.

Eur. Court H.R. 8 February 1996 (John Murray v. the United Kingdom), ECHR Reports 1996-I, para. 54.

25.08   [The presumption of innocence] will be violated if a statement of a public official concerning a person charged with a criminal offence reflects an opinion that he is guilty before he has been proved so according to law. It suffices, even in the absence of any formal finding, that there is some reasoning to suggest that the official regards the accused as guilty. In this regard the Court emphasises the importance of the choice of words by public officials in their statements before a person has been tried and found guilty of an offence.

Eur. Court H.R. 10 October 2000 (Daktaras v. Lithuania, no 42095/98), ECHR Reports 2000-VI, para. 41.

(b)   EU Courts

[T]he presumption of innocence resulting in particular from Article 6(2) of the ECHR **25.09** is one of the fundamental rights which, according to the Court's settled case-law, reaffirmed in the preamble to the Single European Act and in Article F(2) of the Treaty on European Union, are protected in the Community legal order (see, to that effect, *Bosman*, [...], para. 79).

It must also be accepted that, given the nature of the infringements in question and the nature and degree of severity of the ensuing penalties, the principle of the presumption of innocence applies to the procedures relating to infringements of the competition rules applicable to undertakings that may result in the imposition of fines or periodic penalty payments [...].

CoJ 8 July 1999 (Hüls v. Commission, C-199/92 P) [1999] ECR I-4287, paras 149 and 150.

Since the prohibition on participating in anti-competitive agreements and the penalties **25.10** which offenders may incur are well known, it is normal for the activities which those practices and those agreements entail to take place in a clandestine fashion, for meetings to be held in secret, most frequently in a non-member country, and for the associated documentation to be reduced to a minimum.

Even if the Commission discovers evidence explicitly showing unlawful contact between traders, such as the minutes of a meeting, it will normally be only fragmentary and sparse, so that it is often necessary to reconstitute certain details by deduction.

In most cases, the existence of an anti-competitive practice or agreement must be inferred from a number of coincidences and indicia which, taken together, may, in the absence of another plausible explanation, constitute evidence of an infringement of the competition rules.

CoJ 7 January 2004 (Aalborg Portland and others v. Commission, C-204/00 P, C-205/00 P, C-211/00 P, C-213/00 P, C-217/00 P and C-219/00 P) [2004] ECR I-123, paras 55–57.

[I]t is for the party or the authority alleging an infringement of the competition rules to **25.11** prove it and it is for the undertaking or association of undertakings raising a defence against a finding of an infringement of those rules to demonstrate that the conditions for applying the rule on which such defence is based are satisfied, so that the authority will then have to resort to other evidence.

Although according to those principles the legal burden of proof is borne either by the Commission or by the undertaking or association concerned, the factual evidence on which a party relies may be of such a kind as to require the other party to provide an explanation or justification, failing which it is permissible to conclude that the burden of proof has been discharged.

CoJ 7 January 2004 (Aalborg Portland and others v. Commission, C–204/00 P, C–205/00 P, C–211/00 P, C–213/00 P, C–217/00 P and C –219/00 P) [2004] ECR I–123, paras 78 and 79.

25.12   Any doubt in the mind of the Court must operate to the advantage of the undertaking to which the decision finding an infringement was addressed. The Court cannot therefore conclude that the Commission has established the infringement at issue to the requisite legal standard if it still entertains any doubts on that point, in particular in proceedings for annulment of a decision imposing a fine.

General Court 27 September 2006 (Dresdner Bank a.o. v. Commission, Joined Cases T–44/02 OP, T–54/02 OP, T–56/02 OP, T–60/02 OP and T–61/02 OP) [2006] ECR II–3567, para. 60.

25.13   In accordance with settled case-law, in view of the nature of the infringements in question and the nature and degree of severity of the ensuing penalties, the principle of the presumption of innocence, resulting in particular from Article 6(2) of the Convention for the Protection of Human Rights and Fundamental Freedoms and from Article 48(1) of the Charter of Fundamental Rights of the European Union, applies in particular to the procedures relating to infringements of the competition rules applicable to undertakings that may result in the imposition of fines or periodic penalty payments […].

    Thus, the Commission must show precise and consistent evidence in order to establish the existence of the infringement […].

General Court 27 September 2006 (Dresdner Bank a.o. v. Commission, Joined Cases T–44/02 OP, T–54/02 OP, T–56/02 OP, T–60/02 OP and T–61/02 OP) [2006] ECR II–3567, paras 61 and 62.

25.14   However, it is not necessary for every item of evidence produced by the Commission to satisfy those criteria in relation to every aspect of the infringement. It is sufficient if the body of evidence relied on by that institution, viewed as a whole, meets that requirement.

    Therefore, even if, as the appellant asserts, none of the different elements of the infringement in question constitutes, considered separately, an agreement or concerted practice prohibited by Article [101(1) TFEU], such a conclusion does not prevent those elements, considered together, from constituting such an agreement or practice.

CoJ 1 July 2010 (Knauf Gips v. Commission, C–407/08 P) [2010] ECR I–6375, paras 47 and 48.

2. In relation to parental liability

25.15   Recourse to a presumption rule such as that under discussion here [the rule that the Commission as a competition authority can attribute an infringement of a subsidiary to its parent company in case of 100 per cent share holding] does not lead to a reversal of the burden of proof that would be incompatible with the presumption of innocence. On the contrary, only the standard of proof which must be satisfied when attributing responsibility under antitrust law as between a parent company and its subsidiary is being laid down. Since the parent company's 100 per cent shareholding in its subsidiary supports prima facie the conclusion that decisive influence is actually being exercised, it is for the parent company to rebut precisely that conclusion, adducing cogent evidence to the contrary; failing this, that conclusion is adequate to discharge the burden of proof. In other words, there is an interplay between the respective burdens of adducing evidence prior to consideration of the objective burden of proof.

Opinion Advocate General Kokott 23 April 2009 (Akzo Nobel and others v. Commission, C-97/08 P) [2009] ECR I-8237, para. 74, not reflected in the judgment.

It must be borne in mind, first of all, that the concept of undertaking within the **25.16** meaning of Article [101 TFEU] includes economic entities which consist of a unitary organisation of personal, tangible and intangible elements, which pursue a specific economic aim on a long-term basis and can contribute to the Commission of an infringement of the kind referred to in that provision […].

It is therefore not because of a relationship between the parent company and its subsidiary in instigating the infringement or, a fortiori, because the parent company is involved in the infringement, but because they constitute a single undertaking in the sense described above that the Commission is able to address the decision imposing fines to the parent company of a group of companies. It must be borne in mind that Community competition law recognises that different companies belonging to the same group form an economic entity and therefore an undertaking within the meaning of Articles [101 and 102 TFEU] if the companies concerned do not determine independently their own conduct on the market […].

It should also be noted that, for the purpose of applying and enforcing Commission competition law decisions, it is necessary to identify, as addressee, an entity having legal personality […].

In the specific case of a parent company holding 100 per cent of the capital of a subsidiary which has committed an infringement, there is a simple presumption that the parent company exercises decisive influence over the conduct of its subsidiary […]. It is thus for a parent company which disputes before the Community judicature a Commission decision fining it for the conduct of its subsidiary to rebut that presumption by adducing evidence to establish that its subsidiary was independent […].

CoJ 10 September 2009 (Akzo Nobel and others v. Commission, C-97/08 P) [2009] ECR I-8237, paras 58–61.

In their reply, the appellants contest the basis of the case-law resulting from *Akzo Nobel* **25.17** *and Others v Commission* in the light of Article 6 of the ECHR, submitting that the question of the legality, in the light of that provision, of the presumption that the parent company exercises decisive influence over its subsidiary is still not decided. The Court pointed out, however, in *Elf Aquitaine v Commission*, paragraph 62, that a presumption, even where it is difficult to rebut, remains within acceptable limits so long as it is proportionate to the legitimate aim pursued, it is possible to adduce evidence to the contrary and the rights of the defence are safeguarded (see, to this effect, *Case C-45/08 Spector Photo Group and Van Raemdonck* [2009] ECR I-12073, paragraphs 43 and 44, and the judgment of the European Court of Human Rights in *Janosevic v. Sweden, no 34619/97*, § 101 et seq., ECHR 2002-VII).

The presumption that decisive influence is exercised over a subsidiary wholly or almost wholly owned by its parent company is intended, in particular, to strike a balance between, on the one hand, the importance of the objective of combatting conduct contrary to the competition rules, in particular to Article [101 TFEU], and of preventing a repetition of such conduct and, on the other hand, the requirements flowing from certain general principles of European Union law such as the principle of the presumption of innocence, the principle that penalties should be applied solely to the offender and the principle of legal certainty as well as the rights of the defence, including the principle of equality of arms (*Elf Aquitaine v Commission*, para. 59). It follows that such a presumption is proportionate to the legitimate aim pursued.

Furthermore, first, the aforesaid presumption is based on the fact that, save in quite exceptional circumstances, a company holding all, or almost all, the capital of a subsidiary can, by dint merely of holding it, exercise decisive influence over that subsidiary's conduct and, second, it is within the sphere of operations of those entities against which the presumption operates that evidence of the lack of actual exercise of that power to influence is generally apt to be found. The presumption is, however, rebuttable and the entities wishing to rebut it may adduce all factors relating to the economic, organisational and legal links tying the subsidiary to the parent company that they consider to be capable of demonstrating that the subsidiary and the parent company do not constitute a single economic entity, but that the subsidiary acts independently on the market (see *Case C-286/98 P Stora Kopparbergs Bergslags v Commission* [2008] ECR I-9925, para. 29; *Akzo Nobel and Others v Commission*, para. 61; and *Elf Aquitaine v Commission*, paras 57 and 65).

Finally, the parent company must be heard by the Commission before the latter adopts a decision against it and review of that decision may be sought from the European Union judicature which must, in deciding the case, observe the rights of the defence.

Accordingly, the General Court did not make an error of law in adopting [...] the principle that the parent company is presumed to be liable for the conduct of its wholly-owned subsidiary.

CoJ 18 July 2013 (Schindler v. Commission, C-501/11 P) [2013] ECLI:EU: C:2013:522, paras 107–111.

3. In relation to the causal link in case of a concerted practice

25.18   It follows, first, that the concept of a concerted practice, as it results from the actual terms of Article [101(1) TFEU], implies, besides undertakings' concerting with each other, subsequent conduct on the market, and a relationship of cause and effect between the two.

However, subject to proof to the contrary, which the economic operators concerned must adduce, the presumption must be that the undertakings taking part in the concerted action and remaining active on the market take account of the information exchanged with their competitors for the purposes of determining their conduct on that market. That is all the more true where the undertakings concert together on a regular basis over a long period, as was the case here, according to the findings of the [General Court].

Secondly, contrary to Hüls's argument, a concerted practice as defined above is caught by Article [101(1) TFEU], even in the absence of anti-competitive effects on the market. *CoJ 8 July 1999 (Hüls AG v. Commission, C-199/92 P) [1999] ECR I-4287, paras 161–163 and CoJ 8 July 1999 (Commission v. Anic Partecipazioni, C-49/92 P) [1999] ECR I-4125, paras 161–163.*

See also CoJ 4 June 2009 (T-Mobile Netherlands BV, C-8/08) [2009] ECR I-4529, para. 51.

However, the presumption of innocence is not disregarded if in competition proceed- **25.19** ings certain conclusions are drawn on the basis of common experience and the undertakings concerned are at liberty to refute those conclusions. After all, classic criminal proceedings allow for the use of circumstantial evidence and recourse to principles derived from experience.
Opinion Advocate General Kokott 19 February 2009 (T-Mobile a.o., C-8/08) [2009] ECR I-4529, para. 93, not reflected in the judgment.

In those circumstances, it must be held that the presumption of a causal connection **25.20** stems from Article [101 TFEU], as interpreted by the Court, and it consequently forms an integral part of applicable Community law.
CoJ 4 June 2009 (T-Mobile Netherlands BV, C-8/08) [2009] ECR I-4529, para. 52.

4. In relation to participation in a meeting with an anti-competitive character

Since [...] the Commission had been able to establish that Monte had taken part in **25.21** meetings between undertakings of a manifestly anti-competitive nature, the [General Court] was entitled to consider that it was for Monte to provide another explanation of the tenor of those meetings. It follows that the [General Court] did not unduly reverse the burden of proof and did not set aside the presumption of innocence.
CoJ 8 July 1999 (Montecatini v. Commission, C-235/92 P) [1999] ECR I-4539, para. 181.

See also CoJ 8 July 1999 (Hüls v. Commission, C-199/92 P) [1999] ECR 1-4287, para. 155.

C. RIGHTS OF THE DEFENCE – GENERAL

Paragraph 3 of Article 6 contains an enumeration of specific applications of the general **25.22** principle stated in paragraph 1 of the Article. The various rights of which a non-exhaustive list appears in paragraph 3 reflect certain of the aspects of the notion of a fair trial in criminal proceedings.

Eur. Court H.R. 27 February 1980 (Deweer v. Belgium, no 6903/75), Series A no 35, p. 30, para. 56.

25.23   [...] When compliance with paragraph 3 is being reviewed, its basic purpose must not be forgotten nor must it be severed from its roots.

[T]he Convention is intended to guarantee not rights that are theoretical or illusory but rights that are practical and effective; this is particularly so of the rights of the defence in view of the prominent place held in a democratic society by the right to a fair trial, from which they derive [...].

Eur. Court. H.R. 13 May 1980 (Artico v. Italy, no 6694/74), Series A no 37, p. 16, paras 32 and 33.

25.24   The rights of the defence are fundamental rights forming an integral part of the general principles of law, whose observance the Court ensures [...], drawing inspiration for that purpose from the constitutional traditions common to the Member States and from the guidelines supplied by international treaties for the protection of human rights on which the Member States have collaborated or to which they are signatories, such as the European Convention for the Protection of Human Rights and Fundamental Freedoms [...].

CoJ 7 January 2004 (Aalborg Portland and others v. Commission Joined Cases C-204/00 P, C-205/00 P, C-211/00 P, C-213/00 P, C-217/00 P and C-219/00 P) [2004] ECR I-123, para. 64.

D. PRIVILEGE AGAINST SELF-INCRIMINATION AND RIGHT TO REMAIN SILENT

1. Intrinsic to the concept of 'fair trial'

25.25   The special features of customs law [...] cannot justify [...] an infringement of the right of anyone 'charged with a criminal offence', within the autonomous meaning of this expression in Article 6, to remain silent and not to contribute to incriminating himself.

Eur. Court H.R. 25 February 1993 (Funke v. France, no 10828/84), Series A no 256-A, pp. 24–25, para. 44.

25.26   Although not specifically mentioned in Article 6 of the Convention, there can be no doubt that the right to remain silent under police questioning and the privilege against self-incrimination are generally recognised international standards which lie at the heart of the notion of a fair procedure under Article 6 [...]. By providing the accused with protection against improper compulsion by the authorities these immunities contribute to avoiding miscarriages of justice and to securing the aims of Article 6.

Eur. Court H.R. (Grand Chamber) 8 February 1996 (John Murray v. the United Kingdom), ECHR Reports 1996-I, para. 45.

The right not to incriminate oneself, in particular, presupposes that the prosecution in a **25.27** criminal case seek to prove their case against the accused without resort to evidence obtained through methods of coercion or oppression in defiance of the will of the accused. In this sense the right is closely linked to the presumption of innocence contained in Article 6 paragraph 2 of the Convention.

[The Court] considers that the general requirements of fairness contained in Article 6, including the right not to incriminate oneself, apply to criminal proceedings in respect of all types of criminal offences without distinction from the most simple to the most complex. The public interest cannot be invoked to justify the use of answers compulsorily obtained in a non-judicial investigation to incriminate the accused during the trial proceedings.

Eur. Court H.R. (Grand Chamber) 17 December 1996 (Saunders v. the United Kingdom, no 43/1994), ECHR Reports 1996-VI, paras 68 and 74.

2. Scope

[W]hilst the Commission is entitled, in order to preserve the useful effect of Article **25.28** 11(2) and (5) of Regulation No 17 [now Regulation No 1/2003], to compel an undertaking to provide all necessary information concerning such facts as may be known to it and to disclose to it, if necessary, such documents relating thereto as are in its possession, even if the latter may be used to establish, against it or another undertaking, the existence of anti-competitive conduct, it may not, by means of a decision calling for information, undermine the rights of defence of the undertaking concerned.

Thus, the Commission may not compel an undertaking to provide it with answers which might involve an admission on its part of the existence of an infringement which it is incumbent upon the Commission to prove.

CoJ 18 October 1989 (Orkem v. Commission 374/87) [1989] ECR 3283, paras 34 and 35.

See also CoJ 10 November 1993 (Otto v. Postbank, C-60/92) [1993] ECR I-5683.

Bearing in mind the concept of fairness in Article 6, the right not to incriminate oneself **25.29** cannot reasonably be confined to statements of admission of wrongdoing or to remarks which are directly incriminating. Testimony obtained under compulsion which appears on its face to be of a non-incriminating nature – such as exculpatory remarks or mere information on questions of fact – may later be deployed in criminal proceedings in support of the prosecution case, for example to contradict or cast doubt upon other statements of the accused or evidence given by him during the trial or to otherwise undermine his credibility. Where the credibility of an accused must be assessed by a jury the use of such testimony may be especially harmful. It follows that what is of the essence in this context is the use to which evidence obtained under compulsion is put in the course of the criminal trial.

Eur. Court H.R. (Grand Chamber) 17 December 1996 (Saunders v. the United Kingdom, no 43/1994), ECHR Reports 1996-VI, para. 71.

3. Test

25.30   The facts of the present case accordingly fall to be distinguished from those in *Funke* [...] where criminal proceedings were brought against the applicant by the customs authorities in an attempt to compel him to provide evidence of offences he had allegedly committed. Such a degree of compulsion in that case was found by the Court to be incompatible with Article 6 since, in effect, it destroyed the very essence of the privilege against self-incrimination.

Eur. Court H.R. 8 February 1996 (John Murray v. the United Kingdom), ECHR Reports 1996-I, para. 49.

25.31   In order to determine whether the applicant's right not to incriminate himself has been violated, the Court will have regard, in turn, to the following factors: the nature and degree of compulsion used to obtain the evidence; the weight of the public interest in the investigation and punishment of the offence at issue; the existence of any relevant safeguards in the procedure; and the use to which any material so obtained is put.

Eur. Court H.R. (Grand Chamber) 11 July 2006 (Jalloh v. Germany, no 54810/00), para. 117.

25.32   In the light of the principles contained in its *Jalloh* judgment, and in order to determine whether the essence of the applicants' right to remain silent and privilege against self-incrimination was infringed, the Court will focus on the nature and degree of compulsion used to obtain the evidence, the existence of any relevant safeguards in the procedure, and the use to which any material so obtained was put.

Eur. Court H.R. (Grand Chamber) 29 June 2007 (O'Halloran and Francis v. United Kingdom, 15809/02 and 25624/02), para. 55.

4. Right to remain silent *stricto sensu*

25.33   [Obligation to answer questions relating to stock rates] It has not been disputed by the Government that the applicant was subject to legal compulsion to give evidence to the inspectors. He was obliged under sections 434 and 436 of the Companies Act 1985 [...] to answer the questions put to him by the inspectors in the course of nine lengthy interviews of which seven were admissible as evidence at his trial. A refusal by the applicant to answer the questions put to him could have led to a finding of contempt of court and the imposition of a fine or committal to prison for up to two years [...] and it was no defence to such refusal that the questions were of an incriminating nature [...].

Eur. Court H.R. (Grand Chamber) 17 December 1996 (Saunders v. the United Kingdom, no 43/1994), ECHR Reports 1996-VI, para. 70.

[Obligation to indicate one's whereabouts at a given time] Accordingly, the Court finds **25.34** that the 'degree of compulsion' imposed on the applicants by the application of section 52 of the 1939 Act with a view to compelling them to provide information relating to charges against them under that Act in effect destroyed the very essence of their privilege against self-incrimination and their right to remain silent.

Eur. Court H.R. 21 December 2000 (Heaney and McGuiness v. Ireland, no 34720/97), ECHR Reports 2000-XII, para. 55.

[Obligation to answer truthfully under oath] Dans ces circonstances, la Cour estime **25.35** que lorsque le requérant a été placé en garde à vue et a dß prêter serment 'de dire toute la vérité, rien que la vérité', celui-ci faisait l'objet d'une 'accusation en matière pénale' et bénéficiait du droit de ne pas contribuer à sa propre incrimination et de garder le silence garanti par l'article 6 §§ 1 et 3 de la Convention.

La Cour relève ensuite que, lors de sa première déposition le 8 juin 1999, le requérant a fourni certains éléments de preuve pouvant démontrer son implication dans l'agression de B.M: il a en effet livré des détails sur ses conversations avec l'un des individus mis en examen, J.P.G., sur leur entente 'pour faire peur' à B.M. et sur la remise d'une somme d'argent de 100 000 francs français. La Cour note également que ces déclarations ont été ensuite utilisées par les juridictions pénales pour établir les faits et condamner le requérant.

La Cour estime que le fait d'avoir dß prêter serment avant de déposer a constitué pour le requérant – qui faisait déjà depuis la veille l'objet d'une mesure coercitive, la garde à vue – une forme de pression, et que le risque de poursuites pénales en cas de témoignage mensonger a assurément rendu la prestation de serment plus contraignante.

Eur. Court H.R. 14 October 2010 (Brusco v. France, no 1466/07), paras 50–52.

5. Order to submit information or documents

(a) Eur. Court H.R.

[Regarding documents the French customs suspected Funke to have] The Court notes **25.36** that the customs secured Mr Funke's conviction in order to obtain certain documents which they believed must exist, although they were not certain of the fact. Being unable or unwilling to procure them by some other means, they attempted to compel the applicant himself to provide the evidence of offences he had allegedly committed. The special features of customs law […] cannot justify such an infringement of the right of anyone 'charged with a criminal offence', within the autonomous meaning of this expression in Article 6, to remain silent and not to contribute to incriminating himself.

Eur. Court H.R. 25 February 1993 (Funke v. France, no 10828/84), Series A no 256-A, p. 24–25, para. 44.

[Criterion of 'material which has an existence independent of the will of the suspect'] **25.37** The right not to incriminate oneself is primarily concerned […] with respecting the will of an accused person to remain silent. As commonly understood in the legal systems of the Contracting Parties to the Convention and elsewhere, it does not extend to the use in criminal proceedings of material which may be obtained from the accused through the use of compulsory powers but which has an existence independent of the will of the suspect such as, inter alia, documents acquired pursuant to a warrant, breath, blood and urine samples and bodily tissue for the purpose of DNA testing.

Eur. Court H.R. (Grand Chamber) 17 December 1996 (Saunders v. the United Kingdom, no 43/1994), ECHR Reports 1996-VI, para. 69.

25.38   [Regarding an obligation to provide information concerning the origin of certain income] [I]t appears that the authorities were attempting to compel the applicant to submit documents which would have provided information as to his income with a view to the assessment of his taxes. [...]

The Court notes that in its judgment of 7 July 1995 the Federal Court referred to various provisions in criminal law obliging a person to act in a particular way so as to enable the authorities to obtain his conviction, for instance, the obligation to install a tachograph in lorries, or to submit to a blood or a urine test. In the Court's opinion, however, the present case does not involve material of this nature which, like that considered in *Saunders*, has an existence independent of the person concerned and is not, therefore, obtained by means of coercion and in defiance of the will of that person [...]. [...]

As a result, and against the above background, the Court considers that there has been a violation of the right under Article 6(1) of the Convention not to incriminate oneself.

Eur. Court H.R. 3 May 2001 (J.B. v. Switzerland, no 31827/96), paras 66, 68 and 71.

See also *Eur. Court H.R. (Grand Chamber) 29 June 2007 (O'Halloran and Francis v. United Kingdom, 15809/02 and 25624/02), paras 56–63.*

25.39   [Assessment of a UK obligation to give the name of the driver of a registered vehicle when an offence has been found to have taken place with that vehicle] [...] Those who choose to keep and drive motor cars can be taken to have accepted certain responsibilities and obligations as part of the regulatory regime relating to motor vehicles, and in the legal framework of the United Kingdom, these responsibilities include the obligation, in the event of suspected commission of road traffic offences, to inform the authorities of the identity of the driver on that occasion.

Eur. Court H.R. (Grand Chamber) 29 June 2007 (O'Halloran and Francis v. United Kingdom, 15809/02 and 25624/02), para. 57.

(b)   EU Courts

25.40   It is necessary [...] to consider whether certain limitations on the Commission's powers of investigation are implied by the need to safeguard the rights of the defence which the Court has held to be a fundamental principle of the Community legal order [...].

In that connection, the Court observed recently, in its judgment of 21 September 1989 in *Joined Cases 46/87 and 227/88 Hoechst v. Commission* [1989] ECR 2859, paragraph 15, that whilst it is true that the rights of the defence must be observed in administrative procedures which may lead to the imposition of penalties, it is necessary to prevent those rights from being irremediably impaired during preliminary inquiry procedures which may be decisive in providing evidence of the unlawful nature of conduct engaged in by undertakings and for which they may be liable. Consequently, although certain rights of the defence relate only to contentious proceedings which follow the delivery of the statement of objections, other rights must be respected even during the preliminary inquiry.

Accordingly, whilst the Commission is entitled, in order to preserve the useful effect of Article 11(2) and (5) of Regulation No 17, to compel an undertaking to provide all necessary information concerning such facts as may be known to it and to disclose to it, if necessary, such documents relating thereto as are in its possession, even if the latter may be used to establish, against it or another undertaking, the existence of anti-competitive conduct, it may not, by means of a decision calling for information, undermine the rights of defence of the undertaking concerned.

Thus, the Commission may not compel an undertaking to provide it with answers which might involve an admission on its part of the existence of an infringement which it is incumbent upon the Commission to prove.

CoJ 18 October 1989 (Orkem v. Commission, 374/87) [1989] ECR 3283, paras 32–35.

See also CoJ 10 November 1993 (Otto v. Postbank, C-60/92) [1993] ECR I-5683.

It is in application of those principles, which offer, in the specific field of competition **25.41** law, [...], protection equivalent to that guaranteed by Article 6 of the Convention, that the Court of Justice and the [General Court] have consistently held that the recipient of requests sent by the Commission pursuant to Article 11(5) of Regulation No 17 is entitled to confine himself to answering questions of a purely factual nature and to producing only the pre-existing documents [...].

General Court 20 February 2001 (Mannesmannröhren-Werke v. Commission, T-112/98) [2001] ECR II-729, para. 77.

[The *Orkem v. Commission* judgment thus acknowledged] as one of the general **25.42** principles of Community law, of which fundamental rights are an integral part and in the light of which all Community laws must be interpreted, the right of undertakings not to be compelled by the Commission, under Article 11 of Regulation No 17, to admit their participation in an infringement (see *Orkem*, paras 28, 38 in fine and 39). The protection of that right means that, in the event of a dispute as to the scope of a question, it must be determined whether an answer from the undertaking to which the question is addressed is in fact equivalent to the admission of an infringement, such as to undermine the rights of the defence.

The parties agree that, since *Orkem*, there have been further developments in the case-law of the European Court of Human Rights which the Community judicature must take into account when interpreting the fundamental rights, as introduced by the judgment in *Funke* [...] on which the appellants rely, and the judgments of 17 December 1996 in *Saunders v. the United Kingdom* (Reports of Judgments and

Decisions 1996-VI, p. 2044) and of 3 May 2001 in *J.B. v. Switzerland* (not yet published in the Reports of Judgments and Decisions).

However, both the *Orkem* judgment and the recent case-law of the European Court of Human Rights require, first, the exercise of coercion against the suspect in order to obtain information from him and, second, establishment of the existence of an actual interference with the right which they define.

Examined in the light of that finding and the specific circumstances of the present case, the ground of appeal alleging infringement of the privilege against self-incrimination does not permit annulment of the contested judgment on the basis of the developments in the case-law of the European Court of Human Rights.

CoJ 15 October 2002 (Limburgse Vinyl Maatschappij and others v. Commission, Joined cases C-238/99 P, C-244/99 P, C-245/99 P, C-247/99 P, C-250–252/99 P and C-254/99 P) [2002] ECR I-8375, paras 273–276.

25.43   As regards the Commission's powers to make such requests [to provide information pursuant to Article 11(1) Regulation No. 17, currently Article 18(1) Regulation No. 1/2003], it is important to note that, in paragraph 27 of the judgment in *Orkem v. Commission*, the Court pointed out that Regulation No 17 does not give an undertaking which is being investigated under that regulation any right to evade the investigation and that, on the contrary, the undertaking in question is subject to an obligation to cooperate actively, which implies that it must make available to the Commission all information relating to the subject-matter of the investigation.

So far as concerns the question whether that obligation also applies to requests for information which could be used to establish, against the undertaking which provides the information, an infringement of the competition rules, the Court held, in paragraph 34 of that judgment that in order to ensure the effectiveness of Article 11(2) and (5) of Regulation No 17 the Commission is entitled to compel an undertaking, if necessary by adopting a decision, to provide all necessary information concerning such facts as may be known to it and to disclose to it, if necessary, such documents relating thereto as are in that undertaking's possession, even if the latter may be used to establish, against it or another undertaking, the existence of anti-competitive conduct.

By contrast, the situation is completely different where the Commission seeks to obtain answers from an undertaking, which is being investigated, by which that undertaking would be led to admit an infringement which it is incumbent upon the Commission to prove (see *Orkem v. Commission*, para. 35).

It must be added that the Court of Justice, in paragraphs 274–276 of the judgment in *Limburgse Vinyl Maatschappij and others v. Commission*, observed that since the judgment in *Orkem v. Commission* there have been further developments in the case-law of the European Court of Human Rights which the Community judicature must take into account when interpreting the fundamental rights. The Court of Justice stated however in that regard that those developments were not such as to put in question the statements of principle in *Orkem v. Commission*.

It does not follow from that case-law that the Commission's powers of investigation have been limited as regards the production of documents in the possession of an undertaking which is subject to investigation. The undertaking concerned must therefore, if the Commission requests it, provide the Commission with documents which relate to the subject-matter of the investigation, even if those documents could be used by the Commission in order to establish the existence of an infringement. [...]

That obligation to cooperate means that the undertaking may not evade requests for production of documents on the ground that by complying with them it would be required to give evidence against itself.

In addition, [...] while it is evident that the rights of the defence should be respected, the undertaking concerned is still able, either during the administrative procedure or in the proceedings before the Community courts, to contend that the documents produced have a different meaning from that ascribed to them by the Commission.

CoJ 29 June 2006 (Commission v. SGL Carbon and others, C-301/04 P) [2006] ECR I-5915, paras 40–44 and 48–49.

6. Inferences which may be drawn from the exercise of the right to remain silent

[...] What is at stake in the present case is whether these immunities are absolute in the **25.44** sense that the exercise by an accused of the right to silence cannot under any circumstances be used against him at trial or, alternatively, whether informing him in advance that, under certain conditions, his silence may be so used, is always to be regarded as 'improper compulsion'.

On the one hand, it is self-evident that it is incompatible with the immunities under consideration to base a conviction solely or mainly on the accused's silence or on a refusal to answer questions or to give evidence himself. On the other hand, the Court deems it equally obvious that these immunities cannot and should not prevent that the accused's silence, in situations which clearly call for an explanation from him, be taken into account in assessing the persuasiveness of the evidence adduced by the prosecution. Wherever the line between these two extremes is to be drawn, it follows from this understanding of 'the right to silence' that the question whether the right is absolute must be answered in the negative. It cannot be said therefore that an accused's decision to remain silent throughout criminal proceedings should necessarily have no implications when the trial court seeks to evaluate the evidence against him. In particular, as the Government have pointed out, established international standards in this area, while providing for the right to silence and the privilege against self-incrimination, are silent on this point. Whether the drawing of adverse inferences from an accused's silence infringes Article 6 is a matter to be determined in the light of all the circumstances of the case, having particular regard to the situations where inferences may be drawn, the weight attached to them by the national courts in their assessment of the evidence and the degree of compulsion inherent in the situation.

As regards the degree of compulsion involved in the present case, it is recalled that the applicant was in fact able to remain silent. Notwithstanding the repeated warnings as to the possibility that inferences might be drawn from his silence, he did not make any statements to the police and did not give evidence during his trial. Moreover, [...] his insistence in maintaining silence throughout the proceedings did not amount to a criminal offence or contempt of court. Furthermore, as has been stressed in national court decisions, silence, in itself, cannot be regarded as an indication of guilt [...].

Eur. Court H.R. 8 February 1996 (John Murray v. the United Kingdom, no 18731/91), ECHR Reports 1996–I, paras 46 et seq.

25.45 It is true [...] that legal presumptions are not in principle incompatible with Article 6 (see for instance the *Salabiaku v. France* judgment of 7 October 1988, Series A no 141-A, pp. 15–16, § 28); nor is the drawing of inferences from the accused's silence (see the *John Murray* judgment, [...], pp. 49–52, §§ 45–54).

However, the present case does not concern the application of a legal presumption of fact or law, nor is the Court convinced by the Government's argument that the domestic courts could legitimately draw inferences from the applicants' silence. The Court recalls that the above-mentioned *John Murray* judgment concerned a case in which the law allowed for the drawing of common-sense inferences from the accused's silence, where the prosecution had established a case against him, which called for an explanation. Considering that the evidence adduced at the trial constituted a formidable case against the applicant, the Court found that the drawing of such inferences, which was moreover subject to important procedural safeguards, did not violate Article 6 in the circumstances of the case (ibid.). The Court considers that the drawing of inferences from an accused's silence may also be permissible in a system like the Austrian one where the courts freely evaluate the evidence before them, provided that the evidence adduced is such that the only common-sense inference to be drawn from the accused's silence is that he had no answer to the case against him.

Eur. Court H.R. 20 March 2001 (Telfner v. Austria, no 33501/96), ECHR Reports 2001–V, paras 16 and 17.

E. OBLIGATION TO MENTION THE PRIVILEGE AGAINST SELF-INCRIMINATION AND THE RIGHT TO REMAIN SILENT

25.46 Concerning the privilege against self-incrimination and the right to remain silent, the Court has already held that the circumstances of the case disclosed the existence of a suspicion of theft against the applicant after he had failed to prove the fuel purchase. [...] The Convention is intended to guarantee rights that are practical and effective (see *Airey v. Ireland*, 9 October 1979, § 24, Series A no 32). The Court considers that in the circumstances of the case it was incumbent on the police to inform the applicant of the privilege against self-incrimination and the right to remain silent.

Eur. Court H.R. 18 February 2010 (Zaichenko v. Russia, no 39660/02), para. 52.

F. ACCESS TO LEGAL ASSISTANCE AND LEGAL AID

Please refer to Sections K and L of Chapter 24 on Article 47 Charter.

26

ARTICLE 49 CHARTER[*]

PRINCIPLES OF LEGALITY AND PROPORTIONALITY OF CRIMINAL OFFENCES AND PENALTIES

1. No one shall be held guilty of any criminal offence on account of any act or omission which did not constitute a criminal offence under national law or international law at the time when it was committed. Nor shall a heavier penalty be imposed than the one that was applicable at the time the criminal offence was committed. If, subsequent to the commission of a criminal offence, the law provides for a lighter penalty, that penalty shall be applicable.
2. This Article shall not prejudice the trial and punishment of any person for any act or omission which, at the time when it was committed, was criminal according to the general principles recognised by the community of nations.
3. The severity of penalties must not be disproportionate to the criminal offence.

ARTICLE 7 (ECHR) – NO PUNISHMENT WITHOUT PRIOR LAW

1. No one shall be held guilty of any criminal offence on account of any act or omission which did not constitute a criminal offence under national or international law at the time when it was committed. Nor shall a heavier penalty be imposed than the one that was applicable at the time the criminal offence was committed.
2. This Article shall not prejudice the trial and punishment of any person for any act or omission which, at the time when it was committed, was criminal according to the general principles of law recognised by civilised nations.

---

[*] This chapter was written by Herman Speyart.

OVERVIEW

A. EXPLANATION RELATING TO ARTICLE 49 CHARTER	(p.858)	1. Eur. Court H.R.	26.11
		2. EU Courts	26.12
B. LEGALITY PRINCIPLE	26.01	F. FORESEEABILITY	26.13
1. Eur. Court H.R.	26.01	1. Eur. Court H.R.	26.13
2. EU Courts	26.05	2. EU Courts	26.15
C. CONCEPT OF 'PENALTY'	26.08	G. PROPORTIONALITY	26.19
D. NON-RETROACTIVITY OF CRIMINAL SANCTIONS	26.09	H. PRINCIPLE OF PERSONAL LIABILITY	26.24
E. RETROACTIVITY OF THE MORE LENIENT SANCTION	26.11		

A. EXPLANATION RELATING TO ARTICLE 49 CHARTER

This Article follows the traditional rule of the non-retroactivity of laws and criminal sanctions. There has been added the rule of the retroactivity of a more lenient penal law, which exists in a number of Member States and which features in Article 15 of the Covenant on Civil and Political Rights.

Article 7 of the ECHR is worded as follows […].

In paragraph 2, the reference to 'civilised' nations has been deleted; this does not change the meaning of this paragraph, which refers to crimes against humanity in particular. In accordance with Article 52(3), the right guaranteed here therefore has the same meaning and scope as the right guaranteed by the ECHR.

Paragraph 3 states the general principle of proportionality between penalties and criminal offences which is enshrined in the common constitutional traditions of the Member States and in the case-law of the Court of Justice of the Communities.

B. LEGALITY PRINCIPLE

1. Eur. Court H.R.

26.01   The guarantee enshrined in Article 7, which is an essential element of the rule of law, occupies a prominent place in the Convention system of protection, as is underlined by the fact that no derogation from it is permissible under Article 15 in time of war or other public emergency. It should be construed and applied, as follows from its object and purpose, in such a way as to provide effective safeguards against arbitrary prosecution, conviction and punishment.

Accordingly […], Article 7 is not confined to prohibiting the retrospective application of the criminal law to an accused's disadvantage: it also embodies, more generally, the principle that only the law can define a crime and prescribe a penalty (nullum crimen, nulla poena sine lege) and the principle that the criminal law must not be extensively construed to an accused's detriment, for instance by analogy. From these principles it follows that an offence must be clearly defined in the law. [T]his requirement is satisfied where the individual can know from the wording of the relevant provision and, if need be, with the assistance of the courts' interpretation of it, what acts and omissions will make him criminally liable.

Eur. Court H.R. 22 November 1995 (S.W. v. the United Kingdom), Series A no 335-B, p. 41, paras 34 and 35.

See also Eur. Court H.R. 22 November 1995 (C.R. v. the United Kingdom), Series A no 335-C, p. 68, paras 32–34; Eur. Court H.R. 22 June 2000 (Coëme and others v. Belgium, nos. 32492/96, 32547/96, 32548/96, 33209/ 96 and 33210/96), ECHR Reports 2000-VII, para. 145; Eur. Court H.R. (Grand Chamber) 12 February 2008 (Kafkaris v. Cyprus, no 21906/04), paras 137–138, 140; Eur. Court H.R. (Grand Chamber) 17 September 2009 (Scoppola v. Italy, no. 10249/03), unreported, paras 92 and 93.

26.02 However clearly drafted a legal provision may be, in any system of law, including criminal law, there is an inevitable element of judicial interpretation. There will always be a need for elucidation of doubtful points and for adaptation to changing circumstances. Indeed, in […] the […] Convention States, the progressive development of the criminal law through judicial law making is a well-entrenched and necessary part of legal tradition. Article 7 of the Convention cannot be read as outlawing the gradual clarification of the rules of criminal liability through judicial interpretation from case to case, provided that the resultant development is consistent with the essence of the offence and could reasonably be foreseen.

Eur. Court H.R. 22 November 1995 (S.W. v. the United Kingdom), Series A no 335-B, p. 41, para. 35.

26.03 [W]hen speaking of 'law' Article 7 alludes to the very same concept as that to which the Convention refers elsewhere when using that term, a concept which comprises [statute law as well as case-law] [written as well as unwritten law] and implies qualitative requirements, notably those of accessibility and foresee ability […]. In this connection, the Court has always understood the term 'law' in its 'substantive' sense, not its 'formal' one. It has thus included both enactments of lower rank than statutes and unwritten law. In sum, the 'law' is the provision in force as the competent courts have interpreted it.

Eur. Court H.R. 22 June 2000 (Coëme and others v. Belgium, nos. 32492/96, 32547/96, 32548/96, 33209/ 96 and 33210/96), ECHR Reports 2000-VII, para. 145.

See also Eur. Court H.R. (Grand Chamber) 12 February 2008 (Kafkaris v. Cyprus, no 21906/04), para. 139.

26.04   Again, whilst certainty is highly desirable, it may bring in its train excessive rigidity and the law must be able to keep pace with changing circumstances. Accordingly, many laws are inevitably couched in terms which, to a greater or lesser extent, are vague and whose interpretation and application are questions of practice […]. The role of adjudication vested in the courts is precisely to dissipate such interpretational doubts as remain […]. Article 7 of the Convention cannot be read as outlawing the gradual clarification of the rules of criminal liability through judicial interpretation from case to case, 'provided that the resultant development is consistent with the essence of the offence and could reasonably be foreseen' […].

Eur. Court H.R. (Grand Chamber) 12 February 2008 (Kafkaris v. Cyprus, no 21906/04), para. 141.

2. EU Courts

26.05   [L]e principe de légalité des peines, qui fait partie des principes généraux du droit communautaire se trouvant à la base des traditions constitutionnelles communes aux États membres, a également été consacré par différents traités internationaux, et notamment à l'article 7 de la CEDH.

Ce principe exige que la loi définisse clairement les infractions et les peines qui les répriment. Cette condition se trouve remplie lorsque le justiciable peut savoir, à partir du libellé de la disposition pertinente et au besoin à l'aide de l'interprétation qui en est donnée par les tribunaux, quels actes et omissions engagent sa responsabilité pénale.

En outre, selon la jurisprudence de la Cour européenne des droits de l'homme, la clarté de la loi s'apprécie au regard non seulement du libellé de la disposition pertinente, mais également des précisions apportées par une jurisprudence constante et publiée. À cet égard, la Cour a reconnu qu'il découle de cette jurisprudence que la notion de 'droit' au sens de l'article 7, paragraphe 1, de la CEDH correspond à celle de 'loi' utilisée dans d'autres dispositions de la même convention et englobe le droit d'origine tant législative que jurisprudentielle.

CoJ 22 May 2008 (Evonik Degussa, C-266/06 P) [2008] ECR I-81 (summary), paras 38–40.

26.06   [In respect of the fines] Degussa soutient que le Tribunal a, aux points 77 à 82 de l'arrêt attaqué, méconnu le fait que ni les lignes directrices, ni la jurisprudence communautaire, ni les principes généraux du droit n'ont suffisamment réduit l'imprécision de l'article 15, paragraphe 2, du règlement n° 17.

Cet argument ne saurait être accueilli. En effet, s'agissant des lignes directrices, la Cour a déjà jugé, ainsi que le Tribunal l'a rappelé au point 82 de l'arrêt attaqué, que celles-ci déterminent, de manière générale et abstraite, la méthodologie que la Commission s'est imposée aux fins de la fixation du montant des amendes infligées en vertu de l'article 15 du règlement n° 17 et assurent, par conséquent, la sécurité juridique des entreprises […].

De même, il ne saurait être contesté que la jurisprudence bien établie de la Cour et du Tribunal a contribué à clarifier les critères et la méthode de calcul que la Commission doit appliquer dans le cadre de la fixation du montant des amendes. À cet égard, les critères dégagés par cette jurisprudence ont, notamment, été empruntés par la Commission pour la rédaction des lignes directrices et permis à celle-ci de développer une pratique décisionnelle connue et accessible.

CoJ 22 May 2008 (Evonik Degussa, C-266/06 P) [2008] ECR I-81 (summary), paras 59–61.

In paragraph 96 of the judgment under appeal, the General Court, without committing **26.07** an error of law, recalled that the principle of legality requires legislation to define clearly offences and the penalties which they attract (*Case C-413/08 P Lafarge v Commission* [2010] ECR I-5361, para. 94). In paragraph 99 of that judgment, it likewise did not commit an error of law in recalling the criteria for assessing the clarity of the law under the case-law of the European Court of Human Rights, namely that the clarity of a law is assessed having regard not only to the wording of the relevant provision but also to the clarification provided by settled, published case-law (see, to this effect, the judgment of the European Court of Human Rights in *G. v. France*, 27 September 1995, § 25, Series A no 325-B) and that the fact that a law confers a discretion is not in itself inconsistent with the requirement of foreseeability, provided that the scope of the discretion and the manner of its exercise are indicated with sufficient clarity, having regard to the legitimate aim in question, to give the individual adequate protection against arbitrary interference (judgment of the European Court of Human Rights in *Margareta and Roger Andersson v. Sweden*, 25 February 1992, § 75, Series A no 226-A).

According to the case-law of the Court of Justice, although Article 23(2) of Regulation No 1/2003 leaves the Commission a discretion, it nevertheless limits the exercise of that discretion by establishing objective criteria to which the Commission must adhere. Thus, first, the amount of the fine that may be imposed on an undertaking is subject to a quantifiable and absolute ceiling, so that the maximum amount of the fine that can be imposed on a given undertaking can be determined in advance. Second, the exercise of that discretion is also limited by rules of conduct which the Commission imposed on itself in the 2002 Leniency Notice and the 1998 Guidelines. Furthermore, the Commission's well-known and accessible administrative practice is subject to unlimited review by the European Union judicature, whose settled case-law has enabled the concepts that Article 23(2) might contain to be defined. A prudent trader, if need be by taking legal advice, can thus foresee in a sufficiently precise manner the method of calculation and order of magnitude of the fines which he incurs for a given line of conduct, and the fact that that trader cannot know in advance precisely the level of the fines which the Commission will impose in each individual case cannot constitute a breach of the principle that penalties must have a proper legal basis (see also, to this effect, the judgment of 22 May 2008 in *Case C-266/06 P Evonik Degussa v Commission and Council*, paras 50–55).

Having regard to these factors, it must be held that the General Court did not commit an error of law when it examined the Commission's discretion in the light, in particular, of the objective criteria, the general principles of law and the 1998 Guidelines to which the Commission must adhere and concluded, in paragraph 116 of the judgment under appeal, that the objection that Article 23(2) of Regulation No 1/2003 is unlawful in that it breaches the principle that penalties must have a proper legal basis had to be rejected.

CoJ 18 July 2013 (Schindler v. Commission, C-501/11 P), ECLI:EU:C:2013:522, paras 57–59.

C. CONCEPT OF 'PENALTY'

26.08   The concept of 'penalty' in Article 7 is, like the notions of 'civil right and obligations' and 'criminal charge' in Article 6(1) of the Convention, autonomous in scope. To render the protection afforded by Article 7 effective, the Court must remain free to go behind appearances and assess for itself whether a particular measure amounts in substance to a 'penalty' within the meaning of this provision [...]. The wording of Article 7(1), second sentence, indicates that the starting-point in any assessment of the existence of a penalty is whether the measure in question is imposed following conviction for a 'criminal offence'. Other factors that may be taken into account as relevant in this connection are the nature and purpose of the measure in question; its characterisation under national law; the procedures involved in the making and implementation of the measure; and its severity [...].

Eur. Court H.R. (Grand Chamber) 12 February 2008 (Kafkaris v. Cyprus, no 21906/04), para. 142.

D. NON-RETROACTIVITY OF CRIMINAL SANCTIONS

26.09   Although [Article 7(1) ECHR], which enshrines in particular the principle that offences and punishments are to be strictly defined by law (nullum crimen, nulla poena sine lege), cannot be interpreted as precluding the gradual clarification of the rules of criminal liability, it may preclude the retroactive application of a new interpretation of a rule establishing an offence.

That is particularly true [...] of a judicial interpretation which produces a result which was not reasonably foreseeable at the time when the offence was committed, especially in the light of the interpretation put on the provision in the case-law at the material time.

CoJ 28 June 2005 (Dansk Rørindustrie and Others v. Commission, Joined Cases C-189/02 P, C-202/02 P, C-205–208/02 P and C-213/02 P) [2005] ECR I-5425, paras 217 and 218.

See also CoJ 8 February 2007 (Groupe Danone v. Commission, C-3/06 P) [2007] ECR I-1331, paras 87–92.

26.10   As the Court of Justice held in paragraphs 207 and 208 of *Dansk Rørindustri and Others v. Commission*, the premiss of the [General Court] that the Guidelines do not form part of the legal framework that determines the amount of fines, which consists exclusively of Article 15 of Regulation No 17, so that the application of the Guidelines to infringements committed before they were adopted cannot run counter to the principle of non-retroactivity, is incorrect.

A change in an enforcement policy, in this instance the Commission's general competition policy in the matter of fines, especially where it comes about as a result of the adoption of rules of conduct such as the Guidelines, may have an impact from the aspect of the principle of non-retroactivity.

However, the proper application of the Community competition rules requires that the Commission may at any time adjust the level of fines to the needs of that policy.

It follows that undertakings involved in an administrative procedure in which fines may be imposed cannot acquire a legitimate expectation in the fact that the Commission will not exceed the level of fines previously imposed or in a method of calculating the fines.

Consequently, in the present case, the undertakings must take account of the possibility that the Commission may decide at any time to raise the level of the fines by reference to that applied in the past.

That is true not only where the Commission raises the level of the amount of fines in imposing fines in individual decisions but also if that increase takes effect by the application, in particular cases, of rules of conduct of general application, such as the Guidelines.

As in the *Dansk Rørindustri and Others v. Commission* case, it must be concluded that the Guidelines and, in particular, the new method of calculating fines contained therein, on the assumption that this new method had the effect of increasing the level of the fines imposed, were reasonably foreseeable for undertakings such as the appellants at the time when the infringements concerned were committed and that, in applying the Guidelines in the contested decision to infringements committed before they were adopted, the Commission did not breach the principle of non-retroactivity.

Consequently, the [General Court] did not err in law in rejecting the plea of annulment alleging infringement of the principle of non-retroactivity.

CoJ 18 May 2006 (Archer Daniel Midlands v. Commission, C-397/03 P) [2006] ECR I-4429, paras 19–26.

See also CoJ 28 June 2005 (Dansk Rørindustrie and Others v. Commission, Joined Cases C-189/02 P, C-202/02 P, C-205–208/02 P and C-213/02 P) [2005] ECR I-5425, paras 207–208, 222, 227–232; CoJ 8 February 2007 (Groupe Danone v. Commission, C-3/06 P) [2007] ECR I-1331, paras 87–92; CoJ 18 July 2013 (Schindler v. Commission, C-501/11 P), ECLI:EU:C:2013:522, para. 75.

E. RETROACTIVITY OF THE MORE LENIENT SANCTION

1. Eur. Court H.R.

In 1978 the European Commission of Human Rights expressed the opinion that, **26.11** unlike Article 15(1) in fine of the United Nations Covenant on Civil and Political Rights, Article 7 of the Convention did not guarantee the right to a more lenient penalty provided for in a law subsequent to the offence (see *X v. Germany*, no. 7900/77, Commission decision of 6 March 1978, Decisions and Reports (DR) 13, pp. 70–72). It accordingly declared manifestly ill-founded the complaint of an applicant who alleged that, after their commission, some of the offences he had been charged with had been decriminalised. That ruling has been repeated by the Court, which has reiterated that Article 7 does not afford the right of an offender to application of a more favourable criminal law [...]. [...]

The Court considers that a long time has elapsed since the Commission gave the above-mentioned *X v. Germany* decision and that during that time there have been important developments internationally. In particular, apart from the entry into force of the American Convention on Human Rights, Article 9 of which guarantees the retrospective effect of a law providing for a more lenient penalty enacted after the commission of the relevant offence [...], mention should be made of the proclamation of the European Union's Charter of Fundamental Rights. The wording of Article 49(1) of the Charter differs – and this can only be deliberate (see, mutatis mutandis, Christine Goodwin [...] § 100 in fine) – from that of Article 7 of the Convention in that it states: 'If, subsequent to the commission of a criminal offence, the law provides for a lighter penalty, that penalty shall be applicable' (see para. 37 above). In the case of *Berlusconi and Others*, the Court of Justice of the European Communities, whose ruling was endorsed by the French Court of Cassation [...], held that this principle formed part of the constitutional traditions common to the member States [...]. Lastly, the applicability of the more lenient criminal law was set forth in the statute of the International Criminal Court and affirmed in the case-law of the ICTY [...].

The Court therefore concludes that since the *X v. Germany* decision a consensus has gradually emerged in Europe and internationally around the view that application of a criminal law providing for a more lenient penalty, even one enacted after the commission of the offence, has become a fundamental principle of criminal law. It is also significant that the legislation of the respondent State had recognised that principle since 1930 (see Article 2 § 3 of the Criminal Code [...]).

Admittedly, Article 7 of the Convention does not expressly mention an obligation for Contracting States to grant an accused the benefit of a change in the law subsequent to the commission of the offence. It was precisely on the basis of that argument relating to the wording of the Convention that the Commission rejected the applicant's complaint in the case of *X v. Germany*. However, taking into account the developments mentioned above, the Court cannot regard that argument as decisive. Moreover, it observes that in prohibiting the imposition of 'a heavier penalty ... than the one that was applicable at the time the criminal offence was committed', paragraph 1 in fine of Article 7 does not exclude granting the accused the benefit of a more lenient sentence, prescribed by legislation subsequent to the offence.

In the Court's opinion, it is consistent with the principle of the rule of law, of which Article 7 forms an essential part, to expect a trial court to apply to each punishable act the penalty which the legislator considers proportionate. Inflicting a heavier penalty for the sole reason that it was prescribed at the time of the commission of the offence would mean applying to the defendant's detriment the rules governing the succession of criminal laws in time. In addition, it would amount to disregarding any legislative change favourable to the accused which might have come in before the conviction and continuing to impose penalties which the State – and the community it represents – now consider excessive. The Court notes that the obligation to apply, from among several criminal laws, the one whose provisions are the most favourable to the accused is a clarification of the rules on the succession of criminal laws, which is in accord with another essential element of Article 7, namely the foreseeability of penalties.

In the light of the foregoing considerations, the Court takes the view that it is necessary to depart from the case-law established by the Commission in the case of *X v. Germany* and affirm that Article 7(1) of the Convention guarantees not only the principle of non-retrospectiveness of more stringent criminal laws but also, and implicitly, the principle of retrospectiveness of the more lenient criminal law. That principle is embodied in the rule that where there are differences between the criminal law in force at the time of the commission of the offence and subsequent criminal laws enacted before a final judgment is rendered, the courts must apply the law whose provisions are most favourable to the defendant.

Eur. Court H.R. (Grand Chamber) 17 September 2009 (Scoppola v. Italy, no. 10249/03), unreported, paras 103 and 105–109.

2. EU Courts

[T]he principle of the retroactive application of the more lenient penalty forms part of **26.12** the constitutional traditions common to the Member States and, accordingly, must be considered to be one of the general principles of Community law, which the Court ensures are respected and which national courts are required to abide by [...].

CoJ 11 March 2008 (Jager, C–420/06) [2008] ECR I–1315, para. 59.

See also CoJ 3 May 2005 (Berlusconi a.o., Joined Cases C–387/02, C–391/02 and C–403/02) [2005] ECR I–3565, paras 67 and 68; CoJ 14 February 2012 (Toshiba Corporation and Others v. Úřad pro ochranu hospodářské soutěže, C–17/10), ECLI:EU:C:2012:72, para. 64.

F. FORESEEABILITY

1. Eur. Court H.R.

[I]t follows [from the Legality Principle] that an offence must be clearly defined by law. **26.13** This condition is satisfied where the individual can know from the wording of the relevant provision and, if need be, with the assistance of the courts' interpretation of it, what acts and omissions will make him liable.

Eur. Court H.R. 25 May 1993 (Kokkinakis v. Greece, no. 14307/88), Series A no. 260-A, para. 52.

See also Eur. Court H.R. (Grand Chamber) 17 September 2009 (Scoppola v. Italy, no. 10249/03), unreported, para. 94.

When speaking of 'law' Article 7 alludes to the very same concept as that to which the **26.14** Convention refers elsewhere when using that term, a concept which comprises statute law as well as case-law and implies qualitative requirements, including those of accessibility and foreseeability [...].

In consequence of the principle that laws must be of general application, the wording of statutes is not always precise. One of the standard techniques of regulation by rules is to use general categorisations as opposed to exhaustive lists. That means that many laws are inevitably couched in terms which, to a greater or lesser extent are vague, and their interpretation and application depend on practice [...]. Consequently, in any system of law, however clearly drafted a legal provision may be, including a criminal law provision, there is an inevitable element of judicial interpretation. There will always be a need for elucidation of doubtful points and for adaptation to changing circumstances. Again, whilst certainty is highly desirable, it may bring in its train excessive rigidity and the law must be able to keep pace with changing circumstances.

The role of adjudication vested in the courts is precisely to dissipate such interpretational doubts as remain [...]. Moreover, it is a firmly established part of the legal tradition of the States party to the Convention that case-law, as one of the sources of the law, necessarily contributes to the gradual development of the criminal law [...]. Article 7 of the Convention cannot be read as outlawing the gradual clarification of the rules of criminal liability through judicial interpretation from case to case, provided that the resultant development is consistent with the essence of the offence and could reasonably be foreseen [...].

Foreseeability depends to a considerable degree on the content of the law concerned, the field it is designed to cover and the number and status of those to whom it is addressed. A law may still satisfy the requirement of "foreseeability" where the person concerned has to take appropriate legal advice to assess, to a degree that is reasonable in the circumstances, the consequences which a given action may entail [...].

Eur. Court H.R. (Grand Chamber) 17 September 2009 (Scoppola v. Italy, no. 10249/03), unreported, paras 99–102.

2. EU Courts

26.15   [...] Community legislation must be certain and its application foreseeable by those subject to it.

CoJ 15 December 1987 (Ireland v. Commission, 325/85) [1987] ECR 5041, para. 18.

26.16   [I]t is appropriate to refer to the case-law of the European Court of Human Rights on Article 7(1) of the ECHR, which, moreover, is cited by a number of the applicants (see, in particular, Eur. Court H.R., *S.W. v. the United Kingdom and C.R. v. the United Kingdom*, judgments of 22 November 1995, Series A Nos 335-B and 335-C, §§ 34 to 36 and §§ 32 to 34; *Cantoni v. France*, judgment of 15 November 1996, Reports of Judgments and Decisions, 1996-V, §§ 29 to 32, and *Coëme and others v. Belgium*, judgment of 22 June 2000, Reports, 2000-VII, § 145).

It follows from that case-law that the concept of 'law' ('droit') for the purposes of Article 7(1) corresponds to 'law' ('loi') used in other provisions of the ECHR and encompasses both law of legislative origin and that deriving from case-law.

Although that provision, which enshrines in particular the principle that offences and punishments are to be strictly defined by law (nullum crimen, nulla poena sine lege), cannot be interpreted as prohibiting the gradual clarification of the rules of criminal liability, it may, according to that case-law, preclude the retroactive application of a new interpretation of a rule establishing an offence.

That is particularly true, according to that case-law, of a judicial interpretation which produces a result which was not reasonably foreseeable at the time when the offence was committed, especially in the light of the interpretation put on the provision in the case-law at the material time.

It follows from that case-law of the European Court of Human Rights that the scope of the notion of foreseeability depends to a considerable degree on the content of the text in issue, the field it is designed to cover and the number and status of those to whom it is addressed. A law may still satisfy the requirement of foreseeability even if the person concerned has to take appropriate legal advice to assess, to a degree that is reasonable in the circumstances, the consequences which a given action may entail. This is particularly true in relation to persons carrying on a professional activity, who are used to having to proceed with a high degree of caution when pursuing their occupation. They can on this account be expected to take special care in assessing the risks that such an activity entails (see *Cantoni v. France*, […], § 35).

Like that case-law on new developments in case-law, a change in an enforcement policy, in this instance the Commission's general competition policy in the matter of fines, especially where it comes about as a result of the adoption of rules of conduct such as the Guidelines, may have an impact from the aspect of the principle of non-retroactivity.

Having particular regard to their legal effects and to their general application, as indicated at paragraph 211 of this judgment, such rules of conduct come, in principle, within the principle of 'law' for the purposes of Article 7(1) of the ECHR.

As stated at paragraph 219 of this judgment, in order to ensure that the principle of non-retroactivity was observed, it is necessary to ascertain whether the change in question was reasonably foreseeable at the time when the infringements concerned were committed.

In that regard, it should be noted that, as a number of the appellants have pointed out, the main innovation in the Guidelines consisted in taking as a starting-point for the calculation a basic amount, determined on the basis of brackets laid down for that purpose by the Guidelines; those brackets reflect the various degrees of gravity of the infringements but, as such, bear no relation to the relevant turnover. The essential feature of that method is thus that fines are determined on a tariff basis, albeit one that is relative and flexible.

It is therefore necessary to consider whether that new method of calculating fines, on the assumption that it has the effect of increasing the level of fines imposed, was reasonably foreseeable at the time when the infringements concerned were committed.

As already stated at paragraph 169 of this judgment in connection with the pleas alleging breach of the principle of protection of legitimate expectations, it follows from the case-law of the Court that the fact that the Commission, in the past, imposed fines of a certain level for certain types of infringement does not mean that it is stopped from raising that level within the limits indicated in Regulation No 17 if that is necessary to ensure the implementation of Community competition policy. On the contrary, the proper application of the Community competition rules requires that the Commission may at any time adjust the level of fines to the needs of that policy.

It follows, as already held at paragraph 173 of this judgment, that undertakings involved in an administrative procedure in which fines may be imposed cannot acquire a legitimate expectation in the fact that the Commission will not exceed the level of fines previously imposed or in a method of calculating the fines.

Consequently, the undertakings in question must take account of the possibility that the Commission may decide at any time to raise the level of the fines by reference to that applied in the past.

That is true not only where the Commission raises the level of the amount of fines in imposing fines in individual decisions but also if that increase takes effect by the application, in particular cases, of rules of conduct of general application, such as the Guidelines.

It must be concluded that, particularly in the light of the case-law cited at paragraph 219 of this judgment, the Guidelines and, in particular, the new method of calculating fines contained therein, on the assumption that this new method had the effect of increasing the level of the fines imposed, were reasonably foreseeable for undertakings such as the appellants at the time when the infringements concerned were committed.

Accordingly, in applying the Guidelines in the contested decision to infringements committed before they were adopted, the Commission did not breach the principle of non-retroactivity.

CoJ 28 June 2005 (Dansk Rørindustrie a.o. v. Commission, Joined Cases C-189/02 P, C-202/02 P, C-205–208/02 P and C-213/02 P) [2005] ECR I-5425, paras 215–232.

26.17   [S]uffice it to observe that Article 7(1) of the ECHR does not require the terms of the provisions by virtue of which those fines are imposed to be so precise that the potential consequences of an infringement of those provisions should be foreseeable with absolute certainty.

According to the settled case-law of the European Court of Human Rights, the existence of vague terms in a provision does not necessarily entail a violation of Article 7 of the ECHR. [...] The fact that a law confers a discretion is not in itself inconsistent with the requirement of foreseeability, provided that the scope of the discretion and the manner of its exercise are indicated with sufficient clarity, having regard to the legitimate aim in question, to give the individual adequate protection against arbitrary interference (see European Court of Human Rights, *Margareta and Roger Andersson v. Sweden*, judgment of 25 February 1992, Series A no 226-A, § 75). Finally, the European Court of Human Rights states that, in addition to the actual wording of the law, it takes account of the settled and published case-law when deciding whether the concepts used are definite or not (see European Court of Human Rights, *G. v. France*, judgment of 27 September 1995, Series A no 325-B, § 25, and *E.K. v. Turkey*, no 28496/95, 7 February 2002, § 51).

General Court 27 September 2006 (Jungbunzlauer v. Commission, T-43/02) [2006] ECR II-3435, paras 79 and 80.

See also General Court 5 April 2006 (Degussa v. Commission, T 279/02) [2006] ECR II–897, paras 66 et seq.

Generally speaking, that principle [nullum crimen, nulla poena sine lege] requires, inter **26.18** alia, that any Community legislation, in particular where it imposes or permits the imposition of penalties, must be clear and precise so that the persons concerned may know without ambiguity what rights and obligations flow from it and may take steps accordingly. By the same token, that principle must be observed in regard both to provisions of a criminal-law nature and to specific administrative instruments imposing or permitting the imposition of administrative penalties [...], such as penalties imposed under Regulation No 17.

In addition, it is apparent from the consistent interpretation which the Eur. Court H. R. has given to Article 7(1) of the ECHR that the principle of nullum crimen, nulla poena sine lege, which is laid down therein, requires, inter alia, that criminal law not be applied broadly, in particular by analogy, to the detriment of the defendant. It follows that an infringement must be clearly defined by the law, a condition which is satisfied where the individual can know from the wording of the relevant provision – and, if need be, with the assistance of the courts' interpretation – what acts or omissions would make him criminally liable. In that regard, the Eur. Court H. R. has stated that the concept of law used in Article 7 of the ECHR is the same as that to be found in other articles thereof and that it encompasses both law deriving from legislation and that deriving from case-law, and implies qualitative conditions, in particular those of accessibility and foresee ability (see Eur. Court H. R. *Kokkinakis v. Greece*, judgment of 25 May 1993, Series A no 260-A, § 40, 41 and 52; *S.W. v. the United Kingdom*, [...], § 35; *Cantoni v. France*, judgment of 15 November 1996, Reports of Judgments and Decisions, 1996-V, p. 1627, § 29; *Baokaya and Okçuoglu v. Turkey*, judgment of 8 July 1999, Reports of Judgments and Decisions, 1999-IV, p. 308, § 36; *Coëme and others v. Belgium*, judgment of 22 June 2000, Reports of Judgments and Decisions, 2000-VII, p. 1, § 145; *E.K. v. Turkey*, no 28496/95, § 51, 7 February 2002; see also *Dansk Rørindustrie and others v. Commission*, [...], para. 216).

In the light of that case-law, the principle of nullum crimen, nulla poena sine lege cannot be interpreted as prohibiting the gradual clarification of the rules of criminal liability through interpretation by the courts [...]. According to the case-law of the Eur. Court H. R., however clearly a legal provision is drafted, including a provision of criminal law, there is inevitably a need for interpretation by the courts and it will always be necessary to elucidate points of doubt and to adapt the wording to changing circumstances. Moreover, according to the Eur. Court H. R., it is well established in the legal traditions of the contracting parties to the ECHR that case-law, as a source of law, necessarily contributes to the progressive development of the criminal law [...]. In that regard, the Eur. Court H. R. has recognised that even the wording of many statutes is not absolutely precise and that, because of the need to avoid excessive rigidity and to keep pace with changing circumstances, much legislation is inevitably couched in terms which, to a greater or lesser degree, are vague and their interpretation and application depend on practice [...]. Thus, in addition to the actual wording of the legislation, the Eur. Court H. R. also takes account of the settled and published case-law when deciding whether the concepts used are definite or not (*G. v. France*, judgment of 27 September 1995, Series A no 325-B, § 25).

Nevertheless, although the principle of nullum crimen, nulla poena sine lege in principle enables the rules governing criminal liability to be gradually clarified through interpretation by the courts, it may preclude the retroactive application of a new interpretation of a rule establishing an offence. That is particularly true if the result of that interpretation was not reasonably foreseeable at the time when the offence was committed, especially in the light of the interpretation attributed to the provision in the case-law at the material time. Furthermore, the notion of foreseeability depends to a considerable degree on the content of the text in issue, the field it is designed to cover and the number and status of those to whom it applies, and does not preclude the person concerned from taking appropriate legal advice to assess, to a degree that is reasonable in the circumstances, the consequences which a given action may entail. This is particularly true in the case of persons engaged in a professional activity, who are used to having to proceed with a high degree of caution when pursuing their occupation. They can thus be expected to take special care in assessing the risks that such an activity entails [...].

General Court 8 July 2008 (Treuhand v. Commission, T-99/04) [2008] ECR II-1501, paras 139–142.

G. PROPORTIONALITY

Please refer to the case extracts in Chapter 13 on Article 23, Section C.7. Regulation 1/2003 (paras 13.146–13.158).

26.19   Under the terms of Article 15(2) of Regulation No 17, the Commission may impose fines of from 1 000 to 1 000 000 units of account or a sum in excess thereof but not exceeding 10 per cent of the turnover in the preceding business year of each of the undertakings participating in the infringement. Article 15 (2) provides that in fixing the amount of the fine within those limits the gravity and the duration of the infringement are to be taken into consideration.

Thus the only express reference to the turnover of the undertaking concerns the upper limit of a fine exceeding 1 000 000 units of account. In such a case the limit seeks to prevent fines from being disproportionate in relation to the size of the undertaking and, since only the total turnover can effectively give an approximate indication of that size, the aforementioned percentage must, as the Commission has argued, be understood as referring to the total turnover. [...]

CoJ 7 June 1983 (Musique Diffusion française and Others v Commission, Joined Cases 100/80 to 103/80) [1983] ECR 1825, paras 118 and 119.

26.20   [T]he principle of proportionality requires that measures implemented through Community provisions should be appropriate for attaining the objective pursued and must not go beyond what is necessary to achieve it.

CoJ 14 December 2004 (Arnold André, C-434/02) [2004] ECR I-11825, para. 45.

[...] In the exercise of its unlimited jurisdiction, the Court must consider whether **26.21** the amount of the fine imposed is proportionate to the gravity and duration of the infringement [...] and must weigh the seriousness of the infringement with the circumstances invoked by the applicant [...].

[I]t is settled case-law that the gravity of infringements has to be determined by reference to numerous factors, such as, in particular, the actual circumstances of the case, its context and the deterrent effect of fines; moreover, no binding or exhaustive list of the criteria which must be applied has been drawn up [...]. In particular, the gravity of the infringement is to be appraised by taking into account the nature of the restrictions on competition [...]. The Commission must also have regard to the deterrent effect of its action, especially as regards those types of infringement which are particularly harmful to the attainment of the objectives of the Community [...].

General Court 25 October 2005 (Groupe Danone v. Commission, T-38/02) [2005] ECR II-4407, para. 136 and 137.

[I]t is permissible, for the purpose of fixing the fine, to have regard both to the total **26.22** turnover of the undertaking, which gives an indication, albeit approximate and imperfect, of the size of the undertaking and of its economic power, and to the proportion of that turnover accounted for by the goods in respect of which the infringement was committed, which gives an indication of the scale of the infringement. It is important not to confer on one or the other of those figures an importance disproportionate in relation to the other factors and, consequently, that the fixing of an appropriate fine cannot be the result of a simple calculation based on the total turnover. That is particularly the case where the goods concerned account for only a small part of that figure.

By contrast, Community law contains no general principle that the penalty be proportionate to the undertaking's size on the product market in respect of which the infringement was committed.

CoJ 18 May 2006 (Archer Daniel Midlands v. Commission, C-397/03 P) [2006] ECR I-4429, paras 100 and 101.

It is only in so far as the Court of Justice considers that the level of the penalty is not **26.23** merely inappropriate, but also excessive to the point of being disproportionate, that it would have to find that the General Court erred in law, due to the inappropriateness of the amount of a fine (*Case C-89/11P E.ON Energie v Commission* ECLI: EU:C:2012:738, para. 126).

In this instance, the General Court did not merely verify whether the amount of the fines exceeded the ceiling of 10 per cent of turnover, referred to in the second subparagraph of Article 23(2) of Regulation No 1/2003, but carried out an in-depth examination of the proportionality of the fines in paragraphs 368 to 370 of the judgment under appeal.

As to the criticism of the fact that the turnover of Schindler Holding was taken into account, this is based on an incorrect premiss regarding the legality of the recourse to the concept of an undertaking, as has been demonstrated in responding to the seventh plea.

In so far as the reference to the judgment of the European Court of Human Rights in *Mamidakis v. Greece* is relevant in a competition case involving a commercial company and its subsidiaries and not a natural person, it is to be pointed out that, as the Advocate General has observed in point 214 of her Opinion, it is not possible to assess whether a fine entails a disproportionate burden for the person upon whom it is imposed solely on the basis of its nominal amount. That is also dependent, in particular, on the person's ability to pay.

In a situation where fines are imposed on an undertaking which constitutes an economic unit and which is composed only formally of a number of legal persons, those persons' ability to pay cannot be taken into consideration individually. In this context, the General Court was correct in holding in paragraph 370 of the judgment under appeal, having regard to gravity of the practices concerned and to the size and economic strength of the Schindler group, that the total amount of the fines imposed on the appellants represents approximately 2 per cent of their aggregated turnover in 2005, which cannot be regarded as disproportionate in relation to the size of the group concerned.

CoJ 18 July 2013 (Schindler v. Commission, C-501/11 P), ECLI:EU:C:2013:522, paras 165–169.

H. PRINCIPLE OF PERSONAL LIABILITY

26.24   In complaining that the Court of First Instance attributed responsibility for the infringement to it although it had transferred its polypropylene business to Monte, Anic is disregarding the principle of personal responsibility and neglecting the decisive factor, identifiable from the case-law of the Court of Justice [...], that the 'economic continuity' test can only apply where the legal person responsible for running the undertaking has ceased to exist in law after the infringement has been committed. It also follows that the application of these tests is not contrary in any way to the principle of legal certainty.

CoJ 8 July 1999 (Commission v. Anic Partecipazioni, C-49/92 P) [1999] ECR I-4125, para. 145.

26.25   Community competition law refers to the activities of undertakings [...], and [...] the concept of an undertaking covers any entity engaged in an economic activity, regardless of its legal status and the way in which it is financed [...]

[T]he concept of an undertaking, in the same context, must be understood as designating an economic unit even if in law that economic unit consists of several persons, natural or legal [...].

When such an economic entity infringes the competition rules, it falls, according to the principle of personal responsibility, to that entity to answer for that infringement [...].

CoJ 10 September 2009 (Akzo Nobel NV e.a. v. Commission, C-97/08 P) [2009] ECR I-8237, paras 54–56.

See also CoJ 10 April 2014 (Commission v. Siemens AG Österreich e.a., Joined Cases C-231/11 P to C-233/11 P), ECLI:EU:C:2014:256, paras 43 and 44.

[T]he appellants submit that the case-law of the European Union judicature [on **26.26** parental liability] infringes the principle of personal liability of legal persons. However, as the Advocate General has observed in points 65 and 66 of her Opinion, whilst this principle is of particular importance especially as regards liability in the sphere of civil law, it cannot be relevant for defining the perpetrator of an infringement of competition law, which is concerned with the actual conduct of undertakings.

The authors of the Treaties chose to use the concept of an undertaking to designate the perpetrator of an infringement of competition law, who is liable to be punished pursuant to Articles 81 EC and 82 EC, now Articles 101 TFEU and 102 TFEU, and not the concept of a company or firm or of a legal person, used in Article 48 EC, currently Article 54 TFEU. The secondary legislation cited by the appellants is connected with the latter provision and therefore is not relevant to determining the perpetrator of an infringement of competition law.

The concept of an undertaking has been defined by the European Union judicature and designates an economic unit even if in law that economic unit consists of several natural or legal persons (see, to this effect, *Akzo Nobel and Others v Commission*, para. 55, and *Elf Aquitaine v Commission*, para. 53 and the case-law cited).

It follows that, after recalling that case-law in paragraph 66 of the judgment under appeal, the General Court did not commit an error of law in holding, in paragraph 67 of the judgment, that, when an economic entity infringes the competition rules, it falls to that entity to answer for that infringement.

CoJ 18 July 2013 (Schindler v. Commission, C-501/11 P), ECLI:EU:C:2013:522, paras 101–104.

Where, in accordance with Article 23(2) of Regulation No 1/2003, the Commission **26.27** has the possibility of holding jointly and severally liable for payment of a fine a number of legal persons forming part of one and the same undertaking that is responsible for the infringement, the Commission's determination of the amount of that fine—in so far as it is based, in any particular case, on the concept of an undertaking, which is a concept of EU law—is subject to certain limitations, which require due account to be taken of the characteristics of the undertaking concerned, as constituted during the period in which the infringement was committed.

When determining how joint and several liability is to be imposed from an external perspective, the Commission is under an obligation, in particular, to adhere to the principle that the penalty must be specific to the offender and the offence, which requires, in accordance with Article 23(3) of Regulation No 1/2003, the amount of the fine imposed to be determined by reference to the gravity of the infringement for which the undertaking concerned is held individually responsible and the duration of the infringement.

It should be noted in that regard that the factors capable of affecting the assessment of the gravity of infringements and which may, for that purpose, be taken into account in ensuring that the penalty imposed is appropriate to the economic entity in question, include the conduct of each of the undertakings concerned, the role played by each of them in the establishment of the concerted agreements or practices, the profit which they were able to derive from those agreements or practices, their size, the value of the goods concerned and the threat that infringements of that type pose to the objectives of the European Union [...].

In that connection, the General Court was also correct to find, first, at paragraph 153 of the judgment under appeal, that the Commission does not have complete freedom to determine the sums to be paid jointly and severally and, second, at paragraph 154 of the judgment, that, in the present case, the Commission had to take account of the findings which it made in recital 468 of the contested decision regarding the responsibility of the various undertakings for the infringement periods concerning them.

While it is true that a Commission decision imposing fines must necessarily be addressed to the legal persons comprising an undertaking, that limitation, which is of a purely practical nature, does not mean that, where the Commission makes use of its power to hold a number of legal entities jointly and severally liable for payment of a fine, as they formed a single undertaking at the time the infringement was committed, the rules and principles of EU competition law are to be applied not only to the undertaking concerned but also to the legal persons of which the undertaking is made up.

It follows from the foregoing that the rules governing EU competition law, including those relating to the Commission's power to impose penalties, the EU law principle of personal liability for an infringement and the principle that the penalty must be specific to the offender and the offence, which must be complied with when the power to impose penalties is being exercised, relate only to the undertaking per se, not the natural or legal persons forming part of the undertaking.

In particular, in so far as it is merely the manifestation of an ipso jure legal effect of the concept of an 'undertaking', the EU law concept of joint and several liability for payment of a fine concerns only the undertaking itself and not the companies of which it is made up.

CoJ 10 April 2014 (Commission v. Siemens AG Österreich e.a., Joined Cases C-231/11 P to C-233/11 P), ECLI:EU:C:2014:256, paras 51–57.

27

ARTICLE 50 CHARTER*

RIGHT NOT TO BE TRIED OR PUNISHED TWICE IN CRIMINAL PROCEEDINGS FOR THE SAME CRIMINAL OFFENCE

No one shall be liable to be tried or punished again in criminal proceedings for an offence for which he or she has already been finally acquitted or convicted within the Union in accordance with the law.

ARTICLE 4 PROTOCOL 7 ECHR

1. **No one shall be liable to be tried or punished again in criminal proceedings under the jurisdiction of the same State for an offence for which he has already been finally acquitted or convicted in accordance with the law and penal procedure of that State.**
2. **The provisions of the preceding paragraph shall not prevent the re-opening of the case in accordance with the law and the penal procedure of the State concerned, if there is evidence of new or newly discovered facts, or if there has been a fundamental defect in the previous proceedings, which could affect the outcome of the case.**
3. **No derogation from this Article shall be made under Article 15 of the Convention.**

OVERVIEW

A. EXPLANATION RELATING TO ARTICLE 50 CHARTER	(p.876)	D. SAME OFFENCE	27.06
B. PRINCIPLE	27.01	E. FINAL ACQUITTAL OR CONVICTION IN THE FIRST PROCEEDINGS	27.07
C. CRIMINAL PROCEEDINGS	27.03	F. TRIED OR PUNISHED AGAIN	27.09

---

* This chapter was written by Herman Speyart.

A. EXPLANATION RELATING TO ARTICLE 50 CHARTER

Article 4 of Protocol No 7 to the ECHR reads as follows [...].

The 'non bis in idem' rule applies in Union law (see, among the many precedents, the judgment of 5 May 1966, Joined Cases 18/65 and 35/65 Gutmann v. Commission [1966] ECR 149 and a recent case, the decision of the [General Court] of 20 April 1999, Joined Cases T-305/94 and others Limburgse Vinyl Maatschappij v. Commission [1999] ECR II-931). The rule prohibiting cumulation refers to cumulation of two penalties of the same kind, that is to say criminal-law penalties.

In accordance with Article 50, the 'non bis in idem' rule applies not only within the jurisdiction of one State but also between the jurisdictions of several Member States. That corresponds to the acquis in Union law; see Articles 54–58 of the Schengen Convention and the judgment of the Court of Justice of 11 February 2003, C-187/01 Gözütok [2003] ECR I-1345, Article 7 of the Convention on the Protection of the European Communities' Financial Interests and Article 10 of the Convention on the fight against corruption. The very limited exceptions in those Conventions permitting the Member States to derogate from the 'non bis in idem' rule are covered by the horizontal clause in Article 52(1) of the Charter concerning limitations. As regards the situations referred to by Article 4 of Protocol No 7, namely the application of the principle within the same Member State, the guaranteed right has the same meaning and the same scope as the corresponding right in the ECHR.

B. PRINCIPLE

27.01 The principle of non bis in idem, which is a fundamental principle of Community law also enshrined in Article 4(1) of Protocol No 7 to the ECHR [the Convention], precludes, in competition matters, an undertaking from being found guilty or proceedings from being brought against it a second time on the grounds of anti-competitive conduct in respect of which it has been penalised or declared not liable by a previous unappealable decision.

CoJ 15 October 2002 (Limburgse Vinyl Maatschappij a.o. v. Commission, Joined Cases C-238/99 P, C-244/99 P, C-245/99 P, C-247/99 P, C-250/99 P–C-252/99 P and C-254/99 P) [2002] ECR I-8375, para. 59.

See also CoJ 14 February 2012 (Toshiba Corporation and Others v. Úřad pro ochranu hospodářské soutěže, C-17/10), ECLI:EU:C:2012:72, para. 94.

27.02 As regards observance of the principle non bis in idem, the application of that principle is subject to the threefold condition of identity of the facts, unity of offender and unity of the legal interest protected. Under that principle, therefore, the same person cannot be sanctioned more than once for a single unlawful course of conduct designed to protect the same legal asset.

CoJ 7 January 2004 (Aalborg Portland and others v. Commission, C-204/00 P, C-205/00 P, C-211/00 P, C-213/00 P, C-217/00 P and C-219/00 P) [2004] ECR I-123, para. 338.

See also CoJ 14 February 2012 (Toshiba Corporation and Others v. Úřad pro ochranu hospodářské soutěže, C-17/10), ECLI:EU:C:2012:72, para. 97.

C. CRIMINAL PROCEEDINGS

[T]he legal characterisation of the procedure under national law cannot be the sole criterion of relevance for the applicability of the principle of non bis in idem under Article 4(1) of Protocol No 7. Otherwise, the application of this provision would be left to the discretion of the Contracting States to a degree that might lead to results incompatible with the object and purpose of the Convention [...]. The notion of 'penal procedure' in the text of Article 4 of Protocol No. 7 must be interpreted in the light of the general principles concerning the corresponding words 'criminal charge' and 'penalty' in Articles 6 and 7 of the Convention respectively [...]. **27.03**

The Court's established case-law sets out three criteria, commonly known as the 'Engel criteria' (see *Engel and Others*, [...]), to be considered in determining whether or not there was a 'criminal charge'. The first criterion is the legal classification of the offence under national law, the second is the very nature of the offence and the third is the degree of severity of the penalty that the person concerned risks incurring. The second and third criteria are alternative and not necessarily cumulative. This, however, does not exclude a cumulative approach where separate analysis of each criterion does not make it possible to reach a clear conclusion as to the existence of a criminal charge.

Eur. Court H.R. 10 February 2009 (Sergey Zolotukhin v. Russia, no 14939/03), paras 52 and 53.

[T]hree criteria are relevant in this respect. The first criterion is the legal classification of the offence under national law, the second is the very nature of the offence, and the third is the nature and degree of severity of the penalty that the person concerned is liable to incur. **27.04**

CoJ (Grand Chamber) 5 June 2012 (Bonda, C-489/10), ECLI:EU:C:2012:319, para. 37, quoting Eur. Court H.R. 8 June 1976 (Engel and Others v. the Netherlands), Series A no 22, paras 80–82 and Eur. Court H.R. 10 February 2009 (Sergey Zolotukhin v. Russia, no 14939/03), paras 52 and 53.

[I]t is to be noted first of all that Article 50 of the Charter does not preclude a Member State from imposing, for the same acts of non-compliance with declaration obligations in the field of VAT, a combination of tax penalties and criminal penalties. In order to ensure that all VAT revenue is collected and, in so doing, that the financial interests of the European Union are protected, the Member States have freedom to choose the applicable penalties [...]. These penalties may therefore take the form of administrative penalties, criminal penalties or a combination of the two. It is only if the tax penalty is **27.05** criminal in nature for the purposes of Article 50 of the Charter and has become final that that provision precludes criminal proceedings in respect of the same acts from being brought against the same person.

Next, three criteria are relevant for the purpose of assessing whether tax penalties are criminal in nature. The first criterion is the legal classification of the offence under national law, the second is the very nature of the offence, and the third is the nature and degree of severity of the penalty that the person concerned is liable to incur.

It is for the referring court to determine, in the light of those criteria, whether the combining of tax penalties and criminal penalties that is provided for by national law should be examined in relation to the national standards as referred to in paragraph 29 of the present judgment, which could lead it, as the case may be, to regard their combination as contrary to those standards, as long as the remaining penalties are effective, proportionate and dissuasive [...].

It follows from the foregoing considerations that the answer to the second, third and fourth questions is that the non bis in idem principle laid down in Article 50 of the Charter does not preclude a Member State from imposing successively, for the same acts of non-compliance with declaration obligations in the field of VAT, a tax penalty and a criminal penalty in so far as the first penalty is not criminal in nature, a matter which is for the national court to determine.

CoJ (Grand Chamber) 26 February 2013 (Åkerberg Fransson, C-617/10), ECLI: EU:C:2013:105, paras 34–37.

D. SAME OFFENCE

27.06   [Judgment putting an end to the debate on whether the 'idem' criterion should focus on the facts as of themselves or on their legal qualification as an offence:]

The Court considers that the existence of a variety of approaches to ascertain whether the offence for which an applicant has been prosecuted is indeed the same as the one of which he or she was already finally convicted or acquitted engenders legal uncertainty incompatible with a fundamental right, namely the right not to be prosecuted twice for the same offence. It is against this background that the Court is now called upon to provide a harmonised interpretation of the notion of the 'same offence' – the idem element of the non bis in idem principle – for the purposes of Article 4 of Protocol No 7. While it is in the interests of legal certainty, foreseeability and equality before the law that the Court should not depart, without good reason, from precedents laid down in previous cases, a failure by the Court to maintain a dynamic and evolutive approach would risk rendering it a bar to reform or improvement [...].

An analysis of the international instruments incorporating the non bis in idem principle in one or another form reveals the variety of terms in which it is couched. Thus, Article 4 of Protocol No 7 to the Convention, Article 14 § 7 of the United Nations Covenant on Civil and Political Rights and Article 50 of the Charter of Fundamental Rights of the European Union refer to the '[same] offence' ('[même] infraction'), the American Convention on Human Rights speaks of the 'same cause' ('mêmes faits'), the Convention Implementing the Schengen Agreement prohibits prosecution for the 'same acts' ('mêmes faits'), and the Statute of the International

Criminal Court employs the term '[same] conduct' ('[mêmes] actes constitutifs') . The difference between the terms 'same acts' or 'same cause' ('mêmes faits') on the one hand and the term '[same] offence' ('[même] infraction') on the other was held by the Court of Justice of the European Union and the Inter-American Court of Human Rights to be an important element in favour of adopting the approach based strictly on the identity of the material acts and rejecting the legal classification of such acts as irrelevant. In so finding, both tribunals emphasised that such an approach would favour the perpetrator, who would know that, once he had been found guilty and served his sentence or had been acquitted, he need not fear further prosecution for the same act [...].

The Court considers that the use of the word 'offence' in the text of Article 4 of Protocol No 7 cannot justify adhering to a more restrictive approach. It reiterates that the Convention must be interpreted and applied in a manner which renders its rights practical and effective, not theoretical and illusory. It is a living instrument which must be interpreted in the light of present-day conditions [...]. The provisions of an international treaty such as the Convention must be construed in the light of their object and purpose and also in accordance with the principle of effectiveness [...].

The Court further notes that the approach which emphasises the legal character-isation of the two offences is too restrictive on the rights of the individual, for if the Court limits itself to finding that the person was prosecuted for offences having a different legal classification it risks undermining the guarantee enshrined in Article 4 of Protocol No 7 rather than rendering it practical and effective as required by the Convention [...].

Accordingly, the Court takes the view that Article 4 of Protocol No 7 must be understood as prohibiting the prosecution or trial of a second 'offence' in so far as it arises from identical facts or facts which are substantially the same.

The guarantee enshrined in Article 4 of Protocol No 7 becomes relevant on commencement of a new prosecution, where a prior acquittal or conviction has already acquired the force of res judicata. At this juncture the available material will necessarily comprise the decision by which the first 'penal procedure' was concluded and the list of charges levelled against the applicant in the new proceedings. Normally, these docu-ments would contain a statement of facts concerning both the offence for which the applicant has already been tried and the offence of which he or she stands accused. In the Court's view, such statements of fact are an appropriate starting-point for its determination of the issue whether the facts in both proceedings were identical or substantially the same. The Court emphasises that it is irrelevant which parts of the new charges are eventually upheld or dismissed in the subsequent proceedings, because Article 4 of Protocol No 7 contains a safeguard against being tried or being liable to be tried again in new proceedings rather than a prohibition on a second conviction or acquittal.

Eur. Court H.R. 10 February 2009 (Sergey Zolotukhin v. Russia, no 14939/03), paras 78–83.

E. FINAL ACQUITTAL OR CONVICTION IN THE FIRST PROCEEDINGS

27.07   The application of that principle therefore presupposes that a ruling has been given on the question whether an offence has in fact been committed or that the legality of the assessment thereof has been reviewed.

Thus, the principle of non bis in idem merely prohibits a fresh assessment in depth of the alleged commission of an offence which would result in the imposition of either a second penalty, in addition to the first, in the event that liability is established a second time, or a first penalty in the event that liability not established by the first decision is established by the second.

On the other hand, it does not in itself preclude the resumption of proceedings in respect of the same anti-competitive conduct where the first decision was annulled for procedural reasons without any ruling having been given on the substance of the facts alleged, since the annulment decision cannot in such circumstances be regarded as an acquittal within the meaning given to that expression in penal matters. In such a case, the penalties imposed by the new decision are not added to those imposed by the annulled decision but replace them.

Accordingly, since the Court of Justice, in its judgment of 15 June 1994, annulled the PVC I decision, including the penalties imposed thereby, without ruling on any of the substantive pleas raised by the appellants, the [General Court] was correct in finding that the Commission, by adopting the PVC II decision after curing the defect formally declared unlawful, had neither penalised the undertakings twice nor initiated a second procedure against them on the basis of the same facts.

CoJ 15 October 2002 (Limburgse Vinyl Maatschappij a.o. v. Commission, Joined Cases C-238/99 P, C-244/99 P, C-245/99 P, C-247/99 P, C-250–252/99 P and C-254/99 P) [2002] ECR I-8375, paras 60–63.

27.08   [T]he aim of Article 4 of Protocol No 7 is to prohibit the repetition of criminal proceedings that have been concluded by a 'final' decision [...]. According to the Explanatory Report to Protocol No 7, which itself refers back to the European Convention on the International Validity of Criminal Judgments, a 'decision is final "if, according to the traditional expression, it has acquired the force of res judicata. This is the case when it is irrevocable, that is to say when no further ordinary remedies are available or when the parties have exhausted such remedies or have permitted the time-limit to expire without availing themselves of them"'. This approach is well entrenched in the Court's case-law [...].

Decisions against which an ordinary appeal lies are excluded from the scope of the guarantee contained in Article 4 of Protocol No 7 as long as the time-limit for lodging such an appeal has not expired. On the other hand, extraordinary remedies such as a request for the reopening of the proceedings or an application for extension of the expired time-limit are not taken into account for the purposes of determining whether the proceedings have reached a final conclusion [...]. Although these remedies represent a continuation of the first set of proceedings, the 'final' nature of the decision does not depend on their being used. It is important to point out that Article 4 of Protocol No 7 does not preclude the reopening of the proceedings, as stated clearly by the second paragraph of Article 4.

Eur. Court H.R. 10 February 2009 (Sergey Zolotukhin v. Russia, no 14939/03), paras 107 and 108.

F. TRIED OR PUNISHED AGAIN

Article 4 of Protocol No 7 is not confined to the right not to be punished twice but **27.09** extends to the right not to be prosecuted or tried twice [...]. Were this not the case, it would not have been necessary to add the word 'punished' to the word 'tried' since this would be mere duplication. Article 4 of Protocol No 7 applies even where the individual has merely been prosecuted in proceedings that have not resulted in a conviction. The Court reiterates that Article 4 of Protocol No 7 contains three distinct guarantees and provides that no one shall be (i) liable to be tried, (ii) tried or (iii) punished for the same offence [...].

Eur. Court H.R. 10 February 2009 (Sergey Zolotukhin v. Russia, no 14939/03), para. 110.

28

ARTICLE 51 CHARTER*

FIELD OF APPLICATION

1. **The provisions of this Charter are addressed to the institutions, bodies, offices and agencies of the Union with due regard for the principle of subsidiarity and to the Member States only when they are implementing Union law. They shall therefore respect the rights, observe the principles and promote the application thereof in accordance with their respective powers and respecting the limits of the powers of the Union as conferred on it in the Treaties.**

2. **The Charter does not extend the field of application of Union law beyond the powers of the Union or establish any new power or task for the Union, or modify powers and tasks as defined in the Treaties.**

OVERVIEW

A. EXPLANATION RELATING TO ARTICLE 51 CHARTER (p.882)	C. ABILITY OF THE MEMBER STATES TO APPLY NATIONAL FUNDAMENTAL RIGHTS	28.02
B. APPLICABILITY TO THE MEMBER STATES WHEN THEY ARE IMPLEMENTING UNION LAW 28.01		

A. EXPLANATION RELATING TO ARTICLE 51 CHARTER

The aim of Article 51 is to determine the scope of the Charter. It seeks to establish clearly that the Charter applies primarily to the institutions and bodies of the Union, in compliance with the principle of subsidiarity. This provision was drafted in keeping with Article 6(2) of the Treaty on European Union, which required the Union to respect fundamental rights, and with the mandate issued by the Cologne European Council. The term 'institutions' is enshrined in the Treaties. The expression 'bodies, offices and agencies' is commonly used in the Treaties to refer to all the authorities set up by the Treaties or by secondary legislation (see, e.g., Articles 15 or 16 of the Treaty on the Functioning of the European Union).

---

* This chapter was written by Herman Speyart.

As regards the Member States, it follows unambiguously from the case-law of the Court of Justice that the requirement to respect fundamental rights defined in the context of the Union is only binding on the Member States when they act in the scope of Union law (judgment of 13 July 1989, Case 5/88 Wachauf [1989] ECR 2609; judgment of 18 June 1991, Case C-260/89 ERT [1991] ECR I-2925; judgment of 18 December 1997, Case C-309/96 Annibaldi [1997] ECR I-7493). The Court of Justice confirmed this case-law in the following terms: 'In addition, it should be remembered that the requirements flowing from the protection of fundamental rights in the Community legal order are also binding on Member States when they implement Community rules ...' (judgment of 13 April 2000, Case C-292/97 Karlsson [2000] ECR I-2737, paragraph 37 of the grounds). Of course this rule, as enshrined in this Charter, applies to the central authorities as well as to regional or local bodies, and to public organisations, when they are implementing Union law.

Paragraph 2, together with the second sentence of paragraph 1, confirms that the Charter may not have the effect of extending the competences and tasks which the Treaties confer on the Union. Explicit mention is made here of the logical consequences of the principle of subsidiarity and of the fact that the Union only has those powers which have been conferred upon it. The fundamental rights as guaranteed in the Union do not have any effect other than in the context of the powers determined by the Treaties. Consequently, an obligation, pursuant to the second sentence of paragraph 1, for the Union's institutions to promote principles laid down in the Charter may arise only within the limits of these same powers.

Paragraph 2 also confirms that the Charter may not have the effect of extending the field of application of Union law beyond the powers of the Union as established in the Treaties. The Court of Justice has already established this rule with respect to the fundamental rights recognised as part of Union law (judgment of 17 February 1998, C-249/96 Grant [1998] ECR I-621, paragraph 45 of the grounds). In accordance with this rule, it goes without saying that the reference to the Charter in Article 6 of the Treaty on European Union cannot be understood as extending by itself the range of Member State action considered to be 'implementation of Union law' (within the meaning of paragraph 1 and the above-mentioned case-law).

B. APPLICABILITY TO THE MEMBER STATES WHEN THEY ARE IMPLEMENTING UNION LAW

28.01 The Court's settled case-law indeed states, in essence, that the fundamental rights guaranteed in the legal order of the European Union are applicable in all situations governed by European Union law, but not outside such situations. In this respect the Court has already observed that it has no power to examine the compatibility with the Charter of national legislation lying outside the scope of European Union law. On the other hand, if such legislation falls within the scope of European Union law, the Court, when requested to give a preliminary ruling, must provide all the guidance as to interpretation needed in order for the national court to determine whether that legislation is compatible with the fundamental rights the observance of which the Court ensures […].

That definition of the field of application of the fundamental rights of the European Union is borne out by the explanations relating to Article 51 of the Charter […]. According to those explanations, 'the requirement to respect fundamental rights defined in the context of the Union is only binding on the Member States when they act in the scope of Union law'.

Since the fundamental rights guaranteed by the Charter must therefore be complied with where national legislation falls within the scope of European Union law, situations cannot exist which are covered in that way by European Union law without those fundamental rights being applicable. The applicability of European Union law entails applicability of the fundamental rights guaranteed by the Charter.

Where, on the other hand, a legal situation does not come within the scope of European Union law, the Court does not have jurisdiction to rule on it and any provisions of the Charter relied upon cannot, of themselves, form the basis for such jurisdiction (see, to this effect, the order in *Case C-466/11 Currà and others*, ECLI: EU:T:2012:465, para. 26).

These considerations correspond to those underlying Article 6(1) TEU, according to which the provisions of the Charter are not to extend in any way the competences of the European Union as defined in the Treaties. Likewise, the Charter, pursuant to Article 51(2) thereof, does not extend the field of application of European Union law beyond the powers of the European Union or establish any new power or task for the European Union, or modify powers and tasks as defined in the Treaties (see *Dereci and others*, para. 71).

CoJ (Grand Chamber) 26 February 2013 (Åkerberg Fransson, C-617/10), ECLI: EU:C:2013:105, paras 19–23.

C. ABILITY OF THE MEMBER STATES TO APPLY NATIONAL FUNDAMENTAL RIGHTS

28.02   [W]here a court of a Member State is called upon to review whether fundamental rights are complied with by a national provision or measure which, in a situation where action of the Member States is not entirely determined by European Union law, implements the latter for the purposes of Article 51(1) of the Charter, national authorities and courts remain free to apply national standards of protection of fundamental rights, provided that the level of protection provided for by the Charter, as interpreted by the Court, and the primacy, unity and effectiveness of European Union law are not thereby compromised.

CoJ (Grand Chamber) 26 February 2013 (Åkerberg Fransson, C-617/10), ECLI: EU:C:2013:105, para. 44.

See also CoJ (Grand Chamber) 26 February 2013 (Melloni, C-399/11), ECLI: EU:C:2013:107, para. 60.

29

ARTICLE 52 CHARTER[*]

SCOPE AND INTERPRETATION OF RIGHTS AND PRINCIPLES

1. Any limitation on the exercise of the rights and freedoms recognised by this Charter must be provided for by law and respect the essence of those rights and freedoms. Subject to the principle of proportionality, limitations may be made only if they are necessary and genuinely meet objectives of general interest recognised by the Union or the need to protect the rights and freedoms of others.

2. Rights recognised by this Charter for which provision is made in the Treaties shall be exercised under the conditions and within the limits defined by those Treaties.

3. In so far as this Charter contains rights which correspond to rights guaranteed by the Convention for the Protection of Human Rights and Fundamental Freedoms, the meaning and scope of those rights shall be the same as those laid down by the said Convention. This provision shall not prevent Union law providing more extensive protection.

4. In so far as this Charter recognises fundamental rights as they result from the constitutional traditions common to the Member States, those rights shall be interpreted in harmony with those traditions.

5. The provisions of this Charter which contain principles may be implemented by legislative and executive acts taken by institutions, bodies, offices and agencies of the Union, and by acts of Member States when they are implementing Union law, in the exercise of their respective powers. They shall be judicially cognisable only in the interpretation of such acts and in the ruling on their legality.

6. Full account shall be taken of national laws and practices as specified in this Charter.

7. The explanations drawn up as a way of providing guidance in the interpretation of this Charter shall be given due regard by the courts of the Union and of the Member States.

---

[*] This chapter was written by Herman Speyart.

OVERVIEW

A. EXPLANATION RELATING TO   C. EXPLANATIONS   29.04
    ARTICLE 52 CHARTER   (p.886)

B. EXCEPTIONS   29.01

A. EXPLANATION RELATING TO ARTICLE 52 CHARTER

The purpose of Article 52 is to set the scope of the rights and principles of the Charter, and to lay down rules for their interpretation. Paragraph 1 deals with the arrangements for the limitation of rights. The wording is based on the case-law of the Court of Justice: '… it is well established in the case-law of the Court that restrictions may be imposed on the exercise of fundamental rights, in particular in the context of a common organisation of the market, provided that those restrictions in fact correspond to objectives of general interest pursued by the Community and do not constitute, with regard to the aim pursued, disproportionate and unreasonable interference undermining the very substance of those rights' (judgment of 13 April 2000, Case C-292/97, paragraph 45 of the grounds). The reference to general interests recognised by the Union covers both the objectives mentioned in Article 3 of the Treaty on European Union and other interests protected by specific provisions of the Treaties such as Article 4(1) of the Treaty on European Union and Articles 35(3), 36 and 346 of the Treaty on the Functioning of the European Union.

Paragraph 2 refers to rights which were already expressly guaranteed in the Treaty establishing the European Community and have been recognised in the Charter, and which are now found in the Treaties (notably the rights derived from Union citizenship). It clarifies that such rights remain subject to the conditions and limits applicable to the Union law on which they are based, and for which provision is made in the Treaties. The Charter does not alter the system of rights conferred by the EC Treaty and taken over by the Treaties.

Paragraph 3 is intended to ensure the necessary consistency between the Charter and the ECHR by establishing the rule that, in so far as the rights in the present Charter also correspond to rights guaranteed by the ECHR, the meaning and scope of those rights, including authorised limitations, are the same as those laid down by the ECHR. This means in particular that the legislator, in laying down limitations to those rights, must comply with the same standards as are fixed by the detailed limitation arrangements laid down in the ECHR, which are thus made applicable for the rights covered by this paragraph, without thereby adversely affecting the autonomy of Union law and of that of the Court of Justice of the European Union.

The reference to the ECHR covers both the Convention and the Protocols to it. The meaning and the scope of the guaranteed rights are determined not only by the text of those instruments, but also by the case-law of the European Court of Human Rights and by the Court of Justice of the European Union. The last sentence of the paragraph is designed to allow the Union to guarantee more extensive protection. In any event, the level of protection afforded by the Charter may never be lower than that guaranteed by the ECHR.

The Charter does not affect the possibilities of Member States to avail themselves of Article 15 ECHR, allowing derogations from ECHR rights in the event of war or of other public dangers threatening the life of the nation, when they take action in the areas of national defence in the event of war and of the maintenance of law and order, in accordance with their responsibilities recognised in Article 4(1) of the Treaty on European Union and in Articles 72 and 347 of the Treaty on the Functioning of the European Union.

The list of rights which may at the present stage, without precluding developments in the law, legislation and the Treaties, be regarded as corresponding to rights in the ECHR within the meaning of the present paragraph is given hereafter. It does not include rights additional to those in the ECHR.

1. *Articles of the Charter where both the meaning and the scope are the same as the corresponding Articles of the ECHR:*
   - *Article 2 corresponds to Article 2 of the ECHR,*
   - *Article 4 corresponds to Article 3 of the ECHR,*
   - *Article 5(1) and (2) corresponds to Article 4 of the ECHR,*
   - *Article 6 corresponds to Article 5 of the ECHR,*
   - *Article 7 corresponds to Article 8 of the ECHR,*
   - *Article 10(1) corresponds to Article 9 of the ECHR,*
   - *Article 11 corresponds to Article 10 of the ECHR without prejudice to any restrictions which Union law may impose on Member States' right to introduce the licensing arrangements referred to in the third sentence of Article 10(1) of the ECHR,*
   - *Article 17 corresponds to Article 1 of the Protocol to the ECHR,*
   - *Article 19(1) corresponds to Article 4 of Protocol No 4,*
   - *Article 19(2) corresponds to Article 3 of the ECHR as interpreted by the European Court of Human Rights,*
   - *Article 48 corresponds to Article 6(2) and (3) of the ECHR,*
   - *Article 49(1) (with the exception of the last sentence) and (2) correspond to Article 7 of the ECHR.*

2. *Articles where the meaning is the same as the corresponding Articles of the ECHR, but where the scope is wider:*

- *Article 9 covers the same field as Article 12 of the ECHR, but its scope may be extended to other forms of marriage if these are established by national legislation,*
- *Article 12(1) corresponds to Article 11 of the ECHR, but its scope is extended to European Union level,*
- *Article 14(1) corresponds to Article 2 of the Protocol to the ECHR, but its scope is extended to cover access to vocational and continuing training,*
- *Article 14(3) corresponds to Article 2 of the Protocol to the ECHR as regards the rights of parents,*
- *Article 47(2) and (3) corresponds to Article 6(1) of the ECHR, but the limitation to the determination of civil rights and obligations or criminal charges does not apply as regards Union law and its implementation,*
- *Article 50 corresponds to Article 4 of Protocol No 7 to the ECHR, but its scope is extended to European Union level between the courts of the Member States,*
- *Finally, citizens of the European Union may not be considered as aliens in the scope of the application of Union law, because of the prohibition of any discrimination on grounds of nationality. The limitations provided for by Article 16 of the ECHR as regards the rights of aliens therefore do not apply to them in this context.*

The rule of interpretation contained in paragraph 4 has been based on the wording of Article 6(3) of the Treaty on European Union and takes due account of the approach to common constitutional traditions followed by the Court of Justice (e.g., judgment of 13 December 1979, Case 44/79 Hauer [1979] ECR 3727; judgment of 18 May 1982, Case 155/79 AM&S [1982] ECR 1575). Under that rule, rather than following a rigid approach of 'a lowest common denominator', the Charter rights concerned should be interpreted in a way offering a high standard of protection which is adequate for the law of the Union and in harmony with the common constitutional traditions.

Paragraph 5 clarifies the distinction between 'rights' and 'principles' set out in the Charter. According to that distinction, subjective rights shall be respected, whereas principles shall be observed (Article 51(1)). Principles may be implemented through legislative or executive acts (adopted by the Union in accordance with its powers, and by the Member States only when they implement Union law); accordingly, they become significant for the courts only when such acts are interpreted or reviewed. They do not however give rise to direct claims for positive action by the Union's institutions or Member States authorities. This is consistent both with case-law of the Court of Justice (cf. notably case-law on the 'precautionary principle' in Article 191(2) of the Treaty on the Functioning of the European Union: judgment of the [General Court] of 11 September 2002, Case T-13/99 Pfizer v. Council, with numerous references to earlier case-law; and a series of judgments on Article 33 (ex-39) on the principles of agricultural law, e.g. judgment of the Court of Justice in Case 265/85 Van den Berg [1987] ECR 1155: scrutiny of the principle of market stabilisation and of reasonable expectations) and with the approach of the Member States' constitutional systems to 'principles', particularly in the field of social law. For illustration, examples for principles, recognised in the Charter include e.g. Articles 25, 26 and 37. In some cases, an Article of the Charter may contain both elements of a right and of a principle, e.g. Articles 23, 33 and 34.

Paragraph 6 refers to the various Articles in the Charter which, in the spirit of subsidiarity, make reference to national laws and practices.

B. EXCEPTIONS

It should, however, be borne in mind that fundamental rights, such as respect for the **29.01** rights of the defence, do not constitute unfettered prerogatives and may be restricted, provided that the restrictions in fact correspond to objectives of general interest pursued by the measure in question and that they do not constitute, with regard to the objectives pursued, a disproportionate and intolerable interference which infringes upon the very substance of the rights guaranteed.

CoJ 11 July 1989 (Hermann Schräder HS Kraftfutter v. Hauptzollamt Gronau, 265/87) [1989] ECR 2237, para. 15.

See also CoJ 8 April 1992 (Commission v. Germany, C-62/90) [1992] ECR I-2575, para. 23.

In so far as concerns the proportionality of the interference found to exist, the Court **29.02** recalls that, according to settled case-law, the principle of proportionality requires that measures adopted by European Union institutions do not exceed the limits of what is appropriate and necessary in order to attain the objectives legitimately pursued by the legislation in question; when there is a choice between several appropriate measures recourse must be had to the least onerous, and the disadvantages caused must not be disproportionate to the aims pursued [...].

CoJ 22 January 2013 (Sky Österreich, C-283/11), ECLI:EU:2013:28, para. 50.

Where several rights and fundamental freedoms protected by the European Union legal **29.03** order are at issue, the assessment of the possible disproportionate nature of a provision of European Union law must be carried out with a view to reconciling the requirements of the protection of those different rights and freedoms and a fair balance between them [...].

CoJ 22 January 2013 (Sky Österreich, C-283/11), ECLI:EU:2013:28, para. 60.

C. EXPLANATIONS

The explanations referred to in paragraph 7 have been published in OJ 2007 C 303, p. 17.

29.04   [I]n accordance with the third sub-paragraph of Article 6(1) TEU and Article 52(7) of the Charter, [the explanations] have to be taken into consideration for the interpretation of the Charter.
CoJ 22 December 2010 (DEB, C-279/09) [2010] ECR I-13849, para. 32.

30

ARTICLE 53 CHARTER[*]

LEVEL OF PROTECTION

Nothing in this Charter shall be interpreted as restricting or adversely affecting human rights and fundamental freedoms as recognised, in their respective fields of application, by Union law and international law and by international agreements to which the [European] Union or all the Member States are party, including the [ECHR] and by the Member States' constitutions.

OVERVIEW

A. EXPLANATION RELATING TO ARTICLE 53 CHARTER (p.891)	B. GENERAL	30.01

A. EXPLANATION RELATING TO ARTICLE 53 CHARTER

This provision is intended to maintain the level of protection currently afforded within their respective scope by Union law, national law and international law. Owing to its importance, mention is made of the ECHR.

B. GENERAL

30.01 By its third question, the national court asks, in essence, whether Article 53 of the Charter must be interpreted as allowing the executing Member State to make the surrender of a person convicted in absentia conditional upon the conviction being open to review in the issuing Member State, in order to avoid an adverse effect on the right to a fair trial and the rights of the defence guaranteed by its constitution.

The interpretation envisaged by the national court at the outset is that Article 53 of the Charter gives general authorisation to a Member State to apply the standard of protection of fundamental rights guaranteed by its constitution when that standard is

---

[*] This chapter was written by Herman Speyart.

higher than that deriving from the Charter and, where necessary, to give it priority over the application of provisions of EU law. Such an interpretation would, in particular, allow a Member State to make the execution of a European arrest warrant issued for the purposes of executing a sentence rendered in absentia subject to conditions intended to avoid an interpretation which restricts or adversely affects fundamental rights recognised by its constitution, even though the application of such conditions is not allowed under Article 4a(1) of Framework Decision 2002/584.

Such an interpretation of Article 53 of the Charter cannot be accepted.

That interpretation of Article 53 of the Charter would undermine the principle of the primacy of EU law inasmuch as it would allow a Member State to disapply EU legal rules which are fully in compliance with the Charter where they infringe the fundamental rights guaranteed by that State's constitution.

It is settled case-law that, by virtue of the principle of primacy of EU law, which is an essential feature of the EU legal order (see *Opinion 1/91* [1991] ECR I-6079, para. 21, and *Opinion 1/09* [2011] ECR I-1137, para. 65), rules of national law, even of a constitutional order, cannot be allowed to undermine the effectiveness of EU law on the territory of that State (see, to that effect, inter alia, *Case 11/70 Internationale Handelsgesellschaft* [1970] ECR 1125, para. 3, and *Case C-409/06 Winner Wetten* [2010] ECR I-8015, para. 61).

It is true that Article 53 of the Charter confirms that, where an EU legal act calls for national implementing measures, national authorities and courts remain free to apply national standards of protection of fundamental rights, provided that the level of protection provided for by the Charter, as interpreted by the Court, and the primacy, unity and effectiveness of EU law are not thereby compromised.

However, as is apparent from paragraph 40 of this judgment, Article 4a(1) of Framework Decision 2002/584 does not allow Member States to refuse to execute a European arrest warrant when the person concerned is in one of the situations provided for therein. […]

In the light of the foregoing considerations, the answer to the third question is that Article 53 of the Charter must be interpreted as not allowing a Member State to make the surrender of a person convicted in absentia conditional upon the conviction being open to review in the issuing Member State, in order to avoid an adverse effect on the right to a fair trial and the rights of the defence guaranteed by its constitution.

CoJ (Grand Chamber) 26 February 2013 (Melloni, C-399/11), ECLI:EU: C:2013:107, paras 55–61 and 64.

ANNEX

Table A.1   Correlation Table (ECHR – Charter)

Subject	ECHR	Charter
Fair trial	Article 6(1)	Article 47 second indent first sentence
Presumption of innocence	Article 6(2)	Article 48(1)
Rights of the defence	Article 6(3)(a)–(b) and (d)–(e)	Article 48(2)
Representation and legal aid	Article 6(3)(c)	Article 47 second indent second sentence and third indent
Principle of legality of sanctions	Article 7(1) and (2)	Article 49(1) and (2)
Private and family life – Right	Article 8(1)	Article 8
Private and family life – Restriction	Article 8(2)	Article 52(1)
Effective remedy	Article 13	Article 47 first indent
Ne bis in idem	Article 4 Protocol 7	Article 50

INDEX

ability to pay fines 13.175–7, 24.110, 26.27
  see also fines
absence of intention to pay fines 14.175
  see also fines
access
  citizens' right of access to documents
    13.238
  essential facilities and access time 5.95–6
  file in criminal proceedings 24.92–4
  right to access to a lawyer 24.119–25
  rights to courts or tribunals 24.57–61
  service provision and access time 5.94
accessibility of law, ECHR, respect for
    private and family life (Article 8) 19.22
acquisition of brand rights 14.89
  see also brands
acquisition of control *see* control
acquisition by one company of an equity
    interest in a competitor 4.160
acquittal, final, and right not to be tried or
    punished twice for same criminal
    offence 27.07–8
administrative procedure
  ECHR, full review of sanctions by an
    administrative court 24.51–6
  ECHR imposition of fines by an
    administrative body 24.69–75
  representation in administrative procedure,
    Regulation 1/2003 13.204–5
  right to good *see* Charter, right to good
    administration (Article 41)
adversarial proceedings principle *see* ECHR,
    right to a fair trial (Article 6), fair trial,
    adversarial proceedings principle
advertising
  restrictions 4.300
  television advertising 9.01
  trade association campaigns 10.18

agency agreements, cartel prohibition
    4.276–81
agent and principal agreements 4.61, 5.122
aggravating circumstances, implementation
    of rules of competition 13.138–45
agreement conception, cartel prohibition *see*
    TFEU, Article 101 and cartel
    prohibition, agreement concept
agreements, and concerted practice concept
    4.96, 4.114–24
agriculture policy 17.01, 17.02, 17.11
  banana market 4.153, 5.26, 5.34, 5.130
  cartel prohibition 4.07
  cheese market 4.233
  common agricultural policy 17.01, 17.04,
    17.11, 17.14–17
  exclusive supply obligation 17.08
  fertilizer market 4.237, 5.31, 14.15, 14.52
  livestock insemination centres 9.16
  pig meat market 10.76
  potash market 14.15, 14.52
  product markets *see* Regulation
    1308/2013, common organisation of
    markets in agricultural products
  wine production 10.77
  see also fisheries sector; food and drink
    sector
aid notification, TFEU, Article 108 *see*
    TFEU, Article 108, notification of aid
aid prohibition, TFEU, Article 107 *see*
    TFEU, Article 107, aid prohibition
air transport
  air carriers, non-commercially viable
    routes 9.36
  air navigation safety 4.51
  airport charges 9.53, 10.25
  airport management services 5.59, 5.124
  cartel prohibition 4.08–9
  civil air transport installations 4.45

dominance abuse 5.03, 5.47, 5.59
in-flight magazine 14.173
international air transport services
    between Community airports 4.09
Regulation 139/2004, control of
    concentrations between undertakings,
    appraisal of concentrations (Article
    2) 14.13, 14.76
Regulation 139/2004, control of
    concentrations between undertakings,
    turnover calculation (Article 5)
    14.131
tariffs 2.06–7, 2.10
travel agent commission on airline tickets
    5.80
see also transport
annulment decisions
    action, TFEU, Article 108 *see* TFEU,
        Article 108, notification of aid,
        annulment action
    and Commission liability 14.79–81
    contested decision, hearings of parties
        13.226, 13.231
    inspection decision, right to a fair trial
        24.65
    no obligation to remand to a different
        body following 24.75
    Regulation 1/2003 13.04, 13.169, 13.226,
        13.231
another person, proceedings against a
    decision addressed to 11.91, 11.95,
    11.98, 11.97
Anton Piller order, UK 19.20, 19.48
appeal
    sanctions open to 24.69–72
    setting aside of judgment under 24.116
    by third party possible, Regulation
        139/2004, control of concentrations
        between undertakings, referral to
        competent authorities of Member
        States 14.161
    unlimited jurisdiction on 13.249–50
appraisal of concentrations, Regulation
    139/2004 *see* Regulation 139/2004,
    control of concentrations between
    undertakings, appraisal of
    concentrations (Article 2)

ARPU (average revenue per unit)
    calculation, horizontal mergers 14.53
assistance, granting assistance to
    Commission officials, inspection
    powers 13.61
association of undertakings
    calculation turnover 13.168, 13.177
    chartered accountant undertaking training
        4.66
    and competition restriction 4.152,
        4.179–82, 25.11
    concept 4.63–7, 4.125–9, 5.53
    FIFA as 5, 55, 4.139
    and single continuous infringement
        4.116
    trade union association as 4.17
    see also undertakings
atomic energy 4.07
Austria
    home-delivery services 5.41
    judicial searches 19.44
    mobile telephone charges 9.54
automobiles *see* vehicles
autonomy
    concept 24.14–15
    conduct that restricts competition 4.138
    national procedural 8.02
    principle 24.09

banana market 4.153, 5.26, 5.34, 5.130
    see also agricultural policy
banking
    guarantees 13.220
    MasterCard scheme 4.129, 4.227, 4.231
    mergers 14.47
    savings deposits and maximum rates of
        interest 2.09
    sector, TFEU, Article 101 and cartel
        prohibition, competition restriction
        4.150
    transfers 4.11, 4.103
bankruptcy, and aid recovery 11.121–3
beer supply agreements 4.161, 4.206,
    4.311
Belgium
    air tariffs 2.07
    airport charges 10.25
    BMW dealership 4.78, 15.08

CD-Contact Data and Nintendo 4.77
FEDETAB and tobacco imports 4.63,
    4.70, 4.125, 4.239
international removal services 4.121,
    4.197–8
judicial searches 19.42
shipbuilding and ship conversion aid
    10.145
travel agencies 4.276
vehicle approval services 5.16
bidding, collusive 13.108
bidding markets (tenders) 9.34, 10.114,
    14.37–40
block exemptions
  and dominance abuse 5.154
  exclusive supply contract and block
    exemption, Regulation 330/2010,
    vertical agreements 15.15
  hardcore restrictions removing benefit of
    16.09
  restriction removing benefit see Regulation
    330/2010, vertical agreements,
    restrictions removing benefit of block
    exemption (Article 4)
book sales 2.03, 4.10, 14.166
branding
  acquisition of brand rights 14.89
  brand name dominance and refusal to
    supply 5.93
  chocolate brands 14.44
  equity and product differentiation 5.48
  single branding 4.310–11
breach of reserved area, TFEU, Article 106,
    public undertakings 9.09
breach of the rights of the defence
    complaint, Regulation 1/2003,
    implementation of rules of
    competition, hearings of parties,
    complainants and others (Article 27)
    13.223–4
breaking a seal, Regulation 1/2003,
    implementation of rules of
    competition, fines (Article 23)
    13.67
brewery sector, new entry issues, TFEU,
    Article 101 and cartel prohibition,
    competition restriction 4.161

broadcasting
  control of concentrations between
    undertakings 14.128, 14.198
  and dominance abuse 5.20, 9.14
  intellectual property rights and
    broadcaster decoding 4.308
  public undertakings 9.14
  radio equipment, type approval
    requirements 9.17
  television advertising 9.01
  television broadcasting of horse-racing
    5.108
  television broadcasting of musical works
    5.120
  television programme listings 5.20, 5.106
  TV broadcasting market 14.18
  see also media
bundling
  and dominance abuse 5.84–7
  leverage a strong position from one
    market to another 14.66
  of similar contracts and new entrant issues
    4.161
burden of proof see proof, burden of
business
  discrimination between business partners
    5.125
  freedom to conduct 20.01
  premises, right to protection of 19.12–13
  secrets 13.234–5, 13.237, 13.239

call option, control of concentrations
    between undertakings 14.91, 14.113,
    14.134
capital
  injections and aid prohibition 10.91–101
  international movement 4.11
  investment as entry barrier 5.34
  see also economic activity
cars see vehicles
cartel prohibition
  TFEU, Article 101 see TFEU, Article 101
    and cartel prohibition
  TFEU, Article 102 see TFEU, Article
    102, cartel prohibition
carton market 14.67
cash register spares 5.84
censorship, retroactive 4.300

certification
  services for public works contracts 4.54
  systems and standards 4.258–9
chain of substitution 14.27–8
  see also substitution
Charter Article 47 applicability, ECHR,
    right to a fair trial (Article 6) 24.07
Charter, equality before the law (Article 20)
    22.01–7
  finding of an infringement 22.02
  fine calculation by Commission 22.04
  fine review by EU courts and unlimited
    jurisdiction 22.05–7
  leniency rebate 22.03
Charter, field of application (Article 51)
    28.01–2
Charter, freedom to conduct a business
    (Article 16) 20.01
Charter, level of protection (Article 53)
    30.01
Charter, presumption of innocence and
    rights of defence (Article 48) see
    ECHR, presumption of innocence and
    rights of defence (Article 6)
Charter, principles of legality and
    proportionality (Article 49) see ECHR,
    no punishment without proper law
    (Article 7)
Charter, respect for family life (Article 7) see
    ECHR, respect for private and family
    life (Article 8)
Charter, right not to be tried or punished
    twice for same criminal offence
    (Article 50) see ECHR, right not to be
    tried or punished twice for same
    criminal offence (Article 4 Protocol 7)
Charter, right to a fair trial (Article 47) see
    ECHR, right to a fair trial (Article 6)
Charter, right to good administration
    (Article 41) 23.01–30
  exculpatory documents 23.29
  file access 23.25–30
  fines, level of 23.20–21
  legal certainty requirement 23.03
  notification of statement of objections
    23.04
  reasonable period 23.01–9

  reasonable period, assessment in respect of
    administrative proceedings 23.07–8
  reasonable period, consequences of failure
    to adopt decision within a reasonable
    period, EFTA court 23.09
  reasonable period, test 23.02–6
  right to be heard 23.14–15, 23.17–21,
    23.25
  rights of defence 23.10–30
  rights of defence, preliminary enquiries
    applicability 23.13
  statement of objections 23.16–24
  unlimited jurisdiction in reviewing fine
    23.09
Charter, right to property (Article 17) 21.1
Charter, scope and interpretation of rights
    and principle (Article 52) 29.01–4
  exceptions 29.01–3
  explanations 29.04
  proportionality of interference 29.02
chartered accountants 4.53, 4.66
cheese market 4.233
  see also agriculture policy
chemical sector 13.184
chocolate brands 14.44
  see also branding
cigarettes see tobacco
citizens' right of access to documents 13.238
  see also access; documents
civil rights, determination of 24.08–13
clandestine contact between traders 25.10
closeness of competition, horizontal mergers
    14.37–44
closeness of substitution, horizontal mergers
    14.39
coffee espresso machines 14.43
collective bargaining 4.14–17
collective dominance
  dominance abuse 5.49–56, 5.136
  horizontal mergers 14.56, 14.57, 14.58,
    14.81
  theory 14.06
  see also dominance abuse
collusion, collusive bidding 13.108
commercial information exchange 4.100
  see also information
commercial interests, protecting 5.141–4

commercial lease agreement 4.154
commercial vehicle replacement 10.43
  see also vehicles
Commission
  competence in case of amendment of
    proposed concentration 14.02
  competences, Commission versus Member
    States 14.193–5
  decision powers *see* Regulation 139/2004,
    control of concentrations between
    undertakings, powers of Commission
    decision (Article 8)
  failure to provide information within
    period fixed by Commission decision
    14.174
  investigation by 14.139–40
  liability, annulment of decision 14.79–81
  powers 9.46–54, 14.195
  referrals 14.196–8
  right to be heard, after concentration has
    been notified to Commission 14.188
commission income 13.194
common agricultural policy 17.01, 17.04,
    17.11, 17.14–17
  see also agricultural policy
communications apps 14.55
  see also technology
compatibility
  assessment, formal investigation procedure
    11.18–21, 11.23, 11.24, 11.28–9,
    11.36–8
  concentrations with the common market
    14.06
  with internal market 10.126, 10.127–45
  with rule of law 19.24–8
competences, Commission versus Member
    States 14.193–5
competition
  authority searches *see under* ECHR,
    respect for private and family life
    (Article 8), interference justification,
    disproportionate national systems
  closeness, horizontal mergers 14.37–44
  competitors in non-Member countries,
    TFEU, Article 101 and cartel
    prohibition 4.20–21

concept *see* TFEU, Article 101 and cartel
    prohibition, competition concept
  and concerted practice concept 4.109
  distortion 10.54–7
  and EEA Agreement 4.164
  effect to prevent, restrict or distort
    4.156–64
  elimination, and abuse of dominance
    5.05–6
  elimination, horizontal mergers 14.48,
    14.49–52
  non-competition clauses 4.269–71
  restrictions *see* TFEU, Article 101 and
    cartel prohibition, competition
    restriction
  restrictions, and association of
    undertakings 4.152, 4.179–82, 25.11
  ruinous 4.31
  rules, and aid prohibition 10.81
  rules implementation, Regulation 1/2003
    see Regulation 1/2003,
    implementation of rules of
    competition
  rules and State aid 10.81
  uniform application of competition law
    13.36–7
complaints
  obligation of Commission to address
    11.51
  received by Commission, aid notification
    11.123–4
complexity of dispute, right to a fair trial
    24.111–12
compulsion, testimony obtained under
    25.29, 25.30–32, 25.44
computer software and third party licence to
    use a product 5.110
  see also technology
concentrations between undertakings *see*
    Regulation 139/2004, control of
    concentrations between undertakings
concerted practice
  cartel prohibition *see* TFEU, Article 101
    and cartel prohibition, concerted
    practice concept
  causal link, presumption of innocence and
    rights of defence 25.18–20

ECSC Treaty 4.108
  as having anti-competitive object 4.147
concurrence of wills
  as agreement, and cartel prohibition
    4.68–77, 4.84, 4.87
  and vertical agreements 4.274
concurrent sanctions 13.164–5
conduct of applicant and conduct of court,
    right to a fair trial (Article 6) 24.110
conferred powers principle 8.02
confidentiality
  information 13.233, 13.239, 14.181,
    14.189
  lawyer-client 1.55
  procedure protection 13.55–6
  written communications 13.51–2, 13.56
conglomerate mergers 14.64–9
  see also mergers
consecutive acquisitions 14.132–5
constraints associated with use of languages
    24.110
consumers
  consumer protection associations and
    'sufficient interest' 14.187
  customer-sharing and price-fixing 13.153
  direct access to sources of production 4.28
  direct benefit for 4.228–31
  horizontal mergers and cultural diversity
    14.54
  MasterCard scheme and benefit to
    consumers 4.227, 4.231
  price information known by 4.268
contestable market, and abuse of dominance
    5.147
continuing or repeated infringements
    13.17–20, 13.213–14, 13.216
continuity, legal and economic 13.197–203
contract bundling see bundling
contract to contractor other than lowest
    bidder 4.248
contractual relations between suppliers and
    their approved distributors 16.05
contractual veto rights 14.91
control
  acquisition of control by the State
    14.109–10

change from joint to sole control
    14.11–13
  joint control 14.95–8, 14.105–7
  sole control, see Regulation 139/2004,
    control of concentrations between
    undertakings, concentration
    definition (Article 3), sole control
cooperation
  agreement between producer and
    wholesaler 4.232, 4.238
  competition concept 4.29, 4.32
  cooperative purchasing association 4.179
  criteria, concerted practice concept 4.97
  duty of genuine, aid recovery 11.111–12
  implementation of rules of competition,
    inspection powers 13.31–2
  obligation of active cooperation,
    information requests 19.55
  obligation of sincere cooperation 24.36
coordination
  competition concept 4.29, 4.32
  and concerted practice concept 4.97
  effects assessment, appraisal of
    concentrations 14.78
  effects, horizontal mergers 14.56–60
  effects, non-horizontal mergers 14.63
copper market 14.16, 14.21, 14.28, 14.58
copyright
  musical composers 5.102, 5.120
  and refusal to supply 5.99–100, 5.102–3
  sound recordings 5.99
  see also intellectual property rights
correspondence, respect for 19.09–10
  see also documents
cosmetics, internet sales ban 4.305
countervailing buyer power 14.61
  see also mergers
courts
  access rights 24.57–61
  conduct of 24.110
  national courts, cooperation with 13.34–5
  see also national courts; tribunals
credit information exchange 4.267
credit institutions 10.29, 14.127
criminal proceedings
  access to file 24.92–4
  right not to be tried or punished twice for
    same criminal offence 27.03–5

right to a fair trial *see* ECHR, right to a
    fair trial (Article 6), criminal charge
criminal sanctions, non-retroactivity of
    26.09–10, 26.16
crisp bread market 14.41
    see also food and drink sector
cross-subsidisation, aid prohibition 10.105
cultural diversity effects 14.54
customers *see* consumers
customs agents' activities 4.42
customs searches 19.40
Czech Republic
    banking sector 4.150
    competition authority searches 19.46

damages
    and aid notification 10.125
    civil action for 24.36
    claims against EU 24.116
    claims, and failure to adjudicate within a
        reasonable period 24.117
    compensation, and aid prohibition 10.125
data protection 4.52, 13.239
    see also information
dawn raids 24.63–5
de facto control of concentrations *see*
    Regulation 139/2004, control of
    concentrations between undertakings,
    concentration definition (Article 3), de
    facto control
'de facto control/economic dependence'
    arguments, turnover calculation
    (Article 5) 14.137
de facto prohibition on sales via internet in
    selective distribution agreements
    15.06–12
de minimis notice 4.175, 10.65–6, 13.21
dealers, conditions for admission of 17.05
dealing agreements with third country laws
    4.19
    see also third countries
debt arrangement, aid prohibition 10.102,
    10.115
defence
    breach of rights 13.223–4
    respect for the rights of 9.49, 13.87

rights of, inspection powers (Article 20)
    13.47, 13.51
rights of 14.80, 23.10–30, 25.23–4
rights of, preliminary enquiries
    applicability 23.13
rights of, and presumption of innocence
    see ECHR, presumption of
    innocence and rights of defence
    (Article 6)
deferred powers
    decisions of the executive 24.49–50
    Member State responsibility 18.17–25
Deggendorf-doctrine 11.90
democratic society necessity, respect for
    private and family life 19.32–52
Denmark, fertilizer market 5.31
derogation
    exceptional derogation from Treaty rules
        9.26–45
    suspension of concentrations 14.149–52
    TFEU, Article 106, public undertakings,
        exceptional derogation from Treaty
        rules 9.26–45
determination of civil rights 24.08–13
deterrence effect 13.120–22, 13.162, 24.19,
    24.21–2
diamonds and exclusive purchasing 5.72
differentiated markets, dominance abuse
    5.18–20
differentiation, product 5.48, 14.40–44
digital map databases 14.10, 14.63
    see also technology
direct action against decision adopted by a
    Community institution 11.79, 13.12,
    13.219, 13.236, 13.240
direct effect
    aid prohibition 10.71–4
    cartel prohibition 4.01–2, 5.01
disclosure
    relevant evidence 24.93
    to competitor of course of conduct 4.99
    see also information
discounts
    and dominance abuse 5.145–6
    practical effect of thresholds for 5.78

quantity discount effect circumstances 5.79

discretionary powers 4.238, 8.05, 10.37, 10.142, 13.73, 13.75, 13.78, 13.81, 13.151–2

margin of discretion 13.77, 13.243

discrimination between business partners 5.125

discriminatory pricing predation 5.89

disproportionate national systems *see* ECHR, respect for private and family life (Article 8), interference justification, disproportionate national systems

distancing, undertaking publicly distancing itself from agreement or concerted practice 13.06–9

distortion of competition 10.54–7

see also competition

distribution system

contractual relations between suppliers and their approved distributors 16.05

de facto prohibition on sales via internet in selective distribution agreements 15.06–12

exclusive distribution 4.306–9

protection, motor vehicle sector 15.10–11

spare parts 5.17, 5.84–6, 5.104–5

unauthorised distributors definition 15.07

unilateral conduct 4.78–80, 4.82, 4.84–5

divestitures beyond geographical markets 14.147

dock work 9.15, 9.21

see also transportation

documentation

citizens' right of access to documents 13.238

correspondence, respect for 19.09–10

failure to communicate a document 23.29

order to submit information or documents 25.36–43

preparatory documents 13.54

privileged correspondence between lawyer and client 13.53–4

probative data 4.112, 13.13–14

sealed envelope procedure 13.56, 19.59

written communications *see* written communications

see also file access; information

dominance abuse

collective *see* collective dominance

tariff approvals that lead to dominance abuse 9.18

TFEU, Article 102 *see* TFEU, Article 102, and abuse of dominance

double mark-up elimination 14.75

dual membership prohibition 4.179

duration of infringement *see* gravity and duration of infringement

ECHR, *ne bis in idem* principle 13.190

ECHR, no punishment without proper law (Article 7) 26.01–27

'economic continuity' test 26.24

foreseeability, EU courts 26.15–18

foreseeability, European Court of Human Rights 26.13–14, 26.17–18

gravity of infringements, determination of 26.21

joint and several liability 26.27

legality principle 26.01–7

legality principle, EU courts 26.05–7

legality principle, European Court of Human Rights 26.01–4

non-retroactivity of criminal sanctions 26.09–10, 26.16

penalty concept 26.08

personal liability principle 26.24–7

proportionality 26.19–23

retroactivity of the more lenient sanction, EU courts 26.12

retroactivity of the more lenient sanction, European Court of Human Rights 26.11

turnover of undertaking and calculation of fine 26.19, 26.22–3

ECHR, obligation to respect human rights (Article 1) 18.01–25

equivalence finding 18.23

equivalent guarantees 18.21–5

grant of exequatur for Commission Decision imposing a fine 18.24

international law sources 18.13–14

interpretation methods 18.02–14

as living instrument 18.04–5
Member State practice 18.12
Member State responsibility when
    deferring powers to EU 18.17–25
no binding effect vis-à-vis the EU 18.15
no binding effect vis-à-vis the EU as
    holder of powers 18.16
preliminary reference procedure 18.25
right to a fair trial 18.08
supplementary means of interpretation
    18.03, 18.11
supra-national human rights treaty 18.01
two-step test, general level and protection
    in the individual case concerned
    18.22
Vienna Treaty on the Law of Treaties
    18.03, 18.06–13
ECHR, presumption of innocence and
    rights of defence (Article 6) 25.01–46
burden of proof 25.04–7, 25.11, 25.15
causal link in case of a concerted practice
    25.18–20
clandestine contact between traders 25.10
degree of severity of the ensuing penalties
    25.09–10
EU courts 25.09–14
European Court of Human Rights
    25.01–8
legal certainty principle 25.17
obligation to answer truthfully under oath
    25.35
obligation to give the name of the driver
    of a registered vehicle 25.39
obligation to indicate one's whereabouts at
    a given time 25.34
obligation to mention the privilege against
    self-incrimination 25.46
obligation to provide information
    concerning the origin of certain
    income 25.38
order to submit information or documents
    25.36–43
order to submit information or
    documents, EU courts 25.40–43
order to submit information or
    documents, European Court of
    Human Rights 25.36–9

parent company liability 25.16–17
participation in a meeting with an
    anti-competitive character 25.21
privilege against self-incrimination and
    right to remain silent 25.25–45
reversible presumptions of fact or law,
    possibility of use of 25.03
right to remain silent, inferences drawn
    from 25.44–5
right to remain silent *stricto sensu* 25.33–5
rights of defence 25.23–4
testimony obtained under compulsion
    25.29, 25.30–32, 25.44
ECHR, respect for private and family life
    (Article 8) 19.01–59
respect for correspondence 19.09–10
respect for the home 19.01–8
respect for the home, EU Court of
    Human Rights 19.01–4
respect for the home, EU Courts 19.05–8
respect for privacy of telephone calls
    19.11
ECHR, respect for private and family life
    (Article 8), interference justification
    19.13–55
absence of prior judicial search
    authorisation sufficiently
    compensated by other safeguards
    19.55
accessibility 19.22
in accordance with the law 19.17–28
in accordance with national laws
    19.19–21, 19.25, 19.39–53, 19.55,
    19.57
in accordance with national laws,
    non-compliant Finnish system
    19.27–8
Community law guarantees 19.53
compatibility with rule of law 19.24–8
democratic society necessity 19.32–52
EU system assessment 19.53–5
explanatory notes 19.55
foreseeability 19.23
and judicial review 19.53, 19.55
lawyer-client confidentiality 1.55
legal privilege 19.56–9
legal privilege, EU courts 19.57–9

legal privilege, European Court of Human Rights 19.56

legitimate aim 19.29–30

obligation of active cooperation 19.55

penalty payments 19.57, 19.59

prior judicial authorisation, importance of 19.37–8

proportionality test 19.35–6

reasonable suspicion requirement 19.54

right to legal representation 19.53, 19.56, 19.59

right to protection of business premises 19.12–13

safeguards, adequate 19.33–4

sealed envelope procedure 19.59

search and seizure as serious interference 19.26

statement of reasons 19.55

two-step test 19.35–6

written communication between lawyer and client 19.56, 19.57–9

ECHR, respect for private and family life (Article 8), interference justification, disproportionate national systems 19.39–47

Austrian judicial searches 19.44

Belgian judicial searches 19.42

Czech competition authority searches 19.46

French competition authority searches 19.47

French competition searches according to former legislation 19.41

French customs searches 19.40

German judicial searches 19.39

Romanian judicial searches 19.45

Russian judicial searches 19.43

ECHR, respect for private and family life (Article 8), interference justification, proportionate national systems 19.48–52

French competition authority searches 19.52

Swiss searches under telecommunications legislation 19.49

UK Anton Piller order 19.20, 19.48

UK judicial searches 19.50

ECHR, right not to be tried or punished twice for same criminal offence (Article 4 Protocol 7) 27.01–9

criminal proceedings 27.03–5

criteria 27.03–4

final acquittal or conviction in the first proceedings 27.07–8

non bis in idem principle 27.01–2, 27.05–7

same offence, understanding of 27.06

tax penalties and criminal penalties combined 27.05

tried or punished again, understanding of 27.09

ECHR, right to a fair trial (Article 6) 18.08, 23.09, 23.29, 24.01–130

access rights to courts or tribunals 24.57–61

access rights to courts or tribunals, restrictions 24.60–61

autonomy principle 24.09

Charter Article 47 applicability 24.07

civil rights and obligations 24.08–13

right of silence 13.45

right to access to a lawyer 24.119–25

right to public hearing 24.118

social security proceedings 24.118

tax matters 24.12

ECHR, right to a fair trial (Article 6), criminal charge 24.14–27

autonomy concept 24.14–15

EU courts 24.21–7

European Court of Human Rights 24.14–20

fines for infringement of road traffic rules 24.16–17

fines for infringement of tax rules 24.18

hard core criminal law and other criminal charges, distinction between 24.22

moment when charge is brought 24.23–7

nature of offence 24.14

presumption of innocence 24.21

'reasonable time' from arrest to prosecution 24.25

rule of law 24.14

severity of offence, punishment and deterrence objectives 24.19, 24.21–2

ECHR, right to a fair trial (Article 6),
    effective remedy (Article 13) 23.09,
    24.01–6, 24.62–5
  annulment of inspection decision 24.65
  dawn raids 24.63–5
  EU courts 24.03–6, 24.65
  European Court of Human Rights 24.02,
    24.63–4
  legal standard 24.62
ECHR, right to a fair trial (Article 6), fair
    trial 24.66–101
  access to the file in criminal proceedings
    24.92–4
  applicability to pre-trial proceedings,
    European Court of Human Rights
    24.66–8
  effective judicial protection principle
    24.72
  entitlement to disclosure of relevant
    evidence 24.93
  equality of arms 24.88–91
  equality of arms, EU courts 24.91
  equality of arms, European Court of
    Human Rights 24.88–90
  exclusionary rule 24.95–6
  imposition of fines by an administrative
    body 24.69–75
  imposition of fines by an administrative
    body, EU courts 24.72
  imposition of fines by an administrative
    body, European Court of Human
    Rights 24.69–71
  imposition of fines by an administrative
    body, except in relation to serious
    charges 24.73
  inspectors, functions performed by 24.68
  lawfulness of having one and the same
    body investigate and fine 24.74
  legality review 24.72
  no obligation to remand to a different
    body following annulment 24.75
  obligation to comply 24.72
  obligation to state the grounds of a
    judgment 24.97–9
  prosecution and punishment of minor
    offences 24.70
  right to be heard 24.86

  sanction open to appeal 24.69–72
  waiver of rights 24.100–101
ECHR, right to a fair trial (Article 6), fair
    trial, adversarial proceedings principle
    24.76–87
  applicability when the court applies
    grounds of its own motion 24.84–7
  EU courts 24.82–3, 24.85–6
  European Court of Human Rights
    24.76–81, 24.84–5
  exceptions 24.87
ECHR, right to a fair trial (Article 6), full
    jurisdiction 24.43–56
  assessment 24.46–56
  equal treatment principle 24.55
  full review of sanctions by an
    administrative court 24.51–6
  full review of sanctions by an
    administrative court, EU courts
    24.55–6
  full review of sanctions by an
    administrative court, European Court
    of Human Rights 24.51–4
  gravity and duration of infringement, and
    setting of fines 24.55
  insufficiency in case of deference of the
    court to decisions of the executive
    24.49–50
  insufficiency of a pure constitutionality
    review 24.46
  insufficiency of a review restricted to
    points of law 24.47–8
  legal standard 24.43–5
  reciprocity clause 24.50
  unlimited jurisdiction exercise 24.55
ECHR, right to a fair trial (Article 6),
    independent and impartial tribunal
    24.28–42
  civil action for damages 24.36
  economic assessments 24.36
  following remandment 24.40–42
  following remandment, EU courts
    24.42–3
  following remandment, European Court
    of Human Rights 24.40–41, 24.43
  impartiality 24.37–42
  independence 24.35–6

independence, EU courts 24.35–6
independence, European Court of Human
  Rights 24.35
legality review 24.36
objective and subjective test 24.38–9
obligation of sincere cooperation 24.36
tribunal concept 24.28–34
tribunal concept, EU courts 24.32–4
tribunal concept, European Court of
  Human Rights 24.28–31
ECHR, right to a fair trial (Article 6), legal
  aid 24.126–29
assistance by a lawyer and dispensation of
  the cost of proceedings 24.127
availability to a legal person 24.129
grant procedure 24.128
principle of effective judicial protection
  24.129
right to an effective remedy 24.129
ECHR, right to a fair trial (Article 6),
  reasonable period 24.102–18
assessment 24.110–12
complexity of dispute 24.111–12
conduct of applicant 24.110
conduct of court 24.110
constraints associated with use of
  languages 24.110
EU courts 24.103
European Court of Human Rights 24.102
failure to adjudicate within a reasonable
  period 24.113–17
failure to adjudicate within a reasonable
  period, damages claims 24.117
failure to adjudicate within a reasonable
  period, EU courts 24.115–17
failure to adjudicate within a reasonable
  period, European Court of Human
  Rights 24.113–14
legal certainty requirement 24.111
legal standard 24.108–9
relevant period 24.104–7
setting aside of judgment under appeal
  24.116
superseded case law providing for
  immediate redress 24.115
ECHR, right to property (Article 1
  Protocol) 21.01

economic activity
  assessments, independent and impartial
    tribunal 24.36
  and cartel prohibition 4.38–54
  'de facto control/economic dependence'
    arguments 14.137
  development of certain, aid prohibition
    10.142
economic agents, provision of 16.03
economic aim pursued by parties 14.104
'economic continuity' test, ECHR, no
  punishment without proper law
  (Article 7) 26.24
economic progress, promotion of
  4.218–27
economic unit 4.55–62, 4.93–4
economic value and excessive pricing
  5.118, 5.119
financial crisis and emergency aid 10.141
legal and economic continuity 13.197–203
legal and economic links 13.194–6
restrictions inherent to an object of
  economic interest 4.179–82
retail pharmacies and economic progress
  4.222
strength measurement 5.07
value of royalties 5.117
see also capital; investment
ECSC Treaty 4.07, 4.32
  agreement concept 4.71
  concerted practices 4.108
  and exchange of information 4.265
  ne bis in idem principle 13.164
ECUs conversion 13.92
EEA Agreement
  and competition restriction 4.164
  evidence, nature of 13.13
  joint and several liability for infringement
    13.190
effect to prevent, restrict or distort
  competition 4.156–64
effective judicial protection principle 13.244,
  13.246, 24.72, 24.129
effective remedy, right to a fair trial see
  ECHR, right to a fair trial (Article 6),
  effective remedy (Article 13)

efficiencies, and dominance abuse 5.138,
    5.145–6
efficiency defence of mergers 14.74–8
    see also mergers
efficient competitor test 5.83
electricity
    distribution 5.50
    imports 9.39
elimination of competition concerns
    14.45–52, 14.142
employment
    collective bargaining between employers
        and workers 4.14, 4.15
    fixed-term employment contracts 10.122
    procurement activities 4.39, 9.13
    small businesses and protection of workers
        against unfair dismissal 10.06
    standard of living and employment levels
        10.127
energy transport network 5.96
enforcement measures
    limitation period for the enforcement of
        penalties 13.218–20
    TFEU, Article 103 6.01–3
entry barriers
    and cartel prohibition 4.35
    and dominance abuse 5.34–43
    and fixed costs 5.42
    and infrastructure 5.41
    reduction 14.143
    and standardization 5.43
environmental factors
    anti-pollution surveillance 4.41
    pollution and aid prohibition 10.138
    taxation 10.45–6
equal treatment principle 10.19, 13.75,
    13.81, 13.159–63, 24.55
equality of arms, right to a fair trial
    24.88–91
equality before the law see Charter, equality
    before the law (Article 20)
equity
    interest acquisition of competitor 4.160
    veto rights over issuance of fresh 14.114
equivalent guarantees 18.21–5
    see also guarantees
essential facilities and access time 5.95–6

EU Charter see Charter
EU courts
    equality of arms 24.91
    failure to adjudicate within a reasonable
        period 24.115–17
    fine review and unlimited jurisdiction
        22.05–7
    following remandment, EU courts,
        ECHR, right to a fair trial (Article
        6), independent and impartial
        tribunal 24.42–3
    full review of sanctions by an
        administrative court, EU courts,
        ECHR, right to a fair trial (Article
        6), full jurisdiction 24.55–6
    imposition of fines by an administrative
        body 24.72
    independence 24.35–6
    legal privilege 19.57–9
    legality principle 26.05–7
    no punishment without proper law 26.12,
        26.15–18
    order to submit information or documents
        25.40–43
    presumption of innocence and rights of
        defence 25.09–14
    respect for private and family life 19.05–8,
        19.53–5
    right to a fair trial, adversarial proceedings
        principle 24.82–3, 24.85–6
    right to a fair trial, criminal charge
        24.21–7
    right to a fair trial, effective remedy
        24.03–6, 24.65
    right to a fair trial, reasonable period
        24.103
    tribunal concept 24.32–4
European Convention on Human Rights see
    ECHR
European Court of Human Rights
    equality of arms, right to a fair trial
        24.88–90
    legal privilege, respect for private and
        family life 19.56
    no punishment without proper law
        26.01–4, 26.11, 26.13–14, 26.17–18

presumption of innocence and rights of
defence 25.01–8, 25.36–9
respect for private and family life 19.01–4
right to a fair trial, adversarial proceedings
principle 24.76–81, 24.84–5
right to a fair trial, applicability to
pre-trial proceedings 24.66–8
right to a fair trial, criminal charge
24.14–20
right to a fair trial, effective remedy
24.02, 24.63–4
right to a fair trial, failure to adjudicate
within a reasonable period 24.113–14
right to a fair trial, full jurisdiction
24.51–4
right to a fair trial, imposition of fines by
an administrative body 24.69–71
right to a fair trial, independent and
impartial tribunal 24.28–31, 24.35,
24.40–41, 24.43
right to a fair trial, reasonable period
24.102
European Regional Development Fund
10.133
evidence
assessment and standard of proof 4.113,
4.116
entitlement to disclosure of relevant 24.93
probative value of statements 13.13–14
Regulation 1/2003 13.04–5, 13.12–15
sufficient to demonstrate existence of
infringement 13.04
supplemented by inferences 13.05
testimony obtained under compulsion
25.29, 25.30–32, 25.44
examination of notification *see* Regulation
139/2004, control of concentrations
between undertakings, examination of
notification and initiation of
proceedings (Article 7)
exceptional derogation from Treaty rules
derogation 9.26–45
TFEU, Article 106, public undertakings
9.26–45
exceptions
Charter, rights and principle 29.01–3

equality of arms, right to a fair trial
24.88–91
exceptional circumstances for suspension
14.170
exceptional derogation from Treaty rules
9.26–45
right to a fair trial, adversarial proceedings
principle 24.87
serious charge 24.73
excessive pricing 5.116–21
see also pricing
exchange rates and turnover 13.92
exclusionary rule, right to a fair trial 24.95–6
exclusive distribution 4.306–9
see also distribution system
exclusive licence agreement, intellectual
property rights and broadcaster 4.308
see also broadcasting
exclusive purchasing 5.71–2
exclusive rights 5.76, 9.08, 9.15, 9.16, 9.19,
14.195
and state intervention 5.35–40
exclusive supply contract and block
exemption 15.15
exclusive supply obligation, agricultural
products 17.08
see also agricultural policy
exculpatory documents 23.29
see also documentation
exemptions
block *see* block exemptions
individual 5.154
TFEU, Article 101 *see* TFEU, Article 101
and cartel prohibition, exemptions
vertical agreements 15.02, 16.02–8
exequatur, grant of 18.24
exports
dock work 9.15, 9.21
maritime import and export operations
5.58
motor trade restrictions 4.172
port duties 9.20
preferential rediscount rate 10.116
prohibition 4.81–2
extraordinary general meetings insufficient
to create control 14.119
see also meetings

failing firm defence 14.70–73
failure to communicate a document 23.29
    see also documents
failure to notify a concentration 14.176–7
failure to provide information within period
    fixed by Commission decision 14.174
fair trial
    obligation to respect human rights 18.08
    right to *see* ECHR, right to a fair trial
        (Article 6)
    see also presumption of innocence
family life, respect for *see* ECHR, respect for
    private and family life (Article 8)
FEDETAB and tobacco imports 4.63, 4.70,
    4.125, 4.239
    see also tobacco
fees
    airport management services 5.124
    levels charged in other Member States
        5.121, 5.123
    self-employed substitutes 4.17
fertilizer market 4.237, 5.31, 14.15, 14.52
    see also agriculture policy
FIFA *see under* football
file access
    criminal proceedings 24.92–4
    equality of arms, right to a fair trial
        24.88–91
    right to good administration 23.25–30
    see also documentation
final acquittal or conviction in the first
    proceedings 27.07–8
final price composition 4.100
    see also pricing
financial activity *see* economic activity
financial crisis and emergency aid 10.141
financial institutions 4.267, 14.127
fines
    ability to pay 13.175–7, 24.110, 26.27
    absence of intention to pay 14.175
    calculation by Commission 22.04
    grant of exequatur for Commission
        Decision 18.24
    and gravity and duration of infringement
        24.55
    immunity or reduction 13.24

imposition by administrative body
    24.69–75
infringement of road traffic rules
    24.16–17
infringement of tax rules 24.18
lawfulness of having one and the same
    body investigate and fine 24.74
publication of decisions 13.236
Regulation 1/2003 *see* Regulation 1/2003,
    implementation of rules of
    competition, fines (Article 23)
Regulation 139/2004 *see* Regulation
    139/2004, control of concentrations
    between undertakings, fines (Article
    14)
review by EU courts and unlimited
    jurisdiction 22.05–7, 23.09
right to good administration 23.20–21
and turnover of undertaking 26.19,
    26.22–3
    see also sanctions
Finland, non-compliant system 19.27–8
fiscal measures, aid prohibition 10.118–19
fisheries sector 10.78, 11.17
    see also agriculture policy
'fix-it-first' commitment 14.141–2,
    14.147
fixed price agreements 4.71
    see also pricing
fixed-term employment contracts 10.122
    see also employment
fixing amount, fines 13.68–176
flour additives sector 5.14
'follow-my-leader' role in infringement
    13.128, 13.136
food and drink sector
    banana market 4.153, 5.26, 5.34, 5.130
    beer supply agreements 4.161, 4.206,
        4.311
    cheese market 4.233
    crisp bread market 14.41
    flour additives sector 5.14
    lysine market 13.93
    sugar market 4.102, 5.57, 13.197,
        14.25
    wine production 10.77
    see also agriculture policy

football
  broadcast licences for Premier League
    matches 4.149
  FIFA as association of undertakings
    4.139, 5.55
  national associations that are members of
    FIFA 4.128
  see also sports
foreclosure, non-horizontal mergers 14.62
foreseeability
  no punishment without proper law
    26.13–18
  respect for private and family life,
    interference justification 19.23
France
  airport management services 5.59
  competition authority searches 19.41,
    19.47, 19.52
  customs searches 19.40
  Expedia and *de minimis* notice 4.175
  racing companies and PMU 4.136
  social plans and financial assistance 10.36
franchise agreements 4.189, 4.211, 4.312–13,
    14.136–7
free movement of goods 10.80
freedom of establishment and freedom to
    provide services 13.51
freedom of movement, sports and freedom
    of movement, TFEU, Article 46
    4.18
freedom to conduct a business 20.01
  see also business
full jurisdiction, right to a fair trial *see*
    ECHR, right to a fair trial (Article 6),
    full jurisdiction
full review of sanctions by administrative
    court 24.51–6
  see also sanctions
fundamental rights, respect for 13.12
funeral services 9.12

gambling
  horse-racing 4.136, 4.182
  television broadcasting of horse-racing
    5.108
  and unclaimed winnings 10.07
gentlemen's agreement 4.35, 4.68
geographic allocation of power 14.130–31

geographic market
  and dominance abuse 5.22–5
  land sales 10.107–13
  price discrimination 5.127–31
  size and fines 13.105–6
Germany
  copyright laws 5.103
  intellectual property rights 9.33
  judicial searches 19.39
  motor vehicle industry 4.279, 15.09–10
  potash market 14.15
  reunification effects 10.139
  shipbuilding and marine and defence
    electronics 10.62
  statutory health insurance scheme 4.49
  tobacco distribution improvement 4.220
  vehicle leasing contracts 4.277
  zinc sheet manufacture 4.167
glass, float glass trade 14.27
good faith intention 14.129
grant procedure, legal aid 24.128
gravity and duration of infringement
  and fines 13.75, 13.82–5, 13.96, 13.98,
    13.101, 13.107–19, 13.134, 13.139,
    13.148–53, 13.162, 13.173, 13.230,
    24.55
  implementation of rules of competition
    13.03, 13.08, 13.10–11
  limitation periods for the imposition of
    penalties 13.214
  no punishment without proper law 26.21
Greece, maritime transport fares 13.159
green card system 9.11
grounds of judgment, obligation to state
    24.97–9
guarantees
  and aid prohibition 10.104
  equivalent 18.21–5
  respect for private and family life,
    interference justification 19.53
  vertical agreements 4.302, 4.303
gun jumping 14.128
GUPPI (gross upward pricing pressure
    index) test 14.53

hardcore criminal law and other criminal
    charges, distinction between 24.22

hardcore restrictions removing benefit of
    block exemption 16.09
health
    healthcare costs 4.16, 9.45
    hospital building investment 10.68
    insurance scheme 4.49
    patient transport services 9.24
    public ambulance service 9.43
    public health protection and dominance
        abuse 5.140
    services and medical care provision,
        Ireland 9.35
    specialist medical services 4.44, 4.171
heard, right to be *see* right to be heard
hearings of the parties *see* Regulation
    1/2003, implementation of rules of
    competition, hearings of parties,
    complainants and others (Article 27)
high-quality products, vertical agreements
    4.288–9, 4.291
high-technology products 4.80, 5.27
    see also technology
hold-up problem, appraisal of concentrations
    14.75
home, respect for 19.01–8
home-delivery services 5.41
horizontal agreements
    cartel prohibition *see* TFEU, Article 101
        and cartel prohibition, horizontal
        agreements
    mergers *see* Regulation 139/2004, control
        of concentrations between
        undertakings, appraisal of
        concentrations (Article 2), horizontal
        mergers
    see also vertical agreements
horse-racing 4.136, 4.182
    see also gambling; sports
human rights *see* ECHR headings

illegal practices, prices derived from
    13.146–7
immunity, fine immunity or reduction 13.24
    see also fines
impartiality *see* fair trial
implementation of rules of competition *see*
    Regulation 1/2003, implementation of
    rules of competition

imputability
    aid prohibition 10.12–16
    infringement on parent
        company/companies and conduct of
        subsidiaries 13.181–8, 13.195,
        13.204–6
income, obligation to provide information
    concerning origin of certain 25.38
incorrect or misleading information 13.66–7,
    14.173–5
    see also information
independent and impartial tribunal *see*
    ECHR, right to a fair trial (Article 6),
    independent and impartial tribunal
independent lawyer, position and status
    13.51
independent leasing companies 4.83
individual exemption, competition restriction
    5.154
individual legal entity comprising
    undertaking 4.58
individual liability principle 13.157
individual rights, preservation of and aid
    notification 11.84
individualised targets, rebate schemes 5.80,
    5.81
inferences, evidence supplemented by 13.05
information
    confidentiality 13.233, 13.239, 14.181,
        14.189
    data protection 4.52, 13.239
    disclosure effect 4.99, 4.106, 4.108, 4.110,
        4.112–13, 24.93
    exchange 4.100, 4.260–68, 13.33
    incorrect or misleading 13.66–7, 14.173–5
    obligation to give name of driver of
        registered vehicle 25.39
    obligation to provide information
        concerning origin of certain income
        25.38
    order to submit information or documents
        25.36–43
    professional secrecy 13.232–5, 13.237,
        13.239, 14.180–81
    public authority and data storage and
        access 4.52

requests *see* Regulation 1/2003, implementation of rules of competition, information requests (Article 18)

requests, control of concentrations between undertakings 14.171–2

requests, relevance of market tests 14.172

see also documentation

'infringements by object' and 'infringements by effect', distinction between 4.146, 4.175

initiation of proceedings *see* Regulation 139/2004, control of concentrations between undertakings, examination of notification and initiation of proceedings (Article 7)

innocence, presumption of *see* presumption of innocence

input market, and dominance abuse 5.15–17

insolvency or liquidation of credit institution 10.29

inspection, annulment of inspection decision, ECHR, right to a fair trial (Article 6), effective remedy (Article 13) 24.65

inspection powers *see* Regulation 1/2003, implementation of rules of competition, inspection powers (Article 20)

inspectors, functions performed by 24.68

insufficiency, right to a fair trial, full jurisdiction 24.46–50

insurance

agencies' rules 2.13

and cartel prohibition 4.11–12

companies 14.127

contracts and car repairs 4.151

industry supervision 4.133

scheme as economic activity 4.46

transport liability 14.31

intellectual property rights

copyright *see* copyright

and dominance abuse 5.95, 5.97–112, 5.148

exclusive licence agreement and broadcaster 4.308

Germany 9.33

patent rights 5.97, 5.107, 5.111, 5.112, 5.132

and public undertakings 9.32–3

trade-mark rights 5.97, 5.101

see also property rights

inter-trade agreements, TFEU, Article 107, aid prohibition 10.16

interest, savings deposits and maximum rates 2.09

interested parties, notification of aid 11.39–51

interference justification *see* ECHR, respect for private and family life (Article 8), interference justification

interim measures, Regulation 1/2003 13.26–8

International Covenant, right of silence 13.44

international law sources 18.13–14

international movement of capital 4.11

international removal services 4.121, 4.197–8

internet

cosmetics sales ban 4.305

de facto prohibition on sales via internet in selective distribution agreements 15.06–12

see also technology

interpretation

methods 18.02–14

rights and principle *see* Charter, scope and interpretation of rights and principle (Article 52)

interrelated transactions *see* Regulation 139/2004, control of concentrations between undertakings, concentration definition (Article 3), interrelated transactions

interrupted infringement 4.120

interruption of limitation periods for the imposition of penalties 13.215–16

intra-community trade 4.284, 13.106

investigation by authorisation or ordered by decision, choice between 13.58

investment

capital investment as entry barrier 5.34

hospital building investment 10.68

public sector investment funds 10.12
see also economic activity
Ireland
  health services and medical care provision
    9.35
  television programmes and weekly
    programme information 5.20
irreparable damage threat 13.27–8
IT services 14.155
see also technology
Italy
  certification services for public works
    contracts 4.54
  energy transport network 5.96
  motor vehicle manufacturer and supply
    quotas 4.273
  national quota system 4.130

jet engines 14.78
see also transport
joint control *see* control
joint and several liability 13.189–93, 26.27
joint and several liability for infringement,
    EEA Agreement 13.190
joint ventures 4.59, 4.234, 14.121–5
judicial protection principle, effective 13.244,
    13.246, 24.72, 24.129
judicial review
  aid prohibition 10.23, 10.86, 10.139
  cartel prohibition 13.245
  dominance abuse 13.245
  legality review 13.243–6
  prior judicial authorisation, importance of
    19.37–8
  public undertakings 9.52
  Regulation 1/2003 *see* Regulation 1/2003,
    implementation of rules of
    competition, judicial review (Article
    31)
  Regulation 1/2003, implementation of
    rules of competition, fines (Article
    23) 13.86
  Regulation 139/2004, control of
    concentrations between undertakings
    14.178–9
  and respect for private and family life,
    interference justification 19.53, 19.55

judicial searches *see under* ECHR, respect
    for private and family life (Article 8),
    interference justification,
    disproportionate national systems
judicial warrants, Regulation 1/2003,
    implementation of rules of
    competition, inspection powers 13.49

land sales 10.107–13
see also geographic market
language, constraints associated with use of
    24.110
lawfulness principle 13.238
lawyers
  fair trial, right to *see* ECHR, right to a
    fair trial (Article 6)
  lawyer-client confidentiality 1.55
  legal aid *see* ECHR, right to a fair trial
    (Article 6), legal aid
  legal professional privilege 8.02, 13.51–7,
    13.142, 19.55, 19.56–9
  position and status as independent 13.51
  right of access to 24.119–25
  written communication between lawyer
    and client 19.56, 19.57–9
leasing companies 4.83
legal aid *see* ECHR, right to a fair trial
    (Article 6), legal aid
legal certainty principle 11.119, 13.211–13,
    23.03, 24.111, 25.17
legal and economic continuity 13.194–203
legal framework, fines 13.71–5
legal professional privilege 8.02, 13.51–7,
    13.142, 19.55, 19.56–9
see also lawyers
legal representation right 19.53, 19.56, 19.59
legal standard 24.43–5, 24.62, 24.108–9
legality of Commission decision 24.33
legality principle 26.01–7
legality review
  judicial review 13.243–6
  right to a fair trial 24.36, 24.72
  TFEU, Article 263 13.244–6, 19.53,
    24.36, 24.55, 24.65
leisure equipment 4.238, 10.67
see also sports
leniency
  fines 13.131, 13.135, 13.171–4

grounds, Regulation 1/2003 13.14, 13.24, 13.45

judicial review 13.244

rebate 22.03

retroactivity of more lenient sanction 26.11, 26.12

leveraging, non-horizontal markets 14.66

liability, Regulation 1/2003 and fines 13.178–206

lignite deposits 9.10

limitation defence/duration 13.10–11

limitation periods for imposition of penalties see Regulation 1/2003, implementation of rules of competition, limitation periods for the imposition of penalties (Article 25)

limited review, Regulation 139/2004, referral to competent authorities of Member States 14.164

liquid gas distribution 14.49

liquidation of an undertaking 13.176

livestock insemination centres 9.16
    see also agriculture policy

living standards, standard of living and employment levels 10.127

loans and interest rates 10.103

lysine market 13.93
    see also food and drink sector

mail distribution 4.13, 9.09, 9.38, 9.44, 9.49, 14.26, 14.69

manufacturer's guarantee restrictions 4.302

margin of appreciation, aid prohibition 10.85–8

margin of discretion 13.77, 13.243
    see also discretionary powers

margin squeeze, dominance abuse 5.113–15

maritime import and export operations 5.58
    see also exports

maritime transport fares 13.159
    see also transport

markets
    agricultural products see Regulation 1308/2013, common organisation of markets in agricultural products
    bundling, horizontal mergers 14.66
    cartel prohibition, exemptions 4.224

conduct and relationship of cause and effect 4.101–13

contestable 5.147

definition 5.13–26

differentiated 5.18–20

economy investor principle 10.22–39

entry delay of generic undertakings 4.155

entry and potential competition 4.37

exclusion agreements 4.155

foreclosure 5.147

geographic market, relevant 5.22–5

high market share, horizontal mergers 14.31–6

input market 5.15–17

interpenetration of national 4.28

power and dominance abuse 5.29–48

products belonging to different 5.18

relevant see Regulation 139/2004, control of concentrations between undertakings, appraisal of concentrations (Article 2), relevant market

share 14.33–6

share and market power 5.29–33

share threshold 15.03

share and turnover 13.93, 13.95–6, 13.98, 13.103–4, 13.138, 13.140, 13.159–60

shares and competitors, relationship between 5.08–11

sharing negotiations and joint intentions 4.73–7

sharing of 4.253–7

sharing or price-fixing agreements 13.108, 13.110–11

tests 14.172

transparency 14.56

maverick competitive force 14.45–8

maximum aggregate amount, fines 13.63

media
    broadcasting see broadcasting
    newspaper distribution 4.290, 4.295, 5.95
    players and abusive bundling 5.87

meetings
    between minority shareholder and management insufficient to create control 14.117

extraordinary general meetings insufficient to create control 14.119

lack of stable majority at 14.86

participation in a meeting with anti-competitive character 25.21

shareholder attendance rates 14.85

see also shareholders

Member States

acquisition of control by 14.109–10

action defence 5.149

aid notification, requirement to notify and standstill obligation 11.60–61, 11.87

aid prohibition, effect on trade between 10.58–70

aid prohibition, no effect on trade between 10.69–70

competences versus Commission 14.193–5

dominance abuse, effect on trade between 5.150–51

dominance abuse and trade limitations between 5.129–31

human rights obligation 18.12

intervention and exclusive rights 5.35–40

mergers and competent authority referral *see* Regulation 139/2004, control of concentrations between undertakings, referral to competent authorities of Member States

power of competition authorities 13.23–4

responsibility when deferring powers to EU 18.17–25

tariff fixing 10.124

see also national legislation; State aid; trade

mergers

banking 14.47

conglomerate 14.64–9

countervailing buyer power 14.61

efficiency defence of 14.74–8

horizontal *see* Regulation 139/2004, control of concentrations between undertakings, appraisal of concentrations (Article 2), horizontal mergers

rescue 14.70–71

vertical agreements 14.62–3

minimum retail prices 10.123

see also pricing

ministerial orders 2.08–9

minor offences, prosecution and punishment of 24.70

mitigating circumstances 13.80, 13.123–37

mobile telephony 9.54, 14.45, 14.149

see also telecommunications

motivation inspection decision 13.59–60

motor vehicles *see* vehicles

museums, local museum projects 10.70

music

appliances for cleaning gramophone records 4.166

composers' copyright 5.102, 5.120

digital music services 14.54

sound recordings 5.99

television broadcasting of musical works 5.120

national courts

cooperation with 13.34–5

legislation 3.02, 3.07

role 11.83–90

see also courts

national insurance bureaux and green card system 9.11

national legislation

administrations, activity of assisting 4.51

cartel prohibition 4.51, 4.133, 4.136, 4.140

competition laws 13.21–2, 14.192, 17.17

disproportionate national systems *see* ECHR, respect for private and family life (Article 8), interference justification, disproportionate national systems

procedural autonomy 8.02

quota system 4.130

respect for private and family life, interference justification 19.19–21, 19.25, 19.27–8, 19.39–53, 19.55, 19.57

restrictions 2.02–5

and TFEU Article 101 *see* TFEU, Article 101 and cartel prohibition, national law relationship

see also Member States; State aid; trade

national preferences 14.18–19

ne bis in idem principle 13.164–70, 13.190, 27.01–2, 27.05–7
Netherlands
  cheese market cooperative 4.233
  electricity distribution 5.50
  insurance agencies' rules 2.13
  oil products and rebate scheme 5.74
  pension schemes 9.23, 9.42
  postal services 9.49
  professional body as regulatory body 4.65
  standard of living and employment levels 10.127
  TV broadcasting 14.198
  Watts brand and restricted intra-Community trade 4.166
network effects 4.188, 14.55–61
new aid 11.01–3, 11.05–10, 11.12–15
new calculation method, fines 13.158
new entrants, bundle of similar contracts and new entrant issues 4.161
new product markets 4.222, 5.21, 5.106, 5.108, 5.110, 14.14
newspaper distribution 4.290, 4.295, 5.95
  see also media
no binding effect 18.15–16
non-competition clauses 4.269–71
non-contractual liability 14.79
non-disclosure obligation, professional secrecy 14.181
non-discrimination, equal treatment principle 10.19, 13.75, 13.81, 13.159–63, 24.55
non-horizontal mergers *see* Regulation 139/2004, control of concentrations between undertakings, appraisal of concentrations (Article 2), non-horizontal mergers
non-profit-making associations 4.50
non-retroactivity of criminal sanctions 26.09–10, 26.16
Nordic countries
  mail delivery services 14.26
  telecommunications mergers 14.49
notification incorrect and misleading 14.175
notification of statement of objections 23.04

notified transactions 14.102, 14.101–4
nullity of agreements
  agricultural cooperative 17.16
  and cartel prohibition 4.201–9, 15.05
  vertical agreements in the motor vehicle sector 16.02–3
nullum crimen, nulla poena sine lege (no crime without law) principle 26.01, 26.09, 26.16, 26.18

oath, obligation to answer truthfully under 25.35
objections, statement of 23.04, 23.16–24
obligations
  active cooperation 19.55
  answer questions relating to stock rates 25.33
  answer truthfully under oath 25.35
  Commission's obligation to address complaints parties 11.51
  give name of driver of a registered vehicle 25.39
  indicate one's whereabouts at a given time 25.34
  mention privilege against self-incrimination 25.46
  provide information concerning the origin of certain income 25.38
  respect human rights *see* ECHR, obligation to respect human rights (Article 1)
  sincere cooperation 24.36
  state the grounds of a judgment 24.97–9
offence, same offence, understanding of 27.06
oil products 5.74, 15.05, 15.14–18
order to submit information or documents 25.36–43
  see also documents; information

packaging fees 5.123
packaging products 5.13, 14.22
parallel behaviour
  concerted practice concept 4.101, 4.103
  exports 5.143
  imports 4.77, 4.219, 4.294, 4.307, 16.05
  notifications 14.08–10
  trade agreements 4.77, 4.148

parent companies
  decisive influence over subsidiary
    13.180–81, 13.183–8
  imputability of infringement on 13.181–8,
    13.195, 13.204–6
  joint ventures 4.59
  liability 25.16–17
  subsidiary's failure to carry out parent
    company's instructions 4.67
  transfer from parent company to
    subsidiary 4.91–2, 4.94
particle board trade 14.20
patent rights 5.97, 5.107, 5.111, 5.112,
  5.132
  see also intellectual property rights
pay-for-delay, horizontal agreements 4.272
penalties
  concept 26.08
  degree of severity of ensuing 25.09–10
  effectiveness 13.35
  limitation period for enforcement of
    13.218–20
  limitation periods for imposition of see
    Regulation 1/2003, implementation
    of rules of competition, limitation
    periods for the imposition of
    penalties (Article 25)
  precludes penalising more than once
    13.167, 13.190
  respect for private and family life,
    interference justification 19.57, 19.59
  tax penalties and criminal penalties
    combined 27.05
pensions 4.15, 9.23, 9.42
  compulsory membership of occupational
    pension fund 4.180
  sectoral pension funds 4.43
  supplementary pension benefits of medical
    specialists 4.171
personal liability principle 26.24–7
petroleum products 5.74, 15.05, 15.14–18
pharmaceutical products
  company refusal to supply wholesalers
    involved in parallel exports, TFEU,
    Article 102, and abuse of dominance,
    abuse 5.143
  cosmetics, internet sales ban 4.305

and dominance abuse 5.21
  generic products, competition from 5.144
  out of proportion to those previously sold
    5.131
  quinine price fixing 4.243
  retail pharmacies and economic progress
    4.222
photographic equipment dealers 4.294
pig meat market 10.76
  see also agriculture policy
pipe sector, pre-insulated 13.159
plasterboard imports 5.76
plastics sector, TFEU, Article 102, and
    abuse of dominance, dominance 5.14
Poland, TEU, Article 6, Charter and ECHR
    3.15
Portugal
  airport charges 9.53
  chartered accountant regulation 4.53
postal services 4.13, 9.09, 9.38, 9.44, 9.49,
    14.26, 14.69
potash market 14.15, 14.52
  see also agricultural policy
pre-existing agreements 2.09
pre-notification referrals 14.128–9
pre-trial proceedings 24.66–8
predatory pricing 5.88–91
  see also pricing
preferential rediscount rate for exports
    10.116
preferential tariffs 10.21
preliminary examination, aid notification
    11.75–7, 11.87
preliminary reference procedure 18.25
preparatory documents 13.54
  see also documentation
preservation of individual rights 11.84
presumption of causal connection 4.111,
    4.113
presumption of innocence
  criminal charge 24.21
  principle, vertical agreements 4.274
  Regulation 1/2003, implementation of
    rules of competition 13.05, 13.233
  and right to a fair trial, criminal charge
    24.21

and rights of defence *see* ECHR,
   presumption of innocence and rights
   of defence (Article 6)
see also fair trial
pricing
   alignment on those previously charged by
      a competitor 5.142
   announcements as evidence of price
      concertation 4.107
   below average variable cost or below
      average total cost 5.88
   common price list adoption 4.247
   controls 4.135, 4.137
   differences 14.17
   discrimination 5.89, 5.124–8
   excessive 5.116–21
   final price composition 4.100
   fixed price agreements 4.71
   fixing 4.105, 4.121, 4.144, 4.163, 4.243,
      4.250, 13.108, 13.110–11, 13.153,
      17.11
   geographic price discrimination
      5.127–31
   loss recoupment possibility, no
      requirement to show 5.90–91
   minimum retail prices 10.123
   objectives 4.252
   predatory 5.88–91
   production costs and excessive pricing
      5.117
   resale price clauses 4.281, 15.04–5
   retail selling prices 2.04–5
   see also profits; tariffs
prior judicial authorisation, importance of
   19.37–8
prior judicial search, respect for private and
   family life, interference justification
   19.55
prior notification of concentrations and
   pre-notification referrals 14.128–9
privacy
   respect for privacy of telephone calls
      19.11
   respect for private and family life *see*
      ECHR, respect for private and
      family life (Article 8)

private investor
   behaviour in comparable circumstances
      10.28–9
   of comparable size to public body 10.20
   test 10.22, 10.23–5, 10.28, 10.29
      TFEU, Article 108, notification of aid,
         formal investigation procedure
         11.31
privatisation by tendering 10.114
privilege against self-incrimination and right
   to remain silent 25.25–45
privileged correspondence between lawyer
   and client 13.53–4
   see also documentation
probative data 4.112, 13.13–14
   see also documentation
procedure protection confidentiality
   13.55–6
product differentiation 5.48, 14.40–44
product packaging 5.13, 14.22
production capacity increase 10.128
production costs 5.117, 13.100
production and distribution improvement
   4.218–27
products belonging to different markets
   5.18
products related to those covered by an
   agreement or practice 4.196
professional body acting as association of
   undertakings 4.64
professional body as regulatory body 4.65
professional secrecy 13.232–5, 13.237,
   13.239, 14.180–81
profits
   derived from illegal practices 13.146–7
   rebates on retailers' profit margins 4.169
   see also pricing
prohibited measures, public undertakings
   9.11–25
prohibition of sales between authorized
   dealers 4.301
proof
   agreement between undertakings 4.84
   evidence assessment and standard of
      4.113, 4.116
   Regulation 139/204, TFEU, Article 102,
      and abuse of dominance 14.1543

proof, burden
  aid notification of aid, formal
    investigation procedure 11.30
  cartel prohibition 4.216, 4.226
  presumption of innocence and rights of
    defence 25.04–7, 25.11, 25.15
  Regulation 1/2003 13.01–11, 13.13,
    13.181, 13.213–14
property rights 21.1
  see also intellectual property rights
proportionality principle
  cartel prohibition, exemptions 4.232–6
  and interference 29.02
  and legality *see* ECHR, no punishment
    without proper law (Article 7)
  price fixing 17.11
  public undertakings 9.36–45
  Regulation 1/2003, implementation of
    rules of competition 13.30, 13.58,
    13.75, 13.86, 13.97, 13.101, 13.121,
    13.146–58, 13.161
  respect for private and family life *see*
    ECHR, respect for private and
    family life (Article 8), interference
    justification, proportionate national
    systems
  restorative measures 14.156
  test 19.35–6
prosecution, 'reasonable time' from arrest to
    prosecution, ECHR, right to a fair
    trial (Article 6), criminal charge 24.25
prosecution and punishment of minor
    offences, ECHR, right to a fair trial
    (Article 6), fair trial 24.70
protection, Charter, level of protection
    (Article 53) 30.01
protection of business premises 19.12–13
  see also business
protection of written communications
    principle 13.53
  see also documentation
public authorities
  cartel prohibition 4.52
  data storage and access 4.52
  employment procurement activities 4.39,
    9.13

market economy investor principle
    10.22–39
  share capital owned by 10.26
public health *see* health
public hearing, right to 24.118
public interest protection 13.52
public law, trade association governed by
    10.17–18
public sector investment funds 10.12
public service obligations 10.34–5
public undertakings
  TFEU, Article 106 *see* TFEU, Article
    106, public undertakings
  TFEU, Article 107, aid prohibition
    10.13–14, 10.30
public works, certification services for 4.54
publication of decisions *see* Regulation
    1/2003, implementation of rules of
    competition, publication of decisions
    (Article 30)
publishers, book sales 2.03, 4.10, 14.166
punished twice, right not to be tried or
    punished twice for same criminal
    offence *see* ECHR, right not be tried
    or punished twice for same criminal
    offence (Article 4 Protocol 7)
punishment
  minor offences 24.70
  no punishment without proper law *see*
    ECHR, no punishment without
    proper law (Article 7)
  objectives, right to a fair trial, criminal
    charge 24.19, 24.21–2
purchasing
  cooperative purchasing association 4.179
  exclusive purchasing 5.71–2
  goods, economic activity issues 4.48
  Share Purchase Agreement 14.105
PVC market 4.250

quality of control 14.100–3
quantity discounts 5.73, 5.79, 5.82
quinine price fixing 4.243
  see also pharmaceutical products
quota agreements 4.130, 4.273, 13.108

radio equipment, type approval requirements
    9.17

see also broadcasting

raw materials market 5.15, 5.92, 11.43, 13.100, 14.61, 17.10

reasonable grounds, inspection powers 13.48

reasonable period

right to a fair trial *see* ECHR, right to a fair trial (Article 6), reasonable period

right to good administration 23.01–9

reasonable suspicion requirement 19.54

reasonable time from arrest to prosecution 24.25

reasons, statement of, respect for private and family life, interference justification 19.55

rebate schemes *see* TFEU, Article 102, and abuse of dominance, abuse, rebate schemes

rebates on retailers' profit margins 4.169

reciprocity clause, right to a fair trial 24.50

recovery of aid *see* TFEU, Article 108, notification of aid, recovery of aid

reference period calculation, rebate schemes 5.75

referral to competent authorities *see* Regulation 139/2004, control of concentrations between undertakings, referral to competent authorities of the Member States (Article 9)

refusal to supply *see* TFEU, Article 102, and abuse of dominance, abuse, refusal to supply

regional aid 10.133, 10.134–7

regional selectivity, aid prohibition 10.40

Regulation 1/2003, implementation of rules of competition 13.01–252

annulment of decision 13.04

Article 101 and time of entry into force of Treaty 4.27

bank guarantees 13.220

burden and standard of proof (Article 2) 13.01–11, 13.181

commitments (Article 9) 13.29–30

competition rules and State aid 10.81

cooperation (Article 11) 13.31–2

de minimis notice thresholds 13.21

designation of competition authorities of Member States (Article 35) 13.252

dispute concerning existence of infringement 13.11

economic unit and infringement of competition law 4.58

evidence, nature of 13.12–15

evidence, nature of, probative value of statements 13.13–14

evidence sufficient to demonstrate existence of infringement 13.04

evidence supplemented by inferences 13.05

fine immunity or reduction 13.24

fundamental rights, respect for 13.12

information exchange (Article 12) 13.33

infringement duration 13.03, 13.08

infringement, finding and terminating (Article 7) 13.25

insurance industry 4.12

interim measures (Article 8) 13.26–8

irreparable damage threat 13.27–8

leniency grounds 13.14, 13.24, 13.45

limitation defence/duration 13.10–11

limitation period for the enforcement of penalties (Article 26) 13.218–20

Member States, power of competition authorities (Article 5) 13.23–4

national competition laws (Article 3) 13.21–2

national courts, cooperation with (Article 15) 13.34–5

presumption of innocence 13.05, 13.233

prima facie case 13.26

professional secrecy (Article 28) 13.232–3

proportionality principle 13.30

single and continuous or repeated infringement 13.17–20

single and continuous or repeated infringement, continuous versus repeated infringement 13.19–20

tacit approval rules 13.08

transitional provisions (Article 34) 13.251

undertaking publicly distancing itself from agreement or concerted practice 13.06–9

uniform application of Community
    competition law (Article 16) 13.36–7
validity period of commitment decisions
    13.29
Regulation 1/2003, implementation of rules
    of competition, fines (Article 23)
    13.62–206, 24.36
ability to pay 13.175–7, 24.110, 26.27
aggravating circumstances 13.138–45
and annulment decisions 13.169
assessment conduct undertaking in
    relation to gravity infringement
    13.148–53
assessment factors 13.82–122
associations of undertakings, calculation
    turnover 13.177
breaking a seal 13.67
chemical sector 13.184
classification of undertakings by category
    13.161–2
commission income 13.194
compliance programmes 13.124
consequences of infringement 13.116–19
decisive influence by parent over
    subsidiary 13.180–81, 13.183–8
deterrence effect 13.120–22, 13.162
discretionary powers 13.81, 13.151–2
equal treatment or non-discrimination
    principle 13.75, 13.81
equality of treatment 13.159–63
exchange rates and turnover 13.92
fixing amount 13.68–176
'follow-my-leader' role in infringement
    13.128, 13.136
geographic market size 13.105–6
gravity and duration of infringement
    13.75, 13.82–5, 13.96, 13.98, 13.101,
    13.107–19, 13.134, 13.139,
    13.148–53, 13.162, 13.173, 13.230
guidelines on method of setting 13.76–81
imputability of infringement on parent
    company/companies and conduct of
    subsidiaries 13.181–8, 13.195,
    13.204–6
incorrect or misleading information
    13.66–7
individual liability principle 13.157

joint and several liability 13.189–93
judicial review 13.86
legal and economic continuity 13.197–203
legal and economic links 13.194–6
legal framework 13.71–5
legal professional privilege 13.142
leniency grounds 13.131, 13.135,
    13.171–4
liability 13.178–206
liquidation of an undertaking 13.176
lysine market and turnover 13.93
margin of discretion 13.77
maritime transport fares 13.159
market share and turnover 13.93, 13.95–6,
    13.98, 13.103–4, 13.138, 13.140,
    13.159–60
market-sharing or price-fixing agreements
    13.108, 13.110–11
maximum aggregate amount 13.63
mitigating circumstances 13.80,
    13.123–37
ne bis in idem principle (dual procedures)
    13.164–70, 13.190
ne bis in idem principle (dual procedures),
    Member State prior to accession to
    EU 13.170
ne bis in idem principle (dual procedures),
    and turnover of Members 13.168
new calculation method 13.158
number of undertakings committing
    infringement 13.82–3, 13.154–5
pre-insulated pipe sector 13.159
price-fixing and customer-sharing 13.153
prices derived from illegal practices
    13.146–7
production cost exclusions 13.100
proportionality principle 13.75, 13.86,
    13.97, 13.101, 13.121, 13.146–58,
    13.161
quota agreements 13.108
relation fine undertakings involved in the
    same infringement 13.154–7
repeat infringements 13.85–7, 13.144
representation in administrative procedure
    13.204–5
respect for the rights of the defence 13.87

size differences between undertakings
13.159
small- or medium-sized undertakings
13.99, 13.154
sugar market 13.197
transparency of decisions 13.174
turnover of undertaking 13.88–102
vertical relation 13.206
Regulation 1/2003, implementation of rules
of competition, hearings of parties,
complainants and others (Article 27)
13.222–31
annulment of contested decision 13.226,
13.231
breach of the rights of the defence
complaint 13.223–4
right to be heard 13.226, 13.228, 13.232
statement of objections 13.221–5,
13.227–8, 13.231
third-party observations 13.226, 13.229
Regulation 1/2003, implementation of rules
of competition, information requests
(Article 18) 13.38–45
Commission powers 13.39–41
obligation to cooperate 13.44–5
purpose of request, stating 13.43
request by decision 13.42–3
right of silence 13.44–5
specification and time limits 13.43
Regulation 1/2003, implementation of rules
of competition, inspection powers
(Article 20) 13.46–61, 24.65
confidentiality of written communications
13.51–2, 13.56
documents other than privileged
correspondence between lawyer and
client 13.53–4
freedom of establishment and freedom to
provide services 13.51
granting assistance to Commission
officials 13.61
investigation by authorisation or ordered
by decision, choice between 13.58
judicial warrants 13.49
legal professional privilege 13.51–7, 19.55,
19.57, 19.59

legal professional privilege, limitation for
in-house lawyers 13.57
motivation inspection decision 13.59–60
position and status as independent lawyer
13.51
preparatory documents 13.54
principle of protection of written
communications 13.53
procedure protection confidentiality
13.55–6
proportionality principle 13.58
public interest protection 13.52
reasonable grounds 13.48
rights of the defence 13.47, 13.51
sealed envelope procedure 13.56
searches of premises 13.48, 13.50
Regulation 1/2003, implementation of rules
of competition, judicial review (Article
31) 13.240–50, 24.72
economic assessments 13.243
effective judicial protection principle
13.244, 13.246
legality review 13.243–6
leniency grounds 13.244
margin of discretion 13.243
unlimited jurisdiction 13.241–2, 13.244–8
unlimited jurisdiction on appeal
13.249–50
Regulation 1/2003, implementation of rules
of competition, limitation periods for
the imposition of penalties (Article 25)
13.207–17
applicable periods 13.207–10
burden of proof, single and continuous
infringement 13.213–14
continuing or repeated infringements
13.216
court proceedings pending 13.217
gravity and duration of infringement
13.214
information requests 13.215
interruption of 13.215–16
legal certainty principle 13.211–13
repeated infringements 13.208, 13.210
Regulation 1/2003, implementation of rules
of competition, publication of decisions
(Article 30) 13.234–9

appropriateness of amounts of fines
13.236

and business secrets 13.234–5, 13.237,
13.239

citizens' right of access to documents
13.238

principle of lawfulness 13.238

and professional secrecy 13.234–5, 13.237

Regulation 45/2001, business secrets 13.237

Regulation 139/2004, control of
concentrations between undertakings
14.01–200

air transport, in-flight magazine 14.173

Commission competence in case of
amendment of proposed
concentration 14.02

educational material sales 14.166

extraterritorial application 14.01

information requests (Article 11)
14.171–2

information requests (Article 11),
relevance of market tests 14.172

IT services 14.155

judicial review (Article 16) 14.178–9

mobile telephony 14.149

prior notification of concentrations and
pre-notification referrals (Article 4)
14.128–9

prior notification of concentrations and
pre-notification referrals (Article 4),
good faith intention 14.129

prior notification of concentrations and
pre-notification referrals (Article 4),
suspensive effect and gun jumping
14.128

professional secrecy (Article 17)
14.180–81

professional secrecy (Article 17),
incidentally gained information
14.180

professional secrecy (Article 17),
non-disclosure obligation 14.181

referral to Commission (Article 22)
14.196–7

referral to Commission (Article 22),
influence of trade between States
14.197–8

suspension of concentrations (Article 7)
14.148–52

suspension of concentrations (Article 7),
derogation 14.149–52

third country relations (Article 24) 14.200

time limits for initiating proceedings and
for decisions (Article 10) 14.169–70

time limits for initiating proceedings and
for decisions (Article 10), exceptional
circumstances for suspension 14.170

TV broadcasting 14.128, 14.198

'undertakings concerned', notion of 14.03

Regulation 139/2004, control of
concentrations between undertakings,
appraisal of concentrations (Article 2)
14.04–81

air transport 14.13, 14.76

annulment of decision, Commission
liability 14.79–81

bidding markets (tenders) 14.37–40

carton market 14.67

collective dominance theory 14.06

compatibility of concentrations with the
common market 14.06

coordinated effects assessment 14.78

counterfactual in case of change from
joint to sole control 14.11–13

crisp bread trade 14.41

digital map databases 14.10, 14.63

double mark-up elimination 14.75

efficiency defence of mergers 14.74–8

elimination of strong competitive force
('maverick') 14.45–8

failing firm defence 14.70–73

first notification prevails over second
notification 14.09–10

hold-up problem 14.75

incorrect substantive assessment 14.81

jet engines 14.78

liability in case of breach of an
undertaking's right of defence 14.80

liner shipping services 14.12

mobile telephony services 14.45

new product markets 14.14

non-contractual liability 14.79

parallel notifications 14.08–10

parties' products are close substitutes 14.41

price differences 14.17

prohibition decision 14.05

prospective analysis 14.04–5

rescue merger 14.70–71

sealed-bid first price auction 14.40

simultaneous analysis 14.08

standard of proof 14.04–7

telecommunications networks 14.49, 14.53

Regulation 139/2004, control of concentrations between undertakings, appraisal of concentrations (Article 2), horizontal mergers 14.29–61

agricultural potash market 14.52

alpine skis and alpine bindings 14.42

ARPU (average revenue per unit) calculation 14.53

chocolate brands 14.44

closeness of competition 14.37–44

closeness of substitution 14.39

coffee espresso machines 14.43

collective dominance conditions 14.56, 14.81

collective dominance, conditions may be established indirectly 14.57

collective dominance as result of participation in a competitor 14.58

communications apps 14.55

coordinated effects 14.56–58

copper shapes market 14.58

countervailing buyer power 14.61

cruise ship market 14.32, 14.51

effects on consumers and cultural diversity 14.54

elimination of maverick in mergers from four to three players 14.47

elimination of a potential competitor 14.49–52

extending scope of 'important competitive force' 14.48

GUPPI (gross upward pricing pressure index) test 14.53

high market share 14.31–6

high market share and dependence on one customer 14.31

high market share neutralised by immature market without significant expansion barriers 14.32

liquid gas distribution 14.49

market share of 50 per cent + 14.33

market share of 70–80 per cent, combined 14.34

market share (high) not indicative of market power in case of short innovation cycles and free products 14.36

market share relevance 14.35

market transparency 14.56

network effects 14.55–61

oceanic cruises 14.32

parties are close competitors 14.44

parties' products are differentiated 14.43

product differentiation 14.40–44

product differentiation used to rebut high market shares 14.42

recorded music markets 14.54

retaliation mechanisms 14.56

tacit coordination 14.59–60

transport liability insurance 14.31

Regulation 139/2004, control of concentrations between undertakings, appraisal of concentrations (Article 2), non-horizontal mergers 14.62–9

bundling, leverage a strong position from one market to another 14.66

conglomerate mergers 14.64–9

coordinated effects as result of vertical merger 14.63

foreclosure 14.62

mail preparation services 14.69

relation assessment of conglomerate mergers and Art. 102 TFEU 14.67–9

vertical mergers 14.62–3

Regulation 139/2004, control of concentrations between undertakings, appraisal of concentrations (Article 2), relevant market 14.14–28

chain of substitution 14.27–8

copper rod suppliers 14.28

copper scrap trade 14.16, 14.21

float glass trade 14.27

mail delivery services 14.26

motor vehicle parts 14.23, 14.61
national preferences 14.18–19
packaging products 14.22
particle board trade 14.20
potash imports 14.15
regulatory differences 14.24–6
sugar industry and beet quota reduction
   14.25
toy market 14.19
trade patterns 14.15–16
transportation costs and distances
   14.20–23
TV broadcasting market 14.18
Regulation 139/2004, control of
   concentrations between undertakings,
   concentration definition (Article 3)
   14.82–127
acquisition of control by the State
   14.109–10
credit institutions, financial institutions or
   insurance companies 14.127
joint control 14.95–8
joint control, acquisition of indirect 14.98
joint venture creation 14.121–6
joint venture creation, full function
   14.122–6
joint venture creation, not full function
   14.121
lasting structural change, minimum time
   period 14.120
'undertakings concerned' in case of
   acquisition of control by state-owned
   enterprises (SOE) 14.111–12
'undertakings concerned' in case of
   acquisition of control by state-owned
   enterprises (SOE), independent
   power of decision from State 14.111
'undertakings concerned' in case of
   acquisition of control by state-owned
   enterprises (SOE), power to
   coordinate commercial conduct
   14.112
Regulation 139/2004, control of
   concentrations between undertakings,
   concentration definition (Article 3), de
   facto control 14.82–7, 14.137

intent to acquire control by a shareholder
   14.87
lack of stable majority at meetings 14.86
passive acquisition 14.85
shareholder attendance rates 14.85
voting rights 14.82
without de jure control 14.83
Regulation 139/2004, control of
   concentrations between undertakings,
   concentration definition (Article 3),
   interrelated transactions 14.99–108
changes in quality of control 14.100–3
economic aim pursued by the parties
   14.104
joint control acquisition 14.105–7
notified transactions 14.102, 14.101–4
Share Purchase Agreement 14.105
treatment of several transactions as single
   concentration 14.108
unitary nature of transactions 14.104
Regulation 139/2004, control of
   concentrations between undertakings,
   concentration definition (Article 3), no
   control/concentration 14.113–19
call option insufficient to create control
   14.113
meetings between minority shareholder
   and management insufficient to
   create control 14.117
no acquisition of control in case of
   minority shareholdings 14.116
request for extraordinary general meetings
   insufficient to create control 14.119
veto rights over issuance of fresh equity
   and substantial acquisitions
   insufficient to create control 14.114
voting against shareholders' resolutions
   insufficient to create control 14.118
voting in concert 14.115
Regulation 139/2004, control of
   concentrations between undertakings,
   concentration definition (Article 3),
   sole control 14.88–94
acquisition of brand (rights) 14.89
contractual veto rights 14.91
negative 14.92–4

special rights for minority shareholder 14.90

Regulation 139/2004, control of concentrations between undertakings, examination of notification and initiation of proceedings (Article 7) 14.139–47
acceptance of other commitments than divestitures 14.143
commitments 14.141–7
commitments involving pre-existing contractual rights of a third party 14.145
divestitures beyond geographical markets 14.147
elimination of competition concerns 14.142
entry barriers reduction 14.143
'fix-it-first' commitment 14.141–2, 14.147
investigation by Commission 14.139–40
'up-front buyer' commitment 14.141

Regulation 139/2004, control of concentrations between undertakings, fines (Article 14) 14.173–7
absence of intention 14.175
failure to notify a concentration 14.176–7
failure to provide information within period fixed by Commission decision 14.174
notification was incorrect and misleading 14.175
providing incorrect or misleading information 14.173–5
relation between failure to notify and implementation prior to clearance 14.177

Regulation 139/2004, control of concentrations between undertakings, hearing of the parties and of third persons (Article 18) 14.182–9
access to files 14.189
right to be heard 14.187–8
right to be heard, after concentration has been notified to Commission 14.188
right to be heard, 'sufficient interest' in case of consumer protection associations 14.187

Regulation 139/2004, control of concentrations between undertakings, hearing of the parties and of third persons (Article 18), statement of objections 14.182–6
arguments put forward by parties after 14.185
competition problems not mentioned in 14.186
delimits scope of administrative procedure 14.184
functions and requirement 14.183
must be sufficiently clear 14.182
procedures for reviewing concentrations 14.183

Regulation 139/2004, control of concentrations between undertakings, powers of Commission decision (Article 8) 14.153–60
ancillary restraints assessment 14.155
restorative measures 14.156–60
restorative measures, adoption of divestiture decision 14.157
restorative measures, implementation, meaning of 14.160
restorative measures, implementation and relevant point in time 14.158
restorative measures, proportionality principle 14.156
TFEU Article 102 versus remedies 14.154
unnecessary or insufficient commitments 14.153

Regulation 139/2004, control of concentrations between undertakings, referral to competent authorities of the Member States (Article 9) 14.161–7
appeal by third party possible 14.161
Commission decision regarding request for referral 14.163–8
comprehensive review 14.162
explicit rejection of referral request 14.168
limited review 14.164
non-referral decision by Commission may not be contested by third parties 14.167
significant effect within a Member State 14.162

transfer of exclusive competence 14.165

Regulation 139/2004, control of concentrations between undertakings, regulation and jurisdiction application (Article 21) 14.190–95

Commission versus Member States competences 14.193–5

exclusive competence for Commission 14.190–91

merger control without prejudice to separate assessment under State aid rules 14.191

national competition law applicability 14.192

no competence of Commission for decision after abandonment of merger 14.194

transformation into infringement procedure 14.195

Regulation 139/2004, control of concentrations between undertakings, turnover calculation (Article 5) 14.130–38

air transport 14.131

attribution of turnover 14.136–8

consecutive acquisitions 14.132–5

'de facto control/economic dependence' arguments 14.137

franchises 14.136–7

geographic allocation 14.130–31

global assessment 14.133

notified concentration does not meet turnover thresholds 14.132, 14.135

Regulation 169/2009, inland transport services 4.225

Regulation 267/2010, insurance industry 4.12

Regulation 330/2010, vertical agreements 15.01–20

beer supply agreements 4.206

exclusive supply contract and block exemption 15.15

exemption (Article 2) 15.02

market share threshold (Article 3) 15.03

motor vehicle sector 15.01, 15.08–10

non-complete and exclusivity clauses for petroleum products 15.14–18

overview 15.13–18

resale price clauses 4.281, 15.04–5

secondary markets definition 15.03

specified criteria 15.01

transitional period (Article 9) 15.19–20

Regulation 330/2010, vertical agreements, restrictions removing benefit of block exemption (Article 4) 15.04–12

de facto prohibition on sales via internet in selective distribution agreements 15.06–12

integrity of selective distribution system 15.07

resale price clauses 15.04

resale price clauses in vertical agreements for petroleum products 15.05

territorial restrictions 15.08–12

unauthorised distributors definition 15.07

Regulation 461/2010, vertical agreements in the motor vehicle sector 16.01–9

contractual relations between suppliers and their approved distributors 16.05

distribution system protection 15.10–11

exemption (Article 4) 16.02–8

freedom of contract 16.04

hardcore restrictions removing benefit of block exemption (Article 5) 16.09

mandatory provisions directly affecting validity of clauses of a contract 16.08

nullity of agreement 16.02–3

provision of economic agents 16.03

selective distribution system, imperviousness of 16.06

specified criteria 16.01

Regulation 659/1999

existing aid 11.10

new aid 11.14

notification of aid 11.35–7, 11.46, 11.52, 11.93–4, 11.105–6

Regulation 773/2004, professional secrecy 13.239

Regulation 802/2004, request to be heard 14.188

Regulation 1017/68, inland transport services 4.225

Regulation 1049/2001, information confidentiality 13.233, 13.239, 14.181, 14.189

Regulation 1184/2006, common agricultural policy 17.01, 17.04, 17.11, 17.14–17

Regulation 1234/2007, common agricultural policy 17.04

Regulation 1308/2013, common
organisation of markets in agricultural products 17.01–17
conditions for admission of dealers 17.05
division of competence in Regulation 1184/2006 17.14–17
exclusive supply obligation 17.08
farmers and farmers' associations (Article 209) 17.03, 17.05–17
individual earnings in the agricultural sector, jeopardizing 17.10
national competition authorities 17.17
price fixing and proportionality principle 17.11
resignation clauses 17.08
restrictive practices 17.12
scope of articles 206 and 209 17.03

Regulation 1534/91, insurance industry 4.12

Regulation 1768/92, patents and lack of transparency 5.132

Regulation 2759/75, pig meat market 10.76

Regulation 2842/98
infringement, finding and terminating 13.25
professional secrecy 13.239

Regulation 2988/74, legal certainty principle and limitation period 13.211–12, 13.215

relevant market
appraisal of concentrations *see* Regulation 139/2004, control of concentrations between undertakings, appraisal of concentrations (Article 2), relevant market
share definition 4.197–8

relevant period, right to a fair trial 24.104–7

remandment, impartiality following 24.40–42

remedies
effective, and, legal aid 24.129
right to a fair trial *see* ECHR, right to a fair trial (Article 6), effective remedy (Article 13)
versus TFEU Article 102 14.154

renewal application, cartel prohibition, exemptions 4.241

repeat infringements 13.17–20, 13.213–14, 13.216
and fines 13.85–7, 13.144
limitation periods for the imposition of penalties 13.208, 13.210, 13.216

representation in administrative procedure 13.204–5

request to be heard, Regulation 802/2004 14.188

res judicata principle 11.88, 27.06, 27.08

resale price clauses 4.281, 15.04–5
see also pricing

rescue mergers 14.70–71
see also mergers

resignation clauses, common organisation of markets in agricultural products 17.08

respect for private and family life *see* ECHR, respect for private and family life (Article 8)

respect for the rights of the defence 9.49, 13.87

restorative measures 14.156–60

restraints, ancillary restraints assessment 14.155

restrictions
access rights to courts or tribunals 24.60–61
agreement between traders within common market and competitors in third countries 4.187
common organisation of markets in agricultural products 17.12
effect on trade between Member States 4.192
inherent to an object of economic interest 4.179–82
manufacturer's guarantee 4.302

retail selling prices 2.04–5
see also pricing

retaliation mechanisms, horizontal mergers 14.56

retroactive censorship, vertical agreements 4.300

retroactivity of the more lenient sanction 26.11–12

right of access *see* access

right to an effective remedy 24.129

right to a fair trial *see* ECHR, right to a fair trial (Article 6)

right to good administration *see* Charter, right to good administration (Article 41)

right to be heard
  hearing of the parties and of third persons 14.187–8
  right to a fair trial 24.86
  right to good administration 13.226, 13.228, 13.232, 14.188, 23.14–15, 23.17–21, 23.25

right to legal representation 19.53, 19.56, 19.59

right not to be tried or punished twice for same criminal offence *see* ECHR, right not be tried or punished twice for same criminal offence (Article 4 Protocol 7)

right to property 21.1

right to protection of business premises 19.12–13

right to public hearing 24.118

right to silence 13.45, 25.25–45

rights, interpretation of rights and principle *see* Charter, scope and interpretation of rights and principle (Article 52)

rights of defence 13.47, 13.51, 14.80, 23.10–30, 23.13, 25.23–4
  presumption of innocence *see* ECHR, presumption of innocence and rights of defence (Article 6)

road traffic rules, fines for infringement of 24.16–17

Romania, judicial searches 19.45

royalties 5.111, 5.117, 5.120

ruinous competition 4.31
  see also competition

rule of law 19.24–8, 24.14

rule of reason, cartel prohibition 4.176–8

Russia, judicial searches 19.43

safeguard measures
  aid notification 11.85, 11.87
  respect for private and family life, interference justification 19.33–4, 19.55

same offence, right not be tried *see* ECHR, right not be tried or punished twice for same criminal offence (Article 4 Protocol 7)

sanctions
  full review by administrative court 24.51–6
  non-retroactivity of criminal sanctions 26.09–10, 26.16
  open to appeal 24.69–72
  retroactivity of the more lenient sanction 26.11–12
  see also fines

savings deposits and maximum rates of interest 2.09

sealed envelope procedure 13.56, 19.59
  see also documentation

sealed-bid first price auction 14.40

search and seizure as serious interference 19.26

searches of premises 13.48, 13.50

secondary markets 5.134–5, 15.03

secrecy, professional 13.232–5, 13.237, 13.239, 14.180–81

sectoral over-capacity, aid prohibition 10.135

selective distribution
  aid prohibition 10.36–53
  and cartel prohibition 4.80–82
  de facto prohibition on sales via internet 15.06–12
  high-technology products 4.80
  taxation context 10.41–53
  vertical agreements 4.283, 4.285–9, 4.292–9, 4.301–5, 16.06

self-employed substitutes, fees for 4.17

self-incrimination, privilege against, and right to remain silent 25.25–45

serious charge, exceptions 24.73

serious difficulties concept, aid notification 11.27–31

service provision and access time 5.94
services
    and cartel prohibition 4.199
    freedom to provide 13.51
    SGEI (services of general economic
        interest) 9.31–42, 10.30–35
several transactions, treatment as single
    concentration 14.108
severity of offence, punishment and
    deterrence objectives 24.19, 24.21–2
SGEI (services of general economic interest)
    9.31–42, 10.30–35
sham action 5.133
shareholders
    attendance rates 14.85
    intent to acquire control by 14.87
    meetings between minority shareholder
        and management insufficient to
        create control 14.117
    no acquisition of control in case of
        minority shareholdings 14.116
    share capital owned by public authorities
        10.26
    Share Purchase Agreement 14.105
    special rights for minority shareholders
        14.90
    voting against shareholders' resolutions
        insufficient to create control 14.118
    see also meetings
shipping
    cruise ship market 14.32, 14.51
    liners 5.89, 14.12
    merchant vessels in International
        Shipping Register 10.04
    mooring marinas 10.69
    port duties 9.20
    sailboards trade 4.190
    shipbuilding and marine and defence
        electronics 10.62
    shipbuilding and ship conversion aid
        10.145
silent, right to remain 13.45, 25.25–45
single branding 4.310–11
    see also branding
single and continuous infringement
    13.17–20, 13.213–14, 13.216
single undertakings 4.56, 14.126

size differences between undertakings
    13.159
skis, alpine skis and bindings 14.42
    see also sports
Slovak Republic, Postal Regulatory Office
    9.09
SMEs 4.04, 10.06, 13.99, 13.154
social policy 4.14–17, 10.36, 10.82
social security system 4.40, 4.43, 4.49, 10.41,
    10.115, 24.118
    see also taxation
sole control of concentrations see Regulation
    139/2004, control of concentrations
    between undertakings, concentration
    definition (Article 3), sole control
sound recordings 5.99
    see also music; technology
Spain
    commercial vehicle replacement 10.43
    theme park sale 10.107
spare parts distribution 5.17, 5.84–6,
    5.104–5
    see also distribution
special rights see exclusive rights
sports
    alpine skis and bindings 14.42
    football see football
    and freedom of movement 4.18
    horse-racing 4.136, 4.182
    leisure equipment 4.238, 10.67
SSNIP test 5.21
standard of living and employment levels
    10.127
standstill obligation see TFEU, Article 108,
    notification of aid, requirement to
    notify and standstill obligation
State aid
    aid notification 10.05, 10.75–7
    aid prohibition 10.01–11
    and cartel prohibition 9.55
    and competition rules 10.81
    dominance abuse 9.55
    merger control without prejudice to
        separate assessment 14.191
    notification in case of 11.52–4
    public undertakings 9.55–6

see also Member States; national legislation; trade
statement of objections
  and cartel prohibition 14.184
  hearing of the parties *see* Regulation 139/2004, control of concentrations between undertakings, hearing of the parties and of third persons (Article 18), statement of objections
  respect for private and family life (Article 8), interference justification 19.55
  right to good administration 23.16–24
  TFEU, Article 102, and abuse of dominance 14.184
structural change, minimum time period 14.120
subsidiaries *see under* parent companies
subsidiarity principle 4.194
subsidy concept 10.89–90
substitution
  chain 14.27–8
  close 14.39, 14.41
sugar market 4.102, 5.57, 13.197, 14.25
  see also food and drink sector
sui generis protection and databases 4.52
superseded case law providing for immediate redress 24.115
supra-national human rights treaty 18.01
suspensive effect 11.96, 11.98, 14.128, 14.148–52, 14.149–52, 14.170
suspicion, reasonable suspicion requirement, respect for private and family life, interference justification 19.54
Switzerland, telecommunications legislation 19.49

tacit acceptance of agreement, cartel prohibition 4.86, 5.56
tacit approval rules 13.08
tacit coordination 5.56, 14.59–60
tariffs
  air tariffs 2.06–7, 2.10
  approvals that lead to dominance abuse 9.18
  fixed at level lower than normal 10.21
  fixing by Member States 10.124
  long-distance transport of goods by road 2.12

preferential 10.21
public undertakings 9.18
quotas 10.02
see also pricing
taxation
  aid notification of aid and method of financing 11.56–9
  corporate income tax and change of ownership 10.48
  direct business 10.44
  environmental factors 10.45–6
  exemptions 10.119
  fines for infringement of tax rules 24.18
  as integral part of aid measure 10.120
  penalties and criminal penalties combined 27.05
  and right to a fair trial 24.12
  selectivity 10.41–53
  see also social security system
technology
  communications apps 14.55
  computer software and third party licence to use a product 5.110
  digital map databases 14.10, 14.63
  digital music services 14.54
  high-technology products 4.80, 5.27
  internet *see* internet
  IT services 14.155
  sound recordings 5.99
  technologically advanced equipment 10.17
telecommunications
  digital subscriber line 5.114
  end-user access services 5.113
  ex ante regulation 6.04
  legislation 19.49
  mergers 14.49
  mobile telephony 9.54, 14.45, 14.149
  networks 14.49, 14.53
  telephone calls, respect for privacy of 19.11
  telephone equipment market 9.37
  telephone installations 5.24
television broadcasting *see under* broadcasting
tenders 9.34, 10.114, 14.37–40
territoriality principle
  and cartel prohibition 4.19–24
  and dominance abuse 5.04–6

extraterritorial application 14.01
territorial limits, lack of 13.90
vertical agreements 15.08–12
testimony obtained under compulsion 25.29,
    25.30–32, 25.44
see also evidence
TEU, Article 3
    common market establishment 1.01–3
    social policy 4.14
TEU, Article 4 2.01–16
    aeronautical authorities and tariff
        agreements 2.10
    air tariffs 2.06–7, 2.10
    binding domestic and Community rules
        2.16
    collective bargaining and healthcare costs
        4.16
    duty not to jeopardise Union objectives re
        TFEU Articles 101 and 102a
        2.01–13
    duty not to jeopardise Union objectives re
        TFEU articles 107 and 108 2.14,
        11.111
    inspection powers 13.46
    insurance agencies' rules 2.13
    ministerial orders 2.08–9
    national legislation restrictions 2.02–5
    pre-existing agreements 2.09
    procedural aspects 2.15–16
    retail selling prices 2.04–5
    review in context of procedures provided
        for in TFEU Articles 258 and 267
        2.15
    savings deposits and maximum rates of
        interest 2.09
    tariffs for long-distance transport of goods
        by road 2.12
TEU, Article 6, Charter and ECHR
    3.01–15
    Charter 3.01–2
    direct effect in relation to EU law 3.11
    direct effect in relation to national law
        3.12–14
    EHRC application by EU courts 3.03–14
    EHRC application by EU courts, prior to
        Lisbon Treaty 3.03–8
    EHRC as source of law 3.01–10

national court legislation 3.02, 3.07
position of Poland and UK 3.15
TEU, Article 51, competition infringements
    1.03
TFEU, Article 4, social policy 4.14
TFEU, Article 15, citizens' right of access to
    documents 13.238
TFEU, Article 16, data protection 13.239
TFEU, Article 34, exclusive right to
    organize dock work 9.15
TFEU, Article 39, agriculture policy 10.77,
    17.01, 17.11
TFEU, Article 42, agriculture policy 17.02
TFEU, Article 43, agriculture policy 17.01
TFEU, Article 45
    exclusive right to organize dock work 9.15
    sports and freedom of movement 4.18
TFEU, Article 46, sports and freedom of
    movement 4.18
TFEU, Article 49, special or exclusive rights
    9.08, 14.195
TFEU, Article 56, special or exclusive rights
    9.08
TFEU, Article 101 and cartel prohibition
    4.01–313
    agriculture 4.07
    air transport 4.08–9
    atomic energy 4.07
    bank transfers 4.11
    books 4.10
    coal and steel and ECSC Treaty 4.07
    collective bargaining 4.14–17
    competition rules and State aid 10.81
    competitors in non-Member countries
        4.20–21
    direct effect 4.01–2, 5.01
    healthcare costs 4.16
    insurance industry 4.11–12
    judicial review 13.245
    motor vehicles 4.13
    nullity of agreements 4.201–9
    pension funds 4.15
    postal services 4.13
    ratione loci 4.19–24
    ratione materiae 4.07–18
    ratione personae and activities of
        undertakings 4.03–6

ratione temporis 4.25–7
self-employed substitutes, fees for 4.17
selling contractual product outside
    contractual territory assigned to it
    4.23
simultaneous application with TFEU
    Article 102 5.155–6
social policy 4.14–17
sports and freedom of movement 4.18
State aid 9.55
statement of objections and Regulation
    139/2004 14.184
territoriality principle 4.19–24
TFEU Article 102 relation 5.152–6
trade between Member States 4.20–24
transport 4.08–9
TFEU, Article 101 and cartel prohibition,
    agreement concept 4.68–94
agreements no longer in force 4.69–70
between two or more undertakings
    4.88–94
concurrence of wills 4.68–77, 4.84, 4.87
contractual variation acceptance 4.85
export prohibition 4.81–2
fixed price agreements 4.71
gentlemen's agreement 4.68
high-technology products, selective
    distribution services 4.80
independent leasing companies 4.83
market-sharing negotiations and joint
    intentions 4.73–7
motor vehicle dealership 4.78–9, 4.83
parallel trade agreement 4.77
proof of agreement between undertakings
    4.84
selective distribution system 4.80–82
tacit acceptance of agreement 4.86, 5.56
transfer from parent company to
    subsidiary 4.91–2, 4.94
undertakings forming economic unit
    4.93–4
unilateral conduct and apparently
    unilateral conduct 4.78–87
TFEU, Article 101 and cartel prohibition,
    association of undertakings concept
    4.63–7, 4.125–9, 5.53

chartered accountant undertaking training
    4.66
professional body acting as 4.64
professional body as regulatory body 4.65
subsidiary's failure to carry out parent
    company's instructions 4.67
TFEU, Article 101 and cartel prohibition,
    competition concept 4.28–37
coordination and cooperation 4.29, 4.32
and ECSC Treaty 4.32
entry barriers 4.35
function 4.28
Gentlemen's Agreement 4.35
interpenetration of national markets 4.28
market entry and potential competition
    4.37
nature and intensiveness of competition,
    variations in 4.30–31
potential competition 4.33–7
ruinous competition 4.31
TFEU, Article 101 and cartel prohibition,
    competition restriction 4.141–82
acquisition by one company of an equity
    interest in a competitor 4.160
agreement intended to limit parallel trade
    4.148
anti-doping rules 4.182
appliances for cleaning gramophone
    records 4.166
appreciable restriction of competition
    4.174–75
association of undertakings 4.179–82
banking sector 4.150
brewery sector, new entry issues 4.161
bundle of similar contracts and new
    entrant issues 4.161
commercial lease agreement 4.154
compulsory membership of occupational
    pension fund 4.180
concerted practice as having
    anti-competitive object 4.147
cooperative purchasing association 4.179
cross-border transactions 4.198
de minimis notice 4.175
dual membership prohibition 4.179
effect to prevent, restrict or distort
    competition 4.156–64

exclusive licences for the broadcasting of
Premier League football matches
4.149

food sector, quotation prices for bananas
4.153

individual exemption 5.154

'infringements by object' and
'infringements by effect', distinction
between 4.146, 4.175

insurance contracts and car repairs 4.151

market entry delay of generic
undertakings 4.155

market exclusion agreements 4.155

method of analysis required by settled
case-law 4.164

motor trade, export restrictions 4.172

object to prevent, restrict or distort
competition 4.141–55

price fixing 4.144, 4.163

rebates on retailers' profit margins 4.169

restrictions inherent to an object of (non)
economic interest 4.179–82

rule of reason 4.176–8

supplementary pension benefits of medical
specialists 4.171

transport sector, horizontal agreements
between undertakings 4.170

zinc sheet manufacture 4.167

TFEU, Article 101 and cartel prohibition,
concerted practice concept 4.95–124

and agreements, distinction between 4.96

and agreements, single continuous
infringement 4.114–24

and agreements, single continuous
infringement, interrupted
infringement 4.120

and agreements, single continuous
infringement, three conditions 4.121

bank transfers and debiting bank charges
4.103

commercial information exchange 4.100

and competition restriction 4.109

concertation 4.96–100

coordination and cooperation criteria 4.97

disclosure to competitor of course of
conduct 4.99

evidence assessment and standard of proof
4.113, 4.116

final price composition 4.100

information disclosure effect 4.106, 4.108,
4.110, 4.112–13

market conduct and relationship of cause
and effect 4.101–13

parallel behaviour 4.101, 4.103

presumption of causal connection 4.111,
4.113

price announcements as evidence of price
concertation 4.107

price fixing 4.105, 4.120

probative data 4.112

raw sugar transactions 4.102

as substitute for risks of competition
cooperation between undertakings
4.98

travel agencies 4.113

TFEU, Article 101 and cartel prohibition,
decision of associations of undertakings
concept 4.125–9

FEDETAB and tobacco imports 4.125

MasterCard and bank services 4.129

national associations that are members of
FIFA 4.128

TFEU, Article 101 and cartel prohibition,
effect on trade between Member States
4.20–24, 4.183–200

agreement constituting a threat to trade
4.184

applicant's individual participation 4.191

existence of similar contracts 4.185

franchise agreements for the distribution
of goods 4.189

presumption that trade between Member
States is affected 4.195

probability factor 4.193

processed tobacco products 4.196

products that are related to those covered
by an agreement or practice' 4.196

relevant market share definition 4.197–8

restrictive agreement between traders
within common market and
competitors in third countries 4.187

restrictive arrangements, effects of 4.192

sailboards trade 4.190

services 4.199
subsidiarity principle 4.194
traders applying for admission to a
   distribution network 4.188
TFEU, Article 101 and cartel prohibition,
   exemptions 4.210–42
burden and standard of proof 4.216, 4.226
car manufacture and technological
   progress 4.223
cheese market cooperative 4.233
compound potash fertilizers 4.237
cooperation agreement between producer
   and wholesaler 4.232, 4.238
cumulative conditions 4.218–42
demarcation of the market 4.240
direct benefit for consumers 4.228–31
electronic leisure equipment sector and
   cooperation agreements 4.238
FEDETAB and tobacco imports 4.239
franchises 4.211
improvement of production and
   distribution, promotion of technical
   and economic progress 4.218–27
inland transport services 4.225
joint ventures 4.234
market transparency 4.224
MasterCard scheme and benefit to
   consumers 4.227, 4.231
no elimination of competition 4.237–42
proportionality 4.232–6
renewal application 4.241
retail pharmacies and economic progress
   4.222
tobacco distribution improvement 4.220
TFEU, Article 101 and cartel prohibition,
   horizontal agreements 4.253–72
certification systems and standards
   4.258–9
exchange of information 4.260–68
non-competition clauses 4.269–71
pay-for-delay 4.272
sharing of markets 4.253–7
TFEU, Article 101 and cartel prohibition,
   horizontal agreements, agreements
   concerning prices and other trading
   conditions 2.43–52, 4.243–72
common price list adoption 4.247

contract to contractor other than lowest
   bidder 4.248
FETTCSA and customer discounts 4.251
price fixing in PVC market 4.250
price fixing of quinine 4.243
price objectives 4.252
TFEU, Article 101 and cartel prohibition,
   national law relationship 4.130–40
autonomous conduct that restricts
   competition 4.138
FIFA association 4.139
insurance industry supervision 4.133
national quota system 4.130
price controls 4.135, 4.137
racing companies and PMU 4.136
TFEU, Article 101 and cartel prohibition,
   undertaking concept 4.38–62
agent and principals, economic unit
   determination 4.61
air navigation safety 4.51
anti-pollution surveillance 4.41
certification of motor vehicles 4.54
certification services for public works
   contracts 4.54
chartered accountants 4.53
civil air transport installations 4.45
customs agents' activities 4.42
economic activity 4.38–54
economic unit 4.55–62
employee incorporated into economic unit
   4.62
insurance scheme as economic activity
   4.46
joint ventures 4.59
national administrations, activity of
   assisting 4.51
non-profit-making associations 4.50
offer of goods or services without profit
   4.50
public authority and data storage and
   access 4.52
purchasing goods, economic activity issues
   4.48
sectoral pension fund 4.43
service provider acting under control of
   undertaking that is using its services
   4.62

single undertakings 4.56, 14.126
social security system 4.40, 4.43, 4.49
specialist medical services and
    self-employment 4.44
statutory health insurance scheme 4.49
sui generis protection and databases 4.52
transfer of activities date 4.60
TFEU, Article 101 and cartel prohibition,
    vertical agreements 4.273–313,
    15.01–3, 15.12, 15.14, 15.19–20,
    16.01–8
advertising restrictions 4.300
agency 4.276–81
beer supply agreements 4.311
car insurance companies and bilateral
    arrangements with car dealers 4.275
car sales and fuel agencies 4.279–81
concurrence of wills 4.274
exclusive distribution 4.306–9
exclusive licence agreement concluded
    between holder of intellectual
    property rights and broadcaster 4.308
franchising 4.312–13
high-quality products 4.288–9, 4.291
'impervious' guarantee 4.303
internet sales ban for cosmetics 4.305
and intra-community trade 4.284, 13.106
motor vehicle distribution system
    4.273–4, 4.285, 4.298
nature of products 4.288–91
newspaper and periodical distribution
    4.290, 4.295
photographic equipment dealers 4.294
presumption of innocence principle 4.274
price undertaking condition 4.299
prohibition of sales between authorized
    dealers 4.301
restriction of the manufacturer's guarantee
    4.302
retroactive censorship 4.300
selection criteria 4.292–8
selective distribution systems 4.283,
    4.285–9, 4.292–9, 4.301–5
single branding 4.310–11
travel agencies 4.276
vehicle leasing contracts 4.277
verification obligations 4.282

TFEU Article 101 and time of entry into
    force of Treaty, Regulation 1/2003,
    implementation of rules of competition
    4.27
TFEU, Article 102, and abuse of dominance
    5.01–158
air transport 5.03
Community law 5.04
competitor elimination 5.05–6
conglomerate mergers and Regulation
    139/2004 14.67–9
contestable market 5.147
dangerous waste disposal 9.22
direct effect 5.01–2
effect on trade between Member States
    5.150–51
employment procurement activities 9.13
exclusive right to organize dock work 9.15
exercise of the exclusive right necessarily
    leading to abuse 9.16
individual exemption 5.154
judicial review 13.245
mobile telephone charges 9.54
motorcycling events 9.25
proof, and Regulation 139/204 14.154
public undertaking charging unreasonable
    port duties pursuant to national
    regulations 9.20
radio equipment, type approval
    requirements 9.17
ratione loci (territorial jurisdiction) 5.04–6
simultaneous application with TFEU
    Article 101 5.155–6
State aid 9.55
statement of objections and Regulation
    139/2004 14.184
tariff approvals that lead to dominance
    abuse 9.18
TFEU Article 101 relation 5.152–6
TFEU Article 106 relation 5.157–8
TV broadcast services 9.14
waste management 9.30
TFEU, Article 102, and abuse of
    dominance, abuse 5.60–149
agent and principal agreements 5.122
banana ripeners 5.130

capability of restricting competition 5.66–9
cash register spares 5.84
categories 5.70–133
collective dominance 5.136
commercial interests, protecting 5.141–4
dangerous products 5.139
diamonds and exclusive purchasing 5.72
discounts 5.145–6
discrimination between business partners 5.125
discriminatory pricing predation 5.89
economic value and excessive pricing 5.118, 5.119
economic value of royalties 5.117
efficiencies 5.145–6
efficiency gains 5.138
excessive pricing 5.116–21
exclusive purchasing 5.71–2
fee levels charged in other Member States 5.121, 5.123
fee system for airport management services 5.124
geographic price discrimination 5.127–31
intellectual property rights 5.148
justification 5.137–49
knowledge of abusive nature of conduct 5.64–5
liner conference 5.89
margin squeeze 5.113–15
market foreclosure 5.147
media players and abusive bundling 5.87
musical copyright and royalties 5.120
objective concept 5.60–65
objective necessity 5.139–40
packaging fees 5.123
patents and lack of transparency 5.132
pharmaceutical products out of proportion to those previously sold 5.131
pharmaceuticals company refusal to supply wholesalers involved in parallel exports 5.143
pharmaceuticals, competition from generic products 5.144
predatory pricing 5.88–91
price alignment on those previously charged by a competitor 5.142

price discrimination 5.124–8
price loss recoupment possibility, no requirement to show 5.90–91
pricing below average variable cost or below average total cost 5.88
production costs and excessive pricing 5.117
public health protection 5.140
royalties for use of patents 5.111
secondary markets 5.134–5
sham action 5.133
State action defence 5.149
telecommunication end-user access services 5.113
telecommunications digital subscriber line 5.114
trade limitations between Member States 5.129–31
transparency, lack of 5.132
tying and bundling 5.84–7
tying and bundling, conditions for abusive bundling 5.87
tying sales of spare parts to maintenance and repair services 5.84–6
unfair conditions 5.116–23
vehicle industry discount system 5.145
TFEU, Article 102, and abuse of dominance, abuse, rebate schemes 5.69, 5.71, 5.73–83
conditional on exclusivity 5.76
efficient competitor test 5.83
individualised targets 5.80
individualised targets leaving margin of discretion to supplier 5.81
meeting competition 5.77
oil products and rebate scheme 5.74
plasterboard imports 5.76
practical effect of thresholds for discounts 5.78
quantity discount effect circumstances 5.79
Quantity rebate versus Loyalty rebate 5.73, 5.82
reference period calculation 5.75
travel agent commission on airline tickets 5.80
vehicle tyres 5.75, 5.80

TFEU, Article 102, and abuse of
  dominance, abuse, refusal to supply
  5.92–112, 5.115, 16.09
 brand name dominance 5.93
 computer software and third party licence
  to use a product 5.110
 copyright of sound recordings 5.99
 copyrights 5.99–100, 5.102–3
 energy transport network 5.96
 essential facilities and access time 5.95–6
 intellectual property rights 5.95, 5.97–112
 newspaper distribution 5.95
 patent ambush 5.111
 patent rights 5.97, 5.107
 patents, standard essential patents 5.112
 product indispensable for operating on
  secondary market 5.109
 raw materials 5.92
 service provision and access time 5.94
 spare parts 5.104–5
 television broadcasting of horse-racing
  5.108
 television programme listings 5.106
 third party licence to use a product 5.110
 trade-mark rights 5.97, 5.101
TFEU, Article 102, and abuse of
  dominance, dominance 5.07–56
 airport management 5.47
 banana market 5.26, 5.34
 brand equity and product differentiation
  5.48
 cigarette filters 5.44
 collective dominance 5.49–56
 declining market share 5.32–3
 differentiated market 5.18–20
 differentiated products 5.19–20
 economic strength measurement 5.07
 electricity distribution 5.50
 entitlement to discontinue contractual
  relations 5.46
 entry barriers 5.34–43
 fertilizer market 5.31
 FIFA membership and collective
  dominance 5.55
 fixed costs and entry barriers 5.42
 flour additives sector 5.14
 highly technical products 5.27

home-delivery services 5.41
 infrastructure and barriers to entry 5.41
 input market 5.15–17
 market definition 5.13–26
 market power 5.29–48
 market share and market power 5.29–33
 market shares and competitors,
  relationship between 5.08–11
 nail market and transport costs 5.25
 pharmaceutical products 5.21
 plastics sector 5.14
 product packaging, light metal containers
  5.13
 products belonging to different markets
  5.18
 raw materials 5.15
 relevant geographic market 5.22–5
 relevant product market 5.13–21
 spare parts 5.17
 SSNIP test 5.21
 standardization and entry barriers 5.43
 state intervention and exclusive rights
  5.35–40
 tacit coordination 5.56
 telephone installations 5.24
 television programmes and weekly
  programme information 5.20
 temporal markets 5.26
 transport costs 5.25
 unavoidable trading partner 5.45–8
 vehicle approval services 5.16
 vehicle tyres 5.19
 vertical integration 5.44
TFEU, Article 102, and abuse of
  dominance, substantial part of internal
  market 5.57–9
 airport management services 5.59
 maritime import and export operations
  5.58
 sugar market 5.57
TFEU, Article 102, cartel prohibition
 autonomous conduct that restricts
  competition 4.138
 insurance industry 4.11–12
 insurance industry supervision 4.133
 national administrations, activity of
  assisting 4.51

and national law 4.133, 4.136, 4.140
products that are related to those covered
  by an agreement or practice 4.196
public authority and data storage and
  access 4.52
racing companies and PMU 4.136
sports and freedom of movement 4.18
TFEU Article 102 versus remedies,
  Regulation 139/2004, control of
  concentrations between undertakings,
  powers of Commission decision
  (Article 8) 14.154
TFEU, Article 103
  enforcement measures 6.01–3
  ne bis in idem principle 13.164
  regulation regarding application of Article
    101 and 102 6.01–4
  telecommunications market, ex ante
    regulation 6.04
TFEU, Article 104
  air transport 4.09
  Article 101 and time of entry into force
    of Treaty 4.25
TFEU, Article 104, competence of
  authorities in Member States 7.01–2
TFEU, Article 105, air transport 4.09
TFEU, Article 105, application of Articles
  101 and 102 by Commission 8.01–6
  applicability from time of entry into force
    of Treaty 4.25
  conferred powers principle 8.02
  legal professional privilege 8.02
  national procedural autonomy 8.02
  objective impartiality 8.03
TFEU, Article 105, Article 101 and time of
  entry into force of Treaty 4.25
TFEU, Article 106
  bank transfers 4.11
  direct effect 5.02
  exclusive rights 5.38
TFEU, Article 106, public undertakings
  9.01–56
  air carriers, non-commercially viable
    routes 9.36
  airport charges 9.53
  anti-competitive conduct by undertakings
    on their own initiative 9.05–6

breach of reserved area 9.09
Commission powers 9.46–54, 14.195
dangerous waste disposal 9.22
dock-work company, exclusive right to
  supply 9.21
electricity imports 9.39
exceptional derogation from Treaty rules
  9.26–45
exclusive right necessarily leading to abuse
  9.16
exclusive right to organize dock work 9.15
exclusive rights 9.19
funeral services 9.12
health services and medical care provision
  9.35
healthcare costs reimbursement scheme
  9.45
intellectual property rights 9.32–3
judicial review rights 9.52
livestock insemination centres 9.16
mail delivery, universal service provider
  9.44
mobile telephone charges 9.54
motorcycling events 9.25
national insurance bureaux and green card
  system 9.11
patient transport services 9.24
pension schemes 9.23, 9.42
postal services 9.38, 9.49
preferential rights for the exploration and
  exploitation of lignite deposits 9.10
prohibited measures 9.11–25
proportionality test 9.36–45
public ambulance service 9.43
public employment agency including
  executive search 9.13
public undertaking charging unreasonable
  port duties pursuant to national
  regulations 9.20
radio equipment, type approval
  requirements 9.17
respect for the rights of the defence 9.49
State aid 9.55–6
tariff approvals that lead to dominance
  abuse 9.18
telephone equipment market 9.37
television advertising 9.01

tenders 9.34

TFEU Article 107 relation 9.55–6

TV broadcast services 9.14

undertakings entrusted with the operation of services of general economic interest (SGEI) 9.31–43

waste management 9.30

TFEU, Article 106

    TFEU, Article 102 relation 5.157–8, 9.27, 9.29–30, 9.54–5

    transport 4.08

TFEU, Article 107, aid prohibition 9.55–6, 10.01–144, 11.09, 11.19, 11.27, 11.52–3, 11.67, 11.71, 11.87, 11.86–7, 11.94, 11.123

    airport charges 10.25

    amount of aid/de minimis 10.65–6

    behaviour of private investor in comparable circumstances (pari passu) 10.28–9

    capital injections 10.91–101

    commercial vehicle replacement 10.43

    compatibility with internal market 10.126

    compatibility with internal market, may be considered 10.127–45

    competition rules 10.81

    corporate income tax and change of ownership 10.48

    criteria 10.01–70

    cross-subsidisation 10.105

    damages compensation 10.125

    debt arrangement 10.102, 10.115

    development of certain economic activities or of certain economic areas 10.142

    direct business taxation 10.44

    direct effect 10.71–4

    distortion of competition 10.54–7

    ecotax 10.46

    effect on trade between Member States 10.58–70

    environmental pollution 10.138

    environmental protection levy 10.45

    equal treatment principle 10.19

    financial crisis and emergency aid 10.141

    fiscal measures 10.118–19

    fisheries sector 10.78

    fixed-term employment contracts 10.122

    form in which aid is provided 10.83–124

    free movement of goods 10.80

    gambling and unclaimed winnings 10.07

    guarantees 10.104

    hospital building investment 10.68

    imputability 10.12–16

    insolvency or liquidation of credit institution 10.29

    inter-trade agreements 10.16

    judicial review 10.23, 10.86, 10.139

    leisure pool renovation costs 10.67

    loans and interest rates 10.103

    local museum projects 10.70

    margin of appreciation 10.85–8

    market economy investor principle 10.22–39

    merchant vessels in International Shipping Register 10.04

    minimum retail prices 10.123

    mooring marinas 10.69

    no effect on trade between Member States 10.69–70

    non-financial regulatory measures 10.121–22

    operating aid 10.106, 10.129

    and other Treaty provisions 10.75–82

    pig meat market 10.76

    preferential rediscount rate for exports 10.116

    private investor of comparable size to public body 10.20

    private-investor test 10.22, 10.23–5, 10.28, 10.29

    privatisation by tendering 10.114

    production capacity increase 10.128

    public sector investment funds 10.12

    public service obligations 10.34–5

    public undertakings 10.13–14, 10.30

    reductions and non-payment of social security contributions 10.115

    regional aid 10.133, 10.134–7

    regional aid and European Regional Development Fund 10.133

    regional aid and sectoral overcapacity 10.135

    regional selectivity 10.40

    sale of land 10.107–13

selectivity 10.37–53
selectivity in taxation context 10.41–53
services of general economic interest (SGEI) 10.30–35
share capital owned by public authorities 10.26
shipbuilding and marine and defence electronics 10.62
shipbuilding and ship conversion aid 10.145
shipping undertakings and social security contributions 10.121
small businesses and protection of workers against unfair dismissal 10.06
SMEs and de minimis rule 10.65
social measures 10.82
social plans and financial assistance 10.36
social security system 10.41
standard of living and employment levels 10.127
State resources 10.01–11
subsidy concept 10.89–90
tariff fixed at level lower than normal 10.21
tariff fixing by Member States 10.124
tariff quotas 10.02
tax exemptions 10.119
technologically advanced equipment 10.17
TFEU Article 106 relation 9.55–6
trade association advertising campaign 10.18
trade association governed by public law 10.17–18
transnational European programmes 10.138
transport services, local or regional 10.63
venture capital 10.27
wine producers 10.77
TFEU, Article 108, notification of aid 11.01–125
appropriate measures 11.16–17
complaints received by Commission 11.123–4
damages compensation 10.125
existing aid 11.01–12, 11.14–15
extension of period to submit comments 11.45

fisheries sector 10.78
fishing vessel construction 11.17
interested parties 11.39–51
interested parties, rights of 11.44–7
limited role of interested parties 11.48–49
new aid 11.01–3, 11.05–10, 11.12–15
obligation of Commission to address complaints parties 11.51
pig meat market 10.76
State aid 10.05, 10.75–7
supply difficulties and restructuring plan 11.25–6
trade union as interested party 11.42
TFEU, Article 108, notification of aid, annulment action 11.91–9
admissibility 11.91–5
assessment by Union courts 11.97–9
compatibility of State aids with common market 11.99
TFEU, Article 108, notification of aid, formal investigation procedure 11.21–38
alleged unlawful aid 11.22
burden of proof into existence of serious difficulties 11.30
compatibility assessment 11.18–21, 11.23, 11.24, 11.28–9, 11.36–8
decision to initiate 11.36–7
initiation obligation 11.21–23
length and circumstances of preliminary examination procedure 11.38
private investor test 11.31
procedure between Commission and Member State granting aid 11.32–4
serious difficulties concept 11.27–31
withdrawal of act as contested act 11.37
TFEU, Article 108, notification of aid, recovery of aid 11.100–123
absolutely impossible 11.114–15
in accordance with national law 11.110
duty of genuine cooperation 11.111–12
legal certainty principle 11.119
legitimate expectations 11.117–20
objective of recovery 11.108–9
recovery and bankruptcy 11.121–3
tax as integral part of aid measure 10.120

TFEU, Article 108, notification of aid, requirement to notify and standstill obligation 11.52–90
  alterations to existing aid 11.55
  compatibility of aid with common market 11.80, 11.86
  Deggendorf-doctrine 11.90
  direct applicability 11.74
  examination of unlawful aid 11.68–9
  injunction to suspend 11.73
  Member State obligation 11.60–61, 11.87
  national courts role 11.83–90
  no ruling on compatibility of aid 11.89
  notification after the implementation of the aid measure 11.64–7
  notification of aid and method of financing the aid (taxes) 11.56–9
  notification in case of State aid 11.52–4
  notification time 11.62
  preliminary examination 11.75–7, 11.87
  preservation of individual rights 11.84
  res judicata principle 11.88
  safeguard measures 11.85, 11.87
  standstill obligation 11.70–73
TFEU, Article 109, Member State obligation 10.76, 11.87
TFEU, Article 153, collective bargaining between employers and workers 4.14, 4.15
TFEU, Article 155, dialogue between management and labour 4.14, 4.15
TFEU, Article 236, legality of a Commission decision 24.33
TFEU, Article 258, Commission powers 9.48, 14.195
TFEU, Article 258–60, suspension of operation of decision 11.96
TFEU, Article 261, unlimited jurisdiction powers 13.236, 13.240, 13.242, 13.244–6, 24.36, 24.72
TFEU, Article 263
  direct action against decision adopted by a Community institution 11.79, 13.12, 13.219, 13.236, 13.240
  legality review 13.244–6, 19.53, 24.36, 24.55, 24.65

  proceedings against a decision addressed to another person 11.91, 11.95, 11.98, 11.97
TFEU, Article 267, preliminary ruling 18.25
TFEU, Article 278 and 279, compliance with treaty rules on competition 13.55
TFEU, Article 279, suspension of operation of decision 11.98
TFEU, Article 288 4.02
TFEU Article 296
  compliance with duty to state reasons for decision 13.236
  notification of aid, obligation of Commission to address complaints parties 11.51
TFEU, Article 297, citizens' right of access to documents 13.238
TFEU, Article 339
  business secrets 13.237
  professional secrecy 12.232, 13.239, 14.181
third countries
  control of concentrations between undertakings 14.200
  dealing agreements 4.19
  restrictive agreements 4.187
third parties
  appeal by third party possible 14.161
  hearing of the parties *see* Regulation 139/2004, control of concentrations between undertakings, hearing of the parties and of third persons (Article 18)
  licence to use a product 5.110
  non-referral decision by Commission may not be contested by 14.167
  pre-existing contractual rights 14.145
thresholds
  de minimis notice 13.21
  discount 5.78
  market share 15.03
time factors
  aid notification time 11.62
  extension of period to submit comments, aid notification 11.45
  failure to provide information within period fixed by Commission decision 14.174

lasting structural change, minimum time period 14.120

reasonable period, right to good administration 23.01–9

time of entry into force of Treaty 4.27

time limits for initiating proceedings 14.169–70

tobacco products 4.196, 4.220

cigarette filters 5.44

FEDETAB and tobacco imports 4.63, 4.70, 4.125, 4.239

toy market 14.19

trade

association governed by public law 10.17–18

between Member States *see* TFEU, Article 101 and cartel prohibition, effect on trade between Member States

influence of trade between States 14.197–8

limitations between Member States 5.129–31

patterns 14.15–16

unavoidable trading partner 5.45–8

see also Member States; national legislation; State aid

trade unions 4.17, 11.42

trade-mark rights 5.97, 5.101

see also intellectual property rights

transfer of activities date 4.60

transfer of exclusive competence 14.165

transfer from parent company to subsidiary 4.91–2, 4.94

transnational European programmes 10.138

transparency

exemptions 4.224

and fines 13.174

lack of 5.132

market, and horizontal mergers 14.56

transportation

air *see* air transport

and cartel prohibition 4.08–9

costs and distances 14.20–23

dock work 9.15, 9.21

horizontal agreements 4.170

inland transport services 4.225

jet engines 14.78

liability insurance 14.31

local or regional, and aid prohibition 10.63

maritime transport fares 13.159

patient transport services 9.24

public ambulance service 9.43

tariffs for long-distance transport of goods by road 2.12

see also vehicles

travel agencies 4.113, 4.276, 5.80

tribunals

access rights 24.57–61

independent and impartial *see* ECHR, right to a fair trial (Article 6), independent and impartial tribunal

see also courts

tried twice, right not to be *see* ECHR, right not be tried or punished twice for same criminal offence (Article 4 Protocol 7)

truth under oath 25.35

turnover

calculation *see* Regulation 139/2004, control of concentrations between undertakings, turnover calculation (Article 5)

and exchange rates 13.92

fines calculation 13.88–102, 13.177, 26.19, 26.22–3

and lysine market 13.93

and market share 13.93, 13.95–6, 13.98, 13.103–4, 13.138, 13.140, 13.159–60

TV broadcasting *see under* broadcasting

twice, right not to be tried or punished twice for same criminal offence *see* ECHR, right not be tried or punished twice for same criminal offence (Article 4 Protocol 7)

two-step test 18.22, 19.35–6

tying and bundling *see* bundling

UK

Anton Piller order 19.20, 19.48

judicial searches 19.50

obligation to give the name of the driver of a registered vehicle 25.39

oceanic cruises, new entry expansion
14.32
photographic equipment dealers 4.294
TEU, Article 6, Charter and ECHR
applicability 3.15
unauthorised distributors definition 15.07
see also distribution system
unavoidable trading partner 5.45–8
undertakings
and aid prohibition 10.121
and cartel prohibition 4.03–6, 4.84,
4.88–94, 4.98, 4.155, 4.170, 4.299
concept *see* TFEU, Article 101 and cartel
prohibition, undertaking concept
control of concentrations between *see*
Regulation 139/2004, control of
concentrations between undertakings
and dominance abuse 9.20
economic unit formation 4.93–4
and fines 13.99, 13.148–57, 13.159,
13.161–2, 13.176
fines and turnover of undertaking
13.88–102
number committing infringement
13.82–3, 13.154–5
public *see* TFEU, Article 106, public
undertakings
public, and aid prohibition 10.13–14,
10.30
publicly distancing itself from agreement
or concerted practice 13.06–9
single 4.56, 14.126
size differences between undertakings
13.159
'undertakings concerned' notion 14.03,
14.111–12
see also association of undertakings
unfair conditions, TFEU, Article 102, and
abuse of dominance, abuse 5.116–23
unfair dismissal 10.06
see also employment
uniform application of competition law
13.36–7
see also competition
unilateral conduct and apparently unilateral
conduct 4.78–87
unlawful aid 11.68–9

unlimited jurisdiction
on appeal 13.249–50
exercise 24.55
judicial review 13.241–2, 13.244–8
powers 13.236, 13.240, 13.242, 13.244–6,
24.36, 24.72
reviewing fine 23.09
'up-front buyer' commitment 14.141

validity period of commitment decisions
13.29
vehicles
approval services 5.16
car insurance companies and bilateral
arrangements with car dealers 4.275
car manufacture and technological
progress 4.223
car sales and fuel agencies 4.279–81
certification 4.54
commercial vehicle replacement 10.43
dealerships 4.78–9, 4.83
distribution system 4.273–4, 4.285,
4.298
export restrictions 4.172
industry discount system 5.145
industry, Germany 4.279, 15.09–10
insurance contracts and car repairs 4.151
leasing contracts 4.277
manufacture and supply quotas 4.273
motorcycling events 9.25
obligation to give name of driver of
registered vehicle 25.39
obligation to give the name of the driver
of a registered vehicle, UK 25.39
parts 14.23, 14.61
sector vertical agreements 15.01, 15.08–10
TFEU, Article 101 and cartel prohibition
4.13
TFEU, Article 101 and cartel prohibition,
vertical agreements 4.277
TFEU, Article 102, and abuse of
dominance, dominance 5.19
TFEU, Article 106, public undertakings
9.25
tyres, TFEU, Article 102, and abuse of
dominance, abuse, rebate schemes
5.75, 5.80

vertical agreements, Regulation 461/2010 *see* Regulation 461/2010, vertical agreements in the motor vehicle sector

see also transportation

venture capital 10.27

verification obligations, vertical agreements 4.282

vertical agreements
and cartel prohibition *see* TFEU, Article 101 and cartel prohibition, vertical agreements
and fines 13.206
integration and dominance abuse 5.44
mergers 14.62–3
Regulation 330/2010 *see* Regulation 330/2010, vertical agreements
see also horizontal agreements

veto rights 14, 114, 14.91

Vienna Treaty on the Law of Treaties 18.03, 18.06–13

voting rights 14.82, 14.115, 14.118

waiver of rights, and right to a fair trial 24.100–101

waste management 9.22, 9.30

whereabouts, obligation to indicate one's whereabouts at a given time 25.34

wine production 10.77
see also agriculture policy; food and drink sector

written communications
between lawyer and client 19.56, 19.57–9
confidentiality of 13.51–2, 13.56
see also documentation

Zaire, Ogefrem Agreement 5.39

zinc sheet manufacture 4.167